FIELDS OF

WRITING

READINGS ACROSS
THE DISCIPLINES

Third Edition

Nancy R. Comley
QUEENS COLLEGE, CUNY

David Hamilton
UNIVERSITY OF IOWA

Carl H. Klaus
UNIVERSITY OF IOWA

Robert Scholes
BROWN UNIVERSITY

Nancy Sommers
HARVARD UNIVERSITY

St. Martin's Press
NEW YORK

Senior editor: Mark Gallaher
Project editor: Denise Quirk
Production supervisor: Alan Fischer
Cover design: Darby Downey
Cover art: Georgia O'Keeffe, Sky Above Clouds II, 1963. Copyright © 1989
        Estate of Georgia O'Keeffe.
Cover photo: Malcolm Varon, New York City. Copyright © 1987.

For information, write:
St. Martin's Press, Inc.
175 Fifth Avenue
New York, NY 10010

ISBN: 0-312-02111-9

ACKNOWLEDGMENTS

Angelou, Maya. From I Know Why the Caged Bird Sings by Maya Angelou. Copyright © 1969 Maya Angelou. Reprinted by permission of Random House, Inc.

Asimov, Isaac, "The Case against Man," copyright © 1970 by Field Enterprises, Inc. From Science Past-Science Future by Isaac Asimov. Used by permission of Doubleday, a division of Bantam, Doubleday, Dell Publishing Group, Inc.

Avedon, John F., "Tibetan Medicine: The Science of Healing." From In Exile from the Land of Snows, by John F. Avedon. Copyright © 1979, 1984 by John F. Avedon. Reprinted by permission of Alfred A. Knopf, Inc.

Baldwin, James, "Autobiographical Notes." From Notes of a Native Son by James Baldwin. Copyright © 1955, renewed 1983 by James Baldwin. Reprinted by permission of Beacon Press.

Baldwin, James, "If Black English Isn't a Language, Then Tell Me, What Is?" Copyright © 1979 by the New York Times Company. Reprinted by permission.

Barthes, Roland, "Einstein's Brain." From Mythologies by Roland Barthes. Translation copyright © 1972 by Jonathan Cape, Ltd. Reprinted by permission of Hill and Wang, a division of Farrar, Straus and Giroux, Inc. and Georges Borchardt Inc.

Baumrind, Diana, "Review of Stanley Milgram's Experiments on Obedience." From "Some Thoughts on Ethics of Research: After Reading Milgram's 'Behavioral Study of Obedience,'" American Psychologist, 19, 1964, pp. 421–3. Copyright © 1964 by the American Psychological Association. Reprinted by permission.

Acknowledgments and copyrights are continued at the back of the book on pages 781–784, which constitute an extension of the copyright page.

For Instructors

The third edition of *Fields of Writing*, like previous editions, offers a collection of readings designed to reflect the range and variety of thinking and writing across the disciplines. In choosing pieces for this edition, we have been guided by the reactions and suggestions of more than 100 instructors who used the second edition, all of whom asked that we keep the collection wide-ranging and varied in its subject matter. Thus, our table of contents again covers a broad array of topics, from the sculpture of Michelangelo to the paintings of Georgia O'Keefe, from the bubonic plague of the fourteenth century to the atomic bombing of Nagasaki, from the origin of the universe to the evolution of Mickey Mouse. So, too, the table of contents again offers material drawn equally from the arts and humanities, from the social sciences and public affairs, and from the sciences and technologies—from the major areas of the curriculum in both their academic and applied forms. Overall, then, you will find here a total of 82 selections as various in subject, form, and purpose as the different kinds of reading and writing that students are expected to carry on both in undergraduate education and in the world outside the classroom.

In organizing our collection, we have once again grouped selections according to four broad rhetorical categories—"Reflecting," "Reporting," "Explaining," and "Arguing"—that represent essential kinds of reading and writing in virtually every academic or professional area. Within each of these four categories, we have as before grouped the selections according to three broad curricular areas— "Arts and Humanities," "Social Sciences and Public Affairs," and "Sciences and Technologies." This combined system of organization, our reviewers tell us, continues to be a convenient aid to discovering and assigning selections for a variety of classroom purposes.

While maintaining this rhetorical/cross-curricular system of organization, we have been stimulated by the suggestions of instructors who used the second edition to make a substantial number of changes throughout the table of contents, with the result that 33 of the 82 selections are new to this edition. These new selections include pieces by major scholars, critics, artists, and observers, such as Roland Barthes, Umberto Eco, Clifford Geertz, Carol Gilligan, Stephen W. Hawking, Ernest Hemingway, and Oliver Sacks. This new edition also offers two or three selections by each of the following writers: James Baldwin, Bruno Bettelheim, Joan Didion, Stephen Jay Gould, George Orwell, Oliver Sacks, Richard Selzer, Lewis Thomas, Barbara Tuchman, Alice Walker, and E. B. White.

Adding these new selections has also made it possible for us to provide substantially more pairings or sets of topically related pieces throughout the table of contents than in either of our previous editions, so that students will now have numerous opportunities to read and consider different perspectives on a single issue or to explore a particular topic in depth. Wherever possible, we have placed these topically related pieces side by side, so that you can quickly find them in the table of contents. But in some instances, they necessarily appear under different rhetorical headings. To display these thematic connections, we have also prepared a "Topical Guide to the Contents," making it possible to approach all of the selections in terms of particular subjects of study or themes of interest. And in order to encourage students to pursue thematic relationships among the selections, we have provided one or two special questions for each piece, devoted to "Making Connections."

Our critical apparatus, once again, focuses on strategies for reading and writing across the curriculum. These frameworks are discussed in our prefatory note, "For Students," as well as in the detailed introductions to each of the four main sections, "Reflecting," "Reporting," "Explaining," and "Arguing." These sectional introductions, which are illustrated with passages from the anthologized readings, define each type of writing, discuss its relevance within a broad range of fields, compare and contrast its use in differing fields and situations, as well as identify and explain methods of achieving its aims. Thus, the introductions show, for example, how description and narration are basic in reporting or how analogy, comparison and contrast, definition, and illustration are basic to explaining. All of the rhetorical aims and modes that we discuss in the critical apparatus are referenced in a "Rhetorical Index" to the collection that we have provided at the back of the book. Concepts and terms that figure in the sectional introductions are also applied throughout the remainder of our editorial apparatus. For example, you will find that our headnote for each piece identifies its author's professional field and the rhetorical context or source of its original publication. Likewise, our questions following each selection call for reading and writing that relate form and style to purpose, subject, and academic field.

Because the material in this collection is primarily intended to help students develop their reading and writing abilities, we have revised our discussion of these activities that previously appeared as an appendix and relocated it in the front of the book as a three-part general introduction. The first part, "Reading and Rereading," explains and illustrates various approaches to reading through a detailed discussion focusing primarily on an essay by E. B. White. The second part, "Writing and Rewriting," in turn, explains and illustrates the composing process through an in-depth discussion of White's notes and drafts for the piece. Finally in this introduction, we have added a brief but important note for students, "Acknowledging Sources," which explains the purposes of documentation and citation. This introduction, like the rest of the book, is meant to present reading and writing not in abstract terms, but through discussion and examples that vividly demonstrate what is actually involved in each activity.

FOR INSTRUCTORS

ACKNOWLEDGMENTS

Once again, we have many people to thank for helping us to make our way across the disciplines, particularly those who provided detailed reactions to the second edition of *Fields of Writing*. In addition, for their helpful reactions to earlier drafts of this third edition, we are grateful to Catherine Amdahl, Washington State University; Anne Gervasi, Texas Woman's University; Stephen Hahn, William Paterson College; Dusky Loebel, Tulane University; Robert Shelton, Oberlin College; and Louise Smith, University of Massachusetts—Harbor Campus.

For their excellent work in bringing this book into print, we are grateful to the staff at St. Martin's Press, especially Mark Gallaher, Denise Quirk, and Alan Fischer.

N.R.C.
D.H.
C.H.K.
R.S.
N.S.

Contents

CONTENTS

CONTENTS

ix

CONTENTS

CONTENTS

Contents

CONTENTS

CONTENTS

xiv

CONTENTS

CONTENTS

Topical Guide to the Contents

THE EXPERIENCE OF WOMEN

VIOLENCE AND WAR

LIFE AND DEATH

OBSERVING ANIMALS

UNDERSTANDING THE PHYSICAL WORLD

TEACHING, LEARNING, AND SCHOOLING

HEALTH, DISEASE, AND MEDICINE

For Students

Fields of Writing: Readings across the Disciplines, Third Edition, is intended to help you develop the abilities in reading and writing that you will need as you move from one course to another, one field of study to another, throughout your college career. In some senses, of course, all areas of study expect the same things of you—namely, close and careful reading as well as clear and exact writing, with an attentiveness above all to information and ideas. But the particular kinds of information, ideas, and concerns that distinguish each field of study also call for somewhat different reading and writing abilities. A book review for a literature course, for example, requires a different form and style from a lab report in physics. So we have tried to give you a sampling of the varied fields of writing you are likely to encounter in the academic world.

Most undergraduate schools are organized around some version of the traditional division of studies into "the humanities," "the social sciences," and "the sciences." The humanities generally include fields of learning that are thought of as having a cultural orientation, such as language, literature, history, philosophy, and religion. The social sciences, which include such fields as anthropology, economics, education, political science, psychology, and sociology, deal with social institutions and the behavior of their individual members. The sciences include fields of knowledge that are concerned with the natural and physical world, such as astronomy, botany, chemistry, physics, and zoology.

These traditional divisions of study are closely affiliated with applied areas of study and work that also exist in the professional world. The humanities, for example, are closely allied with the arts; the social sciences, with public affairs such as business and government; and the sciences, with technology. These divisions and clusterings of fields—"Arts and Humanities," "Social Sciences and Public Affairs," "Sciences and Technologies"—are so broadly applicable that we have used them as one of the organizing principles in our table of contents.

Like any set of categories, these divisions are a convenient, but by no means foolproof, system of classification. Although the system can help you to understand the academic world, it does not reflect the exact state of affairs in every specialized field at every college and university. Specialists in a particular field sometimes migrate from one area of learning to another, from the social sciences to the sciences, for example, according to the orientation of their research in a particular project. Or specialists from several fields may form an interdisciplinary area of research, such as environmental studies, which involves a wide range of academic disciplines—botany, chemistry, economics, philosophy, political science, and zoology. So, the writing that results from these projects often can be categorized in more than one broad area of learning.

The writing we have collected in *Fields of Writing* can be understood not only in terms of the area of learning that it represents, but also in terms of the particular purpose it is meant to achieve. Every piece of writing, of course, is the product of an author's personal and professional motives, so in a sense the purposes for writing are as varied and ultimately mysterious as are authors themselves. But setting aside the mysteries of human nature, it is possible to identify and define a set of different purposes for writing, which we refer to as "Reflecting," "Reporting," "Explaining," and "Arguing," one or another of which predominates in most academic and professional writing. So, we have used this set of purposes as the major organizing principle in our table of contents.

By "Reflecting," we mean a kind of writing in which authors are concerned with recalling and thinking about their past experience, for personal experience is often an especially valuable source of knowledge and learning. By "Reporting," we mean writing that is concerned primarily with conveying factual information about some particular aspect of the world, past or present. By "Explaining," we mean writing that is concerned primarily with making sense of information or shedding light on a particular subject. By "Arguing," we mean writing that is given to debating controversial explanations, values, or beliefs. Like our other categories, these are convenient, but not rigid, modes of classification. So, they need to be used tactfully, with an awareness that to some degree they are bound to overlap. Most pieces of explanation, for example, will at some point involve reporting, if only to convey the information or subject to be explained. And most pieces of argument will call for some explanation, if only to make clear the issues that are at odds with one another. But generally you will find one or another of these purposes to be dominant in any particular piece of writing.

We think that an awareness of these basic purposes can be especially helpful both in the process of reading and in the process of writing, no matter what academic or professional field is involved. So, we have introduced each section of our collection with an essay on "Reflecting," "Reporting," "Explaining," or "Arguing." In these essays, you will find detailed definitions and examples of each purpose, as well as explanations and illustrations of how to carry it out in differing fields and situations. Each selection is accompanied by a brief headnote, explanatory footnotes where necessary, and questions for you to think about in your reading and writing. In addition, each selection is also followed by questions to help you make connections among related readings in this collection.

Immediately following this preface, you will find an introduction consisting of three parts: In "Reading and Rereading," we discuss various ways to read and understand the pieces in this book or any other material you might encounter in your studies; in "Writing and Rewriting," we show an actual example of how one writer goes through the process of composing a piece of writing, and in "Acknowledging Sources," we explain various forms of documentation and why such acknowledgment is important in every field of study. This introduction, like the headnotes, questions, and sectional introductions, is meant to help you become a thoughtful and responsible reader and writer. The rest is up to your instructor, your classmates, and you.

Introduction

No matter what your field of study, you will probably find that it involves you repeatedly in the activities of reading and writing. Reading, even in the age of the computer, continues to be the primary means of acquiring knowledge, and writing the primary means of sharing ideas with others. So, we have decided to introduce this collection with a discussion of some general ideas that you might find useful in your own reading and writing.

Our discussion of both activities is illustrated primarily by reference to a short essay that appeared in the *New York Times*, September 23, 1967. We suggest that you begin by reading that essay, which follows, and getting the gist of it for yourself, before we begin to discuss it in detail.

Dear Mr. ⑊0 2 14 ⑊ 106 3⑊ ⑊0 2 ⑊ 10 7 30 ⑊ 8 ⑊

By E. B. WHITE

My bank, which I have forgotten the name of in the excitement of the moment, sent me a warning the other day. It was headed: "An important notice to all our checking account customers." The burden of this communication was that I would no longer be allowed to write checks that did not bear the special series of magnetic ink numbers along the base. [1]

My bank said the Federal Reserve System had notified them that it will not accept for processing any checks that don't show these knobby little digits. For example, I would no longer be free to write a check on a blank form, because it would lack a certain magnetism that computers insist on. [2]

Slightly Rheumatoid

I first encountered these spooky numbers a few years back and took a dislike to them. They looked like numbers that had been run over by a dump truck or [3]

1

that had developed rheumatoid arthritis and their joints had swollen. But I kept my mouth shut, as they seemed to be doing me no harm.

Now, however, it appears that we are all going to knuckle under to the machines that admire these numbers. We must all forgo the pleasure and convenience of writing a check on an ordinary nonmagnetic piece of paper. My signature used to be enough to prod my bank into dispatching some of my money to some deserving individual or firm. Not any more.

This, I think, is a defeat for all—a surrender. In order to accommodate the Federal Reserve System, we are asked to put ourselves out.

I Embarrass Easily

The notice I received says that if I try to palm off a check that lacks the magnetic ink numbers, the check cannot be processed without "delay, extra handling charges, and possible embarrassment." I embarrass easily—it doesn't take much, really—and naturally I am eager to learn what form this embarrassment will take if I should decide to write a check using the old blank form that has proved so convenient, for I don't know how many decades, on those occasions when one is stuck without his checkbook or enough lettuce to carry the day.

"The tremendous increase in the use of checks," writes my bank, warming to its subject, "made it necessary for the Federal Reserve to establish a completely computerized operation for processing all checks from all banks. Their computer can function only when proper magnetic numbers are used."

Well, I can believe that last part, about the computer requiring a special diet of malformed numbers; but I am suspicious of that first statement, about how the Federal Reserve would have been unable to carry on unless it went completely over to machines. I suspect that the Federal Reserve simply found machines handy and adventurous. But suppose we had had, in this country, a tremendous increase in the use of checks before anybody had got round to inventing the computer—what would have happened then? Am I expected to believe that the Federal Reserve and all its members would have thrown in the sponge?

I know banks better than that. Banks love money and are not easily deflected from the delicious act of accumulating it. Love would have found a way. Checks would have cleared.

I'm not against machines, as are some people who feel that the computer is leading us back into the jungle. I rather like machines, particularly the egg beater, which is the highest point the machine has yet reached. I'm against machines only when the convenience they afford to some people is regarded as more important than the inconvenience they cause to all.

In short, I don't think computers should wear the pants, or make the decisions. They are deficient in humor, they are not intuitive, and they are not aware of the imponderables. The men who feed them seem to believe that everything is made out of ponderables, which isn't the case. I read a poem once that a computer had written, but didn't care much for it. It seemed to me I could write a better one myself, it I were to put my mind to it.

2

Time to Find Out

And now I must look around for a blank check. It's time I found out what 12 form my new embarrassment is going to take. First, though, I'll have to remember the name of my bank. It'll come to me, if I sit here long enough. Oddly enough, the warning notice I received contained no signature. Imagine a bank forgetting to sign its name!

READING AND REREADING

Reading this essay in a textbook for a course in English composition, as you have just done, is not quite the same as reading it in a daily newspaper. Not only does the format—the layout, the page size, the typeface—of a newspaper differ from that of a textbook, but the reasons we have for reading each and, consequently, the *way* we read will differ, as well.

Think for a moment, though, about the similarities between your reading of this essay here and now and someone's reading of it in the fall of 1967. First of all, both readings are based on recognizing and interpreting an arrangement of printed symbols, symbols most of us were familiar with long before we began to learn them systematically in the first grade. This aspect of reading is so elemental that you probably never stop to consider what a feat it really is. Second, both readings begin with the title and work their way sequentially through the final line of the text (though seeing the process as purely sequential is somewhat misleading; in fact, our minds ordinarily move back and forth, comparing what we read at one point with what we've read at others, as we work to make sense of the text). Third, both readings assume an active, rather than a passive, reader—someone who is responding to everything that White has to say. And responding in a variety of ways—pondering, questioning, nodding, gesturing, laughing, or growling, just to name a few of the reactions that might be provoked in a reader of White's piece.

Responses to Reading

The complexity of such reactions can be seen just by trying to imagine how one might read the title, "Dear Mr. 0214 1063 02 10730 8." The first two words are easy enough: we recognize them immediately as the conventional salutation of a business letter. We could even speak them aloud (taking into account that the unpronounceable *Mr.* is an abbreviated form of *Mister*). But the following series of "knobby little digits" presents a more complicated problem. "What are they?" we might ask. "What do they mean?" Even if we recognize them as the sort of figures that are printed at the bottom of a check, we cannot, in fact *read* them, because the markings between the numbers represent nothing in our language or our grammar. In fact, they are meant to be read not by human beings but by machines. Trying to read such a title, therefore, will set off any number of responses: perhaps an inkling of what White is up to ("Ah, a put-down of computer technology"), perhaps confusion ("I can't imagine what to make of this"), perhaps the desire to read on, and probably a less than fully articulated combination of several of these.

Next, the name of the author will create another round of responses. Perhaps you (and our imaginary reader of the *Times*) will be familiar with the name E. B. White and will associate it with *Charlotte's Web* or *Elements of Style* or a piece in the *New Yorker* magazine or something else you've read by White or know he wrote. You (and our imaginary *Times* reader) might respond positively ("I loved *Charlotte's Web*") or negatively ("I hate that *New Yorker* stuff") or less familiarly ("Is E. B. a man or a woman?"), but you will certainly have some response. This complicated sequence of responses, of course, occurs in just the second or two it takes you to comprehend the symbols on the page.

As you continue to read, you will continue to respond. Thoughts and impressions, no matter how tentative and ill-formed, will play through your consciousness. (You may even feel compelled to jot down some of these responses in the margin of the page.) Our minds can only make sense of the information we receive by testing this information against what we already know and feel. Such testing is a peculiarly human activity—at least we regard it as "human" when we observe it in other species—and only by allowing, even encouraging, ourselves to make these mental connections can we participate fully in the collaboration necessary to create meaning. Reading, as you probably realize, is a *transaction* that spans at least two human minds; reader and writer both must work actively for a meaningful transaction to take place.

If either participant fails to regard the human responsibilities of communication, the transaction will be unsatisfying. White provides a particularly unpleasant example of this: an impersonal letter, written not by a human being but by "a bank," has had an unsettling effect because it indicates to White the abrupt dehumanization of what was previously a human transaction. Readers can fail, as well, when they approach the transaction impersonally, when they ignore their personal reactions and responses, when they don't participate actively in examining and judging what they read. Such passivity is, of course, what impersonal writers hope for from their readers; the impersonal mask is calculated to discourage any questions or objections. Perhaps you have occasionally found yourself intimidated by such all-knowing bureaucratic pronouncements. The surest way to prevent yourself from being cowed ever again is to read inquisitively, ready to respond with all of your mind and all of your feelings to whatever you find in your reading, from the smallest detail to the text as a whole.

As we have said, your reading will always involve responses of some kind. The important step is to move from the responses themselves to a serious examination of them. To read White's reflections on his bank's warning and

4

respond simply with "It's dumb" or "It's funny" or "I agree" or "I disagree" or the implacable "I can't relate to this" is not enough. Examining such responses will reveal a complex interaction between the structures of the text, the intentions and abilities of the writer, and what you as a reader bring to the text from your own experience. You may find White's essay "funny" because his treatment of his bank as a letter-writing entity that forgets to sign its name sets off a particularly exact set of images in your mind. You may "disagree" with White because you find his comment that the egg beater "is the highest point the machine has yet reached" to be overly flippant and because you think the computer's greater accuracy does in fact afford convenience to all. You may feel you "can't relate to" White's experience because you've never known checks *without* the magnetic code and because you've never received a similarly impersonal letter from a bureaucratic institution. Whatever the case, your responses will remain superficial and ill-formed until you examine them closely enough to explain them in detail.

Clearly, our own experiences will deeply affect our reading. Whatever we have seen or done or felt or heard, even the room we are in and our last meal, will contribute to a data bank from which our responses arise. Consider the following excerpt from the memoirs of Frederick Douglass (the complete chapter from which this was taken appears on pp. 71–76). Born into slavery, Douglass managed to learn to read and at the age of twelve saved enough money—fifty cents—to buy his first book, *The Columbian Orator*. This was a popular school book containing speeches by famous orators and dialogues for students of rhetoric to practice and memorize. Here are Douglass's reactions to one of his readings.

I was now about twelve years old, and the thought of being *a slave for life* began to bear heavily upon my heart. Just about this time, I got hold of a book entitled "The Columbian Orator." Every opportunity I got, I used to read this book. Among much of other interesting matter, I found in it a dialogue between a master and his slave. The slave was represented as having run away from his master three times. The dialogue represented the conversation which took place between them, when the slave was retaken the third time. In this dialogue, the whole argument in behalf of slavery was brought forward by the master, all of which was disposed of by the slave. The slave was made to say some very smart as well as impressive things in reply to his master—things which had the desired though unexpected effect; for the conversation resulted in the voluntary emancipation of the slave on the part of the master.

In the same book, I met with one of Sheridan's mighty speeches on and in behalf of Catholic emancipation. These were choice documents to me. I read them over and over again with unabated interest. They gave tongue to interesting thoughts of my own soul, which had frequently flashed through my mind, and died away for want of utterance. The moral which I gained from the dialogue was the power of truth over the conscience of even a slaveholder. What I got from Sheridan was a bold denunciation of slavery, and a powerful vindication of human rights. The reading of these documents enabled me to utter my thoughts, and to meet the arguments brought forward to sustain slavery, but while they relieved me of one difficulty, they brought on another even more painful than the one of which I was relieved. The more I read, the more I was led to abhor and detest my enslavers.

Obviously, Douglass's experience as a slave determined his strong response to his reading. The words he read spoke directly to his condition, shaping his previously inexpressible desires and emotions into language. He was, of course, the perfect audience for Richard Brinsley Sheridan's "bold denunciation of slavery and powerful vindication of human rights." But had Douglass's master and mistress read the same speech, they might well have reacted in a strongly negative way, finding Sheridan subversive of their position as slave owners. They might have characterized his denunciation as "too bold" and his vindication of human rights as "wrongheaded" rather than "powerful." We might read Sheridan today and respond to his speech as an effective piece of eighteenth-century rhetoric or as an interesting historical document. On the other hand, if we have lived in places where human rights are greatly restricted, we might find Sheridan's speech as powerful and bold as Douglass did.

This does not mean, of course, that one's responses are limited to a strictly personal point of view. As we determine the basis for our most personal responses, we can begin to read with greater discipline and to think more systematically about what we read. First of all, we are able to realize that not everyone will have the same responses that we do. This, in turn, can help us recognize what may be limitations in our original responses, limitations imposed perhaps by our *lack* of experience ("Well, sure, I guess if I had been using blank checks all my life and got a letter like that out of the blue, threatening me with 'possible embarrassment' if I didn't start using the magnetically coded ones, I wouldn't have liked it very much either. But what's his point in making a joke of it?"). Opening up a text for ourselves will almost always mean moving beyond those important initial responses to asking ourselves implicit questions about what is being said, how it is being said, and why it is being said in this particular way.

Obviously, we can't fully comprehend what we are reading until we have read through it completely. Not until we reach White's final line ("Imagine a bank forgetting to sign its name!") do all the various strands of thought that he has been pursuing begin to fall clearly into place. At this point a second reading (and maybe a third or a fourth) will allow us to pay more attention to how a writer has presented the material because our curiosity has been satisfied as to what the text is about and we have a sense of it as a whole. In rereading it, we may discover points we have missed or misinterpreted; other of our experiences may begin to come to bear ("This is like that letter I got from the registrar's office informing me that from now on I'd have to have financial aid forms notarized and submit them with my term bill"). Consequently, our responses will be different, and we may significantly revise our initial reading. We can also begin in this second reading to question the text more closely to discover its intentions and its structure. This questioning may take a number of forms (which we'll be considering later in this discussion), but in all cases it's a good idea to write down your responses, beginning with those that arise during the initial reading. Writing helps us to think more clearly and deeply about what we read and to preserve our thoughts for further development.

Elements of Reading

Earlier we pointed out some basic similarities between reading E. B. White's "Dear Mr. . . ." on the editorial page of the *New York Times* and reading the same essay in a textbook as an assignment for an English composition course. However, as you already know from experience, many elements of your reading can vary, depending on the situation. What you read and why you read will always influence the way you read.

For example, a *Times* buyer in the fall of 1967 would have read White's essay primarily for what we can call "pleasure." "Pleasure," of course, can take many forms: we may read for amusement, for escape, for intellectual discovery and stimulation, even to get angry or to make ourselves more depressed. But it's clear that we *choose* to do such reading because of a definite personal interest. No one is asking us to look for anything or remember anything. Ironically, though, we will often remember what we read for pleasure more clearly and more fully than what we read under pressure, because our minds are more relaxed. On such occasions, we have time to pause over a word or a phrase just because we like the sound of it or the feeling it expresses. So, while the pleasure that arises from personal interest may be our primary purpose for reading, we may also be assimilating new information, analyzing a particularly striking passage to understand how it works, or evaluating what a writer has to say, all because we enjoy what we are doing.

Taking account of how you read for pleasure, then, can help you read more effectively in other situations; you can even use your personal reading to help you develop habits that will make you a better reader generally. One way is to take the time to make note of your immediate responses. For example, you may want to remember a particular piece of information or to hold on to a word or phrase that made an impression; to respond evaluatively, agreeing or disagreeing with what the writer has to say; or to explore responses that the writer has triggered. Begin to record such responses in writing. Keep a notebook handy to use as a journal of observations, information, and impressions. You can then refer to this journal for ideas to use in your own writing. Taking pleasure in working with new concepts and new information is an important step in becoming a better reader.

Reading in its broadest sense (as White's bank's computer *reads* his magnetic "code-name") always implies taking in information. We do so whenever and whatever we read. But grasping the most pertinent information in a text requires that we read with an awareness of the author's purpose for writing. An author's primary purpose may be reflective, reportorial, explanatory, or argumentative. Each of these purposes entails a different kind of writing, and thus each calls for a somewhat different kind of reading, as we show in our introductions to the sections "Reflecting," "Reporting," "Explaining," and "Arguing." For example, when we read White's argumentative piece about the computerized numbers on his checks, we must weigh the merits of competing ideas—of his antitechnological outlook versus the technological needs of the bank and its customers. But when we read "'This Is the End of the World: The Black Death'" (pp. 159–168), Barbara Tuchman's reportorial piece about the medieval plague, we concern ourselves not with controversial issues but with the details of a particular historical event. So, whenever you are assigned a piece of reading, you should try to determine the author's primary purpose as quickly as possible. Then you will have a better idea of what to focus on as you read and study the material for class discussions, paper assignments, or tests.

Whatever type of reading you are doing, in whatever field of study, you will generally be called upon to analyze, understand, memorize, and possibly evaluate the most important information and ideas that it contains. In order to sort out the most pertinent information and make sense of it for yourself, you will probably find it helpful to use a combination of the following methods:

(1) *Synoptic Reading.* Begin by reading the piece through from beginning to end primarily to get a quick overall sense of the author's subject, purpose, major ideas, and information. This initial reading is meant to help you get acquainted with the piece as a whole, so don't let yourself get bogged down in details as you make your way through the text. But don't hesitate to underline or check off what seem to be important (or puzzling) words, phrases, sentences, ideas, and points of information that you want to look into later when you examine the piece in detail. Once you have completed your initial reading of the piece, you should jot down a few notes about what you consider to be the gist of the piece—its major subject, purpose, points, and information.

(2) *Annotating.* After you have gathered the gist of the piece, then you should annotate the material for yourself. An annotation consists of explanatory notes. So if the piece contains words, names, titles of works, or other bits of information with which you are unfamiliar, you should consult a dictionary, encyclopedia, or other reference work, jotting down explanatory notes that you can use for future reference. This procedure will help you not only to understand the piece but also to expand both your vocabulary and your storehouse of general knowledge.

(3) *Outlining.* Once you have annotated the piece, then you may find it useful to make an outline of the material that it contains. An outline systematically lists the major ideas, points, and bits of information according to the order that they appear in the piece. The process of making an outline will help

you to understand the piece more reliably and thoroughly than you can by simply reading it over once or twice. And the outline itself will serve as an invaluable aid to remembering the piece at a later date, when you may want to draw upon it for a paper or examination. In preparing an outline, you might be tempted to rely entirely on your initial reading, underlinings, and notes. But just to make sure that your outline is reliable, you should read the piece carefully a second time with an eye to getting down the most important material in a form that is accurately worded and arranged. Here, for example, is an outline of White's piece.

I. White's bank informs him that the Federal Reserve System will no longer process checks written on a "blank form," and that he must, therefore, use checks with computer-legible identification numbers.
II. White opposes this requirement because
    A. It is inconvenient for the individual bank customer, and
    B. It subordinates the needs and desires of the individual to the will of the government banking system.
III. White's bank further informs him that the government's adoption of a computerized check-processing system was necessitated by "the tremendous increase in the use of checks."
IV. White is dissatisfied with this explanation because
    A. He believes it is based on a faulty assumption that the increase in checks could only have been processed by computers, and
    B. He believes that computers lack human mental capacities and thus should not be given influence over human affairs.

(4) *Summarizing.* Instead of outlining the piece, you may prefer to summarize it. A summary, like an outline, offers a highly condensed version of the most important material in a piece. But rather than casting the material in a numbered and lettered list, a summary calls upon you to write a paragraph of continuous prose in which you identify the major purpose, ideas, arguments, and information. The process of summarizing, like that of outlining, is a valuable aid to understanding a piece, and the summary itself will also serve as an aid to remembering the piece at a later date. The ability to summarize is an especially important skill in writing research papers, for they usually call upon you to condense material that you have read and integrate it into your own discussion. So you should try your hand at summarizing a few of the pieces that you read in this collection. Here, for example, is a summary of White's piece.

    White's intention is to challenge the Federal Reserve System's computerized system of processing bank checks. White opposes the changeover from blank forms to checks with computer-legible numbers, because it inconveniences individual citizens and thus subordinates the needs of the individual to the will of the federal banking system. He also opposes the changeover because he considers it to be based on a faulty assumption that the increasing use of checks could only be

9

handled by computers. Finally, he opposes the changeover because he believes that computers lack human mental capacities and thus should not be allowed to have so much influence over human affairs.

A special kind of summary, known as an *abstract*, is also customary in highly specialized professional journals, which require an author to provide a very brief summary at the beginning of an article for the convenience of readers. (For a sample abstract, see Antonio R. Damasio, "Face Perception without Recognition," p. 563. See also the synopsis that comes at the beginning of "Aircraft Accident Report" by the National Transportation Safety Board, p. 287.)

(5) *Analyzing and Evaluating.* Instead of outlining or summarizing a piece, you may find it necessary to analyze and evaluate it, particularly if you need to understand it in detail. In order to analyze a text carefully and thoughtfully, we suggest that you read it over with several key questions in mind that you want to answer for yourself. Each of these questions, as you will see in the following, is designed to focus on a different aspect of the piece—its purpose, organization, evidence, implied audience, and use of language. In the following paragraphs, we will use White's "Dear Mr. . . ." to show how you can analyze a text by asking and answering a set of questions about it.

What is the writer's purpose? White's immediate purpose is to describe his responses to the letter from his bank, ranging from personal annoyance to ironic evaluations of why a change should be required to a note of wry defiance. These personal reflections revolve around a more general and serious point, which he states fairly directly in paragraph 5 and again in paragraph 10: he thinks it is a "defeat," a "surrender" to allow machines to inconvenience "all" (and himself, in particular) for the sake of making life easier for a powerful few. Allied with this idea is White's belief that computers are "deficient" in the qualities which make us human and that, consequently, they should not be allowed to usurp human transactions (paragraph 11). His conclusion is a refusal to "knuckle under" to the dictates of such machines.

How does the writer organize his or her material? White's reflections are organized around the information contained in the letter he received from his bank. His title is an ironic version of the letter's salutation, and his concluding sentence refers to the lack of a closing signature. In paragraphs 1, 2, 6, and 7, he quotes from the letter, directly or indirectly, and goes on to offer his specific responses. Paragraphs 10 and 11 represent a new, more general direction of thought that grows out of his specific responses to the letter. Paragraph 12 returns to the letter and reinforces White's reactionary position on encroaching impersonality.

10

Does the writer use appropriate evidence and logic to support the points he or she is trying to make? White is not offering a formal or systematic argument, but a more personal consideration of his subject, so we should not necessarily expect detailed, enumerated evidence or other methodical forms of support. Instead, he offers imaginative and playful appeals based on personal experience, particularly in paragraphs 3, 4, 8, 9, 10, and 11. Though his appeals are witty, he does not provide any kind of support for his repeated claims of being inconvenienced, nor does he offer even an imaginative or whimsical alternative to computer processing as a means of dealing with the "tremendous increase in the use of checks."

What are the writer's assumptions about his or her audience? White's essay was written for the *New York Times*, so he could assume that his readers would be a reasonably well-informed group, many of whom would have themselves received similar letters from their banks. Even so, he is careful to explain the change the bank is demanding as well as its practical effects. (A further question you might consider is whether the writer assumes his or her readers will be generally sympathetic with, antagonistic toward, or neutral about the ideas being raised. What would you say about White's assumptions?)

What kind of language and imagery does the writer use? White is responding to what he regards as a ridiculous letter with very serious implications. His language is resolutely informal and conversational; phrases like "spooky numbers," "kept my mouth shut," "palm off," "enough lettuce," and "wear the pants" can be contrasted to the kind of communication he is criticizing. Yet when he has a serious point to make (for example, that computers "are deficient in humor, they are not intuitive, and they are not aware of the imponderables"), his language becomes more formal. His images—particularly his personification of the bank as a letter-writing entity—are comic or wryly sarcastic, but, as with his language, they don't overwhelm his underlying seriousness.

In responding to questions such as these, a reader is able to take a piece of writing apart and examine its components to see how it works. In many situations, so careful an analysis won't be necessary: you would have little reason, for example, to analyze a comprehensive textbook in this way. However, analytical skill can be applied to a wide variety of activities and, in particular, can help a reader move beyond simply personal responses to a more systematic evaluation of a piece of writing.

Suppose that your initial response to the White essay was something like, "I enjoyed this; it was funny." A second analytical reading then helped you to understand the workings of the essay and how the tone and imagery contributed to your interest and appreciation. Further analysis of your own initial responses perhaps led you to realize that you share White's suspicion of computers and

11

his subversive reaction to impersonal, bureaucratic pronouncements. This, in turn, has given you a sense of how others, who do not particularly share your views, might respond. Now you may develop a more systematic evaluation of the essay, using topics like the following to assess or judge the essay:

Purpose. White has succeeded well in presenting his own reactions with wit and grace. His conversational tone and his wry imagery allow a reader to sympathize with his very human rebellion against being inconvenienced because of the requirements of a machine.

Organization. Organizing his essay around the letter he received from his bank is an effective way for White to move from his specific responses to his more general considerations about the relationship between technology and human life. This organization also leads him to his important central image of a bank that forgets "to sign its name."

Evidence. Because White is relating his responses rather than arguing a position, the personal evidence he presents (the inconvenience the new rules will cause him, the computer-composed poem, and so on) is sufficient to communicate aptly and forcefully his reason for feeling the way he does. What White's evidence does not do, however, is to convince us that carrying checks with the magnetic code is a terrible inconvenience. White simply assumes that his reader will agree. Consequently, his general comments on computer technology—particularly from the perspective of almost twenty years—don't carry the weight they might.

Summary. White's essay is an entertaining and thought-provoking revelation of what it's like to be told to modify old habits in order to conform to the dictates of new technology. The clarity of his organization, the grace of his style, and the wit of his personality are engaging and continuously appealing. Although we may not finally agree with the specific basis for his objections or with his underlying argument, we can't help but be persuaded by his sincerity, skill, and good sense that his attitudes are admirably humane and that they suggest some of the perils that beset an increasingly complex society.

This, of course, is only the beginning of only one evaluation. These notations—or another set that might be entirely contradictory—could be expanded and developed into an evaluative essay that presents reasons and evidence based on further research, perhaps into other essays by White or studies of computerized banking. Such an essay might be highly supportive (as our sample summary would indicate), or highly critical ("Though White's essay is very clever, the subversive point of view he expresses here is just a few steps from anarchy"), or it might take an intermediate position. It might concentrate on

12

the consequences of the writer's ideas, or the success of the writer's methods, or some combination of the two.

As you may already have begun to realize, becoming a more astute reader can lay the groundwork for becoming a more effective writer. The more reading we do—the more we understand our role as a reader—the more we learn about what it means to be an audience. By paying attention to our responses, by examining them in order to analyze and evaluate what we read, we can begin to see more clearly *why* we feel well or poorly treated by a writer. Transferring such knowledge from our own experience as an audience to the audience for whom we are writing, we become more aware of what that intended audience will require. We become more concerned about the appropriate tone to take, about what does and doesn't need to be said about a topic, given our purpose, and we have a better idea of the organization necessary to gain and hold our audience's interest and bring our work to a satisfactory conclusion. We realize more fully the transaction that must take place, and how we as writers can encourage a reader to collaborate in the making of meaning. In "Writing and Rewriting" we will consider this subject in more detail.

WRITING AND REWRITING

As we discussed in "Reading and Rereading," expressing your ideas will often begin with recording your most immediate responses, jotting them down on a pad, in a journal, or in the margin of a book. Clearly, such jottings are not intended for a reader. You may be surprised to realize, however, that with thought and care and concern for an eventual audience, even the sketchiest notes can evolve into a significant, controlled piece of writing. This process of development and revision is rarely apparent when we read: all we see is the finished product, the piece of writing in its final form. But the polished work that is presented to an audience may, in fact, barely resemble what the writer started out with.

E. B. White didn't simply sit down the afternoon he received the warning from his bank and allow "Dear Mr. . . ." to flow out onto a page (if you haven't yet read White's essay, you'll find it on p. 1). The letter sparked a response, however—a sense of injustice, of annoyance at the threat of "embarrassment" and concern about the effects of technology—and White realized that here was at least the germ of an essay that might eventually find its way into print, earning him a bit of money and the satisfaction of reaching an audience with his concerns. His first thought, though, was merely to provide himself with a rough rendering of his immediate response. Consequently, his original notes (which we include on pp. 14–17) do little more than sketch out his basic intentions and establish a point of view.

White's notes bear almost no resemblance to his polished final draft as it appeared in the *New York Times*. We see White beginning with his immediate

I seldom carry a checkbook because I like to travel light but I always have money in the bank (it is an old habit of mine that I cant seem to break) and I feel that I should be free to dispense this money without any embarrassment to myself. Now, because of the Federal Reserve's knuckly under, I will not be privileged to write a blank check

The ~~only most~~ danger ~~of~~ in a
machine culture is that ~~it~~
in the enjoyment of
the convenience of machines,
~~will to we some~~, will ~~overshadow~~
their disadvantages to others

The danger in a machine
culture is not that ~~machine~~
~~will take over our thinking~~
~~and dominate it in our lives~~, but
~~that even, who~~ the convenience
of machines may come to
overshadow the losses we suffer
~~from their~~ by reason of their
peculiar requirements —

Computers free the Federal Reserve from arduous and voluminous ~~~~ operations in clearing checks. But in so doing they deprive the ^narrow consumer's ^right ~~but the privilege~~ of instructing his bank in a casual, agreeable manner

The man who foresaw all
this was a man named
Orwell. and he foresaw
pretty good. If were
not careful. we may
wake up some morning
and find that what he
predicted has come to
pass.

personal response—his desire to dispense his money without any embarrassment or inconvenience to himself—and then moving on to generalize, to expand his annoyance over the particular letter to the larger issue of "the danger in a machine culture." Thus, he establishes the meaning and purpose that will govern his final essay. But there is little attempt to formulate a coherent design at this point. In fact, it is almost comforting to see how messy these initial notes are, when we realize the product for which they will provide the foundation.

Even as White is scribbling notes to himself, however, with little concern for coherence and the needs of his eventual reader, he is his own critic. He is listening to himself as he writes, thinking about how his words go together, and revising when he's not quite satisfied. He has, for example, reworked the sentence about "the danger in a machine culture" several times, trying to get it right (although, as we'll see in his subsequent drafts, this central idea would continue to give him trouble). But he is not particularly concerned with correctness; for instance, he lets stand a sentence like "The man who foresaw all this was a man named Orwell, and he foresaw pretty good." No sentence like this will, in fact, appear in the final draft, but what White seems to be after here is a kind of aptness. Orwell is a touchstone for White's ideas, a way of getting at what he wants to say and finding the words to generalize about his particular situation.

Based on these very rough notes, White typed a first draft, onto which he wrote in further revisions (see pp. 19–21).

This step from notes to first draft is significant: the essay is actually beginning to take shape here. White has used the letter from his bank to provide an opening and conclusion, but you'll note that he has not yet discovered the precise design that will allow his finished work to revolve around this letter. In fact, he has to wrench his attention back to the letter in the final paragraph, after a digression about his bank statement and balancing his checkbook. Nor has he quite developed the important image of the bank as a letter writer (although he *has* begun to personify the bank in his opening sentence and later on when he writes, "Banks love money . . ."; and he has also—perhaps for very practical reasons—assumed the pose of not being able to remember his bank's name). The idea about "the danger in a machine culture," which he struggled with in his original notes, appears here in a quite different form—a specific reference to the bank accommodating the Federal Reserve rather than customers—and, consequently, the incident has not yet been fully generalized.

Again, though, White is his own critic. The draft is messy and chewed over, with typed emendations as well as handwritten ones. Some of these changes seem to show White trying to capture fleeting thoughts, slapping them down on paper, as he did in his notes, to save and cull from later. Others are based on his concern for how an audience will respond (the deletion of the line about banks employing "retarded children" is a good example), while still others are

which I don't often do but which I
consider a great convenience in
certain circumstances.

My bank, which I have forgotten the name of
in the excitement of the moment, sent me a ~~notice~~ *warning* the other
day. It ~~read~~ *was headed =*: "An important notice to all our checking account
customers." The burden of this communication was ~~this~~ that
~~the Federal Reserve System~~ I would no longer be allowed to
write ~~submit~~ checks that did not bear the special series of
"magnetic ink numbers" along the base. ~~Then~~ My bank said ~~that~~
the Federal Reserve System had notified them that it will not
accept for processing any checks that don't bear these curious *form*
numbers. ~~(That~~ For example, I would not be allowed to write a check on a blank
~~(I've~~ I've never been very fond of these numbers, since
I first laid eyes on them---they look tonme kike numbers that
have been ~~run over~~ *backed into* by a dump truck *that* or have deve,oped rheumoatoid
joints
arthritis, and their knuckles have swollen. But, I have kept my *although the numbers did*
mouth shut, until now.) Now it appears that we are going
to knuckle under to machines, and that I am no longer orivelegd
to write a check on a blank form, because it lacks these ~~magnetic~~ *spooky*
little numbers. This, I thinkm is a defeat, a surrender. (*or mankind*)
~~I plan to go on~~ *It was a clear alternative = whether to accommodate bank customers*
name, to dispense my money in the way I want it dispensed, witjout
any reference to magnetic ink numbers. I will be ~~very~~ iiterested t
to see what gappens. *by letter, then write blank checks, or whether to
accommodate the Federal Reserve.*

palm off
~~put over~~ a check that lacks the magnetic ink numbers, it cannot *the check*
be processed without /delay, extra handling charges, and possible
embarrassment." *to me -* | *am*

The notice I received says that if I try to

rather easily embarrassed---it doesn't take much----and I would like [of course] [am ~~keeps~~ eager]

to ~~know~~ [learn] what form this embarrassment is going to take if I should

decide to write a check using the old blank form that has proved

so convenient for I don't know how many decades, when one is stuck
without one's checkbook or enough lettuce to carry the day.
                    The reason given by my bank for this tightening

of its service is ~~that~~ this: "The tremendous increase in the use of

checks made it necessary for the Federal Reserve to establish a

completely computerized operation for processing all checks from all

banks. Their computer can function only when proper magnetic numbers
            Well, I can believe that   last
are used." ~~Ixcanxbelievexthixxlast~~ part, about the computer requiring

a special diet of funny numbers, ---this I can believe. But I am

suspicious of that first statement, about how the Federal Reserve
would have been unable   had gone over
cou dn't carry on unless it went over to machines. I think the truth
                                    and adventurous
is ~~itxfoundxtt~~ the Federal Reserve found machines handy, and that's
                                    But   we had had, in this country
why it went over to them. Suppose there had been a tremendous increase
                    and nobody had got round to inventing the computer
in the use of checks but the computer hadn't been invented---what would

h va happened then? Would ~~bankingxhavex~~ banks have ~~givenxupxths~~
            [Would the Federal Reserve System have collapsed from exhaustion.] [the]
thrown in the sponge? I know banks better than that---they would [duh.]
                    [and educate them later]
have cleared those checks ~~if they had to employ retarded children~~ to
                    and they are not easily deflected from accumulating it.
~~do it.~~ Banks love money. ~~Soxdoxlyxecomxxtvxvxhintvxnfxttvxvxv~~

Come to think it, I love money, too. I am a lifelong checking account

patron and have had to be ~~trunnxrtn~~ extremely thrifty because of my

refusal to balance my checkbook in the space on the left where you

are supposd to keep track of what you've been spending and depositing.

I've never done that, on the theory that it is a waste of time--also
            [I subtract good]   [misleading]
I don't add good, and my figures would be ~~deceptive~~ because inaccurate.

Instead, I practice thrift and never know my balance until I receive [my]
                    in the days before machines
[month] statement. Speaking of bank statements, mine used to arrive the first

3

of the month and was legible and decipherable and coherent. Now, since machines have taken over, it arrives anywhere from the
largely
first of the month to the eighth of the month, and is indecipherable, except to a man hell bent on deciphering something.

The notice

To get back to the warning from my bank, it ended: "So remember...be sure to use only your own personal checks with pre-encoded magnetic ink numbering. It takes both your account number and your signature for your check to clear properly. Thank you very much."

"improvements," revisions of vocabulary and syntax to clarify meaning or create more graceful, forceful expression.

In his second draft, White continues to revise, to tighten his structure and refine his language (see pp. 23–25).

The pieces have begun to fall more gracefully into place here. Most important, perhaps, White gets rid of the digression about bank statements at the end of his first draft and replaces it with the more general reflections he has been aiming toward all along. Note how the troublesome sentence from his notes about "the danger in a machine culture" has found its place in the penultimate paragraph of this second draft. (Note, as well, how White has continued to rework and refine it.)

In the handwritten emendations of this draft, we also see White sharpening the wit of his reflections, particularly as he develops his wry personification of his bank and computers in general ("a certain magnetism that computers insist on" and "machines that admire these numbers"). And it is not until now, in his attempt to bring the essay to a satisfactory close, that White adds the final, memorable image of "a bank forgetting to sign its name," an image that eventually grows very naturally out of his process of revising, of focusing and clarifying his ideas in order to make his point most vividly for his audience. Names are no longer important; all that matters now is a magnetic code for computers to read.

Reading White's finished essay as it appeared in the *New York Times*, we have a hard time realizing that he didn't know exactly what he had in mind when he sat down to write. When a piece of writing is successful, we do not see the seams; the words carry us along so that we are not aware of the writer's process. But it is clear from White's notes and his drafts that this graceful, carefully conceived essay required a great deal of work: jotting, scratching out, drafting, rewriting, private questions and decisions, moments of inspiration when the connections began to seem clear, when the work seemed to pay off. What we learn from White's manuscripts is that ideas don't spring full blown from a writer's mind into a clear, coherent form. Rather, ideas may tumble out in unformed, fragmented ways that can be developed, modified, and sharpened draft after draft.

Composition is, then, a process, and the practical implications for student writers are readily apparent. It takes time to put what you have to say, your most personal and immediate responses, into a form that an audience can understand and appreciate, into words that will best express your intentions. Waiting to begin a writing assignment until the night before it is due will not allow this sort of time. Fully developed ideas are the result of revising, of working step by step, and require a series of working sessions over the course of several days or several weeks. Only then can you take full advantage of your reading and writing skills in order to produce a final draft that seems to be ready

My bank, which I have forgotten the name of in the excitement of the moment, sent me a warning the other day. It was headed: "An important notice to all our checking account customers." The burden of this communication was that I would no longer be allowed to write checks that did not bear the special series of magnetic ink numbers along the base. My bank said the Federal Reserve System had notified them that it will not accept for processing any checks that don't show these knobby little digits. For example, I would no longer be free to write a check on a blank form, because it would lack ~~the~~ a. ~~magnetic numbers~~ certain magnetism that computers insist on.

I first encountered these spooky numbers a few years back and took a dislike to them. ~~They~~ They looked like numbers that had been run over by a dump truck, or that had developed rheumatoid arthritis and their joints had swollen. But I kept my mouth shut [about them] as they seemed to be doing me no harm. Now, however, it appears that we are all going to knuckle under to machines ~~and will have to forego~~ the that admire these numbers. We must all forego the pleasure and convenience of writing a check on an ordinary, non-magnetic piece of paper. My signature used to be enough to prod my bank into dispatching some of my money to some needy individual or firm, ~~but~~ not any more. This, I think, is a defeat for all---a surrender. In order to accommodate the Federal Reserve system, we are asked ~~going~~ to put ourselves out.

The notice I received says that if I try to

270

2

palm off a check that lacks the magnetic ink numbers, the check
cannot be processed without "delay, extra handling charges, and
possible embarrassment."   I embarrass easy---it doesn't take
much, really---and naturally I am eager to learn what form this
embarrassment will take if I should decide to write a check using
the old blank form that has proved so convenient for I don't know
how many decades on those occasions when one is stuck without
his checkbook or enough lettuce to carry the day.

             "The tremendous increase in the use of checks,"
writes my bank , warming to its subject, "made it necessary for
the Federal Reserve to establish a completely computerized operation for processing all checks from all banks. Their computer
can function only when proper magnetic numbers are used." Well,
I can believe that last part, about the computer requiring a
special diet of ~~deranged numbers~~ malformed numbers; but I am
suspicious of that first statement, about how the Federal Reserve
would have been unable to carry on unless it went over to machines.
I suspect that the Federal Reserve simply found machines useful,
handy, and ~~sustaining to its ego.~~ adventurous But suppose we had had,
in this country, a tremendous increase in the use of checks and
nobody had yet got round to inventing the computer---what would have
happened then? Am I supposed to believe that the Federal Reserve
and all their member banks would have thrown in the sponge? I
know banks better than that. Banks love money and are not easily
deflected from the ~~exhausting~~ delicious business of accumulating
it. ~~Somehow they would have found~~ Love would have found a way.
Checks would have cleared.

             I'm not against machines, as are some people

3

who feel that the computer is leading us down the primrose
trail. I ~~kxxxxxxxxx~~ like machines---particularly the egg
beater, which is the machine at its finest and most mysterious. *the highest point has yet reached*
~~But~~ I8m only against machines when the convenience they afford
to ~~xxxxxxx xxxxxxxxxxxxx~~ overshadwos the ~~in~~inconvience they *some is considered more important than*
cause to ~~xxx xxxx~~. In short, I don't think computers should *all* *50*
wear the pants, or even make the decisions---~~sxxxxxxx~~. They
lack humor, and they are not intuitive--or even aware ofthe
mponderables. I read a poem once written by a computer but,
didn't care much for it. It seemed to me I could write a better
one myself, if I put my mind to it, and my heart in it. *100*

And now I must look around for a blank check.
It's time I found out what form ~~txxxxxxxxxx~~ my new embarrssment
is going to take. First, thoulg, I'll have o remember the
name of my bank. It'll come to me, if I sit here long enough. *150*

Oddly enough, the warning notice I received contained no signature. Imagine a bank forgetting to sign its name!

174
278
270
722

for an audience. What you end with will very likely come a long way from how you begin.

You've just seen, of course, how E. B. White began. You'll find what he ended with on page 1.

ACKNOWLEDGING SOURCES

In most of the writing that you do both during and after college, you will probably find yourself drawing upon the ideas, information, and statements of others, interpreting this material, and putting it together with your own experience, observation, and thought to generate new ideas of your own. Some of this material will come from your reading, some of it from lectures and class discussions, some of it from conversations and interviews. Our thinking about things does not, after all, take place in a vacuum, but is shaped by a wide array of influences and sources. Thus, we invariably have an obligation to others that we can only repay by giving credit where credit is due—that is, by acknowledging the sources we have used in our thinking and writing.

To acknowledge your intellectual debts is by no means a confession that your work is unoriginal or without merit. In fact, original work in every field and profession invariably builds in some way and to some extent on the prior work of other researchers and thinkers. Most pieces that you find in this book, except for those that deal entirely with personal experience, include some kind of acknowledgment or reference to the ideas, information, or statements of others. By acknowledging their sources, the writers of these pieces implicitly establish exactly what is new or special in their own way of thinking about something. Acknowledging sources will also enable readers to corroborate your claims and to find material that they wish to investigate in connection with their own research and writing. For a variety of important reasons, then, you should always make sure that you acknowledge any and all sources that you have used in preparing a piece of writing.

In order to get some idea of the various ways in which sources can be acknowledged, you might find it useful to scan several of the pieces in this collection. Some writers, you will notice, cite only the names of authors or interviewees and/or the titles of works from which they have gathered ideas and information or quoted statements; these citations are incorporated into the written discussion, as you can see by looking at Martin Luther King, Jr.'s "Pilgrimage to Nonviolence," the Associated Press "Report of an Airplane Crash," Susan Fraker's "Why Women Aren't Getting to the Top," or Stephen Jay Gould's "Evolution as Fact and Theory." Other writers use footnotes or endnotes in which they provide not only names of authors or interviewees and titles of works, but also dates of publication or of interviews and specific page references, as you can see by looking at Theodore R. Sizer's "What High School Is," Tania Modleski's "Soap Opera, Melodrama, and Women's Anger," Antonio

R. Damasio's "Face Perception without Recognition," Frances FitzGerald's "America Revised," or Phillip Knightley's "The First Televised War." Finally, some writers, instead of using footnotes, provide author and page references in the text of their discussion, and include more detailed publication data, such as titles and dates of publication, in a complete list of works cited at the end of their discussion, as you can see by looking at Carol Gilligan's "Woman's Place in a Man's Life Cycle."

These various forms of acknowledgment are usually determined by the different purposes and audiences for which authors have written their pieces. For example, personal essays, newspaper reports, and magazine articles, which are written for a general audience, tend to rely on a more casual and shorthand form of acknowledgment, citing only the author and/or title of the source in the body of the discussion. Pieces written for a more specialized audience, such as academic research papers and scholarly articles or books, tend to rely on a more detailed and systematic form of acknowledgment, using either footnotes, or a combination of references in the text with a complete list of works cited at the end of the text. These specialized forms of acknowledgment vary somewhat from one field to another, but in general you will find that research papers in the arts and humanities tend to follow the guidelines set down in the *Modern Language Association Handbook for Writers of Research Papers*, Third Edition (1988), and that research papers in the social sciences and sciences tend to follow the guidelines set down in *The Publication Manual of the American Psychological Association*, Third Edition (1983).

If you are ever in doubt about the form of acknowledgment to be used in any of your courses, don't hesitate to ask your instructor for guidance. Most instructors do have special preferences of one kind or another. But whatever their special preferences may be, they all expect you to acknowledge your sources.

REFLECTING

REFLECTING

Here in "Reflecting," as in other parts of this collection, you will encounter writing that touches upon a wide range of topics—from a high school graduation in Arkansas to a sacred landmark in Oklahoma, from the structure of a grain of salt to the personality of Albert Einstein. But you will also find that the writing in this particular section relies very heavily on personal experience. This personal element may strike you at first as being out of place in a college textbook. However, if you consider the matter just a bit, you will see that personal experience is a basic source of knowledge and understanding. Think for a moment about someone you have known for a long time, or about a long-remembered event in your life; then think about what you have learned from being with that person or going through that event, and you will see that personal experience is, indeed, a valuable source of knowledge. You will probably also notice that in thinking about that person or event you rely very heavily on your remembrance of things past—on your memory of particular words, or deeds, or gestures, or scenes that are especially important to you. Your memory, after all, is the storehouse of your personal knowledge, and whenever you look into this storehouse, you will invariably find an image or impression of your past experience. So, you should not be surprised to find the authors in this section looking into their own memories as they might look into a mirror. Ultimately, the activity of looking back is a hallmark of reflection because it involves writers in recalling and thinking about some aspect of their world in order to make sense of it for themselves and for others.

This essential quality of reflective writing can be seen in the following passage from George Orwell's "Shooting an Elephant":

> One day something happened which in a roundabout way was enlightening. It was a tiny incident in itself, but it gave me a better glimpse than I had had before of the real nature of imperialism—the real motives for which despotic governments act. Early one morning the sub-inspector at a police station the other end of the town rang me up on the 'phone and said that an elephant was ravaging the bazaar. Would I please come and do something about it? I did not know what I could do, but I wanted to see what was happening and I got on to a pony and started out.

This passage, which comes from the third paragraph of Orwell's essay, clearly presents him as being in a reflective frame of mind. In the opening sentence, for example, he looks back to a specific event from his personal experiences in Burma—to "One day" when "something happened." And in the midst of looking back, he also makes clear that this event is important to him because "in a roundabout way" it "was enlightening." Again, in the second sentence, he looks back not only to the event, "a tiny incident in itself," but also to the understanding that he gained from the event—"a better glimpse than I had had before of the real nature of imperialism—the real motives for which despotic governments act." Having announced the general significance of this event, he then returns to looking back at the event itself, to recalling the particular things that happened that day—the phone call informing him "that an elephant was ravaging the bazaar," the request that he "come and do something about it," and his decision to get "on to a pony" in order "to see what was happening."

This alternation between recalling things and commenting on their significance is typical not only of Orwell's piece, but of all the writing in this section. Sometimes, the alternation takes place within a single sentence, as in the opening of the previous passage. Sometimes, the alternation occurs between sentences or clusters of sentences, as in the following paragraph from Loren Eiseley's "The Bird and the Machine":

> I suppose their little bones have years ago been lost among the stones and winds of those high glacial pastures. I suppose their feathers blew eventually into the piles of tumbleweed beneath the straggling cattle fences and rotted there in the mountain snows, along with dead steers and all the other things that drift to an end in the corners of the wire. I do not quite know why I should be thinking of birds over the *New York Times* at breakfast, particularly the birds of my youth half a continent away. It is a funny thing what the brain will do with memories and how it will treasure them and finally bring them into odd juxtapositions with other things, as though it wanted to make a design, or get something out of them, whether you want it or not, or even see it.

The first two sentences of this passage portray Eiseley as being in a contemplative mood, remembering some birds that he had evidently seen years ago in a high mountain pasture and wondering what became of them. But in the third sentence he is no longer wondering about the fate of the birds, so much as about the focus of his thoughts, about why he "should be thinking of birds over the *New York Times* at breakfast." His curiosity about the movement of his own mind then provokes him in the fourth sentence to reflect on the workings of the human brain, especially on "what the brain will do with memories." Though he ranges quite widely here and later in the piece, each image or idea that comes to his mind is occasioned either by a preceding memory or reflection or by some aspect of his immediate situation, such as his reading of the *Times*. His thoughts develop, then, by a process of association and suggestion, one thing leading to another. This linked sequence of memories, images, other bits of information, and ideas is typical of reflection. Reflective writing thus echoes the process that Eiseley attributes to the brain—calling upon memories, bringing them into "odd juxtapositions with other things," in order "to make a design, or get some meaning out of them."

The alternation between recalling and interpreting will vary from writer to writer, and work to work, depending on the details of the experience and the author's reflective purpose. Nevertheless, every piece of reflective writing will contain both kinds of material, for every reflective writer is concerned not only with sharing something memorable, but also with showing why it is memorable. And as it happens, most memorable experiences, images, or bits of information stick in our minds because they give us, as Orwell says, "a better glimpse than [we] had had before of the real nature of" someone, something, or some aspect of the world. So, as a reader of reflective writing, you should always be attentive not only to the details of an author's recollected experience, but also to the "glimpse" that it gives the author, and you, into the "real nature" of things. And in your own reflective writing, you should make sure that you convey both dimensions of your experience—both what happened and what the happenings enabled you to see.

THE RANGE OF REFLECTIVE WRITING

The range of reflective writing is in one sense limitless, for it necessarily includes the full range of things that make up our personal experience or the personal experience of anyone else in the world. Reflecting, in other words, may deal with anything that anyone has ever seen, or heard, or done, or thought about, and considered memorable enough to write about. Though the range of reflective writing is extraordinarily broad, the subject of any particular piece is likely to be very specific, and as it happens, most pieces can be classified in terms of a few recurrent types of subject matter.

A single, memorable event is often the center of attention in reflective writing, as in Maya Angelou's "Graduation," or George Orwell's "Shooting an Elephant." In reflecting on this kind of subject, the author will usually provide not only a meticulous detailing of the event itself, but also some opening background information that serves as a context for making sense of the event. In "Graduation," for example, Maya Angelou tells about all the pregraduation excitement in her home, at school, and around town before turning to the graduation ceremony itself. And in "Shooting an Elephant," Orwell gives an overall description of his life as a colonial officer in Burma before he turns to the story about shooting the elephant. The event, in turn, is of interest not only in itself but also for what it reveals to the author (and the reader) about some significant aspect of experience. Thus for Angelou, graduation remains memorable because it helped her to see how African-American people have been "sustained" by "Black known and unknown poets," and for Orwell, the shooting remains memorable because it helped him to see "the real nature of imperialism."

A notable person is another type of subject that often moves people to reflective writing, as in N. Scott Momaday's recollections of his grandmother, or Banesh Hoffmann's memories of Albert Einstein. In reflecting on a particular individual, most writers naturally seek to discover and convey what they consider to be the most essential or outstanding aspects of that person's character and ideas. In order to do so, they survey a number of memorable incidents or images from the life of that person. Momaday, for example, recalls not only the stories and legends that he heard from his grandmother, but also "the several postures that were peculiar to her" and her "long, rambling prayers." And Hoffmann remembers Einstein in a number of different professional and personal situations. In each case, the recollection of several experiences serves to reveal, define, and illustrate qualities that might otherwise remain obscure or abstract, such as the "ancient awe" of Momaday's grandmother, and the remarkable "simplicity" of Einstein.

Instead of concentrating on a particular person or event, reflective writing may center on a specific problem or significant issue in the past experience of an author, as in Frederick Douglass's "Learning to Read and Write," or Martin Luther King, Jr.'s "Pilgrimage to Nonviolence." A piece with this kind of subject is likely to touch upon a number of persons and events, and to encompass a substantial period of time, in the process of recalling and reflecting upon the problem with which it is concerned. Douglass, for example, covers seven years of his life in his piece about the problem of learning to read and write, and King recalls events and issues throughout his life that led him to espouse the principles of "nonviolent resistance." In each case, the breadth of coverage serves to reveal the scope and complexity of the problem, as well as the author's special understanding of it.

As you can see from just this brief survey of possibilities, reflective writing may deal with a single event, several events, or a whole lifetime of events. It may be as restricted in its attention as a close-up or as all encompassing as a wide-angle shot. But no matter how little, or how much, experience it takes into account, reflective writing is always decisively focused through the author's persistent attempt to make sense of the past, to push memory to the point of understanding the significance of experience.

METHODS OF REFLECTING

Your experience is unique, as is your memory, so in a sense you know the best methods to follow whenever you are of a mind to reflect upon something that interests you. But once you have recalled something in detail and made sense of it for yourself, you are still faced with the problem of how to present it to readers in a way that will also make sense to them. Given the fact that your readers will probably not be familiar with your experience, you will need to be very careful in selecting and organizing your material so that you give them a clearly detailed account of it. By the same token, you will need to give special emphasis to aspects or elements of your experience that will enable them to understand its significance. Usually, you will find that your choice of subject suggests a corresponding method of presenting it clearly and meaningfully to your readers.

If your reflections are focused on a single, circumscribed event, you will probably find it most appropriate to use a narrative presentation, telling your readers what happened in a relatively straightforward chronological order. Though you cover the event from beginning to end, your narrative should be carefully designed to emphasize the details that you consider most striking and significant. In "Shooting an Elephant," for example, Orwell devotes the largest segment in his piece to covering the very, very brief period of a few moments when he finds himself on the verge of having to shoot the elephant despite his strong desire not to do so. In fact, he devotes one-third of his essay to these few moments of inner conflict because they bring about one of his major insights— "that when the white man turns tyrant it is his own freedom that he destroys." So in telling about a memorable event of your own, you should deliberately pace your story to make it build toward some kind of climax or surprise or decisive incident, which in turn leads to a moment of insight for you (and your reader).

If your reflections are focused on a particular person, you will probably find it necessary to use both narrative and descriptive methods of presentation, telling about several events in order to make clear to readers the character and thought of the person in question. Though you rely heavily on narration, you will not be able to cover incidents in as much detail as if you were focusing on a single event. Instead, you will find it necessary to isolate only the most striking and significant details from each incident you choose to recall. In his recollection of Einstein, for example, Banesh Hoffmann includes more than fifteen separate anecdotes, but in each case he touches on only a couple of telling images or a few very memorable statements by Einstein. And Hoffmann isolates these particular details because they vividly reveal Einstein's most remarkable characteristics—"his knack for going instinctively to the heart of a matter" and "his extraordinary feeling for beauty." So, too, in writing about an individual whom you have known, you should carefully select and arrange the details that you recall to make them convey a clear and compelling impression of that person's character and ideas.

If your reflections are focused on a particular problem or issue in your past experience, you will probably need to combine narrative, descriptive, and explanatory methods of presentation, bringing together your recollections of numerous events and persons in order to reveal the nature and significance of

35

the problem. Although you will survey the problem chronologically from beginning to end, you will also need to organize your narrative so that it highlights the essential aspects, elements, or facets of the problem. For example, in "Pilgrimage to Nonviolence," King immediately focuses on the "new and sometimes complex doctrinal lands" through which he traveled. And from this point on, he recalls the various theological and philosophical ideas with which he struggled in formulating his belief in nonviolence. So in writing about a particular problem of your own, your recollections should be deliberately selected and organized to highlight your special understanding of the issue.

No matter what specific combination of methods you use in your reflective writing, you will probably find, as do most writers, that a striking recollection is the most effective way to interest your readers and that a significant observation about experience is the most rewarding means to send them on their way. In the following selections, you will get to see how a wide variety of writers use language to produce some very striking and significant pieces of reflection.

Arts and Humanities

GRADUATION
Maya Angelou

In her four volumes of autobiography, Maya Angelou (b. 1928) has written vividly of her struggles to achieve success as an actor, a dancer, a songwriter, a teacher, and a writer. An active worker in the civil rights movement in the 1960s, Angelou continues to focus much of her writing on racial issues. The following selection is from I Know Why the Caged Bird Sings *(1969), in which she writes, "I speak to the Black experience, but I am always talking about the human condition."*

The children in Stamps trembled visibly and anticipation.[1] Some adults were excited too, but to be certain the whole young population had come down with graduation epidemic. Large classes were graduating from both the grammar school and the high school. Even those who were years removed from their own day of glorious release were anxious to help with preparations as a kind of dry run. The junior students who were moving into the vacating classes' chairs were tradition-bound to show their talents for leadership and management. They strutted through the school and around the campus exerting pressure on the lower grades. Their authority was so new that occasionally if they pressed a little too hard it had to be overlooked. After all, next term was coming, and it never hurt a sixth grader to have a play sister in the eighth grade, or a tenth-year student to be able to call a twelfth grader Bubba. So all was endured in a spirit of shared understanding. But the graduating classes themselves were the nobility. Like travelers with exotic destinations on their minds, the graduates

---
[1] Stamps: a town in Arkansas. [Eds.]

were remarkably forgetful. They came to school without their books, or tablets or even pencils. Volunteers fell over themselves to secure replacements for the missing equipment. When accepted, the willing workers might or might not be thanked, and it was of no importance to the pregraduation rites. Even teachers were respectful of the now quiet and aging seniors, and tended to speak to them, if not as equals, as beings only slightly lower than themselves. After tests were returned and grades given, the student body, which acted like an extended family, knew who did well, who excelled, and what piteous ones had failed.

Unlike the white high school, Lafayette County Training School distin- 2 guished itself by having neither lawn, nor hedges, nor tennis court, nor climbing ivy. Its two buildings (main classrooms, the grade school and home economics) were set on a dirt hill with no fence to limit either its boundaries or those of bordering farms. There was a large expanse to the left of the school which was used alternately as a baseball diamond or basketball court. Rusty hoops on swaying poles represented the permanent recreational equipment, although bats and balls could be borrowed from the P.E. teacher if the borrower was qualified and if the diamond wasn't occupied.

Over this rocky area relieved by a few shady tall persimmon trees the grad- 3 uating class walked. The girls often held hands and no longer bothered to speak to the lower students. There was a sadness about them, as if this old world was not their home and they were bound for higher ground. The boys, on the other hand, had become more friendly, more outgoing. A decided change from the closed attitude they projected while studying for finals. Now they seemed not ready to give up the old school, the familiar paths and classrooms. Only a small percentage would be continuing on to college—one of the South's A & M (agricultural and mechanical) schools, which trained Negro youths to be carpenters, farmers, handymen, masons, maids, cooks and baby nurses. Their future rode heavily on their shoulders, and blinded them to the collective joy that had pervaded the lives of the boys and girls in the grammar school graduating class.

Parents who could afford it had ordered new shoes and ready-made clothes 4 for themselves from Sears and Roebuck or Montgomery Ward. They also engaged the best seamstresses to make the floating graduating dresses and to cut down secondhand pants which would be pressed to a military slickness for the important event.

Oh, it was important, all right. Whitefolks would attend the ceremony, and 5 two or three would speak of God and home, and the Southern way of life, and Mrs. Parsons, the principal's wife, would play the graduation march while the lower-grade graduates paraded down the aisles and took their seats below the platform. The high school seniors would wait in empty classrooms to make their dramatic entrance.

In the Store I was the person of the moment. The birthday girl. The center. 6

Bailey had graduated the year before,[2] although to do so he had had to forfeit all pleasures to make up for his time lost in Baton Rouge.

My class was wearing butter-yellow piqué dresses, and Momma launched out on mine. She smocked the yoke into tiny crisscrossing puckers, then shirred the rest of the bodice. Her dark fingers ducked in and out of the lemony cloth as she embroidered raised daisies around the hem. Before she considered herself finished she had added a crocheted cuff on the puff sleeves, and a point crocheted collar. 7

I was going to be lovely. A walking model of all the various styles of fine hand sewing and it didn't worry me that I was only twelve years old and merely graduating from the eighth grade. Besides, many teachers in Arkansas Negro schools had only that diploma and were licensed to impart wisdom. 8

The days had become longer and more noticeable. The faded beige of former times had been replaced with strong and sure colors. I began to see my classmates' clothes, their skin tones, and the dust that waved off pussy willows. Clouds that lazed across the sky were objects of great concern to me. Their shiftier shapes might have held a message that in my new happiness and with a little bit of time I'd soon decipher. During that period I looked at the arch of heaven so religiously my neck kept a steady ache. I had taken to smiling more often, and my jaws hurt from the unaccustomed activity. Between the two physical sore spots, I suppose I could have been uncomfortable, but that was not the case. As a member of the winning team (the graduating class of 1940) I had outdistanced unpleasant sensations by miles. I was headed for the freedom of open fields. 9

Youth and social approval allied themselves with me and we trammeled memories of slights and insults. The wind of our swift passage remodeled my features. Lost tears were pounded to mud and then to dust. Years of withdrawal were brushed aside and left behind, as hanging ropes of parasitic moss. 10

My work alone had awarded me a top place and I was going to be one of the first called in the graduating ceremonies. On the classroom blackboard, as well as on the bulletin board in the auditorium, there were blue stars and white stars and red stars. No absences, no tardinesses, and my academic work was among the best of the year. I could say the preamble to the Constitution even faster than Bailey. We timed ourselves often: "WethepeopleoftheUnitedStatesinordertoformamoreperfectunion . . ." I had memorized the Presidents of the United States from Washington to Roosevelt in chronological as well as alphabetical order. 11

My hair pleased me too. Gradually the black mass had lengthened and thickened, so that it kept at last to its braided pattern, and I didn't have to yank my scalp off when I tried to comb it. 12

---

[2] Bailey: the brother of the author. [Eds.]

Louise and I had rehearsed the exercises until we tired out ourselves. Henry   13
Reed was class valedictorian. He was a small, very black boy with hooded eyes,
a long, broad nose and an oddly shaped head. I had admired him for years
because each term he and I vied for the best grades in our class. Most often he
bested me, but instead of being disappointed I was pleased that we shared top
places between us. Like many Southern Black children, he lived with his
grandmother, who was as strict as Momma and as kind as she knew how to be.
He was courteous, respectful and soft-spoken to elders, but on the playground
he chose to play the roughest games. I admired him. Anyone, I reckoned,
sufficiently afraid or sufficiently dull could be polite. But to be able to operate
at a top level with both adults and children was admirable.

His valedictory speech was entitled "To Be or Not to Be." The rigid tenth-   14
grade teacher had helped him write it. He'd been working on the dramatic
stresses for months.

The weeks until graduation were filled with heady activities. A group of   15
small children were to be presented in a play about buttercups and daisies and
bunny rabbits. They could be heard throughout the building practicing their
hops and their little songs that sounded like silver bells. The older girls (non-
graduates, of course) were assigned the task of making refreshments for the
night's festivities. A tangy scent of ginger, cinnamon, nutmeg and chocolate
wafted around the home economics building as the budding cooks made samples
for themselves and their teachers.

In every corner of the workshop, axes and saws split fresh timber as the   16
woodshop boys made sets and stage scenery. Only the graduates were left out
of the general bustle. We were free to sit in the library at the back of the
building or look in quite detachedly, naturally, on the measures being taken for
our event.

Even the minister preached on graduation the Sunday before. His subject   17
was, "Let your light so shine that men will see your good works and praise your
Father, Who is in Heaven." Although the sermon was purported to be addressed
to us, he used the occasion to speak to backsliders, gamblers and general ne'er-
do-wells. But since he had called our names at the beginning of the service we
were mollified.

Among Negroes the tradition was to give presents to children going only   18
from one grade to another. How much more important this was when the
person was graduating at the top of the class. Uncle Willie and Momma had
sent away for a Mickey Mouse watch like Bailey's. Louise gave me four embroidered handkerchiefs. (I gave her crocheted doilies.) Mrs. Sneed, the minister's wife, made me an undershirt to wear for graduation, and nearly every
customer gave me a nickel or maybe even a dime with the instruction "Keep
on moving to higher ground," or some such encouragement.

Amazingly the great day finally dawned and I was out of bed before I knew   19 it. I threw open the back door to see it more clearly, but Momma said, "Sister, come away from that door and put your robe on."

I hoped the memory of that morning would never leave me. Sunlight was 20 itself young, and the day had none of the insistence maturity would bring it in a few hours. In my robe and barefoot in the backyard, under cover of going to see about my new beans, I gave myself up to the gentle warmth and thanked God that no matter what evil I had done in my life He had allowed me to live to see this day. Somewhere in my fatalism I had expected to die, accidentally, and never have the chance to walk up the stairs in the auditorium and gracefully receive my hard-earned diploma. Out of God's merciful bosom I had won reprieve.

Bailey came out in his robe and gave me a box wrapped in Christmas paper. 21 He said he had saved his money for months to pay for it. It felt like a box of chocolates, but I knew Bailey wouldn't save money to buy candy when we had all we could want under our noses.

He was as proud of the gift as I. It was a soft-leather-bound copy of a 22 collection of poems by Edgar Allan Poe, or, as Bailey and I called him, "Eap." I turned to "Annabel Lee" and we walked up and down the garden rows, the cool dirt between our toes, reciting the beautifully sad lines.

Momma made a Sunday breakfast although it was only Friday. After we 23 finished the blessing, I opened my eyes to find the watch on my plate. It was a dream of a day. Everything went smoothly and to my credit. I didn't have to be reminded or scolded for anything. Near evening I was too jittery to attend to chores, so Bailey volunteered to do all before his bath.

Days before, we had made a sign for the Store, and as we turned out the 24 lights Momma hung the cardboard over the doorknob. It read clearly: CLOSED. GRADUATION.

My dress fitted perfectly and everyone said that I looked like a sunbeam in 25 it. On the hill, going toward the school, Bailey walked behind with Uncle Willie, who muttered, "Go on, Ju." He wanted him to walk ahead with us because it embarrassed him to have to walk so slowly. Bailey said he'd let the ladies walk together, and the men would bring up the rear. We all laughed, nicely.

Little children dashed by out of the dark like fireflies. Their crepe-paper 26 dresses and butterfly wings were not made for running and we heard more than one rip, dryly, and the regretful "uh uh" that followed.

The school blazed without gaiety. The windows seemed cold and unfriendly 27 from the lower hill. A sense of ill-fated timing crept over me, and if Momma hadn't reached for my hand I would have drifted back to Bailey and Uncle Willie, and possibly beyond. She made a few slow jokes about my feet getting cold, and tugged me along to the now-strange building.

Around the front steps, assurance came back. There were my fellow "greats," 28

41

the graduating class. Hair brushed back, legs oiled, new dresses and pressed pleats, fresh pocket handkerchiefs and little handbags, all homesewn. Oh, we were up to snuff, all right. I joined my comrades and didn't even see my family go in to find seats in the crowded auditorium.

The school band struck up a march and all classes filed in as had been rehearsed. We stood in front of our seats, as assigned, and on a signal from the choir director, we sat. No sooner had this been accomplished than the band started to play the national anthem. We rose again and sang the song, after which we recited the pledge of allegiance. We remained standing for a brief minute before the choir director and the principal signaled to us, rather desperately I thought, to take our seats. The command was so unusual that our carefully rehearsed and smooth-running machine was thrown off. For a full minute we fumbled for our chairs and bumped into each other awkwardly. Habits change or solidify under pressure, so in our state of nervous tension we had been ready to follow our usual assembly pattern: the American national anthem, then the pledge of allegiance, then the song every Black person I knew called the Negro National Anthem. All done in the same key, with the same passion and most often standing on the same foot. 29

Finding my seat at last, I was overcome with a presentiment of worse things to come. Something unrehearsed, unplanned, was going to happen, and we were going to be made to look bad. I distinctly remember being explicit in the choice of pronoun. It was "we," the graduating class, the unit, that concerned me then. 30

The principal welcomed "parents and friends" and asked the Baptist minister to lead us in prayer. His invocation was brief and punchy, and for a second I thought we were getting on the high road to right action. When the principal came back to the dais, however, his voice had changed. Sounds always affected me profoundly and the principal's voice was one of my favorites. During assembly it melted and lowed weakly into the audience. It had not been in my plan to listen to him, but my curiosity was piqued and I straightened up to give him my attention. 31

He was talking about Booker T. Washington, our "late great leader," who said we can be as close as the fingers on the hand, etc. . . . Then he said a few vague things about friendship and the friendship of kindly people to those less fortunate than themselves. With that his voice nearly faded, thin, away. Like a river diminishing to a stream and then to a trickle. But he cleared his throat and said, "Our speaker tonight, who is also our friend, came from Texarkana to deliver the commencement address, but due to the irregularity of the train schedule, he's going to, as they say, 'speak and run.'" He said that we understood and wanted the man to know that we were most grateful for the time he was able to give us and then something about how we were willing always to adjust to another's program, and without more ado—"I give you Mr. Edward Donleavy." 32

Not one but two white men came through the door off-stage. The shorter 33
one walked to the speaker's platform, and the tall one moved to the center seat
and sat down. But that was our principal's seat, and already occupied. The
dislodged gentleman bounced around for a long breath or two before the Baptist
minister gave him his chair, then with more dignity than the situation deserved,
the minister walked off the stage.

Donleavy looked at the audience once (on reflection, I'm sure that he wanted 34
only to reassure himself that we were really there), adjusted his glasses and
began to read from a sheaf of papers.

He was glad "to be here and to see the work going on just as it was in the 35
other schools."

At the first "Amen" from the audience I willed the offender to immediate 36
death by choking on the word. But Amens and Yes, sir's began to fall around
the room like rain through a ragged umbrella.

He told us of the wonderful changes we children in Stamps had in store. 37
The Central School (naturally, the white school was Central) had already been
granted improvements that would be in use in the fall. A well-known artist was
coming from Little Rock to teach art to them. They were going to have the
newest microscopes and chemistry equipment for their laboratory. Mr. Donleavy
didn't leave us long in the dark over who made these improvements available
to Central High. Nor were we to be ignored in the general betterment scheme
he had in mind.

He said that he had pointed out to people at a very high level that one of 38
the first-line football tacklers at Arkansas Agricultural and Mechanical College
had graduated from good old Lafayette County Training School. Here fewer
Amen's were heard. Those few that did break through lay dully in the air with
the heaviness of habit.

He went on to praise us. He went on to say how he had bragged that "one 39
of the best basketball players at Fisk sank his first ball right here at Lafayette
County Training School."

The white kids were going to have a chance to become Galileos and Madame 40
Curies and Edisons and Gauguins, and our boys (the girls weren't even in on
it) would try to be Jesse Owenses and Joe Louises.

Owens and the Brown Bomber were great heroes in our world, but what 41
school official in the white-goddom of Little Rock had the right to decide that
those two men must be our only heroes? Who decided that for Henry Reed to
become a scientist he had to work like George Washington Carver, as a boot-
black, to buy a lousy microscope? Bailey was obviously always going to be too
small to be an athlete, so which concrete angel glued to what country seat had
decided that if my brother wanted to become a lawyer he had to first pay
penance for his skin by picking cotton and hoeing corn and studying correspondence books at night for twenty years?

The man's dead words fell like bricks around the auditorium and too many 42

43

settled in my belly. Constrained by hard-learned manners I couldn't look behind me, but to my left and right the proud graduating class of 1940 had dropped their heads. Every girl in my row had found something new to do with her handkerchief. Some folded the tiny squares into love knots, some into triangles, but most were wadding them, then pressing them flat on their yellow laps.

On the dais, the ancient tragedy was being replayed. Professor Parsons sat, 43 a sculptor's reject, rigid. His large, heavy body seemed devoid of will or willingness, and his eyes said he was no longer with us. The other teachers examined the flag (which was draped stage right) on their notes, or the windows which opened on our now-famous playing diamond.

Graduation, the hush-hush magic time of frills and gifts and congratulations 44 and diplomas, was finished for me before my name was called. The accomplishment was nothing. The meticulous maps, drawn in three colors of ink, learning and spelling decasyllabic words, memorizing the whole of *The Rape of Lucrece*[3]—it was for nothing. Donleavy had exposed us.

We were maids and farmers, handymen and washerwomen, and anything 45 higher that we aspired to was farcical and presumptuous.

Then I wished that Gabriel Prosser and Nat Turner had killed all whitefolks 46 in their beds and that Abraham Lincoln had been assassinated before the signing of the Emancipation Proclamation,[4] and that Harriet Tubman[5] had been killed by that blow on her head and Christopher Columbus had drowned in the *Santa Maria*.

It was awful to be a Negro and have no control over my life. It was brutal 47 to be young and already trained to sit quietly and listen to charges brought against my color with no chance of defense. We should all be dead. I thought I should like to see us all dead, one on top of the other. A pyramid of flesh with the whitefolks on the bottom, as the broad base, then the Indians with their silly tomahawks and teepees and wigwams and treaties, the Negroes with their mops and recipes and cotton sacks and spirituals sticking out of their mouths. The Dutch children should all stumble in their wooden shoes and break their necks. The French should choke to death on the Louisiana Purchase (1803) while silkworms ate all the Chinese with their stupid pigtails. As a species, we were an abomination. All of us.

Donleavy was running for election, and assured our parents that if he won 48 we could count on having the only colored paved playing field in that part of Arkansas. Also—he never looked up to acknowledge the grunts of acceptance— also, we were bound to get some new equipment for the home economics building and the workshop.

---

[3] *The Rape of Lucrece*: an 1,855-line narrative poem by William Shakespeare. [Eds.]
[4] Gabriel Prosser and Nat Turner: leaders of slave rebellions during the early 1800s in Virginia. [Eds.]
[5] Harriet Tubman (ca. 1820–1913): an escaped slave who conducted others to freedom on the Underground Railroad and worked as an abolitionist. [Eds.]

He finished, and since there was no need to give any more than the most 49
perfunctory thank-you's, he nodded to the men on the stage, and the tall white
man who was never introduced joined him at the door. They left with the
attitude that now they were off to something really important. (The graduation
ceremonies at Lafayette County Training School had been a mere preliminary.)

The ugliness they left was palpable. An uninvited guest who wouldn't leave. 50
The choir was summoned and sang a modern arrangement of "Onward, Christian Soldiers," with new words pertaining to graduates seeking their place in
the world. But it didn't work. Elouise, the daughter of the Baptist minister,
recited "Invictus,"[6] and I could have cried at the impertinence of "I am the
master of my fate, I am the captain of my soul."

My name had lost its ring of familiarity and I had to be nudged to go and 51
receive my diploma. All my preparations had fled. I neither marched up to the
stage like a conquering Amazon, nor did I look in the audience for Bailey's
nod of approval. Marguerite Johnson, I heard the name again, my honors were
read, there were noises in the audience of appreciation, and I took my place
on the stage as rehearsed.

I thought about colors I hated: ecru, puce, lavender, beige and black. 52

There was shuffling and rustling around me, then Henry Reed was giving 53
his valedictory address, "To Be or Not to Be." Hadn't he heard the whitefolks?
We couldn't *be*, so the question was a waste of time. Henry's voice came out
clear and strong. I feared to look at him. Hadn't he got the message? There
was no "nobler in the mind" for Negroes because the world didn't think we had
minds, and they let us know it. "Outrageous fortune"? Now, that was a joke.
When the ceremony was over I had to tell Henry Reed some things. That is,
if I still cared. Not "rub," Henry, "erase." "Ah, there's the erase." Us.

Henry had been a good student in elocution. His voice rose on tides of 54
promise and fell on waves of warnings. The English teacher had helped him
to create a sermon winging through Hamlet's soliloquy. To be a man, a doer,
a builder, a leader, or to be a tool, an unfunny joke, a crusher of funky
toadstools. I marveled that Henry could go through with the speech as if we
had a choice.

I had been listening and silently rebutting each sentence with my eyes closed; 55
then there was a hush, which in an audience warns that something unplanned
is happening. I looked up and saw Henry Reed, the conservative, the proper,
the A student, turn his back to the audience and turn to us (the proud graduating
class of 1940) and sing, nearly speaking,

> "Lift ev'ry voice and sing
> Till earth and heaven ring
> Ring with the harmonies of Liberty . . ."

---

[6]"Invictus": a poem by the nineteenth-century English poet, William Ernest Henley. Its inspi-
rational conclusion is quoted here. [Eds.]

It was the poem written by James Weldon Johnson. It was the music composed by J. Rosamond Johnson. It was the Negro National Anthem. Out of habit we were singing it.

Our mothers and fathers stood in the dark hall and joined the hymn of encouragement. A kindergarten teacher led the small children onto the stage and the buttercups and daisies and bunny rabbits marked time and tried to follow: 56

> "Stony the road we trod
> Bitter the chastening rod
> Felt in the days when hope, unborn, had died.
> Yet with a steady beat
> Have not our weary feet
> Come to the place for which our fathers sighed?"

Each child I knew had learned that song with his ABC's and along with "Jesus Loves Me This I Know." But I personally had never heard it before. Never heard the words, despite the thousands of times I had sung them. Never thought they had anything to do with me. 57

On the other hand, the words of Patrick Henry had made such an impression on me that I had been able to stretch myself tall and trembling and say, "I know not what course others may take, but as for me, given me liberty or give me death." 58

And now I heard, really for the first time: 59

> "We have come over a way that with tears
> has been watered,
> We have come, treading our path through
> the blood of the slaughtered."

While echoes of the song shivered in the air, Henry Reed bowed his head, said "Thank you," and returned to his place in the line. The tears that slipped down many faces were not wiped away in shame. 60

We were on top again. As always, again. We survived. The depths had been icy and dark, but now a bright sun spoke to our souls. I was no longer simply a member of the proud graduating class of 1940; I was a proud member of the wonderful, beautiful Negro race. 61

Oh, Black known and unknown poets, how often have your auctioned pains sustained us? Who will compute the only nights made less lonely by your songs, or the empty pots made less tragic by your tales? 62

If we were a people much given to revealing secrets, we might raise monuments and sacrifice to the memories of our poets, but slavery cured us of that weakness. It may be enough, however, to have it said that we survive in exact relationship to the dedication of our poets (include preachers, musicians and blues singers). 63

QUESTIONS

1. Why was graduation such an important event in Stamps, Arkansas? Note the rituals and preparations associated with this event. How do they compare with those accompanying your own junior-high or high school graduation?

2. At the beginning of the graduation ceremony, Angelou was "overcome with a presentiment of worse things to come. Something unrehearsed, unplanned, was going to happen" (paragraph 30). What "unrehearsed, unplanned" event does occur? How does Angelou convey to the reader the meaning of this event?

3. Toward the end of the essay we are told, "I was no longer simply a member of the proud graduating class of 1940; I was a proud member of the wonderful, beautiful Negro race" (paragraph 61). How did the experience of the graduation change Angelou's way of thinking about herself and her people?

4. Understanding the structure of this essay is important for understanding the meaning of the essay. How does Angelou organize her material, and how does this organization reflect her purpose? Why do you think Angelou changes her point of view from third person in the first five paragraphs to first person in the rest of the essay?

5. Think of an event in your life that didn't turn out as you expected. What were your expectations of this event? What was the reality? Write an essay in which you show the significance of this event by contrasting how you planned for the event with how it actually turned out.

6. We have all had experiences that have changed the directions of our lives. These experiences may be momentous, such as moving from one country to another or losing a parent, or they may be experiences that did not loom so large at the time but that changed the way you thought about things, such as finding that your parents disapproved of your best friend because of her race. Recall such a turning point in your life, and present it so as to give the reader a sense of what your life was like before the event and how it changed after the event.

MAKING CONNECTIONS

1. The essays by Loren Eiseley, George Orwell, Martin Luther King, Jr., and Alice Walker presented later in this section pinpoint formative moments in the life of the writer. Identify some of those moments and compare one or more with Angelou's account of her graduation.

2. Compare the points of view taken by Angelou and Walker. How does the "presence" of the valedictorian in Angelou's essay influence the point of view she takes?

3. Two things link this essay with Orwell's "Shooting an Elephant": each essay turns on an unexpected event, and the reflections each event prompts have to do with political domination. Of course they are from dissimilar points of view. But Orwell, when he goes out to meet and shoot the elephant, finds himself forced before a native crowd, in somewhat the same way that Mr. Donleavy stands before Angelou's school. Write an essay in which you compare and contrast these two events.

BEAUTY: WHEN THE OTHER DANCER IS THE SELF

Alice Walker

Born in Eatonton, Georgia, in 1944, Alice Walker is the youngest of eight children. Her father was a sharecropper, and her mother was a maid. A graduate of Sarah Lawrence College, Walker has been an active worker for civil rights. She has been a fellow of the Radcliffe Institute, a contributing and consulting editor for Ms. *magazine, and a teacher of literature and writing at a number of colleges and universities. She has published poetry, essays, short stories, and four novels,* The Third Life of Grange Copeland *(1970),* Meridian *(1976),* The Color Purple *(1982), for which she won the Pulitzer Price, and* The Temple of My Familiar *(1989). "Beauty : When the Other Dancer Is the Self" first appeared in* Ms. *magazine, and later in a collection of essays,* In Search of Our Mothers' Gardens *(1983). When asked why she writes, Walker said, "I'm really paying homage to people I love, the people who are thought to be dumb and backward but who were the ones who first taught me to see beauty."*

It is a bright summer day in 1947. My father, a fat, funny man with beautiful 1
eyes and a subversive wit, is trying to decide which of his eight children he will
take with him to the county fair. My mother, of course, will not go. She is
knocked out from getting most of us ready: I hold my neck stiff against the
pressure of her knuckles as she hastily completes the braiding and then berib-
boning of my hair.

My father is the driver for the rich old white lady up the road. Her name is 2
Miss Mey. She owns all the land for miles around, as well as the house in
which we live. All I remember about her is that she once offered to pay my
mother thirty-five cents for cleaning her house, raking up piles of her magnolia
leaves, and washing her family's clothes, and that my mother—she of no money,
eight children, and a chronic earache—refused it. But I do not think of this in
1947. I am two and a half years old. I want to go everywhere my daddy goes.
I am excited at the prospect of riding in a car. Someone has told me fairs are
fun. That there is room in the car for only three of us doesn't faze me at all.
Whirling happily in my starchy frock, showing off my biscuit-polished patent-
leather shoes and lavender socks, tossing my head in a way that makes my

48

ribbons bounce, I stand, hands on hips, before my father. "Take me, Daddy," I say with assurance; "I'm the prettiest!"

Later, it does not surprise me to find myself in Miss Mey's shiny black car, 3 sharing the back seat with the other lucky ones. Does not surprise me that I thoroughly enjoy the fair. At home that night I tell the unlucky ones all I can remember about the merry-go-round, the man who eats live chickens, and the teddy bears, until they say: that's enough, baby Alice. Shut up now, and go to sleep.

It is Easter Sunday, 1950. I am dressed in a green, flocked, scalloped-hem 4 dress (handmade by my adoring sister, Ruth) that has its own smooth satin petticoat and tiny hot-pink roses tucked into each scallop. My shoes, new T-strap patent leather, again highly biscuit-polished. I am six years old and have learned one of the longest Easter speeches to be heard that day, totally unlike the speech I said when I was two: "Easter lilies / pure and white / blossom in / the morning light." When I rise to give my speech I do so on a great wave of love and pride and expectation. People in the church stop rustling their new crinolines. They seem to hold their breath. I can tell they admire my dress, but it is my spirit, bordering on sassiness (womanishness), they secretly applaud.

"That girl's a little *mess*," they whisper to each other, pleased. 5

Naturally I say my speech without stammer or pause, unlike those who 6 stutter, stammer, or worst of all, forget. This is before the word "beautiful" exists in people's vocabulary, but "Oh, isn't she the *cutest* thing!" frequently floats my way. "And got so much sense!" they gratefully add . . . for which thoughtful addition I thank them to this day.

It was great fun being cute. But then, one day, it ended. 7

I am eight years old and a tomboy. I have a cowboy hat, cowboy boots, 8 checkered shirt and pants, all red. My playmates are my brothers, two and four years older than I. Their colors are black and green, the only difference in the way we are dressed. On Saturday nights we all go to the picture show, even my mother; Westerns are her favorite kind of movie. Back home, "on the ranch," we pretend we are Tom Mix, Hopalong Cassidy, Lash LaRue (we've even named one of our dogs Lash LaRue); we chase each other for hours rustling cattle, being outlaws, delivering damsels from distress. Then my parents decide to buy my brothers guns. These are not "real" guns. They shoot "BBs," copper pellets my brothers say will kill birds. Because I am a girl, I do not get a gun. Instantly I am relegated to the position of Indian. Now there appears a great distance between us. They shoot and shoot at everything with their new guns. I try to keep up with my bow and arrows.

One day while I am standing on top of our makeshift "garage"—pieces of 9 tin nailed across some poles—holding my bow and arrow and looking out toward the fields, I feel an incredible blow in my right eye. I look down just in time to see my brother lower his gun.

Both brothers rush to my side. My eye stings, and I cover it with my hand. "If you tell," they say, "we will get a whipping. You don't want that to happen, do you?" I do not. "Here is a piece of wire," says the older brother, picking it up from the roof; "say you stepped on one end of it and the other flew up and hit you." The pain is beginning to start. "Yes," I say. "Yes, I will say that is what happened." If I do not say this is what happened, I know my brothers will find ways to make me wish I had. But now I will say anything that gets me to my mother. 10

Confronted by our parents we stick to the lie agreed upon. They place me on a bench on the porch and I close my left eye while they examine the right. There is a tree growing from underneath the porch that climbs past the railing to the roof. It is the last thing my right eye sees. I watch as its trunk, its branches, and then its leaves are blotted out by the rising blood. 11

I am in shock. First there is intense fever, which my father tries to break using lily leaves bound around my head. Then there are chills: my mother tries to get me to eat soup. Eventually, I do not know how, my parents learn what has happened. A week after the "accident" they take me to see a doctor "Why did you wait so long to come?" he asks, looking into my eye and shaking his head. "Eyes are sympathetic," he says. "If one is blind, the other will likely become blind too." 12

This comment of the doctor's terrifies me. But it is really how I look that bothers me most. Where the BB pellet struck there is a glob of whitish scar tissue, a hideous cataract, on my eye. Now when I stare at people—a favorite pastime, up to now—they will stare back. Not at the "cute" little girl, but at her scar. For six years I do not stare at anyone, because I do not raise my head. 13

Years later, in the throes of a mid-life crisis, I ask my mother and sister whether I changed after the "accident." "No," they say, puzzled. "What do you mean?" 14

What do I mean? 15

I am eight, and, for the first time, doing poorly in school, where I have been something of a whiz since I was four. We have just moved to the place where the "accident" occurred. We do not know any of the people around us because this is a different county. The only time I see the friends I knew is when we go back to our old church. The new school is the former state penitentiary. It is a large stone building, cold and drafty, crammed to overflowing with boisterous, ill-disciplined children. On the third floor there is a huge circular imprint of some partition that has been torn out. 16

"What used to be here?" I ask a sullen girl next to me on our way past it to lunch. 17

"The electric chair," says she. 18

At night I have nightmares about the electric chair, and about all the people   19
reputedly "fried" in it. I am afraid of the school, where all the students seem
to be budding criminals.

"What's the matter with your eye?" they ask, critically.   20

When I don't answer (I cannot decide whether it was an "accident" or not),   21
they shove me, insist on a fight.

My brother, the one who created the story about the wire, comes to my   22
rescue. But then brags so much about "protecting" me, I become sick.

After months of torture at the school, my parents decide to send me back to   23
our old community, to my old school. I live with my grandparents and the
teacher they board. But there is no room for Phoebe, my cat. By the time my
grandparents decide there *is* room, and I ask for my cat, she cannot be found.
Miss Yarborough, the boarding teacher, takes me under her wing, and begins
to teach me to play the piano. But soon she marries an African—a "prince,"
she says—and is whisked away to his continent.

At my old school there is at least one teacher who loves me. She is the   24
teacher who "knew me before I was born" and bought my first baby clothes. It
is she who makes life bearable. It is her presence that finally helps me turn on
the one child at the school who continually calls me "one-eyed bitch." One
day I simply grab him by his coat and beat him until I am satisfied. It is my
teacher who tells me my mother is ill.

My mother is lying in bed in the middle of the day, something I have never   25
seen. She is in too much pain to speak. She has an abscess in her ear. I stand
looking down on her, knowing that if she dies, I cannot live. She is being
treated with warm oils and hot bricks held against her cheek. Finally a doctor
comes. But I must go back to my grandparents' house. The weeks pass but I
am hardly aware of it. All I know is that my mother might die, my father is
not so jolly, my brothers still have their guns, and I am the one sent away from
home.

"You did not change," they say.   26

Did I imagine the anguish of never looking up?   A Key phrase   27

I am twelve. When relatives come to visit I hide in my room. My cousin   28
Brenda, just my age, whose father works in the post office and whose mother
is a nurse, comes to find me. "Hello," she says. And then she asks, looking at
my recent school picture, which I did not want taken, and on which the "glob,"
as I think of it, is clearly visible, "You still can't see out of that eye?"

"No, " I say, and flop back on the bed over my book.   29

That night, as I do almost every night, I abuse my eye. I rant and rave at   30
it, in front of the mirror. I plead with it to clear up before morning. I tell it I
hate and despise it. I do not pray for sight. I pray for beauty.

"You did not change," they say.   31

51

I am fourteen and baby-sitting for my brother Bill, who lives in Boston. He 32 is my favorite brother and there is a strong bond between us. Understanding my feelings of shame and ugliness he and his wife take me to a local hospital, where the "glob" is removed by a doctor named O. Henry. There is still a small bluish crater where the scar tissue was, but the ugly white stuff is gone. Almost immediately I become a different person from the girl who does not raise her head. Or so I think. Now that I've raised my head I win the boyfriend of my dreams. Now that I've raised my head I have plenty of friends. Now that I've raised my head classwork comes from my lips as faultlessly as Easter speeches did, and I leave high school as valedictorian, most popular student, and *queen*, hardly believing my luck. Ironically, the girl who was voted most beautiful in our class (and was) was later shot twice through the chest by a male companion, using a "real" gun, while she was pregnant. But that's another story in itself. Or is it?

"You did not change," they say. 33

It is now thirty years since the "accident." A beautiful journalist comes to 34 visit and to interview me. She is going to write a cover story for her magazine that focuses on my latest book. "Decide how you want to look on the cover," she says. "Glamorous, or whatever."

Never mind "glamorous," it is the "whatever" that I hear. Suddenly all I can 35 think of is whether I will get enough sleep the night before the photography session: if I don't, my eye will be tired and wander, as blind eyes will.

At night in bed with my lover I think up reasons why I should not appear 36 on the cover of a magazine. "My meanest critics will say I've sold out," I say. "My family will now realize I write scandalous books."

"But what's the real reason you don't want to do this?" he asks. 37

"Because in all probability," I say in a rush, "my eye won't be straight." 38

"It will be straight enough," he says. Then, "Besides, I thought you'd made 39 your peace with that."

And I suddenly remember that I have. 40

I remember: 41

I am talking to my brother Jimmy, asking if he remembers anything unusual 42 about the day I was shot. He does not know I consider that day the last time my father, with his sweet home remedy of cool lily leaves, chose me, and that I suffered and raged inside because of this. "Well," he says, "all I remember is standing by the side of the highway with Daddy, trying to flag down a car. A white man stopped, but when Daddy said he needed somebody to take his little girl to the doctor, he drove off."

I remember: 43

I am in the desert for the first time. I fall totally in love with it. I am so 44 overwhelmed by its beauty, I confront for the first time, consciously, the meaning of the doctor's words years ago: "Eyes are sympathetic. If one is blind, the other will likely become blind too." I realize I have dashed about the world madly, looking at this, looking at that, storing up images against the fading of the light. *But I might have missed seeing the desert!* The shock of that possibility—and gratitude for over twenty-five years of sight—sends me literally to my knees. Poem after poem comes—which is perhaps how poets pray.

ON SIGHT

I am so thankful I have seen
The Desert
And the creatures in the desert
And the desert Itself.

The desert has its own moon
Which I have seen
With my own eye.

There is no flag on it.

Trees of the desert have arms
All of which are always up
That is because the moon is up
The sun is up
Also the sky
The stars
Clouds
None with flags.

If there *were* flags, I doubt
the trees would point.
Would you?

But mostly, I remember this: 45

I am twenty-seven, and my baby daughter is almost three. Since her birth I   46
have worried about her discovery that her mother's eyes are different from other people's. Will she be embarrassed? I think. What will she say? Every day she watches a television program called "Big Blue Marble." It begins with a picture of the earth as it appears from the moon. It is bluish, a little battered-looking, but full of light, with whitish clouds swirling around it. Every time I see it I weep with love, as if it is a picture of Grandma's house. One day when I am putting Rebecca down for her nap, she suddenly focuses on my eye. Something inside me cringes, gets ready to try to protect myself. All children are cruel about physical differences, I know from experience, and that they don't always mean to be is another matter. I assume Rebecca will be the same.

But no-o-o-o. She studies my face intently as we stand, her inside and me 47
outside her crib. She even holds my face maternally between her dimpled little
hands. Then, looking every bit as serious and lawyerlike as her father, she says,
as if it may just possibly have slipped my attention: "Mommy, there's a *world*
in your eye." (As in, "Don't be alarmed, or do anything crazy.") And then,
gently, but with great interest: "Mommy, where did you *get* that world in your
eye?"

For the most part, the pain left then. (So what, if my brothers grew up to 48
buy even more powerful pellet guns for their sons and to carry real guns
themselves. So what, if a young "Morehouse man" once nearly fell off the steps
of Trevor Arnett Library because he thought my eyes were blue.) Crying and
laughing I ran to the bathroom, while Rebecca mumbled and sang herself off
to sleep. Yes indeed, I realized, looking into the mirror. There *was* a world in
my eye. And I saw that it was possible to love it: that in fact, for all it had
taught me of shame and anger and inner vision, I *did* love it. Even to see it
drifting out of orbit in boredom, or rolling up out of fatigue, not to mention
floating back at attention in excitement (bearing witness, a friend has called it),
deeply suitable to my personality, and even characteristic of me.

That night I dream I am dancing to Stevie Wonder's song "Always" (the 49
name of the song is really "As," but I hear it as "Always"). As I dance, whirling
and joyous, happier than I've ever been in my life, another bright-faced dancer
joins me. We dance and kiss each other and hold each other through the night.
The other dancer has obviously come through all right, as I have done. She is
beautiful, whole and free. And she is also me.

QUESTIONS

1. Walker's essay moves forward in time through abrupt, though steadily progressive
descriptions of episodes. What effect on the reader does this structure produce? Why do
you suppose Walker chose this form instead of providing transitions from one episode
to the next?

2. Consider Walker's method of contrasting other people's memories with her own.
What effect is created by the repetition of "You did not change"?

3. Consider Walker's choices of episodes or examples of beauty. How does each one
work toward developing a definition of "beauty"?

4. In what ways does this essay play with the possible meanings of the familiar adage,
"Beauty is in the eye of the beholder?"

5. One theme of this essay could be that of coming to terms with a disfigurement,
an imagined loss of physical beauty. Recall an event (or accident) in your own life that
changed your perception of yourself. Write a reflective narrative in which you use
Walker's method of chronologically arranged episodes, including a reflection on the time
before the change, as well as the change itself, and episodes from the time following.
Like Walker, you may want to contrast (or compare) your memories with those of others.

6. Recall a memorable event that occurred a year or more ago. It might be an event in your family's life, or a public event at which you and your friends were present. Write down your memories of the event, and then interview your family or friends and write down their recollections. Compare the various memories of the event. Come to some conclusion about the differences or similarities you find, and perhaps about the selectivity of memory.

MAKING CONNECTIONS

1. Could Walker's essay be titled "Why I Write," like Didion's essay presented later in this section? Compare and contrast the themes and points of view of these two essays.

2. Walker's daughter's exclamation, "Mommy, there's a *world* in your eye," is obviously a transcendent moment. It is also a metaphor. One or another writer in this section could also be said to have a world in her or his eye. For example, Carl Sagan's description of how insight depends on a degree of restriction is closely related to Walker's theme. Select another essay from this section and show how Walker's reflections on her blind eye can help us understand the discoveries the writer of the other essay is making.

THE IGUANA

Isak Dinesen

Karen Dinesen (1885–1962) was a Danish woman who married a Swedish baron and went to Kenya in East Africa with him in 1914 to manage their coffee plantation. After their divorce she stayed in Kenya, managing the plantation until its failure in 1931. During this time she began to write in English (the language of whites in Kenya), taking the male first name of Isak. Her best-known books are Seven Gothic Tales *(1934), a volume of stories, and* Out of Africa *(1937), her reminiscences of Kenya. The following brief selection from the latter volume appeared in the section called "From an Immigrant's Notebook."*

In the Reserve I have sometimes come upon the Iguana, the big lizards,[1] as they were sunning themselves upon a flat stone in a river-bed. They are not pretty in shape, but nothing can be imagined more beautiful than their coloring. They shine like a heap of precious stones or like a pane cut out of an old church window. When, as you approach, they swish away, there is a flash of azure, green and purple over the stones, the color seems to be standing behind them in the air, like a comet's luminous tail.

Once I shot an Iguana. I thought that I should be able to make some pretty things from his skin. A strange thing happened then, that I have never afterwards forgotten. As I went up to him, where he was lying dead upon his stone, and actually while I was walking a few steps, he faded and grew pale, all color died out of him as in one long sigh, and by the time that I touched him he was grey and dull like a lump of concrete. It was the live impetuous blood pulsating within the animal, which had radiated out all that glow and splendor. Now that the flame was put out, and the soul had flown, the Iguana was as dead as a sandbag.

Often since I have, in some sort, shot an Iguana, and I have remembered the one of the Reserve. Up at Meru I saw a young Native girl with a bracelet on, a leather strap two inches wide, and embroidered all over with very small turquoise-colored beads which varied a little in color and played in green, light blue and ultramarine. It was an extraordinarily live thing; it seemed to draw breath on her arm, so that I wanted it for myself, and made Farah buy it from

---

[1] the Reserve: the game reserve in the Ngong Hills of Kenya, Africa. [Eds.]

56

her.[2] No sooner had it come upon my own arm than it gave up the ghost. It was nothing now, a small, cheap, purchased article of finery. It had been the play of colors, the duet between the turquoise and the "nègre",—that quick, sweet, brownish black, like peat and black pottery, of the Native's skin,—that had created the life of the bracelet.

In the Zoological Museum of Pietermaritzburg, I have seen, in a stuffed   4 deep-water fish in a showcase, the same combination of coloring, which there had survived death; it made me wonder what life can well be like, on the bottom of the sea, to send up something so live and airy. I stood in Meru and looked at my pale hand and at the dead bracelet, it was as if an injustice had been done to a noble thing, as if truth had been suppressed. So sad did it seem that I remembered the saying of the hero in a book that I had read as a child: "I have conquered them all, but I am standing amongst graves."

In a foreign country and with foreign species of life one should take measures   5 to find out whether things will be keeping their value when dead. To the settlers of East Africa I give the advice: "For the sake of your own eyes and heart, shoot not the Iguana."

QUESTIONS

1. In this essay the act of shooting an iguana comes to stand as a type or model of other actions; it becomes a symbolic event. This is expressed explicitly at the beginning of paragraph 3: "Often since I have, *in some sort*, shot an Iguana" (italics added). How do the incidents described in paragraphs 3 and 4 help us to understand the full meaning of the symbolic action of shooting an iguana? Restate this meaning in your own words.

2. An argument that lurks beneath the surface of this meditative essay is made explicit in its last sentence. How do you understand that sentence and that argument?

3. The power of this essay grows from its effective representation—its ability to put us in the picture, to make us see and feel the events represented. Find a phrase of description or comparison that seems to you especially vivid, and explain why it is effective.

4. Dinesen uses three concrete examples here. How are the three related? Why do you suppose she arranged them in the order in which she did?

5. In her meditation, Dinesen moves from lizard, to bracelet, to fish, and then uses these three specific, concrete instances to make the jump to generalizations about foreign species and foreign countries. Try this technique yourself. Find some incident in your own life that reminds you of other similar events, so that they can be brought together as being symbolic of a certain *kind* of event. To what broader point can you leap from these few recollected events?

---

[2] Farah Aden: Dinesen's Somali servant. [Eds.]

ISAK DINESEN

MAKING CONNECTIONS

Consider the deaths and captivities of animals in this essay, in Orwell's "Shooting an Elephant," and in Eiseley's "The Bird and the Machine." Could Dinesen's final sentence and its implied argument be the theme of either of the other essays? Would it fit one better than the other? How would Orwell's or Eiseley's essay change if Dinesen's remark were to guide it?

WHY I WRITE

Joan Didion

*Joan Didion was born in Sacramento, California, in 1934
and graduated with a B.A. in English from the University
of California at Berkeley in 1956. Until the publication of
her first novel,* Run River, *in 1963, she worked as an
associate feature editor for* Vogue *magazine. Since then she
has written three more novels,* Play It As It Lays *(1971),* A
Book of Common Prayer *(1977), and* Democracy *(1984),
as well as four books of essays,* Slouching Towards Bethlehem *(1969),* The White Album *(1982),* Salvador *(1983),
and* Miami *(1987). As an essayist, she has shown herself to
be a trenchant observer and interpreter of American society.
The selection reprinted here is adapted from a lecture given
at the University of California at Berkeley. In reflecting on
this essay, Didion said, "I didn't express confidence [about
the process of writing] so much as blind faith that if you go
in and work every day it will get better."*

Of course I stole the title for this talk, from George Orwell.[1] One reason I
stole it was that I like the sound of the words: Why I Write. There you have
three short unambiguous words that share a sound; and the sound they share is
this:

I

I

I

In many ways writing is the act of saying *I*, of imposing oneself upon other
people, of saying *listen to me, see it my way, change your mind*. It's an aggressive,
even a hostile act. You can disguise its aggressiveness all you want with veils of
subordinate clauses and qualifiers and tentative subjunctives, with ellipses and
evasions—with the whole manner of intimating rather than claiming, of alluding rather than stating—but there's no getting around the fact that setting words
on paper is the tactic of a secret bully, an invasion, an imposition of the writer's
sensibility on the reader's most private space.

I stole the title not only because the words sounded right but because they
seemed to sum up, in a no-nonsense way, all I have to tell you. Like many

---

[1] "Why I Write": one of British writer George Orwell's (1903–1950) best-known essays. [Eds.]

writers I have only this one "subject," this one "area": the act of writing. I can bring you no reports from any other front. I may have other interests: I am "interested," for example, in marine biology, but I don't flatter myself that you would come out to hear me talk about it. I am not a scholar. I am not in the least an intellectual, which is not to say that when I hear the word "intellectual" I reach for my gun, but only to say that I do not think in abstracts. During the years when I was an undergraduate at Berkeley I tried, with a kind of hopeless late-adolescent energy, to buy some temporary visa into the world of ideas, to forge for myself a mind that could deal with the abstract.

In short I tried to think. I failed. My attention veered inexorably back to the specific, to the tangible, to what was generally considered, by everyone I knew then and for that matter have known since, the peripheral. I would try to contemplate the Hegelian dialectic[2] and would find myself concentrating instead on a flowering pear tree outside my window and the particular way the petals fell on my floor. I would try to read linguistic theory and would find myself wondering instead if the lights were on in the bevatron[3] up the hill. When I say that I was wondering if the lights were on in the bevatron you might immediately suspect, if you deal in ideas at all, that I was registering the bevatron as a political symbol, thinking in shorthand about the military-industrial complex and its role in the university community, but you would be wrong. I was only wondering if the lights were on in the bevatron, and how they looked. A physical fact.

I had trouble graduating from Berkeley, not because of this inability to deal with ideas—I was majoring in English, and I could locate the house-and-garden imagery in *The Portrait of a Lady*[4] as well as the next person, "imagery" being by definition the kind of specific that got my attention—but simply because I had neglected to take a course in Milton. For reasons which now sound baroque I needed a degree by the end of that summer, and the English department finally agreed, if I would come down from Sacramento every Friday and talk about the cosmology of *Paradise Lost*, to certify me proficient in Milton. I did this. Some Fridays I took the Greyhound bus, other Fridays I caught the Southern Pacific's City of San Francisco on the last leg of its transcontinental trip. I can no longer tell you whether Milton put the sun or the earth at the center of his universe in *Paradise Lost*, the central question of at least one century and a topic about which I wrote ten thousand words that summer, but

7

8

---

[2]Hegelian dialectic: according to philosopher G. W. F. Hegel (1770–1831), history moves by a process of contradictions. [Eds.]

[3]bevatron: the proton synchroton (a device for accelerating protons) at the University of California at Berkeley. [Eds.]

[4]*The Portrait of a Lady*: a novel by American writer Henry James (1843–1916); frequently taught in literature courses. [Eds.]

I can still recall the exact rancidity of the butter in the City of San Francisco's dining car, and the way the tinted windows on the Greyhound bus cast the oil refineries around Carquinez Straits into a grayed and obscurely sinister light. In short my attention was always on the periphery, on what I could see and taste and touch, on the butter, and the Greyhound bus. During those years I was traveling on what I knew to be a very shaky passport, forged papers: I knew that I was no legitimate resident in any world of ideas. I knew I couldn't think. All I knew then was what I couldn't do. All I knew then was what I wasn't, and it took me some years to discover what I was.

Which was a writer. 9

By which I mean not a "good" writer or a "bad" writer but simply a writer, 10 a person whose most absorbed and passionate hours are spent arranging words on pieces of paper. Had my credentials been in order I would never have become a writer. Had I been blessed with even limited access to my own mind there would have been no reason to write. I write entirely to find out what I'm thinking, what I'm looking at, what I see and what it means. What I want and what I fear. Why did the oil refineries around Carquinez Straits seem sinister to me in the summer of 1956? Why have the night lights in the bevatron burned in my mind for twenty years? *What is going on in these pictures in my mind?*

When I talk about pictures in my mind I am talking, quite specifically, about 11 images that shimmer around the edges. There used to be an illustration in every elementary psychology book showing a cat drawn by a patient in varying stages of schizophrenia. This cat had a shimmer around it. You could see the molecular structure breaking down at the very edges of the cat: the cat became the background and the background the cat, everything interacting, exchanging ions. People on hallucinogens describe the same perception of objects. I'm not a schizophrenic, nor do I take hallucinogens, but certain images do shimmer for me. Look hard enough, and you can't miss the shimmer. It's there. You can't think too much about these pictures that shimmer. You just lie low and let them develop. You stay quiet. You don't talk to many people and you keep your nervous system from shorting out and you try to locate the cat in the shimmer, the grammar in the picture.

Just as I meant "shimmer" literally I mean "grammar" literally. Grammar is 12 a piano I play by ear, since I seem to have been out of school the year the rules were mentioned. All I know about grammar is its infinite power. To shift the structure of a sentence alters the meaning of that sentence, as definitely and inflexibly as the position of a camera alters the meaning of the object photographed. Many people know about camera angles now, but not so many know about sentences. The arrangement of the words matters, and the arrangement you want can be found in the picture in your mind. The picture dictates the arrangement. The picture dictates whether this will be a sentence with or without clauses, a sentence that ends hard or a dying-fall sentence, long or short, active or passive. The picture tells you how to arrange the words and the arrangement of the words tells you, or tells me, what's going on in the picture. *Nota bene:*[5]

It tells you.   13

You don't tell it.   14

Let me show you what I mean by pictures in the mind. I began *Play It As*   15
It Lays just as I have begun each of my novels, with no notion of "character" or "plot" or even "incident." I had only two pictures in my mind, more about which later, and a technical intention, which was to write a novel so elliptical and fast that it would be over before you noticed it, a novel so fast that it would scarcely exist on the page at all. About the pictures: the first was of white space. Empty space. This was clearly the picture that dictated the narrative intention of the book—a book in which anything that happened would happen off the page, a "white" book to which the reader would have to bring his or her own bad dreams—and yet this picture told me no "story," suggested no situation. The second picture did. This second picture was of something actually witnessed. A young woman with long hair and a short white halter dress walks through the casino at the Riviera in Las Vegas at one in the morning. She crosses the casino alone and picks up a house telephone. I watch her because I have heard her paged, and recognize her name: she is a minor actress I see around Los Angeles from time to time, in places like Jax and once in a gynecologist's office in the Beverly Hills Clinic, but have never met. I know nothing about her. Who is paging her? Why is she here to be paged? How exactly did she come to this? It was precisely this moment in Las Vegas that made *Play It As It Lays* begin to tell itself to me, but the moment appears in the novel only obliquely, in a chapter which begins: "Maria made a list of things she would never do. She would never: walk through the Sands or Caesar's alone after midnight. She would never: ball at a party, do S-M unless she wanted to, borrow furs from Abe Lipsey, deal. She would never: carry a Yorkshire in Beverly Hills."

That is the beginning of the chapter and that is also the end of the chapter,   16
which may suggest that I meant by "white space."

I recall having a number of pictures in my mind when I began the novel I   17
just finished, *A Book of Common Prayer.* As a matter of fact one of these pictures was of that bevatron I mentioned, although I would be hard put to tell you a story in which nuclear energy figures. Another was a newspaper photograph of a hijacked 707 burning on the desert in the Middle East. Another was the night view from a room in which I once spent a week with paratyphoid, a hotel room on the Colombian coast. My husband and I seemed to be on the Colombian

---

[5] *Nota bene:* (Latin) note well, or particularly. [Eds.]

coast representing the United States of America at a film festival (I recall invoking the name "Jack Valenti"[6] a lot, as if its reiteration could make me well), and it was a bad place to have fever, not only because my indisposition offended our hosts but because every night in this hotel the generator failed. The lights went out. The elevator stopped. My husband would go to the event of the evening and make excuses for me and I would stay alone in this hotel room, in the dark. I remember standing at the window trying to call Bogotá (the telephone seemed to work on the same principle as the generator) and watching the night wind come up and wondering what I was doing eleven degrees off the equator with a fever of 103. The view from that window definitely figures in A *Book of Common Prayer*, as does the burning 707, and yet none of these pictures told me the story I needed.

The picture that did, the picture that shimmered and made these other 18 images coalesce, was the Panama airport at 6 A.M. I was in this airport only once, on a plane to Bogotá that stopped for an hour to refuel, but the way it looked that morning remained superimposed on everything I saw until the day I finished A *Book of Common Prayer*. I lived in that airport for several years. I can still feel the hot air when I step off the plane, can see the heat already rising off the tarmac at 6 A.M. I can feel my skirt damp and wrinkled on my legs. I can feel the asphalt stick to my sandals. I remember the big tail of a Pan American plane floating motionless down at the end of the tarmac. I remember the sound of a slot machine in the waiting room. I could tell you that I remember a particular woman in the airport, an American woman, a *norte-americana*, a thin *norteamericana* about forty who wore a big square emerald in lieu of a wedding ring, but there was no such woman there.

I put this woman in the airport later. I made this woman up, just as I later 19 made up a country to put the airport in, and a family to run the country. This woman in the airport is neither catching a plane nor meeting one. She is ordering tea in the airport coffee shop. In fact she is not simply "ordering" tea but insisting that the water be boiled, in front of her, for twenty minutes. Why is this woman in this airport? Why is she going nowhere, where has she been? Where did she get that big emerald? What derangement, or disassociation, makes her believe that her will to see the water boiled can possibly prevail?

> She had been going to one airport or another for four months, one could see it, looking at the visas on her passport. All those airports where Charlotte Douglas's passport had been stamped would have looked alike. Sometimes the sign on the tower would say "Bienvenidos" and sometimes the sign on the tower would say "Bienvenue," some places were wet and hot and others dry and hot, but at each of these airports the pastel concrete walls would rust and stain and the swamp off the runway would be littered with the fuselages of cannibalized Fairchild F-227's and the water would need boiling.

---

[6] Jack Valenti: speech writer for President Lyndon B. Johnson. [Eds.]

I knew why Charlotte went to the airport even if Victor did not.
I knew about airports.

These lines appear about halfway through A *Book of Common Prayer,* but I 20
wrote them during the second week I worked on the book, long before I had
any idea where Charlotte Douglas had been or why she went to airports. Until
I wrote these lines I had no character called "Victor" in mind: the necessity for
mentioning a name, and the name "Victor," occurred to me as I wrote the
sentence: *I knew why Charlotte went to the airport* sounded incomplete. *I knew
why Charlotte went to the airport even if Victor did not* carried a little more
narrative drive. Most important of all, until I wrote these lines I did not know
who "I" was, who was telling the story. I had intended until that moment that
the "I" be no more than the voice of the author, a nineteenth-century omniscient
narrator. But there it was:

I knew why Charlotte went to the airport even if Victor did not.
I knew about airports.

This "I" was the voice of no author in my house. This "I" was someone who 21
not only knew why Charlotte went to the airport but also knew someone called
"Victor." Who was Victor? Who was this narrator? Why was this narrator telling
me this story? Let me tell you one thing about why writers write: had I known
the answer to any of these questions I would never have needed to write a novel.

QUESTIONS

1. Didion claims that her writing develops from "pictures in the mind" (paragraphs
10–18), "images that shimmer around the edges." Reflect on your own writing process.
Compare it to Didion's and to your classmates' writing processes.

2. In paragraphs 15–18, Didion tries to show the reader what she means by "pictures
in the mind." To what extent is she successful in illustrating her process? Could this
essay have started from a picture? Can you locate it?

3. In paragraph 8, Didion says, "my attention was always on the periphery, on what
I could see and taste and touch." Does such attention indicate a lack of thought, as she
seems to imply in paragraph 7? Why do you suppose the "specific" and the "tangible"
might be considered "peripheral"? By whom?

4. Consider the structure of Didion's essay. How does it move from the opening "I's"
to the closing "I's"—the voices of the fictional "I" and that of the author?

5. Reflect on a person you know well. Use Didion's method of description in
paragraph 15 which merges visual and cultural information as a model for your own
written description. What does Maria's "list of things she would never do" tell us about
her? Include such a list (though it might be of things your person would *always* do) in
your description.

6. In paragraph 12, Didion talks about the power of grammar. How does she define

it? Look closely at her sentence structure in one or two paragraphs and write a brief analysis of it.

MAKING CONNECTIONS

1. Do you think attention "always on the periphery" describes other writers in this section as Didion says it describes herself? Where do you find examples of peripheral attention in Maya Angelou, Alice Walker, N. Scott Momaday, George Orwell, or Zoë Tracy Hardy? How do you identify it as peripheral? What do those writers make of what they find on the periphery of things?

2. What about peripheral attention in the case of the sciences? Look at one of the essays by a scientist in this section or by Jane van Lawick-Goodall or Farley Mowat in "Reporting," or by Oliver Sacks or Stephen Jay Gould in "Explaining." Of course there are many further examples. After surveying several, write an essay yourself about the contributions of peripheral attention. Would you have any other name for this phenomenon?

AUTOBIOGRAPHICAL NOTES

James Baldwin

James Baldwin was born in Harlem in 1924 and followed his father's vocation, becoming a preacher at age fourteen. At seventeen, he left the ministry and devoted himself to writing until his death in 1987. Baldwin's most frequent subject was the relationship between blacks and whites, about which he wrote, "The color of my skin made me automatically an expert." He wrote five novels, a book of stories, one play, and several collections of essays. This essay, "Autobiographical Notes," introduces his collection, Notes of a Native Son *(1955).*

I was born in Harlem thirty-one years ago. I began plotting novels at about the time I learned to read. The story of my childhood is the usual bleak fantasy, and we can dismiss it with the restrained observation that I certainly would not consider living it again. In those days my mother was given to the exasperating and mysterious habit of having babies. As they were born, I took them over with one hand and held a book with the other. The children probably suffered, though they have since been kind enough to deny it, and in this way I read *Uncle Tom's Cabin* and *A Tale of Two Cities* over and over and over again; in this way, in fact, I read just about everything I could get my hands on—except the Bible, probably because it was the only book I was encouraged to read. I must also confess that I wrote—a great deal—and my first professional triumph, in any case, the first effort of mine to be seen in print, occurred at the age of twelve or thereabouts, when a short story I had written about the Spanish revolution won some sort of prize in an extremely short-lived church newspaper. I remember the story was censored by the lady editor, though I don't remember why, and I was outraged.

I also wrote plays, and songs, for one of which I received a letter of congratulations from Mayor La Guardia, and poetry, about which the less said, the better. My mother was delighted by all these goings-on, but my father wasn't; he wanted me to be a preacher. When I was fourteen I became a preacher, and when I was seventeen I stopped. Very shortly thereafter I left home. For God knows how long I struggled with the world of commerce and industry—I guess they would say they struggled with *me*—and when I was about twenty-one I had enough done of a novel to get a Saxton Fellowship. When I was twenty-two the fellowship was over, the novel turned out to be unsalable, and I started waiting on tables in a Village restaurant and writing book reviews—mostly, as it turned out, about the Negro problem, concerning which the color of my skin made me automatically an expert. Did another book, in company with photographer Theodore Pelatowski, about the store-front churches in Harlem. This book met exactly the same fate as my first—fellowship, but no sale. (It was a Rosenwald Fellowship.) By the time I was twenty-four I had decided to stop reviewing books about the Negro problem—which, by this time, was only slightly less horrible in print than it was in life—and I packed my bags and went to France, where I finished, God knows how, *Go Tell It on the Mountain*.

Any writer, I suppose, feels that the world into which he was born is nothing 3 less than a conspiracy against the cultivation of his talent—which attitude certainly has a great deal to support it. On the other hand, it is only because the world looks on his talent with such a frightening indifference that the artist is compelled to make his talent important. So that any writer, looking back over even so short a span of time as I am here forced to assess, finds that the things which hurt him and the things which helped him cannot be divorced from each other; he could be helped in a certain way only because he was hurt in a certain way; and his help is simply to be enabled to move from one conundrum to the next—one is tempted to say that he moves from one disaster to the next. When one begins looking for influences one finds them by the score. I haven't thought much about my own, not enough anyway; I hazard that the King James Bible, the rhetoric of the store-front church, something ironic and violent and perpetually understated in Negro speech—and something of Dickens' love for bravura—have something to do with me today; but I wouldn't stake my life on it. Likewise, innumerable people have helped me in many ways; but finally, I suppose, the most difficult (and most rewarding) thing in my life has been the fact that I was born a Negro and was forced, therefore, to effect some kind of truce with this reality. (Truce, by the way, is the best one can hope for.)

One of the difficulties about being a Negro writer (and this is not special 4 pleading, since I don't mean to suggest that he has it worse than anybody else) is that the Negro problem is written about so widely. The bookshelves groan under the weight of information, and everyone therefore considers himself informed. And this information, furthermore, operates usually (generally, popularly) to reinforce traditional attitudes. Of traditional attitudes there are only two—For or Against—and I, personally, find it difficult to say which attitude has caused me the most pain. I am speaking as a writer; from a social point of view I am perfectly aware that the change from ill-will to good-will, however motivated, however imperfect, however expressed, is better than no change at all.

But it is part of the business of the writer—as I see it—to examine attitudes, 5 to go beneath the surface, to tap the source. From this point of view the Negro problem is nearly inaccessible. It is not only written about so widely; it is written about so badly. It is quite possible to say that the price a Negro pays for becoming articulate is to find himself, at length, with nothing to be articulate about. ("You taught me language," says Caliban to Prospero,[1] "and my profit on't is I know how to curse.") Consider: the tremendous social activity that this problem generates imposes on whites and Negroes alike the necessity of looking forward, of working to bring about a better day. This is fine, it keeps the waters troubled; it is all, indeed, that has made possible the Negro's progress. Nevertheless, social affairs are not generally speaking the writer's prime concern, whether they ought to be or not; it is absolutely necessary that he establish between himself and these affairs a distance which will allow, at least, for clarity, so that before he can look forward in any meaningful sense, he must first be allowed to take a long look back. In the context of the Negro problem neither whites nor blacks, for excellent reasons of their own, have the faintest desire to look back; but I think that the past is all that makes the present coherent, and further, that the past will remain horrible for exactly as long as we refuse to assess it honestly.

I know, in any case, that the most crucial time in my own development   6 came when I was forced to recognize that I was a kind of bastard of the West; when I followed the line of my past I did not find myself in Europe but in Africa. And this meant that in some subtle way, in a really profound way, I brought to Shakespeare, Bach, Rembrandt, to the stones of Paris, to the cathedral at Chartres, and to the Empire State Building, a special attitude. These were not really my creations, they did not contain my history; I might search in them in vain forever for any reflection of myself. I was an interloper; this was not my heritage. At the same time I had no other heritage which I could possibly hope to use—I had certainly been unfitted for the jungle or the tribe. I would have to appropriate these white centuries, I would have to make them mine—I would have to accept my special attitude, my special place in this scheme—otherwise I would have no place in *any* scheme. What was the most difficult was the fact that I was forced to admit something I had always hidden from myself, which the American Negro has had to hide from himself as the price of his public progress; that I hated and feared white people. This did not mean that I loved black people; on the contrary, I despised them, possibly because they failed to produce Rembrandt. In effect, I hated and feared the world. And this meant, not only that I thus gave the world an altogether murderous power over me, but also that in such a self-destroying limbo I could never hope to write.

One writes out of one thing only—one's own experience. Everything depends   7 on how relentlessly one forces from this experience the last drop, sweet or bitter, it can possibly give. This is the only real concern of the artist, to recreate out of the disorder of life that order which is art. The difficulty then, for me, of being a Negro writer was the fact that I was, in effect, prohibited from examining

---

[1] Caliban to Prospero: characters in Shakespeare's *The Tempest*. Caliban, a savage and deformed creature, is the slave of Prospero, the rightful Duke of Milan. [Eds.]

my own experience too closely by the tremendous demands and the very real dangers of my social situation.

I don't think the dilemma outlined above is uncommon. I do think, since writers work in the disastrously explicit medium of language, that it goes a little way towards explaining why, out of the enormous resources of Negro speech and life, and despite the example of Negro music, prose written by Negroes has been generally speaking so pallid and so harsh. I have not written about being a Negro at such length because I expect that to be my only subject, but only because it was the gate I had to unlock before I could hope to write about anything else. I don't think that the Negro problem in America can be even discussed coherently without bearing in mind its context; its context being the history, traditions, customs, the moral assumptions and preoccupations of the country; in short, the general social fabric. Appearances to the contrary, no one in America escapes its effects and everyone in America bears some responsibility for it. I believe this the more firmly because it is the overwhelming tendency to speak of this problem as though it were a thing apart. But in the work of Faulkner, in the general attitude and certain specific passages in Robert Penn Warren, and, most significantly, in the advent of Ralph Ellison, one sees the beginnings—at least—of a more genuinely penetrating search. Mr. Ellison, by the way, is the first Negro novelist I have ever read to utilize in language, and brilliantly, some of the ambiguity and irony of Negro life. 8

About my interests: I don't know if I have any, unless the morbid desire to own a sixteen-millimeter camera and make experimental movies can be so classified. Otherwise, I love to eat and drink—it's my melancholy conviction that I've scarcely ever had enough to eat (this is because it's *impossible* to eat enough if you're worried about the next meal)—and I love to argue with people who do not disagree with me too profoundly, and I love to laugh. I do *not* like bohemia, or bohemians, I do not like people whose principal aim is pleasure, and I do not like people who are *earnest* about anything. I don't like people who like me because I'm a Negro; neither do I like people who find in the same accident grounds for contempt. I love America more than any other country in the world, and, exactly for this reason, I insist on the right to criticize her perpetually. I think all theories are suspect, that the finest principles may have to be modified, or may even be pulverized by the demands of life, and that one must find, therefore, one's own moral center and move through the world hoping that this center will guide one aright. I consider that I have many responsibilities, but none greater than this: to last, as Hemingway says, and get my work done. 9

I want to be an honest man and a good writer. 10

QUESTIONS

1. What does Baldwin believe is the business of the writer? With what should a writer be concerned?

2. What circumstances have influenced Baldwin as a writer? What does he consider the most important point in his development as a writer?

3. Explain what you think Baldwin means when he writes in paragraph 8: "I have not written about being a Negro at such length because I expect that to be my only subject, but only because it was the gate I had to unlock before I could hope to write about anything else."

4. What is Baldwin's point of view toward himself and his life as a writer? That is, what sense of himself does he project? Find specific passages in the essay to support your answer.

5. What is Baldwin's tone? What is the effect of this tone with an autobiographical topic?

6. Baldwin finds it hard to separate the things that helped him as a writer from those that hurt him. Consider your own experiences with writing, and write an essay in which you reflect on what has been most helpful and most harmful in your development as a writer.

7. What central fact of your life—race, religion, parents, birthplace, special abilities, and so on—has influenced you the most? Write your own "Autobiographical Notes" in which you focus on the influence of this central fact on the shaping of your life.

MAKING CONNECTIONS

1. This is another essay that could be called "Why I Write." Compare it to Joan Didion's and Alice Walker's remarks on this subject. What similarities do you find among the different essays?

2. When Baldwin says on race relations, "the color of my skin made me automatically an expert" (paragraph 2), he is making a fundamental assertion about the relation of experience to knowledge. Locate another writer in this section, not necessarily an African-American writer, and describe the extent to which experience made him or her an expert. Reflect also on Baldwin's modifier, "automatically." What other aspects of Baldwin's life help him *develop* expertise?

LEARNING TO READ
AND WRITE

Frederick Douglass

Frederick Augustus Washington Bailey (1817–1895) was born into slavery on the Eastern Shore of Maryland. His mother was a black slave; his father, a white man. After his escape from the South in 1838, he adopted the name of Douglass and worked to free other slaves and later (after the Civil War) to protect the rights of freed slaves. He was a newspaper editor, a lecturer, United States minister to Haiti, and the author of several books about his life and times. The Narrative of the Life of Frederick Douglass: An American Slave *(1841), from which the following chapter has been taken, is his best-known work.*

I lived in Master Hugh's family about seven years. During this time, I   1
succeeded in learning to read and write. In accomplishing this, I was compelled
to resort to various stratagems. I had no regular teacher. My mistress, who had
kindly commenced to instruct me, had, in compliance with the advice and
direction of her husband, not only ceased to instruct, but had set her face
against my being instructed by any one else. It is due, however, to my mistress
to say of her, that she did not adopt this course of treatment immediately. She
at first lacked the depravity indispensable to shutting me up in mental darkness.
It was at least necessary for her to have some training in the exercise of
irresponsible power, to make her equal to the task of treating me as though I
were a brute.

My mistress was, as I have said, a kind and tender-hearted woman; and in   2
the simplicity of her soul she commenced, when I first went to live with her,
to treat me as she supposed one human being ought to treat another. In entering
upon the duties of a slaveholder, she did not seem to perceive that I sustained
to her the relation of a mere chattel, and that for her to treat me as a human
being was not only wrong, but dangerously so. Slavery proved as injurious to
her as it did to me. When I went there, she was a pious, warm, and tender-
hearted woman. There was no sorrow or suffering for which she had not a tear.
She had bread for the hungry, clothes for the naked, and comfort for every
mourner that came within her reach. Slavery soon proved its ability to divest
her of these heavenly qualities. Under its influence, the tender heart became
stone, and the lamblike disposition gave way to one of tiger-like fierceness. The
first step in her downward course was in her ceasing to instruct me. She now

71

commenced to practise her husband's precepts. She finally became even more violent in her opposition than her husband himself. She was not satisfied with simply doing as well as he had commanded; she seemed anxious to do better. Nothing seemed to make her more angry than to see me with a newspaper. She seemed to think that here lay the danger. I have had her rush at me with a face made all up of fury, and snatch from me a newspaper, in a manner that fully revealed her apprehension. She was an apt woman; and a little experience soon demonstrated, to her satisfaction, that education and slavery were incompatible with each other.

From this time I was most narrowly watched. If I was in a separate room any considerable length of time, I was sure to be suspected of having a book, and was at once called to give an account of myself. All this, however, was too late. The first step had been taken. Mistress, in teaching me the alphabet, had given me the *inch*, and no precaution could prevent me from taking the *ell*. 3

The plan which I adopted, and the one by which I was most successful, was that of making friends of all the little white boys whom I met in the street. As many of these as I could, I converted into teachers. With their kindly aid, obtained at different times and in different places, I finally succeeded in learning to read. When I was sent on errands, I always took my book with me, and by going one part of my errand quickly, I found time to get a lesson before my return. I used also to carry bread with me, enough of which was always in the house, and to which I was always welcome; for I was much better off in this regard than many of the poor white children in our neighborhood. This bread I used to bestow upon the hungry little urchins, who, in return, would give me that more valuable bread of knowledge. I am strongly tempted to give the names of two or three of those little boys, as a testimonial of the gratitude and affection I bear them; but prudence forbids;—not that it would injure me, but it might embarrass them; for it is almost an unpardonable offence to teach slaves to read in this Christian country. It is enough to say of the dear little fellows, that they lived on Philpot Street, very near Durgin and Bailey's ship-yard. I used to talk this matter of slavery over with them. I would sometimes say to them, I wished I could be as free as they would be when they got to be men. "You will be free as soon as you are twenty-one, *but I am a slave for life!* Have not I as good a right to be free as you have?" These words used to trouble them; they would express for me the liveliest sympathy, and console me with the hope that something would occur by which I might be free. 4

I was now about twelve years old, and the thought of being *a slave for life* began to bear heavily upon my heart. Just about this time, I got hold of a book entitled "The Columbian Orator."[1] Every opportunity I got, I used to read this book. Among much of other interesting matter, I found in it a dialogue between 5

---

[1] *The Columbian Orator:* a popular schoolbook designed to introduce students to argument and rhetoric. [Eds.]

a master and his slave. The slave was represented as having run away from his master three times. The dialogue represented the conversation which took place between them, when the slave was retaken the third time. In this dialogue, the whole argument in behalf of slavery was brought forward by the master, all of which was disposed of by the slave. The slave was made to say some very smart as well as impressive things in reply to his master—things which had the desired though unexpected effect; for the conversation resulted in the voluntary emancipation of the slave on the part of the master.

In the same book, I met with one of Sheridan's mighty speeches on and in behalf of Catholic emancipation.[2] These were choice documents to me. I read them over and over again with unabated interest. They gave tongue to interesting thoughts of my own soul, which had frequently flashed through my mind, and died away for want of utterance. The moral which I gained from the dialogue was the power of truth over the conscience of even a slaveholder. What I got from Sheridan was a bold denunciation of slavery, and a powerful vindication of human rights. The reading of these documents enabled me to utter my thoughts, and to meet the arguments brought forward to sustain slavery; but while they relieved me of one difficulty, they brought on another even more painful than the one of which I was relieved. The more I read, the more I was led to abhor and detest my enslavers. I could regard them in no other light than a band of successful robbers, who had left their homes, and gone to Africa, and stolen us from our homes, and in a strange land reduced us to slavery. I loathed them as being the meanest as well as the most wicked of men. As I read and contemplated the subject, behold! that very discontentment which Master Hugh had predicted would follow my learning to read had already come, to torment and sting my soul to unutterable anguish. As I writhed under it, I would at times feel that learning to read had been a curse rather than a blessing. It had given me a view of my wretched condition, without the remedy. It opened my eyes to the horrible pit, but to no ladder upon which to get out. In moments of agony, I envied my fellow-slaves for their stupidity. I have often wished myself a beast. I preferred the condition of the meanest reptile to my own. Any thing, no matter what, to get rid of thinking! It was this everlasting thinking of my condition that tormented me. There was no getting rid of it. It was pressed upon me by every object within sight or hearing, animate or inanimate. The silver trump of freedom had roused my soul to eternal wakefulness. Freedom now appeared, to disappear no more forever. It was heard in every sound, and seen in every thing. It was ever present to torment me with a sense of my wretched condition. I saw nothing without seeing it, I heard nothing without hearing it, and felt nothing without feeling it. It looked from every star, it smiled in every calm, breathed in every wind, and moved in every storm.

6

---

[2] Richard Brinsley Sheridan (1751–1816): British dramatist, orator, and politician. Catholics were not allowed to vote in England until 1829. [Eds.]

I often found myself regretting my own existence, and wishing myself dead; 7 and but for the hope of being free, I have no doubt but that I should have killed myself, or done something for which I should have been killed. While in this state of mind, I was eager to hear any one speak of slavery. I was a ready listener. Every little while, I could hear something about the abolitionists. It was some time before I found what the word meant. It was always used in such connections as to make it an interesting word to me. If a slave ran away and succeeded in getting clear, or if a slave killed his master, set fire to a barn, or did any thing very wrong in the mind of a slaveholder, it was spoken of as the fruit of *abolition*. Hearing the word in this connection very often, I set about learning what it meant. The dictionary afforded me little or no help. I found it was "the act of abolishing"; but then I did not know what was to be abolished. Here I was perplexed. I did not dare to ask any one about its meaning, for I was satisfied that it was something they wanted me to know very little about. After a patient waiting, I got one of our city papers, containing an account of the number of petitions from the north, praying for the abolition of slavery in the District of Columbia, and of the slave trade between the States. From this time I understood the words *abolition* and *abolitionist*, and always drew near when that word was spoken, expecting to hear something of importance to myself and fellow-slaves. The light broke in upon me by degrees. I went one day down on the wharf of Mr. Waters; and seeing two Irishmen unloading a scow of stone, I went, unasked, and helped them. When we had finished, one of them came to me and asked me if I were a slave. I told him I was. He asked, "Are ye a slave for life?" I told him that I was. The good Irishman seemed to be deeply affected by the statement. He said to the other that it was a pity so fine a little fellow as myself should be a slave for life. He said it was a shame to hold me. They both advised me to run away to the north; that I should find friends there, and that I should be free. I pretended not to be interested in what they said, and treated them as if I did not understand them; for I feared they might be treacherous. White men have been known to encourage slaves to escape, and then, to get the reward, catch them and return them to their masters. I was afraid that these seemingly good men might use me so; but I nevertheless remembered their advice, and from that time I resolved to run away. I looked forward to a time at which it would be safe for me to escape. I was too young to think of doing so immediately; besides, I wished to learn how to write, as I might have occasion to write my own pass. I consoled myself with the hope that I should one day find a good chance. Meanwhile, I would learn to write.

The idea as to how I might learn to write was suggested to me by being in 8 Durgin and Bailey's ship-yard, and frequently seeing the ship carpenters, after hewing, and getting a piece of timber ready for use, write on the timber the name of that part of the ship for which it was intended. When a piece of timber was intended for the larboard side, it would be marked thus—"L." When a piece was for the starboard side, it would be marked thus—"S." A piece for the larboard side forward, would be marked thus—"L. F." When a piece was for starboard side forward, it would be marked thus—"S. F." For larboard aft, it would be marked thus—"L. A." For starboard aft, it would be marked thus— "S. A." I soon learned the names of these letters, and for what they were intended when placed upon a piece of timber in the ship-yard. I immediately commenced copying them, and in a short time was able to make the four letters named. After that, when I met with any boy who I knew could write, I would tell him I could write as well as he. The next word would be, "I don't believe you. Let me see you try it." I would then make the letters which I had been so fortunate as to learn, and ask him to beat that. In this way I got a good many lessons in writing, which it is quite possible I should never have gotten in any other way. During this time, my copy-book was the board fence, brick wall, and pavement; my pen and ink was a lump of chalk. With these, I learned mainly how to write. I then commenced and continued copying the Italics in Webster's Spelling Book, until I could make them all without looking on the book. By this time, my little Master Thomas had gone to school, and learned how to write, and had written over a number of copy-books. These had been brought home, and shown to some of our near neighbors, and then laid aside. My mistress used to go to class meeting at the Wilk Street meetinghouse every Monday afternoon, and leave me to take care of the house. When left thus, I used to spend the time in writing in the spaces left in Master Thomas's copy-book, copying what he had written. I continued to do this until I could write a hand very similar to that of Master Thomas. Thus, after a long, tedious effort for years, I finally succeeded in learning how to write.

QUESTIONS

1. As its title proclaims, Douglass's book is a narrative, the story of his life. So, too, is this chapter a narrative, the story of his learning to read and write. Separate out the main events of this story, and list them in chronological order.

2. Douglass is reporting some of the events in his life in this selection, but certain events are not simply reported. Instead, they are described so that we may see, hear, and feel what was experienced by those people who were present on the original occasions. Which events are described most fully in this narrative? How does Douglass seek to engage our interest and direct our feelings through such scenes?

3. In this episode from his life, as in his whole book, Douglass is engaged in evaluating an institution—slavery—and arguing a case against it. Can you locate the points in the text where reflecting gives way to argumentation? How does Douglass support his argument against slavery? What are the sources of his persuasiveness?

4. The situation of Irish Catholics is a subtheme in this essay. You can trace it by locating every mention of the Irish or of Catholicism in the text. How does this theme relate to African-American slavery? Try to locate *The Columbian Orator* in your library,

or find out more about who Sheridan was and why he had to argue on behalf of "Catholic emancipation" (paragraph 6).

5. There is a subnarrative in this text that tells the story of Master Hugh's wife, the "mistress" of the household in which Douglass learned to read and write. Retell *her* story in your own words. Consider how her story relates to Douglass's own story and how it relates to Douglass's larger argument about slavery.

6. Put yourself in the place of Master Hugh's wife, and retell all events in her words and from her point of view. To do so, you will have to decide both what she might have come to know about all these events and how she would feel about them. You will also have to decide when she is writing. Is she keeping a diary during this very time (the early 1830s), or is she looking back from the perspective of later years? Has she been moved to write by reading Douglass's own book, which appeared in 1841? If so, how old would she be then, and what would she think about these past events? Would she be angry, bitter, repentant, embarrassed, indulgent, scornful, or what?

MAKING CONNECTIONS

1. What are the most common themes of the African-American writers in this section? On what issues, when they write about writing, do they have most in common with the artists represented here who are white?

2. For Maya Angelou, Frederick Douglass, and Alice Walker, events of childhood and youth are particularly important. Compare how at least two of these writers view events when they were young, how they present their younger selves or viewpoints, and how they connect childhood experience to adult knowledge.

Social Sciences and Public Affairs

PILGRIMAGE TO NONVIOLENCE
Martin Luther King, Jr.

The son of a minister, Martin Luther King, Jr. (1929–1968) was ordained a Baptist minister in his father's church in Atlanta, Georgia, at the age of eighteen. He sprang into prominence in 1955 when he called a citywide boycott of the segregated bus system in Montgomery, Alabama, and he continued to be the most prominent civil rights activist in America until his assassination on April 4, 1968. During those tumultuous years, he was jailed at least fourteen times and endured countless threats against his life, but he per-severed in his fight against racial discrimination using a synthesis of the nonviolent philosophy of Mahatma Gandhi and the Sermon on the Mount. The 1964 Nobel Peace Prize was only one of the many awards he received, and his several books are characterized as much by their eloquent prose style as by their moral fervor. "Pilgrimage to Nonviolence" orig-inally appeared in the magazine Christian Century *and was revised and updated for a collection of his sermons,* Strength to Love *(1963), the source of the following text.*

In my senior year in theological seminary, I engaged in the exciting reading   1
of various theological theories. Having been raised in a rather strict fundamentalist tradition, I was occasionally shocked when my intellectual journey carried
me through new and sometimes complex doctrinal lands, but the pilgrimage

was always stimulating, gave me a new appreciation for objective appraisal and critical analysis, and knocked me out of my dogmatic slumber.

Liberalism provided me with an intellectual satisfaction that I had never 2 found in fundamentalism. I became so enamored of the insights of liberalism that I almost fell into the trap of accepting uncritically everything it encompassed. I was absolutely convinced of the natural goodness of man and the natural power of human reason.

I

A basic change in my thinking came when I began to question some of the 3 theories that had been associated with so-called liberal theology. Of course, there are aspects of liberalism that I hope to cherish always: its devotion to the search for truth, its insistence on an open and analytical mind, and its refusal to abandon the best lights of reason. The contribution of liberalism to the philosophical-historical criticism of biblical literature has been of immeasurable value and should be defended with religious and scientific passion.

But I began to question the liberal doctrine of man. The more I observed 4 the tragedies of history and man's shameful inclination to choose the low road, the more I came to see the depths and strength of sin. My reading of the works of Reinhold Niebuhr made me aware of the complexity of human motives and the reality of sin on every level of man's existence.[1] Moreover, I came to recognize the complexity of man's social involvement and the glaring reality of collective evil. I realized that liberalism had been all too sentimental concerning human nature and that it leaned toward a false idealism.

I also came to see the superficial optimism of liberalism concerning human 5 nature overlooked the fact that reason is darkened by sin. The more I thought about human nature, the more I saw how our tragic inclination for sin encourages us to rationalize our actions. Liberalism failed to show that reason by itself is little more than an instrument to justify man's defensive ways of thinking. Reason, devoid of the purifying power of faith, can never free itself from distortions and rationalizations.

Although I rejected some aspects of liberalism, I never came to an all-out 6 acceptance of neo-orthodoxy. While I saw neo-orthodoxy as a helpful corrective for a sentimental liberalism, I felt that it did not provide an adequate answer to basic questions. If liberalism was too optimistic concerning human nature, neo-orthodoxy was too pessimistic. Not only on the question of man, but also on other vital issues, the revolt of neo-orthodoxy went too far. In its attempt to

---

[1] Reinhold Niebuhr (1892–1971): American theologian, social activist, and noted writer on social and religious issues. [Eds.]

preserve the transcendence of God, which had been neglected by an overstress of his immanence in liberalism, neo-orthodoxy went to the extreme of stressing a God who was hidden, unknown, and "wholly other." In its revolt against overemphasis on the power of reason in liberalism, neo-orthodoxy fell into a mood of antirationalism and semifundamentalism, stressing a narrow uncritical biblicism. This approach, I felt, was inadequate both for the church and for personal life.

So although liberalism left me unsatisfied on the question of the nature of   7
man, I found no refuge in neo-orthodoxy. I am now convinced that the truth about man is found neither in liberalism nor in neo-orthodoxy. Each represents a partial truth. A large segment of Protestant liberalism defined man only in terms of his essential nature, his capacity for good; neo-orthodoxy tended to define man only in terms of his existential nature, his capacity for evil. An adequate understanding of man is found neither in the thesis of liberalism nor in the antithesis of neo-orthodoxy, but in a synthesis which reconciles the truths of both.

During the intervening years I have gained a new appreciation for the   8
philosophy of existentialism. My first contact with the philosophy came through my reading of Kierkegaard and Nietzsche.[2] Later I turned to a study of Jaspers, Heidegger, and Sartre.[3] These thinkers stimulated my thinking; while questioning each, I nevertheless learned a great deal through a study of them. When I finally engaged in a serious study of the writings of Paul Tillich,[4] I became convinced that existentialism, in spite of the fact that it had become all too fashionable, had grasped certain basic truths about man and his condition that could not be permanently overlooked.

An understanding of the "finite freedom" of man is one of the permanent   9
contributions of existentialism, and its perception of the anxiety and conflict produced in man's personal and social life by the perilous and ambiguous structure of existence is especially meaningful for our time. A common denominator in atheistic or theistic existentialism is that man's existential situation is estranged from his essential nature. In their revolt against Hegel's essentialism,[5] all existentialists contend that the world is fragmented. History is a series of

---

[2] Soren Kierkegaard (1813–1855): Danish religious and aesthetic philosopher, concerned especially with the role of the individual; Friedrich Nietzsche (1844–1900): German philosopher and moralist looking for a heroic, creative rejuvenation of decadent Western civilization. [Eds.]

[3] Karl Jaspers (1883–1969): German philosopher; Martin Heidegger (1899–1976): German philosopher; Jean-Paul Sartre (1905–1980): French philosopher and novelist. All three were existentialists, concerned with the existence and responsibility of the individual in an unknowable universe. [Eds.]

[4] Paul Tillich (1886–1965): German-born American philosopher and theologian whose writings drew on psychology and existentialism. [Eds.]

[5] Georg Friedrich Hegel (1770–1831): German philosopher best known for his dialectic (thesis vs. antithesis produces synthesis). [Eds.]

unreconciled conflicts, and man's existence is filled with anxiety and threatened with meaninglessness. While the ultimate Christian answer is not found in any of these existential assertions, there is much here by which the theologian may describe the true state of man's existence.

Although most of my formal study has been in systematic theology and philosophy, I have become more and more interested in social ethics. During my early teens I was deeply concerned by the problem of racial injustice. I considered segregation both rationally inexplicable and morally unjustifiable. I could never accept my having to sit in the back of a bus or in the segregated section of a train. The first time that I was seated behind a curtain in a dining car I felt as though the curtain had been dropped on my selfhood. I also learned that the inseparable twin of racial injustice is economic injustice. I saw how the systems of segregation exploited both the Negro and the poor whites. These early experiences made me deeply conscious of the varieties of injustice in our society.

II

Not until I entered theological seminary, however, did I begin a serious intellectual quest for a method that would eliminate social evil. I was immediately influenced by the social gospel. In the early 1950s I read Walter Rauschenbusch's *Christianity and the Social Crisis*, a book which left an indelible imprint on my thinking. Of course, there were points at which I differed with Rauschenbusch. I felt that he was a victim of the nineteenth-century "cult of inevitable progress," which led him to an unwarranted optimism concerning human nature. Moreover, he came perilously close to identifying the Kingdom of God with a particular social and economic system, a temptation to which the church must never surrender. But in spite of these shortcomings, Rauschenbusch gave to American Protestantism a sense of social responsibility that it should never lose. The gospel at its best deals with the whole man, not only his soul but also his body, not only his spiritual well-being but also his material well-being. A religion that professes a concern for the souls of men and is not equally concerned about the slums that damn them, the economic conditions that strangle them, and the social conditions that cripple them, is a spiritually moribund religion.

After reading Rauschenbusch, I turned to a serious study of the social and ethical theories of the great philosophers. During this period I had almost despaired of the power of love to solve social problems. The turn-the-other-cheek and the love-your-enemies philosophies are valid, I felt, only when individuals are in conflict with other individuals; when racial groups and nations are in conflict, a more realistic approach is necessary.

Then I was introduced to the life and teachings of Mahatma Gandhi.[6] As I   13
read his works I became deeply fascinated by his campaigns of nonviolent
resistance. The whole Gandhian concept of *satyagraha* (*satya* is truth which
equals love and *graha* is force; *satyagraha* thus means truth-force or love-force)
was profoundly significant to me. As I delved deeper into the philosophy of
Gandhi, my skepticism concerning the power of love gradually diminished, and
I came to see for the first time that the Christian doctrine of love, operating
through the Gandhian method of nonviolence, is one of the most potent
weapons available to an oppressed people in their struggle for freedom. At that
time, however, I acquired only an intellectual understanding and appreciation
of the position, and I had no firm determination to organize it in a socially
effective situation.

When I went to Montgomery, Alabama, as a pastor in 1954, I had not the   14
slightest idea that I would later become involved in a crisis in which nonviolent
resistance would be applicable. After I had lived in the community about a
year, the bus boycott began. The Negro people of Montgomery, exhausted by
the humiliating experience that they had constantly faced on the buses, expressed in a massive act of noncooperation their determination to be free. They
came to see that it was ultimately more honorable to walk the streets in dignity
than to ride the buses in humiliation. At the beginning of the protest, the
people called on me to serve as their spokesman. In accepting this responsibility,
my mind, consciously or unconsciously, was driven back to the Sermon on the
Mount and the Gandhian method of nonviolent resistance. This principle
became the guiding light of our movement. Christ furnished the spirit and
motivation and Gandhi furnished the method.

The experience in Montgomery did more to clarify my thinking in regard to   15
the question of nonviolence than all of the books that I had read. As the days
unfolded, I became more and more convinced of the power of nonviolence.
Nonviolence became more than a method to which I gave intellectual assent;
it became a commitment to a way of life. Many issues I had not cleared up
intellectually concerning nonviolence were now resolved within the sphere of
practical action.

My privilege of traveling to India had a great impact on me personally, for   16
it was invigorating to see firsthand the amazing results of a nonviolent struggle
to achieve independence. The aftermath of hatred and bitterness that usually
follows a violent campaign was found nowhere in India, and a mutual friendship, based on complete equality, existed between the Indian and British people
within the Commonwealth.

I would not wish to give the impression that nonviolence will accomplish   17
miracles overnight. Men are not easily moved from their mental ruts or purged

---

[6]Mahatma Gandhi (1869–1948): Hindu nationalist and spiritual leader. [Eds.]

of their prejudiced and irrational feelings. When the underprivileged demand freedom, the privileged at first react with bitterness and resistance. Even when the demands are couched in nonviolent terms, the initial response is substantially the same. I am sure that many of our white brothers in Montgomery and throughout the South are still bitter toward the Negro leaders, even though these leaders have sought to follow a way of love and nonviolence. But the nonviolent approach does something to the hearts and souls of those committed to it. It gives them new self-respect. It calls up resources of strength and courage that they did not know they had. Finally, it so stirs the conscience of the opponent that reconciliation becomes a reality.

III

More recently I have come to see the need for the method of nonviolence 18 in international relations. Although I was not yet convinced of its efficacy in conflicts between nations, I felt that while war could never be a positive good, it could serve as a negative good by preventing the spread and growth of an evil force. War, horrible as it is, might be preferable to surrender to a totalitarian system. But I now believe that the potential destructiveness of modern weapons totally rules out the possibility of war ever again achieving a negative good. If we assume that mankind has a right to survive, then we must find an alternative to war and destruction. In our day of space vehicles and guided ballistic missiles, the choice is either nonviolence or nonexistence.

I am no doctrinaire pacifist, but I have tried to embrace a realistic pacifism 19 which finds the pacifist position as the lesser evil in the circumstances. I do not claim to be free from the moral dilemmas that the Christian nonpacifist confronts, but I am convinced that the church cannot be silent while mankind faces the threat of nuclear annihilation. If the church is true to her mission, she must call for an end to the arms race.

Some of my personal sufferings over the last few years have also served to 20 shape my thinking. I always hesitate to mention these experiences for fear of conveying the wrong impression. A person who constantly calls attention to his trials and sufferings is in danger of developing a martyr complex and impressing others that he is consciously seeking sympathy. It is possible for one to be self-centered in his self-sacrifice. So I am always reluctant to refer to my personal sacrifices. But I feel somewhat justified in mentioning them in this essay because of the influence they have had upon my thought.

Due to my involvement in the struggle for the freedom of my people, I have 21 known very few quiet days in the last few years. I have been imprisoned in Alabama and Georgia jails twelve times. My home has been bombed twice. A day seldom passes that my family and I are not the recipients of threats of death. I have been the victim of a near-fatal stabbing. So in a real sense I have been battered by the storms of persecution. I must admit that at times I have felt that

I could no longer bear such a heavy burden, and have been tempted to retreat to a more quiet and serene life. But every time such a temptation appeared, something came to strengthen and sustain my determination. I have learned now that the Master's burden is light precisely when we take his yoke upon us.

My personal trials have also taught me the value of unmerited suffering. As 22 my sufferings mounted I soon realized that there were two ways in which I could respond to my situation—either to react with bitterness or seek to transform the suffering into a creative force. I decided to follow the latter course. Recognizing the necessity for suffering, I have tried to make of it a virtue, if only to save myself from bitterness, I have attempted to see my personal ordeals as an opportunity to transfigure myself and heal the people involved in the tragic situation which now obtains. I have lived these last few years with the conviction that unearned suffering is redemptive. There are some who still find the Cross a stumbling block, others consider it foolishness, but I am more convinced than ever before that it is the power of God unto social and individual salvation. So like the Apostle Paul I can now humbly, yet proudly, say, "I bear in my body the marks of the Lord Jesus."

The agonizing moments through which I have passed during the last few 23 years have also drawn me closer to God. More than ever before I am convinced of the reality of a personal God. True, I have always believed in the personality of God. But in the past the idea of a personal God was little more than a metaphysical category that I found theologically and philosophically satisfying. Now it is a living reality that has been validated in the experiences of everyday life. God has been profoundly real to me in recent years. In the midst of outer dangers I have felt an inner calm. In the midst of lonely days and dreary nights I have heard an inner voice saying, "Lo, I will be with you." When the chains of fear and the manacles of frustration have all but stymied my efforts, I have felt the power of God transforming the fatigue of despair into the buoyancy of hope. I am convinced that the universe is under the control of a loving purpose, and that in the struggle for righteousness man has cosmic companionship. Behind the harsh appearances of the world there is a benign power. To say that this God is personal is not to make him a finite object beside other objects or attribute to him the limitations of human personality; it is to take what is finest and noblest in our consciousness and affirm its perfect existence in him. It is certainly true that human personality is limited, but personality as such involves no necessary limitations. It means simply self-consciousness and self-direction. So in the truest sense of the word, God is a living God. In him there is feeling and will, responsive to the deepest yearnings of the human heart: *this* God both evokes and answers prayer.

The past decade has been a most exciting one. In spite of the tensions and 24 uncertainties of this period something profoundly meaningful is taking place. Old systems of exploitation and oppression are passing away; new systems of justice and equality are being born. In a real sense this is a great time to be alive. Therefore, I am not yet discouraged about the future. Granted that the easygoing optimism of yesterday is impossible. Granted that we face a world crisis which leaves us standing so often amid the surging murmur of life's restless sea. But every crisis has both its dangers and its opportunities. It can spell either salvation or doom. In a dark, confused world the Kingdom of God may yet reign in the hearts of men.

QUESTIONS

1. King found the extremes of liberalism on one hand and neo-orthodoxy on the other both unsatisfactory. Why?

2. Existentialism and Rauschenbusch's social gospel proved more useful to King than liberalism or neo-orthodoxy. How did these concepts help shape his outlook?

3. King is interested in religious and philosophical theories not for their own sake but for their usefulness in the social world. How do Gandhi's example and King's own experience in Montgomery (paragraphs 14, 15, and 17) illustrate this concern?

4. How did King's personal faith in God aid in his struggles and sufferings? Is his dream of a better society totally dependent upon the existence of this "benign power" (paragraph 23)?

5. King's intellectual development is described as a pilgrimage from a simple fundamentalist attitude through conflicting theological and philosophical concepts to an intensified belief in a benign God and a commitment to international nonviolence. How is his final set of beliefs superior to his original one? Has he convinced you of the validity of his beliefs?

6. King writes for a general audience rather than one with theological and philosophical training. How successful is King at clarifying religious and philosophical concepts for the general reader? Point out examples that show how he treats such concepts.

7. Again and again King employs the classical rhetorical strategy of concession: the opposition's viewpoint is stated and partially accepted before King gives his own viewpoint. Locate two or three instances of this strategy, and explain how it aids a reader's understanding (if not acceptance) of King's views.

8. King's essay reflects on how he came to accept the method of nonviolence. Have you, over time, changed your thoughts or methods of approaching an issue or problem? Or has someone you know well? If so, write an essay reflecting on the events central to this change and their significance.

9. King's hopes for a better world were expressed in the early 1960s. Based on your knowledge of history since then, write an essay in which you justify or disqualify King's guarded optimism.

MAKING CONNECTIONS

1. Like several other writers in this section, King reflects on a turning point in his life. Consider his essay in relation to two or three others, such as those by Maya Angelou, Alice Walker, George Orwell, Zoë Tracy Hardy, or Loren Eiseley. Compare and contrast

the ways these writers present their turning points. How does each present the crucial moment or event, and how does each show its meaning?

2. One way a writer convinces us is by the authority we sense in the person as he or she writes. What details in King's essay contribute to our sense of him as an authoritative person, a writer we are inclined to believe? What do you find of similar persuasiveness in the essays of Maya Angelou, George Orwell, or Zoë Tracy Hardy?

THE WAY TO
RAINY MOUNTAIN

N. Scott Momaday

N. Scott Momaday was born in Lawton, Oklahoma, in 1934. His father is a full-blooded Kiowa and his mother is part Cherokee. After attending schools on Navaho, Apache, and Pueblo reservations, Momaday graduated from the University of New Mexico and took his Ph.D. at Stanford University. He has published two collections of poetry, Angle of Geese and Other Poems *(1974) and* The Gourd Dancer *(1976), and a memoir,* The Names *(1976). In 1969, his novel* House Made of Dawn *won the Pulitzer Prize. The following essay appeared first in the* Reporter *magazine in 1967 and later as the introduction to* The Way to Rainy Mountain *(1969), a collection of Kiowa legends.*

A single knoll rises out of the plain in Oklahoma, north and west of the   1
Wichita range. For my people, the Kiowas, it is an old landmark, and they
gave it the name Rainy Mountain. The hardest weather in the world is there.
Winter brings blizzards, hot tornadic winds arise in the spring, and in summer
the prairie is an anvil's edge. The grass turns brittle and brown, and it cracks
beneath your feet. There are green belts along the rivers and creeks, linear
groves of hickory and pecan, willow and witch hazel. At a distance in July or
August the steaming foliage seems almost to writhe in fire. Great green and
yellow grasshoppers are everywhere in the tall grass, popping up like corn to
sting the flesh, and tortoises crawl about on the red earth, going nowhere in
the plenty of time. Loneliness is an aspect of the land. All things in the plain
are isolate; there is no confusion of objects in the eye, but *one* hill or *one* tree
or *one* man. To look upon that landscape in the early morning, with the sun
at your back, is to lose the sense of proportion. Your imagination comes to life,
and this, you think, is where Creation was begun.

I returned to Rainy Mountain in July. My grandmother had died in the   2
spring, and I wanted to be at her grave. She had lived to be very old and at last
infirm. Her only living daughter was with her when she died, and I was told
that in death her face was that of a child.

I like to think of her as a child. When she was born, the Kiowas were living   3
the last great moment of their history. For more than a hundred years they had
controlled the open range from the Smoky Hill River to the Red, from the

86

headwaters of the Canadian to the fork of the Arkansas and Cimarron. In alliance with the Comanches, they had ruled the whole of the Southern Plains. War was their sacred business, and they were the finest horsemen the world has ever known. But warfare for the Kiowas was pre-eminently a matter of disposition rather than of survival, and they never understood the grim, unrelenting advance of the U.S. Cavalry. When at last, divided and ill provisioned, they were driven onto the Staked Plains in the cold of autumn, they fell into panic. In Palo Duro Canyon they abandoned their crucial stores to pillage and had nothing then but their lives. In order to save themselves, they surrendered to the soldiers at Fort Sill and were imprisoned in the old stone corral that now stands as a military museum. My grandmother was spared the humiliation of those high gray walls by eight or ten years, but she must have known from birth the affliction of defeat, the dark brooding of old warriors.

Her name was Aho, and she belonged to the last culture to evolve in North   4
America. Her forebears came down from the high country in western Montana nearly three centuries ago. They were a mountain people, a mysterious tribe of hunters whose language has never been classified in any major group. In the late seventeenth century they began a long migration to the south and east. It was a journey toward the dawn, and it led to a golden age. Along the way the Kiowas were befriended by the Crows, who gave them the culture and religion of the Plains. They acquired horses, and their ancient nomadic spirit was suddenly free of the ground. They acquired Tai-me, the sacred sun-dance doll, from that moment the object and symbol of their worship, and so shared in the divinity of the sun. Not least, they acquired the sense of destiny, therefore courage and pride. When they entered upon the Southern Plains they had been transformed. No longer were they slaves to the simple necessity of survival; they were a lordly and dangerous society of fighters and thieves, hunters and priests of the sun. According to their origin myth, they entered the world through a hollow log. From one point of view, their migration was the fruit of an old prophecy, for indeed they emerged from a sunless world.

Though my grandmother lived out her long life in the shadow of Rainy   5
Mountain, the immense landscape of the continental interior lay like memory in her blood. She could tell of the Crows, whom she had never seen, and of the Black Hills, where she had never been. I wanted to see in reality what she had seen more perfectly in the mind's eye, and drove fifteen hundred miles to begin my pilgrimage.

A dark mist lay over the Black Hills, and the land was like iron. At the top   6
of a ridge I caught sight of Devil's Tower upthrust against the gray sky as if in the birth of time the core of the earth had broken through its crust and the motion of the world was begun. There are things in nature that engender an awful quiet in the heart of man; Devil's Tower is one of them. Two centuries

87

ago, because of their need to explain it, the Kiowas made a legend at the base of the rock. My grandmother said:

"Eight children were there at play, seven sisters and their brother. Suddenly the boy was struck dumb; he trembled and began to run upon his hands and feet. His fingers became claws, and his body was covered with fur. There was a bear where the boy had been. The sisters were terrified; they ran, and the bear after them. They came to the stump of a great tree, and the tree spoke to them. It bade them climb upon it, and as they did so, it began to rise into the air. The bear came to kill them, but they were just beyond its reach. It reared against the tree and scored the bark all around with its claws. The seven sisters were borne into the sky, and they became the stars of the Big Dipper." From that moment, and so long as the legend lives, the Kiowas have kinsmen in the night sky. Whatever they were in the mountains, they could be no more. However tenuous their well-being, however much they had suffered and would suffer again, they had found a way out of the wilderness.

My grandmother had a reverence for the sun, a holy regard that now is all but gone out of mankind. There was a wariness in her, and an ancient awe. She was a Christian in her later years, but she had come a long way about, and she never forgot her birthright. As a child she had been to the sun dances; she had taken part in that annual rite, and by it she had learned the restoration of her people in the presence of Tai-me. She was about seven when the last Kiowa sun dance was held in 1887 on the Washita River above Rainy Mountain Creek. The buffalo were gone. In order to consummate the ancient sacrifice—to impale the head of a buffalo bull upon the Tai-me tree—a delegation of old men journeyed into Texas, there to beg and barter for an animal from the Goodnight herd. She was ten when the Kiowas came together for the last time as a living sun-dance culture. They could find no buffalo; they had to hang an old hide from the sacred tree. Before the dance could begin, a company of soldiers rode out from Fort Sill under orders to disperse the tribe. Forbidden without cause the essential act of their faith, having seen the wild herds slaughtered and left to rot upon the ground, the Kiowas backed away forever from the tree. That was July 20, 1890, at the great bend of the Washita. My grandmother was there. Without bitterness, and for as long as she lived, she bore a vision of deicide.[1]

Now that I can have her only in memory, I see my grandmother in the several postures that were peculiar to her: standing at the wood stove on a winter morning and turning meat in a great iron skillet; sitting at the south window, bent above her beadwork, and afterwards, when her vision failed, looking down for a long time into the fold of her hands; going out upon a cane, very slowly as she did when the weight of age came upon her; praying. I remember her

---

[1] deicide: the killing of a deity or god. [Eds.]

most often at prayer. She made long, rambling prayers out of suffering and hope, having seen many things. I was never sure that I had the right to hear, so exclusive were they of all mere custom and company. The last time I saw her she prayed standing by the side of her bed at night, naked to the waist, the light of a kerosene lamp moving upon her dark skin. Her long black hair, always drawn and braided in the day, lay upon her shoulders and against her breasts like a shawl. I do not speak Kiowa, and I never understood her prayers, but there was something inherently sad in the sound, some merest hesitation upon the syllables of sorrow. She began in a high and descending pitch, exhausting her breath to silence; then again and again—and always the same intensity of effort, of something that is, and is not, like urgency in the human voice. Transported so in the dancing light among the shadows of her room, she seemed beyond the reach of time. But that was illusion; I think I knew then that I should not see her again.

Houses are like sentinels in the plain, old keepers of the weather watch. 10 There, in a very little while, wood takes on the appearance of great age. All colors wear soon away in the wind and rain, and then the wood is burned gray and the grain appears and the nails turn red with rust. The window panes are black and opaque; you imagine there is nothing within, and indeed there are many ghosts, bones given up to the land. They stand here and there against the sky, and you approach them for a longer time than you expect. They belong in the distance; it is their domain.

Once there was a lot of sound in my grandmother's house, a lot of coming 11 and going, feasting and talk. The summers there were full of excitement and reunion. The Kiowas are a summer people; they abide the cold and keep to themselves, but when the season turns and the land becomes warm and vital they cannot hold still; an old love of going returns upon them. The aged visitors who came to my grandmother's house when I was a child were made of lean and leather, and they bore themselves upright. They wore great black hats and bright ample shirts that shook in the wind. They rubbed fat upon their hair and wound their braids with strips of colored cloth. Some of them painted their faces and carried the scars of old and cherished enmities. They were an old council of warlords, come to remind and be reminded of who they were. Their wives and daughters served them well. The women might indulge themselves; gossip was at once the mark and compensation of their servitude. They made loud and elaborate talk among themselves, full of jest and gesture, fright and false alarm. They went abroad in fringed and flowered shawls, bright beadwork and German silver. They were at home in the kitchen, and they prepared meals that were banquets.

There were frequent prayer meetings, and nocturnal feasts. When I was a 12 child I played with my cousins outside, where the lamplight fell upon the ground and the singing of the old people rose up around us and carried away into the darkness. There were a lot of good things to eat, a lot of laughter and surprise. And afterwards, when the quiet returned, I lay down with my grandmother and could hear the frogs away by the river and feel the motion of the air.

Now there is a funereal silence in the rooms, the endless wake of some final word. The walls have closed in upon my grandmother's house. When I returned to it in mourning, I saw for the first time in my life how small it was. It was late at night, and there was a white moon, nearly full. I sat for a long time on the stone steps by the kitchen door. From there I could see out across the land; I could see the long row of trees by the creek, the low light upon the rolling plains, and the stars of the Big Dipper. Once I looked at the moon and caught sight of a strange thing. A cricket had perched upon the handrail, only a few inches away. My line of vision was such that the creature filled the moon like a fossil. It had gone there, I thought, to live· and die, for there, of all places, was its small definition made whole and eternal. A warm wind rose up and purled like the longing within me. 13

The next morning, I awoke at dawn and went out on the dirt road to Rainy Mountain. It was already hot, and the grasshoppers began to fill the air. Still, it was early in the morning, and birds sang out of the shadows. The long yellow grass on the mountain shone in the bright light, and a scissortail hied above the land. There, where it ought to be, at the end of a long and legendary way, was my grandmother's grave. She had at last succeeded to that holy ground. Here and there on the dark stones were ancestral names. Looking back once, I saw the mountain and came away. 14

QUESTIONS

1. What is this essay about? Explain whether it is a history of the Kiowas, or a biography of Momaday's grandmother, or a narrative of his journey.

2. Trace the movement in time in this essay. How much takes place in the present, the recent past, the distant past, or legendary time? What effect does such movement create?

3. How much of the essay reports events, and how much of the essay represents a sense of place or of persons through description of what Momaday sees and feels? Trace the pattern of reporting and representing, and consider Momaday's purpose in such an approach to his subject.

4. The first paragraph ends by drawing the reader into the writer's point of view: "Your imagination comes to life, and this, you think, is where Creation was begun." Given the description of the Oklahoma landscape that precedes this in the paragraph, how do you react to Momaday's summarizing statement? Why? What other passages in the essay evoke a sense of place?

5. Visit a place that has historical significance. It may be a place where you or members of your family lived in the past, or it may be a place of local or national historical significance. Describe the place as it appears now, and report on events that

took place there in the past. What, if any, evidence do you find in the present of those events that took place in the past?

6. If you have a grandparent or an older friend living nearby, ask this person about his or her history. What does this person remember about the past that is no longer in the present? Are there also objects—pictures, clothing, medals, and so on—that can speak to you of your subject's past life? Reflect on the person's present life as well as on those events from the past that seem most memorable. Write an essay in which you represent your subject's life by concentrating on the place where he or she lives and the surrounding objects that help you to understand the past and present life.

MAKING CONNECTIONS

1. Compare Momaday's essay to Banesh Hoffmann's for their extended portraits of individuals. How complete is the portrait each writer gives? On what kind of detail or observation is it based? How central is it to the essay in question?

2. Compare Momaday's essay to Alice Walker's for the way each essay moves through time. How do these essayists differ in their conception and representation of time, and how do those differences relate to their individual purposes as writers?

SHOOTING AN ELEPHANT
George Orwell

George Orwell (1903–1950) was the pen name of Eric Blair, the son of a British customs officer serving in Bengal, India. As a boy he was sent home to prestigious schools, where he learned to dislike the rich and powerful. After finishing school at Eton, he served as an officer of the British police in Burma, where he became disillusioned with imperialism. Then he studied conditions among the urban poor and the coal miners of Wigan, a city in northwestern England, which confirmed him as a socialist. He was wounded in the Spanish civil war, defending the lost cause of the left against the fascists. Under the name Orwell, he wrote accounts of all these experiences as well as the anti-Stalinist fable An-imal Farm and the novel 1984. In the following essay, first published in 1936, Orwell attacks the politics of imperialism.

In Moulmein, in Lower Burma, I was hated by large numbers of people— 1 the only time in my life that I have been important enough for this to happen to me. I was sub-divisional police officer of the town, and in an aimless, petty kind of way anti-European feeling was very bitter. No one had the guts to raise a riot, but if a European woman went through the bazaars alone somebody would probably spit betel juice over her dress. As a police officer I was an obvious target and was baited whenever it seemed safe to do so. When a nimble Burman tripped me up on the football field and the referee (another Burman) looked the other way, the crowd yelled with hideous laughter. This happened more than once. In the end the sneering yellow faces of young men that met me everywhere, the insults hooted after me when I was at a safe distance, got badly on my nerves. The young Buddhist priests were the worst of all. There were several thousands of them in the town and none of them seemed to have anything to do except stand on street corners and jeer at Europeans.

All this was perplexing and upsetting. For at that time I had already made 2 up my mind that imperialism was an evil thing and the sooner I chucked up my job and got out of it the better. Theoretically—and secretly, of course—I was all for the Burmese and all against their oppressors, the British. As for the job I was doing, I hated it more bitterly than I can perhaps make clear. In a job like that you see the dirty work of Empire at close quarters. The wretched prisoners huddling in the stinking cages of the lock-ups, the grey, cowed faces of the long-term convicts, the scarred buttocks of the men who had been flogged with bamboos—all these oppressed me with an intolerable sense of guilt. But I could get nothing into perspective. I was young and ill-educated and I had had to think out my problems in the utter silence that is imposed on every Englishman in the East. I did not even know that the British Empire is dying, still less did I know that it is a great deal better than the younger empires that are going to supplant it. All I knew was that I was stuck between my hatred of the empire I served and my rage against the evil-spirited little beasts who tried to make my job impossible. With one part of my mind I thought of the British Raj as an unbreakable tyranny,[1] as something clamped down, in *saecula saeculorum*,[2] upon the will of prostrate peoples; with another part I thought that the greatest joy in the world would be to drive a bayonet into a Buddhist priest's guts. Feelings like these are the normal by-product of imperialism; ask any Anglo-Indian official, if you can catch him off duty.

One day something happened which in a roundabout way was enlightening. 3 It was a tiny incident in itself, but it gave me a better glimpse than I had had before of the real nature of imperialism—the real motives for which despotic governments act. Early one morning the sub-inspector at a police station the other end of the town rang me up on the phone and said that an elephant was ravaging the bazaar. Would I please come and do something about it? I did not know what I could do, but I wanted to see what was happening and I got on to a pony and started out. I took my rifle, an old .44 Winchester and much too small to kill an elephant, but I thought the noise might be useful *in terrorem*.[3] Various Burmans stopped me on the way and told me about the elephant's doings. It was not, of course, a wild elephant, but a tame one which had gone "must." It had been chained up, as tame elephants always are when their attack of "must" is due, but on the previous night it had broken its chain and escaped. Its mahout, the only person who could manage it when it was in that state, had set out in pursuit, but had taken the wrong direction and was now twelve hours' journey away, and in the morning the elephant had suddenly reappeared in town. The Burmese population had no weapons and were quite helpless against it. It had already destroyed somebody's bamboo hut, killed a cow and raided some fruit-stalls and devoured the stock; also it had met the municipal rubbish van and, when the driver jumped out and took to his heels, had turned the van over and inflicted violences upon it.

The Burmese sub-inspector and some Indian constables were waiting for me 4 in the quarter where the elephant had been seen. It was a very poor quarter, a labyrinth of squalid bamboo huts, thatched with palm-leaf, winding all over a steep hillside. I remember that it was a cloudy, stuffy morning at the beginning

---

[1] the British Raj: the imperial government ruling British India and Burma. [Eds.]
[2] *saecula saeculorum*: forever and ever. [Eds.]
[3] *in terrorem*: for fright. [Eds.]

of the rains. We began questioning the people as to where the elephant had gone and, as usual, failed to get any definite information. That is invariably the case in the East; a story always sounds clear enough at a distance, but the nearer you get to the scene of events the vaguer it becomes. Some of the people said that the elephant had gone in one direction, some said that he had gone in another, some professed not even to have heard of any elephant. I had almost made up my mind that the whole story was a pack of lies, when we heard yells a little distance away. There was a loud, scandalized cry of "Go away, child! Go away this instant!" and an old woman with a switch in her hand came round the corner of a hut, violently shooing away a crowd of naked children. Some more women followed, clicking their tongues and exclaiming; evidently there was something that the children ought not to have seen. I rounded the hut and saw a man's dead body sprawling in the mud. He was an Indian, a black Dravidian coolie, almost naked, and he could not have been dead many minutes. The people said that the elephant had come suddenly upon him round the corner of the hut, caught him with its trunk, put its foot on his back and ground him into the earth. This was the rainy season and the ground was soft, and his face had scored a trench a foot deep and a couple of yards long. He was lying on his belly with arms crucified and head sharply twisted to one side. His face was coated with mud, the eyes wide open, the teeth bared and grinning with an expression of unendurable agony. (Never tell me, by the way, that the dead look peaceful. Most of the corpses I have seen looked devilish.) The friction of the great beast's foot had stripped the skin from his back as neatly as one skins a rabbit. As soon as I saw the dead man I sent an orderly to a friend's house nearby to borrow an elephant rifle. I had already sent back the pony, not wanting it to go mad with fright and throw me if it smelt the elephant.

The orderly came back in a few minutes with a rifle and five cartridges, and meanwhile some Burmans had arrived and told us that the elephant was in the paddy fields below, only a few hundred yards away. As I started forward practically the whole population of the quarter flocked out of the houses and followed me. They had seen the rifle and were all shouting excitedly that I was going to shoot the elephant. They had not shown much interest in the elephant when he was merely ravaging their homes, but it was different now that he was to be shot. It was a bit of fun to them, as it would be to an English crowd; besides they wanted the meat. It made me vaguely uneasy. I had no intention of shooting the elephant—I had merely sent for the rifle to defend myself if necessary—and it is always unnerving to have a crowd following you. I marched down the hill, looking and feeling a fool, with the rifle over my shoulder and an ever-growing army of people jostling at my heels. At the bottom, when you got away from the huts, there was a metalled road and beyond that a miry waste of paddy fields a thousand yards across, not yet ploughed but soggy from the first rains and dotted with coarse grass. The elephant was standing eight yards from the road, his left side towards us. He took not the slightest notice of the crowd's approach. He was tearing up bunches of grass, beating them against his knees to clean them and stuffing them into his mouth.

I had halted on the road. As soon as I saw the elephant I knew with perfect   6
certainty that I ought not to shoot him. It is a serious matter to shoot a working elephant—it is comparable to destroying a huge and costly piece of machinery—and obviously one ought not to do it if it can possibly be avoided. And at that distance, peacefully eating, the elephant looked no more dangerous than a cow. I thought then and I think now that his attack of "must" was already passing off; in which case he would merely wander harmlessly about until the mahout came back and caught him. Moreover, I did not in the least want to shoot him. I decided that I would watch him for a little while to make sure that he did not turn savage again, and then go home.

But at that moment I glanced around at the crowd that had followed me. It   7
was an immense crowd, two thousand at the least and growing every minute. It blocked the road for a long distance on either side. I looked at the sea of yellow faces above the garish clothes—faces all happy and excited all over this bit of fun, all certain that the elephant was going to be shot. They were watching me as they would watch a conjurer about to perform a trick. They did not like me, but with the magical rifle in my hands I was momentarily worth watching. And suddenly I realized that I should have to shoot the elephant after all. The people expected it of me and I had got to do it; I could feel their two thousand wills pressing me forward, irresistibly. And it was at this moment, as I stood there with the rifle in my hands, that I first grasped the hollowness, the futility of the white man's dominion in the East. Here was I, the white man with his gun, standing in front of the unarmed native crowd—seemingly the leading actor of the piece; but in reality I was only an absurd puppet pushed to and fro by the will of those yellow faces behind. I perceived in this moment that when the white man turns tyrant it is his own freedom that he destroys. He becomes a sort of hollow, posing dummy, the conventionalized figure of a sahib. For it is the condition of his rule that he shall spend his life in trying to impress the "natives," and so in every crisis he has got to do what the "natives" expect of him. He wears a mask, and his face grows to fit it. I had got to shoot the elephant. I had committed myself to doing it when I sent for the rifle. A sahib has got to act like a sahib; he has got to appear resolute, to know his own mind and do definite things. To come all that way, rifle in hand, with two thousand people marching at my heels, and then to trail feebly away, having done nothing—no, that was impossible. The crowd would laugh at me. And my whole life, every white man's life in the East, was one long struggle not to be laughed at.

But I did not want to shoot the elephant. I watched him beating his bunch   8
of grass against his knees, with that preoccupied grandmotherly air that elephants have. It seemed to me that it would be murder to shoot him. At that age I was not squeamish about killing animals, but I had never shot an elephant and

never wanted to. (Somehow it always seems worse to kill a *large* animal.) Besides, there was the beast's owner to be considered. Alive, the elephant was worth at least a hundred pounds; dead, he would only be worth the value of his tusks, five pounds, possibly. But I had got to act quickly. I turned to some experienced-looking Burmans who had been there when we arrived, and asked them how the elephant had been behaving. They all said the same thing: he took no notice of you if you left him alone, but he might charge if you went too close to him.

It was perfectly clear to me what I ought to do. I ought to walk up to within, say, twenty-five yards of the elephant and test his behavior. If he charged, I could shoot; if he took no notice of me, it would be safe to leave him until the mahout came back. But also I knew that I was going to do no such thing. I was a poor shot with a rifle and the ground was soft mud into which one would sink at every step. If the elephant charged and I missed him, I should have about as much chance as a toad under a steam-roller. But even then I was not thinking particularly of my own skin, only of the watchful yellow faces behind. For at the moment, with the crowd watching me, I was not afraid in the ordinary sense, as I would have been if I had been alone. A white man mustn't be frightened in front of "natives"; and so, in general, he isn't frightened. The sole thought in my mind was that if anything went wrong those two thousand Burmans would see me pursued, caught, trampled on and reduced to a grinning corpse like that Indian up the hill. And if that happened it was quite probable that some of them would laugh. That would never do. There was only one alternative. I shoved the cartridges into the magazine and lay down on the road to get a better aim.

The crowd grew very still, and a deep, low, happy sigh, as of people who see the theatre curtain go up at last, breathed from innumerable throats. They were going to have their bit of fun after all. The rifle was a beautiful German thing with cross-hair sights. I did not then know that in shooting an elephant one would shoot to cut an imaginary bar running from ear-hole to ear-hole. I ought, therefore, as the elephant was sideways on, to have aimed straight at his ear-hole; actually I aimed several inches in front of this, thinking the brain would be further forward.

When I pulled the trigger I did not hear the bang or feel the kick—one never does when a shot goes home—but I heard the devilish roar of glee that went up from the crowd. In that instant, in too short a time, one would have thought, even for the bullet to get there, a mysterious, terrible change had come over the elephant. He neither stirred nor fell, but every line of his body had altered. He looked suddenly stricken, shrunken, immensely old, as though the frightful impact of the bullet had paralyzed him without knocking him down. At last, after what seemed a long time—it might have been five seconds, I dare say— he sagged flabbily to his knees. His mouth slobbered. An enormous senility seemed to have settled upon him. One could have imagined him thousands of years old. I fired again into the same spot. At the second shot he did not collapse but climbed with desperate slowness to his feet and stood weakly upright, with legs sagging and head drooping. I fired a third time. That was the shot that did for him. You could see the agony of it jolt his whole body and knock the last remnant of strength from his legs. But in falling he seemed for a moment to rise, for as his hind legs collapsed beneath him he seemed to tower upward like a huge rock toppling, his trunk reaching skywards like a tree. He trumpeted, for the first and only time. And then down he came, his belly towards me, with a crash that seemed to shake the ground even where I lay.

I got up. The Burmans were already racing past me across the mud. It was 12 obvious that the elephant would never rise again, but he was not dead. He was breathing very rhythmically with long rattling gasps, his great mound of a side painfully rising and falling. His mouth was wide open—I could see far down into caverns of pale pink throat. I waited for a long time for him to die, but his breathing did not weaken. Finally I fired my two remaining shots into the spot where I thought his heart must be. The thick blood welled out of him like red velvet, but still he did not die. His body did not even jerk when the shots hit him, the tortured breathing continued without a pause. He was dying, very slowly and in great agony, but in some world remote from me where not even a bullet could damage him further. I felt that I had got to put an end to that dreadful noise. I seemed dreadful to see the great beast lying there, powerless to move and yet powerless to die, and not even to be able to finish him. I sent back for my small rifle and poured shot after shot into his heart and down his throat. They seemed to make no impression. The tortured gasps continued as steadily as the ticking of a clock.

In the end I could not stand it any longer and went away. I heard later that 13 it took him half an hour to die. Burmans were bringing dahs and baskets even before I left,[4] and I was told they had stripped his body almost to the bones by the afternoon.

Afterwards, of course, there were endless discussions about the shooting of 14 the elephant. The owner was furious, but he was only an Indian and could do nothing. Besides, legally I had done the right thing, for a mad elephant has to be killed, like a mad dog, if its owner fails to control it. Among the Europeans opinion was divided. The older men said I was right, the younger men said it was a damn shame to shoot an elephant for killing a coolie, because an elephant was worth more than any damn Coringhee coolie. And afterwards I was very glad that the coolie had been killed; it put me legally in the right and it gave me a sufficient pretext for shooting the elephant. I often wondered whether any of the others grasped that I had done it solely to avoid looking a fool.

---

[4]dahs: butcher knives. [Eds.]

QUESTIONS

1. Describe Orwell's mixed feelings about serving as a police officer in Burma.

2. How do the natives "force" Orwell to shoot the elephant against his better judgment? How does he relate this personal episode to the larger problems of British imperialism?

3. What is Orwell's final reaction to his deed? How literally can we take his statement that he "was very glad that the coolie had been killed" (paragraph 14)?

4. From the opening sentence Orwell displays a remarkable candor concerning his feelings. How does this personal, candid tone add to or detract from the strength of the essay?

5. Orwell's recollection of shooting the elephant is shaped to support a specific point or thesis. Where does Orwell state this thesis? Is this placement effective?

6. This essay reads more like a short story than an expository essay. In what ways is Orwell's use of narrative and personal experience effective?

7. Orwell often wrote with a political purpose, with a "desire to push the world in a certain direction, to alter other people's idea of the kind of society that they should strive after." To what extent does the "tiny incident" in this essay illuminate "the real nature of imperialism" (paragraph 3)? Does Orwell succeed in altering your idea of imperialism?

8. Using Orwell's essay as a model, write a reflection in which the narration of "a tiny incident" (paragraph 3) illuminates a larger social or political problem.

9. Like "Shooting an Elephant," Orwell's novel *Burmese Days* (1934) takes place in Burma and attacks British imperialism. After reading this novel, write a report comparing it with the essay.

MAKING CONNECTIONS

1. The selections by Maya Angelou, Loren Eiseley, and Zoë Tracy Hardy in this section read somewhat like short stories, as does Orwell's essay. Compare the narrative designs of two of these writers and discuss the usefulness of storytelling in reflective writing.

2. How important is the elephant to this essay? What if Orwell had shot an iguana as Isak Dinesen did, or a sparrow hawk such as Loren Eiseley captured and then released, or one of the chimpanzees studied by Jane van Lawick-Goodall (recounted in her essay in "Reporting")? Read Stephen Jay Gould's essay, "A Biological Homage to Mickey Mouse," in "Explaining" and then write a commentary on the importance of the elephant to this essay.

SIGMUND FREUD

Carl G. Jung

Along with Sigmund Freud, Carl G. Jung (1875–1961) was one of the great pioneers of modern psychology. After receiving his medical degree from the University of Basel in 1900, he studied with Pierre Janet (in Paris) and Eugen Bleuler (in Zuirch) in the new field of depth psychology. His collected works run to twenty volumes and deal with such important psychological concepts as the collective unconscious, introversion and extroversion, the association method, and dream symbolism. An early champion of Freud's controversial ideas, Jung later broke with him for the reasons set forth in the following selection from his autobiography Memories, Dreams, Reflections *(1963, rev. 1973). Of this work, which he undertook reluctantly, Jung said: "A book of mine is always a matter of fate. There is something unpredictable about the process of writing, and I cannot prescribe for myself any predetermined course. Thus this 'autobiography' is now taking a direction quite different from what I had imagined at the beginning. It has become a necessity for me to write down my early memories. If I neglect to do so for a single day, unpleasant physical symptoms immediately follow. As soon as I set to work they vanish and my head feels perfectly clear."*

I embarked on the adventure of my intellectual development by becoming 1
a psychiatrist. In all innocence I began observing mental patients, clinically, from the outside, and thereby came upon psychic processes of a striking nature. I noted and classified these things without the slightest understanding of their contents, which were considered to be adequately evaluated when they were dismissed as "pathological." In the course of time my interest focused more and more upon cases in which I experienced something understandable—that is, cases of paranoia, manic-depressive insanity, and psychogenic disturbances. From the start of my psychiatric career the studies of Breuer and Freud, along with the work of Pierre Janet, provided me with a wealth of suggestions and stimuli.[1] Above all, I found that Freud's technique of dream analysis and dream

---

[1] Josef Breuer (1842–1925): Austrian physician, coauthor with Freud of *Studies in Hysteria* (1895); Pierre Janet (1859–1947): French psychologist and neurologist. [Eds.]

interpretation cast a valuable light upon schizophrenic forms of expression. As early as 1900 I had read Frued's *The Interpretation of Dreams*. I had laid the book aside, at the time, because I did not yet grasp it. At the age of twenty-five I lacked the experience to appreciate Freud's theories. Such experience did not come until later. In 1903 I once more took up *The Interpretation of Dreams* and discovered how it all linked up with my own ideas. What chiefly interested me was the application to dreams of the concept of the repression mechanism, which was derived from the psychology of the neuroses. This was important to me because I had frequently encountered repressions in my experiments with word association; in response to certain stimulus words that patient either had no associative answer or was unduly slow in his reaction time. As was later discovered, such a disturbance occurred each time the stimulus word had touched upon a psychic lesion or conflict. In most cases the patient was unconscious of this. When questioned about the cause of the disturbance, he would often answer in a peculiarly artificial manner. My reading of Freud's *The Interpretation of Dreams* showed me that the repression mechanism was at work here, and that the facts I had observed were consonant with his theory. Thus I was able to corroborate Freud's line of argument.

The situation was different when it came to the content of the repression. 2 Here I could not agree with Freud. He considered the cause of the repression to be a sexual trauma. From my practice, however, I was familiar with numerous cases of neurosis in which the question of sexuality played a subordinate part, other factors standing in the foreground—for example, the problem of social adaptation, of oppression by tragic circumstances of life, prestige considerations, and so on. Later I presented such cases to Freud; but he would not grant that factors other than sexuality could be the cause. That was highly unsatisfactory to me.

At the beginning it was not easy for me to assign Freud the proper place in 3 my life, or to take the right attitude toward him. When I became acquainted with his work I was planning an academic career, and was about to complete a paper that was intended to advance me at the university. But Freud was definitely *persona non grata* in the academic world at the time,[2] and any connection with him would have been damaging in scientific circles. "Important people" at most mentioned him surreptitiously, and at congresses he was discussed only in the corridors, never on the floor. Therefore the discovery that my association experiments were in agreement with Freud's theories was far from pleasant to me.

Once, while I was in my laboratory and reflecting again upon these questions, 4 the devil whispered to me that I would be justified in publishing the results of my experiments and my conclusions without mentioning Freud. After all, I had worked out my experiments long before I understood his work. But then I

---

[2] *persona non grata*: an unacceptable person. [Eds.]

heard the voice of my second personality: "If you do a thing like that, as if you had no knowledge of Freud, it would be a piece of trickery. You cannot build your life upon a lie." With that, the question was settled. From then on I became an open partisan of Freud's and fought for him.

I first took up the cudgels for Freud at a congress in Munich where a lecturer 5 discussed obsessional neuroses but studiously forbore to mention the name of Freud. In 1906, in connection with this incident, I wrote a paper for the *Münchner Medizinische Wochenschrift* on Freud's theory of the neuroses, which had contributed a great deal to the understanding of obsessional neuroses. In response to this article, two German professors wrote to me, warning that if I remained on Freud's side and continued to defend him, I would be endangering my academic career. I replied: "If what Freud says is the truth, I am with him. I don't give a damn for a career if it has to be based on the premise of restricting research and concealing the truth." And I went on defending Freud and his ideas. But on the basis of my own findings I was still unable to feel that all neuroses were caused by sexual repression or sexual traumata. In certain cases that was so, but not in others. Nevertheless, Freud had opened up a new path of investigation, and the shocked outcries against him at the time seemed to me absurd.

I had not met with much sympathy for the ideas expressed in "The Psychology 6 of Dementia Praecox." In fact, my colleagues laughed at me. But through this book I came to know Freud. He invited me to visit him, and our first meeting took place in Vienna in February 1907. We met at one o'clock in the afternoon and talked virtually without a pause for thirteen hours. Freud was the first man of real importance I had encountered; in my experience up to that time, no one else could compare with him. There was nothing the least trivial in his attitude, I found him extremely intelligent, shrewd, and altogether remarkable. And yet my first impressions of him remained somewhat tangled; I could not make him out.

What he said about his sexual theory impressed me. Nevertheless, his words 7 could not remove my hesitations and doubts. I tried to advance these reservations of mine on several occasions, but each time he would attribute them to my lack of experience. Freud was right; in those days I had not enough experience to support my objections. I could see that his sexual theory was enormously important to him, both personally and philosophically. This impressed me, but I could not decide to what extent this strong emphasis upon sexuality was connected with subjective prejudices of his, and to what extent it rested upon verifiable experiences.

Above all, Freud's attitude toward the spirit seemed to me highly question- 8 able. Wherever, in a person or in a work of art, an expression of spirituality (in the intellectual, not the supernatural sense) came to light, he suspected it, and insinuated that it was repressed sexuality. Anything that could not be directly interpreted as sexuality he referred to as "psychosexuality." I protested that this hypothesis, carried to its logical conclusion, would lead to an annihilating judgment upon culture. Culture would then appear as a mere farce, the morbid consequence of repressed sexuality. "Yes," he assented, "so it is, and that is just a curse of fate against which we are powerless to contend." I was by no means disposed to agree, or to let it go at that, but still I did not feel competent to argue it out with him.

There was something else that seemed to me significant at that first meeting.   9
It had to do with things which I was able to think out and understand only after our friendship was over. There was no mistaking the fact that Freud was emotionally involved in his sexual theory to an extraordinary degree. When he spoke of it, his tone became urgent, almost anxious, and all signs of his normally critical and skeptical manner vanished. A strange, deeply moved expression came over his face, the cause of which I was at a loss to understand. I had a strong intuition that for him sexuality was a sort of *numinosum*.³ This was confirmed by a conversation which took place some three years later (in 1910), again in Vienna.

I can still recall vividly how Freud said to me, "My dear Jung, promise me   10
never to abandon the sexual theory. That is the most essential thing of all. You see, we must make a dogma of it, an unshakable bulwark." He said that to me with great emotion, in the tone of a father saying, "And promise me this one thing, my dear son: that you will go to church every Sunday." In some astonishment I asked him, "A bulwark—against what?" To which he replied, "Against the black tide of mud"—and here he hesitated for a moment, then added—"of occultism." First of all, it was the words "bulwark" and "dogma" that alarmed me; for a dogma, that is to say, an undisputable confession of faith, is set up only when the aim is to suppress doubts once and for all. But that no longer has anything to do with scientific judgment; only with a personal power drive.

This was the thing that struck at the heart of our friendship. I knew that I   11
would never be able to accept such an attitude. What Freud seemed to mean by "occultism" was virtually everything that philosophy and religion, including the rising contemporary science of parapsychology, had learned about the psyche. To me the sexual theory was just as occult, that is to say, just as unproven an hypothesis, as many other speculative views. As I saw it, a scientific truth was a hypothesis which might be adequate for the moment but was not to be preserved as an article of faith for all time.

Although I did not properly understand it then, I had observed in Freud the   12
eruption of unconscious religious factors. Evidently he wanted my aid in erecting a barrier against these threatening unconscious contents.

The impression this conversation made upon me added to my confusion;   13

---

³ *numinosum:* spiritual force. [Eds.]

102

until then I had not considered sexuality as a precious and imperiled concept to which one must remain faithful. Sexuality evidently meant more to Freud than to other people. For him it was something to be religiously observed. In the face of such deep convictions one generally becomes shy and reticent. After a few stammering attempts on my part, the conversation soon came to an end.

I was bewildered and embarrassed. I had the feeling that I had caught a glimpse of a new, unknown country from which swarms of new ideas flew to meet me. One thing was clear; Freud, who had always made much of his irreligiosity, had now constructed a dogma; or rather, in the place of a jealous God whom he had lost, he had substituted another compelling image, that of sexuality. It was no less insistent, exacting, domineering, threatening, and morally ambivalent than the original one. Just as the psychically stronger agency is given "divine" or "daemonic" attributes, so the "sexual libido" took over the role of a *deus absconditus*, a hidden or concealed god. The advantage of this transformation for Freud was, apparently, that he was able to regard the new numinous principle as scientifically irreproachable and free from all religious taint. At bottom, however, the numinosity, that is, the psychological qualities of the two rationally incommensurable opposites—Yahweh and sexuality—remained the same. The name alone had changed, and with it, of course, the point of view: the lost god had now to be sought below, not above. But what difference does it make, ultimately, to the stronger agency if it is called now by one name and now by another? If psychology did not exist, but only concrete objects the one would actually have been destroyed and replaced by the other. But in reality, that is to say, in psychological experience, there is not one whit the less of urgency, anxiety, compulsiveness, etc. The problem still remains; how to overcome or escape our anxiety, bad conscience, guilt, compulsion, unconsciousness, and instinctuality. If we cannot do this from the bright, idealistic side, then perhaps we shall have better luck by approaching the problem from the dark, biological side.

Like flames suddenly flaring up, these thoughts darted through my mind. Much later, when I reflected upon Freud's character, they revealed their significance. There was one characteristic of his that preoccupied me above all; his bitterness. It had struck me at our first encounter, but it remained inexplicable to me until I was able to see it in connection with his attitude toward sexuality. Although, for Freud, sexuality was undoubtedly a *numinosum*, his terminology and theory seemed to define it exclusively as a biological function. It was only the emotionality with which he spoke of it that revealed the deeper elements reverberating within him. Basically, he wanted to teach—or so at least it seemed to me—that, regarded from within, sexuality included spirituality and had an intrinsic meaning. But his concretistic terminology was too narrow to express this idea. He gave me the impression that at bottom he was working against his own goal and against himself; and there is, after all, no harsher

14

15

bitterness than that of a person who is his own worst enemy. In his own words, he felt himself menaced by a "black tide of mud"—he who more than anyone else had tried to let down his buckets into those black depths.

Freud never asked himself why he was compelled to talk continually of sex, why this idea had taken such possession of him. He remained unaware that his "monotony of interpretation" expressed a flight from himself, or from that other side of him which might perhaps be called mystical. So long as he refused to acknowledge that side, he could never be reconciled with himself. He was blind toward the paradox and ambiguity of the contents of the unconscious, and did not know that everything which arises out of the unconscious has a top and a bottom, an inside and an outside. When we speak of the outside—and that is what Freud did—we are considering only half of the whole, with the result that a countereffect arises out of the unconscious. 16

There was nothing to be done about this one-sidedness of Freud's. Perhaps some inner experience of his own might have opened his eyes; but then his intellect would have reduced any such experience to "mere sexuality" or "psychosexuality." He remained the victim of the one aspect he could recognize, and for that reason I see him as a tragic figure; for he was a great man, and what is more, a man in the grip of his daimon.[4] 17

QUESTIONS

1. Jung began by supporting Freud but later split from him. Trace the various conflicts that resulted in Jung's abandonment of Freudian psychology.

2. Although Freud considered himself irreligious (paragraph 14), Jung found "unconscious religious factors (paragraph 12) in Freud's attitude toward his own theories. How does Jung explain this apparent contradiction?

3. This essay is as much about Freud the man as it is about his theories. What kind of man emerges from Jung's portrait? On what basis has Jung selected the events and illustrations he uses to create this portrait?

4. Do you trust Jung's evaluation of Freud? What is there in his approach and tone that allows you to trust (or mistrust) him?

5. Read an evaluation by Freud (or by one of his followers) of Jung and his theories. Many, for example, feel Jung was pulled under by the very "'black tide of mud' . . . of 'occultism'" (paragraph 10) that Freud warned against. Write an essay on how this supplementary reading alters your view of Freud.

6. Jung's essay on Freud includes "things which [he] was able to think out and understand only after our friendship was over" (paragraph 9). Write an essay reflecting on one of your former friends, both recalling and commenting on the significance of your experience.

---

[4]daimon: demon. [Eds.]

MAKING CONNECTIONS

1. Compare Jung's portrait of Freud to Banesh Hoffmann's portrait of Einstein. Compare, in particular, the more hidden portraits of Jung and Hoffmann that emerge from their writings. How does each writer present himself? What relation do you find between their self-presentations and the authority you sense in their writing?

2. Read Freud's essay, "The Moses of Michelangelo," in "Explaining." What sense of Freud do you get from that essay? How does it square with Jung's presentation of him here?

WHAT DID YOU DO IN THE WAR, GRANDMA?

A Flashback to August, 1945

Zoë Tracy Hardy

Born in 1927 and raised in the Midwest, Zoë Tracy Hardy was one of millions of young women called "Rosie the Riveters" who worked in defense plants during World War II. Considered at first to be mere surrogates for male workers, these women soon were building bombers that their supervisors declared "equal in the construction [to] those turned out by experienced workmen in the plant's other departments," as a news feature at the time stated. After the eventful summer described in the essay below, Hardy finished college, married, and began teaching college English in Arizona, Guam, and Colorado. This essay first appeared in the August 1985 issue of Ms. magazine—exactly forty years after the end of World War II.

It was unseasonably cool that day in May, 1945, when I left my mother and   1
father and kid brother in eastern Iowa and took the bus all the way to Omaha
to help finish the war. I was 18, and had just completed my first year at the
University of Iowa without distinction. The war in Europe had ended in April;
the war against the Japanese still raged. I wanted to go where something *real*
was being done to end this bitter war that had always been part of my adolescence.

I arrived in Omaha at midnight. The YWCA, where I promised my family   2
I would get a room, was closed until 7 A.M., so I curled up in a cracked maroon
leather chair in the crowded, smoky waiting room of the bus station.

In the morning I set off on foot for the YWCA, dragging a heavy suitcase   3
and carrying my favorite hat trimmed in daisies in a large round hatbox. An
hour of lugging and resting brought me to the Y, a great Victorian house of
dark brick, where I paid two weeks in advance (most of my money) for board
and a single room next to a bathroom that I would share with eight other girls.
I surrendered my red and blue food-ration stamp books and my sugar coupons
to the cook who would keep them as long as I stayed there.

I had eaten nothing but a wartime candy bar since breakfast at home the   4
day before, but breakfast at the Y was already over. So, queasy and light-headed,
I went back out into the cold spring day to find my job. I set out for the
downtown office of the Glenn L. Martin Company. It was at their plant south

106

of the city that thousands of workers, in around-the-clock shifts, built the famous B-29 bombers, the great Superfortresses, which the papers said would end the war.

I filled out an application and thought about the women welders and riveters and those who operated machine presses to help put the Superfortresses together. I grew shakier by the minute, more and more certain I was unqualified for any job here.

My interview was short. The personnel man was unconcerned about my total lack of skills. If I passed the physical, I could have a job in the Reproduction Department, where the blueprints were handled.

Upstairs in a gold-walled banquet room furnished with examination tables and hospital screens, a nurse sat me on a stool to draw a blood sample from my arm. I watched my blood rolling slowly into the needle. The gold walls wilted in the distance, and I slumped forward in a dead faint.

A grandfatherly doctor waved ammonia under my nose, and said if I would go to a café down the street and eat the complete 50-cent breakfast, I had the job.

The first week in the Reproduction Department, I learned to cut and fold enormous blueprints as they rolled from a machine that looked like a giant washing machine wringer. Then I was moved to a tall, metal contraption with a lurid light glowing from its interior. An ammonia guzzler, it spewed out smelly copies of specifications so hot my finger-tips burned when I touched them. I called it the dragon, and when I filled it with ammonia, the fumes reminded me of gold walls dissolving before my eyes. I took all my breaks outdoors, even when it was raining.

My boss, Mr. Johnson,[1] was a sandy-haired man of about 40, who spoke pleasantly when he came around to say hello and to check our work. Elsie, his secretary, a cool redhead, seldom spoke to any of us and spent most of her time in the darkroom developing negatives and reproducing photographs.

One of my coworkers in Reproduction was Mildred, a tall dishwater blond with a horsey, intelligent face. She was the first woman I'd ever met with an earthy unbridled tongue.

When I first arrived, Mildred warned me always to knock on the darkroom door before going in because Mr. Johnson and Elsie did a lot of screwing in there. I didn't believe her, I thought we were supposed to knock to give Elsie time to protect her negatives from the sudden light. "Besides," I said, "there isn't room to lie down in there." Mildred laughed until tears squeezed from the corners of her eyes. "You poor kid," she said. "Don't you *know* you don't have to lie down?"

I was stunned. "But it's easier if you do," I protested, defensive about my

---

[1] All names but the author's have been changed.

sex education. My mother, somewhat ahead of her time, had always been explicit in her explanations, and I had read "Lecture 14," an idyllic description of lovemaking being passed around among freshman girls in every dormitory in the country.

"Sitting, standing, any quick way you can in time of war," Mildred winked 14 wickedly. She was as virginal as I, but what she said reminded us of the steady dearth of any day-to-day presence of young men in our lives.

We were convinced that the war would be over by autumn. We were stepping 15 up the napalm and incendiary bombing of the Japanese islands, the British were now coming to our aid in the Pacific, and the Japanese Navy was being reduced to nothing in some of the most spectacular sea battles in history.

Sometimes, after lunch, I went into the assembly areas to see how the 16 skeletons of the B-29s were growing from our blueprints. At first there were enormous stark ribs surrounded by scaffolding two and three stories high. A few days later there was aluminum flesh over the ribs and wings sprouting from stubs on the fuselage. Women in overalls and turbans, safety glasses, and steel-toed-shoes scrambled around the wings with riveting guns and welding torches, fitting fuel tanks in place. Instructions were shouted at them by hoarse, paunchy old men in hard hats. I cheered myself by thinking how we were pouring it on, a multitude of us together creating this great bird to end the war.

Away from the plant, however, optimism sometimes failed me. My room at 17 the Y was bleak. I wrote letters to my unofficial fiancé and to other young men in the service who had been friends and classmates. Once in a while I attempted to study, thinking I would redeem my mediocre year at the university.

During those moments when I sensed real homesickness lying in wait, I 18 would plan something to do with Betty and Celia, friends from high school, who had moved to Omaha "for the duration" and had jobs as secretaries for a large moving and storage company. Their small apartment was upstairs in an old frame house in Benson, a northwest suburb. Celia and Betty and I cooked, exchanged news from servicemen we all knew and talked about plans for the end of the war. Betty was engaged to her high school sweetheart, a soldier who had been wounded in Germany and who might be coming home soon. We guessed she would be the first one of us to be married, and we speculated, in the careful euphemisms of "well-brought-up girls," about her impending intro-duction to sex.

By the first of July, work and the pace of life had lost momentum. The war 19 news seemed to repeat itself without advancing, as day after day battles were fought around jungly Pacific islands that all seemed identical and unreal.

At the plant, I was moved from the dragon to a desk job, a promotion of 20 sorts. I sat on a high stool in a cubicle of pigeonholed cabinets and filed blueprints, specs, and deviations in the proper holes. While I was working, I saw no one and couldn't talk to anybody.

In mid-July Betty got married. Counsel from our elders was always to wait—   21
wait until things settle down after the war. Harold, still recuperating from
shrapnel wounds, asked Betty not to wait.

Celia and I attended the ceremony on a sizzling afternoon in a musty   22
Presbyterian church. Harold was very serious, gaunt-faced and thin in his loose-
hanging Army uniform. Betty, a fair-skinned, blue-eyed brunet in a white street
dress, looked pale and solemn. After the short ceremony, they left the church
in a borrowed car. Someone had given them enough gasoline stamps for a
honeymoon trip to a far-off cabin on the shore of a piney Minnesota lake.

Celia and I speculated on Betty's introduction to lovemaking. I had "Lecture   23
14" in mind and hoped she would like lovemaking, especially way off in
Minnesota, far from the sweltering city and the war. Celia thought it didn't
matter much whether a girl liked it or not, as long as other important parts of
marriage got off to a good start.

That weekend Celia and I took a walk in a park and watched a grandfather   24
carefully pump a seesaw up and down for his small grandson. We saw a short,
middle-aged sailor walking with a sad-faced young woman who towered over
him. "A whore," Celia said, "Probably one of those from the Hotel Bianca."
Celia had been in Omaha longer than I and knew more of its secrets.

I wanted, right then, to see someone young and male and healthy cross the   25
grass under the trees, someone without wounds and without a cap, someone
with thick disheveled hair that hadn't been militarily peeled down to the green
skin on the back of his skull. Someone wearing tennis shorts to show strong,
hair-matted legs, and a shirt with an open neck and short sleeves revealing
smooth, hard muscles and tanned skin. Someone who would pull me out of
this gloom with a wide spontaneous smile as he passed.

In the next few days, the tempo of the summer changed subtly. From friends   26
stationed in the Pacific, I began to get letters free from rectangular holes where
military censors had snipped out "sensitive" words. Our Navy was getting ready
to surround the Japanese islands with a starvation blockade, and our B-29s had
bombed the industrial heart of the country. We were dropping leaflets warning
the Japanese people that we would incinerate hundreds of thousands of them
by firebombing 11 of their major cities. Rumors rippled through the plant back
in Omaha. The Japanese Empire would collapse in a matter of weeks, at most.

One Friday night, with Celia's help, I moved out of the Y to Celia's   27
apartment in Benson. We moved by streetcar. Celia carried my towels and my
full laundry bag in big rolls, one under each arm, and wore my straw picture
hat with the daisies, which bobbled wildly on top of her head. My hatbox was
crammed with extra underwear and the war letters I was determined to save.
When we climbed aboard the front end of the streetcar, I dropped the hatbox,
spilled an armload of books down the aisle, and banged my suitcase into the
knees of an elderly man who was trying to help me retrieve them.

We began to laugh, at everything, at nothing, and were still laughing when   28

109

we hauled everything off the car and down one block to the apartment, the daisies all the while wheeling recklessly on Celia's head.

It was a good move. Summer nights were cooler near the country, and so 29 quiet I could hear the crickets. The other upstairs apartment was occupied by Celia's older sister, Andrea, and her husband, Bob, who hadn't been drafted.

Late in July, an unusual thing happened at the plant. Mr. Johnson asked us 30 to work double shifts for a few days. The situation was urgent, he said, and he wanted 100 percent cooperation from the Reproduction Department, even if it meant coming to work when we felt sick or postponing something that was personally important to us.

The next morning no one from the day shift was missing, and the place was 31 full of people from the graveyard shift. Some of the time I worked in my cubicle counting out special blueprints and deviations. The rest of the time I helped the crews sweating over the blueprint machine cut out prints that contained odd lines and numbers that I had never seen before. Their shapes were different, too, and there was no place for them in the numbered pigeonholes of my cubicle. Some prints were small, about four inches square. Mildred said they were so cute she might tuck one in her shoe and smuggle it home as a souvenir even if it meant going to the federal pen if she got caught.

During those days I learned to nap on streetcars. I had to get up at 4:30, 32 bolt down breakfast, and catch the first car to rumble out of the darkness at 5:15. The double shift wasn't over until 11:30, so I got home about one in the morning.

The frenzy at the plant ended as suddenly as it had begun. Dazed with 33 fatigue, I slept through most of a weekend and hoped we had pushed ourselves to some limit that would lift us over the last hump of the war.

On Monday the familiar single shift was not quite the same. We didn't know 34 what we had done, but an undercurrent of anticipation ran through the department because of those double shifts—and the news. The papers told of factories that were already gearing up to turn out refrigerators, radios, and automobiles instead of bombs and planes.

In Reproduction, the pace began to slacken. Five hundred thirty-six B-29s, 35 planes we had put together on the Nebraska prairie, had firebombed the principal islands of the Japanese Empire: Hokkaido, Honshu, Kyushu, Shikoku. We had reduced to ashes more than 15 square miles of the heart of Tokyo. The battered and burned Japanese were so near defeat that there couldn't be much left for us to do. With surprising enthusiasm, I began to plan for my return to college.

Going home on the streetcar the first Tuesday afternoon in August, I heard 36 about a puzzling new weapon. Some excited people at the end of the car were jabbering about it, saying the Japanese would be forced to surrender in a matter of hours.

110

When I got home, Andrea, her round bespectacled face flushed, met me at   37
the head of the stairs. "Oh, come and listen to the radio—it's a new bomb—
it's almost over!"

I sat down in her living room and listened. There was news, then music,   38
then expanded news. Over and over the newscaster reported that the United
States had unlocked a secret of the universe and unleased a cosmic force—from
splitting atoms of uranium—on the industrial seaport of Hiroshima. Most of
the city had been leveled to the ground, and many of its inhabitants disintegrated
to dust in an instant by a single bomb. "Our scientists have changed the history
of the world," the newscaster said. He sounded as if he could not believe it
himself.

We ate dinner from our laps and continued to listen as the news pounded   39
on for an hour, then two, then three. I tried, at last, to *think* about it. In high
school physics we had already learned that scientists were close to splitting an
atom. We imagined that a cupful of the tremendous energy from such a
phenomenon might run a car back and forth across the entire country dozens
of times. I could visualize that. But I could not imagine how such energy put
into a small bomb would cause the kind of destruction described on the radio.

About nine, I walked over to McCollum's grocery store to buy an evening   40
paper. The headline said we had harnessed atomic power. I skimmed through
a front page story. Science had ushered us into a strange new world, and
President Truman had made two things clear: the bomb had created a monster
that could wipe out civilization; and some protection against this monster would
have to be found before its secret could be given to the world.

Back out in the dark street, I hesitated. For the first time I could remember,   41
I felt a rush of terror at being out in the night alone.

When I got back to the apartment, I made a pot of coffee and sat down at   42
the kitchen table to read the rest of the paper. President Truman had said: "The
force from which the sun draws its power has been loosed against those who
brought war to the Far East. . . . If they do not now accept our terms they may
expect a rain of ruin from the air the like of which has never been seen on this
earth." New and more powerful bombs were now being developed.

I read everything, looking for some speculation from someone about how   43
we were going to live in this new world. There was nothing. About midnight
Andrea knocked on my open door to get my attention. She stood there a
moment in her nightgown and curlers looking at me rather oddly. She asked if
I was all right.

I said yes, just trying to soak it all in.   44

Gently she told me I had better go to bed and think about how soon the war   45
would be over.

The next day Reproduction was nearly demolished by the spirit of celebra-   46
tion. The *Enola Gay*, the plane that had dropped the bomb, was one of ours.
By Thursday morning the United States had dropped a second atomic bomb,

111

an even bigger one, on an industrial city, Nagasaki, and the Russians had declared war on Japan.

At the end of the day, Mr. Johnson asked us to listen to the radio for   47
announcements about when to return to work, then shook hands all around. "You've all done more than you know to help with the war," he said.

We said tentative good-byes. I went home and over to McCollum's for an   48
evening paper. An Army Strategic Air Forces expert said that there was no comparison between the fire caused by the atomic bomb and that of a normal conflagration. And there were other stories about radiation, like X-rays, that might cripple and poison living things for hours, weeks, maybe years, until they died.

I went to bed late and had nightmares full of flames and strange dry gale   49
winds. The next noon I got up, exhausted, and called Mildred. She said they were still saying not to report to work until further notice. "It's gonna bore our tails off," she moaned. "I don't know how long we can sit around here just playing hearts." I could hear girls laughing in the background.

"Mildred," I blurted anxiously, "do you think we should have done this   50
thing?"

"Why not? Better us than somebody else, kid."   51

I reminded her that we knew the Japanese were finished weeks ago and asked   52
her if it wasn't sort of like kicking a dead horse—brutally.

"Look," she said. "The war is really over even if the bigwigs haven't said so   53
yet. What more do you want?"

The evening paper finally offered a glimmer of relief. One large headline   54
said that serious questions about the morality of *Americans* using such a weapon were being raised by some civilians of note and some churchmen. I went to bed early and lay listening to the crickets and thinking about everyone coming home—unofficial financés, husbands, fathers, brothers—all filling the empty spaces between kids and women and old men, putting a balance in our lives we hadn't known in years.

Yet the bomb haunted me. I was still awake when the windowpanes lightened   55
up at daybreak.

It was all over on August 14, 1945. Unconditional surrender.   56

For hours at a time, the bomb's importance receded in the excitement of   57
that day. Streetcar bells clanged up and down the streets; we heard sirens, whistles, church bells. A newscaster described downtown Omaha as a free-for-all. Perfect strangers were hugging each other in the streets; some were dancing. Churches had thrown open their doors, and people were streaming in and out, offering prayers of thanksgiving. Taverns were giving away free drinks.

Andrew wanted us to have a little whiskey, even though we were under age,   58 because there would never be another day like this as long as we lived. I hated the first taste of it, but as we chattered away, inventing wild, gratifying futures, I welcomed the muffler it wrapped around the ugliness of the bomb.

In the morning Mildred called to say our jobs were over and that we should 59 report to the plant to turn in our badges and get final paychecks. She had just talked to Mr. Johnson, who told her that those funny blueprints we had made during double shift had something to do with the bomb.

"Well, honey," she said, "I don't understand atomic energy, but old jazzy 60 Johnson said we had to work like that to get the *Enola Gay* and the *thing* to go together."

I held my breath, waiting for Mildred to say she was kidding, as usual. 61 Ordinary 19- and 20-year-old girls were not, not in the United States of America, required to work night and day to help launch scientific monsters that would catapult us all into a precarious "strange new world"—forever. But I knew in my bones that Mildred, forthright arrow-straight Mildred, was only telling me what I had already, unwillingly, guessed.

After a long silence she said, "Well, kid, give me your address in Iowa, and 62 I'll send you a Christmas card for auld lang syne."

I wanted to cry as we exchanged addresses. I liked Mildred. I hated the gap 63 that I now sensed would always be between me and people like her.

"It's been nice talking dirty to you all summer," she said. 64

"Thanks," I hung up, slipped down the stairs, and walked past the streetcar 65 line out into the country.

The whole countryside was sundrenched, fragrant with sweet clover and 66 newly mown alfalfa. I leaned against a fence post and tried to think.

The President had said we had unleashed the great secret of the universe in 67 this way, to shorten the war and save American lives. Our commitment to defeat the Japanese was always clear to me. They had attacked us first. But we had already firebombed much of the Japanese Empire to char. That seemed decisive enough, and terrible enough.

If he had asked me whether I would work very hard to help bring this horror 68 into being, knowing it would shorten the war but put the world into jeopardy for all time, how would I have answered?

I would have said, "No. With all due respect, Sir, how could such a thing 69 make a just end to our just cause?"

But the question had never been asked of us. And I stood now, in the warm 70 sun, gripping a splintery fence post, outraged by our final insignificance—all of us who had worked together in absolute trust to end the war.

An old cow stood near the fence switching her tail. I looked at her great, 71 uncomprehending brown eyes and began to sob.

After a while I walked back to the apartment, mentally packing my suitcase 72

113

and tying up my hatbox of war letters. I knew it was going to be very hard, from now on, for the whole world to take care of itself.

I wanted very much to go home.   73

QUESTIONS

1. How does Hardy's attitude toward the war change in the course of this essay? What event causes her to reevaluate her attitude?

2. Describe Hardy's feelings about the introduction of atomic power into her world. Are they optimistic or pessimistic?

3. "You've all done more than you know to help win the war," Hardy's boss tells her (paragraph 47). How does she react to the fact that she was not informed by the authorities of the purpose of her work? How does her reaction differ from that of her coworker Mildred?

4. As Hardy's attitude toward war changes, her attitude toward sex changes as well. Trace this change in attitude; what connection, if any, do you see between the two?

5. Is this essay merely a personal reminiscence, or does the author have a larger purpose? Explain what you think her purpose is.

6. This essay was published forty years after the events it describes. Are Hardy's fears and speculations (on atomic power, on the authority of the government, on sex) dated in any way, or are they still relevant today? Explain your answer.

7. Have you, like Hardy, ever wondered about the larger social implications of any job that you've held or that a friend or parent holds? Write an essay like Hardy's reflecting on that job and describing how your attitude changed as you placed the job in a larger context.

MAKING CONNECTIONS

1. Somewhat like Hemingway in "A New Kind of War" (in "Reporting"), Hardy senses that she stands on the threshold of a new era. Compare these two writers for the sense of the new that each conveys. Which writer is more explicit about what he or she senses? Hardy, of course, writes forty years after the events she describes whereas Hemingway writes from a much closer vantage point. How does this fact complicate your comparison?

2. Could Hardy's essay be described as a "pilgrimage" to a particular intellectual or political position, somewhat like Martin Luther King's "Pilgrimage to Nonviolence"? How fair would that retitling be to Hardy's essay? What aspects of pilgrimage do you find in it?

Sciences and Technologies

MY FRIEND, ALBERT EINSTEIN

Banesh Hoffmann

Born in England, Banesh Hoffmann (1906–1986) came to America to pursue his career as a mathematician and teacher. He took his B.A. at Oxford but finished his graduate education at Princeton. There he became a member of Princeton's Institute for Advanced Study, where he met and worked with Albert Einstein. During his forty years as a mathematics professor at Queens College in Flushing, New York, he wrote such books as The Strange Story of the Quantum *(1959) and* The Tyranny of Testing *(1978), as well as articles for a wide variety of magazines. With Helen Dukas, Einstein's personal secretary, Hoffmann wrote* Albert Einstein: Creator and Rebel *(1973), which won a science writing award, and* Albert Einstein: The Human Side *(1979), a collection of Einstein's letters and personal reflections. The following essay first appeared in* Reader's Digest *and was later reprinted in their anthology* Unforgettable Characters *(1980).*

He was one of the greatest scientists the world has ever known, yet if I had 1 to convey the essence of Albert Einstein in a single word, I would choose *simplicity.* Perhaps an anecdote will help. Once, caught in a downpour, he took off his hat and held it under his coat. Asked why, he explained, with admirable logic, that the rain would damage the hat, but his hair would be none the worse for its wetting. This knack for going instinctively to the heart of a matter was the secret of his major scientific discoveries—this and his extraordinary feeling for beauty.

I first met Albert Einstein in 1935, at the famous Institute for Advanced 2

115

Study in Princeton, N.J. He had been among the first to be invited to the Institute, and was offered *carte blanche* as to salary. To the director's dismay, Einstein asked for an impossible sum: it was far too *small*. The director had to plead with him to accept a larger salary.

I was in awe of Einstein, and hesitated before approaching him about some ideas I had been working on. When I finally knocked on his door, a gentle voice said, "Come"—with a rising inflection that made the single word both a welcome and a question. I entered his office and found him seated at a table, calculating and smoking his pipe. Dressed in ill-fitting clothes, his hair characteristically awry, he smiled a warm welcome. His utter naturalness at once set me at ease.

As I began to explain my ideas, he asked me to write the equations on the blackboard so he could see how they developed. Then came the staggering—and altogether endearing—request: "Please go slowly. I do not understand things quickly." This from Einstein! He said it gently, and I laughed. From then on, all vestiges of fear were gone.

Einstein was born in 1879 in the German city of Ulm. He had been no infant prodigy; indeed, he was so late in learning to speak that his parents feared he was a dullard. In school, though his teachers saw no special talent in him, the signs were already there. He taught himself calculus, for example, and his teachers seemed a little afraid of him because he asked questions they could not answer. At the age of 16, he asked himself whether a light wave would seem stationary if one ran abreast of it. From that innocent question would arise, ten years later, his theory of relativity.

Einstein failed his entrance examinations at the Swiss Federal Polytechnic School, in Zurich, but was admitted a year later. There he went beyond his regular work to study the masterworks of physics on his own. Rejected when he applied for academic positions, he ultimately found work, in 1902, as a patent examiner in Berne, and there in 1905 his genius burst into fabulous flower.

Among the extraordinary things he produced in that memorable year were his theory of relativity, with its famous offshot, $E=mc^2$ (energy equals mass times the speed of light squared), and his quantum theory of light. These two theories were not only revolutionary, but seemingly contradictory: the former was intimately linked to the theory that light consists of waves, while the latter said it consists somehow of particles. Yet this unknown young man boldly proposed both at once—and he was right in both cases, though how he could have been is far too complex a story to tell here.

Collaborating with Einstein was an unforgettable experience. In 1937, the Polish physicist Leopold Infeld and I asked if we could work with him. He was pleased with the proposal, since he had an idea about gravitation waiting to be worked out in detail. Thus we got to know not merely the man and the friend, but also the professional.

The intensity and depth of his concentration were fantastic. When battling   9 a recalcitrant problem, he worried it as an animal worries its prey. Often, when we found ourselves up against a seemingly insuperable difficulty, he would stand up, put his pipe on the table, and say in his quaint English, "I will a little tink" (he could not pronounce "th"). Then he would pace up and down, twirling a lock of his long, graying hair around his forefinger.

A dreamy, faraway and yet inward look would come over his face. There   10 was no appearance of concentration, no furrowing of the brow—only a placid inner communion. The minutes would pass, and then suddenly Einstein would stop pacing as his face relaxed into a gentle smile. He had found the solution to the problem. Sometimes it was so simple that Infeld and I could have kicked ourselves for not having thought of it. But the magic had been performed invisibly in the depths of Einstein's mind, by a process we could not fathom.

When his wife died he was deeply shaken, but insisted that now more than   11 ever was the time to be working hard. I remember going to his house to work with him during that sad time. His face was haggard and grief-lined, but he put forth a great effort to concentrate. To help him, I steered the discussion away from routine matters into more difficult theoretical problems, and Einstein gradually became absorbed in the discussion. We kept at it for some two hours, and at the end his eyes were no longer sad. As I left, he thanked me with moving sincerity. "It was a fun," he said. He had had a moment of surcease from grief, and the groping words expressed a deep emotion.

Although Einstein felt no need for religious ritual and belonged to no formal   12 religious group, he was the most deeply religious man I have known. He once said to me, "Ideas come from God," and one could hear the capital "G" in the reverence with which he pronounced the word. On the marble fireplace in the mathematics building at Princeton University is carved, in the original German, what one might call his scientific credo: "God is subtle, but he is not malicious." By this Einstein meant that scientists could expect to find their task difficult, but not hopeless: the Universe was a Universe of law, and God was not confusing us with deliberate paradoxes and contradictions.

Einstein was an accomplished amateur musician. We used to play duets, he   13 on the violin, I at the piano. One day he surprised me by saying Mozart was the greatest composer of all. Beethoven "created" his music, but the music of Mozart was of such purity and beauty one felt he had merely "found" it—that it had always existed as part of the inner beauty of the Universe, waiting to be revealed.

It was this very Mozartean simplicity that most characterized Einstein's   14 methods. His 1905 theory of relativity, for example, was built on just two simple assumptions. One is the so-called principle of relativity, which means, roughly speaking, that we cannot tell whether we are at rest or moving smoothly. The other assumption is that the speed of light is the same no matter what the speed of the object that produces it. You can see how reasonable this is if you think of agitating a stick in a lake to create waves. Whether you wiggle the stick from a stationary pier, or from a rushing speedboat, the waves, once generated, are on their own, and their speed has nothing to do with that of the stick.

Each of these assumptions, by itself, was so plausible as to seem primitively obvious. But together they were in such violent conflict that a lesser man would have dropped one or the other and fled in panic. Einstein daringly kept both— and by so doing he revolutionized physics. For he demonstrated they could, after all, exist peacefully side by side, provided we gave up cherished beliefs about the nature of time. 15

Science is like a house of cards, with concepts like time and space at the lowest level. Tampering with time brought most of the house tumbling down, and it was this that made Einstein's work so important—and controversial. At a conference in Princeton in honor of his 70th birthday, one of the speakers, a Nobel Prize winner, tried to convey the magical quality of Einstein's achievement. Words failed him, and with a shrug of helplessness he pointed to his wristwatch, and said in tones of awed amazement, "It all came from this." His very ineloquence made this the most eloquent tribute I have heard to Einstein's genius. 16

Although fame had little effect on Einstein as a person, he could not escape it; he was, of course, instantly recognizable. One autumn Saturday, I was walking with him in Princeton discussing some technical matters. Parents and alumni were streaming excitedly toward the stadium, their minds on the coming football game. As they approached us, they paused in sudden recognition, and a momentary air of solemnity came over them as if they had been reminded of a different world. Yet Einstein seemed totally unaware of this effect and went on with the discussion as though they were not there. 17

We think of Einstein as one concerned only with the deepest aspects of science. But he saw scientific principles in everyday things to which most of us would give barely a second thought. He once asked me if I had ever wondered why a man's feet will sink into either dry or completely submerged sand, while sand that is merely damp provides a firm surface. When I could not answer, he offered a simple explanation. 18

It depends, he pointed out, on *surface tension*, the elastic-skin effect of a liquid surface. This is what holds a drop together, or causes two small raindrops on a windowpane to pull into one big drop the moment their surfaces touch. 19

When sand is damp, Einstein explained, there are tiny amounts of water   20
between grains. The surface tensions of these tiny amounts of water pull all the
grains together, and friction then makes them hard to budge. When the sand
is dry, there is obviously no water between grains. If the sand is fully immersed,
there is water between grains, but no water *surface* to pull them together.

This is not as important as relativity; yet there is no telling what seeming   21
trifle will lead an Einstein to a major discovery. And the puzzle of the sand
does give us an inkling of the power and elegance of his mind.

Einstein's work, performed quietly with pencil and paper, seemed remote   22
from the turmoil of everyday life. But his ideas were so revolutionary they
caused violent controversy and irrational anger. Indeed, in order to be able to
award him a belated Nobel Prize, the selection committee had to avoid mentioning relativity, and pretend the prize was awarded primarily for his work on
the quantum theory.

Political events upset the serenity of his life even more. When the Nazis   23
came to power in Germany, his theories were officially declared false because
they had been formulated by a Jew. His property was confiscated, and it is said
a price was put on his head.

When scientists in the United States, fearful that the Nazis might develop   24
an atomic bomb, sought to alert American authorities to the danger, they were
scarcely heeded. In desperation, they drafted a letter which Einstein signed and
sent directly to President Roosevelt. It was this act that led to the fateful decision
to go all-out on the production of an atomic bomb—an endeavor in which
Einstein took no active part. When he heard of the agony and destruction that
his $E=mc^2$ had wrought, he was dismayed beyond measure, and from then on
there was a look of ineffable sadness in his eyes.

There was something elusively whimsical about Einstein. It is illustrated by   25
my favorite anecdote about him. In his first year in Princeton, on Christmas
Eve, so the story goes, some children sang carols outside his house. Having
finished, they knocked on his door and explained they were collecting money
to buy Christmas presents. Einstein listened, then said, "Wait a moment." He
put on his scarf and overcoat, and took his violin from its case. Then, joining
the children as they went from door to door, he accompanied their singing of
"Silent Night" on his violin.

How shall I sum up what it meant to have known Einstein and his works?   26
Like the Nobel Prize winner who pointed helplessly at his watch, I can find no
adequate words. It was akin to the revelation of great art that lets one see what
was formerly hidden. And when, for example, I walk on the sand of a lonely
beach, I am reminded of his ceaseless search for cosmic simplicity—and the
scene takes on a deeper, sadder beauty.

QUESTIONS

1. Simplicity is not often considered an enviable personal trait; how does Hoffmann turn this to Einstein's advantage?

2. Hoffmann alternates between personal anecdotes and scientific anecdotes. Is this alternation confusing, or does it add to the effectiveness of the essay? In what ways?

3. Although primarily about Einstein, the essay reveals a certain amount about Hoffmann himself. What qualities as both a person and a scientist does he possess?

4. Is Hoffmann mainly concerned in this essay with Einstein the person or Einstein the scientist? What is Hoffmann's purpose in writing this essay?

5. Does this essay have a formal structure, or is the essay simply a series of reminiscences? How is the structure consistent with Hoffmann's purpose?

6. Hoffmann's reminiscences all center on Einstein's simplicity. Choose a memorable character you have known, define this character's key attraction (as Hoffmann has done), and then write an essay using a series of reminiscences that illustrate this trait or quality from various angles.

7. Many have written on Einstein's unique personality. Find another biographical account of Einstein, and compare it with Hoffmann's. Do the same qualities emerge?

MAKING CONNECTIONS

1. Keeping in mind the qualities that Hoffmann highlights in Einstein, consider the essays by other scientists that follow in this section. In which scientists do you find qualities that are surprisingly like Einstein's, and in which do you find qualities that are markedly different?

2. Make a similar comparison of the qualities Hoffmann locates in Einstein with those you sense in writers from the "Arts and Humanities" section above. Try to identify who you think would be remarkably congenial with Einstein, as described by Hoffmann, and explain the commonality you find.

CAN WE KNOW THE UNIVERSE? REFLECTIONS ON A GRAIN OF SALT

Carl Sagan

Carl Sagan (b. 1934), David Duncan Professor of Astronomy and Space Sciences at Cornell University, is renowned both as a scientist and a writer. For his work with the National Space Administration's Mariner, Viking, and Voyager expeditions, he was awarded NASA's Medals for Exceptional Scientific Achievement and for Distinguished Public Service. Sagan produced the Cosmos television series for public television and received the Peabody award in 1981. For his book, The Dragons of Eden (1977), he received the Pulitzer Prize for Literature in 1978. Among his recent works is Comet (1985) and a novel, Contact (1985). The following selection is from Broca's Brain: Reflections on the Romance of Science (1979).

> Nothing is rich but the inexhaustible wealth
> of nature. She shows us only surfaces,
> but she is a million fathoms deep.
>
> Ralph Waldo Emerson

Science is a way of thinking much more than it is a body of knowledge. Its goal is to find out how the world works, to seek what regularities there may be, to penetrate to the connections of things—from subnuclear particles, which may be the constituents of all matter, to living organisms, the human social community, and thence to the cosmos as a whole. Our intuition is by no means an infallible guide. Our perceptions may be distorted by training and prejudice or merely because of the limitations of our sense organs, which, of course, perceive directly but a small fraction of the phenomena of the world. Even so straightforward a question as whether in the absence of friction a pound of lead falls faster than a gram of fluff was answered incorrectly by Aristotle and almost everyone else before the time of Galileo. Science is based on experiment, on a willingness to challenge old dogma, on an openness to see the universe as it really is. Accordingly, science sometimes requires courage—at the very least the courage to question the conventional wisdom.

Beyond this the main trick of science is to *really* think of something: the shape of clouds and their occasional sharp bottom edges at the same altitude everywhere in the sky; the formation of a dewdrop on a leaf; the origin of a name or a word—Shakespeare, say, or "philanthropic"; the reason for human social customs—the incest taboo, for example; how it is that a lens in sunlight can make paper burn; how a "walking stick" got to look so much like a twig; why the Moon seems to follow us as we walk; what prevents us from digging a hole down to the center of the Earth; what the definition is of "down" on a spherical Earth; how it is possible for the body to convert yesterday's lunch into today's muscle and sinew; or how far is up—does the universe go on forever, or if it does not, is there any meaning to the question of what lies on the other side? Some of these questions are pretty easy. Others, especially the last, are mysteries to which no one even today knows the answer. They are natural questions to ask. Every culture has posed such questions in one way or another. Almost always the proposed answers are in the nature of "Just So Stories," attempted explanations divorced from experiment, or even from careful comparative observations.

But the scientific cast of mind examines the world critically as if many alternative worlds might exist, as if other things might be here which are not. Then we are forced to ask why what we see is present and not something else. Why are the Sun and the Moon and the planets spheres? Why not pyramids, or cubes, or dodecahedra? Why not irregular, jumbly shapes? Why so symmetrical, worlds? If you spend any time spinning hypotheses, checking to see whether they make sense, whether they conform to what else we know, thinking of tests you can pose to substantiate or deflate your hypotheses, you will find yourself doing science. And as you come to practice this habit of thought more and more you will get better and better at it. To penetrate into the heart of the thing—even a little thing, a blade of grass, as Walt Whitman said—is to experience a kind of exhilaration that, it may be, only human beings of all the beings on this planet can feel. We are an intelligent species and the use of our intelligence quite properly gives us pleasure. In this respect the brain is like a muscle. When we think well, we feel good. Understanding is a kind of ecstasy.

But to what extent can we *really* know the universe around us? Sometimes this question is posed by people who hope the answer will be in the negative, who are fearful of a universe in which everything might one day be known. And sometimes we hear pronouncements from scientists who confidently state that everything worth knowing will soon be known—or even is already known— and who paint pictures of a Dionysian or Polynesian age in which the zest for intellectual discovery has withered, to be replaced by a kind of subdued languor, the lotus eaters drinking fermented coconut milk or some other mild hallucinogen. In addition to maligning both the Polynesians, who were intrepid explorers (and whose brief respite in paradise is now sadly ending), as well as the inducements to intellectual discovery provided by some hallucinogens, this contention turns out to be trivially mistaken.

122

Let us approach a much more modest question: not whether we can know   5
the universe or the Milky Way Galaxy or a star or a world. Can we know,
ultimately and in detail, a grain of salt? Consider one microgram of table salt,
a speck just barely large enough for someone with keen eyesight to make out
without a microscope. In that grain of salt there are about 10^{16} sodium and
chlorine atoms. This is a 1 followed by 16 zeros, 10 million billion atoms. If
we wish to know a grain of salt, we must know at least the three-dimensional
positions of each of these atoms. (In fact, there is much more to be known—
for example, the nature of the forces between the atoms—but we are making
only a modest calculation.) Now, is this number more or less than the number
of things which the brain can know?

How much *can* the brain know? There are perhaps 10^{11} neurons in the   6
brain, the circuit elements and switches that are responsible in their electrical
and chemical activity for the functioning of our minds. A typical brain neuron
has perhaps a thousand little wires, called dendrites, which connect it with its
fellows. If, as seems likely, every bit of information in the brain corresponds to
one of these connections, the total number of things knowable by the brain is
no more than 10^{14}, one hundred trillion. But this number is only one percent
of the number of atoms in our speck of salt.

So in this sense the universe is intractable, astonishingly immune to any   7
human attempt at full knowledge. We cannot on this level understand a grain
of salt, much less the universe.

But let us look more deeply at our microgram of salt. Salt happens to be a   8
crystal in which, except for defects in the structure of the crystal lattice, the
position of every sodium and chlorine atom is predetermined. If we could shrink
ourselves into this crystalline world, we could see rank upon rank of atoms in
an ordered array, a regularly alternating structure—sodium, chlorine, sodium,
chlorine, specifying the sheet of atoms we are standing on and all the sheets
above us and below us. An absolutely pure crystal of salt could have the position
of every atom specified by something like 10 bits of information.[1] This would
not strain the information-carrying capacity of the brain.

If the universe had natural laws that governed its behavior to the same degree   9
of regularity that determines a crystal of salt, then, of course, the universe would
be knowable. Even if there were many such laws, each of considerable complexity, human beings might have the capacity to understand them all. Even if
such knowledge exceeded the information-carrying capacity of the brain, we
might store the additional information outside our bodies—in books, for example, or in computer memories—and still, in some sense, know the universe.

Human beings are, understandably, highly motivated to find regularities,   10

---

[1] Chlorine is a deadly poison gas employed on European battlefields in World War I. Sodium
is a corrosive metal which burns upon contact with water. Together they make a placid and
unpoisonous material, table salt. Why each of these substances has the properties it does is a subject
called chemistry, which requires more than 10 bits of information to understand.

natural laws. The search for rules, the only possible way to understand such a vast and complex universe, is called science. The universe forces those who live in it to understand it. Those creatures who find everyday experience a muddled jumble of events with no predictability, no regularity, are in grave peril. The universe belongs to those who, at least to some degree, have figured it out.

It is an astonishing fact that there *are* laws of nature, rules that summarize conveniently—not just qualitatively but quantitatively—how the world works. We might imagine a universe in which there are no such laws, in which the 10^{80} elementary particles that make up a universe like our own behave with utter and uncompromising abandon. To understand such a universe we would need a brain at least as massive as the universe. It seems unlikely that such a universe could have life and intelligence, because beings and brains require some degree of internal stability and order. But even if in a much more random universe there were such beings with an intelligence much greater than our own, there could not be much knowledge, passion or joy. 11

Fortunately for us, we live in a universe that has at least important parts that are knowable. Our common-sense experience and our evolutionary history have prepared us to understand something of the workaday world. When we go into other realms, however, common sense and ordinary intuition turn out to be highly unreliable guides. It is stunning that as we go close to the speed of light our mass increases indefinitely, we shrink toward zero thickness in the direction of motion, and time for us comes as near to stopping as we would like. Many people think that this is silly, and every week or two I get a letter from someone who complains to me about it. But it is a virtually certain consequence not just of experiment but also of Albert Einstein's brilliant analysis of space and time called the Special Theory of Relativity. It does not matter that these effects seem unreasonable to us. We are not in the habit of traveling close to the speed of light. The testimony of our common sense is suspect at high velocities. 12

Or consider an isolated molecule composed of two atoms shaped something like a dumbbell—a molecule of salt, it might be. Such a molecule rotates about an axis through the line connecting the two atoms. But in the world of quantum mechanics, the realm of the very small, not all orientations of our dumbbell molecule are possible. It might be that the molecule could be oriented in a horizontal position, say, or in a vertical position, but not at many angles in between. Some rotational positions are forbidden. Forbidden by what? By the laws of nature. The universe is built in such a way as to limit, or quantize, rotation. We do not experience this directly in everyday life; we would find it startling as well as awkward in sitting-up exercises, to find arms outstretched from the sides or pointed up to the skies permitted but many intermediate positions forbidden. We do not live in the world of the small, on the scale of 10^{-13} centimeters, in the realm where there are twelve zeros between the decimal place and the one. Our common-sense intuitions do not count. What 13 does count is experiment—in this case observations from the far infrared spectra of molecules. They show molecular rotation to be quantized.

The idea that the world places restrictions on what humans might do is 14 frustrating. Why *shouldn't* we be able to have intermediate rotational positions? Why *can't* we travel faster than the speed of light? But so far as we can tell, this is the way the universe is constructed. Such prohibitions not only press us toward a little humility; they also make the world more knowable. Every restriction corresponds to a law of nature, a regularization of the universe. The more restrictions there are on what matter and energy can do, the more knowledge human beings can attain. Whether in some sense the universe is ultimately knowable depends not only on how many natural laws there are that encompass widely divergent phenomena, but also on whether we have the openness and the intellectual capacity to understand such laws. Our formulations of the regularities of nature are surely dependent on how the brain is built, but also, and to a significant degree, on how the universe is built.

For myself, I like a universe that includes much that is unknown and, at 15 the same time, much that is knowable. A universe in which everything is known would be static and dull, as boring as the heaven of some weakminded theologians. A universe that is unknowable is no fit place for a thinking being. The ideal universe for us is one very much like the universe we inhabit. And I would guess that this is not really much of a coincidence.

QUESTIONS

1. How are *science* and *scientific thinking* defined in the first three paragraphs? What is Sagan's purpose in defining these terms? What does this tell you about Sagan's conception of his audience?

2. Sagan's mode of reflection might be considered less personal than others in this section in that he is reflecting on an idea rather than on an event in his life. How does Sagan keep the tone from becoming abstract? What elements of the personal are present in this essay?

3. Sagan cites scientists who believe that "everything worth knowing will soon be known" (paragraph 4). How does the evidence in this essay challenge that assumption?

4. We might consider paragraph 15 Sagan's most personal statement in his reflections on the universe: he likes "a universe that includes much that is unknown and, at the same time, much that is knowable." Why is this balance important to Sagan? Do you agree with his closing statements?

5. Consider the statement, "The more restrictions there are on what matter and energy can do, the more knowledge human beings can attain" (paragraph 14). Describe an example in your own experience (or another's) when you learned that rules, or laws, were helpful in ensuring your personal freedom.

6. In paragraph 3 Sagan concludes, "Understanding is a kind of ecstasy." Describe a time in your life when you understood something for the first time; when, as they say,

the light went on in your head, shining on a difficult problem, and bringing about a realization. Could your feelings at the time be considered ecstatic, or did you experience some other emotion?

7. What sort of universe would you consider ideal? What would you like to know about the universe that is now unknown to you? Explain.

MAKING CONNECTIONS

1. A number of the writers in this section offer their reflections in order to justify a belief or a strong feeling about a subject. In other words, their reflections become a kind of argument. Isak Dinesen, Martin Luther King, Jr., George Orwell, and Zoë Tracy Hardy come to mind as well as Sagan. How convincing is the argument in each case? How has the writer used purely personal responses to make a persuasive case? How would you go about developing a more objective argument for one of their positions? What would be the difference in effect?

2. Does his concern for "passion" and "joy" (paragraph 11) surprise you in these remarks by Sagan? Where else, especially in the writings by scientists in this section, do you find evidence of the same concerns? Citing several examples from essayists you have read, write an essay on the role of "passion" and "joy" in the work of scientists and other writers.

1933 MEDICINE
Lewis Thomas

Lewis Thomas, a highly regarded medical administrator, is the former chancellor of Memorial Sloan-Kettering Cancer Center in New York City and former chairman of the board of the Scientists' Institute for Public Information. His engaging essay collections are mentioned in the headnote on page 741. This piece introduces an account of his medical education at Harvard.

I was admitted to medical school under circumstances that would have been impossible today. There was not a lot of competition; not more than thirty of my four hundred classmates, most of these the sons of doctors, planned on medicine. There was no special curriculum; elementary physics and two courses in chemistry were the only fixed requirements; the term "premedical" had not yet been invented. My academic record at Princeton was middling fair; I had entered college at fifteen, having been a bright enough high-school student, but then I turned into a moult of dullness and laziness, average or below average in the courses requiring real work. It was not until my senior year, when I ventured a course in advanced biology under Professor Swingle, who had just discovered a hormone of the adrenal cortex, that I became a reasonably alert scholar, but by that time my grade averages had me solidly fixed in the dead center, the "gentlemen's third," of the class. Today, I would have been turned down by every place, except perhaps one of the proprietary medical schools in the Caribbean.

I got into Harvard, by luck and also, I suspect, by pull. Hans Zinsser, the professor of bacteriology, had interned with my father at Roosevelt and had admired my mother, and when I went to Boston to be interviewed in the winter of 1933, I was instructed by the dean's secretary to go have a talk with Dr. Zinsser. It was the briefest of interviews, but satisfactory from my point of view. Zinsser looked at me carefully, as at a specimen, then informed me that my father and mother were good friends of his, and if I wanted to come to Harvard he would try to help, but because of them, not me; he was entirely good-natured, but clear on this point. It was favoritism, but not all that personal, I was to understand.

My medical education was, in principle, much like that of my father. The details had changed a lot since his time, especially in the fields of medical science relating to disease mechanisms; physiology and biochemistry had become far more complex and also more illuminating; microbiology and immunology had already, by the early 1930s, transformed our understanding of the causation of the major infectious diseases. But the *purpose* of the curriculum was, if anything, even more conservative than thirty years earlier. It was to teach the recognition of disease entities, their classification, their signs, symptoms, and laboratory manifestations, and how to make an accurate diagnosis. The treatment of disease was the most minor part of the curriculum, almost left out altogether. There was, to be sure, a course in pharmacology in the second year, mostly concerned with the mode of action of a handful of everyday drugs: aspirin, morphine, various cathartics, bromides, barbiturates, digitalis, a few others. Vitamin B was coming into fashion as a treatment for delirium tremens, later given up. We were provided with a thin, pocket-size book called *Useful Drugs*, one hundred pages or so, and we carried this around in our white coats when we entered the teaching wards and clinics in the third year, but I cannot recall any of our instructors ever referring to this volume. Nor do I remember much talk about treating disease at any time in the four years of medical school except by the surgeons, and most of their discussions dealt with the management of injuries, the drainage or removal of infected organs and tissues, and, to a very limited extent, the excision of cancers.

The medicine we were trained to practice was, essentially, Osler's medicine.[1] 4
Our task for the future was to be diagnosis and explanation. Explanation was the real business of medicine. What the ill patient and his family wanted most was to know the name of the illness, and then, if possible, what had caused it, and finally, most important of all, how it was likely to turn out.

The successes possible in diagnosis and prognosis were regarded as the 5
triumph of medical science, and so they were. It had taken long decades of careful, painstaking observation of many patients; the publication of countless papers describing the detailed aspects of one clinical syndrome after another; more science, in the correlation of the clinical features of disease with the gross and microscopic abnormalities, contributed by several generations of pathologists. By the 1930s we thought we knew as much as could ever be known about the dominant clinical problems of the time: syphilis, tuberculosis, lobar pneumonia, typhoid, rheumatic fever, erysipelas, poliomyelitis. Most of the known varieties of cancer had been meticulously classified, and estimates of the duration of life could be made with some accuracy. The electrocardiogram had arrived, adding to the fair precision already possible in the diagnosis of heart disease. Neurology possessed methods for the localization of disease processes anywhere in the nervous system. When we had learned all that, we were ready for our M.D. degrees, and it was expected that we would find out about the

---

[1] Sir William Osler (1849–1919): Canadian-born physician and teacher. [Eds.]

actual day-to-day management of illness during our internship and residency years.

During the third and fourth years of school we also began to learn something that worried us all, although it was not much talked about. On the wards of the great Boston teaching hospitals—the Peter Bent Brigham, the Massachusetts General, the Boston City Hospital, and Beth Israel—it gradually dawned on us that we didn't know much that was really useful, that we could do nothing to change the course of the great majority of the diseases we were so busy analyzing, that medicine, for all its façade as a learned profession, was in real life a profoundly ignorant occupation.

Some of this we were actually taught by our clinical professors, much more we learned from each other in late-night discussions. When I am asked, as happens occasionally, which member of the Harvard faculty had the greatest influence on my education in medicine, I no longer grope for a name on that distinguished roster. What I remember now, from this distance, is the influence of my classmates. We taught each other; we may even have set careers for each other without realizing at the time that so fundamental an education process was even going on. I am not so troubled as I used to be by the need to reform the medical school curriculum. What worries me these days is that the curriculum, whatever its sequential arrangement, has become so crowded with lectures and seminars, with such masses of data to be learned, that the students may not be having enough time to instruct each other in what may lie ahead.

The most important period for discovering what medicine would be like was a three-month ward clerkship in internal medicine that was a required part of the fourth year of medical school. I applied for the clerkship at the Beth Israel Hospital, partly because of the reputation of Professor Hermann Blumgart and partly because several of my best friends were also going there. Ward rounds with Dr. Blumgart were an intellectual pleasure, also good for the soul. I became considerably less anxious about the scale of medical ignorance as we followed him from bed to bed around the open circular wards of the B.I. I've seen his match only three or four times since then. He was a tall, thin, quick-moving man, with a look of high intelligence, austerity, and warmth all at the same time. He had the special gift of perceiving, almost instantaneously, while still approaching the bedside of a new patient, whether the problem was a serious one or not. He seemed to do this by something like intuition; at times when there were no particular reasons for alarm that could be sensed by others in the retinue, Blumgart would become extremely alert and attentive, requiring the resident to present every last detail of the history, and then moving closer to the bedside, asking his own questions of the patient, finally performing his physical examination. To watch a master of physical diagnosis in the execution of a complete physical examination is something of an aesthetic experience, rather like observing a great ballet dancer or a concert cellist. Blumgart did all this swiftly, then asked a few more questions, then drew us away to the corridor outside the ward for his discussion, and then his diagnosis, sometimes a death sentence. Then back to the bedside for a brief private talk with the patient, inaudible to the rest of us, obviously reassuring to the patient, and on to the next bed. So far as I know, from that three months of close contact with Blumgart for three hours every morning, he was never wrong, not once. But I can recall only three or four patients for whom the diagnosis resulted in the possibility of doing something to change the course of the illness, and each of these involved calling in the surgeons to do the something—removal of a thyroid nodule, a gallbladder, an adrenal tumor. For the majority, the disease had to be left to run its own course, for better or worse.

There were other masters of medicine, each as unique in his way as Blum- 9 gart, surrounded every day by interns and medical students on the wards of the other Boston hospitals.

The Boston City Hospital, the city's largest, committed to the care of indigent 10 Bostonians, was divided into five separate clinical services, two staffed by Harvard Medical School (officially designated as the Second and Fourth services), two by Tufts, and one by Boston University. The most spectacular chiefs on the Harvard faculty were aggregated on the City Hospital wards, drawn there in the 1920s by the creation of the Thorndike Memorial Laboratories, a separate research institute on the hospital grounds, directly attached by a series of ramps and tunnels to the buildings containing the teaching wards. The Thorndike was founded by Dr. Francis Weld Peabody, still remembered in Boston as perhaps the best of Harvard physicians. Peabody was convinced that the study of human disease should not be conducted solely by bedside observations, as had been largely the case for the research done by physicians up to that time, nor by pure bench research in the university laboratories; he believed that the installation of a fully equipped research institute, containing laboratories for investigations of any promising line of inquiry, directly in communication with the hospital wards, offered the best opportunity for moving the field forward.

Peabody was also responsible for the initial staffing of the Thorndike. By the 11 time I arrived, in 1937, the array of talent was formidable: George Minot (who had already received his Nobel prize for the discovery of liver extract as a cure for pernicious anemia), William Castle (who discovered the underlying deficiency in pernicious anemia), Chester Keefer, Soma Weiss, Maxwell Finland, John Dingle, Eugene Stead—each of them running a laboratory, teaching on the wards, and providing research training for young doctors who came from two- and three-year fellowship stints from teaching hospitals across the country. The Thorndike was a marvelous experiment, a model for what were to become the major departments of medicine in other medical schools, matched at the time only by the hospital of the Rockefeller Institute in New York.

Max Finland built and then ran the infectious disease service. He and his 12 associates had done most of the definitive work on antipneumococcal sera in the treatment of lobar pneumonia, testing each new preparation of rabbit antiserum as it arrived from the Lederle Laboratories. Later, Finland's laboratories were to become a national center for the clinical evaluation of penicillin, streptomycin, cholromycetin, and all the other antibiotics which followed during the 1950s and 1960s. As early as 1937, medicine was changing into a technology based on genuine science. The signs of change were there, hard to see because of the overwhelming numbers of patients for whom we could do nothing but stand by, but unmistakably there all the same. Syphilis could be treated in its early stages, and eventually cured, by Paul Ehrlich's arsphenamine; the treatment took a long time, many months, sometimes several years. If arsphenamine was started in the late stages of the disease, when the greatest damage was under way—the central nervous system and the major arteries— the results were rarely satisfactory—but in the earliest stages, the chancre and then the rash of secondary syphilis, the spirochete could be killed off and the Wassermann reaction reversed.[2] The treatment was difficult and hazardous, the side effects of the arsenical drugs were appalling, sometimes fatal (I cannot imagine such a therapy being introduced and accepted by any of today's FDA or other regulatory agencies), but it did work in many cases, and it carried a powerful message for the future: it was possible to destroy an invading microorganism, intimately embedded within the cells and tissues, without destroying the cells themselves. Chemotherapy for infectious disease in general lay somewhere ahead, and we should have known this.

Immunology was beginning to become an applied science. Thanks to the basic research launched twenty years earlier by Avery, Heidelberger, and Goebbel, it was known that pneumococci possessed specific carbohydrates in their capsules which gave rise to highly specific antibodies.[3] By the mid-1930s, rabbit antipneumococcal sera were available for the treatment of the commonest forms of lobar pneumonia. The sera were difficult and expensive to prepare, and sometimes caused overwhelming anaphylactic reactions in patients already moribund from their infection,[4] but they produced outright cures in many patients. Pernicious anemia, a uniformly fatal disease, was spectacularly reversed by liver extract (much later found to be due to the presence of vitamin B_{12} in the extracts). Diabetes mellitus could be treated—at least to the extent of reducing the elevated blood sugar and correcting the acidosis that otherwise led to diabetic coma and death—by the insulin preparation isolated by Banting and Best. Pellagra, a common cause of death among the impoverished rural populations in the South, had become curable with Goldberger's discovery of the vitamin B complex and the subsequent identification of nicotinic acid. Diphtheria could

13

---

[2] spirochete: type of bacteria including the one that produces syphilis; Wassermann reaction: the reaction to the test used to diagnose syphilis. [Eds.]

[3] pneumococci: bacteria that cause pneumonia. [Eds.]

[4] anaphylactic reactions: severe toxic reactions by certain individuals who are hypersensitive to a drug; moribund: approaching death. [Eds.]

131

be prevented by immunization against the toxin of diphtheria bacilli and, when it occurred, treated more or less effectively with diphtheria antitoxin.

All these things were known at the time of my internship at the Boston City   14
Hospital, but they seemed small advances indeed. The major diseases, which filled the wards to overflowing during the long winter months, were infections for which there was no treatment at all.

The two great hazards of life were tuberculosis and tertiary syphilis. These   15
were feared by everyone, in the same way that cancer is feared today. There was nothing to be done for tuberculosis except to wait it out, hoping that the body's own defense mechanisms would eventually hold the tubercle bacillus in check. Some patients were helped by collapsing the affected lung (by injecting air into the pleural space, or by removing the ribs overlying the lung), and any number of fads were introduced for therapy—mountain resorts, fresh air, sun-shine, nutritious diets—but for most patients tuberculosis simply ran its own long debilitating course despite all efforts. Tertiary syphilis was even worse. The wards of insane asylums were filled with psychotic patients permanently inca-pacitated by this disease—"general paresis of the insane";[5] some benefit was claimed for fever therapy; but there were few real cures. Rheumatic fever, the commonest cause of fatal heart disease in children, was shown by Coburn to be the result of infection by hemolytic streptococci; aspirin, the only treatment available, relieved the painful arthritis in this disease but had no effect on the heart lesions. For most of the infectious diseases on the wards of the Boston City Hospital in 1937, there was nothing to be done beyond bed rest and good nursing care.

Then came the explosive news of sulfanilamide, and the start of the real   16
revolution in medicine.

I remember the astonishment when the first cases of pneumococcal and   17
streptococcal septicemia were treated in Boston in 1937. The phenomenon was almost beyond belief. Here were moribund patients, who would surely have died without treatment, improving in their appearance within a matter of hours of being given the medicine and feeling entirely well within the next day or so.

The professionals most deeply affected by these extraordinary events were, I   18
think, the interns. The older physicians were equally surprised, but took the news in stride. For an intern, it was the opening of a whole new world. We had been raised to be ready for one kind of profession, and we sensed that the profession itself had changed at the moment of our entry. We knew that other molecular variations of sulfanilamide were on their way from industry, and we heard about the possibility of penicillin and other antibiotics; we became con-vinced, overnight, that nothing lay beyond reach for the future. Medicine was off and running.

---

[5] general paresis of the insane: name for the type of insanity caused by syphilis. [Eds.]

QUESTIONS

1. "We had been raised to be ready for one kind of profession," Thomas writes in the final paragraph. What was the purpose of a medical education in the 1930s?

2. How had the purpose of medicine changed since the 1930s? Where is the major emphasis now? Have today's standards changed the quality of medical education?

3. Thomas claims to have learned more from his classmates than from his professors. What did he learn from his fellow students?

4. Although Thomas doesn't make any direct criticism of 1933 medicine, he manages to demonstrate its limitations in contrast to modern practice. How does he achieve this? Would the essay be more effective had Thomas been more directly critical?

5. What qualities of Dr. Blumgart did Thomas admire? What techniques does Thomas use to describe Dr. Blumgart so that a reader can see those admirable qualities?

6. Which half of the essay relies more heavily on technical descriptions? Trace the way in which the changing vocabulary of the essay parallels Thomas's education as a physician.

7. Thomas expected one profession but found another. Write an essay in which you reflect on changes in your expectations in a certain field as you learned more about the subject.

8. Write an essay in which you describe a person (such as Dr. Blumgart) whom you admire. Create a dominant impression for your readers by using vivid details that show why you admire this person.

MAKING CONNECTIONS

1. Compare the medical education Thomas describes with the one John F. Avedon details in "Tibetan Medicine: The Science of Healing," in "Reporting." Do you think Thomas would agree with the remarks in that essay about the two kinds of medicine having much to learn from each other?

2. Compare Thomas's essay with one from each of the other disciplinary areas of this section, with Joan Didion and Carl G. Jung, for example. How does each writer seem to be led from one thought to the next? Explore the similarities and differences you find among the three writers you select. Can you draw any conclusion about the relationship between a writer's field of interest and his or her writing?

WHY A SURGEON WOULD WRITE

Richard Selzer

Richard Selzer (b. 1928) is a surgeon and professor of surgery at the Yale University Medical School. His articles on various aspects of medicine have appeared in Harper's, Esquire, *and* Redbook. *In 1975 he won the National Magazine Award for his articles. His books include a volume of short stories,* Rituals of Surgery, *and a collection of autobiographical essays,* Mortal Lessons, *from which this selection is taken.*

Someone asked me why a surgeon would write. Why, when the shelves are 1 already too full? They sag under the deadweight of books. To add a single adverb is to risk exceeding the strength of the boards. A surgeon should abstain. A surgeon, whose fingers are more at home in the steamy gullies of the body than they are tapping the dry keys of a typewriter. A surgeon, who feels the slow slide of intestines against the back of his hands and is no more alarmed than were a family of snakes taking their comfort from such an indolent rubbing. A surgeon, who palms the human heart as though it were some captured bird.

Why should he write? Is it vanity that urges him? There is glory enough in 2 the knife. Is it for money? One can make too much money. No. It is to search for some meaning in the ritual of surgery, which is at once murderous, painful, healing, and full of love. It is a devilish hard thing to transmit—to find, even. Perhaps if one were to cut out a heart, a lobe of the liver, a single convolution of the brain, and paste it to a page, it would speak with more eloquence than all the words of Balzac.[1] Such a piece would need no literary style, no mass of erudition or history, but in its very shape and feel would tell all the frailty and strength, the despair and nobility of man. What? Publish a heart? A little piece of bone? Preposterous. Still I fear that is what it may require to reveal the truth that lies hidden in the body. Not all the undressings of Rabelais, Chekhov, or even William Carlos Williams have wrested it free,[2] although God knows each one of those doctors made a heroic assault upon it.

---

[1] Honoré de Balzac (1799–1850): French novelist. [Eds.]

[2] François Rabelais (1494?–1553): French writer and satirist; Anton Pavlovich Chekhov (1860–1904): Russian dramatist and short-story writer; William Carlos Williams (1883–1963): American poet; all three writers also were physicians. [Eds.]

I have come to believe that it is the flesh alone that counts. The rest is that   3
with which we distract ourselves when we are not hungry or cold, in pain or
ecstasy. In the recesses of the body I search for the philosophers' stone.[3] I know
it is there, hidden in the deepest, dampest cul-de-sac. It awaits discovery. To
find it would be like the harnessing of fire. It would illuminate the world. Such
a quest is not without pain. Who can gaze on so much misery, and feel no
hurt? Emerson has written that the poet is the only true doctor.[4] I believe him,
for the poet, lacking the impediment of speech with which the rest of us are
afflicted, gazes, records, diagnoses, and prophesies.

I invited a young diabetic woman to the operating room to amputate her   4
leg. She could not see the great shaggy black ulcer upon her foot and ankle
that threatened to encroach upon the rest of her body, for she was blind as well.
There upon her foot was a Mississippi Delta brimming with corruption, sending
its raw tributaries down between her toes. Gone were all the little web spaces
that when fresh and whole are such a delight to loving men. She could not see
her wound, but she could feel it. There is no pain like that of the bloodless
limb turned rotten and festering. There is neither unguent or anodyne to kill
such a pain yet leave intact the body.[5]

For over a year I trimmed away the putrid flesh, cleansed, anointed, and   5
dressed the foot, staving off, delaying. Three times each week, in her darkness,
she sat upon my table, rocking back and forth, holding her extended leg by the
thigh, gripping it as though it were a rocket that must be steadied lest it explode
and scatter her toes about the room. And I would cut away a bit here, a bit
there, of the swollen blue leather that was her tissue.

At last we gave up, she and I. We could no longer run ahead of the gangrene.   6
We had not the legs for it. There must be an amputation in order that she
might live—and I as well. It was to heal us both that I must take up knife and
saw, and cut the leg off. And when I could feel it drop from her body to the
table, see the blessed *space* appear between her and that leg, I too would be
well.

Now it is the day of the operation. I stand by while the anesthetist administers   7
the drugs, watch as the tense familiar body relaxes into narcosis. I turn then to
uncover the leg. There, upon her kneecap, she has drawn, blindly, upside
down for me to see, a face; just a circle with two ears, two eyes, a nose, and a
smiling upturned mouth. Under it she had printed SMILE, DOCTOR. Minutes
later I listen to the sound of the saw, until a little crack at the end tells me it
is done.

So, I have learned that man is not ugly, but that he is Beauty itself. There   8
is no other his equal. Are we not all dying, none faster or more slowly than

---

[3]philosophers' stone: an imaginary substance supposed to turn other metals to gold. [Eds.]
[4]Ralph Waldo Emerson (1803–1882): American essayist and poet. [Eds.]
[5]unguent: salve or ointment; anodyne: soothing medicine that relieves pain. [Eds.]

any other? I have become receptive to the possibilities of love (for it is love, this thing that happens in the operating room), and each day I wait, trembling in the busy air. Perhaps today it will come. Perhaps today I will find it, take part in it, this love that blooms in the stoniest desert.

All through literature, the doctor is portrayed as a figure of fun. Shaw was   9
splenetic about him,[6] Molière delighted in pricking his pompous medicine men,[7] and well they deserved it. The doctor is ripe for caricature. But I believe that the truly great writing about doctors has not yet been done. I think it must be done *by* a doctor, one who is through with the love affair with his technique, who recognizes that he has played Narcissus,[8] raining kisses on a mirror, and who now, out of the impacted masses of his guilt, has expanded into self-doubt, and finally into the high state of wonderment. Perhaps he will be a nonbeliever who, after a lifetime of grand gestures and mighty deeds, comes upon the knowledge that he has done no more than meddle in the lives of his fellows, and that he has done at least as much harm as good. Yet he may continue to pretend, at least, that there is nothing to fear, that death will not come, so long as people depend on his authority. Later, after his patients have left, he may closet himself in his darkened office, sweating and afraid.

There is a story by Unamuno in which a priest,[9] living in a small Spanish   10
village, is adored by all the people for his piety, kindness, and the majesty with which he celebrates the Mass each Sunday. To them he is already a saint. It is a foregone conclusion, and they speak of him as Saint Immanuel. He helps them with their plowing and planting, tends them when they are sick, confesses them, comforts them in death, and every Sunday, in his rich, thrilling voice, transports them to paradise with his chanting. The fact is that Don Immanuel is not so much a saint as a martyr. Long ago his own faith left him. He is an atheist, a good man doomed to suffer the life of a hypocrite, pretending to a faith he does not have. As he raises the chalice of wine, his hands tremble, and a cold sweat pours from him. He cannot stop for he knows that the people need this of him, that their need is greater than his sacrifice. Still . . . still . . . could it be that Don Immanuel's whole life is a kind of prayer, a paean to God?

A writing doctor would treat men and women with equal reverence, for what   11
is the "liberation" of either sex to him who knows the diagrams, the inner geographies of each? I love the solid heft of men as much as I adore the heated capaciousness of women—women in whose penetralia is found the repository

---

[6]George Bernard Shaw (1856–1950): British playwright and critic. [Eds.]

[7]Jean-Baptiste Poquelin Molière (1622–1673): French playwright and actor. [Eds.]

[8]Narcissus: After rejecting the love of Echo, this character in Greek mythology pined away for his own beautiful reflection in a pool, and then was turned into the flower that bears his name. [Eds.]

[9]Miguel de Unamuno (1864–1936): Spanish writer and philosopher. [Eds.]

of existence. I would have them glory in that. Women are physics and chemistry. They are matter. It is their bodies that tell of the frailty of men. Men have not their cellular, enzymatic wisdom. Man is albuminoid, proteinaceous, laked pearl; woman is yolky, ovoid, rich. Both are exuberant bloody growths. I would use the defects and deformities of each for my sacred purpose of writing, for I know that it is the marred and scarred and faulty that are subject to grace. I would seek the soul in the facts of animal economy and profligacy. Yes, it is the exact location of the soul that I am after. The smell of it is in my nostrils. I have caught glimpses of it in the body diseased. If only I could tell it. Is there no mathematical equation that can guide me? So much pain and pus equals so much truth? It is elusive as the whippoorwill that one hears calling incessantly from out the night window, but which, nesting as it does low in the brush, no one sees. No one but the poet, for he sees what no one else can. He was born with the eye for it.

Once I thought I had it: Ten o'clock one night, the end room off a long   12
corridor in a college infirmary, my last patient of the day, degree of exhaustion suitable for the appearance of a vision, some manifestation. The patient is a young man recently returned from Guatemala, from the excavation of Mayan ruins. His left upper arm wears a gauze dressing which, when removed, reveals a clean punched-out hole the size of a dime. The tissues about the opening are swollen and tense. A thin brownish fluid lips the edge, and now and then a lazy drop of the overflow spills down the arm. An abscess, inadequately drained. I will enlarge the opening to allow better egress of the pus. Nurse, will you get me a scalpel and some . . . ?

What happens next is enough to lay Francis Drake avomit in his cabin.[10]   13
No explorer ever stared in wilder surmise than I into that crater from which there now emerges a narrow gray head whose sole distinguishing feature is a pair of black pincers. The head sits atop a longish flexible neck arching now this way, now that, testing the air. Alternately it folds back upon itself, then advances in new boldness. And all the while, with dreadful rhythmicity, the unspeakable pincers open and close. Abscess? Pus? Never. Here is the lair of a beast at whose malignant purpose I could but guess. A Mayan devil, I think, that would soon burst free to fly about the room, with horrid blanket-wings and iridescent scales, raking, pinching, injecting God knows what acid juice. And even now the irony does not escape me, the irony of my patient as excavator excavated.

With all the ritual deliberation of a high priest I advance a surgical clamp   14
toward the hole. The surgeon's heart is become a bat hanging upside down from his rib cage. The rim achieved—now thrust—and the ratchets of the

---

[10] Francis Drake (1540?–1596): English admiral who raided the Spanish treasures from the New World and circumnavigated the world. [Eds.]

clamp close upon the empty air. The devil has retracted. Evil mocking laughter bangs back and forth in the brain. More stealth. Lying in wait. One must skulk. Minutes pass, perhaps an hour. . . . A faint disturbance in the lake, and once again the thing upraises, farther and farther, hovering. Acrouch, strung, the surgeon is one with his instrument; there is no longer any boundary between its metal and his flesh. They are joined in single perfect tool of extirpation. It is just for this that he was born. Now—thrust—and clamp—and *yes*. Got him!

Transmitted to the fingers comes the wild thrashing of the creature. Pinned   15 and wriggling, he is mine. I hear the dry brittle scream of the dragon, and a hatred seizes me, but such a detestation as would make of Iago a drooling sucktit.[11] It is the demented hatred of the victor for the vanquished, the warden for his prisoner. It is the hatred of fear. Within the jaws of my hemostat is the whole of the evil of the world, the dark concentrate itself, and I shall kill it. For mankind. And, in so doing, will open the way into a thousand years of perfect peace. Here is Surgeon as Savior indeed.

Tight grip now . . . steady, relentless pull. How it scrabbles to keep its   16 tentacle-hold. With an abrupt moist plop the extraction is complete. There, writhing in the teeth of the clamp, is a dirty gray body, the size and shape of an English walnut. He is hung everywhere with tiny black hooklets. Quickly . . . into the specimen jar of saline . . . the lid screwed tight. Crazily he swims round and round, wiping his slimy head against the glass, then slowly sinks to the bottom, the mass of hooks in frantic agonal wave.

"You are going to be all right," I say to my patient. "We are *all* going to be   17 all right from now on."

The next day I take the jar to the medical school. "That's the larva of the   18 botfly," says a pathologist. "The fly usually bites a cow and deposits its eggs beneath the skin. There, the egg develops into the larval form which, when ready, burrows its way to the outside through the hide and falls to the ground. In time it matures into a fullgrown botfly. This one happened to bite a man. It was about to come out on its own, and, of course, it would have died."

The words *imposter, sorehead, servant of Satan* sprang to my lips. But now   19 he has been joined by other scientists. They nod in agreement. I gaze from one gray eminence to another, and know the mallet-blow of glory pulverized. I tried to save the world, but it didn't work out.

No, it is not the surgeon who is God's darling. He is the victim of vanity. It   20 is the poet who heals with his words, stanches the flow of blood, stills the rattling breath, applies poultice to the scalded flesh.

Did you ask me why a surgeon writes? I think it is because I wish to be a   21 doctor.

---

[11] Iago: the villain in Shakespeare's *Othello*. [Eds.]

QUESTIONS

1. What are Selzer's reasons for writing? In what ways do his reasons surprise you?

2. Throughout this essay, Selzer compares the doctor with the poet. Why does he believe that the poet "sees what no one else can" (paragraph 11)? What is his reason for comparing the doctor with the poet?

3. Why does Selzer introduce the examples of his patients, the diabetic amputee (paragraphs 4 through 7) or the excavator (paragraphs 12 through 19)? How do these examples enhance the meaning of Selzer's reflections?

4. Trace the movement of Selzer's thoughts from any one paragraph to the next.

5. Ask one or two people in the field you plan to enter about the kind of writing that is required in that profession. Find out if the writing they do is helpful in understanding the profession and their place in it. Ask them what they would write if they were asked to write about what they do and why they do it. Use this information in an essay considering the importance of writing in your chosen field.

6. Write a reflective essay that considers why writing is important to you. If writing is not important to you, consider why this is so.

MAKING CONNECTIONS

1. Compare Selzer's account of removing the botfly from his patient to Roy C. Selby, Jr.'s "A Delicate Operation," in "Reporting," an essay on a brain operation. How studied and how vivid do you find their essays to be? Selzer writes in the first person and Selby in the third. What difference does that make in these essays?

2. Compare Selzer's writings on why a surgeon would write to Joan Didion on why she writes and perhaps to George Orwell, since Didion took her title from one of his essays. How similar do you find their motives for writing? Would you say that similarities or differences are more essential to all three?

THE BIRD AND
THE MACHINE

Loren Eiseley

Loren Eiseley (1907–1977) rode the rails as a young hobo before he finished college, went to graduate school at the University of Pennsylvania, and began a distinguished career as an anthropologist, archaeologist, essayist, and poet. Through his writing, Eiseley made the ideas and findings of anthropology comprehensible to the public. He found significance in small incidents—the flights of birds, the web of a spider, and the chance encounter with a young fox. Eiseley once wrote that animals understand their roles, but that man, "bereft of instinct, must search continually for meanings." This essay is taken from his collection The Immense Journey *(1957).*

I suppose their little bones have years ago been lost among the stones and winds of those high glacial pastures. I suppose their feathers blew eventually into the piles of tumbleweed beneath the straggling cattle fences and rotted there in the mountain snows, along with dead steers and all the other things that drift to an end in the corners of the wire. I do not quite know why I should be thinking of birds over the *New York Times* at breakfast, particularly the birds of my youth half a continent away. It is a funny thing what the brain will do with memories and how it will treasure them and finally bring them into odd juxtapositions with other things, as though I wanted to make a design, or get some meaning out of them, whether you want it or not, or even see it.

It used to seem marvelous to me, but I read now that there are machines that can do these things in a small way, machines that can crawl about like animals, and that it may not be long now until they do more things—maybe even make themselves—I saw that piece in the *Times* just now. And then they will, maybe—well, who knows—but you read about it more and more with no one making any protest, and already they can add better than we and reach up and hear things through the dark and finger the guns over the night sky.

This is the new world that I read about at breakfast. This is the world that confronts me in my biological books and journals, until there are times when I sit quietly in my chair and try to hear the little purr of the cogs in my head and the tubes flaring and dying as the messages go through them and the circuits snap shut or open. This is the great age, make no mistake about it; the robot has been born somewhat appropriately along with the atom bomb, and the

140

brain they say now is just another type of more complicated feedback system. The engineers have its basic principles worked out; it's mechanical, you know; nothing to get superstitious about; and man can always improve on nature once he gets the idea. Well, he's got it all right and that's why, I guess, that I sit here in my chair, with the article crunched in my hand, remembering those two birds and that blue mountain sunlight. There is another magazine article on my desk that reads "Machines Are Getting Smarter Every Day." I don't deny it, but I'll still stick with the birds. It's life I believe in, not machines.

Maybe you don't believe there is any difference. A skeleton is all joints and pulleys, I'll admit. And when man was in his simpler stages of machine building in the eighteenth century, he quickly saw the resemblances. "What," wrote Hobbes, "is the heart but a spring, and the nerves but so many strings, and the joints but so many wheels, giving motion to the whole body?" Tinkering about in their shops it was inevitable in the end that men would see the world as a huge machine "subdivided into an infinite number of lesser machines."

The idea took on with a vengeance. Little automatons toured the country— dolls controlled by clockwork. Clocks described as little worlds were taken on tours by their designers. They were made up of moving figures, shifting scenes and other remarkable devices. The life of the cell was unknown. Man, whether he was conceived as possessing a soul or not, moved and jerked about like these tiny puppets. A human being thought of himself in terms of his own tools and implements. He had been fashioned like the puppets he produced and was only a more clever model made by a greater designer.

Then in the nineteenth century, the cell was discovered, and the single machine in its turn was found to be the product of millions of infinitesimal machines—the cells. Now, finally, the cell itself dissolves away into an abstract chemical machine—and that into some intangible, inexpressible flow of energy. The secret seems to lurk all about, the wheels get smaller and smaller, and they turn more rapidly, but when you try to seize it the life is gone—and so, by popular definition, some would say that life was never there in the first place. The wheels and the cogs are the secret and we can make them better in time— machines that will run faster and more accurately than real mice to real cheese.

I have no doubt it can be done, though a mouse harvesting seeds on an autumn thistle is to me a fine sight and more complicated, I think, in his multiform activity, than a machine "mouse" running a maze. Also, I like to think of the possible shape of the future brooding in mice, just as it brooded once in a rather ordinary mousy insectivore who became a man. It leaves a nice fine indeterminate sense of wonder that even an electronic brain hasn't got, because you know perfectly well that if the electronic brain changes, it will be because of something man has done to it. But what man will do to himself he doesn't really know. A certain scale of time and a ghostly intangible thing called change are ticking in him. Powers and potentialities like the oak in the seed, or a red and awful ruin. Either way, it's impressive; and the mouse has it, too. Or those birds, I'll never forget those birds—yet before I measured their significance, I learned the lesson of time first of all. I was young then and left alone in a great desert—part of an expedition that had scattered its men over several hundred miles in order to carry on research more effectively. I learned there that time is a series of planes existing superficially in the same universe. The tempo is a human illusion, a subjective clock ticking in our own kind of protoplasm.

As the long months passed, I began to live on the slower planes and to observe more readily what passed for life there. I sauntered, I passed more and more slowly up and down the canyons in the dry baking heat of midsummer. I slumbered for long hours in the shade of huge brown boulders that had gathered in tilted companies out on the flats. I had forgotten the world of men and the world had forgotten me. Now and then I found a skull in the canyons, and these justified my remaining there. I took a serene cold interest in these discoveries. I had come, like many a naturalist before me, to view life with a wary and subdued attention. I had grown to take pleasure in the divested bone. 8

I sat once on a high ridge that fell away before me into a waste of sand dunes. I sat through hours of a long afternoon. Finally, as I glanced beside my boot an indistinct configuration caught my eye. It was a coiled rattlesnake, a big one. How long he had sat with me I do not know. I had not frightened him. We were both locked in the sleep-walking tempo of the earlier world, baking in the same high air and sunshine. Perhaps he had been there when I came. He slept on as I left, his coils, so ill discerned by me, dissolving once more among the stones and gravel from which I had barely made him out. 9

Another time I got on a higher ridge, among some tough little wind-warped pines half covered over with sand in a basin-like depression that caught everything carried by the air up to those heights. There were a few thin bones of birds, some cracked shells of indeterminable age, and the knotty fingers of pine roots bulged out of shape from their long and agonizing grasp upon the crevices of the rock. I lay under the pines in the sparse shade and went to sleep once more. 10

It grew cold finally, for autumn was in the air by then, and the few things that lived thereabouts were sinking down into an even chillier scale of time. In the moments between sleeping and waking I saw the roots about me and slowly, slowly, a foot in what seemed many centuries, I moved my sleep-stiffened hands over the scaling bark and lifted my numbed face after the vanishing sun. I was a great awkward thing of knots and aching limbs, trapped up there in some long, patient endurance that involved the necessity of putting living fingers into rock and by slow, aching expansion bursting those rocks asunder. I suppose, so thin and slow was the time of my pulse by then, that I might have stayed on to drift still deeper into the lower cadences of the frost, or the crystalline life 11 that glitters in pebbles, or shines in a snowflake, or dreams in the meteoric iron between the worlds.

It was a dim descent, but time was present in it. Somewhere far down in $\quad$ 12 that scale the notion struck me that one might come the other way. Not many months thereafter I joined some colleagues heading higher into a remote windy tableland where huge bones were reputed to protrude like boulders from the turf. I had drowsed with reptiles and moved with the century-long pulse of trees; now, lethargically, I was climbing back up some invisible ladder of quickening hours. There had been talk of birds in connection with my duties. Birds are intense, fast-living creatures—reptiles, I suppose one might say, that have escaped out of the heavy sleep of time, transformed fairy creatures dancing over sunlit meadows. It is a youthful fancy, no doubt, but because of something that happened up there among the escarpments of that range, it remains with me a lifelong impression. I can never bear to see a bird imprisoned.

We came into that valley through the trailing mists of a spring night. It was $\quad$ 13 a place that looked as though it might never have known the foot of man, but our scouts had been ahead of us and we knew all about the abandoned cabin of stone that lay far up on one hillside. It had been built in the land rush of the last century and then lost to the cattlemen again as the marginal soils failed to take to the plow.

There were spots like this all over that country. Lost graves marked by $\quad$ 14 unlettered stones and old corroding rim-fire cartridge cases lying where somebody had made a stand among the boulders that rimmed the valley. They are all that remain of the range wars; the men are under the stones now. I could see our cavalcade winding in and out through the mist below us: torches, the reflection of the truck lights on our collecting tins, and the far-off bumping of a loose dinosaur thigh bone in the bottom of a trailer. I stood on a rock a moment looking down and thinking what it cost in money and equipment to capture the past.

We had, in addition, instructions to lay hands on the present. The word $\quad$ 15 had come through to get them alive—birds, reptiles, anything. A zoo somewhere abroad needed restocking. It was one of those reciprocal matters in which science involves itself. Maybe our museum needed a stray ostrich egg and this was the payoff. Anyhow, my job was to help capture some birds and that was why I was there before the trucks.

The cabin had not been occupied for years. We intended to clean it out and $\quad$ 16 live in it, but there were holes in the roof and the birds had come in and were roosting in the rafters. You could depend on it in a place like this where everything blew away, and even a bird needed some place out of the weather and away from coyotes. A cabin going back to nature in a wild place draws them till they come in, listening at the eaves, I imagine, pecking softly among the shingles till they find a hole and then suddenly the place is theirs and man is forgotten.

Sometimes of late years I find myself thinking the most beautiful sight in   17
the world might be the birds taking over New York after the last man has run
away to the hills. I will never live to see it, of course, but I know just how it
will sound because I've lived up high and I know the sort of watch birds keep
on us. I've listened to sparrows tapping tentatively on the outside of air condi-
tioners when they thought no one was listening, and I know how other birds
test the vibrations that come up to them through the television aerials.

"Is he gone?" they ask, and the vibrations come up from below, "Not yet,   18
not yet."

Well, to come back, I got the door open softly and I had the spotlight all   19
ready to turn on and blind whatever birds there were so they couldn't see to get
out through the roof. I had a short piece of ladder to put against the far wall
where there was a shelf on which I expected to make the biggest haul. I had
all the information I needed just like any skilled assassin. I pushed the door
open, the hinges squeaking only a little. A bird or two stirred—I could hear
them—but nothing flew and there was a faint starlight through the holes in the
roof.

I padded across the floor, got the ladder up and the light ready, and slithered   20
up the ladder till my head and arms were over the shelf. Everything was dark
as pitch except for the starlight at the little place back of the shelf near the
eaves. With the light to blind them, they'd never make it. I had them. I reached
my arm carefully over in order to be ready to seize whatever was there and I
put the flash on the edge of the shelf where it would stand by itself when I
turned it on. That way I'd be able to use both hands.

Everything worked perfectly except for one detail—I didn't know what kind   21
of birds were there. I never thought about it at all, and it wouldn't have mattered
if I had. My orders were to get something interesting. I snapped on the flash
and sure enough there was a great beating and feathers flying, but instead of
my having them, they, or rather he, had me. He had my hand, that is, and
for a small hawk not much bigger than my fist he was doing all right. I heard
him give one short metallic cry when the light went on and my hand descended
on the bird beside him; after that he was busy with his claws and his beak was
sunk in my thumb. In the struggle I knocked the lamp over on the shelf, and
his mate got her sight back and whisked neatly through the hole in the roof
and off among the stars outside. It all happened in fifteen seconds and you
might think I would have fallen down the ladder, but no, I had a professional
assassin's reputation to keep up, and the bird, of course, made the mistake of
thinking the hand was the enemy and not the eyes behind it. He chewed my
thumb up pretty effectively and lacerated my hand with his claws, but in the
end I got him, having two hands to work with.

He was a sparrow hawk and a fine young male in the prime of life. I was   22
sorry not to catch the pair of them, but as I dripped blood and folded his wings
carefully, holding him by the back so that he couldn't strike again, I had to

144

admit the two of them might have been more than I could have handled under the circumstances. The little fellow had saved his mate by diverting me, and that was that. He was born to it, and made no outcry now, resting in my hand hopelessly, but peering toward me in the shadows behind the lamp with a fierce, almost indifferent glance. He neither gave nor expected mercy and something out of the high air passed from him to me, stirring a faint embarrassment.

I quit looking into that eye and managed to get my huge carcass with its fist full of prey back down the ladder. I put the bird in a box too small to allow him to injure himself by struggle and walked out to welcome the arriving trucks. It had been a long day, and camp still to make in the darkness. In the morning that bird would be just another episode. He would go back with the bones in the truck to a small cage in a city where he would spend the rest of his life. And a good thing, too. I sucked my aching thumb and spat out some blood. An assassin has to get used to these things. I had a professional reputation to keep up. 23

In the morning, with the change that comes on suddenly in that high country, the mist that had hovered below us in the valley was gone. The sky was a deep blue, and one could see for miles over the high outcroppings of stone. I was up early and brought the box in which the little hawk was imprisoned out onto the grass where I was building a cage. A wind as cool as a mountain spring ran over the grass and stirred my hair. It was a fine day to be alive. I looked up and all around and at the hole in the cabin roof out of which the other little hawk had fled. There was no sign of her anywhere that I could see. 24

"Probably in the next county by now," I thought cynically, but before beginning work I decided I'd have a look at my last night's capture. 25

Secretively, I looked again all around the camp and up and down and opened the box. I got him right out in my hand with his wings folded properly and I was careful not to startle him. He lay limp in my grasp and I could feel his heart pound under the feathers but he only looked beyond me and up. 26

I saw him look that last look away beyond me into a sky so full of light that I could not follow his gaze. The little breeze flowed over me again, and nearby a mountain aspen shook all its tiny leaves. I suppose I must have had an idea then of what I was going to do, but I never let it come up into consciousness. I just reached over and laid the hawk on the grass. 27

He lay there a long minute without hope, unmoving, his eyes still fixed on that blue vault above him. It must have been that he was already so far away in heart that he never felt the release from my hand. He never even stood. He just lay with his breast against the grass. 28

In the next second after that long minute he was gone. Like a flicker of light, he had vanished with my eyes full on him, but without actually seeing even a premonitory wing beat. He was gone straight into that towering emptiness of 29 light and crystal that my eyes could scarcely bear to penetrate. For another long moment there was silence. I could not see him. The light was too intense. Then from far up somewhere a cry came ringing down.

I was young then and had seen little of the world, but when I heard that cry my heart turned over. It was not the cry of the hawk I had captured; for, by shifting my position against the sun, I was now seeing further up. Straight out of the sun's eye, where she must have been soaring restlessly above us for untold hours, hurtled his mate. And from far up, ringing from peak to peak of the summits over us, came a cry of such unutterable and ecstatic joy that it sounds down across the years and tingles among the cups on my quiet breakfast table.

I saw them both now. He was rising fast to meet her. They met in a great soaring gyre that turned to a whirling circle and a dance of wings. Once more, just once, their two voices, joined in a harsh wild medley of question and response, struck and echoed the pinnacles of the valley. Then they were gone forever somewhere into those upper regions beyond the eyes of men.

I am older now, and sleep less, and have seen most of what there is to see and am not very much impressed any more, I suppose, by anything. "What Next in the Attributes of Machines?" my morning headline runs. "It Might Be the Power to Reproduce Themselves."

I lay the paper down and across my mind a phrase floats insinuatingly: "It does not seem that there is anything in the construction, constituents, or behavior of the human being which it is essentially impossible for science to duplicate and synthesize. On the other hand . . ."

All over the city the cogs in the hard, bright mechanisms have begun to turn. Figures move through computers, names are spelled out, a thoughtful machine selects the fingerprints of a wanted criminal from an array of thousands. In the laboratory an electronic mouse runs swiftly through a maze toward the cheese it can neither taste nor enjoy. On the second run it does better than a living mouse.

"On the other hand . . ." Ah, my mind takes up, on the other hand the machine does not bleed, ache, hang for hours in the empty sky in a torment of hope to learn the fate of another machine, nor does it cry out with joy nor dance in the air with the fierce passion of a bird. Far off, over a distance greater than space, that remote cry from the heart of heaven makes a faint buzzing among my breakfast dishes and passes on and away.

QUESTIONS

1. According to Eiseley, what is the difference between birds and machines?
2. Why does Eiseley tell the story about his experience as a young anthropologist exploring life in the American desert? How does this story relate to the rest of the essay?

3. Trace the associative movement of Eiseley's mind. How does one thought suggest another? How does this movement help illustrate his point?

4. Eiseley projects himself from the beginning as someone remembering and reflecting upon his experience. How did the meditative process of this essay, with its various twists and turns of thought, affect you as a reader?

5. Eiseley writes: "It is a funny thing what the brain will do with memories and how it will treasure and finally bring them into odd juxtapositions with other things, as though it wanted to make a design, or get some meaning out of them, whether you want it or not, or even see it" (paragraph 1). Begin reflecting on some important memories from your past, and see where these reflections take you. As your mind wanders between past and present, see if any kind of design or meaning emerges for you. See what associations can be shaped into your own essay.

MAKING CONNECTIONS

1. One of the themes of the essays in this section concerns not just knowing things but reflecting on how we know them. Consider two or three writers, such as N. Scott Momaday, Joan Didion, Alice Walker, or Richard Selzer, in relation to Loren Eiseley. Compare their ideas about knowing and their techniques for conveying these ideas to readers.

2. Consider Carl Sagan's title, "Can We Know the Universe? Reflections on a Grain of Salt" and Alice Walker's, "Beauty: When the Other Dancer Is the Self," in relation to this essay by Loren Eiseley. Could either of those titles be appropriate here? In the second case, "Beauty" might indicate the sparrow hawk and the "Other Dancer" the author. Would that work? Write a commentary on Eiseley's essay supposing that one of the other titles (and the themes it suggests) applies to this essay as well.

REPORTING

REPORTING

Here in "Reporting" you will find writing that reflects a wide array of academic and professional situations—a naturalist describing the tool-using behavior of chimpanzees, a brain surgeon detailing the progress of a delicate operation, a historian telling about the plague that swept through medieval Europe, a journalist recounting the brief life of a runaway girl in New York City. Informative writing is basic to every field of endeavor, and the writers in this section seek to fulfill that basic need by reporting material drawn from various sources—a data recorder, a voice recorder, a telescope, articles, books, public records, or firsthand observation. Working from such various sources, these writers aim to provide detailed and reliable accounts of things—to give the background of a case, to convey the look and smell and feel of a place, to describe the appearance and behavior of people, to tell the story of recent or ancient events.

Though reporting depends on a careful gathering of information, it is by no means a mechanical and routine activity that consists simply of getting some facts and writing them up. Newspaper editors and criminal investigators, to be sure, often say that they want "just the facts," but they know that in one way or another the facts are substantially shaped by the point of view of the person who is gathering and reporting them. By point of view, we mean both the physical and the mental standpoints from which a person observes or investigates something. Each of us, after all, stands at a particular point in space and time, as well as in thought and feeling, whenever we look at any subject. And wherever we stand in relation to the subject—whether we observe it close up or at a distance, in sunlight or in shadows, from one angle or another—will determine the particular aspects of it that we perceive and bring out in an account.

The influence that point of view exerts on reporting can be seen in the following passage from an article about an airline crash that took place outside of Washington, D.C., on December 1, 1974:

> According to the National Transportation Safety Board, today's was the first fatal crash by an airliner approaching Dulles, which opened in 1962.
> A T.W.A. spokesman said 85 passengers and a crew of seven were aboard the flight, which originated in Indianapolis. He said 46 persons got on at Columbus.
> The plane crashed about one and one-half miles from an underground complex that reportedly is designed to serve as a headquarters for high government officials

in the event of nuclear war. A Federal spokesman acknowledged only that the facility was operated by the little known Office of Preparedness, whose responsibilities, he said, include "continuity of government in a time of national disaster."

This report by the Associated Press, (AP), which appeared in the *New York Times* on December 2, 1974, was evidently written by someone who had ready access to a number of sources, for virtually every bit of information in this excerpt comes from a different agency or "spokesman." In fact, the AP report as a whole refers not only to the three sources that are explicitly identified in this passage—namely, the "National Transportation Safety Board," a "T.W.A. spokesman," and a "Federal spokesman"—but also to twelve others, including a county medical examiner, a telephone worker, a state police officer, a T.W.A. ground maintenance employee, and the Dulles control tower. Drawing upon these sources, the writer of this report is able not only to cover the vital statistics, such as the origin of the flight, the number of people aboard, and the location of the crash, but also to give a vividly detailed impression of the weather, the scarred landscape, and the scattered wreckage at and around the scene of the crash, as well as to reveal some fascinating details about the "underground complex" near the site of the crash. As you read through this piece, however, you will discover that it reports very little about the events leading up to the crash or about the circumstances that caused it, for the anonymous writer was evidently not in a position either to track the plane before the crash or to speculate about the cause of the crash only hours after it had taken place.

But an extensive investigation of the crash was carried out by the National Transportation Safety Board (NTSB), a federal agency that is charged with tracing the causes of airline accidents. Almost one year later, on November 26, 1975, the Board issued an elaborately detailed, forty-two-page report of its findings, a segment of which is reprinted in our collection. If you look at this segment of the NTSB "Aircraft Accident Report," you will see that it grew out of a completely different point of view from the one that produced the AP report. The NTSB report, for example, does not make any reference to the "secret government installation" that is highlighted in the AP report; nor does it contain any vividly descriptive passages, like those in the AP report, about the weather, or the scarred landscape, or the scattered wreckage at the site of the crash; nor does it even mention some of the sources who figure prominently in the AP report, such as Captain William Carvello of the state police; Bill Smith of the Marshall, Virginia, Rescue Squad; Vance Berry of Bluemont, Virginia; and Richard Eastman, a ground maintenance employee of TWA. Conversely, some matters that are barely touched upon in the AP report are extensively covered in the NTSB report. In particular, the NTSB report provides a detailed "History of the Flight," which includes summaries of cockpit conversation and navigational information at key points during the flight, as well as excerpts of the conversation that took place among members of the flight crew during the last five minutes of the flight. And the NTSB report provides detailed information about some topics that are not mentioned at all in the AP report, such as "Aids to Navigation" and "Aerodrome and Ground Facilities."

Given such striking differences in the emphases of these two pieces, you might wonder which one offers a more accurate report of the crash. Actually, both are true to the crash within the limits of their points of view on it. The AP report, for example, concentrates on the scene at the site of the crash, drawing material from a number of firsthand observers, and this standpoint brings into focus the appalling spectacle that must have been visible on the mountainside where the crash took place. The NTSB report, by contrast, views the crash within a much broader context that takes into account not only a detailed history of the flight itself, but also the complex system of navigational rules and procedures that were in effect at the time of the flight. And this perspective enables the NTSB to reveal that the mountainside crash resulted in part from serious "inadequacies and lack of clarity in the air traffic control procedures. . . ." Thus each point of view affords a special angle on the crash, obscuring some aspects of it, revealing others. And these are only two of many standpoints from which the crash might have been seen and reported. Imagine, for example, how the crash might have been viewed by workers who scoured the mountainside for remains of the passengers, or by specialists who identified their remains, or by relatives and friends of the victims, or by crews and passengers aboard other flights into Dulles that day.

Once you try to imagine the various perspectives from which anything can be observed or investigated, you will see that no one person can possibly uncover everything there is to be known about something. For this reason, above all, point of view is an important aspect of reporting to be kept in mind by both readers and writers. As a reader of reportorial writing, you should always attempt to identify the point of view from which the information was gathered so as to help yourself assess the special strengths and weaknesses in the reporting that arise from that point of view as distinct from other possible points of view. By the same token, in your own reporting you should carefully decide upon the point of view that you already have or plan to use in observing or gathering information about something. Once you begin to pay deliberate attention to point of view, you will come to see that it is closely related to the various purposes for which people gather and report information in writing.

THE RANGE OF REPORTORIAL WRITING

The purpose of reporting is in one sense straightforward and self-evident, particularly when it is defined in terms of its commonly accepted value to readers. Whether it involves a firsthand account of some recent happening or the documented record of a long-past sequence of events, reportorial writing informs readers about the various subjects that may interest them but that they cannot possibly observe or investigate on their own. You may never get to see chimpanzees in their native African habitats, but you can get a glimpse of their behavior through the firsthand account of Jane van Lawick-Goodall. So, too, you will probably never have occasion to make your way through the many public records and personal reports of the bubonic plague that beset Europe in the mid-fourteenth century, but you can get a synoptic view of the plague from Barbara Tuchman's account, which is based on a thorough investigation of those sources. Reporting expands the range of its readers' perceptions and knowledge beyond the limits of their own immediate experience. From the outlook of readers, then, the function of reporting does seem to be very clear-cut.

But if we shift our focus and look at reporting in terms of the purposes to which it is evidently put by writers, it often turns out to serve a more complex function than might at first be supposed. An example of this complexity can be seen in the following passage from van Lawick-Goodall's account:

> Suddenly I stopped, for I saw a slight movement in the long grass about sixty yards away. Quickly focusing my binoculars I saw that it was a single chimpanzee, and just then he turned in my direction. I recognized David Graybeard.
>
> Cautiously I moved around so that I could see what he was doing. He was squatting beside the red earth mound of a termite nest, and as I watched I saw him carefully push a long grass stem down into a hole in the mound. After a moment he withdrew it and picked something from the end with his mouth.

This passage seems on the whole to be a very neutral bit of scientific reporting that details van Lawick-Goodall's observation of a particular chimpanzee probing for food in a termite nest. The only unusual aspect of the report is her naming of the creature, which has the unscientific effect of personifying the animal. Otherwise, she is careful in the opening part of the description to establish the physical point of view from which she observed the chimpanzee—sixty yards away, looking at him through binoculars. And at the end of the passage she is equally careful not to identify or even conjecture about "something" beyond her range of detailed vision. As it turns out, however, this passage is a record not only of her observations but also of a pivotal moment in the story of how she came to make an important discovery about chimpanzees—that they are tool users—and thus how she came to regard their behavior as being much closer to that of human beings than had previously been supposed. So, she climaxes her previous description of the chimpanzee with this sentence:

> I was too far away to make out what he was eating, but it was obvious that he was actually using a grass stem as a tool.

Here as elsewhere, then, her reporting is thoughtfully worded and structured to make a strong case for her ideas about chimpanzee and human behavior. Thus, she evidently intends her report to be both informative and persuasive.

A different set of purposes can be seen in yet another firsthand account—this time of a medical patient, as observed by his doctor, Richard Selzer:

> From the doorway of Room 542 the man in the bed seems deeply tanned. Blue eyes and close-cropped white hair give him the appearance of vigor and good health. But I know that his skin is not brown from the sun. It is rusted rather, in the last stage of containing the vile repose within. And the blue eyes are frosted, looking inward like the windows of a snowbound cottage. This man is blind. This man is also legless—the right leg missing from midthigh down, the left from just below the knee. It gives him the look of a bonsai, roots and branches pruned into the dwarfed facsimile of a great tree.

In this passage, Selzer seeks to describe both the seemingly healthy visual appearance of his patient and the actually decaying physical condition of the patient. Thus he begins by reporting visual details, such as the "deeply tanned" skin as well as the "blue eyes and close-cropped white hair," that convey "the appearance of vigor and good health." Then in the sentences that follow, Selzer relies heavily on figurative language, on a striking sequence of metaphors and similes, each of which reverses the initial impression so as to convey the drastically impaired condition of the patient. The patient's skin turns out to be "rusted," his eyes "frosted," and his body like "the dwarfed facsimile of a great tree." Yet it is also clear from these and other bits of figurative language in the passage that Selzer is not only trying to convey the dire physical condition of his patient, but also to suggest his own intense personal feelings about the patient. Clearly, he intends his report to be provocative as well as informative.

For yet another combination of purposes, you might look at Farley Mowat's informative, entertaining, and self-mocking account of his firsthand encounter with the territorial behavior of wolves. Or you might look at Dennis Hevesi's vivid, evocative, and disturbing report about a runaway teenager. Or you might turn to the NTSB report we discussed earlier in this introduction, and you will see that it is clearly intended not only to convey information pertaining to the cause of the airline crash, but also to make a case for various procedural changes that might prevent similar accidents in the future.

As is apparent from just this handful of selections, writers invariably seem to use reporting for a combination of purposes—not only to provide information but also to convey their attitudes, beliefs, or ideas about it, as well as to influence the views of their readers. This joining of purposes is hardly surprising, given the factors involved in any decision to report on something. After all, whenever we make a report, we do so presumably because we believe that the subject of our report is important enough for others to be told about it. And presumably we believe the subject to be important because of what we have come to know and think about it. So, when we are faced with deciding what information to report and how to report it, we inevitably base our decisions on these ideas. At every point in the process of planning and writing a report, we act on the basis of our particular motives and priorities for conveying information about the subject. And how could we do otherwise? How else could van Lawick-Goodall have decided what information to report out of all she must have observed during her first few months in Africa? How else could Selzer have decided what to emphasize out of all the information that he must gathered from the time he first met his patient until the time of the patient's death? Without specific purposes to control our reporting, our records of events would be as long as the events themselves.

Reporting, as you can see, necessarily serves a widely varied range of purposes—as varied as are writers and their subjects. Thus, whenever you read a piece of reportorial writing, you should always try to discover for yourself what appear to be its guiding purposes by examining its structure, its phrasing, and its wording, much as we have earlier in this discussion. And once you have identified the purpose, you should then consider how it has influenced the selection, arrangement, and weighting of information in the report. When you turn to doing your own writing, you should be equally careful in determining your purposes for reporting as well as in organizing your report so as to put the information in a form that is true to what you know and think about the subject.

METHODS OF REPORTING

In planning a piece of reportorial writing, you should be sure to keep in mind not only your ideas about the subject, but also the needs of your readers. Given the fact that most of your readers will probably not be familiar with your information, you should be very careful in selecting and organizing it so that you give them a clear and orderly report of it. Usually, you will find that the nature of your information suggests a corresponding method of presenting it most clearly and conveniently to your readers.

If the information concerns a single, detailed event or covers a set of events spread over time, then the most effective method probably is narration—the form of story telling—in a more or less chronological order. This is the basic form that van Lawick-Goodall uses in recounting her first few months of observation in Africa, and it proves to be a very clear and persuasive form for gradually unfolding her discovery about the behavior of chimpanzees. If the information concerns a particular place, or scene, or spectacle, then the most convenient method is description, presenting your information in a clear-cut spatial order so as to help your reader visualize both the overall scene and its important details. This is the method that Selzer uses not only in describing his patient's condition, but also in detailing the patient's posture and his hospital room. If the information is meant to provide a synoptic body of knowledge about a particular subject, then the clearest form will be a topical summation, using a set of categories appropriate to the subject at hand. This is the basic form that is used in the NTSB report, which takes us through a comprehensive survey of material about the airline crash, methodically organized under clearly defined topical headings: "History of the Flight," "Meteorological Information," "Aids to Navigation," "Wreckage," "Medical and Pathological Information," and "Survival Aspects."

Although narration, description, topical summation, and other forms of reporting are often treated separately for purposes of convenience in identifying each of them, it is well to keep in mind that they usually end up working in some sort of combination with one another. Narratives, after all, involve not only events but also people and places, so it is natural that they include descriptive passages. Similarly, descriptions of places frequently entail stories about events taking place in them, so it is not surprising that they include bits of narration. And given the synoptic nature of topical summations, they are likely to involve both descriptive and narrative elements. In writing, as in most other activities, form should follow function, rather than being forced to fit arbitrary rules of behavior.

Once you have settled upon a basic form, you should then devise a way of managing your information within that form—of selecting, arranging, and proportioning it—so as to achieve your purposes most effectively. To carry out this task, you will need to review all of the material you have gathered with an eye to determining what you consider to be the most important information to report. Some bits or kinds of information inevitably will strike you as more significant than others, and these are the ones that you should feature in your report. Likewise, you will probably find that some information is simply not important enough even to be mentioned. Van Lawick-Goodall, for example, produces a striking account of her first few months in Africa because she focuses primarily on her observation of chimpanzees, subordinating all the other material she reports to her discoveries about their behavior. Thus, only on a couple of occasions does she include observations about the behavior of animals other than chimpanzees—in particular about the timidities of a bushbuck and a leopard. And she only includes these observations to point up by contrast the distinctively sociable behavior of chimpanzees. For much the same reasons, she proportions her coverage of the several chimpanzee episodes she reports so as to give the greatest amount of detail to the one that provides the most compelling indication of their advanced intelligence—namely, the final episode, which shows the chimpanzees to be tool-users and makers, a behavior previously attributed only to human beings.

To help achieve your purposes, you should also give special thought to deciding on the perspective from which you present your information to the reader. Do you want to present the material in first or third person? Do you want to be present in the piece, as are van Lawick-Goodall and Selzer? Or do you want to be invisible, as are the authors of the AP and NTSB reports? To some extent, of course, your answer to these questions will depend upon whether you gathered the information through your own firsthand observation and then

157

want to convey your firsthand reactions to your observations, as van Lawick-Goodall and Selzer do in their pieces. But just to show that there are no hard-and-fast rules on this score, you might look at "A Delicate Operation" by Roy C. Selby, Jr. You will notice at once that although Selby must have written this piece on the basis of firsthand experience, he tells the story in third person, removing himself almost completely from it except for such distant-sounding references to himself as "the surgeon." Clearly, Selby is important to the information in this report, yet he evidently decided to de-emphasize himself in writing the report. In order to see just how important it is to consider these alternatives in planning any report, you might compare Selby's report with Selzer's, which is written throughout in first person. If the perspectives of these two reports were reversed—you might take a stab at changing them around yourself—you would find the contents and effects of both reports to be surprisingly different. Ultimately, then, the nature of a report is substantially determined not only by *what* a writer gathers from various sources but also by *how* a writer presents the information.

In the reports that follow in this section, you will have an opportunity to see various ways of presenting things in writing. In later sections, you will see how reporting combines with other kinds of writing—explaining and arguing.

Arts and Humanities

"THIS IS THE END OF THE WORLD": THE BLACK DEATH

Barbara Tuchman

For over twenty-five years Barbara Wertheim Tuchman (1912–1989) wrote books on historical subjects, ranging over the centuries from the Middle Ages to World War II. Her combination of careful research and lively writing enabled her to produce books like The Guns of August *(1962), A* Distant Mirror *(1978), and* The March of Folly, From Troy to Vietnam *(1984), which please not only the general public but many professional historians as well. She twice won the Pulitzer Prize. A Distant Mirror, from which the following selection has been taken, was on the* New York Times *best-seller list for over nine months. Her final book,* The First Salute *(1988), is notable for the presence of Tuchman's characteristic scholarship and wit.*

In October 1347, two months after the fall of Calais, Genoese trading ships 1 put into the harbor of Messina in Sicily with dead and dying men at the oars. The ships had come from the Black Sea port of Caffa (now Feodosiya) in the Crimea, where the Genoese maintained a trading post. The diseased sailors showed strange black swellings about the size of an egg or an apple in the armpits and groin. The swellings oozed blood and pus and were followed by spreading boils and black blotches on the skin from internal bleeding. The sick suffered severe pain and died quickly within five days of the first symptoms. As the disease spread, other symptoms of continuous fever and spitting of blood appeared instead of the swellings or buboes. These victims coughed and sweated heavily and died even more quickly, within three days or less, sometimes in 24 hours. In both types everything that issued from the body—breath, sweat, blood from the buboes and lungs, bloody urine, and blood-blackened excrement—smelled foul. Depression and despair accompanied the physical symptoms, and before the end "death is seen seated on the face."

The disease was bubonic plague, present in two forms: one that infected the bloodstream, causing the buboes and internal bleeding, and was spread by contact; and a second, more virulent pneumonic type that infected the lungs and was spread by respiratory infection. The presence of both at once caused the high mortality and speed of contagion. So lethal was the disease that cases were known of persons going to bed well and dying before they woke, of doctors catching the illness at a bedside and dying before the patient. So rapidly did it spread from one to another that to a French physician, Simon de Covino, it seemed as if one sick person "could infect the whole world." The malignity of the pestilence appeared more terrible because its victims knew no prevention and no remedy.

The physical suffering of the disease and its aspects of evil mystery were expressed in a strange Welsh lament which saw "death coming into our midst like black smoke, a plague which cuts off the young, a rootless phantom which has no mercy for fair countenance. Woe is me of the shilling in the armpit! It is seething, terrible . . . a head that gives pain and causes a loud cry . . . a painful angry knob . . . Great is its seething like a burning cinder . . . a grievous thing of ashy color." Its eruption is ugly like the "seeds of black peas, broken fragments of brittle sea-coal . . . the early ornaments of black death, cinders of the peelings of the cockle weed, a mixed multitude, a black plague like half-pence, like berries. . . ."

Rumors of a terrible plague supposedly arising in China and spreading through Tartary (Central Asia) to India and Persia, Mesopotamia, Syria, Egypt, and all of Asia Minor had reached Europe in 1346. They told of a death toll so devastating that all of India was said to be depopulated, whole territories covered by dead bodies, other areas with no one left alive. As added up by Pope Clement VI at Avignon, the total of reported dead reached 23,840,000. In the absence of a concept of contagion, no serious alarm was felt in Europe until the trading ships brought their black burden of pestilence into Messina while other infected ships from the Levant carried it to Genoa and Venice.

By January 1348 it penetrated France via Marseille, and North Africa via Tunis. Shipborne along coasts and navigable rivers, it spread westward from Marseille through the ports of Languedoc to Spain and northward up the Rhône to Avignon, where it arrived in March. It reached Narbonne, Montpellier, Carcassonne, and Toulouse between February and May, and at the same time in Italy spread to Rome and Florence and their hinterlands. Between June and August it reached Bordeaux, Lyon, and Paris, spread to Burgundy and Normandy, and crossed the Channel from Normandy into southern England. From Italy during the same summer it crossed the Alps into Switzerland and reached eastward to Hungary.

In a given area the plague accomplished its kill within four to six months 6
and then faded, except in the larger cities, where, rooting into the close-
quartered population, it abated during the winter, only to reappear in spring
and rage for another six months.

In 1349 it resumed in Paris, spread to Picardy, Flanders, and the Low 7
Countries, and from England to Scotland and Ireland as well as to Norway,
where a ghost ship with a cargo of wool and a dead crew drifted offshore until
it ran aground near Bergen. From there the plague passed into Sweden, Denmark, Prussia, Iceland, and as far as Greenland. Leaving a strange pocket of
immunity in Bohemia, and Russia unattacked until 1351, it had passed from
most of Europe by mid-1350. Although the mortality rate was erratic, ranging
from one fifth in some places to nine tenths or almost total elimination in
others, the overall estimate of modern demographers has settled—for the area
extending from India to Iceland—around the same figure expressed in Froissart's
casual words: "a third of the world died." His estimate, the common one at the
time, was not an inspired guess but a borrowing of St. John's figure for mortality
from plague in Revelation, the favorite guide to human affairs of the Middle
Ages.

A third of Europe would have meant about 20 million deaths. No one knows 8
in truth how many died. Contemporary reports were an awed impression, not
an accurate count. In crowded Avignon, it was said, 400 died daily; 7,000
houses emptied by death were shut up; a single graveyard received 11,000
corpses in six weeks; half the city's inhabitants reportedly died, including 9
cardinals or one third of the total, and 70 lesser prelates. Watching the endlessly
passing death carts, chroniclers let normal exaggeration take wings and put the
Avignon death toll at 62,000 and even at 120,000, although the city's total
population was probably less then 50,000.

When graveyards filled up, bodies at Avignon were thrown into the Rhône 9
until mass burial pits were dug for dumping the corpses. In London in such
pits corpses piled up in layers until they overflowed. Everywhere reports speak
of the sick dying too fast for the living to bury. Corpses were dragged out of
homes and left in front of doorways. Morning light revealed new piles of bodies.
In Florence the dead were gathered up by the Compagnia della Misericordia—
founded in 1244 to care for the sick—whose members wore red robes and hoods
masking the face except for the eyes. When their efforts failed, the dead lay
putrid in the streets for days at a time. When no coffins were to be had, the
bodies were laid on boards, two or three at once, to be carried to graveyards or
common pits. Families dumped their own relatives into the pits, or buried them
so hastily and thinly "that dogs dragged them forth and devoured their bodies."

Amid accumulating death and fear of contagion, people died without last 10
rites and were buried without prayers, a prospect that terrified the last hours of
the stricken. A bishop in England gave permission to laymen to make confession
to each other as was done by the Apostles, "or if no man is present then even

to a woman," and if no priest could be found to administer extreme unction, "then faith must suffice." Clement VI found it necessary to grant remissions of sin to all who died of the plague because so many were unattended by priests. "And no bells tolled," wrote a chronicler of Siena, "and nobody wept no matter what his loss because almost everyone expected death. . . . And people said and believed, 'This is the end of the world.'"

In Paris, where the plague lasted through 1349, the reported death rate was   11
800 a day, in Pisa 500, in Vienna 500 to 600. The total dead in Paris numbered 50,000 or half the population. Florence, weakened by the famine of 1347, lost three to four fifths of its citizens, Venice two thirds, Hamburg and Bremen, though smaller in size, about the same proportion. Cities, as centers of transportation, were more likely to be affected than villages, although once a village was infected, its death rate was equally high. At Givry, a prosperous village in Burgundy of 1,200 to 1,500 people, the parish register records 615 deaths in the space of fourteen weeks, compared to an average of thirty deaths a year in the previous decade. In three villages of Cambridgeshire, manorial records show a death rate of 47 percent, 57 percent, and in one case 70 percent. When the last survivors, too few to carry on, moved away, a deserted village sank back into the wilderness and disappeared from the map altogether, leaving only a grass-covered ghostly outline to show where mortals once had lived.

In enclosed places such as monasteries and prisons, the infection of one   12
person usually meant that of all, as happened in the Franciscan convents of Carcassonne and Marseille, where every inmate without exception died. Of the 140 Dominicans at Montpellier only seven survived. Petrarch's brother Gherardo, member of a Carthusian monastery, buried the prior and 34 fellow monks one by one, sometimes three a day, until he was left alone with his dog and fled to look for a place that would take him in. Watching every comrade die, men in such places could not but wonder whether the strange peril that filled the air had not been sent to exterminate the human race. In Kilkenny, Ireland, Brother John Clyn of the Friars Minor, another monk left alone among dead men, kept a record of what had happened lest "things which should be remembered perish with time and vanish from the memory of those who come after us." Sensing "the whole world, as it were, placed within the grasp of the Evil One," and waiting for death to visit him too, he wrote, "I leave parchment to continue this work, if perchance any man survive and any of the race of Adam escape this pestilence and carry on the work which I have begun." Brother John, as noted by another hand, died of the pestilence, but he foiled oblivion.

The largest cities of Europe, with populations of about 100,000, were Paris   13
and Florence, Venice and Genoa. At the next level, with more than 50,000, were Ghent and Bruges in Flanders, Milan, Bologna, Rome, Naples, and Palermo, and Cologne. London hovered below 50,000, the only city in England except York with more than 10,000. At the level of 20,000 to 50,000 were

Bordeaux, Toulouse, Montpellier, Marseille, and Lyon in France, Barcelona, Seville, and Toledo in Spain, Siena, Pisa, and other secondary cities in Italy, and the Hanseatic trading cities of the Empire. The plague raged through them all, killing anywhere from one third to two thirds of their inhabitants. Italy, with a total population of 10 to 11 million, probably suffered the heaviest toll. Following the Florentine bankruptcies, the crop failures and workers' riots of 1346–47, the revolt of Cola di Rienzi that plunged Rome into anarchy, the plague came as the peak of successive calamities. As if the world were indeed in the grasp of the Evil One, its first appearance on the European mainland in January 1348 coincided with a fearsome earthquake that carved a path of wreckage from Naples up to Venice. Houses collapsed, church towers toppled, villages were crushed, and the destruction reached as far as Germany and Greece. Emotional response, dulled by horrors, underwent a kind of atrophy epitomized by the chronicler who wrote, "And in these days was burying without sorrowe and wedding without friendschippe."

In Siena, where more than half the inhabitants died of the plague, work was 14 abandoned on the great cathedral, planned to be the largest in the world, and never resumed, owing to loss of workers and master masons and "the melancholy and grief" of the survivors. The cathedral's truncated transept still stands in permanent witness to the sweep of death's scythe. Agnolo di Tura, a chronicler of Siena, recorded the fear of contagion that froze every other instinct. "Father abandoned child, wife husband, one brother another," he wrote, "for this plague seemed to strike through the breath and sight. And so they died. And no one could be found to bury the dead for money or friendship. . . . And I, Angolo di Tura, called the Fat, buried my five children with my own hands, and so did many others likewise."

There were many to echo his account of inhumanity and few to balance it, 15 for the plague was not the kind of calamity that inspired mutual help. Its loathsomeness and deadliness did not herd people together in mutual distress, but only prompted their desire to escape each other. "Magistrates and notaries refused to come and make the wills of the dying," reported a Franciscan friar of Piazza in Sicily; what was worse, "even the priests did not come to hear their confessions." A clerk of the Archbishop of Canterbury reported the same of English priests who "turned away from the care of their benefices from fear of death." Cases of parents deserting children and children their parents were reported across Europe from Scotland to Russia. The calamity chilled the hearts of men, wrote Boccaccio in his famous account of the plague in Florence that serves as introduction to the *Decameron*. "One man shunned another . . . kinsfolk held aloof, brother was forsaken by brother, oftentimes husband by wife; nay, what is more, and scarcely to be believed, fathers and mothers were found to abandon their own children to their fate, untended, unvisited as if they had been strangers." Exaggeration and literary pessimism were common in the 14th century, but the Pope's physician, Guy de Chauliac, was a sober, careful observer who reported the same phenomenon: "A father did not visit his son, nor the son his father. Charity was dead."

Yet not entirely. In Paris, according to the chronicler Jean de Venette, the   16
nuns of the Hotel Dieu or municipal hospital, "having no fear of death, tended the sick with all sweetness and humility." New nuns repeatedly took the places of those who died, until the majority "many times renewed by death now rest in peace with Christ as we may piously believe."

When the plague entered northern France in July 1348, it settled first in   17
Normandy and, checked by winter, gave Picardy a deceptive interim until the next summer. Either in mourning or warning, black flags were flown from church towers of the worst-stricken villages of Normandy. "And in that time," wrote a monk of the abbey of Fourcarment, "the mortality was so great among the people of Normandy that those of Picardy mocked them." The same un-neighborly reaction was reported of the Scots, separated by a winter's immunity from the English. Delighted to hear of the disease that was scourging the "southrons," they gathered forces for an invasion, "laughing at their enemies." Before they could move, the savage mortality fell upon them too, scattering some in death and the rest in panic to spread the infection as they fled.

In Picardy in the summer of 1349 the pestilence penetrated the castle of   18
Coucy to kill Enguerrand's mother,[1] Catherine, and her new husband. Whether her nine-year-old son escaped by chance or was perhaps living elsewhere with one of his guardians is unrecorded. In nearby Amiens, tannery workers, re-sponding quickly to losses in the labor force, combined to bargain for higher wages. In another place villagers were seen dancing to drums and trumpets, and on being asked the reason, answered that, seeing their neighbors die day by day while their village remained immune, they believed that they could keep the plague from entering "by the jollity that is in us. That is why we dance." Further north in Tournai on the border of Flanders, Gilles li Muisis, Abbot of St. Martin's, kept one of the epidemic's most vivid accounts. The passing bells rang all day and all night, he recorded, because sextons were anxious to obtain their fees while they could. Filled with the sound of mourning, the city became oppressed by fear, so that the authorities forbade the tolling of bells and the wearing of black and restricted funeral services to two mourners. The silencing of funeral bells and of criers' announcements of deaths was ordained by most cities. Siena imposed a fine on the wearing of mourning clothes by all except widows.

Flight was the chief recourse of those who could afford it or arrange it. The   19
rich fled to their country places like Boccaccio's young patricians of Florence, who settled in a pastoral palace "removed on every side from the roads" with

---

[1] Enguerrand de Coucy: the French nobleman whose life is followed by Tuchman as a way of unifying her study of the fourteenth century. [Eds.]

"wells of cool water and vaults of rare wines." The urban poor died in their burrows, "and only the stench of their bodies informed neighbors of their deaths." That the poor were more heavily afflicted than the rich was clearly remarked at the time, in the north as in the south. A Scottish chronicler, John of Fordun, stated flatly that the pest "attacked especially the meaner sort and common people—seldom the magnates." Simon de Covino of Montpellier made the same observation. He ascribed it to the misery and want and hard lives that made the poor more susceptible, which was half the truth. Close contact and lack of sanitation was the unrecognized other half. It was noticed too that the young died in greater proportion than the old; Simon de Covino compared the disappearance of youth to the withering of flowers in the fields.

In the countryside peasants dropped dead on the roads, in the fields, in their houses. Survivors in growing helplessness fell into apathy, leaving ripe wheat uncut and livestock untended. Oxen and asses, sheep and goats, pigs and chickens ran wild and they too, according to local reports, succumbed to the pest. English sheep, bearers of the precious wool, died throughout the country. The chronicler Henry Knighton, canon of Leicester Abbey, reported 5,000 dead in one field alone, "their bodies so corrupted by the plague that neither beast nor bird would touch them," and spreading an appalling stench. In the Austrian Alps wolves came down to prey upon sheep and then, "as if alarmed by some invisible warning, turned and fled back into the wilderness." In remote Dalmatia bolder wolves descended upon a plague-stricken city and attacked human survivors. For want of herdsmen, cattle strayed from place to place and died in hedgerows and ditches. Dogs and cats fell like the rest.

The dearth of labor held a fearful prospect because the 14th century lived close to the annual harvest both for food and for next year's seed. "So few servants and laborers were left," wrote Knighton, "that no one knew where to turn for help." The sense of a vanishing future created a kind of dementia of despair. A Bavarian chronicler of Neuberg on the Danube recorded that "Men and women . . . wandered around as if mad" and let their cattle stray "because no one had any inclination to concern themselves about the future." Fields went uncultivated, spring seed unsown. Second growth with nature's awful energy crept back over cleared land, dikes crumbled, salt water reinvaded and soured the lowlands. With so few hands remaining to restore the work of centuries, people felt, in Walsingham's words, that "the world could never again regain its former prosperity."

Though the death rate was higher among the anonymous poor, the known and the great died too. King Alfonso XI of Castile was the only reigning monarch killed by the pest, but his neighbor King Pedro of Aragon lost his wife, Queen Leonora, his daughter Marie, and a niece in the space of six months. John Cantacuzene, Emperor of Byzantium, lost his son. In France the lame Queen Jeanne and her daughter-in-law Bonne de Luxemburg, wife of the Dauphin, both died in 1349 in the same phase that took the life of Enguerrand's mother.

Jeanne, Queen of Navarre, daughter of Louis X, was another victim. Edward III's second daughter, Joanna, who was on her way to marry Pedro, the heir of Castile, died in Bordeaux. Women appear to have been more vulnerable than men, perhaps because, being more housebound, they were more exposed to fleas. Boccaccio's mistress Fiammetta, illegitimate daughter of the King of Naples, died, as did Laura, the beloved—whether real or fictional—of Petrarch. Reaching out to us in the future, Petrarch cried, "Oh happy posterity who will not experience such abysmal woe and will look upon our testimony as a fable."

In Florence Giovanni Villani, the great historian of his time, died at 68 in the midst of an unfinished sentence: ". . . e dure questo pistolenza fino a . . . (in the midst of this pestilence there came to an end . . .)." Siena's master painters, the brothers Ambrogio and Pietro Lorenzetti, whose names never appear after 1348, presumably perished in the plague, as did Andrea Pisano, architect and sculptor of Florence. William of Ockham and the English mystic Richard Rolle of Hampole both disappear from mention after 1349. Francisco Datini, merchant of Prato, lost both his parents and two siblings. Curious sweeps of mortality afflicted certain bodies of merchants in London. All eight wardens of the Company of Cutters, all six wardens of the Hatters, and four wardens of the Goldsmiths died before July 1350. Sir John Pulteney, master draper and four times Mayor of London, was a victim, likewise Sir John Montgomery, Governor of Calais. 23

Among the clergy and doctors the mortality was naturally high because of the nature of their professions. Out of 24 physicians in Venice, 20 were said to have lost their lives in the plague, although, according to another account, some were believed to have fled or to have shut themselves up in their houses. At Montpellier, site of the leading medieval medical school, the physician Simon de Covino reported that, despite the great number of doctors, "hardly one of them escaped." In Avignon, Guy de Chauliac confessed that he performed his medical visits only because he dared not stay away for fear of infamy, but "I was in continual fear." He claimed to have contracted the disease but to have cured himself by his own treatment; if so, he was one of the few who recovered. 24

Clerical mortality varied with rank. Although the one-third toll of cardinals reflects the same proportion as the whole, this was probably due to their concentration in Avignon. In England, in strange and almost sinister procession, the Archbishop of Canterbury, John Stratford, died in August 1348, his appointed successor died in May 1349, and the next appointee three months later, all three within a year. Despite such weird vagaries, prelates in general managed to sustain a higher survival rate than the lesser clergy. Among bishops the deaths have been estimated at about one in twenty. The loss of priests, even if many avoided their fearful duty of attending the dying, was about the same as among the population as a whole. 25

Government officials, whose loss contributed to the general chaos, found, 26 on the whole, no special shelter. In Siena four of the nine members of the governing oligarchy died, in France one third of the royal notaries, in Bristol 15 out of the 52 members of the Town Council or almost one third. Tax-collecting obviously suffered, with the result that Philip VI was unable to collect more than a fraction of the subsidy granted him by the Estates in the winter of 1347–48.

Lawlessness and debauchery accompanied the plague as they had during the great plague of Athens of 430 B.C., when according to Thucydides, men grew bold in the indulgence of pleasure: "For seeing how the rich died in a moment and those who had nothing immediately inherited their property, they reflected that life and riches were alike transitory and they resolved to enjoy themselves while they could." Human behavior is timeless. When St. John had his vision of plague in Revelation, he knew from some experience or race memory that those who survived "repented not of the work of their hands. . . . Neither repented they of their murders, nor of their sorceries, nor of their fornication, nor of their thefts." 27

NOTES[2]

1: "Death Is Seen Seated": Simon de Covino, q. Campbell, 80.
2: "Could Infect the World": q. Gasquet, 41.
3: Welsh Lament: q. Ziegler, 190.
9: "Dogs Dragged Them Forth": Agnolo di Tura, q. Ziegler, 58.
10: "Or If No Man Is Present": Bishop of Bath and Wells, q. Ziegler, 125. "No Bells Tolled": Agnolo di Tura, q. Schevill, *Siena*, 211. The same observation was made by Gabriel de Muisis, notary of Piacenza, q. Crawfurd, 113.
11: Givry Parish Register: Renouard, 111. Three Villages Of Cambridgeshire: Salt-marsh.
12: Petrarch's Brother: Bishop, 273. Brother John Clyn: q. Ziegler, 195.
13: Atrophy; "and in These Days": q. Deaux, 143, citing only "an old northern chronicle."
14: Agnolo Di Tura, "Father Abandoned Child": q. Ziegler, 58.
15: "Magistrates And Notaries": q. Deaux, 49. English Priests Turned away: Ziegler, 261. Parents Deserting Children: Hecker, 30. Guy De Chauliac, "A Father": q. Gasquet, 50–51.
16: Nuns of the Hotel Dieu: *Chron. Jean de Venette*, 49.
17: Picards and Scots Mock Mortality of Neighbors: Gasquet, 53, and Ziegler, 198.
18: Catherine de Coucy: *L'Art de vérifier*, 237. Amiens Tanners: Gasquet, 57. "By the Jollity That is in Us": *Grandes Chrôns.*, VI, 486–87.
19: John Of Fordun: q. Ziegler, 199. Simon de Covino on the Poor: Gasquet, 42. On Youth: Cazelles, *Peste*.

---

[2]Tuchman does not use numbered footnotes, but at the back of her book she identifies the source of every quotation or citation. The works cited follow in a bibliography. Although Tuchman's notes are labeled by page number, the numbers here refer to the paragraphs in which the sources are mentioned. [Eds.]

BARBARA TUCHMAN

20: Knighton On Sheep: q. Ziegler, 175. Wolves of Austria and Dalmatia: ibid., 84, 111. Dogs and Cats: Muisis, q. Gasquet, 44, 61.

21: Bavarian Chronicler of Neuberg: q. Ziegler, 84. Walsingham, "The World Could Never": Denifle, 273.

22: "Oh Happy Posterity": q. Ziegler, 45.

23: Giovanni Villani, *"e dure questo"*: q. Snell, 334.

24: Physicians of Venice: Campbell, 98. Simon de Covino: ibid., 31. Guy de Chauliac, "I Was in Fear": q. Thompson *Ec. and Soc.*, 379.

27: Thucydides: q. Crawfurd, 30–31.

BIBLIOGRAPHY

L'Art de vérifier les dates des faits historiques, par un Religieux de la Congregation de St.-Maur, vol XII. Paris, 1818.
Bishop, Morris. *Petrarch and His World*. Indiana University Press, 1963.
Campbell, Anna M. *The Black Death and Men of Learning*. Columbia University Press, 1931.
Cazelles, Raymond. *"La Peste de 1348–49 en Langue d'oil: épidémie prolitarienne et enfantine." Bull philologique et historique*, 1962, pp. 293–305.
Chronicle of Jean de Venette. Trans. Jean Birdsall. Ed. Richard A. Newhall. Columbia University Press, 1853.
Crawfurd, Raymond. *Plague and Pestilence in Literature and Art*. Oxford, 1914.
Deaux, George. *The Black Death*, 1347. London, 1969.
Denifle, Henri. *La Dèsolation des églises, monastères et hopitaux en France pendant la guerre de cent ans*, vol. I. Paris, 1899.
Gasquet, Francis Aidan, Abbot. *The Black Death of 1348 and 1349*, 2nd ed. London, 1908.
Grandes Chroniques de France, vol. VI (to 1380). Ed. Paulin Paris. Paris, 1838.
Hecker, J. F. C. *The Epidemics of the Middle Ages*. London, 1844.
Renouard, Yves. *"La Peste noirs de 1348–50." Rev. de Paris*, March, 1950.
Saltmarsh, John. "Plague and Economic Decline in England in the Later Middle Ages," *Cambridge Historical Journal*, vol. VII, no. 1, 1941.
Schevill, Ferdinand. *Siena: The History of a Medieval Commune*. New York, 1909.
Snell, Frederick. *The Fourteenth Century*. Edinburgh, 1899.
Thompson, James Westfall. *Economic and Social History of Europe in the Later Middle Ages*. New York, 1931.
Ziegler, Philip. *The Black Death*. New York, 1969. (The best modern study.)

QUESTIONS

1. Try to imagine yourself in Tuchman's position. If you were assigned the task of reporting on the black plague in Europe, how would you go about it? What problems would you expect to encounter in the research and in the composition of your report?

2. The notes and bibliography reveal a broad scholarly base: Tuchman's research was clearly prodigious. But so were the problems of organization after the research had been done. Tuchman had to find a way to present her information to readers that would be clear and interesting. How has she solved her problem? What overall patterns of

organization do you find in this selection? Can you mark off subsections with topics of their own?

3. How does Tuchman organize her paragraphs? Consider paragraph 20, for example. What is the topic? What are the subtopics? Why does the paragraph begin and end as it does? Consider paragraph 22. How does the first sentence serve as a transition from the previous paragraph? How is the rest of the paragraph ordered? Does the next paragraph start a new topic or continue developing the topic announced at the beginning of paragraph 22?

4. Many paragraphs end with direct quotations. Examine some of these. What do they have in common? Why do you suppose Tuchman closes so many paragraphs in this way?

5. Much of this essay is devoted to the reporting of facts and figures. This could be supremely dull, but Tuchman is an expert at avoiding dullness. How does she help the reader see and feel the awfulness of the plague? Locate specific examples in the text, and discuss their effectiveness.

6. We have included the notes for the chapter reprinted here. Examine Tuchman's list of sources, and explain how she has used them. Does she quote directly from each source, or does she paraphrase it? Does she use a source to illustrate a point, or as evidence for argument, or in some other way? Describe Tuchman's general method of using sources.

7. Taking Tuchman as a model, write a report on some other catastrophe, blending factual reporting with description of what it was like to be there. This will require both careful research and artful selection and arrangement of the fruits of that research.

8. Using Tuchman's notes to A *Distant Mirror* as a reference guide, find out more about some specific place or event mentioned by Tuchman. Write a report of your findings.

MAKING CONNECTIONS

1. Compare this account of the black death to the writings by Farley Mowat or Jane van Lawick-Goodall, included in this section. Make your comparison in terms of the points of view established and sustained in the reports you compare. What is Tuchman's point of view toward her subject?

2. Using the terms of our introduction to this section, would you say Tuchman's basic method of reporting is narrative, or that it emphasizes spatial order, or that it makes a topical summation of categories appropriate to its subject? How does her handling of sources compare to Dennis Hevesi's "Running Away" or to the National Transportation Safety Board's report on an airplane crash?

A NEW KIND OF WAR

Ernest Hemingway

Ernest Hemingway (1899–1961) was born in Oak Park, Illinois. After serving as an ambulance driver in Italy in World War I, Hemingway became a writer and correspondent for the Toronto Star. *His early collection of short fiction,* In Our Time *(1925), shows clear evidence of his journalistic background and his war experience. The latter also informs his novel* A Farewell to Arms *(1929); another novel,* For Whom the Bell Tolls *(1940), is set during the Spanish Civil War (1936–1938). In that war, volunteers from other nations, including anarchists and communists, came to fight with the loyalists, the duly elected government of Spain, against the fascists, led by the rebel Francisco Franco and his generals, who were supported by Italian troops. Hemingway covered the war for the North American Newspaper Alliance. The following piece is a dispatch of April 14, 1937.*

Madrid.—The window of the hotel is open and, as you lie in bed, you hear the firing in the front line seventeen blocks away. There is a rifle fire all night long. The rifles go tacrong, capong, craang, tacrong, and then a machine gun opens up. It has a bigger calibre and is much louder, rong, cararong, rong, rong. Then there is the incoming boom of a trench mortar shell and a burst of machine gun fire. You lie and listen to it and it is a great thing to be in bed with your feet stretched out gradually warming the cold foot of the bed and not out there in University City or Carabanchel. A man is singing hard-voiced in the street below and three drunks are arguing when you fall asleep.

In the morning, before your call comes from the desk, the roaring burst of a high explosive shell wakes you and you go to the window and look out to see a man, his head down, his coat collar up, sprinting desperately across the paved square. There is the acrid smell of high explosive you hoped you'd never smell again, and, in a bathrobe and bedroom slippers, you hurry down the marble stairs and almost into a middle-aged woman, wounded in the abdomen, who is being helped into the hotel entrance by two men in blue workmen's smocks. She has her two hands crossed below her big, old-style Spanish bosom and from between her fingers the blood is spurting in a thin stream. On the corner, twenty yards away, is a heap of rubble, smashed cement and thrown up dirt, a single dead man, his torn clothes dusty, and a great hole in the sidewalk from

170

which the gas from a broken main is rising, looking like a heat mirage in the cold morning air.

"How many dead?" you ask a policeman.   3

"Only one," he says. "It went through the sidewalk and burst below. If it   4
would have burst on the solid stone of the road there might have been fifty."

A policeman covers the top of the trunk, from which the head is missing;   5
they send for someone to repair the gas main and you go in to breakfast. A
charwoman, her eyes red, is scrubbing the blood off the marble floor of the
corridor. The dead man wasn't you nor anyone you know and everyone is very
hungry in the morning after a cold night and a long day the day before up at
the Guadalajara front.

"Did you see him?" asked someone else at breakfast.   6

"Sure," you say.   7

"That's where we pass a dozen times a day. Right on that corner." Someone   8
makes a joke about missing teeth and someone else says not to make that joke.
And everyone has the feeling that characterizes war. It wasn't me, see? It wasn't
me.

The Italian dead up on the Guadalajara front weren't you, although Italian   9
dead, because of where you had spent your boyhood, always seemed, still, like
our dead. No. You went to the front early in the morning in a miserable little
car with a more miserable little chauffeur who suffered visibly the closer he
came to the fighting. But at night, sometimes late, without lights, with the big
trucks roaring past, you came on back to sleep in a bed with sheets in a good
hotel, paying a dollar a day for the best rooms on the front. The smaller rooms
in the back, on the side away from the shelling, were considerably more
expensive. After the shell that lit on the sidewalk in front of the hotel you got
a beautiful double corner room on that side, twice the size of the one you had
had, for less than a dollar. It wasn't me they killed. See? No. Not me. It wasn't
me anymore.

Then, in a hospital given by the American Friends of Spanish Democracy,   10
located out behind the Morata front along the road to Valencia, they said,
"Raven wants to see you."

"Do I know him?"   11

"I don't think so," they said, "but he wants to see you."   12

"Where is he?"   13

"Upstairs."   14

In the room upstairs they are giving a blood transfusion to a man with a very   15
gray face who lay on a cot with his arm out, looking away from the gurgling
bottle and moaning in a very impersonal way. He moaned mechanically and
at regular intervals and it did not seem to be him that made the sound. His lips
did not move.

"Where's Raven?" I asked.   16

"I'm here," said Raven.   17

171

The voice came from a high mound covered by a shoddy gray blanket. There 18
were two arms crossed on the top of the mound and at one end there was
something that had been a face, but now was a yellow scabby area with a wide
bandage across where the eyes had been.

"Who is it?" asked Raven. He didn't have lips, but he talked pretty well 19
without them and with a pleasant voice.

"Hemingway," I said. "I came up to see how you were doing." 20

"My face was pretty bad," he said. "It got sort of burned from the grenade, 21
but it's peeled a couple of times and it's doing better."

"It looks swell," I said. "It's doing fine." 22

I wasn't looking at it when I spoke. 23

"How are things in America?" he asked. "What do they think of us over 24
there?"

"Sentiment's changed a lot," I said. "They're beginning to realize the gov- 25
ernment is going to win this war."

"Do you think so?" 26

"Sure," I said. 27

"I'm awfully glad," he said. "You know, I wouldn't mind any of this if I 28
could just watch what was going on. I don't mind the pain, you know. It never
seemed important really. But I was always awfully interested in things and I
really wouldn't mind the pain at all if I could just sort of follow things intelli-
gently. I could even be some use. You know, I didn't mind the war at all. I did
all right in the war. I got hit once before and I was back and rejoined the
battalion in two weeks. I couldn't stand to be away. Then I got this."

He had put his hand in mine. It was not a worker's hand. There were no 29
callouses and the nails on the long, spatulate fingers were smooth and rounded.

"How did you get it?" I asked. 30

"Well, there were some troops that were routed and we went over to sort of 31
reform them and we did and then we had quite a fight with the fascists and we
beat them. It was quite a bad fight, you know, but we beat them and then
someone threw this grenade at me."

Holding his hand and hearing him tell it, I did not believe a word of it. 32
What was left of him did not sound like the wreckage of a soldier somehow. I
did not know how he had been wounded, but the story did not sound right. It
was the sort of way everyone would like to have been wounded. But I wanted
him to think I believed it.

"Where did you come from?" I asked. 33

"From Pittsburgh. I went to the University there." 34

"What did you do before you joined up here?" 35

"I was a social worker," he said. Then I knew it couldn't be true and I 36
wondered how he had really been so frightfully wounded and I didn't care. In
the war that I had known, men often lied about the manner of their wounding.
Not at first; but later. I'd lied a little myself in my time. Especially late in the

evening. But I was glad he thought I believed it, and we talked about books, he wanted to be a writer, and I told him about what happened north of Guadalajara and promised to bring some things from Madrid next time we got out that way. I hoped maybe I could get a radio.

"They tell me Dos Passos and Sinclair Lewis[1] are coming over, too," he said.   37

"Yes," I said. "And when they come I'll bring them up to see you."   38

"Gee, that will be great," he said. "You don't know what that will mean to me."   39

"I'll bring them," I said.   40

"Will they be here pretty soon?"   41

"Just as soon as they come I'll bring them."   42

"Good boy, Ernest," he said. "You don't mind if I call you Ernest, do you?"   43

The voice came very clear and gentle from that face that looked like some hill that had been fought over in muddy weather and then baked in the sun.   44

"Hell, no," I said. "Please. Listen, old-timer, you're going to be fine. You'll be a lot of good, you know. You can talk on the radio."   45

"Maybe," he said. "You'll be back?"   46

"Sure," I said. "Absolutely."   47

"Goodbye, Ernest," he said.   48

"Goodbye," I told him.   49

Downstairs they told me he'd lost both eyes as well as his face and was also badly wounded all through the legs and in the feet.   50

"He's lost some toes, too," the doctor said, "but he doesn't know that."   51

"I wonder if he'll ever know it."   52

"Oh, sure he will," the doctor said. "He's going to get well."   53

And it still isn't you that gets hit but it is your countryman now. Your countryman from Pennsylvania, where once we fought at Gettysburg.   54

Then, walking along the road, with his left arm in an airplane splint, walking with the gamecock walk of the professional British soldier that neither ten years of militant party work nor the projecting metal wings of the splint could destroy, I met Raven's commanding officer, Jock Cunningham, who had three fresh rifle wounds through his upper left arm (I looked at them, one was septic) and another rifle bullet under his shoulder blade that had entered his left chest, passed through, and lodged there. He told me, in military terms, the history of the attempt to rally retiring troops on his battalion's right flank, of his bombing raid down a trench which was held at one end by the fascists and at the other end by the government troops, of the taking of this trench and, with six men and a Lewis gun, cutting off a group of some eighty fascists from their own lines, and of the final desperate defense of their impossible position his six men put up until the government troops came up and, attacking, straightened out the line again. He told it clearly, completely convincingly, and with a strong   55

[1] John Dos Passos (1896–1970) and Sinclair Lewis (1885–1951): American writers. [Eds.]

Glasgow accent. He had deep, piercing eyes sheltered like an eagle's, and, hearing him talk, you could tell the sort of soldier he was. For what he had done he would have had a V.C.[2] in the last war. In this war there are no decorations. Wounds are the only decorations and they do not award wound stripes.

"Raven was in the same show," he said. "I didn't know he'd been hit. Ay,   56 he's a good mon. He got his after I got mine. The fascists we'd cut off were very good troops. They never fired a useless shot when we were in that bad spot. They waited in the dark there until they had us located and then opened with volley fire. That's how I got four in the same place."

We talked for a while and he told me many things. They were all important,   57 but nothing was as important as what Jay Raven, the social worker from Pittsburgh with no military training, had told me was true. This is a strange new kind of war where you learn just as much as you are able to believe.

QUESTIONS

1. Hemingway's use of the second person tends to draw the reader into the text. What other effects does he use to place "you" there?

2. Hemingway's own responses to events are very much a part of this dispatch. Are there any sections of relatively objective reporting present? Can dialogue be considered objective reporting?

3. Why is so much space allotted to Hemingway's meeting with Raven? What does Raven represent?

4. Hemingway is comparing the Spanish Civil War with his experience in World War I. What is "new" about this war?

5. How does Hemingway want his readers to perceive him?

6. Using Hemingway's approach to draw readers into a situation (the second person, present tense, sensual information), report on your most recent battle: a subway commute, a department store sale, registration for classes, for example.

MAKING CONNECTIONS

1. Compare Hemingway's essay to Virginia Woolf's or Richard Selzer's in this section. Make your comparison in terms of the points of view of the writers. How important is each writer's point of view to the essential purpose of his or her writing? How do these points of view differ?

2. Could Hemingway's account of "a new kind of war" be an example of "peripheral attention" as Joan Didion describes that in her essay, "Why I Write"? Why or why not? Note, in particular, Hemingway's last paragraph, and comment on the quality of attention he pays in this report.

---

[2] V.C.: the Victoria Cross, Great Britain's highest military decoration, is awarded for exceptional valor. [Eds.]

HATSUYO NAKAMURA
John Hersey

John Hersey was born in 1914 in Tientsin, China, where his father was a YMCA secretary and his mother a missionary. After graduating from Yale in 1936, Hersey was a war correspondent in China and Japan. When the United States entered World War II, Hersey covered the war in the South Pacific, the Mediterranean, and Moscow. In 1945, he won the Pulitzer Prize for his novel, A Bell for Adano. In 1946, Hiroshima, a report about the effects of the atomic bomb on the lives of six people, was widely acclaimed. Almost forty years later, Hersey went back to Japan to find those six people to see what their lives had been like. Their stories form the final chapter of the 1985 edition of Hiroshima. The selection presented here first appeared in the New Yorker, as did the first edition of Hiroshima. A prolific writer of fiction and nonfiction, Hersey believes that "journalism allows its readers to witness history; fiction gives its readers an opportunity to live it."

In August, 1946, a year after the bombing of Hiroshima, Hatsuyo Nakamura   1
was weak and destitute. Her husband, a tailor, had been taken into the Army and had been killed at Singapore on the day of the city's capture, February 15, 1942. She lost her mother, a brother, and a sister to the atomic bomb. Her son and two daughters—ten, eight, and five years old—were buried in rubble when the blast of the bomb flung her house down. In a frenzy, she dug them out alive. A month after the bombing, she came down with radiation sickness; she lost most of her hair and lay in bed for weeks with a high fever in the house of her sister-in-law in the suburb of Kabe, worrying all the time about how to support her children. She was too poor to go to a doctor. Gradually, the worst of the symptoms abated, but she remained feeble; the slightest exertion wore her out.

She was near the end of her resources. Fleeing from her house through the   2
fires on the day of the bombing, she had saved nothing but a rucksack of emergency clothing, a blanket, an umbrella, and a suitcase of things she had stored in her air-raid shelter; she had much earlier evacuated a few kimonos to Kabe in fear of a bombing. Around the time her hair started to grow in again, her brother-in-law went back to the ruins of her house and recovered her late husband's Sankoku sewing machine, which needed repairs. And though she

had lost the certificates of a few bonds and other meagre wartime savings, she had luckily copied off their numbers before the bombing and taken the record to Kabe, so she was eventually able to cash them in. This money enabled her to rent for fifty yen a month—the equivalent then of less than fifteen cents—a small wooden shack built by a carpenter in the Nobori-cho neighborhood, near the site of her former home. In this way, she could free herself from the charity of her in-laws and begin a courageous struggle, which would last for many years, to keep her children and herself alive.

The hut had a dirt floor and was dark inside, but it was a home of sorts. 3 Raking back some rubble next to it, she planted a garden. From the debris of collapsed houses she scavenged cooking utensils and a few dishes. She had the Sankoku fixed and began to take in some sewing, and from time to time she did cleaning and laundry and washed dishes for neighbors who were somewhat better off than she was. But she got so tired that she had to take two days' rest for every three days she worked, and if she was obliged for some reason to work for a whole week she then had to rest for three or four days. She soon ran through her savings and was forced to sell her best kimono.

At that precarious time, she fell ill. Her belly began to swell up, and she 4 had diarrhea and so much pain she could no longer work at all. A doctor who lived nearby came to see her and told her she had roundworm, and he said, incorrectly, "If it bites your intestine, you'll die." In those days, there was a shortage of chemical fertilizers in Japan, so farmers were using night soil, and as a consequence many people began to harbor parasites, which were not fatal in themselves but were seriously debilitating to those who had had radiation sickness. The doctor treated Nakamura-san (as he would have addressed her) with santonin, a somewhat dangerous medicine derived from certain varieties of artemisia.[1] To pay the doctor, she was forced to sell her last valuable possession, her husband's sewing machine. She came to think of that as marking the lowest and saddest moment of her whole life.

In referring to those who went through the Hiroshima and Nagasaki bomb- 5 ings, the Japanese tended to shy away from the term "survivors," because in its focus on being alive it might suggest some slight to the sacred dead. The class of people to which Nakamura-san belonged came, therefore, to be called by a more neutral name, "hibakusha"—literally, "explosion-affected persons." For more than a decade after the bombings, the hibakusha lived in an economic limbo, apparently because the Japanese government did not want to find itself saddled with anything like moral responsibility for heinous acts of the victorious United States. Although it soon became clear that many hibakusha suffered consequences of their exposure to the bombs which were quite different in

---

[1] artemisia: a genus of herbs and shrubs, including sagebrush and wormwood, distinguished by strong-smelling foliage. [Eds.]

nature and degree from those of survivors even of the ghastly fire bombings in Tokyo and elsewhere, the government made no special provision for their relief—until, ironically, after the storm of rage that swept across Japan when the twenty-three crewmen of a fishing vessel, the Lucky Dragon No. 5, and its cargo of tuna were irradiated by the American test of a hydrogen bomb at Bikini in 1954. It took three years even then for a relief law for the hibakusha to pass the Diet.

Though Nakamura-san could not know it, she thus had a bleak period ahead 6
of her. In Hiroshima, the early postwar years were, besides, a time, especially painful for poor people like her, of disorder, hunger, greed, thievery, black markets. Non-hibakusha employers developed a prejudice against the survivors as word got around that they were prone to all sorts of ailments, and that even those like Nakamura-san, who were not cruelly maimed and had not developed any serious overt symptoms, were unreliable workers, since most of them seemed to suffer, as she did, from the mysterious but real malaise that came to be known as one kind of lasting "A-bomb sickness": a nagging weakness and weariness, dizziness now and then, digestive troubles, all aggravated by a feeling of oppression, a sense of doom, for it was said that unspeakable diseases might at any time plant nasty flowers in their bodies, and even in those of their descendants.

As Nakamura-san struggled to get from day to day, she had no time for 7
attitudinizing about the bomb or anything else. She was sustained, curiously, by a kind of passivity, summed up in a phrase she herself sometimes used—"*Shikata ga-nai,*" meaning, loosely, "It can't be helped." She was not religious, but she lived in a culture long colored by the Buddhist belief that resignation might lead to clear vision; she had shared with other citizens a deep feeling of powerlessness in the face of a state authority that had been divinely strong ever since the Meiji Restoration, in 1868; and the hell she had witnessed and the terrible aftermath unfolding around her reached so far beyond human understanding that it was impossible to think of them as the work of resentable human beings, such as the pilot of the Enola Gay, or President Truman, or the scientists who had made the bomb[2]—or even, nearer at hand, the Japanese militarists who had helped to bring on the war. The bombing almost seemed a natural disaster—one that it had simply been her bad luck, her fate (which must be accepted), to suffer.

When she had been wormed and felt slightly better, she made an arrangement 8
to deliver bread for a baker named Takahashi, whose bakery was in Nobori-cho. On days when she had the strength to do it, she would take orders for bread from retail shops in her neighborhood, and the next morning she would

---

[2] Enola Gay: name of the airplane that dropped the atomic bomb on Hiroshima; Harry S. Truman (1884–1972): president of the United States who made the decision to drop the bomb. [Eds.]

pick up the requisite number of loaves and carry them in baskets and boxes through the streets to the stores. It was exhausting work, for which she earned the equivalent of about fifty cents a day. She had to take frequent rest days.

After some time, when she was feeling a bit stronger, she took up another 9 kind of peddling. She would get up in the dark and trundle a borrowed two-wheeled pushcart for two hours across the city to a section called Eba, at the mouth of one of the seven estuarial rivers that branch from the Ota River through Hiroshima. There, at daylight, fishermen would cast their leaded skirt-like nets for sardines, and she would help them to gather up the catch when they hauled it in. Then she would push the cart back to Nobori-cho and sell the fish for them from door to door. She earned just enough for food.

A couple of years later, she found work that was better suited to her need 10 for occasional rest, because within certain limits she could do it on her own time. This was a job of collecting money for deliveries of the Hiroshima paper, the *Chugoku Shimbun*, which most people in the city read. She had to cover a big territory, and often her clients were not at home or pleaded that they couldn't pay just then, so she would have to go back again and again. She earned the equivalent of about twenty dollars a month at this job. Every day, her will power and her weariness seemed to fight to an uneasy draw.

In 1951, after years of this drudgery, it was Nakamura-san's good luck, her 11 fate (which must be accepted), to become eligible to move into a better house. Two years earlier, a Quaker professor of dendrology from the University of Washington named Floyd W. Schmoe, driven, apparently, by deep urges for expiation and reconciliation, had come to Hiroshima, assembled a team of carpenters, and, with his own hands and theirs, begun building a series of Japanese-style houses for victims of the bomb; in all, his team eventually built twenty-one. It was to one of these houses that Nakamura-san had the good fortune to be assigned. The Japanese measure their houses by multiples of the area of the floor-covering *tsubo* mat, a little less than four square yards, and the Dr. Shum-o houses, as the Hiroshimans called them, had two rooms of six mats each. This was a big step up for the Nakamuras. This home was redolent of new wood and clean matting. The rent, payable to the city government, was the equivalent of about a dollar month.

Despite the family's poverty, the children seemed to be growing normally. 12 Yaeko and Myeko, the two daughters, were anemic, but all three had so far escaped any of the more serious complications that so many young hibakusha were suffering. Yaeko, now fourteen, and Myeko, eleven, were in middle school. The boy, Toshio, ready to enter high school, was going to have to earn money to attend it, so he took up delivering papers to the places from which his mother was collecting. These were some distance from their Dr. Shum-o house, and they had to commute at odd hours by streetcar.

The old hut in Nobori-cho stood empty for a time, and, while continuing 13 with her newspaper collections, Nakamura-san converted it into a small street shop for children, selling sweet potatoes, which she roasted, and *dagashi,* or little candies and rice cakes, and cheap toys, which she bought from a wholesaler.

All along, she had been collecting for papers from a small company, Suyama   14
Chemical, that made mothballs sold under the trade name Paragen. A friend of hers worked there, and one day she suggested to Nakamura-san that she join the company, helping wrap the product in its packages. The owner, Nakamura-san learned, was a compassionate man, who did not share the bias of many employers against hibakusha; he had several on his staff of twenty women wrappers. Nakamura-san objected that she couldn't work more than a few days at a time; the friend persuaded her that Suyama would understand that.

So she began. Dressed in company uniforms, the women stood, somewhat   15
bent over, on either side of a couple of conveyor belts, working as fast as possible to wrap two kinds of Paragen in cellophane. Paragen had a dizzying odor, and at first it made one's eyes smart. Its substance, powdered paradichlorobenzene, had been compressed into lozenge-shaped mothballs and into larger spheres, the size of small oranges, to be hung in Japanese-style toilets, where their rank pseudomedicinal smell would offset the unpleasantness of non-flushing facilities.

Nakamura-san was paid, as a beginner, a hundred and seventy yen—then   16
less than fifty cents—a day. At first, the work was confusing, terribly tiring, and a bit sickening. Her boss worried about her paleness. She had to take many days off. But little by little she became used to the factory. She made friends. There was a family atmosphere. She got raises. In the two ten-minute breaks, morning and afternoon, when the moving belt stopped, there was a birdsong of gossip and laughter, in which she joined. It appeared that all along there had been, deep in her temperament, a core of cheerfulness, which must have fuelled her long fight against A-bomb lassitude, something warmer and more vivifying than mere submission, than saying "*Shikata ga-nai.*" The other women took to her; she was constantly doing them small favors. They began calling her, affectionately, *Oba-san*—roughly, "Auntie."

She worked at Suyama for thirteen years. Though her energy still paid its   17
dues, from time to time, to the A-bomb syndrome, the searing experiences of that day in 1945 seemed gradually to be receding from the front of her mind.

The Lucky Dragon No. 5 episode took place the year after Nakamura-san   18
started working for Suyama Chemical. In the ensuing fever of outrage in the country, the provision of adequate medical care for the victims of the Hiroshima and Nagasaki bombs finally became a political issue. Almost every year since 1946, on the anniversary of the Hiroshima bombing, a Peace Memorial Meeting had been held in a park that the city planners had set aside, during the city's rebuilding, as a center of remembrance, and on August 6, 1955, delegates from

179

all over the world gathered there for the first World Conference Against Atomic and Hydrogen Bombs. On its second day, a number of hibakusha tearfully testified to the government's neglect of their plight. Japanese political parties took up the cause, and in 1957 the Diet at last passed the A-Bomb Victims Medical Care Law. This law and its subsequent modifications defined four classes of people who would be eligible for support: those who had been in the city limits on the day of the bombing; those who had entered an area within two kilometers of the hypocenter in the first fourteen days after it; those who had come into physical contact with bomb victims, in administering first aid or in disposing of their bodies; and those who had been embryos in the wombs of women in any of the first three categories. These hibakusha were entitled to receive so-called health books, which would entitle them to free medical treatment. Later revisions of the law provided for monthly allowances to victims suffering from various aftereffects.

Like a great many hibakusha, Nakamura-san had kept away from all the 19
agitation, and, in fact, also like many other survivors, she did not even bother to get a health book for a couple of years after they were issued. She had been too poor to keep going to doctors, so she had got into the habit of coping alone, as best she could, with her physical difficulties. Besides, she shared with some other survivors a suspicion of ulterior motives on the part of the political-minded people who took part in the annual ceremonies and conferences.

Nakamura-san's son, Toshio, right after his graduation from high school, 20
went to work for the bus division of the Japanese National Railways. He was in the administrative offices, working first on timetables, later in accounting. When he was in his midtwenties, a marriage was arranged for him, through a relative who knew the bride's family. He built an addition to the Dr. Shum-o house, moved in, and began to contribute to his mother's support. He made her a present of a new sewing machine.

Yaeko, the older daughter, left Hiroshima when she was fifteen, right after 21
graduating from middle school, to help an ailing aunt who ran a *ryo-kan*, a Japanese-style inn. There, in due course, she fell in love with a man who ate at the inn's restaurant, and she made a love marriage.

After graduating from high school, Myeko, the most susceptible of the three 22
children to the A-bomb syndrome, eventually became an expert typist and took up instructing at typing schools. In time, a marriage was arranged for her.

Like their mother, all three children avoided pro-hibakusha and antinuclear 23
agitation.

In 1966, Nakamura-san, having reached the age of fifty-five, retired from 24
Suyama Chemical. At the end, she was being paid thirty thousand yen, or about eighty-five dollars, a month. Her children were no longer dependent on her, and Toshio was ready to take on a son's responsibility for his aging mother. She felt at home in her body now; she rested when she needed to, and she had

no worries about the cost of medical care, for she had finally picked up Health Book No. 1023993. It was time for her to enjoy life. For her pleasure in being able to give gifts, she took up embroidery and the dressing of traditional *kimekomi* dolls, which are supposed to bring good luck. Wearing a bright kimono, she went once a week to dance at the Study Group of Japanese Folk Music. In set movements, with expressive gestures, her hands now and then tucking up the long folds of the kimono sleeves, and with head held high, she danced, moving as if floating, with thirty agreeable women to a song of celebration of entrance into a house:

> May your family flourish
> For a thousand generations,
> For eight thousand generations.

A year or so after Nakamura-san retired, she was invited by an organization called the Bereaved Families' Association to take a train trip with about a hundred other war widows to visit the Yasukuni Shrine, in Tokyo. This holy place, established in 1869, was dedicated to the spirits of all the Japanese who had died in wars against foreign powers, and could be thought roughly analogous, in terms of its symbolism for the nation, to the Arlington National Cemetery—with the difference that souls, not bodies, were hallowed there. The shrine was considered by many Japanese to be a focus of a still smoldering Japanese militarism, but Nakamura-san, who had never seen her husband's ashes and had held on to a belief that he would return to her someday, was oblivious of all that. She found the visit baffling. Besides the Hiroshima hundred, there were huge crowds of women from other cities on the shrine grounds. It was impossible for her to summon up a sense of her dead husband's presence, and she returned home in an uneasy state of mind.

Japan was booming. Things were still rather tight for the Nakamuras, and Toshio had to work very long hours, but the old days of bitter struggle began to seem remote. In 1975, one of the laws providing support to the hibakusha was revised, and Nakamura-san began to receive a so-called health-protection allowance of six thousand yen, then about twenty dollars, a month; this would gradually be increased to more than twice that amount. She also received a pension, toward which she had contributed at Suyama, of twenty thousand yen, or about sixty-five dollars, a month; and for several years she had been receiving a war widow's pension of another twenty thousand yen a month. With the economic upswing, prices had, of course, risen steeply (in a few years Tokyo would become the most expensive city in the world), but Toshio managed to buy a small Mitsubishi car, and occasionally he got up before dawn and rode a train for two hours to play golf with business associates. Yaeko's husband ran a shop for sales and service of air-conditioners and heaters, and Myeko's husband ran a newsstand and candy shop near the railroad station.

181

JOHN HERSEY

In May each year, around the time of the Emperor's birthday, when the   27
trees along broad Peace Boulevard were at their feathery best and banked azaleas
were everywhere in bloom, Hiroshima celebrated a flower festival. Entertainment booths lined the boulevard, and there were long parades, with floats and
bands and thousands of marchers. This year, Nakamura-san danced with the
women of the folk-dance association, six dancers in each of sixty rows. They
danced to "Oiwai-Ondo," a song of happiness, lifting their arms in gestures of
joy and clapping in rhythms of threes:

> Green pine trees, cranes and turtles . . .
> You must tell a story of your hard times
> And laugh twice.

The bombing had been four decades ago. How far away it seemed!   28

The sun blazed that day. The measured steps and the constant lifting of the   29
arms for hours at a time were tiring. In midafternoon, Nakamura-san suddenly
felt woozy. The next thing she knew, she was being lifted, to her great embarrassment and in spite of begging to be let alone, into an ambulance. At the
hospital, she said she was fine; all she wanted was to go home. She was allowed
to leave.

QUESTIONS

1. What does Hatsuyo Nakamura's story tell us about the larger group of atomic-
bomb survivors?

2. Why do you think Hersey chose Hatsuyo Nakamura as a subject to report on?
How is she presented to us? How are we meant to feel about her?

3. In composing his article, Hersey presumably interviewed Nakamura and reports
from her point of view. At what points does he augment her story? For example, look
at paragraph 5. What material probably comes from Nakamura? What material probably
comes from other sources?

4. How has Hersey arranged his material? He has covered forty years of Hatsuyo
Nakamura's life in twenty-nine paragraphs. Make a list of the events he chose to report.
At what points does he condense large blocks of time?

5. Interview a relative or someone you know who participated in World War II or
in some other war, such as Vietnam. How did the war change the person's life? What
events does the person consider most important in the intervening years?

6. No doubt every person then in Hiroshima remembers the day of the bombing
just as Americans of certain ages remember days of critical national events—the attack
on Pearl Harbor, the Kennedy or King assassinations, the space shuttle disaster, and so
on. Interview several people about one such day, finding out where they were when
they first learned of the event, how they reacted, what long-term impact they felt, and
how they view that day now. Use the information from your interviews to write a report.

MAKING CONNECTIONS

1. Imagine an encounter between Hatsuyo Nakamura and either Zoë Tracy Hardy ("What Did You Do in the War, Grandma?") or William L. Laurence ("Atomic Bombing of Nagasaki Told by Flight Member"). What could those persons say to each other? Write the dialogue for a possible conversation between them.

2. One characteristic of reports is to be tentative or even oblique in drawing conclusions. Compare Hersey's report to one by Hemingway, Hevesi, Selby, or Selzer, all presented in this section, and assess their differing methods of coming to a conclusion. What would you say the points are of the two reports you chose to compare?

SINGING WITH
THE FUNDAMENTALISTS
Annie Dillard

Annie Dillard, naturalist, writer, and poet, is known for her poetic descriptions and meditations on the natural world. Her writings reflect her curiosity about nature, and she describes her nature voyages by saying: "I am an explorer, and I am also a stalker." Born in 1945 in Pittsburgh, Dillard received a B.A. (1967) and an M.A. (1968) from Hollins College in the Blue Ridge Mountains of Virginia. Dillard settled in the area to investigate the natural world and to write. Her first book, Tickets for a Prayer Wheel *(1974), was closely followed by* A Pilgrim at Tinker Creek *(1974), for which she won a Pulitzer Prize. Her most recent book is an autobiography,* An American Childhood *(1987). The following selection appeared in 1985 in the* Yale Review *under the heading "Comment." Here Dillard's curiosity is focused on religious behavior in the academic world.*

It is early spring. I have a temporary office at a state university on the West Coast. The office is on the third floor. It looks down on the Square, the enormous open courtyard at the center of campus. From my desk I see hundreds of people moving between classes. There is a large circular fountain in the Square's center. 1

Early one morning, on the first day of spring quarter, I hear singing. A pack of students has gathered at the fountain. They are singing something which, at this distance, and through the heavy window, sounds good. 2

I know who these singing students are: they are the Fundamentalists. This campus has a lot of them. Mornings they sing on the Square; it is their only perceptible activity. What are they singing? Whatever it is, I want to join them, for I like to sing; whatever it is, I want to take my stand with them, for I am drawn to their very absurdity, their innocent indifference to what people think. My colleagues and students here, and my friends everywhere, dislike and fear Christian fundamentalists. You may never have met such people, but you've heard what they do: they pile up money, vote in blocs, and elect right-wing crazies; they censor books; they carry handguns; they fight fluoride in the drinking water and evolution in the schools; probably they would lynch people if they could get away with it. I'm not sure my friends are correct. I close my pen and join the singers on the Square. 3

There is a clapping song in progress. I have to concentrate to follow it: 4

> Come on, rejoice,
> And let your heart sing,
> Come on, rejoice,
> Give praise to the king.
> Singing alleluia—
> He is the king of kings;
> Singing alleluia—
> He is the king of kings.

Two song leaders are standing on the broad rim of the fountain; the water is splashing just behind them. The boy is short, hard-faced, with a moustache. He bangs his guitar with the backs of his fingers. The blonde girl, who leads the clapping, is bouncy; she wears a bit of make-up. Both are wearing blue jeans.

The students beside me are wearing blue jeans, too—and athletic jerseys,   5
parkas, football jackets, turtlenecks, and hiking shoes or jogging shoes. They all have canvas or nylon book bags. They look like any random batch of seventy or eighty students at this university. They are grubby or scrubbed, mostly scrubbed; they are tall, fair, or red-headed in large proportions. Their parents are white-collar workers, blue-collar workers, farmers, loggers, orchardists, merchants, fishermen; their names are, I'll bet, Olsen, Jensen, Seversen, Hansen, Klokker, Sigurdsen.

Despite the vigor of the clapping song, no one seems to be giving it much   6
effort. And no one looks at anyone else; there are no sentimental glances and smiles, no glances even of recognition. These kids don't seem to know each other. We stand at the fountain's side, out on the broad, bricked Square in front of the science building, and sing the clapping song through three times.

It is quarter to nine in the morning. Hundreds of people are crossing the   7
Square. These passersby—faculty, staff, students—pay very little attention to us; this morning singing has gone on for years. Most of them look at us directly, then ignore us, for there is nothing to see: no animal sacrifices, no lynchings, no collection plate for Jesse Helms, no seizures, snake handling, healing, or glossolalia. There is barely anything to hear. I suspect the people glance at us to learn if we are really singing: how could so many people make so little sound? My fellow singers, who ignore each other, certainly ignore passersby as well. Within a week, most of them will have their eyes closed anyway.

We move directly to another song, a slower one.   8

> He is my peace
> Who has broken down every wall;
> He is my peace,
> He is my peace.

> Cast all your cares on him,
> For he careth for you—oo—oo
> He is my peace,
> He is my peace.

I am paying strict attention to the song leaders, for I am singing at the top 9
of my lungs and I've never heard any of these songs before. They are not the
old American low-church Protestant hymns; they are not the old European
high-church Protestant hymns. These hymns seem to have been written just
yesterday, apparently by the same people who put out lyrical Christian greeting
cards and bookmarks.

"Where do these songs come from?" I ask a girl standing next to me. She 10
seems appalled to be addressed at all, and startled by the question. "They're
from the praise albums!" she explains, and moves away.

The songs' melodies run dominant, subdominant, dominant, tonic, domi- 11
nant. The pace is slow, about the pace of "Tell Laura I Love Her," and with
that song's quavering, long notes. The lyrics are simple and repetitive; there are
very few of them to which a devout Jew or Mohammedan could not give
wholehearted assent. These songs are similar to the things Catholics sing in
church these days. I don't know if any studies have been done to correlate the
introduction of contemporary songs into Catholic churches with those churches'
decline in membership, or with the phenomenon of Catholic converts' applying
to enter cloistered monasteries directly, without passing through parish churches.

> I'm set free to worship,
> I'm set free to praise him,
> I'm set free to dance before the Lord . . .

At nine o'clock sharp we quit and scatter. I hear a few quiet "see you's." 12
Mostly the students leave quickly, as if they didn't want to be seen. The Square
empties.

The next day we show up again, at twenty to nine. The same two leaders 13
stand on the fountain's rim; the fountain is pouring down behind them.

After the first song, the boy with the moustache hollers, "Move on up! Some 14
of you guys aren't paying attention back there! You're talking to each other. I
want you to concentrate!" The students laugh, embarrassed for him. He sounds
like a teacher. No one moves. The girl breaks into the next song, which we
join at once:

> In my life, Lord,
> Be glorified, be glorified, be glorified;
> In my life, Lord,
> Be glorified, be glorified, today.

At the end of this singularly monotonous verse, which is straining my tolerance for singing virtually anything, the boy with the moustache startles me by shouting, "Classes!"

At once, without skipping a beat, we sing, "In my classes, Lord, be glorified, be glorified . . ." I give fleet thought to the class I'm teaching this afternoon. We're reading a little "Talk of the Town"[1] piece called "Eggbag," about a cat in a magic store on Eighth Avenue. "Relationships!" the boy calls. The students seem to sing "In my relationships, Lord," more easily than they sang "classes." They seemed embarrassed by "classes." In fact, to my fascination, they seem embarrassed by almost everything. Why are they here? I will sing with the Fundamentalists every weekday morning all spring; I will decide, tentatively, that they come pretty much for the same reasons I do: each has a private relationship with "the Lord" and will put up with a lot of junk for it.

I have taught some Fundamentalist students here, and know a bit of what they think. They are college students above all, worried about their love lives, their grades, and finding jobs. Some support moderate Democrats; some support moderate Republicans. Like their classmates, most support nuclear freeze, ERA, and an end to the draft. I believe they are divided on abortion and busing. They are not particularly political. They read *Christianity Today* and *Campus Life* and *Eternity*—moderate, sensible magazines, I think; they read a lot of C. S. Lewis. (One such student, who seemed perfectly tolerant of me and my shoddy Christianity, introduced me to C. S. Lewis's critical book on Charles Williams.) They read the Bible. I think they all "believe in" organic evolution. The main thing about them is this: there isn't any "them." Their views vary. They don't know each other.

Their common Christianity puts them, if anywhere, to the left of their classmates. I believe they also tend to be more able than their classmates to think well in the abstract, and also to recognize the complexity of moral issues. But I may be wrong.

In 1980, the media were certainly wrong about television evangelists. Printed estimates of Jerry Falwell's television audience ranged from 18 million to 30 million people. In fact, according to Arbitron's actual counts, fewer than 1.5 million people were watching Falwell. And, according to an Emory University study, those who did watch television evangelists didn't necessarily vote with them. Emory University sociologist G. Melton Mobley reports, "When that message turns political, they cut it off." Analysis of the 1982 off-year elections turned up no Fundamentalist bloc voting. The media were wrong, but no one printed retractions.

The media were wrong, too, in a tendency to identify all fundamentalist

---

[1] The regular introductory section of the *New Yorker*. [Eds.]

Christians with Falwell and his ilk, and to attribute to them, across the board, conservative views.

Someone has sent me two recent issues of *Eternity: The Evangelical Monthly.* 20 One lead article criticizes a television preacher for saying that the United States had never used military might to take land from another nation. The same article censures Newspeak, saying that government rhetoric would have us believe in a "clean bomb," would have us believe that we "defend" America by invading foreign soil, and would have us believe that the dictatorships we support are "democracies." "When the President of the United States says that one reason to support defense spending is because it creates jobs," this lead article says, "a little bit of *1984* begins to surface." Another article criticizes a "heavy-handed" opinion of Jerry Falwell Ministries—in this case a broadside attack on artificial insemination, surrogate motherhood, and lesbian motherhood. Browsing through *Eternity*, I find a double crosstic. I find an intelligent, analytical, and enthusiastic review of the new London Philharmonic recording of Mahler's second symphony—a review which stresses the "glorious truth" of the Jewish composer's magnificent work, and cites its recent performance in Jerusalem to celebrate the recapture of the Western Wall following the Six Day War. Surely, the evangelical Christians who read this magazine are not book-burners. If by chance they vote with the magazine's editors, then it looks to me as if they vote with the American Civil Liberties Union and Americans for Democratic Action.

Every few years some bold and sincere Christian student at this university 21 disagrees with a professor in class—usually about the professor's out-of-hand dismissal of Christianity. Members of the faculty, outraged, repeat the stories of these rare and uneven encounters for years on end, as if to prove that the crazies are everywhere, and gaining ground. The notion is, apparently, that these kids can't think for themselves. Or they wouldn't disagree.

Now again the moustached leader asks us to move up. There is no harangue, 22 so we move up. (This will be a theme all spring. The leaders want us closer together. Our instinct is to stand alone.) From behind the tall fountain comes a wind; on several gusts we get sprayed. No one seems to notice.

We have time for one more song. The leader, perhaps sensing that no one 23 likes him, blunders on. "I want you to pray this one through," he says. "We have a lot of people here from a lot of different fellowships, but we're all one body. Amen?" They don't like it. He gets a few polite Amens. We sing:

> Bind us together, Lord,
> With a bond that can't be broken;
> Bind us together, Lord,
> With love.

Everyone seems to be in a remarkably foul mood today. We don't like this song. There is no one here under seventeen, and, I think, no one here who

188

believes that love is a bond that can't be broken. We sing the song through three times; then it is time to go.

The leader calls after our retreating backs, "Hey, have a good day! Praise 24
Him all day!" The kids around me roll up their eyes privately. Some groan; all
flee.

The next morning is very cold. I am here early. Two girls are talking on the 25
fountain's rim; one is part Indian. She says, "I've got all the Old Testament,
but I can't get the New. I screw up the New." She takes a breath and rattles off
a long list, ending with "Jonah, Micah, Nahum, Habakkuk, Zephaniah, Hag-
gai, Zechariah, Malachi." The other girl produces a slow, sarcastic applause. I
ask one of the girls to help me with the words to a song. She is agreeable, but
says, "I'm sorry, I can't. I just became a Christian this year, so I don't know all
the words yet."

The others are coming; we stand and separate. The boy with the moustache 26
is gone, replaced by a big, serious fellow in a green down jacket. The bouncy
girl is back with her guitar; she's wearing a skirt and wool knee socks. We begin,
without any preamble, by singing a song that has so few words that we actually
stretch one syllable over eleven separate notes. Then we sing a song in which
the men sing one phrase and the women echo it. Everyone seems to know just
what to do. In the context of our vapid songs, the lyrics of this one are
extraordinary:

> I was nothing before you found me.
> Heartache! Broken people! Ruined lives
> Is why you died on Calvary.

The last line rises in a regular series of half-notes. Now at last some people are
actually singing; they throw some breath into the business. There is a seriousness
and urgency to it: "Heartache! Broken people! Ruined lives . . . I was nothing."

We don't look like nothing. We look like a bunch of students of every stripe, 27
ill-shaven or well-shaven, dressed up or down, but dressed warmly against the
cold: jeans and parkas, jeans and heavy sweaters, jeans and scarves and blow-
dried hair. We look ordinary. But I think, quite on my own, that we are here
because we know this business of nothingness, brokenness, and ruination. We
sing this song over and over.

Something catches my eye. Behind us, up in the science building, professors 28
are standing alone at opened windows.

The long brick science building has three upper floors of faculty offices, 29
thirty-two windows. At one window stands a bearded man, about forty; his
opening his window is what caught my eye. He stands full in the open window,
his hands on his hips, his head cocked down toward the fountain. He is drawn
to look, as I was drawn to come. Up on the building's top floor, at the far right
window, there is another: an Asian-American professor, wearing a white shirt,

is sitting with one hip on his desk, looking out and down. In the middle of the row of windows, another one, an old professor in a checked shirt, stands sideways to the opened window, stands stock-still, his long, old ear to the air. Now another window cranks open, another professor—or maybe a graduate student—leans out, his hands on the sill.

We are all singing, and I am watching these five still men, my colleagues, 30 whose office doors are surely shut—for that is the custom here: five of them alone in their offices in the science building who have opened their windows on this very cold morning, who motionless hear the Fundamentalists sing, utterly unknown to each other.

We sing another four songs, including the clapping song, and one which 31 repeats, "This is the day which the Lord hath made; rejoice and be glad in it." All the professors but one stay still by their opened windows, figures in a frieze. When after ten minutes we break off and scatter, each cranks his window shut. Maybe they have nine o'clock classes too.

I miss a few sessions. One morning of the following week, I rejoin the 32 Fundamentalists on the Square. The wind is blowing from the north: it is sunny and cold. There are several new developments.

Someone has blown up rubber gloves and floated them in the fountain. I 33 saw them yesterday afternoon from my high office window, and couldn't quite make them out: I seemed to see hands in the fountain waving from side to side, like those hands wagging on springs which people stick in the back windows of their cars. I saw these many years ago in Quito and Guayaquil, where they were a great fad long before they showed here. The cardboard hands said, on their palms, HOLA GENTE, hello people. Some of them just said HOLA, hello, with a little wave to the universe at large, in case anybody happened to be looking. It is like our sending radio signals to planets in other galaxies: HOLA, if anyone is listening. Jolly folk, these Ecuadorians, I thought.

Now, waiting by the fountain for the singing, I see that these particular 34 hands are long surgical gloves, yellow and white, ten of them, tied off at the cuff. They float upright and they wave, *hola, hola, hola*; they mill around like a crowd, bobbing under the fountain's spray and back again to the pool's rim, *hola*. It is a good prank. It is far too cold for the university's maintenance crew to retrieve them without turning off the fountain and putting on rubber boots.

From all around the Square, people are gathering for the singing. There is 35 no way I can guess which kids, from among the masses crossing the Square, will veer off to the fountain. When they get here, I never recognize anybody except the leaders.

The singing begins without ado as usual, but there is something different 36 about it. The students are growing prayerful, and they show it this morning with a peculiar gesture. I'm glad they weren't like this when I first joined them, or I never would have stayed.

Last night there was an educational television special, part of "Middletown." 37
It was a segment called "Community of Praise," and I watched it because it
was about Fundamentalists. It showed a Jesus-loving family in the Midwest; the
treatment was good and complex. This family attended the prayer meetings,
healing sessions, and church services of an unnamed sect—a very low-church
sect, whose doctrine and culture were much more low-church than those of
the kids I sing with. When the members of this sect prayed, they held their
arms over their heads and raised their palms, as if to feel or receive a blessing
or energy from above.

Now today on the Square there is a new serious mood. The leaders are 38
singing with their eyes shut. I am impressed that they can bang their guitars,
keep their balance, and not fall into the pool. It is the same bouncy girl and
earnest boy. Their eyeballs are rolled back a bit. I look around and see that
almost everyone in this crowd of eighty or so has his eyes shut and is apparently
praying some other prayer.

Now as the chorus rises, as it gets louder and higher and simpler in melody— 39

> I exalt thee,
> I exalt thee,
> I exalt thee,
> Thou art the Lord—

then, at this moment, hands start rising. All around me, hands are going up—
that tall girl, that blond boy with his head back, the redheaded boy up front,
the girl with the McDonald's jacket. Their arms rise as if pulled on strings.
Some few of them have raised their arms very high over their heads and are
tilting back their palms. Many, many more of them, as inconspicuously as
possible, have raised their hands to the level of their chins.

What is going on? Why are these students today raising their palms in this 40
gesture, when nobody did it last week? Is it because the leaders have set a
prayerful tone this morning? Is it because this gesture always accompanies this
song, just as clapping accompanies other songs? Or is it, as I suspect, that these
kids watched the widely publicized documentary last night just as I did, and
are adopting, or trying out, the gesture?

It is a sunny morning, and the sun is rising behind the leaders and the 41
fountain, so those students have their heads tilted, eyes closed, and palms
upraised toward the sun. I glance up at the science building and think my own
prayer: thank God no one is watching this.

The leaders cannot move around much on the fountain's rim. The girl has 42
her eyes shut; the boy opens his eyes from time to time, glances at the neck of
his guitar, and closes his eyes again.

When the song is over, the hands go down, and there is some desultory 43
chatting in the crowd, as usual: can I borrow your library card? And, as usual,
nobody looks at anybody.

191

All our songs today are serious. There is a feudal theme to them, or a feudal   44
analogue:

> I will eat from abundance of your household.
> I will dream beside your streams of righteousness.

> You are my king.

> Enter his gates
> with thanksgiving in your heart;
> come before his courts with praise.

> He is the king of kings.

> Thou art the Lord.

All around me, eyes are closed and hands are raised. There is no social   45
pressure to do this, or anything else. I've never known any group to be less
cohesive, imposing fewer controls. Since no one looks at anyone, and since
passersby no longer look, everyone out here is inconspicuous and free. Perhaps
the palm-raising has begun because the kids realize by now that they are not
on display; they're praying in their closets, right out here on the Square. Over
the course of the next weeks, I will learn that the palm-raising is here to stay.

The sun is rising higher. We are singing our last song. we are praying. We   46
are alone together.

> He is my peace
> Who has broken down every wall . . .

When the song is over, the hands go down. The heads lower, the eyes open   47
and blink. We stay still a second before we break up. We have been standing
in a broad current; now we have stepped aside. We have dismantled the radar
cups; we have closed the telescope's vault. Students gather their book bags and
go. The two leaders step down from the fountain's rim and pack away their
guitars. Everyone scatters. I am in no hurry, so I stay after everyone is gone. It
is after nine o'clock, and the Square is deserted. The fountain is playing to an
empty house. In the pool the cheerful hands are waving over the water, bobbing
under the fountain's veil and out again in the current, *hola*.

QUESTIONS

1. Why do you suppose Dillard chose to write predominantly in the present tense?
What effect does this have on the reader?

2. What is Dillard's purpose for writing? Is this article a piece of investigative
reporting? Can it be considered a defense of Christian fundamentalists?

3. Dillard criticizes the media for biased reporting in 1980. Does she avoid bias in her article?

4. How would you describe Dillard's attitude toward the fundamentalists? Does her perception of them change during the time she sings with them?

5. Dillard strongly suggests that the behavior of the student fundamentalists was affected by a television program about fundamentalists (paragraphs 37–40). Write a report on a similar example of media influence on the behavior (dress, speech, eating, and so on) of a person or group you know.

6. Investigate a group on your campus or in your community about which you are curious. Observe what they do, and interview some members of the group. Write a report of your experience.

MAKING CONNECTIONS

1. How do Dillard's procedures in her study of fundamentalists compare with those of Farley Mowat and Jane van Lawick-Goodall in their studies of creatures in a natural habitat? To what extent are their procedures similar? How are they different? How do their procedures influence what they find and how they present their findings?

2. Describe Dillard's point of view in comparison with Ernest Hemingway's and Virginia Woolf's in essays in this section. Try to be as particular as you can about each writer's point of view. How close to his or her subject does each writer get? How carefully do these writers keep some distance? What do their points of view enable them to see?

THE DEATH
OF THE MOTH
Virginia Woolf

*Born in 1882, Virginia Woolf became one of England's
major modern novelists before her death in 1941. She is also
known as the author of important critical essays and such
personal documents as letters, journals, and familiar essays.
This selection combines the reporting of a naturalist with
the reflecting of an essayist. Ironically, this selection was
first published for a wide audience in the posthumous collection* The Death of the Moth and Other Essays *(1942),
seen into print by her husband, Leonard Woolf.*

Moths that fly by day are not properly to be called moths; they do not excite   1
that pleasant sense of dark autumn nights and ivy-blossom which the commonest
yellow-underwing asleep in the shadow of the curtain never fails to rouse in us.
They are hybrid creatures, neither gay like butterflies nor sombre like their own
species. Nevertheless the present specimen, with his narrow hay-colored wings,
fringed with a tassel of the same color, seemed to be content with life. It was a
pleasant morning, mid-September, mild, benignant, yet with a keener breath
than that of the summer months. The plough was already scoring the field
opposite the window, and where the share had been, the earth was pressed flat
and gleamed with moisture. Such vigor came rolling in from the fields and the
down beyond that it was difficult to keep the eyes strictly turned upon the book.
The rooks too were keeping one of their annual festivities;[1] soaring round the
tree tops until it looked as if a vast net with thousands of black knots in it had
been cast up into the air; which, after a few moments sank slowly down upon
the trees until every twig seemed to have a knot at the end of it. Then, suddenly,
the net would be thrown into the air again in a wider circle this time, with the
utmost clamor and vociferation, as though to be thrown into the air and settle
slowly down upon the tree tops were a tremendously exciting experience.

The same energy which inspired the rooks, the ploughmen, the horses, and   2
even, it seemed, the lean bare-backed downs, sent the moth fluttering from
side to side of his square of the window-pane. One could not help watching
him. One was, indeed, conscious of a queer feeling of pity for him. The
possibilities of pleasure seemed that morning so enormous and various that to
have only a moth's part in life, and a day moth's at that, appeared a hard fate,

---

[1] rooks: European birds, similar to American crows. [Eds.]

194

and his zest in enjoying his meagre opportunities to the full, pathetic. He flew vigorously to one corner of his compartment, and, after waiting there a second, flew across to the other. What remained for him but to fly to a third corner and then to a fourth? That was all he could do, in spite of the size of the downs, the width of the sky, the far-off smoke of houses, and the romantic voice, now and then, of a steamer out at sea. What he could do he did. Watching him, it seemed as if a fibre, very thin but pure, of the enormous energy of the world had been thrust into his frail and diminutive body. As often as he crossed the pane, I could fancy that a thread of vital light became visible. He was little or nothing but life.

Yet, because he was so small, and so simple a form of the energy that was   3 rolling in at the open window and driving its way through so many narrow and intricate corridors in my own brain and in those of other human beings, there was something marvelous as well as pathetic about him. It was as if someone had taken a tiny bead of pure life and decking it as lightly as possible with down and feathers, had set it dancing and zigzagging to show us the true nature of life. Thus displayed one could not get over the strangeness of it. One is apt to forget all about life, seeing it humped and bossed and garnished and cumbered so that it has to move with the greatest circumspection and dignity. Again, the thought of all that life might have been had he been born in any other shape caused one to view his simple activities with a kind of pity.

After a time, tired by his dancing apparently, he settled on the window ledge   4 in the sun, and, the queer spectacle being at an end, I forgot about him. Then, looking up, my eye was caught by him. He was trying to resume his dancing, but seemed either so stiff or so awkward that he could only flutter to the bottom of the window-pane; and when he tried to fly across it he failed. Being intent on other matters I watched these futile attempts for a time without thinking, unconsciously waiting for him to resume his flight, as one waits for a machine, that has stopped momentarily, to start again without considering the reason of its failure. After perhaps a seventh attempt he slipped from the wooden ledge and fell, fluttering his wings, onto his back on the window sill. The helplessness of his attitude roused me. It flashed upon me he was in difficulties; he could no longer raise himself; his legs struggled vainly. But, as I stretched out a pencil, meaning to help him to right himself, it came over me that the failure and awkwardness were the approach of death. I laid the pencil down again.

The legs agitated themselves once more. I looked as if for the enemy against   5 which he struggled. I looked out of doors. What had happened there? Presumably it was midday, and work in the fields had stopped. Stillness and quiet had replaced the previous animation. The birds had taken themselves off to feed in the brooks. The horses stood still. Yet the power was there all the same, massed outside indifferent, impersonal, not attending to anything in particular. Somehow it was opposed to the little hay-colored moth. It was useless to try to do anything. One could only watch the extraordinary efforts made by those tiny legs against an oncoming doom which could, had it chosen, have submerged an entire city, not merely a city, but masses of human beings; nothing, I knew, had any chance against death. Nevertheless after a pause of exhaustion the legs fluttered again. It was superb this last protest, and so frantic that he succeeded at last in righting himself. One's sympathies, of course, were all on the side of life. Also, when there was nobody to care or to know, this gigantic effort on the part of an insignificant little moth, against a power of such magnitude, to retain what no one else valued or desired to keep, moved one strangely. Again, somehow, one saw life, a pure bead. I lifted the pencil again, useless though I knew it to be. But even as I did so, the unmistakable tokens of death showed themselves. The body relaxed, and instantly grew stiff. The struggle was over. The insignificant little creature now knew death. As I looked at the dead moth, this minute wayside triumph of so great a force over so mean an antagonist filled me with wonder. Just as life had been strange for a few minutes before, so death was now as strange. The moth having righted himself now lay most decently and uncomplainingly composed. O yes, he seemed to say, death is stronger than I am.

QUESTIONS

1. A moth is a creature so small and seemingly insignificant that most of us would not pay attention to its dying. Why does Woolf pay attention? How does she engage our attention?

2. What most impresses Woolf as she watches the moth?

3. Why does Woolf describe in paragraph 1 the scene beyond the window? How does this description connect with her purpose in writing this essay?

4. In this essay, Woolf reports the sequence of events in the death of the moth as well as her thoughts concerning its dying. Trace the way in which she has chosen to weave the two strands of reporting and commenting together throughout the essay. How else might she have arranged her material? Why do you think she has chosen to arrange it as she has?

5. If you have witnessed a hopeless but valiant struggle on a human, animal, or insect scale, write a report of your observations. Decide how you will make a reader aware of your thoughts about what you observed.

MAKING CONNECTIONS

1. Woolf's essay is one of those that might have as easily appeared in another section, for example, "Reflecting." Compare it to one or more of the pieces by Isak Dinesen, George Orwell, and Loren Eiseley in that section. Each of those pieces deals with the

death or near death of an animal. Does any one of them seem a particularly good candidate for "Reporting?" If so, why?

2. Is this essay another example of "peripheral attention" as described by Joan Didion in "Reflecting"? If so, what is at the periphery and what is at the center of Woolf's attention? How does that change over the course of her essay? Do you think Didion took some lessons from Woolf, not just in "why" but in "how" to write?

Social Sciences and Public Affairs

RUNNING AWAY

Dennis Hevesi

Dennis Hevesi, born in New York City in 1943, is a reporter for the New York Times *whose interest in reporting began when he found that "I was too small to make the basketball team in high school, so I started to write about the team for the school paper." In 1984, as a reporter for* Newsday, *Hevesi was a member of the team who won the Pulitzer Prize for their coverage of the "Baby Jane Doe" case. While covering the problem of the homeless in New York City, Hevesi several times met and interviewed April Savino, the subject of the piece presented here. "I was always intrigued by this young, bright girl who so obviously did not belong in the bowels of Grand Central," he says. "When I heard that she had killed herself, I felt compelled to tell her story."*

The tragedy of April Savino's abbreviated life is that when she finally found 1
a home it was among the homeless—on the benches and in the bleak recesses
of Grand Central Terminal. There, at last, she felt needed and even, by the
strange code of the streets, respected.

To the old women with sores on their legs, walking with canes, she was an 2
angel who fed them sandwiches and covered them with blankets. To other teen-
agers, she was "a wildcat" who "wouldn't take nothing from nobody."

April Savino was 15 years old when she became another of those children 3
who live, by their whims and wits in and around Grand Central. There, she
finally felt free—from the ordeal of living in a broken home, from the frenzy
of a psychiatric ward, from the constraints of residential treatment facilities.

But Grand Central is no home. For those who are not just passing through,   4
it is, ultimately, a hellish pit of violence, drugs and despair. Fourteen months
ago, April Savino sat down on the steps of a church, half a block from the
terminal, and put a bullet through her head.

There are approximately 1.2 million runaway and so-called "throw-away"   5
children in the nation, according to June Bucy, the executive director of the
National Network of Runaway and Youth Services in Washington. In New
York City alone, a study by the Coalition for the Homeless estimates, there are
20,000 children under 18 living on the streets.

April Savino was not much different from most of those others. Like many   6
of them, she had been robbed of her birthright—a family and, consequently, a
foundation for trust. Like many of them, she had waged the pitched battles of
adolescent rebellion.

Still, April was special. Where others, victimized by emotional if not physical   7
battering and hardened by the streets, might have turned vicious, April remained, essentially, a sweet kid. Sweet and sassy.

"She'd annoy the hell out of you, but you couldn't really stay mad at her,"   8
says Sgt. Frank Dowd, a Metro-North Commuter Railroad police officer who
knew April throughout the four years that she lived in the terminal. "She knew
everybody in the place, every railroad employee, every cop. She had nicknames
for all of us, some not very complimentary."

Unlike many of the other youths in Grand Central, April had a lot going   9
for her. Her parents, both beauticians, were not poor—not rich, but not poor.
Her grandmother obviously cared about her. And April—a slim, 5-foot-6-inch,
pug-nosed brunette—was intelligent, pretty and quick-witted. Even toward the
end, when she was wasting away, she could be clever.

"After she became addicted to crack, other people would criticize me for   10
giving her money," says George McDonald, the founder of the Doe Fund Inc.,
an organization set up to aid homeless people. "One night, I asked her, 'April,
what do I tell people who say I shouldn't give you money because you only use
it to buy crack?' She said, 'Tell them you're saving me from prostitution.' What
can you do?"

What, in fact, could anyone do?   11

Many people came in contact with April, including some people of power   12
and influence. Many tried to assist her. Could not someone, some agency, have
done something to alter the course of her seemingly inexorable destruction? In
many ways, April chose the way she lived; she chose to stay in the terminal.
But that's too simple; she was a victim.

Now, more than a year since the end, her life and death still pose some   13
questions: Was April Savino beyond saving? If parents cannot or will not be
parents, who is responsible for the children? What can be done to close a gap
that now exists in the legal system—a gap that allows teen-agers to destroy

themselves without intervention? According to New York State law, individuals between the ages of 16 and 18 cannot be held against their wishes for more than 72 hours unless their guardian moves to have them committed or two physicians determine that they pose an immediate danger to themselves or others. How can this system be reformed? And perhaps the most essential question: Where are our priorities?

April Candy Savino was born on July 27, 1968, the second child of Karin and Michael Savino of Fresh Meadows, Queens. "They were good parents," insists April's grandmother, Frances Savino, who lives in the Coney Island section of Brooklyn. "The kids were their life." In 1972, when April was 4 and her brother, Rodney, was 7, the Savinos moved to California. "They bought a camper and left," recalls Mrs. Savino, the mother of April's father.   14

"He wasn't happy here," April's mother, Karin Savino, says of her former husband. "He thought California would be better. I had to give him that shot."   15

Six months after the Savinos settled in Tarzana, Calif., the marriage collapsed. "He left a note," Karin Savino recalls, sitting at the kitchen table of her co-op apartment in Long Beach, L.I. "It said he'd come home once a year or once a month and I'd have to live with that. So I packed up and took April on the bus to New York." (Michael Savino declined to be interviewed for this story.)   16

"They started with drugs when they went to California," Frances Savino says of her son and daughter-in-law. "I would say drugs were the start. Once they were on the dope, they couldn't handle things right. Dope must be very influential."   17

Asked about drugs, April's mother admits: "That was another reason I felt I had to leave. Yeah, I was smoking marijuana."   18

When she got on the bus with April, she left Rodney with a cousin in California. Within weeks of her return to Queens, she had a job as a beautician. And within a few months, she had opened her own beauty parlor in Fresh Meadows. "Instead of an apartment, I rented a store," she says. One day, her husband called and announced, "Your son is at the airport, pick him up." For several months, Mrs. Savino and the children slept in the store on air mattresses.   19

The business prospered, and within a year, she and her children were living in North Shore Towers, an expensive apartment complex near the Queens-Nassau border. The children attended P.S. 205 in Bayside, and did well, according to their mother. But when April was in third grade, she recalls, "they started to complain that she lost her temper, that she threw chairs. She was immature. Her father wasn't around. I felt I had to show her I loved her more. I sent her to private school—Highland in Jamaica Estates."   20

For several years, things seemed normal. "When you sat on her," April's mother says, "she performed. She got 95s, 100s." But there were hints of trouble.   21

"She was 9 when her grandfather died," April's grandmother remembers,   22

201

shuffling through family photographs in her tidy 20th-floor co-op in a high-rise, moderate-income housing project in Coney Island. "He was an idol to her. She was born on his birthday. And he was more affectionate than me. She was very hurt because she couldn't go to the funeral. None of the grandchildren were allowed to go.

"When we came back from the cemetery, April stood with a pad and pencil and took everybody's name at the table—the aunts, the cousins. She wanted to know who they were and who she was to them. She wanted family. Unfortunately, she wasn't getting it."   23

Sometimes, at her mother's beauty parlor, April would act spitefully. "She'd wait until I'm with a client and walk over and say, 'You didn't feed me today,'" Karin Savino recalls.   24

In 1978, April's brother, Rodney, moved back to California to live with his father. It was another loss for April. "The children were very close," according to April's grandmother. Real problems began when April was 12 and visited her father and brother.   25

"I couldn't postpone her any more," says Karin Savino. "She wanted to know her father. She pushed the issue. For a while, I said I don't know his phone number, because I knew he didn't want her." Eventually he relented. "Michael told me he would let her come for one week, if I paid for it."   26

Michael Savino had remarried. "They had a wonderful time at the Big Sur," April's grandmother says, "and when April came home, she'd brag about the things her father and his wife did. It made the mother angry. April came home very elated and spoiled. So she fought her mother."   27

After that week in California, Karin Savino says, "it was a complete turnaround. Everything I did was bad. I was stupid. Her whole personality was negative. She wanted to go outside late at night, hang out at the pizza place. She disappeared for three, four days."   28

Finally, there was an explosion. "When she came at me," Mrs. Savino said, "the knife was an inch from my face. I ducked. She threw the TV at me and screamed, 'What are you gonna do now?' Eventually, I got exhausted. I sent her to Elmhurst."   29

On Oct. 31, 1981, April was committed to the psychiatric ward at the City Hospital Center in Elmhurst, Queens. When Frances Savino visited her granddaughter, "April was medicated, very quiet. There were kids there, screaming, yelling. She'd say, 'I'm crazy. You know I'm crazy. That's why I'm here.' I'd say, 'Don't talk like that.'"   30

April spent two months on the psychiatric ward. It was the start of three years during which she bounced between the hospital, her home, the Pleasantville Cottage School (a residential treatment center in Pleasantville, N.Y.), High Point Hospital in Port Chester, N.Y., and ultimately, the Linden Hill Residential Treatment Facility in Hawthorne, N.Y.   31

Fred Steffen is director of Linden Hill. "In some ways," he says, "we didn't   32
get to know April well enough." She was always running away. Usually, she
came back on her own. "The fact is that when April was with us," Steffen says,
"though she was not our best kid," she was far from the worst. "She was
immensely appealing—charming, bright, warm-hearted. But when she became
anxious, depressed, she would go into action—typically, run away. During her
runaways, since her judgment was bad, she would hook up with people who
exploited her—drugs, sex."

Before she was sent to Linden Hill in March 1984, April was a resident at   33
the Pleasantville school. Fred Steffen says reports from Pleasantville indicated
that April had a discipline problem. She was always "a difficult young lady,"
he recalls. "But my hypothesis is that she became more difficult when her
brother died."

At 3:30 A.M. on Oct. 17, 1982, a car driven by Rodney Savino ran off the   34
shoulder of Interstate Highway 15, south of Barstow, Calif. Rodney died of head
injuries two days later. He was 17.

"It was a bad turning point," April's grandmother says. "She would talk to   35
Rodney after he was dead. "April's mother agrees: "She didn't want to live after
her brother died. She was fascinated with anybody who died."

Young people like April, who get overwhelmed by stress, "feel they're entitled   36
to be destructive to themselves or others," Steffen speculates. "They may have
been subject to a subtle form of exploitation that results from some parents'
inability or unwillingness to parent them. It destroys a kid's foundation of
trust.

"Paradoxically, when she got close to staff, if you reached her heart, it stirred   37
up anxiety. And her way of dealing was to run.

"It is significant," Steffen says, "that April winds up in Grand Central Station   38
mothering everybody, when what she so desperately needed was that kind of
parenting." The last time April ran away from Linden Hall was on December
12, 1984.

It was in the "Living Room" at Grand Central that George McDonald first   39
met April. That's what the homeless people call it. For commuters, it's the
waiting room.

"I was standing there talking to a Metro-North police officer, and he asked   40
if I had met April," recalls McDonald, who was then one of the volunteers
from the Coalition for the Homeless who hand out sandwiches at the terminal
night after night. April was over by the benches, flitting like a chatty hostess
among her homeless friends. "She was awful pretty, and she had that baseball
cap on, backward, like she always did. I went and talked to her. I immediately
loved her, and she knew it. She started to con me. She asked, 'Would you buy
me a pack of cigarettes?' I told her she shouldn't smoke."

"She wound up with a pack of cigarettes," McDonald says. "I was never able   41
to say no to her."

If April could get what she wanted, she could also give. McDonald began   42
to notice that April "would always come to the food truck and get a sandwich
for somebody down in the tunnels who might be sick."

"The old women with the sores and the canes, they couldn't get the food,"   43
says Sgt. Frank Dowd of the Metro-North Railroad police. "She would bring it
to them, open the wrappers for them. She'd get blankets, cover them over. She
was like a spark. She got all the old women laughing, brought a little life to a
dreary place."

Rick Haber of Los Angeles, a former friend of April's father, used to visit   44
April at Grand Central during business trips to New York. Even toward the
end, he said, she did things for others. "Whenever I took her to dinner she
would get candy to pass out," Haber says. "She actually believed there were
people less fortunate than her."

When she was still new to the terminal, April shunned drugs. "When she   45
saw the others using drugs, she would tell you they are killing themselves,"
Sergeant Dowd recalls. Despite her surroundings, she always managed to appear
clean and presentable. When reporters came to the terminal they repeatedly
sought her out. "They wanted homeless folks who are articulate, personable, to
speak with them about why they were there," says McDonald.

For April, it was always a temporary thing, she insisted. In an interview on   46
the "CBS Evening News With Dan Rather" in March 1986, she declared: "I
want a big house, one as big as this one. I'm going to marry a rich man."

But for the time being, the terminal represented both a home and a liberation   47
of sorts. "It was a wonderland for April," Sergeant Dowd says. "She could run
like a deer. Sometimes we'd chase her, but she knew more about the lower
depths than most employees did. It was futile to chase her."

It was April's turf.   48

Angel Rivera, 27, was April's boyfriend for one of her four years in Grand   49
Central. "We had a room, below the tracks," he says. "It was a bathroom for
janitors. But it was closed. We cleaned it up and what-not. We brought
mattresses down there. She put up pictures. She had teddy bears and stuff."

Finally, he says, "the police took us out. I told April not to bring anyone   50
there, but she brought her girlfriend and, before you knew it, messed up
everything."

April was "no angel," Rivera asserts. "I remember when she broke a bottle   51
on the guy, just broke it on his head. The guy looks at me and laughs. She
ran. I caught up to her and said, 'What was that about?' She said he cursed
her. She wouldn't take nothing from nobody. She was a wildcat."

Occasionally, April would take a subway to Coney Island to stay with her   52
grandmother.

"She always talked nice about her grandmother," Rivera says. "She said the   53
grandmother was the only one who loved her, really. As a matter of fact, she
stayed with her grandmother for a while, until she robbed her. Can you believe
that?"

Several times, April tried to assume a normal life with her grandmother in   54
Coney Island. "First mistake is I registered her in school," recalls Frances
Savino. "I took her to Lincoln High School. I wanted to treat her as a child
should be treated. She said, 'Look, Grandma, I really want to go back to Grand
Central. I don't want to go to school.' I didn't realize that she hadn't been to
school since seventh grade. And all those kids had all those nice clothes."

Mrs. Savino owned two sets of jewelry—some costume jewelry from Mexico   55
and "the good stuff." April stole the costume jewelry and pawned it for a few
dollars. "I didn't think that she could steal."

Eventually, Mrs. Savino says, "I couldn't handle her no more." April left.   56

A few weeks later, Frances Savino went to Grand Central to see how her   57
granddaughter was getting along. "I followed her. She got very nasty." April's
mother also sought out her daughter at the terminal. "Sure, I said come home,
but she wasn't going to come," Karin Savino says. "I didn't want to lecture. At
this point, she was big; she'll belt me one."

The last time Frances Savino heard about her granddaughter—before the   58
end—"she was with that crippled boy, when she stole a truck."

George McDonald remembers: "I get a call from a woman at Traveler's Aid   59
in Washington. She said, 'I have a little girl here who says she lives in Grand
Central Station.' I said, 'You don't have to tell me, it's April Savino.'" Early
one morning in February 1986, April and two young men—one of them in a
wheelchair—had spotted an unattended bagel truck parked on Third Avenue.
On the spur of the moment, they climbed in and headed south with the load
of hot bagels. Outside Washington, the truck broke down.

"Her friend disappeared, the guy in the wheelchair tried to molest her and   60
she wound up at Traveler's Aid," McDonald recounts.

By then, April had tried crack.   61

"When I first met her, she was smoking," says Angel Rivera. "I paid for   62
my habit and her habit. But we weren't smoking that much." A few months
after he broke up with April, her addiction grew worse. "It began fading her
away."

Rick Haber saw the change and became so alarmed that he made a special   63
appointment to warn April's father. Haber is a clothing manufacturer from Los
Angeles whose company has offices in New York. He met Michael Savino in
1974, when April's father was "one of the few haircutters who would come to
your house."

Over the years, they became friends. "We're no longer friends," Haber says.   64
"It's relevant to what happened."

Early in 1985, Haber asked his friend whether he should visit April at Grand Central. "I said, 'I'm in New York once a month.' He said, 'Well, if you're around there, look her up.' I must say, he thought it was incredibly cool that she was living there, sort of a chip off the old block." When he went to the terminal, "I saw this girl that looked like Rodney's twin. I said, 'You're April?' She says, 'Who's asking?' I told her and she asked, 'Did my father send you?' I said, 'In a manner of speaking.'

"We sat and talked for an hour. We talked about Rodney, and she cried. Then she got angry with herself for crying."

Over the next two years, Haber went to see April about once a month. "Everybody there got to know me. I was 'Hollywood.' I went down to the tracks and she showed me where she would crawl up into this maze of tunnels. She always needed candles. I would come with candles. And then I came in and she was all screwed up. She was losing meat off her bones."

Several times, Haber says, he offered to fly April out to California. "She would say, 'Does my father want me there?' I told her, call and ask him." On one occasion, Haber thought April was in such bad shape that he called Michael Savino himself. "He got very angry, told me I was meddling. He said, in fact, if I brought April to California, whatever happened to her would be on my hands. I thought that was cold, because she was desperate.

"She would say, 'That's my father.' I think she loved him very much and needed him and she wanted him to ask. He just never asked."

Back in California, Haber confronted Savino. "I told him that she's terrible, she looks like she's going to die. He maintained his coolness. And that's pretty much when I started feeling angry at him, because I come from a divorce, and if I didn't see my kid in 10 years I'd be on a plane."

After his daughter's funeral, Michael Savino was interviewed by CBS News. "I told her that she's in something that's very, very difficult to get out of," he told the reporter. "And she said that she'd like to get out of it but didn't know how to get out of it. And I didn't know how to get her out of it. I didn't offer her to live with me. I didn't feel I could give her what she needed or what I thought she needed."

No one, it seemed, could give April what she needed.

She went to see a priest, Msgr. Eugene Clark, pastor of the Church of St. Agnes at 43d Street between Lexington and Third Avenues. "When she was talking sensibly, she was quite a sweet youngster, and this underlined the horror of the whole situation," he recalls. "She seemed to know her situation. She was clearheaded in a macabre sort of way. But you're dealing with a youngster whose nervous system was probably shattered."

It would be hard to say why April suddenly turned to crack. But the ending of her relationship with Angel Rivera played a part.

"She loved him, not normally," says her grandmother. "If ever she had a love affair or a fight, the whole world was ended. She had a fixation with love. And if they showed her any kind of attention, she went for them."

After the break, April swallowed 75 Tylenol pills and was hospitalized at the Bellevue Hospital Center in Manhattan. 76

"She was haunted over the Puerto Rican—what's his name?" April's mother 77 says. In the hospital, she painted a heart with a split in it and hung it over her bed. The inscription read: "Here lies a broken heart."

Several months later, Karen Savino asked April why she was using crack. 78 "She said that's the only way she feels good. I think she used it to try to kill herself—like the Tylenol."

George McDonald often talked to April about crack, trying to get her to seek 79 help. "She would say she loved crack more than anybody or anything. She just loved it. That's the word she used over and over."

Before April started using drugs, McDonald says, she was very concerned 80 about being arrested. Once she was addicted, all she cared about was getting her next hit. "It consumed her. Her face was sucked out, like a sucked orange. I would tell her, 'April, you're dead.' And Frank Dowd told her that they had a body bag waiting for her, with her name on it."

By this time, April was breaking into cars and burglarizing stores in Grand 81 Central to support her habit. "They would put her up to it, the older ones, have her crawl through the air ducts," says Sergeant Dowd. "God, she was skinny."

Whatever trouble she might get into, April drew the line at prostitution. 82 "One time she took an old guy down underneath the tunnels at night, when the trains aren't running," McDonald says. "She got his pants off and ran away with them. He had a couple hundred dollars in his pocket. She told me this." But when a friend began prostituting herself, April was appalled and regularly berated the younger girl.

Frances Savino wonders whether someone—someone besides herself or 83 April's parents—couldn't have helped. "I'm not blaming," she insists, "but I really feel that all these times she was picked up they really let her slip through. The cop who loved her. George loved her. The priest. They watched her go down the drain." Mrs. Savino poured another cup of coffee. "Before she took all this stuff, when Gabe Pressman interviewed her, the other press guys—it was just a story for them?"

Officials from the residential treatment facilities didn't pursue April, Mrs. 84 Savino points out, even though they knew she was living in the terminal.

Fred Steffen, the director of Linden Hill, doesn't dispute Mrs. Savino's 85 version. "We got wind that April was in Grand Central." Neither does Richard Altman, the director of the Pleasantville school. "April didn't just vanish," he says. "Many professionals who knew her knew where she was." But legally, there was nothing they could do.

The last time George McDonald intervened was in the summer of 1987. He went to Grand Central and tried to persuade April to enter Samaritan Village, a drug rehabilitation center in Queens. It was July 27—her 19th birthday. "I thought it would be a moment when she might think about her life. Nothing came of it."

Thirteen days later, on Aug. 9, April stole a gun.

"She grabbed it from another homeless person," McDonald recalls, piecing together details from his sources on the street. "It was cheap, a little .25-caliber automatic—no clip, no bullets except for one in the chamber. It didn't have the black handle, just the metal. It looked like what it was, junk."

All that day April tried to sell the gun. Nobody would buy it. "She wanted $25 for it," McDonald says. "For crack."

At about 7:30 that night, April sat down on the steps of the Church of St. Agnes, 143 East 43d Street. A few feet away sat a homeless man known only as Mexico. "She said to him, 'Say goodbye to Angel, and say goodbye to yourself.' And then she put the gun to her head and pulled the trigger." April died the next day.

"So young, so beautiful," says Sergeant Dowd. "A lot of cops went home that night and hugged their kids tighter."

McDonald identified the body at the medical examiner's office. "They take you into an outer room, where you fill out the forms. There's a smaller, adjoining room, and it has a lift that brings the body up from the basement. A light goes on when the body is there.

"The attendant goes in first. I could tell by the look on her face, the attendant's face, that it wasn't a pleasant sight. April's eyes were closed and her mouth was wide open, in a primal scream."

In an interview in November of 1985, April Savino said: "I ran away from a group home. It's in Westchester. I like this. I feel comfortable here. I panhandle. Panhandling is a tax-free job. It's very easy living out here."

"I tried to kill myself. See, I had this boyfriend—or I had delusions that he was my boyfriend."

"When you're in a home, you're always complaining. While you're out here you learn to appreciate the little things: like a shower or a warm bed. Lots of things. Like opening up the refrigerator."

"See my mother knows I'm here. My brother died. My mother didn't talk to me for a year. I wasn't a problem. I went to school. But I can't go home. My mother paid me $10 to get out of the house. My father's in California. My parents aren't the right parents. They shouldn't have had kids."

"I'm not going to be here when I'm older. See, Prince Charming is not going to meet me here. I saw somebody get shot. I've seen people robbed. When I'm older, I'll be a better person because I understand everything."

QUESTIONS

1. This article opens with a sentence that can be considered evaluative or subjective, since Hevesi considers his subject's life a tragedy. How much of the article is presented relatively objectively? What sections reveal Hevesi's point of view?

2. How is April Savino being used in this article? She is called "special." Why? Why would her case appeal to the media?

3. Does Hevesi try to place the blame for April's death? Does he expect you to?

4. How many people did Hevesi interview for this article? Note the amount of direct quotation. Why did he choose to use other people's words directly instead of reporting the facts they offered?

5. Much of the article is chronologically arranged. Where does Hevesi deviate from the chronological arrangement. Why? What effect is he after?

6. Why do you suppose Hevesi ended his article with April's own words?

7. If there are homeless people in your area, find out what percentage of them are children. Investigate and write a report of the help available in your area for someone like April Savino.

MAKING CONNECTIONS

1. Compare Hevesi's account of April Savino's childhood and youth with the first-person accounts by Maya Angelou and Alice Walker of aspects of their own growing up. Then imagine April telling part of her own story and try to tell it for her. Select one or two incidents from Hevesi's report and tell that story as you imagine April might have told it herself.

2. Read Jan Harold Brunvand's "Urban Legends: 'The Boyfriend's Death'" in "Explaining," and write an "urban legend" based on Hevesi's report. Then add a comment on what you gain and lose in relation to the report when you write a good "urban legend."

ATOMIC BOMBING OF NAGASAKI
TOLD BY FLIGHT MEMBER

William L. Laurence

William L. Laurence was born in Lithuania and came to the United States in 1905. He studied at Harvard and the Boston University Law School. His main interest, however, had always been in science, and after working at the New York World *for five years, Laurence went to the* New York Times *as a science reporter. During World War II, Laurence was the only reporter to know about the top-secret testing of the atomic bomb. On August 9, 1945, he was permitted to fly with the mission to drop the second atomic bomb on Nagasaki. Three days earlier, over one hundred thousand people had been killed in the Hiroshima bombing. Laurence won the Pulitzer Prize for this account of the bombing of Nagasaki. The article appeared in the* New York Times, *September 9, 1945.*

With the atomic-bomb mission to Japan, August 9 (Delayed)—We are on 1 our way to bomb the mainland of Japan. Our flying contingent consists of three specially designed B-29 Superforts, and two of these carry no bombs. But our lead plane is on its way with another atomic bomb, the second in three days, concentrating in its active substance an explosive energy equivalent to twenty thousand and, under favorable conditions, forty thousand tons of TNT.

We have several chosen targets. One of these is the great industrial and 2 shipping center of Nagasaki, on the western shore of Kyushu, one of the main islands of the Japanese homeland.

I watched the assembly of this man-made meteor during the past two days 3 and was among the small group of scientists and Army and Navy representatives privileged to be present at the ritual of its loading in the Superfort last night, against a background of threatening black skies torn open at intervals by great lightning flashes.

It is a thing of beauty to behold, this "gadget." Into its design went millions 4 of man-hours of what is without doubt the most concentrated intellectual effort in history. Never before had so much brain power been focused on a single problem.

This atomic bomb is different from the bomb used three days ago with such 5 devastating results on Hiroshima.

I saw the atomic substance before it was placed inside the bomb. By itself it 6
is not at all dangerous to handle. It is only under certain conditions, produced
in the bomb assembly, that it can be made to yield up its energy, and even
then it gives only a small fraction of its total contents—a fraction, however,
large enough to produce the greatest explosion on earth.

The briefing at midnight revealed the extreme care and the tremendous 7
amount of preparation that had been made to take care of every detail of the
mission, to make certain that the atomic bomb fully served the purpose for
which it was intended. Each target in turn was shown in detailed maps and in
aerial photographs. Every detail of the course was rehearsed—navigation, altitude, weather, where to land in emergencies. It came out that the Navy had
rescue craft, known as Dumbos and Superdumbos, stationed at various strategic
points in the vicinity of the targets, ready to rescue the fliers in case they were
forced to bail out.

The briefing period ended with a moving prayer by the chaplain. We then 8
proceeded to the mess hall for the traditional early-morning breakfast before
departure on a bombing mission.

A convoy of trucks took us to the supply building for the special equipment 9
carried on combat missions. This included the Mae West,[1] a parachute, a
lifeboat, an oxygen mask, a flak suit, and a survival vest. We still had a few
hours before take-off time, but we all went to the flying field and stood around
in little groups or sat in jeeps talking rather casually about our mission to the
Empire, as the Japanese home islands are known hereabouts.

In command of our mission is Major Charles W. Sweeney, twenty-five, of 10
124 Hamilton Avenue, North Quincy, Massachusetts. His flagship, carrying
the atomic bomb, is named *The Great Artiste,* but the name does not appear
on the body of the great silver ship, with its unusually long, four-bladed, orange-
tipped propellers. Instead, it carries the number 77, and someone remarks that
it was "Red" Grange's winning number on the gridiron.

We took off at 3:50 this morning and headed northwest on a straight line for 11
the Empire. The night was cloudy and threatening, with only a few stars here
and there breaking through the overcast. The weather report had predicted
storms ahead part of the way but clear sailing for the final and climactic stages
of our odyssey.

We were about an hour away from our base when the storm broke. Our 12
great ship took some heavy dips through the abysmal darkness around us, but
it took these dips much more gracefully than a large commercial air liner,
producing a sensation more in the nature of a glide than a "bump," like a great
ocean liner riding the waves except that in this case the air waves were much
higher and the rhythmic tempo of the glide was much faster.

---

[1] Mae West: an inflatable life jacket named for the actor. [Eds.]

I noticed a strange eerie light coming through the window high above the 13
navigator's cabin, and as I peered through the dark all around us I saw a startling
phenomenon. The whirling giant propellers had somehow become great luminous disks of blue flame. The same luminous blue flame appeared on the
plexiglas windows in the nose of the ship, and on the tips of the giant wings.
It looked as though we were riding the whirlwind through space on a chariot
of blue fire.

It was, I surmised, a surcharge of static electricity that had accumulated on 14
the tips of the propellers and on the di-electric material of the plastic windows.
One's thoughts dwelt anxiously on the precious cargo in the invisible ship ahead
of us. Was there any likelihood of danger that this heavy electric tension in the
atmosphere all about us might set it off?

I expressed my fears to Captain Bock, who seems nonchalant and unper- 15
turbed at the controls. He quickly reassured me.

"It is a familiar phenomenon seen often on ships. I have seen it many times 16
on bombing missions. It is known as St. Elmo's fire."

On we went through the night. We soon rode out the storm and our ship 17
was once again sailing on a smooth courses straight ahead, on a direct line to
the Empire.

Our altimeter showed that we were traveling through space at a height of 18
seventeen thousand feet. The thermometer registered an outside temperature of
thirty-three degrees below zero Centigrade, about thirty below Fahrenheit.
Inside our pressurized cabin the temperature was that of a comfortable air-
conditioned room and a pressure corresponding to an altitude of eight thousand
feet. Captain Bock cautioned me, however, to keep my oxygen mask handy in
case of emergency. This, he explained, might mean either something going
wrong with the pressure equipment inside the ship or a hole through the cabin
by flak.

The first signs of dawn came shortly after five o'clock. Sergeant Curry, of 19
Hoopeston, Illinois, who had been listening steadily on his earphones for radio
reports, while maintaining a strict radio silence himself, greeted it by rising to
his feet and gazing out the window.

"It's good to see the day," he told me. "I get a feeling of claustrophobia 20
hemmed in this cabin at night."

He is a typical American youth, looking even younger than his twenty years. 21
It takes no mind reader to read his thoughts.

"It's a long way from Hoopeston," I find myself remarking. 22

"Yep," he replies, as he busies himself decoding a message from outer space. 23

"Think this atomic bomb will end the war?" he asks hopefully. 24

"There is a very good chance that this one may do the trick," I assured him, 25
"but if not, then the next one or two surely will. Its power is such that no
nation can stand up against it very long." This was not my own view. I had
heard it expressed all around a few hours earlier, before we took off. To anyone

who had seen this manmade fireball in action, as I had less than a month ago in the desert of New Mexico, this view did not sound overoptimistic.

By 5:50 it was really light outside. We had lost our lead ship, but Lieutenant   26
Godfrey, our navigator, informs me that we had arranged for that contingency. We have an assembly point in the sky above the little island of Yakushima, southeast of Kyushu, at 9:10. We are to circle there and wait for the rest of our formation.

Our genial bombardier, Lieutenant Levy, comes over to invite me to take   27
his front-row seat in the transparent nose of the ship, and I accept eagerly. From that vantage point in space, seventeen thousand feet above the Pacific, one gets a view of hundreds of miles on all sides, horizontally and vertically. At that height the vast ocean below and the sky above seem to merge into one great sphere.

I was on the inside of that firmament, riding above the giant mountains of   28
white cumulus clouds, letting myself be suspended in infinite space. One hears the whirl of the motors behind one, but it soon becomes insignificant against the immensity all around and is before long swallowed by it. There comes a point where space also swallows time and one lives through eternal moments filled with an oppressive loneliness, as though all life had suddenly vanished from the earth and you are the only one left, a lone survivor traveling endlessly through interplanetary space.

My mind soon returns to the mission I am on. Somewhere beyond these   29
vast mountains of white clouds ahead of me there lies Japan, the land of our enemy. In about four hours from now one of its cities, making weapons of war for use against us, will be wiped off the map by the greatest weapon ever made by man: In one tenth of a millionth of a second, a fraction of time immeasurable by any clock, a whirlwind from the skies will pulverize thousands of its buildings and tens of thousands of its inhabitants.

But at this moment no one yet knows which one of the several cities chosen   30
as targets is to be annihilated. The final choice lies with destiny. The winds over Japan will make the decision. If they carry heavy clouds over our primary target, the city will be saved, at least for the time being. None of its inhabitants will ever know that the wind of a benevolent destiny had passed over their heads. But that same wind will doom another city.

Our weather planes ahead of us are on their way to find out where the wind   31
blows. Half an hour before target time we will know what the winds have decided.

Does one feel any pity or compassion for the poor devils about to die? Not   32
when one thinks of Pearl Harbor and of the Death March on Bataan.[2]

2 Pearl Harbor: on December 7, 1941, a surprise bombing attack by the Japanese on this United States naval base in Hawaii caused the death of 1,177 people and prompted the United States to enter World War II; the Death March on Bataan: physically weakened American and Filipino

Captain Bock informs me that we are about to start our climb to bombing 33
altitude.

He manipulates a few knobs on his control panel to the right of him, and I 34
alternately watch the white clouds and ocean below me and the altimeter on
the bombardier's panel. We reached our altitude at nine o'clock. We were then
over Japanese waters, close to their mainland. Lieutenant Godfrey motioned to
me to look through his radar scope. Before me was the outline of our assembly
point. We shall soon meet our lead ship and proceed to the final stage of our
journey.

We reached Yakushima at 9:12 and there, about four thousand feet ahead 35
of us, was *The Great Artiste* with its precious load. I saw Lieutenant Godfrey
and Sergeant Curry strap on their parachutes and I decided to do likewise.

We started circling. We saw little towns on the coastline, heedless of our 36
presence. We kept on circling, waiting for the third ship in our formation.

It was 9:56 when we began heading for the coastline. Our weather scouts 37
had sent us code messages, deciphered by Sergeant Curry, informing us that
both the primary target as well as the secondary were clearly visible.

The winds of destiny seemed to favor certain Japanese cities that must remain 38
nameless. We circled about them again and again and found no opening in
the thick umbrella of clouds that covered them. Destiny chose Nagasaki as the
ultimate target.

We had been circling for some time when we noticed black puffs of smoke 39
coming through the white clouds directly at us. There were fifteen bursts of
flak in rapid succession, all too low. Captain Bock changed his course. There
soon followed eight more bursts of flak, right up to our altitude, but by this
time were too far to the left.

We flew southward down the channel and at 11:33 crossed the coastline and 40
headed straight for Nagasaki, about one hundred miles to the west. Here again
we circled until we found an opening in the clouds. It was 12:01 and the goal
of our mission had arrived.

We heard the prearranged signal on our radio, put on our arc welder's 41
glasses, and watched tensely the maneuverings of the strike ship about half a
mile in front of us.

"There she goes!" someone said. 42

Out of the belly of *The Great Artiste* what looked like a black object went 43
downward.

Captain Bock swung to get out of range; but even though we were turning 44
away in the opposite direction, and despite the fact that it was broad daylight
in our cabin, all of us became aware of a giant flash that broke through the
dark barrier of our arc welder's lenses and flooded our cabin with intense light.

defenders of the Bataan peninsula were forced by their Japanese captors to march ninety miles
under brutal conditions to a prisoner of war camp in Manila. Many did not survive. [Eds.]

We removed our glasses after the first flash, but the light still lingered on, a 45
bluish-green light that illuminated the entire sky all around. A tremendous blast
wave struck our ship and made it tremble from nose to tail. This was followed
by four more blasts in rapid succession, each resounding like the boom of
cannon fire hitting our plane from all directions.

Observers in the tail of our ship saw a giant ball of fire rise as though from 46
the bowels of the earth, belching forth enormous white smoke rings. Next they
saw a giant pillar of purple fire, ten thousand feet high, shooting skyward with
enormous speed.

By the time our ship had made another turn in the direction of the atomic 47
explosion the pillar of purple fire had reached the level of our altitude. Only
about forty-five seconds had passed. Awe-struck, we watched it shoot upward
like a meteor coming from the earth instead of from outer space, becoming
ever more alive as it climbed skyward through the white clouds. It was no
longer smoke, or dust, or even a cloud of fire. It was a living thing, a new
species of being, born right before our incredulous eyes.

At one stage of its evolution, covering millions of years in terms of seconds, 48
the entity assumed the form of a giant square totem pole, with its base about
three miles long, tapering off to about a mile at the top. Its bottom was brown,
its center was amber, its top white. But it was a living totem pole, carved with
many grotesque masks grimacing at the earth.

Then, just when it appeared as though the thing had settled down into a 49
state of permanence, there came shooting out of the top a giant mushroom that
increased the height of the pillar to a total of forty-five thousand feet. The
mushroom top was even more alive than the pillar, seething and boiling in a
white fury of creamy foam, sizzling upward and then descending earthward, a
thousand Old Faithful geysers rolled into one.

It kept struggling in an elemental fury, like a creature in the act of breaking 50
the bonds that held it down. In a few seconds it had freed itself from its gigantic
stem and floated upward with tremendous speed, its momentum carrying it into
the stratosphere to a height of about sixty thousand feet.

But no sooner did this happen when another mushroom, smaller in size 51
than the first one, began emerging out of the pillar. It was as though the
decapitated monster was growing a new head.

As the first mushroom floated off into the blue it changed its shape into a 52
flowerlike form, its giant petals curving downward, creamy white outside, rose-
colored inside. It still retained that shape when we last gazed at it from a
distance of about two hundred miles. The boiling pillar of many colors could
also be seen at that distance, a giant mountain of jumbled rainbows, in travail.
Much living substance had gone into those rainbows. The quivering top of the
pillar was protruding to a great height through the white clouds, giving the
appearance of a monstrous prehistoric creature with a ruff around its neck, a
fleecy ruff extending in all directions, as far as the eye could see.

215

QUESTIONS

1. What do we learn about the crew members on *The Great Artiste*? Why has Laurence bothered to tell us about them?

2. Laurence's description of the bomb as "a thing of beauty" (paragraph 4) suggests that this eyewitness report is not wholly objective. What is Laurence's moral stance on this mission?

3. Consider Laurence's arrangement of time in his narrative. What effect do you think he wishes to create by switching back and forth between past and present tense?

4. Consider Laurence's description of the blast and its resulting cloud (paragraphs 44 through 52). His challenge as a writer is to help his readers to see this strange and awesome thing. What familiar images does he use to represent this unfamiliar sight? What do those images say—especially the last one—about Laurence's feelings as he watched the cloud transform itself?

5. Write an eyewitness report on an event that you consider important. Present the preparations or actions leading up to the event, and include information about others involved. What imagery can you use to describe the glorious, funny, or chaotic event itself?

6. For a report on the basis for Laurence's attitude toward the bombings of Hiroshima and Nagasaki, look at as many newspapers as you can for August 6 through 10 in 1945. Be sure to look at the editorial pages as well as the front pages. If possible, you might also interview relatives and friends who are old enough to remember the war or who might have fought in it. What attitudes toward the bomb and its use were expressed then? How do these compare or contrast with Laurence's attitude?

MAKING CONNECTIONS

1. Describe the differences in point of view taken toward this cataclysmic event by Laurence, John Hersey, and Zoë Tracy Hardy. How does each writer respond to this unparalleled story? Which responses do you find most unusual, most believable, most sympathetic? Why?

2. Imagine a meeting today between Laurence and Hatsuyo Nakamura. What might they say to one another? How might Laurence reflect today on his feelings forty years ago? Imagine this meeting and write a report of it. Or, if you prefer, substitute Zoë Tracy Hardy for Hatsuyo Nakamura.

A DAY IN SAMOA
Margaret Mead

Margaret Mead (1901–1978) was a cultural anthropologist for almost sixty years. She is the author of many books and articles in the field and is especially known for her studies of the South Sea Islanders. Coming of Age in Samoa *(1928) was her first book, based on her first field trip as a working anthropologist. The essay reprinted here is chapter 2 from that book, which is a study of adolescent girls in Samoa. In the introduction to the fifth edition of the book in 1973, Mead wrote, "The little girls whom I studied are buxom grandmothers, still dancing light-footed as Samoan matrons do. . . . And I, instead of being a dutiful granddaughter writing letters home . . . am now a grandmother delighting in a dancing grandchild."*

The life of the day begins at dawn, or if the moon has shown until daylight, the shouts of the young men may be heard before dawn from the hillside. Uneasy in the night, populous with ghosts, they shout lustily to one another as they hasten with their work. As the dawn begins to fall among the soft brown roofs and the slender palm trees stand out against the colourless, gleaming sea, lovers slip home from trysts beneath the palm trees or in the shadow of beached canoes, that the light may find each sleeper in his appointed place. Cocks crow, negligently, and a shrill-voiced bird cries from the breadfruit trees. The insistent roar of the reef seems muted to an undertone for the sounds of a waking village. Babies cry, a few short wails before sleepy mothers give them the breast. Restless little children roll out of their sheets and wander drowsily down to the beach to freshen their faces in the sea. Boys, bent upon an early fishing, start collecting their tackle and go to rouse their more laggard companions. Fires are lit, here and there, the white smoke hardly visible against the paleness of the dawn. The whole village, sheeted and frowsy, stirs, rubs its eyes, and stumbles towards the beach. "Talofa!" "Talofa!" "Will the journey start to-day?" "Is it bonito fishing your lordship is going?" Girls stop to giggle over some young ne'er-do-well who escaped during the night from an angry father's pursuit and to venture a shrewd guess that the daughter knew more about his presence than she told. The boy who is taunted by another, who has succeeded him in his sweetheart's favour, grapples with his rival, his foot slipping in the wet sand. From the other end of the village comes a long drawn-out, piercing wail. A messenger has just brought word of the death of some relative in another village. Half-clad, un-

217

hurried women, with babies at their breasts, or astride their hips, pause in their tale of Losa's outraged departure from her father's house to the greater kindness in the home of her uncle, to wonder who is dead. Poor relatives whisper their requests to rich relatives, men make plans to set a fish trap together, a woman begs a bit of yellow dye from a kinswoman, and through the village sounds the rhythmic tattoo which calls the young men together. They gather from all parts of the village, digging sticks in hand, ready to start inland to the plantation. The older men set off upon their more lonely occupations, and each household, reassembled under its peaked roof, settles down to the routine of the morning. Little children, too hungry to wait for the late breakfast, beg lumps of cold taro which they munch greedily. Women carry piles of washing to the sea or to the spring at the far end of the village, or set off inland after weaving materials. The older girls go fishing on the reef, or perhaps set themselves to weaving a new set of Venetian blinds.

In the houses, where the pebbly floors have been swept bare with a stiff long- 2 handled broom, the women great with child and the nursing mothers, sit and gossip with one another. Old men sit apart, unceasingly twisting palm husk on their bare thighs and muttering old tales under their breath. The carpenters begin work on the new house, while the owner bustles about trying to keep them in good humour. Families who will cook to-day are hard at work; the taro, yams and bananas have already been brought from inland; the children are scuttling back and forth, fetching sea water, or leaves to stuff the pig. As the sun rises higher in the sky, the shadows deepen under the thatched roofs, the sand is burning to the touch, the hibiscus flowers wilt on the hedges, and little children bid the smaller ones, "Come out of the sun." Those whose excursions have been short return to the village, the women with strings of crimson jelly fish, or baskets of shell fish, the men with cocoanuts, carried in baskets slung on a shoulder pole. The women and children eat their breakfasts, just hot from the oven, if this is cook day, and the young men work swiftly in the midday heat, preparing the noon feast for their elders.

It is high noon. The sand burns the feet of the little children, who leave 3 their palm leaf balls and their pin-wheels of frangipani blossoms to wither in the sun, as they creep into the shade of the houses. The women who must go abroad carry great banana leaves as sun-shades or wind wet cloths about their heads. Lowering a few blinds against the slanting sun, all who are left in the village wrap their heads in sheets and go to sleep. Only a few adventurous children may slip away for a swim in the shadow of a high rock, some industrious woman continues with her weaving, or a close little group of women bend anxiously over a woman in labour. The village is dazzling and dead; any sound seems oddly loud and out of place. Words have to cut through the solid heat slowly. And then the sun gradually sinks over the sea.

A second time, the sleeping people stir, roused perhaps by the cry of "a 4 boat," resounding through the village. The fishermen beach their canoes, weary and spent from the heat, in spite of the slaked lime on their heads, with which they have sought to cool their brains and redden their hair. The brightly coloured fishes are spread out on the floor, or piled in front of the houses until the women pour water over them to free them from taboo. Regretfully, the young fishermen separate out the "Taboo fish," which must be sent to the chief, or proudly they pack the little palm leaf baskets with offerings of fish to take to their sweethearts. Men come home from the bush, grimy and heavy laden, shouting as they come, greeted in a sonorous rising cadence by those who have remained at home. They gather in the guest house for their evening kava drinking. The soft clapping of hands, the high-pitched intoning of the talking chief who serves the kava echoes through the village. Girls gather flowers to weave into necklaces; children, lusty from their naps and bound to no particular task, play circular games in the half shade of the late afternoon. Finally the sun sets, in a flame which stretches from the mountain behind to the horizon on the sea, the last bather comes up from the beach, children straggle home, dark little figures etched against the sky; lights shine in the houses, and each household gathers for its evening meal. The suitor humbly presents his offering, the children have been summoned from their noisy play, perhaps there is an honoured guest who must be served first, after the soft, barbaric singing of Christian hymns and the brief and graceful evening prayer. In front of a house at the end of the village, a father cries out the birth of a son. In some family circles a face is missing, in others little runaways have found a haven! Again quiet settles upon the village, as first the head of the household, then the women and children, and last of all the patient boys, eat their supper.

After supper the old people and the little children are bundled off to bed. If the young people have guests the front of the house is yielded to them. For day is the time for the councils of old men and the labours of youth, and night is the time for lighter things. Two kinsmen, or a chief and his councillor, sit and gossip over the day's events or make plans for the morrow. Outside a crier goes through the village announcing that the communal breadfruit pit will be opened in the morning, or that the village will make a great fish trap. If it is moonlight, groups of young men, women by twos and threes, wander through the village, and crowds of children hunt for land crabs or chase each other among the breadfruit trees. Half the village may go fishing by torchlight and the curving reef will gleam with wavering lights and echo with shouts of triumph or disappointment, teasing words or smothered cries of outraged modesty. Or a group of youths may dance for the pleasure of some visiting maiden. Many of those who have retired to sleep, drawn by the merry music, will wrap their sheets about them and set out to find the dancing. A white-clad, ghostly throng will gather in a circle about the gaily lit house, a circle from which every now and then a few will detach themselves and wander away among the trees. Sometimes sleep will not descend upon the village until long past midnight; then at last there is only the mellow thunder of the reef and the whisper of lovers, as the village rests until dawn.

QUESTIONS

1. Go through the essay, and note every word or phrase that indicates the time of day. When you have found them all, consider what they reveal about the way Mead has organized her material.

2. There are five paragraphs in this essay. How has Mead used the paragraph in shaping her material? That is, what principle or method of selection has determined what should go in each of the five paragraphs?

3. Is this a report of a specific day or a representation of a typical day? Can you find places where Mead seems to be reporting a particular event? Can you also find places where she is clearly speaking of various events that *might* happen on a typical day? How and why does she mix these two modes of writing?

4. Does this essay have an evaluative dimension? Is Samoan life presented neutrally? Is it made especially attractive or unattractive at any points? Consider specific events or episodes.

5. How does Mead achieve the representational quality of this essay? That is, how does she attempt to make the Samoan day available to us as a sensory experience? How does she convey the "feel" of it?

6. Write an essay in which you represent for the reader "A Day in ———." Study Mead's way of selecting details and organizing them as you plan and compose your own essay on a day in a place you know well.

MAKING CONNECTIONS

1. Many of the essays in "Reporting" are written by firsthand observers who reveal their own roles as reporters. Select three of these observers and write an essay about how the role each chooses to play affects the report finally written. Choose your observers from among Annie Dillard, Ernest Hemingway, William L. Laurence, Farley Mowat, Jane van Lawick-Goodall, Roy C. Selby, Jr., Richard Selzer, and of course Margaret Mead.

2. Compare Mead's essay to Barbara Tuchman's account of the black death. Each tries to give an overall picture of a time and place. Which element—time or space—predominates in each essay? Compare these two essays by considering how one element or the other becomes an organizing principle for the essay.

OBSERVING WOLVES
Farley Mowat

Farley Mowat was born in Ontario, Canada, in 1921 and finished college at the University of Toronto in 1949, after wartime service and two years living in the Arctic. He makes his living as a writer rather than a scientist, but he works in the same areas covered by anthropologists and zoologists. Often he writes more as a partisan of primitive people and animals rather than as an "objective" scientist, and his work has reached a wide audience. He has written engagingly about the strange animals he grew up with in Owls in the Family *(1963) and about wolves in* Never Cry Wolf *(1963), from which the following selection is taken.*

During the next several weeks I put my decision into effect with the thoroughness for which I have always been noted. I went completely to the wolves. To begin with I set up a den of my own as near to the wolves as I could conveniently get without disturbing the even tenor of their lives too much. After all, I *was* a stranger, and an unwolflike one, so I did not feel I should go too far too fast. 1

Abandoning Mike's cabin (with considerable relief, since as the days warmed up so did the smell) I took a tiny tent and set it up on the shore of the bay immediately opposite to the den esker.[1] I kept my camping gear to the barest minimum—a small primus stove, a stew pot, a teakettle, and a sleeping bag were the essentials. I took no weapons of any kind, although there were times when I regretted this omission, even if only fleetingly. The big telescope was set up in the mouth of the tent in such a way that I could observe the den by day or night without even getting out of my sleeping bag. 2

During the first few days of my sojourn with the wolves I stayed inside the tent except for brief and necessary visits to the out-of-doors which I always undertook when the wolves were not in sight. The point of this personal concealment was to allow the animals to get used to the tent and to accept it as only another bump on a very bumpy piece of terrain. Later, when the mosquito population reached full flowering, I stayed in the tent practically all of the time unless there was a strong wind blowing, for the most bloodthirsty beasts in the Arctic are not wolves, but the insatiable mosquitoes. 3

My precautions against disturbing the wolves were superfluous. It had re- 4

---

[1] esker: a long, narrow deposit of gravel and sand left by a stream flowing from a glacier. [Eds.]

quired a week for me to get their measure, but they must have taken mine at our first meeting; and, while there was nothing overtly disdainful in their evident assessment of me, they managed to ignore my presence, and indeed my very existence, with a thoroughness which was somehow disconcerting.

Quite by accident I had pitched my tent within ten yards of one of the major paths used by the wolves when they were going to, or coming from, their hunting grounds to the westward; and only a few hours after I had taken up residence one of the wolves came back from a trip and discovered me and my tent. He was at the end of a hard night's work and was clearly tired and anxious to go home to bed. He came over a small rise fifty yards from me with his head down, his eyes half-closed, and a preoccupied air about him. Far from being the preternaturally alert and suspicious beast of fiction, this wolf was so self-engrossed that he came straight on to within fifteen yards of me, and might have gone right past the tent without seeing it at all, had I not banged my elbow against the teakettle, making a resounding clank. The wolf's head came up and his eyes opened wide, but he did not stop or falter in his pace. One brief, sidelong glance was all he vouchsafed to me as he continued on his way.

It was true that I wanted to be inconspicuous, but I felt uncomfortable at being so totally ignored. Nevertheless, during the two weeks which followed, one or more wolves used the track past my tent almost every night—and never, except on one memorable occasion, did they evince the slightest interest in me.

By the time this happened I had learned a good deal about my wolfish neighbors, and one of the facts which had emerged was that they were not nomadic roamers, as is almost universally believed, but were settled beasts and the possessors of a large permanent estate with very definite boundaries.

The territory owned by my wolf family comprised more than a hundred square miles, bounded on one side by a river but otherwise not delimited by geographical features. Nevertheless there *were* boundaries, clearly indicated in wolfish fashion.

Anyone who has observed a dog doing his neighborhood rounds and leaving his personal mark on each convenient post will have already guessed how the wolves marked out *their* property. Once a week, more or less, the clan made the rounds of the family lands and freshened up the boundary markers—a sort of lupine beating of the bounds. This careful attention to property rights was perhaps made necessary by the presence of two other wolf families whose lands abutted on ours, although I never discovered any evidence of bickering or disagreements between the owners of the various adjoining estates. I suspect, therefore, that it was more of a ritual activity.

In any event, once I had become aware of the strong feeling of property rights which existed amongst the wolves, I decided to use this knowledge to make them at least recognize my existence. One evening, after they had gone off for their regular nightly hunt, I staked out a property claim of my own, embracing perhaps three acres, with the tent at the middle, and *including a hundred-yard long section of the wolves' path.*

Staking the land turned out to be rather more difficult than I had anticipated. In order to ensure that my claim would not be overlooked, I felt obliged to make a property mark on stones, clumps of moss, and patches of vegetation at intervals of not more than fifteen feet around the circumference of my claim. This took most of the night and required frequent returns to the tent to consume copious quantities of tea; but before dawn brought the hunters home the task was done, and I retired, somewhat exhausted, to observe results.   11

I had not long to wait. At 0814 hours, according to my wolf log, the leading male of the clan appeared over the ridge behind me, padding homeward with his usual air of preoccupation. As usual he did not deign to glance at the tent; but when he reached the point where my property line intersected the trail, he stopped as abruptly as if he had run into an invisible wall. He was only fifty yards from me and with my binoculars I could see his expression very clearly.   12

His attitude of fatigue vanished and was replaced by a look of bewilderment. Cautiously he extended his nose and sniffed at one of my marked bushes. He did not seem to know what to make of it or what to do about it. After a minute of complete indecision he backed away a few yards and sat down. And then, finally, he looked directly at the tent and at me. It was a long, thoughtful, considering sort of look.   13

Having achieved my object—that of forcing at least one of the wolves to take cognizance of my existence—I now began to wonder if, in my ignorance, I had transgressed some unknown wolf law of major importance and would have to pay for my temerity. I found myself regretting the absence of a weapon as the look I was getting became longer, yet more thoughtful, and still more intent.   14

I began to grow decidedly fidgety, for I dislike staring matches, and in this particular case I was up against a master, whose yellow glare seemed to become more baleful as I attempted to stare him down.   15

The situation was becoming intolerable. In an effort to break the impasse I loudly cleared my throat and turned my back on the wolf (for a tenth of a second) to indicate as clearly as possible that I found his continued scrutiny impolite, if not actually offensive.   16

He appeared to take the hint. Getting to his feet he had another sniff at my marker, and then he seemed to make up his mind. Briskly, and with an air of decision, he turned his attention away from me and began a systematic tour of the area I had staked out as my own. As he came to each boundary marker he sniffed it once or twice, then carefully placed *his* mark on the outside of each clump of grass or stone. As I watched I saw where I, in my ignorance, had erred. He made his mark with such economy that he was able to complete the entire circuit without having to reload once, or, to change the simile slightly, he did it all on one tank of fuel.   17

The task completed—and it had taken him no longer than fifteen minutes—   18

223

he rejoined the path at the point where it left my property and trotted off towards his home—leaving me with a good deal to occupy my thoughts.

QUESTIONS

1. What did you know about wolves before reading this piece? What was the most surprising—or amusing—information you acquired from reading about Mowat's experience?

2. Write a paragraph summarizing the information about wolves that you can infer from this selection.

3. How would you describe the narrator of this piece? What does he tell us about himself, and how do his actions describe him?

4. Mowat concludes by saying that he was left "with a good deal to occupy my thoughts" (paragraph 18). What, do you suppose, were these thoughts?

5. Find a more objective, "scientific" account of wolves. Which of Mowat's observations are substantiated there?

6. Rewrite the main events in this piece from the wolf's point of view.

7. Observe the actions of a dog or a cat as it roams your neighborhood. Write an objective report of the animal's actions. Conclude with your reactions to the animal's behavior and, if pertinent, the animal's reactions to your behavior.

MAKING CONNECTIONS

1. Several of the essays in this section deal with the intricacies of placing humans in relation to specific animals and not only observing but sometimes interfering with their lives. Consider the essays by Virginia Woolf, Jane van Lawick-Goodall, and Loren Eiseley as well as this one by Mowat. Then, choosing two essays, compare the degrees of intervention taken by the writers and how that intervention affects the stories they tell.

2. Compare and contrast the similarities and differences in procedure of Mowat's study of wolves and Annie Dillard's study of fundamentalists.

FIRST OBSERVATIONS
Jane van Lawick-Goodall

Jane van Lawick-Goodall (b. 1934), British student of animal behavior, began her work as an assistant to Louis Leakey, an anthropologist and paleontologist who has studied human origins. In 1960, with his help, she settled in Tanzania, East Africa, in the Gombe Stream Game Reserve to investigate the behavior of chimpanzees in their natural habitat. Her discoveries have been widely published in professional journals and in a number of books for more general audiences. The selection reprinted here is taken from In the Shadow of Man *(1971), a popular work in which she is careful to report her own behavior as well as that of her chimpanzee subjects.*

For about a month I spent most of each day either on the Peak or overlooking Mlinda Valley where the chimps, before or after stuffing themselves with figs, ate large quantities of small purple fruits that tasted, like so many of their foods, as bitter and astringent as sloes or crab apples. Piece by piece, I began to form my first somewhat crude picture of chimpanzee life.

The impression that I had gained when I watched the chimps at the msulula tree of temporary, constantly changing associations of individuals within the community was substantiated. Most often I saw small groups of four to eight moving about together. Sometimes I saw one or two chimpanzees leave such a group and wander off on their own or join up with a different association. On other occasions I watched two or three small groups joining to form a larger one.

Often, as one group crossed the grassy ridge separating the Kasekela Valley from the fig trees on the home valley, the male chimpanzee, or chimpanzees, of the party would break into a run, sometimes moving in an upright position, sometimes dragging a fallen branch, sometimes stamping or slapping the hard earth. These charging displays were always accompanied by loud pant-hoots and afterward the chimpanzee frequently would swing up into a tree overlooking the valley he was about to enter and sit quietly, peering down and obviously listening for a response from below. If there were chimps feeding in the fig trees they nearly always hooted back, as though in answer. Then the new arrivals would hurry down the steep slope and, with more calling and screaming, the two groups would meet in the fig trees. When groups of females and youngsters with no males present joined other feeding chimpanzees, usually there was none of this excitement; the newcomers merely climbed up into the trees, greeted some of those already there, and began to stuff themselves with figs.

While many details of their social behavior were hidden from me by the foliage, I did get occasional fascinating glimpses. I saw one female, newly arrived in a group, hurry up to a big male and hold her hand toward him. Almost regally he reached out, clasped her hand in his, drew it toward him, and kissed it with his lips. I saw two adult males embrace each other in greeting. I saw youngsters having wild games through the treetops, chasing around after each other or jumping again and again, one after the other, from a branch to a springy bough below. I watched small infants dangling happily by themselves for minutes on end, patting at their toes with one hand, rotating gently from side to side. Once two tiny infants pulled on opposite ends of a twig in a gentle tug-of-war. Often, during the heat of midday or after a long spell of feeding, I saw two or more adults grooming each other, carefully looking through the hair of their companions.

At that time of year the chimps usually went to bed late, making their nests when it was too dark to see properly through binoculars, but sometimes they nested earlier and I could watch them from the Peak. I found that every individual, except for infants who slept with their mothers, made his own nest each night. Generally this took about three minutes: the chimp chose a firm foundation such as an upright fork or crotch, or two horizontal branches. Then he reached out and bent over smaller branches onto this foundation, keeping each one in place with his feet. Finally he tucked in the small leafy twigs growing around the rim of his nest and lay down. Quite often a chimp sat up after a few minutes and picked a handful of leafy twigs, which he put under his head or some other part of his body before settling down again for the night. One young female I watched went on and on bending down branches until she had constructed a huge mound of greenery on which she finally curled up.

I climbed up into some of the nests after the chimpanzees had left them. Most of them were built in trees that for me were almost impossible to climb. I found that there was quite complicated interweaving of the branches in some of them. I found, too, that the nests were fouled with dung; and later, when I was able to get closer to the chimps, I saw how they were always careful to defecate and urinate over the edge of their nests, even in the middle of the night.

During that month I really came to know the country well, for I often went on expeditions from the Peak, sometimes to examine nests, more frequently to collect specimens of the chimpanzees' food plants, which Bernard Verdcourt had kindly offered to identify for me. Soon I could find my way around the sheer ravines and up and down the steep slopes of three valleys—the home valley, the Pocket, and Mlinda Valley—as well as a taxi driver finds his way about in the main streets and byways of London. It is a period I remember vividly, not only because I was beginning to accomplish something at last, but also because of the delight I felt in being completely by myself. For those who love to be alone with nature I need add nothing further; for those who do not, no words of mine could ever convey, even in part, the almost mystical awareness of beauty and eternity that accompanies certain treasured moments. And, though the beauty was always there, those moments came upon me unaware: when I was watching the pale flush preceding dawn; or looking up through the rustling leaves of some giant forest tree into the greens and browns and black shadows that occasionally ensnared a bright fleck of the blue sky; or when I stood, as darkness fell, with one hand on the still-warm trunk of a tree and looked at the sparkling of an early moon on the never still, sighing water of the lake.

One day, when I was sitting by the trickle of water in Buffalo Wood, pausing 8
for a moment in the coolness before returning from a scramble in Mlinda Valley, I saw a female bushbuck moving slowly along the nearly dry streambed. Occasionally she paused to pick off some plant and crunch it. I kept absolutely still, and she was not aware of my presence until she was little more than ten yards away. Suddenly she tensed and stood staring at me, one small forefoot raised. Because I did not move, she did not know what I was—only that my outline was somehow strange. I saw her velvet nostrils dilate as she sniffed the air, but I was downwind and her nose gave her no answer. Slowly she came closer, and closer—one step at a time, her neck craned forward—always poised for instant flight. I can still scarcely believe that her nose actually touched my knee; yet if I close my eyes I can feel again, in imagination, the warmth of her breath and the silken impact of her skin. Unexpectedly I blinked and she was gone in a flash, bounding away with loud barks of alarm until the vegetation hid her completely from my view.

It was rather different when, as I was sitting on the Peak, I saw a leopard 9
coming toward me, his tail held up straight. He was at a slightly lower level than I, and obviously had no idea I was there. Ever since arrival in Africa I had had an ingrained, illogical fear of leopards. Already, while working at the Gombe, I had several times nearly turned back when, crawling through some thick undergrowth, I had suddenly smelled the rank smell of cat. I had forced myself on, telling myself that my fear was foolish, that only wounded leopards charged humans with savage ferocity.

On this occasion, though, the leopard went out of sight as it started to climb 10
up the hill—the hill on the peak of which I sat. I quickly hastened to climb a tree, but halfway there I realized that leopards can climb trees. So I uttered a sort of halfhearted squawk. The leopard, my logical mind told me, would be just as frightened of me if he knew I was there. Sure enough, there was a thudding of startled feet and then silence. I returned to the Peak, but the feeling of unseen eyes watching me was too much. I decided to watch for the chimps in Mlinda Valley. And, when I returned to the Peak several hours later, there, on the very rock which had been my seat, was a neat pile of leopard dung. He

must have watched me go and then, very carefully, examined the place where such a frightening creature had been and tried to exterminate my alien scent with his own.

As the weeks went by the chimpanzees became less and less afraid. Quite 11 often when I was on one of my food-collecting expeditions I came across chimpanzees unexpectedly, and after a time I found that some of them would tolerate my presence provided they were in fairly thick forest and I sat still and did not try to move closer than sixty to eighty yards. And so, during my second month of watching from the Peak, when I saw a group settle down to feed I sometimes moved closer and was thus able to make more detailed observations.

It was at this time that I began to recognize a number of different individuals. 12 As soon as I was sure of knowing a chimpanzee if I saw it again, I named it. Some scientists feel that animals should be labeled by numbers—that to name them is anthropomorphic—but I have always been interested in the *differences* between individuals, and a name is not only more individual than a number but also far easier to remember. Most names were simply those which, for some reason or other, seemed to suit the individuals to whom I attached them. A few chimps were named because some facial expression or mannerism reminded me of human acquaintances.

The easiest individual to recognize was old Mr. McGregor. The crown of 13 his head, his neck, and his shoulders were almost entirely devoid of hair, but a slight frill remained around his head rather like a monk's tonsure. He was an old male—perhaps between thirty and forty years of age (the longevity record of a captive chimp is forty-seven years). During the early months of my acquaintance with him, Mr. McGregor was somewhat belligerent. If I accidentally came across him at close quarters he would threaten me with an upward and backward jerk of his head and a shaking of branches before climbing down and vanishing from my sight. He reminded me, for some reason, of Beatrix Potter's old gardener in *The Tale of Peter Rabbit*.

Ancient Flo with her deformed, bulbous nose and ragged ears was equally 14 easy to recognize. Her youngest offspring at that time were two-year-old Fifi, who still rode everywhere on her mother's back, and her juvenile son, Figan, who was always to be seen wandering around with his mother and little sister. He was then about six years old; it was approximately a year before he would attain puberty. Flo often traveled with another old mother, Olly. Olly's long face was also distinctive; the fluff of hair on the back of her head—though no other feature—reminded me of my aunt, Olwen. Olly, like Flo, was accompanied by two children, a daughter younger than Fifi, and an adolescent son about a year older than Figan.

Then there was William, who, I am certain, must have been Olly's blood 15 brother. I never saw any special signs of friendship between them, but their faces were amazingly alike. They both had long upper lips that wobbled when they suddenly turned their heads. William had the added distinction of several thin, deeply etched scar marks running down his upper lip from his nose.

Two of the other chimpanzees I knew well by sight at that time were David Graybeard and Goliath. Like David and Goliath in the Bible, these two individuals were closely associated in my mind because they were very often together. Goliath, even in those days of his prime, was not a giant, but he had a splendid physique and the springy movements of an athlete. He probably weighed about one hundred pounds. David Graybeard was less afraid of me from the start than were any of the other chimps. I was always pleased when I picked out his handsome face and well-marked silvery beard in a chimpanzee group, for with David to calm the others, I had a better chance of approaching to observe them more closely.

Before the end of my trial period in the field I made two really exciting discoveries—discoveries that made the previous months of frustration well worth while. And for both of them I had David Graybeard to thank.

One day I arrived on the Peak and found a small group of chimps just below me in the upper branches of a thick tree. As I watched I saw that one of them was holding a pink-looking object from which he was from time to time pulling pieces with his teeth. There was a female and a youngster and they were both reaching out toward the male, their hands actually touching his mouth. Presently the female picked up a piece of the pink thing and put it to her mouth: it was at this moment that I realized the chimps were eating meat.

After each bite of meat the male picked off some leaves with his lips and chewed them with the flesh. Often, when he had chewed for several minutes on this leafy wad, he spat out the remains into the waiting hands of the female. Suddenly he dropped a small piece of meat, and like a flash the youngster swung after it to the ground. Even as he reached to pick it up the undergrowth exploded and an adult bushpig charged toward him. Screaming, the juvenile leaped back into the tree. The pig remained in the open, snorting and moving backward and forward. Soon I made out the shapes of three small striped piglets. Obviously the chimps were eating a baby pig. The size was right and later, when I realized that the male was David Graybeard, I moved closer and saw that he was indeed eating piglet.

For three hours I watched the chimps feeding. David occasionally let the female bite pieces from the carcass and once he actually detached a small piece of flesh and placed it in her outstretched hand. When he finally climbed down there was still meat left on the carcass; he carried it away in one hand, followed by the others.

Of course I was not sure, then, that David Graybeard had caught the pig for himself, but even so, it was tremendously exciting to know that these chimpanzees actually ate meat. Previously scientists had believed that although these apes might occasionally supplement their diet with a few insects or small rodents and the like they were primarily vegetarians and fruit eaters. No one had suspected that they might hunt larger mammals.

It was within two weeks of this observation that I saw something that excited 22 me even more. By then it was October and the short rains had begun. The blackened slopes were softened by feathery new grass shoots and in some places the ground was carpeted by a variety of flowers. The Chimpanzees' Spring, I called it. I had had a frustrating morning, tramping up and down three valleys with never a sign or sound of a chimpanzee. Hauling myself up the steep slope of Mlinda Valley I headed for the Peak, not only weary but soaking wet from crawling through dense undergrowth. Suddenly I stopped, for I saw a slight movement in the long grass about sixty yards away. Quickly focusing my binoculars I saw that it was a single chimpanzee, and just then he turned in my direction. I recognized David Graybeard.

Cautiously I moved around so that I could see what he was doing. He was 23 squatting beside the red earth mound of a termite nest, and as I watched I saw him carefully push a long grass stem down into a hole in the mound. After a moment he withdrew it and picked something from the end with his mouth. I was too far away to make out what he was eating, but it was obvious that he was actually using a grass stem as a tool.

I knew that on two occasions casual observers in West Africa had seen 24 chimpanzees using objects as tools: one had broken open palm-nut kernels by using a rock as a hammer, and a group of chimps had been observed pushing sticks into an underground bees' nest and licking off the honey. Somehow I had never dreamed of seeing anything so exciting myself.

For an hour David feasted at the termite mound and then he wandered 25 slowly away. When I was sure he had gone I went over to examine the mound. I found a few crushed insects strewn about, and a swarm of worker termites sealing the entrances of the nest passages into which David had obviously been poking his stems. I picked up one of his discarded tools and carefully pushed it into a hole myself. Immediately I felt the pull of several termites as they seized the grass, and when I pulled it out there were a number of worker termites and a few soldiers, with big red heads, clinging on with their mandibles. There they remained, sticking out at right angles to the stem with their legs waving in the air.

Before I left I trampled down some of the tall dry grass and constructed a 26 rough hide—just a few palm fonds leaned up against the low branch of a tree and tied together at the top. I planned to wait there the next day. But it was another week before I was able to watch a chimpanzee "fishing" for termites again. Twice chimps arrived, but each time they saw me and moved off immediately. Once a swarm of fertile winged termites—the princes and princesses, as they are called—flew off on their nuptial flight, their huge white wings fluttering frantically as they carried the insects higher and higher. Later I realized that it is at this time of year, during the short rains, when the worker termites extend the passages of the nest to the surface, preparing for these emigrations. Several such swarms emerge between October and January. It is principally during these months that the chimpanzees feed on termites.

On the eighth day of my watch David Graybeard arrived again, together   27
with Goliath, and the pair worked there for two hours. I could see much better: I observed how they scratched open the sealed-over passage entrances with a thumb or forefinger. I watched how they bit the end off their tools when they became bent, or used the other end, or discarded them in favor of new ones. Goliath once moved at least fifteen yards from the heap to select a firm-looking piece of vine, and both males often picked three or four stems while they were collecting tools, and put the spares beside them on the ground until they wanted them.

Most exciting of all, on several occasions they picked small leafy twigs and   28
prepared them for use by stripping off the leaves. This was the first recorded example of a wild animal not merely *using* an object as a tool, but actually modifying an object and thus showing the crude beginnings of tool*making*.

Previously man had been regarded as the only tool-making animal. Indeed,   29
one of the clauses commonly accepted in the definition of man was that he was a creature who "made tools to a regular and set pattern." The chimpanzees, obviously, had not made tools to any set pattern. Nevertheless, my early observations of their primitive toolmaking abilities convinced a number of scientists that it was necessary to redefine man in a more complex manner than before. Or else, as Louis Leakey put it, we should by definition have to accept the chimpanzee as Man.

QUESTIONS

1. This essay is an example, principally, of reporting; that is, it is a gathering of facts by a clearheaded, unbiased observer. Identify passages in the essay in which this kind of reporting clearly takes place.

2. Although van Lawick-Goodall, in the main, is a neutral observer of chimpanzee behavior, that neutrality is in fact impossible in any absolute sense. It is clear that she writes, for example, with an eye always on comparisons of chimpanzee and human behavior. Make a list of words, just from paragraphs 3 and 4, that reveal that particular bias.

3. Describe how van Lawick-Goodall's comparison of chimpanzee with human behavior becomes increasingly prominent in the course of her essay.

4. Paraphrase the last discovery van Lawick-Goodall reports toward the end of her essay. What, exactly, was her contribution to science in this instance? What other activities, described earlier in the piece, make that discovery understandable, perhaps even unsurprising once we come to it?

5. What do you make of the choice outlined in paragraph 29? Which choice do you suppose the scientists made? Why?

6. Van Lawick-Goodall's scientific work resembles that of an anthropologist in that she goes into the field to observe the behavior of another social group. Even from this short piece we can learn a good deal about the practices and the way of life of such a worker in the field. Describe van Lawick-Goodall's life in the field as best you can, making whatever inferences you can from this single essay.

7. Amplify your description of van Lawick-Goodall's life in the field, done for question 6, by reading whatever articles you can find that tell more about her and about her work.

8. Place yourself somewhere and observe behavior more or less as van Lawick-Goodall does. You might observe wildlife—pigeons, sparrows, crows, squirrels, or whatever is available—or you might observe some aspect of human behavior. If you choose the latter, look for behavior that is unfamiliar to you, such as that of children at play, of workers on the job, or of persons in a social group very different from your own. Write a report detailing your observations.

9. After you have completed question 8, write a second, shorter report in which you comment on the nature of your task as an observer. Was it difficult to watch? Was it difficult to decide what was meaningful behavior? Did you influence what you saw so that you could not be confident that the behavior was representative? Looking back on your experience as a field worker, what else seems questionable to you now?

MAKING CONNECTIONS

1. Both van Lawick-Goodall and Farley Mowat study a specific kind of animal in its natural habitat. How are their procedures similar? How are they different? What kinds of refinement do they venture in their studies as they proceed? How do their procedures influence both their findings and their presentation of those findings?

2. Compare and contrast van Lawick-Goodall's account of observing the chimpanzees with Clifford Geertz's "Of Cocks and Men" in "Explaining." To what extent are both writers ethnographers, studying and describing behavior in a technologically more primitive society?

3. One of the tools Dennis Hevesi has at his disposal in writing "Running Away" and that van Lawick-Goodall lacks in her writing is the ability to interview relevant parties. Don't you imagine she would have liked to interview Mr. McGregor, Goliath, or David Graybeard? Imagine her doing so. What questions would she be likely to ask? What would you like to know from one of those individuals were you able to interview him? Write out the interview that you can imagine.

BODY RITUAL AMONG
THE NACIREMA

Horace Miner

*Horace Miner (b. 1912) has been a cultural anthropologist
and a professor of anthropology at the University of Michigan in Ann Arbor for many years. The topics of his published studies have ranged from Timbuktu to French
Canada. The following selection appeared first in a professional journal, the* American Anthropologist, *in 1956. Reprinted far and wide, it has now become a classic joke among
social scientists.*

The anthropologist has become so familiar with the diversity of ways in 1
which different peoples behave in similar situations that he is not apt to be
surprised by even the most exotic customs. In fact, if all of the logically possible
combinations of behavior have not been found somewhere in the world, he is
apt to suspect that they must be present in some yet undescribed tribe. This
point has, in fact, been expressed with respect to clan organization by Murdock
(1949:71). In this light, the magical beliefs and practices of the Nacirema present
such unusual aspects that it seems desirable to describe them as an example of
the extremes to which human behavior can go.

Professor Linton first brought the ritual of the Nacirema to the attention of 2
anthropologists twenty years ago (1936:326), but the culture of this people is
still very poorly understood. They are a North American group living in the
territory between the Canadian Cree, the Yaqui and Tarahumare of Mexico,
and the Carib and Arawak of the Antilles. Little is known of their origin,
although tradition states that they came from the east. According to Nacirema
mythology, their nation was originated by a culture hero, Notgnihsaw, who is
otherwise known for two great feats of strength—the throwing of a piece of
wampum across the river Pa-To-Mac and the chopping down of a cherry tree
in which the Spirit of Truth resided.

Nacirema culture is characterized by a highly developed market economy 3
which has evolved in a rich natural habitat. While much of the people's time
is devoted to economic pursuits, a large part of the fruits of these labors and a
considerable portion of the day are spent in ritual activity. The focus of this
activity is the human body, the appearance and health of which loom as a
dominant concern in the ethos of the people. While such a concern is certainly
not unusual, its ceremonial aspects and associated philosophy are unique.

The fundamental belief underlying the whole system appears to be that the 4 human body is ugly and that its natural tendency is to debility and disease. Incarcerated in such a body, man's only hope is to avert these characteristics through the use of the powerful influences of ritual and ceremony. Every household has one or more shrines devoted to this purpose. The more powerful individuals in the society have several shrines in their houses and, in fact, the opulence of a house is often referred to in terms of the number of such ritual centers it possesses. Most houses are of wattle and daub construction, but the shrine rooms of the more wealthy are walled with stone. Poorer families imitate the rich by applying pottery plaques to their shrine walls.

While each family has at least one such shrine, the rituals associated with it   5
are not family ceremonies but are private and secret. The rites are normally only discussed with children, and then only during the period when they are being initiated into these mysteries. I was able, however, to establish sufficient rapport with the natives to examine these shrines and to have the rituals described to me.

The focal point of the shrine is a box or chest which is built into the wall.   6
In this chest are kept the many charms and magical potions without which no native believes he could live. These preparations are secured from a variety of specialized practitioners. The most powerful of these are the medicine men, whose assistance must be rewarded with substantial gifts. However, the medicine men do not provide the curative potions for their clients, but decide what the ingredients should be and then write them down in an ancient and secret language. This writing is understood only by the medicine men and by the herbalists who, for another gift, provide the required charm.

The charm is not disposed of after it has served its purpose, but is placed in   7
the charm-box of the household shrine. As these magical materials are specific for certain ills, and the real or imagined maladies of the people are many, the charm-box is usually full to overflowing. The magical packets are so numerous that people forget what their purposes were and fear to use them again. While the natives are very vague on this point, we can only assume that the idea in retaining all the old magical materials is that their presence in the charm-box, before which the body rituals are conducted, will in some way protect the worshipper.

Beneath the charm-box is a small font. Each day every member of the   8
family, in succession, enters the shrine room, bows his head before the charm-box, mingles different sorts of holy water in the font, and proceeds with a brief rite of ablution. The holy waters are secured from the Water Temple of the community, where the priests conduct elaborate ceremonies to make the liquid ritually pure.

In the hierarchy of magical practitioners, and below the medicine men in   9
prestige, are specialists whose designation is best translated "holy-mouth-men." The Nacirema have an almost pathological horror of and fascination with the

mouth, the condition of which is believed to have a supernatural influence on all social relationships. Were it not for the rituals of the mouth, they believe that their teeth would fall out, their gums bleed, their jaws shrink, their friends desert them, and their lovers reject them. They also believe that a strong relationship exists between oral and moral characteristics. For example, there is a ritual ablution of the mouth for children which is supposed to improve their moral fiber.

The daily body ritual performed by everyone includes a mouth-rite. Despite   10
the fact that these people are so punctilious about care of the mouth, this rite involves a practice which strikes the uninitiated stranger as revolting. It was reported to me that the ritual consists of inserting a small bundle of hog hairs into the mouth, along with certain magical powders, and then moving the bundle in a highly formalized series of gestures.

In addition to the private mouth-rite, the people seek out a holy-mouth-man   11
once or twice a year. These practitioners have an impressive set of paraphernalia, consisting of a variety of augers, awls, probes, and prods. The use of these objects in the exorcism of the evils of the mouth involves almost unbelievable ritual torture of the client. The holy-mouth-man opens the client's mouth and, using the above mentioned tools, enlarges any holes which decay may have created in the teeth. Magical materials are put into these holes. If there are no naturally occurring holes in the teeth, large sections of one or more teeth are gouged out so that the supernatural substance can be applied. In the client's view, the purpose of these ministrations is to arrest decay and to draw friends. The extremely sacred and traditional character of the rite is evident in the fact that the natives return to the holy-mouth-men year after year, despite the fact that their teeth continue to decay.

It is to be hoped that, when a thorough study of the Nacirema is made,   12
there will be careful inquiry into the personality structure of these people. One has but to watch the gleam in the eye of a holy-mouth-man, as he jabs an awl into an exposed nerve, to suspect that a certain amount of sadism is involved. If this can be established, a very interesting pattern emerges, for most of the population shows definite masochistic tendencies. It was to these that Professor Linton referred in discussing a distinctive part of the daily body ritual which is performed only by men. This part of the rite involves scraping and lacerating the surface of the face with a sharp instrument. Special women's rites are performed only four times during each lunar month, but what they lack in frequency is made up in barbarity. As part of this ceremony, women bake their heads in small ovens for about an hour. The theoretically interesting point is that what seems to be a preponderantly masochistic people have developed sadistic specialists.

The medicine men have an imposing temple, or *latipso*, in every community   13
of any size. The more elaborate ceremonies required to treat very sick patients

can only be performed at this temple. These ceremonies involve not only the thaumaturge but a permanent group of vestal maidens who move sedately about the temple chambers in distinctive costume and headdress.

The *latipso* ceremonies are so harsh that it is phenomenal that a fair pro- 14 portion of the really sick natives who enter the temple ever recover. Small children whose indoctrination is still incomplete have been known to resist attempts to take them to the temple because "that is where you go to die." Despite this fact, sick adults are not only willing but eager to undergo the protracted ritual purification, if they can afford to do so. No matter how ill the supplicant or how grave the emergency, the guardians of many temples will not admit a client if he cannot give a rich gift to the custodian. Even after one has gained admission and survived the ceremonies, the guardians will not permit the neophyte to leave until he makes still another gift.

The supplicant entering the temple is first stripped of all his or her clothes. 15 In every-day life the Nacirema avoids exposure of his body and its natural functions. Bathing and excretory acts are performed only in the secrecy of the household shrine, where they are ritualized as part of the body-rites. Psycho- logical shock results from the fact that body secrecy is suddenly lost upon entry into the *latipso*. A man, whose own wife has never seen him in an excretory act, suddenly finds himself naked and assisted by a vestal maiden while he performs his natural functions into a sacred vessel. This sort of ceremonial treatment is necessitated by the fact that the excreta are used by a diviner to ascertain the course and nature of the client's sickness. Female clients, on the other hand, find their naked bodies are subjected to the scrutiny, manipulation and prodding of the medicine men.

Few supplicants in the temple are well enough to do anything but lie on 16 their hard beds. The daily ceremonies, like the rites of the holy-mouth-men, involve discomfort and torture. With ritual precision, the vestals awaken their miserable charges each dawn and roll them about on their beds of pain while performing ablutions, in the formal movements of which the maidens are highly trained. At other times they insert magic wands in the supplicant's mouth or force him to eat substances which are supposed to be healing. From time to time the medicine men come to their clients and jab magically treated needles into their flesh. The fact that these temple ceremonies may not cure, and may even kill the neophyte, in no way decreases the people's faith in the medicine men.

There remains one other kind of practitioner, known as a "listener." This 18 witch-doctor has the power to exorcise the devils that lodge in the heads of people who have been bewitched. The Nacirema believe that parents bewitch their own children. Mothers are particularly suspected of putting a curse on children while teaching them the secret body rituals. The counter-magic of the witch-doctor is unusual in its lack of ritual. The patient simply tells the "listener" all his troubles and fears, beginning with the earliest difficulties he can remember. The memory displayed by the Nacirema in these exorcism sessions is truly remarkable. It is not uncommon for the patient to bemoan the rejection he felt upon being weaned as a babe, and a few individuals even see their troubles going back to the traumatic effects of their own birth.

In conclusion, mention must be made of certain practices which have their base in native esthetics but which depend upon the pervasive aversion to the natural body and its functions. There are ritual fasts to make fat people thin and ceremonial feasts to make thin people fat. Still other rites are used to make women's breasts larger if they are small, and smaller if they are large. General dissatisfaction with breast shape is symbolized in the fact that the ideal form is virtually outside the range of human variation. A few women afflicted with almost inhuman hypermammary development are so idolized that they make a handsome living by simply going from village to village and permitting the natives to stare at them for a fee. [19]

Reference has already been made to the fact that excretory functions are ritualized, routinized, and relegated to secrecy. Natural reproductive functions are similarly distorted. Intercourse is taboo as a topic and scheduled as an act. Efforts are made to avoid pregnancy by the use of magical materials or by limiting intercourse to certain phases of the moon. Conception is actually very infrequent. When pregnant, women dress so as to hide their condition. Parturition takes place in secret, without friends or relatives to assist, and the majority of women do not nurse their infants. [20]

Our review of the ritual life of the Nacirema has certainly shown them to be magic-ridden people. It is hard to understand how they have managed to exist so long under the burdens which they have imposed upon themselves. But even such exotic customs as these take on real meaning when they are viewed with the insight provided by Malinowski when he wrote (1948:70): [21]

> Looking from far and above, from our high places of safety in the developed civilization, it is easy to see all the crudity and irrelevance of magic. But without its power and guidance early man could not have mastered his practical difficulties as he has done, nor could man have advanced to the higher stages of civilization.

REFERENCES CITED

LINTON, RALPH
 1936   The Study of Man. New York, D. Appleton-Century Co.
MALINOWSKI, BRONISLAW
 1948   Magic, Science, and Religion. Glencoe, The Free Press.
MURDOCK, GEORGE P.
 1949   Social Structure. New York, The Macmillan Co.

QUESTIONS

1. Where do the Nacirema live? Why would an anthropologist want to study their culture? Do the Nacirema sound like people you would want to know more about?

2. What is Miner's attitude toward his subject? Is his report objective, or is there evaluative language present?

3. What evidence is presented to support the writer's claim in paragraph 12 that "most of the population shows definite masochistic tendencies"? How is the evidence organized? Is enough evidence presented to substantiate this claim?

4. Miner's report was written in 1956. Have you seen in your community any more recent evidence that would indicate that the Nacirema's belief in magical powers has enabled them to advance to a higher stage of civilization, as Malinowski suggests it might?

5. Miner concentrates on the body rituals of the Nacirema. Obviously, the Nacirema must have other rituals, and surely some of these are more pleasurable than those described here. On the other hand, Miner may not have included other barbaric customs of the Nacirema. Do some field research of your own, and write a report of another Nacirema ritual that you have observed.

6. Nonanthropologists find this piece humorous because of Professor Miner's treatment of the Nacirema. Might anthropologists find this piece more humorous than nonanthropologists find it? Use your answer to draw some conclusions about how different audiences respond to humor.

MAKING CONNECTIONS

1. Read Joan Didion's essay, "Why I Write," in "Reflecting" and think about her motivations for writing in relation to Miner's probable motivations. To what extent to you think their motivations are similar? To what extent are they different? What particular points in Miner's essay suggest some connection on his part to the kinds of motives Didion expresses?

2. Miner, Farley Mowat, and Clifford Geertz all write with a noticeable sense of humor. How does their humor affect the stances they take toward their subjects, and toward themselves as they write?

Sciences and Technologies

LOVE CANAL AND
THE POISONING OF AMERICA
Michael Brown

Michael Brown is a free-lance writer interested in environmental issues. His investigations into the dumping of toxic waste, which have appeared in newspaper and magazine articles, have won him three Pulitzer Prize nominations and a special award from the Environmental Protection Agency. This essay is taken from his book Laying Waste: The Poisoning of America by Toxic Chemicals *(1980).*

Niagara Falls is a city of unmatched natural beauty; it is also a tired industrial   1
workhorse, beaten often and with a hard hand. A magnificent river—a strait, really—connecting Lake Erie to Lake Ontario flows hurriedly north, at a pace of a half-million tons a minute, widening into a smooth expanse near the city before breaking into whitecaps and taking its famous 186-foot plunge. Then it cascades through a gorge of overhung shale and limestone to rapids higher and swifter than anywhere else on the continent.

The falls attract long lines of newlyweds and other tourists. At the same   2
time, the river provides cheap electricity for industry; a good stretch of its shore is now filled with the spiraled pipes of distilleries, and the odors of chlorine and sulfides hang in the air.

Many who live in the city of Niagara Falls work in chemical plants, the   3
largest of which is owned by the Hooker Chemical Company, a subsidiary of Occidental Petroleum since the 1960s. Timothy Schroeder did not. He was a cement technician by trade, dealing with the factories only if they needed a pathway poured, or a small foundation set. Tim and his wife, Karen, lived in a ranch-style home with a brick and wood exterior at 460 99th Street. One of the Schroeder's most cherished purchases was a Fiberglas pool, built into the ground and enclosed by a red-wood fence.

Karen looked from a back window one morning in October 1974, noting   4

239

with distress that the pool had suddenly risen two feet above the ground. She called Tim to tell him about it. Karen then had no way of knowing that this was the first sign of what would prove to be a punishing family and economic tragedy.

Mrs. Schroeder believed that the cause of the uplift was the unusual ground- 5 water flow of the area. Twenty-one years before, an abandoned hydroelectric canal directly behind their house had been backfilled with industrial rubble. The underground breaches created by this disturbance, aided by the marshland nature of the region's surficial layer, collected large volumes of rainfall and undermined the back yard. The Schroeders allowed the pool to remain in its precarious position until the following summer and then pulled it from the ground, intending to pour a new pool, cast in cement. This they were unable to do, for the gaping excavation immediately filled with what Karen called "chemical water," rancid liquids of yellow and orchid and blue. These same chemicals had mixed with the groundwater and flooded the entire yard, attacking the redwood posts with such a caustic bite that one day the fence simply collapsed. When the chemicals receded in the dry weather, they left the gardens and shrubs withered and scorched, as if by a brush fire.

How the chemicals got there was no mystery. In the late 1930s, or perhaps 6 early 1940s, the Hooker Company, whose many processes included the man- ufacture of pesticides, plasticizers, and caustic soda, began using the abandoned canal as a dump for at least 20,000 tons of waste residues—"still-bottoms," in the language of the trade.

Karen Schroeder's parents had been the first to experience problems with the 7 canal's seepage. In 1959, her mother, Aileen Voorhees, encountered a strange black sludge bleeding through the basement walls. For the next twenty years, she and her husband, Edwin, tried various methods of halting the irritating intrusion, pasting the cinder-block wall with sealants and even constructing a gutter along the walls to intercept the inflow. Nothing could stop the chemical smell from permeating the entire household, and neighborhood calls to the city for help were fruitless. One day, when Edwin punched a hole in the wall to see what was happening, quantities of black liquid poured from the block. The cinder blocks were full of the stuff.

More ominous than the Voorhees basement was an event that occurred at 8 11:12 P.M. on November 21, 1968, when Karen Schroeder gave birth to her third child, a seven-pound girl named Sheri. No sense of elation filled the delivery room. The child was born with a heart that beat irregularly and had a hole in it, bone blockages of the nose, partial deafness, deformed ear exteriors, and a cleft palate. Within two years, the Schroeders realized Sheri was also mentally retarded. When her teeth came in, a double row of them appeared on her lower jaw. And she developed an enlarged liver.

The Schroeders considered these health problems, as well as illnesses among 9 their other children, as acts of capricious genes—a vicious quirk of nature. Like

Mrs. Schroeder's parents, they were concerned that the chemicals were devaluing their property. The crab apple tree and evergreens in the back were dead, and even the oak in front of the home was sick; one year, the leaves had fallen off on Father's Day.

The canal had been dug with much fanfare in the late nineteenth century   10
by a flamboyant entrepreneur named William T. Love, who wanted to construct an industrial city with ready access to water power, and major markets. The setting for Love's dream was to be a navigable power channel that would extend seven miles from the Upper Niagara before falling two hundred feet, circumventing the treacherous falls and at the same time providing cheap power. A city would be constructed near the point where the canal fed back into the river, and he promised it would accommodate half a million people.

So taken with his imagination were the state's leaders that they gave Love a   11
free hand to condemn as much property as he liked, and to divert whatever amounts of water. Love's dream, however, proved grander than his resources, and he was eventually forced to abandon the project after a mile-long trench, ten to forty feet deep and generally twenty yards wide, had been scoured perpendicular to the Niagara River. Eventually, the trench was purchased by Hooker.

Few of those who, in 1977, lived in the numerous houses that had sprung   12
up by the site were aware that the large and barren field behind them was a burial ground for toxic waste. Both the Niagara County Health Department and the city said it was a nuisance condition, but not serious danger to the people. Officials of the Hooker Company refused comment, claiming only that they had no records of the chemical burials and that the problem was not their responsibility. Indeed, Hooker had deeded the land to the Niagara Falls Board of Education in 1953, for a token $1. With it the company issued no detailed warnings of the chemicals, only a brief paragraph in the quitclaim document that disclaimed company liability for any injuries or deaths which might occur at the site.

Though Hooker was undoubtedly relieved to rid itself of the contaminated   13
land, the company was so vague about the hazards involved that one might have thought the wastes would cause harm only if touched, because they irritated the skin; otherwise, they were not of great concern. In reality, as the company must have known, the dangers of these wastes far exceeded those of acids or alkalines or inert salts. We now know that the drums Hooker had dumped in the canal contained a veritable witch's brew—compounds of truly remarkable toxicity. There were solvents that attacked the heart and liver, and residues from pesticides so dangerous that their commercial sale was shortly thereafter restricted outright by the government; some of them were already suspected of causing cancer.

Yet Hooker gave no hint of that. When the board of education, which   14
wanted the parcel for a new school, approached Hooker, B. Kaussen, at the

241

time Hooker's executive vice president, said in a letter to the board. "Our officers have carefully considered your request. We are very conscious of the need for new elementary schools and realize that the sites must be carefully selected. We will be willing to donate the entire strip of property which we own between Colvin Boulevard and Frontier Avenue to be used for the erection of a school at a location to be determined. . . ."

The board built the school and playground at the canal's midsection. Con- 15
struction progressed despite the contractor's hitting a drainage trench that gave off a strong chemical odor and the discovery of a waste pit nearby. Instead of halting the work, the authorities simply moved the school eighty feet away. Young families began to settle in increasing numbers alongside the dump, many of them having been told that the field was to be a park and recreation area for their children.

Children found the "playground" interesting, but at times painful. They 16
sneezed, and their eyes teared. In the days when the dumping was still in progress, they swam at the opposite end of the canal, occasionally arriving home with hard pimples all over their bodies. Hooker knew children were playing on its spoils. In 1958, three children were burned by exposed residues on the canal's surface, much of which, according to residents, had been covered with nothing more than fly ash and loose dirt. Because it wished to avoid legal repercussions, the company chose not to issue a public warning of the dangers it knew were there, nor to have its chemists explain to the people that their homes would have been better placed elsewhere.

The Love Canal was simply unfit as a container for hazardous substances, 17
poor even by the standards of the day, and now, in 1977, local authorities were belatedly finding that out. Several years of heavy snowfall and rain had filled the sparingly covered channel like a bathtub. The contents were overflowing at a frightening rate.

The city of Niagara Falls, I was assured, was planning a remedial drainage 18
program to halt in some measure the chemical migration off the site. But no sense of urgency had been attached to the plan, and it was stalled in red tape. No one could agree on who should pay the bill—the city, Hooker, or the board of education—and engineers seemed confused over what exactly needed to be done.

Niagara Falls City Manager Donald O'Hara persisted in his view that, 19
however displeasing to the eyes and nose, the Love Canal was not a crisis matter, mainly a question of aesthetics. O'Hara reminded me that Dr. Francis Clifford, county health commissioner, supported that opinion.

With the city, the board, and Hooker unwilling to commit themselves to a 20
remedy, conditions degenerated in the area between 97th and 99th streets, until, by early 1978, the land was a quagmire of sludge that oozed from the canal's every pore. Melting snow drained the surface soot onto the private yards, while on the dump itself the ground had softened to the point of collapse, exposing

the crushed tops of barrels. Beneath the surface, masses of sludge were finding their way out at a quickening rate, constantly forming springs of contaminated liquid. The Schroeder back yard, once featured in a local newspaper for its beauty, had reached the point where it was unfit even to walk upon. Of course, the Schroeders could not leave. No one would think of buying the property. They still owed on their mortgage and, with Tim's salary, could not afford to maintain the house while they moved into a safer setting. They and their four children were stuck.

Apprehension about large costs was not the only reason the city was reluctant   21
to help the Schroeders and the one hundred or so other families whose properties abutted the covered trench. The city may also have feared distressing Hooker. To an economically depressed area, the company provided desperately needed employment—as many as 3000 blue-collar jobs and a substantial number of tax dollars. Hooker was speaking of building a $17 million headquarters in downtown Niagara Falls. So anxious were city officials to receive the new building that they and the state granted the company highly lucrative tax and loan incentives, and made available to the firm a prime parcel of property near the most popular tourist park on the American side.

City Manager O'Hara and other authorities were aware of the nature of   22
Hooker's chemicals. In fact, in the privacy of his office, O'Hara, after receiving a report on the chemical tests at the canal, had informed the people at Hooker that it was an extremely serious problem. Even earlier, in 1976, the New York State Department of Environmental Conservation had been made aware that dangerous compounds were present in the basement sump pump of at least one 97th Street home, and soon after, its own testing had revealed that highly injurious halogenated hydrocarbons were flowing from the canal into adjoining sewers. Among them were the notorious PCBs; quantities as low as one part PCBs to a million parts normal water were enough to create serious environmental concerns; in the sewers of Niagara Falls, the quantities of halogenated compounds were thousands of times higher. The other materials tracked, in sump pumps or sewers, were just as toxic as PCBs, or more so. Prime among the more hazardous ones was residue from hexachlorocyclopentadiene, or C-56, which was deployed as an intermediate in the manufacture of several pesticides. In certain dosages, the chemical could damage every organ in the body.

While the mere presence of C-56 should have been cause for alarm, gov-   23
ernment remained inactive. Not until early 1978—a full eighteen months after C-56 was first detected—was testing conducted in basements along 97th and 99th streets to see if the chemicals had vaporized off the sump pumps and walls and were present in the household air.

While the basement tests were in progress, the rains of spring arrived at the   24
canal, further worsening the situation. Heavier fumes rose above the barrels. More than before, the residents were suffering from headaches, respiratory

243

discomforts, and skin ailments. Many of them felt constantly fatigued and irritable, and the children had reddened eyes. In the Schroeder home, Tim developed a rash along the backs of his legs. Karen could not rid herself of throbbing pains in her head. Their daughter, Laurie, seemed to be losing some of her hair.

The EPA test revealed that benzene, a known cause of cancer in humans,   25 had been readily detected in the household air up and down the streets. A widely used solvent, benzene was known in chronic-exposure cases to cause headaches, fatigue, loss of weight, and dizziness followed by pallor, nose-bleeds, and damage to the bone marrow.

No public announcement was made of the benzene hazard. Instead, officials   26 appeared to shield the finding until they could agree among themselves on how to present it.

Dr. Clifford, the county health commissioner, seemed unconcerned by the   27 detection of benzene in the air. His health department refused to conduct a formal study of the people's health, despite the air-monitoring results. For this reason, and because of the resistance growing among the local authorities, I went to the southern end of 99th Street to take an informal health survey of my own. I arranged a meeting with six neighbors, all of them instructed beforehand to list the illnesses they were aware of on their block, with names and ages specified for presentation at the session.

The residents' list was startling. Though unafflicted before they moved there,   28 many people were now plagued with ear infections, nervous disorders, rashes, and headaches. One young man, James Gizzarelli, said he had missed four months of work owing to breathing troubles. His wife was suffering epileptic-like seizures which her doctor was unable to explain. Meanwhile, freshly applied paint was inexplicably peeling from the exterior of their house. Pets too were suffering, most seriously if they had been penned in the back yards nearest to the canal, cosntantly breathing air that smelled like mothballs and weedkiller. They lost their fur, exhibited skin lesions, and, while still quite young, developed internal tumors. A great many cases of cancer were reported among the women, along with much deafness. On both 97th and 99th streets, traffic signs warned passing motorists to watch for deaf children playing near the road.

Evidence continued to mount that a large group of people, perhaps all of   29 the one hundred families immediately by the canal, perhaps many more, were in imminent danger. While watching television, while gardening or doing a wash, in their sleeping hours, they were inhaling a mixture of damaging chemicals. Their hours of exposure were far longer than those of a chemical factory worker, and they wore no respirators or goggles. Nor could they simply open a door and escape. Helplessness and despair were the main responses to the blackened craters and scattered cinders behind their back yards.

But public officials often characterized the residents as hypochondriacs. Every   30 agent of government had been called on the phone or sent pleas for help, but none offered aid.

Commissioner Clifford expressed irritation at my printed reports of illness, 31 and disagreement began to surface in the newsroom on how the stories should be printed. "There's a high rate of cancer among my friends," Dr. Clifford argued. "It doesn't mean anything."

Yet as interest in the small community increased, further revelations shook 32 the neighborhood. In addition to benzene, eighty or more other compounds were found in the makeshift dump, ten of them potential carcinogens. The physiological effects they could cause were profound and diverse. At least fourteen of them could impact on the brain and central nervous system. Two of them, carbon tetrachloride and chlorobenzene, could readily cause narcotic and anesthetic consequences. Many others were known to cause headaches, seizures, loss of hair, anemia, or skin rashes. Together, the compounds were capable of inflicting innumerable illnesses, and no one knew what new concoctions were being formulated by their mixture underground.

Edwin and Aileen Voorhees had the most to be concerned about. When a 33 state biophysicist analyzed the air content of their basement, he determined that the safe exposure time there was less than 2.4 minutes—the toxicity in the basement was thousands of times the acceptable limit for twenty-four-hour-breathing. This did not mean they would necessarily become permanently ill, but their chances of contracting cancer, for example, had been measurably increased. In July, I visited Mrs. Voorhees for further discussion of her problems, and as we sat in the kitchen, drinking coffee, the industrial odors were apparent. Aileen, usually chipper and feisty, was visibly anxious. She stared down at the table, talking only in a lowered voice. Everything now looked different to her. The home she and Edwin had built had become their jail cell. Their yard was but a pathway through which toxicants entered the cellar walls. The field out back, that proposed "park," seemed destined to be the ruin of their lives.

On July 14 I received a call from the state health department with some 34 shocking news. A preliminary review showed that women living at the southern end had suffered a high rate of miscarriages and had given birth to an abnormally high number of children with birth defects. In one age group, 35.3 percent had records of spontaneous abortions. That was far in excess of the norm. The odds against it happening by chance were 250 to one. These tallies, it was stressed, were "conservative" figures. Four children in one small section of the neighborhood had documentable birth defects, club feet, retardation, and deafness. Those who lived there the longest suffered the highest rates.

The data on miscarriages and birth defects, coupled with the other accounts 35 of illness, finally pushed the state's bureaucracy into motion. A meeting was scheduled for August 2, at which time the state health commissioner, Dr.

Robert Whalen, would formally address the issue. The day before the meeting, Dr. Nicholas Vianna, a state epidemiologist, told me that the residents were also incurring some degree of liver damage. Blood analyses had shown hepatitis-like symptoms in enzyme levels. Dozens if not hundreds of people, apparently, had been adversely affected.

In Albany, on August 2, Dr. Whalen read a lengthy statement in which he 36 urged that pregnant women and children under two years of age leave the southern end of the dump site immediately. He declared the Love Canal an official emergency, citing it as a "great and imminent peril to the health of the general public."

When Commissioner Whalen's words hit 97th and 99th streets, by way of 37 one of the largest banner headlines in the Niagara *Gazette's* 125-year history, dozens of people massed on the streets, shouting into bullhorns and micro-phones to voice frustrations that had been accumulating for months. Many of them vowed a tax strike because their homes were rendered unmarketable and unsafe. They attacked their government for ignoring their welfare. A man of high authority, a physician with a title, had confirmed that their lives were in danger. Most wanted to leave the neighborhood immediately.

Terror and anger roiled together, exacerbated by Dr. Whalen's failure to 38 provide a government-funded evacuation plan. His words were only a recom-mendation: individual families had to choose whether to risk their health and remain, or abandon their houses and, in so doing, write off a lifetime of work and savings.

On August 3, Dr. Whalen decided he should speak to the people. He arrived 39 with Dr. David Axelrod, a deputy who had directed the state's investigation, and Thomas Frey, a key aide to Governor Hugh Carey.

At a public meeting, held in the 99th Street School auditorium, Frey was 40 given the grueling task of controlling the crowd of 500 angry and frightened people. In an attempt to calm them, he announced that a meeting between the state and the White House had been scheduled for the following week. The state would propose that Love Canal be classified a national disaster, thereby freeing federal funds. For now, however, he could promise no more. Neither could Dr. Whalen and his staff of experts. All they could say was what was already known: twenty-five organic compounds, some of them capable of caus-ing cancer, were in their homes, and because young children were especially prone to toxic effects, they should be moved to another area.

Dr. Whalen's order had applied only to those living at the canal's southern 41 end, on its immediate periphery. But families living across the street from the dump site, or at the northern portion, where the chemicals were not so visible at the surface, reported afflictions remarkably similar to those suffered by families whose yards abutted the southern end. Serious respiratory problems, nervous disorders, and rectal bleeding were reported by many who were not covered by the order.

Throughout the following day, residents posted signs of protest on their front   42
fences or porch posts. "Love Canal Kills," they said, or "Give Me Liberty, I've
Got Death." Emotionally exhausted and uncertain about their future, men
stayed home from work, congregating on the streets or comforting their wives.
By this time the board of education had announced it was closing the 99th
Street School for the following year, because of its proximity to the exposed
toxicants. Still, no public relief was provided for the residents.

Another meeting was held that evening, at a firehall on 102nd Street. It was   43
unruly, but the people, who had called the session in an effort to organize
themselves, managed to form an alliance, the Love Canal Homeowners Association, and to elect as president Lois Gibbs, a pretty, twenty-seven-year-old
woman with jet-black hair who proved remarkably adept at dealing with experienced politicians and at keeping the matter in the news. After Mrs. Gibbs'
election, Congressman John LaFalce entered the hall and announced, to wild
applause, that the Federal Disaster Assistance Administration would be represented the next morning, and that the state's two senators, Daniel Patrick
Moynihan and Jacob Javits, were working with him in an attempt to get funds
from Congress.

With the Love Canal story now attracting attention from the national media,   44
the Governor's office announced that Hugh Carey would be at the 99th Street
School on August 7 to address the people. Decisions were being made in Albany
and Washington. Hours before the Governor's arrival, a sudden burst of "urgent"
reports from Washington came across the newswires. President Jimmy Carter
had officially declared the Hooker dump site a national emergency.

Hugh Carey was applauded on his arrival. The Governor announced that   45
the state, through its Urban Development Corporation, planned to purchase,
at fair market value, those homes rendered uninhabitable by the marauding
chemicals. He spared no promises. "You will not have to make mortgage
payments on homes you don't want or cannot occupy. Don't worry about the
banks. The state will take care of them." By the standards of Niagara Falls,
where the real estate market was depressed, the houses were in the middle-class
range, worth from $20,000 to $40,000 apiece. The state would assess each
house and purchase it, and also pay the costs of moving, temporary housing
during the transition period, and special items not covered by the usual real
estate assessment, such as installation of telephones.

First in a trickle and then, by September, in droves, the families gathered   46
their belongings and carted them away. Moving vans crowded 97th and 99th
streets. Linesmen went from house to house disconnecting the telephones and
electrical wires, while carpenters pounded plywood over the windows to keep
vandals away. By the following spring, 237 families were gone; 170 of them
had moved into new houses. In time the state erected around a six-block

residential area a green chain-link fence, eight feet in height, clearly demarcating the contamination zone.

In October 1978, the long-awaited remedial drainage program began at the 47 south end. Trees were uprooted, fences and garages torn down, and swimming pools removed from the area. So great were residents' apprehensions that dangerous fumes would be released over the surrounding area that the state, at a cost of $500,000, placed seventy-five buses at emergency evacuation pickup spots during the months of work, in the event that outlying homes had to be vacated quickly because of an explosion. The plan was to construct drain tiles around the channel's periphery, where the back yards had been located, in order to divert leakage to seventeen-foot-deep wet wells from which contaminated groundwater could be drawn and treated by filtration through activated carbon. (Removing the chemicals themselves would have been financially prohibitive, perhaps costing as much as $100 million—and even then the materials would have to be buried elsewhere.) After the trenching was complete, and the sewers installed, the canal was to be covered by a sloping mound of clay and planted with grass. One day, city officials hoped, the wasteland would become a park.

In spite of the corrective measures and the enormous effort by the state health 48 department, which took thousands of blood samples from past and current residents and made uncounted analyses of soil, water, and air, the full range of the effects remained unknown. In neighborhoods immediately outside the official "zone of contamination," more than 500 families were left near the desolate setting, their health still in jeopardy. The state announced it would buy no more homes.

The first public indication that chemical contamination had probably 49 reached streets to the east and west of 97th and 99th streets, and to the north and south as well, came on August 11, 1978, when sump-pump samples I had taken from 100th and 101st streets, analyzed in a laboratory, showed the trace presence of a number of chemicals found in the canal itself, including lindane, a restricted pesticide that had been suspected of causing cancer in laboratory animals. While probing 100th Street, I knocked on the door of Patricia Pino, thirty-four, a blond divorcee with a young son and daughter. I had noticed that some of the leaves on a large tree in front of her house exhibited a black oiliness much like that on the trees and shrubs of 99th Street; she was located near what had been a drainage swale.

After I had extracted a jar of sediment from her sump pump for the analysis, 50 we conversed about her family situation and what the trauma now unfolding meant to them. Ms. Pino was extremely depressed and embittered. Both of her children had what appeared to be slight liver abnormalities, and her son had been plagued with "non-specific" allergies, teary eyes, sinus trouble, which improved markedly when he was sent away from home. Patricia told of times, during the heat of summer, when fumes were readily noticeable in her basement and sometimes even upstairs. She herself had been treated for a possibly cancerous condition of her cervix. But, like others, her family was now trapped.

On September 24, 1978, I obtained a state memorandum that said chemical 51 infiltration of the outer regions was significant indeed. The letter, sent from the state laboratories to the U.S. Environmental Protection Agency, said, "Preliminary analysis of soil samples demonstrates extensive migration of potentially toxic materials outside the immediate canal area." There it was, in the state's own words. Not long afterward, the state medical investigator, Dr. Nicholas Vianna, reported indications that residents from 93rd to 103rd streets might also have incurred liver damage.

On October 4, a young boy, John Allen Kenny, who lived quite a distance 52 north of the evacuation zone, died. The fatality was due to the failure of another organ that can be readily affected by toxicants, the kidney. Naturally, suspicions were raised that his death was in some way related to a creek that still flowed behind his house and carried, near an outfall, the odor of chlorinated compounds. Because the creek served as a catch basin for a portion of the Love Canal, the state studied an autopsy of the boy. No conclusions were reached. John Allen's parents, Norman, a chemist, and Luella, a medical research assistant, were unsatisfied with the state's investigation, which they felt was "superficial." Luella said, "He played in the creek all the time. There had been restrictions on the older boys, but he was the youngest and played with them when they were old enough to go to the creek. We let him do what the other boys did. He died of nephrosis. Proteins were passing through his urine. Well, in reading the literature, we discovered that chemicals can trigger this. There was no evidence of infection, which there should have been, and there was damage to his thymus and brain. He also had nosebleeds and headaches, and dry heaves. So our feeling is that chemicals probably triggered it."

The likelihood that water-carried chemicals had escaped from the canal's 53 deteriorating bounds and were causing problems quite a distance from the site was not lost upon the Love Canal Homeowners Association and its president, Lois Gibbs, who was attempting to have additional families relocated. Because she lived on 101st Street, she was one of those left behind, with no means of moving despite persistent medical difficulties in her six-year-old son, Michael, who had been operated on twice for urethral strictures. [Mrs. Gibbs's husband, a worker at a chemical plant, brought home only $150 a week, she told me, and when they subtracted from that the $90 a week for food and other necessities, clothing costs for their two children, $125 a month for mortgage payments and taxes, utility and phone expenses, and medical bills, they had hardly enough cash to buy gas and cigarettes, let alone vacate their house.]

Assisted by two other stranded residents, Marie Pozniak and Grace McCoulf, 54 and with the professional analysis of a Buffalo scientist named Beverly Paigen, Lois Gibbs mapped out the swale and creekbed areas, many of them long ago filled, and set about interviewing the numerous people who lived on or near

249

formerly wet ground. The survey indicated that these people were suffering from an abnormal number of kidney and bladder aggravations and problems of the reproductive system. In a report to the state, Dr. Paigen claimed to have found, in 245 homes outside the evacuation zone, thirty-four miscarriages, eighteen birth defects, nineteen nervous breakdowns, ten cases of epilepsy, and high rates of hyperactivity and suicide.

In their roundabout way, the state health experts, after an elaborate investigation, confirmed some of the homeowners' worst fears. On February 8, 1979, Dr. David Axelrod, who by then had been appointed health commissioner, and whose excellence as a scientist was widely acknowledged, issued a new order that officially extended the health emergency of the previous August, citing high incidences of birth deformities and miscarriages in the areas where creeks and swales had once flowed, or where swamps had been. With that, the state offered to evacuate temporarily those families with pregnant women or children under the age of two from the outer areas of contamination, up to 103rd Street. But no additional homes would be purchased; nor was another large-scale evacuation, temporary or otherwise, under consideration. Those who left under the new plan would have to return when their children passed the age limit. 55

Twenty-three families accepted the state's offer. Another seven families, ineligible under the plan but of adequate financial means to do so, simply left their homes and took the huge loss of investment. Soon boarded windows speckled the outlying neighborhoods. 56

The previous November and December, not long after the evacuation of 97th and 99th streets, I became interested in the possibility that Hooker might have buried in the Love Canal waste residues from the manufacture of what is known as 2,4,5-trichlorophenol. My curiosity was keen because I knew that this substance, which Hooker produced for the manufacture of the antibacterial agent hexachlorophene, and which was also used to make defoliants such as Agent Orange, the herbicide employed in Vietnam, carries with it an unwanted by-product technically called 2,3,7,8-tetrachlorodibenzo-para-dioxin, or tetra dioxin. The potency of dioxin of this isomer is nearly beyond imagination. Although its toxicological effects are not fully known, the few experts on the subject estimate that if three ounces were evenly distributed and subsequently ingested among a million people, or perhaps more than that, all of them would die. It compares in toxicity to the botulinum toxin. On skin contact, dioxin causes a disfiguration called "chloracne," which begins as pimples, lesions, and cysts, but can lead to calamitous internal damage. Some scientists suspect that dioxin causes cancer, perhaps even malignancies that occur, in galloping fashion, within a short time of contact. At least two (some estimates went as high as eleven) pounds of dioxin were dispersed over Seveso, Italy, in 1976, after an explosion of a trichlorophenol plant: dead animals littered the streets, and more than 300 acres of land were immediately evacuated. In Vietnam, the spraying 57

250

of Agent Orange, because of the dioxin contaminant, was banned in 1970, when the first effects on human beings began to surface, including dioxin's powerful teratogenic, or fetus-deforming, effects.

I posed two questions concerning trichlorophenol: Were wastes from the process buried in the canal? If so, what were the quantities? 58

On November 8, before Hooker answered my queries, I learned that, indeed, trichlorophenol had been found in liquids pumped from the remedial drain ditches. No dioxin had been found yet, and some officials, ever wary of more emotionalism among the people, argued that, because the compound was not soluble in water, there was little chance it had migrated off-site. Officials at Newco Chemical Waste Systems, a local waste disposal firm, at the same time claimed that if dioxin had been there, it had probably been photolytically destroyed. Its half-life, they contended, was just a few short years. 59

I knew from Whiteside, however, that in every known case, waste from 2,4,5-trichlorophenol carried dioxin with it. I also knew that dioxin *could* become soluble in groundwater and migrate into the neighborhood upon mixing with solvents such as benzene. Moreover, because it had been buried, sunlight would not break it down. 60

On Friday, November 10, I called Hooker again to urge that they answer my questions. Their spokesman, Bruce Davis, came to the phone and, in a controlled tone, gave me the answer: His firm had indeed buried trichlorophenol in the canal—200 tons of it. 61

Immediately I called Whiteside. His voice took on an urgent tone. According to his calculation, if 200 tons of trichlorophenol were there, in all likelihood they were accompanied by 130 pounds of tetra dioxin, an amount equaling the estimated total content of dioxin in the thousands of tons of Agent Orange rained upon Vietnamese jungles. The seriousness of the crisis had deepened, for now the Love Canal was not only a dump for highly dangerous solvents and pesticides; it was also the broken container for one of the most toxic substances ever synthesized by man. 62

I reckoned that the main danger was to those working on the remedial project, digging in the trenches. The literature on dioxin indicated that, even in quantities at times too small to detect, the substance possessed vicious characteristics. In one case, workers in a trichlorophenol plant had developed chloracne, although the substance could not be traced on the equipment with which they worked. The mere tracking of minuscule amounts of dioxin on a pedestrian's shoes in Seveso led to major concerns, and, according to Whiteside, a plant in Amsterdam, upon being found contaminated with dioxin, had been "dismantled, brick by brick, and the material embedded in concrete, loaded at a specially constructed dock, on ships, and dumped at sea, in deep water near the Azores." Workers in trichlorophenol plants had died of cancer or severe liver damage, or had suffered emotional and sexual disturbances. 63

Less than a month after the first suspicions arose, on the evening of December   64
9, I received a call from Dr. Axelrod. "We found it. The dioxin. In a drainage
trench behind 97th Street. It was in the part-per-trillion range."

The state remained firm in its plans to continue the construction, and,   65
despite the ominous new findings, no further evacuations were announced.
During the next several weeks, small incidents of vandalism occurred along
97th and 99th streets. Tacks were spread on the road, causing numerous flat
tires on the trucks. Signs of protest were hung in the school. Meetings of the
Love Canal Homeowners Association became more vociferous. Christmas was
near, and in the association's office at the 99th Street School, a holiday tree
was decorated with bulbs arranged to spell "DIOXIN."

The Love Canal people chanted and cursed at meetings with the state   66
officials, cried on the telephone, burned an effigy of the health commissioner,
traveled to Albany with a makeshift child's coffin, threatened to hold officials
hostage, sent letters and telegrams to the White House, held days of mourning
and nights of prayer. On Mother's Day this year, they marched down the
industrial corridor and waved signs denouncing Hooker, which had issued not
so much as a statement of remorse. But no happy ending was in store for them.
The federal government was clearly not planning to come to their rescue, and
the state felt it had already done more than its share. City Hall was silent and
remains silent today. Some residents still hoped that, miraculously, an agency
of government would move them. All of them watched with anxiety as each
newborn came to the neighborhood, and they looked at their bodies for signs
of cancer.

One hundred and thirty families from the Love Canal area began leaving   67
their homes last August and September, seeking temporary refuge in local hotel
rooms under a relocation plan funded by the state which had been implemented
after fumes became so strong, during remedial trenching operations, that the
United Way abandoned a care center it had opened in the neighborhood.

As soon as remedial construction is complete, the people will probably be   68
forced to return home, as the state will no longer pay for their lodging. Some
have threatened to barricade themselves in the hotels. Some have mentioned
violence. Anne Hillis of 102nd Street, who told reporters her first child had
been born so badly decomposed that doctors could not determine its sex, was
so bitter that she threw table knives and a soda can at the state's on-site
coordinator.

In October, Governor Carey announced that the state probably would buy   69
an additional 200 to 240 homes, at an expense of some $5 million. In the
meantime, lawyers have prepared lawsuits totaling about $2.65 billion and have
sought court action for permanent relocation. Even if the latter action is successful, and they are allowed to move, the residents' plight will not necessarily
have ended. The psychological scars are bound to remain among them and

their children, along with the knowledge that, because they have already been exposed, they may never fully escape the Love Canal's insidious grasp.

QUESTIONS

1. What caused the poisoning of Love Canal? Why did it take so long for both local and state officials to acknowledge the seriousness of the condition of Love Canal?

2. What kind of information does Brown provide to document the tragedy of Love Canal? What role did he play in uncovering this information?

3. Consider the introduction to this article. Why did Brown choose to tell the story of the Schroeder family in the opening paragraphs?

4. The power of this essay has much to do with the overwhelming tragedy and horror it relates. Find passages in the essay that you feel are especially effective. Explain how Brown creates this effect on the reader.

5. In this essay, Brown relies primarily on the factual data he has collected to tell the story of Love Canal. Compare this writer's approach with that found in newspapers featuring sensational headlines. Analyze one of the headlined stories. How much factual evidence is present? How would such a newspaper's treatment of the story of the Schroeder family differ from Brown's treatment?

6. Environmental calamities such as Love Canal or Three Mile Island have become a permanent part of our lives. The Environmental Protection Agency reports that in most communities the groundwater has become so laced with toxic chemicals that it is no longer safe to drink. Investigate some aspect of the environment in your community such as the water supply or the quality of the air. Write a report based on your investigation.

MAKING CONNECTIONS

1. Compare Brown's position as a reporter in relation to his topic with that of Dennis Hevesi in "Running Away" or with Barbara Tuchman in "'This is the End of the World': The Black Death." What similarities and differences can you find in the ways Brown, Hevesi, and Tuchman gather their information? How do their presentations of that information compare? Try to come to some conclusion about the most effective way to present stories of disasters and similarly provocative subject matter.

2. As a reporter, Brown is obviously involved with his subject and participating in the story he tells. To what extent do you think that jeopardizes his credibility? Compare Brown's study to that of a more obviously detached reporter. Ernest Hemingway and Virginia Woolf are examples. Rewrite a section of Brown's report in the manner of either Woolf or Hemingway.

THE SOCIAL LIVES
OF DOLPHINS

William Booth

Born in 1959 in Flushing, New York, William Booth majored in English and American literature at the University of Texas at Austin. While working as a journalist on a daily newspaper, he developed an increasing interest in science, and is now a senior writer at Science, the journal published by the American Association for the Advancement of Science. "Science writing allows me to write about ideas, hard facts, people, political battles, things real and immediate (acid rain, AIDS), or things that are just fascinating to know, just to know (black holes)." Booth says he learned about the dolphin site described in this article "from anthropologist Irven DeVore while working on another article about controversy surrounding the creation of zombies with tetrodotoxin from puffer fish."

On the shores of Shark Bay in Western Australia, there is a beach where 1 wild bottlenosed dolphins swim into knee-deep water and allow tourists to stroke their flanks and feed them frozen fish. Often, the dolphins return the favor by tossing the onlookers a fresh herring or nice piece of seaweed.

Fascinated by tales of Shark Bay and intrigued by the research potential of 2 such a place, two undergraduate students traveled to Western Australia in the summer of 1982 to have a look for themselves. What Richard Connor and Rachel Smolker found was a mixed group of eight bottle-nosed dolphins so habituated to humans that they daily swam onto a beach "so shallow that they could be seen using their pectoral fins as braces against the bottom while lifting their heads out of the water."

With only $1000 in funding from the New York Explorers Club and no boat 3 their first summer, Connor and Smolker simply watched the dolphins from the shore, yet they made a number of unique observations, including evidence of begging behavior among dolphins similar to that exhibited by wild chimpanzees. "It was like watching a soap opera," says Connor, who along with Smolker, is now a graduate student at the University of Michigan in Ann Arbor.

In addition to amusing the tourists in a remote part of Australia, the habit- 4 uated dolphins often brought other, more shy and retiring, dolphins with them. As Connor and Smolker began identifying individuals, it became clear that the

254

eight friendly dolphins were part of a larger community of over 200 animals residing in the shallow, clear waters of Shark Bay.

This remarkable site is now being compared to the Gombe Stream Reserve, a flattering allusion to the chimpanzee habitat on the shores of Lake Tanganyika so richly worked by Jane Goodall, who originally encouraged the habituation of wild chimpanzees by feeding them bananas. Says Irven DeVore, an anthropologist and primatologist from Harvard University who has visited Shark Bay: "These youngsters are sitting on the motherlode."

The comparison between Gombe Stream and Shark Bay does not end with the habituation of the residents. The dolphins are attracting some of the very same scientists whose previous work focused on the chimpanzees of Gombe and who now hope to compare the social lives of these two big-brained mammals, animals which live in such different media and are separated by at least 60 million years of evolution yet seem to share many social adaptations.

The first reports from Shark Bay, which are built upon nearly two decades of research on a community of dolphins in Florida, are revealing "a striking and remarkable convergence between the social systems of dolphins and chimpanzees," says Barbara Smuts of the University of Michigan who studied chimpanzees with Goodall in Tanzania and is now launching projects at Shark Bay with Richard Wrangham, another primatologist who cut his teeth at Gombe. The two will oversee the work of Connor and Smolker and a third graduate student.

In the past, says Smuts, researchers have been frustrated in their attempts to make comparisons between terrestrial and aquatic mammals because of their inability to observe wild dolphins with the same intimacy and intensity that they could achieve with wild chimpanzees at sites such as Gombe. Such richly textured observations of individual and group behavior are crucial if comparisons between higher primates and dolphins are to be made. Captive populations of dolphins, with their small numbers of mixed animals in cramped aquaria, have been of limited value in unraveling social structures, says Smuts.

Until now, the study of dolphin social organization in the wild has been pioneered by Randy Wells of Woods Hole Oceanographic Institution and the Long Marine Laboratory at the University of California at Santa Cruz. Since 1970, when he began his dolphin days while still in high school, Wells has gathered an enormous amount of data on a dolphin community living in the warm, grassy shallows around Sarasota, Florida. In particular, by tagging, radiotracking, and taking blood samples, Wells has pieced together much of what is known about the range and demographics of a stable community of dolphins.

"Randy has given us incredible information about who associates with whom, but not as much on who does *what* with whom," says Smuts. For unfortunately, the inshore waters of Sarasota are a murky green soup, making detailed observations of interactions difficult. In contrast, the water at Shark Bay is relatively clear and the animals allow boats to pursue them at distances of only a few meters. The dolphins at Shark Bay are so cooperative that they often roll over while riding the research boat's bow wave, giving observers a chance to sex the animals with a quick glance at the animal's genital slits. (Unlike Wells and his colleagues, who capture and quickly release animals, the researchers at Shark Bay will not handle the dolphins.)

What makes dolphins so appealing to primate researchers is the fact that both dolphins and chimpanzees evolved to possess such big brains while adapting to very different environments. Says Smuts: "Once you start comparing chimpanzees and dolphins—and large brains and social systems separated by millions of years of evolution—you can ask some pretty interesting questions." The forebears of both animals were terrestrial mammals. About 60 million years ago, the ancestors of modern cetaceans[1] were primitive ungulates[2] with small bodies and small brains that returned to the sea, from which two extant suborders of cetaceans eventually evolved, one being toothed whales and dolphins. As Smuts notes, it is the dolphins alone among the cetaceans that exhibit such a dramatic increase in brain size. When compared to body size, the brain of *Tursiops truncatus* is below that of humans but roughly double the size value of higher primates. Like humans, both dolphins and chimpanzees possess brains with an expanded neocortex and with extensive convolution, and much development is completed after birth.   11

Based on the work of Wells and as yet unpublished observations made at Shark Bay, a picture of the social lives of wild dolphins is beginning to emerge. Though the primatologists believe the social system employed by dolphins might prove remarkably similar to chimpanzees, Wells himself is not completely convinced. "I think anyone who tries to pin the dolphins on any one terrestrial animal will probably be disappointed," says Wells. Yet Smuts maintains that, combined, the social systems of dolphins and chimps are not shared by other mammals.   12

Like chimpanzees, for example, dolphin communities occupy a common home range, says Smuts. In Florida, Wells has established that his Sarasota community of 100 individuals lives along a 40-kilometer stretch of shallow bays and inlets that hug the barrier islands separating the Gulf of Mexico from the mainland, with the total range amounting to about 100 square kilometers.   13

Within their home range, both dolphins and chimpanzees live in an extremely fluid and flexible community, referred to as a "fusion-fission society," where individuals may join temporary parties of varying sizes, instead of operating in one relatively closed or rigid group. The females in both chimpanzee and dolphin communities have a tendency to travel in more limited, "core areas" within the home range, while the males roam to the periphery. The   14

---

[1] cetaceans: an order of aquatic mammals, including whales and dolphins. [Eds.]
[2] ungulates: hoofed quadrupeds. [Eds.]

wandering males probably occasionally succeed in mating with a female from another community, thus keeping the populations from being reproductively isolated, says Wells.

Within the community, dolphins have a tendency to associate with members   15
of the same sex and age, except in the case of females and young calves. Mothers and offspring form some of the tightest bonds in the community, remaining together until the calf is weaned between the ages of 3 and 4 years.

Indeed, like chimpanzees, sons and daughters may often closely associate   16
with their mothers years after weaning. Wells reports that he has watched older offspring return to their mother's side for the birth of a sibling. "They seem to want to check out the new arrival," says Wells.

Female dolphins with calves are extremely cooperative. The mothers will   17
often form "playpens" around youngsters and allow them to interact within the protective enclave. Episodes of "baby-sitting" are also common, where one female will watch another's calf while the mother is occupied elsewhere. In many cases, Wells says that the cooperating females are related.

As females tend to associate together, so do males. Perhaps the most intrigu-   18
ing of all male groups is the existence of persistent pairs or trios. Wells has seen many such pairings of both juvenile and adult males. In one case, two large, older, and heavily scarred males have been observed in each other's constant company since 1975. Connor is also seeing what he calls "coalitions" of two and three males in Shark Bay and is preparing several papers on the subject. "I can say the coalitions of males that I am seeing are extremely exciting," says Connor.

The rationale behind such behavior is only just emerging. Wells believes   19
that the male pairs may protect each other from predation and cooperate in hunting. According to Wells, the teams are also capable of working in tandem to separate individual females from groups. In one anecdote published in 1987 by Wells, he describes two males flanking a female and chasing her.

At Shark Bay, Connor has repeatedly witnessed a behavior he considers   20
"sexual herding," in which two or three males in a coalition will cooperate to intimidate a female and keep her close by their sides. Connor suspects the males intend to mate with their captive. In Sarasota, this hypothesis is supported somewhat by the presence of closely bonded male pairs even during the mating season.

Using DNA fingerprinting techniques and chromosome band analysis, Wells   21
and Debbie Duffield of Portland State University in Oregon are currently examining blood samples taken from many of his male pairs in Sarasota to find out whether or not the males are related. The reason for the blood analysis is that it would be almost impossible to discern in the wild which male is fruitfully mating with which female because sexual encounters among dolphins are so common, says Wells.

The mating system for dolphins, like chimpanzees, is a promiscuous one.   22

Males and females do not form long-term bonds. Females may mate with a number of different males. Among the males in Shark Bay, Connor observes constant sexual interaction, both heterosexual and homosexual. "There'll be a group of 4 or 5 males and it seems like one of them goes, 'Let's go get Pointer!' And the other males start mounting him with erections," says Connor. "So much of the sexual interaction appears to be purely social. The males are constantly mounting each other and mounting females not in estrus."

Indeed, Wells reports that male bottle-nosed dolphins have unusually large 23 testes and that the sperm concentrations in their ejaculate is 300 times the mean concentration for humans and 100 times the concentration for chimpanzees. Two-day old dolphins have exhibited erections, and dolphins in both captivity and the wild masturbate. In Sarasota, males have been reported to mount sailboats. Says Wells: "The early development of sexual behavior, many years before sexual maturity, suggests that sex is quite important in the lives of these animals." It appears that large brains may have something to do with the amount of sexual behavior that is pursued outside of any reproductive context, says Smuts.[3]

QUESTIONS

1. Consider Booth's purpose for writing. How does this article end? Does Booth reach any conclusion about his material?

2. Summarize the similarities between chimpanzees and dolphins as Booth presents them in this article.

3. One of the dolphin-watchers says of his experience, "It was like watching a soap opera" (paragraph 3). What does he mean by this? What evidence of "soap opera" behavior is reported in this article?

4. How many sources does Booth use? How frequently does he rely on direct quotation of his sources? How much synthesizing and paraphrasing of information does he do?

5. Find a prime area for observing the courting or herding behavior other large-brained mammals, such as college students. Write a report in which you tell why the site you chose is a particularly good one, what types of behavior you observed, and what your findings suggest for further investigation.

6. In groups, compare reports written for question 5. Draw up a report in each group based on your combined findings. Discuss these reports in class to see what general patterns of behavior emerge, and what these patterns suggest about the socialization of college students (or whatever group you've chosen to study).

---

[3] Booth later emphasized that the theory relating large brains and sexual behavior is speculative and not original with Smuts. [Eds.]

MAKING CONNECTIONS

1. The Shark Bay site is compared to the Gombe Stream Game Reserve (paragraphs 5–8). In what ways are these sites comparable? Read Jane van Lawick-Goodall's "First Observations" and compare the methods of observation at the two sites.

2. Consider the various animals reported and reflected upon by Booth, Farley Mowat, Jane van Lawick-Goodall, Virginia Woolf, Loren Eiseley, George Orwell, and Isak Dinesen. Do you find any patterns in the kinds of animals found for study and the attitudes of various writers toward them? What are some of the reasons we find animals so interesting? Which of these accounts do you find most interesting, and why? Is it the subject itself or the writer's handling of the subject that most attracts you? Explain.

A DELICATE OPERATION

Roy C. Selby, Jr.

Roy C. Selby, Jr., (b. 1930) graduated from Louisiana State University and the University of Arkansas Medical School, where he specialized in neurology and neurosurgery. He now practices in the Chicago area and is the author of numerous professional articles on neurosurgery. "A Delicate Operation," which first appeared in Harper's *magazine in 1975, reports for a more general audience the details of a difficult brain operation.*

In the autumn of 1973 a woman in her early fifties noticed, upon closing   1
one eye while reading, that she was unable to see clearly. Her eyesight grew slowly worse. Changing her eyeglasses did not help. She saw an ophthalmologist, who found that her vision was seriously impaired in both eyes. She then saw a neurologist, who confirmed the finding and obtained X rays of the skull and an EMI scan—a photograph of the patient's head. The latter revealed a tumor growing between the optic nerves at the base of the brain. The woman was admitted to the hospital by a neurosurgeon.

Further diagnosis, based on angiography, a detailed X-ray study of the cir-   2
culatory system, showed the tumor to be about two inches in diameter and supplied by many small blood vessels. It rested beneath the brain, just above the pituitary gland, stretching the the optic nerves to either side and intimately close to the major blood vessels supplying the brain. Removing it would pose many technical problems. Probably benign and slow-growing, it may have been present for several years. If left alone it would continue to grow and produce blindness and might become impossible to remove completely. Removing it, however, might not improve the patient's vision and could make it worse. A major blood vessel could be damaged, causing a stroke. Damage to the undersurface of the brain could cause impairment of memory and changes in mood and personality. The hypothalamus, a most important structure of the brain, could be injured, causing coma, high fever, bleeding from the stomach, and death.

The neurosurgeon met with the patient and her husband and discussed the   3
various possibilities. The common decision was to operate.

The patient's hair was shampooed for two nights before surgery. She was   4
given a cortisonelike drug to reduce the risk of damage to the brain during surgery. Five units of blood were cross-matched, as a contingency against

hemorrhage. At 1:00 P.M. the operation began. After the patient was anesthetized her hair was completely clipped and shaved from the scalp. Her head was prepped with an organic iodine solution for ten minutes. Drapes were placed over her, leaving exposed only the forehead and crown of the skull. All the routine instruments were brought up—the electrocautery used to coagulate areas of bleeding, bipolar coagulation forceps to arrest bleeding from individual blood vessels without damaging adjacent tissues, and small suction tubes to remove blood and cerebrospinal fluid from the head, thus giving the surgeon a better view of the tumor and surrounding areas.

A curved incision was made behind the hairline so it would be concealed when the hair grew back. It extended almost from ear to ear. Plastic clips were applied to the cut edges of the scalp to arrest bleeding. The scalp was folded back to the level of the eyebrows. Incisions were made in the muscle of the right temple, and three sets of holes were drilled near the temple and the top of the head because the tumor had to be approached from directly in front. The drill, powered by nitrogen, was replaced with a fluted steel blade, and the holes were connected. The incised piece of skull was pried loose and held out of the way by a large sponge.

Beneath the bone is a yellowish leatherlike membrane, the dura, that surrounds the brain. Down the middle of the head the dura carries a large vein, but in the area near the nose the vein is small. At that point the vein and dura were cut, and clips made of tantalum, a hard metal, were applied to arrest and prevent bleeding. Sutures were put into the dura and tied to the scalp to keep the dura open and retracted. A malleable silver retractor, resembling the blade of a butter knife, was inserted between the brain and skull. The anesthesiologist began to administer a drug to relax the brain by removing some of its water, making it easier for the surgeon to manipulate the retractor, hold the brain back, and see the tumor. The nerve tracts for smell were cut on both sides to provide additional room. The tumor was seen approximately two-and-one-half inches behind the base of the nose. It was pink in color. On touching it, it proved to be very fibrous and tough. A special retractor was attached to the skull, enabling the other retractor blades to be held automatically and freeing the surgeon's hands. With further displacement of the frontal lobes of the brain, the tumor could be seen better, but no normal structures—the carotid arteries, their branches, and the optic nerves—were visible. The tumor obscured them.

A surgical microscope was placed above the wound. The surgeon had selected the lenses and focal length prior to the operation. Looking through the microscope, he could see some of the small vessels supplying the tumor and he coagulated them. He incised the tumor to attempt to remove its core and thus collapse it, but the substance of the tumor was too firm to be removed in this fashion. He then began to slowly dissect the tumor from the adjacent brain tissue and from where he believed the normal structures to be.

Using small squares of cotton, he began to separate the tumor from very loose fibrous bands connecting it to the brain and to the right side of the part of the skull where the pituitary gland lies. The right optic nerve and carotid artery came into view, both displaced considerably to the right. The optic nerve had a normal appearance. He protected these structures with cotton compresses placed between them and the tumor. He began to raise the tumor from the skull and slowly to reach the point of its origin and attachment—just in front of the pituitary gland and medial to the left optic nerve, which still could not be seen. The small blood vessels entering the tumor were cauterized. The upper portion of the tumor was gradually separated from the brain, and the branches of the carotid arteries and the branches to the tumor were coagulated. The tumor was slowly and gently lifted from its bed, and for the first time the left carotid artery and optic nerve could be seen. Part of the tumor adhered to this nerve. The bulk of the tumor was amputated, leaving a small bit attached to the nerve. Very slowly and carefully the tumor fragment was resected.

The tumor now removed, a most impressive sight came into view—the 9 pituitary gland and its stalk of attachment to the hypothalamus, the hypothalamus itself, and the brainstem, which conveys nerve impulses between the body and the brain. As far as could be determined, no damage had been done to these structures or other vital centers, but the left optic nerve, from chronic pressure of the tumor, appeared gray and thin. Probably it would not completely recover its function.

After making certain there was no bleeding, the surgeon closed the wounds 10 and placed wire mesh over the holes in the skull to prevent dimpling of the scalp over the points that had been drilled. A gauze dressing was applied to the patient's head. She was awakened and sent to the recovery room.

Even with the microscope, damage might still have occurred to the cerebral 11 cortex and hypothalamus. It would require at least a day to be reasonably certain there was none, and about seventy-two hours to monitor for the major postoperative dangers—swelling of the brain and blood clots forming over the surface of the brain. The surgeon explained this to the patient's husband, and both of them waited anxiously. The operation had required seven hours. A glass of orange juice had given the surgeon some additional energy during the closure of the wound. Though exhausted, he could not fall asleep until after two in the morning, momentarily expecting a call from the nurse in the intensive care unit announcing deterioration of the patient's condition.

At 8:00 A.M. the surgeon saw the patient in the intensive care unit. She was 12 alert, oriented, and showed no sign of additional damage to the optic nerves or the brain. She appeared to be in better shape than the surgeon or her husband.

QUESTIONS

1. Why did the neurosurgeon decide to operate? What could have happened if the patient chose not to have the operation? What effect does knowing this information have on the reader?

2. Although the essay is probably based on the writer's experience, it is reported in the third person. What effect does this have on the information reported? How would the report have come across if it had been written in the first person?

3. Selby uses different methods of reporting to create the drama of "A Delicate Operation." At what point in the essay does he provide background information? How much of the essay reports events before, during, and after the operation? At what points does the writer explain terms and procedures for the reader?

4. Which passages in this essay do you find especially powerful? How did Selby create this effect?

5. Write a report of a procedure with which you are familiar and which calls for some expertise or sensitivity or a combination of these because there is always the chance that something could go wrong. You should proceed step by step, giving the reader as much information as necessary to understand and follow the procedure. At appropriate points, also include the problems you face. Suggestions are trimming a Christmas tree, carrying out a chemistry experiment, getting a child off to school, or preparing a gourmet meal.

MAKING CONNECTIONS

1. Compare Selby's essay with Richard Selzer's "The Discus Thrower." Whereas Selby writes in the third person, Selzer uses the first. How do those choices affect the resulting essays?

2. Rewrite several paragraphs of Selby's and Selzer's essays, changing one from third to first person and the other from first to third. How do these changes alter the nature of the information presented and the effect of each report?

THE DISCUS THROWER
Richard Selzer

*Richard Selzer is a surgeon who has written widely, pub-
lishing articles in popular magazines as well as occasional
short fiction. (See earlier biographical note, page 134, for
additional details.) In the essay reprinted here, which first
appeared in* Harper's *magazine in 1977, Selzer reports on
the visits he made to one of his patients.*

I spy on my patients. Ought not a doctor to observe his patients by any   1
means and from any stance, that he might the more fully assemble evidence?
So I stand in the doorways of hospital rooms and gaze. Oh, it is not all that
furtive an act. Those in bed need only look up to discover me. But they never
do.

From the doorway of Room 542 the man in the bed seems deeply tanned.   2
Blue eyes and close-cropped white hair give him the appearance of vigor and
good health. But I know that his skin is not brown from the sun. It is rusted,
rather, in the last stage of containing the vile repose within. And the blue eyes
are frosted, looking inward like the windows of a snowbound cottage. This man
is blind. This man is also legless—the right leg missing from midthigh down,
the left from just below the knee. It gives him the look of a bonsai, roots and
branches pruned into the dwarfed facsimile of a great tree.

Propped on pillows, he cups his right thigh in both hands. Now and then   3
he shakes his head as though acknowledging the intensity of his suffering. In
all of this he makes no sound. Is he mute as well as blind?

The room in which he dwells is empty of all possessions—no get-well cards,   4
small, private caches of food, day-old flowers, slippers, all the usual kickshaws
of the sickroom. There is only the bed, a chair, a nightstand, and a tray on
wheels that can be swung across his lap for meals.

"What time is it?" he asks.   5
"Three o'clock."   6
"Morning or afternoon?"   7
"Afternoon."   8
He is silent. There is nothing else he wants to know.   9
"How are you?" I say.   10
"Who is it?" he asks.   11
"It's the doctor. How do you feel?"   12
He does not answer right away.   13

"Feel?" he says.   14

"I hope you feel better," I say.   15

I press the button at the side of the bed.   16

"Down you go," I say.   17

"Yes, down," he says.   18

He falls back upon the bed awkwardly. His stumps, unweighted by legs and   19
feet, rise in the air, presenting themselves. I unwrap the bandages from the
stumps, and begin to cut away the black scabs and the dead, glazed fat with
scissors and forceps. A shard of white bone comes loose. I pick it away. I wash
the wounds with disinfectant and redress the stumps. All this while, he does
not speak. What is he thinking behind those lids that do not blink? Is he
remembering a time when he was whole? Does he dream of feet? Of when his
body was not a rotting log?

He lies solid and inert. In spite of everything, he remains impressive, as   20
though he were a sailor standing athwart a slanting deck.

"Anything more I can do for you?" I ask.   21

For a long moment he is silent.   22

"Yes," he says at last and without the least irony. "You can bring me a pair   23
of shoes."

In the corridor, the head nurse is waiting for me.   24

"We have to do something about him," she says. "Every morning he orders   25
scrambled eggs for breakfast, and, instead of eating them, he picks up the plate
and throws it against the wall."

"Throws his plate?"   26

"Nasty. That's what he is. No wonder his family doesn't come to visit. They   27
probably can't stand him any more than we can."

She is waiting for me to do something.   28

"Well?"   29

"We'll see," I say.   30

The next morning I am waiting in the corridor when the kitchen delivers   31
his breakfast. I watch the aide place the tray on the stand and swing it across
his lap. She presses the button to raise the head of the bed. Then she leaves.

In time the man reaches to find the rim of the tray, then on to find the   32
dome of the covered dish. He lifts off the cover and places it on the stand. He
fingers across the plate until he probes the eggs. He lifts the plate in both hands,
sets it on the palm of his right hand, centers it, balances it. He hefts it up and
down slightly, getting the feel of it. Abruptly, he draws back his right arm as
far as he can.

There is the crack of the plate breaking against the wall at the foot of his   33
bed and the small wet sound of the scrambled eggs dropping to the floor.

And then he laughs. It is a sound you have never heard. It is something   34
new under he sun. It could cure cancer.

Out in the corridor, the eyes of the head nurse narrow.   35
"Laughed, did he?"   36
She writes something down on her clipboard.   37
A second aide arrives, brings a second breakfast tray, puts it on the nightstand,   38
out of his reach. She looks over at me shaking her head and making her mouth
go. I see that we are to be accomplices.
"I've got to feed you," she says to the man.   39
"Oh, no you don't," the man says.   40
"Oh, yes I do," the aide says, "after the way you just did. Nurse says so."   41
"Get me my shoes," the man says.   42
"Here's oatmeal," the aide says. "Open." And she touches the spoon to his   43
lower lip.
"I ordered scrambled eggs," says the man.   44
"That's right," the aide says.   45
I step forward.   46
"Is there anything I can do?" I say.   47
"Who are you?" the man asks.   48

In the evening I go once more to that ward to make my rounds. The head   49
nurse reports to me that Room 542 is deceased. She has discovered this quite
by accident, she says. No, there had been no sound. Nothing. It's a blessing,
she says.

I go into his room, a spy looking for secrets. He is still there in his bed. His   50
face is relaxed, grave, dignified. After a while, I turn to leave. My gaze sweeps
the wall at the foot of the bed, and I see the place where it has been repeatedly
washed, where the wall looks very clean and very white.

QUESTIONS

1. Why does the writer say, "I spy on my patients" (paragraph 1)? Don't doctors
usually "look in on" their patients? What effect does Selzer hope to achieve by starting
with such a statement?

2. The writer uses the present tense throughout this piece. Would the past tense be
just as effective? Explain your answer.

3. Selzer writes in the first person. Why might he have decided to make himself
prominent in the report in that way? How would his report have come across if it had
been written in the third person rather than the first person?

4. How would you describe this doctor's attitude toward his patient? How would you
describe the nurse's attitude toward the patient? How does the narrator manage to
characterize himself in one way and the nurse in another?

5. Is the title, "The Discus Thrower," appropriate for this piece? In a slightly revised
version, the title was changed to "Four Appointments with the Discus Thrower." Is this
a better title?

6. What do you think Selzer's purpose was in writing this essay? Did he simply wish to shock us, or is there a message in this piece for the medical profession or for those of us who fear illness and death?

7. The essay reports on four visits to the patient by the doctor. Write a shorter version reporting on two or more visits by the head nurse. How would she react to the patient's request for shoes? How might her own point of view explain some of her reactions?

8. For many of us, knowledge of hospitals is limited, perhaps to television shows in which the hospital functions as a backdrop for the romances of its staff. Write a short essay in which you present your conception of what a hospital is and in which you consider how Selzer's essay either made you revise that conception or reaffirmed what you know through experience.

MAKING CONNECTIONS

1. Consider the writers included here who treat one person as their subjects. Besides Selzer, Dennis Hevesi, Ernest Hemingway, and Banesh Hoffmann offer examples. How close to their subjects do these writers get? Compare two of these writers closely, one who seems to get quite close to his subject and another who maintains more of a distance. Do you think that closeness or distance is unavoidable or more a matter of strategy? What effect does the difference have on the resulting reflective essay or report?

2. Selzer and Roy C. Selby, Jr., write of human subjects. Farley Mowat and Jane van Lawick-Goodall write of animals. Does this choice of subject seem to affect the distance the writer maintains, achieves, or overcomes in offering his or her report? Do you find any common denominators here? How do you account for them?

TIBETAN MEDICINE:
THE SCIENCE OF HEALING

John F. Avedon

John F. Avedon is a writer whose interest in Tibet began in 1973, on his first trip to Asia, when he toured a Tibetan refugee camp in New Delhi, India. The material presented here is a chapter from his book on present-day Tibet, In Exile from the Land of Snows. *His intent was "to tell Tibet's tale through the lives of those who have both defined and been governed by the major developments in recent history." Avedon also included "some measure of Tibetan civilization, the spiritual underpinnings of which permeate every facet of the country's political life." In the following selection, the life of Dr. Yeshi Donden, physician to the Dalai Lama, the ruler of the Tibetans, serves to illuminate the ancient science of Tibetan medicine.*

Dr. Yeshi Dhonden pressed the three middle fingers of his right hand gently   1
along the inside of William Schneider's left wrist, bowed his head and listened. The fifty-two-year-old patient smiled, perplexed. The physician before him wore neither a white coat nor a name tag. He asked no questions and carried no charts or instruments. Dressed in maroon robes, head shaved, a turquoise-studded charm box bulging beneath his orange shirt, Dr. Dhonden remained motionless, deep in concentration. A minute later, he took the patient's right arm and briefly pressed the radial artery as if to confirm his findings. Ushering Mr. Schneider into an adjacent room, the doctor gestured for him to undress, whereupon he pressed selected points along his spine. With each touch, Mr. Schneider cried out in pain. Dr. Dhonden nodded sympathetically and told him to get dressed.

In his guest suite at the University of Virginia, Dr. Yeshi Dhonden offered   2
his diagnosis of William Schneider, a man he knew nothing of and had met only minutes before. "Many years ago you lifted a heavy object," he said, speaking through an interpreter. "At that time you damaged a channel in the vicinity of your right kidney, blocking the normal flow of wind through your back. The wind has accumulated outside the channel, there is bone deterioration and the disease has become quite severe." Mr. Schneider was stunned. For three years, he confirmed, he had suffered from acute arthritis along the neck and lower back. The illness had caused incapacitating pain, and he had been

forced to give up his job. But he was even more astonished at Dr. Dhonden's ability to reconstruct his past. "In 1946," he recalled, "I injured my back lifting a milk can out of a cooler. I was in bed a week, and as soon as I got up I reinjured it and was bed-ridden again. That must have been the start of the whole problem."

It was a diagnosis that Western physicians could arrive at simply by using an X ray, but Dr. Yeshi Dhonden, the Dalai Lama's personal physician, sent by him in the winter of 1980 to introduce Tibetan medicine to the West, enthralled American doctors and patients alike with his unique skills. "It's quite conceivable that in our attempt to be scientific, some of our powers of observation have atrophied," said Dr. Gerald Goldstein, a professor at the University of Virginia's Medical Oncology Department, who worked closely with the Tibetan physician during his stay. "Dr. Dhonden, on the other hand, is totally attuned to everything that is going on. He uses all of his senses as his medical instrument. Our patients have been very impressed." Dr. Richard Selzer, assistant professor of surgery at Yale University, met Yeshi Dhonden in 1974 on his first visit to the United States. "I went to observe Dr. Dhonden with some healthy skepticism," he recounted. "I was surprised and elated by what I found. It was as if he was a human electrocardiogram machine interpreting the component parts of the pulse. We have nothing like it in the West. It's a dimension of medicine that we have not yet realized." "Western scientific documentation of Tibetan claims is nonexistent," observed Dr. Herbert Benson, leader of a team of Harvard researchers that visited the Tibetan Medical Center in 1981. "It would be nice, though, to discover the worth of what they have developed over thousands of years. If their claims are only partly true they would be worthy of investigation. Therefore, can we really afford to ignore this?"

To test the efficacy of Tibetan drugs by laboratory standards, Yeshi Dhonden agreed, while in Virginia, to engage in an experiment with cancerous mice. On the basis of a visual examination alone, he prescribed a general Tibetan cancer drug, comprised of over sixty ingredients, for nine tumor-implanted mice in a lab in the University of Virginia's vivarium. Six mice refused the medicine and died within thirty-five days. Three mice accepted it and survived up to fifty-three days. A second experiment involving sixteen animals confirmed the findings, producing the most successful results since work with the particular tumor involved began in 1967. Of even greater interest, though, was the fact that Dr. Dhonden had no knowledge of the nature of the cancer he was dealing with. "There are literally hundreds of kinds of tumors," commented Dr. Donald Baker, the researcher in charge of the experiment. "How often has Dr. Dhonden encountered a KHT anaplastic sarcoma growing in a highly inbred strain of 3CH/HEJ female mice? It would be utterly unreasonable to ask him to decide what would be the best treatment. If he had been familiar with these conditions he might well have effected a complete cure." "There is no question that this is a very fertile area for cancer quacks," added Dr. Goldstein. "In the end, though, things either work or they don't work. Dr. Dhonden has things that work."

Sitting cross-legged over a cup of butter tea in his Virginia apartment, Dr. Dhonden offered a brief description of cancer in Tibetan terms. "I've treated perhaps one thousand cancer patients of which sixty to seventy percent have been cured," he maintained. "Our medical texts specify fifty-four types of tumors which appear at eighteen places in the body in one of three forms. We consider cancer to be a disease of the blood. It begins with pollutants in the environment. These, in turn, affect seven types of sentient beings in the body, two of which are most susceptible. They are extremely minute, but if you could see them, they would be round, red and flat. They can travel through the bloodstream in an instant, are formed with the embryo in the womb and normally function to maintain strength. In general the Buddha predicted that eighteen diseases would become prevalent in our time due to two causes, low moral conduct and pollution. Cancer is one of the eighteen."

Based on the results of his first experiment those physicians working with Yeshi Dhonden hoped to initiate a broader study of Tibetan medicine in the West. Dr. Dhonden, too, was eager to undertake an in-depth exchange of medical lore. "If Western medicine can come to understand the Tibetan view of the human organism," he commented toward the close of his stay in Virginia, "I feel it will be of inestimable value. Our medicine has many cures for diseases which Western doctors currently don't understand or have incorrectly identified. We successfully treat diabetes, various forms of coronary disease, arthritis, hepatitis, Parkinson's disease, cancers, ulcers and the common cold. We have difficulty treating epilepsy and paralysis. But because the Tibetan system is scientific, Western physicians, as scientists, will see what is of value and what is not." To illuminate an ancient science hidden behind the Himalayas for over two thousand years, Yeshi Dhonden described his own life and training as a Tibetan doctor.

Dr. Dhonden was born in 1929 into a wealthy family of farmers living in the small village of Namro, south of the Tsangpo River, one day's ride from Lhasa. Much of the land surrounding Namro belonged to the Dhonden family and their relatives. Five thousand sheep, yaks and horses and many fields of *chingko* or mountain barley were owned by Yeshi Dhonden's aunt and uncle, who, not having a male child, assumed he would grow up to run the estate. Dr. Dhonden's parents, however, felt differently. As their only child, they decided that Yeshi Dhonden should devote his life to the Dharma.[1] Accordingly, at the age of six, their son left his home and traveled a short way up the mountain behind Namro, to be accepted as a novice monk in the local mon-

[1] Dharma: the corpus of Buddhist teaching. [Eds.]

astery of Shedrup Ling. "I remember it all," recollected Dr. Dhonden. "Becoming a monk, entering into the comfort of the group, living with my teacher. I had a strong wish to learn quickly and my mind was very clear. I could memorize four of our long pages in a single day." Yeshi Dhonden's facility for memorization earned him a high position among his peers, on the basis of which he was selected at the age of eleven to represent Shedrup Ling at Mendzekhang, the larger of Lhasa's two state-run medical colleges. Like all monasteries, district headquarters and military camps, Shedrup Ling was required by the government to send medical students to Lhasa. Upon the completion of their training, they would then return to practice in their region. But while the monastery's superiors were not averse to receiving the government salary paid to them for their students' attendance, the four hundred monks were less than enthusiastic at the prospect of medical studies. "Everyone in the monastery was afraid that he would be selected," recalled Dr. Dhonden, laughing. "No one wanted to become a doctor. You have to spend at least eleven years in classes and there is a tremendous amount of memorization. But because I liked to memorize, when my parents told me that I had been chosen, I was eager to go."

The medical system Yeshi Dhonden was to study had begun as one of the ten branches of learning originally pursued by all Mahayana Buddhist monks. It flourished for over a thousand years in the great monastic universities of northern India, from whence it was taken to Tibet by two Indian pandits in the first century B.C. Thereafter, it was the province for almost seven hundred years of a single family of physicians attendant on the Royal Tibetan Court. With the introduction of over a hundred Buddhist medical texts in the sixth century, however, it grew into a widespread practice and was ultimately acclaimed by a conference of physicians from nine nations convened in Tibet, as the preeminent medical science of its time. Subsequently, Tibet's first medical college, called Melung or "Country of Medicine," was built in the eighth century by King Trisong Detsen in Kongpo, south of Lhasa. Melung inspired the founding of scores of medical schools, most contained in *dratsangs* or colleges appended to the country's larger monasteries. In the mid-seventeenth century, the Fifth Dalai Lama built Tibet's second medical college, called Chokpori, atop Iron Hill, just across from the Potala.[2] There, doctors from all across Tibet and Mongolia were trained to practice a composite of the various schools of medicine that had developed over the years. The need for more physicians in modern times resulted in the Thirteenth Dalai Lama's construction of Tibet's most recent central medical college, Mendzekhang or "Medicine House," in 1916.

Mendzekhang lay on the west side of Lhasa, next to the Tibetan government's newly built post and telegraph office. It was centered on a flagstone courtyard, with dormitories for students, both lay and monk, occupying two long wings, at the head of which, facing the main gate, stood the classrooms, assembly hall

8

9

---

[2] Potala: the winter palace of the Dalai Lama. [Eds.]

and the Master's quarters. Outside, the college walls were lined with display beds of frequently used medicinal plants. Inside, life at Mendzekhang followed a spartan schedule. At four each morning a bell sounded in the main temple at the head of the courtyard. Yeshi Dhonden had a few minutes to wash and roll up his bedding before hurrying to his classroom to begin memorizing by the soft light of butter lamps. As the mind was believed to be most fresh on waking, the first three hours before sunrise were given over to the memorization of the 1,140 pages of the four medical tantras, the root texts, preached by the Buddha, which, together with hundreds of commentaries and pharmacological catalogues, were the basis of Tibetan medicine. At seven o'clock instructors quizzed their students on the morning's work, after which they would return to their rooms for the day's first bowl of tea. A second bell then rang, and the whole college gathered to pray in long seated rows running the length of the pillared assembly hall, its walls hung with *thankas* illustrating herbs, anatomy, embryonic development and surgical instruments. On the way back to his room, Yeshi Dhonden would pass patients lined up for treatment beneath the apartments of Kenrab Norbu, the Master of Mendzekhang. Under their instructors' observation, senior students examined the sick while other professors, along with all the doctors of Chokpori, fanned out into the city on morning house calls, visiting those too ill to come to the colleges. As always in Tibet, medical treatment was free, only the medicines themselves having to be paid for.

Although Yeshi Dhonden's day was spent mainly in memorization, he often looked in on Mendzekhang's chief pharmacist and his staff. Two doors east of the front gate, they carried out the first step in the preparation of medicines, pounding into a fine powder the various roots, stems, leaves and branches as well as the numerous gems, minerals and animal products used in the 2,000 drugs routinely made by the college. The demands of their work were so great that Mendzekhang was covered with the raw materials of the trade. Hundreds of pungent medicinal plants, collected on expeditions into the mountains, were laid out to dry throughout the school's hallways, classrooms and rooftops. Subsequently they were administered either in powder form or as shiny black and brown pills.

Following an early dinner at five o'clock, the student body once again assembled, this time to practice debate. Seated by class in the courtyard, the college would, on the Master's signal, break into a cacophony of shouts, claps and loud retorts as attackers queried their respondents on the correct interpretation of the tantras' description of the causes, conditions and treatments of various illnesses. Often debates became so heated that when the five-hour session had concluded, individual pairs, a small group of entranced onlookers seated around them, their *sens* or outer robes wrapped tightly against the chill, continued debating far into the night.

After two years and four months, Yeshi Dhonden completed memorizing the medical tantras. He then recited for a full day before his teacher, declining to divide his first test over a period of time, as was customary. Promoted, despite his youth, to be senior student among the five in his room, he went on to take his official examination. The mornings of four days were set aside. His parents came from Namro to attend, while his home monastery, Shedrup Ling, offered a tea service at each session. Yeshi Dhonden, aged thirteen and a half, then appeared in the Assembly Hall before the Master of Mendzekhang, the faculty and the entire student body and after prostrating three times to the images of the Medicine Buddha and Tibet's most famous doctor, Yuthok Yonten Gonpo, on the main altar, recited verbatim the one hundred fifty-six chapters of the four tantras—in and out of sequence—as he was requested. Only minor mistakes were accepted—a lapse of any kind being considered grounds for failure. On the afternoon of the fourth day Yeshi Dhonden was informed that he had passed in good standing. Rewarded with a white scarf and a set of brocade book covers, he was admitted into the college to commence his formal education.

Dr. Dhonden spent the next four years absorbed in eleven divisions of study. To provide an overview of the medical system, Mendzekhang's curriculum began with the Illustrated Tree of Medicine, a diagram wherein each field of learning found its proper place in relation to the whole. Yeshi Dhonden and his fellow students spent long hours laying out on the large flagstones before their rooms the three roots, nine trunks, forty-two branches, two hundred twenty-four leaves, three fruits and two flowers of the tree, using colored thread, sticks and bright plastic buttons from the Barkhor or marketplace. After they had mastered the diagram, they were taught how to collate the appropriate chapters of the tantras with the various parts of the tree, following which they entered into the study of root one, trunk one, branch one, explaining the most important topic in Tibetan medicine, the theoretical basis for the entire system, that of the three bodily humors.

As explained by the Buddha in the First or Root Tantra, three humors govern the condition of all sentient beings: wind, bile and phlegm. Wind is described as rough, hard, cold, subtle and motile in nature; bile as light, oily, acrid and hot; phlegm as sticky, cool, heavy and gentle. Five kinds of each orchestrate the human organism. The five winds control movement, respiration, circulation, secretions and the joining of consciousness to the body; the five biles, digestion, sight and skin tone; the five phlegms, among other functions, the body's cohesiveness. The quantity of wind in an average adult is said to fill a bladder, that of bile a scrotum, that of phlegm, three double handfuls. Although active throughout the body, wind predominates in the pelvis, bile in the middle torso and phlegm in the upper torso. Wind moves through the skeleton, bile in the blood, phlegm in the chyle, flesh, fat and regenerative fluid. Phlegm prevails in youth, bile in adulthood, wind in old age. When all the humors are in balance, health exists. The smallest imbalance, however, produces disease. Every illness—of which the tantras account for 84,000 in 1,616 divisions— owes its cure to the correction of a humoral imbalance. Equipped with such

273

an all-inclusive theory, the medical system could address itself to any disease, known or unknown, including mental illness, as not just the body but also the personality of each individual was said to be governed by the balance of humors in his makeup.

With a working knowledge of the humors, Dr. Dhonden went on to study 15 embryology, anatomy, metabolic function, signs of death, pathology, treatment and diagnosis. In embryology, conception, followed by the weekly growth of the embryo (including the nature of its consciousness at critical stages of development), was described in texts predating Western medicine's own findings by 2,000 years. Techniques for determining the sex of the child prior to birth were demonstrated, along with medicines which would reduce labor to between two and four hours, guard against postpartum infection and ease pain. Anatomy was the next subject. As autopsies were performed only if attending physicians disagreed on the cause of death, Mendzekhang's students obtained their anatomical knowledge from detailed charts first drawn up late in the eighth century when the practice of surgery in Tibetan medicine was at its height. At that time Tibetan surgeons had routinely performed heart and brain surgery until the mother of King Muni Tsenpo, Tibet's thirty-eighth monarch, died during an operation to lessen swelling from water retention around the heart. Following her death, surgery was officially banned. Nevertheless, minor operations continued to be performed and the use of surgical instruments as well as that of anesthetizing drugs remained part of the Mendzekhang program. While metabolic function and signs of death were relatively brief topics, pathology, treatment and diagnosis were immense undertakings, requiring Yeshi Dhonden's greatest efforts. Pathology alone dealt with in the ninety-two chapters of the Third or Oral Tradition Tantra, entailed individual descriptions of the categories, causes, symptoms and complications of thousands of diseases, supplemented by their treatments under varying conditions. It was here that memorization of the tantras proved invaluable as, equipped with commentaries written by Tibet's long line of physicians, Yeshi Dhonden gradually built up an intricate picture of the entire range of human illness through its expression in single, double and triple humoral imbalances. The study of diagnostic procedure, though, was even more difficult. Unlike academic topics, the three trunks, eight branches and thirty-eight leaves of the Diagnostic Root of the Tree of Medicine could be thoroughly understood only through actual practice. Questioning the patient and analyzing nine aspects of his urine were essential to diagnosis. But it was mastery of the third trunk, pulse diagnosis, that was the hallmark of a leading physician.

Although pulse diagnosis was taught for an entire year in Mendzekhang, it 16 was believed to take a decade or more to fully comprehend. The basics were laid out in thirteen sections of the Last Tantra. The first four detail eight guidelines for the evening before an examination. To prepare themselves, both patient and doctor should refrain from the consumption of tea, alcohol and overly nutritious food, also avoiding exercise, sex and any anxiety-producing encounter. The following morning, after the sun has risen but, as the Tantra says, before "its rays have fallen on the mountaintop," the pulse should be read. In this brief period, two definitive factors characterizing every pulse, disease and medicine—the forces of hot and cold—are believed to be most in equilibrium. Prior to dawn, lunar influences, manifested in an enhanced cold or negative pulse, accentuate wind and phlegm; after dawn, solar influences augment the hot or positive pulse of bile and blood (sometimes spoken of as the fourth humor). Because the patient has not yet eaten, digestion does not obscure other functions, while all the winds have subsided during sleep into the heart of the central channel, where, according to tantric theory, the mind and body are joined.

The best place to read the pulse is said to be on the patient's wrist, just over 17 the radial artery. The Last Trantra queries itself: "Why is the radial artery used?" It replies that listening to arteries close to the vital organs "is like talking to someone by a waterfall," whereas using those in the extremities is like receiving "messages brought by distant merchants." The radial artery is the optimum position and is likened to "a voice in summer shouting across an open field." "How is it possible to read the quality of the twelve organs at the radial artery?" the tantra continues. "Just as a successful businessman can discern the place of origin and make of wares at a marketplace, so the pulse if read at the radial artery can exhibit the condition of the hollow and solid organs." Only in children below the age of eight and terminally ill patients is the pulse to be read elsewhere: in the former, on the blood vessels in the lobe of the ear; in the latter, to determine how many days of life remain, at the posterior tibial artery behind the ankle.

The doctor is now instructed in the technique for taking the pulse. If the 18 patient is male, the left arm is examined first; if female, the right. Switching hands, the physician then examines the patient's other arm. In both cases he uses the three middle fingers of either hand spaced apart the width "of a grain," while to overcome the thickness of the forearm's muscle, his index finger presses the skin, his middle finger the flesh and his ring finger the bone. The essential ingredient of pulse diagnosis is explained next. Each of the six fingers used is to be divided into an "inner" and "outer" half. These twelve positions monitor the organs; hollow organs are read on the outer half, solid on the inner. For example, the outside of the physician's right index finger reads the heart; the inside, the small intestine; the outside of his middle finger, the spleen; the inside, the stomach. The correspondence of all six fingers is the same for both men and women save for one instance. In a male patient the doctor's right index finger registers the heart; his left, the lung. With a female patient the reverse applies. They are switched because the consciousness of a woman is believed to enter the center of the ovum and sperm at a slightly different position than that of a man at the time of conception. The text then admonishes the

275

doctor to always keep his fingertips "smooth, sensitive, without scars and pliable."

There is one final consideration before the pulse can be read. One of three [19] "constitutional pulses," corresponding to the three humors, is said to dominate every person. The male pulse, similar to wind, is bulky and prominent; the female, similar to bile, subtle and rapid; the neuter, similar to phlegm, slow and smooth. Unless the patient's particular type—any of which can be had by either a man or a woman—is known to the physician (either by examining the patient when healthy or by being told), a diagnostic error can easily be made. Furthermore, once the constitutional pulse is known, it is crucial to factor in the "seasonal pulse"—each season manifesting an influence on the characteristic pulse imprint of a particular organ, such as heat in summer, which affects the heart, and cold in winter, which affects the kidneys.

The doctor begins by ascertaining whether the illness is hot or cold in nature. [20] He does so by using his own respiratory cycle, to determine the rate of the patient's pulse. If the pulse beats five times per breath, the person is in perfect health. More than five beats denotes a hot disorder; less than five, a cold. Above eight in a hot disorder or below three in a cold disease means an extremely severe, usually uncurable problem.

One of twelve general pulse types is now sought. The six hot beats are strong, [21] ample, rolling, swift, tight and hard. The six cold beats are weak, deep, declining, slow, loose and hollow. If the moment all his fingers touch the radial artery a hot beat is superficially felt, the physician knows that the disorder is new and minor. If, after pressure is applied, they are felt deeply, the illness is chronic and complex. The reverse holds true for cold disorders; superficial pulses reveal old, serious ailments; deep ones indicate new, minor imbalances. From this second step the history of an ailment is known.

The state of the three humors in the body is now explored. Each humor, as [22] well as its combinations, possesses a characteristic pulse type. When it has been identified, the individual pulse of one of a huge number of conditions is sought. If the patient is pregnant, the "pregnancy pulse" will reveal it, as well as, after the sixth week, the sex of the child. If worms are present, the pulse is "flat" and seems to knot as it beats; if bacteria, it is incomplete, with "sudden, irregular and unpredictable cessation in the rhythm of the beat." In leprosy, the pulsebeat is "quivering," and contracting at its conclusion "like a person who limps." Wounds manifest a "bulky, hard and quick" pulse. A bullet lodged in the body produces a "limping and double" pulse as if there were two arteries, not one, being read. After describing tests to distinguish pulse types, the tantra instructs the physician to investigate the individual organs through the twelve positions on the fingertips. His exam complete, over a period of roughly one hundred breaths, the doctor knows what the humoral imbalance is, its severity, which organs are affected and in what manner.

As Yeshi Dhonden and his classmates discovered, however, the topic of pulse   23
diagnosis was far from exhausted. In the remaining sections numerous exceptions to the rules were cited as well as the uses of the pulse in determining
lifespan, spirit possession and, in an extremely complex section known as the
"Seven Amazing Pulses," the future course of an illness. In the eleventh section,
those pulses which reveal that a disease will be terminal are described, showing
how vivid the tantra's descriptions can be.

The "changing" death pulse is said to "flutter like a flag in the wind"; while   24
the "irregular" death pulse appears "like a vulture attacking a bird, who stops,
plunges, beats its wings quickly, stops again and then resumes flight." In a
combined wind-bile disorder, the patient's pulse will resemble "a fish leaping
out of water to catch a fly, who quickly shimmers back." Accumulation of
phlegm and wind producing death are like "the pecking of a hen eating grain";
that of a triple humoral imbalance, like "the saliva of a drooling cow, moving
in the wind." The text then enumerates death pulses unrelated to the humors.
If a healthy person who has had an accident has a thin pulse, he will die
shortly. If in a person who has been sick for some time the pulse suddenly turns
strong or violent, death is imminent. The amount of time left to live, within a
period of eight days, is shown by the absence of pulse. Death will occur in
three days if the liver or gallbladder pulse is missing; in two if the lung or large
intestine pulse is absent; in one if the tongue is black, the eyes are in a fixed
stare and the pulse of either the heart or the small intestine is gone.

Dr. Dhonden's true education in pulse diagnosis came only after his studies   25
were completed. At the age of eighteen he was sent to Kenrab Norbu, Mendzekhang's principal, to undertake a four-year internship with a master physician
practicing in Lhoka, who was already surrounded by many disciples. During
this second stage in his training, Dr. Dhonden rose before dawn each day to
take pulse, analyze urine and present his diagnosis of patients' ailments to his
new teacher. While his understanding of the myriad pulse types grew, he came
to have a profound regard for the efficacy of the entire medical system. Although
patients in advanced states of illness could not be cured, others, afflicted by a
number of usually fatal degenerative diseases, such as cancer and diabetes,
responded with complete remission. In the case of diabetes, seen in one out of
every two to three hundred patients, he witnessed many cures occurring within
six to nine months. When medicine proved ineffective, he and his teacher used
accessory treatments: emetics, purgatives, moxabustion, cauterization, blood-
letting and acupuncture or "Golden Needle" therapy, which, according to
Tibetan medical histories, originated in Tibet and spread to China via Mongolia.
Among the most successful treatments Yeshi Dhonden found were those for
senility (employing memory pills), those included in the divisions covering
women's and children's diseases as well as those in the eight branches of
infertility, itself an entire category of medical practice. Although rarely pre-

277

scribed, due to Buddhist ethics, two types of birth-control pill existed. One had to be taken for a few consecutive days, whereafter its effect lasted for a year; the other eliminated fertility for life.

A related specialty known as *chu-len* or "Extracting the Essence" dealt with rejuvenation. By using its medicines, religious practitioners on three-, nine-, or twelve-year retreats were able to survive, it was believed, on a single seed or flower a day. For lay people *chu-len* could restore hair and teeth while increasing lifespan by many decades. As Dr. Dhonden explained, "Each of us breathes 21,000 times a day; 500 of these breaths are associated with lifespan. *Chu-len* medicines, taken in conjunction with the correct meditation practices, increase the number of these breaths. From my own experience I can definitely say they work. I've known people in their hundreds who have undergone the full course of treatment, beginning at the age of fifty, and been restored to a state of middle age. I met one lama when he was 170 years old. He had gray hair but the face of a forty-year old."

Having administered rejuvenation treatment for two millennia, Tibetan physicians considered it a normal component of their medical practice. However, one group of drugs, as venerable as those of *chu-len*, excited particular interest— *rinchen ribus* or "Precious Pills." Whenver Dr. Dhonden returned to Mendzekhang to replenish his professor's medicines, he made sure to inquire which Precious Pills had most recently been manufactured in the college's pharmacy. Seven types existed, the weakest composed of eighteen ingredients, the strongest, known as the King of Medicines, of one hundred sixty-five. Wrapped in colored cotton, tied with rainbow-hued thread and sealed with wax, the Precious Pills received their name for two reasons: for their contents—gold, silver, mercury, pearl, ruby, sapphire and diamond, specially treated and then mixed with various medicinal plants—and for their function—as panaceas for the entire body. Precious Pills, it was believed, could cure the most intractable ailments. As their manufacture sometimes took up to three months of around-the-clock labor by a team of twenty druggists, they were extremely potent and administered only under strict conditions. The stronger ones often incapacitated the patient for a day, while toxins were eliminated and imbalances in the body corrected. Though Yeshi Dhonden was familiar with their ingredients, his internship was primarily geared toward expanding his knowledge of Tibetan medicine's vast pharmacopoeia. To check his progress, Kenrab Norbu required Dr. Dhonden to accompany the college each year on its annual outing to pick herbs in the mountains.

The journey commenced at the start of July and was attended by those who had completed memorization, generally 300 students and faculty in all. As a rule, each traveler brought three changes of clothing, the Buddha having stressed the importance of cleanliness while collecting medicinal substances. With one pack animal and a groom serving every two students, the caravan left Mendzekhang and, skirting Lhasa, proceeded a day north to Dhakyaba, a region of peaks and alpine meadows considered ideal for herb gathering. A large tent camp provided by the government, staffed with cooks and fully provisioned, already awaited the college. For seven weeks, changing location every three days, small groups of students and teachers set off at eight o'clock each morning to collect herbs just below the snow line. While harvesting, they recited prayers to the Medicine Buddha, intent on keeping the mind as well as the body pure. Thirty classes of plants, subdivided into fifty-nine categories, with each plant having nine divisions, were initially sought. Hundreds of herbs with less universal value were also taken. With the waxing of vegetative processes and the onset of pollination, barks and plant secretions received less attention; flowers, fruits, seeds and leaves, more.

Halfway through the summer, large wooden crates began arriving from Lhasa. Ordered from district governors months in advance, the crates contained dozens of medicinal plants that were unavailable in Central Tibet. They had been carefully picked with earth still around their roots and immediately packed in snow and ice. By the end of August, when all had arrived, the students had completed their own collections and were ready to take the year-end test on the identification of plants. 29

The exam took place inside a large tent surrounded by a high cloth wall. Within, stacks of wood covered with white cotton lined the enclosure, two hundred selected plants laid out haphazardly on top. With Kenrab Norbu presiding from a high seat at the far end, three faculty members, each assisted by a secretary, escorted students past the tables. While the secretaries recorded their replies, the students were asked to describe each specimen by type, species and the medicinal power of the active part. Guided out the tent's rear, they were separated from those yet to be examined, and the next group of three took their places. While they did, the scores were tabulated and given to the Master, who had them announced to the whole gathering—a procedure guaranteed to increase the tremendous tension the students alrady felt. The test completed, students once more were taken around, this time to have their mistakes pointed out. 30

Most of Mendzekhang's aspiring physicians took up to five exams before they could correctly identify a majority of each year's plants. In his first and second attempts, Yeshi Dhonden placed sixty-second, then forty-fifth in the ranking. By the age of twenty, though, with his internship completed, he captured third place. By coincidence his old roommates took first and second, giving the three friends a clean sweep of the top positions. Because their scores were so close, Kenrab Norbu ordered a retest. This time the young men were taken around the tables blindfolded. One by one their examiners held up plants, requesting that they be identified by odor and taste alone. As Yeshi Dhonden recalled, "This was very difficult, but fortunately all of us were able to answer correctly. 31

When the test was over, it was announced that I had come in number one. Later, though," he added, laughing, "I found out there had been a catch. Because I was graduating, my friends had pretended to make little mistakes. In reality I was number three, but thanks to their trick I was chosen as the best student in the college."

Following the exam, a large celebration, equivalent to graduation day, was 32 held. Hundreds of people came from Lhasa and the surrounding villages to watch as the students were publicly ranked. Those who took first and second places received long silk scarves embroidered with the words "Luck in the Day. Luck in the Night." Those who came in last didn't fare so well. The fifth from last was pronounced "Carrier of the Medicines"—a barb equivalent to "nurse"— and given a blue doctor's bag to hold, of the kind used by every physician's assistant. The fourth from last, called "The Doorman," was dressed in the black robes of a government servant and placed at the entrance to the tent; the third from last, costumed as a muleteer, escorted the second from last and the last— banished not from the race of physicians but that of men—known, respectively, as the "White" and "Black Donkeys." With bells, reins and halters on their necks and medicines loaded across their backs, the "donkeys" were driven around the camp, bellowing and braying, to the great amusement of the crowd, after which a picnic was shared by all. The next day the college returned to Lhasa, where a ceremony at the Central Cathedral took place and the year ended for a week's vacation.

After graduating, Dr. Dhonden served as Kenrab Norbu's special assistant 33 for three years. In the evenings he continued to debate with Mendzekhang's senior students and faculty members. Once a month he went to the Lingkhor, Lhasa's Holy Walk, to treat the hundreds of poor pilgrims and beggars who rarely came on their own for help. In conjunction with this, he paid special attention to cultivating the eleven vows of the physicians' code which attempted to instill an altruistic motive as the basis of a doctor's practice. As Yeshi Dhonden commented, concerning his own application of the ancient code, "I am just an ordinary person afflicted by desire, hatred and ignorance. But through contemplating the suffering I see in my work, I have tried to increase my compassion. As doctors we are expected to put kindness before all else." Out of his own curiosity, Dr. Dhonden also went, two hours a day, to the British Legation, to acquaint himself with Western medicine. Finally, in 1951, Kenrab Norbu sent Yeshi Dhonden's diploma to the office of the Cabinet, where it was officially confirmed. The Kashag then dispatched letters to district officials in Lhoka, as well as the government transport center, from which Yeshi Dhonden received free passage home. Thirteen years after his education began, Dr. Dhonden left Lhasa, looking forward to taking up practice on his own.

He didn't have long to wait. An epidemic had broken out along the Bhutanese 34 border, imported—along with chocolate, batteries, silks and the beloved fedora hats—by traders returning from India. In Tibet's high, germ-scarce environ-ment, those who contracted the disease—a form of intestinal influenza—died quickly. Scores of doctors had already flocked to the area.

Traveling to a monastery called Sungroling Gonpa, Dr. Dhonden joined 35 three physicians who had been attempting, unsuccessfully, to check the epi-demic. Nine of the monastery's 300 monks had already died, as well as many of the inhabitants of the village below its walls. Arriving just before nightfall, Dr. Dhonden was shown to a private room, where, after his regular evening meditation session, he went to sleep, expecting to see his first patients in the morning. During the night, however, he experienced an unusual dream, one which, though seemingly inexplicable by Western standards, demonstrated the close relationship of religion to science in Tibetan medicine. "In the night I dreamt that a naked woman came before me, a *khadroma*," said Dr. Dhonden, referring to a spiritual being believed, in a manner similar to that of an angel, to aid practitioners in meditation. "In her right hand she held a tantric drum; in her left hand she held a skull. She carried a bag of medicine under her left arm. A white tin cup with a red design and a slight crack on its rim, filled with urine, appeared before her. Then the woman asked me, 'After examining this urine can you tell me the disease of the patient? What is your diagnosis?' In the dream I looked at the urine and replied, 'This is today's epidemic, one of sixty-five types of the eighteen new diseases predicted in the tantras for this era.' 'What is its cause?' she asked. I responded that it was due, as the tantras state, to environmental pollution and that it was a hot disease. 'You said that externally it is a fever, but are you sure that internally it's not cold?' she said. At that time, because my memory was fresh from constant study, I recalled that the thirteenth and fourteenth chapters of the third Tantra address the topic of cold and hot diseases together. I answered her in debate form, quoting the text as proof, stating that there was no hidden cold fever, but that the ailment was hot both inside and out. We debated back and forth for some time and finally she said, 'What treatment will you give?' I replied, 'Because the bacteria causing the disease have mixed the blood and bile, medicine should be given to separate them.' Then she asked what the patient's behavior and diet should be—two aspects of treatment that always accompany medicine. I answered and she said, 'Tell me again. How will you cut the tail of this disease?' Once more we debated vigorously and then she laughed and suddenly disappeared. There was complete silence and I woke up."

In a short while, as the day began, Dr. Dhonden was brought tea. Afterwards 36 he was asked to visit his first patient, a twenty-three-year-old monk, infected by the illness, languishing in his room. "I went to see the young man," continued Dr. Dhonden. "It was a very serious case. The room he lay in stank. Diarrhea mixed with blood was pouring from him onto the bed and he was semi-comatose; he couldn't talk. I asked for his urine specimen and it was brought to me in a tin cup. All of a sudden I remembered my dream. It was the exact cup, even with the crack on the rim. 'Oh, I have already examined this before,' I thought. I was amazed. Then the whole dream came back. I recalled the debate and the treatment and immediately I prepared the correct medicines. The man recovered and after that, the epidemic in the village was completely stopped. Now when I look back on it," Dr. Dhonden said, "I feel that whoever came to me in the form of a *khadroma* that night was actually administering my true final examination."

As Dr. Dhonden's reputation spread, he spent the remainder of the 1950s 37 traveling from one district to another. "Each day I rode from village to village, returning periodically to Lhasa to obtain medicines," he recounted. "I was able to cure three quarters of my patients. And because I gave penicillin injections for skin disease—a great novelty among Tibetans—my reputation continued to increase. I never had a free day." A group of young relations began to study with him but before long the uprising against the nine-year-old Chinese occupation broke out in Lhasa and the Dalai Lama fled. "I saw His Holiness when his party came through my area," recalled Dr. Dhonden. "Those who weren't following him had joined the guerrillas to put up a last fight for our freedom. My students all had family members whom they couldn't leave. My own mother's legs were too poor for her to walk out and my father had said that he was too old to cross the high passes into Bhutan. As a monk, I wouldn't fight. So I felt that I had no other choice but to leave. I borrowed a horse, said farewell and set off."

Though Namro was only a few days from the border, the presence of Chinese 38 troops forced Dr. Dhonden to hide for over a month before finally, in the company of eighty other refugees, he descended a steep snow-covered slope, trekked through a valley and crossed a glacial stream into the forests of Bhutan. With only a few texts, instruments and medicines in his possession, he then walked across Bhutan begging day to day. "After I was forced to flee my homeland, I was overwhelmed by a deep sense of renunciation," reflected Dr. Dhonden. "I saw life as essenceless, without real stability. I only wanted to practice religion." Arriving at Buxa, Yeshi Dhonden requested permission to remain with the monks there while the rest of his group was transferred to road work. The Tibetan government official in charge replied, "You have the right to practice religion and you are also young and fit to work on the roads. However, if the Kashag asks me, 'Has any doctor come out of Tibet?' and I've sent you elsewhere, what will I say? Therefore, you studied medicine at the government's expense, and now the time has come for you to help us."

Dr. Dhonden was sent to Dalhousie, where 3,000 refugees, including the 39 elite monks of Lhasa's two Tantric colleges, Gyudto and Gyudme, were camped in squalid conditions. Tuberculosis, hepatitis and amoebic dysentery were rampant. Preparing what medicines he could from the few herbs available in Indian stores, he set up a clinic and went to work. "One day a sweeper in my clinic was bitten by a poisonous snake," he related. "Just as I was applying a Tibetan tourniquet, an Indian doctor arrived. He examined the bite and declared that unless his leg was amputated immediately the man would die in half an hour. I told him this was unnecessary; I had already given the man Tibetan medicine effective for poison. The doctor turned to the sweeper and said, 'You will die within minutes unless I operate, but this Tibetan'—indicating me—'thinks otherwise.' He asked him whose diagnosis he wished to accept. The sweeper had seen my work and so he replied mine. The doctor then compelled me to sign a paper releasing him from all responsibility in the case. There were many aspects to my treatment, but after ten days the sweeper could move about and in a month he was completely cured."

Despite the man's recovery, the episode proved to be the start of a serious conflict. Once a week Indian doctors came to inspect the refugees, in the course of which they dropped by Dr. Dhonden's clinic to demand that, as he was not certified in India, he discontinue practice. "During one of their visits I was examining a patient with skin disease," continued Dr. Dhonden. "The physicians saw this woman and together announced that she had chicken pox. They claimed that unless she was isolated an epidemic would sweep over all the refugees. I said bluntly that they were wrong. It was a minor heat disorder and no more. They departed, leaving medicine for her to take. I forbade her to. In a short while they came back and tried to remove her to an isolated house in the forest. I refused to let her go. They asked if I was willing to have an outbreak of chicken pox on my hands and I replied, 'The Tibetans are my own people. How could I ever harm them?' I then demanded that now *they* sign a paper, just as I had been made to, certifying that indeed this woman had chicken pox. They stalled and within a few days the woman was cured." Despite this minor victory, more battles ensued, until, in mid-1960, Yeshi Dhonden was unexpectedly summoned to Dharamsala. Word had reached the government-in-exile that a Mendzekhang-trained physician had escaped. Apprised of his existence, the Dalai Lama had called for Dr. Dhonden personally.

"I arrived in Dharamsala just before sunset," Dr. Dhonden remembered. "The hills were covered with tents. People were living in very poor conditions. They had refused to leave His Holiness and were going wherever he went." Directed to the kitchen area of the Secretariat compound at Mortimer Hall, Yeshi Dhonden sat and waited. He was finishing his tea when the Dalai Lama arrived. "Suddenly I heard His Holiness in the other room. 'Where is the doctor?' he said. I stood up, folding my hands in prayer, praying for his long life. I had a very strong mind of faith. But when he entered the room I began to weep. I had never wept upon meeting someone before. I must have been thinking of Tibet . . ."

The Dalai Lama questioned Dr. Dhonden on his escape and then requested

283

him to treat those camped around Dharamsala. Working out of the Nursery at Conium House, Dr. Dhonden began seeing patients under the observation of Tibetan government officials. Having met with their approval, he was summoned to the Dalai Lama once more, this time in the capacity of examining physician. After curing the Dalai Lama of a skin disorder, he was asked to see Kyabjé Ling Rinpoché, the Dalai Lama's senior tutor and head of the Gelugpa sect, who was bedridden in a hospital in Calcutta suffering from a severe case of pericarditis, an inflammation and swelling around the heart. In little over a year Ling Rinpoché was cured and Dr. Dhonden was officially appointed to be the Dalai Lama's personal physician, a post normally filled by up to four doctors in Tibet. His enthusiasm for his practice now fully recovered, he set about the momumental task of preserving Tibetan medicine in exile.

Only two other doctors had escaped from Tibet, neither of whom could assist Dr. Dhonden in Dharamsala. Alone, he began to train ten students in the rudiments of his science, their progress hampered by an almost total lack of funds. Yeshi Dhonden could do little until, one day in 1963, his many run-ins with Indian doctors yielded an ironically positive result.

Responding to repeated complaints from local physicians that the Tibetan was "stealing" their patients, a senior minister in the Indian Health Department arrived in Dharamsala to investigate. For a week he watched Dr. Dhonden diagnose patients by their pulse and urine, after which he carefully asked each individual his ailment. At one point, five officers from the nearby army cantonment came in to refill prescriptions. "When the minister saw them he exploded in rage," recalled Dr. Dhonden. 'We give you the best health care in India and now you've come here to eat shit from a Tibetan!' he yelled." The officers replied that in many cases they had been ill for fifteen years or more. Where Western medicine had failed, Tibetan medicine had succeeded. "Unlike other doctors," they said, "we don't have to tell Dr. Dhonden what's wrong. He tells us." The day before he departed for New Delhi, the minister came to Yeshi Dhonden's office. "You are doing very good work here," he said. "There is only one problem. You don't have enough students. I'm going to give you thirty thousand rupees a year and a twenty-bed hospital." In this manner, the Tibetan Medical Center was formally organized.

Dr. Dhonden assumed the roles of director and pharmacologist as well as chief examining physician. In 1965 he was joined by a second physician, who assisted in teaching the now seven-year curriculum, leading expeditions into the mountains behind Dharamsala to collect herbs and manufacturing 165 principal drugs. With 15 students graduating to join the 150 or so doctors practicing Tibetan medicine outside of Tibet and plans underway for a research wing, a museum and nine outpatient clinics in the settlements, Dr. Dhonden resigned from the Center in 1969. Opening a private practice in McLeod Ganj, he continued to see the Dalai Lama, taking his pulse each day just after sunrise, until in 1978 another physician was appointed to assist him. Dr. Dhonden was then freed to introduce Tibetan medicine to the West.

"The information required before Tibetan medicines could be approved for   46
use in the United States would take an army of lab technicians years to develop,"
commented Dr. Gerald Goldstein, speculating on the future of an exchange
between Tibetan and Western doctors as Yeshi Dhonden's visit in Virginia drew
to an end. "Each ingredient must be individually identified, purified from its
crude state and then thoroughly tested. Who is going to pay for it?" "Research
today is a cost-benefit situation," concurred Dr. Donald Baker. "How is a drug
company going to collect all of these medicines in northern India and still make
a profit at it?" "The impetus for the work, though, is clear," added Dr. Goldstein.
"Over one third of our pharmacopoeia comes from plants and microorganisms,
specifically some of our oldest and most effective cancer drugs. These are just
the sort of materials Tibetans have acquired experience with over centuries of
use. Personally, I think the drug companies are missing a bet. Some of these
medicines are definitely going to be active."

In the East, the bet has not been missed. Whereas Peking destroyed every   47
institution of the old Tibet soon after 1959, it preserved and later expanded
Mendzekhang. Now called the Hospital of Tibetan Medicine, Mendzekhang's
127-member staff treats 700 to 800 patients a day. Though the doctors have
been forced to curtail their unique knowledge of the mind's relation to the body
(considered, as a basic component of Buddhist teachings, anathema), volumes
of color photographs cataloguing medicinal plants have been compiled, while
many of the most valuable herbs indigenous to the Himalayas have begun to
be cultivated on high-altitude farms. Concurrently, Tibetan drugs are in widespread use throughout mainland China though they are referred to as Chinese
in origin and not Tibetan.

"Tibetan and Western medicine begin from completely opposite standpoints,"   48
said Dr. Dhonden, summing up his view of the two sciences after visiting the
United States. "To start with, a Western scientist looks though a microscope to
examine the cause of a disease in terms of its molecular particles. Only then
does he take into account the particular patient. Tibetan doctors begin with the
patient. We consider his disposition in terms of wind, bile and phlegm. And
then we approach the disease. The difference, I feel, makes for weakness and
strength in both. We lack many of the symptomatic treatments modern physicians possess. On the other hand, it would be useful for Western doctors to
understand the Tibetan presentation of the humors, their balance and imbalance
in the human body. Without this, their medical system remains incomplete. It
cannot establish a clear view of the correct causes and conditions governing all
disease. If young Western doctors would come and train with us for a period

of years—as well as relating their own system's analysis of disease—then, I feel, a true exchange could occur. So each of us it seems," he concluded, judiciously, "has something of value to learn from the other."

QUESTIONS

1. For most readers, Tibetan medicine is an exotic subject. How does Avedon help readers acclimate themselves to such a subject and a foreign sensibility? For example, how does he deal with the many Tibetan terms he uses?

2. Yeshi Dhonden's career can be called a medical success story. What are its highlights? How many times must he prove his ability? How would an American medical success story compare with Dhonden's?

3. What aspects of Tibetan medicine do you think would be useful to Western medicine?

4. Compare your most recent encounter with the processes of a Western doctor to Dhonden's approach. Would you agree with his assessment of Western medicine as starting with a microscope and not a patient?

5. Because Dhonden was so good at memorization he was chosen to represent his monastery at medical school. What particular talent might distinguish a student hoping for a career in Western medicine?

6. The story of Dhonden's education and career is framed by the account of his more recent trip to Virginia. What other essays in this collection use a similar framing device? What purpose does the frame serve?

7. Upon what sources other than Dhonden has Avedon drawn?

8. At a crucial moment in Dhonden's early career, the cure for intestinal flu comes to him in a dream (paragraphs 34–36). Describe a time in your life when the help you desired came from an unexpected source, such as a dream.

MAKING CONNECTIONS

1. Read Lewis Thomas's reflective essay, "1933 Medicine," and write a comparison of the Western and Tibetan systems of medical education. Of course Avedon attempts to be more comprehensive in outlining Tibetan medicine than Thomas ever pretends to be in outlining Western medicine. Still, Thomas gives enough detail to suggest some similarities and more differences. What surprises you most in reading the two accounts of medical education?

2. Read Richard Selzer's reflective essay, "Why a Surgeon Would Write." Notice that Selzer is quoted in Avedon's account, too (paragraph 3). What connections do you think Selzer would find between his own orientation to medicine and that of Dhonden?

3. Avedon and Michael Brown both assemble and organize a large body of relatively technical information. Compare their methods of managing such material and making it presentable to readers. What similarities do you find between them? What differences?

TWO REPORTS OF AN AIRPLANE CRASH

The Associated Press
The National Transportation Safety Board

The crash of a TWA jetliner on its way into Dulles International Airport outside Washington, D.C., was the lead story in the New York Times *on December 2, 1974. Almost a year later, the National Transportation Safety Board (NTSB) reported the results of their investigation into the causes of that crash. The work of the NTSB, which is also responsible for investigating rail, highway, marine, and pipeline accidents, has contributed significantly to the low rate of airline accidents in this country. We present here the newspaper article and the first part of the NTSB report, which reviews the accident itself, as examples of two different approaches to the reporting of the same event.*

BY THE ASSOCIATED PRESS

Upperville, Va., Dec. 1—

A Trans World Airlines 727, battling a driving rainstorm, slammed into a wooded slope near a secret government installation today, killing all 92 persons aboard. It was the worst air disaster of the year in the United States. 1

Capt. William Carvello of the state police declared "there are no survivors" after rescue workers had combed for hours through the wreckage on Mount Weather, a foothill of the Blue Ridge Mountains. 2

The plane, Flight 514, was bound for Washington from Columbus, Ohio, and was approaching Dulles International Airport when the tower lost radar contact at 11:10 A.M. 3

The crash site was about five miles north of Upperville, a tiny community in the tip of the state and about 20 miles northwest of Dulles. 4

First on Dulles Approach

According to the National Transportation Safety Board, today's was the first fatal crash by an airliner approaching Dulles, which opened in 1962. 5

A T.W.A. spokesman said 85 passengers and a crew of seven were aboard the flight, which originated in Indianapolis. He said 46 persons got on at Columbus. 6

The plane crashed about one and one-half miles from an underground 7
complex that reportedly is designed to serve as a headquarters for high government officials in the event of nuclear war. A Federal spokesman ackowledged only that the facility was operated by the little known Office of Preparedness, whose responsibilities, he said, include "continuity of government in a time of national disaster."

All of Mount Weather, a peak of about 2000 feet, is owned by the Federal 8
Government. One official confirmed that several government employees were at work at the building complex, and helped in search and rescue efforts.

The airlines released a list of the victims' names tonight after relatives had 9
been notified. The remains were taken to a makeshift morgue at the Bluemont Community Center, five miles from the site. Rescue operations were halted at 8:15 P.M. because of fog, high winds, and rain.

Dr. George Hocker, Loudoun County medical examiner, said the plane hit 10
just below the summit and cut a swath 60 to 70 yards wide and about a quarter of a mile long.

"There were just chunks of metal and total destruction," he said. 11

The police initially sealed off an area within a five-mile radius of the site to 12
all but law enforcement and rescue officials. A reporter who viewed the wreckage several hours later said that much of it was still burning and the largest piece of metal he could find measured only 5 by 10 feet.

The Federal Aviation Administration said there were no unusual commu- 13
nications from the plane before the crash, "just routine flight conversation."

The flight had been scheduled to land at National Airport near Washington 14
at 10:23 A.M. but was diverted to Dulles, a larger facility about 20 miles west of the capital, because of high winds.

When the Dulles tower lost radar contact 37 minutes later, it notified the 15
local authorities to begin a search. Captain Carvello said two state troopers found the wreckage almost immediately.

Apparently no one on the ground was hit by the crash nor were any buildings. 16
But a worker for the Chesapeake and Potomac Telephone Company said the wreckage had severed the main underground phone line into the secret government installation. It was restored after two-and-a-half hours.

According to Federal aviation experts examining the wreckage, the airliner 17
broke down through the treetops and its underbelly was apparently ripped off by a 10-foot high rock ledge at the end of a secondary road.

Visibility on the ground was only about 100 feet, with snow flurries mixed 18
with rain and some fog. The Dulles tower said that at the proper altitude, visibility would have been up to five miles, despite the rain.

John Reed, chairman of the National Transportation Safety Board, said "it 19
was impossible to say" what the cause of the crash was, outside of "an obviously premature descent." He said his team of accident investigators was still searching for the cockpit voice recorder and the aircraft's technical data recorder.

Mr. Reed said it was hoped that when these instruments were recovered, they would provide a clue to the fateful last minutes. 20

Bill Smith, a member of the Marshall, Va. Rescue Squad, said the plane hit "well below" the peak and there was "quite a bit of fire" at the site. He said the plane devastated about 700 to 800 yards of the mountain's surface. 21

Vance Berry of Bluemont, who said he lived about three miles from the scene, walked to it about an hour after the crash. 22

"There was nothing left but what looked like a bunch of crumpled up tinfoil," he said. "You couldn't tell it had been a plane. What was left of the fuselage was burning fiercely with a blue flame, even in the rain. For 100 yards the tops of the trees had been cut off." 23

Mr. Berry added, "The weather was fierce—winds up to 50 miles per hour, raining and foggy. I'd say the visibility was about 100 or 150 yards." 24

Richard Eastman, a ground maintenance employee of T.W.A., said after viewing the wreckage, "If you didn't know it was an airplane you could never guess it. The parts of the plane were scattered all over the area. There's no tail or wing that you could make out." 25

In Washington, relatives and friends of the victims waited in despair at private lounges at National and Dulles Airports for news from the crash site. 26

Carl Zwisler, a lawyer who said he believed his parents were on the plane, said Senator Birch Bayh, Democrat of Indiana, who had planned to take the plane back to Indianapolis, came into the lounge "and was very comforting." 27

"He was very helpful," Mr. Zwisler said. "He gave us his number and offered to try to help us any way he could." 28

T.W.A. said the seven crew members included three pilots, all based in Los Angeles, three stewardesses from Chicago and one from Kansas City. 29

AIRCRAFT ACCIDENT REPORT
NATIONAL TRANSPORATION SAFETY BOARD

At 1110 e.s.t., December 1, 1974, Trans World Airlines, Inc., Flight 514, a Boeing 727-231, N54328, crashed 25 nautical miles northwest of Dulles International Airport, Washington, D.C. The accident occurred while the flight was descending for a VOR/DME approach to runway 12 at Dulles during instrument meteorological conditions.[1] The 92 occupants—85 passengers and 7 crewmembers—were killed and the aircraft was destroyed. 1

The National Transportation Safety Board determines that the probable cause of the accident was the crew's decision to descend to 1,800 feet before the aircraft had reached the approach segment where that minimum altitude ap- 2

---

[1] VOR: very high frequency omnidirectional radio range, a radio navigation aid supplying bearing information; DME: distance measuring equipment, a radio navigation aid that provides distance information. VOR/DME is basic equipment used for an instrument landing in bad weather. [Eds.]

plied. The crew's decision to descend was a result of inadequacies and lack of clarity in the air traffic control procedures which led to a misunderstanding on the part of the pilots and of the controllers regarding each other's responsibilities during operations in terminal areas under instrument meteorological conditions. Nevertheless, the examination of the plan view of the approach chart should have disclosed to the captain that a minimum altitude of 1,800 feet was not a safe altitude.

Contributing factors were: 3

(1) The failure of the FAA to take timely action to resolve the confusion and misinterpretation of air traffic terminology although the Agency had been aware of the problem for several years;

(2) The issuance of the approach clearance when the flight was 44 miles from the airport on an unpublished route without clearly defined minimum altitudes; and

(3) Inadequate depiction of altitude restrictions on the profile view of the approach chart for the VOR/DME approach to runway 12 at Dulles International Airport.

1. INVESTIGATION

1.1 *History of the Flight*

Trans World Airlines, Inc., Flight 514 was a regularly scheduled flight from 4 Indianapolis, Indiana, to Washington, D.C., with an intermediate stop at Columbus, Ohio. There were 85 passengers and 7 crewmembers aboard the aircraft when it departed Columbus.

The flight was dispatched by TWA's dispatch office in New York through 5 the operations office in Indianapolis. The captain received a dispatch package which included en route and destination weather information. The flight operated under a computer-stored instrument flight rules (IFR) flight plan.

Flight 514 departed Indianapolis at 0853 e.s.t.[2] and arrived in Columbus at 6 0932. The crew obtained weather and aircraft load information. The flight departed Columbus at 1024, 11 minutes late.

At 1036, the Cleveland Air Route Traffic Control Center (ARTCC) informed 7 the crew of Flight 514 that no landings were being made at Washington National Airport because of high crosswinds, and that flights destined for that airport were either being held or being diverted to Dulles International Airport.

At 1038, the captain of Flight 514 communicated with the dispatcher in 8

---

[2] All times are eastern standard times expressed on 24-hour clock.

New York and advised him of the information he had received. The dispatcher, with the captain's concurrence, subsequently amended Flight 514's release to allow the flight to proceed to Dulles.

At 1042, Cleveland ARTCC cleared Flight 514 to Dulles Airport via the Front Royal VOR, and to maintain flight level (FL) 290.[3] At 1043, the controller cleared the flight to descend to FL 230 and to cross a point 40 miles west of Front Royal at that altitude. Control of the flight was then transferred to the Washington ARTCC and communication were established with that facility at 1048.

During the period between receipt of the amended flight release and the transfer of control of Washington ARTCC, the flightcrew discussed the instrument approach to runway 12, the navigational aids, and the runways at Dulles, and the captain turned the flight controls over to the first officer.

When radio communications were established with Washington ARTCC, the controller affirmed that he knew the flight was proceeding to Dulles. Following this contract, the cockpit voice recorder (CVR) indicated that the crew discussed the various routings they might receive to conduct a VOR/DME approach to runway 12 at Dulles. They considered the possibilities of proceeding via Front Royal VOR, via Martinsburg VOR, or proceeding on a "straight-in" clearance.

At 1501, the Washington ARTCC controller requested the flight's heading. After being told that the flight was on a heading of 100°, the controller cleared the crew to change to a heading of 090°, to intercept the 300° radial of the Armel VOR, to cross a point 25 miles northwest of Armel to maintain 8,000 feet,[4] and ". . . the 300° radial will be for a VOR approach to runway 12 at Dulles." He gave the crew an altimeter setting of 29.74 for Dulles.[5] The crew acknowledged this clearance. The CVR recording indicated that the Armel VOR was then tuned on a navigational receiver. The pilots again discussed the VOR/DME approach to runway 12 at Dulles.

At 1055, the landing preliminary checklist was read by the flight engineer and the other crewmembers responded to the calls. A reference speed of 127 kn was calculated and set on the airspeed indicator reference pointers. The altimeters were set at 29.74.

At 1057, the crew again discussed items on the instrument approach chart including the Round Hill intersection, the final approach fix, the visual approach slope indicator and runway lights, and the airport diagram.

At 1059, the captain commented that the flight was descending from 11,000 feet to 8,000 feet. He then asked the controller if there were any weather obstructions between the flight and the airport. The controller replied that he

9

10

11

12

13

14

15

---

[3] Altitude reference used above 18,000 feet m.s.l., using an altimeter setting of 29.92.
[4] All altitudes and elevations are expressed in feet above mean sea level unless otherwise noted.
[5] altimeter: instrument which shows the altitude of the airplace with respect to a fixed level, such as sea level. [Eds.]

did not see any significant weather along the route. The captain replied that the crew also did not see any weather on the aircraft weather radar. The CVR recording indicated that the captain then turned on the anti-icing system.

At 1101, the controller cleared the flight to descend to and maintain 7,000 feet and to contact Dulles approach control. Twenty-six seconds later, the captain initiated a conversation with Dulles approach control and reported that the aircaft was descending from 10,000 feet to maintain 7,000 feet. He also reported having received the information "Charlie" transmitted on the ATIS broadcast.[6] 16

The controller replied with a clearance to proceed inbound to Armel and to expect a VOR/DME approach to runway 12. The controller then informed the crew that ATIS information Delta was current and read the data to them. The crew determined that the difference between information Charlie and Delta was the altimeter setting which was given in Delta as 29.70. There was no information on the CVR to indicate that the pilots reset their altimeters from 29.74. 17

At 1104, the flight reported it was level at 7,000 feet. Five seconds after receiving that report, the controller said, "TWA 514, you're cleared for a VOR/DME approach to runway 12." This clearance was acknowledged by the captain. The CVR recorded the sound of the landing gear warning horn followed by a comment from the captain that "Eighteen hundred is the bottom." The first officer then said, "Start down." The flight engineer said, "We're out here quite a ways. I better turn the heat down." 18

At 1105:06, the captain reviewed the field elevation, the minimum descent altitude, and the final approach fix and discussed the reason that no time to the missed approach point was published. At 1106:15, the first officer commented that, "I hate the altitude jumping around." Then he commented that the instrument panel was bouncing around. At 1106:15, the captain said, "We have a discrepancy in our VOR's, a little but not much." He continued, "Fly yours, not mine." At 1106:27, the captain discussed the last reported ceiling and minimum descent altitude. He concluded, ". . . should break out." 19

At 1106:42, the first officer said, "Gives you a headache after a while, watching this jumping around like that." At 1107:27, he said, ". . . you can feel that wind down here now." A few seconds later, the captain said, "You know, according to this dumb sheet it says thirty-four hundred to Round Hill— is our minimum altitude." The flight engineer then asked where the captain saw that and the captain replied, "Well, here. Round Hill is eleven and a half DME." The first officer said, "Well, but—" and the captain replied, "When he clears you, that means you can go to your—" An unidentified voice said, "Initial approach," and another unidentified voice said, "Yeah!" Then the captain said "Initial approach altitude." The flight engineer then said, "We're 20

---

[6] ATIS—Automatic Terminal Information Service.

out a—twenty-eight for eighteen." An unidentified voice said, "Right," and someone said, "One to go."

At 1108:14, the flight engineer said, "Dark in here," and the first officer   21
stated, "And bumpy too." At 1108:25, the sound of an altitude alert horn was recorded. The captain said, "I had ground contact a minute ago," and the first officer replied, "Yeah, I did too." At 1108:29, the first officer said, "* power on this #."[7] The captain said "Yeah—you got a high sink rate." The first officer replied, "Yeah." An unidentified voice said, "We're going uphill," and the flight engineer replied, "We're right there, we're on course." Two voices responded, "Yeah!" The captain then said, "You ought to see ground outside in just a minute.—Hang in there boy." The flight engineer said, "We're getting seasick."

At 1108:57, the altitude alert sounded. Then the first officer said, "Boy, it   22
was—wanted to go right down through there, man," to which an unidentified voice replied, "Yeah!" Then the first officer said, "Must have had a # of a downdraft."

At 1109:14, the radio altimeter warning horn sounded and stopped. The first   23
officer said, "Boy!" At 1109:20, the captain said, "Get some power on." The radio altimeter warning horn sounded again and stopped. At 1109:22, the sound of impact was recorded.

At 1109:54, the approach controller called Flight 514 and said, "TWA 514,   24
say your altitude." There was no response to this or subsequent calls.

The controller subsequently testified that he noticed on the radarscope that   25
the flight's altitude was about 2,000 feet just before he called them.

The flight data recorder (FDR) readout indicated that after the aircraft left   26
7,000 feet, the descent was continuous with little rate variation until the indicated altitude was about 1,750 feet. The altitude increased about 150 feet over a 15-second period and then decreased about 200 feet during a 20-second period. The recorded altitude remained about 1,750 feet until impact.

During that same portion of the flight, the indicated airspeed varied from   27
240 kn to 230 kn until the altitude trace leveled off about 1,750 feet after which the airspeed decreased and fluctuated between 222 kn to 248 kn. Some of the fluctuations occurred within short time spans while others were within longer spans.

The heading trace showed little variation during the latter portion of the   28
flight. As the aircraft left 7,000 feet, the heading changed from an indication of 112° to about 120° in about 2.5 minutes. The heading did not vary more than 2° to 4° from that indication until impact.

As the aircraft left 7,000 feet, the vertical acceleration (g) trace was smooth   29
with little fluctuation. After 40 seconds, the g trace activity increased to about ± 0.1 g. This continued for about 1 minute and then increased in amplitude to about ± 0.2 g for about 70 seconds. At this point there was a blank in the

---

[7] * Indicates unintelligible word(s); # indicates nonpertinent word(s).

g trace. When the trace reappeared, it was still active, with variations in indicated g ranging from ± 0.2 to 0.5 g, until impact.

The accident occurred on the west slope of Mount Weather, Virginia, about   30 25 nmi from Dulles, at an elevation of about 1,670 feet. The latitude was 39° 04.6ᴵN and the longitude was 77° 52.9°W.

31

1.2 Injuries to Persons

Injuries	Crew	Passengers	Others
Fatal	7	85	0
Nonfatal	0	0	0
None	0	0	

1.3 Damage to Aircraft

The aircraft was destroyed.   32

1.4 Other Damage

Power and communications lines were damaged.   33

1.5 Crew Information

The flightcrew was qualified and certificated in accordance with the existing   34 FAA requirements. The captain was qualified to operate into Dulles under the provisions of 14 CFR 121.443.

1.6 Aircraft Information

The aircraft was certified and maintained in accordance with FAA-approved   35 procedures. The aircraft weight and balance were calculated to be within limits at takeoff and at the time of the accident. The aircraft was serviced with Jet A fuel, and there were 29,700 pounds of fuel aboard when the flight departed Columbus. There were about 19,300 pounds of fuel aboard at impact.

1.7 Meteorological Information

The weather in the area where the accident occurred was characterized by   36 low clouds, rain mixed with occasional wet snow, and strong, gusty easterly winds. A complex low-pressure system extended from western Kentucky to southeastern Virginia and the eastern Carolinas with small low centers located in western Kentucky and south-central Virginia. An occluded front extended from the Kentucky low through North Carolina into the Virginia low.[8] A warm front extended northeastward from the Virginia low into the Atlantic, while a cold front extended from the same low to the Virginia coast, then southward into the Atlantic. A large area of low cloudiness and precipitation extended from the mid-Atlantic states to the Great Lakes, and southward to Tennessee. High gusty winds extended from the Middle Atlantic States to the Great Lakes.

The aviation weather observations taken at Washington National Airport   37
between 0853 and 1054 reported scattered clouds at 700 feet, overcast at 1,200 feet, and visibility of 5 or more miles with very light to light rain. The winds were blowing from 70°, and the velocity varied from 25 to 28 kn with gusts of 35 kn reported at 0853, 44 kn reported at 0953, and 49 kn reported at 1054.

The aviation weather observations taken at Dulles International Airport be-   38
tween 0858 and 1055 reported an overcast at 900 feet with visibility varying from 3 to 7 miles in light rain. The winds were from: 080° to 20 kn gusting to 32 kn reported at 0858; 090° at 26 kn, gusting to 40 kn reported at 0955; and, 080° at 25 kn, gusting to 36 kn, reported at 1055.

The 1131 radar weather observation from Patuxent, Maryland, showed a   39
large area of weather echoes which included the accident area. One-tenth of the area was covered with thunderstorms which were producing moderate rain showers, and five-tenths of the area was covered with moderate rain. The thunderstorm cells were moving from 170° at 45 kn. The maximum cloud tops were at 24,000 feet between Charlottesville, Virginia, and the accident site.

There were three SIGMETS[9] in effect at the time of the accident. They   40
recommended caution due to ". . . moderate to severe mixed icing in clouds and precipitation above the freezing level" and embedded thunderstorms with tops near 40,000 feet. The cells were moving northeastward at 25 to 30 kn.

Although there were numerous pilot reports of weather conditions in the   41
area around Washington, none was received from pilots flying in the area where the accident occurred.

Ground witnesses in the accident area stated that, at about the time of the   42
accident, the local weather was characterized by low ceilings with visibilities ranging from 50 to 100 feet at the crash site. The wind was estimated at 40 mph with stronger gusts. There was a steady drizzle in the accident area.

At the request of the Safety Board, the National Weather Service (NWS)   43
studied the possibility of pressure changes in the accident area which could have contributed to the cause of the accident. Based on the observed wind direction and velocity at Dulles at 1025 (43 kn), the NWS calculated that a pressure drop of 0.4 millibars, equivalent to 0.012 in. Hg., could have occurred

---

[8] occluded front: when a warm front is overtaken by a cold front, the warm air is forced upward from the surface of the earth. [Eds.]

[9] SIGMETS are advisory warnings of weather severe enough to be potentially hazardous to all aircraft. They are broadcast on navigation aid voice frequencies and by flight service stations. They are also transmitted on the Service A weather teletype circuits.

if the wind conditions in the accident area were the same as the winds at Dulles.[10] This pressure change could result in an aircraft altimeter reading 13 feet higher than the actual altitude of the aircraft. They further calculated that if the wind velocity was 60 kn, the resulting pressure change could be 3.2 millibars (0.094 in. Hg.) causing an altimeter reading 95 feet higher than the actual altitude. A wind velocity of 80 kn could result in an altitude indication 218 feet higher than the aircraft altitude.

The accident occurred in clouds and during the hours of daylight.   44

1.8 Aids to Navigation

The navigational aids in use for the VOR/DME approach to runway 12 at   45
Dulles included the Martinsburg, Front Royal, Linden, and Armel VOR's. These navigational aids were flightchecked after the accident and were operating within the prescribed tolerances. The distance measuring function of Armel had been inoperative about 2 hours before the accident, but it was operating without reported malfunction shortly before and after the accident.

Automated radar terminal system equipment (ARTS III) was used by the   46
approach controller to observe and control the traffic. The ARTS III is a system which automatically processes the transponder beacon return from all transponder-equipped aircraft.[11] The computed data are selectively presented on a data block next to each aircraft's updated position on the air traffic controller's radar display. The information provided on the video display is aircraft identification, groundspeed in knots, and, when the transponder of the aircraft being tracked has Mode C capability, pressure altitude in 100-foot increments. The aircraft's transponder has this capability. The position accuracy of these data is limited to about $\frac{1}{4}°$ in azimuth and $\frac{1}{16}$ nmi in range.[12] Altitude is presented with a tolerance of ± 100 feet.

The controller's radarscopes are equipped with video maps which depict   47
various terrain features, the position of navigational aids, and other pertinent data. In this case, the video map did not display the Round Hill intersection which is the intermediate approach fix for this approach, nor did it display the high terrain northwest of that fix. The updated video maps depicting the Round Hill intersection had been ordered but had not been received at the time of the accident.

There was no current letter of agreement between Dulles Approach Control   48
and the adjacent ARTCC's regarding the use of the Armel VOR/DME approach to runway 12 at Dulles.

---

[10] Hg.: mercury, used to measure atmospheric changes and thus changes in altitude. [Eds.]

[11] transponder: a radio transmitter-receiver. [Eds.]

[12] azimuth: the horizontal direction of a celestial point from a terrestrial point; range: a line of bearing defined by a radio range. [Eds.]

1.9 *Communications*

No air-to-ground radio communication difficulties were reported.   49

1.10 *Aerodrome and Ground Facilities*

Dulles International Airport is equipped with three primary runways: 12/30,   50
1L/19R, and 1R/19L. The north-south runways (1L/19R and 1R/19L) are
11,500 feet long and 12/30 (runway 12) is 10,000 feet long. There are provisions
for ILS approaches to the north-south runways. Runway 12 is served by a VOR/
DME approach. In addition, a surveillance radar approach is available to all
runways. Runway 12 is equipped with high intensity runway lights but not with
approach lights. There is a visual approach slope indicator (VASI) installed on
the left side of the runway.

1.11 *Flight Recorders*

N54328 was equipped with Lockheed Aircraft Service Model 109-D flight   51
data recorder, serial No. 117, and a Fairchild Model A-100 cockpit voice
recorder, serial No. 1123. Both recorders were installed in a nonpressurized
area aft of the pressure bulkhead.

The flight data recorder parameter traces were clearly recorded. There were   52
no recorder malfunctions. A readout was made of the last 15 minutes 25 seconds
of the flight. There was a small gap in the vertical acceleration trace shown on
the data graph at time 13 minutes 30 seconds because of foil damage which
obliterated the trace.

The cockpit voice recorder remained intact and the recording was clear. A   53
composite flight track was prepared by correlating the recorder data.

1.12 *Wreckage*

The wreckage was contained within an area about 900 feet long and 200 feet   54
wide. The evidence of first impact was trees whose tops were cut off about 70
feet above the ground. The elevation at the base of the trees was 1,605 feet.
The wreckage path was oriented along a line 118° magnetic. Calculations
indicated that the left wing went down about 6° as the aircraft passed through
the trees and the aircraft was descending at an angle of about 1°. After about
500 feet of travel through the trees, the aircraft struck a rock outcropping at an
elevation of about 1,675 feet. Numerous heavy components of the aircraft were
thrown forward of the outcropping.

The wing flaps, wing leading edge devices, and the landing gears were   55
retracted. The condition of the flight control system could not be determined

because of impact and fire damage. No evidence was found of preimpact structural failure or control system malfunction.

All three engines separated from the aircraft and were damaged.   56

The major rotating compressor components were bent or broken in a direction opposite to normal rotation. There was no evidence found of preimpact engine fire or malfunction.   57

Most of the instruments on the pilots' instrument panels were destroyed, as were most of the aircraft navigational and flight instrument systems' components. Among those that were recovered and from which useful information could be obtained were the first officer's DME indicator which read 12 miles; the first officer's course deviation indicator which showed a selected course of 123°; and the first officer's altimeter, set at 29.70 in. Hg., with an internal indication of 1,818 feet. The first officer's flight director indicator showed the altitude marker at "0" feet, and the pitch display showed 5° aircraft noseup. An airspeed indicator was recovered with the reference pointer set at 123 kn; and a radio altimeter was found which indicated 10 feet. One distance measuring equipment interrogator unit was recovered; it showed a mileage indication of 12 miles and was tuned to a channel paired with 115.3 MHz., the frequency of the Front Royal VOR.[13]   58

1.13 *Medical and Pathological Information*

All of the occupants of the aircraft died of traumatic injuries. Post-mortem examinations and toxicological and histological analyses were conducted on all flight crewmembers. No evidence of disease was found and the analyses were negative. The medical histories of the flight crewmembers disclosed no evidence of abnormal conditions.   59

1.14 *Fire*

No evidence of in-flight fire was found. Scattered intense ground fires occurred throughout the wreckage area. Local fire departments were notified of the location of the wreckage about 1145 and about 150 fire and rescue personnel responded with six pumpers and several rescue vehicles.   60

1.15 *Survival Aspects*

This was not a survivable accident.   61

---

[13] Mhz.: megahertz, a unit of frequency equal to one million hertz, or cycles per second. [Eds.]

QUESTIONS

1. What information is present in the *Times* article but missing in the NTSB report? What does the NTSB report include that the newspaper account does not?

2. What does this difference in information tell you about the writers' conceptions of audience and purpose? Look back at the first two paragraphs of each report. How do these two openings reflect these conceptions?

3. The editors had to go to a library reference room to look up terms not explained by the writers of the NTSB report. Choose a term from the report that is not glossed or that is not explained clearly. Then find the best source in your library that explains the term better than the editors (or the NTSB) did.

4. Using the NTSB report, write an article for the *New York Times* in which you summarize the information in the report. Be sure to provide a headline.

5. Select an event familiar to you, and write a report about it aimed at a general audience that will need key terms explained. You might choose an event such as participating in a bicycle race or tour, entering a pet in a show, participating in a band concert or a wrestling match, preparing a special meal, or building a dog house. Give your report to a classmate for comments on any areas that may need revision for clarity.

MAKING CONNECTIONS

1. Compare the NTSB account of this crash with Horace Miner's "Body Ritual among the Nacirema." Although Miner's report is a parody, both reports exhibit formal features that show them prepared for specialized, professional audiences. Describe several formal features of each report. What can you infer about the audience and purpose of each report?

2. Compare the AP report of this crash with William Booth's "The Social Lives of Dolphins." How similar and how different are the methods of each report? What does your comparison tell you about the purpose of each writer?

EXPLAINING

EXPLAINING

Here in "Explaining" you will find writing by specialists from a wide range of fields seeking to account for matters as various as the color of the sky, the origin of the universe, the content of urban legends, and the art of Georgia O'Keeffe. Explanation is an essential kind of writing in every academic field and profession. Facts, after all, do not speak for themselves, nor do figures add up on their own. Even the most vividly detailed report or computer printout requires someone to make sense of the information it contains. To make sense of a subject, we need to see it in terms of something that is related to it—the color of the sky in terms of light waves from the sun, the content of urban legends in terms of the immediate circumstances in which they are told. To understand a subject, in other words, we must examine it in terms of some relevant context that will shed light on its origin and development, or its nature and design, or its elements and functions, or its causes and effects, or its meaning and significance. For this reason, you will repeatedly find the writers in this section drawing on specific bodies of knowledge and systems of interpretation to explain the problems and subjects that they address.

This essential element of explaining can be seen in connection with the following passage from James Jeans's "Why the Sky Is Blue":

> We know that sunlight is a blend of lights of many colors—as we can prove for ourselves by passing it through a prism, or even through a jug of water, or as Nature demonstrates to us when she passes it through the raindrops of a summer shower and produces a rainbow. We also know that light consists of waves and that the different colors of light are produced by waves of different lengths, red light by long waves and blue light by short waves. The mixture of waves which constitutes sunlight has to struggle through the obstacles it meets in the atmosphere, just as the mixture of waves at the seaside has to struggle past the columns of the pier. And these obstacles treat the light-waves much as the columns of the pier treat the sea-waves. The long waves which constitute red light are hardly affected, but the short waves which constitute blue light are scattered in all directions.
>
> Thus, the different constituents of sunlight are treated in different ways as they struggle through the earth's atmosphere. A wave of blue light may be scattered by a dust particle, and turned out of its course. After a time a second dust particle again turns it out of its course, and so on, until finally it enters our eyes by a

path as zigzag as that of a flash of lightning. Consequently the blue waves of the sunlight enter our eyes from all directions. And that is why the sky looks blue.

Jeans's purpose here is to explain "why the sky looks blue," and as you can see from the opening sentence of the passage, he systematically establishes an explanatory context by setting forth directly relevant information about the nature and properties of sunlight, light, and light-waves. That is, he approaches the explanatory problem in terms of knowledge drawn from his specialized fields of astronomy and physics. With this knowledge in hand, he then proceeds to show how "the different constituents of sunlight are treated in different ways as they struggle through the earth's atmosphere." In this way, he develops his explanation according to the analytic framework one would expect of an astronomer and physicist, concerning himself with the interaction of the atmosphere and light-waves. Having formulated a cause-and-effect analysis demonstrating that blue light is scattered "in all directions," Jeans is able to conclude that "the blue waves of the sunlight enter our eyes from all directions. And that is why the sky looks blue." Thus, the particular body of information that Jeans draws upon from astronomy and physics makes it possible for him to offer a knowledgeable, systematic, and instructive explanation.

To appreciate how significant an explanatory context can be, you need only consider how knowledge from other fields might influence an understanding of "why the sky looks blue." A zoologist specializing in optics, for example, might note the importance of the retinal organs known as cones, which in animals are thought to be the mechanism primarily responsible for the reception of color. Given this crucial bit of information, a zoologist might observe that the sky looks blue to human beings because their eyes are equipped with cones, whereas it does not look blue to animals lacking cones, such as guinea pigs, owls, and armadillos. An anthropologist, in turn, might think it worth noting that coastal and island cultures, given their maritime environments, tend to develop unusually rich vocabularies for describing how the sea looks and how the sky looks. Thus, an anthropologist might conclude that members of maritime cultures are likely to be especially discerning about the colors of the sea and sky.

Our hypothetical zoologist and anthropologist would both differ from Jeans in their explanatory approaches to the blue sky. Whereas Jeans approached it in terms of accounting for the source and prevalence of blue color, our zoologist and anthropologist would take the color for granted and seek instead to account for the human ability to perceive the color or the propensity of some cultures to be especially discriminating in their perception of it. Their differing approaches, in this case as in others, would result from their differing fields of study. Each academic area, after all, involves a distinctive body of knowledge, a distinctive array of interests, and a distinctive set of methods for making sense of the subjects that fall within its field of interest. Thus it follows that each area is likely to approach problems from different angles and arrive at different kinds of explanations. It follows, too, that no area can lay claim to the ultimate truth about things. But, as the case of the blue sky illustrates, each field does have a special angle on the truth, particularly about subjects that fall within its area of specialization. Our zoologist and anthropologist could be as valid and as enlightening in this case as the astronomer-physicist. In a broader sense, you can see from the case of the blue sky that in trying to explain a particular subject or problem one always has to look at it or approach it from a particular angle or a combination of viewpoints and that any particular approach brings a corresponding body of knowledge to bear upon an understanding of the subject. Relevant knowledge, quite simply, is the most essential element of explaining.

But knowledge alone is not sufficient to produce intelligible and effective explanation. Jeans's explanation, for example, depends not only upon a body of information about the properties and movement of light and light-waves but also, as you will see, upon the form and style in which the information is presented. To develop your ability in explaining, then, you will need to develop a resourcefulness in putting your knowledge to use. One way to do that is to familiarize yourself with some of the many different forms that explanatory writing can take in different academic and professional situations.

THE RANGE OF EXPLANATORY WRITING

Explanatory writing serves a wide range of academic, professional, and public purposes. Rules and regulations, guidelines and instructions—all these are familiar examples of explanation in the service of telling people how to carry on many of the practical and public activities of their lives. Textbooks, such as the one you are reading right now, as well as popularized presentations of highly specialized research or theory are common examples of explanatory writing in the service of helping people to understand a particular body of information and ideas. Scholarly research papers, government documents, and other highly technical presentations of data and analysis, though less familiar to the general reader, are important kinds of explanation that advance knowledge and informed decision making.

To serve the differing needs of such varied purposes and audiences, explanatory writing necessarily incorporates various forms and styles of presentation. Jeans's piece about the sky, for example, comes from a book intended as an introduction to astronomy. Thus, he writes in a style that depends on a vocabulary accessible to most readers. And to make sure that beginners will understand the important concepts in his explanation, Jeans repeatedly illustrates his discussion with analogies and references to familiar experience. In fact, if you look at the whole of Jeans's piece, you will see that he establishes his analogy of light-waves to sea-waves at the very beginning of his discussion and then systematically uses it to organize and clarify the rest of his explanation.

By contrast, the scientific paper by Antonio R. Damasio, "Face Perception without Recognition," is written for a highly specialized audience of researchers, as you can tell immediately from the abstract that precedes it as well as from its highly technical language and scholarly reference notes. Thus, Damasio does not structure his explanation in terms of a familiar analogy but instead uses a highly methodological format for reviewing research on a particular problem. According to this format, his review begins with a definition of the research topic and a summary of established knowledge, then moves into a detailed discussion of research on issues about which there has been "considerable controversy," and finally concludes with a look at some "new developments" in the study of the problem. In each of these sections of his review, Damasio refers to specific pieces of published research, which he enumerates and documents at the end of his article. Thus, the review of research not only provides readers with an explanatory overview of investigation, but it also tells them where to look for more detailed information on the subject.

For yet another variation in the format and style of explanatory writing, we need only shift our attention from the sciences to the social sciences and look at Bruno Bettelheim's "Joey: A 'Mechanical Boy.'" Here Bettelheim is not reviewing investigative research, but is offering the results of a case study, which entails the close observation of an individual subject over time. Because the subject of a case study is by definition unique, the study cannot be replicated by other researchers. A case study, therefore, must be written up in sufficient detail not only to document the observer's understanding of the subject but also to enable other researchers to draw their own conclusions about the subject. So, you will find that Bettelheim provides an extensively detailed description, history, and analysis of Joey's behavior. You will also find that Bettelheim writes on the whole in a standard rather than specialized style, as befits the audience of generally educated readers who are the predominant subscribers to *Scientific American*, the magazine in which his article first appeared.

However, we need only look at the following passage from the first paragraph of Joan Didion's essay, "Georgia O'Keeffe" to see that style and format do not always adhere to audience and purpose exactly as one might expect:

> I recall an August afternoon in Chicago in 1973 when I took my daughter, then seven, to see what Georgia O'Keeffe had done with where she had been. One of the vast O'Keeffe "Sky Above Clouds" canvases floated over the back stairs in the Chicago Art Institute that day, dominating what seemed to be several stories of empty light, and my daughter looked at it once, ran to the landing, and kept on looking. "Who drew it," she whispered after a while. I told her. "I need to talk to her," she said finally.

Judging from the plain style as well as the personal aspects of the story that Didion tells about her daughter's reaction to O'Keeffe's painting, you might think that this piece belongs in "Reflecting" rather than here in "Explaining."

306

But if you read the whole of Didion's essay, you will discover that it is a highly informed piece, in which she also tells some surprising stories about O'Keeffe in order to identify and explain what she perceives to be the most distinctive elements and qualities in O'Keeffe's work. You will also discover that Didion organizes her material and tells her stories in a way that is often quite surprising, yet also quite appropriate to what she considers to be most distinctive about O'Keeffe.

As you can see from our brief discussion of just this handful of selections, explanation is a widely varied form of writing, involving as it does in every case a delicate mix of adjustments to the audience, purpose, specialized field, and subject matter. Thus as a reader of explanation, you will have to be very flexible in your approach, always willing to make your way through unfamiliar territory on the way to a clear understanding of the subject being discussed, or perhaps to a clear recognition that understanding may be beyond the scope of your knowledge in a particular field. And as a writer, you will have to be equally flexible in your choice of language, as well as in your selection and arrangement of material, so as to put your knowledge and understanding in a form that not only satisfies you but also fulfills the complex set of conditions to which your explanation is addressed.

METHODS OF EXPLAINING

In planning a piece of explanatory writing, you should begin by reviewing your material with an eye to deciding upon the overall approach that you intend to use. As our previous discussion has indicated, you should aim to develop an approach that is adjusted to all the conditions of your explanatory situation. Some methods, you will find, are inescapable, no matter what your subject, audience, or purpose. Every piece of explanation requires that ideas be clarified and demonstrated through *illustration*—that is, through the citing of specific examples, as you can see from the earlier passage by Jeans and in the following excerpt from Bettelheim's essay on Joey:

> During Joey's first weeks with us we would watch absorbedly as this at once fragile-looking and imperious nine-year-old went about his mechanical existence. Entering the dining room, for example, he would string an imaginary wire from his "energy source"—an imaginary electric outlet—to the table. There he "insulated" himself with paper napkins and finally plugged himself in. Only then could Joey eat, for he firmly believed that the "current" ran his ingestive apparatus.

Bettelheim's obligation to illustrate and demonstrate Joey's machine-centered behavior leads him here, as elsewhere in his piece, to turn to a detailed *description* and *narration* of Joey's actions. So it is that reporting constitutes an essential element of explaining. And not only for reasons of clarity, but also for purposes of reliability and credibility. If an explanation cannot be illustrated, or can only be weakly documented, then it is likely to be much less reliable and therefore much less credible to readers than one that can be amply and vividly detailed.

Some methods, while not required in every case, are often so important that they should be kept in mind as being potentially necessary in any piece of explanation. An essay that depends on the use of special terms or concepts almost certainly will call for a *definition* of each term and concept, in order to assure that the reader understands them exactly as the writer intends them to be understood. In "Urban Legends: 'The Boyfriend's Death,'" for example, Jan Harold Brunvand begins his study by carefully defining urban legends as a subclass of folklore, and by defining in turn what is entailed in the study of folklore. Likewise, in his essay about Joey, Bettelheim introduces a special term and concept in the phrase "mechanical boy," and thus he immediately defines it at the beginning of his piece by citing examples of it in Joey's behavior, in his self-conception, and in the perception of him by others. Bettelheim also uses some relatively familiar terms in his discussion of Joey, such as "disturbed children," but he evidently recognizes that familiar terms, too, need to be defined, especially if they are being used in a specialized way. Familiar terms, after all, are commonly understood in different ways by different readers and writers. And the more varied are the understandings of a particular word or concept, the greater are the chances of it being misunderstood if it is not defined. Thus, Bettelheim defines the exact sense in which he means us to understand "disturbed children" by identifying an essential quality or character-istic of their disturbed behavior—"they remain withdrawn, prisoners of the inner world of delusion and fantasy." And just to make sure that we are clear about his definition, he sharpens it by distinguishing the fantasy life of "disturbed children" from that of "normal children." Definition, in other words, can be carried out in a variety of ways—by citing examples, by identifying essential qualities or characteristics, by offering synonyms, by making distinctions.

Other methods, while not necessarily imperative, can be very effective in a broad range of explanatory situations. If you are trying to explain the character, design, elements, or nature of something, you will often do best to *compare and contrast* it with something to which it is logically and self-evidently related. Comparison calls attention to similarities, contrast focuses on differences, and together the methods work to clarify and emphasize important points by playing related subjects against each other. In his study of urban legends, for example, Brunvand attempts to shed light on the complex circumstances that influence the content of such folktales by comparing and contrasting several versions of the same legendary story. His comparison and contrast enables him to show that popular urban legends, such as "The Boyfriend's Death," retain a basically unvarying situation and plot as they travel from one storyteller and locale to another, but that specific details are altered by individual storytellers to make them fit the circumstances of a particular audience. Like Brunvand's piece,

308

some examples of comparison and contrast rely on a strategic balancing of similarities and differences. Other pieces, such as Murray Ross's "Football Red and Baseball Green," which explains the differing appeal of two well-known American spectator sports, depend largely on a sustained contrast. And still other pieces might work primarily in terms of comparison. The mix within each piece is adjusted to the needs of its explanatory situation. By the same token, you should make sure that whenever you use comparison and contrast, your attention to similarities and differences is adjusted to the needs of your explanatory situation.

A special form of comparison, namely *analogy*, can also be useful in many explanatory situations. Analogies help readers to understand difficult or unfamiliar ideas by putting them in tangible and familiar terms. In "Why the Sky Is Blue," for example, Jeans's analogy of light-waves to sea-waves enables us to visualize a process that we could not otherwise see. And in "Times and Distances, Large and Small," Francis Crick discusses a variety of analogies that scientists have used in order to help people grasp measurements of space and time that are either so vast or so diminutive as to be otherwise quite difficult to comprehend. Useful as analogies are, however, they rely at last upon drawing particular resemblances between things that are otherwise unlike. Sea-waves, after all, are not light-waves, and the dimensions of the universe are not the same as anything within the range of ordinary human experience. Thus, whenever you develop an analogy, you should be careful in applying it to your explanatory situation, so as to make sure that the analogy fits and that it does not involve misleading implications.

Some explanatory methods are especially suited to a particular kind of situation. If you are trying to show how to do something, or how something works, or how something was done, you will find it best to use a method known as *process analysis*. In analyzing a process, your aim is to make it clear to a reader by providing a narrative breakdown and presentation of it step-by-step, by identifying and describing each step or stage in the process, by showing how each step leads to the next, and by explaining how the process as a whole leads to its final result. Jeans's piece, for example, analyzes the process by which light-waves from the sun make their way through the earth's atmosphere and determine human perception of the color of the sky. And Stephen Jay Gould in "A Biological Homage to Mickey Mouse" explains and illustrates the surprising process by which Mickey's "appearance became more youthful" over a period of fifty years.

A method related to process analysis is *causal analysis*. As the term suggests, this type of analysis seeks to get at the causes of things, particularly ones that are sufficiently complex as to be open to various lines of explanation. Usually, then, a causal analysis involves a careful investigation that works backward from something difficult to account for—such as the popularity of soap opera, the machinelike behavior of Joey, or the corporate career problems of aspiring women—through an examination of various causes that might account for the situation. Sometimes, however, an analysis might work forward from a particular cause to the various effects it has produced; Carol Gilligan uses this method in "Woman's Place in Man's Life Cycle" when she shows the numerous and quite different ways in which male and female children are shaped by the fact "that for both sexes the primary caretaker in the first three years of life is typically female." Because no two things can be identically accounted for, no set method exists for carrying out a causal analysis. Keep in mind, however, a few cautionary procedures. You should review other possible causes and other related circumstances before attempting to assert the priority of one cause or set of causes over another, and you should present enough evidence to demonstrate the reliability of your explanation. By doing so, you will be avoiding the temptation to oversimplify things.

As you can probably tell by now, almost any piece of writing that aims to make sense of something will invariably have to combine several methods of explanation. But this should come as no surprise if you stop to think about the way people usually explain even the simplest things in their day-to-day conversations with each other. Just ask someone, for example, to give you directions for getting from one place to another, and you will probably find that the person gives you both an overview of where the place is situated and a step-by-step set of movements to follow and places to look for, as well as brief descriptions of the most prominent guideposts along the way, and possibly even a review of the original directions, together with a brief remark or two about misleading spots to avoid. Whenever we ask for directions, after all, we want not only to get reliable information but also to get it in a form that cannot be misunderstood. So, whenever people give directions, they try not only to give them accurately but also to give them so clearly and fully from start to finish that they cannot be mistaken. By the same token, whenever people try to explain something in writing, they want to help readers get from one place to another in a particular subject matter. Thus, in the midst of giving a process analysis or causal analysis, a writer might feel compelled to illustrate this point, or define that term, or offer a telling analogy.

In the several pieces that make up this section, you will get to see how writers in different fields combine various methods of explaining things. And in the next section, you will see how explaining also contributes to arguing.

Arts and Humanities

URBAN LEGENDS:
"THE BOYFRIEND'S DEATH"

Jan Harold Brunvand

Trained in the study of folklore, Jan Harold Brunvand has become a leading collector and interpreter of contemporary legends. These "urban legends" are stories told around camp-fires and in college dormitories, often as true experiences that happened to somebody other than the teller of the tale. Presently a professor at the University of Utah, Brunvand has been the editor of The Journal of American Folklore *and is the author of the standard introduction to the field,* The Study of American Folklore: An Introduction. *The following selection is taken from the first of his several collections of urban legends,* The Vanishing Hitchhiker: American Urban Legends and Their Meanings (1981). *Here he defines* urban legend, *gives one striking example, and offers some explanations about how and why such stories flourish even in the midst of a highly technologized society. The selection as reprinted is complete, except for the deletion of a few brief references to other discussions elsewhere in Brunvand's book.*

We are not aware of our own folklore any more than we are of the gram- 1
matical rules of our language. When we follow the ancient practice of informally
transmitting "lore"—wisdom, knowledge, or accepted modes of behavior—by
word of mouth and customary example from person to person, we do not
concentrate on the form or content of our folklore; instead, we simply listen to
information that others tell us and then pass it on—more or less accurately—
to other listeners. In this stream of unselfconscious oral tradition the information
that acquires a clear story line is called *narrative folklore*, and those stories
alleged to be true are *legends*. This, in broad summary, is the typical process

311

of legend formation and transmission as it has existed from time immemorial and continues to operate today. It works about the same way whether the legendary plot concerns a dragon in a cave or a mouse in a Coke bottle.

It might seem unlikely that legends—*urban* legends at that—would continue to be created in an age of widespread literacy, rapid mass communications, and restless travel. While our pioneer ancestors may have had to rely heavily on oral traditions to pass the news along about changing events and frontier dangers, surely we no longer need mere "folk" reports of what's happening, with all their tendencies to distort the facts. A moment's reflection, however, reminds us of the many weird, fascinating, but unverified rumors and tales that so frequently come to our ears—killers and madmen on the loose, shocking or funny personal experiences, unsafe manufactured products, and many other unexplained mysteries of daily life. Sometimes we encounter different oral versions of such stories, and on occasion we may read about similar events in newspapers or magazines; but seldom do we find, or even seek after, reliable documentation. The lack of verification in no way diminishes the appeal urban legends have for us. We enjoy them merely as stories, and we tend at least to half-believe them as possibly accurate reports. And the legends we tell, as with any folklore, reflect many of the hopes, fears, and anxieties of our time. In short, legends are definitely part of our modern folklore—legends which are as traditional, variable, and functional as those of the past.

Folklore study consists of collecting, classifying, and interpreting in their full cultural context the many products of everyday human interaction that have acquired a somewhat stable underlying form and that are passed traditionally from person to person, group to group, and generation to generation. Legend study is a most revealing area of such research because the stories that people believe to be true hold an important place in their worldview. "If it's true, it's important" is an axiom to be trusted, whether or not the lore really *is* true or not. Simply becoming aware of this modern folklore which we all possess to some degree is a revelation in itself, but going beyond this to compare the tales, isolate their consistent themes, and relate them to the rest of the culture can yield rich insights into the state of our current civilization. . . .

URBAN LEGENDS AS FOLKLORE

Folklore subsists on oral tradition, but not all oral communication is folklore. The vast amounts of human interchange, from casual daily conversations to formal discussions in business or industry, law, or teaching, rarely constitute straight oral folklore. However, all such "communicative events" (as scholars dub them) are punctuated routinely by various units of traditional material that are memorable, repeatable, and that fit recurring social situations well enough to serve in place of original remarks. "Tradition" is the key idea that links together such utterances as nicknames, proverbs, greeting and leave-taking formulas, wisecracks, anecdotes, and jokes as "folklore"; indeed, these are a few of the best known "conversational genres" of American folklore. Longer and more complex folk forms—fairy tales, epics, myths, legends, or ballads, for example—may thrive only in certain special situations of oral transmission. All true folklore ultimately depends upon continued oral dissemination, usually within fairly homogeneous "folk groups," and upon the retention through time of internal patterns and motifs that become traditional in the oral exchanges. The corollary of this rule of stability in oral tradition is that all items of folklore, while retaining a fixed central core, are constantly changing as they are transmitted, so as to create countless "variants" differing in length, detail, style, and performance technique. Folklore, in short, consists of oral tradition in variants.

Urban legends belong to the subclass of folk narratives, legends, that—unlike   5
fairy tales—are believed, or at least believable, and that—unlike myths—are set in the recent past and involve normal human beings rather than ancient gods or demigods. Legends are folk history, or rather quasi-history. As with any folk legends, urban legends gain credibility from specific details of time and place or from references to source authorities. For instance, a popular western pioneer legend often begins something like, "My great-grandmother had this strange experience when she was a young girl on a wagon train going through Wyoming when an Indian chief wanted to adopt her . . ." Even though hundreds of different great-grandmothers are supposed to have had the same doubtful experience (being desired by the chief because of her beautiful long blond hair), the fact seldom reaches legend-tellers; if it does, they assume that the family lore has indeed spread far and wide. This particular popular tradition, known as "Goldilocks on the Oregon Trail," interests folklorists because of the racist implications of a dark Indian savage coveting a fair young civilized woman— this legend is familiar in the *white* folklore only—and it is of little concern that the story seems to be entirely apocryphal.

In the world of modern urban legends there is usually no geographical or   6
generational gap between teller and event. The story is *true*; it really occurred, and recently, and always to someone else who is quite close to the narrator, or at least "a friend of a friend." Urban legends are told both in the course of casual conversations and in such special situations as campfires, slumber parties, and college dormitory bull sessions. The legends' physical settings are often close by, real, and sometimes even locally renowned for other such happenings. Though the characters in the stories are usually nameless, they are true-to-life examples of the kind of people the narrators and their audience know firsthand.

One of the great mysteries of folklore research is where oral traditions orig-   7
inate and who invents them. One might expect that at least in modern folklore we could come up with answers to such questions, but this is seldom, if ever, the case. . . .

THE PERFORMANCE OF LEGENDS

Whatever the origins of urban legends, their dissemination is no mystery.   8
The tales have traveled far and wide, and have been told and retold from person
to person in the same manner that myths, fairy tales, or ballads spread in earlier
cultures, with the important difference that today's legends are also disseminated
by the mass media. Groups of age-mates, especially adolescents, are one important American legend channel, but other paths of transmission are among
office workers and club members, as well as among religious, recreational, and
regional groups. Some individuals make a point of learning every recent rumor
or tale, and they can enliven any coffee break, party, or trip with the latest
supposed "news." The telling of one story inspires other people to share what
they have read or heard, and in a short time a lively exchange of details occurs
and perhaps new variants are created.

Tellers of these legends, of course, are seldom aware of their roles as "per-   9
formers of folklore." The conscious purpose of this kind of storytelling is to
convey a true event, and only incidentally to entertain an audience. Nevertheless, the speaker's demeanor is carefully orchestrated, and his or her delivery is
low-key and soft-sell. With subtle gestures, eye movements, and vocal inflections
the stories are made dramatic, pointed, and suspenseful. But, just as with jokes,
some can tell them and some can't. Passive tellers of urban legends may just
report them as odd rumors, but the more active legend tellers re-create them
as dramatic stories of suspense and, perhaps, humor.

"THE BOYFRIEND'S DEATH"

With all these points in mind folklore's subject-matter style, and oral per-   10
formance, consider this typical version of a well-known urban legend that
folklorists have named "The Boyfriend's Death," collected in 1964 (the earliest
documented instance of the story) by folklorist Daniel R. Barnes from an
eighteen-year-old freshman at the University of Kansas. The usual tellers of the
story are adolescents, and the normal setting for the narration is a college
dormitory room with fellow students sprawled on the furniture and floors.

> This happened just a few years ago out on the road that turns off 59 highway by
> the Holiday Inn. This couple were parked under a tree out on this road. Well, it
> got to be time for the girl to be back at the dorm, so she told her boyfriend that
> they should start back. But the car wouldn't start, so he told her to lock herself
> in the car and he would go down to the Holiday Inn and call for help. Well, he
> didn't come back and he didn't come back, and pretty soon she started hearing a
> scratching noise on the roof of the car. "Scratch, scratch . . . scratch, scratch."
> She got scareder and scareder, but he didn't come back. Finally, when it was
> almost daylight, some people came along and stopped and helped her out of the
> car, and she looked up and there was her boyfriend hanging from the tree, and

his feet were scraping against the roof of the car. This is why the road is called "Hangman's Road."

Here is a story that has traveled rapidly to reach nationwide oral circulation, in the process becoming structured in the typical manner of folk narratives. The traditional and fairly stable elements are the parked couple, the abandoned girl, the mysterious scratching (sometimes joined by a dripping sound and ghostly shadows on the windshield), the daybreak rescue, and the horrible climax. Variable traits are the precise location, the reason for her abandonment, the nature of the rescuers, murder details, and the concluding placename explanation. While "The Boyfriend's Death" seems to have captured teenagers' imaginations as a separate legend only since the early 1960s, it is clearly related to at least two older yarns, "The Hook" and "The Roommate's Death." All three legends have been widely collected by American folklorists, although only scattered examples have been published, mostly in professional journals. Examination of some of these variations helps to make clear the status of the story as folklore and its possible meanings. 11

At Indiana University, a leading American center of folklore research, folk-narrative specialist Linda Dégh and her students have gathered voluminous data on urban legends, especially those popular with adolescents. Dégh's preliminary published report on "The Boyfriend's Death" concerned nineteen texts collected from IU students from 1964 to 1968. Several storytellers had heard it in high school, often at parties; others had picked it up in college dormitories or elsewhere on campus. Several students expressed some belief in the legend, supposing either that it had happened in their own hometowns, or possibly in other states, once as far distant as "a remote part of Alabama." One informant reported that "she had been sworn to that the incident actually happened," but another, who had heard some variations of the tale, felt that "it seemed too horrible to be true." Some versions had incorporated motifs from other popular teenage horror legends or local ghost stories. . . . 12

One of the Indiana texts, told in the state of Washington, localizes the story there near Moses Lake, "in the country on a road that leads to a dead-end right under a big weeping willow tree . . . about four or five miles from town." As in most American versions of the story, these specific local touches make believable what is essentially a traveling legend. In a detail familiar from other variants of "The Boyfriend's Death," the body—now decapitated—is left hanging upside down from a branch of the willow tree with the fingernails scraping the top of the car. Another version studied by the Indiana researcher is somewhat aberrant, perhaps because the student was told the story by a friend's parents who claimed that "it happened a long time ago, probably thirty or forty years." Here a murderer is introduced, a "crazy old lady" on whose property the couple has parked. The victim this time is skinned rather than decapitated, and his head scrapes the car as the corpse swings to and fro in the breezy night. 13

315

A developing motif in "The Boyfriend's Death" is the character and role of   14
the rescuers, who in the 1964 Kansas version are merely "some people." The
standard identification later becomes "the police," authority figures whose presence lends further credence to the story. They are either called by the missing
teenagers' parents, or simply appear on the scene in the morning to check the
car. In a 1969 variant from Leonardtown, Maryland, the police give a warning,
"Miss, please get out of the car and walk to the police car with us, but don't
look back." . . . In a version from Texas collected in 1971, set "at this lake
somewhere way out in nowhere," a policeman gets an even longer line: "Young
lady, we want you to get out of the car and come with us. Whatever you do,
don't turn, don't turn around, just keep walking, just keep going straight and
don't look back at the car." The more detailed the police instructions are, the
more plausible the tale seems to become. Of course the standard rule of folk-
narrative plot development now applies: the taboo must be broken (or the
"interdiction violated" as some scholars put it). The girl always *does* look back,
like Orpheus in the underworld, and in a number of versions her hair turns
white from the shock of what she sees, as in a dozen other American legends.

In a Canadian version of "The Boyfriend's Death," told by a fourteen-year-   15
old boy from Willowdale, Ontario, in 1973, the words of the policemen are
merely summarized, but the opening scene of the legend is developed more
fully, with several special details, including . . . a warning heard on the car
radio. The girl's behavior when left behind is also described in more detail.

> A guy and his girlfriend are on the way to a party when their car starts to give
> them some trouble. At that same time they catch a news flash on the radio
> warning all people in the area that a lunatic killer has escaped from a local
> criminal asylum. The girl becomes very upset and at that point the car stalls
> completely on the highway. The boyfriend gets out and tinkers around with the
> engine but can't get the car to start again. He decides that he is going to have to
> walk on up the road to a gas station and get a tow truck but wants his girlfriend
> to stay behind in the car. She is frightened and pleads with him to take her, but
> he says that she'll be safe on the floor of the car covered with a blanket so that
> anyone passing will think it is an abandoned car and not bother her. Besides he
> can sprint along the road and get back more quickly than if she comes with him
> in her high-heeled shoes and evening dress. She finally agrees and he tells her
> not to come out unless she hears his signal of three knocks on the window. . . .

She does hear knocks on the car, but they continue eerily beyond three; the
sound is later explained as the shoes of the boyfriend's corpse bumping the car
as the body swings from a limb above the car.

The style in which oral narratives are told deserves attention, for the live   16
telling that is dramatic, fluid, and often quite gripping in actual folk performance
before a sympathetic audience may seem stiff, repetitious, and awkward on the
printed page. Lacking in all our examples of "The Boyfriend's Death" is the
essential ingredient of immediate context—the setting of the legend-telling, the

316

storyteller's vocal and facial expression and gestures, the audience's reaction, and the texts of other similar tales narrated at the same session. Several of the informants explained that the story was told to them in spooky situations, late at night, near a cemetery, out camping, or even "while on a hayride or out parked," occasionally near the site of the supposed murder. Some students refer to such macabre legends, therefore, as "scary stories," "screamers," or "horrors."

A widely-distributed folk legend of this kind as it travels in oral tradition acquires a good deal of its credibility and effect from the localized details inserted by individual tellers. The highway and motel identification in the Kansas text are good examples of this, and in a New Orleans version, "The Boyfriend's Death" is absorbed into a local teenage tradition about "The Grunch"—a half-sheep, half-human monster that haunts specific local sites. One teenager there reported, "A man and lady went out by the lake and in the morning they found 'em hanging upside down on a tree and they said grunches did it." Finally, rumors or news stories about missing persons or violent crimes (as mentioned in the Canadian version) can merge with urban legends, helping to support their air of truth, or giving them renewed circulation after a period of less frequent occurrence. 17

Even the bare printed texts retain some earmarks of effective oral tradition. Witness in the Kansas text the artful use of repetition (typical of folk narrative style): "Well, he didn't come back and he didn't come back . . . but he didn't come back." The repeated use of "well" and the building of lengthy sentences with "and" are other hallmarks of oral style which give the narrator complete control over his performance, tending to squeeze out interruptions or prevent lapses in attention among the listeners. The scene that is set for the incident— lonely road, night, a tree looming over the car, out of gas—and the sound effects—scratches or bumps on the car—contribute to the style, as does the dramatic part played by the policeman and the abrupt ending line: "She looked back, and she saw . . . !" Since the typical narrators and auditors of "The Boyfriend's Death" themselves like to "park" and may have been alarmed by rumors, strange sights and noises, or automobile emergencies (all intensified in their effects by the audience's knowing other parking legends), the abrupt, unresolved ending leaves open the possibilities of what "really happened." 18

URBAN LEGENDS AS CULTURAL SYMBOLS

Legends can survive in our culture as living narrative folklore if they contain three essential elements: a strong basic story-appeal, a foundation in actual belief, and a meaningful message or "moral." That is, popular stories like "The Boyfriend's Death" are not only engrossing tales, but also "true," or at least so people think, and they teach valuable lessons. Jokes are a living part of oral tradition, despite being fictional and often silly, because of their humor, brevity, and snappy punch lines, but legends are by nature longer, slower, and more 19 serious. Since more effort is needed to tell and appreciate a legend than a joke, it needs more than just verbal art to carry it along. Jokes have significant "messages" too, but these tend to be disguised or implied. People tell jokes primarily for amusement, and they seldom sense their underlying themes. In legends the primary messages are quite clear and straightforward; often they take the form of explicit warnings or good examples of "poetic justice." Secondary messages in urban legends tend to be suggested metaphorically or symbolically; these may provide deeper criticisms of human behavior or social condition.

People still tell legends, therefore, and other folk take time to listen to them, not only because of their inherent plot interest but because they seem to convey true, worthwhile, and relevant information, albeit partly in a subconscious mode. In other words, such stories are "news" presented to us in an attractive way, with hints of larger meanings. Without this multiple appeal few legends would get a hearing in the modern world, so filled with other distractions. Legends survive by being as lively and "factual" as the television evening news, and, like the daily news broadcasts, they tend to concern deaths, injuries, kidnappings, tragedies, and scandals. Apparently the basic human need for meaningful personal contact cannot be entirely replaced by the mass media and popular culture. A portion of our interest in what is occurring in the world must be filled by some face-to-face reports from other human beings. 20

On a literal level a story like "The Boyfriend's Death" simply warns young people to avoid situations in which they may be endangered, but at a more symbolic level the story reveals society's broader fears of people, especially women and the young, being alone and among strangers in the darkened world outside the security of their own home or car. Note that the young woman in the story (characterized by "her high-heeled shoes and evening dress") is shown as especially helpless and passive, cowering under the blanket in the car until she is rescued by men. Such themes recur in various forms in many other urban legends. . . . 21

In order to be retained in a culture, any form of folklore must fill some genuine need, whether this be the need for an entertaining escape from reality, or a desire to validate by anecdotal examples some of the culture's ideals and institutions. For legends in general, a major function has always been the attempt to explain unusual and supernatural happenings in the natural world. To some degree this remains a purpose for urban legends, but their more common role nowadays seems to be to show that the prosaic contemporary scene is capable of producing shocking or amazing occurrences which may actually have happened to friends or to near-acquaintances but which are nevertheless explainable in some reasonably logical terms. On the one hand we want our factual lore to inspire awe, and at the same time we wish to have the most fantastic tales include at least the hint of a rational explanation and perhaps even a conclusion. Thus an escaped lunatic, a possibly *real* character, not a fantastic invader from outer space or Frankenstein's monster, is said to be 22 responsible for the atrocities committed in the gruesome tales that teenagers tell. As sometimes happens in real life, the car radio gives warning, and the police get the situation back under control. (The policemen's role, in fact, becomes larger and more commanding as the story grows in oral tradition.) Only when the young lovers are still alone and scared are they vulnerable, but society's adults and guardians come to their rescue presently.

In common with brief unverified reports ("rumors"), to which they are often 23 closely related, urban legends gratify our desire to know about and to try to understand bizarre, frightening, and potentially dangerous or embarrassing events that *may* have happened. (In rumors and legends there is always some element of doubt concerning where and when these things *did* occur.) These floating stories appeal to our morbid curiosity and satisfy our sensation-seeking minds that demand gratification through frequent infusions of new information, "sanitized" somewhat by the positive messages. Informal rumors and stories fill in the gaps left by professional news reporting, and these marvelous, though generally false, "true" tales may be said to be carrying the folk-news—along with some editorial matter—from person to person even in today's technological world.

QUESTIONS

1. In your own words, define *urban legend*.
2. Have you ever heard the story of "The Boyfriend's Death" before? Did you believe it was true? Can you remember the circumstances in which you first heard this legend (or a similar one)? Describe your first encounter with this tale or a similar one. How does your experience compare with those described by Brunvand?
3. Below is a list of other tales collected by Brunvand. Do you know any stories that might correspond to these titles?

> The Vanishing Hitchhiker
> The Hook
> The Baby-sitter and the Man Upstairs
> The Pet (or Baby) in the Oven
> The Spider in the Hairdo
> Alligators in the Sewers
> The Nude in the RV
> The Economical Car

Compare the various versions produced by members of the class. What are the variables in the tale and what seem to be the common features?

4. Do you know a story that looks like an urban legend but really is true? Can you prove it?
5. What urban legend are you most aware of at the present time? Write down the best version of it that you can, then analyze what you have written as an urban legend.

319

That is, explain what features mark it as an urban legend and discuss the elements in it that have made it interesting or appealing to you.

6. Can you remember someone who told you something as a "true" story that you now recognize as an urban legend? Write an essay in which you first describe that person and report on the legend he or she told you, and then go on to explain to that person that the story he or she told is not actually true but is an urban legend. If you think that your explanation would not convince the person in question, try to explain why this is so. Describe the resistance you might encounter and indicate how you might modify your explanation to make it more persuasive.

MAKING CONNECTIONS

1. Several of the pieces in "Reporting" deal with events that could provide the material for an urban legend. The AP report of the air crash, Richard Selzer's "The Discus Thrower," and Dennis Hevesi's "Running Away" are examples. What elements of those stories would qualify them as urban legends? In what ways do they not qualify as such a legend?

2. Rewrite either the AP report of the air crash, "The Discus Thrower," or "Running Away" as an urban legend. Make any changes you find necessary to make it read like an urban legend. Then write a few paragraphs of explanation, discussing the changes you made and why you made them.

CASABLANCA, OR THE CLICHÉS ARE HAVING A BALL

Umberto Eco

Umberto Eco (b. 1932) is professor of semiotics at the University of Bologna, Italy. He is widely known in the United States and throughout the world for his novel, The Name of the Rose, *which won a number of prizes and was an international best-seller. Like the French critic Roland Barthes, Eco uses the discipline of semiotics (the study of signs and symbols) as a way of discussing a wide range of topics from comic strips to medieval philosophy; Eco has been especially effective in writing about contemporary popular culture and media. He has written about Superman and James Bond (the hero of spy novels and films). In the essay reprinted here, Eco writes about the most enduringly popular film made during World War II,* Casablanca. *This essay first appeared in an Italian collection of Eco's work in 1977.*

When people in their fifties sit down before their television sets for a rerun   1
of *Casablanca*, it is an ordinary matter of nostalgia. However, when the film is
shown in American universities, the boys and girls greet each scene and can-
onical line of dialogue ("Round up the usual suspects," "Was that cannon fire,
or is it my heart pounding?"—or even every time that Bogey says "kid") with
ovations usually reserved for football games. And I have seen the youthful
audience in an Italian art cinema react in the same way. What then is the
fascination of *Casablanca*?

The question is a legitimate one, for aesthetically speaking (or by any strict   2
critical standards) *Casablanca* is a very mediocre film. It is a comic strip, a
hotch-potch, low on psychological credibility, and with little continuity in its
dramatic effects. And we know the reason for this: the film was made up as the
shooting went along, and it was not until the last moment that the director and
scriptwriters knew whether Ilse would leave with Victor or with Rick. So all
those moments of inspired direction that wring bursts of applause for their
unexpected boldness actually represent decisions taken out of desperation. What
then accounts for the success of this chain of accidents, a film that even today,
seen for a second, third or fourth time, draws forth the applause reserved for
the operatic aria we love to hear repeated, or the enthusiasm we accord to an
exciting discovery? There is a cast of formidable hams. But that is not enough.

Here are the romantic lovers—he bitter, she tender—but both have been   3
seen to better advantage. And *Casablanca* is not *Stagecoach*, another film
periodically revived. *Stagecoach* is a masterpiece in every respect. Every element
is in its proper place, the characters are consistent from one moment to the
next, and the plot (this too is important) comes from Maupassant—at least the
first part of it. And so? So one is tempted to read *Casablanca* the way T. S.
Eliot reread *Hamlet*. He attributed its fascination not to its being a successful
work (actually he considered it one of Shakespeare's less fortunate plays) but to
something quite the opposite: *Hamlet* was the result of an unsuccessful fusion
of several earlier Hamlets, one in which the theme was revenge (with madness
as only a strategem), and another whose theme was the crisis brought on by the
mother's sin, with the consequent discrepancy between Hamlet's nervous ex-
citation and the vagueness and implausibility of Gertrude's crime. So critics
and public alike find *Hamlet* beautiful because it is interesting, and believe it
to be interesting because it is beautiful.

On a smaller scale, the same thing happened to *Casablanca*. Forced to   4
improvise a plot, the authors mixed in a little of everything, and everything
they chose came from a repertoire of the tried and true. When the choice of
the tried and true is limited, the result is a trite or mass-produced film, or
simply kitsch. But when the tried and true repertoire is used wholesale, the
result is an architecture like Gaudi's Sagrada Familia in Barcelona. There is a
sense of dizziness, a stroke of brilliance.

But now let us forget how the film was made and see what it has to show   5
us. It opens in a place already magical in itself—Morocco, the Exotic—and
begins with a hint of Arab music that fades into "La Marseillaise." Then as we
enter Rick's Place we hear Gershwin. Africa, France, America. At once a tangle
of Eternal Archetypes comes into play. These are situations that have presided
over stories throughout the ages. But usually to make a good story a single
archetypal situation is enough. More than enough. Unhappy Love, for example,
or Flight. But *Casablanca* is not satisfied with that: it uses them all. The city
is the setting for a Passage, the passage to the Promised Land (or a Northwest
Passage, if you like). But to make the passage one must submit to a test, the
Wait ("they wait and wait and wait," says the off-screen voice at the beginning).
The passage from the waiting room to the Promised Land requires a Magic
Key, the visa. It is around the winning of this Key that passions are unleashed.
Money (which appears at various points, usually in the form of the Fatal Game,
roulette) would seem to be the means for obtaining the Key. But eventually we
discover that the Key can be obtained only through a Gift—the gift of the visa,
but also the gift Rick makes of his Desire by sacrificing himself. For this is also
the story of a round of Desires, only two of which are satisfied: that of Victor
Laszlo, the purest of heroes, and that of the Bulgarian couple. All those whose
passions are impure fail.

Thus, we have another archetype: the Triumph of Purity. The impure do   6 not reach the Promised Land; we lose sight of them before that. But they do achieve purity through sacrifice—and this means Redemption. Rick is redeemed and so is the French police captain. We come to realize that underneath it all there are two Promised Lands: one is America (though for many it is a false goal), and the other is the Resistance—the Holy War. That is where Victor has come from, and that is where Rick and the captain are going to join de Gaulle. And if the recurring symbol of the aeroplane seems every so often to emphasize the flight to America, the Cross of Lorraine, which appears only once, anticipates the other symbolic gesture of the captain, when at the end he throws away the bottle of Vichy water as the plane is leaving. On the other hand the myth of sacrifice runs through the whole film: Ilse's sacrifice in Paris when she abandons the man she loves to return to the wounded hero, the Bulgarian bride's sacrifice when she is ready to yield herself to help her husband, Victor's sacrifice when he is prepared to let Ilse go with Rick so long as she is saved.

Into this orgy of sacrificial archetypes (accompanied by the Faithful Servant 7 theme in the relationship of Bogey and the black man Dooley Wilson) is inserted the theme of Unhappy Love: unhappy for Rick, who loves Ilse and cannot have her; unhappy for Ilse, who loves Rick and cannot leave with him; unhappy for Victor, who understands that he has not really kept Ilse. The interplay of unhappy loves produces various twists and turns: in the beginning Rick is unhappy because he does not understand why Ilse leaves him; then Victor is unhappy because he does not understand why Ilse is attracted to Rick; finally Ilse is unhappy because she does not understand why Rick makes her leave with her husband. These three unhappy (or Impossible) loves take the form of a Triangle. But in the archetypal love-triangle, there is a Betrayed Husband and a Victorious Lover. Here instead both men are betrayed and suffer a loss, but, in this defeat (and over and above it) an additional element plays a part, so subtly that one is hardly aware of it. It is that, quite subliminally, a hint of male or Socratic love is established. Rick admires Victor, Victor is ambiguously attracted to Rick, and it almost seems at a certain point as if each of the two were playing out the duel of sacrifice in order to please the other. In any case, as in Rousseau's *Confessions*, the woman places herself as Intermediary between the two men. She herself is not a bearer of positive values; only the men are.

Against the background of these intertwined ambiguities, the characters are 8 stock figures, either all good or all bad. Victor plays a double role, as an agent of ambiguity in the love story, and an agent of clarity in the political intrigue— he is Beauty against the Nazi Beast. This theme of Civilization against Barbarism becomes entangled with the others, and to the melancholy of an Odyssean Return is added the warlike daring of an *Iliad* on open ground.

Surrounding this dance of eternal myths, we see the historical myths, or 9 rather the myths of the movies, duly served up again. Bogart himself embodies at least three: the Ambiguous Adventurer, compounded of cynicism and generosity; the Lovelorn Ascetic; and at the same time the Redeemed Drunkard (he has to be made a drunkard so that all of a sudden he can be redeemed, while he was already an ascetic, disappointed in love). Ingrid Bergman is the Enigmatic Woman, or *Femme Fatale*. Then such myths as: They're Playing Our Song; the Last Day in Paris; America, Africa, Lisbon as a Free Port; and the Border Station or Last Outpost on the Edge of the Desert. There is the Foreign Legion (each character has a different nationality and a different story to tell), and finally there is the Grand Hotel (people coming and going). Rick's Place is a magic circle where everything can (and does) happen: love, death, pursuit, espionage, games of chance, seductions, music, patriotism. (The theatrical origin of the plot, and its poverty of means, led to an admirable condensation of events in a single setting.) This place is *Hong Kong, Macao, l'Enfer du Jeu*, an anticipation of *Lisbon*, and even *Showboat*.

But precisely because *all* the archetypes are here, precisely because *Casablanca* cites countless other films, and each actor repeats a part played on other occasions, the resonance of intertextuality plays upon the spectator. *Casablanca* brings with it, like a trail of perfume, other situations that the viewer brings to bear on it quite readily, taking them without realizing it from films that only appeared later, such as *To Have and Have Not*, where Bogart actually plays a Hemingway hero, while here in *Casablanca* he already attracts Hemingway-esque connotations by the simple fact that Rick, so we are told, fought in Spain (and, like Malraux, helped the Chinese Revolution). Peter Lorre drags in reminiscences of Fritz Lang; Conrad Veidt envelops his German officer in a faint aroma of *The Cabinet of Dr Caligari*—he is not a ruthless, technological Nazi, but a nocturnal and diabolical Caesar. 10

Thus *Casablanca* is not just one film. It is many films, an anthology. Made haphazardly, it probably made itself, it not actually against the will of its authors and actors, then at least beyond their control. And this is the reason it works, in spite of aesthetic theories and theories of film making. For in it there unfolds with almost telluric force the power of Narrative in its natural state, without Art intervening to discipline it.[1] And so we can accept it when characters change mood, morality and psychology from one moment to the next, when conspirators cough to interrupt the conversation if a spy is approaching, when whores weep at the sound of "La Marseillaise." When all the archetypes burst in shamelessly, we reach Homeric depths. Two clichés make us laugh. A hundred clichés move us. For we sense dimly that the clichés are talking *among themselves*, and celebrating a reunion. Just as the height of pain may encounter sensual pleasure, and the height of perversion border on mystical energy, so too the height of banality allows us to catch a glimpse of the sublime. Something has spoken in place of the director. If nothing else, it is a phenomenon worthy of awe. 11

---

[1] telluric force: with the power of the earth turning on its axis; irresistible, fundamental power. [Eds.]

QUESTIONS

1. The question Eco raises in his first two paragraphs is why a film that is "very mediocre" should have been as popular as *Casablanca* has proved to be. Have you seen this film? What is your own evaluation of it? Compare your view to Eco's.

2. Eco answers the question he poses at the beginning of the essay in the remaining paragraphs. How would you summarize Eco's explanation of the appeal of the film in a sentence or two?

3. Part of Eco's answer is based on the concept of "archetypes." What does he mean by an archetype? If you have not encountered the word before, try to define it by the way Eco uses the word and the examples he mentions. Literally, the word means something that is typical in a deep and widespread way, a pattern that occurs in many times and places. Refine that general meaning so that it applies specifically to the kinds of examples Eco presents.

4. What does Eco mean by the word *myth*? What examples of myth does he provide in explaining the film's appeal?

5. What does Eco mean by the word *cliché*? What, exactly, do clichés have to do with the success of *Casablanca*, as Eco explains this success? Do you agree with him?

6. In paragraph 10, Eco speaks of "the resonance of intertextuality." If you are unfamiliar with this concept, try to figure out what he means by rereading the explanation given in this paragraph. Once you understand the concept as it applies here, consider the "intertextual resonance" in other cultural products, such as advertising, television shows, and the like. Select a text from one of these media and develop a discussion of the ways in which its meaning is generated by the way it reminds you of other texts.

7. Perhaps you have a favorite film or television show that you have watched many times with pleasure. Write an essay in which you try to explain exactly and convincingly why this particular text appeals to you. It may be for reasons similar to those advanced by Eco or it may be for quite different reasons. If you know that your choice would be the choice of many others, try to say why this is so—not just why you like it, but why it is popular. If, on the other hand, you know your choice is widely regarded as peculiar, try to explain the negative reaction of others and why yours is an exception to the general opinion.

8. Eco uses the structure of a short question and a long answer to organize his essay. Use that structure yourself in explaining some feature of contemporary life that seems odd or unusual, such as the popularity of a certain personality, style of dress, musical group, food, or place. You don't have to agree or disagree with the standard evaluation. Your explanation should simply account for the popularity—not in absolute terms ("they like it because it's good"), but in cultural terms ("they like it because it offers A, B, and C, which appeal to X, Y, and Z in our society").

MAKING CONNECTIONS

1. Eco uses the terms *myth* and *cliché,* and to understand his essay, you need to define them. Jan Harold Brunvand similarly uses the word *legend*. How does a legend differ from a myth and a cliché? Given the examples that accumulate in these two

essays, redefine *legend*. Is there an element of myth in legend? Is there an element of cliché? How do these terms sort themselves out?

2. Can you find "archetypes" in other essays collected in this collection? Richard Selzer's "The Discus Thrower," Dennis Hevesi's "Running Away," Ernest Hemingway's "A New Kind of War," Banesh Hoffmann's "My Friend, Albert Einstein," George Orwell's "Shooting an Elephant," and Maya Angelou's "Graduation" all provide plausible examples; but there are no doubt others. Describe several of the archetypes you find and use them to provide a more detailed explanation of what an archetype is.

EINSTEIN'S BRAIN
Roland Barthes

Roland Barthes (1915–1980) was a major force in the intellectual life of France until his death in 1980. His reputation as a writer continues to grow as his works are translated into more and more languages. He wrote frequently on literary subjects and popular culture from the perspective known as semiotics: the study of signs and symbols. In his writing, Barthes favored short and personal forms such as the essay and the fragment; he wrote for newspapers and magazines in addition to producing the more formal articles expected of a French professor. Among his most accessible pieces are the brief discussions he called Mythologies: *studies in the various ways that myths are created in the modern world. In his view the popular media, while seeming to report facts about the contemporary world, actually make myths that people find comforting. He believed, and demonstrated many times over, that myths could be made from almost anything—wrestling, striptease, tourism, advertising—even the brain of Albert Einstein. Like most of the other pieces collected in* Mythologies, *the following essay was written in the mid-1950s for the French magazine,* les Lettres Nouvelles.

Einstein's brain is a mythical object: paradoxically, the greatest intelligence of all provides an image of the most up-to-date machine, the man who is too powerful is removed from psychology, and introduced into a world of robots; as is well known, the supermen of science-fiction always have something reified about them. So has Einstein: he is commonly signified by his brain, which is like an object for anthologies, a true museum exhibit. Perhaps because of his mathematical specialization, superman is here divested of every magical character; no diffuse power in him, no mystery other than mechanical: he is a superior, a prodigious organ, but a real, even a physiological one. Mythologically, Einstein is matter, his power does not spontaneously draw one towards the spiritual, it needs the help of an independent morality, a reminder about the scientist's "conscience" (*Science without conscience,*[1] they said . . .).

---

[1] "Science without conscience is but the ruin of the Soul" (Rabelais, *Pantagruel* II, ch. 8).

Einstein himself has to some extent been a party to the legend by bequeathing   2
his brain, for the possession of which two hospitals are still fighting as if it were
an unusual piece of machinery which it will at last be possible to dismantle. A
photograph shows him lying down, his head bristling with electric wires: the
waves of his brain are being recorded, while he is requested to "think of
relativity." (But for that matter, what does "to think of" mean, exactly?) What
this is meant to convey is probably that the seismograms will be all the more
violent since "relativity" is an arduous subject. Thought itself is thus represented
as an energetic material, the measurable product of a complex (quasi-electrical)
apparatus which transforms cerebral substance into power. The mythology of
Einstein shows him as a genius so lacking in magic that one speaks about his
thoughts as of a functional labour analogous to the mechanical making of
sausages, the grinding of corn or the crushing of ore: he used to produce thought,
continuously, as a mill makes flour, and death was above all, for him, the
cessation of a localized function: *the most powerful brain of all has stopped
thinking.*

What this machine of genius was supposed to produce was equations.   3
Through the mythology of Einstein, the world blissfully regained the image of
knowledge reduced to a formula. Paradoxically, the more the genius of the man
was materialized under the guise of his brain, the more the product of his
inventiveness came to acquire a magical dimension, and gave a new incarnation
to the old esoteric image of a science entirely contained in a few letters. There
is a single secret to the world, and this secret is held in one word; the universe
is a safe of which humanity seeks the combination: Einstein almost found it,
this is the myth of Einstein. In it, we find all the Gnostic themes: the unity of
nature, the ideal possibility of a fundamental reduction of the world, the
unfastening power of the word, the age-old struggle between a secret and an
utterance, the idea that total knowledge can only be discovered all at once, like
a lock which suddenly opens after a thousand unsuccessful attempts. The
historic equation $E = mc^2$, by its unexpected simplicity, almost embodies the
pure idea of the key, bare, linear, made of one metal, opening with a wholly
magical ease a door which had resisted the desperate efforts of centuries. Popular
imagery faithfully expresses this: *photographs* of Einstein show him standing
next to a blackboard covered with mathematical signs of obvious complexity;
but *cartoons* of Einstein (the sign that he has become a legend) show him chalk
still in hand, and having just written on an empty blackboard, as if without
preparation, the magic formula of the world. In this way mythology shows an
awareness of the nature of the various tasks: research proper brings into play
clockwork-like mechanisms and has its seat in a wholly material organ which
is monstrous only by its cybernetic complication; discovery, on the contrary,
has a magical essence, it is simple like a basic element, a principal substance,

like the philosphers' stone of hermetists, tar-water for Berkeley, or oxygen for Schelling. [2]

But since the world is still going on, since research is proliferating, and on the other hand since God's share must be preserved, some failure on the part of Einstein is necessary: Einstein died, it is said, without having been able to verify *"the equation in which the secret of the world was enclosed."* So in the end the word resisted; hardly opened, the secret closed again, the code was incomplete. In this way Einstein fulfills all the conditions of myth, which could not care less about contradictions so long as it establishes a euphoric security: at once magician and machine, eternal researcher and unfulfilled discoverer, unleashing the best and the worst, brain and conscience, Einstein embodies the most contradictory dreams, and mythically reconciles the infinite power of man over nature with the "fatality" of the sacrosanct, which man cannot yet do without.

4

QUESTIONS

1. By a common figure of speech (synecdoche), one part of Einstein—his brain—has come to stand for the whole person. Can you think of other public figures who are normally perceived in terms of some part of their anatomy or by something regularly associated with them (metonymy)? Why do you suppose this practice is so common in our media?

2. Examine how Barthes reports on the way Einstein has been represented visually through photographs and cartoons. How does Barthes move from description of the image to interpretation? That is, how does he move from a picture or image to its meaning?

3. In paragraph 4, Barthes says that myths establish for us a "euphoric security." Talk this phrase over with your classmates. What does *euphoric* mean? What does the phrase mean as a whole way of thinking about myth? If Barthes is right about the function of myth, then we can see the media not so much as distorting the truth, but rather as simply giving us what we want, which is not truth but comfort. Is he right?

4. What relationship between science and magic does Barthes present in this essay? Consider especially paragraphs 2 and 3 in answering this question.

5. Barthes says that the "supermen" of science fiction always have something "reified" about them. (*Reified* comes from the Latin word for "thing," *res*; to be reified is to be turned into a thing.) What Barthes means is that the supermen—and superwomen—of science fiction always have something thinglike or machinelike about them. Einstein, Barthes suggests, is understood by our connecting him to the superfigures of science

---

[2] hermetists: alchemists, prescientific dabblers in chemical matters; George Berkeley (1685–1753) and Friedrich Willem Joseph von Schelling (1775–1854): early philosphers of science. [Eds.]

fiction. Such understanding is part of the mythologizing process. Do you agree with Barthes about this?

6. Using Barthes's essay as a model, consider the way we have mythologized some other public figure. That is, discuss the way that our images of this person simplify and reduce him or her to the proportions of a comforting myth. Make your essay about the same length as Barthes's and try, like him, to consider typical representations of this person (in newsphotos, cartoons, etc.), moving from these images to the way we understand them and the reasons behind our understanding.

MAKING CONNECTIONS

1. There is a different view of Einstein presented in Banesh Hoffmann's essay in "Reflecting." Write a paper in which you discuss the differences between the two essays and try to explain why they are so different. Is one view of Einstein more true than the other? If this question makes you uncomfortable, try to explain why. In considering the two essays, look not only at what the writers say but also at the way they say it.

2. Draw a cartoon to illustrate "The Boyfriend's Death" as related in Jan Harold Brunvand's essay on Urban Legends. Try to make your cartoon parallel to the one described in paragraph 3 in this essay, of Einstein at the blackboard. Then write an explanation of your cartoon, drawing out and interpreting the representation of "The Boyfriend's Death" that your cartoon offers.

FOOTBALL RED AND BASEBALL GREEN

Murray Ross

Murray Ross (b. 1942) was born in Pasadena, California, and educated at Williams College in Massachusetts and the University of California at Berkeley. He is now artistic director of the theater program at the University of Colorado, Colorado Springs. This essay was first published in the Chicago Review *in 1971 when Ross was a graduate student at Berkeley. Though not a study of a usual academic subject, "Football Red and Baseball Green" shows Ross thinking about those sports much as a critic might think about one of the performing arts.*

The Super Bowl, the final game of the professional football season, draws a   1
larger television audience than any of the moon walks or Tiny Tim's wedding.
This revelation is one way of indicating just how popular spectator sports are
in this country. Americans, or American men anyway, seem to care about the
games they watch as the Elizabethans cared about their plays, and I suspect for
some of the same reasons. There is, in sport, some of the rudimentary drama
found in popular theater: familiar plots, type characters, heroic and comic
action spiced with new and unpredictable variations. And common to watching
both activities is the sense of participation in a shared tradition and in shared
fantasies. If sport exploits these fantasies, without significantly transcending
them, it seems no less satisfying for all that.

It is my guess that sport spectating involves something more than the vicarious   2
pleasures of identifying with athletic prowess. I suspect that each sport contains
a fundamental myth which it elaborates for its fans, and that our pleasure in
watching such games derives in part from belonging briefly to the mythical
world which the game and its players bring to life. I am especially interested in
baseball and football because they are so popular and so uniquely *American*;
they began here and unlike basketball they have not been widely exported. Thus
whatever can be said, mythically, about these games would seem to apply to
our culture.

Baseball's myth may be the easier to identify since we have a greater historical   3
perspective on the game. It was an instant success during the Industrialization,
and most probably it was a reaction to the squalor, the faster pace and the
dreariness of the new conditions. Baseball was old-fashioned right from the
start; it seems conceived in nostalgia, in the resuscitation of the Jeffersonian

331

dream. It established an artificial rural environment, one removed from the toil of an urban life, which spectators could be admitted to and temporarily breathe in. Baseball is a *pastoral* sport, and I think the game can be best understood as this kind of art. For baseball does what all good pastoral does—it creates an atmosphere in which everything exists in harmony.

Consider, for instance, the spatial organization of the game. A kind of controlled openness is created by having everything fan out from home plate, and the crowd sees the game through an arranged perspective that is rarely violated. Visually this means that the game is always seen as a constant, rather calm whole, and that the players and the playing field are viewed in relationship to each other. Each player has a certain position, a special area to tend, and the game often seems to be as much a dialogue between the fielders and the field as it is a contest between players themselves; will that ball get through the hole? Can the outfielder run under that fly? As a moral genre, pastoral asserts the virtue of communion with nature. As a competitive game, baseball asserts that the team which best relates to the playing field (by hitting the ball in the right places) will win. 4

I suspect baseball's space has a subliminal function too, for topographically it is a sentimental mirror of older America. Most of the game is played between the pitcher and the hitter in the extreme corner of the playing area. This is the busiest, most sophisticated part of the ball park, where something is always happening, and from which all subsequent action originates. From this urban corner we move to a supporting infield, active but a little less crowded, and from there we come to the vast stretches of the outfield. As is traditional in American lore, danger increases with distance, and the outfield action is often the most spectacular in the game. The long throw, the double off the wall, the leaping catch—these plays take place in remote territory, and they belong, like most legendary feats, to the frontier. 5

Having established its landscape, pastoral art operates to eliminate any reference to that bigger, more disturbing, more real world it has left behind. All games are to some extent insulated from the outside by having their own rules, but baseball has a circular structure as well which furthers its comfortable feeling of self-sufficiency. By this I mean that every motion of extension is also one of return—a ball hit outside is a *home* run, a full circle. Home—familiar, peaceful, secure—it is the beginning and end. You must go out and come back; only the completed movement is registered. 6

Time is a serious threat to any form of pastoral. The genre poses a timeless world of perpetual spring, and it does its best to silence the ticking of clocks which remind us that in time the green world fades into winter. One's sense of time is directly related to what happens in it, and baseball is so structured as to stretch out and ritualize whatever action it contains. Dramatic moments are few, and they are almost always isolated by the routine texture of normal play. It is certainly a game of climax and drama, but it is perhaps more a game of 7 repeated and predictable action: the foul balls, the walks, the pitcher fussing around on the mound, the lazy fly ball to centerfield. This is, I think, as it should be, for baseball exists as an alternative to a world of too much action, struggle and change. It is a merciful release from a more grinding and insistent tempo, and its time, as William Carlos Williams suggests, makes a virtue out of idleness simply by providing it:[1]

> The crowd at the ball game
> is moved uniformly
> by a spirit of uselessness
> Which delights them . . .

Within this expanded and idle time the baseball fan is at liberty to become 8
a ceremonial participant and a lover of style. Because the action is normalized, how something is done becomes as important as the action itself. Thus baseball's most delicate and detailed aspects are often, to the spectator, the most interesting. The pitcher's windup, the anticipatory crouch of the infielders, the quick waggle of the bat as it poises for the pitch—these subtle miniature movements are as meaningful as the home runs and the strikeouts. It somehow matters in baseball that all the tiny rituals are observed: the shortstop must kick the dirt and the umpire must brush the plate with his pocket broom. In a sense baseball is largely a continuous series of small gestures, and I think it characteristic that the game's most treasured moment came when Babe Ruth pointed to where he subsequently hit a home run.

Baseball is a game where the little things mean a lot, and this, together with 9
its clean serenity, its open space, and its ritualized action is enough to place it in a world of yesterday. Baseball evokes for us a past which may never have been ours, but which we believe was, and certainly that is enough. In the Second World War, supposedly, we fought for "Baseball, Mom and Apple Pie," and considering what baseball means that phrase is a good one. We fought then for the right to believe in a green world of tranquillity and uninterrupted contentment, where the little things would count. But now the possibilities of such a world are more remote, and it seems that while the entertainment of such a dream has an enduring appeal, it is no longer sufficient for our fantasies. I think this may be why baseball is no longer our preeminent national pastime, and why its myth is being replaced by another more appropriate to the new realities (and fantasies) of our time.

Football, especially professional football, is the embodiment of a newer myth, 10
one which in many respects is opposed to baseball's. The fundamental difference is that football is not a pastoral game; it is a heroic one. One way of seeing the difference between the two is by the juxtaposition of Babe Ruth and Jim Brown, both legendary players in their separate genres. Ruth, baseball's most powerful

---

[1] William Carlos Williams (1883–1963): American poet, short-story writer, and physician. [Eds.]

hitter, was a hero maternalized (his name), an epic figure destined for a second immortality as a candy bar. His image was impressive but comfortable and altogether human: round, dressed in a baggy uniform, with a schoolboy's cap and a bat which looked tiny next to him. His spindly legs supported a Santa-sized torso, and this comic disproportion would increase when he was in motion. He ran delicately, with quick, very short steps, since he felt that stretching your stride slowed you down. This sort of superstition is typical of baseball players, and typical too is the way in which a personal quirk or mannerism mitigates their awesome skill and makes them poignant and vulnerable.

There was nothing funny about Jim Brown. His muscular and almost perfect physique was emphasized further by the uniform which armored him. Babe Ruth had a tough face, but boyish and innocent; Brown has an expressionless mask under the helmet. In action he seemed invincible, the embodiment of speed and power in an inflated human shape. One can describe Brown accurately only with superlatives, for as a player he was a kind of Superman, undisguised. 11

Brown and Ruth are caricatures, yet they represent their games. Baseball is part of a comic tradition which insists that its participants be humans, while football, in the heroic mode, asks that its players be more than that. Football converts men into gods, and suggests that magnificence and glory are as desirable as happiness. Football is designed, therefore, to impress its audience rather differently than baseball. 12

As a pastoral game, baseball attempts to close the gap between the players and the crowd. It creates the illusion, for instance, that with a lot of hard work, a little luck, and possibly some extra talent, the average spectator might well be playing; not watching. For most of us can do a few of the things the ball players do: catch a pop-up, field a ground ball, and maybe get a hit once in a while. Chance is allotted a good deal of play in the game. There is no guarantee, for instance, that a good pitch will not be looped over the infield, or that a solidly batted ball will not turn into a double play. In addition to all of this, almost every fan feels he can make the manager's decision for him, and not entirely without reason. Baseball's statistics are easily calculated and rather meaningful; and the game itself, though a subtle one, is relatively lucid and comprehendible. 13

As a heroic game football is not concerned with a shared community of near-equals. It seeks almost the opposite relationship between its spectators and players, one which stresses the distance between them. We are not allowed to identify directly with Jim Brown any more than we are with Zeus, because to do so would undercut his stature as something more than human. The players do much of the distancing themselves by their own excesses of speed, size and strength. When Bob Brown, the giant all-pro tackle says that he could "block King Kong all day," we look at him and believe. But the game itself contributes to the players' heroic isolation. As George Plimpton has graphically illustrated 14 in *Paper Lion*,[2] it is almost impossible to imagine yourself in a professional football game without also considering your imminent humiliation and possible injury. There is scarcely a single play that the average spectator could hope to perform adequately, and there is even a difficulty in really understanding what is going on. In baseball what happens is what meets the eye, but in football each action is the result of eleven men acting simultaneously against eleven other men, and clearly this is too much for the eye to totally comprehend. Football has become a game of staggering complexity, and coaches are now wired in to several "spotters" during the games so they can find out what is happening.

If football is distanced from its fans by its intricacy and its "superhuman"   15
play, it nonetheless remains an intense spectacle. Baseball, as I have implied, dissolves time and urgency in a green expanse, thereby creating a luxurious and peaceful sense of leisure. As is appropriate to a heroic enterprise, football reverses this procedure and converts space into time. The game is ideally played in an oval stadium, not in a "park," and the difference is the elimination of perspective. This makes football a perfect television game, because even at first hand it offers a flat, perpetually moving foreground (wherever the ball is). The eye in baseball viewing opens up; in football it zeroes in. There is no democratic vista in football, and spectators are not asked to relax, but to concentrate. You are encouraged to watch the drama, not a medley of ubiquitous gestures, and you are constantly reminded that this event is taking place in time. The third element in baseball is the field; in football this element is the clock. Traditionally heroes do reckon with time, and football players are no exceptions. Time in football is wound up inexorably until it reaches the breaking point in the last minutes of a close game. More often than not it is the clock which emerges as the real enemy, and it is the sense of time running out that regularly produces a pitch of tension uncommon in baseball.

A further reason for football's intensity is that the game is played like a war.   16
The idea is to win by going through, around or over the opposing team and the battle lines, quite literally, are drawn on every play. Violence is somewhere at the heart of the game, and the combat quality is reflected in football's army language ("blitz," "trap," "zone," "bomb," "trenches," etc.). Coaches often sound like generals when they discuss their strategy. Woody Hayes of Ohio State, for instance, explains his quarterback option play as if it had been conceived in the Pentagon: "You know," he says, "the most effective kind of warfare is siege. You have to attack on broad fronts. And that's all the option is—attacking on a broad front. You know General Sherman ran an option through the south."

[2] George Plimpton (b. 1927): best-selling author and journalist, founder of the *Paris Review*; he wrote in *Paper Lion* about his experiences in training with the Detroit Lions. [Eds.]

Football like war is an arena for action, and like war football leaves little   17
room for personal style. It seems to be a game which projects "character" more
than personality, and for the most part football heroes, publicly, are a rather
similar lot. They tend to become personifications rather than individuals, and,
with certain exceptions, they are easily read emblematically as embodiments of
heroic qualities such as "strength," "confidence," "perfection," etc.—clichés
really, but forceful enough when represented by the play of a Dick Butkus, a
Johnny Unitas or a Bart Starr. Perhaps this simplification of personality results
in part from the heroes' total identification with their mission, to the extent
that they become more characterized by their work than by what they intrinsically "are." At any rate football does not make allowances for the idiosyncracies
that baseball actually seems to encourage, and as a result there have been few
football players as uniquely crazy or human as, say, Casey Stengel or Dizzy
Dean.

A further reason for the underdeveloped qualities of football personalities,   18
and one which gets us to the heart of the game's modernity, is that football is
very much a game of modern technology. Football's action is largely interaction,
and the game's complexity requires that its players mold themselves into a
perfectly coordinated unit. Jerry Kramer, the veteran guard and author of *Instant
Replay*, writes how Lombardi would work to develop such integration:

> He makes us execute the same players over and over, a hundred times, two
> hundred times, until we do every little thing automatically. He works to make the
> kickoff-team perfect, the punt-return perfect, the field-goal team perfect. He
> ignores nothing. Technique, technique, technique, over and over and over, until
> we feel like we're going crazy. But we win.

Mike Garrett, the halfback, gives the player's version:

> After a while you train your mind like a computer—put the ideas in, and the
> body acts accordingly.

As the quotations imply, pro football is insatiably preoccupied with the   19
smoothness and precision of play execution, and most coaches believe that the
team which makes the fewest mistakes will be the team that wins. Individual
identity thus comes to be associated with the team or unit that one plays for to
a much greater extent than in baseball. To use a reductive analogy, it is the
difference between *Bonanza* and *Mission Impossible*. Ted Williams is mostly
Ted Williams, but Bart Starr is mostly the Green Bay Packers. The latter
metaphor is a precise one, since football heroes stand out not because of purely
individual acts, but because they epitomize the action and style of the groups
they are connected to. Kramer cites the obvious if somewhat self-glorifying
historical precedent: "Perhaps," he writes, "we're living in Camelot." Ideally a
football team should be what Camelot was supposed to have been, a group of

men who function as equal parts of a larger whole, dependent on each other for total meaning.

The humanized machine as hero is something very new in sport, for in 20 baseball anything approaching a machine has always been suspect. The famous Yankee teams of the fifties were almost flawlessly perfect and never very popular. Their admirers took pains to romanticize their precision into something more natural than plain mechanics—Joe DiMaggio, for instance, was the "Yankee Clipper." Even so, most people hoped fervently the Brooklyn Dodgers (the "bums") would thrash them in every World Series. To take a more recent example, the victory of the Mets in 1969 was so compelling largely because it was at the expense of a superbly homogenized team, the Baltimore Orioles, and it was accomplished by a somewhat random collection of inspired leftovers. In baseball, machinery seems tantamount to villainy, whereas in football this smooth perfection is part of the expected integration a championship team must attain.

It is not surprising, really, that we should have a game which asserts the 21 heroic function of a mechanized group, since we have become a country where collective identity is a reality. Football as a game of groups is appealing to us as a people of groups, and for this reason football is very much an "establishment" game—since it is in the corporate business and government structures that group America is most developed. The game comments on the culture, and vice versa:

> President Nixon, an ardent football fan, got a football team picture as an inaugural anniversary present from his cabinet. . . .
> Superimposed on the faces of real gridiron players were the faces of cabinet members. (A.P.)

This is not to say that football appeals only to a certain class, for group America is visible everywhere. A sign held high in the San Francisco Peace Moratorium . . . read: "49er Fans against War, Poverty and the Baltimore Colts."

Football's collective pattern is only one aspect of the way in which it seems 22 to echo our contemporary environment. The game, like our society, can be thought of as a cluster of people living under great tension in a state of perpetual flux. The potential for sudden disaster or triumph is as great in football as it is in our own age, and although there is something ludicrous in equating interceptions with assassinations and long passes with moonshots, there is also something valid and appealing in the analogies. It seems to me that football does successfully reflect those salient and common conditions which affect us all, and it does so with the end of making us feel better about them and our lot. For one thing, it makes us feel that something can be released and connected in all this chaos; out of the accumulated pile of bodies something can emerge— a runner breaks into the clear or a pass finds its way to a receiver. To the spectator plays such as these are human and dazzling. They suggest to the audience what it has hoped for (and been told) all along, that technology is still a tool and not a master. Fans get living proof of this every time a long pass is completed; they see at once that it is the result of careful planning, perfect integration and an effective "pattern," but they see too that it is human and that what counts as well is man, his desire, his natural skill and his "grace under pressure." Football metaphysically yokes heroic action and technology by violence to suggest that they are mutually supportive. It's a doubtful proposition, but given how we live it has its attractions.

Football, like the space program, is a game in the grand manner, yet it is a rather sober sport and often seems to lack that positive, comic vision of what baseball's pastoral mannerisms are a part. It is a winter game, as those fans who saw the Minnesota Vikings play the Detroit Lions one Thanksgiving were graphically reminded. The two teams played in a blinding snowstorm, and except for the small flags in the corners of the end zones, and a patch of mud wherever the ball was downed, the field was totally obscured. Even through the magnified television lenses the players were difficult to identify; you saw only huge shapes come out of the gloom, thump against each other and fall in a heap. The movement was repeated endlessly and silently in a muffled stadium, interrupted once or twice by a shot of a bare-legged girl who fluttered her pompons in the cold. The spectacle was by turns pathetic, compelling and absurd; a kind of theater of oblivion. 23

Games such as this are by no means unusual, and it is not difficult to see why for many football is a gladiatorial sport of pointless bludgeoning played by armored monsters. However accurate this description may be, I still believe that even in the worst of circumstances football can be a liberating activity. In the game I have just described, for instance, there was one play, the turning point of the game, which more than compensated for the sluggishness of most of the action. Jim Marshall, the huge defensive end (who hunts on dogsleds during the off season), intercepted a pass deep in his own territory and rumbled upfield like a dinosaur through the mud, the snow, and the opposing team, lateraling at the last minute to another lineman who took the ball in for a touchdown. It was a supreme moment because Marshall's principal occupation is falling on quarterbacks, not catching the ball and running with it. His triumphant jaunt, something that went unequaled during the rest of that dark afternoon, was a hearty burlesque of the entire sport, an occasion for epic laughter in bars everywhere (though especially in Minnesota), and it was more than enough to rescue the game from the snowbound limbo it was in. 24

In the end I suppose both football and baseball could be seen as varieties of decadence. In its preoccupation with mechanization, and in its open display of violence, football is the more obvious target for social moralists, but I wonder if this is finally more "corrupt" than the seductive picture of sanctuary and tranquillity that baseball has so artfully drawn for us. Almost all sport is vulnerable to such criticism because it is not strictly ethical in intent, and for this 25 reason there will always be room for puritans like the Elizabethan John Stubbes who howled at the "wanton fruits which these cursed pastimes bring forth." As a long-time dedicated fan of almost anything athletic, I confess myself out of sympathy with most of this; which is to say, I guess, that I am vulnerable to those fantasies which these games support, and that I find happiness in the company of people who feel as I do.

A final note. It is interesting that the heroic and pastoral conventions which 26 underlie our most popular sports are almost classically opposed. The contrasts are familiar: city versus country, aspirations versus contentment, activity versus peace and so on. Judging from the rise of professional football we seem to be slowly relinquishing that unfettered rural vision of ourselves that baseball so beautifully mirrors, and we have come to cast ourselves in a genre more reflective of a nation confronted by constant and unavoidable challenges. Right now, like the Elizabethans, we seem to share both heroic and pastoral yearnings, and we reach out to both. Perhaps these divided needs account in part for the enormous attention we as a nation now give to spectator sports. For sport provides one place where we can have our football and our baseball too.

QUESTIONS

1. Summarize each of the "fundamental myths" of baseball and football. Do you find Ross's interpretations justifiable?

2. In discussing two games, Ross makes use of several other fields of human activity and modes of behavior, both ancient and modern. Make lists of the chief terms he draws upon in characterizing baseball and football. How do those terms help you understand Ross's explanation of baseball and football?

3. How would you describe the audience for whom Ross is writing? How much knowledge of baseball and football does he expect of his readers? How much knowledge of other matters, such as literary conventions and patterns in American cultural history, does he assume?

4. From what viewpoint does Ross look at baseball and football? Contrast his particular approach with that of the writer of a typical sports article.

5. Ross structures his essay mostly by means of comparison and contrast. At what points does he discuss his subjects (baseball and football) separately and at what points together? What is his purpose in such an arrangement?

6. Are there other popular pastimes which could be said to "echo our contemporary environment" (paragraph 22) as Ross claims football does? Are there others which reflect our yearnings for a simpler, more pastoral America?

7. More than a decade has passed since Ross published this essay. Do you think his evaluations of baseball and football have stood the test of time? Write a short paper expressing your opinion on this matter.

8. Despite its exportation to the world, we still think of basketball as mainly an American game. Write an essay in which you compare and contrast basketball with

either football or baseball. As you prepare your essay, see which of Ross's interpretations remain useful to you, which fade away, and which you change.

9. Compare and contrast another pair of fantasies, perhaps of those who watch horror movies with those who watch westerns, of those who play poker with those who play chess, or of those who prefer one electronic game to another.

10. Research the public response to baseball and football since Ross's essay was first published. Investigate how the public responded to the World Series and the Super Bowl in 1971 (the date of Ross's essay), 1976 (our bicentennial year), and last season. Write a paper explaining whatever trends you discover.

MAKING CONNECTIONS

1. To what extent are the myths of baseball and football that Ross outlines male myths and male myths alone? Taking hints from Tania Modleski's "Soap Opera, Melodrama, and Women's Anger," Susan Fraker's "Why Women Aren't Getting to the Top," and Carol Gilligan's "Woman's Place in Man's Life Cycle," and perhaps even from Joan Didion's "Georgia O'Keeffe," rewrite Ross's explanation of football and baseball from a point of view that is more explicitly female.

2. How do Ross's interpretations of baseball and football relate to Theodore R. Sizer's essay of "What High School Is"? How does the context of high school (or college, if you prefer) complicate the view Ross offers? Write an essay in which you interpret either baseball or football, or another sport, in the school context that you best know for it.

WHAT HIGH SCHOOL IS
Theodore R. Sizer

*Born in New Haven, Connecticut, and educated at Yale
and Harvard, Theodore R. Sizer has been headmaster at
Phillips Academy, Andover, dean of the Graduate School of
Education at Harvard University, and chairman of the
Education Department at Brown University. Besides being
the author of several books on American secondary schools,
in recent years he has also worked on a study of American
high schools sponsored by the National Association of Secondary School Principals and the National Association of
Independent Schools. His book* Horace's Compromise: The
Dilemma of the American High School *(1984) reports the
results of that study. The selection reprinted here is the first
chapter of the second section of that book, "The Program."*

Mark, sixteen and a genial eleventh-grader, rides a bus to Franklin High   1
School, arriving at 7:45. It is an Assembly Day, so the schedule is adapted to
allow for a meeting of the entire school. He hangs out with his friends, first
outside school and then inside, by his locker. He carries a pile of textbooks and
notebooks; in all, it weighs eight and a half pounds.

From 7:30 to 8:19, with nineteen other students, he is in Room 304 for   2
English class. The Shakespeare play being read this year by the eleventh grade
is *Romeo and Juliet*. The teacher, Ms. Viola, has various students in turn take
parts and read out loud. Periodically, she interrupts the (usually halting) reci-
tations to ask whether the thread of the conversation in the play is clear. Mark
is entertained by the stumbling readings of some of his classmates. He hopes
he will not be asked to be Romeo, particularly if his current steady, Sally, is
Juliet. There is a good deal of giggling in class, and much attention paid to
who may be called on next. Ms. Viola reminds the class of a test on this part
of the play to be given next week.

The bell rings at 8:19. Mark goes to the boys' room, where he sees a classmate   3
who he thinks is a wimp but who constantly tries to be a buddy. Mark avoids
the leech by rushing off. On the way, he notices two boys engaged in some sort
of transaction, probably over marijuana. He pays them no attention. 8:24.
Typing class. The rows of desks that embrace big office machines are almost
filled before the bell. Mark is uncomfortable here: typing class is girl country.
The teacher constantly threatens what to Mark is a humiliatingly female future:
"Your employer won't like these erasures." The minutes during the period are

spent copying a letter from a handbook onto business stationery. Mark struggles to keep from looking at his work; the teacher wants him to watch only the material from which he is copying. Mark is frustrated, uncomfortable, and scared that he will not complete his letter by the class's end, which would be embarrassing.

Nine tenths of the students present at school that day are assembled in the auditorium by the 9:18 bell. The dilatory tenth still stumble in, running down aisles. Annoyed class deans try to get the mob settled. The curtains part; the program is a concert by a student rock group. Their electronic gear flashes under the lights, and the five boys and one girl in the group work hard at being casual. Their movements on stage are studiously at three-quarter time, and they chat with one another as though the tumultuous screaming of their schoolmates were totally inaudible. The girl balances on a stool; the boys crank up the music. It is very soft rock, the sanitized lyrics surely cleared with the assistant principal. The girl sings, holding the mike close to her mouth, but can scarcely be heard. Her light voice is tentative, and the lyrics indecipherable. The guitars, amplified, are tuneful, however, and the drums are played with energy.

The students around Mark—all juniors, since they are seated by class—alternately slouch in their upholstered, hinged seats, talking to one another, or sit forward, leaning on the chair backs in front of them, watching the band. A boy near Mark shouts noisily at the microphone-fondling singer, "Bite it . . . ohhh," and the area around Mark explodes in vulgar male laughter, but quickly subsides. A teacher walks down the aisle. Songs continue, to great applause. Assembly is over at 9:46, two minutes early.

9:53 and biology class. Mark was at a different high school last year and did not take this course there as a tenth-grader. He is in it now, and all but one of his classmates are a year younger than he. He sits on the side, not taking part in the chatter that goes on after the bell. At 9:57, the public address system goes on, with the announcements of the day. After a few words from the principal ("Here's today's cheers and jeers . . ." with a cheer for the winning basketball team and a jeer for the spectators who made a ruckus at the gymnasium), the task is taken over by officers of ASB (Associated Student Bodies). There is an appeal for "bat bunnies." Carnations are for sale by the Girls' League. Miss Indian American is coming. Students are auctioning off their services (background catcalls are heard) to earn money for the prom. Nominees are needed for the ballot for school bachelor and school bachelorette. The announcements end with a "thought for the day. When you throw a little mud, you lose a little ground."

At 10:04 the biology class finally turns to science. The teacher, Mr. Robbins, has placed one of several labeled laboratory specimens—some are pinned in frames, others swim in formaldehyde—on each of the classroom's eight laboratory tables. The three or so students whose chairs circle each of these benches are to study the specimen and make notes about it or drawings of it. After a few minutes each group of three will move to another table. The teacher points out that these specimens are of organisms already studied in previous classes. He says that the period-long test set for the following day will involve observing some of these specimens—then to be without labels—and writing an identifying paragraph on each. Mr. Robbins points out that some of the printed labels ascribe the specimens names different from those given in the textbook. He explains that biologists often give several names to the same organism.

The class now falls to peering, writing, and quiet talking. Mr. Robbins comes over to Mark, and in whispered words asks him to carry a requisition form for science department materials to the business office. Mark, because of his "older" status, is usually chosen by Robbins for this kind of errand. Robbins gives Mark the form and a green hall pass to show to any teacher who might challenge him, on his way to the office, for being out of a classroom. The errand takes Mark four minutes. Meanwhile Mark's group is hard at work but gets to only three of the specimens before the bell rings at 10:42. As the students surge out, Robbins shouts a reminder about a "double" laboratory period on Thursday. 8

Between classes one of the seniors asks Mark whether he plans to be a candidate for schoolwide office next year. Mark says no. He starts to explain. The 10:47 bell rings, meaning that he is late for French class. 9

There are fifteen students in Monsieur Bates's language class. He hands out tests taken the day before: *"C'est bien fait, Etienne . . . c'est mieux, Marie . . . Tch, tch, Robert . . ."* Mark notes his C+ and peeks at the A− in front of Susanna, next to him. The class has been assigned seats by M. Bates; Mark resents sitting next to prissy, brainy Susanna. Bates starts by asking a student to read a question and give the correct answer. *"James, question un."* James haltingly reads the question and gives an answer that Bates, now speaking English, says is incomplete. In due course: *"Mark, question cinq."* Mark does his bit, and the sequence goes on, the eight quiz questions and answers filling about twenty minutes of time. 10

"Turn to page forty-nine. *Maintenant, lisez après moi . . ."* and Bates reads a sentence and has the class echo it. Mark is embarrassed by this and mumbles with a barely audible sound. Others, like Susanna, keep the decibel count up, so Mark can hide. This I-say-you-repeat drill is interrupted once by the public address system, with an announcement about a meeting for the cheerleaders. Bates finishes the class, almost precisely at the bell, with a homework assignment. The students are to review these sentences for a brief quiz the following day. Mark takes note of the assignment, because he knows that tomorrow will be a day of busy-work in French class. Much though he dislikes oral drills, they are better than the workbook stuff that Bates hands out. Write, write, write, for Bates to throw away, Mark thinks. 11

11:36. Down to the cafeteria, talking noisily, hanging, munching. Getting to room 104 by 12:17: U.S. history. The teacher is sitting cross-legged on his desk when Mark comes in, heatedly arguing with three students over the fracas 12

343

that had followed the previous night's basketball game. The teacher, Mr. Suslovic, while agreeing that the spectators from their school certainly were provoked, argues that they should neither have been so obviously obscene in yelling at the opposing cheerleaders nor have allowed Coke cans to be rolled out on the floor. The three students keep saying that "it isn't fair." Apparently they and some others had been assigned "Saturday mornings" (detentions) by the principal for the ruckus.

At 12:34, the argument appears to subside. The uninvolved students, including Mark, are in their seats, chatting amiably. Mr. Suslovic climbs off his desk and starts talking: "We've almost finished this unit, chapters nine and ten . . ." The students stop chattering among themselves and turn toward Suslovic. Several slouch down in their chairs. Some open notebooks. Most have the five-pound textbook on their desks. 13

Suslovic lectures on the cattle drives, from north Texas to railroads west of St. Louis. He breaks up this narrative with questions ("Why were the railroad lines laid largely east to west?"), directed at nobody in particular and eventually answered by Suslovic himself. Some students take notes. Mark doesn't. A student walks in the open door, hands Mr. Suslovic a list, and starts whispering with him. Suslovic turns from the class and hears out this messenger. He then asks, "Does anyone know where Maggie Sharp is?" Some one answers, "Sick at home"; someone else says, "I thought I saw her at lunch." Genial consternation. Finally Suslovic tells the messenger, "Sorry, we can't help you," and returns to the class: "Now, where were we?" He goes on for some minutes. The bell rings. Suslovic forgets to give the homework assignment. 14

1:11 and Algebra II. There is a commotion in the hallway: someone's locker is rumored to have been opened by the assistant principle and a narcotics agent. In the five-minute passing time, Mark hears the story three times and three ways. A locker had been broken into by another student. It was Mr. Gregory and a narc. It was the cops, and they did it without Gregory's knowing. Mrs. Ames, the mathematics teacher, has not heard anything about it. Several of the nineteen students try to tell her and start arguing among themselves. "O.K., that's enough." She hands out the day's problem, one sheet to each student. Mark sees with dismay that it is a single, complicated "word" problem about some train that, while traveling at 84 mph, due west, passes a car that was going due east at 55mph. Mark struggles: Is it $d = rt$ or $t = rd$? The class becomes quiet, writing, while Mrs. Ames writes some additional, short problems on the blackboard. "Time's up." A sigh; most students still writing. A muffled "Shit." Mrs. Ames frowns. "Come on, now." She collects papers, but it takes four minutes for her to corral them all. 15

"Copy down the problems from the board." A minute passes. "William, try number one." William suggests an approach. Mrs. Ames corrects and cajoles, and William finally gets it right. Mark watches two kids to his right passing notes; he tries to read them, but the handwriting is illegible from his distance. 16

He hopes he is not called on, and he isn't. Only three students are asked to puzzle out an answer. The bell rings at 2:00. Mrs. Ames shouts a homework assignment over the resulting hubbub.

Mark leaves his books in his locker. He remembers that he has homework, but figures that he can do it during English class the next day. He knows that there will be an in-class presentation of one of the *Romeo and Juliet* scenes and that he will not be in it. The teacher will not notice his homework writing, or won't do anything about it if she does. 17

Mark passes various friends heading toward the gym, members of the basketball teams. Like most students, Mark isn't an active school athlete. However, he is associated with the yearbook staff. Although he is not taking "Yearbook" for credit as an English course, he is contributing photographs. Mark takes twenty minutes checking into the yearbook staff's headquarters (the classroom of its faculty adviser) and getting some assignments of pictures from his boss, the senior who is the photography editor. Mark knows that if he pleases his boss and the faculty adviser, he'll take that editor's post for the next year. He'll get English credit for his work then. 18

After gossiping a bit with the yearbook staff, Mark will leave school by 2:35 and go home. His grocery market bagger's job is from 4:45 to 8:00, the rush hour for the store. He'll have a snack at 4:30, and his mother will save him some supper to eat at 8:30. She will ask whether he has any homework, and he'll tell her no. Tomorrow, and virtually every other tomorrow, will be the same for Mark, save for the lack of the assembly: each period then will be five minutes longer. 19

Most Americans have an uncomplicated vision of what secondary education should be. Their conception of high school is remarkably uniform across the country, a striking fact, given the size and diversity of the United States and the politically decentralized character of the schools. This uniformity is of several generations' standing. It has, however, two appearances, each quite different from the other, one of words and the other of practice, a world of political rhetoric and Mark's world. 20

A California high school's general goals, set out in 1979, could serve equally well most of America's high schools, public and private. This school had as its ends: 21

· Fundamental scholastic achievement . . . to acquire knowledge and share in the traditionally academic fundamentals . . . to develop the ability to make decisions, to solve problems, to reason independently, and to accept responsibility for self-evaluation and continuing self-improvement.
· Career and economic competence . . .
· Citizenship and civil responsibility . . .
· Competence in human and social relations . . .

- Moral and ethical values . . .
- Self-realization and mental and physical health . . .
- Aesthetic awareness . . .
- Cultural diversity . . .[1]

In addition to its optimistic rhetoric, what distinguishes this list is its comprehensiveness. The high school is to touch most aspects of an adolescent's existence—mind, body, morals, values, career. No one of these areas is given especial prominence. School people arrogate to themselves an obligation to all.

An example of the wide acceptability of thse goals is found in the courts. Forced to present a detailed definition of "thorough and efficient education," elementary as well as secondary, a West Virginia judge sampled the best of conventional wisdom and concluded that

> there are eight general elements of a thorough and efficient system of education: (a) Literacy, (b) The ability to add, subtract, multiply, and divide numbers, (c) Knowledge of government to the extent the child will be equipped as a citizen to make informed choices among persons and issues that affect his own governance, (d) Self-knowledge and knowledge of his or her total environment to allow the child to intelligently choose life work—to know his or her options, (e) Work-training and advanced academic training as the child may intelligently choose, (f) Recreational pursuits, (g) Interests in all creative arts such as music, theater, literature, and the visual arts, and (h) Social ethics, both behavioral and abstract, to facilitate compatibility with others in this society.[2]

That these eight—now powerfully part of the debate over the purpose and practice of education in West Virginia—are reminiscent of the influential list, "The Seven Cardinal Principles of Secondary Education," promulgated in 1918 by the National Education Association, is no surprise.[3] The rhetoric of high school purpose has been uniform and consistent for decades. Americans agree on the goals for their high schools.

That agreement is convenient, but it masks the fact that virtually all the words in these goal statements beg definition. Some schools have labored long to identify specific criteria beyond them; the result has been lists of daunting

---

[1] Shasta High School, Redding, California. An eloquent and analogous statement, "The Essentials of Education," one stressing explicitly the "interdependence of skills and content" that is implicit in the Shasta High School statement, was issued in 1980 by a coalition of educational associations. Organizations for the Essentials of Education (Urbana, Illinois).

[2] Judge Arthur M. Recht, in his order resulting from *Pauley v. Kelly*, 1979, as reprinted in *Education Week*, May 26, 1982, p. 10. See also, in *Education Week*, January 16, 1983, pp. 21, 24, Jonathan P. Sher, "The Struggle to Fulfill a Judicial Mandate: How Not to 'Reconstruct' Education in W. Va."

[3] Bureau of Education, Department of the Interior, "Cardinal Principles of Secondary Education: A Report of the Commission on the Reorganization of Secondary Education, appointed by the National Education Association," *Bulletin*, no. 35 (Washington: U.S. Government Printing Office, 1918).

pseudospecificity and numbing earnestness. However, most leave the words undefined and let the momentum of traditional practice speak for itself. That is why analyzing how Mark spends his time is important: from watching him one uncovers the important purposes of education, the ones that shape practice. Mark's day is similar to that of other high school students across the country, as similar as the rhetoric of one goal statement to others'. Of course, there are variations, but the extent of consistency in the shape of school routine for a large and diverse adolescent population is extraordinary, indicating more graphically than any rhetoric the measure of agreement in America about what one does in high school, and, by implication, what it is for.

The basic organizing structures in schools are familiar. Above all, students 24 are grouped by age (that is, freshman, sophomore, junior, senior), and all are expected to take precisely the same time—around 720 school days over four years, to be precise—to meet the requirements for a diploma. When one is out of his grade level, he can feel odd, as Mark did in his biology class. The goals are the same for all, and the means to achieve them are also similar.

Young males and females are treated remarkably alike; the schools' goals are 25 the same for each gender. In execution, there are differences, as those pressing sex discrimination suits have made educators intensely aware. The students in metalworking classes are mostly male; those in home economics, mostly female. But it is revealing how much less sex discrimination there is in high schools than in other American institutions. For many young women, the most liberated hours of their week are in school.

School is to be like a job: you start in the morning and end in the afternoon, 26 five days a week. You don't get much of a lunch hour, so you go home early, unless you are an athlete or are involved in some special school or extracurricular activity. School is conceived of as the children's workplace, and it takes young people off parents' hands and out of the labor market during prime-time work hours. Not surprisingly, many students see going to school as little more than a dogged necessity. They perceive the day-to-day routine, a Minnesota study reports, as one of "boredom and lethargy." One of the students summarizes: School is "boring, restless, tiresome, puts ya to sleep, tedious, monotonous, pain in the neck."[4]

The school schedule is a series of units of time: the clock is king. The base 27 time block is about fifty minutes in length. Some schools, on what they call modular scheduling, split that fifty-minute block into two or even three pieces. Most schools are double periods for laboratory work, especially in the sciences, or four-hour units for the small numbers of students involved in intensive

---

[4]Diane Hedin, Paula Simon, and Michael Robin, *Minnesota Youth Poll: Youth's Views on School and School Discipline*, Minnesota Report 184 (1983), Agricultural Experiment Station, University of Minnesota, p. 13.

vocational or other work-study programs. The flow of all school activity arises from or is blocked by these time units. "How much time do I have with my kids" is the teacher's key question.

Because there are many claims for those fifty-minute blocks, there is little   28
time set aside for rest between them, usually no more than three to ten minutes, depending on how big the school is and, consequently, how far students and teachers have to walk from class to class. As a result, there is a frenetic quality to the school day, a sense of sustained restlessness. For the adolescents, there are frequent changes of room and fellow students, each change giving tempting opportunities for distraction, which are stoutly resisted by teachers. Some schools play soft music during these "passing times," to quiet the multitude, one principal told me.

Many teachers have a chance for a coffee break. Few students do. In some   29
city schools where security is a problem, students must be in class for seven consecutive periods, interrupted by a heavily monitored twenty-minute lunch period for small groups, starting as early as 10:30 A.M. and running to after 1:00 P.M. A high premium is placed on punctuality and on "being where you're supposed to be." Obviously, a low premium is placed on reflection and repose. The students rush from class to class to collect knowledge. Savoring it, it is implied, is not to be done much in school, nor is such meditation really much admired. The picture that these familiar patterns yield is that of an academic supermarket. The purpose of going to school is to pick things up, in an organized and predictable way, the faster the better.

What is supposed to be picked up is remarkably consistent among all sorts   30
of high schools. Most schools specifically mandate three out of every five courses a student selects. Nearly all of these mandates fall into five areas—English, social studies, mathematics, science, and physical education. On the average, English is required to be taken each year, social studies and physical education three out of the four high school years, and mathematics and science one or two years. Trends indicate that in the mid-eighties there is likely to be an increase in the time allocated to these last two subjects. Most students take classes in these four major academic areas beyond the minimum requirements, sometimes in such special areas as journalism and "yearbook," offshoots of English departments.[5]

Press most adults about what high school is for, and you hear these subjects   31
listed. *High school? That's where you learn English and math and that sort of thing.* Ask students, and you get the same answer. High school is to "teach" these "subjects."

---

[5] I am indebted to Harold F. Sizer and Lyde E. Sizer for a survey of the diploma requirements of fifty representative secondary schools, completed for A Study of High Schools.

What is often absent is any definition of these subjects or any rationale for 32 them. They are just there, labels. Under those labels lie a multitude of things. A great deal of material is supposed to be "covered"; most of these courses are surveys, great sweeps of the stuff of their parent disciplines.

While there is often a sequence *within* subjects—algebra before trigonometry, 33 "first-year" French before "second-year" French—there is rarely a coherent relationship or sequence *across* subjects. Even the most logically related matters—reading ability as a precondition for the reading of history books, and certain mathematical concepts or skills before the study of some of physics— are only loosely coordinated, if at all. There is little demand for a synthesis of it all; English, mathematics, and the rest are discrete items, to be picked up individually. The incentive for picking them up is largely through tests and, with success at these, in credits earned.

Coverage within subjects is the key priority. If some imaginative teacher 34 makes a proposal to force the marriage of, say, mathematics and physics or to require some culminating challenges to students to use several subjects in the solution of a complex problem, and if this proposal will take "time" away from other things, opposition is usually phrased in terms of what may be thus forgone. If we do that, we'll have to give up colonial history. We won't be able to get to programming. We'll not be able to read *Death of a Salesman*. There isn't time. The protesters usually win out.

The subjects come at a student like Mark in random order, a kaleidoscope 35 of worlds: algebraic formulae to poetry to French verbs to Ping-Pong to the War of the Spanish Succession, all before lunch. Pupils are to pick up these things. Tests measure whether the picking up has been successful.

The lack of connection between stated goals, such as those of the California 36 high school cited earlier, and the goals inherent in school practice is obvious and, curiously, tolerated. Most striking is the gap between statements about "self-realization and mental and physical growth" or "moral and ethical values"—common rhetoric in school documents—and practice. Most physical education programs have neither the time nor the focus really to ensure fitness. Mental health is rarely defined. Neither are ethical values, save at the negative extremes, such as opposition to assault or dishonesty. Nothing in the regimen of a day like Mark's signals direct or implicit teaching in this area. The "school boy code" (not ratting on a fellow student) protects the marijuana pusher, and a leechlike associate is shrugged off without concern. The issue of the locker search was pushed aside, as not appropriate for class time.

Most students, like Mark, go to class in groups of twenty to twenty-seven 37 students. The expected attendance in some schools, particularly those in low-income areas, is usually higher, often thirty-five students per class, but high absentee rates push the actual numbers down. About twenty-five per class is an average figure for expected attendance, and the actual numbers are somewhat lower. There are remarkably few students who go to class in groups much larger or smaller than twenty-five.[6]

A student such as Mark sees five or six teachers per day; their differing styles   38 and expectations are part of his kaleidoscope. High school staffs are highly specialized: guidance counselors rarely teach mathematics, mathematics teachers rarely teach English, principals rarely do any classroom instruction. Mark, then, is known a little bit by a number of people, each of whom sees him in one specialized situation. No one may know him as a "whole person"—unless he becomes a special problem or has special needs.

Save in extracurricular or coaching situations, such as in athletics, drama,   39 or shop classes, there is little opportunity for sustained conversation between student and teacher. The mode is a one-sentence or two-sentence exchange: *Mark, when was Grover Cleveland president? Let's see, was 1890 . . . or something . . . wasn't he the one . . . he was elected twice, wasn't he . . . Yes . . . Gloria, can you get the dates right?* Dialogue is strikingly absent, and as a result the opportunity of teachers to challenge students' ideas in a systematic and logical way is limited. Given the rushed, full quality of the school day, it can seldom happen. One must infer that careful probing of students' thinking is not a high priority. How one gains (to quote the California school's statement of goals again) "the ability to make decisions, to solve problems, to reason independently, and to accept responsibility for self-evaluation and continuing self-improvement" without being challenged is difficult to imagine. One certainly doesn't learn these things merely from lectures and textbooks.

Most schools are nice places. Mark and his friends enjoy being in theirs.   40 The adults who work in schools generally like adolescents. The academic pressures are limited, and the accommodations to students are substantial. For example, if many members of an English class have jobs after school, the English teacher's expectations for them are adjusted, downward. In a word, school is sensitively accommodating, as long as students are punctual, where they are supposed to be, and minimally dutiful about picking things up from the clutch of courses in which they enroll.

This characterization is not pretty, but it is accurate, and it serves to describe   41 the vast majority of American secondary schools. "Taking subjects" in a systematized, conveyer-belt way is what one does in high school. That this process is, in substantial respects, not related to the rhetorical purposes of education is tolerated by most people, perhaps because they do not really either believe in those ill-defined goals or, in their heart of hearts, believe that schools can or should even try to achieve them. The students are happy taking subjects. The parents are happy, because that's what they did in high school. The rituals, the most important of which is graduation, remain intact. The adolescents are

---

[6]Education Research Service, Inc., *Class Size: A Summary of Research* (Arlington, Virginia, 1978); and *Class Size Research: A Critique of Recent Meta-Analyses* (Arlington, Virginia, 1980).

supervised safely and constructively most of the time, during the morning and afternoon hours, and they are off the labor market. That is what high school is all about.

QUESTIONS

1. The first half of this essay (the first nineteen paragraphs, to be exact) is a report. What do you think of this report? Given your own experience, how accurate is it? What attitude does the report convey, or is it objective?

2. Paragraph 19 is the conclusion of the report. It ends the story of Mark's day. Does it draw or imply any conclusions from the events reported?

3. How is the explanatory section of the essay (paragraphs 20 through 41) organized? If the first subtopic discussed is the goals of high school, what are the other subtopics?

4. What is the major conclusion of this explanation? To what extent do you agree with the last sentence of the essay and what it implies?

5. How does the report (paragraphs 1 through 19) function in the explanation that follows? What would be lost if the report were omitted? In considering how the two sections of the essay relate, note especially places where the explanation specifically refers to the report.

6. If you have a different view of high school, or went to a different kind of school, write an essay that is organized like Sizer's but that presents your own report and explanation of what school is.

7. Using the basic outline of Sizer's essay, write your own explanation of the workings of some institution: store, family, church or temple, club, team, or whatever else you know well. Think of your project in terms of Sizer's title: "What X Is."

MAKING CONNECTIONS

1. How do you suppose Sizer got this information about Mark and "what high school is"? Compare his approach to that of Dennis Hevesi, Farley Mowat, Jane van Lawick-Goodall, and Horace Miner. Which one comes closest, do you think, to Sizer's method for researching his essay? Explain the resemblances and differences.

2. Compare Sizer's interpretation of Mark's high-school experience to Umberto Eco's interpretation of *Casablanca* or Murray Ross's interpretation of baseball and football. To what extent does Sizer share a way of seeing things with either or both of them? Try to define, with examples from at least two of these writers, the method of interpretation they share.

SOAP OPERA, MELODRAMA, AND WOMEN'S ANGER

Tania Modleski

Tania Modleski (b. 1949) is associate professor of film and literature at the University of Wisconsin/Milwaukee. Her book Loving with a Vengeance: Mass-Produced Fantasies for Women *(1982) is a powerful demonstration of her conviction that "it is crucial to understand soap operas and other forms of mass art" in order "to let their very omissions and distortions speak, informing us of the contradictions they are meant to conceal and, equally importantly, of the fears that lie behind them." The material reprinted here from that book discusses the differences between soap opera and literary forms such as romance and melodrama, while it also explores the ways in which soap opera expresses or redirects the frustration and anger of the women in its audience. Modleski's work contributes to the rapidly developing academic field of cultural studies, in which texts drawn from the popular media are studied with the care formerly lavished only on works of high art.*

I

Approximately twelve soap operas are shown daily, each half an hour to an hour and a half long. The first of them goes on the air at about 10:00 A.M., and they run almost continuously until about 3:30 P.M. (of course, the times vary according to local programming schedules). In 1975 the *New York Times Magazine* reported that 20 million people watch soap operas daily, the average program attacting 6.7 million viewers, almost 90 percent of them female. Further:

> The households break down economically and educationally in proportions similar to the population as a whole—51.3 percent with household incomes under $10,000, for instance, and 23.9 percent with incomes over $15,000. About 24.8 percent of household heads have only an elementary school education, while 56.2 percent have a high school education or better. . . . The programs gross more than $300-million a year from the makers of soaps, deodorants, cake mixes and other household products, providing a disproportionate share of network profits though nighttime budgets are much larger.[1]

With the exception of "Ryan's Hope," which takes place in a big city, the soap operas are set in small towns and involve two or three families intimately connected with one another. Families are often composed of several generations, and the proliferation of generations is accelerated by the propensity of soap opera characters to mature at an incredibly rapid rate; thus, the matriarch on "Days of Our Lives," who looks to be about 65, has managed over the years to become a great-great-grandmother. Sometimes on a soap opera one of the families will be fairly well to do, and another somewhat lower on the social scale though still, as a rule, identifiably middle-class. In any case, since there is so much intermingling and intermarrying, class distinctions quickly become hopelessly blurred. Children figure largely in many of the plots, but they don't appear on the screen all that often; nor do the very old. Blacks and other minorities are almost completely excluded.

Women as well as men frequently work outside the home, usually in profes- 2
sions such as law and medicine, and women are generally on a professional par with men. But most of everyone's time is spent experiencing and discussing personal and domestic crises. Kathryn Weibel lists "some of the most frequent themes":

the evil woman
the great sacrifice
the winning back of an estranged lover/spouse
marrying her for her money, respectability, etc.
the unwed mother
deceptions about the paternity of children
career vs. housewife
the alcoholic woman (and occasionally man).[2]

Controversial social problems are introduced from time to time: rape was recently an issue on several soap operas and was, for the most part, handled in a sensitive manner. In spite of the fact that soap operas contain more references to social problems than do most other forms of mass entertainment, critics tend to fault them heavily for their lack of social realism.

If television is considered by some to be a vast wasteland, soap operas are 3
thought to be the least nourishing spot in the desert. The surest way to damn a film, a television program, or even a situation in real life is to invoke an analogy to soap operas. In the same way that men are often concerned to show that what they are, above all, is not women, not "feminine," so television programs and movies will, surprisingly often, tell us that they are not soap operas. On a recent "Phil Donahue Show," a group of handicapped Vietnam War Veterans were bitterly relating their experiences; at one point Donahue interrupted the conversation to assure his audience (comprised almost entirely of women) that he was not giving them soap opera, but he thought it important to "personalize" the war experience. An afternoon "Money Movie," *Middle of the Night*, an interminable Paddy Chayevsky affair starring Frederick March, dealt with one man's life-crisis as, on the brink of old age, he falls in love with

a very young Kim Novak and struggles against the petty and destructive jealousy of his sister and daughter. "This is *not* a soap opera," he reprimands the sister at one point. Since to me it had all the ingredients of one, I could only conclude that men's soap operas are not to be thought of as soap operas only because they are *for men* (or about men).

It is refreshing, therefore, to read Horace Newcomb's book, *T.V.: The Most Popular Art*, in which he suggests that far from being the nadir of art forms, as most people take them to be, soap operas represent in some ways the furthest advance of T.V. art. In other words, for all their stereotypical qualities, they combine to the highest degree two of the most important elements of the television aesthetic: "intimacy" and "continuity." Television, says Newcomb, is uniquely suited to deal with character and interpersonal relations rather than with action and setting. Soap operas, of course, play exclusively on the intimate properties of the medium. Newcomb also points out that because of the serial nature of the programs television can offer us depictions of people in situations which grow and change over time, allowing for a greater "audience involvement, a sense of becoming a part of the lives and actions of the characters they see."[3] Thus far it is mainly soap opera which has taken advantage of these possibilities for continuity, nighttime programs, by and large, tending to "forget" from week to week all of the conflicts and lessons which have gone before.

Newcomb's book is important in that, by refusing to indulge in an anti-feminine bias against soap operas, it reveals a new way of seeing these programs which allows them to be placed in the vanguard of T.V. aesthetics (dubious as this distinction may seem to many people). My approach is different from, though in no sense opposed to Newcomb's. I propose not to ignore what is "feminine" about soap operas but to focus on it, to show how they provide a unique narrative pleasure which, while it has become thoroughly adapted to the rhymths of women's lives in the home, provides an alternative to the dominant "pleasures of the text" analyzed by Roland Barthes and others. Soap operas may be in the vanguard not just of T.V. art but of all popular narrative art.

II

Whereas the meaning of Harlequin Romances depends almost entirely on the sense of an ending, soap operas are important to their viewers in part because they never end. Whereas Harlequins encourage our identification with one character, soap operas invite identification with numerous personalities. And whereas Harlequins are structured around two basic enigmas, in soap operas, the enigmas proliferate: "Will Bill find out that his wife's sister's baby is really his by artificial insemination? Will his wife submit to her sister's blackmail attempts, or will she finally let Bill know the truth? If he discovers the truth, will this lead to another nervous breakdown, causing him to go back to Spring General where his ex-wife and his illegitimate daughter are both doctors and sworn enemies?" Tune in tomorrow, not in order to find out the answers, but to see what further complications will defer the resolutions and introduce new questions. Thus the narrative, by placing ever more complex obstacles between desire and fulfillment, makes anticipation of an end an end in itself. Soap operas invest exquisite pleasure in the central condition of a woman's life: waiting—whether for her phone to ring, for the baby to take its nap, or for the family to be reunited shortly after the day's final soap opera has left *its* family still struggling against dissolution.

According to Roland Barthes, the hermeneutic code,[4] which propounds the enigmas, functions by making "expectation . . . the basic condition for truth: truth, these narratives tell us, is what is *at the end* of expectation. This design implies a return to order, for expectation is a disorder."[5] But, of course, soap operas do not end. Consequently, truth for women is seen to lie not "at the end of expectation," but *in* expectation, not in the "return to order," but in (familial) disorder.

Many critics have considered endings to be crucial to narratives. Frank [8] Kermode speculates that fictive ends are probably "figures" for death.[6] In his essay on "The Storyteller," Walter Benjamin comes to a similar conclusion:

> The novel is significant . . . not because it presents someone else's fate to us, perhaps didactically, but because this stranger's fate by virtue of the flame which consumes it yields us the warmth which we never draw from our own fate. What draws the reader to the novel is the hope of warming his shivering life with a death he reads about.[7]

But soap operas offer the promise of immortality and eternal return—same time tomorrow. Although at first glance, soap opera seems in this respect to be diametrically opposed to the female domestic novels of the nineteenth century, which were preoccupied with death, especially the deaths of infants and small children, a second look tells us that the fantasy of immortality embodied in modern melodrama is not so very different from the fantasies expressed in the older works. In the latter, it is not the case that, in Benjamin's words, "the 'meaning' of a character's life is revealed only in his death";[8] rather, for women writers and readers, forced to endure repeatedly the premature loss of their children, it was the meaning of the character's death that had to be ascertained, and this meaning was revealed only in the afterlife, only in projections of eternity.

"[T]racts of time unpunctuated by meaning derived from the end are not to [9] be borne," says Frank Kermode, confidently.[9] But perhaps for women (no doubt for men too) certain kinds of endings are attended by a sense of meaninglessness even less capable of being borne than limitless expanses of time which at least hold open the possibility that something may sometime happen to confer sense upon the present. The loss of a child was, for nineteenth century women, an example of such an unbearable ending: it was, as Helen Papashvily has called it, "a double tragedy—the loss of a precious individual and the negation of her creativity,"[10] and it threatened, perhaps more than any other experience, to give the lie to the belief in a benevolent God and the ultimate rightness of the world order. And so, it was necessary to believe that the child would join a heavenly family for all eternity.

For twentieth-century woman, the loss of her family, not through death, but through abandonment (children growing up and leaving home) is perhaps another "ending" which is feared because it leaves women lonely and isolated and without significant purpose in life. The fear, as Barbara Easton persuasively argues, is not without foundation:

> With the geographical mobility and breakdown of communities of the twentieth century, women's support networks outside the family have weakened, and they are likely to turn to their husbands for intimacy that earlier generations would have found elsewhere.[11]

The family is, for many women, their only support, and soap operas offer the assurance of its immortality.[12] They present the viewer with a picture of a family which, though it is always in the process of breaking down, stays together no matter how intolerable its situation may get. Or, perhaps more accurately, the family remains close precisely because it is perpetually in a chaotic state. The unhappiness generated by the family can only be solved in the family. Misery becomes not, as in many nineteenth-century women's novels, the consequence and sign of the family's breakdown, but the very means of its functioning and perpetuation. As long as the children are unhappy, as long as things *don't* come to a satisfying conclusion, the mother will be needed as confidante and adviser, and her function will never end.

One critic of soap opera remarks, "If . . . as Aristotle so reasonably claimed, drama is the imitation of a human action that has a beginning, a middle, and an end, soap opera belongs to a separate genus that is entirely composed of an indefinitely expandable middle."[13] It is not only that successful soap operas do not end, it is also that they cannot end. In *The Complete Soap Opera Book*, an interesting and lively work on the subject, the authors show how a radio serial forced off the air by television tried to wrap up its story.[14] It was an impossible task. Most of the storyline had to be discarded and only one element could be followed through to its end—an important example of a situation in which what Barthes calls the "discourse's instinct for preservation" has virtually triumphed over authorial control.[15] Furthermore, it is not simply that the story's completion would have taken too long for the amount of time allotted by the producers. More importantly, I believe it would have been impossible to resolve the contradiction between the imperatives of melodrama—the good must be rewarded and the wicked punished—and the latent message of soap operas— everyone cannot be happy at the same time, no matter how deserving they are.

The claims of any two people, especially in love matters, are often mutually exclusive.

John Cawelti defines melodrama as having   12

> at its center the moral fantasy of showing forth the essential 'rightness' of the world
> order. . . . Because of this, melodramas are usually rather complicated in plot
> and character; instead of identifying with a single protagonist through his line of
> action, the melodrama typically makes us intersect imaginatively with many lives.
> Subplots multiply, and the point of view continually shifts in order to involve us
> in a complex of destinies. Through this complex of characters and plots we see
> not so much the working of individual fates but the underlying moral process of
> the world.[16]

It is scarcely an accident that this essentially nineteenth-century form continues to appeal strongly to women, whereas the classic (male) narrative film is, as Laura Mulvey points out, structured "around a main controlling figure with whom the spectator can identify."[17] Soap operas continually insist on the insignificance of the individual life. A viewer might at one moment be asked to identify with a woman finally reunited with her love, only to have that identification broken in a moment of intensity and attention focused on the sufferings of the woman's rival.

If, as Mulvey claims, the identification of the spectator with "a main male   13
protagonist" results in the spectator's becoming "the representative of power,"[18] the multiple identification which occurs in soap opera results in the spectator's being divested of power. For the spectator is never permitted to identify with a character completing an entire action. Instead of giving us one "powerful ideal ego . . . who can make things happen and control events better than the subject/ spectator can,"[19] soap operas present us with numerous limited egos, each in conflict with the others, and continually thwarted in its attempts to control events because of inadequate knowledge of other peoples' plans, motivations, and schemes. Sometimes, indeed, the spectator, frustrated by the sense of powerlessness induced by soap operas, will, like an interfering mother, try to control events directly:

> Thousands and thousands of letters [from soap fans to actors] give advice, warn
> the heroine of impending doom, caution the innocent to beware of the nasties
> ("Can't you see that your brother-in-law is up to no good?"), inform one character
> of another's doings, or reprimand a character for unseemly behavior.[20]

Presumably, this intervention is ineffectual, and feminine powerlessness is reinforced on yet another level.

The subject/spectator of soap operas, it could be said, is constituted as a sort   14
of ideal mother: a person who possesses greater wisdom than all her children, whose sympathy is large enough to encompass the conflicting claims of her family (she identifies with them all), and who has no demands or claims of her own (she identifies with no one character exclusively). The connection between

melodrama and mothers is an old one. Harriet Beecher Stowe, of course, made it explicit in *Uncle Tom's Cabin*, believing that if her book could bring its female readers to see the world as one extended family, the world would be vastly improved. But in Stowe's novel, the frequent shifting of perspective identifies the reader with a variety of characters in order ultimately to ally her with the mother/author and with God who, in their higher wisdom and understanding, can make all the hurts of the world go away, thus insuring the "essential 'rightness' of the world order." Soap opera, however, denies the "mother" this extremely flattering illusion of her power. On the one hand, it plays upon the spectator's expectation of the melodramatic form, continually stimulating (by means of the Hermeneutic code) the desire for a just conclusion to the story, and, on the other hand, it constantly presents the desire as unrealizable, by showing that conclusions only lead to further tension and suffering. Thus soap operas convince women that their highest goal is to see their families united and happy, while consoling them for their inability to realize this ideal and bring about familial harmony.

This is reinforced by the character of the good mother on soap operas. In contrast to the manipulating mother who tries to interfere with her children's lives, the good mother must sit helplessly by as her children's lives disintegrate; her advice, which she gives only when asked, is temporarily soothing, but usually ineffectual. Her primary function is to be sympathetic, to tolerate the foibles and errors of others. Maeve Ryan, the mother on "Ryan's Hope," is a perfect example. "Ryan's Hope," a soap opera centered around an Irish-Catholic, bar-owning family which, unlike the majority of soap families, lives in a large city, was originally intended to be more "realistic," more socially oriented than the majority of soap operas.[21] Nevertheless, the function of the mother is unchanged: she is there to console her children and try to understand them as they have illegitimate babies, separate from their spouses (miraculously obtaining annulments instead of divorces), and dispense birth control information in the poor neighborhoods.

It is important to recognize that soap operas serve to affirm the primacy of the family not by presenting an ideal family, but by portraying a family in constant turmoil and appealing to the spectator to be understanding and tolerant of the many evils which go on within that family. The spectator/mother, identifying with each character in turn, is made to see "the larger picture" and extend her sympathy to both the sinner and the victim. She is thus in a position to forgive all. As a rule, only those issues which can be tolerated and ultimately pardoned are introduced on soap operas. The list includes careers for women, abortions, premarital and extramarital sex, alcoholism, divorce, mental and even physical cruelty. An issue like homosexuality, which could explode the family structure rather than temporarily disrupt it, is simply ignored. Soap operas, contrary to many people's conception of them, are not conservative but liberal, and the mother is the liberal par excellence. By constantly presenting her with the many-sidedness of any question, by never reaching a permanent conclusion, soap operas undermine her capacity to form unambiguous judgments.

In this respect, soap opera melodrama can be said to create in the spectator a divisiveness of feeling totally different from the "monopathic" feeling Robert Heilman sees as constituting the appeal of traditional melodrama. There, he writes, "one enjoys the wholeness of a practical competence that leads to swift and sure action; one is untroubled by psychic fumbling, by indecisiveness, by awareness of alternate courses, by weak muscles or strong counterimperatives."[22] But in soap operas, we are constantly troubled by "psychic fumbling" and by "strong counterimperatives." To take one example, Trish, on "Days of Our Lives," takes her small son and runs away from her husband David in order to advance her singing career. When she gets an opportunity to go to London to star in a show, she leaves the child with her mother. When the show folds, she becomes desperate to get back home to see her child, but since she has no money, she has to prostitute herself. Finally she is able to return, and after experiencing a series of difficulties, she locates her son, who is now staying with his father. Once she is in town, a number of people, angry at the suffering she has caused David, are hostile and cruel towards her. Thus far, the story seems to bear out the contention of the critics who claim that soap opera characters who leave the protection of the family are unequivocally punished. But the matter is not so simple. For the unforgiving people are shown to have limited perspectives. The larger view is summed up by Margo, a woman who has a mysterious and perhaps fatal disease and who, moreover, has every reason to be jealous of Trish since Trish was the first love of Margo's husband. Margo claims that no one can ever fully know what private motives drove Trish to abandon her family; besides, she says, life is too short to bear grudges and inflict pain. The spectator, who sees the extremity of Trish's sorrow, assents. And at the same time, the spectator is made to forgive and understand the unforgiving characters, for she is intimately drawn into their anguish and suffering as well.

These remarks must be qualified. If soap operas keep us caring about everyone; if they refuse to allow us to condemn most characters and actions until all the evidence is in (and, of course, it never is), there is one character whom we are allowed to hate unreservedly: the villainess, the negative image of the spectator's ideal self.[23] Although much of the suffering on soap opera is presented as unavoidable, the surplus suffering is often the fault of the villainess who tries to "make things happen and control events better than the subject/spectator can." The villainess might very possibly be a mother trying to manipulate her children's lives or ruin their marriages. Or perhaps she is a woman avenging herself on her husband's family because it has never fully accepted her.

This character cannot be dismissed as easily as many critics seem to think.[24] The extreme delight viewers apparently take in despising the villainess testifies to the enormous amount of energy involved in the spectator's repression and to her (albeit unconscious) resentment at being constituted as an egoless receptacle for the suffering of others.[25] The villainess embodies the "split-off fury" which, in the words of Dorothy Dinnerstein, is "the underside of the 'truly feminine' woman's monstrously overdeveloped talent for unreciprocated empathy."[26] This aspect of melodrama can be traced back to the middle of the nineteenth century when *Lady Audley's Secret*, a drama based on Mary Elizabeth Braddon's novel about a governess turned bigamist and murderess, became one of the most popular stage melodramas of all time.[27] In her discussion of the novel, Elaine Showalter shows how the author, while paying lipservice to conventional notions about the feminine role, managed to appeal to "thwarted female energy":

> The brilliance of *Lady Audley's Secret* is that Braddon makes her would-be murderess the fragile blond angel of domestic realism. . . . The dangerous woman is not the rebel or the bluestocking, but the "pretty little girl" whose indoctrination in the female role has taught her secrecy and deceitfulness, almost as secondary sex characteristics.[28]

Thus the villainess is able to transform traditional feminine weaknesses into the sources of her strength.

Similarly, on soap operas, the villainess seizes those aspects of a woman's life which normally render her most helpless and tries to turn them into weapons for manipulating other characters. She is, for instance, especially good at manipulating pregnancy, unlike most women, who, as Mary Ellmann wittily points out, tend to feel manipulated by it:

> At the same time, women cannot help observing that conception (their highest virtue, by all reports) simply happens or doesn't. It lacks the style of enterprise. It can be prevented by foresight and device (though success here, as abortion rates show, is exaggerated), but it is accomplished by luck (good or bad). Purpose often seems if anything, a deterrent. A devious business benefitting by indirection, by pretending not to care, as though the self must trick the body. In the regrettable conception, the body instead tricks the self—much as it does in illness or death.[29]

In contrast to the numerous women on soap operas who are either trying unsuccessfully to become pregnant or who have become pregnant as a consequence of a single unguarded moment in their lives, the villainess manages, for a time at least, to make pregnancy work for her. She gives it the "style of enterprise." If she decides she wants to marry a man, she will take advantage of him one night when he is feeling especially vulnerable and seduce him. And if she doesn't achieve the hoped-for pregnancy, undaunted, she simply lies to her lover about being pregnant. The villainess thus reverses male/female roles: anxiety about conception is transferred to the male. He is the one who had better watch his step and curb his promiscuous desires or he will find himself burdened with an unwanted child.

Some episodes on "The Young and the Restless" perfectly illustrate the point.

Lori's sister Leslie engages in a one night sexual encounter with Lori's husband, Lance. Of course, she becomes pregnant as a result. Meanwhile Lori and Lance have been having marital difficulties, and Lori tries to conceive a child, hoping this will bring her closer to her husband. When she finds out about her sister and Lance, she becomes frantic about her inability to conceive, realizing that if Lance ever finds out he is the father of Leslie's child, he will be drawn to Leslie and reject her. Vanessa, Lance's mother and a classic villainess, uses her knowledge of the situation to play on Lori's insecurities and drive a wedge between her and Lance. At the same time, Lori's father has been seduced by Jill Foster, another villainess, who immediately becomes pregnant, thus forcing him to marry her.

Furthermore, the villainess, far from allowing her children to rule her life, 22 often uses them in order to further her own selfish ambitions. One of her typical ploys is to threaten the father or the woman possessing custody of the child with the deprivation of that child. She is the opposite of the woman at home, who at first is forced to have her children constantly with her, and later is forced to let them go—for a time on a daily recurring basis and then permanently. The villainess enacts for the spectator a kind of reverse *fort-da* game, in which the mother is the one who attempts to send the child away and bring it back at will, striving to overcome feminine passivity in the process of the child's appearance and loss. [30] Into the bargain, she also tries to manipulate the man's disappearance and return by keeping the fate of his child always hanging in the balance. And again, male and female roles tend to get reversed: the male suffers the typically feminine anxiety over the threatened absence of his children. On "Ryan's Hope," for example, Delia continually uses her son to control her husband and his family. At one point she clashes with another villainess, Raye Woodward, over the child and the child's father, Frank Ryan, from whom Delia is divorced. Raye realizes that the best way to get Frank interested in her is by taking a maternal interest in his child. When Delia uncovers Raye's scheme, she becomes determined to foil it by regaining custody of the boy. On "The Young and the Restless," to take another example, Derek is on his way out of the house to try to intercept Jill Foster on her way to the altar and persuade her to marry him instead of Stuart Brooks. Derek's ex-wife Suzanne thwarts the attempt by choosing that moment to inform him that their son is in a mental hospital.

The villainess thus continually works to make the most out of events which 23 render other characters totally helpless. Literal paralysis turns out, for one villainess, to be an active blessing, since it prevents her husband from carrying out his plans to leave her; when she gets back the use of her legs, therefore, she doesn't tell anyone. And even death doesn't stop another villainess from wreaking havoc; she returns to haunt her husband and convince him to try to kill his new wife.

The popularity of the villainess would seem to be explained in part by the   24
theory of repetition compulsion, which Freud saw as resulting from the individual's attempt to become an active manipulator of her/his own powerlessness.[31] The spectator, it might be thought, continually tunes into soap operas
to watch the villainess as she tries to gain control over her feminine passivity,
thereby acting out the spectator's fantasies of power. Of course, most formula
stories (like the Western) appeal to the spectator/reader's compulsion to repeat:
the spectator constantly returns to the same story in order to identify with the
main character and achieve, temporarily, the illusion of mastery denied him or
her in real life. But soap operas refuse the spectator even this temporary illusion
of mastery. The villainess's painstaking attempts to turn her powerlessness to
her own advantage are always thwarted just when victory seems most assured,
and she must begin her machinations all over again. Moreover, the spectator
does not comfortably identify with the villainess. Since the spectator despises
the villainess as the negative image of her ideal self, she not only watches the
villainess act out her own hidden wishes, but simultaneously sides with the
forces conspiring against fulfillment of those wishes. As a result of this "internal
contestation,"[32] the spectator comes to enjoy repetition for its own sake and
takes her adequate pleasure in the building up and tearing down of the plot. In
this way, perhaps, soap operas help reconcile her to the meaningless, repetitive
nature of much of her life and work within the home.

Soap operas, then, while constituting the spectator as a "good mother,"   25
provide in the person of the villainess an outlet for feminine anger: in particular,
as we have seen, the spectator has the satisfaction of seeing men suffer the same
anxieties and guilt that women usually experience and seeing them receive
similar kinds of punishment for their transgressions. But that anger is neutralized
at every moment in that it is the special object of the spectator's hatred. The
spectator, encouraged to sympathize with almost everyone, can vent her frustration on the one character who refuses to accept her own powerlessness, who
is unashamedly self-seeking. Woman's anger is directed at woman's anger, and
an eternal cycle is created.

And yet, if the villainess never succeeds, if, in accordance with the spectator's   26
conflicting desires, she is doomed to eternal repetition, then she obviously never
permanently fails either. When, as occasionally happens, a villainess reforms,
a new one immediately supplants her. Generally, however, a popular villainess
will remain true to her character for most or all of the soap opera's duration.
And if the villainess constantly suffers because she is always foiled, we should
remember that she suffers no more than the good characters, who don't even
try to interfere with their fates. Again, this may be contrasted to the usual
imperatives of melodrama, which demand an ending to justify the suffering of
the good and punish the wicked. While soap operas thrive they present a
continual reminder that women's anger is alive, if not exactly well.

NOTES

1. Anthony Astrachan, quoted in Dan Wakefield, *All Her Children*, p. 149.
2. Weibel, p. 56.
3. Horace Newcomb, *T.V.: The Most Popular Art*, p. 253.
4. hermeneutic code: In Roland Barthes's theory of fiction, everything in a story is understood in terms of one or more of five codes. One of these, the hermeneutic code, organizes the reader's desire to find out the truth about the characters and events in any story. This code is very active in detective stories, of course, but it is present in every kind of narrative. Modleski's point, in the present case, is that soap operas are different from most kinds of narrative, in that they will never reach that conclusion in which everything is revealed. If there is truth in them, it cannot be the kind of truth we learn only at the end of the tale. [Eds.]
5. Barthes, *S/Z*, p. 76.
6. Frank Kermode, *The Sense of an Ending*, p. 7.
7. Walter Benjamin, "The Storyteller," in his *Illuminations*, p. 101.
8. Benjamin, "The Storyteller," pp. 100–101.
9. Kermode, p. 162.
10. Papashvily, p. 194.
11. Barbara Easton, "Feminism and the Contemporary Family," p. 30.
12. Not only can women count on a never ending story line, they can also, to a great extent, rely upon the fact that their favorite characters will never desert them. To take a rather extreme example: when, on one soap opera, the writers killed off a popular female character and viewers were unhappy, the actress was brought back to portray the character's twin sister. See Madeleine Edmondson and David Rounds, *From Mary Noble to Mary Hartman: The Complete Soap Opera Book*, p. 208.
13. Dennis Porter, "Soap Time: Thoughts on a Commodity Art Form," p. 783.
14. Edmondson and Rounds, *The Complete Soap Opera Book*, pp. 104–110.
15. Barthes, *S/Z*, p. 135.
16. John G. Cawelti, *Adventure, Mystery and Romance*, pp. 45–46.
17. Laura Mulvey, "Visual Pleasure and Narrative Cinema," p. 420.
18. Mulvey, p. 420.
19. Mulvey, p. 420.
20. Edmondson and Rounds, p. 193.
21. See Paul Mayer, "Creating 'Ryan's Hope.'"
22. Robert B. Heilman, *Tragedy and Melodrama*, p. 85.
23. There are still villains on soap operas, but their numbers have declined considerably since radio days—to the point where they are no longer indispensable to the formula. "The Young and the Restless," for example, does without them.
24. According to Weibel, we quite simply "deplore" the victimizers and totally identify with the victim (p. 62).
25. "A soap opera without a bitch is a soap opera that doesn't get watched. The more hateful the bitch the better. Erica of 'All My Children' is a classic. If you want to hear some hairy rap, just listen to a bunch of women discussing Erica.
'Girl, that Erica needs her tail whipped.'
'I wish she'd try to steal my man and plant some marijuana in my purse. I'd be mopping up the street with her new hairdo.'" Bebe Moore Campbell, "Hooked on Soaps," p. 103.
26. Dorothy Dinnerstein, *The Mermaid and The Minotaur*, p. 236.
27. "The author, Mary Elizabeth Braddon, belonged to that class of writers called

by Charles Reade 'obstacles to domestic industry.'" Frank Rahill, *The World of Melodrama*, p. 204.

28. Elaine Showalter, *A Literature of Their Own*, p. 204.

29. Mary Ellmann, *Thinking About Women*, p. 181. Molly Haskell makes a similar point in her discussion of "The Woman's Film," in *From Reverence to Rape*, pp. 172–73.

30. The game, observed by Freud, in which the child plays "disappearance and return" with a wooden reel tied to a string. "What he did was to hold the reel by the string and very skilfully throw it over the edge of his curtained cot, so that it disappeared into it, at the same time uttering his expressive 'O-O-O-O'. [Freud speculates that this represents the German word *'fort'* or *'gone.'*] He then pulled the reel out of the cot again by the string and hailed its reappearance with a joyful *'da'* ['there']." According to Freud, "Throwing away the object so that it was 'gone' might satisfy an impulse of the child's, which was suppressed in his actual life, to revenge himself on his mother for going away from him. In that case it would have a defiant meaning: 'All right then, go away! I don't need you. I'm sending you away myself.'" Sigmund Freud, *Beyond the Pleasure Principle*, pp. 10–11.

31. Speaking of the child's *fort-da* game, Freud notes, "At the outset he was in a passive situation—he was overpowered by experience; but by repeating it, unpleasurable though it was, as a game, he took on an *active* part. These efforts might be put down to an instinct for mastery that was acting independently of whether the memory was in itself pleasurable or not." In *Beyond the Pleasure Principle*, p. 10.

32. Jean-Paul Sartre's phrase for the tension surrealism's created object sets up in the spectator is remarkably appropriate here. See *What Is Literature?*, p. 133n.

WORKS CITED

Barthes, Roland. *S/Z*. Translated by Richard Miller. New York: Hill and Wang, 1974.

Benjamin, Walter. *Illuminations*. Translated by Harry Zohn, Edited by Hannah Arendt. New York: Schocken Books, 1969.

Campbell, Bebe Moore. "Hooked on Soaps." *Essence*, November 1978, pp. 100–103.

Cawelti, John G. *Adventure, Mystery, and Romance*. Chicago: University of Chicago Press, 1976.

Dinnerstein, Dorothy. *The Mermaid and the Minotaur: Sexual Arrangements and Human Malaise*. New York: Harper & Row, 1976.

Easton, Barbara. "Feminism and the Contemporary Family." *Socialist Review* 8, no. 3 (1978), pp. 11–36.

Edmondson, Madeleine, and Rounds, David. *From Mary Noble to Mary Hartmann: The Complete Soap Opera Book*. New York: Stein and Day, 1976.

Ellmann, Mary. *Thinking about Women*. New York: Harvest Books, 1968.

Freud, Sigmund. *Beyond the Pleasure Principle*. Translated by James Strachey. New York: W. W. Norton Co., 1961.

Haskell, Molly. *From Reverence to Rape: The Treatment of Women in the Movies*. New York: Penguin, 1974.

Heilman, Robert B. *Tragedy and Melodrama: Versions of Experience*. Seattle: University of Washington Press, 1968.

Kermode, Frank. *The Sense of an Ending: Studies in the Theory of Fiction*. New York: Oxford University Press, 1967.

Mayer, Paul. "Creating 'Ryan's Hope.'" In *T.V. Book*. Edited by Judy Fireman. New York: Workman Publishing Co., 1977.

Mulvey, Laura. "Visual Pleasure and Narrative Cinema." In *Women and the Cinema*. Edited by Karyn Kay and Gerald Peary. New York: E. P. Dutton, 1977.

Newcome, Horace. *T.V.: The Most Popular Art*. New York: Anchor Books, 1974.

Papashvily, Helen Waite. *All the Happy Endings, A Study of the Domestic Novel in America, the Women Who Wrote It, the Women Who Read It, in the Nineteenth Century*. New York: Harper & Brothers, 1956.

Porter, Dennis. "Soap Time: Thoughts on a Commodity Art Form." *College English* 38 (1977): 782–88.

Rahill, Frank. *The World of Melodrama*. University Park: Pennsylvania State University Press, 1967.

Sartre, Jean-Paul. *What Is Literature?* Translated by Bernard Frechtman. New York: Washington Square Press, 1966.

Showalter, Elaine. *A Literature of Their Own*. Princeton: Princeton University Press, 1977.

Wakefield, Dan. *All Her Children*. Garden City, N.Y.: Doubleday & Co., 1976.

Weibel, Kathryn. *Mirror, Mirror: Images of Women Reflected in Popular Culture*. Garden City, N.Y.: Anchor Books, 1977.

QUESTIONS

1. Before discussing Modleski's essay, take a survey in your class and find out how many class members watch soap operas with some regularity. If only some watch, see if you can explain why some do and some do not. Is gender a significant discriminator here? That is, can you tell by someone's gender whether he or she is more or less likely to watch soap operas? Do your findings support or contradict Modleski's views?

2. The first short section of Modleski's text gives some background to her study and explains what she is attempting to do. Summarize her intentions, especially as she presents them in paragraph 5.

3. The long second section of her essay begins with a comparison of soap opera with books like Harlequin Romances. If you have no experience of such books, ask a classmate who has read them to tell you what they are like. Summarize in your own words Modleski's point about the difference between the plots of these novels and the plots of soap operas.

4. Modleski says in paragraph 14 that the "subject/spectator" is conceived as a sort of "ideal mother." What does she mean by this? What point is she making in this and the surrounding paragraphs about the relationship between what goes on in the video lives of characters and in the real lives of viewers? Consider this question as not just a matter of one sort of life resembling or failing to resemble the other, but as a matter of what aspects of real life predispose viewers to respond to certain aspects of video life.

5. Modleski gives considerable attention to the character of the typical soap-opera "villainess." Why does she take this character so seriously? Do you remember any such characters clearly enough to test her explanation against your own impressions? Pick one of the villainesses known best by members of the class and make a list of her deeds and qualities. Use this as a way of supporting or contradicting Modleski.

6. Write an essay in which you discuss some soap-opera villainess in relation to Modleski's explanation of the significance of this figure. Try to analyze your own emotions as you contemplate the villainess. To what extent are they as Modleski suggests

they will be? To what extent do you think they differ? Do some research among other viewers, outside of your class, who have not read Modleski. Ask them how they feel about your chosen villainess. Use this information to enrich your discussion. Aim at a conclusion that supports, contradicts, or modifies in some way Modleski's view of the function of the villainess in the mind and emotions of the viewer.

7. Select a particular soap opera, either a regular day-time program or a prime-time drama. Concentrating on this one show, select certain features of it that seem to you especially interesting or appealing, and write an essay in which you attempt to explain just what it is in this feature of the show that appeals to you. Does it match up in some interesting way with our own hopes and fears? Your project is to produce an explanation of what you feel, not a defense of your position. Our reasons for liking things are not always admirable or worthy. Try to use this exercise as a way of deepening your understanding of the appeal that the medium or this particular aspect of it has for you.

8. Consider some other television show, film, comic strip, or other form of popular art that seems aimed at a particular kind of audience. Write a paper in which you analyze the appeal your subject holds for the audience that it seems designed to reach. For whom are the *Rambo* films designed, for instance, or others like them? What is the nature of the appeal that they make to their target audience? What about sporting events? What do wrestling matches provide for their audience? Try to choose a subject that will allow you some room for thought and analysis.

MAKING CONNECTIONS

1. Insofar as Modleski is correct in equating one of the appeals of soap opera with its quality of "waiting," of never ending, of "an indefinitely expandable middle," the soaps would seem to be in a much more comfortable relation to baseball than to football, as Murray Ross explains each of those sports. Do you find this to be true? Survey a number of followers of soap operas and see which sport they prefer, football or baseball. Try to explain the results you find.

2. Read Umberto Eco's essay on *Casablanca*. Are "the clichés having a ball" in the soaps? Or are the soaps, to draw upon Jan Harold Brunvand's studies, a fertile ground for discovering new urban legends? Write an essay in which you bring either Eco's or Brunvand's work to bear upon soap opera, as you know it both from Modleski's article and, perhaps, from your own experience as a viewer.

GEORGIA O'KEEFFE

Joan Didion

As the headnote on page 59 explains, Joan Didion's novels have been published to critical acclaim, but the highest praises have been reserved for her essays and other journalistic studies, such as Slouching Towards Bethlehem *(1969),* The White Album *(1979), and* Salvador *(1983), of which the novelist Jerzy Kosinski wrote in a review, "She is always at the center. . . . Our quintessential essayist." The following essay on Georgia O'Keeffe, a major American painter, is taken from* The White Album.

"Where I was born and where and how I have lived is unimportant," Georgia   1
O'Keeffe told us in the book of paintings and words published in her ninetieth year on earth. She seemed to be advising us to forget the beautiful face in the Stieglitz photographs. She appeared to be dismissing the rather condescending romance that had attached to her by then, the romance of extreme good looks and advanced age and deliberate isolation. "It is what I have done with where I have been that should be of interest." I recall an August afternoon in Chicago in 1973 when I took my daughter, then seven, to see what Georgia O'Keeffe had done with where she had been. One of the vast O'Keeffe "Sky Above Clouds" canvases floated over the back stairs in the Chicago Art Institute that day, dominating what seemed to be several stories of empty light, and my daughter looked at it once, ran to the landing, and kept on looking. "Who drew it," she whispered after a while. I told her. "I need to talk to her," she said finally.

My daughter was making, that day in Chicago, an entirely unconscious but   2
quite basic assumption about people and the work they do. She was assuming that the glory she saw in the work reflected a glory in its maker, that the painting was the painter as the poem is the poet, that every choice one made alone— every word chosen or rejected, every brush stroke laid or not laid down— betrayed one's character. *Style is character.* It seemed to me that afternoon that I had rarely seen so instinctive an application of this familiar principle, and I recall being pleased not only that my daughter responded to style as character but that it was Georgia O'Keeffe's particular style to which she responded: this was a hard woman who had imposed her 192 square feet of clouds on Chicago.

"Hardness" has not been in our century a quality much admired in women,   3
nor in the past twenty years has it even been in official favor for men. When

367

hardness surfaces in the very old we tend to transform it into "crustiness" or eccentricity, some tonic pepperiness to be indulged at a distance. On the evidence of her work and what she has said about it, Georgia O'Keeffe is neither "crusty" nor eccentric. She is simply hard, a straight shooter, a woman clean of received wisdom and open to what she sees. This is a woman who could early on dismiss most of her contemporaries as "dreamy," and would later single out one she liked as "a very poor painter." (And then add, apparently by way of softening the judgment: "I guess he wasn't a painter at all. He had no courage and I believe that to create one's own world in any of the arts takes courage.") This is a woman who in 1939 could advise her admirers that they were missing her point, that their appreciation of her famous flowers was merely sentimental. "When I paint a red hill," she observed coolly in the catalogue for an exhibition that year, "you say it is too bad that I don't always paint flowers. A flower touches almost everyone's heart. A red hill doesn't touch everyone's heart." This is a woman who could describe the genesis of one of her most well-known paintings—the "Cow's Skull: Red, White and Blue" owned by the Metropolitan—as an act of quite deliberate and derisive orneriness. "I thought of the city men I had been seeing in the East," she wrote. "They talked so often of writing the Great American Novel—the Great American Play—the Great American Poetry. . . . So as I was painting my cow's head on blue I thought to myself, "I'll make it an American painting. They will not think it great with the red stripes down the sides—Red, White and Blue—but they will notice it.'"

The city men. The men. They. The words crop up again and again as this   4
astonishingly aggressive woman tells us what was on her mind when she was making her astonishingly aggressive paintings. It was those city men who stood accused of sentimentalizing her flowers: "I made you take time to look at what I saw and when you took time to really notice my flower you hung all your associations with flowers on my flower and you write about my flower as if I think and see what you think and see—and I don't." *And I don't.* Imagine those words spoken, and the sound you hear is *don't tread on me.* "The men" believed it impossible to paint New York, so Georgia O'Keeffe painted New York. "The men" didn't think much of her bright color, so she made it brighter. The men yearned toward Europe so she went to Texas, and then New Mexico. The men talked about Cézanne, "long involved remarks about the 'plastic quality' of his form and color," and took one another's long involved remarks, in the view of his angelic rattlesnake in their midst, altogether too seriously. "I can paint one of those dismal-colored paintings like the men," the woman who regarded herself always as an outsider remembers thinking one day in 1922, and she did: a painting of a shed "all low-toned and dreary with the tree beside the door." She called this act of rancor "The Shanty" and hung it in her next show. "The men seemed to approve of it," she reported fifty-four years later, her contempt undimmed. "They seemed to think that maybe I was beginning to paint. That was my only low-toned dismal-colored painting."

Some women fight and others do not. Like so many successful guerrillas in 5 the war between the sexes, Georgia O'Keeffe seems to have been equipped early with an immutable sense of who she was and a fairly clear understanding that she would be required to prove it. On the surface her upbringing was conventional. She was a child on the Wisconsin prairie who played with china dolls and painted watercolors with cloudy skies because sunlight was too hard to paint and with her brother and sisters, listened every night to her mother read stories of the Wild West, of Texas, of Kit Carson and Billy the Kid. She told adults that she wanted to be an artist and was embarrassed when they asked what kind of artist she wanted to be: she had no idea "what kind." She had no idea what artists did. She had never seen a picture that interested her, other than a pen-and-ink Maid of Athens in one of her mother's books, some Mother Goose illustrations printed on cloth, a tablet cover that showed a little girl with pink roses, and the painting of Arabs on horseback that hung in her grandmother's parlor. At thirteen, in a Dominican convent, she was mortified when the sister corrected her drawing. At Chatham Episcopal Institute in Virginia she painted lilacs and sneaked time alone to walk out to where she could see the line of the Blue Ridge Mountains on the horizon. At the Art Institute in Chicago she was shocked by the presence of live models and wanted to abandon anatomy lessons. At the Art Students League in New York one of her fellow students advised her that, since he would be a great painter and she would end up teaching painting in a girls' school, any work of hers was less important than modeling for him. Another painted over her work to show her how the Impressionists did trees. She had not before heard how the Impressionists did trees and she did not much care.

At twenty-four she left all those opinions behind and went for the first time 6 to live in Texas, where there were no trees to paint and no one to tell her how not to paint them. In Texas there was only the horizon she craved. In Texas she had her sister Claudia with her for a while, and in the late afternoons they would walk away from town and toward the horizon and watch the evening star come out. "The evening star fascinated me," she wrote. "It was in some way very exciting to me. My sister had a gun, and as we walked she would throw bottles into the air and shoot as many as she could before they hit the ground. I had nothing but to walk into nowhere and the wide sunset space with the star. Ten watercolors were made from that star." In a way one's interest is compelled as much by the sister Claudia with the gun as by the painter Georgia with the star, but only the painter left us this shining record. Ten watercolors were made from that star.

369

QUESTIONS

1. Summarize the qualities of O'Keeffe's paintings as they are enumerated in this essay. Then study the painting on the cover, which is also by Georgia O'Keeffe. Do the qualities mentioned in Didion's essay square with what you see on the cover?

2. Didion's first paragraph brings together two kinds of material, research and personal experience. In doing this, Didion quotes from two sources, a ninety-year-old woman and a seven-year-old child. The result is that we encounter three "I"s in the first paragraph—all female—and we also encounter a mixture of the personal and the impersonal. What is the effect of all this? How did you personally react to this mixture of research and personal experience? What connections can you make among the three "I"s?

3. Paragraph 3 opens with "Hardness." Comment on the importance of this word to Didion's essay. What does this concept add to her mixture of research and personal experience? What would the essay be like without this concept?

4. Extend your study of O'Keeffe by locating a book in the library that reproduces more of her paintings. What qualities do you find in her work? Write an essay of your own in which you describe her essential style, as you see it.

5. Select a visual artist (or an artist in any other medium) whose work interests you. Find out about this person's life and career. Then, write an essay in which you explain what you like in this artist's work and why you like it, connecting the life and work through some metaphor or concept that organizes your feelings and your essay the way that "hardness" organizes Didion's.

MAKING CONNECTIONS

1. Compare Didion's account of Georgia O'Keeffe to the several other representations of women artists collected in this anthology, such as Maya Angelou's "Graduation," Alice Walker's "Beauty: When the Other Dancer Is the Self," Isak Dinesen's, "The Iguana," Didion's other essay, "Why I Write," Annie Dillard's "Singing with the Fundamentalists," and Virginia Woolf's "The Death of the Moth." What themes and concerns seem common to these women?

2. Compare Didion's account of Georgia O'Keeffe to Virginia Woolf's essay, "The Death of the Moth." Does O'Keeffe, as Didion represents her, bear any relation to Woolf, as she represents herself in her essay? What, if anything, seems similar in the stances of these two artists? What seems most different? Although O'Keeffe (1887–1986) lived much longer, she and Woolf (1882–1940) were of the same generation. Would you expect them to have been compatible?

THE MOSES OF MICHELANGELO[1]
Sigmund Freud

Sidmund Freud (1856–1939) spent most of his life in Vienna and would have died there if he had not, like many other Jews, had to leave Austria when Nazi Germany invaded in 1938. As a young man he studied medicine in Vienna, became a doctor, and specialized in mental illness. His researches in this area led him to the study of unconscious mental processes and to the development of psychoanalysis as a way of understanding and treating certain emotional problems. Though most of his many books dealt with case studies and various problems relating to emotional disorders, his lifelong interest in art occasionally led him to discuss the works of writers, painters, and sculptors. In the interpretative essay reprinted here, Freud turns his thoughts to the study of a particular sculpture by the Italian Renaissance artist Michelangelo.

I may say at once that I am no connoisseur in art, but simply a layman. I have often observed that the subject-matter of works of art has a stronger attraction for me than their formal and technical qualities, though to the artist their value lies first and foremost in these latter. I am unable rightly to appreciate many of the methods used and the effects obtained in art. I state this so as to secure the reader's indulgence for the attempt I propose to make here. 1

Nevertheless, works of art do exercise a powerful effect on me, especially those of literature and sculpture, less often of painting. This has occasioned me, when I have been contemplating such things, to spend a long time before them trying to apprehend them in my own way, *i.e.* to explain to myself what their effect is due to. Wherever I cannot do this, as for instance with music, I am almost incapable of obtaining any pleasure. Some rationalistic, or perhaps analytic, turn of mind in me rebels against being moved by a thing without knowing why I am thus affected and what it is that affects me. 2

This has brought me to recognize the apparently paradoxical fact that precisely some of the grandest and most overwhelming creations of art are still 3

---

[1] Originally published anonymously in *Imago*, Bd. III, 1914, prefaced by the following editorial note: *Although this paper does not, strictly speaking, conform to the conditions under which contributions are accepted for publication in this Journal, the editors have decided to print it, since the author, who is personally known to them, belongs to psychoanalytical circles, and since his mode of thought has in point of fact a certain resemblance to the methodology of psychoanalysis.* [Translated by Alix Strachey.]

unsolved riddles to our understanding. We admire them, we feel overawed by them, but we are unable to say what they represent to us. I am not sufficiently well-read to know whether this fact has already been remarked upon; possibly, indeed, some writer on aesthetics has discovered that this state of intellectual bewilderment is a necessary condition when a work of art is to achieve its greatest effects. It would be only with the greatest reluctance that I could bring myself to believe in any such necessity.

I do not mean that connoisseurs and lovers of art find no words with which   4
to praise such objects to us. They are eloquent enough, it seems to me. But usually in the presence of a greater work of art each says something different from the other; and none of them says anything that solves the problem for the unpretending admirer. In my opinion, it can only be the artist's intention, in so far as he succeeded in expressing it in his work and in conveying it to us, that grips us so powerfully. I realize that it cannot be merely a matter of intellectual comprehension; what he aims at is to awaken in us the same emotional attitude, the same mental constellation as that which in him produced the impetus to create. But why should the artist's intention not be capable of being communicated and comprehended in words like any other fact of mental life? Perhaps where great works of art are concerned this would never be possible without the application of psychoanalysis. The product itself after all must admit of such an analysis, if it really is an effective expression of the intentions and emotional activities of the artist. To discover his intention, though, I must first find out the meaning and content of what is represented in his work; I must, in other words, be able to *interpret* it. It is possible, therefore, that a work of art of this kind needs interpretation, and that until I have accomplished that interpretation I cannot come to know why I have been so powerfully affected. I even venture to hope that the effect of the work will undergo no diminution after we have succeeded in thus analysing it.

Let us consider Shakespeare's masterpiece, *Hamlet*, a play now over three   5
centuries old.[2] I have followed the literature of psychoanalysis closely, and I accept its claim that it was not until the material of the tragedy had been traced back analytically to the Oedipus theme that the mystery of its effect was at last explained. But before this was done, what a mass of differing and contradictory interpretative attempts, what a variety of opinions about the hero's character and the dramatist's design! Does Shakespeare claim our sympathies on behalf of a sick man, or of an ineffectual weakling, or of an idealist who is only too good for the real world? And how many of these interpretations leave us cold— so cold that they do nothing to explain the effect of the play and rather incline us to the view that its magical appeal rests solely upon the impressive thoughts in it and the splendour of its language. And yet, do not those very endeavours

[2] Probably first performed in 1602.

speak for the fact that we feel the need of discovering in it some source of power beyond these alone?

Another of these inscrutable and wonderful works of art is the marble statue   6
of Moses, by Michelangelo . . . , in the Church of S. Pietro in Vincoli in Rome. As we know, it was only a fragment of the gigantic tomb which the artist was to have erected for the powerful Pope Julius II.[3] It always delights me to read an appreciatory sentence about this statute, such as that it is "the crown of modern sculpture" (Hermann Grimm). For no piece of statuary has ever made a stronger impression on me than this. How often have I mounted the steep steps of the unlovely Corso Cavour to the lonely place where the deserted church stands, and have essayed to support the angry scorn of the hero's glance! Sometimes I have crept cautiously out of the half-gloom of the interior as though I myself belonged to the mob upon whom his eye is turned—the mob which can hold fast no conviction, which has neither faith nor patience and which rejoices when it has regained its illusory idols.

But why do I call this statue inscrutable? There is not the slightest doubt   7
that it represents Moses, the Law-giver of the Jews, holding the Tables of the Ten Commandments. That much is certain, but that is all. As recently as 1912 an art critic, Max Sauerlandt, has said, "No other work of art in the world has been judged so diversely as the Moses with the head of Pan. The mere interpretation of the figure has given rise to completely opposed views. . . ." Basing myself on an essay published only five years ago,[4] I will first set out what are the doubts associated with this figure of Moses; and it will not be difficult to show that behind them lies concealed all that is most essential and valuable for the comprehension of this work of art.

1

The Moses of Michelangelo is represented as seated; his body faces forward,   8
his head with its mighty beard looks to the left, his right foot rests on the ground and his left leg is raised so that only the toes touch the ground. His right arm links the Tables of the Law with a portion of his beard; his left arm lies in his lap. [See photographs.] Were I to give a more detailed description of his attitude, I should have to anticipate what I want to say later on. The descriptions of the figure given by various writers are, by the way, curiously inapt. What has not been understood has been inaccurately perceived or reproduced. Grimm says that the right hand "under whose arm the Tables rest, grasps his beard." So also Lübke: "Profoundly shaken, he grasps with his right hand his magnificent streaming beard . . ."; and Springer: "Moses presses one (the left) hand against his body, and thrusts the other, as though unconsciously, into the mighty locks

---

[3] According to Henry Thode, the statue was made between the years 1512 and 1516.
[4] Henry Thode, *Michelangelo: kritische Untersuchungen über seine Werke*, Bd. I., 1908.

of his beard." Justi thinks that the fingers of his (right) hand are playing with his beard, "as an agitated man nowadays might play with his watch-chain." Müntz, too, lays stress on this playing with the beard. Thode speaks of the "calm, firm posture of the right hand upon the Tables resting against his side." He does not recognize any sign of excitement even in the right hand, as Justi and also Boito do. "The hand remains grasping his beard, in the position it was before the Titan turned his head to one side." Jacob Burckhardt complains that "the celebrated left arm has no other functions in reality than to press his beard to his body."

If mere descriptions do not agree we shall not be surprised to find a divergence   9 of view as to the meaning of various features of the statue. In my opinion we cannot better characterize the facial expression of Moses than in the words of Thode, who reads in it "a mixture of wrath, pain and contempt,"—"wrath in his threatening contracted brows, pain in his glance, and contempt in his protruded under lip and in the down-drawn corners of his mouth." But other admirers must have seen with other eyes. Thus Dupaty says, "His august brow seems to be but a transparent veil only half concealing his great mind."[5] Lübke, on the other hand, declares that "one would look in vain in that head for an expression of higher intelligence; his down-drawn brow speaks of nothing but a capacity of infinite wrath and an all-compelling energy." Guillaume (1875) differs still more widely in his interpretation of the expression of the face. He finds no emotion in it, "only a proud simplicity, an inspired dignity, a living faith. The eye of Moses looks into the future, he foresees the lasting survival of his people, the immutability of his law." Similarly, to Müntz, "the eyes of Moses rove far beyond the race of men. They are turned towards those mysteries which he alone has descried." To Steinmann, indeed, this Moses is "no longer the stern Law-giver, no longer the terrible enemy of sin, armed with the wrath of Jehovah, but the royal priest, whom age may not approach, beneficent and prophetic, with the reflection of eternity upon his brow, taking his last farewell of his people."

There have even been some for whom the Moses of Michelangelo had   10 nothing at all to say, and who are honest enough to admit it. Thus a critic in the *Quarterly Review* of 1858: "There is an absence of meaning in the general conception, which precludes the idea of a self-sufficing whole. . . ." And we are astonished to learn that there are yet others who find nothing to admire in the Moses, but who revolt against it and complain of the brutality of the figure and the animal cast of the head.

Has then the master-hand indeed traced such a vague or ambiguous script   11 in the stone, that so many different readings of it are possible?

Another question, however, arises, which covers the first one. Did Michel-   12 angelo intend to create a "timeless study of character and mood" in this Moses,

---

[5] Thode, *loc. cit.* p. 197.

or did he portray him at a particular and, if so, at a highly significant moment of his life? The majority of judges have decided in the latter sense and are able to tell us what episode in his life it is which the artist has immortalized in stone. It is the descent from Mount Sinai, where Moses has received the Tables from God, and it is the moment when he perceives that the people have meanwhile made themselves a Golden Calf and are dancing around it and rejoicing. This is the scene upon which his eyes are turned, this the spectacle which calls out the feelings depicted in his countenance—those feelings which in the next instant will launch his great frame to violent action. Michelangelo has chosen this last moment of hesitation, of calm before the storm, for his representation. In the next instant Moses will spring to his feet—his left foot is already raised from the ground—hurl the Tables to the ground, and let loose his rage upon his faithless people.

Once more many individual differences of opinion exist among those who support this interpretation. 13

Jacob Burckhardt writes: "Moses seems to be shown in that moment in which he catches sight of the worship of the Golden Calf, and is springing to his feet. His form is animated by the inception of a mighty movement and the physical strength with which he is endowed causes us to await it with fear and trembling." 14

And Lübke says: "As if at this moment his flashing eye were perceiving the sin of the worship of the Golden Calf and a mighty inward movement were running through his whole frame. Profoundly shaken, he grasps with his right hand his magnificent, streaming beard, as though to master his actions for one instant longer, only for the explosion of his wrath to burst with more annihilation the next." 15

Springer agrees with this view, but not without mentioning one misgiving, which will engage our attention later in the course of this paper. He says, "Burning with energy and zeal, it is with difficulty that the hero subdues his inward emotion. . . . We are thus involuntarily reminded of a dramatic situation and are brought to believe that Moses is represented in that moment when he sees the people of Israel worshipping the Golden Calf and is about to start up in wrath. Such an impression, it is true, is not easy to reconcile with the artist's real intention, since the figure of Moses, like the other five seated figures on the upper part of the Papal tomb, is meant primarily to have a decorative effect. But it testifies very convincingly to the vitality and individuality portrayed in the figure of Moses." 16

One or two writers, without actually accepting the Golden Calf theory, do nevertheless agree on its main point, namely, that Moses is just about to spring to his feet and take action. 17

According to Hermann Grimm, "The form (of Moses) is filled with a majesty, a consciousness of self, a feeling that all the thunders of heaven are at his command, and that yet he is holding himself in check before loosing them, waiting to see whether his foes whom he means to annihilate will dare to attack 18 him. He sits there as if on the point of starting to his feet, his proud head carried high on his shoulders; the hand under whose arm the Tables rest grasps his beard which falls in heavy waves over his breast, his nostrils distended and his lips shaped as though words were trembling upon them."

Heath Wilson declares that Moses' attention has been excited by something, 19 and he is about to leap to his feet, but is still hesitating; and that his glance of mingled scorn and indignation is still capable of changing into one of compassion.

Wölfflin speaks of "inhibited movement." The cause of this inhibition, he 20 says, lies in the will of the man himself; it is the last moment of self-control before he lets himself go and leaps to his feet.

Justi has gone the furthest of all in his interpretation of the statue as Moses 21 in the act of perceiving the Golden Calf, and he has pointed out details hitherto unobserved in it and worked them into his hypothesis. He directs our attention to the position of the two Tables, and it is indeed an unusual one, for they are about to slip down on to the stone seat. "He (Moses) might therefore be looking in the direction from which the clamour was coming with an expression of evil foreboding, or it might be the actual sight of the abomination which has dealt him a stunning blow. Quivering with horror and pain he has sunk down.[6] He has sojourned on the mountain forty days and nights and he is weary. A horror, a great turn of fortune, a crime, even happiness itself, can be perceived in a single moment, but not grasped in its essence, its depths or its consequences. For an instant it seems to Moses that his work is destroyed and he despairs of his people. In such moments the inner emotions betray themselves involuntarily in small movements. He lets the Tables slip from his right hand on to the stone seat; they have been brought up sideways there, pressed by his forearm against the side of his body. His hand, however, comes in contact with his breast and beard and thus, by the turning of the head to the spectator's right, it draws the beard to the left and breaks the symmetry of that masculine ornament. It looks as though his fingers were playing with his beard as an agitated man nowadays might play with his watch-chain. His left hand is buried in his garment over the lower part of his body—in the Old Testament the viscera are the seat of the emotions—but the left leg is already drawn back and the right put forward; in the next instant he will leap up, his mental energy will be transposed from feeling into action, his right arm will move, the Tables will fall to the ground, and the shameful trespass will be expiated in torrents of blood. . . ." "Here is not yet the moment of tension of a physical act. The pain of mind still dominates him almost like a paralysis."

Fritz Knapp takes exactly the same view, except that he does not introduce 22

---

[6] It should be remarked that the careful arrangement of the mantle over the knees of the sitting figure invalidates this first part of Justi's view. On the contrary, this would lead us to suppose that Moses is represented as sitting there in calm repose until he is startled by some sudden perception.

the doubtful point at the beginning of the description,[7] and carries the idea of the sliding Tables further. "He who just now was alone with his God is distracted by earthly sounds. He hears a noise; voices shouting to dance and music wake him from his dream; he turns his eyes and his head in the direction of the clamour. In one instant fear, rage and unbridled passion traverse his huge frame. The Tables begin to slip down, and will fall to the ground and break when he leaps to his feet and hurls the angry thunder of his words into the midst of his back-sliding people. . . . This is the moment of highest tension which is chosen. . . ." Knapp, therefore, emphasizes the element of preparation for action, and disagrees with the view that what is being represented is an initial inhibition due to an overmastering agitation.

It cannot be denied that there is something extraordinarily attractive about attempts at an interpretation of the kind made by Justi and Knapp. This is because they do not stop short at the general effect of the figure, but are based on separate features in it; these we usually fail to notice, being overcome by the total impression of the statue and as it were paralysed by it. The marked turn of the head and eyes to the left, whereas the body faces forwards, supports the view that the resting Moses has suddenly seen somethiing on that side to rivet his attention. His lifted foot can hardly mean anything else but that he is preparing to spring up,[8] and the very unusual way in which the Tables are held (for they are most sacred objects and are not to be introduced into the composition like any other belonging) is fully accounted for if we suppose that they have slipped down as a result of the agitation of their bearer and will fall to the ground. According to this view we should believe that the statue represents a special and important moment in the life of Moses, and we should be left in no doubt of what that moment is. 23

But two remarks of Thode's deprive us of the knowledge we thought to have gained. This critic says that to his eye the Tables are not slipping down but are "firmly lodged." He notes the "calm, firm pose of the right hand upon the resting Tables." If we look for ourselves we cannot but admit unreservedly that Thode is right. The Tables are firmly placed and in no danger of slipping. Moses' right hand supports them or is supported by them. This does not explain the position in which they are held, it is true, but the interpretation of Justi and others cannot be based upon it. 24

The second observation is still more final. Thode reminds us that "this statue was planned as one out of six, and is intended to be seated. Both facts contradict the view that Michelangelo meant to record a particular historical moment. For as to the first consideration, the plan of representing a row of seated figures as types of human beings—as the *vita activa* and the *vita contemplativa*— 25

---

[7][Cf. previous note.—Trans.]

[8]Although the left foot of the reposeful seated figure of Giuliano in the Medici Chapel is similarly raised from the ground.

excluded a representation of particular historic episodes. And as to the second, the representation of a seated posture—a posture necessitated by the artistic conception of the whole monument—contradicts the nature of that episode, namely, the descent of Moses from Mount Sinai into the camp."

If we accept Thode's objection we shall find that we can add to its weight. 26 The figure of Moses was to have decorated the base of the tomb together with five other statues (in a later sketch, with three). Its immediate complement was to have been a figure of Paul. One other pair, representing the *vita activa* and the *vita contemplativa* in the shape of Leah and Rachel—standing, it is true—has been executed on the tomb as it still exists in its mournfully aborted form. The Moses thus forms part of a whole and we cannot imagine that the figure was meant to arouse an expectation in the spectator that it was on the point of leaping up from its seat and rushing away to create a disturbance on its own account. If the other figures are not also represented as about to take violent action—and this seems very improbable—then it would create a very bad impression for one of them to give us the illusion that it was going to leave its place and its companions, in fact to abandon its rôle in the general scheme. Such an intention would have a chaotic effect and we could not charge a great artist with it unless the facts drove us to it. A figure in the act of instant departure would be utterly at variance with the state of mind which the tomb is meant to induce in us.

The figure of Moses, therefore, cannot be supposed to be springing to his 27 feet; he must be allowed to remain as he is in sublime repose like the other figures and like the proposed statue of the Pope (which was not, however, executed by Michelangelo himself). But then the statue we see before us cannot be that of a man filled with wrath, of Moses when he came down from Mount Sinai and found his people faithless and threw down the Holy Tables so that they were broken. And, indeed, I can recollect my own disillusionment when, during my first visits to the church, I used to sit down in front of the statue in the expectation that I should now see how it would start up on its raised foot, hurl the Tables of the Law to the ground and let fly its wrath. Nothing of the kind happened. Instead, the stone image became more and more transfixed, an almost oppressively solemn calm emanated from it, and I was obliged to realize that something was represented here that could stay without change; that this Moses would remain sitting like this in his wrath for ever.

But if we have to abandon our interpretation of the statue as showing Moses 28 just before his outburst of wrath at the sight of the Golden Calf, we have no alternative but to accept one of those hypotheses which regard it as a study of character. Thode's view seems to be the least arbitrary and to have the closest reference to the meaning of its movements. He says, "Here, as always, he is concerned with representing a certain type of character. He creates the image of a passionate leader of mankind who, conscious of his divine mission as Law-giver, meets the uncomprehending opposition of men. The only means of representing a man of action of this kind was to accentuate the power of his will, and this was done by a rendering of movement pervading the whole of his apparent quiet, as we see in the turn of his head, the tension of his muscles and the position of his left foot. These are the same distinguishing marks that we find again in the *vir activus* of the Medici chapel in Florence. This general character of the figure is further heightened by laying stress on the conflict which is bound to arise between such a reforming genius and the rest of mankind. Emotions of anger, contempt and pain are typified in him. Without them it would not have been possible to portray the nature of a superman of this kind. Michelangelo has created, not an historical figure, but a character-type, embodying an inexhaustible inner force which tames the recalcitrant world; and he has given a form not only to the Biblical narrative of Moses, but to his own inner experiences, and to his impressions both of the individuality of Julius himself, and also, I believe, of the underlying springs of Savonarola's perpetual conflicts."

This view may be brought into connection with Knackfuss's remark that the great secret of the effect produced by the Moses lies in the artistic contrast between the inward fire and the outer calm of his bearing. 29

For myself, I see nothing to object to in Thode's explanation; but I feel the lack of something in it. Perhaps it is the need to discover a closer parallel between the state of mind of the hero as expressed in his attitude, and the above-mentioned contrast between his "outward" calm and "inward" emotion. 30

2

Long before I had any opportunity of hearing about psychoanalysis, I learnt that a Russian art-connoisseur, Ivan Lermolieff,[9] had caused a revolution in the art galleries of Europe by questioning the authorship of many pictures, showing how to distinguish copies from originals with certainty, and constructing hypothetical artists for those works of art whose former supposed authorship had been discredited. He achieved this by insisting that attention should be diverted from the general impression and main features of a picture, and he laid stress on the significance of minor details, of things like the drawing of the finger-nails, of the lobe of an ear, of aureoles and such unconsidered trifles which the copyist neglects to imitate and yet which every artist executes in his own characteristic way. I was then greatly interested to learn that the Russian pseudonym concealed the identity of an Italian physician called Morelli, who died in 1891 with the rank of Senator of the Kingdom of Italy. It seems to me that his method of inquiry is closely related to the technique of psychoanalysis. It, too, is accustomed to divine secret and concealed things from unconsidered or unnoticed details, from the rubbish-heap, as it were, of our observations. 31

---

[9] His first essays were published in German between 1874 and 1876.

Now in two places in the figure of Moses there are certain details which 32
have hitherto not only escaped notice—but, in fact, have not even been properly
described. These are the attitude of his right hand and the position of the two
Tables of the Law. We may say that this hand forms a very singular, unnatural
link, and one which calls for explanation, between the Tables and the wrathful
hero's beard. He has been described as running his fingers through his beard
and playing with its locks, while the outer edge of his hand rests on the Tables.
But this is plainly not so. It is worth while examining more closely what those
fingers of the right hand are doing, and describing more minutely the mighty
beard with which they are in contact. [10]

We now quite clearly perceive the following things: the thumb of the hand 33
is concealed and the index finger alone is in effective contact with the beard.
It is pressed so deeply against the soft masses of hair that they bulge out beyond
it both above and below, that is, both towards the head and towards the
abdomen. The other three fingers are propped upon the wall of his chest and
are bent at the upper joints; they are barely touched by the extreme right-hand
lock of the beard which falls past them. They have, as it were, withdrawn
themselves from the beard. It is therefore not correct to say that the right hand
is playing with the beard or plunged in it; the simple truth is that the index
finger is laid over a part of the beard and makes a deep trough in it. To press
one's beard with one finger is assuredly an extraordinary gesture and one not
easy to understand.

The much-admired beard of Moses flows from his cheeks, chin and upper 34
lip in a number of waving strands which are kept distinct from one another all
the way down. One of the strands on the extreme right, growing from the
cheek, flows down to the inward-pressing index finger, where it stops. We may
assume that it resumes its course between that finger and the concealed thumb.
The corresponding strand on the left side falls practically unimpeded far down
over his breast. What has received the most unusual treatment is the thick mass
of hair on the inside of this latter strand, the part between it and the middle
line. It is not suffered to follow the turn of the head to the left; it is forced to
roll over loosely and form part of a kind of scroll which lies across and over the
strands on the inner right side of the beard. This is because it is held fast by
the pressure of the right index finger, although it grows from the left side of the
face and is, in fact, the main portion of the whole left side of the beard. Thus,
the main mass of the beard is thrown to the right of the figure, whereas the
head is sharply turned to the left. At the place where the right index finger is
pressed in, a kind of whorl of hairs is formed; strands of hair coming from the
left lie over strands coming from the right, both caught in by that despotic
finger. It is only beyond this place that the masses of hair deflected from their

---

[10] Cf. the photo insert.

course, flow freely once more, and now they fall vertically until their ends are gathered up in Moses' left hand as it lies open on his lap.

I have no illusions as to the clarity of my description, and venture no opinion whether the sculptor really does invite us to solve the riddle of that knot in the beard of his statue. But apart from this, the fact remains that the pressure of the *right* index-finger affects mainly the strands of hair from the *left* side; and that this oblique hold prevents the beard from accompanying the turn of the head and eyes to the left. Now we may be allowed to ask what this arrangement means and to what motives it owes its existence. Were they indeed considerations of linear and spatial design which caused the sculptor to draw the downward-streaming wealth of hair across to the right of the figure which is looking to its left, how strangely unsuitable as a means appears the pressure of a single finger! And what man who, for some reason or other, has drawn his beard over to the other side, would take it into his head to hold down the one half across the other by the pressure of a single finger? Yet may not these minute particulars mean nothing in reality, and may we not be racking our brains about things which were of no moment to their creator? 35

Let us proceed on the assumption that even these details have significance. There is a solution which will remove our difficulties and afford a glimpse of a new meaning. If the *left* side of Moses' beard lies under the pressure of his *right* finger, we may perhaps take this pose as the last stage of some connection between his right hand and the left half of his beard, a connection which was a much more intimate one at some moment before that chosen for representation. Perhaps his hand had seized his beard with far more energy, had reached across to its left edge, and, in returning to that position in which the statue shows it, had been followed by a part of his beard which now testifies to the movement which has just taken place. The loop of the beard would thus be an indication of the path taken by this hand. 36

Thus we shall have inferred that there had been retreating motion of the right hand. This one assumption necessarily brings others with it. In imagination we complete the scene of which this movement, established by the evidence of the beard, is a part; and we are brought back quite naturally to the hypothesis according to which the resting Moses is startled by the clamour of the people and the spectacle of the Golden Calf. He was sitting there calmly, we will suppose, his head with its flowing beard facing forward, and his hand in all probability not near it at all. Suddenly the clamour strikes his ear; he turns his head and eyes in the direction from which the disturbance comes, sees the scene and takes it in. Now wrath and indignation seize him; and he would fain leap up and punish the wrongdoers, annihilate them. His rage, distant as yet from its object, is meanwhile directed in a gesture against his own body. His impatient hand, ready to act, clutches at his beard which has moved with the turn of his head, and shuts it down with his fingers between the thumb and the palm in an iron grasp—it is a gesture whose power and vehemence remind 37 us of other creations of Michelangelo's. But now an alteration takes place, as yet we do not know how or why. The hand that had been put forward and had sunk into his beard is hastily withdrawn and unclasped, and the fingers let go their hold; but so deeply have they been plunged in that in their withdrawal they drag a great piece of the left side of the beard across to the right, and this piece remains lodged over the hair of the right under the weight of one finger, the longest and uppermost one of the hand. And this new position, which can only be understood with reference to the former one, is now retained.

It is time now to pause and reflect. We have assumed that the right hand   38
was, to begin with, away from the beard; that then it reached across the left of the figure in a moment of great emotional tension and seized the beard; and that it was finally drawn back again, taking a part of the beard with it. We have disposed of this right hand as though we had the free use of it. But may we do this? Is the hand indeed so free? Must.it not hold or support the Tables? Are not such mimetic evolutions as these prohibited by its important function? And furthermore, what could have occasioned its withdrawal if such a powerful motive caused its first displacement?

Here are indeed fresh difficulties. It is undeniable that the right hand is   39
responsible for the Tables; and also that we have no motive to account for the withdrawal we have ascribed to it. But what if both difficulties could be solved together, then and then only presenting a clear and connected sequence of events? What if it is precisely something which is happening to the Tables that explains the movements of the hand?

If we look at the drawing in Fig. 1 we shall see that the Tables present one   40
or two notable features hitherto not deemed worthy of remark. It has been said

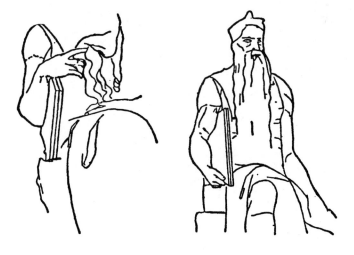

FIG. 1   FIG. 2

that the right hand rests upon the Tables; or again that it supports them. And we can see at once that the two apposed, rectangular tablets are standing on edge. If we look closer we shall notice that the lower edge is a different shape from the upper one, which is obliquely inclined forward. The top edge is straight, whereas the bottom one has a protuberance like a horn on the part nearest to us, and the Tables touch the stone seat precisely with this protuberance. What can be the meaning of this detail?[11] It can hardly be doubted that this projection is meant to mark the actual upper side of the Tables, as regards the writing. It is only the upper edge of rectangular tablets of this kind that is curved or notched. Thus we see that the Tables are upside-down. This is a singular way to treat such sacred objects. They are stood on their heads and practically balanced on one corner. What consideration of form could have led to such an attitude? Or was this detail, too, of no importance to the artist Michelangelo?

The view begins to form in us that the Tables also have arrived at their present position as the result of a previous movement; that this movement depended on the inferred change of place of the right hand and then in its turn compelled that hand to make its subsequent retreat. The movements of the hand and of the Tables can be co-ordinated in this way: at first the figure of Moses, while it was still sitting quietly, carried the Tables upright under its right arm. Its right hand grasped their bottom edge and found a hold in the projection of their front part. The greater ease thereby gained sufficiently accounts for the 41

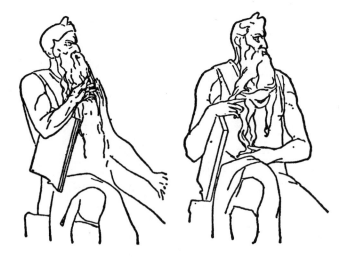

FIG. 3 FIG. 4

[11] Which, by the way, is quite incorrectly reproduced in a large plaster cast in the collection of the Vienna Academy of Plastic Arts.

reversed position in which the Tables are held. Then came the moment when Moses' calm was broken by the disturbance. He turns his head in its direction, and when he sees the spectacle he lifts his foot preparatory to starting up, lets go the Tables with his hand and throws it to the left and upwards into his beard, as though to turn his vehemence against his own body. The Tables were now consigned to the pressure of his arm, which had to squeeze them against his side. But this support was not sufficient and the Tables began to slip in a forward and downward direction. The upper edge, which had been held horizontally, now began to face forwards and downwards; and the lower edge, deprived of its stay, was nearing the stone seat with its front corner. Another instant and the Tables would have pivoted upon this new point of support, have hit the ground with the upper edge foremost, and been shattered to pieces. It is *to prevent this* that the right hand retreats, lets go the beard, a part of which is drawn back with it unintentionally, comes against the top edge of the Tables in time and grips them near the hind corner, which has now come uppermost. Thus the singularly constrained air of the whole—beard, hand and tilted Tables—can be traced to that one passionate movement of the hand and its natural consequences. If we wish to reverse the effects of those stormy movements, we must raise the upper front corner of the Tables and push it back, thus lifting their lower front corner (the one with the protuberance) from the stone seat; and then lower the right hand and bring it under the now horizontal bottom edge of the Tables.

I have procured from the hand of an artist four drawings to illustrate my meaning. Fig. 4 reproduces the statue as it actually is; Figs. 2 and 3 represent the preceding stages according to my hypothesis—the first that of calm, the second that of highest tension, in which the figure is preparing to spring up and has abandoned its hold of the Tables, so that these are beginning to slip down. Now it is remarkable how the two postures in the supplementary drawings vindicate the incorrect descriptions of earlier writers. Condivi, a contemporary of Michelangelo's, says: "Moses, the captain and leader of the Hebrews, is seated in the attitude of a contemplative sage, holding the Tables of the Law under his right arm, and leaning his chin on his left hand (!), as one who is weary and full of care." No such attitude is to be seen in Michelangelo's statue, but it describes almost exactly the view on which the first drawing is based. Lübke writes, together with other critics: "Profoundly shaken, he grasps with his right hand his magnificent, streaming beard." This is incorrect if we look at the reproduction of the actual statue, but it is true of the second sketch (Fig. 3). Justi and Knapp have observed, as we have seen, that the Tables are about to slip down and are in danger of being broken. Thode set them right and showed that the Tables were securely held by the right hand; yet they would have been correct if they had been describing not the statue itself but the middle stage of our reconstructed action. It almost seems as if they had emancipated themselves from the visual image of the statue and had unconsciously begun an analysis of the motive forces behind it, and that that analysis had led them to make the same claim as we, more consciously and more explicitly, have done.

3

We may now, I believe, permit ourselves to reap the fruits of our endeavours.   43
We have seen how many of those who have felt the influence of this statue have been impelled to interpret it as representing Moses agitated by the spectacle of his people fallen from grace and dancing round an idol. But this interpretation had to be given up, for it made us expect to see him spring up in the next moment, break the Tables and accomplish the work of vengeance. Such a conception, however, would fail to harmonize with the design of making this figure, together with three or five more seated figures, a part of the tomb of Julius II. We may now take up again the abandoned interpretation, for the Moses we have reconstructed will neither leap up nor cast the Tables from him. What we see before us is not the inception of a violent action but the remains of a movement that has already taken place. In his first transport of fury, Moses desired to act, to spring up and take vengeance and forget the Tables; but he has overcome the temptation, and he will now remain seated and still in his frozen wrath and in his pain mingled with contempt. Nor will he throw away the Tables so that they will break on the stones, for it is on their especial account that he has controlled his anger; it was to preserve them that he kept his passion in check. In giving way to his rage and indignation, he had to neglect the Tables, and the hand which upheld them was withdrawn. They began to slide down and were in danger of being broken. This brought him to himself. He remembered his mission and renounced for its sake an indulgence of his feeling. His hand returned and saved the unsupported Tables before they had actually fallen to the ground. In this attitude he remained immobilized, and in this attitude Michelangelo has portrayed him as the guardian of the tomb.

Viewed from above downwards, the figure exhibits three distinct emotional   44
strata. The lines of the face reflect the feelings which have become predominant; the middle of the figure shows the traces of suppressed movement; and the foot still retains the attitude of the projected action. It is as though the controlling influence had proceeded downwards from above. No mention has been made so far of the left arm, and it seems to claim a share in our interpretation. The hand is laid in his lap in a mild gesture and holds as though in a caress the end of his flowing beard. It seems as if it is meant to counteract the violence with which the other hand had misused the beard a few moments ago.

But here it will be objected that after this is not the Moses of the Bible. For   45
that Moses did actually fall into a fit of rage and did throw away the Tables and break them. This Moses must be a quite different man, a new Moses of the artist's conception; so that Michelangelo must have had the presumption to

388

emend the sacred text and to falsify the character of that holy man. Can we think him capable of a boldness which might almost be said to approach an act of blasphemy?

The passage in the Holy Scriptures which describes Moses' action at the scene of the Golden Calf is as follows: (Exodus xxxii. 7) "And the Lord said unto Moses, Go, get thee down; for thy people, which thou broughtest out of the land of Egypt, have corrupted themselves: (8) They have turned aside quickly out of the way which I commanded them: they have made them a molten calf, and have worshipped it, and have sacrificed thereunto, and said, These be thy gods, O Israel, which brought thee up out of the land of Egypt. (9) And the Lord said unto Moses, I have seen this people, and, behold, it is a stiff-necked people: (10) Now therefore let me alone, that my wrath may wax hot against them, and that I may consume them; and I will make of thee a great nation. (11) And Moses besought the Lord his God, and said, Lord why doth thy wrath wax hot against thy people, which thou hast brought forth out of the land of Egypt with great power, and with a mighty hand? . . .

"(14) And the Lord repented of the evil which he thought to do unto his people. (15) And Moses turned, and went down from the mount, and the two tables of the testimony were in his hand: the tables were written on both their sides; on the one side and on the other were they written. (16) And the Tables were the work of God, and the writing was the writing of God, graven upon the tables. (17) And when Joshua heard the noise of the people as they shouted, he said unto Moses, There is a noise of war in the camp. (18) And he said, It is not the voice of them that shout for mastery, neither is it the voice of them that cry for being overcome; but the noise of them that sing do I hear. (19) And it came to pass, as soon as he came nigh unto the camp, that he saw the calf, and the dancing: and Moses' anger waxed hot, and he cast the tables out of his hands, and brake them beneath the mount. (20) And he took the calf which they had made, and burnt it in the fire, and ground it to powder, and strewed it upon the water, and made the children of Israel drink of it. . . .

"(30) And it came to pass on the morrow, that Moses said unto the people, Ye have sinned a great sin: and now I will go up unto the Lord; peradventure I shall make an atonement for your sin. (31) And Moses returned unto the Lord, and said, Oh! this people have sinned a great sin, and have made them gods of gold! (32) Yet now, if thou wilt forgive their sin—; and if not, blot me, I pray thee, out of thy book which thou hast written. (33) And the Lord said unto Moses, Whosoever hath sinned against me, him will I blot out of my book. (34) Therefore now go, lead the people unto the place of which I have spoken unto thee. Behold, mine Angel shall go before thee: nevertheless, in the day when I visit, I will visit their sin upon them. (35) And the Lord plagued the people, because they made the calf which Aaron made."

It is impossible to read the above passage in the light of modern criticism of the Bible without finding evidence that it has been clumsily put together from

389

various sources. In verse 8 the Lord Himself tells Moses that his people have
fallen away and made themselves an idol; and Moses intercedes for the wrongdoers. And yet he speaks to Joshua as though he knew nothing of this (18), and
is suddenly aroused to wrath as he sees the scene of the worshipping of the
Golden Calf (19). In verse 14 he has already gained a pardon from God for his
erring people, yet in verse 31 he returns into the mountains to implore this
forgiveness, tells God about his people's sin and is assured of the postponement
of the punishment. Verse 35 speaks of a visitation of his people by the Lord
about which nothing more is told us; whereas the verses 20–30 describe the
punishment which Moses himself dealt with. It is well known that the historical
parts of the Bible, dealing with the Exodus, are crowded with still more glaring
incongruities and contradictions.

The age of the Renaissance had naturally no such critical attitude towards 50
the text of the Bible, but had to accept it as a consistent whole, with the result
that the passage in question was not a very good subject for representation.
According to the Scriptures Moses was already instructed about the idolatry of
his people and had ranged himself on the side of mildness and forgiveness;
nevertheless, when he saw the Golden Calf and the dancing crowd, he was
overcome by a sudden frenzy of rage. It would therefore not surprise us to find
that the artist, in depicting the reaction of his hero to that painful surprise, had
deviated from the text from inner motives. Moreover, such deviations from the
scriptural text on a much slighter pretext were by no means unusual or disal-
lowed to artists. A celebrated picture of Parmigiano possessed by his native town
depicts Moses sitting on the top of a mountain and hurling the Tables to the
ground, although the Bible expressly says that he broke them "beneath the
mount." Even the representation of a seated Moses finds no support in the text,
and seems rather to bear out those critics who maintain that Michelangelo's
statue is not meant to record any particular moment in the prophet's life.

More important than his infidelity to the text of the Scriptures is the alteration 51
which Michelangelo has, in our supposition, made in the character of Moses.
The Moses of legend and tradition had a hasty temper and was subject to fits
of passion. It was in a transport of divine wrath of this kind that he slew an
Egyptian who was maltreating an Israelite, and had to flee out of the land into
the wilderness; and it was in a similar passion that he broke the Tables of the
Law, inscribed by God Himself. Tradition, in recording such a characteristic,
is unbiased, and preserves the impression of a great personality who once lived.
But Michelangelo has placed a different Moses on the tomb of the Pope, one
superior to the historical or traditional Moses. He has modified the theme of
the broken Tables; he does not let Moses break them in his wrath, but makes
him be influenced by the danger that they will be broken and calm that wrath,
or at any rate prevent it from becoming an act. In this way he has added
something new and more than human to the figure of Moses; so that the giant
frame with its tremendous physical power becomes only a concrete expression

of the highest mental achievement that is possible in a man, that of struggling successfully against an inward passion for the sake of a cause to which he has devoted himself.

We have now completed our interpretation of the statue of Moses. It can still be asked what motives prompted the sculptor to select the figure of Moses, and a so much altered Moses, as an ornament for the tomb of Julius II. In the opinion of many these motives are to be found in the character of the Pope and in Michelangelo's relations with him. Julius II was akin to Michelangelo in this, that he attempted to realize great and mighty ends, especially designs on a large scale. He was a man of action and he had a definite purpose, which was to unite Italy under the Papal supremacy. He desired to bring about single-handed what was not to happen for several centuries, and then only through the conjunction of many alien forces; and he worked alone, with impatience, in the short span of sovereignty allowed him, and used violent means. He could appreciate Michelangelo as a man of his own kind, but he often made him smart under his sudden anger and his utter lack of consideration for others. The artist felt the same violent force of will in himself, and, as the more introspective thinker, may have had a premonition of the failure to which they were both doomed. And so he carved his Moses on the Pope's tomb, not without a reproach against the dead pontiff, as a warning to himself, thus rising in self-criticism superior to his own nature.

In 1863 an Englishman, Watkiss Lloyd, devoted a little book to the Moses of Michelangelo.[12] I succeeded in getting hold of this short essay of forty-six pages, and read it with mixed feelings. I once more had occasion to experience in myself what unworthy and puerile motives enter into our thoughts and acts even in a serious cause. My first feeling was one of regret that the author should have anticipated so much of my thought, which seemed precious to me because it was the result of my own efforts; and it was only in the second instance that I was able to get pleasure from its unexpected confirmation of my opinion. Our views, however, diverge on one very important point.

It was Lloyd who first remarked that the usual descriptions of the figure are incorrect, and that Moses is not in the act of rising up[13]—that the right hand is not grasping the beard, but that the index-finger alone is resting upon it.[14] Lloyd has also recognized, and this is much more important, that the attitude portrayed can only be explained by postulating a foregoing one, which is not represented, and that the drawing of the left lock of the beard across to the right

---

[12] W. Watkiss Lloyd, *The Moses of Michelangelo* (London, 1863).

[13] "But he is not rising or preparing to rise; the bust is fully upright, not thrown forward for the alteration of balance preparatory for such a movement. . . ." (p. 10).

[14] "Such a description is altogether erroneous; the fillets of the beard are detained by the right hand but they are not held, nor grasped, enclosed or taken hold of. They are even detained but momentarily—momentarily engaged, they are on the point of being free for disengagement" (p. 11).

signifies that the right hand and the left side of the beard have been in closer and more natural contact before. But he suggests another way of reconstructing that logically inferred earlier contact. According to him, it was not the hand which had been plunged into the beard, but the beard which had been where the hand now is. We must, he says, imagine that the head of the statue was turned far round to its right just before the sudden interruption and rose right over the hand which, then as now, was holding the Tables of the Law. The pressure (of the Tables) against the palm of the hand caused the fingers to open naturally beneath the flowing locks of the beard, and the sudden turn of the head to the other side had the result that a part of the beard was detained for an instant by the motionless hand and formed that loop of hair which is to be looked on as a mark of the course it has taken—its "wake," to use Lloyd's own word.

In rejecting the other possibility, that of the right hand having previously 55 been in contact with the left side of the beard, Lloyd allows himself to be influenced by a consideration which shows how near he came to our interpretation. He says that it was not possible for the prophet, even in very great agitation, to have put out his hand to draw his beard across to the right. For in that case his fingers would have been in an entirely different position; and, moreover, such a movement would have allowed the Tables to slip down, since they are only supported by the pressure of the right arm—unless, in Moses' endeavour to save them at the last moment, we think of them as being "clutched by a gesture so awkward that to imagine it is profanation."

It is easy to see what the writer overlooked. He has correctly interpreted the 56 anomalies of the beard as indicating a movement that has gone before, but he has omitted to apply the same explanation to the no less unnatural details in the position of the Tables. He examines only the data connected with the beard and not those connected with the Tables, whose position he assumes to be the original one. In this way he closes the door to a conception like ours which, by examining certain insignificant details, has arrived at an unexpected interpretation of the meaning and aim of the figure as a whole.

But what if we have both strayed on to a wrong path? What if we have taken 57 too serious and profound a view of details which were nothing to the artist, details which he had introduced quite arbitrarily or for some purely formal reasons with no hidden intention behind? What if we have shared the fate of so many interpreters who have thought to see quite clearly things which the artist did not intend either consciously or unconsciously? I cannot tell. I cannot say whether it is reasonable to credit Michelangelo—that artist in whose works there is so much thought striving for expression—with such an elementary want of precision, especially whether this could be assumed in regard to the striking and singular features of the statue under discussion. And finally we may be allowed to point out, in all modesty, that the artist is no less responsible than his interpreters for the obscurity which surrounds his work. In his creations

Michelangelo has often enough gone to the utmost limit of what is expressible in art; and perhaps in his statue of Moses he has not completely succeeded, if his design was to trace the passage of a violent gust of passion in the signs left by it on the ensuing calm.

QUESTIONS

1. Freud's opening paragraphs tell us that he is not an expert on art but an interested amateur. As such, he needs to find out what the "experts" have said on this subject and then see if there is room for his own views. In the first part of his essay (paragraphs 8–30), Freud uses sources to open up his subject, summarizes and disagrees without being disagreeable, and sets the stage for his own contribution to the question under discussion. Later (in paragraph 53), Freud tells us that only when well into his studies he came across some work that partly anticipated his own view. Take a good look at this part of his essay and compare his use of this source with the earlier ones. Consider, among other things, why he mentions this one at this point rather than earlier.

2. Do you find Freud's explanation/interpretation of the sculpture convincing? What would you say are the weak points in his view?

3. What impression of Freud himself do you get from this essay? What kind of person do you sense behind this writing? What in the writing has led you to this feeling about the writer?

4. Do you think Freud is making too much fuss about a mere piece of stone? What is it about certain objects that seems to provoke so much interpretation? Why were all those other people as well as Freud himself so concerned to find the right interpretation of this Moses? Is this a matter of religion or art or something else?

5. How do you suppose Michelangelo would feel if he were to read Freud's essay? How do you suppose Moses would feel about both the sculpture and the essay? Imagine that these three figures have just met and are discussing these matters. Write their dialogue.

6. Using Freud's essay as a model, select some work of art or literature and produce your own interpretation of it, looking at some other interpretations by "experts" and finding some place for your own view. If you agree with one or more of the experts, explain your own reasons for finding one view more persuasive than another. If you find your own view different from all the others you read, explain why you stand by yours, treating the others in a manner similar to Freud's. That is, summarize the other views clearly and present your reasons for thinking them imperfect, without being unfair in your treatment of them.

MAKING CONNECTIONS

1. Like Umberto Eco's essay on *Casablanca*, Freud's essay attempts to account for the power and interest generated by a particular object: in one case a popular film and in the other a sculpture. Do you find any similarities in the two approaches? Why does Shakespeare's *Hamlet* appear in each essay at about the same point in the discussion?

2. Virtually all the essays in this "Arts and Humanities" section are interpretive. Compare at least two other essays with Freud's and describe the common denominators of interpretation that you find in them. For example, Tania Modleski's "Soap Opera, Melodrama, and Women's Anger" and Murray Ross's "Football Red and Baseball Green" would be particularly good comparisons because each one forces us to reevaluate something we probably thought we knew and understood on our own, much as Freud forces viewers familiar with the Moses to reevaluate it.

Social Sciences and Public Affairs

JOEY: A "MECHANICAL BOY"

Bruno Bettelheim

Born in 1903 and educated in Vienna, Bruno Bettelheim's psychoanalytic work was strongly influenced by Sigmund Freud. During 1938 and 1939, he was a prisoner in Nazi concentration camps; he wrote about those experiences in The Informed Heart *after coming to the United States in 1939. Bettelheim has described his major work with emotionally disturbed children in books addressed to the general reader as well as to his fellow psychoanalysts. His other work includes* Children of the Dream, *a study of children raised in an Israeli kibbutz, and a study of fairy tales called* The Uses of Enchantment. *This essay on Joey was first published in* Scientific American *in 1959.*

Joey, when we began our work with him, was a mechanical boy. He functioned as if by remote control, run by machines of his own powerfully creative fantasy. Not only did he himself believe that he was a machine but, more remarkably, he created this impression in others. Even while he performed actions that are intrinsically human, they never appeared to be other than machine-started and executed. On the other hand, when the machine was not working we had to concentrate on recollecting his presence, for he seemed not to exist. A human body that functions as if it were a machine and a machine that duplicates human functions are equally fascinating and frightening. Perhaps they are so uncanny because they remind us that the human body can operate without a human spirit, that body can exist without soul. And Joey was a child who had been robbed of his humanity.

395

Not every child who possesses a fantasy world is possessed by it. Normal 2
children may retreat into realms of imaginary glory or magic powers, but they
are easily recalled from these excursions. Disturbed children are not always able
to make the return trip; they remain withdrawn, prisoners of the inner world of
delusion and fantasy. In many ways Joey presented a classic example of this
state of infantile autism.[1]

At the Sonia Shankman Orthogenic School of the University of Chicago it 3
is our function to provide a therapeutic environment in which such children
may start life over again. I have previously described in this magazine the
rehabilitation of another of our patients ["Schizoprehenic Art: A Case Study";
SCIENTIFIC AMERICAN, April 1952]. This time I shall concentrate upon the
illness, rather than the treatment. In any age, when the individual has escaped
into a delusional world, he has usually fashioned it from bits and pieces of the
world at hand. Joey, in his time and world, chose the machine and froze himself
in its image. His story has a general relevance to the understanding of emotional
development in a machine age.

Joey's delusion is not uncommon among schizophrenic children today.[2] He 4
wanted to be rid of his unbearable humanity, to become completely automatic.
He so nearly succeeded in attaining this goal that he could almost convince
others, as well as himself, of his mechanical character. The descriptions of
autistic children in the literature take for their point of departure and comparison
the normal or abnormal human being. To do justice to Joey I would have to
compare him simultaneously to a most inept infant and a highly complex piece
of machinery. Often we had to force ourselves by a conscious act of will to
realize that Joey was a child. Again and again his acting-out of his delusions
froze our own ability to respond as human beings.

During Joey's first weeks with us we would watch absorbedly as this at once 5
fragile-looking and imperious nine-year-old went about his mechanical existence. Entering the dining room, for example, he would string an imaginary
wire from his "energy source"—an imaginary electric outlet—to the table. There
he "insulated" himself with paper napkins and finally plugged himself in. Only
then could Joey eat, for he firmly believed that the "current" ran his ingestive
apparatus. So skillful was the pantomime that one had to look twice to be sure
there was neither wire nor outlet nor plug. Children and members of our staff
spontaneously avoided stepping on the "wires" for fear of interrupting what
seemed the source of his very life.

For long periods of time, when his "machinery" was idle, he would sit so 6
quietly that he would disappear from the focus of the most conscientious

---

[1] autism: a form of psychosis characterized by an inability to relate to and perceive the environment in a realistic manner. Autistic thinking is characterized by withdrawal and detachment from
reality, fantasies, delusions, and hallucinations. [Eds.]

[2] schizophrenic: severe mental disorder characterized by unrealistic behavior, bizarre actions,
and a tendency to live in an inner world dominated by private fantasies. [Eds.]

observation. Yet in the next moment he might be "working" and the center of our captivated attention. Many times a day he would turn himself on and shift noisily through a sequence of higher and higher gears until he "exploded," screaming "Crash, crash!" and hurling items from his ever present apparatus—radio tubes, light bulbs, even motors or, lacking these, any handy breakable object. (Joey had an astonishing knack for snatching bulbs and tubes unobserved.) As soon as the object thrown had shattered, he would cease his screaming and wild jumping and retire to mute, motionless nonexistence.

Our maids, inured to difficult children, were exceptionally attentive to Joey; they were apparently moved by his extreme infantile fragility, so strangely coupled with megalomaniacal superiority. Occasionally some of the apparatus he fixed to his bed to "live him" during his sleep would fall down in disarray. This machinery he contrived from masking tape, cardboard, wire and other paraphernalia. Usually the maids would pick up such things and leave them on a table for the children to find, or disregard them entirely. But Joey's machine they carefully restored: "Joey must have the carburetor so he can breathe." Similarly they were on the alert to pick up and preserve the motors that ran him during the day and the exhaust pipes through which he exhaled. 7

How had Joey become a human machine? From intensive interviews with his parents we learned that the process had begun even before birth. Schizophrenia often results from parental rejection, sometimes combined ambivalently with love. Joey, on the other hand, had been completely ignored. 8

"I never knew I was pregnant," his mother said, meaning that she had already excluded Joey from her consciousness. His birth, she said, "did not make any difference." Joey's father, a rootless draftee in the wartime civilian army, was equally unready for parenthood. So, of course, are many young couples. Fortunately most such parents lose their indifference upon the baby's birth. But not Joey's parents. "I did not want to see or nurse him," his mother declared. "I had no feeling of actual dislike—I simply didn't want to take care of him." For the first three months of his life Joey "cried most of the time." A colicky baby, he was kept on a rigid four-hour feeding schedule, was not touched unless necessary and was never cuddled or played with. The mother, preoccupied with herself, usually left Joey alone in the crib or playpen during the day. The father discharged his frustration by punishing Joey when the child cried at night. 9

Soon the father left for overseas duty, and the mother took Joey, now a year and a half old, to live with her at her parents' home. On his arrival the grandparents noticed that ominous changes had occurred in the child. Strong and healthy at birth, he had become frail and irritable; a responsive baby, he had become remote and inaccessible. When he began to master speech, he talked only to himself. At an early date he became preoccupied with machinery, including an old electric fan which he could take apart and put together again with surprising deftness. 10

Joey's mother impressed us with a fey quality that expressed her insecurity, 11

GROWING SELF-ESTEEM is shown in this sequence of drawings. At left Joey portrays himself as an electrical "papoose," completely enclosed, suspended in empty space and operated by wireless signals. In center drawing his figure is much larger, though still under wireless control. At right he is able to picture the machine which controls him, and he has acquired hands with which he can manipulate his immediate environment.

her detachment from the world and her low physical vitality. We were struck especially by her total indifference as she talked about Joey. This seemed much more remarkable than the actual mistakes she made in handling him. Certainly he was left to cry for hours when hungry, because she fed him on a rigid schedule; he was toilet-trained with great rigidity so that he would give no trouble. These things happen to many children. But Joey's existence never registered with his mother. In her recollections he was fused at one moment with one event or person; at another, with something or somebody else. When she told us about his birth and infancy, it was as if she were talking about some vague acquaintance, and soon her thoughts would wander off to another person or to herself.

When Joey was not yet four, his nursery school suggested that he enter a special school for disturbed children. At the new school his autism was immediately recognized. During his three years there he experienced a slow improvement. Unfortunately a subsequent two years in a parochial school destroyed this progress. He began to develop compulsive defenses, which he called his "preventions." He could not drink, for example, except through elaborate piping systems built of straws. Liquids had to be "pumped" into him, in his fantasy, or he could not suck. Eventually his behavior became so upsetting that he could not be kept in the parochial school. At home things did not improve. Three months before entering the Orthogenic School he made a serious attempt at suicide.

12

398

To us Joey's pathological behavior seemed the external expression of an 13
overwhelming effort to remain almost nonexistent as a person. For weeks Joey's
only reply when addressed was "Bam." Unless he thus neutralized whatever we
said, there would be an explosion, for Joey plainly wished to close off every
form of contact not mediated by machinery. Even when he was bathed he
rocked back and forth with mute, engine-like regularity, flooding the bathroom.
If he stopped rocking, he did this like a machine too; suddenly he went
completely rigid. Only once, after months of being lifted from his bath and
carried to bed, did a small expression of puzzled pleasure appear on his face as
he said very softly: "They even carry you to your bed here."

For a long time after he began to talk he would never refer to anyone by 14
name, but only as "that person" or "the little person" or "the big person." He
was unable to designate by its true name anything to which he attached feelings.
Nor could he name his anxieties except through neologisms or word contaminations.[3] For a long time he spoke about "master paintings" and "a master
painting room" (i.e., masturbating and masturbating room). One of his machines, the "criticizer," prevented him from "saying words which have unpleasant feelings." Yet he gave personal names to the tubes and motors in his
collection of machinery. Moreover, these dead things had feelings; the tubes
bled when hurt and sometimes got sick. He consistently maintained this reversal
between animate and inanimate objects.

In Joey's machine world everything, on pain of instant destruction, obeyed 15
inhibitory laws much more stringent than those of physics. When we came to
know him better, it was plain that in his moments of silent withdrawal, with
his machine switched off, Joey was absorbed in pondering the compulsive laws
of his private universe. His preoccupation with machinery made it difficult to
establish even practical contacts with him. If he wanted to do something with
a counselor, such as play with a toy that had caught his vague attention, he
could not do so: "I'd like this very much, but first I have to turn off the
machine." But by the time he had fulfilled all the requirements of his preventions, he had lost interest. When a toy was offered to him, he could not touch
it because his motors and his tubes did not leave him a hand free. Even certain
colors were dangerous and had to be strictly avoided in toys and clothing,
because "some colors turn off the current, and I can't touch them because I
can't live without the current."

Joey was convinced that machines were better than people. Once when he 16
bumped into one of the pipes on our jungle gym he kicked it so violently that
his teacher had to restrain him to keep him from injuring himself. When she
explained that the pipe was much harder than his foot, Joey replied: "That
proves it. Machines are better than the body. They don't break; they're much

---

[3]neologisms or word contaminations: words that Joey made up or words that he peculiarly
altered. [Eds.]

ELABORATE SEWAGE SYSTEM in Joey's drawing of a house reflects his long preoccupation with excretion. His obsession with sewage reflected intense anxieties produced by his early toilet-training, which was not only rigid but also completely impersonal.

harder and stronger." If he lost or forgot something, it merely proved that this brain ought to be thrown away and replaced by machinery. If he spilled something, his arm should be broken and twisted off because it did not work properly. When his head or arm failed to work as it should, he tried to punish it by hitting it. Even Joey's feelings were mechanical. Much later in his therapy, when he had formed a timid attachment to another child and had been rebuffed, Joey cried: "He broke my feelings."

Gradually we began to understand what had seemed to be contradictory in Joey's behavior—why he held on to the motors and tubes, then suddenly destroyed them in a fury, then set out immediately and urgently to equip himself with new and larger tubes. Joey had created these machines to run his body and mind because it was too painful to be human. But again and again he became dissatisfied with their failure to meet his need and rebellious at the way they frustrated his will. In a recurrent frenzy he "exploded" his light bulbs and tubes, and for a moment became a human being—for one crowning instant he came alive. But as soon as he had asserted his dominance through the self-created explosion, he felt his life ebbing away. To keep on existing he had immediately to restore his machines and replenish the electricity that supplied his life energy.

What deep-seated fears and needs underlay Joey's delusional system? We were long in finding out, for Joey's preventions effectively concealed the secret

400

of his autistic behavior. In the meantime we dealt with his peripheral problems one by one.

During his first year with us Joey's most trying problem was toilet behavior. 19 This surprised us, for Joey's personality was not "anal" in the Freudian sense; his original personality damage had antedated the period of his toilet-training. Rigid and early toilet-training, however, had certainly contributed to his anxieties. It was our effort to help Joey with this problem that led to his first recognition of us as human beings.

Going to the toilet, like everything else in Joey's life, was surrounded by 20 elaborate preventions. We had to accompany him; he had to take off all his clothes; he could only squat, not sit, on the toilet seat; he had to touch the wall with one hand, in which he also clutched frantically the vacuum tubes that powered his elimination. He was terrified lest his whole body be sucked down.

To counteract this fear we gave him a metal wastebasket in lieu of a toilet. 21 Eventually, when eliminating into the wastebasket, he no longer needed to take off all his clothes, nor to hold on to the wall. He still needed the tubes and motors which, he believed, moved his bowels for him. But here again the all-important machinery was itself a source of new terrors. In Joey's world the gadgets had to move their bowels, too. He was terribly concerned that they should, but since they were so much more powerful than men, he was also terrified that if his tubes moved their bowels, their feces would fill all of space and leave him no room to live. He was thus always caught in some fearful contradiction.

Our readiness to accept his toilet habits, which obviously entailed some 22 hardship for our counselors, gave Joey the confidence to express his obsessions in drawings. Drawing these fantasies was a first step toward letting us in, however distantly, to what concerned him most deeply. It was the first step in a yearlong process of externalizing his anal preoccupations. As a result he began seeing feces everywhere; the whole world became to him a mire of excrement. At the same time he began to eliminate freely wherever he happened to be. But with this release from his infantile imprisonment in compulsive rules, the toilet and the whole process of elimination became less dangerous. Thus far it had been beyond Joey's comprehension that anybody could possibly move his bowels without mechanical aid. Now Joey took a further step forward; defecation became the first physiological process he could perform without the help of vacuum tubes. It must not be thought that he was proud of this ability. Taking pride in an achievement presupposes that one accomplishes it of one's own free will. He still did not feel himself an autonomous person who could do things on his own. To Joey defecation still seemed enslaved to some incomprehensible but utterly binding cosmic law, perhaps the law his parents had imposed on him when he was being toilet-trained.

It was not simply that his parents had subjected him to rigid, early training. 23 Many children are so trained. But in some cases the parents have a deep

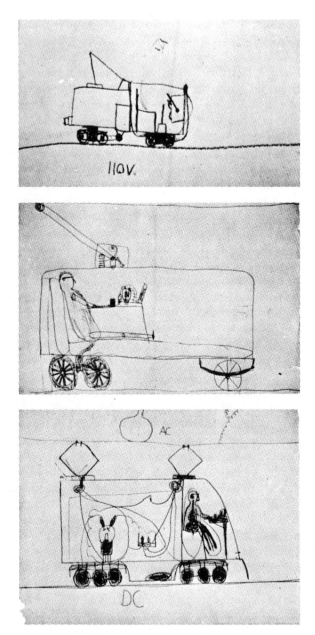

GROWING AUTONOMY is shown in Joey's drawings of the imaginary "Carr" (car) family. Top drawing shows a machine which can move but is unoccupied. Machine in center is occupied, but by a passive figure. In bottom drawing figure has gained control of machine.

emotional investment in the child's performance. The child's response in turn makes training an occasion for interaction between them and for the building of genuine relationships. Joey's parents had no emotional investment in him. His obedience gave them no satisfaction and won him no affection or approval. As a toilet-trained child he saved his mother labor, just as household machines saved her labor. As a machine he was not loved for his performance, nor could he love himself.

So it had been with all other aspects of Joey's existence with his parents. 24 Their reactions to his eating or noneating, sleeping or wakening, urinating or defecating, being dressed or undressed, washed or bathed did not flow from any unitary interest in him, deeply embedded in their personalities. By treating him mechanically his parents made him a machine. The various functions of life— even the parts of his body—bore no integrating relationship to one another or to any sense of self that was acknowledged and confirmed by others. Though he had acquired mastery over some functions, such as toilet-training and speech, he had acquired them separately and kept them isolated from each other. Toilet-training had thus not gained him a pleasant feeling of body mastery; speech had not led to communication of thought or feeling. On the contrary, each achievement only steered him away from self-mastery and integration. Toilet-training had enslaved him. Speech left him talking in neologisms that obstructed his and our ability to relate to each other. In Joey's development the normal process of growth had been made to run backward. Whatever he had learned put him not at the end of his infantile development toward integration but, on the contrary, farther behind than he was at its very beginning. Had we understood this sooner, his first years with us would have been less baffling.

It is unlikely that Joey's calamity could befall a child in any time and culture 25 but our own. He suffered no physical deprivation; he starved for human contact. Just to be taken care of is not enough for relating. It is a necessary but not a sufficient condition. At the extreme where utter scarcity reigns, the forming of relationships is certainly hampered. But our society of mechanized plenty often makes for equal difficulties in a child's learning to relate. Where parents can provide the simple creature-comforts for their children only at the cost of significant effort, it is likely that they will feel pleasure in being able to provide for them; it is this, the parents' pleasure, that gives children a sense of personal worth and sets the process of relating in motion. But if comfort is so readily available that the parents feel no particular pleasure in winning it for their children, then the children cannot develop the feeling of being worthwhile around the satisfaction of their basic needs. Of course parent and children can and do develop relationships around other situations. But matters are then no longer so simple and direct. The child must be on the receiving end of care and concern given with pleasure and without the exaction of return if he is to feel loved and worthy of respect and consideration. This feeling gives him the ability to trust; he can entrust his well-being to persons to whom he is so

important. Out of such trust the child learns to form close and stable relationships.

For Joey relationship with his parents was empty of pleasure in comfort-   26
giving as in all other situations. His was an extreme instance of a plight that
sends many schizophrenic children to our clinics and hospitals. Many months
passed before he could relate to us; his despair that anybody could like him
made contact impossible.

When Joey could finally trust us enough to let himself become more infan-   27
tile, he began to play at being a papoose. There was a corresponding change
in his fantasies. He drew endless pictures of himself as an electrical papoose.
Totally enclosed, suspended in empty space, he is run by unknown, unseen
powers through wireless electricity [*see illustration at left on page 398*].

As we eventually came to understand, the heart of Joey's delusional system   28
was the artificial, mechanical womb he had created and into which he had
locked himself. In his papoose fantasies lay the wish to be entirely reborn in a
womb. His new experiences in the school suggested that life, at all, might be

GENTLE LANDSCAPE painted by Joey after his recovery symbolizes the human emotions
he had regained. At 12, having learned to express his feelings, he was no longer a
machine.

worth living. Now he was searching for a way to be reborn in a better way. Since machines were better than men, what was more natural than to try rebirth through them? This was the deeper meaning of his electrical papoose.

As Joey made progress, his pictures of himself became more dominant in his drawings. Though still machine-operated, he has grown in self-importance [*see illustration at center on page* 398]. Another great step forward is represented in the picture at right. . . . Now he has acquired hands that do something, and he has had the courage to make a picture of the machine that runs him. Later still the papoose became a person, rather than a robot encased in glass.

Eventually Joey began to create an imaginary family at the school: the "Carr" family. Why the Carr family? In the car he was enclosed as he had been in his papoose, but at least the car was not stationary; it could move. More important, in a car one was not only driven but also could drive. The Carr family was Joey's way of exploring the possibility of leaving the school, of living with a good family in a safe, protecting car [*see illustrations on page* 402].

Joey at last broke through his prison. In this brief account it has not been possible to trace the painfully slow process of his first true relations with other human beings. Suffice it to say that he ceased to be a mechanical boy and became a human child. This newborn child was, however, nearly 12 years old. To recover the lost time is a tremendous task. That work has occupied Joey and us ever since. Sometimes he sets to it with a will; at other times the difficulty of real life makes him regret that he ever came out of his shell. But he has never wanted to return to his mechanical life.

One last detail and this fragment of Joey's story has been told. When Joey was 12, he made a float for our Memorial Day parade. It carried the slogan: "Feelings are more important than anything under the sun." Feelings, Joey had learned, are what make for humanity; their absence, for a mechanical existence. With this knowledge Joey entered the human condition.

QUESTIONS

1. Bettelheim's task was to explain Joey's behavior as best he could. What did he and his colleagues do, what did they examine, and how did they behave in order to develop their explanation of Joey?

2. Joey, of course, had already come to some conclusions about himself and about the world he inhabited. These explanations seem to have become fixed as interpretations, by which we mean simply that he had come to understand himself in terms of something else. In which passages does Bettelheim come closest to presenting Joey as his own interpreter? Summarize Joey's interpretation of himself—the structure or set of principles by which he understands himself.

3. In order to begin to be cured, Joey had to *reinterpret* his life. What were the major steps toward that reinterpretation? What changed for Joey?

4. Even to say *cured*, as we just did in question 3, involves an unexamined interpretation. What assumptions guide our use of that word? Do you find *cured* a satisfying explanation of what begins to happen to Joey?

5. The introduction to this section mentions this essay as an example of a case study, that is, a close examination of a unique person, event, or situation over time in a set of circumstances that are probably not replicable. Using this essay as your example, what else might characterize a case study? What makes a case study believable?

6. Quite a few people play roles or assume characterizations that deviate from what we think we know about them. Describe a person who does that. Offer your own limited case study. Try to indicate the extent to which that person's understanding of himself or herself is based on reality and the extent to which it isn't.

7. College can lead you to reinterpret yourself. In fact, that traditionally has been a large part of the experience of going to college. Write an explanation of yourself or of someone else you know well who is undergoing such a reinterpretation. What were the terms that prevailed earlier? What happened to call them into question? What kind of change has occurred, and what is at stake in this matter?

MAKING CONNECTIONS

1. If Bettelheim's essay is a kind of a case study, what other essays in this collection present something like it? Could you call Dennis Hevesi's "Running Away" a case study? What about Richard Selzer's "The Discus Thrower"? Or what about one of the early pieces in "Reflections," such as essays by Maya Angelou, Alice Walker, Joan Didion, or Frederick Douglass? Pick two or three pieces that seem close to being case studies and describe how they are like and unlike this example by Bettelheim.

2. What does it mean to be human? Taking into account several essays besides Bettelheim's—essays by Robert Jay Lifton, Carol Gilligan, Stephen Jay Gould, Jane van Lawick-Goodall, Dennis Hevesi, Richard Selzer, and Alice Walker are all possibilities—take a stab at defining our essential human nature. What if anything seems invariable within a wealth of human possibilities? Is Joey's slogan (paragraph 32) a convincing expression of what is essentially human, or would you point to something else?

THE AUTIST ARTIST
Oliver Sacks

Oliver Sacks was born in London, England, in 1933, and educated in London and Oxford before coming to the United States to complete his education in California and New York. At present he is professor of clinical neurology at Albert Einstein College of Medicine. He is best known, however, for his extraordinary writing on matters related to his medical studies, in such books as Awakenings (1974), A Leg to Stand On (1984), *and his national best-seller,* The Man Who Mistook His Wife for a Hat (1986), *in which the following selection appeared after its earlier publication in the* New York Review of Books. *Interested in the art of story telling as well as in clinical neurology, Sacks subtitled the book in which this essay appeared,* and Other Clinical Tales. *He insists that his essays are not just case studies, though they are that, but also tales or fables of "heroes, victims, martyrs, warriors." In his writing, he says, "the scientific and romantic . . . come together at the intersection of fact and fable."*

"Draw this," I said, and gave José my pocket watch. 1

He was about 21, said to be hopelessly retarded, and had earlier had one of 2 the violent seizures from which he suffers. He was thin, fragile-looking.

His distraction, his restlessness, suddenly ceased. He took the watch carefully, 3 as if it were a talisman or jewel, laid it before him, and stared at it in motionless concentration.

"He's an idiot," the attendant broke in. "Don't even ask him. He don't know 4 what it is—he can't tell time. He can't even talk. They says he's 'autistic,' but he's just an idiot." José turned pale, perhaps more at the attendant's tone than at his words—the attendant had said earlier that José didn't use words.

"Go on," I said. "I know you can do it." 5

José drew with an absolute stillness, concentrating completely on the little 6 clock before him, everything else shut out. Now, for the first time, he was bold, without hesitation, composed, not distracted. He drew swiftly but minutely, with a clear line, without erasures.

I nearly always ask patients, if it is possible for them, to write and draw, 7 partly as a rough-and-ready index of various competences, but also as an expression of "character" or "style."

407

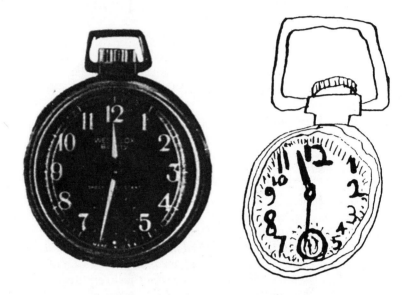

José had drawn the watch with remarkable fidelity, putting in every feature (at least every essential feature—he did not put in "Westclox, shock resistant, made in USA"), not just "the time" (though this was faithfully registered at 11:31), but every second as well, and the inset seconds dial, and, not least, the knurled winder and trapezoid clip of the watch, used to attach it to a chain. The clip was strikingly amplified, though everything else remained in due proportion. And the figures, now that I came to look at them, were of different sizes, different shapes, different styles—some thick, some thin; some aligned, some inset; some plain and some elaborated, even a bit "gothic." And the inset second hand, rather inconspicuous in the original, had been given a striking prominence, like the small inner dials of star clocks, or astrolabes.

The general grasp of the thing, its "feel," had been strikingly brought out— all the more strikingly if, as the attendant said, José had no idea of time. And otherwise there was an odd mixture of close, even obsessive, accuracy, with curious (and, I felt, droll) elaborations and variations.

I was puzzled by this, haunted by it as I drove home. An "idiot"? Autism? No. Something else was going on here.

I was not called to see José again. The first call, on a Sunday evening, had been for an emergency. He had been having seizures the entire weekend, and I had prescribed changes in his anticonvulsants, over the phone, in the afternoon. Now that his seizures were "controlled," further neurological advice was not requested. But I was still troubled by the problems presented by the clock,

408

and felt an unresolved sense of mystery about it. I needed to see him again. So I arranged a further visit, and to see his entire chart—I had been given only a consultation slip, not very informative, when I saw him before.

José came casually into the clinic—he had no idea (and perhaps did not care) why he'd been called—but his face lit up with a smile when he saw me. The dull, indifferent look, the mask I remembered, was lifted. There was a sudden, shy smile, like a glimpse through a door. 12

"I have been thinking about you, José." I said. He might not understand my words, but he understood my tone. "I want to see more drawing"—and I gave him my pen. 13

What should I ask him to draw this time? I had, as always, a copy of *Arizona Highways* with me, a richly illustrated magazine which I especially delight in, and which I carry around for neurological purposes, for testing my patients. The cover depicted an idyllic scene of people canoeing on a lake, against a backdrop of mountains and sunset. José started with the foreground, a mass of near-black silhouetted against the water, outlined this with extreme accuracy, and started to block it in. But this was clearly a job for a paintbrush, not a fine pen. "Skip it," I said, then pointing, "Go on to the canoe." Rapidly, unhesitatingly, José outlined the silhouetted figures and the canoe. He looked at them, then looked away, their forms fixed in his mind—then swiftly blocked them in with the side of the pen. 14

Here again, and more impressively, because an entire scene was involved, I 15

409

was amazed at the swiftness and the minute accuracy of reproduction, the more so since José had gazed at the canoe and then away, having taken it in. This argued strongly against any mere copying—the attendant had said earlier, "He's just a Xerox"—and suggested that he had apprehended it as an image, exhibiting a striking power not just of copying but of perception. For the image had a dramatic quality not present in the original. The tiny figures, enlarged, were more intense, more alive, had a feeling of involvement and purpose not at all clear in the original. All the hallmarks of what Richard Wollheim[1] calls "iconicity"—subjectivity, intentionality, dramatization—were present. Thus, over and above the powers of mere facsimile, striking as these were, he seemed to have clear powers of imagination and creativity. It was not *a* canoe but *his* canoe that emerged in the drawing.

I turned to another page in the magazine, to an article on trout fishing, with a pastel watercolour of a trout stream, a background of rocks and trees, and in the foreground a rainbow trout about to take a fly. "Draw this," I said, pointing to the fish. He gazed at it intently, seemed to smile to himself, and then turned away—and now, with obvious enjoyment, his smile growing broader and broader, he drew a fish of his own. 16

I smiled myself, involuntarily, as he drew it, because now, feeling comfortable with me, he was letting himself go, and what was emerging, slyly, was not just a fish, but a fish with a "character" of sorts. 17

The original had lacked character, had looked lifeless, two-dimensional, even stuffed. José's fish, by contrast, tilted and poised, was richly three-dimensional, 18

---

[1]Richard Wollheim: Philosopher and art historian. [Eds.]

far more like a real fish than the original. It was not only verisimilitude and animation that had been added but something else, something richly expressive, though not wholly fishlike: a great, cavernous, whalelike mouth; a slightly crocodilian snout; an eye, one had to say, which was distinctly human, and with altogether a positively roguish look. It was a very funny fish—no wonder he had smiled—a sort of fish-person, a nursery character, like the frog-footman in *Alice*.[2]

Now I had something to go on. The picture of the clock had startled me, stimulated my interest, but did not, in itself, allow any thoughts or conclusions. The canoe had shown that José had an impressive visual memory, and more. The fish showed a lively and distinctive imagination, a sense of humour, and something akin to fairy-tale art. Certainly not great art, it was "primitive," perhaps it was child-art; but, without doubt, it was art of a sort. And imagination, playfulness, art are precisely what one does not expect in idiots, or *idiots savants*, or in the autistic either. Such at least is the prevailing opinion.

My friend and colleague Isabelle Rapin had actually seen José years before, when he was presented with "intractable seizures" in the child neurology clinic—and she, with her great experience, did not doubt that he was "autistic." Of autism in general she had written:

> A small number of autistic children are exceedingly proficient at decoding written language and become hyperlexic or preoccupied with numbers . . . Extraordinary proficiencies of some autistic children for putting together puzzles, taking apart mechanical toys, or decoding written texts may reflect the consequences of attention and learning being inordinately focused on non-verbal visual-spatial tasks to

---

[2] *Alice*: Lewis Carroll's *Alice in Wonderland*. [Eds.]

the exclusion of, or perhaps because of, the lack of demand for learning verbal skills. (1982, pp. 146–50)

Somewhat similar observations, specifically about drawing, are made by Lorna Selfe in her astonishing book *Nadia* (1978). All *idiot savant* or autistic proficiencies and performances, Dr Selfe gathered from the literature, were apparently based on calculation and memory alone, never on anything imaginative or personal. And if these children could draw—supposedly a very rare occurrence—their drawings too were merely mechanical. "Isolated islands of proficiency" and "splinter skills" are spoken of in the literature. No allowance is made for an individual, let alone a creative, personality. 21

What then was José, I had to ask myself. What sort of being? What went on inside him? How had he arrived at the state he was in? And what state was it— and might anything be done? 22

I was both assisted and bewildered by the available information—the mass of "data" that had been gathered since the first onset of his strange illness, his "state." I had a lengthy chart available to me, containing early descriptions of his original illness: a very high fever at the age of eight, associated with the onset of incessant, and subsequently continuing, seizures, and the rapid appearance of a brain-damaged or autistic condition. (There had been doubt from the start about what, exactly, was going on.) 23

His spinal fluid had been abnormal during the acute stage of the illness. The consensus was that he had probably suffered an encephalitis of sorts. His seizures were of many different types—*petit mal, grand mal*, "akinetic," and "psychomotor," these last being seizures of an exceptionally complex type. 24

Psychomotor seizures can also be associated with sudden passion and violence, and the occurrence of peculiar behaviour-states even between seizures (the so-called psychomotor personality). They are invariably associated with disorder in, or damage to, the temporal lobes, and severe temporal-lobe disorder, both left-sided and right-sided, had been demonstrated in José by innumerable EEGs. 25

The temporal lobes are also associated with the auditory capacities, and, in particular, the perception and production of speech. Dr Rapin had not only considered José "autistic," but had wondered whether a temporal-lobe disorder had caused a "verbal auditory agnosia"—an inability to recognise speech sounds that interfered with his capacity to use or understand the spoken word. For what was striking, however it was to be interpreted (and both psychiatric and neurological interpretations were offered), was the loss or regression of speech, so that José, previously "normal" (or so his parents avowed), became "mute," and ceased talking to others when he became ill. 26

One capacity was apparently "spared"—perhaps in a compensatory way enhanced: an unusual passion and power to draw, which had been evident since early childhood, and seemed to some extent hereditary or familial, for his father 27 had always been fond of sketching, and his (much) older brother was a successful artist. With the onset of his illness; with his seemingly intractable seizures (he might have twenty or thirty major convulsions a day, and uncounted "little seizures," falls, "blanks," or "dreamy states"); with the loss of speech and his general intellectual and emotional "regression," José found himself in a strange and tragic state. His schooling was discontinued, though a private tutor was provided for a while, and he was returned permanently to his family, as a "fulltime" epileptic, autistic, perhaps aphasic, retarded child. He was considered ineducable, untreatable and generally hopeless. At the age of nine, he "dropped out"—out of school, out of society, out of almost all of what for a normal child would be "reality."

For fifteen years he scarcely emerged from the house, ostensibly because of "intractable seizures," his mother maintaining she dared not take him out, otherwise he would have twenty or thirty seizures in the street every day. All sorts of anticonvulsants were tried, but his epilepsy seemed "untreatable": this, at least, was the stated opinion in his chart. There were older brothers and sisters, but José was much the youngest—the "big baby" of a woman approaching fifty.

We have far too little information about these intervening years. José, in effect, disappeared from the world, was "lost to follow-up," not only medically but generally, and might have been lost forever, confined and convulsing in his cellar room, had he not "blown up" violently very recently and been taken to the hospital for the first time. He was not entirely without inner life, in the cellar. He showed a passion for pictorial magazines, especially of natural history, of the *National Geographic* type, and when he was able, between seizures and scoldings, would find stumps of pencil and draw what he saw.

These drawings were perhaps his only link with the outside world, and especially the world of animals and plants, of nature, which he had so loved as a child, especially when he went out sketching with his father. This, and this only, he was permitted to retain, his one remaining link with reality.

This, then was the tale I received, or, rather, put together from his chart or charts, documents as remarkable for what they lacked as for what they con- tained—the documentation, through default, of a fifteen-year "gap": from a social worker who had visited the house, taken an interest in him, but could do nothing; and from his now aged and ailing parents as well. But none of this would have come to light had there not been a rage of sudden, unprecedented, and frightening violence—a fit in which objects were smashed—which brought José to a state hospital for the first time.

It was far from clear what had caused this rage, whether it was an eruption of epileptic violence (such as one may see, on rare occasions, with very severe temporal-lobe seizures), or whether it was, in the simplistic terms of his admis- sion note, simply "a psychosis," or whether it represented some final, desperate

28

29

30

31

32

call for help, from a tortured soul who was mute and had no direct way of expressing his predicament, his needs.

What was clear was that coming to the hospital and having his seizures 33 "controlled" by powerful new drugs, for the first time, gave him some space and freedom, a "release," both physiological and psychological, of a sort he had not known since the age of eight.

Hospitals, state hospitals, are often seen as "total institutions" in Erving 34 Goffman's sense, geared mainly to the degradation of patients. Doubtless this happens, and on a vast scale. But they may also be "asylums" in the best sense of the word, a sense perhaps scarcely allowed by Goffman: places that provide a refuge for the tormented, storm-tossed soul, provide it with just that mixture of order and freedom of which it stands in such need. José had suffered from confusion and chaos—partly organic epilepsy, partly the disorder of his life—and from confinement and bondage, also both epileptic and existential. Hospital was good for José, perhaps lifesaving, at this point in his life, and there is no doubt that he himself felt this fully.

Suddenly too, after the moral closeness, the febrile intimacy of his house, 35 he now found others, found a world, both "professional" and concerned: un-judging, unmoralistic, unaccusing, detached, but at the same time with a real feeling both for him and for his problems. At this point, therefore (he had now been in hospital for four weeks), he started to have hope; to become more animated, to turn to others as he had never done before—not, at least, since the onset of autism, when he was eight.

But hope, turning to others, interaction, was "forbidden," and no doubt 36 frighteningly complex and "dangerous" as well. José had lived for fifteen years in a guarded, closed world—in what Bruno Bettelheim in his book on autism called the "empty fortress." But it was not, it had never been, for him, entirely empty; there had always been his love for nature, for animals and plants. *This* part of him, *this* door, had always remained open. But now there was tempta-tion, and pressure, to "interact," pressure that was often too much, came too soon. And precisely at such time José would "relapse"; would turn again, as if for comfort and security, to the isolation, to the primitive rocking movements, he had at first shown.

The third time I saw José, I did not send for him in the clinic, but went up, 37 without warning, to the admission ward. He was sitting, rocking, in the frightful day room, his face and eyes closed, a picture of regression. I had a qualm of horror when I saw him like this, for I had imagined, had indulged, the notion of "a steady recovery." I had to see José in a regressed condition (as I was to do again and again) to see that there was no simple "awakening" for him, but a path fraught with a sense of danger, double jeopardy, terrifying as well as exciting—because he had come to love his prison bars.

As soon as I called him, he jumped up, and eagerly, hungrily, followed me 38 to the art room. Once more I took a fine pen from my pocket, for he seemed

414

to have an aversion to crayons, which was all they used on the ward. "That fish you drew," I hinted it with a gesture in the air, not knowing how much of my words he might understand, "that fish, can you remember it, can you draw it again?" He nodded eagerly, and took the pen from my hands. It was three weeks since he had seen it. What would he draw now?

He closed his eyes for a moment—summoning an image?—and then drew. 39 It was still a trout, rainbow-spotted, with fringy fins and a forked tail, but, this time, with egregiously human features, an odd nostril (what fish has nostrils?), and a pair of ripely human lips. I was about to take the pen, but, no, he was not finished. What had he in mind? The image was complete. The image, perhaps, but not the scene. The fish before had existed—as an icon—in isolation: now it was to become part of a world, a scene. Rapidly he sketched in a little fish, a companion, swooping into the water, gambolling, obviously in play. And then the surface of the water was sketched in, rising to a sudden, tumultuous wave. As he drew the wave, he became excited, and emitted a strange, mysterious cry.

I couldn't avoid the feeling, perhaps a facile one, that this drawing was 40 symbolic—the little fish and the big fish, perhaps him and me? But what was so important and exciting was the spontaneous representation, the impulse, not my suggestion, entirely from himself, to introduce this new element—a living interplay in what he drew. In his drawings as in his life hitherto, interaction had always been absent. Now, if only in play, a symbol, it was allowed back. Or was it? What was that angry, avenging wave?

Best to go back to safe ground, I felt; no more free association. I had seen 41

potential, but I had seen, and heard, danger too. Back to safe, Edenic, prelapsarian Mother Nature.[3] I found a Christmas card lying on the table, a robin redbreast on a tree trunk, snow and stark twigs all around. I gestured to the bird, and gave José the pen. The bird was finely drawn, and he used a red pen for the breast. The feet were somewhat taloned, grasping the bark (I was struck, here and later, by his need to emphasise the grasping power of hands and feet,

[3] Prelapsarian: belonging to the time before the "fall" of humans. [Eds.]

416

to make contact sure, almost gripping, obsessed). But—what was happening?—the dry winter twiglet, next to the tree trunk, had shot up in his drawing, expanded into florid open bloom. There were other things that were perhaps symbolic, although I could not be sure. But the salient and exciting and most significant transformation was this: that José had changed winter into spring.

Now, finally, he started to speak—though "speak" is much too strong a term for the strange-sounding, stumbling, largely unintelligible utterances that came out, on occasion startling him as much as they startled us—for all of us, José 42

417

included, had regarded him as wholly and incorrigibly mute, whether from incapacity, indisposition, or both (there had been the *attitude*, as well as the fact, of not speaking). And here, too, we found it impossible to say how much was "organic," how much was a matter of "motivation." We had reduced, though not annulled, his temporal-lobe disorders—his electro-encephalograms (EEGs) were never normal; they still showed in these lobes a sort of low-grade electrical muttering, occasional spikes, dysrhythmia, slow waves. But they were immensely improved compared with what they were when he came in. If he could remove their convulsiveness, he could not reverse the damage they had sustained.

We had improved, it could not be doubted, his physiological *potentials* for 43 speech, though there was an impairment of his abilities to use, understand, and recognise speech, with which, doubtless, he would always have to contend. But, equally important, he now was fighting for the recovery of his understanding and speech (egged on by all of us, and guided by the speech therapist in particular), where previously he had accepted it, hopelessly or masochistically, and indeed had turned against virtually all communication with others, verbal and otherwise. Speech impairment and the refusal to speak had coupled before in the double malignancy of disease; now, recovery of speech and attempts to speak were being happily coupled in the double benignity of beginning to get well. Even to the most sanguine of us it was very apparent that José would never speak with any facility approaching normal, that speech could never, for him, be a real vehicle for self-expression, could serve only to express his simpler needs. And he himself seemed to feel this too and, while he continued to fight for speech, turned more fiercely to drawing for self-expression.

One final episode. José had been moved off the frenzied admission ward to 44 a calmer, quieter special ward, more homelike, less prisonlike, than the rest of the hospital: a ward with an exceptional number and quality of staff, designed especially, as Bettelheim would say, as "a home for the heart," for patients with autism who seem to require a kind of loving and dedicated attention that few hospitals can give. When I went up to this new ward, he waved his hand lustily as soon as he saw me—an outgoing, open gesture. I could not imagine him having done this before. He pointed to the locked door, he wanted it open, he wanted to go outside.

He led the way downstairs, outside, into the overgrown, sunlit garden. So 45 far as I could learn, he had not, voluntarily, gone outside since he was eight, since the very start of his illness and withdrawal. Nor did I have to offer him a pen—he took one himself. We walked around the hospital grounds, José sometimes gazing at the sky and trees, but more often down at his feet, at the mauve and yellow carpet of clover and dandelions beneath us. He had a very quick eye for plant forms and colours, rapidly saw and picked a rare white clover, and found a still rarer four-leaved one. He found seven different types of grass, no

418

less, seemed to recognise, to greet, each one as a friend. He was delighted most of all by the great yellow dandelions, open, all their florets flung open to the sun. This was his plant—it was how he felt, and to show his feeling he would draw it. The need to draw, to pay graphic reverence, was immediate and strong: he knelt down, placed his clipboard on the ground, and, holding the dandelion, drew it.

This, I think, is the first drawing from real life that José had done since his father took him sketching as a child, before he became ill. It is a splendid drawing, accurate and alive. It shows his love for reality, for another form of life. It is, to my mind, rather similar to, and not inferior to, the fine vivid flowers one finds in medieval botanies and herbals—fastidiously, botanically exact, even though José has no formal knowledge of botany, and could not be taught it or understand it if he tried. His mind is not built for the abstract, the conceptual. *That* is not available to him as a path to truth. But he has a passion and a real power for the particular—he loves it, he enters into it, he re-creates it. And the particular, if one is particular enough, is also a road—one might say nature's road—to reality and truth.

The abstract, the categorical, has no interest for the autistic person—the concrete, the particular, the singular, is all. Whether this is a question of capacity or disposition, it is strikingly the case. Lacking, or indisposed to, the

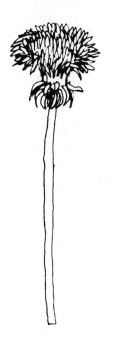

419

general, the autistic seem to compose their world picture entirely of particulars. Thus they live, not in a universe, but in what William James called a "multiverse," of innumerable, exact, and passionately intense particulars. It is a mode of mind at the opposite extreme from the generalising, the scientific, but still "real," equally real, in a quite different way. Such a mind has been imagined in Borges's story "Funes the Memorious" (so like Luria's *Mnemonist*):

> He was, let us not forget, almost incapable of ideas of a general, Platonic sort . . . In the teeming world of Funes, there were only details, almost immediate in their presence . . . No one . . . has felt the heat and pressure of a reality as indefatigable as that which day and night converged upon the hapless Ireneo.

As for Borges's Ireneo, so for José. But it is not necessarily a hapless circumstance: there may be a deep satisfaction in particulars, especially if they shine, as they may do for José, with an emblematic radiance.

I think José, an autist, a simpleton too, has such a gift for the concrete, for *form*, that he is, in his way, a naturalist and natural artist. He grasps the world as forms—directly and intensely felt forms—and reproduces them. He has fine lateral powers, but he has figurative powers too. He can draw a flower or fish with remarkable accuracy, but he can also make one which is a personification, an emblem, a dream, or a joke. And the autistic are supposed to lack imagination, playfulness, art!

Creatures like José are not supposed to exist. Autistic child-artists like "Nadia" were not supposed to exist. Are they indeed so rare, or are they overlooked? Nigel Dennis, in a brilliant essay on Nadia in the *New York Review of Books* (4 May 1978), wonders how many of the world's "Nadias" may be dismissed or overlooked, their remarkable productions crumpled up and consigned to the trash can, or simply, like José, treated without thought, as an odd talent, isolated, irrelevant, of no interest. But the autistic artist or (to be less lofty) the autistic imagination is by no means rare. I have seen a dozen examples of it in as many years, and this without making any particular effort to find them.

The autistic, by their nature, are seldom open to influence. It is their fate to be isolated, and thus original. Their "vision," if it can be glimpsed, comes from within and appears aboriginal. They seem to me, as I see more of them, to be a strange species in our midst, odd, original, wholly inwardly directed, unlike others.

Autism was once seen as a childhood schizophrenia, but phenomenologically the reverse is the case. The schizophrenic's complaint is always of "influence" from the outside: he is passive, he is played upon, he cannot be himself. The autistic would complain—if they complained—of absence of influence, of absolute isolation.

"No man is an island, entire of itself," wrote Donne. But this is precisely what autism is—an island, cut off from the main. In "classical" autism, which is manifest, and often total, by the third year of life, the cutting off is so early there may be no memory of the main. In "secondary" autism, like José's, caused by brain disease at a later stage in life, there is some memory, perhaps some nostalgia, for the main. This may explain why José was more accessible than most, and why, at least in drawing, he may show interplay taking place.

Is being an island, being cut off, necessarily a death? It may be a death, but 54 it is not necessarily so. For though "horizontal" connections with others, with society and culture, are lost, yet there may be vital and intensified "vertical" connections, direct connections with nature, with reality, uninfluenced, unmediated, untouchable, by any others. This "vertical" contact is very striking with José, hence the piercing directness, the absolute clarity of his perceptions and drawings, without a hint or shade of ambiguity or indirection, a rocklike power uninfluenced by others.

This brings us to our final question: is there any "place" in the world for a 55 man who is like an island, who cannot be acculturated, made part of the main? Can "the main" accommodate, make room for, the singular? There are similarities here to the social and cultural reactions to genius. (Of course I do not suggest that all autists have genius, only that they share with genius the problem of singularity.) Specifically: what does the future hold for José? Is there some "place" for him in the world which will *employ* his autonomy, but leave it intact?

Could he, with his fine eye, and great love of plants, make illustrations for 56 botanical works or herbals? Be an illustrator for zoology or anatomy texts? (See the drawing overleaf he made for me when I showed him a textbook illustration of the layered tissue called "ciliated epithelium.") Could he accompany scientific expeditions, and make drawings (he paints and makes models with equal facility) of rare species? His pure concentration on the thing before him would make him ideal in such situations.

Or, to take a strange but not illogical leap, could he, with his peculiarities, 57 his idiosyncrasy, do drawings for fairy tales, nursery tales, Bible tales, myths? Or (since he cannot read, and sees letters only as pure and beautiful forms) could he not illustrate, and elaborate, the gorgeous capitals of manuscript breviaries and missals? He has done beautiful altarpieces, in mosaic and stained wood, for churches. He has carved exquisite lettering on tombstones. His current "job" is hand-printing sundry notices for the ward, which he does with the flourishes and elaborations of a latter-day Magna Carta. All this he could do, and do very well. And it would be of use and delight to others, and delight him too. He could do all of these—but, alas, he will do none, unless someone very understanding, and with opportunities and means, can guide and employ him. For, as the stars stand, he will probably do nothing, and spend a useless, fruitless life, as so many other autistic people do, overlooked, unconsidered, in the back ward of a state hospital.

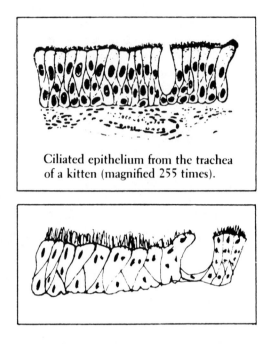

Ciliated epithelium from the trachea
of a kitten (magnified 255 times).

QUESTIONS

1. In this essay, Sacks presents two stories along with an explanation of autism: the story of José's life and the story of his treatment by Sacks and his colleagues. Retell these two stories in your own words.

2. Does Sacks think of himself as a storyteller? Discuss paragraph 31 in this connection.

3. In paragraph 45, Sacks not only tells us what José did, but what he was feeling and almost what he was thinking as well. How does he *know* this? Is it proper for him to present such material as part of a case study? Is the use of such material justified or not?

4. As indicated in question 1, this essays offers an explanation of autism as well as two stories. The explanation is limited and incomplete because the state of our knowledge about this condition is itself far from complete. Paragraphs 47–54 in particular sum up the gist of this explanation. Drawing upon these paragraphs, construct your own tentative definition of autism.

5. Sacks is a successful writer on medical subjects, no doubt because of both the information he presents, which many people find interesting, and the way he presents it. Look at his presentation in the beginning of the essay. How would you characterize the way the first ten paragraphs are written? Be specific. Look carefully at paragraph 4, for instance. What is the function of this paragraph? Compare these paragraphs to the beginning of Bettleheim's essay on Joey. What are the differences between these two ways of starting an essay on similar subjects?

6. Both Bettelheim and Sacks use art in their essays. Write an essay in which you discuss the ways in which they both use art. Consider such things as the ways in which art functions in the treatment of certain mental ailments and the different ways in which Bettelheim and Sacks interpret the artworks of their patients. Do not hesitate to offer your own interpretations of these works in the course of your discussion. You need not argue a preference for one or the other of the two essays. Rather, use them as the basis for a discussion of the uses of art in studying mental illness.

7. Drawing on the two essays by Bettelheim and Sacks, write an essay in which you discuss autism and what we can learn from it about the way that the human mind works. Consider, for instance, how such an illness helps us to understanding what we mean by a "healthy" mind. If your instructor wishes, you can do more research into autism, but you should be able to find enough material in these two pieces to support a short, interesting discussion of the topic. Indicate what you have learned from these essays that you did not know before—and express whatever feelings you have about this knowledge. If anything in these essays disturbs you or makes you feel uneasy, try to include that in your own essay.

MAKING CONNECTIONS

1. This essay is mainly about autism, but it is also about art. Drawing upon this and other essays that touch on the nature of visual art (by Joan Didion, or Sigmund Freud, for example) write an essay in which you explain the nature and function of visual art. How does it affect us? How should we respond to it? What role does it play in your life? What role should it play in our lives? Quote from the essays you use as sources, but try to describe your own explanation of what art is and should be.

2. If Bettelheim offers a case study and Sacks a medical tale, Sacks's work must share characteristics with both Bettelheim and with other storytellers included in this collection. Maya Angelou, Alice Walker, George Orwell, Annie Dillard, and Dennis Hevesi offer examples. Do you think Sacks's work is closer to a case study or closer to a story? What makes the difference?

WHAT MADE THIS MAN?
MENGELE

Robert Jay Lifton

Born in New York City in 1926, Robert Jay Lifton received his M.D. in 1948 and is presently Distinguished Professor of Psychiatry and Psychology at John Jay College of Criminal Justice in the City University of New York. The author of books on "brainwashing" and Vietnam veterans, his study of Nazi doctors, The Nazi Doctors: Killing and the Psychology of Genocide *was published in 1986. The following essay was adapted from that book for the* New York Times Magazine *in July 1985. This essay appeared in the* Times *just after Mengele's body—or what most people believe to be his body—was found in a South American grave.*

His bones do not satisfy. Josef Mengele had come to symbolize the entire   1
Nazi killing project. The need was to capture him and put him on trial, hear
his confession, put *him* at *our* mercy. For many, that anticipated event took on
the significance of confronting the Holocaust and restoring a moral universe.

For Mengele has long been the focus of what could be called a cult of   2
demonic personality. He has been seen as the embodiment of absolute evil, a
doctor pledged to heal who kills instead. But this demonization made him
something of a deity, a nonhuman or even superhuman force, and served as a
barrier to any explanation of his behavior. One reason Auschwitz survivors have
hungered for his capture and trial is to divest him of this status. One of them,
for instance, spoke to me of his yearning to see "this metamorphosis of turning
him back into a person instead of God Almighty."

Mengele was a man, not a demon, and that is our problem.   3

Indeed, during recent weeks he had already begun to fall from grace as a   4
symbol of pure evil. The most notorious Nazi fugitive, unsuccessfully pursued
for decades, had suddenly appeared—as bones in a Brazilian grave. The world
watched in fascination as scientific examination seemed to confirm that these
were the right bones.

It was reported that Mengele had lived out much of his last 25 years in   5
lonely, despairing isolation, that he had fallen in love with a housemaid. An
exemplar of pure evil is not supposed to experience loneliness or to care for
another person.

What has been lost in the preoccupation with the corpse has been the nature   6 of the man: What made Mengele Mengele? How can we explain his murderous behavior in Auschwitz?

Over the last eight years, while conducting research for a book on Nazi doctors, I have sought answers to these questions. I have conducted psychological interviews with 28 former Nazi doctors; a number of Nazi lawyers, economists and other nonmedical professionals, and also with more than 80 former Auschwitz inmates who were engaged in medical work in the camp. The study has required me to probe moral as well as psychological issues and to raise questions about the nature of evil.   7

Hannah Arendt gave currency to a concept of the banality of evil in her portrayal of Adolf Eichmann as a rather unremarkable bureaucrat who killed by meeting schedules and quotas. She is surely correct in her claim that an ordinary person is capable of extreme evil. But over the course of committing evil acts, an ordinary person becomes something different. In a process I call "doubling," a new self takes shape that adapts to the evil environment, and the evil acts become part of that self. At this point, the person and his behavior are anything but banal.   8

Mengele possessed unusually intense destructive potential, but there were no apparent signs of aberrant behavior prior to the Nazis and Auschwitz. Without Auschwitz, he would probably have kept his destructive potential under control. As a wise former inmate physician told me, "In ordinary times, Mengele could have been a slightly sadistic German professor."   9

It was the coming together of the man and the place, the "fit" between the two, that created the Auschwitz Mengele.   10

What we know about the man who arrived in Auschwitz in May 1943 is not especially remarkable. The son of a well to-do Bavarian industrialist, Mengele is remembered by an acquaintance as a popular young man, an enthusiastic friend. He was also intelligent, a serious student who showed "a very distinct ambitiousness."   11

In 1931, at the age of 20, Mengele joined a right-wing, nationalistic organization. He was an early Nazi enthusiast, enlisting with the SA (the storm troopers) in 1933, applying for party membrship in 1937 and for SS membership the following year. There are rumors that, while studying in Munich, he met such high-ranking Nazis as Alfred Rosenberg, a leading ideologue, and even Hitler himself.   12

Mengele became a true ideologue: a man who understood his life to be in the service of a larger vision.   13

According to an Auschwitz friend and fellow-SS physician, Mengele espoused the visionary SS ideology that the Nordic race was the only truly creative race, that it had been weakened by Christian morality of Jewish origin, and that Germany needed to revert to ancient German myths in creating an SS "order" to purify the Nordic race. According to his friend, Mengele was an extreme anti-Semite, "fully convinced that the annihilation of the Jews is a   14 provision for the recovery of the world and Germany." And Mengele considered these views to be scientifically derived. (I have preserved the anonymity of the people I interviewed. Those who are identified had previously made themselves known in books or other public documents.)

Mengele's ideology considerably influenced his intellectual choices. Matriculating not only at Munich but also at Bonn, Vienna and Frankfurt, he came to concentrate on physical anthropology and genetics, eventually working under Professor Freiherr Otmar von Verschuer at the Institute of Hereditary Biology and Racial Hygiene at Frankfurt. He earned a degree in anthropology as well as medicine. 15

Mengele produced three publications before he came to Auschwitz. They dealt with physical characteristics and abnormalities and, in each case, emphasized the role of heredity—an emphasis in keeping with trends in German and international scholarship at the time. Though jammed with charts, diagrams and photographs that claim more than they prove, the papers are relatively respectable scientific works of that era. But their conclusions uniformly reflect Mengele's commitment to bringing science into the service of the Nazi vision. 16

Mengele seemed well on his way toward an academic career. He had the strong backing of Verschuer who, in a letter of recommendation, praised his reliability and his capacity for clear verbal presentation of difficult intellectual problems. Mengele's marriage to a professor's daughter was in keeping with his academic aspirations. 17

His military experience loomed large in his idea of himself. In 1938–39, Mengele served six months with a specially trained mountain light-infantry regiment, followed by a year in the reserve medical corps. He spent three years with a Waffen SS unit, mostly in the East, including action in Russia, where, according to SS records, he was wounded and declared medically unfit for combat. A commendation declared that he had "acquitted himself brilliantly in the face of the enemy," and he received five decorations, including the Iron Cross First Class and Second Class. 18

Mengele, his friend said, was the only doctor in Auschwitz who possessed that array of medals, and he was enormously proud of them; he frequently referred to his combat experience to bolster his arguments on a variety of matters. According to his friend, Mengele arrived at the camp with a special aura because he was coming more or less directly from the front. 19

His friend suggests something else special about Mengele. He had asked to be sent to the Auschwitz death camp because of the opportunities it could provide for his research. He continued to have the support and collaboration of his teacher, Verschuer, who convinced the German Research Society to provide financial support for Mengele's work. 20

Auschwitz was both an annihilation camp and a work camp for German industry. Like other SS doctors there, Mengele had the task of "selecting" prisoners for the gas chamber—the vast majority—and for the slave labor force. 21

SS doctors also controlled and supervised the inmate doctors who alone did whatever actual medical treatment was done. Mengele was the chief doctor of Birkenau, an Auschwitz subcamp, but seemed to many inmates to have authority beyond his position. Dr. Olga Lengyel, an inmate doctor, described Mengele as "far and away the chief provider for the gas chamber and the crematory ovens." Another inmate doctor spoke of Mengele's role as "very important, more than that of the others."

One reason he appeared to be especially important was that he was extraordinarily energetic. While many SS doctors did no more than what was required of them, Mengele was always on the move, busy with his work, initiating new projects. More than any other SS doctor, he seemed to find his calling in Auschwitz.   22

Many inmates thought that Mengele alone conducted the large "selections." When they arrived at Auschwitz, packed by the hundreds into freight and cattle cars, they were unloaded and herded down a ramp. The Nazi doctors were assigned, on a rotating basis, to stand on the ramp and select those prisoners who would live, as workers at the camp, and those who would be killed.   23

The evidence is that Mengele took his turn at the ramp, like everyone else, but he also appeared there frequently to make sure that any twins in a "transport," as the trains were called, would be collected and saved for his research. But the prisoners saw it differently. At a trial of former Auschwitz personnel, in Frankfurt in 1964, an inmate who had been assigned to unload the transports recalled only the name of Mengele. When the judge commented, "Mengele cannot have been there all the time," the witness answered: "In my opinion, always. Night and day." Mengele brought such flamboyance and posturing to the selections task that it was his image inmates remembered.   24

He was an elegant figure on the ramp—handsome, well groomed, extremely upright in posture. Prisoners sometimes described him as "very Aryan looking" or "tall and blond," when he was actually of medium height, with dark hair and a dark complexion. Inmates said Mengele "conveyed the impression of a gentle and cultured man" and spoke of the "cheerful expression on his face . . . almost like he had fun . . . he was very playful."   25

There was an easy rhythm in his approach to selections. He walked back and forth, an inmate recalled, "a nice-looking man" with a riding crop in his hand who "looked at the bodies and the faces just a couple of seconds" and said, *"Links* [left], *Rechts* [right], *Links, Rechts . . . Rechts . . . Links, Rechts."*   26

Prisoners were struck by the stark contrast between his calm, playful manner and the horror of what he was doing. Occasionally, though, his detachment could give way to outbreaks of rage and violence, especially when he encountered resistance to his sense of "the rules." In one instance, a mother refused to be separated from her teen-age daughter and scratched the face of the SS trooper who tried to enforce Mengele's decision. Mengele drew his gun and shot both the woman and her child. Still raging, he ordered that all the people   27 from that transport whom he had previously selected as workers be sent to the gas chamber.

In the hospital blocks where medical treatment was given to prisoners in order to maintain the workforce, there was another kind of "selection" process. Nazi doctors would weed out for the gas chamber the weakest patients, those thought unlikely to recover in two or three weeks. Mengele, Dr. Lengyel recalled, "could show up suddenly at any hour, day or night. . . . when we least expected him." The prisoners would "march before him with their arms in the air while he continued to whistle his Wagner—or it might be Verdi or Johann Strauss." 28

Though usually cool in his conduct of selections, Mengele was passionate in pursuing his "scientific research." His main interest was the study of twins, but he carried out a variety of projects with different groups of human subjects. 29

· He collected and studied dwarfs in an effort to determine the genetic reasons for their condition. 30

· He investigated a gangrenous condition of the face and mouth called noma. Though ordinarily a rare condition, it was common among gypsy inmates of Auschwitz. It was known to be caused by the kind of debilitation that inmates were subject to, but Mengele focused on what he deemed to be genetic and racial factors. 31

· He sought out inmates with a condition known as heterochromia of the iris—in which the two eyes are of different colors—and, after their death, sent their eyes to his old professor, Verschuer, at the Berlin-Dahlem Institute of Racial Biology. With some of these inmates, Mengele took the bizarre step of attempting to change eye color in an Aryan direction by injecting methylene blue into the brown eyes of blond inmate children. 32

But the research that most occupied Mengele, to which he devoted the greatest time and energy, was his study of twins. In fact, he probably came to Auschwitz for that specific purpose—as a continuation of work he had done under Verschuer at the University of Frankfurt a few years earlier. 33

As early as 1935, Verschuer had written of the absolute necessity of research on twins to achieve "complete and reliable determination of what is hereditary in man." 34

Because identical twins (derived from the same ovum) possess the same genetic constitution, they have traditionally been used in research on hereditary influences. Their shared physical and sometimes psychological characteristics, normal and abnormal, can be assumed to be genetically determined. Such characteristics can be assumed to be genetically determined in other people as well. 35

428

Mengele recognized that Auschwitz would permit him to pursue his mentor's 36
dream. From the hundreds of thousands of prisoners, he could collect twins in
quantities never before available to a scientist. What is more, he could exercise
total control over them.

He could compare measurements and bodily features. He could try medi- 37
cations meant to prevent, treat or induce a particular illness on an individual
twin, or both of a pair of twins. He could then make comparisons of various
kinds, in which he sought to demonstrate the importance of heredity rather
than environment. He had no need or inclination to concern himself with
ethical considerations, sharing as he did the general SS doctor's view that one
was doing no harm since Auschwitz inmates, especially Jews, were in any case
doomed.

Mengele had a fanatic's commitment to twin research. A number of survivors 38
reported seeing him on the transport ramp, shouting "Zwillinge heraus! [Twins
out!], Zwillinge heraustreten! [Twins step forward!]." An inmate anthropologist
whom Mengele had eagerly recruited to assist him described the arrival of a
group of Hungarian Jews "like a river . . . women, men, women with children,
and suddenly I saw Mengele going quickly . . . the same speed [as] the crowd
[crying out] only 'Zwillinge heraus!' . . . with such a face that I would think
he's mad."

Mengele had the same frenzied attitude in carrying out his research. To 39
inmates, he seemed to have an inner compulsion to get a great deal accomplished quickly in a personal race against time. He undoubtedly came to
recognize increasingly that the days of the Auschwitz research bonanza were
numbered.

Mainly to pursue his studies of twins, Mengele set up an Auschwitz caricature 40
of an academic research institute. Inmate doctors, mostly Jewish, with specialized training in various laboratory and clinical areas, were called upon to
contribute to his work by diagnosing, sometimes treating, X-raying and performing post-mortem examinations of his research subjects. For his pathologist, Dr.
Miklos Nyiszli, he provided a special dissection room complete with porcelain
sinks and a dissecting table of polished marble. The overall arrangement, as
Dr. Nyiszli later wrote, was "the exact replica of any large city's institute of
pathology." In addition to the area used by SS physicians, Mengele had three
offices of his own, mainly for work with twins.

The precise number of twins Mengele studied is not known, but during the 41
spring and summer of 1944, the time of the influx and mass murder of enormous
numbers of Hungarian Jews, he accumulated what inmates of the men's and
women's camps estimated to be a total of 175 sets of twins; it was an extraordinarily large number to have available simultaneously in a single place. Most
were children, but the twins ranged up to the age of 70. The relative number
of identical twins, as opposed to nonidentical twins, is also uncertain. (Nonidentical twins come from different ova and are genetically similar only to the

429

extent of ordinary siblings.) Mengele's capacity or inclination to maintain, in his work, the crucial distinction between these two kinds of twins is unclear. Since it is known that a few ordinary siblings masqueraded as twins, upon discovering the advantages of doing so, there is reason to doubt the reliability of Mengele's research.

Being a twin gave one a much better chance to survive. That was especially true for children, who were otherwise routinely selected for the gas chamber on arrival. 42

Twins had unique status. They felt themselves, as one put it, "completely elevated, segregated from the hurly-burly of the camp." They lived in special blocks, usually within medical units. They were frequently permitted to keep their own clothing. Their heads were not shaved. Their diet was rich by Auschwitz standards, often including white bread and milk. They were never beaten, as one surviving twin explained—even if they were caught in such a normally "ultimate sin" as stealing food—because the word was out "not to ruin us physically." 43

Mothers of young female twins were sometimes allowed to stay with their children, though usually only temporarily, in order to help the twins remain in good physical and mental condition—and on occasion to contribute to information about heredity and family history. We may say that the lives of twins had unique existential value in Auschwitz. 44

Mengele's research method, according to the inmate anthropologist, was standard for the time—and much the same as that used by her own well-regarded professor at the Polish university where she had obtained her advanced degree. That professor, she said, stressed "the biological foundaion of [the] social environment" and the delineation of "racial types." Mengele's approach was different only in being "terribly detailed." 45

Measurements were taken of the twins' skulls and bodies and various characteristics of the nose, lips, ears, hair and eyes. The inmate anthropologist used quality Swiss instruments and wore a white coat "like a physician." 46

Identical twins, Mengele's most treasured research objects, were often examined together. As one of them described: "It was like a laboratory. . . . There isn't a piece of body that wasn't measured and compared. . . . We were always sitting together—always nude. . . . We would sit for hours together." 47

When Mengele himself performed the examination, they said, he was very proper and methodical: "He concentrated on one part of the body at one time . . . like [one day] he measured our eyes for about two hours." They spoke of being examined as frequently as twice a week for a period of five months in late 1944, and also remembered vividly a special visit to the Auschwitz main camp for photographs. 48

There were less benign research programs on twins. One twin survivor, for example, told how he and his 12-year-old twin sister would be examined and subjected to such procedures as the injection of material into their spines or 49 the clamping of some part of the body "to see how long you could stand the pressure."

The twin survivor also spoke of Mengele's supervising "a lot of research with chemicals" and of how Mengele's assistants "might stick a needle in various places from behind," including the performing of spinal taps. These procedures, when done on young children, resulted sometimes in loss of consciousness, deafness and—among the smaller children—death. 50

The final step in Mengele's research on a number of the twins was dissection. Auschwitz enabled him not only to observe and measure twins to compare them in life, but to arrange for them to die together. He could thereby obtain comparisons of healthy or diseased organs to show the effects of heredity. 51

Sometimes Mengele himself presided over the murder of his twins. A deposition given by Dr. Nyiszli in 1945 described one such event: 52

> "In the work room next to the dissecting room, 14 gypsy twins were waiting . . . and crying bitterly. Dr. Mengele didn't say a single word to us, and prepared a 10cc. and 5cc. syringe. From a box he took evipan, and from another box he took chloroform, which was in 20 cubic-centimeter glass containers, and put these on the operating table. After that, the first twin was brought in . . . a 14-year-old girl. Dr. Mengele ordered me to undress the girl and put her on the dissecting table. Then he injected the evipan into her right arm intravenously. After the child had fallen asleep, he felt for the left ventricle of the heart and injected 10cc. of chloroform. After one little twitch the child was dead, whereupon Dr. Mengele had it taken into the corpse chamber. In this manner, all 14 twins were killed during the night."

Mengele could be totally arbitrary in his killings. An inmate radiologist told of a pair of gypsy twins, "two splendid boys of 7 or 8, whom we were studying from all aspects—from the 16 or 18 different specialties we represented." The boys both had symptoms in their joints that, according to a belief at that time, could be linked to tuberculosis. Mengele was convinced that the boys were tubercular, but the various inmate doctors, including the radiologist, found no trace of that disease. 53

Mengele was outraged, and he left the room, ordering the radiologist to remain. When he returned about an hour later, Mengele said calmly: "You are right. There was nothing." After some silence, Mengele added, "Yes, I dissected them." Later, the radiologist said, he heard from Dr. Nyiszli that Mengele had shot the two boys in the neck and that "while they were still warm, began to examine them: lungs first, then each organ." 54

The two boys, the radiologist added, had been favorites with all the doctors— including Mengele. They had been treated very well, he added, "spoiled in all respects . . . these two especially . . . they fascinated him considerably." But their post-mortem study had still greater fascination for him. 55

Mengele's fanatically brutal approach to his research can be understood mainly in terms of his combination of ideological zealotry and scientific am- 56

431

bition. Verschuer, his mentor, was taking science in a Nazi direction when he declared that research with twins would demonstrate "the extent of the damage caused by adverse hereditary influences" as well as "relations between disease, racial types, and miscegenation." In Auschwitz, Mengele saw an opportunity to deepen and extend the Nazi racial vision by means of systematic research "evidence."

He was also intent upon gaining personal recognition as a scientist. Indeed, 57 his Auschwitz friend told me that Mengele planned to use his research with twins as the basis for his Habilitation, the presentation necessary for a formal university appointment. Mengele's ideological worship, then, included the worship of Nazified "science," and from that standpoint he told his friend that "it would be a sin, a crime . . . and irresponsible not to utilize the possiblities that Auschwitz had for twin research," and that "there would never be another chance like it."

Mengele saw himself as a biological revolutionary, part of a vanguard devoted 58 to the bold scientific task of remaking his people and ultimately the people of the world. The German race would have to be cured and its genes improved. Many believed, as one inmate doctor said, that Mengele wanted to make use of his research on twins "to find the cause of multiple pregnancies" in order to increase such events among Aryan women. In any case, he did wish to apply his results toward German-centered racial goals.

Mengele's friend revealed something of this motivation when he told me 59 that Mengele saw his work as having bearing on selecting national leaders "not on a political basis but on a biological basis." He might well have been unclear himself about his exact motivations, but we have reason to see in them a combination of distorted scientific claims and related ideological fantasies.

Mengele's treatment of twins provides important additional clues to his 60 psychology. There we see displayed the full range of his adaptation to the Auschwitz environment. Survivors repeatedly commented on his confusing duality of affection and violence, an extreme manifestation of the process I call "doubling."

The twins lived in an atmosphere that combined sanctuary with terror. As 61 one recalled, they never forgot they were in Auschwitz where, starting in the summer of 1944, they could clearly see "flames really coming up every day, every night" from the open pits in which bodies were burned, and they could "hear every evening a cacophony of screams" and breathe in "the unbearable smell."

Yet most of the twins were safe, under the protection of Mengele, and much 62 of the time he treated them lovingly. According to an inmate doctor, Mengele in his contacts with the children was "as gentle as a father," talking to them and patting them on the head "in a loving way." He could be playful, jumping about to please them. The twin children frequently called him "Uncle Pepi." Sometimes, though, as the inmate doctor reported, Mengele would bring some gypsy twins sweets and invite them for a ride in his car which turned out to be "a little drive with Uncle Pepi, to the gas chamber."

For many of the twins, the strength of their warm feelings toward Mengele 63 was such that they found it impossible in later years to believe the evil things they heard about him. "For us," one said, he was "like a papa, like a mama."

One inmate doctor, in his own excruciating struggles to come to terms with 64 Mengele, thought of him as "the double man" who had "all the human feelings, pity and so on," but also had in his psyche an "impenetrable, indestructible cell, which is obedience to the received order."

He was describing Mengele's Auschwitz self, the new self that can take shape 65 in virtually anyone in adapting to an extreme environment. With the Auschwitz self, Mengele's potential for evil became actual, even as he maintained elements of his prior self that included affection toward children. In this process, each part-self behaved as a functioning whole: the Auschwitz self enabling him to function in that murderous environment and to exploit its human resources with considerable efficiency; the prior self enabling him to maintain a sense of decency. His powerful commitment to Nazi ideology served as a bridge, a necessary connection between the two.

Mengele's Auschwitz behavior reflects important pre-existing psychological 66 tendencies that contributed greatly to that doubling process. His inclinations toward omnipotence and total control over others could be given extreme expression in Auschwitz.

The man and the place were dramatically summed up by a survivor who did 67 art work for him and spoke of herself as Mengele's "pet," someone who was pleasant to have around. The death camp, she said, was like a city dog pound, with Mengele as the inspector checking up on the keepers—the inmate doctors—and on the dogs—the inmates.

The inspector, she recalled, would often admonish the keepers to "wash up 68 the excrement" in the pound, "to keep it clean, to keep the dogs healthy." Then he would examine "these chambers where they are killed" and he would inquire about the dog population: "How many are you? Well, it's too crowded—you better put in two more [gas chambers] today."

This image, with its blending of omnipotence and sadism, was relevant to 69 much of Mengele's relationship to twins. "It was an axiom," one of them told me, "that Mengele is God. He used to come always with an entourage, very well decked out, very elegant. He always carried around him an aura of some terrifying threat, which is, I suspect, unexplainable to normal human beings who didn't see this." It was "literally impossible," the survivor said, "to transmit the edge of this terror."

Only in Auschwitz could Mengele assume that aura and become what the 70 inmate artist described as "a very charismatic man" with "star quality." But when she added, "Marilyn Monroe flashed through my mind," she was perhaps suggesting the strong element of mannered self-display, what is loosely called "narcissism"—and perhaps a certain amount of kitsch and absurdity—contained in Mengele's assumption of omnipotence.

Another prior trait, Mengele's schizoid tendencies, were reflected in survivors' accounts of his "dead eyes"—eyes that showed no emotion, that avoided looking into the eyes of others. The inmate artist described him as so distant from others that "he seemed to be from a different planet." That kind of schizoid person, however friendly or affectionate at times, remains fundamentally removed from others, with inner divisions that can contribute to the doubling process. 71

Mengele's exaggerated immaculateness was consistent with such tendencies toward withdrawal. He was "very sensitive about bad smells," an inmate doctor reported, so that before he arrived, "the doors and windows had to be opened." He was "Clean, clean, clean!" one survivor said. This passion for cleanliness actually became part of Mengele's selection esthetic. He often sent prisoners with skin blemishes—even those with small abscesses or old appendectomy scars—to the gas chamber. 72

All people are capable of psychic numbing, a diminished tendency or inclination to feel. But Mengele's version of the Auschwitz self—his ease in harming and killing—carried psychic numbing to a remarkable exteme. "The main thing about him," an observant inmate-doctor stated, "was that he totally lacked feeling." He was enabled to feel nothing in killing a young twin, even one he had been fond of, to make a medical point. 73

Mengele's sadism was of a piece with these other traits. The pleasure he could take in causing pain was an aspect of his omnipotence, a means of maintaining his schizoid withdrawal and his renunciation of anything in the realm of fellow-feeling toward his victims. That kind of sadism was manifest in his smiling enthusiasm at selections. It was present in his remark to a Jewish woman doctor who was pleading vainly for the life of her father: "Your father is 70 years old. Don't you think he has lived long enough?" And survivors tell of Mengele's proclaiming on Tisha B'Av, the commemoration of the destruction of the first and second temples, "We will have a concert." There was a concert, then a roll-call, then an enormous selection for the gas chamber. 74

In his play "The Deputy," Rolf Hochhuth creates a fiendish Nazi character known only as "the Doctor," modeled after Mengele, who is described as having "the stature of Absolute Evil," as "only playing the part of a human being." 75

Some inmate-doctors also viewed Mengele as a demon and wished to divest him of his professional status. One described him as "a monster, period," and another as "no more doctor than anything else." 76

But being a doctor was part of Mengele's demonology: he took on the dark side of the omnipotent Svengali-like physician-shaman. 77

The myth of Mengele's demonic stature was given added support by the often misleading rumors about his life after Auschwitz. He was said to be living in comfort in South America, advising dictators such as Gen. Alfredo Stroessner 78

434

of Paraguay on how to annihilate the Indian population, growing wealthy in an extensive drug trade run by former Nazis. Nobody could touch Mengele.

We have seen that his death has partly dispelled this demonology. His continuing "metamorphosis" into an ordinary mortal can be enhanced by probing his motivations and behavior. 79

The psychological traits Mengele brought to Auschwitz exist in many of us, but in him they took exaggerated form. His impulse toward omnipotence and total control of the world around him were means of fending off anxiety and doubt, fears of falling apart—ultimately, fear of death. That fear also activated his sadism and extreme psychic numbing. He could quiet his fears of death in that death-dominated environment by performing the ultimate act of power over another person: murder. 80

Yet, as far as we know, he had neither killed nor maimed prior to Auschwitz, and had in fact functioned in a more or less integrated way. 81

The perfect match between Mengele and Auschwitz changed all that. Through doubling, he could call forth his evil potential. That evil, generally speaking, is neither inherent in any self nor foreign to it. Under certain kinds of psychological and moral conditions it can emerge. Crucial to that emergence is an ideology or world view, a theory or vision that justifies or demands evil actions. 82

Viewed in this light, Josef Mengele emerges as he really was: a visionary ideologue, an efficiently murderous functionary, a diligent careerist—and disturbingly human. 83

QUESTIONS

1. As paragraph 6 makes clear, this essay means to "explain" Mengele. Summarize in your own words the explanation that it offers.

2. Why were twins so important to Mengele? Are the reasons psychological, scientific, or both? What has his interest in twins got to do with the process Lifton calls "doubling" in paragraph 8?

3. Much of this essay is devoted to reporting. Where do these reports come from? What sources does Lifton identify in the article?

4. In paragraph 70 Lifton speaks of "narcissism." In what ways does Mengele seem to conform to this psychological type or depart from it?

5. "Viewed in this light," Lifton concludes, "Josef Mengele emerges as he really was: a visionary ideologue, an efficiently murderous functionary, a diligent careerist—and disturbingly human." Do you agree? Would you like to offer a different interpretation?

6. Do some research on another person supposed to have been a human monster such as the Roman emperors Nero or Caligula or some more modern tyrant, terrorist, or torturer. (You may find legend at odds with history as you look into things.) Incorporate your research in an essay considering the kind of figure that humans find horrifying. What is it that makes these creatures both terrible and fascinating?

MAKING CONNECTIONS

Lifton speaks in paragraph 73 of "psychic numbing." Can you think of other instances of this phenomenon that you have encountered in your reading or in your experience? Is a play like Shakespeare's *Macbeth*, for instance, about "psychic numbing"? Is Bettelheim's "Joey," discussed above, another example? Write an essay in which you discuss this phenomenon, defining and illustrating the concept.

SOME CONDITIONS OF OBEDIENCE AND DISOBEDIENCE TO AUTHORITY

Stanley Milgram

Stanley Milgram (1933–1984) was born in New York, went to Queens College and Harvard University, and was a professor of social psychology at the Graduate Center of the City University of New York. The following explanation of Milgram's experiment first appeared in the professional journal Human Relations *in 1965 and made him famous, causing a storm of controversy over his method of experimentation and the results of his experiment. Milgram has said of his work, "As a social psychologist, I look at the world not to master it in any practical sense, but to understand it and to communicate that understanding to others."*

The situation in which one agent commands another to hurt a third turns up time and again as a significant theme in human relations.[1] It is powerfully expressed in the story of Abraham, who is commanded by God to kill his son. It is no accident that Kierkegaard,[2] seeking to orient his thought to the central themes of human experience, chose Abraham's conflict as the springboard to his philosophy.

War too moves forward on the triad of an authority which commands a person to destroy the enemy, and perhaps all organized hostility may be viewed as a theme and variation on the three elements of authority, executant, and victim.[3] We describe an experimental program, recently concluded at Yale

---

[1]This research was supported by two grants from the National Science Foundation: NSF G-17916 and NSF G-24152. Exploratory studies carried out in 1960 were financed by a grant from the Higgins Funds of Yale University. I am grateful to John T. Williams, James J. McDonough, and Emil Elges for the important part they played in the project. Thanks are due also to Alan Elms, James Miller, Taketo Murata, and Stephen Stier for their aid as graduate assistants. My wife, Sasha, performed many valuable services. Finally, I owe a profound debt to the many persons in New Haven and Bridgeport who served as subjects.

[2]Søren Kierkegaard (1813–1855): Danish philosopher and theologian. [Eds.]

[3]Consider, for example, J. P. Scott's analysis of war in his monograph on aggression:

. . . while the actions of key individuals in a war may be explained in terms of direct stimulation to aggression, vast numbers of other people are involved simply by being part of an organized society.

. . . For example, at the beginning of World War I an Austrian archduke was assassinated in Sarajevo. A few days later soldiers from all over Europe were marching toward each other, not

University, in which a particular expression of this conflict is studied by experimental means.

In its most general form the problem may be defined thus: if X tells Y to   3
hurt Z, under what conditions will Y carry out the command of X and under what conditions will he refuse? In the more limited form possible in laboratory research, the question becomes: If an experimenter tells a subject to hurt another person, under what conditions will the subject go along with this instruction, and under what conditions will he refuse to obey? The laboratory problem is not so much a dilution of the general statement as one concrete expression of the many particular forms this question may assume.

One aim of the research was to study behavior in a strong situation of deep   4
consequence to the participants, for the psychological forces operative in powerful and lifelike forms of the conflict may not be brought into play under diluted conditions.

This approach meant, first, that we had a special obligation to protect the   5
welfare and dignity of the persons who took part in the study; subjects were, of necessity, placed in a difficult predicament, and steps had to be taken to ensure their wellbeing before they were discharged from the laboratory. Toward this end, a careful, post-experimental treatment was devised and has been carried through for subjects in all conditions.[4]

TERMINOLOGY

If Y follows the command of X we shall say that he has obeyed X; if he fails   6
to carry out the command of X, we shall say that he has disobeyed X. The terms to *obey* and to *disobey*, as used here, refer to the subject's overt action only, and carry no implication for the motive or experiential states accompanying the action.[5]

---

because they were stimulated by the archduke's misfortune, but because they had been trained to obey orders.

(Slightly rearranged from Scott (1958), *Aggression*, p. 103.)

[4] It consisted of an extended discussion with the experimenter and, of equal importance, a friendly reconciliation with the victim. It is made clear that the victim did *not* receive painful electric shocks. After the completion of the experimental series, subjects were sent a detailed report of the results and full purposes of the experimental program. A formal assessment of this procedure points to its overall effectiveness. Of the subjects, 83.7 percent indicated that they were glad to have taken part in the study; 15.1 percent reported neutral feelings; and 1.3 percent stated that they were sorry to have participated. A large number of subjects spontaneously requested that they be used in further experimentation. Four-fifths of the subjects felt that more experiments of this sort should be carried out, and 74 percent indicated that they had learned something of personal importance as a result of being in the study. Furthermore, a university psychiatrist, experienced in outpatient treatment, interviewed a sample of experimental subjects with the aim of uncovering possible injurious effects resulting from participation. No such effects were in evidence. Indeed, subjects typically felt that their participation was instructive and enriching. A more detailed discussion of this question can be found in Milgram (1964).

[5] To *obey* and to *disobey* are not the only terms one could use in describing the critical action

To be sure, the everyday use of the word *obedience* is not entirely free from 7 complexities. It refers to action within varying situations, and connotes diverse motives within those situations: a child's obedience differs from a soldier's obedience, or the love, honor, and *obey* of the marriage vow. However, a consistent behavioral relationship is indicated in most uses of the term: in the act of obeying, a person does what another person tells him to do. Y obeys X if he carries out the prescription for action which X has addressed to him; the term suggests, moreover, that some form of dominance-subordination, or hierarchical element, is part of the situation in which the transaction between X and Y occurs.

A subject who complies with the entire series of experimental commands 8 will be termed an *obedient* subject; one who at any point in the command series defies the experimenter will be called a *disobedient* or *defiant* subject. As used in this report the terms refer only to the subject's performance in the experiment, and do not necessarily imply a general personality disposition to submit to or reject authority.

SUBJECT POPULATION

The subjects used in all experimental conditions were male adults, residing 9 in the greater New Haven and Bridgeport areas, aged 20 to 50 years, and engaged in a wide variety of occupations. Each experimental condition described in this report employed 40 fresh subjects and was carefully balanced for age and occupational types. The occupational composition for each experiment was:

---

of Y. One could say that Y is cooperating with X, or displays conformity with regard to X's commands. However, *cooperation* suggests that X agrees with Y's ends, and understands the relationship between his own behavior and the attainment of those ends. (But the experimental procedure, and, in particular, the experimenter's command that the subject shock the victim even in the absence of a response from the victim, preclude such understanding.) Moreover, cooperation implies status parity for the co-acting agents, and neglects the asymmetrical, dominance-subordination element prominent in the laboratory relationship between experimenter and subject. *Conformity* has been used in other important contexts in social psychology, and most frequently refers to imitating the judgments or actions of others when no explicit requirement for imitation has been made. Furthermore, in the present study there are two sources of social pressure; pressure from the experimenter issuing the commands, and pressure from the victim to stop the punishment. It is the pitting of a common man (the victim) against an authority (the experimenter) that is the distinctive feature of the conflict. At a point in the experiment the victim demands that he be let free. The experimenter insists that the subject continue to administer shocks. Which act of the subject can be interpreted as conformity? The subject may conform to the wishes of his peer or to the wishes of the experimenter, and conformity in one direction means the absence of conformity in the other. Thus the word has no useful reference in this setting, for the dual and conflicting social pressures cancel out its meaning.

In the final analysis, the linguistic symbol representing the subject's action must take its meaning from the concrete context in which that action occurs; and there is probably no word in everyday language that covers the experimental situation exactly, without omissions or irrelevant connotations. It is partly for convenience, therefore, that the terms *obey* and *disobey* are used to describe the subject's actions. At the same time, our use of the words is highly congruent with dictionary meaning.

workers, skilled and unskilled: 40 percent; white collar, sales, business: 40 percent; professionals: 20 percent. The occupations were intersected with three age categories (subjects in 20's, 30's, and 40's, assigned to each condition in the proportions of 20, 40, and 40 percent, respectively).

THE GENERAL LABORATORY PROCEDURE[6]

The focus of the study concerns the amount of electric shock a subject is willing to administer to another person when ordered by an experimenter to give the "victim" increasingly more severe punishment. The act of administering shock is set in the context of a learning experiment, ostensibly designed to study the effect of punishment on memory. Aside from the experimenter, one naïve subject and one accomplice perform in each session. On arrival each subject is paid $4.50. After a general talk by the experimenter, telling how little scientists know about the effect of punishment on memory, subjects are informed that one member of the pair will serve as teacher and one as learner. A rigged drawing is held so that the naïve subject is always the teacher, and the accomplice becomes the learner. The learner is taken to an adjacent room and strapped into an "electric chair."

The naïve subject is told that it is his task to teach the learner a list of paired associates, to test him on the list, and to administer punishment whenever the learner errs in the test. Punishment takes the form of electric shock, delivered to the learner by means of a shock generator controlled by the naïve subject. The teacher is instructed to increase the intensity of electric shock one step on the generator on each error. The learner, according to plan, provides many wrong answers, so that before long the naïve subject must give him the strongest shock on the generator. Increases in shock level are met by increasingly insistent demands from the learner that the experiment be stopped because of the growing discomfort to him. However, in clear terms the experimenter orders the teacher to continue with the procedure in disregard of the learner's protests. *Thus, the naïve subject must resolve a conflict between two mutually incompatible demands from the social field. He may continue to follow the orders of the experimenter and shock the learner with increasing severity, or he may refuse to follow the orders of the experimenter and heed the learner's pleas. The experimenter's authority operates not in a free field, but against ever-mounting countervailing pressure from the person being punished.*

A few technical points need to be considered before the findings of the study are described. For the purpose of delivering shock, a simulated shock generator

---

[6]A more detailed account of the laboratory procedure can be found in Milgram (1963). A similar and independently evolved experimental procedure, employing a shock generator, victim, and learning task, was reported by Buss (1961). Buss used the technique for studying aggression, not obedience, and did not make use of the fundamental measure employed in the present study: breakoff points.

is used, with 30 clearly marked voltage levels that range from 15 to 450 volts. (Each level is activated by one of 30 individual lever switches set in a horizontal line.) The naïve subject is given a sample shock of 45 volts to convince him of the authenticity of the instrument. The generator bears verbal designations that range from "Slight Shock" to "Danger: Severe Shock."

The responses of the victim are standardized on tape, and each protest is 13 coordinated to a particular voltage level on the shock generator. Starting with 75 volts the learner begins to grunt and moan. At 150 volts he demands to be let out of the experiment. At 180 volts he cries out that he can no longer stand the pain. At 300 volts he refuses to provide any more answers to the memory test, insisting that he is no longer a participant in the experiment and must be freed. In response to this last tactic, the experimenter instructs the naïve subject to treat the absence of an answer as equivalent to a wrong answer, and to follow the usual shock procedure. The experimenter reinforces his demand with the statement: "You have no other choice, you must go on!" (This imperative is used whenever the naïve subject tries to break off the experiment.) If the subject refuses to give the next higher level of shock, the experiment is considered at an end. A quantitative value is assigned to the subject's performance based on the maximum-intensity shock he administered before breaking off. Thus any subject's score may range from zero (for a subject unwilling to administer the first shock level) to 30 (for a subject who proceeds to the highest voltage level on the board). For any particular subject and for any particular experimental condition, the degree to which participants have followed the experimenter's orders may be specified with a numerical value, corresponding to the metric on the shock generator.

This laboratory situation gives us a framework in which to study the subject's 14 reactions to the principal conflict of the experiment. Again, this conflict is between the experimenter's demands that he continue to administer the electric shock, and the learner's demands, which become increasingly more insistent, that the experiment be stopped. The crux of the study is to vary systematically the factors believed to alter the degree of obedience to the experimental commands, to learn under what conditions submission to authority is most probable and under what conditions defiance is brought to the fore.

PILOT STUDIES

Pilot studies for the present research were completed in the winter of 1960; 15 they differed from the regular experiments in a few details: for one, the victim was placed behind a silvered glass, with the light balance on the glass such that the victim could be dimly perceived by the subject (Milgram, 1961).

Though essentially qualitative in treatment, these studies pointed to several 16 significant features of the experimental situation. At first no vocal feedback was used from the victim. It was thought that the verbal and voltage designations on the control panel would create sufficient pressure to curtail the subject's obedience. However, this was not the case. In the absence of protests from the learner, virtually all subjects, once commanded, went blithely to the end of the board, seemingly indifferent to the verbal designations ("Extreme Shock" and "Danger: Severe Shock"). This deprived us of an adequate basis for scaling obedient tendencies. A force had to be introduced that would strengthen the subject's resistance to the experimenter's commands, and reveal individual differences in terms of a distribution of break-off points.

This force took the form of protests from the victim. Initially, mild protests 17 were used, but proved inadequate. Subsequently, more vehement protests were inserted into the experimental procedure. To our consternation, even the strongest protests from the victim did not prevent all subjects from administering the harshest punishment ordered by the experimenter; but the protests did lower the mean maximum shock somewhat and created some spread in the subject's performance; therefore, the victim's cries were standardized on tape and incorporated into the regular experimental procedure.

The situation did more than highlight the technical difficulties of finding a 18 *workable experimental procedure: It indicated that subjects would obey authority to a greater extent than we had supposed.* It also pointed to the importance of feedback from the victim in controlling the subject's behavior.

One further aspect of the pilot study was that subjects frequently averted 19 their eyes from the person they were shocking, often turning their heads in an awkward and conspicuous manner. One subject explained: "I didn't want to see the consequences of what I had done." Observers wrote:

> . . . subjects showed a reluctance to look at the victim, whom they could see through the glass in front of them. When this fact was brought to their attention they indicated that it caused them discomfort to see the victim in agony. We note, however, that although the subject refuses to look at the victim, he continues to administer shocks.

This suggested that the salience of the victim may have, in some degree, 20 regulated the subject's performance. If, in obeying the experimenter, the subject found it necessary to avoid scrutiny of the victim, would the converse be true? If the victim were rendered increasingly more salient to the subject, would obedience diminish? The first set of regular experiments was designed to answer this question.

IMMEDIACY OF THE VICTIM

This series consisted of four experimental conditions. In each condition the 21 victim was brought "psychologically" closer to the subject giving him shocks.

In the first condition (Remote Feedback) the victim was placed in another 22 room and could not be heard or seen by the subject, except that, at 300 volts, he pounded on the wall in protest. After 315 volts he no longer answered or was heard from.

The second condition (Voice Feedback) was identical to the first except that voice protests were introduced. As in the first condition the victim was placed in an adjacent room, but his complaints could be heard clearly through a door left slightly ajar and through the walls of the laboratory.[7]   23

The third experimental condition (Proximity) was similar to the second, except that the victim was now placed in the same room as the subject, and 1½ feet from him. Thus he was visible as well as audible, and voice cues were provided.   24

The fourth, and final, condition of this series (Touch-Proximity) was identical to the third, with this exception: The victim received a shock only when his hand rested on a shockplate. At the 150-volt level the victim again demanded to be let free and, in this condition, refused to place his hand on the shockplate. The experimenter ordered the naïve subject to force the victim's hand onto the plate. Thus obedience in this condition required that the subject have physical contact with the victim in order to give him punishment beyond the 150-volt level.   25

Forty adult subjects were studied in each condition. The data revealed that obedience was significantly reduced as the victim was rendered more immedi-   26

---

[7] It is difficult to convey on the printed page the full tenor of the victim's responses, for we have no adequate notation for vocal intensity, timing, and general qualities of delivery. Yet these features are crucial to producing the effect of an increasingly severe reaction to mounting voltage levels. (They can be communicated fully only by sending interested parties the recorded tapes.) In general terms, however, the victim indicates no discomfort until the 75-volt shock is administered, at which time there is a light grunt in response to the punishment. Similar reactions follow the 90- and 105-volt shocks, and at 120 volts the victim shouts to the experimenter that the shocks are becoming painful. Painful groans are heard on administration of the 135-volt shock, and at 150 volts the victim cries out, 'Experimenter, get me out of here! I won't be in the experiment any more! I refuse to go on!' Cries of this type continue with generally rising intensity, so that at 180 volts the victim cries out, 'I can't stand the pain,' and by 270 volts his response to the shock is definitely an agonized scream. Throughout, he insists that he be let out of the experiment. At 300 volts the victim shouts in desperation that he will no longer provide answers to the memory test; and at 315 volts, after a violent scream, he reaffirms with vehemence that he is no longer a participant. From this point on, he provides no answers, but shrieks in agony whenever a shock is administered; this continues through 450 volts. Of course, many subjects will have broken off before this point.

A revised and stronger set of protests was used in all experiments outside the Proximity series. Naturally, new baseline measures were established for all comparisons using the new set of protests.

There is overwhelming evidence that the great majority of subjects, both obedient and defiant, accepted the victims' reactions as genuine. The evidence takes the form of: (a) tension created in the subjects (see discussion of tension); (b) scores on "estimated-pain" scales filled out by subjects immediately after the experiment; (c) subjects' accounts of their feelings in post-experimental interviews; and (d) quantifiable responses to questionnaires distributed to subjects several months after their participation in the experiments. This matter will be treated fully in a forthcoming monograph.

(The procedure in all experimental conditions was to have the naïve subject announce the voltage level before administering each shock, so that—independently of the victim's responses—he was continually reminded of delivering punishment of ever-increasing severity.)

ate to the subject. The mean maximum shock for the conditions is shown in Figure 1.

Expressed in terms of the proportion of obedient to defiant subjects, the findings are that 34 percent of the subjects defied the experimenter in the Remote condition, 37.5 percent in Voice Feedback, 60 percent in Proximity, and 70 percent in Touch-Proximity.   27

How are we to account for this effect? A first conjecture might be that as the victim was brought closer the subject became more aware of the intensity of his suffering and regulated his behavior accordingly. This makes sense, but our evidence does not support the interpretation. There are no consistent differences in the attributed level of pain across the four conditions (i.e. the amount of pain experienced by the victim as estimated by the subject and expressed on a 14-point scale). But it is easy to speculate about alternative mechanisms: 28

> *Empathic cues.* In the Remote and to a lesser extent the Voice Feedback condi-   29
> tions, the victim's suffering possesses an abstract, remote quality for the subject.
> He is aware, but only in a conceptual sense, that his actions cause pain to another

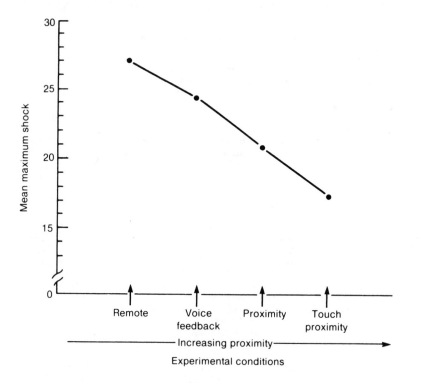

FIGURE 1. Mean maxima in proximity series.

person; the fact is apprehended, but not felt. The phenomenon is common enough. The bombardier can reasonably suppose that his weapons will inflict suffering and death, yet this knowledge is divested of affect and does not move him to a felt, emotional response to the suffering resulting from his actions. Similar observations have been made in wartime. It is possible that the visual cues associated with the victim's suffering trigger empathic responses in the subject and provide him with a more complete grasp of the victim's experience. Or it is possible that the empathic responses are themselves unpleasant, possessing drive properties which cause the subject to terminate the arousal situation. Diminishing obedience, then, would be explained by the enrichment of empathic cues in the successive experimental conditions.

Denial and narrowing of the cognitive field. The Remote condition allows a 30
narrowing of the cognitive field so that the victim is put out of mind. The subject no longer considers the act of depressing a lever relevant to moral judgment, for it is no longer associated with the victim's suffering. When the victim is close it is more difficult to exclude him phenomenologically. He necessarily intrudes on the subject's awareness since he is continuously visible. In the Remote condition his existence and reactions are made known only after the shock has been administered. The auditory feedback is sporadic and discontinuous. In the Proximity conditions his inclusion in the immediate visual field renders him a continuously salient element for the subject. The mechanism of denial can no longer be brought into play. One subject in the Remote condition said: "It's funny how you really begin to forget that there's a guy out there, even though you can hear him. For a long time I just concentrated on pressing the switches and reading the words."

Reciprocal fields. If in the Proximity condition the subject is in an improved 31
position to observe the victim, the reverse is also true. The actions of the subject now come under proximal scrutiny by the victim. Possibly, it is easier to harm a person when he is unable to observe our actions than when he can see what we are doing. His surveillance of the action directed against him may give rise to shame, or guilt, which may then serve to curtail the action. Many expressions of language refer to the discomfort or inhibitions that arise in face-to-face confrontation. It is often said that it is easier to criticize a man "behind his back" than to "attack him to his face." If we are in the process of lying to a person it is reputedly difficult to "stare him in the eye." We "turn away from others in shame" or in "embarrassment" and this action serves to reduce our discomfort. The manifest function of allowing the victim of a firing squad to be blindfolded is to make the occasion less stressful for him, but it may also serve a latent function of reducing the stress of the executioner. In short, in the Proximity conditions, the subject may sense that he has become more salient in the victim's field of awareness. Possibly he becomes more self-conscious, embarrassed, and inhibited in his punishment of the victim.

Phenomenal unity of act. In the Remote condition it is more difficult for the 32
subject to gain a sense of *relatedness* between his own actions and the consequences

445

of these actions for the victim. There is a physical and spatial separation of the act and its consequences. The subject depresses a lever in one room, and protests and cries are heard from another. The two events are in correlation, yet they lack a compelling phenomenological unity. The structure of a meaningful act—*I am hurting a man* — breaks down because of the spatial arrangements, in a manner somewhat analogous to the disappearance of phi phenomena[8] when the blinking lights are spaced too far apart. The unity is more fully achieved in the Proximity condition as the victim is brought closer to the action that causes him pain. It is rendered complete in Touch-Proximity.

Incipient group formation. Placing the victim in another room not only takes him further from the subject, but the subject and the experimenter are drawn relatively closer. There is incipient group formation between the experimenter and the subject, from which the victim is excluded. The wall between the victim and the others deprives him of an intimacy which the experimenter and subject feel. In the Remote condition, the victim is truly an outsider, who stands alone, physically and psychologically. 33

When the victim is placed close to the subject, it becomes easier to form an alliance with him against the experimenter. Subjects no longer have to face the experimenter alone. They have an ally who is close at hand and eager to collaborate in a revolt against the experimenter. Thus, the changing set of spatial relations leads to a potentially shifting set of alliances over the several experimental conditions. 34

Acquired behavior dispositions. It is commonly observed that laboratory mice will rarely fight with their litter mates. Scott (1958) explains this in terms of passive inhibition. He writes: "By doing nothing under . . . circumstances [the animal] learns to do nothing, and this may be spoken of as passive inhibition . . . this principle has great importance in teaching an individual to be peaceful, for it means that he can learn not to fight simply by not fighting." Similarly, we may learn not to harm others simply by not harming them in everyday life. Yet this learning occurs in a context of proximal relations with others, and may not be generalized to that situation in which the person is physically removed from us. Or possibly, in the past, aggressive actions against others who were physically close resulted in retaliatory punishment which extinguished the original form of response. In contrast, aggression against others at a distance may have only sporadically led to retaliation. Thus the organism learns that it is safer to be aggressive toward others at a distance, and precarious to be so when the parties are within arm's reach. Through a pattern of rewards and punishments, he acquires a disposition to avoid aggression at close quarters, a disposition which does not extend to harming others at a distance. And this may account for experimental findings in the remote and proximal experiments. 35

---

[8]phi phenomena: the optical impression of motion generated when similar stationary objects are presented one after another at a certain interval. [Eds.]

Proximity as a variable in psychological research has received far less attention 36
than it deserves. If men were sessile[9] it would be easy to understand this neglect.
But we move about; our spatial relations shift from one situation to the next,
and the fact that we are near or remote may have a powerful effect on the
psychological processes that mediate our behavior toward others. In the present
situation, as the victim is brought closer to the subject ordered to give him
shocks, increasing numbers of subjects break off the experiment, refusing to
obey. The concrete, visible, and proximal presence of the victim acts in an
important way to counteract the experimenter's power to generate disobedience.[10]

CLOSENESS OF AUTHORITY

If the spatial relationship of the subject and victim is relevant to the degree 37
of obedience, would not the relationship of subject to experimenter also play a
part?

There are reasons to feel that, on arrival, the subject is oriented primarily to 38
the experimenter rather than to the victim. He has come to the laboratory to
fit into the structure that the experimenter—not the victim—would provide.
He has come less to understand his behavior than to *reveal* that behavior to a
competent scientist, and he is willing to display himself as the scientist's purposes
require. Most subjects seem quite concerned about the appearance they are
making before the experimenter, and one could argue that this preoccupation
in a relatively new and strange setting makes the subject somewhat insensitive
to the triadic nature of the social situation. In other words, the subject is so
concerned about the show he is putting on for the experimenter that influences
from other parts of the social field do not receive as much weight as they
ordinarily would. This overdetermined orientation to the experimenter would
account for the relative insensitivity of the subject to the victim, and would also
lead us to believe that alterations in the relationship between subject and
experimenter would have important consequences for obedience.

In a series of experiments we varied the physical closeness and degree of 39
surveillance of the experimenter. In one condition the experimenter sat just a
few feet away from the subject. In a second condition, after giving initial
instructions, the experimenter left the laboratory and gave his orders by tele-

---

[9] sessile: permanently attached. [Eds.]

[10] Admittedly, the terms *proximity, immediacy, closeness,* and *salience-of-the-victim* are used in
a loose sense, and the experiments themselves represent a very coarse treatment of the variable.
Further experiments are needed to refine the notion and tease out such diverse factors as spatial
distance, visibility, audibility, barrier interposition, etc.

The Proximity and Touch-Proximity experiments were the only conditions where we were
unable to use taped feedback from the victim. Instead, the victim was trained to respond in these
conditions as he had in Experiment 2 (which employed taped feedback). Some improvement is
possible here, for it should be technically feasible to do a proximity series using taped feedback.

phone. In still a third condition the experimenter was never seen, providing instructions by means of a tape recording activated when the subjects entered the laboratory.

Obedience dropped sharply as the experimenter was physically removed from the laboratory. The number of obedient subjects in the first condition (Experimenter Present) was almost three times as great as in the second, where the experimenter gave his orders by telephone. Twenty-six subjects were fully obedient in the first condition, and only nine in the second (Chi square obedient *vs.* defiant in the two conditions, df = 14.7; $p < 0.001$). Subjects seemed able to take a far stronger stand against the experimenter when they did not have to encounter him face to face, and the experimenter's power over the subject was severely curtailed.[11]

Moreover, when the experimenter was absent, subjects displayed an interesting form of behavior that had not occurred under his surveillance. Though continuing with the experiment, several subjects administered lower shocks than were required and never informed the experimenter of their deviation from the correct procedure. (Unknown to the subjects, shock levels were automatically recorded by an Esterline-Angus event recorder wired directly into the shock generator; the instrument provided us with an objective record of the subjects' performance.) Indeed, in telephone conversations some subjects specifically assured the experimenter that they were raising the shock level according to instruction, whereas in fact they were repeatedly using the lowest shock on the board. This form of behavior is particularly interesting: although these subjects acted in a way that clearly undermined the avowed purposes of the experiment, they found it easier to handle the conflict in this manner than to precipitate an open break with authority.

Other conditions were completed in which the experimenter was absent during the first segment of the experiment, but reappeared at the point that the subject definitely refused to give higher shocks when commanded by telephone. Although he had exhausted his power via telephone, the experimenter could frequently force further obedience when he reappeared in the laboratory.

Experiments in this series show that the *physical presence* of an authority is an important force contributing to the subject's obedience or defiance. Taken together with the first experimental series on the proximity of the victim, it would appear that something akin to fields of force, diminishing in effectiveness with increasing psychological distance from their source, have a controlling effect on the subject's performance. As the victim is brought closer, the subject finds it harder to administer shocks to him. When the victim's position is held constant relative to the subject, and the authority is made more remote, the subject finds it easier to break off the experiment. This effect is substantial in

---

[11] The third condition also led to significantly lower obedience than this first situation in which the experimenter was present, but it contains technical difficulties that require extensive discussion.

both cases, but manipulation of the experimenter's position yielded the more powerful results. Obedience to destructive commands is highly dependent on the proximal relations between authority and subject.

TENSIONS

The description of final scores does not fully convey the character of the 44 subjects' performance, and it would be useful to interrupt our reporting of quantitative relationships to remark on the subjects' general reaction to the situation.

One might suppose that a subject would simply break off or continue as his 45 conscience and temperament dictated. Yet this is very far from what happened. There were powerful reactions of tension and emotional strain in a substantial proportion of the participants. Persons were observed to sweat, tremble, stutter, bite their lips, and groan as they found themselves increasingly implicated in the experimental conflict. Some sense of the subjects' mood can be found in a transcript of their remarks at break-off point. Here are the remarks of two defiant subjects:

> Is he banging? . . . Is he hurt out there? Well, I don't want to be responsible for anything that happens to him. No, I can't go on with it. I don't know whether he's all right or not. I mean he may have a heart condition or something; I wouldn't feel right doing it. He's banging for help. He's evidently in trouble or he wouldn't bang . . . I don't see any sense to this—to knocking him out or something. I just can't see it.
> [*Subject refuses to administer shocks*]   [*Subject 0108*]

> The man is banging. He wants to get out . . . I'm sorry. If the man wants to get out I'd just as soon stop . . . I don't want to administer any more [extremely excited] . . . I will gladly refund the check, but I will not harm this man . . . I'm sorry, I will not give him any more if he obviously wants to get out. There is no money in the world that will make me hurt another individual.
> [*Subject 010X*]

And here is a transcript from an obedient subject. He began the experiment 46 calmly, but became increasingly tense as the experiment proceeded. After administering the 150-volt shock, he began to address the experimenter in agitated tones:

> *150 volts delivered.* You want me to keep going?
> *165 volts delivered.* That guy is hollering in there. There's a lot of them here. He's liable to have heart condition. You want me to go?
> *180 volts delivered.* He can't stand it! I'm not going to kill that man in there! You hear him hollering? He's hollering. He can't stand it. What if something happens to him? . . . I'm not going to get that man sick in there. He's hollering in there. You know what I mean? I mean I refuse to take responsibility. He's getting hurt

449

in there. He's in there hollering. Too many left here. Geez, if he gets them wrong. There's too many of them left. I mean who is going to take responsibility if anything happens to that gentleman?
[*The experimenter accepts responsibility.*] All right.
195 volts delivered. You see he's hollering. Hear that. Gee, I don't know.
[*The experimenter says: 'The experiment requires that you go on.'*]—I know it does, sir, but I mean—hugh—he don't know what he's in for. He's up to 195 volts.
210 volts delivered.
225 volts delivered.
240 volts delivered. Aw, no. You mean I've got to keep going up with the scale? No sir. I'm not going to kill that man! I'm not going to give him 450 volts!
[*The experimenter says: 'The experiment requires that you go on.'*]—I know it does, but that man is hollering there, sir . . .

Despite his numerous, agitated objections, which were constant accompaniments to his actions, the subject unfailingly obeyed the experimenter, proceeding to the highest shock level on the generator. He displayed a curious dissociation between word and action. Although at the verbal level he had resolved not to go on, his actions were fully in accord with the experimenter's commands. This subject did not want to shock the victim, and he found it an extremely disagreeable task, but he was unable to invent a response that would free him from E's authority. Many subjects cannot find the specific verbal formula that would enable them to reject the role assigned to them by the experimenter. Perhaps our culture does not provide adequate models for disobedience.

One puzzling sign of tension was the regular occurrence of nervous laughing 47 fits. In the first four conditions 71 of the 160 subjects showed definite signs of nervous laughter and smiling. The laughter seemed entirely out of place, even bizarre. Full-blown, uncontrollable seizures were observed for 15 of these subjects. On one occasion we observed a seizure so violently convulsive that it was necessary to call a halt to the experiment. In the post-experimental interviews subjects took pains to point out that they were not sadistic types and that the laughter did not mean they enjoyed shocking the victim.

In the interview following the experiment subjects were asked to indicate on 48 a 14-point scale just how nervous or tense they felt at the point of maximum tension (Figure 2). The scale ranged from "not at all tense and nervous" to "extremely tense and nervous." Self-reports of this sort are of limited precision and at best provide only a rough indication of the subject's emotional response. Still, taking the reports for what they are worth, it can be seen that the distribution of responses spans the entire range of the scale, with the majority of subjects concentrated at the center and upper extreme. A further breakdown showed that obedient subjects reported themselves as having been slightly more tense and nervous than the defiant subjects at the point of maximum tension.

How is the occurrence of tension to be interpreted? First, it points to the 49 presence of conflict. If a tendency to comply with authority were the only psychological force operating in the situation, all subjects would have continued to the end and there would have been no tension. Tension, it is assumed, results from the simultaneous presence of two or more incompatible response tendencies (Miller, 1944). If sympathetic concern for the victim were the exclusive force, all subjects would have calmly defied the experimenter. Instead, there were both obedient and defiant outcomes, frequently accompanied by extreme tension. A conflict develops between the deeply ingrained disposition not to harm others and the equally compelling tendency to obey others who are in authority. The subject is quickly drawn into a dilemma of a deeply dynamic character, and the presence of high tension points to the considerable strength of each of the antagonistic vectors.

Moreover, tension defines the strength of the aversive state from which the subject is unable to escape through disobedience. When a person is uncomfortable, tense, or stressed, he tries to take some action that will allow him to terminate this unpleasant state. Thus tension may serve as a drive that leads to

50

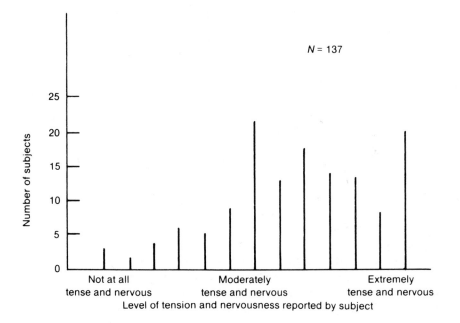

FIGURE 2. Level of tension and nervousness: the self-reports on "tension and nervousness" for 137 subjects in the Proximity experiments. Subjects were given a scale with 14 values ranging from "not at all tense and nervous" to "extremely tense and nervous." They were instructed: "Thinking back to that point in the experiment when you felt the most tense and nervous, indicate just how you felt by placing an X at the appropriate point on the scale." The results are shown in terms of midpoint values.

451

escape behavior. But in the present situation, even where tension is extreme, many subjects are unable to perform the response that will bring about relief. Therefore there must be a competing drive, tendency, or inhibition that precludes activation of the disobedient response. The strength of this inhibiting factor must be of greater magnitude than the stress experienced, or else the terminating act would occur. Every evidence of extreme tension is at the same time an indication of the strength of the forces that keep the subject in the situation.

Finally, tension may be taken as evidence of the reality of the situations for the subjects. Normal subjects do not tremble and sweat unless they are implicated in a deep and genuinely felt predicament.   51

BACKGROUND AUTHORITY

In psychophysics, animal learning, and other branches of psychology, the fact that measures are obtained at one institution rather than another is irrelevant to the interpretation of the findings, so long as the technical facilities for measurement are adequate and the operations are carried out with competence.   52

But it cannot be assumed that this holds true for the present study. The effectiveness of the experimenter's commands may depend in an important way on the larger institutional context in which they are issued. The experiments described thus far were conducted at Yale University, an organization which most subjects regarded with respect and sometimes awe. In post-experimental interviews several participants remarked that the locale and sponsorship of the study gave them confidence in the integrity, competence, and benign purposes of the personnel; many indicated that they would not have shocked the learner if the experiments had been done elsewhere.   53

This issue of background authority seemed to us important for an interpretation of the results that had been obtained thus far; moreover it is highly relevant to any comprehensive theory of human obedience. Consider, for example, how closely our compliance with the imperatives of others is tied to particular institutions and locales in our day-to-day activities. On request, we expose our throats to a man with a razor blade in the barber shop, but would not do so in a shoe store; in the latter setting we willingly follow the clerk's request to stand in our stockinged feet, but resist the command in a bank. In the laboratory of a great university, subjects may comply with a set of commands that would be resisted if given elsewhere. *One must always question the relationship of obedience to a person's sense of the context in which he is operating.*   54

To explore the problem we moved our apparatus to an office building in industrial Bridgeport and replicated experimental conditions, without any visible tie to the university.   55

Bridgeport subjects were invited to the experiment through a mail circular similar to the one used in the Yale study, with appropriate changes in letterhead,   56

452

etc. As in the earlier study, subjects were paid $4.50 for coming to the laboratory. The same age and occupational distributions used at Yale and the identical personnel were employed.

The purpose in relocating in Bridgeport was to assure a complete dissociation 57 from Yale, and in this regard we were fully successful. On the surface, the study appeared to be conducted by Research Associates of Bridgeport, an organization of unknown character (the title had been concocted exclusively for use in this study).

The experiments were conducted in a three-room office suite in a somewhat 58 run-down commercial building located in the downtown shopping area. The laboratory was sparsely furnished, though clean, and marginally respectable in appearance. When subjects inquired about professional affiliations, they were informed only that we were a private firm conducting research for industry.

Some subjects displayed skepticism concerning the motives of the Bridgeport 59 experimenter. One gentleman gave us a written account of the thoughts he experienced at the control board:

> . . . Should I quit this damn test? Maybe he passed out? What dopes we were not to check up on this deal. How do we know that these guys are legit? No furniture, bare walls, no telephone. We could of called the Police up or the Better Business Bureau. I learned a lesson tonight. How do I know that Mr. Williams [the experimenter] is telling the truth . . . I wish I knew how many volts a person could take before lapsing into unconsciousness . . .   [*Subject 2414*]

Another subject stated:

> I questioned on my arrival my own judgment [about coming]. I had doubts as to the legitimacy of the operation and the consequences of participation. I felt it was a heartless way to conduct memory or learning processes on human beings and certainly dangerous without the presence of a medical doctor.   [*Subject 2440V*]

There was no noticeable reduction in tension for the Bridgeport subjects. 60 And the subjects' estimation of the amount of pain felt by the victim was slightly, though not significantly, higher than in the Yale study.

A failure to obtain complete obedience in Bridgeport would indicate that the 61 extreme compliance found in New Haven subjects was tied closely to the background authority of Yale University; if a large proportion of the subjects remained fully obedient, very different conclusions would be called for.

As it turned out, the level of obedience in Bridgeport, although somewhat 62 reduced, was not significantly lower than that obtained at Yale. A large proportion of the Bridgeport subjects were fully obedient to the experimenter's commands (48 percent of the Bridgeport subjects delivered the maximum shock versus 65 percent in the corresponding condition at Yale).

How are these findings to be interpreted? It is possible that if commands of 63 a potentially harmful or destructive sort are to be perceived as legitimate they must occur within some sort of institutional structure. But it is clear from the study that it need not be a particularly reputable or distinguished institution. The Bridgeport experiments were conducted by an unimpressive firm lacking any credentials; the laboratory was set up in a respectable office building with title listed in the building directory. Beyond that, there was no evidence of benevolence or competence. It is possible that the *category* of institution, judged according to its professed function, rather than its qualitative position within that category, wins our compliance. Persons deposit money in elegant, but also in seedy-looking banks, without giving much thought to the differences in security they offer. Similarly, our subjects may consider one laboratory to be as competent as another, so long as it is a scientific laboratory.

It would be valuable to study the subjects' performance in other contexts which go even further than the Bridgeport study in denying institutional support to the experimenter. It is possible that, beyond a certain point, obedience disappears completely. But that point had not been reached in the Bridgeport office: almost half the subjects obeyed the experimenter fully.

FURTHER EXPERIMENTS

We may mention briefly some additional experiments undertaken in the Yale series. A considerable amount of obedience and defiance in everyday life occurs in connection with groups. And we had reason to feel in light of the many group studies already done in psychology that group forces would have a profound effect on reactions to authority. A series of experiments was run to examine these effects. In all cases only one naïve subject was studied per hour, but he performed in the midst of actors who, unknown to him, were employed by the experimenter. In one experiment (Groups for Disobedience) two actors broke off in the middle of the experiment. When this happened 90 percent of the subjects followed suit and defied the experimenter. In another condition the actors followed the orders obediently; this strengthened the experimenter's power only slightly. In still a third experiment the job of pushing the switch to shock the learner was given to one of the actors, while the naïve subject performed a subsidiary act. We wanted to see how the teacher would respond if he were involved in the situation but did not actually give the shocks. In this situation only three subjects out of forty broke off. In a final group experiment the subjects themselves determined the shock level they were going to use. Two actors suggested higher and higher shock levels; some subjects insisted, despite group pressure, that the shock level be kept low; others followed along with the group.

Further experiments were completed using women as subjects, as well as a set dealing with the effects of dual, unsanctioned, and conflicting authority. A final experiment concerned the personal relationship between victim and subject. These will have to be described elsewhere, lest the present report be extended to monographic length.

It goes without saying that future research can proceed in many different   67
directions. What kinds of response from the victim are most effective in causing
disobedience in the subject? Perhaps passive resistance is more effective than
vehement protest. What conditions of entry into an authority system lead to
greater or lesser obedience? What is the effect of anonymity and masking on
the subject's behavior? What conditions lead to the subject's perception of
responsibility for his own actions? Each of these could be a major research topic
in itself, and can readily be incorporated into the general experimental procedure
described here.

LEVELS OF OBEDIENCE AND DEFIANCE

One general finding that merits attention is the high level of obedience   68
manifested in the experimental situation. Subjects often expressed deep disap-
proval of shocking a man in the face of his objections, and others denounced
it as senseless and stupid. Yet many subjects complied even while they protested.
The proportion of obedient subjects greatly exceeded the expectations of the
experimenter and his colleagues. At the outset, we had conjectured that subjects
would not, in general, go above the level of "Strong Shock." In practice, many
subjects were willing to administer the most extreme shocks available when
commanded by the experimenter. For some subjects the experiment provided
an occasion for aggressive release. And for others it demonstrated the extent to
which obedient dispositions are deeply ingrained and engaged, irrespective of
their consequences for others. Yet this is not the whole story. Somehow, the
subject becomes implicated in a situation from which he cannot disengage
himself.

The departure of the experimental results from intelligent expectation, to   69
some extent, has been formalized. The procedure was to describe the experimental situation in concrete detail to a group of competent persons, and to ask
them to predict the performance of 100 hypothetical subjects. For purposes of
indicating the distribution of break-off points, judges were provided with a
diagram of the shock generator and recorded their predictions before being
informed of the actual results. Judges typically underestimated the amount of
obedience demonstrated by subjects.

In Figure 3, we compare the predictions of forty psychiatrists at a leading   70
medical school with the actual performance of subjects in the experiment. The
psychiatrists predicted that most subjects would not go beyond the tenth shock
level (150 volts; at this point the victim makes his first explicit demand to be
freed). They further predicted that by the twentieth shock level (300 volts; the
victim refuses to answer) 3.73 percent of the subjects would still be obedient;
and that only a little over one-tenth of one percent of the subjects would
administer the highest shock on the board. But, as the graph indicates, the
obtained behavior was very different. Sixty-two percent of the subjects obeyed

455

the experimenter's commands fully. Between expectation and occurrence there is a whopping discrepancy.

Why did the psychiatrists underestimate the level of obedience? Possibly, [71] because their predictions were based on an inadequate conception of the determinants of human action, a conception that focuses on motives *in vacuo*. This orientation may be entirely adequate for the repair of bruised impulses as revealed on the psychiatrist's couch, but as soon as our interest turns to action in larger settings, attention must be paid to the situations in which motives are expressed. A situation exerts an important press on the individual. It exercises constraints and may provide push. In certain circumstances it is not so much the kind of person a man is, as the kind of situation in which he is placed, that determines his actions.

Many people, not knowing much about the experiment, claim that subjects [72] who go to the end of the board are sadistic. Nothing could be more foolish than an overall characterization of these persons. It is like saying that a person thrown into a swift-flowing stream is necessarily a fast swimmer, or that he has great stamina because he moves so rapidly relative to the bank. The context of action must always be considered. The individual, upon entering the laboratory,

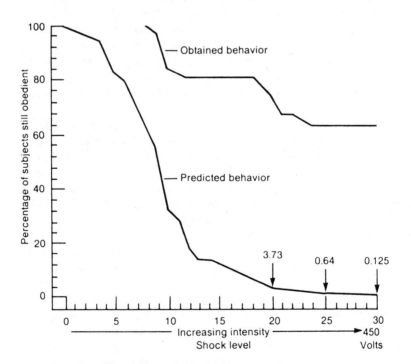

FIGURE 3. Predicted and obtained behavior in voice feedback.

becomes integrated into a situation that carries its own momentum. The subject's problem then is how to become disengaged from a situation which is moving in an altogether ugly direction.

The fact that disengagement is so difficult testifies to the potency of the forces that keep the subject at the control board. Are these forces to be conceptualized as individual motives and expressed in the language of personality dynamics, or are they to be seen as the effects of social structure and pressures arising from the situational field?

A full understanding of the subject's action will, I feel, require that both perspectives be adopted. The person brings to the laboratory enduring dispositions toward authority and aggression, and at the same time he becomes enmeshed in a social structure that is no less an objective fact of the case. From the standpoint of personality theory one may ask: What mechanisms of personality enable a person to transfer responsibility to authority? What are the motives underlying obedient and disobedient performance? Does orientation to authority lead to a short-circuiting of the shame-guilt system? What cognitive and emotional defenses are brought into play in the case of obedient and defiant subjects?

The present experiments are not, however, directed toward an exploration of the motives engaged when the subject obeys the experimenter's commands. Instead, they examine the situational variables responsible for the elicitation of obedience. Elsewhere, we have attempted to spell out some of the structural properties of the experimental situation that account for high obedience, and this analysis need not be repeated here (Milgram, 1963). The experimental variations themselves represent our attempt to probe that structure, by systematically changing it and noting the consequences for behavior. It is clear that some situations produce greater compliance with the experimenter's commands than others. However, this does not necessarily imply an increase or decrease in the strength of any single definable motive. Situations producing the greatest obedience could do so by triggering the most powerful, yet perhaps the most idiosyncratic, of motives in each subject confronted by the setting. Or they may simply recruit a greater number and variety of motives in their service. But whatever the motives involved—and it is far from certain that they can ever be known—action may be studied as a direct function of the situation in which it occurs. This has been the approach of the present study, where we sought to plot behavioral regularities against manipulated properties of the social field. Ultimately, social psychology would like to have a compelling *theory of situations* which will, first, present a language in terms of which situations can be defined; proceed to a typology of situations; and then point to the manner in which definable properties of situations are transformed into psychological forces in the individual.[12]

---

[12] My thanks to Professor Howard Leventhal of Yale for strengthening the writing in this paragraph.

POSTSCRIPT

Almost a thousand adults were individually studied in the obedience research, 76 and there were many specific conclusions regarding the variables that control obedience and disobedience to authority. Some of these have been discussed briefly in the preceding sections, and more detailed reports will be released subsequently.

There are now some other generalizations I should like to make, which do 77 not derive in any strictly logical fashion from the experiments as carried out, but which, I feel, ought to be made. They are formulations of an intuitive sort that have been forced on me by observation of many subjects responding to the pressures of authority. The assertions represent a painful alteration in my own thinking; and since they were acquired only under the repeated impact of direct observation, I have no illusion that they will be generally accepted by persons who have not had the same experience.

With numbing regularity good people were seen to knuckle under the de- 78 mands of authority and perform actions that were callous and severe. Men who are in everyday life responsible and decent were seduced by the trappings of authority, by the control of their perceptions, and by the uncritical acceptance of the experimenter's definition of the situation, into performing harsh acts.

What is the limit of such obedience? At many points we attempted to establish 79 a boundary. Cries from the victim were inserted; not good enough. The victim claimed heart trouble; subjects still shocked him on command. The victim pleaded that he be let free, and his answers no longer registered on the signal box; subjects continued to shock him. At the outset we had not conceived that such drastic procedures would be needed to generate disobedience, and each step was added only as the ineffectiveness of the earlier techniques became clear. The final effort to establish a limit was the Touch-Proximity condition. But the very first subject in this condition subdued the victim on command, and proceeded to the highest shock level. A quarter of the subjects in this condition performed similarly.

The results, as seen and felt in the laboratory, are to this author disturbing. 80 They raise the possibility that human nature or, more specifically, the kind of character produced in American democratic society cannot be counted on to insulate its citizens from brutality and inhumane treatment at the direction of malevolent authority. A substantial proportion of people do what they are told to do, irrespective of the content of the act and without limitations of conscience, so long as they perceive that the command comes from a legitimate authority. If in this study an anonymous experimenter could successfully command adults to subdue a fifty-year-old man and force on him painful electric shocks against his protests, one can only wonder what government, with its vastly greater authority and prestige, can command of its subjects. There is, of course, the extremely important question of whether malevolent political institutions could

or would arise in American society. The present research contributes nothing to this issue.

In an article titled "The Danger of Obedience," Harold J. Laski wrote: 81

> . . . civilization means, above all, an unwillingness to inflict unnecessary pain. Within the ambit of that definition, those of us who heedlessly accept the commands of authority cannot yet claim to be civilized men.
>
> . . . Our business, if we desire to live a life, not utterly devoid of meaning and significance, is to accept nothing which contradicts our basic experience merely because it comes to us from tradition or convention or authority. It may well be that we shall be wrong; but our self-expression is thwarted at the root unless the certainties we are asked to accept coincide with the certainties we experience. That is why the condition of freedom in any state is always a widespread and consistent skepticism of the canons upon which power insists.

REFERENCES

BUSS, ARNOLD H.
1961.   *The Psychology of Aggression.* New York and London: John Wiley.

KIERKEGAARD, S.
1843.   *Fear and Trembling.* English edition, Princeton: Princeton University Press, 1941.

LASKI, HAROLD J.
1929.   "The dangers of obedience." *Harper's Monthly Magazine*, 15 June, 1–10.

MILGRAM, S.
1961.   "Dynamics of obedience: experiments in social psychology." Mimeographed report, *National Science Foundation*, January 25.

———
1963. "Behavioral study of obedience." *J. Abnorm. Soc. Psychol.* 67, 371–378.

———
1964. "Issues in the study of obedience: a reply to Baumrind." *Amer. Psychol.* 1, 848–852.

MILLER, N.E.
1944.   "Experimental studies of conflict." In J. McV. Hunt (ed.), *Personality and the Behavior Disorders.* New York: Ronald Press.

SCOTT, J.P.
1958.   *Aggression.* Chicago: University of Chicago Press.

QUESTIONS

1. What did Milgram want to determine by his experiment? What were his anticipated outcomes?

2. What conclusions did Milgram reach about the extent to which ordinary individuals would obey the orders of an authority figure? Under what conditions is this submission most probable? Under what conditions is defiance most likely?

3. Describe the general procedures of this experiment. Some persons have questioned Milgram's methods. Do you think it is ethical to expose subjects without warning to experiments that might have a lasting effect on them? What such effects might this experiment have had?

4. One characteristic of this paper is Milgram's willingness to consider several possible explanations of the same phenomenon. Study the interpretations in paragraphs 28 through 35. What do you make of the range of interpretation there and elsewhere in the essay? How does Milgram achieve such a range?

5. A report such as Milgram's is not structured in the same way as a conventional essay. His research is really a collection of separate but related experiments, each one of which requires its own interpretation. Describe the groups into which these experiments fall. Which results seemed most surprising to you? Which were easiest to anticipate?

6. In Milgram's experiment, people who are responsible and decent in everyday life were seduced, he says, by trappings of authority. Most of us, however, like to believe that we would neither engage in brutality on our own nor obey directions of this kind. Has Milgram succeeded in getting you to question your own behavior? Would you go so far as to say that he forces you to question your own human nature?

7. In paragraph 46 Milgram comments, "Perhaps our culture does not provide adequate models for disobedience." What do you think of this hypothesis? Are there such models? Ought there to be? Have there appeared such models in the time since the experiment was conducted? Explain your stand on Milgram's statement.

8. If research in social psychology takes place in your school today, there is probably a panel of some sort that enforces guidelines on research with human subjects. Locate that board, if it exists, and find out whether this experiment could take place today. Report to your class on the rules that guide researchers today. Do you think those rules are wise?

9. What, in your opinion, should be the guidelines for psychological research with human subjects? List the guidelines you think are appropriate, and compare your list with the lists of your classmates. Would your guidelines have allowed Milgram's experiment?

10. Think of a situation in which you were faced with the moral and ethical dilemma of whether or not to obey a figure of authority. How did you behave? Did your behavior surprise you? Describe and explain that experience.

MAKING CONNECTIONS

1. One of the conditions of valid scientific research is the replicability of its experiments. When we are persuaded results are replicable, we are inclined to believe them valid. What provisions for replicability does Milgram make in his experiments? Compare his stance to that of Bruno Bettelheim, Oliver Sacks, or Clifford Geertz, whose observations are not replicable but who are also concerned with writing authoritative science.

2. Think of other essays in this collection in which ethical matters are at issue, particularly the ethics of composing some kind of story. Consider Annie Dillard's "Singing with the Fundamentalists," Dennis Hevesi's "Running Away," and Michael Brown's

"Love Canal and the Poisoning of America." In each of those studies, human subjects seem manipulated a little for the sake of the writer's interests. Perhaps you would prefer to offer another example. Whatever study you choose, compare it to Milgram's and discuss the two writers' sensitivity to their human subjects. Note also the last sentence of Milgram's first footnote. What choices does the writer have in the cases that interest you most?

WHY WOMEN AREN'T GETTING TO THE TOP

Susan Fraker

Susan Fraker is an associate editor at Fortune *magazine. Assisted by research associate David Weld Stevens, she wrote this essay for the April 16, 1984, issue of the magazine, where it appeared as the cover story. In the magazine's format, the title appeared in very heavy type. It was followed by a subheading in smaller type, designed to attract the reader's attention: "No women are on the fast track to the chief executive's job at any* Fortune *500 corporation. That's incongruous, given the number of years women have been working in management. The reasons are elusive and tough for management to deal with."*

Ten years have passed since U.S. corporations began hiring more than token 1 numbers of women for jobs at the bottom rung of the management ladder. A decade into their careers, how far up have these women climbed? The answer: not as far as their male counterparts. Despite impressive progress at the entry level and in middle management, women are having trouble breaking into senior management. "There is an invisible ceiling for women at that level," says Janet Jones-Parker, executive director of the Association of Executive Search Consultants Inc. "After eight or ten years, they hit a barrier."

The trouble begins at about the $75,000 to $100,000 salary level, and seems 2 to get worse the higher one looks. Only one company on *Fortune*'s list of the 500 largest U.S. industrial corporations has a woman chief executive. That woman, Katharine Graham of the Washington Post Co. (No. 342), readily admits she got the job because her family owns a controlling share of the corporation.

More surprising, given that women have been on the ladder for ten years, 3 is that none currently seems to have a shot at the top rung. Executive recruiters, asked to identify women who might become presidents or chief executives of *Fortune* 500 companies, draw a blank. Even companies that have women in senior management privately concede that these women aren't going to occupy the chairman's office.

Women have only four of the 154 spots this year at the Harvard Business 4 School's Advanced Management Program—a prestigious 13-week conclave to

462

which companies send executives they are grooming for the corridors of power. The numbers aren't much better at comparable programs at Stanford and at Dartmouth's Tuck School. But perhaps the most telling admission of trouble comes from men at the top. "The women aren't making it," confessed the chief executive of a *Fortune* 500 company to a consultant. "Can you help us find out why?"

All explanations are controversial to one faction or another in this highly charged debate. At one extreme, many women—and some men—maintain that women are the victims of blatant sexism. At the other extreme, many men— and a few women—believe women are unsuitable for the highest managerial jobs: they lack the necessary assertiveness, they don't know how to get along in this rarefied world, or they have children and lose interest in—or time for— their careers. Somewhere in between is a surprisingly large group of men and women who see "discrimination" as the major problem, but who often can't define precisely what they mean by the term.

The discrimination they talk about is not the simple-minded sexism of dirty jokes and references to "girls." It is not born of hatred, or indeed of any ill will that the bearer may be conscious of. What they call discrimination consists simply of treating women differently from men. The notion dumbfounds some male managers. You mean to say, they ask, that managerial women don't want to be treated differently from men in any respect, and that by acting otherwise— as I was raised to think only decent and gentlemanly—I'm somehow prejudicing their chances for success? Yes, the women respond.

"Men I talk to would like to see more women in senior management," says Ann Carol Brown, a consultant to several *Fortune* 500 companies. "But they don't recognize the subtle barriers that stand in the way." Brown thinks the biggest hurdle is a matter of comfort, not competence. "At senior management levels, competence is assumed," she says. "What you're looking for is someone who fits, someone who gets along, someone you trust. Now that's subtle stuff. How does a group of men feel that a woman is going to fit? I think it's very hard."

The experience of an executive at a large Northeastern bank illustrates how many managerial women see the problem. Promoted to senior vice president several years ago, she was the first woman named to that position. But she now believes it will be many years before the bank appoints a woman executive vice president. "The men just don't feel comfortable," she says. "They make all sorts of excuses—that I'm not a banker [she worked as a consultant originally], that I don't know the culture. There's a smoke screen four miles thick. I attribute it to being a woman." Similarly, 117 to 300 women executives polled recently by UCLA's Graduate School of Management and Korn/Ferry International, an executive search firm, felt that being a woman was the greatest obstacle to their success.

A common concern among women, particularly in law and investment 9
banking, is that the best assignments go to men. "Some departments—like sales
and trading or mergers and acquisitions — are considered more macho, hence
more prestigious," says a woman at a New York investment bank. "It's nothing
explicit. But if women can't get the assignments that allow them to shine, how
can they advance?"

Women also worry that they don't receive the same kind of constructive 10
criticism that men do. While these women probably overestimate the amount
of feedback their male colleagues receive, even some men acknowledge widespread male reluctance to criticize a woman. "There are vast numbers of men
who can't do it," says Eugene Jennings, professor of business administration at
Michigan State University and a consultant to a dozen large companies. A male
banking executive agrees: "A male boss will haul a guy aside and just kick ass
if the subordinate performs badly in front of a client. But I heard about a
woman here who gets nervous and tends to giggle in front of customers. She's
unaware of it and her boss hasn't told her. But behind her back he downgrades
her for not being smooth with customers."

Sometimes the message that has to be conveyed to a woman manager is 11
much more sensitive. An executive at a large company says he once had to tell
a woman that she should either cross her legs or keep her legs together when
she sat. The encounter was obviously painful for him. "She listened to me and
thanked me and expressed shock at what she was doing," he recalls, with a
touch of agony in his voice. "My God, this is something only your mother tells
you. I'm a fairly direct person and a great believer in equal opportunity. But it
was damn difficult for me to say this to a woman whom I view to be very proper
in all other respects."

Research by Anne Harlan, a human resource manager at the Federal Aviation 12
Administration, and Carol Weiss, a managing associate of Charles Hamilton
Associates, a Boston consulting firm, suggests that the situation doesn't necessarily improve as the number of women in an organization increases. Their
study, conducted at the Wellesley College Center for Research on Women and
completed in 1982, challenges the theory advanced by some experts that when
a corporation attained a "critical mass" of executive women—defined as somewhere between 30% and 35%—job discrimination would vanish naturally as
men and women began to take each other for granted.

Harlan and Weiss observed the effects of different numbers of women in an 13
organization during a three-year study of 100 men and women managers at two
Northeastern retailing corporations. While their sample of companies was not
large, after their results were published, other companies said they had similar
experiences. Harlan and Weiss found that while overt resistance drops quickly
after the first few women become managers, it seems to pick up again as the
number of women reaches 15%. In one company they studied, only 6% of the

managers were women, compared with 19% in the second company. But more women in the second company complained of discrimination, ranging from sexual harassment to inadequate feedback. Could something other than discrimination—very different corporate cultures, say—have accounted for the result? Harland and Weiss say no, that the two companies were eminently comparable.

Consultants and executives who think discrimination is the problem tend to 14 believe it persists in part because the government has relaxed its commitment to affirmative action, which they define more narrowly than some advocates do. "We're not talking about quotas or preferential treatment," says Margaret Hennig who, along with Anne Jardim, heads the Simmons College Graduate School of Management. "That's stupid management. We just mean the chance to compete equally." Again, a semantic chasm separates women and men. Women like Hennig and Jardim think of affirmative action as a vigorous effort on the part of companies to ensure that women are treated equally and that sexist prejudices aren't permitted to operate. Men think the term means reverse discrimination, giving women preferential treatment.

Legislation such as the Equal Employment Opportunity Act of 1972 prohibits 15 companies from discriminating against women in hiring. The laws worked well—indeed, almost too well. After seven or eight years, says Jennings of Michigan State, the pressure was off and no one pushed hard to see that discrimination was eliminated in selecting people for senior management. Jennings thinks the problem began in the latter days of the Carter Administration, when the economy was lagging and companies worried more about making money than about how their women managers were doing. The Reagan Administration hasn't made equal opportunity a priority either.

What about the belief that women fall behind not because of discrimination, 16 but because they are cautious, unaggressive, and differently motivated than men—or less motivated? Even some female executives believe that women derail their careers by choosing staff jobs over high-risk, high-reward line positions. One woman, formerly with a large consumer goods company and now president of a market research firm, urges women to worry less about sexism and more about whether the jobs they take are the right route to the top. "I spent five years thinking the only reason I didn't become a corporate officer at my former company was because of my sex," she says. "I finally had to come to grips with the fact that I overemphasized being a woman and underemphasized what I did for a living. I was in a staff function—the company didn't live and die by what I did."

Men and women alike tend to believe that because women are raised differ- 17 ently they must manage differently. Research to support this belief is hard to come by, though. The women retail managers studied by Harlan and Weiss, while never quarterbacks or catchers, had no trouble playing on management teams. Nor did they perform less well on standardized tests measuring qualities like assertiveness and leadership. "Women don't manage differently," Harlan says flatly.

In a much larger study specifically addressing management styles, psychol-   18
ogists Jay Hall and Susan Donnell of Teleometrics International Inc., a management training company, reached the same conclusion. They matched nearly 2,000 men and women managers according to age, rank in their organization, kind of organization, and the number of people they supervised. The psychologists ran tests to assess everything from managerial philosophies to the ability to get along with people, even quizzing subordinates on their views of the boss. Donnell and Hall concluded, "Male and female managers do not differ in the way they manage the organization's technical and human resources."

Data on how women's expectations—and therefore, arguably, their perfor-   19
mance—may differ from men's are more confusing. Stanford Professor Myra Strober studied 150 men and 26 women who graduated from the Stanford Business School in 1974. When she and a colleague, Francine Gordon, polled the MBAs shortly before graduation, they discovered that the women had much lower expectations for their peak earnings. The top salary the women expected during their careers was only 60% of the men's. Four years later the ratio had fallen to 40%.

Did this mean that women were less ambitious or were willing to take lower   20
salaries to get management jobs? Strober doesn't think so. She says a major reason for the women's lower salary expectations was that they took jobs in industries that traditionally pay less, but which, the women thought, offered opportunities for advancement. Almost 20% of the women in her sample went into government, compared with 3% of the men. On the other hand, no women went into investment banking or real estate development, which each employed about 6% of the men. Strober points out, however, that investment banking and big-time real estate were all but closed to women in the early 1970s. "One way people decide what their aspirations are," she says, "is to look around and see what seems realistic. If you look at a field and see no women advancing, you may modify your goals."

Some of what Mary Anne Devanna found in her examination of MBAs   21
contradicts Strober's conclusions. Devanna, research coordinator of the Columbia Business School's Center for Research in Career Development, matched 45 men and 45 women who graduated from the Columbia Business School from 1969 to 1972. Each paired man and woman had similar backgrounds, credentials, and marital status. The starting salaries of the women were 98% of the men's. Using data collected in 1980, Devanna found a big difference in the salaries men and women ultimately achieved, though. In manufacturing, the highest paying sector, women earned $41,818 after ten years vs. $59,733 for the men. Women in finance had salaries of $42,867 vs. $46,786 for the men.

The gap in the service industries was smallest: $36,666 vs. $38,600. She then tested four hypotheses in seeking to explain the salary differences: (1) that women are less successful because they are motivated differently than men, (2) that motherhood causes women to divert attention from their careers, (3) that women seek jobs in low-paying industries, and (4) that women seek types of jobs — in human resources, say—that pay less.

Devanna found no major differences between the sexes in the importance   22 they attached to the psychic or monetary rewards of work. "The women did not expect to earn less than the men," she says. Nor did she find that motherhood led women to abandon their careers. Although several women took maternity leaves, all returned to work full time within six months. Finally, Devanna found no big differences in the MBAs' choice of industry or function, either when they took their first jobs or ten years later.

Devanna concluded that discrimination, not level of motivation or choice   23 of job, accounted for the pay differences. Could the problem simply have been performance—that the women didn't manage as well as men? Devanna claims that while she couldn't take this variable into account specifically, she controlled for all the variables that should have made for a difference in performance— from family background to grades in business school.

In their discussions with male executives, researchers like Devanna hear a   24 recurrent theme—a conviction that women don't take their careers seriously. Even though most female managers were regarded as extremely competent, the men thought they would eventually leave—either to have children or because the tensions of work became too much. Both are legitimate concerns. A woman on the fast track is under intense pressure. Many corporate types believe that she gets much more scrutiny than a man and must work harder to succeed. The pressures increase geometrically if she has small children at home.

Perhaps as a result, thousands of women have careers rather than husbands   25 and children. In the UCLA-Korn/Ferry study of executive women, 52% had never married, were divorced, or were widowed, and 61% had no children. A similar study of male executives done in 1979 found that only 5% of the men had never married or were divorced and even fewer—3%—had no children.

Statistics on how many women bear children and then leave the corporation   26 are incomplete. Catalyst, a nonprofit organization that encourages the participation of women in business, studied 815 two-career families in 1980. It found that 37% of the new mothers in the study returned to work within two months; 68% were back after 4½ months; 87% in eight months. To a company, of course, an eight-month absence is a long time. Moreover, the 10% or so who never come back—most males are convinced the figure is higher—represent a substantial capital investment lost. It would be naive to think that companies don't crank this into their calculation of how much the women who remain are worth.

Motherhood clearly slows the progress of women who decide to take long   27 maternity leaves or who choose to work part time. But even those committed to working full time on their return believe they are sometimes held back—purposely or inadvertently. "Men make too many assumptions that women with children aren't free to take on time-consuming tasks," says Gene Kofke, director of human resources at AT&T. Karen Gonçalves, 34, quit her job as a consultant when she was denied challenging assignments after the birth of her daughter. "I was told clearly that I couldn't expect to move ahead as fast as I had been," she says. Later, when Gonçalves began working at the consulting firm of Arthur D. Little Inc. in Cambridge, Massachusetts, she intentionally avoided discussions of family and children: "I didn't keep a picture of my daughter in the office, and I would travel anywhere, no matter how hard it was for me."

Sometimes pregnancy is more of an issue for the men who witness it than   28
for the women who go through it. Karol Emmerich, 35, now treasurer of Dayton Hudson Corp., was the first high-level woman at the department-store company to become pregnant. "The men didn't really know what to do," she recalls. "They were worried when I wanted to take three months off. But they wanted to encourage me to come back. So they promoted me to treasurer when I was seven months pregnant. Management got a lot of good feedback." Emmerich's experience would please Simmons Dean Anne Jardim, who worries that most organizations aren't doing enough to keep women who want to have children. "It's mind-boggling," she argues. "Either some of the brightest women in this country aren't going to reproduce or the companies are going to write off women in whom they have a tremendous investment."

To the corporation it may seem wasteful to train a woman and then be   29
unable to promote her because she won't move to take the new job. The Catalyst study found that 40% of the men surveyed had moved for their jobs, vs. only 21% of the women. An argument can be made that an immobile executive is worth less to the corporation—and hence may be paid less.

Where women frequently do go is out of the company and into business for   30
themselves. "When the achievements you want aren't forthcoming, it makes going out on your own easier," says a woman who has set up her own consultancy. "I was told I wouldn't make it into senior management at my bank. Maybe I just didn't have it. But the bank never found any woman who did. They were operating under a consent decree and they brought in a lot of women at the vice president level. Every single one of them left." Karen Gonçalves left Arthur D. Little to do part-time teaching and consulting when she was pregnant with her second child. "I didn't think I would get the professional satisfaction I wanted at ADL," she says.

From 1977 to 1980, according to the Small Business Administration, the   31
number of businesses owned by women increased 33%, compared with an 11% increase for men—though admittedly the women's increase started from a much

smaller base. While it's not clear from the numbers that women are entering the entrepreneurial ranks in greater numbers than they are joining corporations, some experts think so. "It's ironic," says Strober of Stanford. "The problem of the 1970s was bringing women into the corporation. The problem of the 1980s is keeping them there."

A few companies, convinced that women face special problems and that it's   32
in the corporation's interest to help overcome them, are working hard at solutions. At Penn Mutual Life Insurance Co. in Philadelphia, where nearly half the managers are women, executives conducted a series of off-site seminars on gender issues and sex-role stereotypes. Dayton Hudson provides support (moral and financial) for a program whereby women in the company trade information on issues like personal financial planning and child care.

What women need most, the experts say, are loud, clear, continuing state-   33
ments of support from senior management. Women have come a long way at Merck, says B. Lawrence Branch, the company's director of equal employment affairs, because Chairman John J. Horan insisted that their progress be watched. Merck has a program that identifies 10% of its women and 10% of minorities as "most promising." The company prepares a written agenda of what it will take for them to move to the next level. Progress upward may mean changing jobs or switching functions, so Merck circulates their credentials throughout the company. "We have a timetable and we track these women carefully," says Branch. Since 1979 almost 40% of the net growth in Merck's managerial staff has been women.

Sensitive to charges of reverse discrimination, Branch explains that Merck   34
has for years singled out the best employees to make sure they get opportunities to advance. Women, he notes, were consistently underrepresented in that group. In his view the tracking program simply allows women to get into the competition with fast-track men. Others might not be so charitable. Any company that undertakes to do something on behalf of its managerial women leaves itself open to the charge that it too is discriminating—treating women and men differently.

What everyone may be able to agree on is that opening corporations to   35
competition in the executive ranks is clearly good for performance and profits. But how can a company do this? It can try to find productive part-time work for all employees who want to work part time—even managers. It can structure promotions so that fewer careers are derailed by an absence of a few months or the unwillingness to relocate. It can make sure that the right information, particularly on job openings, reaches everyone. Perhaps most importantly, it can reward its managers for developing talent of all sorts and sexes, penalize them if they don't, and vigilantly supervise the process.

QUESTIONS

1. The title of the essay implies that it will answer the question, "Why aren't women getting to the top?" Does it? What, if anything, have you learned about the problem?

2. Where there's a problem, there may be a solution. What does Fraker offer the reader beyond an explanation of the problem and an exploration of its possible causes?

3. The format of *Fortune* does not allow for footnotes, but Fraker mentions her sources regularly, and it is obvious that this essay is a version of a research paper. List the sources you can identify, in the order in which they are mentioned, to see how many sources were consulted and what range and variety of material it takes to produce an informative essay of this kind. How much of the information Fraker presents is based on private conversations or interviews, and how much comes from published documents or public records?

4. Fraker has to present a lot of information in this essay. What does she do to enliven and humanize her data? Look at particular passages that seem to you successful in turning abstractions into concrete form. How do different *kinds* of information work to prevent this from turning into a recital of dry abstractions?

5. How has Fraker organized the essay? What are the large subdivisions of the main topic?

6. Extend Fraker's study to your own school. Are women getting to the top there? Can you discover changes over the past ten years in numbers of women on the faculty, promotions to higher ranks, and so on? Are any women among your school's senior administrators, such as president, deans, or department heads? Write an essay in which you describe the situation, explain it, and, if it seems appropriate, suggest ways to change it. (Check on whether any plans for change are now in operation—and how they are working.) Use a mixture of statistical data and personal interviews as Fraker has.

7. Choose any minority group and consider their progress to the top in some organization for which you can obtain the relevant data. Using Fraker as a model, try to identify a problem, if there is one, explain its sources, and suggest solutions. If what you find is not a problem but a success story, try to explain how it happened and suggest how it might be repeated in other areas.

MAKING CONNECTIONS

1. Fraker, Tania Modleski, in "Soap Opera, Melodrama, and Women's Anger," and Carol Gilligan, in "Woman's Place in Man's Life Cycle," all express a feminist viewpoint. How similar are these viewpoints? Using these essays as examples, how unified do you take their positions to be?

2. Write an essay in which you define *feminism* and explain what you take to be its aims, using as evidence the essays by Fraker, Modleski, Gilligan, and any other specific examples you wish to cite. You might consider such subjects as what feminism is, what motivates feminists, what feminist goals and methods are, and what differences of approach you find within feminist studies.

WOMAN'S PLACE
IN MAN'S LIFE CYCLE
Carol Gilligan

Carol Gilligan (b. 1936) is a professor of education at Harvard University. The selection reprinted below is the first chapter of her book, In a Different Voice: Psychological Theory and Women's Development *(1982), which brought her to wide attention in the academic community and beyond it. In that book, as she says in her introduction, she reports on "research in progress whose aim is to provide, in the field of human development, a clearer representation of women's development which will enable psychologists and others to follow its course and understand some of the apparent puzzles it presents, especially those that pertain to women's identity formation and their moral development in adolescence and adulthood." Since publishing* In a Different Voice, *Gilligan has edited a collection of related studies,* Mapping the Moral Domain: A Contribution of Women's Thinking to Psychological Theory and Education *(1988).*

In the second act of *The Cherry Orchard*, Lopahin, a young merchant, 1 describes his life of hard work and success. Failing to convince Madame Ranevskaya to cut down the cherry orchard to save her estate, he will go on in the next act to buy it himself. He is the self-made man who, in purchasing the estate where his father and grandfather were slaves, seeks to eradicate the "awkward, unhappy life" of the past, replacing the cherry orchard with summer cottages where coming generations "will see a new life." In elaborating this developmental vision, he reveals the image of man that underlies and supports his activity: "At times when I can't go to sleep, I think: Lord, thou gavest us immense forests, unbounded fields and the widest horizons, and living in the midst of them we should indeed be giants"—at which point, Madame Ranevskaya interrupts him, saying, "You feel the need for giants—They are good only in fairy tales, anywhere else they only frighten us."

Conceptions of the human life cycle represent attempts to order and make 2 coherent the unfolding experiences and perceptions, the changing wishes and realities of everyday life. But the nature of such conceptions depends in part on the position of the observer. The brief excerpt from Chekhov's play suggests that when the observer is a woman, the perspective may be of a different sort.

471

Different judgments of the image of man as giant imply different ideas about human development, different ways of imagining the human condition, different notions of what is of value in life.

At a time when efforts are being made to eradicate discrimination between   3
the sexes in the search for social equality and justice, the differences between the sexes are being rediscovered in the social sciences. This discovery occurs when theories formerly considered to be sexually neutral in their scientific objectivity are found instead to reflect a consistent observational and evaluative bias. Then the presumed neutrality of science, like that of language itself, gives way to the recognition that the categories of knowledge are human constructions. The fascination with point of view that has informed the fiction of the twentieth century and the corresponding recognition of the relativity of judgment infuse our scientific understanding as well when we begin to notice how accustomed we have become to seeing life through men's eyes.

A recent discovery of this sort pertains to the apparently innocent classic *The*   4
Elements of Style by William Strunk and E. B. White. A Supreme Court ruling on the subject of sex discrimination led one teacher of English to notice that the elementary rules of English usage were being taught through examples which counterposed the birth of Napoleon, the writings of Coleridge, and statements such as "He was an interesting talker. A man who had traveled all over the world and lived in half a dozen countries," with "Well, Susan, this is a fine mess you are in" or, less drastically, "He saw a woman, accompanied by two children, walking slowly down the road."

Psychological theorists have fallen as innocently as Strunk and White into   5
the same observational bias. Implicitly adopting the male life as the norm, they have tried to fashion women out of a masculine cloth. It all goes back, of course, to Adam and Eve—a story which shows, among other things, that if you make a woman out of a man, you are bound to get into trouble. In the life cycle, as in the Garden of Eden, the woman has been the deviant.

The penchant of developmental theorists to project a masculine image, and   6
one that appears frightening to women, goes back at least to Freud (1905), who built his theory of psychosexual development around the experiences of the male child that culminate in the Oedipus complex. In the 1920s, Freud struggled to resolve the contradictions posed for his theory by the differences in female anatomy and the different configuration of the young girl's early family relationships. After trying to fit women into his masculine conception, seeing them as envying that which they missed, he came instead to acknowledge, in the strength and persistence of women's pre-Oedipal attachments to their mothers, a developmental difference. He considered this difference in women's development to be responsible for what he saw as women's developmental failure.

Having tied the formation of the superego or conscience to castration anxiety,   7
Freud considered women to be deprived by nature of the impetus for a clear-

cut Oedipal resolution. Consequently, women's superego—the heir to the Oedipus complex — was compromised: it was never "so inexorable, so impersonal, so independent of its emotional origins as we require it to be in men." From this observation of difference, that "for women the level of what is ethically normal is different from what it is in men," Freud concluded that women "show less sense of justice than men, that they are less ready to submit to the great exigencies of life, that they are more often influenced in their judgements by feelings of affection or hostility" (1925, pp. 257–258).

Thus a problem in theory became cast as a problem in women's development, and the problem in women's development was located in their experience of relationships. Nancy Chodorow (1974), attempting to account for "the reproduction within each generation of certain general and nearly universal differences that characterize masculine and feminine personality and roles," attributes these differences between the sexes not to anatomy but rather to "the fact that women, universally, are largely responsible for early child care." Because this early social environment differs for and is experienced differently by male and female children, basic sex differences recur in personality development. As a result, "in any given society, feminine personality comes to define itself in relation and connection to other people more than masculine personality does" (pp. 43–44). 8

In her analysis, Chodorow relies primarily on Robert Stoller's studies which indicate that gender identity, the unchanging core of personality formation, is "with rare exception firmly and irreversibly established for both sexes by the time a child is around three." Given that for both sexes the primary caretaker in the first three years of life is typically female, the interpersonal dynamics of gender identity formation are different for boys and girls. Female identity formation takes place in a context of ongoing relationship since "mothers tend to experience their daughters as more like, and continuous with, themselves." Correspondingly, girls, in identifying themselves as female, experience themselves as like their mothers, thus fusing the experience of attachment with the process of identity formation. In contrast, "mothers experience their sons as a male opposite," and boys, in defining themselves as masculine, separate their mothers from themselves, thus curtailing "their primary love and sense of empathic tie." Consequently, male development entails a "more emphatic individuation and a more defensive firming of experienced ego boundaries." For boys, but not girls, "issues of differentiation have become intertwined with sexual issues" (1978, pp. 150, 166–167). 9

Writing against the masculine bias of psychoanalytic theory, Chodorow argues that the existence of sex differences in the early experiences of individuation and relationship "does not mean that women have 'weaker' ego boundaries than men or are more prone to psychosis." It means instead that "girls emerge from this period with a basis for 'empathy' built into their primary definition of self in a way that boys do not." Chodorow thus replaces Freud's 10 negative and derivative description of female psychology with a positive and direct account of her own: "Girls emerge with a stronger basis for experiencing another's needs or feelings as one's own (or of thinking that one is so experiencing another's needs and feelings). Furthermore, girls do not define themselves in terms of the denial of preoedipal relational modes to the same extent as do boys. Therefore, regression to these modes tends not to feel as much a basic threat to their ego. From very early, then, because they are parented by a person of the same gender . . . girls come to experience themselves as less differentiated than boys, as more continuous with and related to the external object-world, and as differently oriented to their inner object-world as well" (p. 167).

Consequently, relationships, and particularly issues of dependency, are experienced differently by women and men. For boys and men, separation and individuation are critically tied to gender identity since separation from the mother is essential for the development of masculinity. For girls and women, issues of femininity or feminine identity do not depend on the achievement of separation from the mother or on the progress of individuation. Since masculinity is defined through separation while femininity is defined through attachment, male gender identity is threatened by intimacy while female gender identity is threatened by separation. Thus males tend to have difficulty with relationships, while females tend to have problems with individuation. The quality of embeddedness in social interaction and personal relationships that characterizes women's lives in contrast to men's, however, becomes not only a descriptive difference but also a developmental liability when the milestones of childhood and adolescent development in the psychological literature are markers of increasing separation. Women's failure to separate then becomes by definition a failure to develop.   11

The sex differences in personality formation that Chodorow describes in early childhood appear during the middle childhood years in studies of children's games. Children's games are considered by George Herbert Mead (1934) and Jean Piaget (1932) as the crucible of social development during the school years. In games, children learn to take the role of the other and come to see themselves through another's eyes. In games, they learn respect for rules and come to understand the ways rules can be made and changed.   12

Janet Lever (1976), considering the peer group to be the agent of socialization during the elementary school years and play to be a major activity of socialization at that time, set out to discover whether there are sex differences in the games that children play. Studying 181 fifth-grade, white, middle-class children, ages ten and eleven, she observed the organization and structure of their playtime activities. She watched the children as they played at school during recess and in physical education class, and in addition kept diaries of their accounts as to how they spent their out-of-school time. From this study, Lever reports sex   13 differences: boys play out of doors more often than girls do; boys play more often in large and age-heterogeneous groups; they play competitive games more often, and their games last longer than girls' games. The last is in some ways the most interesting finding. Boys' games appeared to last longer not only because they required a higher level of skill and were thus less likely to become boring, but also because, when disputes arose in the course of a game, boys were able to resolve the disputes more effectively than girls: "During the course of this study, boys were seen quarrelling all the time, but not once was a game terminated because of a quarrel and no game was interrupted for more than seven minutes. In the gravest debates, the final word was always, to 'repeat the play,' generally followed by a chorus of 'cheater's proof' " (p. 482). In fact, it seemed that the boys enjoyed the legal debates as much as they did the game itself, and even marginal players of lesser size or skill participated equally in these recurrent squabbles. In contrast, the eruption of disputes among girls tended to end the game.

Thus Lever extends and corroborates the observations of Piaget in his study 14 of the rules of the game, where he finds boys becoming through childhood increasingly fascinated with the legal elaboration of rules and the development of fair procedures for adjudicating conflicts, a fascination that, he notes, does not hold for girls. Girls, Piaget observes, have a more "pragmatic" attitude toward rules, "regarding a rule as good as long as the game repaid it" (p. 83). Girls are more tolerant in their attitudes toward rules, more willing to make exceptions, and more easily reconciled to innovations. As a result, the legal sense, which Piaget considers essential to moral development, "is far less developed in little girls than in boys" (p. 77).

The bias that leads Piaget to equate male development with child develop- 15 ment also colors Lever's work. The assumption that shapes her discussion of results is that the male model is the better one since it fits the requirements for modern corporate success. In contrast, the sensitivity and care for the feelings of others that girls develop through their play have little market value and can even impede professional success. Lever implies that, given the realities of adult life, if a girl does not want to be left dependent on men, she will have to learn to play like a boy.

To Piaget's argument that children learn the respect for rules necessary for 16 moral development by playing rule-bound games, Lawrence Kohlberg (1969) adds that these lessons are most effectively learned through the opportunities for role-taking that arise in the course of resolving disputes. Consequently, the moral lessons inherent in girls' play appear to be fewer than in boys'. Traditional girls' games like jump rope and hopscotch are turn-taking games, where competition is indirect since one person's success does not necessarily signify another's failure. Consequently, disputes requiring adjudication are less likely to occur. In fact, most of the girls whom Lever interviewed claimed that when a quarrel broke out, they ended the game. Rather than elaborating a system of rules for resolving disputes, girls subordinated the continuation of the game to the continuation of relationships.

Lever concludes that from the games they play, boys learn both the inde-   17
pendence and the organizational skills necessary for coordinating the activities of large and diverse groups of people. By participating in controlled and socially approved competitive situations, they learn to deal with competition in a relatively forthright manner—to play with their enemies and to compete with their friends—all in accordance with the rules of the game. In contrast, girls' play tends to occur in smaller, more intimate groups, often the best-friend dyad, and in private places. This play replicates the social pattern of primary human relationships in that its organization is more cooperative. Thus, it points less, in Mead's terms, toward learning to take the role of "the generalized other," less toward the abstraction of human relationships. But it fosters the development of the empathy and sensitivity necessary for taking the role of "the particular other" and points more toward knowing the other as different from the self.

The sex differences in personality formation in early childhood that Cho-   18
dorow derives from her analysis of the mother-child relationship are thus extended by Lever's observations of sex differences in the play activities of middle childhood. Together these accounts suggest that boys and girls arrive at puberty with a different interpersonal orientation and a different range of social experiences. Yet, since adolescence is considered a crucial time for separation, the period of "the second individuation process" (Blos, 1967), female development has appeared most divergent and thus most problematic at this time.

"Puberty," Freud says, "which brings about so great an accession of libido in   19
boys, is marked in girls by a fresh wave of *repression*," necessary for the transformation of the young girl's "masculine sexuality" into the specifically feminine sexuality of her adulthood (1905, pp. 220–221). Freud posits this transformation on the girl's acknowledgment and acceptance of "the fact of her castration" (1931, p. 229). To the girl, Freud explains, puberty brings a new awareness of "the wound to her narcissism" and leads her to develop, "like a scar, a sense of inferiority" (1925, p. 253). Since in Erik Erikson's expansion of Freud's psychoanalytic account, adolescence is the time when development hinges on identity, the girl arrives at this juncture either psychologically at risk or with a different agenda.

The problem that female adolescence presents for theorists of human devel-   20
opment is apparent in Erikson's scheme. Erikson (1950) charts eight stages of psychosocial development, of which adolescence is the fifth. The task at this stage is to forge a coherent sense of self, to verify an identity that can span the discontinuity of puberty and make possible the adult capacity to love and work. The preparation for the successful resolution of the adolescent identity crisis is delineated in Erikson's description of the crises that characterize the preceding four stages. Although the initial crisis in infancy of "trust versus mistrust"

anchors development in the experience of relationship, the task then clearly becomes one of individuation. Erikson's second stage centers on the crisis of "autonomy versus shame and doubt," which marks the walking child's emerging sense of separateness and agency. From there, development goes on through the crisis of "initiative versus guilt," successful resolution of which represents a further move in the direction of autonomy. Next, following the inevitable disappointment of the magical wishes of the Oedipal period, children realize that to compete with their parents, they must first join them and learn to do what they do so well. Thus in the middle childhood years, development turns on the crisis of "industry versus inferiority," as the demonstration of competence becomes critical to the child's developing self-esteem. This is the time when children strive to learn and master the technology of their culture, in order to recognize themselves and to be recognized by others as capable of becoming adults. Next comes adolescence, the celebration of the autonomous, initiating, industrious self through the forging of an identity based on an ideology that can support and justify adult commitments. But about whom is Erikson talking?

Once again it turns out to be the male child. For the female, Erikson (1968) says, the sequence is a bit different. She holds her identity in abeyance as she prepares to attract the man by whose name she will be known, by whose status she will be defined, the man who will rescue her from emptiness and loneliness by filling "the inner space." While for men, identity precedes intimacy and generativity in the optimal cycle of human separation and attachment, for women these tasks seem instead to be fused. Intimacy goes along with identity, as the female comes to know herself as she is known, through her relationships with others.   21

Yet despite Erikson's observation of sex differences, his chart of life-cycle stages remains unchanged: identity continues to precede intimacy as male experience continues to define his life-cycle conception. But in this male life-cycle there is little preparation for the intimacy of the first adult stage. Only the initial stage of trust versus mistrust suggests the type of mutuality that Erikson means by intimacy and generativity and Freud means by genitality. The rest is separateness, with the result that development itself comes to be identified with separation, and attachments appear to be developmental impediments, as is repeatedly the case in the assessment of women.   22

Erikson's description of male identity as forged in relation to the world and of female identity as awakened in a relationship of intimacy with another person is hardly new. In the fairy tales that Bruno Bettelheim (1976) describes an identical portrayal appears. The dynamics of male adolescence are illustrated archetypically by the conflict between father and son in "The Three Languages." Here a son, considered hopelessly stupid by his father, is given one last chance at education and sent for a year to study with a master. But when he returns, all he has learned is "what the dogs bark." After two further attempts of this sort, the father gives up in disgust and orders his servants to take the child into   23 the forest and kill him. But the servants, those perpetual rescuers of disowned and abandoned children, take pity on the child and decide simply to leave him in the forest. From there, his wanderings take him to a land beset by furious dogs whose barking permits nobody to rest and who periodically devour one of the inhabitants. Now it turns out that our hero has learned just the right thing: he can talk with the dogs and is able to quiet them, thus restoring peace to the land. Since the other knowledge he acquires serves him equally well, he emerges triumphant from his adolescent confrontation with his father, a giant of the life-cycle conception.

In contrast, the dynamics of female adolescence are depicted through the telling of a very different story. In the world of the fairy tale, the girl's first bleeding is followed by a period of intense passivity in which nothing seems to be happening. Yet in the deep sleeps of Snow White and Sleeping Beauty, Bettelheim sees that inner concentration which he considers to be the necessary counterpart to the activity of adventure. Since the adolescent heroines awake from their sleep, not to conquer the world, but to marry the prince, their identity is inwardly and interpersonally defined. For women, in Bettelheim's as in Erikson's account, identity and intimacy are intricately conjoined. The sex differences depicted in the world of fairy tales, like the fantasy of the woman warrior in Maxine Hong Kingston's (1977) recent autobiographical novel which echoes the old stories of Troilus and Cressida and Tancred and Chlorinda, indicate repeatedly that active adventure is a male activity, and that if a woman is to embark on such endeavors, she must at least dress like a man. [24]

These observations about sex difference support the conclusion reached by David McClelland (1975) that "sex role turns out to be one of the most important determinants of human behavior; psychologists have found sex differences in their studies from the moment they started doing empirical research." But since it is difficult to say "different" without saying "better" or "worse," since there is a tendency to construct a single scale of measurement, and since that scale has generally been derived from and standardized on the basis of men's interpretations of research data drawn predominantly or exclusively from studies of males, psychologists "have tended to regard male behavior as the 'norm' and female behavior as some kind of deviation from that norm" (p. 81). Thus, when women do not conform to the standards of psychological expectation, the conclusion has generally been that something is wrong with the women. [25]

What Matina Horner (1972) found to be wrong with women was the anxiety they showed about competitive achievement. From the beginning, research on human motivation using the Thematic Apperception Test (TAT) was plagued by evidence of sex differences which appeared to confuse and complicate data analysis. The TAT presents for interpretation an ambiguous cue—a picture about which a story is to be written or a segment of a story that is to be completed. Such stories, in reflecting projective imagination, are considered by psychologists to reveal the ways in which people construe what they perceive, [26] that is, the concepts and interpretations they bring to their experience and thus presumably the kind of sense that they make of their lives. Prior to Horner's work it was clear that women made a different kind of sense than men of situations of competitive achievement, that in some way they saw the situations differently or the situations aroused in them some different response.

On the basis of his studies of men, McClelland divided the concept of 27 achievement motivation into what appeared to be its two logical components, a motive to approach success ("hope success") and a motive to avoid failure ("fear failure"). From her studies of women, Horner identified as a third category the unlikely motivation to avoid success ("fear success"). Women appeared to have a problem with competitive achievement, and that problem seemed to emanate from a perceived conflict between femininity and success, the dilemma of the female adolescent who struggles to integrate her feminine aspirations and the identifications of her early childhood with the more masculine competence she has acquired at school. From her analysis of women's completions of a story that began, "after first term finals, Anne finds herself at the top of her medical school class," and from her observation of women's performance in competitive achievement situations, Horner reports that, "when success is likely or possible, threatened by the negative consequences they expect to follow success, young women become anxious and their positive achievement strivings become thwarted" (p. 171). She concludes that this fear "exists because for most women, the anticipation of success in competitive achievement activity, especially against men, produces anticipation of certain negative consequences, for example, threat of social rejection and loss of femininity" (1968, p. 125).

Such conflicts about success, however, may be viewed in a different light. 28 Georgia Sassen (1980) suggests that the conflicts expressed by the women might instead indicate "a heightened perception of the 'other side' of competitive success, that is, the great emotional costs at which success achieved through competition is often gained—an understanding which, though confused, indicates some underlying sense that something is rotten in the state in which success is defined as having better grades than everyone else" (p. 15). Sassen points out that Horner found success anxiety to be present in women only when achievement was directly competitive, that is, when one person's success was at the expense of another's failure.

In his elaboration of the identity crisis, Erikson (1968) cites the life of George 29 Bernard Shaw to illustrate the young person's sense of being co-opted prematurely by success in a career he cannot wholeheartedly endorse. Shaw at seventy, reflecting upon his life, described his crisis at the age of twenty as having been caused not by the lack of success or the absence of recognition, but by too much of both: "I made good in spite of myself, and found, to my dismay, that Business, instead of expelling me as the worthless imposter I was, was fastening upon me with no intention of letting me go. Behold me, therefore, in my twentieth year, with a business training, in an occupation which I detested as cordially as any sane person lets himself detest anything he cannot escape from. In March 1876 I broke loose" (p. 143). At this point Shaw settled down to study and write as he pleased. Hardly interpreted as evidence of neurotic anxiety about achievement and competition, Shaw's refusal suggests to Erikson "the extraordinary workings of an extraordinary personality [coming] to the fore" (p. 144).

We might on these grounds begin to ask, not why women have conflicts 30 about competitive success, but why men show such readiness to adopt and celebrate a rather narrow vision of success. Remembering Piaget's observation, corroborated by Lever, that boys in their games are more concerned with rules while girls are more concerned with relationships, often at the expense of the game itself—and given Chodorow's conclusion that men's social orientation is positional while women's is personal—we begin to understand why, when "Anne" becomes "John" in Horner's tale of competitive success and the story is completed by men, fear of success tends to disappear. John is considered to have played by the rules and won. He has the *right* to feel good about his success. Confirmed in the sense of his own identity as separate from those who, compared to him, are less competent, his positional sense of self is affirmed. For Anne, it is possible that the position she could obtain by being at the top of her medical school class may not, in fact, be what she wants.

"It is obvious," Virginia Woolf says, "that the values of women differ very 31 often from the values which have been made by the other sex" (1929, p. 76). Yet, she adds, "it is the masculine values that prevail." As a result, women come to question the normality of their feelings and to alter their judgments in deference to the opinion of others. In the nineteenth century novels written by women, Woolf sees at work "a mind which was slightly pulled from the straight and made to alter its clear vision in deference to external authority." The same deference to the values and opinions of others can be seen in the judgments of twentieth century women. The difficulty women experience in finding or speaking publicly in their own voices emerges repeatedly in the form of qualification and self-doubt, but also in intimations of a divided judgment, a public assessment and private assessment which are fundamentally at odds.

Yet the deference and confusion that Woolf criticizes in women derive from 32 the values she sees as their strength. Women's deference is rooted not only in their social subordination but also in the substance of their moral concern. Sensitivity to the needs of others and the assumption of responsibility for taking care lead women to attend to voices other than their own and to include in their judgment other points of view. Women's moral weakness, manifest in an apparent diffusion and confusion of judgment, is thus inseparable from women's moral strength, an overriding concern with relationships and responsibilities. The reluctance to judge may itself be indicative of the care and concern for others that infuse the psychology of women's development and are responsible for what is generally seen as problematic in its nature.

Thus women not only define themselves in a context of human relationship   33
but also judge themselves in terms of their ability to care. Woman's place in
man's life cycle has been that of nurturer, caretaker, and helpmate, the weaver
of those networks of relationships on which she in turn relies. But while women
have thus taken care of men, men have, in their theories of psychological
development, as in their economic arrangements, tended to assume or devalue
that care. When the focus on individuation and individual achievement extends
into adulthood and maturity is equated with personal autonomy, concern with
relationships appears as a weakness of women rather than as a human strength
(Miller, 1976).

The discrepancy between womanhood and adulthood is nowhere more evi-   34
dent than in the studies on sex-role stereotypes reported by Broverman, Vogel,
Broverman, Clarkson, and Rosenkrantz (1972). The repeated finding of these
studies is that the qualities deemed necessary for adulthood—the capacity for
autonomous thinking, clear decision-making, and responsible action—are those
associated with masculinity and considered undesirable as attributes of the
feminine self. The stereotypes suggest a splitting of love and work that relegates
expressive capacities to women while placing instrumental abilities in the masculine domain. Yet looked at from a different perspective, these stereotypes
reflect a conception of adulthood that is itself out of balance, favoring the
separateness of the individual self over connection to others, and leaning more
toward an autonomous life of work than toward the interdependence of love
and care.

The discovery now being celebrated by men in mid-life of the importance   35
of intimacy, relationships, and care is something that women have known from
the beginning. However, because that knowledge in women has been considered
"intuitive" or "instinctive," a function of anatomy coupled with destiny, psychologists have neglected to describe its development. In my research, I have
found that women's moral development centers on the elaboration of that
knowledge and thus delineates a critical line of psychological development in
the lives of both of the sexes. The subject of moral development not only
provides the final illustration of the reiterative pattern in the observation and
assessment of sex differences in the literature on human development, but also
indicates more particularly why the nature and significance of women's development has been for so long obscured and shrouded in mystery.

The criticism that Freud makes of women's sense of justice, seeing it as   36
compromised in its refusal of blind impartiality, reappears not only in the work
of Piaget but also in that of Kohlberg. While in Piaget's account (1932) of the
moral judgment of the child, girls are an aside, a curiosity to whom he devotes
four brief entries in an index that omits "boys" altogether because "the child"
is assumed to be male, in the research from which Kohlberg derives his theory,
females simply do not exist. Kohlberg's (1958, 1981) six stages that describe the
development of moral judgment from childhood to adulthood are based empir-

481

ically on a study of eighty-four boys whose development Kohlberg has followed for a period of over twenty years. Although Kohlberg claims universality for his stage sequence, those groups not included in his original sample rarely reach his higher stages (Edwards, 1975; Holstein, 1976; Simpson, 1974). Prominent among those who thus appear to be deficient in moral development when measured by Kohlberg's scale are women, whose judgments seem to exemplify the third stage of his six-stage sequence. At this stage morality is conceived in interpersonal terms and goodness is equated with helping and pleasing others. This conception of goodness is considered by Kohlberg and Kramer (1969) to be functional in the lives of mature women insofar as their lives take place in the home. Kohlberg and Kramer imply that only if women enter the traditional arena of male activity will they recognize the inadequacy of this moral perspective and progress like men toward higher stages where relationships are subordinated to rules (stage four) and rules to universal principles of justice (stages five and six).

Yet herein lies a paradox, for the very traits that traditionally have defined   37 the "goodness" of women, their care for and sensitivity to the needs of others, are those that mark them as deficient in moral development. In this version of moral development, however, the conception of maturity is derived from the study of men's lives and reflects the importance of individuation in their development. Piaget (1970), challenging the common impression that a developmental theory is built like a pyramid from its base in infancy, points out that a conception of development instead hangs from its vertex of maturity, the point toward which progress is traced. Thus, a change in the definition of maturity does not simply alter the description of the highest stage but recasts the understanding of development, changing the entire account.

When one begins with the study of women and derives developmental   38 constructs from their lives, the outline of a moral conception different from that described by Freud, Piaget, or Kohlberg begins to emerge and informs a different description of development. In this conception, the moral problem arises from conflicting responsibilities rather than from competing rights and requires for its resolution a mode of thinking that is contextual and narrative rather than formal and abstract. This conception of morality as concerned with the activity of care centers moral development around the understanding of responsibility and relationships, just as the conception of morality as fairness ties moral development to the understanding of rights and rules.

This different construction of the moral problem by women may be seen as   39 the critical reason for their failure to develop within the constraints of Kohlberg's system. Regarding all constructions of responsibility as evidence of a conventional moral understanding, Kohlberg defines the highest stages of moral development as deriving from a reflective understanding of human rights. That the morality of rights differs from the morality of responsibility in its emphasis on separation rather than connection, in its consideration of the individual rather than the relationship as primary, is illustrated by two responses to interview questions about the nature of morality. The first comes from a twenty-five-year-old man, one of the participants in Kohlberg's study:

> [*What does the word morality mean to you?*] Nobody in the world knows the answer. I think it is recognizing the right of the individual, the rights of other individuals, not interfering with those rights. Act as fairly as you would have them treat you. I think it is basically to preserve the human being's right to existence. I think that is the most important. Secondly, the human being's right to do as he pleases, again without interfering with somebody else's rights.
>
> [*How have your views on morality changed since the last interview?*] I think I am more aware of an individual's rights now. I used to be looking at it strictly from my point of view, just for me. Now I think I am more aware of what the individual has a right to.

Kohlberg (1973) cites this man's response as illustrative of the principled conception of human rights that exemplifies his fifth and sixth stages. Commenting on the response, Kohlberg says: "Moving to a perspective outside of that of his society, he identifies morality with justice (fairness, rights, the Golden Rule), with recognition of the rights of others as these are defined naturally or intrinsically. The human being's right to do as he pleases without interfering with somebody else's rights is a formula defining rights prior to social legislation" (pp. 29–30).

The second response comes from a woman who participated in the rights and responsibilities study. She also was twenty-five and, at the time, a third-year law student:

> [*Is there really some correct solution to moral problems, or is everybody's opinion equally right?*] No, I don't think everybody's opinion is equally right. I think that in some situations there may be opinions that are equally valid, and one could conscientiously adopt one of several courses of action. But there are other situations in which I think there are right and wrong answers, that sort of inhere in the nature of existence, of all individuals here who need to live with each other to live. We need to depend on each other, and hopefully it is not only a physical need but a need of fulfillment in ourselves, that a person's life is enriched by cooperating with other people and striving to live in harmony with everybody else, and to that end, there are right and wrong, there are things which promote that end and that move away from it, and in that way it is possible to choose in certain cases among different courses of action that obviously promote or harm that goal.
>
> [*Is there a time in the past when you would have thought about these things differently?*] Oh, yeah, I think that I went through a time when I thought that things were pretty relative, that I can't tell you what to do and you can't tell me what to do, because you've got your conscience and I've got mine.

[*When was that?*] When I was in high school. I guess that it just sort of dawned on me that my own ideas changed, and because my own judgment changed, I felt I couldn't judge another person's judgment. But now I think even when it is only the person himself who is going to be affected, I say it is wrong to the extent it doesn't cohere with what I know about human nature and what I know about you, and just from what I think is true about the operation of the universe, I could say I think you are making a mistake.

[*What led you to change, do you think?*] Just seeing more of life, just recognizing that there are an awful lot of things that are common among people. There are certain things that you come to learn promote a better life and better relationships and more personal fulfillment than other things that in general tend to do the opposite, and the things that promote these things, you would call morally right.

This response also represents a personal reconstruction of morality following 41 a period of questioning and doubt, but the reconstruction of moral understanding is based not on the primacy and universality of individual rights, but rather on what she describes as a "very strong sense of being responsible to the world." Within this construction, the moral dilemma changes from how to exercise one's rights without interfering with the rights of others to how "to lead a moral life which includes obligations to myself and my family and people in general." The problem then becomes one of limiting responsibilities without abandoning moral concern. When asked to describe herself, this woman says that she values "having other people that I am tied to, and also having people that I am responsible to. I have a very strong sense of being responsible to the world, that I can't just live for my enjoyment, but just the fact of being in the world gives me an obligation to do what I can to make the world a better place to live in, no matter how small a scale that may be on." Thus while Kohlberg's subject worries about people interfering with each other's rights, this woman worries about "the possibility of omission, of your not helping others when you could help them."

The issue that this woman raises is addressed by Jane Loevinger's fifth 42 "autonomous" stage of ego development, where autonomy, placed in a context of relationships, is defined as modulating an excessive sense of responsibility through the recognition that other people have responsibility for their own destiny. The autonomous stage in Loevinger's account (1970) witnesses a relinquishing of moral dichotomies and their replacement with "a feeling for the complexity and multifaceted character of real people and real situations" (p. 6). Whereas the rights conception of morality that informs Kohlberg's principled level (stages five and six) is geared to arriving at an objectively fair or just resolution to moral dilemmas upon which all rational persons could agree, the responsibility conception focuses instead on the limitations of any particular resolution and describes the conflicts that remain.

Thus it becomes clear why a morality of rights and noninterference may   43
appear frightening to women in its potential justification of indifference and
unconcern. At the same time, it becomes clear why, from a male perspective,
a morality of responsibility appears inconclusive and diffuse, given its insistent
contextual relativism. Women's moral judgments thus elucidate the pattern
observed in the description of the developmental differences between the sexes,
but they also provide an alternative conception of maturity by which these
differences can be assessed and their implications traced. The psychology of
women that has consistently been described as distinctive in its greater orientation toward relationships and interdependence implies a more contextual mode
of judgment and a different moral understanding. Given the differences in
women's conceptions of self and morality, women bring to the life cycle a
different point of view and order human experience in terms of different priorities.

The myth of Demeter and Persephone, which McClelland (1975) cites as   44
exemplifying the feminine attitude toward power, was associated with the Eleu-
sinian Mysteries celebrated in ancient Greece for over two thousand years. As
told in the Homeric *Hymn to Demeter*, the story of Persephone indicates the
strengths of interdependence, building up resources and giving, that McClelland
found in his research on power motivation to characterize the mature feminine
style. Although, McClelland says, "it is fashionable to conclude that no one
knows what went on in the Mysteries, it is known that they were probably the
most important religious ceremonies, even partly on the historical record, which
were organized by and for women, especially at the onset before men by means
of the cult of Dionysos began to take them over." Thus McClelland regards the
myth as "a special presentation of feminine psychology" (p. 96). It is, as well,
a life-cycle story par excellence.

Persephone, the daughter of Demeter, while playing in a meadow with her   45
girlfriends, sees a beautiful narcissus which she runs to pick. As she does so,
the earth opens and she is snatched away by Hades, who takes her to his
underworld kingdom. Demeter, goddess of the earth, so mourns the loss of her
daughter that she refuses to allow anything to grow. The crops that sustain life
on earth shrivel up, killing men and animals alike, until Zeus takes pity on
man's suffering and persuades his brother to return Persephone to her mother.
But before she leaves, Persephone eats some pomegranate seeds, which ensures
that she will spend part of every year with Hades in the underworld.

The elusive mystery of women's development lies in its recognition of the   46
continuing importance of attachment in the human life cycle. Woman's place
in man's life cycle is to protect this recognition while the developmental litany
intones the celebration of separation, autonomy, individuation, and natural
rights. The myth of Persephone speaks directly to the distortion in this view by
reminding us that narcissism leads to death, that the fertility of the earth is in

some mysterious way tied to the continuation of the mother-daughter relationship, and that the life cycle itself arises from an alternation between the world of women and that of men. Only when life-cycle theorists divide their attention and begin to live with women as they have lived with men will their vision encompass the experience of both sexes and their theories become correspondingly more fertile.

REFERENCES

Bettelheim, Bruno. *The Uses of Enchantment*. New York: Alfred A. Knopf, 1976.

Blos, Peter. "The Second Individuation Process of Adolescence." In A. Freud, ed., *The Psychoanalytic Study of the Child*, vol. 22. New York: International Universities Press, 1967.

Broverman, I., Vogel, S., Broverman, D., Clarkson, F., and Rosenkrantz, P. "Sex-role Stereotypes: A Current Appraisal." *Journal of Social Issues* 28 (1972): 59–78.

Chekhov, Anton. *The Cherry Orchard* (1904). In *Best Plays by Chekhov*, trans. Stark Young. New York: The Modern Library, 1956.

Chodorow, Nancy. "Family Structure and Feminine Personality." In M. Z. Rosaldo and L. Lamphere, eds., *Woman, Culture and Society*. Stanford: Stanford University Press, 1974.

Edwards, Carolyn P. "Societal Complexity and Moral Development: A Kenyan Study." *Ethos* 3 (1975): 505–527.

Erikson, Erik H. *Childhood and Society*. New York: W. W. Norton, 1950.

———. *Identity: Youth and Crisis*. New York: W. W. Norton, 1968.

Freud, Sigmund. *The Standard Edition of the Complete Psychological Works of Sigmund Freud*, trans. and ed. James Strachey. London: The Hogarth Press, 1961.

———. *Three Essays on the Theory of Sexuality* (1905). Vol. VII.

———. "Some Psychical Consequences of the Anatomical Distinction Between the Sexes" (1925). Vol. XIX.

———. "Female Sexuality" (1931). Vol. XXI.

Holstein, Constance. "Development of Moral Judgment: A Longitudinal Study of Males and Females." *Child Development* 47 (1976): 51–61.

Horner, Matina S. "Sex Differences in Achievement Motivation and Performance in Competitive and Noncompetitive Situations." Ph.D. Diss., University of Michigan, 1968. University Microfilms #6912135.

———. "Toward an Understanding of Achievement-related Conflicts in Women," *Journal of Social Issues* 28 (1972): 157–175.

Kingston, Maxine Hong. *The Woman Warrior*. New York: Alfred A. Knopf, 1977.

Kohlberg, Lawrence. "The Development of Modes of Thinking and Choices in Years 10 to 16." Ph.D. Diss., University of Chicago, 1958.

———. "Stage and Sequence: The Cognitive-Development Approach to Socialization." In D. A. Goslin, ed., *Handbook of Socialization Theory and Research*. Chicago: Rand McNally, 1969.

———. "Continuities and Discontinuities in Childhood and Adult Moral Development Revisited." In *Collected Papers on Moral Development and Moral Education*. Moral Education Research Foundation, Harvard University, 1973.

———. *The Philosophy of Moral Development*. San Francisco: Harper and Row, 1981.

Kohlberg, L., and Kramer, R. "Continuities and Discontinuities in Child and Adult Moral Development." *Human Development* 12 (1969): 93–120.
Lever, Janet. "Sex Differences in the Games Children Play." *Social Problems* 23 (1976): 478–487.
Loevinger, Jane, and Wessler, Ruth. *Measuring Ego Development.* San Francisco: Jossey-Bass, 1970.
McClelland, David C. *Power: The Inner Experience.* New York: Irvington, 1975.
Mead, George Herbert. *Mind, Self, and Society.* Chicago: University of Chicago Press, 1934.
Miller, Jean Baker. *Toward a New Psychology of Women.* Boston: Beacon Press, 1976.
Piaget, Jean. *The Moral Judgment of the Child* (1932). New York: The Free Press, 1965.
———. *Structuralism.* New York: Basic Books, 1970.
Sassen, Georgia. "Success Anxiety in Women: A Constructivist Interpretation of Its Sources and Its Significance." *Harvard Educational Review* 50 (1980): 13–25.
Simpson, Elizabeth L. "Moral Development Research: A Case Study of Scientific Cultural Bias." *Human Development* 17 (1974): 81–106.
Stoller, Robert J. "A Contribution to the Study of Gender Identity." *International Journal of Psycho-Analysis* 45 (1964): 220–226.
Strunk, William, Jr., and White, E. B. *The Elements of Style* (1918). New York: Macmillan, 1958.
Woolf, Virginia. *A Room of One's Own.* New York: Harcourt, Brace and World, 1929.

QUESTIONS

1. How would you summarize the main conclusions of this rather full and complex essay?

2. In its organization and procedures, this essay is similar to college research papers. Gilligan pursues a particular topic, the development of social values in women, and follows it through the research of many people. She uses the method of documentation considered standard in the social sciences: instead of footnotes, she mentions in her text the name of any author she cites, adding the publication date if she is using more than one work by that author, and giving a page reference for any direct quotation. A list of references gives the full title and publication data for each work cited. What are the advantages and disadvantages of this method as opposed to endnotes or footnotes?

3. Notice that Gilligan does not simply accept whatever her sources say. Find one or more examples of a source that she criticizes and a source that she accepts without criticism. How is she making these decisions? What are her grounds for criticizing or accepting her sources? Is it just a matter of whether she likes what they say, or does she have some principles that you can work out by looking at some specific examples?

4. Gilligan begins with fairy tales and ends with myths, but most of her essay draws upon social-science research. How do you account for her choice of opening and closing material?

5. How does Gilligan organize her essay? Is she making an argument, telling a story, surveying a field? What method does she use to order her many sources? Try to describe the structure that enables her to decide which sources go together. Can you divide the essay into sections with subtitles?

CAROL GILLIGAN

MAKING CONNECTIONS

1. Look at some of the other essays in this collection that are about the social or intellectual development of women (essays by Didion and Walker, for instance). Write an essay in which you test Gilligan's views against the specific material presented in some of these other essays. How does Didion's view of the life of Georgia O'Keefe support or qualify Gilligan's explanation of women's development?

2. Write an essay in which you apply Gilligan's conclusions about the differences between men and women to the problem Fraker examines in "Why Women Aren't Getting to the Top." Is it possible that there is something in the developed ethical values of most women that prevents them from succeeding in corporate America? If so, what do you think should be changed? What other relationships can be found between Gilligan's study and Fraker's?

OF COCKS AND MEN
Clifford Geertz

*Clifford Geertz (b. 1926) has been professor of social science
at the Institute for Advanced Study, Princeton, since 1970.
He is a noted anthropologist, whose published works have
helped to make a major change in the way anthropologists
conceive of their task. In particular, Geertz has argued that
social structures can be seen as "texts," akin to literary texts,
which must be interpreted not mechanically and statistically
but in a manner that fully engages the creative and interpretive powers of the analyst. His own researches began
with fieldwork in Java and Bali. He is especially interested
in economic and religious structures. Among his books are*
Negara: The Theatre State in Nineteenth-Century Bali
(1980) *and* Works and Lives: The Anthropologist as Author
(1988). *The following selection comes from "Deep Play," a
chapter from an earlier work,* The Interpretation of Cultures
(1973). *A still earlier version of this essay on the Balinese
cockfight appeared in* Daedalus *in 1972.*

Bali, mainly because it is Bali, is a well-studied place. Its mythology, art, 1
ritual, social organization, patterns of child rearing, forms of law, even styles
of trance, have all been microscopically examined for traces of that elusive
substance Jane Belo called "The Balinese Temper."[1] But, aside from a few
passing remarks, the cockfight has barely been noticed, although as a popular
obsession of consuming power it is at least as important a revelation of what
being a Balinese "is really like" as these more celebrated phenomena.[2] As much
of America surfaces in a ball park, on a golf links, at a race track, or around a
poker table, much of Bali surfaces in a cock ring. For it is only apparently cocks
that are fighting there. Actually, it is men.

To anyone who has been in Bali any length of time, the deep psychological 2
identification of Balinese men with their cocks is unmistakable. The double
entendre here is deliberate. It works in exactly the same way in Balinese as it
does in English, even to producing the same tired jokes, strained puns, and
uninventive obscenities. Bateson and Mead have even suggested that, in line

---

[1] J. Belo, "The Balinese Temper," in *Traditional Balinese Culture*, ed. J. Belo (New York,
1970) (originally published in 1935), pp. 85–110.
[2] The best discussion of cockfighting is again Bateson and Mead's *Balinese Character*, pp. 24–
25, 140; but it, too, is general and abbreviated.

with the Balinese conception of the body as a set of separately animated parts, cocks are viewed as detachable, self-operating penises, ambulant genitals with a life of their own.[3] And while I do not have the kind of unconscious material either to confirm or disconfirm this intriguing notion, the fact that they are masculine symbols par excellence is about as indubitable, and to the Balinese about as evident, as the fact that water runs downhill.

The language of everyday moralism is shot through, on the male side of it, with roosterish imagery. *Sabung*, the word for cock (and one which appears in inscriptions as early as A.D. 922), is used metaphorically to mean "hero," "warrior," "champion," "man of parts," "political candidate," "bachelor," "dandy," "lady-killer," or "tough guy." A pompous man whose behavior presumes above his station is compared to a tailless cock who struts about as though he had a large, spectacular one. A desperate man who makes a last, irrational effort to extricate himself from an impossible situation is likened to a dying cock who makes one final lunge at his tormentor to drag him along to a common destruction. A stingy man, who promises much, gives little, and begrudges that, is compared to a cock which, held by the tail, leaps at another without in fact engaging him. A marriageable young man still shy with the opposite sex or someone in a new job anxious to make a good impression is called "a fighting cock caged for the first time."[4] Court trials, wars, political contests, inheritance disputes, and street arguments are all compared to cockfights.[5] Even the very island itself is perceived from its shape as a small, proud cock, poised, neck extended, back taut, tail raised, in eternal challenge to large, feckless, shapeless Java.[6]

But the intimacy of men with their cocks is more than metaphorical. Balinese

---

[3] Ibid., pp. 25–26. The cockfight is unusual within Balinese culture in being a single-sex public activity from which the other sex is totally and expressly excluded. Sexual differentiation is culturally extremely played down in Bali and most activities, formal and informal, involve the participation of men and women on equal ground, commonly as linked couples. From religion, to politics, to economics, to kinship, to dress, Bali is a rather "unisex" society, a fact both its customs and its symbolism clearly express. Even in contexts where women do not in fact play much of a role— music, painting, certain agricultural activities—their absence, which is only relative in any case, is more a mere matter of fact than socially enforced. To this general pattern, the cockfight, entirely of, by, and for men (women—at least *Balinese* women—do not even watch), is the most striking exception.

[4] C. Hooykaas, *The Lay of the Jaya Prana* (London, 1958), p. 39. The lay has a stanza (no. 17) with the reluctant bridegroom use. Jaya Prana, the subject of a Balinese Uriah myth, responds to the lord who has offered him the loveliest of six hundred servant girls: "Godly King, my Lord and Master / I beg you, give me leave to go / such things are not yet in my mind; / like a fighting cock encaged / indeed I am on my mettle / I am alone / as yet the flame has not been fanned."

[5] For these, see V. E. Korn, *Het Adatrecht van Bali*, 2d ed. (The Hague, 1932), index under *toh.*

[6] There is indeed a legend to the effect that the separation of Java and Bali is due to the action of a powerful Javanese religious figure who wished to protect himself against a Balinese culture hero (the ancestor of two Ksatria castes) who was a passionate cockfighting gambler. See C. Hooykaas, *Agama Tirtha* (Amsterdam, 1964), p. 184.

men, or anyway a large majority of Balinese men, spend an enormous amount of time with their favorites, grooming them, feeding them, discussing them, trying them out against one another, or just gazing at them with a mixture of rapt admiration and dreamy self-absorption. Whenever you see a group of Balinese men squatting idly in the council shed or along the road in their hips down, shoulders forward, knees up fashion, half or more of them will have a rooster in his hands, holding it between his thighs, bouncing it gently up and down to strengthen its legs, ruffling its feathers with abstract sensuality, pushing it out against a neighbor's rooster to rouse its spirit, withdrawing it toward his loins to calm it again. Now and then, to get a feel for another bird, a man will fiddle this way with someone else's cock for a while, but usually by moving around to squat in place behind it, rather than just having it passed across to him as though it were merely an animal.

In the houseyard, the high-walled enclosures where the people live, fighting cocks are kept in wicker cages, moved frequently about so as to maintain the optimum balance of sun and shade. They are fed a special diet, which varies somewhat according to individual theories but which is mostly maize, sifted for impurities with far more care than it is when mere humans are going to eat it, and offered to the animal kernel by kernel. Red pepper is stuffed down their beaks and up their anuses to give them spirit. They are bathed in the same ceremonial preparation of tepid water, medicinal herbs, flowers, and onions in which infants are bathed, and for a prize cock just about as often. Their combs are cropped, their plumage dressed, their spurs trimmed, and their legs massaged, and they are inspected for flaws with the squinted concentration of a diamond merchant. A man who has a passion for cocks, an enthusiast in the literal sense of the term, can spend most of his life with them, and even those, the overwhelming majority, whose passion though intense has not entirely run away with them, can and do spend what seems not only to an outsider, but also to themselves, an inordinate amount of time with them. "I am cock crazy," my landlord, a quite ordinary *afficionado* by Balinese standards, used to moan as he went to move another cage, give another bath, or conduct another feeding. "We're all cock crazy."

The madness has some less visible dimensions, however, because although it is true that cocks are symbolic expressions or magnifications of their owner's self, the narcissistic male ego writ out in Aesopian terms, they are also expressions—and rather more immediate ones—of what the Balinese regard as the direct inversion, aesthetically, morally, and metaphysically, of human status: animality.

The Balinese revulsion against any behavior regarded as animal-like can hardly be overstressed. Babies are not allowed to crawl for that reason. Incest, though hardly approved, is a much less horrifying crime than bestiality. (The appropriate punishment for the second is death by drowning, for the first being forced to live like an animal.)[7] Most demons are represented—in sculpture, dance, ritual, myth—in some real or fantastic animal form. The main puberty rite consists in filing the child's teeth so they will not look like animal fangs. Not only defecation but eating is regarded as a disgusting, almost obscene activity, to be conducted hurriedly and privately, because of its association with animality. Even falling down or any form of clumsiness is considered to be bad for these reasons. Aside from cocks and a few domestic animals—oxen, ducks— of no emotional significance, the Balinese are aversive to animals and treat their large number of dogs not merely callously but with a phobic cruelty. In identifying with his cock, the Balinese man is identifying not just with his ideal self, or even his penis, but also, and at the same time, with what he most fears, hates, and ambivalence being what it is, is fascinated by—"The Powers of Darkness."

The connection of cocks and cockfighting with such Powers, with the ani- 8 malistic demons that threaten constantly to invade the small, cleared-off space in which the Balinese have so carefully built their lives and devour its inhabitants, is quite explicit. A cockfight, any cockfight, is in the first instance a blood sacrifice offered, with the appropriate chants and oblations, to the demons in order to pacify their ravenous, cannibal hunger. No temple festival should be conducted until one is made. (If it is omitted, someone will inevitably fall into a trance and command with the voice of an angered spirit that the oversight be immediately corrected.) Collective responses to natural evils—illness, crop failure, volcanic eruptions—almost always involve them. And that famous holiday in Bali, "The Day of Silence" (*Njepi*), when everyone sits silent and immobile all day long in order to avoid contact with a sudden influx of demons chased momentarily out of hell, is preceded the previous day by large-scale cockfights (in this case legal) in almost every village on the island.

In the cockfight, man and beast, good and evil, ego and id, the creative 9 power of aroused masculinity and the destructive power of loosened animality fuse in a bloody drama of hatred, cruelty, violence, and death. It is little wonder that when, as is the invariable rule, the owner of the winning cock takes the carcass of the loser—often torn limb from limb by its enraged owner—home to eat, he does so with a mixture of social embarrassment, moral satisfaction, aesthetic disgust, and cannibal joy. Or that a man who has lost an important fight is sometimes driven to wreck his family shrines and curse the gods, an act of metaphysical (and social) suicide. Or that in seeking earthly analogues for heaven and hell the Balinese compare the former to the mood of a man whose cock has just won, the latter to that of a man whose cock has just lost.

---

[7] An incestuous couple is forced to wear pig yokes over their necks and crawl to a pig trough and eat with their mouths there. On this, see J. Belo, "Customs Pertaining to Twins in Bali," in *Traditional Balinese Culture*, ed. J. Belo, p. 49; on the abhorrence of animality generally, Bateson and Mead, *Balinese Character*, p. 22.

QUESTIONS

1. Geertz's first paragraph is typical of many explanations, such as are found in professional writing and student research papers. Analyze this paragraph into sections and indicate what Geertz is trying to accomplish in each section. It may help you to pay particular attention to the conjunctions that divide and connect sentences. In particular, *but*, *as*, and *for*.

2. In paragraph 2, Geertz mentions "tired jokes, strained puns, and uninventive obscenities." What does he mean by these expressions? Why, in particular, do you suppose he uses the adjectives *tired*, *strained*, and *uninventive?*

3. In paragraph 6, Geertz refers to "the narcissistic male ego writ out in Aesopian terms." What do you think this means? In particular, discuss the words *narcissistic* and *Aesopian*. Where do those words come from? What does each mean—in general and in this context?

4. In this short essay (one of a series of "notes" on the subject of the Balinese cockfight) Geertz is neither telling a story nor making an argument. Thus, he adopts no ready-made pattern of organization for his material. How, in fact, does he organize it? Can you give certain sections or paragraphs titles that will reveal the structure of the essay?

5. Consider the description of Balinese men and their cocks in paragraph 4. What is the role of innuendo in this passage, and in the essay as a whole? How important is it in developing Geertz's explanation?

6. Do we have in American culture anything analogous to the Balinese cockfight—any form of "deep play" that reveals important things about the values of the whole society? Try to think of such a thing—some form of sport, game, or play—that is both popular and revealing about our lives. Write an essay in which you explain how this is.

MAKING CONNECTIONS

1. Compare Geertz's discussion of cockfighting with Ross's discussion of football and baseball given in the "Arts and Humanities" section. What similarities in method do you find in the two essays? Do the essays show significant differences either in approach or conclusions? Discuss the ways in which American sporting culture is like and unlike that of Bali. Are we different because we have different sports, or do we have different sports because we are unlike? Or are we not so unlike after all?

2. Compare Geertz's essay with Bruno Bettelheim's "Joey: A 'Mechanical Boy.'" Both essays describe carefully the particular behavior of a person or persons. Bettelheim's essay is a case study of a particular individual whereas Geertz's is a more generalized piece. Compare and contrast the needs of each kind of writing. Consider the "landlord" Geertz mentions in paragraph 5. Does that paragraph bear traces of a case study?

ON THE FEAR OF DEATH
Elizabeth Kübler-Ross

Elizabeth Kübler-Ross (b. 1926), a Swiss-American psychiatrist, is one of the leaders of the movement that may help change the way Americans think about death. Born in Zurich, she received her M.D. from the University of Zurich in 1957 and came to the United States as an intern the following year. Kübler-Ross began her work with terminally ill patients while teaching psychiatry at the University of Chicago Medical School. She now heads "Shanti Nilaya" (Sanskrit for "home of peace"), an organization she founded north of Escondido, California, in 1976, "dedicated to the promotion of physical, emotional, and spiritual health." "On the Fear of Death" is taken from her first and most famous book, On Death and Dying *(1969).*

Let me not pray to be sheltered from
dangers but to be fearless in facing
them.
Let me not beg for the stilling of
my pain but for the heart to conquer it.
Let me not look for allies in life's
battlefield but to my own strength.
Let me not crave in anxious fear to
be saved but hope for the patience to
win my freedom.
Grant me that I may not be a
coward, feeling your mercy in my
success alone; but let me find the grasp
of your hand in my failure.

Rabindranath Tagore, *Fruit-Gathering*

Epidemics have taken a great toll of lives in past generations. Death in   1
infancy and early childhood was frequent and there were few families who
didn't lose a member of the family at an early age. Medicine has changed
greatly in the last decades. Widespread vaccinations have practically eradicated
many illnesses, at least in western Europe and the United States. The use of
chemotherapy, especially the antibiotics, has contributed to an ever-decreasing
number of fatalities in infectious diseases. Better child care and education has

effected a low morbidity and mortality among children. The many diseases that have taken an impressive toll among the young and middle-aged have been conquered. The number of old people is on the rise, and with this fact come the number of people with malignancies and chronic diseases associated more with old age.

Pediatricians have less work with acute and life-threatening situations as they have an ever-increasing number of patients with psychosomatic disturbances and adjustment and behavior problems. Physicians have more people in their waiting rooms with emotional problems than they have ever had before, but they also have more elderly patients who not only try to live with their decreased physical abilities and limitations but who also face loneliness and isolation with all its pains and anguish. The majority of these people are not seen by a psychiatrist. Their needs have to be elicited and gratified by other professional people, for instance, chaplains and social workers. It is for them that I am trying to outline the changes that have taken place in the last few decades, changes that are ultimately responsible for the increased fear of death, the rising number of emotional problems, and the greater need for understanding of and coping with the problems of death and dying.

When we look back in time and study old cultures and people, we are impressed that death has always been distasteful to man and will probably always be. From a psychiatrist's point of view this is very understandable and can perhaps best be explained by our basic knowledge that, in our unconscious, death is never possible in regard to ourselves. It is inconceivable for our unconscious to imagine an actual ending of our own life here on earth, and if this life of ours has to end, the ending is always attributed to a malicious intervention from the outside by someone else. In simple terms, in our unconscious mind we can only be killed; it is inconceivable to die of a natural cause or of old age. Therefore death in itself is associated with a bad act, a frightening happening, something that in itself calls for retribution and punishment.

One is wise to remember these fundamental facts as they are essential in understanding some of the most important, otherwise unintelligible communications of our patients.

The second fact that we have to comprehend is that in our unconscious mind we cannot distinguish between a wish and a deed. We are all aware of some of our illogical dreams in which two completely opposite statements can exist side by side—very acceptable in our dreams but unthinkable and illogical in our wakening state. Just as our unconscious mind cannot differentiate between the wish to kill somebody in anger and the act of having done so, the young child is unable to make this distinction. The child who angrily wishes his mother to drop dead for not having gratified his needs will be traumatized greatly by the actual death of his mother—even if this event is not linked closely in time with his destructive wishes. He will always take part or the whole blame for the loss of his mother. He will always say to himself—rarely to others—"I did it, I am responsible, I was bad, therefore Mommy left me." It is well to remember that the child will react in the same manner if he loses a parent by divorce, separation, or desertion. Death is often seen by a child as an impermanent thing and has therefore little distinction from a divorce in which he may have an opportunity to see a parent again.

Many a parent will remember remarks of their children such as, "I will bury 6 my doggy now and next spring when the flowers come up again, he will get up." Maybe it was the same wish that motivated the ancient Egyptians to supply their dead with food and goods to keep them happy and the old American Indians to bury their relatives with their belongings.

When we grow older and begin to realize that our omnipotence is really not 7 so omnipotent, that our strongest wishes are not powerful enough to make the impossible possible, the fear that we have contributed to the death of a loved one diminishes—and with it the guilt. The fear remains diminished, however, only so long as it is not challenged too strongly. Its vestiges can be seen daily in hospital corridors and in people associated with the bereaved.

A husband and wife may have been fighting for years, but when the partner 8 dies, the survivor will pull his hair, whine and cry louder and beat his chest in regret, fear and anguish, and will hence fear his own death more than before, still believing in the law of talion—an eye for an eye, a tooth for a tooth—"I am responsible for her death, I will have to die a pitiful death in retribution."

Maybe this knowledge will help us understand many of the old customs and 9 rituals which have lasted over the centuries and whose purpose is to diminish the anger of the gods or the people as the case may be, thus decreasing the anticipated punishment. I am thinking of the ashes, the torn clothes, the veil, the *Klage Weiber* of the old days[1]—they are all means to ask you to take pity on them, the mourners, and are expressions of sorrow, grief, and shame. If someone grieves, beats his chest, tears his hair, or refuses to eat, it is an attempt at self-punishment to avoid or reduce the anticipated punishment for the blame that he takes on the death of a loved one.

This grief, shame, and guilt are not very far removed from feelings of anger 10 and rage. The process of grief always includes some qualities of anger. Since none of us likes to admit anger at a deceased person, these emotions are often disguised or repressed and prolong the period of grief or show up in other ways. It is well to remember that it is not up to us to judge such feelings as bad or shameful but to understand their true meaning and origin as something very human. In order to illustrate this I will again use the example of the child— and the child in us. The five-year-old who loses his mother is both blaming himself for her disappearance and being angry at her for having deserted him and for no longer gratifying his needs. The dead person then turns into some-

---

[1] *Klage Weiber:* wailing wives. [Eds.]

thing the child loves and wants very much but also hates with equal intensity for this severe deprivation.

The ancient Hebrews regarded the body of a dead person as something unclean and not to be touched. The early American Indians talked about the evil spirits and shot arrows in the air to drive the spirits away. Many other cultures have rituals to take care of the "bad" dead person, and they all originate in this feeling of anger which still exists in all of us, though we dislike admitting it. The tradition of the tombstone may originate in the wish to keep the bad spirits deep down in the ground, and the pebbles that many mourners put on the grave are leftover symbols of the same wish. Though we call the firing of guns at military funerals a last salute, it is the same symbolic ritual as the Indian used when he shot his spears and arrows into the skies. 11

I give these examples to emphasize that man has not basically changed. Death is still a fearful, frightening happening, and the fear of death is a universal fear even if we think we have mastered it on many levels. 12

What has changed is our way of coping and dealing with death and dying and our dying patients. 13

Having been raised in a country in Europe where science is not so advanced, where modern techniques have just started to find their way into medicine, and where people still live as they did in this country half a century ago, I may have had an opportunity to study a part of the evolution of mankind in a shorter period. 14

I remember as a child the death of a farmer. He fell from a tree and was not expected to live. He asked simply to die at home, a wish that was granted without question. He called his daughters into the bedroom and spoke with each one of them alone for a few moments. He arranged his affairs quietly, though he was in great pain, and distributed his belongings and his land, none of which was to be split until his wife should follow him in death. He also asked each of his children to share in the work, duties, and tasks that he had carried on until the time of the accident. He asked his friends to visit him once more, to bid goodbye to them. Although I was a small child at the time, he did not exclude me or my siblings. We were allowed to share in the preparations of the family just as we were permitted to grieve with them until he died. When he did die, he was left at home, in his own beloved home which he had built, and among his friends and neighbors who went to take a last look at him where he lay in the midst of flowers in the place he had lived in and loved so much. In that country today there is still no make-believe slumber room, no embalming, no false makeup to pretend sleep. Only the signs of very disfiguring illnesses are covered up with bandages and only infectious cases are removed from the home prior to the burial. 15

Why do I describe such "old-fashioned" customs? I think they are an indication of our acceptance of a fatal outcome, and they help the dying patient as well as his family to accept the loss of a loved one. If a patient is allowed to 16

497

terminate his life in the familiar and beloved environment, it requires less adjustment for him. His own family knows him well enough to replace a sedative with a glass of his favorite wine; or the smell of a home-cooked soup may give him the appetite to sip a few spoons of fluid which, I think, is still more enjoyable than an infusion. I will not minimize the need for sedatives and infusions and realize full well from my own experience as a country doctor that they are sometimes life-saving and often unavoidable. But I also know that patience and familiar people and foods could replace many a bottle of intravenous fluids given for the simple reason that it fulfills the physiological need without involving too many people and/or individual nursing care.

The fact that children are allowed to stay at home where a fatality has struck 17 and are included in the talk, discussions, and fears gives them the feeling that they are not alone in their grief and gives them the comfort of shared responsibility and shared mourning. It prepares them gradually and helps them view death as part of life, an experience which may help them grow and mature.

This is in great contrast to a society in which death is viewed as taboo, 18 discussion of it is regarded as morbid, and children are excluded with the presumption and pretext that it would be "too much" for them. They are then sent off to relatives, often accompanied by some unconvincing lies of "Mother has gone on a long trip" or other unbelievable stories. The child senses that something is wrong, and his distrust in adults will only multiply if other relatives add new variations of the story, avoid his questions or suspicions, shower him with gifts as a meager substitute for a loss he is not permitted to deal with. Sooner or later the child will become aware of the changed family situation and, depending on the age and personality of the child, will have an unresolved grief and regard this incident as a frightening, mysterious, in any case very traumatic experience with untrustworthy grownups, which he has no way to cope with.

It is equally unwise to tell a little child who lost her brother that God loved 19 little boys so much that he took little Johnny to heaven. When this little girl grew up to be a woman she never solved her anger at God, which resulted in a psychotic depression when she lost her own little son three decades later.

We would think that our great emancipation, our knowledge of science and 20 of man, has given us better ways and means to prepare ourselves and our families for this inevitable happening. Instead the days are gone when a man was allowed to die in peace and dignity in his own home.

The more we are making advancements in science, the more we seem to 21 fear and deny the reality of death. How is this possible?

We use euphemisms, we make the dead look as if they were asleep, we ship 22 the children off to protect them from the anxiety and turmoil around the house if the patient is fortunate enough to die at home, we don't allow children to visit their dying parents in the hospitals, we have long and controversial discussions about whether patients should be told the truth—a question that rarely arises when the dying person is tended by the family physician who has known him from delivery to death and who knows the weaknesses and strengths of each member of the family.

I think there are many reasons for this flight away from facing death calmly. One of the most important facts is that dying nowadays is more gruesome in many ways, namely, more lonely, mechanical, and dehumanized; at times it is even difficult to determine technically when the time of death has occurred. 23

Dying becomes lonely and impersonal because the patient is often taken out of his familiar environment and rushed to an emergency room. Whoever has been very sick and has required rest and comfort especially may recall his experience of being put on a stretcher and enduring the noise of the ambulance siren and hectic rush until the hospital gates open. Only those who have lived through this may appreciate the discomfort and cold necessity of such transportation which is only the beginning of a long ordeal—hard to endure when you are well, difficult to express in words when noise, light, pumps, and voices are all too much to put up with. It may well be that we might consider more the patient under the sheets and blankets and perhaps stop our well-meant efficiency and rush in order to hold the patient's hand, to smile, or to listen to a question. I include the trip to the hospital as the first episode in dying, as it is for many. I am putting it exaggeratedly in contrast to the sick man who is left at home—not to say that lives should not be saved if they can be saved by a hospitalization but to keep the focus on the patient's experience, his needs and his reactions. 24

When a patient is severely ill, he is often treated like a person with no right to an opinion. It is often someone else who makes the decision if and when and where a patient should be hospitalized. It would take so little to remember that the sick person too has feelings, has wishes and opinions, and has—most important of all—the right to be heard. 25

Well, our presumed patient has now reached the emergency room. He will be surrounded by busy nurses, orderlies, interns, residents, a lab technician perhaps who will take some blood, an electrocardiogram technician who takes the cardiogram. He may be moved to X-ray and he will overhear opinions of his condition and discussions and questions to members of the family. He slowly but surely is beginning to be treated like a thing. He is no longer a person. Decisions are made often without his opinion. If he tries to rebel he will be sedated and after hours of waiting and wondering whether he has the strength, he will be wheeled into the operating room or intensive treatment unit and become an object of great concern and great financial investment. 26

He may cry for rest, peace, and dignity, but he will get infusions, transfusions, a heart machine, or tracheotomy if necessary. He may want one single person to stop for one single minute so that he can ask one single question—but he will get a dozen people around the clock, all busily preoccupied with his heart rate, pulse, electrocardiogram or pulmonary functions, his secretions or excre- 27 tions but not with him as a human being. He may wish to fight it all but it is going to be a useless fight since all this is done in the fight for his life, and if they can save his life they can consider the person afterwards. Those who consider the person first may lose precious time to save his life! At least this seems to be the rationale or justification behind all this—or is it? Is the reason for this increasingly mechanical, depersonalized approach our own defensiveness? Is this approach our own way to cope with and repress the anxieties that a terminally or critically ill patient evokes in us? Is our concentration on equipment, on blood pressure, our desperate attempt to deny the impending death which is so frightening and discomforting to us that we displace all our knowledge onto machines, since they are less close to us than the suffering face of another human being which would remind us once more of our lack of omnipotence, our own limits and failures, and last but not least perhaps our own mortality?

Maybe the question has to be raised: Are we becoming less human or more human? . . . it is clear that whatever the answer may be, the patient is suffering more—not physically, perhaps, but emotionally. And his needs have not changed over the centuries, only our ability to gratify them. 28

QUESTIONS

1. Why does Kübler-Ross describe the death of a farmer? What point is she making in explaining "such 'old-fashioned' customs" (paragraph 16)?

2. To what extent is this essay explanatory? Summarize a particular explanation of hers that you find intriguing. Do you find it persuasive?

3. At what point in this essay does Kübler-Ross turn from explanation toward argument? Do you think she has taken a stand on her subject? How sympathetic are you to her position?

4. In paragraphs 2 and 10, Kübler-Ross indicates a specialized audience for her writing. Who is that audience, and how do you relate to it?

5. Think of the audience you described in question 4 as a primary audience and of yourself as a member of a secondary audience. To what extent do the two audiences overlap? How thoroughly can you divide one from the other?

6. What experience of death have you had so far? Write of a death that you know something about, even if your relation to it is distant, perhaps only through the media. Can you locate elements of fear and anger in your own behavior or in the behavior of other persons involved? Does Kübler-Ross's interpretation of those reactions help you come to terms with the experience?

7. What kind of balance do you think best between prolonging life and allowing a person to die with dignity? What does the phrase "dying with dignity" mean?

8. If you were told you had a limited time to live, how would that news change the way you are living? Or would it? Offer an explanation for your position.

MAKING CONNECTIONS

1. Read Richard Selzer's "The Discus Thrower" and Ernest Hemingway's "A New Kind of War." What, if any, intimations of Kübler-Ross's position do those essays show? What do you think Kübler-Ross would describe as optimum behavior in either of those cases?

2. Compare Kübler-Ross's account of our dealing with death and dying to Carol Gilligan's "Woman's Place in Man's Life Cycle." Kübler-Ross explains her own point of view as deriving from her European background coupled with moving to America and so having "had an opportunity to study a part of the evolution of mankind in a shorter period" (paragraph 14). But Gilligan might describe Kübler-Ross's point of view differently. What explanations does Gilligan offer that may also account for Kübler-Ross's point of view? How important do you think those factors are? Are they more or less important than Kübler-Ross's self-assessment of her position?

EDUCATION TO PREVENT AIDS: PROSPECTS AND OBSTACLES

Harvey V. Fineberg

Harvey V. Fineberg (b. 1945) is dean of the Harvard School of Public Health at Harvard University. An M.D. as well as a Ph.D., Fineberg has been active in clinical medicine and is the author of a number of articles on medical subjects and coauthor of two books, Clinical Decision Analysis *(1980) and* The Epidemic That Never Was *(1983). The article reprinted below appeared first in* Science *magazine in 1988. It follows the* Science *format, beginning with an abstract and using citations that refer to a numbered list of sources at the end of the text rather than footnotes.*

[Abstract.] *A number of obstacles thwart effective education to prevent AIDS in the United States. These include the biological basis and social complexity of the behaviors that must be changed, disagreement about the propriety of educational messages to prevent AIDS, uncertainty about the degree of risk to the majority of Americans, and dual messages of reassurance and alarm from responsible officials. Long-term protection of an individual from infection requires extreme changes in risk-taking behavior. Partial shifts toward safer practices may be epidemiologically important in retarding the rate and extent of spread of infection. Though some striking changes in behavior have occurred, especially in homosexual populations in areas with high prevalence of AIDS, educational efforts to date have succeeded more in raising awareness and knowledge about AIDS than in producing sufficient changes in behavior. The United States has yet to mount a nationwide comprehensive, intensive, and targeted education program to prevent AIDS.*

Today, most Americans view the acquired immunodeficiency syndrome (AIDS) as the most serious health threat confronting the United States (1). Approximately 50,000 Americans have been diagnosed with the disease since 1981 (2). More than half are dead, and no one with AIDS has yet been cured. While researchers seek more effective therapies and biological preventives, education and behavior change have been repeatedly and correctly cited as the only available means of curtailing the spread of the human immunodeficiency virus type 1 (HIV-1) responsible for AIDS. [1]

Extensive epidemiologic investigation has affirmed the principal means by [2] which HIV-1 is spread—blood, sex, and birth (3). In the United States, the major groups who have developed AIDS are men exposed by homosexual contact, intravenous drug users who use contaminated needles, hemophiliacs and blood recipients prior to institution of protective measures, and the offspring of infected mothers.

The virus can be transmitted sexually from men to women and from women to men, though those exposed exclusively by heterosexual contact represent a small fraction of the current U.S. case load (3). Transmission through occupational exposure in health workers and in laboratory technicians handling high concentrations of the virus has also been documented (4).

Understanding of the modes of spread of HIV-1, though incomplete, does provide assurance that individuals have the ability to eliminate or greatly reduce the risk that they will contract AIDS. The key recommendations are by now familiar to the informed public: sexually active men and women should maintain a mutually monogamous relationship, or practice exclusively safer sex (for example, avoiding semen contact of mucous membranes) or use a latex condom for every sexual intercourse, preferably in conjunction with a spermicide containing nonoxynol-9. Intravenous drug users can protect themselves by abstaining from drugs or by relying exclusively on sterile or properly cleaned needles and syringes with no sharing.

Thus, with AIDS, there are a number of ingredients that would appear to favor behavior change to protect health: a dreadful disease perceived as a major threat to the nation, appreciation of behavior change as the sole current means of stemming further spread of HIV-1, firm knowledge of modes of transmission, and clear-cut steps that individuals at risk can take to protect themselves. At the same time, formidable obstacles stand in the way of the kind of behavior change that will help prevent HIV-1 transmission. Here I review several of these obstacles and set expectations for AIDS education in the light of early experience in AIDS prevention. While health education has had some striking successes, the experience to date provides little assurance that current efforts will accomplish the sustained and extensive change needed to stem the AIDS epidemic with a high degree of certainty.

OBSTACLES TO EFFECTIVE AIDS EDUCATION

To be effective, AIDS education must lead to changes in behavior that eliminate or substantially reduce the risk of transmission of HIV-1. Communication of information is clearly an essential part of effective education, and is also alone clearly inadequate. The individual must also have the motivation and means to effect the desired changes. Sustained change also typically requires a reinforcing social environment that supports the new pattern of behavior. Five key obstacles to effective education are as follows.

1) Sexual practices and drug use are biologically based, socially complex

503

behaviors. Both derive from biological impulses that are hard to resist. Sexual attractiveness is a standard widely touted in our youth-oriented culture. Sexual activity may be spontaneous and unplanned and take place when judgment is clouded by alcohol consumption. Condoms may be rejected as unfamiliar, embarrassing, inappropriate, or compromising of pleasure. Sharing of needles has traditionally been part of the subculture among drug addicts. Addicts driven by withdrawal are likely to use the first available injection equipment. Such factors would tend to undermine efforts to change the most important behaviors that allow transmission of HIV-1.

2) There is fundamental disagreement about the propriety of educational messages to prevent AIDS. AIDS touches upon deep-seated fears and inhibitions in American society. For some, the only socially acceptable change is to have people altogether abandon certain behaviors. In this moralist view, it is wrong to have sexual relations outside of marriage and it is wrong to use drugs, hence it is wrong to advocate or even discuss anything (such as use of condoms or sterile needles) that would appear to condone these activities. Others take what might be called a rationalist view: behaviors that will occur and are dangerous should be modified so as to make them safer. Such philosophical differences underlie the reticence of many national leaders about AIDS education, controversies over the propriety of specific educational materials, and debates among Catholic prelates over teaching about condoms. Of course, there are numerous shadings of view in a pluralistic society such as ours. Some condone heterosexual relations among unmarried young adults yet judge homosexual relations as morally unacceptable. Some rationalists oppose teaching addicts to clean their injection equipment on the grounds that illicit drug use has many dangers apart from AIDS and therefore should only be discouraged. Insofar as a major public commitment is required for a potentially successful education effort, these differences in view must be confronted, itself a politically unattractive prospect.

3) The degree of risk to the majority of Americans is currently a matter of debate. In terms of the natural history of an epidemic, AIDS in the United States is still at an early stage. Available data on the changing prevalence of clinical disease are consistent with a wide range of models of the antecedent spread of HIV-1 infection (5). Reliable and pertinent data on the incidence of HIV-1 infection are relatively sparse, though data from testing of military recruits and blood donors would suggest the rates of infection may be leveling off in some groups (2). While the disease has reached saturation levels in some sexually active homosexual populations, it is not certain whether conditions in the United States will sustain an epidemic in the heterosexual population. The circumstances in some urban areas and geographic regions may be more conducive to a sustained epidemic than in other areas. While the prospect of widespread disease is sufficiently daunting and the possibility sufficiently high to make it prudent to act as though the epidemic can be sustained, it is not possible at this time to state with confidence the likelihood of that occurrence.

504

4) The feeling conveyed to the public from responsible officials about AIDS   10
in fact is ambivalent, both reassuring and alarming. Public health authorities
insist that HIV-1 is not transmitted through the air, by mosquito bites, or
through everyday interaction. At the same time, the public is told that AIDS is
everyone's problem, that women as well as men are at risk, and that taking
protective action is wise. The public is told that HIV-1 has been isolated from
saliva and tears, and that kissing on the cheek or even the lips will not transmit
AIDS. To the physician or epidemiologist schooled in the transmission of viral
disease, the dual message is eminently sensible. The layperson runs an understandable risk of confusion.

5) Long-term protection of an individual from infection requires extreme   11
changes in risk-taking behavior. To illustrate, let us consider a simple model
for sexual transmission of HIV-1 and examine the effects of reduction in the
number of partners and increased use of condoms. One can think of the model
as applying, for example, to the homosexual population in a city, though the
same reasoning would pertain to heterosexual transmission. Let us estimate the
cumulative risk of becoming infected with HIV-1 over a period of time involving
1000 sexual encounters. The risk of infection from a single unprotected exposure
to an infected person is assumed to be 0.01 and condoms are assumed to be
90% effective in stopping transmission (6). The actual risk of infection per
exposure would be expected to depend on the type of sexual activity and may
depend on the presence of genital lesions, specific viral strain and stage of
infection, and host genetic factors (3). The cumulative risk depends also on the
probability of selecting a partner who is infected, the number of different
partners, and the frequency of condom use. Table 1 shows the results for various
combinations of a number of partners, prevalence of infection in the population
of prospective sexual partners, and frequency of condom use.

Several observations stand out from these results. First, the cumulative   12
probabilities of infection are high because an individual can escape infection
only by successfully avoiding transmission at every sexual encounter; even one
failure is a failure for life. Perhaps more surprising is the fact that the increment
in risk when one goes from one to five or ten partners is much greater than the
increment in going from five or ten to fifty partners. Put another way, a sexually
active individual who may have 50 partners in the next 10 or 20 years, has less
to gain by reducing the number to five or ten than by going from five or ten
all the way to monogamy. Condom use is beneficial in reducing the cumulative
risk, though if the prevalence of infection in the population of prospective
partners is sufficiently high, even consistent condom use may not afford an
adequate measure of protection over the long term. The benefit gained from
use of condoms is more substantial in moving from half-time to every-time use
than in moving from no use to half-time use.

The main conclusions persist when various assumptions in the model are   13
modified. For example, if the population of potential partners contains a mi-

TABLE 1. Cumulative probability of HIV-1 infection from 1000 sexual exposures. For interpretation see text. Assumptions and calculation: (i) Risk (r) of infection from a single unprotected exposure = 0.01. (ii) Reduction in risk per exposure through use of condoms (c) = 0.90. (iii) Prevalence (p) of HIV-1 among potential partners is constant and selection of partners is random with respect to their probability of being infected. (iv) The number of exposures per partner using a condom (C) is the total number of exposures (1000) divided by the number of partners (m), the result multiplied by the frequency of condom use (0, 0.5, or 1.0). (v) The number of exposurers per partner without using a condom (NC) is the total number of exposures (1000) divided by the number of partners (m), the result multiplied by the frequency of condom nonuse (1.0, 0.5, or 0). Cumulative probability of infection = $1 - [p(1 - r)^{NC}(1 - \{1 - c\}r)^{C} + (1 - p)]^{m}$.

Prevalence of HIV-1 among potential partners	Frequency of condom use		
	NEVER	HALF-TIME	ALWAYS
One partner			
0.001	0.001	0.001	0.0006
0.01	0.01	0.01	0.006
0.05	0.05	0.05	0.03
0.25	0.25	0.25	0.16
0.50	0.50	0.50	0.32
Five partners			
0.001	0.004	0.003	0.0009
0.01	0.04	0.03	0.009
0.05	0.20	0.16	0.04
0.25	0.70	0.60	0.21
0.50	0.94	0.87	0.38
Ten partners			
0.001	0.006	0.004	0.001
0.01	0.06	.0.4	0.01
0.05	0.28	0.19	0.05
0.04			
0.25	0.82	0.67	0.21
0.50	0.98	0.91	0.39
Fifty partners			
0.001	0.009	0.005	0.001
0.01	0.09	0.05	0.01
0.05	0.37	0.23	0.05
0.25	0.90	0.73	0.22
0.50	0.99	0.93	0.39

nority who if infected are ten times as likely as others to transmit the virus, then as the number of partners increases, the cumulative probability of infection rises less steeply than in the case of uniform infectivity, yet the jump in risk from one partner to five or ten is still much greater than the jump from five or ten partners to fifty. If condoms are assumed to be more than 90% effective, this would accentuate the advantage in moving from half-time to every-time use compared to the smaller gain going from never used to half-time use. If the risk of transmission per exposure is very small (for example, 0.001) then the cumulative probability of infection is lowered much more by the consistent use of condoms than by reducing the number of partners. The implication overall is that if the goal of education and behavior change is individual long-term protection from risk of infection, the changes toward safer sex must be rather extreme.

Degrees of change in behavior that fail adequately to protect the individual   14
over a long period may nevertheless be beneficial in retarding the spread of HIV-1 infection in a population. Behavior change such as part-time use of condoms would tend to increase the number of contacts (that is, lengthen the time) required on average to transmit the virus. If the net rate of additions (transmission plus imports) to the infected pool falls below the rate of loss from the infected pool, then an epidemic will not be sustained. Short of stifling the epidemic altogether, prolonging the course of its development can provide time for other strategies of control and treatment to come into being. The precise impact on the course of the epidemic from a partial shift toward safer behavior in different populations at risk remains highly speculative at this time.

EVIDENCE OF THE EFFECTIVENESS OF AIDS EDUCATION

The homosexual communities in cities such as San Francisco and New   15
York, hardest hit by AIDS, were earliest to organize patient support services and an extensive array of educational interventions aimed at preventing spread of infection. These have included community outreach to promote wide participation, distribution of educational literature, broadcast media campaigns, individual counseling and testing, telephone hotlines, and peer discussion and support groups to reinforce change. A number of studies in San Francisco document dramatic changes in behavior (7–10). For example, 90% of a cohort of 125 homosexual men followed at the San Francisco City Clinic between 1978 and 1985 had reduced the reported number of nonsteady partners from a median of 16 to a median of 1 (7, 8). (It is interesting that men who seroconverted during the 7-year period showed a pattern of reduction in high-risk sexual practices similar to that for men who remained seronegative.) The AIDS Behavioral Research Project in San Francisco found substantial changes in reported behavior in a cohort of 454 homosexual men (9). Between November 1982 and May 1984, the average number of male partners in the preceding month

declined from 6.3 to 3.9, and the frequency of anal intercourse without using a condom dropped by more than 50%.

In view of my earlier comments about the limited long-term protection 16 afforded by partial movement toward safer sexual practices, it may be particularly useful to distinguish results in terms of the proportion of individuals who make extreme changes in behavior and the average change made by a group of individuals at risk. Study results reported on a cohort of 745 homosexual men in New York City permits such a distinction (11). In assessing behavior change between 1981 and 1985, Martin found that 40% had made some change toward safer sexual practices. While there was a decline of 72% in the mean reported number of partners, the proportion of the cohort who had become monogamous had increased only from 8 to 14%. Also, of those who reported being mono- gamous in 1981, only 9% had remained so by 1985. Monogamy, of course, refers to a state that is sustained over time, and the proportion of individuals reporting monogamy for a limited time should be regarded as the upper estimate of the number who remain monogamous.

Studies of homosexual men in other cities have also revealed evidence of 17 change toward safer sexual practices, though less striking than in San Francisco. For example, the Multicenter AIDS Cohort Study is following nearly 5000 homosexual or bisexual men (12). Between 1984 and 1986, the proportion reporting either celibacy or monogamy increased from 14 to 39%, and the proportion not practicing receptive anal intercourse increased from 26 to 49%. While the use of condoms doubled, fewer than one-third reported using them in 1986. In a Pittsburgh study of a cohort of homosexual and bisexual men in 1986, more than 60% reported they never or hardly ever used a condom, even though 90% had agreed that condoms can reduce the spread of AIDS (13). More than 70% of the men reported having two or more sexual partners in the preceding 6 months.

Overall, it seems clear that substantial changes in behavior can be effected 18 in populations of homosexual and bisexual men, particularly in geographic areas with relatively large numbers of AIDS cases and a well-organized gay community. Less clear is whether behavior change can be accomplished suffi- ciently soon, by sufficient numbers of individuals, and in sufficient degree and duration to be personally significant (in terms of an individual's long-term risk of infection) and epidemiologically significant (in terms of stifling spread of the virus). The reduction in HIV-1 transmission found in recent years in the homosexual population of San Francisco (10) brings scant comfort when half or more are already infected.

A number of U.S. cities have introduced educational and behavior change 19 programs intended to reduce dependence on intravenous drugs and to reduce the risk of HIV-1 transmission among intravenous drug abusers. These programs have included expanded methadone and residential treatment programs, vouch- ers for entry into detoxification programs, and various outreach efforts to addicts

(14–16). The National Institute on Drug Abuse recently inaugurated a $10-million program in six cities to test various strategies for reducing risk behaviors among intravenous drug abusers, their sexual partners, and prostitutes.

U.S. officials have been reluctant to undertake needle exchange programs,   20
though these have been conducted in the Netherlands apparently without increasing the number of addicts or reducing entry into treatment programs (17). There is evidence for widespread awareness of AIDS among addicts in New York and for an increase in demand for needles believed to be sterile (18).

The outreach efforts in American cities, some utilizing ex-addicts, aim to   21
increase understanding of risks and of ways to clean needles and syringes. In one such program among Baltimore addicts, knowledge about AIDS and risks of transmission increased significantly, though there were no significant changes in needle-sharing behavior (15). Despite a belief by 93% of addicts in a Sacramento study that they would eventually acquire HIV-1 infection from sharing injection equipment, more than three-fourths continued to share needles and syringes (19). Preliminary evidence from a study of San Francisco addicts suggests that providing bleach or other cleaning agents as well as instruction in their use may be more successful in promoting cleaning of injection equipment (16).

Overall, where measured effects have been reported, behavior change to   22
reduce risk of HIV-1 transmission has been less widely adopted among intravenous drug abusers than among some homosexual populations. This is consistent with an analysis of changes in the incidence patterns of hepatitis B in four disparate U.S. counties showing a decline in cases associated with homosexual behavior (from 20% of cases in 1985 to 9% of cases in 1986) at the same time as the number of cases related to intravenous drug abuse rose in absolute numbers and as a proportion of the total (from 16 to 27% of cases) (20).

The general public has been barraged with information about AIDS from   23
the print and broadcast media. Orchestrated campaigns sponsored by the Centers for Disease Control and others conducted in various communities represent only a small fraction of the total coverage given to the many facets of AIDS. By early 1987, more than half of the nation's 73 largest school districts had in place some form of AIDS education program (21). Recently, the Centers for Disease Control provided more than $7 million to state and local agencies to improve AIDS education in the schools. According to preliminary results from the National Center for Health Statistics National Health Interview Survey of August 1987, 92% of the public know that a person can get AIDS by having sex with someone who is infected, and more than 80% believe condoms are a somewhat or very effective way to avoid getting the disease (22). Misunderstandings about transmission persist: shared eating utensils are considered a likely mode of transmission by 47%, mosquito bites by 38%, public toilets by 31%, donating blood by 25%, and working near someone with AIDS by 21%.

To date, relatively few assessments have examined the impact of specific   24

509

communication campaigns on the reported behavior (as distinct from knowledge and attitudes) of the heterosexual population. An advertising campaign in New York City in 1987 was directed especially at AIDS prevention in unmarried, sexually active men and women between the ages of 18 and 34. One purpose of the campaign was to convince sexually active young people that condoms will add a measure of protection against HIV-1. A telephone survey designed to sample the distribution by age, race, and ethnic groups in the target population was carried out before and after the campaign (23). Awareness of sexual transmission of HIV-1 was increased and more than 80% agreed that sexually active people should carry condoms and women should tell their sexual partner to use a condom. Yet, the reported numbers and frequency of sexual contacts in the preceding month had not changed and more than 60% failed to use a condom more than just some of the time.

The burden of AIDS is being borne disproportionately among the black and   25
Hispanic communities, where the prevalence of disease is more than double that for whites. National attention to the problem was catalyzed by a conference at the Centers for Disease Control in August 1987, and a number of programs targeted specifically to the minority community are beginning. The effects on behavior of preventive interventions in minority populations will be especially important. AIDS education in minority communities must deal with all the major risk activities because all contribute to the burden of illness. The special needs of the minority population, itself a composite of many communities, will require culturally specific interventions. If AIDS can become a self-sustaining epidemic in some heterosexual U.S. populations, it is reasonable to expect that this will become evident first in the urban minority areas where the disease is currently most prevalent.

PROSPECTS FOR THE FUTURE

For the most part, those who will develop AIDS in the next 5 years have   26
already been infected with HIV-1. Even a spectacularly successful AIDs education program could not alter the course of the epidemic in the near term. The best that prevention of virus transmission can achieve is a reduction in cases of clinical disease in the intermediate and long terms.

Communicating accurate information to everyone at risk of infection is   27
difficult enough and yet is only a first step in the educational task ahead. Most people who can already answer questions correctly about sexual transmission of HIV-1 and the risks of sharing needles are not modifying their sexual activity and drug behavior accordingly.

Changes in behavior that will reduce risk of acquiring HIV-1 depend upon   28
individual motivation and a reinforcing social environment. In the August 1987 National Health Interview Survey, nine out of ten Americans reportedly viewed their own risk of getting AIDS as low or nonexistent (22, 24). Lacking perceived

vulnerability, a person is unlikely to change customary habits and behaviors, especially ones that are biologically driven. Aware as we are of biological drives, we are usually unconscious of the powerful social and psychological factors that shape our everyday behavior—how we dress, when and what we eat, what we say to one another, and so forth. If there is to be a widespread and persistent shift in behavior related to sex and drugs, it must be grounded in a shift in social norms. Is it imaginable that one day an unmarried couple will find unthinkable the prospect of sexual relations without a condom? That every homosexual couple will practice exclusively safer sex? That every intravenous drug user who cannot quit will incorporate needle cleaning procedures into the ritual of drug use?

The honest answer to such questions must be: not soon and only with a 29 sustained struggle, if at all. To the strict moralist, these are not even the right questions because they concede: unacceptable activities—sexual relations outside of marriage, homosexuality, and illicit drug use.

The history of sexually transmitted disease in the United States is replete 30 with clashes between moral and pragmatic approaches (25). During World War II, the Army aggressively warned troops about the dangers of venereal disease and actively promoted condoms with the slogan, "If you can't say no, take a pro [a prophylactic or condom]." Outraged critics did force withdrawal of several graphic educational films which were said to promote promiscuity. Still, the military sold or distributed freely as many as 50 million condoms each month during the war, and between 1940 and 1943 (prior to the introduction of penicillin), the venereal disease rate in the Army fell from 42.5 to 25 per thousand (26).

When social change occurs, the evolution of life-style and habit can unfold 31 over a period of decades, or longer. Since the first Surgeon General's Report on the Health Consequences of Smoking in 1964, for example, more than 37 million Americans have given up smoking, and the proportion of adults who smoke has declined from 42% in 1965 to less than 30% today (27). Progress has been uneven in that the rate of smoking among women aged 20 to 24 years actually increased in the early 1980's, smoking is disproportionately prevalent in lower socioeconomic groups, and adults who continue to smoke appear to be smoking more than the average smoker in the past (27). Yet, social attitudes are clearly turning against smoking. One can envision the day in a smoke-free society when medical historians will look back quizzically on the 20th century as the age of tobacco.

The capacity to mobilize a social and personal will to prevent AIDS may 32 depend critically on evidence about the rapidity and extent of spread of HIV-1. Active and sensitive surveillance systems for tracking the incidence of HIV-1 infection therefore are an essential underpinning of AIDS prevention. The proportion of Americans who report they know someone with AIDS grew from 4 to 6% between October 1986 and October 1987 (28). Perhaps, as more people are touched personally by AIDS, our collective resolve to stem the epidemic will be fortified. These considerations point to a sad, and somewhat paradoxical, impression: our country may have to experience more spread of infection in order to prevent spread.

A realistic appreciation of the many obstacles besetting AIDS prevention [33] must not deter those who value human life from pressing ahead with every ounce of skill, vigor, imagination, and determination to inform, empower the individual, and create a social environment supportive of behavior changes. Although partial shifts toward safer behaviors will not assure adequate long-term protection to every individual at risk, such changes may nevertheless spell the difference between a serious and a catastrophic epidemic. In the United States and many other countries, the AIDS epidemic is an unprecedented threat in modern times, and it demands an unprecedented response. Despite many hundreds of dedicated individuals working on AIDS prevention in communities throughout the United States, despite the federal and state investments beginning to be made in AIDS education, our nation has yet to mount a coordinated, intensive, and comprehensive AIDS prevention program. In this sense, education to prevent AIDS has not been given the full-scale test it deserves. The best we can do in AIDS education offers no guarantee of success. To do less invites failure.

REFERENCES AND NOTES

1. Gallup poll conducted October 1987. *The New York Times*, 29 November 1987, p. 26.
2. Centers for Disease Control (CDC), *Morbid. Mortal. Wkly. Rep.* 36, 801 (1987).
3. G. H. Friedland and R. S. Klein, *N. Engl. J. Med.* 317, 1125 (1987).
4. CDC, *Morbid. Mortal. Wkly. Rep.* 36, 285 (1987); S. H. Weiss *et. al.*, *Science* 239, 68 (1988).
5. V. De Gruttola and K. H. Mayer, *Rev. Infect. Dis.* 10, 138 (1988).
6. The risk of infection from a single sexual exposure to an infected person and the degree of infection afforded in practice by use of a condom are uncertain. Later discussion takes account of possible ranges in these estimates.
7. L. S. Doll *et al.*, in (8), p. 213.
8. Third International Conference on AIDS, Washington DC, 1 to 5 June 1987, Abstracts Volume.
9. L. McKusick *et al.*, *Public Health Rep.* 100, 622 (1985).
10. W. Winkelstein, Jr., *et al.*, *Am. J. Public Health* 76, 685 (1987).
11. J. L. Martin, *Health Education Quarterly* 13, 347 (1986); *Am. J. Public Health* 77, 578 (1987).
12. R. Fox *et al.*, in (8), p. 213.
13. R. O. Valdiserri *et al.*, in (8), p. 213.
14. J. Jackson *et al.*, in (8), p. 45.
15. W. E. McCauliffe *et al.*, (8), p. 40.
16. J. K. Watters, in (8), p. 60.

17. E. C. Buning, in (8), p. 40.

18. D. C. Des Jarlais, S. R. Friedman, W. Hopkins, *Ann. Intern. Med.* 103, 755 (1985).

19. N. M. Flynn *et al.*, (8), p. 93.

20. M. J. Alter, D. Francis, CDC Sentinel County study group, in (8), p. 156.

21. *AIDS Record*, 15 February 1987, p. 3.

22. D. A. Dawson, M. Cynamon, J. E. Fitti, *NCHS Advance Data* (No. 146), 19 November 1987.

23. Poll conducted by Yankelovich, Skelly & White/Clancy, Shulman, Inc., as part of the Anti-AIDS campaign developed by Saatchi & Saatchi DFS Compton for the New York City Health Department with financial support provided by New York Life; results reported November 1987.

24. A Gallup poll [see (1)] reported more than 40% of Americans said they were very concerned or somewhat concerned that they will contract AIDS. The difference from the August 1987 National Health Interview Survey may represent a trend, difference in sample selected, or the effect of different framing of the question—expected risk versus degree of concern.

25. A. M. Brandt, *No Magic Bullet* (Oxford Univ. Press, New York, 1985).

26. ———, *ibid.*, pp. 163–170.

27. Public Health Service, U.S. Department of Health and Human Services, *The 1990 Health Objectives for the Nation: A Midcourse Review*, November 1986, pp. 177–192.

28. S.R.I.—Gallup poll conducted October 1987. *The New York Times*, 8 January 1988, p. B6.

29. I thank T. Grodner Mendoza for assistance and P. D. Cleary, V. G. De Gruttola, M. E. Wilson, and J. A. Winsten for helpful comments. Supported by a grant from the Helena Rubinstein Foundation.

QUESTIONS

1. The abstract gives a brief outline of the major points of the essay. If you were going to tell people you know what you learned from the piece, however, you would probably not hand them the abstract. How would you summarize Fineberg's article? What, from your own point of view, is the most important information in the essay?

2. Fineberg includes a statistical table relating to probabilities of infection under various circumstances. In the course of his essay, he draws certain conclusions from the table (starting with paragraph 12). Since he presents the conclusions in the body of his text, why does he include the table? That is, what functions are performed by the table?

3. Present in your own words the information given in paragraph 26. What are the implications of this information for the future of AIDS?

4. Paragraph 27 offers some very discouraging conclusions. Assuming they are true, what can be done about this? What should be done about it?

5. Suppose you were on a commission making recommendations to the mayor of your hometown or governor of your state. Based on the information presented here, what recommendations would you urge other commission members to make about AIDS education?

6. In paragraph 33, Fineberg says that we must press ahead with education about AIDS despite the obstacles and problems he explains in his essay. Suppose you were put

in charge of a program to educate college students about AIDS with the hope of reducing possibilities of an epidemic. Write an essay in which you outline what your goals would be and describe the methods you would adopt to reach those goals. Take care that your goals are realistic, given the problems Fineberg describes—and in particular the problem of people who know about AIDS not acting in accordance with that knowledge. Take care, also, to attend to the problem (paragraph 33) of creating a social environment that will support changes in behavior. It is not enough to tell people what they should do; you need to think of ways to make it easy for them to do it. How, for instance, might you make it popular to do the right thing? And what things, if any, are so unlikely that there is no point in trying to persuade people to do them? Your problem involves understanding the realities of the situation, deciding what kinds of behavior can actually be encouraged in a meaningful way, and indicating just what sort of steps you would take to educate college students about risks and possibilities and to persuade them to act on the information you are giving them.

MAKING CONNECTIONS

1. Fineberg observes that not only do we need changes in behavior but we also need changes in the environment making appropriate behavior more likely. What sorts of things is he talking about here? Consider the essays by Murray Ross, Theodore R. Sizer, and Tania Modleski in "Arts and Humanities" section, or the articles by Susan Fraker, Carol Gilligan, and Elizabeth Kübler-Ross in this section. What aspects of the environment do they touch upon that contribute to the problem Fineberg discusses?

2. Compare Fineberg's essay to Michael Brown's "Love Canal and the Poisoning of America." What are their similarities and their differences in the ways they gather and use information? To what extent are they reporting on and describing situations, and to what extent are they advancing arguments about those situations? Would you say they are advancing or implying arguments?

Sciences and Technologies

WHY THE SKY IS BLUE
James Jeans

Sir James Jeans (1877–1946) was a British physicist and astronomer. Educated at Trinity College, Cambridge, he lectured there and was a professor of applied mathematics at Princeton University from 1905 to 1909. He later did research at Mount Wilson Observatory in California. Jeans won many honors for his work and wrote a number of scholarly and popular scientific books. The following selection is from The Stars in Their Courses (1931), *a written version of what began as a series of radio talks for an audience assumed to have no special knowledge of science.*

Imagine that we stand on any ordinary seaside pier, and watch the waves 1
rolling in and striking against the iron columns of the pier. Large waves pay
very little attention to the columns — they divide right and left and re-unite
after passing each column, much as a regiment of soldiers would if a tree stood
in their road; it is almost as though the columns had not been there. But the
short waves and ripples find the columns of the pier a much more formidable
obstacle. When the short waves impinge on the columns, they are reflected
back and spread as new ripples in all directions. To use the technical term,
they are "scattered." The obstacle provided by the iron columns hardly affects
the long waves at all, but scatters the short ripples.

We have been watching a sort of working model of the way in which sunlight 2
struggles through the earth's atmosphere. Between us on earth and outer space
the atmosphere interposes innumerable obstacles in the form of molecules of
air, tiny droplets of water, and small particles of dust. These are represented by
the columns of the pier.

The waves of the sea represent the sunlight. We know that sunlight is a 3

515

blend of lights of many colors—as we can prove for ourselves by passing it through a prism, or even through a jug of water, or as Nature demonstrates to us when she passes it through the raindrops of a summer shower and produces a rainbow. We also know that light consists of waves, and that the different colors of light are produced by waves of different lengths, red light by long waves and blue light by short waves. The mixture of waves which constitutes sunlight has to struggle through the obstacles it meets in the atmosphere, just as the mixture of waves at the seaside has to struggle past the columns of the pier. And these obstacles treat the light-waves much as the columns of the pier treat the sea-waves. The long waves which constitute red light are hardly affected, but the short waves which constitute blue light are scattered in all directions.

Thus, the different constituents of sunlight are treated in different ways as they struggle through the earth's atmosphere. A wave of blue light may be scattered by a dust particle, and turned out of its course. After a time a second dust particle again turns it out of its course, and so on, until finally it enters our eyes by a path as zigzag as that of a flash of lightning. Consequently the blue waves of the sunlight enter our eyes from all directions. And that is why the sky looks blue.

QUESTIONS

1. Analogy, the comparison of something familiar with something less familiar, occurs frequently in scientific explanation. Jeans introduces an analogy in his first paragraph. How does he develop that analogy as he develops his explanation?

2. The analogy Jeans provides enables him to explain the process by which the blue light-waves scatter throughout the sky. Hence he gives us a brief process analysis of that phenomenon. Summarize that process in your own words.

3. Try rewriting this essay without the analogy. Remove paragraph 1 and all the references to ocean waves and pier columns in paragraphs 2 and 3. How clear an explanation is left?

4. Besides the sea-waves, what other familiar examples does Jeans use in his explanation?

5. This piece opens with "Imagine that we stand. . . ." Suppose that every *we* was replaced with a *you*. How would the tone of the essay change?

6. While analogy can be effective in helping to explain difficult scientific concepts, it can be equally useful in explaining and interpreting familiar things by juxtaposing them in new ways. Suppose, for example, that you wished to explain to a friend why you dislike a course you are taking. Select one of the following ideas for an analogy (or find a better one): a forced-labor camp, a three-ring circus, squirrels on a treadmill, a tea party, a group-therapy session. Think through the analogy to your course, and write a few paragraphs of explanation. Let Jeans's essay guide you in organizing your own.

MAKING CONNECTIONS

1. Jeans's essay is a clear explanation of a complex phenomenon. And it is quite short. Where else in this volume have you found explanations as clear? A number of short passages in the essays by Francis Crick, Stephen W. Hawking, Bruno Bettelheim, Murray Ross, Horace Miner, and Farley Mowat could provide examples. Choose a descriptive passage that you find clear and compare it to Jeans's. Is an analogy central to the passage you selected? If not, what are the differences in the authors' explanation?

2. Describe the audience Jeans seems to have in mind for his explanation. How does that sense of audience differ for Francis Crick, Clifford Geertz, Susan Fraker, or Umberto Eco? Compare one or two of those essays with Jeans's account of "Why the Sky Is Blue" and discuss how the task of explaining shifts according to your assumptions about an audience.

TIMES AND DISTANCES,
LARGE AND SMALL

Francis Crick

Francis Crick (b. 1916), British molecular biologist, shared the Nobel prize for medicine in 1962 with James D. Watson for their report on the structure of DNA. Their work probably constitutes the single most important scientific discovery of the century, having generated revolutions in biology, chemistry, physics, and medicine. Crick, known for an incessant inquisitiveness that has taken him into many fields, was recently described in the pages of Nature *as "fractious," a quality that shows in his current research in neuroscience on brain modeling. Both Watson and Crick have made special efforts to explain their studies to the general public. The essay reprinted here is the first chapter of Crick's book,* Life Itself *(1981). A second book, again intended for a larger audience, is* What Mad Pursuit *(1988).*

There is one fact about the origin of life which is reasonably certain. Whenever and wherever it happened, it started a very long time ago, so long ago that it is extremely difficult to form any realistic idea of such vast stretches of time. Our own personal experience extends back over tens of years, yet even for that limited period we are apt to forget precisely what the world was like when we were young. A hundred years ago the earth was also full of people, bustling about their business, eating and sleeping, walking and talking, making love and earning a living, each one steadily pursuing his own affairs, and yet (with very rare exceptions) not one of them is left alive today. Instead, a totally different set of persons inhabits the earth around us. The shortness of human life necessarily limits the span of direct personal recollection. 1

Human culture has given us the illusion that our memories go further back than that. Before writing was invented, the experience of earlier generations, embodied in stories, myths and moral precepts to guide behavior, was passed down verbally or, to a lesser extent, in pictures, carvings and statues. Writing has made more precise and more extensive the transmission of such information and in recent times photography has sharpened our images of the immediate past. Cinematography will give future generations a more direct and vivid impression of their forebears than we can now easily get from the written word. 2

518

What a pity we don't have a talking picture of Cleopatra;[1] it would not only reveal the true length of her nose but would make more explicit the essence of her charm.

We can, with an effort, project ourselves back to the time of Plato and Aristotle,[2] and even beyond to Homer's Bronze Age heroes.[3] We can learn something of the highly organized civilizations of Egypt, the Middle East, Central America and China and a little about other primitive and scattered habitations. Even so, we have difficulty in contemplating steadily the march of history, from the beginnings of civilization to the present day, in such a way that we can truly experience the slow passage of time. Our minds are not built to deal comfortably with periods as long as hundreds or thousands of years.

Yet when we come to consider the origin of life, the time scales we must deal with make the whole span of human history seem but the blink of an eyelid. There is no simple way to adjust one's thinking to such vast stretches of time. The immensity of time passed is beyond our ready comprehension. One can only construct an impression of it from indirect and incomplete descriptions, much as a blind man laboriously builds up, by touch and sound, a picture of his immediate surroundings.

The customary way to provide a convenient framework for one's thoughts is to compare the age of the universe with the length of a single earthly day. Perhaps a better comparison, along the same lines, would be to equate the age of our earth with a single week. On such a scale the age of the universe, since the Big Bang,[4] would be about two or three weeks. The oldest macroscopic fossils (those from the start of the Cambrian)[5] would have been alive just one day ago. Modern man would have appeared in the last ten seconds and agriculture in the last one or two. Odysseus would have lived only half a second before the present time.[6]

Even this comparison hardly makes the longer time scale comprehensible to us. Another alternative is to draw a linear map of time, with the different events marked on it. The problem here is to make the line long enough to show our own experience on a reasonable scale, and yet short enough for convenient reproduction and examination. For easy reference such a map has been printed

---

[1]Cleopatra (69 B.C.–30 B.C.): Egyptian queen who charmed Julius Caesar and Marc Antony. [Eds.]

[2]Plato (428 B.C.?–348 B.C.) and Aristotle (384 B.C.–322 B.C.): Greek philosophers. [Eds.]

[3]Homer's Bronze Age heroes: the heroes of *The Iliad* and *The Odyssey*, epic poems written by the Greek poet Homer about 750 B.C. Homer's heroes fought in the Trojan war (ca. 1200 B.C.) at the end of the Bronze Age (3500 B.C.–1000 B.C.). [Eds.]

[4]Big Bang: a cosmological model in which all matter in the universe originated in a giant explosion about 18 billion years ago. [Eds.]

[5]Cambrian: the earliest period in the Paleozoic era, beginning about 600 million years ago. [Eds.]

[6]Odysseus: the most famous Greek hero of antiquity; he is the hero of Homer's *Odyssey* and a prominent character in the *Iliad*. [Eds.]

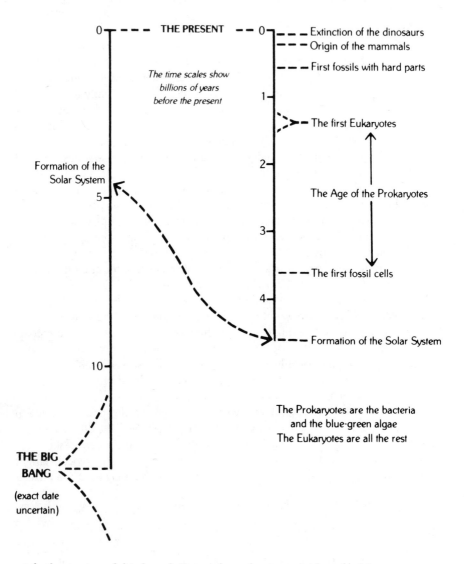

THE UNIVERSE

THE SOLAR SYSTEM

0 — — — THE PRESENT — — 0

The time scales show billions of years before the present

Extinction of the dinosaurs
Origin of the mammals
First fossils with hard parts

1

The first Eukaryotes

Formation of the Solar System
5

2

The Age of the Prokaryotes

3

The first fossil cells

4

10

Formation of the Solar System

The Prokaryotes are the bacteria and the blue-green algae
The Eukaryotes are all the rest

THE BIG BANG

(exact date uncertain)

at the beginning of this [page]. But perhaps the most vivid method is to compare time to the lines of print themselves. Let us make [a 200-page] book equal in length to the time from the start of the Cambrian to the present; that is, about 600 million years. Then each full page will represent roughly 3 million years, each line about ninety thousand years and each letter or small space about fifteen hundred years. The origin of the earth would be about seven books ago and the origin of the universe (which has been dated only approximately) ten or so books before that. Almost the whole of recorded human history would be covered by the last two or three letters of the book.

If you now turn back the pages of the book, slowly reading *one letter at a time*—remember, each letter is fifteen hundred years—then this may convey to you something of the immense stretches of time we shall have to consider. On this scale the span of your own life would be less than the width of a comma. 7

If life really started here we need hardly be concerned with the rest of the universe, but if it started elsewhere the magnitude of large distances must be squarely faced. Though it is difficult to convey a vivid and precise impression of the age of the universe, to grasp its size is almost beyond human comprehension, however we try to express it. The main stumbling block is the extreme emptiness of space; not merely the few atoms in between the stars but the immense distance from one star to another. The visible world close to us is cluttered with objects and our intuitive estimates of their distance depend mainly on various clues provided by their apparent size and their visual interrelationships. It is much more difficult to judge the distance of an unfamiliar object floating in the emptiness of the clear, blue sky. I once heard a Canadian radio interviewer say, when challenged, that he thought the moon "was about the size of a balloon," though admittedly this was before the days of space travel. 8

This is how two astronomers, Jastrow and Thompson, try to describe, by analogy, the size and the distance of objects in space: 9

> Let the sun be the size of an orange; on that scale the earth is a grain of sand circling in orbit around the sun at a distance of thirty feet; Jupiter, eleven times larger than the earth, is a cherry pit revolving at a distance of 200 feet or one city block from the sun. The galaxy on this scale is 100 billion oranges, each orange separated from its neighbors by an average distance of 1,000 miles.[7]

The difficulty with an analogy of this type is that it is almost impossible for us to estimate distances in empty space. A comparison with a city block is misleading, because we too easily visualize the buildings in it, and in doing so lose the idea of emptiness. If you try to imagine an orange floating even a mile up in the sky you will find that its distance seems to become indefinite. An "orange" a thousand miles away would be too small to see unless it were incandescent. 10

Another possible method is to convert distances to time. Pretend you are on a spaceship which is traveling faster than any present-day spaceship. For various reasons, which will become clear later, let us take its speed to be one-hundredth the velocity of light; that is, about 1,800 miles per second. At this speed one 11

---

[7] Robert Jastrow and Malcolm M. Thompson, *Astronomy: Fundamentals and Frontiers*, 2nd ed. (New York: Wiley, 1972).

could go from New York to Europe in about three seconds (Concorde takes roughly three hours), so we are certainly traveling fairly fast by everyday standards. It would take us two minutes to reach the moon and fifteen hours to reach the sun. To go right across the solar system from one side to the other—let us take this distance rather arbitrarily as the diameter of the orbit of Neptune—would take us almost three and half weeks. The main point to grasp is that this journey is not unlike a very long train journey, rather longer than the distance from Moscow to Vladivostok and back. Such a trip would probably be monotonous enough, even though the landscape were constantly flowing past the train window. While going across the solar system, there would be nothing at all just outside the window of the spaceship. Very slowly, day after day, the sun would change in size and position. As we traveled farther away from it, its apparent diameter would decrease, till near the orbit of Neptune it would look "little bigger than a pin's head," as I have previously described it, assuming that its apparent size, as viewed from the earth, corresponds roughly to that of a silver dollar. In spite of traveling so fast—remember that at this speed we could travel from any spot to any other on the earth's surface in less than seven seconds—this journey would be tedious in the extreme. Our main impression would be of the almost total emptiness of space. At this distance a planet would appear to be little more than an occasional speck in this vast wilderness.

This feeling of an immense three-dimensional emptiness is bad enough while 12 we are focusing on the solar system. (Almost all of the scale models of the solar system one sees in museums are grossly misleading. The sun and the planets are almost always shown as far too big by comparison with the distances between them.) It is when we try to go farther afield that the enormity of space really hits us. To reach the nearest star—actually a group of three stars fairly close together—would take our spaceship 430 years and the chances are we would pass nothing significant on the way there. A whole lifetime of one hundred years, traveling at this very high speed, would take us less than a quarter of the way there. We would be constantly traveling from emptiness to emptiness with nothing but a few gas molecules and an occasional tiny speck of dust to show that we were not always in the same place. Very, very slowly a few of the nearest stars would change their positions slightly, while the sun itself would fade imperceptibly until it was just another star in the brilliant panorama of stars visible on all sides of the spaceship. Long though it would seem, this journey to the nearest star is, by astronomical standards, a very short one. To cross our own galaxy from side to side would take no less than ten million years. Such distances are beyond anything we can conceive except in the most abstract way. And yet, on a cosmic scale, the distance across the galaxy is hardly any distance at all. Admittedly it is only about twenty times as far to Andromeda, the nearest large galaxy, but to reach the limits of space visible to us in our giant telescopes we would have to travel more than a thousand times farther than that. To me it is remarkable that this astonishing discovery, the vastness and the emptiness of space, has not attracted the imaginative attention of poets and religious thinkers. People are happy to contemplate the limitless powers of God—a doubtful proposition at best—but quite unwilling to meditate creatively on the size of this extraordinary universe in which, through no virtue of their own, they find themselves. Naïvely one might have thought that both poets and priests would be so utterly astonished by these scientific revelations that they would be working with a white-hot fury to try to embody them in the foundation of our culture. The psalmist who said, "When I consider Thy heavens, the work of Thy fingers, the moon and the stars, which Thou hast ordained; what is man, that Thou art mindful of him? . . ." was at least trying, within the limitations of his beliefs, to express his wonder at the universe visible to the naked eye and the pettiness of man by comparison. And yet *his* universe was a small, almost cozy affair compared to the one modern science has revealed to us. It is almost as if the utter insignificance of the earth and the thin film of its biosphere has totally paralyzed the imagination, as if it were too dreadful to contemplate and therefore best ignored.

I shall not discuss here how these very large distances are estimated. The distance of the main objects in the solar system can now be obtained very accurately by a combination of the theory of solar mechanics and radar ranging, the distances of the nearest stars by the way their relative positions change slightly when viewed from the different positions of the earth in its yearly orbit around the sun. After that the arguments are more technical and less precise. But that the distances are the sort of size astronomers estimate there is not the slightest doubt. 13

So far we have been considering very large magnitudes. Fortunately, when we turn to very small distances and times things are not quite so bad. We need to know the size of atoms—the size and contents of the tiny nucleus within each atom will concern us less—compared to everyday things. This we can manage in two relatively small hops. Let us start with a millimeter. This distance (about a twenty-fifty of an inch) is easy for us to see with the naked eye. One-thousandth part of this is called a micron. A bacteria cell is about two microns long. The wavelength of visible light (which limits what we can see in a high-powered light microscope) is about half a micron long. 14

We now go down by another factor of a thousand to reach a length known as a nanometer. The typical distance between adjacent atoms bonded strongly together in an organic compound lies between a tenth and a fifth of this. Under the best conditions we can see distances of a nanometer, or a little less, using an electron microscope, provided the specimen can be suitably prepared. Moreover, it is possible to exhibit pictures of a whole series of natural objects at every scale between a small group of atoms and a flea, so that with a little practice we can feel one scale merging into another. By contrast with the emptiness of 15 space, the living world is crammed with detail at every level. The ease with which we can go from one scale to another should not blind us to the fact that the numbers of objects within a *volume* can be uncomfortably large. For example, a drop of water contains rather more than a thousand billion billion water molecules.

The short time we shall be concerned with will rarely be less than a pico- 16 second, that is, one-millionth of a millionth of a second, though very much shorter times occur in nuclear reactions and in studies of subatomic particles. This minute interval is the sort of time scale on which molecules are vibrating, but looked at another way, it does not seem so outlandish. Consider the velocity of sound. In air this is relatively slow—little faster than most jet planes—being about a thousand feet per second. If a flash of lightning is only a mile away, it will take a full five seconds for its sound to reach us. This velocity is, incidentally, approximately the same as the average speed of the molecules of gas in the air, in between their collisions with each other. The speed of sound in most solids is usually a little faster.

Now we ask, how long will it take a sound wave to pass over a small molecule? 17 A simple calculation shows this time to be in the picosecond range. This is just what one would expect, since this is about the time scale on which the atoms of the molecule are vibrating against one another. What is important is that this is, roughly speaking, the pulse rate *underlying* chemical reactions. An enzyme—an organic catalyst—can react a thousand or more times a second. This may appear fast to us but this rate is really rather slow on the time scale of atomic vibration.

Unfortunately, it is not so easy to convey the time scales in between a second 18 and a picosecond, though a physical chemist can learn to feel at home over this fairly large range. Fortunately, we shall not be concerned directly with these very short times, though we shall see their effects indirectly. Most chemical reactions are really very rare events. The molecules usually move around intermittently and barge against one another many times before a rare lucky encounter allows them to hit each other strongly enough and in the correct direction to surmount their protective barriers and produce a chemical reaction. It is only because there are usually so many molecules in one small volume, all doing this at the same time, that the rate of chemical reaction appears to proceed quite smoothly. The chance variations are smoothed out by the large numbers involved.

When we stand back and review once again these very different scales—the 19 minute size of an atom and the almost unimaginable size of the universe; the pulse rate of chemical reaction compared to the deserts of vast eternity since the Big Bang—we see that in all these instances our intuitions, based on our experience of everyday life, are likely to be highly misleading. By themselves, large numbers mean very little to us. There is only one way to overcome this handicap, so natural to our human condition. We must calculate and recalculate, even though only approximately, to check and recheck our initial impressions until slowly, with time and constant application, the real world, the world of the immensely small and the immensely great, becomes as familiar to us as the simple cradle of our common earthly experience.

QUESTIONS

1. Study the diagram that accompanies the essay. How does one line relate to the other? What is the diagram trying to convey?

2. Why are the first three paragraphs devoted to the history and historical memory of humankind?

3. Compare the analogies Crick uses to explain the long passage of universal time in paragraphs 5, 6, and 7. What does the analogy of the book add to that of the week?

4. In paragraph 8, what is the implication of *elsewhere* in its first sentence? This essay is the first chapter of a book called *Life Itself*. What do you imagine to be at least one idea treated in the rest of the book?

5. Paragraph 11 is an extremely long paragraph, and paragraph 12 is even longer. Their lengths seem to correspond to the subjects they take up. Can you think of other ways to imagine the kind of emptiness those paragraphs describe?

6. Paragraph 11 implies an unusual definition of *wilderness*, its last word. Explain why you consider Crick's idea of wilderness the essential one or an eccentric notion.

7. Why do you think that priests and poets have not, as Crick observes, been "working with a white-hot fury to try to embody [these scientific revelations] in the foundation of our culture" (paragraph 12)? What does that last phrase, "foundation of our culture," mean in this context?

8. Why do you think Crick treats the very large before the very small? Which are the more astonishing measurements?

9. Think of a way of estimating, closely but reasonably, something quite numerous— for example, the number of grasses in a yard, the number of leaves or pine needles on a tree, the number of hairs on the tail of a cat, or the number of cars on all the roads, during a single day, in your state or city. Describe your system of estimation, and explain the answer it yields.

MAKING CONNECTIONS

1. Compare the diagrams and illustrations in the articles by Crick, Stephen W. Hawking, Stephen Jay Gould, Oliver Sacks, and Bruno Bettelheim. What differences do you find in the purposes for those diagrams and illustrations? Identify one that you find particularly successful and explain its success. Is there one you find less useful?

2. Consider several of the following essays: Virginia Woolf's "The Death of the

Moth," Annie Dillard's "Singing with the Fundamentalists," Isak Dinesen's "The Iguana," Alice Walker's "Beauty: When the Other Dancer Is the Self," George Orwell's "Shooting an Elephant," N. Scott Momaday's "The Way to Rainy Mountain," and Joan Didion's "Georgia O'Keeffe." How do you think one or more of these writers would respond to Crick's assertion in paragraph 12 that our poets and priests are not trying to deal with the wonders of the universe?

OUR PICTURE OF THE UNIVERSE
Stephen W. Hawking

Stephen W. Hawking (b. 1942) is the Lucasian Professor of Mathematics at Cambridge University, and one of the world's leading theoretical physicists. Carl Sagan has described the moment in 1974, when he observed "an ancient rite, the investiture of new fellows into the Royal Society, one of the most ancient scholarly organizations on the planet. In the front row a young man in a wheelchair was, very slowly, signing his name in a book that bore on its earliest pages the signature of Isaac Newton. When at last he finished, there was a stirring ovation. Stephen Hawking was a legend even then." Hawking suffers from the serious physical disabilities associated with Lou Gehrig's disease, making his extraordinary achievements an inspiration to all disabled people. Hawking is known especially for his work on "black holes" and their implications for a unified theory of physical phenomena. His recent book A Brief History of Time *has made his thinking available to the general reader and has become a best-seller. The essay reprinted below is the first chapter of that book, unchanged except for the removal of references to the book as a whole.*

A well-known scientist (some say it was Bertrand Russell) once gave a public 1
lecture on astronomy. He described how the earth orbits around the sun and how the sun, in turn, orbits around the center of a vast collection of stars called our galaxy. At the end of the lecture, a little old lady at the back of the room got up and said: "What you have told us is rubbish. The world is really a flat plate supported on the back of a giant tortoise." The scientist gave a superior smile before replying, "What is the tortoise standing on?" "You're very clever, young man, very clever," said the old lady. "But it's turtles all the way down!"

Most people would find the picture of our universe as an infinite tower of 2
tortoises rather ridiculous, but why do we think we know better? What do we know about the universe, and how do we know it? Where did the universe come from, and where is it going? Did the universe have a beginning, and if so, what happened *before* then? What is the nature of time? Will it ever come to an end? Recent breakthroughs in physics, made possible in part by fantastic new technologies, suggest answers to some of these longstanding questions. Someday these answers may seem as obvious to us as the earth orbiting the

527

sun—or perhaps as ridiculous as a tower of tortoises. Only time (whatever that may be) will tell.

As long ago as 340 B.C. the Greek philosopher Aristotle, in his book *On the Heavens,* was able to put forward two good arguments for believing that the earth was a round sphere rather than a flat plate. First, he realized that eclipses of the moon were caused by the earth coming between the sun and the moon. The earth's shadow on the moon was always round, which would be true only if the earth was spherical. If the earth had been a flat disk, the shadow would have been elongated and elliptical, unless the eclipse always occurred at a time when the sun was directly under the center of the disk. Second, the Greeks knew from their travels that the North Star appeared lower in the sky when viewed in the south than it did in more northerly regions. (Since the North Star lies over the North Pole, it appears to be directly above an observer at the North Pole, but to someone looking from the equator, it appears to lie just at the horizon.) From the difference in the apparent position of the North Star in Egypt and Greece, Aristotle even quoted an estimate that the distance around the earth was 400,000 stadia. It is not known exactly what length a stadium was, but it may have been about 200 yards, which would make Aristotle's estimate about twice the currently accepted figure. The Greeks even had a third argument that the earth must be round, for why else does one first see the sails of a ship coming over the horizon, and only later see the hull?

Aristotle thought that the earth was stationary and that the sun, the moon, the planets, and the stars moved in circular orbits about the earth. He believed this because he felt, for mystical reasons, that the earth was the center of the universe, and that circular motion was the most perfect. This idea was elaborated by Ptolemy in the second century A.D. into a complete cosmological model. The earth stood at the center, surrounded by eight spheres that carried the moon, the sun, the stars, and the five planets known at the time, Mercury, Venus, Mars, Jupiter, and Saturn (Fig. 1). The planets themselves moved on smaller circles attached to their respective spheres in order to account for their rather complicated observed paths in the sky. The outermost sphere carried the so-called fixed stars, which always stay in the same positions relative to each other but which rotate together across the sky. What lay beyond the last sphere was never made very clear, but it certainly was not part of mankind's observable universe.

Ptolemy's model provided a reasonably accurate system for predicting the positions of heavenly bodies in the sky. But in order to predict these positions correctly, Ptolemy had to make an assumption that the moon followed a path that sometimes brought it twice as close to the earth as at other times. And that meant that the moon ought sometimes to appear twice as big as at other times! Ptolemy recognized this flaw, but nevertheless his model was generally, although not universally, accepted. It was adopted by the Christian church as the picture of the universe that was in accordance with Scripture, for it had the great advantage that it left lots of room outside the sphere of fixed stars for heaven and hell.

A simpler model, however, was proposed in 1514 by a Polish priest, Nicholas Copernicus. (At first, perhaps for fear of being branded a heretic by his church, Copernicus circulated his model anonymously.) His idea was that the sun was stationary at the center and that the earth and the planets moved in circular orbits around the sun. Nearly a century passed before this idea was taken seriously. Then two astronomers—the German, Johannes Kepler, and the Italian, Galileo Galilei—started publicly to support the Copernican theory, despite the fact that the orbits it predicted did not quite match the ones observed. The death blow to the Aristotelian/Ptolemaic theory came in 1609. In that year, Galileo started observing the night sky with a telescope, which had just been invented. When he looked at the planet Jupiter, Galileo found that it was accompanied by several small satellites or moons that orbited around it. This implied that everything did *not* have to orbit directly around the earth, as Aristotle and Ptolemy had thought. (It was, of course, still possible to believe that the earth was stationary at the center of the universe and that the moons of Jupiter moved on extremely complicated paths around the earth, giving the *appearance* that they orbited Jupiter. However, Copernicus's theory was much simpler.) At the same time, Johannes Kepler had modified Copernicus's theory,

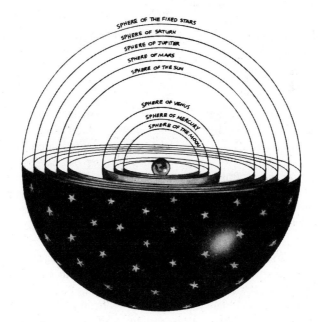

FIGURE 1

suggesting that the planets moved not in circles but in ellipses (an ellipse is an elongated circle). The predictions now finally matched the observations.

As far as Kepler was concerned, elliptical orbits were merely an ad hoc   7
hypothesis, and a rather repugnant one at that, because ellipses were clearly less perfect than circles. Having discovered almost by accident that elliptical orbits fit the observations well, he could not reconcile them with his idea that the planets were made to orbit the sun by magnetic forces. An explanation was provided only much later, in 1687, when Sir Isaac Newton published his *Philosophiae Naturalis Principia Mathematica*, probably the most important single work ever published in the physical sciences. In it Newton not only put forward a theory of how bodies move in space and time, but he also developed the complicated mathematics needed to analyse those motions. In addition, Newton postulated a law of universal gravitation according to which each body in the universe was attracted toward every other body by a force that was stronger the more massive the bodies and the closer they were to each other. It was this same force that caused objects to fall to the ground. (The story that Newton was inspired by an apple hitting his head is almost certainly apocryphal. All Newton himself ever said was that the idea of gravity came to him as he sat "in a contemplative mood" and "was occasioned by the fall of an apple.") Newton went on to show that, according to his law, gravity causes the moon to move in an elliptical orbit around the earth and causes the earth and the planets to follow elliptical paths around the sun.

The Copernican model got rid of Ptolemy's celestial spheres, and with them,   8
the idea that the universe had a natural boundary. Since "fixed stars" did not appear to change their positions apart from a rotation across the sky caused by the earth spinning on its axis, it became natural to suppose that the fixed stars were objects like our sun but very much farther away.

Newton realized that, according to his theory of gravity, the stars should   9
attract each other, so it seemed they could not remain essentially motionless. Would they not fall together at some point? In a letter in 1691 to Richard Bentley, another leading thinker of his day, Newton argued that this would indeed happen if there were only a finite number of stars distributed over a finite region of space. But he reasoned that if, on the other hand, there were an infinite number of stars, distributed more or less uniformly over infinite space, this would not happen, because there would not be any central point for them to fall to.

This argument is an instance of the pitfalls that you can encounter in talking   10
about infinity. In an infinite universe, every point can be regarded as the center, because every point has an infinite number of stars on each side of it. The correct approach, it was realized only much later, is to consider the finite situation, in which the stars all fall in on each other, and then to ask how things change if one adds more stars roughly uniformly distributed outside this region. According to Newton's law, the extra stars would make no difference at

all to the original ones on average, so the stars would fall in just as fast. We can add as many stars as we like, but they will still always collapse in on themselves. We now know it is impossible to have an infinite static model of the universe in which gravity is always attractive.

It is an interesting reflection on the general climate of thought before the 11 twentieth century that no one had suggested that the universe was expanding or contracting. It was generally accepted that either the universe had existed forever in an unchanging state, or that it had been created at a finite time in the past more or less as we observe it today. In part this may have been due to people's tendency to believe in eternal truths, as well as the comfort they found in the thought that even though they may grow old and die, the universe is eternal and unchanging.

Even those who realized that Newton's theory of gravity showed that the 12 universe could not be static did not think to suggest that it might be expanding. Instead, they attempted to modify the theory by making the gravitational force repulsive at very large distances. This did not significantly affect their predictions of the motions of the planets, but it allowed an infinite distribution of stars to remain in equilibrium—with the attractive forces between nearby stars balanced by the repulsive forces from those that were farther away. However, we now believe such an equilibrium would be unstable: if the stars in some region got only slightly nearer each other, the attractive forces between them would become stronger and dominate over the repulsive forces so that the stars would continue to fall toward each other. On the other hand, if the stars got a bit farther away from each other, the repulsive forces would dominate and drive them farther apart.

Another objection to an infinite static universe is normally ascribed to the 13 German philosopher Heinrich Olbers, who wrote about this theory in 1823. In fact, various contemporaries of Newton had raised the problem, and the Olbers article was not even the first to contain plausible arguments against it. It was, however, the first to be widely noted. The difficulty is that in an infinite static universe nearly every line of sight would end on the surface of a star. Thus one would expect that the whole sky would be as bright as the sun, even at night. Olbers's counterargument was that the light from distant stars would be dimmed by absorption by intervening matter. However, if that happened the intervening matter would eventually heat up until it glowed as brightly as the stars. The only way of avoiding the conclusion that the whole of the night sky should be as bright as the surface of the sun would be to assume that the stars had not been shining forever but had turned on at some finite time in the past. In that case the absorbing matter might not have heated up yet or the light from distant stars might not yet have reached us. And that brings us to the question of what could have caused the stars to have turned on in the first place.

The beginning of the universe had, of course, been discussed long before 14 this. According to a number of early cosmologies and the Jewish/Christian/

531

Muslim tradition, the universe started at a finite, and not very distant, time in the past. One argument for such a beginning was the feeling that it was necessary to have "First Cause" to explain the existence of the universe. (Within the universe, you always explained one event as being caused by some earlier event, but the existence of the universe itself could be explained in this way only if it had some beginning.) Another argument was put forward by St. Augustine in his book *The City of God*. He pointed out that civilization is progressing and we remember who performed this deed or developed that technique. Thus man, and so also perhaps the universe, could not have been around all that long. St. Augustine accepted a date of about 5000 B.C. for the Creation of the universe according to the book of Genesis. (It is interesting that this is not so far from the end of the last Ice Age, about 10,000 B.C., which is when archaeologists tell us that civilization really began.)

Aristotle, and most of the other Greek philosophers, on the other hand, did 15 not like the idea of a creation because it smacked too much of divine intervention. They believed, therefore, that the human race and the world around it had existed, and would exist, forever. The ancients had already considered the argument about progress described above, and answered it by saying that there had been periodic floods or other disasters that repeatedly set the human race right back to the beginning of civilization.

The questions of whether the universe had a beginning in time and whether 16 it is limited in space were later extensively examined by the philosopher Immanuel Kant in his monumental (and very obscure) work, *Critique of Pure Reason*, published in 1781. He called these questions antinomies (that is, contradictions) of pure reason because he felt that there were equally compelling arguments for believing the thesis, that the universe had a beginning, and the antithesis, that it had existed forever. His argument for the thesis was that if the universe did not have a beginning, there would be an infinite period of time before any event, which he considered absurd. The argument for the antithesis was that if the universe had a beginning, there would be an infinite period of time before it, so why should the universe begin at any one particular time? In fact, his cases for both the thesis and the antithesis are really the same argument. They are both based on his unspoken assumption that time continues back forever, whether or not the universe had existed forever. As we shall see, the concept of time has no meaning before the beginning of the universe. This was first pointed out by St. Augustine. When asked: What did God do before he created the universe? Augustine didn't reply: He was preparing Hell for people who asked such questions. Instead, he said that time was a property of the universe that God created, and that time did not exist before the beginning of the universe.

When most people believed in an essentially static and unchanging universe, 17 the question of whether or not it had a beginning was really one of metaphysics or theology. One could account for what was observed equally well on the theory that the universe had existed forever or on the theory that it was set in motion at some finite time in such a manner as to look as though it had existed forever. But in 1929, Edwin Hubble made the landmark observation that wherever you look, distant galaxies are moving rapidly away from us. In other words, the universe is expanding. This means that at earlier times objects would have been closer together. In fact, it seemed that there was a time, about ten or twenty thousand million years ago, when they were all at exactly the same place and when, therefore, the density of the universe was infinite. This discovery finally brought the question of the beginning of the universe into the realm of science.

Hubble's observations suggested that there was a time, called the big bang, when the universe was infinitesimally small and infinitely dense. Under such conditions all the laws of science, and therefore all ability to predict the future, would break down. If there were events earlier than this time, then they could not affect what happens at the present time. Their existence can be ignored because it would have no observational consequences. One may say that time had a beginning at the big bang, in the sense that earlier times simply would not be defined. It should be emphasized that this beginning in time is very different from those that had been considered previously. In an unchanging universe a beginning in time is something that has to be imposed by some being outside the universe; there is no physical necessity for a beginning. One can imagine that God created the universe at literally any time in the past. On the other hand, if the universe is expanding, there may be physical reasons why there had to be a beginning. One could still imagine that God created the universe at the instant of the big bang, or even afterwards in just such a way as to make it look as though there had been a big bang, but it would be meaningless to suppose that it was created *before* the big bang. An expanding universe does not preclude a creator, but it does place limits on when he might have carried out his job! 18

In order to talk about the nature of the universe and to discuss questions such as whether it has a beginning or an end, you have to be clear about what a scientific theory is. I shall take the simpleminded view that a theory is just a model of the universe, or a restricted part of it, and a set of rules that relate quantities in the model to observations that we make. It exists only in our minds and does not have any other reality (whatever that might mean). A theory is a good theory if it satisfies two requirements: It must accurately describe a large class of observations on the basis of a model that contains only a few arbitrary elements, and it must make definite predictions about the results of future observations. For example, Aristotle's theory that everything was made out of four elements, earth, air, fire, and water, was simple enough to qualify, but it did not make any definite predictions. On the other hand, Newton's theory of gravity was based on an even simpler model, in which bodies attracted each 19 other with a force that was proportional to a quantity called their mass and inversely proportional to the square of the distance between them. Yet it predicts the motions of the sun, the moon, and the planets to a high degree of accuracy.

Any physical theory is always provisional, in the sense that it is only a hypothesis: you can never prove it. No matter how many times the results of experiments agree with some theory, you can never be sure that the next time the result will not contradict the theory. On the other hand, you can disprove a theory by finding even a single observation that disagrees with the predictions of the theory. As philosopher of science Karl Popper has emphasized, a good theory is characterized by the fact that it makes a number of predictions that could in principle be disproved or falsified by observation. Each time new experiments are observed to agree with the predictions the theory survives, and our confidence in it is increased; but if ever a new observation is found to disagree, we have to abandon or modify the theory. At least that is what is supposed to happen, but you can always question the competence of the person who carried out the observation. 20

In practice, what often happens is that a new theory is devised that is really an extension of the previous theory. For example, very accurate observations of the planet Mercury revealed a small difference between its motion and the predictions of Newton's theory of gravity. Einstein's general theory of relativity predicted a slightly different motion from Newton's theory. The fact that Einstein's predictions matched what was seen, while Newton's did not, was one of the crucial confirmations of the new theory. However, we still use Newton's theory for all practical purposes because the difference between its predictions and those of general relativity is very small in the situations that we normally deal with. (Newton's theory also has the great advantage that it is much simpler to work with than Einstein's!) 21

The eventual goal of science is to provide a single theory that describes the whole universe. However, the approach most scientists actually follow is to separate the problem into two parts. First, there are the laws that tell us how the universe changes with time. (If we know what the universe is like at any one time, these physical laws tell us how it will look at any later time.) Second, there is the question of the initial state of the universe. Some people feel that science should be concerned with only the first part; they regard the question of the initial situation as a matter for metaphysics or religion. They would say that God, being omnipotent, could have started the universe off any way he wanted. That may be so, but in that case he also could have made it develop in a completely arbitrary way. Yet it appears that he chose to make it evolve in a very regular way according to certain laws. It therefore seems equally reasonable to suppose that there are also laws governing the initial state. 22

It turns out to be very difficult to devise a theory to describe the universe all in one go. Instead, we break the problem up into bits and invent a number of partial theories. Each of these partial theories describes and predicts a certain 23 limited class of observations, neglecting the effects of other quantities, or representing them by simple sets of numbers. It may be that this approach is completely wrong. If everything in the universe depends on everything else in a fundamental way, it might be impossible to get close to a full solution by investigating parts of the problem in isolation. Nevertheless, it is certainly the way that we have made progress in the past. The classic example again is the Newtonian theory of gravity, which tells us that the gravitational force between two bodies depends only on one number associated with each body, its mass, but is otherwise independent of what the bodies are made of. Thus one does not need to have a theory of the structure and constitution of the sun and the planets in order to calculate their orbits.

Today scientists describe the universe in terms of two basic partial theories— 24
the general theory of relativity and quantum mechanics. They are the great intellectual achievements of the first half of this century. The general theory of relativity describes the force of gravity and the large-scale structure of the universe, that is, the structure on scales from only a few miles to as large as a million million million million (1 with twenty-four zeros after it) miles, the size of the observable universe. Quantum mechanics, on the other hand, deals with phenomena on extremely small scales, such as a millionth of a millionth of an inch. Unfortunately, however, these two theories are known to be inconsistent with each other—they cannot both be correct. One of the major endeavors in physics today . . . is the search for a new theory that will incorporate them both—a quantum theory of gravity. We do not yet have such a theory, and we may still be a long way from having one, but we do already know many of the properties that it must have. And . . . we already know a fair amount about the predictions a quantum theory of gravity must make.

Now, if you believe that the universe is not arbitrary, but is governed by 25
definite laws, you ultimately have to combine the partial theories into a complete unified theory that will describe everything in the universe. But there is a fundamental paradox in the search for such a complete unified theory. The ideas about scientific theories outlined above assume we are rational beings who are free to observe the universe as we want and to draw logical deductions from what we see. In such a scheme it is reasonable to suppose that we might progress even closer toward the laws that govern our universe. Yet if there really is a complete unified theory, it would also presumably determine our actions. And so the theory itself would determine the outcome of our search for it! And why should it determine that we come to the right conclusions from the evidence? Might it not equally well determine that we draw the wrong conclusion? Or no conclusion at all?

The only answer that I can give to this problem is based on Darwin's principle 26
of natural selection. The idea is that in any population of self-reproducing organisms, there will be variations in the genetic material and upbringing that different individuals have. These differences will mean that some individuals

535

are better able than others to draw the right conclusions about the world around them and to act accordingly. These individuals will be more likely to survive and reproduce and so their pattern of behavior and thought will come to dominate. It has certainly been true in the past that what we call intelligence and scientific discovery has conveyed a survival advantage. It is not so clear that this is still the case: our scientific discoveries may well destroy us all, and even if they don't, a complete unified theory may not make much difference to our chances of survival. However, provided the universe has evolved in a regular way, we might expect that the reasoning abilities that natural selection has given us would be valid also in our search for a complete unified theory, and so would not lead us to the wrong conclusions.

Because the partial theories that we already have are sufficient to make 27 accurate predictions in all but the most extreme situations, the search for the ultimate theory of the universe seems difficult to justify on practical grounds. (It is worth noting, though, that similar arguments could have been used against both relativity and quantum mechanics, and these theories have given us both nuclear energy and the microelectronics revolution!) The discovery of a complete unified theory, therefore, may not aid the survival of our species. It may not even affect our life-style. But ever since the dawn of civilization, people have not been content to see events as unconnected and inexplicable. They have craved an understanding of the underlying order in the world. Today we still yearn to know why we are here and where we came from. Humanity's deepest desire for knowledge is justification enough for our continuing quest. And our goal is nothing less than a complete description of the universe we live in.

QUESTIONS

1. There is a break in the essay after paragraph 18, indicated by extra space between paragraphs. If you had to provide a subtitle for each of the two sections demarcated by that break, what would these subtitles be?

2. What is the function of the anecdote in paragraph 1? Why do you suppose Hawking begins with that story?

3. What is the function of paragraph 2? What kind of sentence structure predominates in this paragraph? Why?

4. The first date mentioned in the essay comes in paragraph 3. Make a list of all the other exact dates that are given, noting the paragraphs in which they appear. Discuss any patterns (or violations of pattern) that you note. What does this list tell you about the organization of the essay?

5. Hawking uses the word *God* with some frequency. How would you describe the notion of *God* generated by his text? Is it different from your own views? How important is *God* to Hawking's view of the universe?

6. What is the notion of *science* that can be derived from Hawking's uses of that

word? That is, with what definition or concept of science is he working? Is it the same as your own, or different? Discuss.

7. In the later part of his essay, Hawking takes up the philosophical question of how we can know that we know what we know. Describe and discuss the view that he presents, bringing in any other theories of knowledge that you have encountered in your studies or reading on the subject.

MAKING CONNECTIONS

1. Read Carl Sagan's essay, "Can We Know the Universe? Reflections on a Grain of Salt" in "Reflecting." Are Sagan and Hawking talking about the same universe? Note Sagan's strongest beliefs as expressed in his final paragraphs. Are Sagan and Hawking thinking along the same lines? To what extent does Hawking seem to be answering the call that Sagan makes?

2. Banesh Hoffmann, in his essay on Einstein, makes the observation that Einstein, perhaps above all else, was marked by an extraordinary simplicity. Does simplicity characterize Hawking's thought as well? What can we mean by simplicity in cases like these? What are some examples of it in this essay?

THE ORIGIN OF THE UNIVERSE
Victor Weisskopf

Victor Weisskopf was born in Vienna in 1908 and came to the United States in 1937. He is now the Institute Professor Emeritus at Massachusetts Institute of Technology. A physicist of international distinction, he was awarded the U.S. Department of Energy's Enrico Fermi Award in 1988, which is only the latest in a series of major awards from many countries. He is a member of the National Academy of Sciences, as well as of the corresponding academies of France, Austria, Denmark, Spain, Germany, Scotland, Bavaria, and the Soviet Union. His several books include Knowledge and Wonder *(1962),* Physics in the Twentieth Century *(1972), and, most recently,* The Privilege of Being a Physicist *(1988). From 1943 to 1946, Weisskopf worked on the Manhattan Project in Los Alamos, New Mexico, developing the atomic bomb. After the war, he became a professor of physics at MIT. The essay reprinted here is based on a talk he gave to the American Academy of Arts and Sciences in Cambridge, Massachusetts.*

1.

How did the universe begin about 12 billion years ago? The question concerns the very large—space, galaxies, etc.—but also the very small, namely the innermost structure of matter. The reason is that the early universe was very hot, so that matter was then decomposed into its constituents. These two topics hang together, and this is what makes them so interesting. 1

One must start with a few words about the innermost structure of matter. The sketch in Figure 1 indicates, on the very left, a piece of metal. It is made of atoms. To the right of it you see one of the atoms symbolically designed with a nucleus in the middle and with electrons around it. Here we proceed toward the innermost structure of matter in steps. That's why I call it the quantum ladder. Further to the right you see the nucleus, consisting of protons and neutrons, which I will call nucleons from now on. We have found out that the nucleons themselves are composite; they are made up of quarks, as seen in Figure 1. 2

Let us look at the forces that keep the constituents together in the four steps of the quantum ladder. The deeper you go, the stronger the forces become. In the piece of metal, the chemical force that keeps the atoms together has the 3

538

strength of a few electron volts (this is a measure of force strength). In the atom, the electrons are bound to the nucleus by a few tens of electron volts. The protons and neutrons are bound within the nucleus by millions of electron volts, and the forces between the quarks in a nucleus are in the billions of electron volts. This leads us to the concept of conditional elementarity. When we apply small amounts of energy, we cannot overcome the forces that keep the constituents together. For example, if energies of less than a few electron volts are available, atoms cannot be decomposed into electrons and nuclei. They seem to be elementary, which means stable, or unchangeable. When energies above a few hundred but below a million electron volts are available, atoms may be decomposed, but nuclei and electrons seem elementary. For energies over a million electron volts, nuclei are decomposed, but the protons and neutrons are elementary. At a billion electron volts, the nucleons appear to be composed of quarks. Electrons, so far, have never been shown to be composite.

It will be important later on to understand the connection between energy and temperature. Heating a piece of material is equivalent to increasing the energy of motion of the constituents of that piece, be they atoms or electrons or other particles. In a hot material, the atoms or the electrons perform all kinds of motions, oscillations, straight flights, etc. The greater the temperature, the higher the energy of the motions. Thus, temperature is equivalent to energy. For example, one electron volt corresponds to about 12,000 degrees Celsius (about 22,000 degrees Fahrenheit). The temperature at which atomic nuclei

4

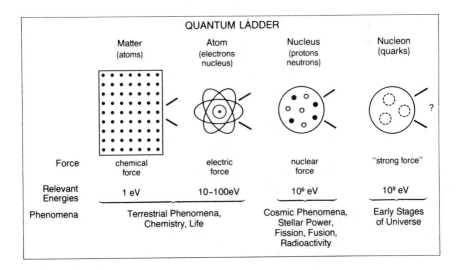

FIGURE 1

decompose is about 20 billion degrees. A billion electron volts would be about 20 trillion degrees Celsius.

On the last rung of the quantum ladder, when billions of electron volts are available—by means of accelerators or when the universe was very hot—new phenomena appear. Let us call it the subnuclear realm. Antimatter plays an important role at that stage. What is it? In the last fifty years it was discovered that there is an antiparticle to every particle; an antielectron called a positron, an antiproton and antineutron, an antiquark. They carry the opposite charge of the actual particle. Thus there ought to exist antiatoms, antimolecules, antimatter of all sorts, made of antielectrons and antinuclei. Why do we not find antimatter in our environment? Because of an important fact: when an antiparticle hits a particle, they "annihilate." A small explosion occurs, and the two entities disappear in a burst of light energy or other forms of energy. This is in agreement with the famous Einstein formula $E=mc^2$, which says that mass—in this case, the masses of the particle and the antiparticle—is a form of energy. The opposite process also occurs: a high concentration of energy can give rise to the birth of a particle and antiparticle. This is called pair creation.

To summarize the quantum ladder, let me quote a prophetic statement by Newton, who wrote three hundred years ago; it describes Figure 1 from the right to the left, as it were:

> Now the smallest particles of matter may cohere by the strongest attractions, and compose bigger particles of weaker virtue. And many of these may cohere, and compose bigger particles whose virtue is still weaker. And so on for universe successions, until the progression ends in the biggest particles on which the operation in chemistry and the colors of natural bodies depend, which by cohering compose bodies of a sensible magnitude. . . .

. . . like that piece of metal. He foresaw the ideas of the structure of matter that were developed centuries after his time.

2.

Let us now turn to our main subject: the universe. Let's first look at the universe as we see it today. There are six facts that are important to us. First, most of the stars we see in the universe consist of 93 percent hydrogen, 6 percent helium, and only 1 percent all other elements. This has been determined by analyzing the light from the stars. Here on earth, things—including our bodies—consist mainly of other elements besides hydrogen. But this is a special case; the stars are made mostly of hydrogen. I have to mention something of which astronomers should be very much ashamed. It turned out that visible matter, the one that sends light to us, is only 10 percent of the total matter. Ninety percent of the matter of the universe is what is now called dark matter— dark because we don't see it; dark because we don't know what it is. How do we know that it is there? The dark matter, like any matter, attracts other matter by gravity. One has found motions of stars and galaxies that could not be explained by the gravitational attraction of the visible, luminous matter. For example, stars in the neighborhood of galaxies move much faster than they would if they were attracted only by the visible stars. So far the nature of that dark matter is unknown. We do not have the slightest idea of what 90 percent of the world is made of.

The second fact concerns the distribution of matter in space. We know that 8 it is very uneven. We see stars, but nothing in between; we see galaxies and clusters of galaxies. However, if we average over a large part of space containing many stars and galaxies, we find that luminous matter is very thinly distributed, only about one hydrogen atom per cubic meter. To this we must add ten times as much dark matter.

The third fact is the expansion of the universe. The following astounding 9 observation was made about sixty years ago, first by the American astronomer E. P. Hubble. It was Hubble who found that faraway objects like galaxies move away from us; the greater the distance, the faster they move away. For example, a galaxy that is as far as one million light years moves away from us with a speed of about twenty kilometers per second. Another galaxy, at a distance of two million light years, moves away at forty kilometers per second; another, at three million light years, moves away at sixty kilometers per second; and so on. As a consequence, the distances between objects in space increase as time goes on. The universe gets more dilute with time. It is a kind of decompression of matter.

A most dramatic conclusion must be drawn from this: if we go backward in 10 time, we conclude that galaxies were nearer to each other in the past. Therefore, at a certain time in the far distant past, the matter in the universe must have been extremely dense. Matter must have been highly compressed, far more than any compression achievable on earth by technical means. At that time there were no galaxies or stars: matter was so thoroughly compressed that everything merged. A little calculation shows that this happened about 12 billion years ago.

In this calculation, one has taken into account that the expansion was faster 11 at an earlier time, since the gravitational attraction acts like a brake and slows down the expansion. Today's rate of expansion, the so-called Hubble constant, is not very well established. It could be fifteen or thirty, instead of twenty, kilometers per second at a million light years. Therefore, the time of extreme compression—this is the time of the beginning of our universe, of the Big Bang—may not have been 12 billion years ago, but perhaps 10 or 15 billion years ago. Still, we can introduce a new chronology: the zero time is the time of extreme compression, the time of the Big Bang. Today is about 12 billion years since the beginning.

We now approach the fourth point regarding our present universe. How far 12 can we see into space? Since the universe is about 12 billion years old, we cannot see farther than about 12 billion light years. We call this distance the cosmic horizon of today. As we will see later in more detail, the Big Bang was a tremendous explosion in which space expanded almost infinitely fast, creating matter over a region probably much larger than what is visible today. Light from those farther regions has not had enough time to reach us today but may do so in the future.

There is another interesting consequence: the farther we look within the cosmic horizons, the younger are the objects we see. After all, it took time for the light to reach us. The light we see of a galaxy, say, 100 million light years away, was emitted 100 million years ago. A picture of the galaxy shows how it was 100 million years back. Figure 2 shows this schematically. The outer circle is the cosmic horizon. The broken circle is about six billion light years away, and objects there appear to us only six billion years old. What about objects at or very near the horizon? What we see there is matter in its first moments, matter just or almost just born. Thus, if we had very good telescopes, we could see the whole history of matter in the universe, starting far out and ending near us. 13

Beware of the following misunderstanding. One could wrongly argue that, say, the regions that are six billion light years away were much nearer to us when they did send out their light, and therefore we should see them earlier than six billion years after emission. This conclusion is false, because the light velocity must be understood as relative to the expanding space. Seen from a nonexpanding frame, a light beam running against the expansion—that is, toward us—moves slower than the usual light velocity. As it were, light is dragged along with the expansion. 14

Our fifth question has to do with the temperature in the universe. How hot is it out there? Let us consider a kiln, such as potters use, to understand the 15

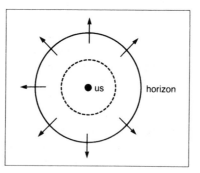

Figure 2

situation. Take a kiln and heat it up. First you can see no light, but the kiln radiates microwaves. When it gets hotter it radiates infrared radiation, which we do not see but can feel as heat radiation. At higher temperatures it becomes red, then yellow and white, then ultraviolet; at millions of degrees it will radiate X-rays.

Today, in the immediate surroundings within a few million light years, the temperature is very low in space. It was measured a few decades ago when two Princeton physicists, A. Penzias and R. Wilson, found a very cool microwave radiation in space corresponding to heat radiation of only five degrees above absolute zero—the lowest possible temperature, which is minus 460°F. An appropriate measure of very low temperatures is the Kelvin scale. Zero degree Kelvin is absolute zero. The Kelvin scale uses Celsius degrees above absolute zero. Thus, the space temperature in our neighborhood is 3°K. This is the temperature in space between the stars. The stars are much hotter inside, but there is so much space between them that their higher temperature does not count. 16

Was the temperature always 3°K? No, it was much warmer at earlier times, a fact that is related to the expansion of the universe. Let us go back to the kiln again. Imagine a kiln made in such a way that we can expand or contract its volume at will. The laws of physics tell us that the temperature of a kiln drops when it expands and rises when it contracts. Thus, we must conclude that the expansion of the universe lowers the temperature. It must have been hotter at earlier times. For example, about six million years ago, the temperature was roughly twice as high—that is, near 6°K. At the very beginning, about 12 billion years ago, when space was extremely contracted, the temperature must have been extremely high. This has interesting consequences. 17

We know from the physics of radiation that matter is transparent for light when the temperature is below 1,000°C. This is true only for very dilute matter, such as that found in the space between the stars. Matter of ordinary density, such as a piece of iron or wood, is not transparent, of course. But if the temperature is raised from 1,000°C, even very dilute matter becomes opaque. Thus light from those outer regions near the cosmic horizon, which are so young that the temperature is over 1,000°C, cannot penetrate space and will not reach us. We should emphasize that these regions are very near the cosmic horizon. A temperature of 1,000°C was reached when the universe was about 300,000 years old, an age that is very young compared with 12 billion years. Hence, light reaches us not from the cosmic horizon but from a distance that is almost as far as the cosmic horizon. We see only matter older than 300,000 years, which is nevertheless pretty young. Even younger matter, younger than that, is hidden by the opaque space. 18

Figure 3 illustrates this schematically. The outermost circle is the cosmic horizon, where matter is just born at extreme density and extreme heat. But already a little nearer to us at the center, the temperature has fallen to and 19 below 1,000°C, and we can see it, since space inside that second circle is transparent.

But why do we not see that part of the universe glowing white-hot at 1,000°C? The reason is the famous Doppler effect. That part of the universe moves away from us at a terrific speed according to the law of expansion, which states that the greater the distance of an object, the faster it moves away from us. The Doppler effect reduces the frequency of light if the emitting object moves away from us. Everybody has observed how the whistle of a fire engine lowers its pitch as the engine moves away. Reducing the frequency is equivalent to lowering the temperature. Red's frequency is lower than yellow's and much lower than violet's. Therefore, the heat radiation from that faraway region of 1,000°K is much cooled down because it moves away from us so fast. Indeed, it is cooled down from 1,000°K to 3°K. Thus, the cool radiation that Penzias and Wilson have observed is indeed the radiation from the hot universe 300,000 years after the Big Bang. The 3°K radiation can be considered the optical reverberation of the Big Bang. This is not quite correct, because it was emitted a little later. That is the explanation of the cool radiation of today.

3.

So far we have discussed the present state of the universe and what one can deduce from it as to its past. Now we will recount the speculations and hypotheses as to the history of the universe from the Big Bang to today, and perhaps also what was before the Big Bang. Usually history does not enter physics. One studies the properties of matter as it is today. Other sciences, such as geology, anthropology, and biology, are historical sciences; the first one deals with the history of the earth, anthropology with the history of the human animal, and biology with the history of animal and plant species.

When physics becomes historical, it deals with the history of matter—that

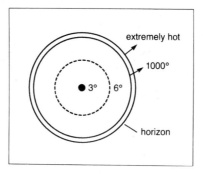

Figure 3

is, with the history of the universe. It is then called cosmology. It must be emphasized that most of the conclusions are much less reliable than those in other fields of physics. Facts are scarce and not known with any accuracy. The Russian physicist Lev Landau said that the cosmologists have very weak facts to work with but very strong convictions about what they think is going on. Whatever will be told here may turn out to be wrong in the near future. Nevertheless, it is so impressive that it is worth reporting.

As we have seen, our universe is expanding and cooling down. We are in   23
principle able to see parts of the universe in earlier periods just by looking at distant objects. We have seen that this is possible to a point in time in the past 300,000 years after the Big Bang. Let us therefore call the time from 300,000 years after the Bang up to today the period of observable history. Of course, the history is observable only in principle. Actually, our instruments are not good enough to get detailed information regarding very distant objects.

We will not say much about that period; the preobservable history is more   24
interesting. At the beginning of observable history the temperature was around 1,000°K, which was low enough so that atoms were not destroyed and robbed of their electrons. Therefore, space was filled mainly with hydrogen and helium atoms forming a hot gas. The density of things never was completely uniform. There were gas accumulations here and more dilute parts somewhere else. The accumulations grew because of gravity. They had more concentration of mass and therefore attracted the surrounding gas more strongly than the dilute parts. The further this accumulative process went, the more effective the gravitational pull became. Such accumulations finally formed "protostars" of much higher density than elsewhere. These protostars also became much hotter than the rest, since compression produces heat. When it became hot enough at the center of such protostars, nuclear reactions were ignited, producing even more energy. The protostar became a real star like the sun, whose radiation energy comes from the nuclear reactions at the center. Furthermore, the early deviations from complete uniformity caused the stars to be not uniformly distributed but to form agglomerations that we see today as galaxies.

The nuclear reactions inside a star produce helium out of hydrogen. When   25
a star has used up its primary nuclear fuel—hydrogen—at its center, other nuclear processes form heavier elements, such as carbon, oxygen, up to iron. Finally the star explodes and becomes a supernova. In this process most other elements are formed and expelled into space. Then new accumulations and protostars are formed from the gases in space, which now contain traces of other heavier elements, such as oxygen, carbon, iron, gold, and uranium. The sun is an example of a "second-generation" star. Some of the stars are surrounded by planets like the sun. In some of the planets, such as the earth, heavier elements are present in higher concentration. This is because most hydrogen and helium atoms escape from smaller planets, since those atoms are light and planets exert only weak gravitational pull. The hydrogen found on earth is

bound in molecules to heavier atoms. Life may develop under the mild warming of the nearby star. So much for the observable history.

Now let us turn to the period between the Big Bang and the onset of observable history at about 300,000 years. Let us call it preobservable history. Nothing about that period can be observed; space was opaque because the temperature was higher than 1,000°C. But we are able to conclude from our knowledge of physics what happened during that period, at least for times that are not too near to the Big Bang. Pursuing the picture of an expanding and cooling universe, one comes to the conclusion that a microsecond after the Big Bang, the temperature must have reached about 10 trillion degrees, or a thermal energy of a billion electron volts. Our present knowledge is good enough that we can guess what has happened in the universe between a microsecond and 300,000 years. But conclusions about events at earlier times, when the energy concentrations were higher, are very uncertain. 26

Let us tell the story in reverse, going back in time from 300,000 years to a microsecond. In that inverse sense, the universe must be regarded as contracting and getting hotter. When the temperature was hotter than 10,000°K, the atoms were decomposed and formed a "plasma," a dense gas of nuclei and electrons. The plasma was bathed in shining light, visible light, during the time when the temperature was between a thousand and a few ten thousand degrees. 27

That light was more and more ultraviolet (that is, of a higher frequency) at earlier times, when the temperature was higher. This radiation should be considered the same as today's 3°K radiation but enormously compressed at the early seconds of the expansion. Compression makes light hotter and of higher frequency. Going back in time, we come to a moment at about one second after the Big Bang, when the temperature was about 10 billion degrees, corresponding to an energy concentration of about a few million electron volts. At that point the thermal energy is high enough for creating pairs of electrons and antielectrons (positrons). This is the process of matter-antimatter formation mentioned before. Hence, at one second and earlier, when the temperature was even higher, space was filled by a plasma composed not only of hydrogen and helium nuclei and their electrons but also of a rather dense gas of electrons and positrons. 28

At a fraction of a second after the Bang, the temperature was high enough to split the helium and nuclei into neutrons and protons. Finally, when our backward history reaches the microsecond after the Bang, the heat and the corresponding energy concentration were high enough not only to decompose protons and neutrons into quarks but also to produce quark-antiquark pairs. At this point of our backward journey in time, the universe was filled with hot, dense gases of quarks and antiquarks, electrons and positrons, and a very intense, high-frequency thermal light radiation. There was also a hot, dense gas of neutrinos, which survived the whole evolution and should be present even 29 today, though much less hot and dense, together with the cool three-degree light radiation. We stop at this point, which is a millionth of a second after the Big Bang. We are practically at it anyway.

The prehistory described here is based on a relatively firm knowledge of the 30 properties of matter at energy concentrations up to several billion electron volts. This knowledge stems from experiments made with accelerators producing particle beams at these energies. The largest of these machines, the ones in Geneva, Switzerland, and in Batavia, Illinois, have reached energies of several hundred billion electron volts. It would be hard to guess what happened much earlier than a microsecond, since the energy concentrations were much higher than the ones reached with our accelerators, and we have no way to know how matter behaves at these enormous compressions and temperatures.

4.

We now have reached the point where we should ask the great questions: 31 What was the Big Bang? What caused it? And what existed before? When facing these exciting questions, it must be said that we have no reliable answers. There are speculation, guesswork led by intuition, and a great deal of imagination that may turn out to be wrong in a few years. However, the answers that are discussed in these days are so unusual and impressive that it is worthwhile to describe them in simple terms. The underlying ideas came mostly from four persons whom one might call the four apostles of the new story of Genesis: Alan Guth of MIT, Alexander Vilenkin of Tufts University, Andrei Linde in the USSR, and Stephen Hawking in England. Paul Steinhardt of the University of Pennsylvania also contributed to it.

In order to understand the basic ideas, we must introduce a concept that is 32 suggested by some of the latest developments in particle physics. It is the so-called false vacuum. According to these ideas, there are two types of vacuum: the true vacuum and the false vacuum. The true one is very much what one would imagine: it is empty space, empty of matter and empty of energy. The false vacuum, however, is also empty of matter, but not of energy. The energy of the false vacuum is supposed to be none of the ordinary forms of energy, such as electric fields or gravity fields. It is imagined to be a new kind of field, of a type encountered in the current theories of radioactive processes. The most characteristic feature of the false vacuum follows directly from Einstein's general relativity theory. A region filled with energy but not with matter is bound to expand suddenly and explosively, filling more and more space with false vacuum. Alan Guth has called it, succinctly, an inflationary expansion, with a speed very much faster than the previously considered expansion of our universe at any time in its development. According to our four apostles, this sudden explosion is nothing else but the Big Bang.

How does this sudden inflationary expansion of a false vacuum start? Before 33

547

the event, all space was in the state of a true vacuum. "The world was without form and void, and darkness was upon the face of the deep," as the Bible says. Now we must introduce a concept that is typical for quantum mechanics. According to the fundamental tenets of this well-established theory, there is nothing in nature that remains quiet. Everything, including the true vacuum, is subject to fluctuations—in particular to energy fluctuations. The field that provides the energy to the false vacuum is absent in the true vacuum, but not completely. There must be fluctuations of the field. Thus, at one moment a small region somewhere in space may have fluctuated into a false vacuum. It would happen very rarely but cannot be excluded. That region almost instantly expands tremendously and creates a large space filled with energy according to the properties of a false vacuum. That is supposed to be the Big Bang!

One might wonder where the energy comes from that fills the expanding false vacuum. There is no need to worry about conservation of energy. According to Einstein, energy is subject to gravity. The newly created energies interact via gravity, an effect that produces negative energy, so that the net energy remains essentially constant. 34

When a certain large size is reached, the inflationary explosion stops and a true vacuum emerges. But the vast amount of energy contained in the false vacuum must have shown up in some form. It filled the true vacuum with hot light, quark-antiquark pairs, electron-antielectron pairs, neutrinos, etc.—in other words, with all the stuff we have described as filling the space at a microsecond after the Big Bang. Our universe is born, the slow expansion takes over, the temperature falls, and the preobservable history develops and is followed by the observable history. 35

In short, the history of our universe started with a fluctuation of the empty true vacuum into a small region of false vacuum, which exploded, almost immediately, into a very much larger region of false vacuum. That was the primal Bang. Then it changed to a true vacuum, but the energy of the false vacuum created all light, all particles and antiparticles, which developed into what existed at about a microsecond after the explosion. Then the ordinary expansion of the universe took over; it cooled down; quarks and antiquarks as well as electrons and antielectrons were annihilated, but a few supernumerary quarks and electrons remained. The quarks formed protons and neutrons. Then some of these nucleons formed helium nuclei. After 300,000 years it was cool enough that the protons and helium nuclei could grab and retain electrons and become atoms. A hot gas of hydrogen and helium appeared. The gas of atoms condensed to protostars, which became hot inside, allowing nuclear processes to start. Stars were born, grouping themselves in galaxies. The nuclear reactions in the center of the stars and in exploding supernovas produced heavier elements. The expelled gases of exploding stars condensed to protostars and then to stars containing traces of all elements, not only hydrogen and helium. The sun is one of these second-generation stars. It is surrounded by planets, some 36 of which—such as the earth—are special concentrations of heavier elements, benignly supplied with energy from the nearby sun, so that life can start and develop the strange human animal that pretends to understand the whole process.

An interesting conclusion follows from this view of the birth of our universe, as the consequence of an energy fluctuation in the true vacuum. Such intense fluctuations creating a speck of false vacuum are very rare, but it may have happened at other places in infinite space at other times and may have developed into other universes. Thus, we may conclude that our universe is not the only one. It is not the center and the stage of everything in this world. There may be other universes much older or much younger or even not yet born somewhere else. Remember that our universe today is most probably considerably larger than our present cosmic horizon of about 12 billion light years, but there is room and time enough for many other universes. Maybe, in a few billion years, another universe will penetrate ours. Until then we cannot check this hypothesis. Our own universe, of which we see only a small part today, may not be unique. Its beginning is not the beginning of everything. Other universes may exist at an earlier or later stage. 37

It must be emphasized again that these are unproven hypotheses. They may turn out to be pure fantasies, but the ideas are impressively grandiose. 38

The origin of the universe is not only of scientific interest. It always was the subject of mythology, art, and religion. Such approaches are complementary to scientific ones. Most familiarly, the Old Testament describes the beginning of the world with the creation of light on the first day. It seemed contradictory that the sun, our terrestrial source of light, was only created on day four, but it turns out to be in line with current scientific thought, according to which the early universe was full of various kinds of radiation long before the sun appeared. 39

Those first days have been depicted in various forms, in pictures and poetry, but to me, Franz Josef Haydn's oratorio *The Creation* is the most remarkable rendition of the Big Bang. At the beginning we hear a choir of angels singing mysteriously and softly, "And God Said Let There Be Light." And at the words "And There Was Light" the entire choir and the orchestra explode into a blazing C major chord. There is no more beautiful and impressive presentation of the beginning of everything. 40

QUESTIONS

1. Reread the quotation from Newton given in paragraph 6, near the end of section 1. How nearly does it summarize Weisskopf's explanation in that section? Why is it useful for Weisskopf to provide that summary?

2. Notice how Weisskopf structures section 1 by reviewing four related structures; then he opens section 2 by saying he will explain six facts. What are some further examples of orderliness in his presentation?

3. What implications do you find in Weisskopf's claim in paragraph 7 that "ninety percent of the matter of the universe is what is now called dark matter"? What later claims seem related to it?

4. Explain how Weisskopf sets up the "dramatic conclusion" drawn after the "third fact" presented in paragraph 9.

5. One of Weisskopf's themes is how much we don't know, ranging beyond what we do know or can conjecture. List several examples he gives of what we do not know. What relations do you find among these ideas?

6. In paragraph 33, Weisskopf says, "Thus, at one moment a small region somewhere in space may have fluctuated into a false vacuum." Three paragraphs later, he adds, "In short, the history of our universe started with a fluctuation of the empty true vacuum into a small region of false vacuum." How do you understand the terms *fluctuated* and *fluctuation* in these sentences? Is *fluctuate* a technical term? What are some consequences of that term for understanding "the origin of our universe"?

7. Weisskopf makes several mentions of the Bible in his account of the origins of the universe and even, with a trace of humor, mentions "the four apostles of the new story of Genesis" (paragraph 31). Reread the story of creation in Genesis. How many points of convergence do you find between Genesis and Weisskopf's explanation? Note especially Weisskopf's mention of the creation of the sun on the fourth day, according to Genesis (paragraph 39). How do you account for such detail in Genesis?

8. Go to the library and look up several more creation stories according to various religions and mythological systems. Compare two or three such stories, looking especially for surprising convergences with Weisskopf's summary of contemporary scientific thinking.

MAKING CONNECTIONS

1. Taking Weisskopf's essay together with the essays by Stephen W. Hawking and Francis Crick, you can get a pretty good introduction to contemporary cosmological thinking. What attitudes of mind unify these thinkers? How do they stand in relation to Banesh Hoffmann's observation of the extraordinary "simplicity" of Einstein?

2. Choose a two- or three-paragraph sequence of close explanation in at least two of the three writers, Crick, Hawking, and Weisskopf, and compare their explanations. Choose passages that you find especially clear. What accounts for that clarity? Are diagrams especially helpful? Do the explanations follow an orderly list of subtopics? Are the sentences particularly vivid and precise? Using the two or three good examples you locate, try to draw some conclusions about effective presentation of technical material.

THE MAN WHO MISTOOK
HIS WIFE FOR A HAT

Oliver Sacks

The following essay is taken from Sacks's collection, The
Man Who Mistook His Wife for a Hat and Other Clinical
Tales. *As the headnote on page 407 details, Sacks's writing
deals not only with textbook cases in clinical neurology, but
also with the bizarre, sometimes tragic and funny stories
the neurologist observes and catalogues. For that reason,
Sacks's prose style is lyrical as well as accurate; his explanation of prosopagnosia seeks to engage our interest and
emotions at the same time it defines and illustrates a syndrome unfamiliar to many readers.*

Dr P. was a musician of distinction, well-known for many years as a singer, 1
and then, at the local School of Music, as a teacher. It was here, in relation to
his students, that certain strange problems were first observed. Sometimes a
student would present himself, and Dr P. would not recognise him; or, specifically, would not recognise his face. The moment the student spoke, he would
be recognised by his voice. Such incidents multiplied, causing embarrassment,
perplexity, fear—and, sometimes, comedy. For not only did Dr P. increasingly
fail to see faces, but he saw faces when there were no faces to see: genially,
Magoo-like, when in the street he might pat the heads of water hydrants and
parking meters, taking these to be the heads of children; he would amiably
address carved knobs on the furniture and be astounded when they did not
reply. At first these odd mistakes were laughed off as jokes, not least by Dr P.
himself. Had he not always had a quirky sense of humour and been given to
Zen-like paradoxes and jests? His musical powers were as dazzling as ever; he
did not feel ill—he had never felt better; and the mistakes were so ludicrous—
and so ingenious—that they could hardly be serious or betoken anything serious.
The notion of there being "something the matter" did not emerge until some
three years later, when diabetes developed. Well aware that diabetes could affect
his eyes, Dr P. consulted an ophthalmologist, who took a careful history and
examined his eyes closely. "There's nothing the matter with your eyes," the
doctor concluded. "But there is trouble with the visual parts of your brain. You
don't need my help, you must see a neurologist." And so, as a result of this
referral, Dr P. came to me.

It was obvious within a few seconds of meeting him that there was no trace 2

551

of dementia in the ordinary sense. He was a man of great cultivation and charm who talked well and fluently, with imagination and humour. I couldn't think why he had been referred to our clinic.

And yet there *was* something a bit odd. He faced me as he spoke, was 3 oriented towards me, and yet there was something the matter—it was difficult to formulate. He faced me with his *ears*, I came to think, but not with his eyes. These, instead of looking, gazing, at me, "taking me in," in the normal way, made sudden strange fixations—on my nose, on my right ear, down to my chin, up to my right eye—as if noting (even studying) these individual features, but not seeing my whole face, its changing expressions, "me," as a whole. I am not sure that I fully realised this at the time—there was just a teasing strangeness, some failure in the normal interplay of gaze and expression. He saw me, he *scanned* me, and yet . . .

"What seems to be the matter?" I asked him at length. 4

"Nothing that I know of," he replied with a smile, "but people seem to think 5 there's something wrong with my eyes."

"But *you* don't recognise any visual problems?" 6

"No, not directly, but I occasionally make mistakes." 7

I left the room briefly to talk to his wife. When I came back, Dr P. was 8 sitting placidly by the window, attentive, listening rather than looking out. "Traffic," he said, "street sounds, distant trains—they make a sort of symphony, do they not? You know Honegger's *Pacific 234?*"

What a lovely man, I thought to myself. How can there be anything seriously 9 the matter? Would he permit me to examine him?

"Yes, of course, Dr Sacks." 10

I stilled my disquiet, his perhaps, too, in the soothing routine of a neuro- 11 logical exam—muscle strength, coordination, reflexes, tone. . . . It was while examining his reflexes—a trifle abnormal on the left side—that the first bizarre experience occurred. I had taken off his left shoe and scratched the sole of his foot with a key—a frivolous-seeming but essential test of a reflex—and then, excusing myself to screw my ophthalmoscope together, left him to put on the shoe himself. To my surprise, a minute later, he had not done this.

"Can I help?" I asked. 12

"Help what? Help whom?" 13

"Help you put on your shoe." 14

"Ach," he said, "I had forgotten the shoe," adding, *sotto voce,* "The shoe? 15 The shoe?" He seemed baffled.

"Your shoe," I repeated. "Perhaps you'd put it on." 16

He continued to look downwards, though not at the shoe, with an intense 17 but misplaced concentration. Finally his gaze settled on his foot: "That is my shoe, yes?"

Did I mis-hear? Did he mis-see? 18

"My eyes," he explained, and put a hand to his foot. "*This* is my shoe, no?" 19

552

"No, it is not. That is your foot. *There* is your shoe." 20

"Ah! I thought that was my foot." 21

Was he joking? Was he mad? Was he blind? If this was one of his "strange 22 mistakes," it was the strangest mistake I had ever come across.

I helped him on with his shoe (his foot), to avoid further complication. Dr 23 P. himself seemed untroubled, indifferent, maybe amused. I resumed my examination. His visual acuity was good: he had no difficulty seeing a pin on the floor, though sometimes he missed it if it was placed to his left.

He saw all right, but what did he see? I opened out a copy of the *National* 24 *Geographic Magazine* and asked him to describe some pictures in it.

His responses here were very curious. His eyes would dart from one thing 25 to another, picking up tiny features, individual features, as they had done with my face. A striking brightness, a colour, a shape would arrest his attention and elicit comment—but in no case did he get the scene-as-a-whole. He failed to see the whole, seeing only details, which he spotted like blips on a radar screen. He never entered into relation with the picture as a whole—never faced, so to speak, *its* physiognomy. He had no sense whatever of a landscape or scene.

I showed him the cover, an unbroken expanse of Sahara dunes. 26

"What do you see here?" I asked. 27

"I see a river," he said. "And a little guest-house with its terrace on the water. 28 People are dining out on the terrace. I see coloured parasols here and there." He was looking, if it was "looking," right off the cover into mid-air and confabulating nonexistent features, as if the absence of features in the actual picture had driven him to imagine the river and the terrace and the coloured parasols.

I must have looked aghast, but he seemed to think he had done rather well. 29 There was a hint of a smile on his face. He also appeared to have decided that the examination was over and started to look around for his hat. He reached out his hand and took hold of his wife's head, tried to lift it off, to put it on. He had apparently mistaken his wife for a hat! His wife looked as if she was used to such things.

I could make no sense of what had occurred in terms of conventional 30 neurology (or neuropsychology). In some ways he seemed perfectly preserved, and in others absolutely, incomprehensibly devastated. How could he, on the one hand, mistake his wife for a hat and, on the other, function, as apparently he still did, as a teacher at the Music School?

I had to think, to see him again—and to see him in his own familiar habitat, 31 at home.

A few days later I called on Dr P. and his wife at home, with the score of 32 the *Dichterliebe* in my briefcase (I knew he liked Schumann), and a variety of odd objects for the testing of perception. Mrs P. showed me into a lofty apartment, which recalled fin-de-siècle Berlin. A magnificent old Bösendorfer stood in state in the centre of the room, and all around it were music stands, instruments, scores. . . . There were books, there were paintings, but the music was central. Dr P. came in, a little bowed, and, distracted, advanced with outstretched hands to the grandfather clock, but, hearing my voice, corrected himself, and shook hands with me. We exchanged greetings and chatted a little of current concerts and performances. Diffidently, I asked him if he would sing.

"The *Dichterliebe!*" he exclaimed. "But I can no longer read music. You will play them, yes?"

I said I would try. On that wonderful old piano even my playing sounded right, and Dr P. was an aged but infinitely mellow Fischer-Dieskau, combining a perfect ear and voice with the most incisive musical intelligence. It was clear that the Music School was not keeping him on out of charity.

Dr P.'s temporal lobes were obviously intact: he had a wonderful musical cortex. What, I wondered, was going on in his parietal and occipital lobes, especially in those areas where visual processing occurred? I carry the Platonic solids in my neurological kit and decided to start with these.

"What is this?" I asked, drawing out the first one.

"A cube, of course."

"Now this?" I asked, brandishing another.

He asked if he might examine it, which he did swiftly and systematically: "A dodecahedron, of course. And don't bother with the others—I'll get the icosahedron, too."

Abstract shapes clearly presented no problems. What about faces? I took out a pack of cards. All of these he identified instantly, including the jacks, queens, kings, and the joker. But these, after all, are stylised designs, and it was impossible to tell whether he saw faces or merely patterns. I decided I would show him a volume of cartoons which I had in my briefcase. Here, again, for the most part, he did well. Churchill's cigar, Schnozzle's nose: as soon as he had picked out a key feature he could identify the face. But cartoons, again, are formal and schematic. It remained to be seen how he would do with real faces, realistically represented.

I turned on the television, keeping the sound off, and found an early Bette Davis film. A love scene was in progress. Dr P. failed to identify the actress—but this could have been because she had never entered his world. What was more striking was that he failed to identify the expressions on her face or her partner's, though in the course of a single torrid scene these passed from sultry yearning through passion, surprise, disgust, and fury to a melting reconciliation. Dr P. could make nothing of any of this. He was very unclear as to what was going on, or who was who or even what sex they were. His comments on the scene were positively Martian.

It was just possible that some of his difficulties were associated with the unreality of a celluloid, Hollywood world; and it occurred to me that he might be more successful in identifying faces from his own life. On the walls of the apartment there were photographs of his family, his colleagues, his pupils, himself. I gathered a pile of these together and, with some misgivings, presented them to him. What had been funny, or farcical, in relation to the movie, was tragic in relation to real life. By and large, he recognised nobody: neither his family, nor his colleagues, nor his pupils, nor himself. He recognised a portrait of Einstein because he picked up the characteristic hair and moustache; and the same thing happened with one or two other people. "Ach, Paul!" he said, when shown a portrait of his brother. "That square jaw, those big teeth—I would know Paul anywhere!" But was it Paul he recognised, or one or two of his features, on the basis of which he could make a reasonable guess as to the subject's identity? In the absence of obvious "markers," he was utterly lost. But it was not merely the cognition, the *gnosis*, at fault; there was something radically wrong with the whole way he proceeded. For he approached these faces—even of those near and dear—as if they were abstract puzzles or tests. He did not relate to them, he did not behold. No face was familiar to him, seen as a "thou," being just identified as a set of features, an "it." Thus, there was formal, but no trace of personal, gnosis. And with this went his indifference, or blindness, to expression. A face, to us, is a person looking out—we see, as it were, the person through his *persona*, his face. But for Dr P. there was no *persona* in this sense—no outward *persona*, and no person within.

I had stopped at a florist on my way to his apartment and bought myself an   43
extravagant red rose for my buttonhole. Now I removed this and handed it to him. He took it like a botanist or morphologist given a specimen, not like a person given a flower.

"About six inches in length," he commented. "A convoluted red form with   44
a linear green attachment."

"Yes," I said encouragingly, "and what do you think it *is*, Dr P.?"   45

"Not easy to say." He seemed perplexed. "It lacks the simple symmetry of   46
the Platonic solids, although it may have a higher symmetry of its own. . . . I think this could be an inflorescence or flower."

"Could be?" I queried.   47

"Could be," he confirmed.   48

"Smell it," I suggested, and he again looked somewhat puzzled, as if I had   49
asked him to smell a higher symmetry. But he complied courteously, and took it to his nose. Now, suddenly, he came to life.

"Beautiful!" he exclaimed. "An early rose. What a heavenly smell!" He   50
started to hum "*Die Rose, die Lillie . . .*" Reality, it seemed, might be conveyed by smell, not by sight.

I tried one final test. It was still a cold day, in early spring, and I had thrown   51
my coat and gloves on the sofa.

"What is this?" I asked, holding up a glove.   52

"May I examine it?" he asked, and, taking it from me, he proceeded to   53
examine it as he had examined the geometrical shapes.

"A continuous surface," he announced at last, "infolded on itself. It appears   54
to have"—he hesitated—"five outpouchings, if this is the word."

"Yes," I said cautiously. "You have given me a description. Now tell me   55
what it is."

"A container of some sort?"   56

"Yes," I said, "and what would it contain?"   57

"It would contain its contents!" said Dr P., with a laugh. "There are many   58
possibilities. It could be a change purse, for example, for coins of five sizes. It
could . . ."

I interrupted the barmy flow. "Does it not look familiar? Do you think it   59
might contain, might fit, a part of your body?"

No light of recognition dawned on his face.[1]   60

No child would have the power to see and speak of "a continuous surface   61
. . . infolded on itself," but any child, any infant, would immediately know a
glove as a glove, see it as familiar, as going with a hand. Dr P. didn't. He saw
nothing as familiar. Visually, he was lost in a world of lifeless abstractions.
Indeed, he did not have a real visual world, as he did not have a real visual
self. He could speak about things, but did not see them face-to-face. Hughlings
Jackson, discussing patients with aphasia and left-hemisphere lesions, says they
have lost "abstract" and "propositional" thought—and compares them with dogs
(or, rather, he compares dogs to patients with aphasia). Dr P., on the other
hand, functioned precisely as a machine functions. It wasn't merely that he
displayed the same indifference to the visual world as a computer but—even
more strikingly—he construed the world as a computer construes it, by means
of key features and schematic relationships. The scheme might be identified—
in an "identi-kit" way—without the reality being grasped at all.

The testing I had done so far told me nothing about Dr P.'s inner world.   62
Was it possible that his visual memory and imagination were still intact? I asked
him to imagine entering one of our local squares from the north side, to walk
through it, in imagination or in memory, and tell me the buildings he might
pass as he walked. He listed the buildings on his right side, but none of those
on his left. I then asked him to imagine entering the square from the south.
Again he mentioned only those buildings that were on the right side, although
these were the very buildings he had omitted before. Those he had "seen"
internally before were not mentioned now; presumably, they were no longer
"seen." It was evident that his difficulties with leftness, his visual field deficits,
were as much internal as external, bisecting his visual memory and imagination.

What, at a higher level, of his internal visualisation? Thinking of the almost   63
hallucinatory intensity with which Tolstoy visualises and animates his characters, I questioned Dr P. about *Anna Karenina*. He could remember incidents

---

[1] Later, by accident, he got it on, and exclaimed, "My God, it's a glove!" This was reminiscent
of Kurt Goldstein's patient "Lanuti," who could only recognise objects by trying to use them in
action.

without difficulty, had an undiminished grasp of the plot, but completely omitted visual characteristics, visual narrative, and scenes. He remembered the words of the characters but not their faces; and though, when asked, he could quote, with his remarkable and almost verbatim memory, the original visual descriptions, these were, it became apparent, quite empty for him and lacked sensorial, imaginal, or emotional reality. Thus, there was an internal agnosia as well.[2]

But this was only the case, it became clear, with certain sorts of visualisation. The visualisation of faces and scenes, of visual narrative and drama—this was profoundly impaired, almost absent. But the visualisation of *schemata* was preserved, perhaps enhanced. Thus, when I engaged him in a game of mental chess, he had no difficulty visualising the chessboard or the moves—indeed, no difficulty in beating me soundly. 64

Luria said of Zazetsky that he had entirely lost his capacity to play games but that his "vivid imagination" was unimpaired. Zazetsky and Dr P. lived in worlds which were mirror images of each other. But the saddest difference between them was that Zazetsky, as Luria said, "fought to regain his lost faculties with the indomitable tenacity of the damned," whereas Dr P. was not fighting, did not know what was lost, did not indeed know that anything was lost. But who was more tragic, or who was more damned—the man who knew it, or the man who did not? 65

When the examination was over, Mrs P. called us to the table, where there was coffee and a delicious spread of little cakes. Hungrily, hummingly, Dr P. started on the cakes. Swiftly, fluently, unthinkingly, melodiously, he pulled the plates towards him and took this and that in a great gurgling stream, an edible song of food, until, suddenly, there came an interruption: a loud, peremptory rat-tat-tat at the door. Startled, taken aback, arrested by the interruption, Dr P. stopped eating and sat frozen, motionless, at the table, with an indifferent, blind bewilderment on his face. He saw, but no longer saw, the table; no longer perceived it as a table laden with cakes. His wife poured him some coffee: the smell titillated his nose and brought him back to reality. The melody of eating resumed. 66

How does he do anything? I wondered to myself. What happens when he's dressing, goes to the lavatory, has a bath? I followed his wife into the kitchen and asked her how, for instance, he managed to dress himself. "It's just like the 67

---

[2] I have often wondered about Helen Keller's visual descriptions, whether these, for all their eloquence, are somehow empty as well? Or whether, by the transference of images from the tactile to the visual, or, yet more extraordinarily, from the verbal and the metaphorical to the sensorial and the visual, she *did* achieve a power of visual imagery, even though her visual cortex had never been stimulated, directly, by the eyes? But in Dr P.'s case it is precisely the cortex that was damaged, the organic prerequisite of all pictorial imagery. Interestingly and typically he no longer dreamed pictorially—the "message" of the dream being conveyed in nonvisual terms.

eating," she explained. "I put his usual clothes out, in all the usual places, and he dresses without difficulty, singing to himself. He does everything singing to himself. But if he is interrupted and loses the thread, he comes to a complete stop, doesn't know his clothes—or his own body. He sings all the time—eating songs, dressing songs, bathing songs, everything. He can't do anything unless he makes it a song."

While we were talking my attention was caught by the pictures on the walls. 68

"Yes," Mrs P. said, "he was a gifted painter as well as a singer. The School 69
exhibited his pictures every year."

I strolled past them curiously—they were in chronological order. All his 70
earlier work was naturalistic and realistic, with vivid mood and atmosphere, but finely detailed and concrete. Then, years later, they became less vivid, less concrete, less realistic and naturalistic, but far more abstract, even geometrical and cubist. Finally, in the last paintings, the canvasses became nonsense, or nonsense to me—mere chaotic lines and blotches of paint. I commented to this to Mrs P.

"Ach, you doctors, you're such Philistines!" she exclaimed. "Can you not 71
see *artistic development*—how he renounced the realism of his earlier years, and advanced into abstract, nonrepresentational art?"

"No, that's not it," I said to myself (but forbore to say it to poor Mrs P.). He 72
had indeed moved from realism to nonrepresentation to the abstract, yet this was not the artist, but the pathology, advancing—advancing towards a profound visual agnosia, in which all powers of representation and imagery, all sense of the concrete, all sense of reality, were being destroyed. This wall of paintings was a tragic pathological exhibit, which belonged to neurology, not art.

And yet, I wondered, was she not partly right? For there is often a struggle, 73
and sometimes, even more interestingly, a collusion between the powers of pathology and creation. Perhaps, in his cubist period, there might have been both artistic and pathological development, colluding to engender an original form; for as he lost the concrete, so he might have gained in the abstract, developing a greater sensitivity to all the structural elements of line, boundary, contour—an almost Picasso-like power to see, and equally depict, those abstract organisations embedded in, and normally lost in, the concrete. . . . Though in the final pictures, I feared, there was only chaos and agnosia.

We returned to the great music room, with the Bösendorfer in the centre, 74
and Dr P. humming the last torte.

"Well, Dr Sacks," he said to me. "You find me an interesting case, I perceive. 75
Can you tell me what you find wrong, make recommendations?"

"I can't tell you what I find wrong," I replied, "but I'll say what I find right. 76
You are a wonderful musician, and music is your life. What I would prescribe, in a case such as yours, is a life which consists entirely of music. Music has been the centre, now make it the whole, of your life."

This was four years ago—I never saw him again, but I often wondered about 77 how he apprehended the world, given his strange loss of image, visuality, and the perfect preservation of a great musicality. I think that music, for him, had taken the place of image. He had no body-image, he had body-music: this is why he could move and act as fluently as he did, but came to a total confused stop if the "inner music" stopped. And equally with the outside, the world . . .[3]

In *The World as Representation and Will*, Schopenhauer speaks of music as "pure will." How fascinated he would have been by Dr P., a man who had wholly lost the world as representation, but wholly preserved it as music or will.

And this, mercifully, held to the end—for despite the gradual advance of his disease (a massive tumour or degenerative process in the visual parts of his brain) Dr P. lived and taught music to the last days of his life.

POSTSCRIPT

How should one interpret Dr P.'s pecular inability to interpret, to judge, a glove as a glove? Manifestly, here, he could not make a cognitive judgment, though he was prolific in the production of cognitive hypotheses. A judgment is intuitive, personal, comprehensive, and concrete—we "see" how things stand, in relation to one another and oneself. It was precisely this setting, this relating, that Dr P. lacked (though his judging, in all other spheres, was prompt and normal). Was this due to lack of visual information, or faulty processing of visual information? (This would be the explanation given by a classical, sche-matic neurology.) Or was there something amiss in Dr P.'s attitude, so that he could not relate what he saw to himself?

These explanations, or modes of explanation, are not mutually exclusive— being in different modes they could coexist and both be true. And this is acknowledged, implicitly or explicitly, in classical neurology: implicitly, by Macrae, when he finds the explanation of defective schemata, or defective visual processing and integration, inadequate; explicitly, by Goldstein, when he speaks of "abstract attitude." But abstract attitude, which allows "categorisation," also misses the mark with Dr P.—and, perhaps, with the concept of "judgment" in general. For Dr P. *had* abstract attitude—indeed, nothing else. And it was precisely this, his absurd abstractness of attitude—absurd because unleavened with anything else—which rendered him incapable of perceiving identity, or particulars, rendered him incapable of judgment.

Neurology and psychology, curiously, though they talk of everything else, almost never talk of "judgment"—and yet it is precisely the downfall of judgment . . . which constitutes the essence of so many neuropsychological disorders.

---

[3] Thus, as I learned later from his wife, though he could not recognise his students if they sat still, if they were merely "images," he might suddenly recognise them if they *moved*. "That's Karl," he would cry. "I know his movements, his body-music."

Judgment and identity may be casualties—but neuropsychology never speaks of them.

And yet, whether in a philosophic sense (Kant's sense), or an empirical and evolutionary sense, judgment is the most important faculty we have. An animal, or a man, may get on very well without "abstract attitude" but will speedily perish if deprived of judgment. Judgment must be the *first* faculty of higher life or mind—yet it is ignored, or misinterpreted, by classical (computational) neurology. And if we wonder how such an absurdity can arise, we find it in the assumptions, or the evolution, of neurology itself. For classical neurology (like classical physics) has always been mechanical—from Hughlings Jackson's mechanical analogies to the computer analogies of today. 83

Of course, the brain *is* a machine and a computer—everything in classical neurology is correct. But our mental processes, which constitute our being and life, are not just abstract and mechanical, but personal, as well—and, as such, involve not just classifying and categorising, but continual judging and feeling also. If this is missing, we become computer-like, as Dr P. was. And, by the same token, if we delete feeling and judging, the personal, from the cognitive sciences, we reduce *them* to something as defective as Dr P.—and we reduce *our* apprehension of the concrete and real. 84

By a sort of comic and awful analogy, our current cognitive neurology and psychology resemble nothing so much as poor Dr P.! We need the concrete and real, as he did; and we fail to see this, as he failed to see it. Our cognitive sciences are themselves suffering from an agnosia essentially similar to Dr P.'s. Dr P. may therefore serve as a warning and parable—of what happens to a science which eschews the judgmental, the particular, the personal, and becomes entirely abstract and computational. 85

It was always a matter of great regret to me that, owing to circumstances beyond my control, I was not able to follow his case further, either in the sort of observations and investigations described, or in ascertaining the actual disease pathology. 86

One always fears that a case is "unique," especially if it has such extraordinary features as those of Dr P. It was, therefore, with a sense of great interest and delight, not unmixed with relief, that I found, quite by chance—looking through the periodical *Brain* for 1956—a detailed description of an almost comically similar case, similar (indeed identical) neuropsychologically and phenomenologically, though the underlying pathology (an acute head injury) and all personal circumstances were wholly different. The authors speak of their case as "unique in the documented history of this disorder"—and evidently experienced, as I did, amazement at their own findings.[4] The interested reader is referred to 87

---

[4]Only since the completion of this book have I found that there is, in fact, a rather extensive literature on visual agnosia in general, and prosopagnosia in particular. In particular I had the great pleasure recently of meeting Dr Andrew Kertesz, who has himself published some extremely detailed studies of patients with such agnosias (see, for example, his paper on visual agnosia, Kertesz 1979).

the original paper, Macrae and Trolle (1956), of which I here subjoin a brief paraphrase, with quotations from the original.

Their patient was a young man of 32, who, following a severe automobile accident, with unconsciousness for three weeks, ". . . complained, exclusively, of an inability to recognise faces, even those of his wife and children." Not a single face was "familiar" to him, but there were three he could identify; these were workmates: one with an eye-blinking tic, one with a large mole on his cheek, and a third "because he was so tall and thin that no one else was like him." Each of these, Macrae and Trolle bring out, was "recognised solely by the single prominent feature mentioned." In general (like Dr P.) he recognised familiars only by their voices.

He had difficulty even recognising himself in a mirror, as Macrae and Trolle describe in detail: "In the early convalescent phase he frequently, especially when shaving, questioned whether the face gazing at him was really his own, and even though he knew it could physically be none other, on several occasions grimaced or stuck out his tongue 'just to make sure.' By carefully studying his face in the mirror he slowly began to recognise it, but 'not in a flash' as in the past—he relied on the hair and facial outline, and on two small moles on his left cheek."

In general he could not recognise objects "at a glance," but would have to seek out, and guess from, one or two features—occasionally his guesses were absurdly wrong. In particular, the authors note, there was difficulty with the *animate*.

On the other hand, simple schematic objects—scissors, watch, key, etc.— presented no difficulties. Macrae and Trolle also note that: "His *topographical memory* was strange: the seeming paradox existed that he could find his way from home to hospital and around the hospital, but yet could not name streets *en route* [unlike Dr P., he also had some aphasia] or appear to visualize the topography."

It was also evident that visual memories of people, even from long before the accident, were severely impaired—there was memory of conduct, or perhaps a mannerism, but not of visual appearance or face. Similarly, it appeared, when he was questioned closely, that he no longer had visual images in his *dreams*. Thus, as with Dr P., it was not just visual perception, but visual imagination and memory, the fundamental powers of visual representation, which were essentially damaged in this patient—at least those powers insofar as they pertained to the personal, the familiar, the concrete.

Dr Kertesz mentioned to me a case known to him of a farmer who had developed prosopagnosia and in consequence could no longer distinguish (the faces of) his *cows*, and of another such patient, an attendant in a Natural History Museum, who mistook his own reflection for the diorama of an *ape*. As with Dr P., and as with Macrae and Trolle's patient, it is especially the animate which is so absurdly misperceived. The most important studies of such agnosias, and of visual processing in general, are now being undertaken by A. R. and H. Damasio.

A final, humorous point. Where Dr P. might mistake his wife for a hat, $\quad$ 93
Macrae's patient, also unable to recognise his wife, needed her to identify
herself by a visual *marker*, by ". . . a conspicuous article of clothing, such as a
large hat."

QUESTIONS

1. Summarize as clearly as you can the nature of Dr. P.'s problem. What are the
symptoms? What seems to have caused them?

2. What conclusions can be drawn from the case of Dr. P. about the way our visual
systems work? Using what Sacks himself says and whatever additional conclusions you
yourself can draw, what does the case of Dr. P. tell us about the way we "see" things
and what it means to "recognize" what we see?

3. Sacks has a way of drawing readers into his case studies, of making them concerned
about the individuals whose cases he presents. How does he do this? That is, considering
him as a writer rather than as a doctor, what aspects of his writing arouse interest and
concern? Look at the opening paragraphs of his essay in particular.

4. Is this essay to any degree a story with a plot? Most people find Sacks a very
compelling writer. What is it about his way of writing that causes this response? How
does he keep readers reading?

5. This essay is not only a single case history and an explanation of some very curious
behavior. It also contains or sketches out an argument about the nature of the cognitive
sciences—how they should and should not proceed. What is that argument? Do you
agree or disagree with the view of cognitive science that Sacks is advocating? Write an
essay in which you present his position and develop one of your own on this matter.

6. This is the second essay by Sacks in this book. (The other is on p. 407.) Write
an essay in which you discuss him as a writer and a scientist. Consider such matters as
his style of writing, his interest in the arts, his clinical procedures, and the values he
expresses or implies in his work. If your instructor wishes, you may look further into his
work in order to write this essay.

MAKING CONNECTIONS

1. Compare Sacks's essay with Bruno Bettelheim's case study: "Joey: A 'Mechanical
Boy.'" How do they differ as case studies? What kinds of evidence do they call upon?
How do they evaluate it? What kinds of stories do they tell? Do you find evidence in
this comparison for what was said about Sacks in our introductory note, that his essays
are "not just case studies . . . but also tales or fables of 'heroes, victims, martyrs,
warriors'"?

2. Compare Sacks's essay to the reports of Annie Dillard ("Singing with the Fundamentalists") and Dennis Hevesi ("Running Away"). What elements of a case study do
those reports contain? Are they also tales or fables similar to Sacks's essay or are they
closer in spirit to the work of Bettelheim?

FACE PERCEPTION WITHOUT RECOGNITION

Antonio R. Damasio

Antonio R. Damasio was born in Portugal in 1944, where he studied medicine, receiving both an M.D. and Ph.D. from the University of Lisbon. He is professor and head of the Department of Neurology at the University of Iowa College of Medicine and adjunct professor at the Salk Institute in La Jolla, California. Most of Damasio's publications are on anatomical aspects of higher brain functions, Parkinsonism, and dementia. His research focuses on understanding the cerebral basis of vision, language, and memory. Oliver Sacks has written that "The most important studies of . . . agnosias, and of visual processing in general, are now being undertaken by A. R. and H. Damasio." In 1989, Damasio was one of four American scientists and scholars named to review progress in Western studies of consciousness for the Dalai Lama. The essay here, a review of research on "prosopagnosia," the phenomenon of perception without recognition, first appeared in Trends in NeuroScience *(March 1985).*

REVIEW OF RESEARCH ON PROSOPAGNOSIA

[Abstract.] *The impaired recognition of previously known familiar faces (prosopagnosia), when it appears in isolation, is one of the most extreme forms of behavioral dissociation encountered in human pathology. Its research provides an outstanding opportunity to understand better the organization of the visual system and of memory mechanisms in humans. Recent evidence indicates that the disorder is associated with bilateral lesions of the central visual system, located in the mesial occipito-temporal region. These lesions either destroy a specific sector of the visual association cortex or disconnect it from limbic structures located anteriorly in the temporal lobe. This evidence is in keeping with the demonstration, in normals, that both hemispheres are capable of facial recognition, but should not be seen to indicate that each hemisphere uses the same mechanisms to process faces or is equally efficient in the process. Cognitive analysis of prosopagnosia reveals that the defect is not specific to human faces* 1 *but also appears in relation to other visual stimuli whose recognition depends on the evocation of specific contextual attributes and associations, and which are visually "ambiguous" (different stimuli belonging to the same group but having similar physical structure). Physiopathologically, prosopagnosia is the result of a failure to activate, on the basis of visual stimuli, memories pertinent to those stimuli.*

The description of prosopagnosia dates from the turn of the century although 2 the designation was only coined in 1947 by Bodamer.[1] In isolation, the condition is so extreme and infrequent that many investigators doubted its reality. Otherwise normal individuals suddenly lose their ability to recognize the faces of relatives, friends, and even their own faces in the mirror, while being able to recognize other objects visually. They also lose the ability to learn to identify the faces of new persons they come into contact with. In short, the visual inspection of these familiar faces no longer generates an experience of even vague familiarity and thus facial recognition is forever precluded. The patients can still recognize, by the sound of their voices, the people whose faces have become meaningless. All the remote memories that pertain to those people remain intact. Cognitive skills also remain intact and so do complex visual abilities, i.e. most prosopagnosic patients describe their visual environment accurately, localize stimuli in space flawlessly, inspect visual arrays in normal fashion, and some can even read. Needless to say, their visual acuity is normal. The only symptoms that commonly accompany prosopagnosia are achromatopsia, an acquired defect in color perception which may affect part or all of the visual field, an acquired defect in the appreciation of textures visually, and some partial field cut for the vision of forms. (Prosopagnosia may also be found as a component of global amnesic syndrome. In such instances no field defects for color or form accompany the manifestation, and visual perception is manifestly intact.)

Even after it became clear that the condition was indeed real, considerable 3 controversy surfaced regarding its physiopathological nature and anatomical basis. This review focuses on some of these issues as well as on new developments in the understanding of prosopagnosia.

ANATOMICAL BASIS

The early descriptions of prosopagnosia indicated that the condition was 4 associated with the bilateral damage to the occipital lobes.[26,3] But when after decades of neglect, there was a resurgence of interest in prosopagnosia, several investigators conceptualized it as a sign of unilateral damage of the right hemisphere. At the time, the 1960s, fresh neuropsychological investigations had revealed the major role of the right hemisphere in visual processing and it appeared reasonable to assume that the right hemisphere might possess the sole key to a refined visual process such as facial recognition. Hecaen and Angelergues[2] added strength to this hypothesis by noting that most prosopagnosic patients had exclusive left visual field defects, and suggesting that this was due to exclusive right hemisphere damage. Later, in a comprehensive review of the data available in 1974, Meadows concluded "that patients with prosopagnosia have right anterior inferior occipital lesions in the region of the occipital temporal junction. Many if not all cases have an additional lesion in the left hemisphere."[4] Although these interpretations were consonant with the anatomical localization methods at the time, the evidence uncovered in the years that followed revealed that they were not supportable. The current view is that bilateral lesions are indeed necessary, a notion that is based on: (1) a critical review of the meaning of visual field data: (2) a reassessment of post-mortem studies of prosopagnosic patients; (3) Computed Tomography (CT), Nuclear Magnetic Resonance (NMR) and Emission Tomography (ET) studies of patients with and without prosopagnosia; (4) a study of patients with cerebral hemispherectomy, callosal surgery and amnesic syndromes. The fundamental evidence is as follows:

(1) The one patient of Hecaen and Angelergues to come to post-mortem, turned out to have a bilateral lesion.[2] The lesion in the left hemisphere was "silent" as far as visual field findings were concerned. Similar "silent" lesions were uncovered at autopsy in patients described by Benson[5] and by Lhermitte.[6] It is now apparent that when lesions of the central visual system fail to involve optic radiations or primary visual cortex they do not produce an overt defect of form vision even when they can cause major disturbances of complex visual processing such as a defect in recognition or color processing.[7] While the presence of a field defect correctly indicates the presence of a lesion, its absence does not exclude focal damage. Thus while the detailed study of field defects is mandatory for the appropriate study of visual agnosia, its details cannot be used for the prediction of lesion localization.

(2) Analysis of the post-mortem records of all patients that have come to autopsy[8,9] indicate that they all have bilateral lesions. Furthermore, it is clear that those lesions preferably involve the inferior visual association cortices, i.e. the occipito-temporal region. Finally, patients with bilateral lesions involving the superior visual association cortices, i.e. the occipito-parietal region, never develop prosopagnosia, presenting instead either a full Balint syndrome or some of its components, i.e. visual disorientation, optic ataxia or ocular apraxia.[7] Patients with Balint syndrome can recognize faces provided their attention is properly directed to the stimuli.

(3) Computed Tomography (CT) has permitted the study of many cases of

prosopagnosia and of numerous controls with unilateral lesions of the left or right occipito-temporal region, or with bilateral lesions of the occipito-parietal region. With one exception all the instances of permanent prosopagnosia studied in appropriate patients with technically advanced scanning techniques, have shown bilateral lesions.[8-11] Furthermore, numerous instances of unilateral lesion in the right and left hemispheres have been described and there has been no report of prosopagnosia appearing in those circumstances. (The possible exception was reported in a hypertensive patient on the basis of a single cut of an acute CT scan;[12] it is important to consider the possibility of an undetected lesion in the opposite hemisphere.)

Patients with bilateral occipito-parietal lesions consistently show Balint syndrome or its components but not prosopagnosia.[7] In the only two cases studies with Nuclear Magnetic Resonance (NMR) the lesions were bilateral. In the only two cases studies with Single Photon Emission Tomography there were bilateral regions of diminished cerebral blood flow.[7]

(4) Evidence from hemispherectomy and from cases of surgical callosal section has also been helpful. Patients with right hemispherectomy maintain their ability to recognize faces with their single left hemisphere.[13] The split-brain subjects continue to recognize faces with each isolated hemisphere although, as expected, the mechanisms of recognition appear to be different on the left and on the right.[27]

Final evidence for the bilaterality of damage in prosopagnosia comes from the analysis of patients with amnesic syndromes. Patients with global amnesic syndromes associated with temporal lobe damage have prosopagnosia as a component. All have bilateral lesions.[15,16] The finding simply underscores the fact that memory processing of the type involved in facial recognition is of crucial importance for the individual and is clearly operated by both hemispheres. This is not to say that the left and right hemispheres perform the task in the same way or equally well. On the contrary, we believe each hemisphere learns, recognizes and recalls faces with different strategies and that the right hemisphere's approach is probably more efficient than the left.

THE NATURE OF THE DEFECT

The bizarre nature of prosopagnosia, when it appears in isolation, has prompted all sorts of explanations for the phenomenon. Those who have never seen a prosopagnosic patient may be tempted to dismiss the phenomenon as the result of psychiatric illness or dementia. None of these interpretations obtain, considering that these patients show no evidence of language impairment, have intact cognitive skills and do not have psychiatric symptomatology before or after the onset of prosopagnosia. In his review of the neuropsychological investigation of prosopagnosia, Benton noted how some authors have seen prosopagnosia as a primary perceptual defect that would preclude the analysis and synthesis of complex visual stimuli; how others have postulated an incapacity to perceive individuality within a single class of objects; and yet others have proposed a material specific defect in memory, that is, a defect of integrating current facial percepts with past experience of them.[17]

Some of these issues are more clear today. There is substantial evidence against the notion that prosopagnosia is due to a primary perceptual disturbance. Firstly, prosopagnosic patients can discriminate unfamiliar faces well. Some of these patients perform normally in Benton and Van Allen's test of facial discrimination—a difficult task in which they are called to match unfamiliar and differently lit photographs of faces but obviously not asked to recognize any of them;[8,17] they can perform complex visual tasks such as the anomalous contours test and they have normal stereopsis,[8] they can draw accurately complex figures shown in photographs, drawings or in real models;[8,17] more importantly, they can recognize, at a generic level, any visual stimulus provided that no contextual memory cues are required.[6,8] Secondly, severe disorders of visual perception such as seen in patients with Balint syndrome or comparable disorders, do not have prosopagnosia.[7,18,19] Patients with prosopagnosia can perceive and recognize accurately many stimuli that are visually more complex than human faces, i.e., that have a greater number of individual components arranged in just as complicated a manner but crowded in smaller areas or volumes.[8] On the other hand, there is evidence that the particular class of visual stimuli, as well as the ability to integrate facial percepts with pertinent past experience, are important factors in the physiopathology of prosopagnosia. The evidence is as follows. [12]

Prosopagnosia does not occur in relation to human faces alone. All of the patients with prosopagnosia have defects of recognition for other stimuli.[4,6,8] The types of stimuli for which they have agnosia, however, are rather special. They include: (a) automobiles (prosopagnosics cannot recognize their own car and do not recognize different makes of cars; however, these patients can recognize different types of car, such as a passenger car, a fire engine, an ambulance, or a funeral car); (b) clothes of the same type and general shape, i.e. dresses, suits, shirts, etc.; (c) food ingredients with similar forms and volumes; (d) specific animals within a group (a farmer suddenly became unable to recognize, within a herd, specific animals that he could easily recognize before; birdwatchers have become unable to recognize different birds, etc.). In all of these instances, the process of recognition operates normally up to the point in which specific recognition of a given member within the group is required. In other words, all of these patients can recognize an automobile as an automobile, a cow as a cow, or a dress as a dress. They can also recognize all of the subcomponents of these stimuli correctly, i.e. eyes, noses, windshields, wheels, sleeves, etc. But when, as is the case with human faces, the patient is requested [13] to identify precisely the specific possessor of that visual appearance, the process breaks down and the within-class-membership of the stimulus cannot be ascertained.

An analysis of the shared characteristics of the stimuli which can cause prosopagnosia reveals that: (a) these are stimuli for which a specific recognition is mandatory and for which a generic recognition is either socially unacceptable (human faces), or incompatible with normal activity (cars, clothing, foodstuffs); (b) the specific recognition of all of the stimuli depends on contextual (episodic) memory, i.e. it depends on the evocation of multiple traces of memory previously associated with the currently perceived stimulus; those traces depend on a personal, temporally and spatially bound, memory process; (c) that all of the stimuli belong to groups in which numerous members are physically *similar* (in visual terms), and yet individually *different*; we have designated these stimuli as visually "ambiguous" (an operational definition of visual ambiguity is the presence in a group of numerous *different* members with *similar* visual characteristics). Prosopagnosia patients have no difficulty with the correct, individual recognition of "non-ambiguous" stimuli, i.e. visual stimuli that belong to groups with numerous members but in which *different* individual members have a *different* (distinctive) visual structure.[8]

According to the analysis above, the basic perceptual mechanisms in prosopagnosic patients are normal. There is no evidence that the varied partial defects of color, texture or form perception, alone or in combination, can cause prosopagnosia. When patients are called on to recognize stimuli that belong to visually ambiguous classes, they fail to evoke the pertinent, associated traces of contextual memory on the basis of which familiarity and recognition of the stimulus would be based. Seen in this light, the defect must be described, physiopathologically, as a disorder of visually-triggered contextual memory. It is important to distinguish this from a disorder of memory in general (memory traces can be normally activated through other sensory channels) and even from a disorder of visual memory (auditory stimulation can bring forward numerous traces of visual memory testifying to the intactness of many visual memory stores). The malfunction is in the triggering system for the associated evocations. We believe this defect can be explained by one of three possible mechanisms: (1) a defect in the highest level of visual analysis, that which permits the distinction of finest structural details necessary for the separation of visually "ambiguous" stimuli but unnecessary for visually unambiguous ones; (2) a defect of the plotting of the ongoing percept into the pre-existing, templated information, acquired for each specific stimulus (this mechanism would assume the normalcy of the perceptual step referred to above); (3) a defect in the activation of pertinent associated memories occurring after both steps above operate normally. Current research in our laboratory and others is aimed at investigating the validity of these possible mechanisms.

568

NEW DEVELOPMENTS

Autonomic evidence for nonconscious recognition

One of the intriguing problems posed by visual agnosia and, more generally, [16] by amnesia has to do with the level at which the failure of recognition occurs. Some investigators have hypothesized that the failure to evoke both non-verbal and verbal memories capable of generating recognition, does not preclude some process of recognition at a lower, nonconscious level of processing. In other words, it is possible that some part of the brain does recognize stimulus even if the subject is not aware of that process taking place. Patients with prosopagnosia are ideal subjects to test this hypothesis and that is what has recently been accomplished using paradigms aimed at detecting autonomic responses to stimuli that patients are clearly not aware of recognizing. In available studies (Ref. 20 and Tranel, D., and Damasio, A.), there is persuading evidence that at a nonconscious level, faces of relatives, friends, and self, generated strong psychophysiological responses clearly different from the weak or nonexistent responses to faces unfamiliar to the subject. The implications of this discovery are far-reaching. The findings support the notion that perception and recognition processes evolve by steps and that failure at the top of the cascade does not necessarily imply failure at more elementary levels. On the issue of facial recognition itself, they argue for the existence of a template system for each individual familiar face, and suggest that, at least in some of the patients, such a template system is intact. It is important to note that in our model the template system is not conceived in the Humian sense, as a static facsimile of a given face, but rather as a dynamic, evolving record of computations built on multiple exposure to the stimulus and probably stored at multiple levels of CNS, but especially anchored in visual association cortices.

Ocular motor activity in visual recognition

It has been suggested that patients with prosopagnosia might have an impairment of the proper scanning of the face, a disturbance of the ability to [17] search appropriately for elements crucial to facial perception, i.e. eyes, nose, mouth, hairline, facial contour. A recent study carried out in prosopagnosic patients shows that this is not the case (Rizzo, M., Hurtig, R. and Damasio, A., unpublished observations). Using electro-oculographic techniques the investigators showed that prosopagnosic patients scan fundamental elements of the face as do controls, using a natural progression in their scanning and spending comparable times in the analysis of separate features. The prosopagnosic patients also scan a complex picture (e.g. the Cookie Theft plate from the Boston Diagnostic Battery) in exactly the same manner as controls. Once again, the results lend credence to the notion that basic perception proceeds normally and that prosopagnosic subjects search and accumulate information as do normal individuals but fail, at a later stage, either to bring that information together in an integrated pattern, or to lead the integrated pattern to activate the pertinent associated memories.

Perception of contrast sensitivity in visual agnosia

It has been suggested that object recognition may be especially dependent [18] on the processing of low visuospatial frequencies.[21] It might follow that prosopagnosia would be caused by selective impairment of low spatial frequency vision. A recent study investigated this possibility in a prosopagnosic patient and has revealed exactly the contrary: the patient's processing of low spatial frequencies was intact, entirely comparable to matched controls, while the processing of high spatial frequencies showed a defect (Rizzo, M., Hurtig, R. and Damasio, A., unpublished observations). Further studies are necessary to clarify the role of different spatial frequencies in the recognition of objects and faces, in both normals and agnosics. Nonetheless, there is evidence to suggest that normal facial recognition calls for both low and high visuospatial frequencies.[22]

Cognitive strategies in facial processing

While it is clear that both hemispheres can learn, recognize and recall faces, [19] recent investigations demonstrate that, as one might have expected, the left and the right hemispheres utilize different strategies to accomplish the task. The findings obtained in patients with callosal surgery,[14] or in normals,[23–25] suggest that the right hemisphere of most individuals is likely to be the most efficient processor of faces and of comparable visual stimuli.

Studies in animals

The electrophysiological study of neurons responsive to visual stimuli in [20] nonhuman primates is likely to shed some light on the mechanisms of facial recognition and prosopagnosia. E. T. Rolls and E. Perrett have reported the presence of neurons in the temporal lobe of the monkey that respond powerfully to faces.[28]

SELECTED REFERENCES

These references work somewhat in the manner of normal footnotes. That is, they are listed roughly in order of their citation in the text. Number 1 is the first cited, and so on, but there are many exceptions to this and sometimes more than one reference is cited as bearing on a particular statement made in the text. The second citation in the text, for instance, is 26, 3, indicating that both references 26 and 3 bear on the issue under discussion. The third citation is numbered 2, the fourth 4, and the fifth is 2 again. This method avoids the needless proliferation of numbers. Why 3 comes before 2, however, is one of the mysteries of science. [Eds.]

1. Bodamer, J. (1947) *Arch. Psychiatr. Nervenkr.* 179, 6–54
2. Hecaen, H. and Angelergues, R. (1962) *Soc. for Inf. Disp. Arch. Neurol.* 7, 92–100
3. Wilbrand, H. (1892) *Deutche Z Nervenheilkd.* 2, 361–387
4. Meadows, J. C. (1974) *J. Neurol. Neurosurg. Psychiatry* 37, 498–501
5. Benson, D., Segarra, J. and Albert, M. L. (1974) *Arch. Neurol. (Chicago)* 30, 307–310
6. Lhermitte, J., Chain, F., Escourolle, R., Ducarne, B. and Pillon, B. (1972) *Rev. Neurol.* 126, 329–346
7. Damasio, A. R. (1985) in *Principles of Behavioral Neurology* (Mesulam, M. M., ed.), Davis, Philadelphia
8. Damasio, A. R., Damasio, H. and Van Hoesen, G. W. (1982) *Neurology* 32, 331–341
9. Nardelli, E., Buonanno, F., Coccia, G., Fiaschi, A., Terzian, H. and Rizzuto, N. (1982) *Eur. Neurol.* 21, 289–297
10. Brazis, P. W., Biller, J. and Fine, M. (1981) *Neurology* 31, 920
11. Bruyer, R., Laterre, C., Seron, X., Feyereisen, P., Strypstein, E., Pierrand, E. and Rectem, D. (1983) *Brain Cognition* 2, 257–284
12. Whitely, A. M. and Warrington, E. K. (1977) *J. Neurol. Neurosurg. Psychiatry* 40, 395–403
13. Damasio, A. R., Lima, P. A. and Damasio, H. (1975) *Neurology* 25, 89–93
14. Gazzaniga, M. S., Smylie, C. S. (1983) *Ann Neurol.* 13, 537–540
15. Corkin, S. (1984) *Semin. Neurol.* 4, 249–259
16. Damasio, A. R., Eslinger, P. J., Damasio, H., Van Hoesen, G. W. and Cornell, S. (1985) *Arch. Neurol.* 42, 252–259
17. Benton, A. (1980) *Am. Psychol.* 35, 176–186
18. Meier, M. J. and French, L. A. (1965) *Neuropsychologia* 3, 261–272
19. Orgass, B., Poeck, K., Kerchensteiner, M. and Hartje, W. (1972) *Z. Neurol.* 202, 177–195
20. Bauer, R. M. (1984) *Neuropsychologia* 22, 457–469; Tranel, D. and Damasio, A. (1985) *Science* 228, 1453–1454
21. Ginsburg, A. P. (1980) *Proc. of the Soc. for Inf. Dis.* 21, 219–227
22. Fiorentini, A., Maffei, L. and Sandini, G. (1983) *Perception* 12, 195–201
23. Ellis, H. D. (1983) in *Functions of the Right Cerebral Hemisphere*, (Young, A. W., ed.), Academic Press, London
24. Sergent, J. and Bindra, D. (1981) *Psycol. Bull.* 89, 541—554
25. Warrington, E. K. and James, M. (1967) *Cortex* 3, 317–326
26. Heidenhain, A. (1927) *Monatschr. Psychiatr. Neurol.* 66, 61–116
27. Levy, J., Trevarthen, C. and Sperry, R. W. (1972) *Brain* 95, 61–78
28. Perrett, D. I., Rolls, E. T. and Caan, W. (1982) *Exp. Brain. Res.* 47, 329–342

QUESTIONS

1. This article is a review of research on prosopagnosia. Analyze how it is organized. Divide the text into sections and explain the function of each. How do you account for the order or arrangement of the sections?

2. Like many pieces written for scientific journals, this one begins with an abstract. What does the full text provide that is not in the abstract?

3. Consider the relationship between the style of this essay (format, vocabulary, sentence structure, and so on) and the audience for whom it was written. Does audience always have an effect on style? Explain why or why not.

4. What portions of this article give you the most vivid sense of prosopagnosia, the condition under review? What accounts for your clearer understanding of those sections?

5. Using this essay as a model, write a review of research in a field that you know something about. What is the purpose of such a review? What does your own review of research put you in a position to do?

MAKING CONNECTIONS

1. Consider this essay along with Oliver Sacks's "The Man Who Mistook His Wife for a Hat." Obviously, Sacks generates a good deal of interest in a case similar to the problem Damasio describes. Damasio, on the other hand, gives us a good deal of additional information on the problem. Describe the differences in form and content between the two essays.

2. Although Oliver Sacks mentions "agnosia" and frequently refers to Dr. P.'s case as an example of "prosopagnosia" (see footnote 4), some of the details he gives do not square with the description of prosopagnosia that Damasio offers. Make a list of those differences, and describe the ways in which Dr. P. does not behave as a prosopagnosiac would.

3. Compare Damasio's article with Carol Gilligan's "Woman's Place in Man's Life Cycle" and Tania Modleski's "Soap Opera, Melodrama, and Women's Anger." All three articles arrange and interpret an array of complex information. What are their common denominators of arrangement and explanation? What kinds of passages do you find most difficult? To what do you attribute those difficulties?

A BIOLOGICAL HOMAGE TO MICKEY MOUSE

Stephen Jay Gould

Born in 1941 in New York City, Stephen Jay Gould has degrees from Antioch College and Columbia University. For the past fifteen years he has been teaching geology at Harvard University, but he is best known for his monthly column in Natural History *magazine. The author of over a hundred scientific articles, he has been enormously successful in making scientific ideas and values available and interesting to a wide readership. His best known books are* Ever Since Darwin *(1977),* The Panda's Thumb *(1980),* The Mismeasure of Man *(1981), and* The Flamingo's Smile *(1985). The essay reprinted here appeared first in* Natural History.

Age often turns fire to placidity. Lytton Strachey, in his incisive portrait of 1 Florence Nightingale, writes of her declining years:

> Destiny, having waited very patiently, played a queer trick on Miss Nightingale. The benevolence and public spirit of that long life had only been equalled by its acerbity. Her virtue had dwelt in hardness. . . . And now the sarcastic years brought the proud woman her punishment. She was not to die as she had lived. The sting was to be taken out of her; she was to be made soft; she was to be reduced to compliance and complacency.

I was therefore not surprised—although the analogy may strike some people 2 as sacrilegious—to discover that the creature who gave his name as a synonym for insipidity had a gutsier youth. Mickey Mouse turned a respectable fifty last year. To mark the occasion, many theaters replayed his debut performance in *Steamboat Willie* (1928). The original Mickey was a rambunctious, even slightly sadistic fellow. In a remarkable sequence, exploiting the exciting new development of sound, Mickey and Minnie pummel, squeeze, and twist the animals on board to produce a rousing chorus of "Turkey in the Straw." They honk a duck with a tight embrace, crank a goat's tail, tweak a pig's nipples, bang a cow's teeth as a stand-in xylophone, and play bagpipe on her udder.

Christopher Finch, in his semiofficial pictorial history of Disney's work, 3 comments: "The Mickey Mouse who hit the movie houses in the late twenties was not quite the well-behaved character most of us are familiar with today. He was mischievous, to say the least, and even displayed a streak of cruelty." But Mickey soon cleaned up his act, leaving to gossip and speculation only his unresolved relationship with Minnie and the status of Morty and Ferdie. Finch continues: "Mickey . . . had become virtually a national symbol, and as such he was expected to behave properly at all times. If he occasionally stepped out of line, any number of letters would arrive at the Studio from citizens and organizations who felt that the nation's moral well-being was in their hands. . . . Eventually he would be pressured into the role of straight man."

As Mickey's personality softened, his appearance changed. Many Disney fans   4 are aware of this transformation through time, but few (I suspect) have recognized the coordinating theme behind all the alterations—in fact, I am not sure that the Disney artists themselves explicitly realized what they were doing, since the changes appeared in such a halting and piecemeal fashion. In short, the blander and inoffensive Mickey became progressively more juvenile in appearance. (Since Mickey's chronological age never altered—like most cartoon characters he stands impervious to the ravages of time—this change in appearance at a constant age is a true evolutionary transformation. Progressive juvenilization as an evolutionary phenomenon is called neoteny. More on this later.)

The characteristic changes of form during human growth have inspired a   5 substantial biological literature. Since the head-end of an embryo differentiates first and grows more rapidly in utero than the foot-end (an antero-posterior gradient, in technical language), a newborn child possesses a relatively large head attached to a medium-sized body with diminutive legs and feet. This gradient is reversed through growth as legs and feet overtake the front end. Heads continue to grow but so much more slowly than the rest of the body that relative head size decreases.

In addition, a suite of changes pervades the head itself during human growth.   6

MICKEY'S EVOLUTION during 50 years (left to right). As Mickey became increasingly well behaved over the years, his appearance became more youthful. Measurements of three stages in his development revealed a larger relative head size, larger eyes, and an enlarged cranium—all traits of juvenility. © Walt Disney Productions

The brain grows very slowly after age three, and the bulbous cranium of a young child gives way to the more slanted, lower-browed configuration of adulthood. The eyes scarcely grow at all and relative eye size declines precipitously. But the jaw gets bigger and bigger. Children, compared with adults, have larger heads and eyes, smaller jaws, a more prominent, bulging cranium, and smaller, pudgier legs and feet. Adult heads are altogether more apish, I'm sorry to say.

Mickey, however, has traveled this ontogenetic pathway in reverse during his   7 fifty years among us. He has assumed an ever more childlike appearance as the ratty character of *Steamboat Willie* became the cute and inoffensive host to a magic kingdom. By 1940, the former tweaker of pig's nipples gets a kick in the ass for insubordination (as the *Sorcerer's Apprentice* in *Fantasia*). By 1953, his last cartoon, he has gone fishing and cannot even subdue a squirting clam.

The Disney artists transformed Mickey in clever silence, often using sugges-   8 tive devices that mimic nature's own changes by different routes. To give him the shorter and pudgier legs of youth, they lowered his pants line and covered his spindly legs with a baggy outfit. (His arms and legs also thickened substantially—and acquired joints for a floppier appearance.) His head grew relatively larger and its features more youthful. The length of Mickey's snout has not altered, but decreasing protrusion is more subtly suggested by a pronounced thickening. Mickey's eye has grown in two modes: first, by a major, discontinuous evolutionary shift as the entire eye of ancestral Mickey became the pupil of his descendants, and second, by gradual increase thereafter.

Mickey's improvement in cranial bulging followed an interesting path since   9 his evolution has always been constrained by the unaltered convention of representing his head as a circle with appended ears and an oblong snout. The circle's form could not be altered to provide a bulging cranium directly. Instead, Mickey's ears moved back, increasing the distance between nose and ears, and giving him a rounded, rather than a sloping, forehead.

To give these observations the cachet of quantitative science, I applied my   10 best pair of dial calipers to three stages of the official phylogeny—the thin-nosed, ears-forward figure of the early 1930s (stage 1), the latter-day Jack of Mickey and the Beanstalk (1947, stage 2), and the modern mouse (stage 3). I measured three signs of Mickey's creeping juvenility: increasing eye size (maximum height) as a percentage of head length (base of the nose to the top of rear ear); increasing head length as a percentage of body length; and increasing cranial vault size measured by rearward displacement of the front ear (base of the nose to top of front ear as a percentage of base of the nose to top of rear ear).

All three percentages increased steadily—eye size from 27 to 42 percent of   11 head length; head length from 42.7 to 48.1 percent of body length; and nose to front ear from 71.7 to a whopping 95.6 percent of nose to rear ear. For comparison, I measured Mickey's young "nephew" Morty Mouse. In each case, Mickey has clearly been evolving toward youthful stages of his stock, although he still has a way to go for head length.

You may, indeed, now ask what an at least marginally respectable scientist 12 has been doing with a mouse like that. In part, fiddling around and having fun, of course. (I still prefer *Pinocchio* to *Citizen Kane*.) But I do have a serious point—two, in fact— to make. We must first ask why Disney chose to change his most famous character so gradually and persistently in the same direction? National symbols are not altered capriciously and market researchers (for the doll industry in particular) have spent a good deal of time and practical effort learning what features appeal to people as cute and friendly. Biologists also have spent a great deal of time studying a similar subject in a wide range of animals.

In one of his most famous articles, Konrad Lorenz argues that humans use 13 the characteristic differences in form between babies and adults as important behavioral cues. He believes that features of juvenility trigger "innate releasing mechanisms" for affection and nurturing in adult humans. When we see a living creature with babyish features, we feel an automatic surge of disarming tenderness. The adaptive value of this response can scarcely be questioned, for we must nurture our babies. Lorenz, by the way, lists among his releasers the very features of babyhood that Disney affixed progressively to Mickey: "a relatively large head, predominance of the brain capsule, large and low-lying eyes, bulging cheek region, short and thick extremities, a springy elastic consistency, and clumsy movements." (I propose to leave aside for this article the contentious issue of whether or not our affectionate response to babyish features is truly innate and inherited directly from ancestral primates—as Lorenz argues—or whether it is simply learned from our immediate experience with babies and grafted upon an evolutionary predisposition for attaching ties of affection to

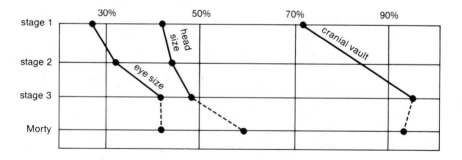

At an early stage in his evolution, Mickey had a smaller head, cranial vault, and eyes. He evolved toward the characteristics of his young nephew Morty (connected to Mickey by a dotted line).

certain learned signals. My argument works equally well in either case for I only claim that babyish features tend to elicit strong feelings of affection in adult humans, whether the biological basis be direct programming or the capacity to learn and fix upon signals. I also treat as collateral to my point the major thesis of Lorenz's article—that we respond not to the totality or *Gestalt*, but to a set of specific features acting as releasers. This argument is important to Lorenz because he wants to argue for evolutionary identity in modes of behavior between other vertebrates and humans, and we know that many birds, for example, often respond to abstract features rather than *Gestalten*. Lorenz's article, published in 1950, bears the title *Ganzheit und Teil in der tierischen und menschlichen Gemeinschaft*—"Entirety and part in animal and human society." Disney's piecemeal change of Mickey's appearance does make sense in this context—he operated in sequential fashion upon Lorenz's primary releasers.)

Lorenz emphasizes the power that juvenile features hold over us, and the abstract quality of their influence, by pointing out that we judge other animals by the same criteria—although the judgment may be utterly inappropriate in an evolutionary context. We are, in short, fooled by an evolved response to our own babies, and we transfer our reaction to the same set of features in other animals. 14

Many animals, for reasons having nothing to do with the inspiration of affection in humans, possess some features also shared by human babies but not by human adults—large eyes and a bulging forehead with retreating chin, in particular. We are drawn to them, we cultivate them as pets, we stop and admire them in the wild—while we reject their small-eyed, long-snouted relatives who might make more affectionate companions or objects of admiration. Lorenz points out that the German names of many animals with features mimicking human babies end in the diminutive suffix *chen*, even though the animals are often larger than close relatives without such features—*Rotkehlchen* (robin), *Eichhörnchen* (squirrel), and *Kaninchen* (rabbit), for example. 15

In a fascinating section, Lorenz then enlarges upon our capacity for biologically inappropriate response to other animals, or even to inanimate objects that mimic human features. "The most amazing objects can acquire remarkable, highly emotional values by 'experiential attachment' of human properties. . . . Steeply rising, somewhat overhanging cliff faces or dark storm-clouds piling up have the same, immediate display value as a human being who is standing at full height and leaning slightly forwards"—that is, threatening. 16

We cannot help regarding a camel as aloof and unfriendly because it mimics, quite unwittingly and for other reasons, the "gesture of haughty rejection" common to so many human cultures. In this gesture, we raise our heads, placing our nose above our eyes. We than half-close our eyes and blow out through our nose—the "harumph" of the stereo-typed upperclass Englishman 17

577

or his well-trained servant. "All this," Lorenz argues quite cogently, "symbolizes resistance against all sensory modalities emanating from the disdained counterpart." But the poor camel cannot help carrying its nose above its elongate eyes, with mouth drawn down. As Lorenz reminds us, if you wish to know whether a camel will eat out of your hand or spit, look at its ears, not the rest of its face.

In his important book *Expression of the Emotions in Man and Animals*, [18] published in 1872, Charles Darwin traced the evolutionary basis of many common gestures to originally adaptive actions in animals later internalized as symbols in humans. Thus, he argued for evolutionary continuity of emotion, not only of form. We snarl and raise our upper lip in fierce anger—to expose our nonexistent fighting canine tooth. Our gesture of disgust repeats the facial actions associated with the highly adaptive act of vomiting in necessary circumstances. Darwin concluded, much to the distress of many Victorian contemporaries: "With mankind some expressions, such as the bristling of the hair under the influence of extreme terror, or the uncovering of the teeth under that

HUMANS FEEL AFFECTION for animals with juvenile features: large eyes, bulging craniums, retreating chins (left column). Small-eyed, long-snouted animals (right column) do not elicit the same response. From *Studies in Animal and Human Behavior*, vol. II, by Konrad Lorenz, 1971. Methuen & Co. Ltd.

of furious rage, can hardly be understood, except on the belief that man once existed in a much lower and animal-like condition."

In any case, the abstract features of human childhood elicit powerful emo- 19 tional responses in us, even when they occur in other animals. I submit that Mickey Mouse's evolutionary road down the course of his own growth in reverse reflects the unconscious discovery of this biological principle by Disney and his artists. In fact, the emotional status of most Disney characters rests on the same set of distinctions. To this extent, the magic kingdom trades on a biological illusion—our ability to abstract and our propensity to transfer inappropriately to other animals the fitting responses we make to changing form in the growth of our own bodies.

Donald Duck also adopts more juvenile features through time. His elongated 20 beak recedes and his eyes enlarge; he converges on Huey, Louie, and Dewey as surely as Mickey approaches Morty. But Donald, having inherited the mantle of Mickey's original misbehavior, remains more adult in form with his projecting beak and more sloping forehead.

Mouse villains or sharpies, contrasted with Mickey, are always more adult 21

DANDIFIED, DISREPUTABLE MORTIMER (here stealing Minnie's affections) has strikingly more adult features than Mickey. His head is smaller in proportion to body length; his nose is a full 80 percent of head length. © Walt Disney Productions

in appearance, although they often share Mickey's chronological age. In 1936, for example, Disney made a short entitled *Mickey's Rival*. Mortimer, a dandy in a yellow sports car, intrudes upon Mickey and Minnie's quiet country picnic. The thoroughly disreputable Mortimer has a head only 29 percent of body length, to Mickey's 45, and a snout 80 percent of head length, compared with Mickey's 49. (Nonetheless, and was it ever different, Minnie transfers her affection until an obliging bull from a neighboring field dispatches Mickey's rival.) Consider also the exaggerated adult features of other Disney characters— the swaggering bully Peg-leg Pete or the simple, if lovable, dolt Goofy.

As a second, serious biological comment on Mickey's odyssey in form, I   22
note that his path to eternal youth repeats, in epitome, our own evolutionary story. For humans are neotenic. We have evolved by retaining to adulthood the originally juvenile features of our ancestors. Our australopithecine forebears, like Mickey in *Steamboat Willie*, had projecting jaws and low vaulted craniums.

Our embryonic skulls scarcely differ from those of chimpanzees. And we   23
follow the same path of changing form through growth: relative decrease of the cranial vault since brains grow so much more slowly than bodies after birth, and continuous relative increase of the jaw. But while chimps accentuate these changes, producing an adult strikingly different in form from a baby, we proceed much more slowly down the same path and never get nearly so far. Thus, as adults, we retain juvenile features. To be sure, we change enough to produce

CARTOON VILLAINS are not the only Disney characters with exaggerated adult features. Goofy, like Mortimer, has a small head relative to body length and a prominent snout. © Walt Disney Productions

580

a notable difference between baby and adult, but our alteration is far smaller than that experienced by chimps and other primates.

A marked slowdown of developmental rates has triggered our neoteny. Primates are slow developers among mammals, but we have accentuated the trend to a degree matched by no other mammal. We have very long periods of gestation, markedly extended childhoods, and the longest life span of any mammal. The morphological features of eternal youth have served us well. Our enlarged brain is, at least in part, a result of extending rapid prenatal growth rates to later ages. (In all mammals, the brain grows rapidly in utero but often very little after birth. We have extended this fetal phase into postnatal life.) 24

But the changes in timing themselves have been just as important. We are preeminently learning animals, and our extended childhood permits the transference of culture by education. Many animals display flexibility and play in childhood but follow rigidly programmed patterns as adults. Lorenz writes, in the same article above: "The characteristic which is so vital for the human peculiarity of the true man—that of always remaining in a state of development—is quite certainly a gift which we owe to the neotenous nature of mankind. 25

In short, we, like Mickey, never grow up although we, alas, do grow old. Best wishes to you, Mickey, for your next half-century. May we stay as young as you, but grow a bit wiser. 26

QUESTIONS

1. Gould admits he is having fun in this essay, but he also says (in paragraph 12) that he has two serious points to make. What are they?

2. What is the function of the very long parenthesis in paragraph 13? How do the remarks in parentheses relate to Gould's presentation of his views as those of "an at least marginally respectable scientist" (paragraph 12). What does he intend by referring to himself in that way?

3. How important are the charts and illustrations to this essay? Consider each of them separately.

4. What would be lost if the essay used no exact measurements but relied instead on the author's impressions?

5. Gould does not consider only the visual images of the cartoon figures he is studying. What other evidence does he mention, and how does he connect it to his major points?

6. Does this essay use biology and psychology to explain popular culture, or popular culture to illustate biological and psychological principles? What do you feel you have learned from reading Gould's essay?

7. Consider another cartoon character (not a Disney figure) that has existed for a long period of time. Examine this figure to see if it has evolved (as opposed to aged) in any way over time—either pictorially or in terms of speech and action. Write an essay explaining this cartoon character's change (or lack of change), being as precise and careful ("scientific"?) as you can.

MAKING CONNECTIONS

1. Read George Orwell's "Shooting an Elephant." What do we learn from Gould that puts new light on Orwell's essay, and that helps us see how much more can be made of his episode with an elephant than of Isak Dinesen's reflections on shooting an iguana?

2. Gould's essay should also add to our understanding of Bruno Bettelheim's "Joey: A 'Mechanical Boy.'" What can we add to Bettelheim's interpretation of Joey's case given this explanation of Gould's? Note particularly Joey's drawings. How does Gould's essay affect your understanding of Joey?

THE ACTION OF NATURAL SELECTION

Charles Darwin

Charles Darwin (1809–1882), British botanist, geologist, and naturalist, is best known for his discovery that natural selection was responsible for changes in organisms during evolution. After an undistinguished academic career and a five-year voyage to South America with a British survey ship, he began keeping his Transmutation Notebooks *(1837–1839), developing the idea of "selection owing to struggle." In 1842 and 1844 he published short accounts of his views and in 1859 published* On the Origin of Species, *which made him famous—even notorious—as the father of the "Theory of Evolution." He preferred to avoid controversy and left the debates over his theories to others whenever possible. But he was a keen observer and continued to study and write on natural history all his life. The essay that follows here is a brief excerpt from* On the Origin of Species, *in which Darwin explains his principle of "natural selection."*

In order to make it clear how, as I believe, natural selection acts, I must beg permission to give one or two imaginary illustrations. Let us take the case of a wolf, which preys on various animals, securing some by craft, some by strength, and some by fleetness; and let us suppose that the fleetest prey, a deer for instance, had from any change in the country increased in numbers, or that other prey had decreased in numbers, during that season of the year when the wolf is hardest pressed for food. I can under such circumstances see no reason to doubt that the swiftest and slimmest wolves would have the best chance for surviving, and so be preserved or selected,—provided always that they retained strength to master their prey at this or at some other period of the year, when they might be compelled to prey on other animals. I can see no more reason to doubt this, than that man can improve the fleetness of his greyhounds by careful and methodical selection, or by that unconscious selection which results from each man trying to keep the best dogs without any thought of modifying the breed.

Even without any change in the proportional numbers of the animals on which our wolf preyed, a cub might be born with an innate tendency to pursue certain kinds of prey. Nor can this be thought very improbable; for we often observe great differences in the natural tendencies of our domestic animals; one cat, for instance, taking to catch rats, another mice; one cat, according to Mr. St. John, bringing home winged game, another hares or rabbits, and another hunting on marshy ground and almost nightly catching woodcocks or snipes. The tendency to catch rats rather than mice is known to be inherited. Now, if any slight innate change of habit or of structure benefited an individual wolf, it would have the best chance of surviving and of leaving offspring. Some of its young would probably inherit the same habits or structure, and by the repetition of this process, a new variety might be formed which would either supplant or coexist with the parent-form of wolf. Or, again, the wolves inhabiting a mountainous district, and those frequenting the lowlands, would naturally be forced to hunt different prey; and from the continued preservation of the individuals best fitted for the two sites, two varieties might slowly be formed. These varieties would cross and blend where they met; but to this subject of intercrossing we shall soon have to return. I may add, that, according to Mr. Pierce, there are two varieties of the wolf inhabiting the Catskill Mountains in the United States, one with a light greyhound-like form, which pursues deer, and the other more bulky, with shorter legs, which more frequently attacks the shepherd's flocks.

Let us now take a more complex case. Certain plants excrete a sweet juice, apparently for the sake of eliminating something injurious from their sap: this is effected by glands at the base of the stipules in some Leguminosae, and at the back of the leaf of the common laurel. This juice, though small in quantity, is greedily sought by insects. Let us now suppose a little sweet juice or nectar to be excreted by the inner bases of the petals of a flower. In this case insects in seeking the nectar would get dusted with pollen, and would certainly often transport the pollen from one flower to the stigma of another flower. The flowers of two distinct individuals of the same species would thus get crossed; and the act of crossing, we have good reason to believe (as will hereafter be more fully alluded to), would produce very vigorous seedlings, which consequently would have the best chance of flourishing and surviving. Some of these seedlings would probably inherit the nectar-excreting power. Those individual flowers which had the largest glands or nectaries, and which excreted most nectar, would be oftenest visited by insects, and would be oftenest crossed; and so in the long-run would gain the upper hand. Those flowers, also, which had their stamens and pistils placed, in relation to the size and habits of the particular insects which visited them, so as to favor in any degree the transportal of their pollen from flower to flower, would likewise be favored or selected. We might have taken the case of insects visiting flowers for the sake of collecting pollen instead of nectar; and as pollen is formed for the sole object of fertilization, its destruction appears a simple loss to the plant; yet if a little pollen were carried, at first occasionally and then habitually, by the pollen-devouring insects from flower to flower, and a cross thus effected, although nine-tenths of the pollen were destroyed, it might still be a great gain to the plant; and those individuals which produced more and more pollen, and had larger and larger anthers, would be selected.

When our plant, by this process of the continued preservation or natural selection of more and more attractive flowers, had been rendered highly attractive to insects, they would unintentionally on their part, regularly carry pollen from flower to flower; and that they can most effectually do this, I could easily show by many striking instances. I will give only one—not as a very striking case, but as likewise illustrating one step in the separation of the sexes of plants, presently to be alluded to. Some holly-trees bear only male flowers, which have four stamens producing rather a small quantity of pollen, and a rudimentary pistil; other holly-trees bear only female flowers; these have a full-sized pistil and four stamens with shrivelled anthers, in which not a grain of pollen can be detected. Having found a female tree exactly sixty yards from a male tree, I put the stigmas of twenty flowers, taken from different branches, under the microscope, and on all, without exception, there were pollen-grains, and on some a profusion of pollen. As the wind had set for several days from the female to the male tree, the pollen could not thus have been carried. The weather had been cold and boisterous, and therefore not favorable to bees, nevertheless every female flower which I examined had been effectually fertilized by the bees, accidentally dusted with pollen, having flown from tree to tree in search of nectar. But to return to our imaginary case: as soon as the plant had been rendered so highly attractive to insects that pollen was regularly carried from flower to flower, another process might commence. No naturalist doubts the advantage of what has been called the "physiological division of labor;" hence we may believe that it would be advantageous to a plant to produce stamens alone in one flower or on one whole plant, and pistils alone in another flower or on one whole plant. In plants under culture and placed under new conditions of life, sometimes the male organs and sometimes the female organs become more or less impotent; now if we suppose this to occur in ever so slight a degree under nature, then as pollen is already carried regularly from flower to flower, and as a more complete separation of the sexes of our plant would be advantageous on the principle of the division of labor, individuals with this tendency more and more increased would be continually favored or selected, until at last a complete separation of the sexes would be effected.

Let us now turn to the nectar-feeding insects in our imaginary case: we may suppose the plant of which we have been slowly increasing the nectar by continued selection, to be a common plant; and that certain insects depended in main part on its nectar for food. I could give many facts, showing how anxious bees are to save time; for instance, their habit of cutting holes and sucking the nectar at the bases of certain flowers, which they can, with a very little more trouble, enter by the mouth. Bearing such facts in mind, I can see no reason to doubt that an accidental deviation in the size and form of the body, or in the curvature and length of the proboscis, &c., far too slight to be

585

appreciated by us, might profit a bee or other insect, so that an individual so characterized would be able to obtain its food more quickly, and so have a better chance of living and leaving descendants. Its descendants would probably inherit a tendency to a similar slight deviation of structure. The tubes of the corollas of the common red and incarnate clovers (Trifolium pratense and incarnatum) do not on a hasty glance appear to differ in length; yet the hive-bee can easily suck the nectar out of the incarnate clover, but not out of the common red clover, which is visited by humble-bees alone; so that whole fields of the red clover offer in vain an abundant supply of precious nectar to the hive-bee. Thus it might be a great advantage to the hive-bee to have a slightly longer or differently constructed proboscis. On the other hand, I have found by experiment that the fertility of clover greatly depends on bees visiting and moving parts of the corolla, so as to push the pollen on to the stigmatic surface. Hence, again, if humble-bees were to become rare in any country, it might be a great advantage to the red clover to have a shorter or more deeply divided tube to its corolla, so that the hive-bee could visit its flowers. Thus I can understand how a flower and a bee might slowly become, either simultaneously or one after the other, modified and adapted in the most perfect manner to each other, by the continued preservation of individuals presenting mutual and slightly favorable deviations of structure.

I am well aware that this doctrine of natural selection, exemplified in the above imaginary instances, is open to the same objections which were at first urged against Sir Charles Lyell's nobel views on "the modern changes of the earth, as illustrative of geology;" but we now very seldom hear the action, for instance, of the coast-waves, called a trifling and insignificant cause, when applied to the excavation of gigantic valleys or to the formation of the longest lines of inland cliffs. Natural selection can act only by the preservation and accumulation of infinitesimally small inherited modifications, each profitable to the preserved being; and as modern geology has almost banished such views as the excavation of a great valley by a single diluvial wave, so will natural selection, if it be a true principle, banish the belief of the continued creation of new organic beings, or of any great and sudden modification in their structure. 6

QUESTIONS

1. What does Darwin mean by "natural selection"?

2. The short title of Darwin's major book is often mistakenly given as *The Origin of the Species*. What is the difference between that and the book's correct title, *On the Origin of Species*? Why do you suppose so many people get it wrong?

3. Why does Darwin "beg permission" in the first sentence? In the same sentence, what does he mean by "imaginary" illustrations? Are they untrue, or what?

4. We use the name "bumblebee" for what Darwin (and other English writers before

him) called a "humble-bee." Find out something about the word *humble* and about the different kinds of bees. (What is the difference between a hive-bee and a humble-bee, anyway?) For the word *humble*, go to a good dictionary, but don't depend on a dictionary for information about different kinds of bees. Play with the words *humble* and *bumble* to see which of their meanings can be appropriately applied to bees.

5. Darwin's illustrative explanations are excellent examples of process analysis, a type of writing that presents a complicated chain of events as clearly as possible. Select some subject that you know well and that involves an intricate linkage of events. Explain an "imaginary" process taken from that subject. That is, imagine how some little change in an intricate pattern of events would lead to other changes that would cause other changes, until a whole new pattern was established. For example, how would some change in your behavior, appearance, or abilities change the patterns of school and family life around you? Explain the process you imagine as accurately and "scientifically" as you can. Complete your explanation by drawing some conclusion about the principles exemplified by the process you have described.

MAKING CONNECTIONS

1. To what extent could you read Francis Crick's "Times and Distances, Large and Small," as a commentary on this explanation of Darwin's? Or could you just as well read Darwin as a commentary on Crick?

2. Compare Darwin's illustrations of the wolf, the bee, and the flower to James Jeans's explanation in "Why the Sky Is Blue." What are some similarities of their explanations? Are there any striking differences?

ARGUING

ARGUING

Here in "Arguing" you will find authors taking positions on a wide range of controversial subjects—from the labeling of alcoholic beverages to the status of black English, from the nature of evolution to the use of animals in psychological research. No matter what their academic fields or professions, these authors energetically defend their stands on the issues and questions they address. But this should come as no surprise. None of us, after all, holds lightly to our beliefs and ideas about what is true or beautiful or good. Indeed, most of us get especially fired up when our views are pitted against the ideas and beliefs of others. So, you will find these authors vigorously engaged in the give-and-take of argument. And as a consequence, you will repeatedly find yourself having to weigh the merits of competing positions in a debate or disagreement about some controversial issue.

The distinctive quality of arguing can be seen in the following passage from Frederick A. King's "Animals in Research: The Case for Experimentation":

> A recent pamphlet published by the MFA [Mobilization for Animals Coalition] stated, "Of all experiments, those conducted in psychology are the most painful, pointless, and repulsive.". . .
>
> Such irresponsible accusations of research cruelty have consistently characterized the publications of the MFA. However, a recent study by psychologists D. Caroline Coile and Neal F. Miller of Rockefeller University counters these charges. Coile and Miller looked at every article (a total of 608) appearing in the past five years in journals of the American Psychological Association that report animal research. They concluded that none of the extreme allegations made by the MFA could be supported. . . .
>
> Furthermore, there are standards and mechanisms to ensure that research animals are treated in a humane and scientifically sensible way. These mechanisms include the Federal Animal Welfare Act of 1966 (amended in Congress in 1970, 1976, and 1979); periodic inspection of all animal-research facilities by the Department of Agriculture. . . .

This excerpt comes from the opening section of a piece in which King attempts to defend the use of animals in psychological research. In taking this view, King realizes that he is at odds with "more than 400 animal-protectionist organizations" that are united by "an adamant opposition to animal research." Given the significant disagreements that exist between his view and those of the animal protectionists, he is not free just to make a straightforward case for his own position on the matter. He must instead contend with his opponents, refuting their positions, while also providing evidence in support of his own. He is, in short, engaged in arguing. The argumentative situation is immediately reflected in the subtitle of his piece, which implicitly acknowledges that there is a case *against* experimentation, and in the debatelike structure of the paragraphs that follow. Accordingly, King begins by identifying the views of his opponents, namely that the use of animals in psychological research is "painful, pointless, and repulsive." He then moves into a discussion intended to refute those claims. So it is that argument puts ideas to the test by forcing them to stand up against opposing beliefs or theories.

As the King passage also reveals, argument naturally arises over significant issues or questions that are open to sharply differing points of view. Questions about the use of animals in research, for example, are of crucial interest to persons in a wide range of fields—not only to experimental psychologists such as King, but also to medical researchers, zoologists, environmentalists, and naturalists in general, as well as to philosophers, theologians, social planners, lawyers, and politicians. And persons in each of these fields might well be inclined to approach the question from markedly different points of view that involve different assumptions as well as different bodies of knowledge and experience. Many experimental psychologists and medical researchers, for example, perceive animals as being absolutely necessary in their investigations, whereas a number of philosophers, lawyers, and specialists in biomedical ethics are intensely committed to establishing and protecting the rights of animals, and thus with defining the point at which those rights have been violated by researchers. Each point of view necessarily leads to substantially different claims about the use of animals in research, and none of the claims can be conclusively proven to be true. Indeed, if conclusive evidence had existed for one view or another, the argument would never have arisen, or it would have been resolved as quickly as the evidence had been discovered. So, like all controversial issues, the question remains open to debate, and anyone involved in such an argument can at best hope to make a persuasive case for a particular viewpoint—a case that will move thoughtful readers to consider that position seriously and possibly even convince them to accept it.

As readers of argumentative writing, we in turn should try to be as impartial as the members of a jury. We should try to set aside any biases or prejudices that we might have about one view or another. Then, we should weigh all the evidence, logic, claims, and appeals for each viewpoint before arriving at a decision about which one we find most convincing. By the same token, as writers of argument we should assume that readers are not likely to be persuaded by a one-sided view of a complex situation. Thus, we should be ready to present a case that not only will support our position but will respond to the crucial challenges of views that differ from our own. Both as readers and writers, then, we should strive to understand the balanced methods of persuasion that can be found throughout the broad range of argumentative writing.

THE RANGE OF ARGUMENTATIVE WRITING

Argumentative writing so pervades our lives that we may not even recognize it as such in the many brochures and leaflets that come our way, urging us to vote for one candidate rather than another or to support one cause rather than another. Argumentative writing also figures heavily in newspaper editorials, syndicated columns, and letters to the editor, which are typically given over to debating the pros and cons of one public issue or another, from local taxes to national defense policies. Argument, of course, is fundamental in the judicial process, providing as it does the basic procedure for conducting all courtroom trials. And it is crucial in the legislative process, for it offers a systematic means of exploring the strengths and weaknesses of differing policies and programs. In a similar way, argument serves the basic aims of the academic world, enabling different ideas and theories to be tested by pitting them against each other. Whatever the field or profession, argument is an important activity in the advancement of knowledge and society.

The broad range of argumentative writing may conveniently be understood by considering the kinds of issues and questions that typically give rise to disagreement and debate. Surely, the most basic sources of controversy are questions of fact—the who, what, when, and where of things, as well as how much. Questions such as these are most commonly at issue in criminal trials. But intense arguments over questions of fact can also develop in any academic or professional field, especially when the facts in question have a significant bearing on the explanation or judgment of a particular subject, body of material, or type of investigation. In his piece on animals in research, for example, King, as we have seen, cites a study conducted by Coile and Miller who "looked at every article (a total of 608) appearing in the past five years in journals of the American Psychological Association that report animal research," in which "[t]hey concluded that none of the extreme allegations made by the MFA could be supported." So, in a very real sense, the argument in this piece arises over questions of fact as well as questions of how to interpret the facts.

Even when there is no question about the facts themselves, there are likely to be arguments about how to explain the facts. Disagreements of this kind abound across the full range of academic and professional fields. And the arguments inevitably arise out of sharply differing points of view on the facts, as can be seen in Stephen Jay Gould's "Racist Arguments and IQ." As he notes in his piece, standardized tests have indicated that "the average difference between American whites and blacks is 15 IQ points. . . ." But the question of whether this difference is the result of inheritance, environment, or flaws in the design and interpretation of IQ tests themselves remains open to debate.

So, Gould and his opponents approach the facts from sharply differing explanatory viewpoints, and an argument naturally ensues.

Differing viewpoints, of course, ultimately reflect differing beliefs and values. The way we view any particular subject is, after all, a matter of personal choice, an outgrowth of what our experience and knowledge have led us to hold as being self-evident. In this sense, beliefs and values are always to some extent at issue in any argumentative situation, even when they remain more or less in the background. But in some cases the conflicting values themselves are so clearly at the heart of the argument that they become a central focus in the debate, as you can see in this well-known passage from The Declaration of Independence.

> We hold these truths to be self-evident, that all men are created equal, that they are endowed by their Creator with certain unalienable Rights, that among these are Life, Liberty, and the pursuit of Happiness. That to secure these rights, Governments are instituted among Men, deriving their just powers from the consent of the governed, That whenever any Form of Government becomes destructive of these ends, it is the Right of the People to alter or to abolish it, and to institute new Government, laying its foundation on such principles and organizing its powers in such form, as to them shall seem most likely to affect their Safety and Happiness.

In this crucial passage that comes at the opening of the second paragraph of the Declaration, Thomas Jefferson and his congressional colleagues directly challenged several fundamental assumptions about the rights of people and the sources of government power that were then held not only by the British king but also by many British people and others throughout the world. Only in this way was it possible for them to make the compelling case for their ultimate claim that the colonies should be "FREE AND INDEPENDENT STATES . . . Absolved from all Allegiance to the British Crown."

Though Jefferson and his colleagues did not outline a new system of government in the Declaration itself, the document does enable us to see that conflicts over beliefs and values can, and often do, have a decisive bearing on questions of policy and planning. For a clear-cut example of how conflicts over beliefs lead to debates over policy, you need only look at Lewis Thomas's "The Art of Teaching Science." In the early section of his piece, Thomas challenges conventional beliefs about the certitude of scientific knowledge with his claim that "The conclusions reached in science are always, when looked at closely, far more provisional and tentative than are most of the assumptions arrived at by our colleagues in the humanities." Based on this and related claims, Thomas then proceeds in a later portion of his piece to outline a completely new method of teaching science:

> I suggest that the introductory courses in science, at all levels from grade school through college, be radically revised. Leave the fundamentals, the so-called basics,

594

aside for a while, and concentrate the attention of all students on the things that are not known. . . . At the outset, before any of the fundamentals, teach the still imponderable puzzles of cosmology. Describe as clearly as possible, for the youngest minds, that there are some things going on in the universe that lie still beyond comprehension, and make it plain how little is known.

Introductory science teachers might not respond too favorably to this proposal, especially since it would oblige them to deal "systematically with ignorance in science." But can you imagine what it would be like to take such a course? Can you imagine how such courses might influence the thinking of future scientists? Can you imagine how such a proposal might affect our contemporary attitudes toward science? None of these questions, of course, can be answered with certitude, for certainty is not possible in deliberations about the future. But Thomas does attempt to address these and other such questions, since in arguing on behalf of a proposal for change he is obligated to explore the possible consequences of his proposed change.

Just as his argument for a new mode of scientific education requires Thomas to consider and defend the possible effects of his proposed change, so every other kind of question imposes on writers a particular set of argumentative obligations. King's argument in favor of using animals in research, for example, obliges him to cite extensive data concerning the humaneness and purposefulness of psychological research on animals, and Gould's argument against the racial significance of IQ tests compels him to refute systematically the statistical evidence of those who believe in the validity of such tests. A writer who aims to be persuasive cannot simply assert that something is or is not the case, for readers in general are not willing to be bullied, hoodwinked, or otherwise manipulated into accepting a particular claim. But they are capable of being reached by civilized and rational methods of persuasion that are appropriate to controversial issues—by evidence, logic, and eloquence.

METHODS OF ARGUING

In any piece of argumentative writing, no matter what field or subject it concerns, your primary purpose is to bring readers around to your point of view rather than another. Some readers, of course, will agree with you in advance, but others will disagree, and still others will be undecided. So, in planning a piece of argumentative writing, you should begin by examining your material with an eye to discovering the issues that have to be addressed and the points that have to be made in order to present your case most persuasively to readers, especially those who oppose you or who are undecided. This means that you will have to deal not only with issues that you consider relevant but also with matters that have been raised by your opponents. In other words, you will have to show readers that you have considered both sides of the controversy. In arguing about the use of animals in research, for example, King repeatedly takes into account the views of his opponents. Likewise, Thomas not only presents his method of teaching science, but also seeks to refute the premises upon which the existing methods are based.

After you have identified the crucial points to be addressed, you should then decide upon the methods that will be necessary to make a convincing case with respect to each of the points. Some methods, of course, are imperative no matter what point you are trying to prove. Every piece of argumentation requires that you offer readers evidence to support your position. To do so, you will need to gather and present specific details that bear on each of the points you are trying to make. This basic concern for providing readers with appropriate evidence will lead you inevitably into the activity of reporting. Jefferson, for example, provides a lengthy and detailed list of "injuries" that the king of Great Britain inflicted on the colonies in order to demonstrate the right of the colonies "to throw off such Government"; and Thomas reports a striking array of unsolved scientific questions to demonstrate the scope of scientific ignorance. Reporting appropriate evidence constitutes the most basic means of making a persuasive case for any point under consideration. So, any point for which evidence cannot be provided, or for which only weak or limited evidence can be offered, is likely to be much less convincing to readers than one that can be amply and vividly substantiated.

But evidence alone will not be persuasive to readers unless it is brought to bear on a point in a reasonable or logical way. In one of its most familiar forms, known as *induction*, logic involves the process of moving from bits of evidence to a generalization or a conclusion that is based upon them. King, for example, tells in detail about several different kinds of psychological experiments involving animals in order to refute the charge of his opponents that animal research is "pointless." Although this evidence is appropriate for showing that some research on animals has been purposeful and beneficial, it does not demonstrate the necessity of using animals in research. In order to do that, King attempts to show that certain kinds of research problems "do not lend themselves" to alternative methods of investigation. Based on this evidence, he claims that in some instances "animals are necessary if the research is to be done at all." This particular claim appears reasonable not just because King has gathered and presented evidence that pertains to the issue at hand, but also because he has carefully worded his claim, so as not to overstate the case. But like all generalizations, it is a hypothesis and not a certainty. In order to prove his claim beyond any doubt, King would have had to examine every instance of animal research that had ever been conducted and consider alternative methods that might have been available at the time. So, he has no choice but to make what is known as an inductive leap from a reasonable, but necessarily limited, body of evidence to a generalization. So, too, his generalization is at best a statement of probability.

Another form of logic, known as *deduction*, involves the movement from general assumptions or hypotheses to particular conclusions that can be derived from them. For example, having made the general claim that "a long train of abuses" entitles people "to throw off such Government," and having cited, in turn, a long list of abuses that Great Britain had inflicted upon the colonies, Jefferson is able to reach the conclusion that the colonies "are Absolved from all Allegiance to the British Crown." Given his initial assumptions about government and the rights of the people together with his evidence about British abuse of the colonists, Jefferson's deduction seems to be a logical conclusion, as indeed it is. But as in any case of deductive logic, the conclusion is only as convincing as the premises on which it is based. Great Britain, obviously, did not accept Jefferson's premises, so it did not accept his conclusions, logical though they were. Other countries of the time, just as obviously, took a different view of the matter. So, in developing an argument deductively, you need to keep in mind not only the logic of your case, but also the appeal its premises are likely to have for those whom you are most interested in convincing.

As you can see just from the cases of Jefferson, King, and Thomas, presenting evidence and using it in a logical way can take a variety of common forms, and all of these forms are likely to be present in subtle and complicated ways in virtually every piece of argumentative writing. For arguing calls upon writers to be especially resourceful in developing and presenting their positions. Actually, logic is a necessary—and powerful—tool in every field and profession, because it serves to fill in gaps where evidence does not exist or, as in a court case, to move beyond the accumulated evidence to conclusions that follow from it. But like any powerful tool it must be used with care. One weak link in a logical chain of reasoning can lead, after all, to a string of falsehood.

Some situations, of course, call not only for logic, but also for an eloquent appeal to the basic truths of human experience. When Thomas challenges the traditional approach to teaching science, he does not rely just on evidence and reasoning about the state of scientific knowledge and ignorance, but also on an inherent appeal to the sense of wonder that most human beings have felt at one time or another in the face of the beauty, the power, or the mystery of existence. And he makes that appeal explicit in the sentence with which he concludes his piece:

> Part of the intellectual equipment of an educated person, however his or her time is to be spent, ought to be a feel for the queernesses of nature, the inexplicable thing, the side of life for which informed bewilderment will be the best way of getting through the day.

Most readers, as Thomas knows, have probably been puzzled occasionally by the mysterious nature of things and wondered what to make of their puzzlement. So, in the climax of this final sentence, he appeals to that common experience through a sequence of three roughly parallel phrases, each of which conveys the idea of mystery, "the inexplicable thing," in an expressively arresting way.

Explanatory techniques, such as we discussed in our introduction to the preceding section, also can play a role in argument, as you may already have inferred from the passages we have just been discussing. Thomas's argument about teaching science, for example, is based on a comparison and contrast of two different conceptions of scientific knowledge, as well as two different approaches to teaching students about those differing conceptions. And Gould's attack on the claim that differences in IQ are attributable to racially genetic differences involves him in using cause-and-effect analysis to debunk such "racist arguments." Any piece of argument, in other words, is likely to draw upon a wide range of techniques, for argument is always attempting to achieve the complex purpose not only of getting at the truth about something, and making that truth intelligible to readers, but also of persuading them to accept it as such.

No matter what particular combination of techniques a writer favors, you will probably find that most authors, when carrying out an argument, save a very telling point or bit of evidence or well-turned phrase for last. Like effective storytellers or successful courtroom lawyers, they know that a memorable detail makes for a powerful climax. In the pieces that follow in this section, you will see how different writers use the various resources of language to produce some very striking and compelling pieces of argument.

Arts and Humanities

AM I BLUE?
Alice Walker

As the headnote on page 48 explains, Alice Walker is an essayist, poet, novelist, and short-story writer. The following essay comes from her collection, Living by the Word: Selected Writings, 1973-1987 *(1988). About this collection, Walker writes: "In my travels I found many people sitting and thinking thoughts similar to my own. In this study I was taught by these other people, by the art and history of past cultures, by the elements, and by the trees, the flowers, and most especially, the animals." In the essay reprinted here, Walker questions the distinctions commonly made between human and animal.*

For about three years my companion and I rented a small house in the country that stood on the edge of a large meadow that appeared to run from the end of our deck straight into the mountains. The mountains, however, were quite far away, and between us and them there was, in fact, a town. It was one of the many pleasant aspects of the house that you never really were aware of this.

It was a house of many windows, low, wide, nearly floor to ceiling in the living room, which faced the meadow, and it was from one of these that I first saw our closest neighbor, a large white horse, cropping grass, flipping its mane, and ambling about—not over the entire meadow, which stretched well out of sight of the house, but over the five or so fenced-in acres that were next to the twenty-odd that we had rented. I soon learned that the horse, whose name was Blue, belonged to a man who lived in another town, but was boarded by our neighbors next door. Occasionally, one of the children, usually a stocky teenager, but sometimes a much younger girl or boy, could be seen riding Blue.

599

They would appear in the meadow, climb up on his back, ride furiously for ten or fifteen minutes, then get off, slap Blue on the flanks, and not be seen again for a month or more.

There were many apple trees in our yard, and one by the fence that Blue   3
could almost reach. We were soon in the habit of feeding him apples, which he relished, especially because by the middle of summer the meadow grasses— so green and succulent since January—had dried out from lack of rain, and Blue stumbled about munching the dried stalks half-heartedly. Sometimes he would stand very still just by the apple tree, and when one of us came out he would whinny, snort loudly, or stamp the ground. This meant, of course: I want an apple.

It was quite wonderful to pick a few apples, or collect those that had fallen   4
to the ground overnight, and patiently hold them, one by one, up to his large, toothy mouth. I remained as thrilled as a child by his flexible dark lips, huge, cubelike teeth that crunched the apples, core and all, with such finality, and his high, broad-breasted *enormity*; beside which, I felt small indeed. When I was a child, I used to ride horses, and was especially friendly with one named Nan until the day I was riding and my brother deliberately spooked her and I was thrown, head first, against the trunk of a tree. When I came to, I was in bed and my mother was bending worriedly over me; we silently agreed that perhaps horseback riding was not the safest sport for me. Since then I have walked, and prefer walking to horseback riding—but I had forgotten the depth of feeling one could see in horses' eyes.

I was therefore unprepared for the expression in Blue's. Blue was lonely.   5
Blue was horribly lonely and bored. I was not shocked that this should be the case; five acres to tramp by yourself, endlessly, even in the most beautiful of meadows—and his was—cannot provide many interesting events, and once rainy season turned to dry that was about it. No, I was shocked that I had forgotten that human animals and nonhuman animals can communicate quite well; if we are brought up around animals as children we take this for granted. By the time we are adults we no longer remember. However, the animals have not changed. They are in fact *completed* creations (at least they seem to be, so much more than we) who are not likely *to* change; it is their nature to express themselves. What else are they going to express? And they do. And, generally speaking, they are ignored.

After giving Blue the apples, I would wander back to the house, aware that   6
he was observing me. Were more apples not forthcoming then? Was that to be his sole entertainment for the day? My partner's small son had decided he wanted to learn how to piece a quilt; we worked in silence on our respective squares as I thought . . .

Well, about slavery: about white children, who were raised by black people,   7
who knew their first all-accepting love from black women, and then, when they

were twelve or so, were told they must "forget" the deep levels of communication between themselves and "mammy" that they knew. Later they would be able to relate quite calmly, "My old mammy was sold to another good family." "My old mammy was ———— ————." Fill in the blank. Many more years later a white woman would say: "I can't understand these Negroes, these blacks. What do they want? They're so different from us."

And about the Indians, considered to be "like animals" by the "settlers" (a   8
very benign euphemism for what they actually were), who did not understand their description as a compliment.

And about the thousands of American men who marry Japanese, Korean,   9
Filipina, and other non–English-speaking women and of how happy they report they are, *"blissfully,"* until their brides learn to speak English, at which point the marriages tend to fall apart. What then did the men see, when they looked into the eyes of the women they married, before they could speak English? Apparently only their own reflections.

I thought of society's impatience with the young. "Why are they playing the   10
music so loud?" Perhaps the children have listened to much of the music of oppressed people their parents danced to before they were born, with its passionate but soft cries for acceptance and love, and they have wondered why their parents failed to hear.

I do not know how long Blue had inhabited his five beautiful, boring acres   11
before we moved into our house; a year after we had arrived—and had also traveled to other valleys, other cities, other worlds—he was still there.

But then, in our second year at the house, something happened in Blue's   12
life. One morning, looking out the window at the fog that lay like a ribbon over the meadow, I saw another horse, a brown one, at the other end of Blue's field. Blue appeared to be afraid of it, and for several days made no attempt to go near. We went away for a week. When we returned, Blue had decided to make friends and the two horses ambled or galloped along together, and Blue did not come nearly as often to the fence underneath the apple tree.

When he did, bringing his new friend with him, there was a different look   13
in his eyes. A look of independence, of self-possession, of inalienable *horse*ness. His friend eventually became pregnant. For months and months there was, it seemed to me, a mutual feeling between me and the horses of justice, of peace. I fed apples to them both. The look in Blue's eyes was one of unabashed "this is *it*ness."

It did not, however, last forever. One day, after a visit to the city, I went out   14
to give Blue some apples. He stood waiting, or so I thought, though not beneath the tree. When I shook the tree and jumped back from the shower of apples, he made no move. I carried some over to him. He managed to half-crunch one. The rest he let fall to the ground. I dreaded looking into his eyes—because I had of course noticed that Brown, his partner, had gone—but I did look. If I

601

had been born into slavery, and my partner had been sold or killed, my eyes would have looked like that. The children next door explained that Blue's partner had been "put with him" (the same expression that old people used, I had noticed, when speaking of an ancestor during slavery who had been impregnated by her owner) so that they could mate and she conceive. Since that was accomplished, she had been taken back by her owner, who lived somewhere else.

Will she be back? I asked. 15

They didn't know. 16

Blue was like a crazed person. Blue *was*, to me, a crazed person. He galloped 17 furiously, as if he were being ridden, around and around his five beautiful acres. He whinnied until he couldn't. He tore at the ground with his hooves. He butted himself against his single shade tree. He looked always and always toward the road down which his partner had gone. And then, occasionally, when he came up for apples, or I took apples to him, he looked at me. It was a look so piercing, so full of grief, a look so *human*, I almost laughed (I felt too sad to cry) to think there are people who do not know that animals suffer. People like me who have forgotten, and daily forget, all that animals try to tell us. "Everything you do to us will happen to you; we are your teachers, as you are ours. We are one lesson" is essentially it, I think. There are those who never once have even considered animals' rights: those who have been taught that animals actually want to be used and abused by us, as small children "love" to be frightened, or women "love" to be mutilated and raped. . . . They are the great-grandchildren of those who honestly thought, because someone taught them this: "Woman can't think" and "niggers can't faint." But most disturbing of all, in Blue's large brown eyes was a new look, more painful than the look of despair: the look of disgust with human beings, with life; the look of hatred. And it was odd what the look of hatred did. It gave him, for the first time, the look of a beast. And what that meant was that he had put up a barrier within to protect himself from further violence; all the apples in the world wouldn't change that fact.

And so Blue remained, a beautiful part of our landscape, very peaceful to 18 look at from the window, white against the grass. Once a friend came to visit and said, looking out on the soothing view: "And it *would* have to be a *white* horse; the very image of freedom." And I thought, yes, the animals are forced to become for us merely "images" of what they once so beautifully expressed. And we are used to drinking milk from containers showing "contented" cows, whose real lives we want to hear nothing about, eating eggs and drumsticks from "happy" hens, and munching hamburgers advertised by bulls of integrity who seem to command their fate.

As we talked of freedom and justice one day for all, we sat down to steaks. 19 I am eating misery, I thought, as I took the first bite. And spit it out.

QUESTIONS

1. Why does Walker begin her argument by setting the scene ("We rented a small house in the country . . .") and by leisurely describing the meadow where she first saw Blue?

2. Walker takes great pleasure in describing Blue for her readers. In paragraph 4 she tells us: "I remained as thrilled as a child by his flexible dark lips, huge, cubelike teeth that crunched the apples, core and all, with such finality, and his high, broad-breasted *enormity*; beside which, I felt small indeed." What does Blue represent to Walker? What does she learn from observing him?

3. In paragraph 7, Walker switches from thinking about Blue to thinking about slavery. This kind of transition is the work of the essayist—to link together through language horses, slavery, Indians, and non–English-speaking women. How does Walker make these various connections? What is her argument?

4. Walker writes in paragraph 18, "And I thought, yes, the animals are forced to become for us merely "images" of what they once so beautifully expressed. And we are used to drinking milk from containers showing "contented" cows, whose real lives we want to hear nothing about, eating eggs and drumsticks from "happy" hens, and munching hamburgers advertised by bulls of integrity who seem to command their fate." How would you respond to this comment? Write a response to Walker's essay in which you argue your position.

5. Some animal rights activists argue that animal rights will emerge as the civil rights movement of the twenty-first century. A central issue in this movement is the question, What distinguishes humans from other animals? Write an essay in which you argue your position on this issue.

MAKING CONNECTIONS

1. Walker's strategies for arguing differ from those of a more formal argument such as Thomas Jefferson's The Declaration of Independence or Stephen Jay Gould's "Racist Arguments and IQ." Describe the strategies Walker uses and how they differ from Jefferson's or Gould's or those of another writer of your choice from this section.

2. Walker's other essay in this volume, "Beauty: When the Other Dancer Is the Self," is categorized as reflective rather than argumentative. Presumably, her approaches to these two essays differ. Compare her two essays. In what passages in "Am I Blue?" do you find Walker most intensely absorbed in arguing? How do those passages stand out? How are they prepared for? Is there an argument embedded in the earlier essay as well? If so, how can you describe it?

3. In paragraph 17, Walker says there are "those who have been taught that animals actually want to be used and abused by us." To what extent does the theme of that passage connect with Tania Modleski's "Soap Opera, Melodrama, and Women's Anger" or Carol Gilligan's "Woman's Place in Man's Life Cycle," both in "Explaining"? Write an essay explaining the common denominator you find among these three essays.

HIROSHIMA

John Berger

*After beginning his career as a painter and drawing instruc-
tor, John Berger (b. 1926) has come to be one of Britain's
most influential art critics. He has achieved recognition as
a screenwriter, novelist, and documentary writer. He now
lives in a small French peasant community and is working
on a project that traces the peasant's journey from village
to city. As a Marxist, he is concerned with the ideological
and technological conditioning of our ways of seeing both
art and the world. In* Ways of Seeing *(1972), he explores
the interrelation between words and images, between verbal
and visual meaning. "Hiroshima" first appeared in 1981 in
the journal* New Society, *and later in a collection of essays,*
The Sense of Sight *(1985). Berger examines how the facts
of nuclear holocaust have been hidden through "a systematic, slow and thorough process of suppression and elimination . . . within the reality of politics." Images, rather
than words, Berger asserts, can help us to see through the
"mask of innocence" that evil wears.*

The whole incredible problem begins with the need to reinsert those events 1
of 6 August 1945 back into living consciousness.

I was shown a book last year at the Frankfurt Book Fair. The editor asked 2
me some question about what I thought of its format. I glanced at it quickly
and gave some reply. Three months ago I was sent a finished copy of the book.
It lay on my desk unopened. Occasionally its title and cover picture caught my
eye, but I did not respond. I didn't consider the book urgent, for I believed that
I already knew about what I would find within it.

Did I not clearly remember the day—I was in the army in Belfast—when 3
we first heard the news of the bomb dropped on Hiroshima? At how many
meetings during the first nuclear disarmament movement had I and others not
recalled the meaning of that bomb?

And then, one morning last week, I received a letter from America, accom- 4
panying an article written by a friend. This friend is a doctor of philosophy and
a Marxist. Furthermore, she is a very generous and warm-hearted woman. The
article was about the possibilities of a third world war. Vis-à-vis the Soviet Union

she took, I was surprised to read, a position very close to Reagan's. She concluded by evoking the likely scale of destruction which would be caused by nuclear weapons, and then welcomed the positive possibilities that this would offer the socialist revolution in the United States.

It was on that morning that I opened and read the book on my desk. It is 5 called *Unforgettable Fire*.[1]

The book consists of drawings and paintings made by people who were in 6 Hiroshima on the day that the bomb was dropped, thirty-six years ago today. Often the pictures are accompanied by a verbal record of what the image represents. None of them is by a professional artist. In 1974, an old man went to the television centre in Hiroshima to show to whoever was interested a picture he had painted, entitled "At about 4 pm, 6th August 1945, near Yurozuyo bridge."

This prompted an idea of launching a television appeal to other survivors of 7 that day to paint or draw their memories of it. Nearly a thousand pictures were sent in, and these were made into an exhibition. The appeal was worded: "Let us leave for posterity pictures about the atomic bomb, drawn by citizens."

Clearly, my interest in these pictures cannot be an art-critical one. One does 8 not musically analyse screams. But after repeatedly looking at them, what began as an impression became a certainty. These were images of hell.

I am not using the word as hyperbole. Between these paintings by women 9 and men who have never painted anything else since leaving school, and who

HOW SURVIVORS SAW IT. A painting by Kazuhiro Ishizu, aged 68

have surely, for the most part, never travelled outside Japan, between these traced memories which had to be exorcised, and the numerous representations of hell in European medieval art, there is a very close affinity.

This affinity is both stylistic and fundamental. And fundamentally it is to do with the situations depicted. The affinity lies in the degree of the multiplication of pain, in the lack of appeal or aid, in the pitilessness, in the equality of wretchedness, and in the disappearance of time.   10

> I am 78 years old. I was living at Midorimachi on the day of the A-bomb blast. Around 9 am that morning, when I looked out of my window, I saw several women coming along the street one after another towards the Hiroshima prefectural hospital. I realized for the first time, as it is sometimes said, that when people are very much frightened hair really does stand on end. The women's hair was, in fact, standing straight up and the skin of their arms was peeled off. I suppose they were around 30 years old.

Time and again, the sober eyewitness accounts recall the surprise and horror of Dante's verses about the Inferno. The temperature at the centre of the Hiroshima fireball was 300,000 degrees centigrade. The survivors are called in Japanese *hibakuska*—"those who have seen hell."   11

> Suddenly, one man who was stark naked came up to me and said in a quavering voice, 'Please help me!' He was burned and swollen all over from the effects of the A-bomb. Since I did not recognize him as my neighbour, I asked who he was. He answered that he was Mr. Sasaki, the son of Mr Ennosuke Sasaki, who had a lumber shop in Funairi town. That morning he had been doing volunteer

At the Aioi bridge, by Sawami Katagiri, aged 76

606

labour service, evacuating the houses near the prefectural office in Kato town. He had been burned black all over and had started back to his home in Funairi. He looked miserable—burned and sore, and naked with only pieces of his gaiters trailing behind as he walked. Only the part of his hair covered by his soldier's hat was left, as if he was wearing a bowl. When I touched him, his burned skin slipped off. I did not know what to do, so I asked a passing driver to take him to Eba hospital.

Does not this evocation of hell make it easier to forget that these scenes belonged to life? Is there not something conveniently unreal about hell? The whole history of the twentieth century proves otherwise.

Very systematically in Europe the conditions of hells have been constructed. 12 It is not even necessary to list the sites. It is not even necessary to repeat the calculations of the organizers. We know this, and we choose to forget it.

We find it ridiculous or shocking that most of the pages concerning, for 13 example, Trotsky were torn out of official Soviet history. What has been torn out of our history are the pages concerning the experience of the two atom bombs dropped on Japan.

Of course, the facts are there in the textbooks. It may even be that school 14 children learn the dates. But what these facts mean—and originally their meaning was so clear, so monstrously vivid, that every commentator in the world was shocked, and every politician was obliged to say (whilst planning differently), "Never again"—what these facts mean has now been torn out. It has been a systematic, slow and thorough process of suppression and elimination. This process has been hidden within the reality of politics.

Do not misunderstand me. I am not here using the word "reality" ironically, 15 I am not politically naïve. I have the greatest respect for political reality, and I believe that the innocence of political idealists is often very dangerous. What we are considering is how in this case in the West—not in Japan for obvious reasons and not in the Soviet Union for different reasons—political and military realities have eliminated another reality.

The eliminated reality is both physical— 16

Yokogawa bridge above Tenma river, 6th August 1945, 8.30 am.
People crying and moaning were running towards the city. I did not know why.
Steam engines were burning at Yokogawa station.
Skin of cow tied to wire.
Skin of girl's hip was hanging down.
"My baby is dead, isn't she?"

and moral.

The political and military arguments have concerned such issues as deter- 17 rence, defence systems, relative strike parity, tactical nuclear weapons and— pathetically—so-called civil defence. Any movement for nuclear disarmament today has to contend with those considerations and dispute their false interpretation. To lose sight of them is to become as apocalyptic as the Bomb and all utopias. (The construction of hells on earth was accompanied in Europe by plans for heavens on earth.)

What has to be redeemed, reinserted, disclosed and never be allowed to be   18
forgotten, is the other reality. Most of the mass means of communication are close to what has been suppressed.

These paintings were shown on Japanese television. Is it conceivable that   19
the BBC would show these pictures on channel one at a peak hour? Without any reference "political" and "military" realities, under the straight title, *This is How It Was, 6th August 1945?* I challenge them to do so.

What happened on that day was, of course, neither the beginning nor the   20
end of the act. It began months, years before, with the planning of the action, and the eventual final decision to drop two bombs on Japan. However much the world was shocked and surprised by the bomb dropped on Hiroshima, it has to be emphasized that it was not a miscalculation, an error, or the result (as can happen in war) of a situation deteriorating so rapidly that it gets out of hand. What happened was consciously and precisely planned. Small scenes like this were part of the plan:

> I was walking along the Hihiyama bridge about 3 pm on 7th August. A woman, who looked like an expectant mother, was dead. At her side, a girl of about three years of age brought some water in an empty can she had found. She was trying to let her mother drink from it.
>
> As soon as I saw this miserable scene with the pitiful child, I embraced the girl close to me and cried with her, telling her that her mother was dead.

There was a preparation. And there was an aftermath. The latter included   21
long, lingering deaths, radiation sickness, many fatal illnesses which developed later as a result of exposure to the bomb, and tragic genetical effects on generations yet to be born.

I refrain from giving the statistics: how many hundreds of thousands of dead,   22
how many injured, how many deformed children. Just as I refrain from pointing out how comparatively "small" were the atomic bombs dropped on Japan. Such statistics tend to distract. We consider numbers instead of pain. We calculate instead of judging. We relativize instead of refusing.

It is possible today to arouse popular indignation or anger by speaking of the   23
threat and immorality of terrorism. Indeed, this appears to be the central plank of the rhetoric of the new American foreign policy ("Moscow is the world-base of all terrorism") and of British policy towards Ireland. What is able to shock people about terrorist acts is that often their targets are unselected and innocent—a crowd in a railway station, people waiting for a bus to go home after work. The victims are chosen indiscriminately in the hope of producing a shock effect on political decision-making by their government.

The two bombs dropped on Japan were terrorist actions. The calculation was   24

terrorist. The indiscriminacy was terrorist. The small groups of terrorists operating today are, by comparison, humane killers.

Another comparison needs to be made. Today terrorist groups mostly rep- 25
resent small nations or groupings, who are disputing large powers in a position
of strength. Whereas Hiroshima was perpetrated by the most powerful alliance
in the world against an enemy who was already prepared to negotiate, and was
admitting defeat.

To apply the epithet "terrorist" to the acts of bombing Hiroshima and Na- 26
gasaki is logically justifiable, and I do so because it may help to re-insert that
act into living consciousness today. Yet the word changes nothing in itself.

The first-hand evidence of the victims, the reading of the pages which have 27
been torn out, provokes a sense of outrage. This outrage has two natural faces.
One is a sense of horror and pity at what happened; the other face is self-
defensive and declares: *this should not happen again (here)*. For some the *here*
is in brackets, for others it is not.

The face of horror, the reaction which has now been mostly suppressed, 28
forces us to comprehend the reality of what happened. The second reaction,
unfortunately, distances us from that reality. Although it begins as a straight
declaration, it quickly leads into the labyrinth of defence policies, military
arguments and global strategies. Finally it leads to the sordid commercial
absurdity of private fall-out shelters.

This split of the sense of outrage into, on one hand, horror and, on the 29
other hand, expediency occurs because the concept of evil has been abandoned.
Every culture, except our own in recent times, has had such a concept.

That its religious or philosophical bases vary is unimportant. The concept 30
of evil implies a force or forces which have to be continually struggled against
so that they do not triumph over life and destroy it. One of the very first written
texts from Mesopotamia, 1,500 years before Homer, speaks of this struggle,
which was the first condition of human life. In public thinking nowadays, the
concept of evil has been reduced to a little adjective to support an opinion or
hypothesis (abortions, terrorism, ayatollahs).

Nobody can confront the reality of 6th August 1945 without being forced to 31
acknowledge that what happened was evil. It is not a question of opinion or
interpretation, but of events.

The memory of these events should be continually before our eyes. This is 32
why the thousand citizens of Hiroshima started to draw on their little scraps of
paper. We need to show their drawings everywhere. These terrible images can
now release an energy for opposing evil and for the life-long struggle of that
opposition.

And from this a very old lesson may be drawn. My friend in the United 33
States is, in a sense, innocent. She looks beyond a nuclear holocaust without
considering its reality. This reality includes not only its victims but also its
planners and those who support them. Evil from time immemorial has often

worn a mask of innocence. One of evil's principal modes of being is *looking beyond* (with indifference) that which is before the eyes.

> August 9th: On the west embankment of a military training field was a young boy four or five years old. He was burned black, lying on his back, with his arms pointing towards heaven.

Only by looking beyond or away can one come to believe that such evil is   34
relative, and therefore under certain conditions justifiable. In reality—the reality to which the survivors and the dead bear witness—it can never be justified.

NOTES

1. Edited by Japan Broadcasting Corporation, London, Wildwood House, 1981; New York, Pantheon, 1981.

QUESTIONS

1. Berger begins his essay with this powerful sentence: "The whole incredible problem begins with the need to reinsert those events of 6 August 1945 into living consciousness." What is "the whole incredible problem" as Berger describes and defines it?

2. Berger argues that what happened on August 6, 1945, was "consciously and precisely planned." What evidence does he present to support this claim? How does this argument advance his larger purpose?

3. Berger tells his readers that he refrains from giving statistics because "statistics tend to distract." What do statistics distance us from understanding about Hiroshima?

4. The content in Berger's essay ranges from thoughts about Hiroshima, to images of hell, to political realities, to terrorist actions, to concepts of evil. How does he connect these various subjects? What is the chain of reasoning?

5. Berger offers various images from the book *Unforgettable Fire*, such as "August 9th: On the west embankment of a military training field was a young boy four or five years old. He was burned black, lying on his back, with his arms pointing towards heaven" (paragraph 33). Look at the various places in the essay where Berger presents such images from *Unforgettable Fire*. What effect does this evidence have on you? How does this evidence strengthen Berger's argument?

6. Spend some time looking at and thinking about the paintings by the survivors, Kazuhiro Ishizu and Sawami Katagiri, reprinted on pages 605 and 606. What do you *see* in these paintings? What do these images represent to you?

MAKING CONNECTIONS

1. Berger insists on closing the distance between ourselves and the essential horror of Hiroshima. Look at some other essays that struggle with issues of distance. Jonathan Swift's "A Modest Proposal," Phillip Knightley's "The First Televised War," and Alice

Walker's "Am I Blue?" would all be examples; but you might propose another. To what an extent is "distance" an issue in arguing? Compare how two or three arguers handle problems of distance in their essays.

2. One of Berger's strategies in this essay is to challenge and invert popular definitions, as of *terrorism* and *terrorists*, for example (paragraphs 23–26). Similar inversions take place or are hinted at in Horace Miner's "Body Ritual among the Nacirema," Jane van Lawick-Goodall's "First Observations," Stephen Jay Gould's "A Biological Homage to Mickey Mouse," and Alice Walker's "Am I Blue?" In those examples, the inversion always involves humans and animals. Write an argument in which you invert the definition of a key term, of *safe* and *unsafe*, for example, or *capitalist* and *communist*, or *fair* and *foul*, or *villain* and *victim*. Experiment with the leverage for arguing you find in such a radical redefinition.

CALCULATING MACHINE
E. B. White

*E. B. White (1899–1985) began writing in various capac-
ities for the* New Yorker *in 1926, soon after the magazine's
inception. In 1957 he retired to his farm in Maine, where
he continued to write. While he is well known for his children's books, namely* Charlotte's Web *and* Stuart Little, *he
has been called with some justice "the finest essayist in the
United States" because of the grace and clarity of his writing
and the range of his interests. As White himself said, the
essayist thoroughly enjoys his work because "he can pull on
any sort of shirt, be any sort of person, according to his
mood or his subject matter." Here in "Calculating Machine," White pokes fun at the genre of "how to write" books
as he argues that "writing is an act of faith, not a trick of
grammar."*

A publisher in Chicago has sent me a pocket calculating machine by which 1
I may test my writing to see whether it is intelligible. The calculator was
developed by General Motors, who, not satisfied with giving the world a Cad-
illac, now dream of bringing perfect understanding to men. The machine (it is
simply a celluloid card with a dial) is called the Reading-Ease Calculator and
shows four grades of "reading ease"—Very Easy, Easy, Hard, and Very Hard.
You count your words and syllables, set the dial, and an indicator lets you
know whether anybody is going to understand what you have written. An
instruction book came with it, and after mastering the simple rules I lost no
time in running a test on the instruction book itself, to see how *that* writer was
doing. The poor fellow! His leading essay, the one on the front cover, tested
Very Hard.

My next step was to study the first phrase on the face of the calculator: "How 2
to test Reading-Ease of written matter." There is, of course, no such thing as
reading ease of written matter. There is the ease with which matter can be read,
but that is a condition of the reader, not of the matter. Thus the inventors and
distributors of this calculator get off to a poor start, with a Very Hard instruction
book and a slovenly phrase. Already they have one foot caught in the brier
patch of English usage.

Not only did the author of the instruction book score badly on the front 3

612

cover, but inside the book he used the word "personalize" in an essay on how to improve one's writing. A man who likes the word "personalize" is entitled to his choice, but I wonder whether he should be in the business of giving advice to writers. "Whenever possible," he wrote, "personalize your writing by directing it to the reader." As for me, I would as lief simonize my grandmother as personalize my writing.

In the same envelope with the calculator, I received another training aid for   4
writers—a booklet called "How to Write Better," by Rudolf Flesch. This, too, I studied, and it quickly demonstrated the broncolike ability of the English language to throw whoever leaps cocksurely into the saddle. The language not only can toss a rider but knows a thousand tricks for tossing him, each more gay than the last. Dr. Flesch stayed in the saddle only a moment or two. Under the heading "Think Before You Write," he wrote, "The main thing to consider is your *purpose* in writing. Why are you sitting down to write?" And Echo answered: Because, sir, it is more comfortable than standing up.

Communication by the written word is a subtler (and more beautiful) thing   5
than Dr. Flesch and General Motors imagine. They contend that the "average reader" is capable of reading only what tests Easy, and that the writer should write at or below this level. This is a presumptuous and degrading idea. There is no average reader, and to reach down toward this mythical character is to deny that each of us is on the way up, is ascending. ("Ascending," by the way, is a word Dr. Flesch advises writers to stay away from. Too unusual.)

It is my belief that no writer can improve his work until he discards the   6
dulcet notion that the reader is feebleminded, for writing is an act of faith, not a trick of grammar. Ascent is at the heart of the matter. A country whose writers are following a calculating machine downstairs is not ascending—if you will pardon the expression—and a writer who questions the capacity of the person at the other end of the line is not a writer at all, merely a schemer. The movies long ago decided that a wider communication could be achieved by a deliberate descent to a lower level, and they walked proudly down until they reached the cellar. Now they are groping for the light switch, hoping to find the way out.

I have studied Dr. Flesch's instructions diligently, but I return for guidance   7
in these matters to an earlier American, who wrote with more patience, more confidence. "I fear chiefly," he wrote, "lest my expression may not be *extravagant* enough, may not wander far enough beyond the narrow limits of my daily experience, so as to be adequate to the truth of which I have been convinced. . . . Why level downward to our dullest perception always, and praise that as common sense? The commonest sense is the sense of men asleep, which they express by snoring."

Run that through your calculator! It may come out Hard, it may come out   8
Easy. But it will come out whole, and it will last forever.

QUESTIONS

1. What is the "calculating machine"?

2. Why does White object to this machine? Why doesn't he think that writing can be calculated?

3. What methods of arguing does White use to bring readers to his point of view?

4. How would you characterize the evidence White presents to support his position? Where in the essay does White present the most persuasive evidence?

5. White writes in paragraph 6, "It is my belief that no writer can improve his work until he discards the dulcet notion that the reader is feebleminded, for writing is an act of faith, not a trick of grammar." Who is White's reader in this essay? Is White's essay an "act of faith"?

6. Read White's essay, "Dear Mr. 0214 1063 02 10730 8" in the introduction. What similarities do you find between these two essays? What do you learn about White the essayist from reading these two essays?

7. Think about a machine or appliance that promises to do one thing, but, in fact, does the very opposite. Using White's essay as a model, argue against the intent of the machine, and show how the machine is symbolic of some larger problem in our culture.

MAKING CONNECTIONS

1. Look up *extravagant* (paragraph 7) in a dictionary. What is its root meaning? Do you agree that a writer should worry about not being extravagant enough? What examples of extravagance have impressed you in this collection? Choose two or three and compare them, summoning some extravagance of your own to the purpose.

2. To what extent is White's essay parallel to Joan Didion's "Why I Write" or Richard Selzer's "Why a Surgeon Would Write" in "Reflecting"?

3. Read George Orwell's "Politics and the English Language" in this section. Do you think White and Orwell are in agreement or not? Which one seems to you the better guide to being a writer? Argue for the advantages found in the essay you prefer.

IF BLACK ENGLISH ISN'T A LANGUAGE, THEN TELL ME, WHAT IS?

James Baldwin

As the headnote on page 66 indicates, James Baldwin's writings stand as important explorations of the relationship between blacks and whites. Baldwin himself might add that his life's work lay in defining and legitimizing the black voice; like Orwell, Baldwin argued that language is "a political instrument, means, and proof of power." The following essay on language and legitimacy first appeared in 1979 in the New York Times *and later was included in* The Price of the Ticket: Collected Nonfiction 1948–1985 *(1985).*

The argument concerning the use, or the status, or the reality, of black 1 English is rooted in American history and has absolutely nothing to do with the question the argument supposes itself to be posing. The argument has nothing to do with language itself but with the role of language. Language, incontestably, reveals the speaker. Language, also, far more dubiously, is meant to define the other—and, in this case, the other is refusing to be defined by a language that has never been able to recognize him.

People evolve a language in order to describe and thus control their circum- 2 stances or in order not to be submerged by a situation that they cannot articulate. (And if they cannot articulate it, they are submerged.) A Frenchman living in Paris speaks a subtly and crucially different language from that of the man living in Marseilles; neither sounds very much like a man living in Quebec; and they would all have great difficulty in apprehending what the man from Guadeloupe, or Martinique, is saying, to say nothing of the man from Senegal—although the "common" language of all these areas is French. But each has paid, and is paying, a different price for this "common" language, in which, as it turns out, they are not saying, and cannot be saying, the same things: They each have very different realities to articulate, or control.

What joins all languages, and all men, is the necessity to confront life, in 3 order, not inconceivably, to outwit death: The price for this is the acceptance, and achievement, of one's temporal identity. So that, for example, though it is

615

not taught in the schools (and this has the potential of becoming a political issue) the south of France still clings to its ancient and musical Provençal, which resists being described as a "dialect." And much of the tension in the Basque countries, and in Wales, is due to the Basque and Welsh determination not to allow their languages to be destroyed. This determination also feeds the flames in Ireland for among the many indignities the Irish have been forced to undergo at English hands is the English contempt for their language.

It goes without saying, then, that language is also a political instrument, means, and proof of power. It is the most vivid and crucial key to identity: It reveals the private identity, and connects one with, or divorces one from, the larger, public, or communal identity. There have been, and are, times and places, when to speak a certain language could be dangerous, even fatal. Or, one may speak the same language, but in such a way that one's antecedents are revealed, or (one hopes) hidden. This is true in France, and is absolutely true in England: The range (and reign) of accents on that damp little island make England coherent for the English and totally incomprehensible for everyone else. To open your mouth in England is (if I may use black English) to "put your business in the street." You have confessed your parents, your youth, your school, your salary, your self-esteem, and, alas, your future.

Now, I do not know what white Americans would sound like if there had never been any black people in the United States, but they would not sound the way they sound. *Jazz*, for example, is a very specific sexual term, as in *jazz me, baby*, but white people purified it into the Jazz Age. *Sock it to me*, which means, roughly, the same thing, has been adopted by Nathaniel Hawthorne's descendants with no qualms or hesitations at all, along with *let it all hang out* and *right on! Beat to his socks*, which was once the black's most total and despairing image of poverty, was transformed into a thing called the Beat Generation, which phenomenon was, largely, composed of *uptight*, middle-class white people, imitating poverty, trying to *get down*, to get *with it*, doing their *thing*, doing their despairing best to be *funky*, which we, the blacks, never dreamed of doing—we were funky, baby, like *funk* was going out of style.

Now, no one can eat his cake, and have it, too, and it is late in the day to attempt to penalize black people for having created a language that permits the nation its only glimpse of reality, a language without which the nation would be even more *whipped* than it is.

I say that the present skirmish is rooted in American history, and it is. Black English is the creation of the black diaspora. Blacks came to the United States chained to each other, but from different tribes. Neither could speak the other's language. If two black people, at that bitter hour of the world's history, had been able to speak to each other, the institution of chattel slavery could never have lasted as long as it did. Subsequently, the slave was given, under the eye, and the gun, of his master, Congo Square, and the Bible—or, in other words, and under those conditions, the slave began the formation of the black church, and it is within this unprecedented tabernacle that black English began to be formed. This was not, merely, as in the European example, the adoption of a foreign tongue, but an alchemy that transformed ancient elements into a new language: *A language comes into existence by means of brutal necessity, and the rules of the language are dictated by what the language must convey.*

There was a moment, in time, and in this place, when my brother, or my mother, or my father, or my sister, had to convey to me, for example, the danger in which I was standing from the white man standing just behind me, and to convey this with a speed and in a language, that the white man could not possibly understand, and that, indeed, he cannot understand, until today. He cannot afford to understand it. This understanding would reveal to him too much about himself and smash that mirror before which he has been frozen for so long. 8

Now, if this passion, this skill, this (to quote Toni Morrison) "sheer intelligence," this incredible music, the mighty achievement of having brought a people utterly unknown to, or despised by "history"—to have brought this people to their present, troubled, troubling, and unassailable and unanswerable place— if this absolutely unprecedented journey does not indicate that black English is a language, I am curious to know what definition of languages is to be trusted. 9

A people at the center of the western world, and in the midst of so hostile a population, has not endured and transcended by means of what is patronizingly called a "dialect." We, the blacks, are in trouble, certainly, but we are not inarticulate because we are not compelled to defend a morality that we know to be a lie. 10

The brutal truth is that the bulk of the white people in America never had any interest in educating black people, except as this could serve white purposes. It is not the black child's language that is despised. It is his experience. A child cannot be taught by anyone who despises him, and a child cannot afford to be fooled. A child cannot be taught by anyone whose demand, essentially, is that the child repudiate his experience, and all that gives him sustenance, and enter a limbo in which he will no longer be black, and in which he knows that he can never become white. Black people have lost too many black children that way. 11

And, after all, finally, in a country with standards so untrustworthy, a country that makes heroes of so many criminal mediocrities, a country unable to face why so many of the nonwhite are in prison, or on the needle, or standing, futureless, in the streets—it may very well be that both the child, and his elder, have concluded that they have nothing whatever to learn from the people of a country that has managed to learn so little. 12

QUESTIONS

1. Baldwin begins his essay by challenging the standard argument concerning black English: "The argument has nothing to do with language itself but with the role of language." What distinctions does Baldwin create between "language itself" and "the role of language"? Why is this distinction central to his argument?

2. Baldwin's position on black English is at odds with those who would like to deny black English status as a language. Summarize Baldwin's position. Summarize the position of Baldwin's opponents.

3. In paragraph 4 Baldwin writes, "It goes without saying, then, that language is also a political instrument, means, and proof of power." How, according to Baldwin, does language connect or divide one from "public or communal identity"? What evidence does he provide to support this claim that "language is a political instrument"?

4. Baldwin asks his readers "What is language?" and thus leads them to define for themselves "what definition of languages is to be trusted" (paragraph 9). Do you find Baldwin's definition and position persuasive?

5. Baldwin's conclusion is a memorable one. Reread it. How does he prepare you for this conclusion? What are you left to contemplate?

6. How has Baldwin's essay made you think about your own use of language and the role language plays in your identity? Baldwin makes an important distinction between *dialect* and *language*. Write an essay in which you take a position on the role of language in shaping your identity.

7. Select a dialect with which you are familiar. Analyze the features of this dialect. Write an essay in which you develop a position showing how this dialect reflects the richness of its culture.

MAKING CONNECTIONS

1. Read Alice Walker's essay, "Am I Blue?," paying particular attention to paragraph 17 on Blue's language and to Walker's sense of Blue's power of communication. To what extent does her argument support Baldwin's position on black English?

2. Consider Baldwin's argument about language as a political instrument that forges and reveals identity in relation to the writings of several women writers in "Explaining"— Tania Modleski, Joan Didion, Susan Fraker, and Carol Gilligan, in particular. Can you find and describe in those writings evidence of a women's English parallel in some ways to black English? Or is there a men's English you would prefer to describe, drawing on another set of writers?

POLITICS AND THE ENGLISH LANGUAGE

George Orwell

The rise of totalitarianism in Europe led George Orwell (see the headnote on page 92 for more biographical information) to write about its causes in his most famous novels 1984 *(1949) and* Animal Farm *(1945) and in essays such as "Politics and the English Language." In this essay, written in 1946, Orwell tells his readers that "In our time, political speech and writing are largely the defense of the indefensible." He attacks language that consists "largely of euphemism, question begging, and sheer cloudy vagueness." Orwell, like John Berger, is concerned with the ways in which language is often used to conceal unpleasant and horrifying realities.*

Most people who bother with the matter at all would admit that the English 1
language is in a bad way, but it is generally assumed that we cannot by conscious action do anything about it. Our civilization is decadent and our language—so the argument runs—must inevitably share in the general collapse. It follows that any struggle against the abuse of language is a sentimental archaism, like preferring candles to electric light or hansom cabs to aeroplanes. Underneath this lies the half-conscious belief that language is a natural growth and not an instrument which we shape for our own purposes.

Now, it is clear that the decline of a language must ultimately have political 2
and economic causes: it is not due simply to the bad influence of this or that individual writer. But an effect can become a cause, reinforcing the original cause and producing the same effect in an intensified form, and so on indefinitely. A man may take to drink because he feels himself to be a failure, and then fail all the more completely because he drinks. It is rather the same thing that is happening to the English language. It becomes ugly and inaccurate because our thoughts are foolish, but the slovenliness of our language makes it easier for us to have foolish thoughts. The point is that the process is reversible. Modern English, especially written English, is full of bad habits which spread by imitation and which can be avoided if one is willing to take the necessary trouble. If one gets rid of these habits one can think more clearly, and to think clearly is a necessary first step towards political regeneration: so that the fight

against bad English is not frivolous and is not the exclusive concern of professional writers. I will come back to this presently, and I hope that by the time the meaning of what I have said here will have become clearer. Meanwhile, here are five specimens of the English language as it is now habitually written.

These five passages have not been picked out because they are especially 3 bad—I could have quoted far worse if I had chosen—but because they illustrate various of the mental vices from which we now suffer. They are a little below the average, but are fairly representative samples. I number them so that I can refer back to them when necessary:

"(1) I am not, indeed, sure whether it is not true to say that the Milton who once seemed not unlike a seventeenth-century Shelley had not become, out of an experience ever more bitter in each year, more alien [*sic*] to the founder of that Jesuit sect which nothing could induce him to tolerate."

Professor Harold Laski (Essay in *Freedom of Expression*)

"(2) Above all, we cannot play ducks and drakes with a native battery of idioms which prescribes such egregious collocations of vocables as the Basic *put up with* for *tolerate* or *put at a loss* for *bewilder*."

Professor Lancelot Hogben (*Interglossa*)

"(3) On the one side we have the free personality: by definition it is not neurotic, for it has neither conflict nor dream. Its desires, such as they are, are transparent, for they are just what institutional approval keeps in the forefront of consciousness; another institutional pattern would alter their number and intensity; there is little in them that is natural, irreducible, or culturally dangerous. But *on the other* side, the social bond itself is nothing but the mutual reflection of these self-secure integrities. Recall the definition of love. Is not this the very picture of a small academic? Where is there a place in this hall of mirrors for either personality or fraternity?"

Essay on psychology in *Politics* (New York)

"(4) All the 'best people' from the gentlemen's clubs, and all the frantic fascist captains, united in common hatred of Socialism and bestial horror of the rising tide of the mass revolutionary movement, have turned to acts of provocation, to foul incendiarism, to medieval legends of poisoned wells, to legalize their own destruction of proletarian organizations, and rouse the agitated petty-bourgeoisie to chauvinistic fervour on behalf of the fight against the revolutionary way out of the crisis."

Communist pamphlet

"(5) If a new spirit *is* to be infused into this old country, there is one thorny and contentious reform which must be tackled, and that is the humanization and galvanization of the B.B.C. Timidity here will bespeak cancer and atrophy of the soul. The heart of Britain may be sound and of strong beat, for instance, but the British lion's roar at present is like that of Bottom in Shakespeare's *Midsummer Night's Dream*—as gentle as any sucking dove. A virile new Britain cannot continue indefinitely to be traduced in the eyes or rather ears, of the world by the effete languors of Langham Place, brazenly masquerading as 'standard English.' When the Voice of Britain is heard at nine o'clock, better far and infinitely less ludicrous to hear aitches honestly dropped than the present priggish, inflated, inhibited, school-ma'amish arch braying of blameless bashful mewing maidens!"

Letter in Tribune

Each of these passages has faults of its own, but, quite apart from avoidable ugliness, two qualities are common to all of them. The first is staleness of imagery: the other is lack of precision. The writer either has a meaning and cannot express it, or he inadvertently says something else, or he is almost indifferent as to whether his words mean anything or not. This mixture of vagueness and sheer incompetence is the most marked characteristic of modern English prose, and especially of any kind of political writing. As soon as certain topics are raised, the concrete melts into the abstract and no one seems able to think of turns of speech that are not hackneyed: prose consists less and less of *words* chosen for the sake of their meaning, and more and more of *phrases* tacked together like the sections of a prefabricated hen-house. I list below, with notes and examples, various of the tricks by means of which the work of prose-construction is habitually dodged:

DYING METAPHORS

A newly invented metaphor assists thought by evoking a visual image, while on the other hand a metaphor which is technically "dead" (e.g. *iron resolution*) has in effect reverted to being an ordinary word and can generally be used without loss of vividness. But in between these two classes there is a huge dump of worn-out metaphors which have lost all evocative power and are merely used because they save people the trouble of inventing phrases for themselves. Examples are: *Ring the changes on, take up the cudgels for, toe the line, ride roughshod over, stand shoulder to shoulder with, play into the hands of, no axe to grind, grist to the mill, fishing in troubled waters, on the order of the day, Achilles' heel, swan song, hotbed.* Many of these are used without knowledge of their meaning (what is a "rift," for instance?), and incompatible metaphors are frequently mixed, a sure sign that the writer is not interested in what he is saying. Some metaphors now current have been twisted out of their original meaning without those who use them even being aware of the fact. For example, *toe the line* is sometimes written *tow the line.* Another example is *the hammer and the anvil,* now always used with the implication that the anvil gets the worst of it. In real life it is always the anvil that breaks the hammer, never the other way about: a writer who stopped to think what he was saying would be aware of this, and would avoid preverting the original phrase.

621

OPERATORS OR VERBAL FALSE LIMBS

These save the trouble of picking out appropriate verbs and nouns, and at 6 the same time pad each sentence with extra syllables which give it an appearance of symmetry. Characteristic phrases are: *render inoperative, militate against, make contact with, be subjected to, give rise to, give grounds for, have the effect of, play a leading part (role) in, make itself felt, take effect, exhibit a tendency to, serve the purpose of, etc., etc.* The keynote is the elimination of simple verbs. Instead of being a single word, such as *break, stop, spoil, mend, kill,* a verb becomes a *phrase,* made up of a noun or adjective tacked on to some general-purposes verb such as *prove, serve, form, play, render.* In addition, the passive voice is wherever possible used in preference to the active, and noun constructions are used instead of gerunds (*by examination of* instead of *by examining*). The range of verbs is further cut down by means of the *-ize* and *de-* formation, and the banal statements are given an appearance of profundity by means of the *not un-* formation. Simple conjunctions and prepositions are replaced by such phrases as *with respect to, having regard to, the fact that, by dint of, in view of, in the interests of, on the hypothesis that;* and the ends of sentences are saved from anticlimax by such resounding commonplaces as *greatly to be desired, cannot be left out of account, a development to be expected in the near future, deserving of serious consideration, brought to a satisfactory conclusion,* and so on and so forth.

PRETENTIOUS DICTION

Words like *phenomenon, element, individual* (as noun), *objective, categorical,* 7 *effective, virtual, basic, primary, promote, constitute, exhibit, exploit, utilize, eliminate, liquidate,* are used to dress up simple statements and give an air of scientific impartiality to biased judgments. Adjectives like *epoch-making, epic, historic, unforgettable, triumphant, age-old, inevitable, inexorable, veritable,* are used to dignify the sordid processes of international politics, while writing that aims at glorifying war usually takes on an archaic colour, its characteristic words being: *realm, throne, chariot, mailed fist, trident, sword, shield, buckler, banner, jackboot, clarion.* Foreign words and expressions such as *cul de sac, ancien régime, deus ex machina, mutatis mutandis, status quo, gleichschaltung, weltanschauung,* are used to give an air of culture and elegance. Except for the useful abbreviations *i.e., e.g.,* and *etc.,* there is no real need for any of the hundreds of foreign phrases now current in English. Bad writers, and especially scientific, political and sociological writers, are nearly always haunted by the notion that Latin or Greek words are grander than Saxon ones, and unnecessary words like *expedite, ameliorate, predict, extraneous, deracinated, clandestine, subaqueous* and hundreds of others constantly gain ground from their Anglo-

622

Saxon opposite numbers.[1] The jargon peculiar to Marxist writing (*hyena, hangman, cannibal, petty bourgeois, these gentry, lacquey, flunkey, mad dog, White Guard*, etc.) consists largely of words and phrases translated from Russian, German or French; but the normal way of coining a new word is to use a Latin or Greek root with the appropriate affix and, where necessary, the *-ize* formation. It is often easier to make up words of this kind (*deregionalize, impermissible, extramarital, nonfragmentatory* and so forth) than to think up the English words that will cover one's meaning. The result, in general, is an increase in slovenliness and vagueness.

MEANINGLESS WORDS

In certain kinds of writing, particularly in art criticism and literary criticism, it is normal to come across long passages which are almost completely lacking in meaning.[2] Words like *romantic, plastic, values, human, dead, sentimental, natural, vitality*, as used in art criticism, are strictly meaningless in the sense that they not only do not point to any discoverable object, but are hardly ever expected to do so by the reader. When one critic writes, "The outstanding feature of Mr. X's work is its living quality," while another writes, "The immediately striking thing about Mr. X's work is its peculiar deadness," the reader accepts this as a simple difference of opinion. If words like *black* and *white* were involved, instead of the jargon words *dead* and *living*, he would see at once that language was being used in an improper way. Many political words are similarly abused. The word *Fascism* has now no meaning except in so far as it signifies "something not desirable." The words *democracy, socialism, freedom, patriotic, realistic, justice*, have each of them several different meanings which cannot be reconciled with one another. In the case of a word like *democracy*, not only is there no agreed definition, but the attempt to make one is resisted from all sides. It is almost universally felt that when we call a country democratic we are praising it: consequently the defenders of every kind of régime claim that it is a democracy, and fear that they might have to stop using the word if it were tied down to any one meaning. Words of this kind are often used in a consciously dishonest way. That is, the person who uses them has his

8

---

[1] An interesting illustration of this is the way in which the English flower names which were in use till very recently are being ousted by Greek ones, *snapdragon* becoming *antirrhinum, forget-me-not* becoming *myosotis*, etc. It is hard to see any practical reason for this change of fashion: it is probably due to an instinctive turning-away from the more homely word and a vague feeling that the Greek word is scientific.

[2] Example: "Comfort's catholicity of perception and image, strangely Whitmanesque in range, almost the exact opposite in aesthetic compulsion, continues to evoke that trembling atmospheric accumulative hinting at a cruel, an inexorably serene timelessness . . . Wrey Gardiner scores by aiming at simple bull's-eyes with precision. Only they are not so simple, and through this contented sadness runs more than the surface bittersweet of resignation" (*Poetry Quarterly*).

own private definition, but allows his hearer to think he means something quite different. Statements like *Marshal Pétain was a true patriot, The Soviet Press is the freest in the world, The Catholic Church is opposed to persecution,* are almost always made with intent to deceive. Other words used in variable meanings, in most cases more or less dishonestly, are: *class, totalitarian, science, progressive, reactionary, bourgeois, equality.*

Now that I have made this catalogue of swindles and perversions, let me give another example of the kind of writing that they lead to. This time it must of its nature be an imaginary one. I am going to translate a passage of good English into modern English of the worst sort. Here is a well-known verse from *Ecclesiastes:* 9

> "I returned and saw under the sun, that the race is not to the swift, nor the battle to the strong, neither yet bread to the wise, nor yet riches to men of understanding, nor yet favour to men of skill; but time and chance happeneth to them all."

Here it is in modern English: 10

> "Objective consideration of contemporary phenomena compels the conclusion that success or failure in competitive activities exhibits no tendency to be commensurate with innate capacity, but that a considerable element of the unpredictable must invariably be taken into account."

This is a parody, but not a very gross one. Exhibit (3), above, for instance, contains several patches of the same kind of English. It will be seen that I have not made a full translation. The beginning and ending of the sentence follow the original meaning fairly closely, but in the middle the concrete illustrations— race, battle, bread—dissolve into the vague phrase "success or failure in competitive activities." This had to be so, because no modern writer of the kind I am discussing—no one capable of using phrases like "objective consideration of contemporary phenomena"—would ever tabulate his thoughts in that precise and detailed way. The whole tendency of modern prose is away from concreteness. Now analyse these two sentences a little more closely. The first contains forty-nine words but only sixty syllables, and all its words are those of everyday life. The second contains thirty-eight words of ninety syllables: eighteen of its words are from Latin roots, and one from Greek. The first sentence contains six vivid images, and only one phrase ("time and chance") that could be called vague. The second contains not a single fresh, arresting phrase, and in spite of its ninety syllables it gives only a shortened version of the meaning contained in the first. Yet without a doubt it is the second kind of sentence that is gaining ground in modern English. I do not want to exaggerate. This kind of writing is not yet universal, and outcrops of simplicity will occur here and there in the worst-written page. Still, if you or I were told to write a few lines on the 11 uncertainty of human fortunes, we should probably come much nearer to my imaginary sentence than to the one from *Ecclesiastes*.

As I have tried to show, modern writing at its worst does not consist in picking out words for the sake of their meaning and inventing images in order to make the meaning clearer. It consists in gumming together long strips of words which have already been set in order by someone else, and making the results presentable by sheer humbug. The attraction of this way of writing is that it is easy. It is easier—even quicker, once you have the habit—to say *In my opinion it is a not unjustifiable assumption that* than to say *I think*. If you use ready-made phrases, you not only don't have to hunt about for words; you also don't have to bother with the rhythms of your sentences, since these phrases are generally so arranged as to be more or less euphonious. When you are composing in a hurry—when you are dictating to a stenographer, for instance, or making a public speech—it is natural to fall into a pretentious, Latinized style. Tags like *a consideration which we should do well to bear in mind* or *a conclusion to which all of us would readily assent* will save many a sentence from coming down with a bump. By using stale metaphors, similes and idioms, you save much mental effort, at the cost of leaving your meaning vague, not only for your reader but for yourself. This is the significance of mixed metaphors. The sole aim of a metaphor is to call up a visual image. When these images clash—as in *The Fascist octopus has sung its swan song, the jackboot is thrown into the melting pot*— it can be taken as certain that the writer is not seeing a mental image of the objects he is naming; in other words he is not really thinking. Look again at the examples I gave at the beginning of this essay. Professor Laski (1) uses five negatives in fifty-three words. One of these is superfluous, making nonsense of the whole passage, and in addition there is the slip *alien* for akin, making further nonsense, and several avoidable pieces of clumsiness which increase the general vagueness. Professor Hogben (2) plays ducks and drakes with a battery which is able to write prescriptions, and, while disapproving of the everyday phrase *put up with*, is unwilling to look *egregious* up in the dictionary and see what it means. (3), if one takes an uncharitable attitude towards it, is simply meaningless: probably one could work out its intended meaning by reading the whole of the article in which it occurs. In (4), the writer knows more or less what he wants to say, but an accumulation of stale phrases chokes him like tea leaves blocking a sink. In (5), words and meaning have almost parted company. People who write in this manner usually have a general emotional meaning—they dislike one thing and want to express solidarity with another—but they are not interested in the detail of what they are saying. A scrupulous writer, in every sentence that he writes, will ask himself at least four questions, thus: What am I trying to say? What words will express it? What image or idiom will make it clearer? Is this image fresh enough to have an effect? And he will probably ask himself two more: Could I put it more shortly? Have I said anything that is avoidably ugly? But you are not obliged to go to all this trouble. You can shirk it by simply throwing your mind open and letting the ready-made phrases come crowding in. They will construct your sentences for you—even think your thoughts for you, to a certain extent—and at need they will perform the important service of partially concealing your meaning even from yourself. It is at this point that the special connection between politics and the debasement of language becomes clear.

In our time it is broadly true that political writing is bad writing. Where it is not true, it will generally be found that the writer is some kind of rebel, expressing his private opinions and not a "party line." Orthodoxy, of whatever colour, seems to demand a lifeless, imitative style. The political dialects to be found in pamphlets, leading articles, manifestos, White Papers and the speeches of under-secretaries do, of course, vary from party to party, but they are all alike in that one almost never finds in them a fresh, vivid, home-made turn of speech. When one watches some tired hack on the platform mechanically repeating the familiar phrases—*bestial atrocities, iron heel, bloodstained tyranny, free peoples of the world, stand shoulder to shoulder*—one often has a curious feeling that one is not watching a live human being but some kind of dummy: a feeling which suddenly becomes stronger at moments when the light catches the speaker's spectacles and turns them into blank discs which seems to have no eyes behind them. And this is not altogether fanciful. A speaker who uses that kind of phraseology has gone some distance towards turning himself into a machine. The appropriate noises are coming out of his larynx, but his brain is not involved as it would be if he were choosing his words for himself. If the speech he is making is one that he is accustomed to make over and over again, he may be almost unconscious of what he is saying, as one is when one utters the responses in church. And this reduced state of consciousness, if not indispensable, is at any rate favourable to political conformity. 13

In our time, political speech and writing are largely the defence of the indefensible. Things like the continuance of British rule in India, the Russian purges and deportations, the dropping of the atom bombs on Japan, can indeed be defended, but only by arguments which are too brutal for most people to face, and which do not square with the professed aims of political parties. Thus political language has to consist largely of euphemism, question-begging and sheer cloudy vagueness. Defenceless villages are bombarded from the air, the inhabitants driven out into the countryside, the cattle machine-gunned, the huts set on fire with incendiary bullets: this is called *pacification*. Millions of peasants are robbed of their farms and sent trudging along the roads with no more than they can carry: this is called *transfer of population* or *rectification of frontiers*. People are imprisoned for years without trial, or shot in the back of the neck or sent to die of scurvy in Arctic lumber camps: this is called *elimination of unreliable elements*. Such phraseology is needed if one wants to name things without calling up mental pictures of them. Consider for instance some comfortable English professor defending Russian totalitarianism. He cannot say 14 outright, "I believe in killing off your opponents when you can get good results by doing so." Probably, therefore, he will say something like this:

"While freely conceding that the Soviet régime exhibits certain features which the humanitarian may be inclined to deplore, we must, I think, agree that a certain curtailment of the right to political opposition is an unavoidable concomitant of transitional periods, and that the rigors which the Russian people have been called upon to undergo have been amply justified in the sphere of concrete achievement."

The inflated style is itself a kind of euphemism. A mass of Latin words falls upon the facts like soft snow, blurring the outlines and covering up all the details. The great enemy of clear language is insincerity. When there is a gap between one's real and one's declared aims, one turns as it were instinctively to long words and exhausted idioms, like a cuttlefish squirting out ink. In our age there is no such thing as "keeping out of politics." All issues are political issues, and politics itself is a mass of lies, evasions, folly, hatred and schizophrenia. When the general atmosphere is bad, language must suffer. I should expect to find—this is a guess which I have not sufficient knowledge to verify— that the German, Russian and Italian languages have all deteriorated in the last ten or fifteen years, as a result of dictatorship.

But if thought corrupts language, language can also corrupt thought. A bad usage can spread by tradition and imitation, even among people who should and do know better. The debased language that I have been discussing is in some ways very convenient. Phrases like *a not unjustifiable assumption, leaves much to be desired, would serve no good purpose, a consideration which we should do well to bear in mind,* are a continuous temptation, a packet of aspirins always at one's elbow. Look back through this essay, and for certain you will find that I have again and again committed the very faults I am protesting against. By this morning's post I have received a pamphlet dealing with conditions in Germany. The author tells me that he "felt impelled" to write it. I open it at random, and here is almost the first sentence that I see: "(The Allies) have an opportunity not only of achieving a radical transformation of Germany's social and political structure in such a way as to avoid a nationalistic reaction in Germany itself, but at the same time of laying the foundations of a cooperative and unified Europe." You see, he "feels impelled" to write—feels, presumably, that he has something new to say—and yet his words, like cavalry horses answering the bugle, group themselves automatically into the familiar dreary pattern. This invasion of one's mind by ready-made phrases (*lay the foundations, achieve a radical transformation*) can only be prevented if one is constantly on guard against them, and every such phrase anaesthetizes a portion of one's brain.

I said earlier that the decadence of our language is probably curable. Those who deny this would argue, if they produced an argument at all, that language merely reflects existing social conditions, and that we cannot influence its development by any direct tinkering with words and constructions. So far as the general tone or spirit of a language goes, this may be true, but it is not true in detail. Silly words and expressions have often disappeared, not through any evolutionary process but owing to the conscious action of a minority. Two recent examples were *explore every avenue* and *leave no stone unturned*, which were killed by the jeers of a few journalists. There is a long list of flyblown metaphors which could similarly be got rid of if enough people would interest themselves in the job; and it should also be possible to laugh the *not un-*formation out of existence,[3] to reduce the amount of Latin and Greek in the average sentence, to drive out foreign phrases and strayed scientific words, and, in general, to make pretentiousness unfashionable. But all these are minor points. The defence of the English language implies more than this, and perhaps it is best to start by saying what it does *not* imply.

To begin with it has nothing to do with archaism, with the salvaging of   19 obsolete words and turns of speech, or with the setting up of a "standard English" which must never be departed from. On the contrary, it is especially concerned with the scrapping of every word or idiom which has outworn its usefulness. It has nothing to do with correct grammar and syntax, which are of no importance so long as one makes one's meaning clear, or with the avoidance of American-isms, or with having what is called a "good prose style." On the other hand it is not concerned with fake simplicity and the attempt to make written English colloquial. Nor does it even imply in every case preferring the Saxon word to the Latin one, though it does imply using the fewest and shortest words that will cover one's meaning. What is above all needed is to let the meaning choose the word, and not the other way about. In prose, the worst thing one can do with words is to surrender to them. When you think of a concrete object, you think wordlessly, and then, if you want to describe the thing you have been visualizing you probably hunt about till you find the exact words that seem to fit. When you think of something abstract you are more inclined to use words from the start, and unless you make a conscious effort to prevent it, the existing dialect will come rushing in and do the job for you, at the expense of blurring or even changing your meaning. Probably it is better to put off using words as long as possible and get one's meaning as clear as one can through pictures or sensations. Afterwards one can choose—not simply *accept*—the phrases that will best cover the meaning, and then switch round and decide what impression one's words are likely to make on another person. This last effort of the mind cuts out all stale or mixed images, all prefabricated phrases, needless repetitions, and humbug and vagueness generally. But one can often be in doubt about the effect of a word or a phrase, and one needs rules that one can rely on when instinct fails. I think the following rules will cover most cases:

---

[3] One can cure oneself of the *not un-* formation by memorizing this sentence: A *not unblack dog was chasing a not unsmall rabbit across a not ungreen field.*

(i) Never use a metaphor, simile or other figure of speech which you are used to seeing in print.

(ii) Never use a long word where a short one will do.

(iii) If it is possible to cut a word out, always cut it out.

(iv) Never use the passive where you can use the active.

(v) Never use a foreign phrase, a scientific word or a jargon word if you can think of an everyday English equivalent.

(vi) Break any of these rules sooner than say anything outright barbarous.

These rules sound elementary, and so they are, but they demand a deep change of attitude in anyone who has grown used to writing in the style now fashionable. One could keep all of them and still write bad English, but one could not write the kind of stuff that I quoted in those five specimens at the beginning of this article.

I have not here been considering the literary use of language, but merely 20 language as an instrument for expressing and not for concealing or preventing thought. Stuart Chase and others have come near to claiming that all abstract words are meaningless, and have used this as a pretext for advocating a kind of political quietism. Since you don't know what Fascism is, how can you struggle against Fascism? One need not swallow such absurdities as this, but one ought to recognize that the present political chaos is connected with the decay of language, and that one can probably bring about some improvement by starting at the verbal end. If you simplify your English, you are freed from the worst follies of orthodoxy. You cannot speak any of the necessary dialects, and when you make a stupid remark its stupidity will be obvious, even to yourself. Political language—and with variations this is true of all political parties, from Conservatives to Anarchists—is designed to make lies sound truthful and murder respectable, and to give an appearance of solidity to pure wind. One cannot change this all in a moment, but one can at least change one's own habits, and from time to time one can even, if one jeers loudly enough, send some worn-out and useless phrase—some *jackboot, Achilles' heel, hotbed, melting pot, acid test, veritable inferno* or other lump of verbal refuse—into the dustbin where it belongs.

QUESTIONS

1. What is Orwell's position on the ways in which modern writers are destroying the English language?

2. Orwell argues that "thought corrupts language" but he also argues that "language can also corrupt thought" (paragraph 17). What argument is he making? How does language corrupt thought?

3. Orwell writes in paragraph 17, "Look back through this essay, and for certain you will find that I have again and again committed the very faults I am protesting against."

Does Orwell, in fact, break his own rules? If so, what might his purpose be in doing so?

4. What sense of himself does Orwell present to his readers? How would you describe his persona, his character?

5. Why do people write badly, according to Orwell? What causes does he identify in his essay? Do you agree with him?

6. Orwell presents guidelines for good writing in paragraph 18. Take one of your recent essays and analyze how your writing measures up to Orwell's standards.

7. Spend one week developing a list of examples of bad writing from newspapers or popular magazines. Use this material as the basis for an essay in which you develop a thesis to argue your position on politics and language.

8. Written more than forty years ago, this is probably the best known of all Orwell's essays. How insightful and current do you find it today? Take five examples from your reading, as Orwell takes from his, and use them as evidence in an argument of your own about the state of contemporary written English. Take your examples from anything you like, including this book—even this question—if you wish. Be careful to choose recent pieces of writing.

MAKING CONNECTIONS

1. Read Orwell's essay, "Shooting an Elephant," in "Reflecting." What do you learn about Orwell, the essayist, from reading these two essays?

2. John Berger and James Baldwin, as represented by their essays in this section, are likely to be two writers influenced by this essay of Orwell's. Choose the essay you responded to more strongly of those two, and write an essay of your own explaining the connections that you find between either Berger or Baldwin and Orwell.

THE FIRST
TELEVISED WAR

Phillip Knightley

Phillip Knightley was born in Australia in 1929. He began his career as a copyboy on a newspaper in Sydney, later becoming a reporter and an editor. For over twenty years he has lived and worked in London as a journalist and historian of journalism, acting as a special correspondent for the Sunday Times *of London.* Knightley's recent work includes The Second Oldest Profession: Spies and Spying in the 20th Century *and a book coauthored with Caroline Kennedy. The following selection is taken from chapter 16 of his book* The First Casualty: From the Crimea to Vietnam: The War Correspondent as Hero, Propagandist, and Myth Maker *(1975). The title of the book is based on a statement made by United States Senator Hiram Johnson in 1917: "The first casualty when war comes is truth."*

The most intrusive medium in Vietnam was television, and, as the war went on, the hunger of editors for combat footage increased. "Before they were satisfied with a corpse," Richard Lindley, a British television reporter, said. "Then they had to have people dying in action."[1] Michael Herr described a truck carrying a dying ARVN soldier that stopped near a group of correspondents. The soldier, who was only nineteen or twenty, had been shot in the chest. A television cameraman leaned over the Vietnamese and began filming. The other correspondents watched. "He opened his eyes briefly a few times and looked back at us. The first time he tried to smile . . . then it left him. I'm sure he didn't even see us the last time he looked, but we all knew what it was that he had seen just before that."[2] The Vietnamese had seen the zoom lens of a sixteen-millimeter converted Auricon sound camera capturing his last moments of life on film that, if the flight connections worked and the editors back at the network liked it, would be shown in American living rooms within forty-eight hours.

This little item would not be exceptional. During the Tet offensive,[3] a Vietnamese in a checked shirt appeared on television being walked—that is,

---

[1] *London Sunday Times*, November 26, 1967.
[2] *Christian Science Monitor*, May 29–June 30, 1970.
[3] Tet offensive: the campaign by the Vietcong begun during the Tet (lunar new year) festival in January 1968. [Eds.]

dragged—between two soldiers. The soldiers took him over to a man holding a pistol, who held it to the head of the man in the checked shirt and blew his brains out. All of it was seen in full color on television (and later in a memorable series of photographs taken by Eddie Adams of the AP).

Any viewer of the United States who watched regularly the television re- 3 porting from Vietnam—and it was from television that 60 per cent of Americans got most of their war news—would agree that he saw scenes of real-life violence, death, and horror on his screen that would have been unthinkable before Vietnam. The risk and intrusion that such filming involved could, perhaps, be justified if it could be shown that television had been particularly effective in revealing the true nature of the war and thus had been able to change people's attitudes to it. Is there any evidence to this effect?

The director of CBS News in Washington, William Small, wrote: "When 4 television covered its 'first war' in Vietnam it showed a terrible truth of war in a manner new to mass audiences. A case can be made, and certainly should be examined, that this was cardinal to the disillusionment of Americans with this war, the cynicism of many young people towards America, and the destruction of Lyndon Johnson's tenure of office."[4] A *Washington Post* reporter, Don Oberdorfer, amply documents, in his book *Tet*, the number of commentators and editors (including those of Time Inc.) who had to re-examine their attitudes after extensive television—and press—coverage brought home to them the bewildering contradictions of a seemingly unending war.

Television's power seems to have impressed British observers even more than 5 American. The director-general of the Royal United Service Institution, Air Vice-Marshal S. W. B. Menaul, believes that television had "a lot to answer for [in] the collapse of American morale in relation to the Vietnam war." The then editor of the *Economist*, Alistair Burnet, wrote that the television reporting of Vietnam had made it very difficult for two American administrations to continue that war, "which was going on in American homes," irrespective of the merits or demerits of why the United States was actually involved in Vietnam. Robin Day, the BBC commentator, told a seminar of the Royal United Service Institution that the war on color-television screens in American living rooms had made Americans far more anti-militarist and anti-war than anything else: "One wonders if in the future a democracy which has uninhibited television coverage in every home will ever be able to fight a war, however just. . . . The full brutality of the combat will be there in close up and color, and blood looks very red on the color television screen." And the Director of Defence Operations, Plans and Supplies at the Ministry of Defence, Brigadier F. G. Caldwell, said that the American experience in Vietnam meant that if

---

[4] *Sunday Times*, October 19 and October 10, 1971; *The Times*, July 12, 1971.

Britain were to go to war again, "we would have to start saying to ourselves, are we going to let the television cameras loose on the battlefield?"[5]

All this seems very persuasive, and it would be difficult to believe that the sight, day after day, of American soldiers and Vietnamese civilians dying in a war that seemed to make no progress could not have had *some* effect on the viewer. Yet a survey conducted for *Newsweek* in 1967 suggested a remarkably different conclusion: that television had encouraged a majority of viewers to *support* the war. When faced with deciding whether television coverage had made them feel more like "backing up the boys in Vietnam" or like opposing the war, 64 per cent of viewers replied that they were moved to support the soldiers and only 26 per cent to oppose the war. A prominent American psychiatrist, Fredric Wertham, said, in the same year, that television had the effect of conditioning its audience to accept war, and a further *Newsweek* enquiry, in 1972, suggested that the public was developing a tolerance of horror in the newscasts from Vietnam—"The only way we can possibly tolerate it is by turning off a part of ourselves instead of the television set."

Edward Jay Epstein's survey of television producers and news editors, for his book *News from Nowhere*, showed that more than two-thirds of those he interviewed felt that television had had little effect in changing public opinion on Vietnam. An opinion commonly expressed was that people saw exactly what they wanted to in a news report and that television only served to reinforce existing views. *The New Yorker's* television critic, Michael J. Arlen, reported, on several occasions, that viewers had a vague, unhappy feeling that they were not getting "the true picture" of Vietnam from the medium.[6] So if it was true that television did not radically change public opinion about the war, could it have been because of the quality of the coverage?

Television is a comparatively new medium. There were 10,000 sets in the United States in 1941; at the time of Korea there were 10 million, and at the peak of the Vietnam War 100 million. There was some television reporting in Korea, a lot of it daring—an American general had to order the BBC cameraman Cyril Page to get down off the front of a tank to which he had tied himself so as to get a grandstand view of the battle as the tank went into action. But, until Vietnam, no one knew what problems the prolonged day-by-day coverage of a war by television would produce. The first was surprising—a lack of reality. It had been believed that when battle scenes were brought into the living room the reality of war would at last be brought home to a civilian audience. But Arlen was quick to point out, in *The New Yorker*, that by the same process battle scenes are made less real, "diminished in part by the physical size of the television screen, which, for all the industry's advances, still shows one a picture

[5] J. Lucas, *Dateline Vietnam* (New York: Award Books, 1967), p. 15.
[6] F. Harvey, *Air War Vietnam* (New York: Bantam, 1967), p. 115.

of men three inches tall shooting at other men three inches tall."[7] Sandy Gall of ITN found shooting combat footage difficult and dangerous, and the end result very disappointing. "I think you lose one dimension on television's small screen and things look smaller than life; the sound of battle, for example, never coming across. I am always let down when I eventually see my footage and think, Is that all? The sense of danger never comes across on television and you, the correspondent, always look as though you had an easy time of it."[8]

For many Americans in Vietnam, there emerged a strange side to the war that became directly related to television—the fact that the war seemed so unreal that sometimes it became almost possible to believe that everything was taking place on some giant Hollywood set and all the participants were extras playing a remake of *Back to Bataan*.[9] GIs—and even correspondents—brought up on Second World War movies shown on television, used to seeing Errol Flynn sweeping to victory through the jungles of Burma or Brian Donlevy giving the Japanese hell in the Coral Sea,[10] tended to relate their experiences in Vietnam to the Hollywood version of America at war.[11] Michael Herr, making a dash, with David Greenway of *Time*, from one position at Hué to another, caught himself saying to a Marine a line from a hundred Hollywood war films: "We're going to cut out now. Will you cover us?" One should not be surprised, therefore, to find the GIs sometimes behaved, in the presence of television cameras, as if they were making *Dispatch from Da Nang*. Herr describes soldiers running about during a fight because they knew there was a television crew nearby. "They were actually making war movies in their heads, doing little guts and glory Leatherneck tap dancers under fire, getting their pimples shot off for the networks."[12]

So it is not difficult to understand how, when seen on a small screen, in the enveloping and cosy atmosphere of the household, sometime between the afternoon soap-box drama and the late-night war movie, the television version of the war in Vietnam could appear as just another drama, in which the hero is the correspondent and everything will come out all right at the end. Jack Laurence of CBS, an experienced war correspondent, who spent a lot of time in Vietnam, had this possibility brought home to him in Israel during the 1973 conflict. He was in a hotel lobby, and a couple who had just arrived from the United States recognized him and said, "We saw you on television and we knew everything was going to be all right because you were there."[13] There is not much a television correspondent can do about such a situation as that; it seems

9

10

---

[7] Harvey, p. 184.

[8] *Washington Post*, February 23, 1966.

[9] *Back to Bataan*: a 1945 John Wayne film about the retaking of Bataan in the Philippines during World War II. [Eds.]

[10] Errol Flynn (1909–1959) and Brian Donlevy (1899–1972): Hollywood filmstars. [Eds.]

[11] The arrival in 1965 of Flynn's son, Sean, as a correspondent tended to confirm this feeling.

[12] Interview with John Shaw.

[13] Harvey, p. 104.

inherent in the nature of the medium. However, correspondents, or, more fairly, their editors, do have something to answer for in their selection of news in Vietnam.

Years of television news of the war have left viewers with a blur of images 11 consisting mainly of helicopters landing in jungle clearings, soldiers charging into undergrowth, wounded being loaded onto helicopters, artillery and mortar fire, air strikes on distant targets, napalm canisters turning slowly in the sky, and a breathless correspondent poking a stick microphone under an army officer's nose and asking, "What's happening up there, Colonel?" (The only honest answer came, in 1972, from a captain on Highway 13. "I wish the hell I knew," he said.) The networks claimed that combat footage was what the public wanted; that concentrating on combat prevented the film's being out of date if it was delayed in transmission; that it was difficult to shoot anything other than combat film when only three or four minutes were available in the average news program for events in Vietnam; and that the illusion of American progress created by combat footage shot from only one side was balanced by what the correspondent had to say.

This is simply not true. To begin with, combat footage fails to convey all 12 aspects of combat. "A camerman feels so inadequate, being able to record only a minute part of the misery, a minute part of the fighting," said Kurt Volkert, a CBS cameraman. "You have to decide what the most important action is. Is it the woman holding her crying baby? Is is the young girl cringing near her house because of the exploding grenades? Or is it the defiant looking Vietcong with blood on his face just after capture?[14] When the cameraman's thirty minutes of combat footage are edited down to three minutes—not an unusual editing ratio—the result is a segment of action that bears about as much relation to the reality in Vietnam as a battle scene shot in Hollywood does. In fact, the Hollywood version would probably appear more realistic.

The American viewer who hoped to learn something serious about Vietnam 13 was subjected, instead, to a television course in the techniques of war, and he was not sufficiently exposed either to what the war meant to the people over whose land it was being fought, or to the political complexities of the situation, or even to the considered personal views of reporters who had spent years covering the situation. Yet, even by the networks' own standards, the limited aspects of the war that the viewer was permitted to see could produce excellent television. One of the most dramatic pieces of film on the war was shot by a CBS team on Highway 13 late in April 1972. A South Vietnamese mine, intended to stop advancing enemy tanks, had caught a truck loaded with refugees. The film showed deaf children, distressed babies, and a woman weeping over the body of her son. The reporter, Bob Simon, described what had happened and then, with perhaps the best sign-off from Vietnam, said

---

[14] P. Jones Griffiths, *Vietnam Inc.* (New York: Macmillan, 1971), p. 60.

simply, "There's nothing left to say about this war, nothing at all." "Morley Safer's Vietnam," an hour-long report by the CBS correspondent in Saigon, was Safer's own explicit view, and was hailed by *The New Yorker's* critic, Michael J. Arlen, as "one of the best pieces of journalism to come out of the Vietnam war in any medium." But film like this was rare.

Competition for combat footage was so intense that it not only forced American television teams to follow each other into what the BBC's correspondent Michael Clayton called "appallingly dangerous situations," but it also made editors reluctant to risk allowing a team the time and the freedom to make its own film of the war. Where were the television equivalents of Martha Gellhorn's series on Vietnamese orphanages and hospitals, or Philip Jones Griffiths' searing book on the nature of the war, *Vietnam Inc.?* True, television was handicapped by its mechanics—a three-man, or even a two-man, team loaded with camera, sound equipment, and film is less mobile and more dependent on military transport, and in a dangerous situation more vulnerable, than a journalist or a photographer. In its presentation, too, television is sometimes handicapped by its commercial associations. The Vietnamese cameraman Vo Suu filmed the brutal shooting of a Vietcong suspect by General Nguyen Ngoc Loan during the Tet offensive. NBC blacked out the screen for three seconds after the dead man hit the ground, so as to provide a buffer before the commercial that followed. (What television *really* wanted was action in which the men died cleanly and not too bloodily. "When they get a film which shows what a mortar does to a man, really shows the flesh torn and the blood flowing, they get squeamish," says Richard Lindley. "They want it to be just so. They want television to be cinema."[15])

American television executives showed too little courage in their approach to Vietnam. They followed each other into paths the army had chosen for them. They saw the war as "an American war in Asia—and that's the only story the American audience is interested in," and they let other, equally important, aspects of Vietnam go uncovered.

QUESTIONS

1. What is the meaning of the incident Knightley describes in his first paragraph?
2. What is Knightley's thesis? Where do you find the clearest statement of it? What position is Knightley arguing *against?*
3. Paragraphs 4 and 5 summarize a position frequently heard about the Vietnam War, yet it turns out to be a position Knightley attacks. What are his major points of disagreement with that position? How convincingly does Knightley develop them?

---

[15] Jones Griffiths, p. 62.

4. Trace the theme of Hollywood as it develops in this essay. What does it add to Knightley's argument? How does it relate to his thesis?

5. Knightley isn't the first person to observe that the movies and television have taught us how to behave in certain critical situations, not always having to do with war. Can you think of a time when your behavior was not just influenced but almost defined by how people in movies act? Write an essay about that event. What were you doing or what did you need to do? What models of behavior influenced your own? How well did that learning enable you to meet the demands of the moment?

6. For a week or more, study television coverage of an important political event. Write a report on the coverage as you find it. How realistic and thorough do you judge it to be? What hints of distortion and misunderstanding do you find? Try to develop a thesis about the success or failure of the coverage of this event.

7. Compare television and newspaper coverage of any significant event. To what extent do the different media focus on different features of the event? What are the values, as you see them, of the differences you find?

MAKING CONNECTIONS

1. Reread Knightley's concluding paragraph. Can a version of his complaint be made for all reporting? Choose an article from "Reporting," for which a version of that complaint might be true, and choose another one for which it seems less true. Compare them. What defines the audiences in those two articles? What, if any, "equally important aspects" of the potential story go "uncovered" in them?

2. In "Hiroshima," John Berger argues that we must insert terrible events "into living consciousness." One would think that television would have that capacity. Yet Knightley argues that television does not really make that happen. Read Berger's essay and compare his argument with Knightley's. Can you compare the drawings by survivors of the bombing with television reporting that Knightley describes? Consider the "brutal shooting of a Vietcong suspect" that Knightley mentions twice (paragraphs 2 and 14). Perhaps you have seen the photograph of it. How did it affect you? What was NBC trying to do with its presentation of the shooting as described in paragraph 14? After rereading and reflecting on Knightley's and Berger's arguments, write an argument of your own suggesting policy for television coverage of a future war. How free would you want that coverage to be, and why?

AMERICA REVISED
Frances FitzGerald

Frances FitzGerald (b. 1940), an American free-lance jour-
nalist, won a Pulitzer Prize in general nonfiction for her
reporting of the Vietnam War. Her writing about the war,
first published in the New Yorker, *was collected in* Fire in
the Lake: The Vietnamese and Americans in Vietnam
(1973). The book did much to turn American public opinion
against military intervention in Vietnam. She then turned
to the study of American history and an investigation of
how history books change with the needs and prejudices of
the time. FitzGerald asserts that "since the progressive era,
those responsible for the majority of American history texts
have been paying mere lip service to the truism that one
must know history in order to understand the present and
know the future." This work resulted in FitzGerald's second
book, America Revised *(1979), where the following essay*
appears as the first chapter. Here, FitzGerald is concerned
with language that defuses problems and turns conflicts into
"bland fictions." Her most recent book, Cities on a Hill: A
Journey through Contemporary American Cultures *(1986),*
examines the American impulse to cut ties and reinvent the
self without any reference to the past.

Those of us who grew up in the fifties believed in the permanence of our   1
American-history textbooks. To us as children, those texts were the truth of
things: they were American history. It was not just that we read them before we
understood that not everything that is printed is the truth, or the whole truth.
It was that they, much more than other books, had the demeanor and trappings
of authority. They were weighty volumes. They spoke in measured cadences:
imperturbable, humorless, and as distant as Chinese emperors. Our teachers
treated them with respect, and we paid them abject homage by memorizing a
chapter a week. But now the textbook histories have changed, some of them to
such an extent that an adult would find them unrecognizable.

One current junior-high-school American history begins with a story about   2
a Negro cowboy called George McJunkin. It appears that when McJunkin was
riding down a lonely trail in New Mexico one cold spring morning in 1925 he

discovered a mound containing bones and stone implements, which scientists later proved belonged to an Indian civilization ten thousand years old. The book goes on to say that scientists now believe there were people in the Americas at least twenty thousand years ago. It discusses the Aztec, Mayan, and Incan civilizations and the meaning of the word "culture" before introducing the European explorers.[1]

Another history text—this one for the fifth grade—begins with the story of how Henry B. Gonzalez, who is a member of Congress from Texas, learned about his own nationality. When he was ten years old, his teacher told him he was an American because he was born in the United States. His grandmother, however, said, "The cat was born in the oven. Does that make him bread?" After reporting that Mr. Gonzalez eventually went to college and law school, the book explains that "the melting pot idea hasn't worked out as some thought it would," and that now "some people say that the people of the United States are more like a salad bowl than a melting pot."[2]

Poor Columbus! He is a minor character now, a walk-on in the middle of American history. Even those books that have not replaced his picture with a Mayan temple or an Iroquois mask do not credit him with discovering America—even for the Europeans. The Vikings, they say, preceded him to the New World, and after that the Europeans, having lost or forgotten their maps, simply neglected to cross the ocean again for five hundred years. Columbus is far from being the only personage to have suffered from time and revision. Captain John Smith, Daniel Boone, and Wild Bill Hickok—the great self-promoters of American history—have all but disappeared, taking with them a good deal of the romance of the American frontier. General Custer has given way to Chief Crazy Horse; General Eisenhower no longer liberates Europe single-handed; and, indeed, most generals, even to Washington and Lee, have faded away, as old soldiers do, giving place to social reformers such as William Lloyd Garrison and Jacob Riis. A number of black Americans have risen to prominence: not only George Washington Carver but Frederick Douglass and Martin Luther King, Jr. W. E. B. Du Bois now invariably accompanies Booker T. Washington. In addition, there is a mystery man called Crispus Attucks, a fugitive slave about whom nothing seems to be known for certain except that he was a victim of the Boston Massacre and thus became one of the first casualties of the American Revolution. Thaddeus Stevens has been reconstructed[3]—his character

---

[1] Wood, Gabriel, and Biller, *America* (1975), p. 3.

[2] King and Anderson, *The United States* (sixth level), Houghton Mifflin Social Studies Program (1976), pp. 15–16.

[3] Thaddeus Stevens (1792–1868): Republican congressman from Pennsylvania. A leader in the House during and after the Civil War, he was a determined abolitionist who hated the South and violently opposed Lincoln's moderate reconstruction plan. Stevens dominated the committee that impeached Andrew Johnson.

changed, as it were, from black to white, from cruel and vindictive to persistent and sincere. As for Teddy Roosevelt, he now champions the issue of conservation instead of charging up San Juan Hill. No single President really stands out as a hero, but all Presidents—except certain unmentionables in the second half of the nineteenth century—seem to have done as well as could be expected, given difficult circumstances.

Of course, when one thinks about it, it is hardly surprising that modern   5
scholarship and modern perspectives have found their way into children's books. Yet the changes remain shocking. Those who in the sixties complained of the bland optimism, the chauvinism, and the materialism of their old civics texts did so in the belief that, for all their protests, the texts would never change. The thought must have had something reassuring about it, for that generation never noticed when its complaints began to take effect and the songs about radioactive rainfall and houses made of ticky-tacky began to appear in the textbooks. But this is what happened.

The history texts now hint at a certain level of unpleasantness in American   6
history. Several books, for instance, tell the story of Ishi, the last "wild" Indian in the continental United States, who, captured in 1911 after the massacre of his tribe, spent the final four and a half years of his life in the University of California's museum of anthropology, in San Francisco. At least three books show the same stunning picture of the breaker boys, the child coal miners of Pennsylvania—ancient children with deformed bodies and blackened faces who stare stupidly out from the entrance to a mine. One book quotes a soldier on the use of torture in the American campaign to pacify the Philippines at the beginning of the century. A number of books say that during the American Revolution the patriots tarred and feathered those who did not support them, and drove many of the loyalists from the country. Almost all the present-day history books note that the United States interned Japanese-Americans in detention camps during the Second World War.

Ideologically speaking, the histories of the fifties were implacable, seamless.   7
Inside their covers, America was perfect: the greatest nation in the world, and the embodiment of democracy, freedom, and technological progress. For them, the country never changed in any important way: its values and its political institutions remained constant from the time of the American Revolution. To my generation—the children of the fifties—these texts appeared permanent just because they were so self-contained. Their orthodoxy, it seemed, left no handholds for attack, no lodging for decay. Who, after all, would dispute the wonders of technology or the superiority of the English colonists over the Spanish? Who would find fault with the pastorale of the West or the Old South? Who would question the anti-Communist crusade? There was, it seemed, no point in comparing these visions with reality, since they were the public truth and were thus quite irrelevant to what existed and to what anyone privately believed.

They were—or so it seemed—the permanent expression of mass culture in America.

But now the texts have changed, and with them the country that American 8 children are growing up into. The society that was once uniform is now a patchwork of rich and poor, old and young, men and women, blacks, whites, Hispanics, and Indians. The system that ran so smoothly by means of the Constitution under the guidance of benevolent conductor Presidents is now a rattletrap affair. The past is no highway to the present; it is a collection of issues and events that do not fit together and that lead in no single direction. The word "progress" has been replaced by the word "change": children, the modern texts insist, should learn history so that they can adapt to the rapid changes taking place around them. History is proceeding in spite of us. The present, which was once portrayed in the concluding chapters as a peaceful haven of scientific advances and Presidential inaugurations, is now a tangle of problems: race problems, urban problems, foreign-policy problems, problems of pollution, poverty, energy depletion, youthful rebellion, assassination, and drugs. Some books illustrate these problems dramatically. One, for instance, contains a picture of a doll half buried in a mass of untreated sewage; the caption reads, "Are we in danger of being overwhelmed by the products of our society and wastage created by their production? Would you agree with this photographer's interpretation?"[4] Two books show the same picture of an old black woman sitting in a straight chair in a dingy room, her hands folded in graceful resignation;[5] the surrounding text discusses the problems faced by the urban poor and by the aged who depend on Social Security. Other books present current problems less starkly. One of the texts concludes sagely:

> Problems are part of life. Nations face them, just as people face them, and try to solve them. And today's Americans have one great advantage over past generations. Never before have Americans been so well equipped to solve their problems. They have today the means to conquer poverty, disease, and ignorance. The technetronic age has put that power into their hands.[6]

Such passages have a familiar ring. Amid all the problems, the deus ex machina of science still dodders around in the gloaming of pious hope.

Even more surprising than the emergence of problems is the discovery that 9 the great unity of the texts has broken. Whereas in the fifties all texts represented the same political view, current texts follow no pattern of orthodoxy. Some books, for instance, portray civil-rights legislation as a series of actions taken by a wise, paternal government; others convey some suggestion of the social up-

---

[4] Sellers et al., *As It Happened* (1975), p. 812.
[5] Graff, *The Free and the Brave*, 2nd ed. (1972), p. 696; and Graff and Krout, *The Adventure*, 2nd ed. (1973), p. 784.
[6] Wood, Gabriel, and Biller, *America* (1975), p. 812.

heaval involved and make mention of such people as Stokely Carmichael and
Malcolm X. In some books, the Cold War has ended; in others, it continues,
with Communism threatening the free nations of the earth.

The political diversity in the books is matched by a diversity of pedagogical   10
approach. In addition to the traditional narrative histories, with their endless
streams of facts, there are so-called "discovery," or "inquiry," texts, which deal
with a limited number of specific issues in American history. These texts do
not pretend to cover the past; they focus on particular topics, such as "stratifi-
cation in Colonial society" or "slavery and the American Revolution," and
illustrate them with documents from primary and secondary sources. The chapters in these books amount to something like case studies, in that they include
testimony from people with different perspectives or conflicting views on a single
subject. In addition, the chapters provide background information, explanatory
notes, and a series of questions for the student. The questions are the heart of
the matter, for when they are carefully selected they force students to think
much as historians think: to define the point of view of the speaker, analyze the
ideas presented, question the relationship between events, and so on. One text,
for example, quotes Washington, Jefferson, and John Adams on the question
of foreign alliances and then asks, "What did John Adams assume that the
international situation would be after the American Revolution? What did
Washington's attitude toward the French alliance seem to be? How do you
account for his attitude?" Finally, it asks, "Should a nation adopt a policy toward
alliances and cling to it consistently, or should it vary its policies toward other
countries as circumstances change?"[7] In these books, history is clearly not a list
of agreed-upon facts or a sermon on politics but a babble of voices and a welter
of events which must be ordered by the historian.

In matters of pedagogy, as in matters of politics, there are not two sharply   11
differentiated categories of books; rather, there is a spectrum. Politically, the
books run from moderate left to moderate right; pedagogically, they run from
the traditional history sermons, through a middle ground of narrative texts with
inquiry-style questions and of inquiry texts with long stretches of narrative, to
the most rigorous of case-study books. What is common to the current texts—
and makes all of them different from those of the fifties—is their engagement
with the social sciences. In eighth-grade histories, the "concepts" of social
science make fleeting appearances. But these "concepts" are the very foundation
stones of various elementary-school social-studies series. The 1970 Harcourt
Brace Jovanovich series, for example, boasts in its preface of "a horizontal base
or ordering of conceptual schemes" to match its "vertical arm of behavioral
themes."[8] What this means is not entirely clear, but the books do proceed from
easy questions to hard ones, such as—in the sixth-grade book—"How was

---

[7] Fenton, gen. ed., A New History of the United States, grade eleven (1969), p. 170.
[8] Brandwein et al., The Social Sciences (1975), introductions to all books.

interaction between merchants and citizens different in the Athenian and Spartan social systems?" Virtually all the American-history texts for older children include discussions of "role," "status," and "culture." Some of them stage debates between eminent social scientists in roped-off sections of the text; some include essays on economics or sociology; some contain pictures and short biographies of social scientists of both sexes and of diverse races. Many books seem to accord social scientists a higher status than American Presidents.

Quite as striking as these political and pedagogical alterations is the change 12 in the physical appearance of the texts. The schoolbooks of the fifties showed some effort in the matter of design: they had maps, charts, cartoons, photographs, and an occasional four-color picture to break up the columns of print. But beside the current texts they look as naïve as Soviet fashion magazines. The print in the fifties books is heavy and far too black, the colors muddy. The photographs are conventional news shots—portraits of Presidents in three-quarters profile, posed "action" shots of soldiers. The other illustrations tend to be Socialist-realist-style drawings (there are a lot of hefty farmers with hoes in the Colonial-period chapters) or incredibly vulgar made-for-children paintings of patriotic events. One painting shows Columbus standing in full court dress on a beach in the New World from a perspective that could have belonged only to the Arawaks.[9] By contrast, the current texts are paragons of sophisticated modern design. They look not like *People* or *Family Circle* but, rather, like *Architectural Digest* or *Vogue*. One of them has an Abstract Expressionist design on its cover, another a Rauschenberg-style collage, a third a reproduction of an American primitive painting. Inside, almost all of them have a full-page reproduction of a painting of the New York school—a Jasper Johns flag, say, or "The Boston Massacre," by Larry Rivers. But these reproductions are separated only with difficulty from the over-all design, for the time charts in the books look like Noland stripe paintings, and the distribution charts are as punctilious as Albers' squares in their color gradings. The amount of space given to illustrations is far greater than it was in the fifties; in fact, in certain "slow-learner" books the pictures far outweigh the text in importance. However, the illustrations have a much greater historical value. Instead of made-up paintings or anachronistic sketches, there are cartoons, photographs, and paintings drawn from the periods being treated. The chapters on the Colonial period will show, for instance, a ship's carved prow, a Revere bowl, a Copley painting—a whole gallery of Early Americana. The nineteenth century is illustrated with nineteenth-century cartoons and photographs—and the photographs are all of high artistic quality. As for the twentieth-century chapters, they are adorned with the contents of a modern-art museum.

The use of all this art and high-quality design contains some irony. The 13 nineteenth-century photographs of child laborers or urban slum apartments are

---

[9] Arawaks: Native American then inhabiting the Caribbean area. [Eds.]

so beautiful that they transcend their subjects. To look at them, or at the Victor Gatto painting of the Triangle shirtwaist-factory fire, is to see not misery or ugliness but an art object. In the modern chapters, the contrast between style and content is just as great: the color photographs of junkyards or polluted rivers look as enticing as *Gourmet's* photographs of food. The book that is perhaps the most stark in its description of modern problems illustrates the horrors of nuclear testing with a pretty Ben Shahn picture of the Bikini explosion,[10] and the potential for global ecological disaster with a color photograph of the planet swirling its mantle of white clouds.[11] Whereas in the nineteen-fifties the texts were childish in the sense that they were naïve and clumsy, they are now childish in the sense that they are polymorphous-perverse. American history is not dull any longer; it is a sensuous experience.

The surprise that adults feel in seeing the changes in history texts must come   14 from the lingering hope that there is, somewhere out there, an objective truth. The hope is, of course, foolish. All of us children of the twentieth century know, or should know, that there are no absolutes in human affairs, and thus there can be no such thing as perfect objectivity. We know that each historian in some degree creates the world anew and that all history is in some degree contemporary history. But beyond this knowledge there is still a hope for some reliable authority, for some fixed stars in the universe. We may know journalists cannot be wholly unbiased and that "balance" is an imaginary point between two extremes, and yet we hope that Walter Cronkite will tell us the truth of things. In the same way, we hope that our history will not change—that we learned the truth of things as children. The texts, with their impersonal voices, encourage this hope, and therefore it is particularly disturbing to see how they change, and how fast.

Slippery history! Not every generation but every few years the content of   15 American-history books for children changes appreciably. Schoolbooks are not, like trade books,[12] written and left to their fate. To stay in step with the cycles of "adoption" in school districts across the country, the publishers revise most of their old texts or substitute new ones every three or four years. In the process of revision, they not only bring history up to date but make changes—often substantial changes—in the body of the work. History books for children are thus more contemporary than any other form of history. How should it be otherwise? Should students read histories written ten, fifteen, thirty years ago? In theory, the system is reasonable—except that each generation of children reads only one generation of schoolbooks. That transient history is those children's history forever—their particular version of America.

---

[10] Bikini explosion: the Bikini atoll in the Pacific Ocean was the site of American nuclear-bomb testing from 1946 to 1958. [Eds.]

[11] Ver Steeg and Hofstadter, *A People* (1974), pp. 722–23.

[12] trade books: not textbooks but books written for a general audience. [Eds.]

QUESTIONS

1. What does FitzGerald say are the main differences between the history textbooks of the fifties and those of the period in which she writes (the seventies)? What are the main points of her comparison?

2. What evidence does FitzGerald offer to support her claim of these differences? Can you think of other illustrations that she might have used, perhaps from a textbook that you have read?

3. FitzGerald identifies her primary audience in the first sentence: "Those of us who grew up in the fifties believed in the permanence of our American-history textbooks." What techniques does FitzGerald use to involve that audience? What role is she inviting her readers to play?

4. Assuming you did not grow up in the fifties, how do you relate to this essay? Are you left out, or does FitzGerald include you in some way? At what other times have you not been directly addressed as a primary audience but been spoken to clearly and forcefully nevertheless?

5. How does FitzGerald organize her discussion of the textbooks? What topics does she discuss? How does one topic connect to the next? How does she organize the movement back and forth between textbooks of the seventies and those of the fifties?

6. What are some of the major historical events in your lifetime? Which of these events are likely to remain classified as "major historical events"? Why is this likely? How might these events be revised and presented in history textbooks a hundred years from now?

7. See if your library has some older textbooks for a course you are taking or have taken. If so, compare your textbook with the older one to see what has changed. Look, as FitzGerald did, at the opening, the major figures or topics, the attitudes, the pedagogical types, the physical appearance, and any other major features of each book. Write an essay explaining what you find.

8. Locate a current textbook in American history. How does it compare to your memory of American history as you learned it in junior high or high school? What was America "like," according to your old text? What is it "like" now?

MAKING CONNECTIONS

1. Read Linda Simon's "The Naked Source," and ask her question (paragraph 15), "What do historians do after breakfast?" in the context of this essay by FitzGerald. What do you find some of the historians FitzGerald refers to must have been doing "after breakfast"? Describe their activity by refering to specific examples.

2. Read Barbara Tuchman's essay, "'This Is the End of the World': The Black Death," in the light of both FitzGerald's and Simon's essays. Write a commentary on her work as an historian, as you infer that from reading her essay, and as you can be guided toward imagining her work by having read both FitzGerald and Simon.

THE NAKED SOURCE
Linda Simon

Linda Simon (b. 1946) is the author of the textbook, Good
Writing, *as well as several biographies. She is currently the
director of the Writing Center at Harvard University. Her
biographies include* Of Virtue Rare: Margaret Beaufort—
Matriarch of the House of Tudor, Thorton Wilder: His
World, *and* The Biography of Alice B. Toklas. *In the
following article, originally published in 1988 in the* Michigan Quarterly Review, *Simon discusses the practice of history. She argues that often the way in which history is taught
fails to give students "a sense of historical mindedness, a
sense that lives were lived in a context." It is by working
with primary sources that students can learn that the practice of history involves "weighing evidence and making inferences" instead of merely gathering information.*

It is true that my students do not know history. That annals of the American   1
past, as students tell it, are compressed into a compact chronicle: John Kennedy
and Martin Luther King flourish just a breath away from FDR and Woodrow
Wilson, who themselves come right on the heels of Jefferson and Lincoln. The
far and distant past is more obscure still.

Some, because they are bright and inquisitive, have learned names, dates,   2
and the titles of major events. But even these masters of Trivial Pursuit often
betray their ignorance of a real sense of the past. Teachers all have favorite one-
liners that point to an abyss in historical knowledge. Mine is: Sputnik *who?*

There is no debate here. Students do not know history. Students should   3
learn history. There is less agreement about what they should know, why they
should know it, and far less agreement about how they should pursue this study
of the past.

When I ask my students why they need to know history, they reply earnestly: 4
We need to learn history because those who do not know history are doomed
to repeat the mistakes of the past. They have heard this somewhere, although
no one can attribute the remark. And if they are told that George Santayana
said it, they know not who Santayana was, although if you care to inform them
they will dutifully record his name, dates (1863–1952), and the title of the work
(*The Life of Reason*) in which the remark was made.

Is that so? I ask. What will not be repeated?   5

Inevitably they respond emotionally with the example of the Holocaust.   6

646

Some have watched an episode of a PBS series. Some have seen the film *The Diary of Anne Frank*. Such genocide, they reply, will not be repeated because we know about it. Undaunted by examples of contemporary genocide, they remain firm in their conviction. Genocide, they maintain. And the Great Depression.

The Great Depression has made a big impact on the adolescent imagination. 7 Given any work of literature written at any time during the 1930s, some students will explain it as a direct response to the Great Depression. Wasn't everyone depressed, after all? And aren't most serious works of literature grim, glum, dark, and deep. There you have it.

But now we know about the Great Depression. And so it will not, cannot, 8 happen again.

I am not persuaded that requiring students to read Tacitus or Thucydides, 9 Carl Becker or Francis Parkman, Samuel Eliot Morison or Arnold Toynbee will remedy this situation, although I believe that students, and we, might well benefit from these writers' illumination. What students lack, after all, is a sense of historical-mindedness, a sense that lives were lived in a context, a sense that events (the Battle of Barnet, for example) had consequences (if men were slain on the battlefield, they could not return to the farm), a sense that answers must generate questions, more questions, and still more subtle questions.

As it is, students learning history, especially in the early grades, are asked 10 prescribed questions and are given little opportunity to pursue their own inquiry or satisfy their own curiosity. The following questions are from current high school texts:

Has the role of the present United Nations proved that the hopes and dreams of Woodrow Wilson were achievable? If so, how? If not, why?

What were the advantages of an isolationist policy for the United States in the nineteenth century? Were there disadvantages?

Questions such as these perpetuate the idea that history is a body of knowledge 11 on which students will be tested. The first question, in other words, asks students: Did you read the section in the text on the role of the United Nations? Did you read the section on Wilson's aims in proposing the League of Nations? Can you put these two sections together?

The second question asks students: Did you understand the term *isolationist?* 12 Did you read the section on U.S. foreign relations in the nineteenth century? Can you summarize the debate that the authors of the textbook recount?

Questions such as these perpetuate the idea that history can uncover "facts" 13 and "truth," that history is objective, and that students, if only they are diligent, can recover "right answers" about the past. Questions such as these ignore the role of historians. Even those bright students who can recall dates and events rarely can recall the name of a historian, much less any feeling about who this particular man or woman was. For many students, historical facts are things out there, like sea shells or autumn leaves, and it hardly matters who fetches them. The sea shell will look the same whether it is gathered in Charles Beard's pocket or Henri Pirenne's.

What students really need to learn, more than "history," is a sense of the historical method of inquiry. They need to know what it is that historians do and how they do it. They need to understand the role of imagination and intuition in the telling of histories, they need to practice, themselves, confronting sources, making judgments, and defending conclusions. 14

When I ask my freshmen what they think historians do, they usually offer me some lofty phrases about "influencing the course of future events." But what I mean is: what do historians do after breakfast? That is a question few of my students can answer. And they are surprised when I read them the following passage by British historian A. L. Rowse from his book *The Use of History*. 15

> You might think that in order to learn history you need a library of books to begin with. Not at all: that only comes at the end. What you need at the beginning is a pair of stout walking shoes, a pencil and a notebook; perhaps I should add a good county guide covering the area you mean to explore . . . and a map of the country . . . that gives you field footpaths and a wealth of things of interest, marks churches and historic buildings and ruins, wayside crosses and holy wells, prehistoric camps and dykes, the sites of battles. When you can't go for a walk, it is a quite a good thing to study the map and plan where you would like to go. I am all in favour of the open-air approach to history; the most delightful and enjoyable, the most imaginative and informative, and—what not everybody understands—the best training.

It is the best training because it gives the would-be historian an encounter with the things that all historians look at and puzzle over; primary sources about the past. Historians look at battlefields and old buildings, read letters and diaries and documents, interview eyewitnesses or participants in events. And they ask questions of these sources. Gradually, after asking increasingly sophisticated questions, they make some sense, for themselves, of what once happened. 16

What professional historians do, however, is not what most students do when they set out to learn history within the confines of a course. Instead of putting students face to face with primary sources, instructors are more likely to send them to read what other people say about the past. Students begin with a library of books of secondary sources, or they may begin with a text. But that, cautions Rowse, should come "at the end." Instead of allowing students to gain experience in weighing evidence and making inferences, the structures of many courses encourage them to amass information. "I found it!" exclaim enthusiastic students. They need to ask, "But what does it mean?" 17

They need to ask that question of the kinds of sources that historians actually use. Instead of reading Morison's rendering of Columbus's voyages, for example, 18 students might read Columbus himself: his journal, his letters to the Spanish monarchs. Then they can begin to decide for themselves what sort of man this was and what sort of experience he had. Morison—as excellent a historian as he is—comes later. With some sense of the sources that Morison used, students can begin to evaluate his contribution to history, to understand how he drew conclusions from the material available to him, to see how "facts" are augmented by historical intuition. They can begin to understand, too, that the reconstruction of the past is slow and painstaking work.

Courses that cover several decades or even millennia may give students a   19
false impression of historical inquiry. Historians, like archaeologists or epidemiologists, move slowly through bumpy and perilous terrain. They are used to travelling for miles only to find themselves stranded at a dead end. Once, in the archives of Westminster Abbey, I eagerly awaited reading a fragment of a letter from King Henry VI (after all, that is how it was described in the card catalog), only to lift out of an envelope the corner of a page, about an inch across, with the faintest ink-mark the only evidence that it had, five hundred years before, been a letter at all.

Slowly the historian assembles pieces of the past. A household expense record   20
might be the only artifact proving that a certain medieval woman existed. How much can be known about her? How much can be known by examining someone's checkbook today? Yet historians must make do with just such odd legacies: wills and land deeds, maps and drawings, family portraits or photographs. Can you imagine the excitement over the discovery of a diary or a cache of letters? At last, a text. But the diary may prove a disappointment, a frustration. William James recorded the title of a book he may have been reading or the name of a visitor. Didn't he understand that a historian or biographer would need the deep, reflective ruminations of which we know he was more than capable?

Students have not had these experiences. When they are asked to write, they   21
write *about* history. The research paper or the term paper seems to many of them another form of test—this time a take-home drawn out over weeks. Even if they have learned that "voice" and "audience" are important for a writer, they see history papers as different. They must be objective; they must learn proper footnoting and documentation. They must compile an impressive bibliography. Most important, they must find something out. The research paper produces nothing so much as anxiety, and the student often feels overwhelmed by the project.

They might, instead, be asked to write history as historians do it. They might   22
be introduced to archives—in their college, in their community, in their state capital. They might be encouraged to interview people, and to interview them again and again until they begin to get the kind of information that will enlighten them about a particular time or event. They might be encouraged to read

newspapers on microfilm or the bound volumes of old magazines that are yellowing in the basement of their local library. And then they might be asked to write in that most challenging form: the historical narrative.

"I can recall experiencing upon the completing of my first work of history," George Kennan wrote once, ". . . a moment of panic when the question suddenly presented itself to me: What is it that I have done here? Perhaps what I have written is not really history but rather some sort of novel, the product of my own imagination,—an imagination stimulated, inspired and informed, let us hope, by the documents I have been reading, but imagination nevertheless." Most historians share Kennan's reaction. 23

Students, of course, can never discover the boundary between "fact" and imaginative construction unless they have contact with primary sources. They cannot know where the historian has intervened to analyze the information he or she has discovered. "Most of the facts that you excavate," Morison wrote in "History as A Literary Art," "are dumb things; it is for you to make them speak by proper selection, arrangement, and emphasis." Morison suggested that beginning historians look to such writers as Sherwood Anderson and Henry James for examples of the kind of palpable description and intense characterization that can make literature—historical or fictional—come alive. 24

Students need to be persuaded that they are writing literature, not taking a test, when they set out to be historians. Their writing needs to be read and evaluated not only for the facts that they have managed to compile, but for the sense of the past that they have conveyed. They need to discover that the past was not only battles and elections, Major Forces and Charismatic Leaders, but ordinary people, growing up, courting, dancing to a different beat, camping by a river that has long since dried up, lighting out for a territory that no longer exists. Except in the imagination of historians, as they confront the naked source, unaided. 25

QUESTIONS

1. Why, according to Simon, do students not know history?

2. What does Simon argue is wrong with the way in which history is currently taught?

3. In paragraph 15 Simon writes; "When I ask my freshmen what they think historians do, they usually offer me some lofty phrases about 'influencing the course of future events.' But what I mean is: what do historians do after breakfast?" What, according to Simon, do historians do after breakfast? With what kinds of documents do they work? How do they assemble pieces of the past?

4. What strategies of arguing does Simon use to bring her readers to understand the value of the "naked source"?

5. Simon encourages students to seek out "wills and land deeds, maps and drawings, family portraits or photographs." Find some primary source material about a historical

figure in your community. Use these materials to help you read and understand something about this person's life.

MAKING CONNECTIONS

1. In "America Revised," Frances FitzGerald's writes, "All of us . . . know, or should know, that there are no absolutes in human affairs and thus there can be no such thing as perfect objectivity. We know that each historian in some degree creates the world anew and that all history is in some degree contemporary history." How would Simon respond to this claim?

2. Several essays elsewhere in this collection offer primary material useful to a writer of modern American history. Martin Luther King, Jr.'s "Pilgrimage to Nonviolence," or Zoë Tracy Hardy's "What Did You Do in the War, Grandma?" or Dennis Hevesi's "Running Away" could be examples. Each writer has an angle on an event that you might want to consider part of our history. Imagine writing that history yourself. How might you interview that writer or the people mentioned in these essays? What questions would you want to ask? What other information would you want to gather to make your own account convincing? Write an essay on what you take that event to be and the problems you foresee in writing its history.

THE HISTORIAN
AND HIS FACTS

Edward Hallet Carr

E. H. Carr (1892–1982) was a distinguished British historian whose major work was The History of Soviet Russia, *in fourteen volumes. A fellow of Trinity College, Cambridge, Carr delivered a series of lectures there in 1961 under the general title of "What Is History?" The lectures were later published in a book, which opened with the selection reprinted here. It is addressed to the general question—What Is history?—in terms of a more specific question: What Is a historical fact? Like Linda Simon's "The Naked Source" and Barbara Tuchman's "When Does History Happen?" Carr's essay addresses the practice of history. He warns against a "fetishism of facts," and urges that more attention be given to the way that the historian processes the facts.*

What is history? Lest anyone think the question meaningless or superfluous, 1
I will take as my text two passages relating respectively to the first and second incarnations of *The Cambridge Modern History.* Here is Acton in his report of October 1896 to the Syndics of the Cambridge University Press on the work which he had undertaken to edit.[1]

> It is a unique opportunity of recording, in the way most useful to the greatest number, the fullness of the knowledge which the nineteenth century is about to bequeath. . . . By the judicious division of labour we should be able to do it, and to bring home to every man the last document, and the ripest conclusions of international research.
>
> Ultimate history we cannot have in this generation; but we can dispose of conventional history, and show the point we have reached on the road from one to the other, now that all information is within reach, and every problem has become capable of solution.[2]

And almost exactly sixty years later Professor Sir George Clark, in his general introduction to the second *Cambridge Modern History,* commented on this

---

[1] John Dalberg Acton (1834–1902): British historian and editor of the first *Cambridge Modern History.* [Eds.]
[2] *The Cambridge Modern History: Its Origin, Authorship and Production* (Cambridge University Press; 1907), pp. 10–12.

belief of Acton and his collaborators that it would one day be possible to produce "ultimate history," and went on:

> Historians of a later generation do not look forward to any such prospect. They expect their work to be superseded again and again. They consider that knowledge of the past has come down through one or more human minds, has been "processed" by them, and therefore cannot consist of elemental and impersonal atoms which nothing can alter. . . . The exploration seems to be endless, and some impatient scholars take refuge in scepticism, or at least in the doctrine that, since all historical judgments involve persons and points of view, one is as good as another and there is no "objective" historical truth.[3]

Where the pundits contradict each other so flagrantly the field is open to enquiry. I hope that I am sufficiently up-to-date to recognize that anything written in the 1890's must be nonsense. But I am not yet advanced enough to be committed to the view that anything written in the 1950's necessarily makes sense. Indeed, it may already have occurred to you that this enquiry is liable to stray into something even broader than the nature of history. The clash between Acton and Sir George Clark is a reflection of the change in our total outlook on society over the interval between these two pronouncements. Acton speaks out of the positive belief, the clear-eyed self-confidence of the later Victorian age; Sir George Clark echoes the bewilderment and distracted scepticism of the beat generation. When we attempt to answer the question, What is history?, our answer, consciously or unconsciously, reflects our own position in time, and forms part of our answer to the broader question, what view we take of the society in which we live. I have no fear that my subject may, on closer inspection, seem trivial. I am afraid only that I may seem presumptuous to have broached a question so vast and so important.

The nineteenth century was a great age for facts. "What I want," said Mr. Gradgrind in *Hard Times*,[4] "is Facts. . . . Facts alone are wanted in life." Nineteenth-century historians on the whole agreed with him. When Ranke in the 1830's,[5] in legitimate protest against moralizing history, remarked that the task of the historian was "simply to show how it really was (*wie es eigentlich gewesen*)" this not very profound aphorism had an astonishing success. Three generations of German, British, and even French historians marched into battle intoning the magic words, *"Wie es eigentlich gewesen"* like an incantation— designed, like most incantations, to save them from the tiresome obligation to think for themselves. The Positivists, anxious to stake out their claim for history as a science, contributed the weight of their influence to this cult of facts. First ascertain the facts, said the positivists, then draw your conclusions from them.

2

---

[3] *The New Cambridge Modern History*, I (Cambridge University Press; 1957), pp. xxiv–xxv.
[4] *Hard Times:* a novel by Charles Dickens. [Eds.]
[5] Leopold von Ranke (1795–1886): German historian. [Eds.]

In Great Britain, this view of history fitted in perfectly with the empiricist tradition which was the dominant strain in British philosophy from Locke to Bertrand Russell.[6] The empirical theory of knowledge presupposes a complete separation between subject and object. Facts, like sense-impressions, impinge on the observer from outside, and are independent of his consciousness. The process of reception is passive: having received the data, he then acts on them. *The Shorter Oxford English Dictionary,* a useful but tendentious work of the empirical school, clearly marks the separateness of the two processes by defining a fact as "a datum of experience as distinct from conclusions." This is what may be called the common-sense view of history. History consists of a corpus of ascertained facts. The facts are available to the historian in documents, inscriptions, and so on, like fish on the fishmonger's slab. The historian collects them, takes them home, and cooks and serves them in whatever style appeals to him. Acton, whose culinary tastes were austere, wanted them served plain. In his letter of instructions to contributors to the first *Cambridge Modern History* he announced the requirement "that our Waterloo must be one that satisfies French and English, German and Dutch alike; that nobody can tell, without examining the list of authors where the Bishop of Oxford laid down the pen, and whether Fairbairn or Gasquet, Liebermann or Harrison took it up."[7] Even Sir George Clark, critical as he was of Acton's attitude, himself contrasted the "hard core of facts" in history with the "surrounding pulp of disputable interpretation"[8]— forgetting perhaps that the pulpy part of the fruit is more rewarding than the hard core. First get your facts straight, then plunge at your peril into the shifting sands of interpretation—that is the ultimate wisdom of the empirical, common-sense school of history. It recalls the favorite dictum of the great liberal journalist C. P. Scott: "Facts are sacred, opinion is free."

Now this clearly will not do. I shall not embark on a philosophical discussion of the nature of our knowledge of the past. Let us assume for present purposes that the fact that Caesar crossed the Rubicon and the fact that there is a table in the middle of the room are facts of the same or of a comparable order, that both these facts enter our consciousness in the same or in a comparable manner, and that both have the same objective character in relation to the person who knows them. But, even on this bold and not very plausible assumption, our argument at once runs into the difficulty that not all facts about the past are historical facts, or are treated as such by the historian. What is the criterion which distinguishes the facts of history from other facts about the past?

What is a historical fact? This is a crucial question into which we must look a little more closely. According to the common-sense view, there are certain basic facts which are the same for all historians and which form, so to speak,

---

[6] John Locke (1632–1704): English philosopher; Bertrand Russell (1872–1970): English philosopher and mathematician. [Eds.]

[7] Acton: *Lectures on Modern History* (London: Macmillan & Co.; 1906), p. 318.

[8] Quoted in *The Listener* (June 19, 1952), p. 992.

the backbone of history—the fact, for example, that the Battle of Hastings was fought in 1066. But this view calls for two observations. In the first place, it is not with facts like these that the historian is primarily concerned. It is no doubt important to know that the great battle was fought in 1066 and not in 1065 or 1067, and that it was fought at Hastings and not at Eastbourne or Brighton. The historian must not get these things wrong. But when points of this kind are raised, I am reminded of Housman's remark that "accuracy is a duty, not a virtue."[9] To praise a historian for his accuracy is like praising an architect for using well-seasoned timber or properly mixed concrete in his building. It is a necessary condition of his work, but not his essential function. It is precisely for matters of this kind that the historian is entitled to rely on what have been called the "auxiliary sciences" of history—archaeology, epigraphy, numismatics, chronology, and so forth. The historian is not required to have the special skills which enable the expert to determine the origin and period of a fragment of pottery or marble, to decipher an obscure inscription, or to make the elaborate astronomical calculations necessary to establish a precise date. These so-called basic facts which are the same for all historians commonly belong to the category of the raw materials of the historian rather than of history itself. The second observation is that the necessity to establish these basic facts rests not on any quality in the facts themselves, but on an *a priori* decision of the historian. In spite of C. P. Scott's motto, every journalist knows today that the most effective way to influence opinion is by the selection and arrangement of the appropriate facts. It used to be said that facts speak for themselves. This is, of course, untrue. The facts speak only when the historian calls on them: it is he who decides to which facts to give the floor, and in what order or context. It was, I think, one of Pirandello's characters who said that a fact is like a sack[10]—it won't stand up till you've put something in it. The only reason why we are interested to know that the battle was fought at Hastings in 1066 is that historians regard it as a major historical event. It is the historian who has decided for his own reasons that Caesar's crossing of that petty stream, the Rubicon, is a fact of history, whereas the crossing of the Rubicon by millions of other people before or since interests nobody at all. The fact that you arrived in this building half an hour ago on foot, or on a bicycle, or in a car, is just as much a fact about the past as the fact that Caesar crossed the Rubicon. But it will probably be ignored by historians. Professor Talcott Parsons once called science "a selective system of cognitive orientations to reality."[11] It might perhaps have been put more simply. But history is, among other things, that. The historian is necessarily selective. The belief in a hard core of historical facts existing objec-

---

[9] M. Manilius: *Astronomicon: Liber Primus*, 2nd ed. (Cambridge University Press; 1937), p. 87. (A. E. Housman [1859–1936]: poet and classical scholar who edited Manilius. [Eds.])

[10] Luigi Pirandello (1867–1936): Italian playwright. [Eds.]

[11] Talcott Parsons and Edward A. Shils: *Toward a General Theory of Action*, 3rd ed. (Cambridge, Mass.: Harvard University Press; 1954), p. 167.

tively and independently of the interpretation of the historian is a preposterous fallacy, but one which it is very hard to eradicate.

Let us take a look at the process by which a mere fact about the past is transformed into a fact of history. At Stalybridge Wakes in 1850, a vendor of gingerbread, as the result of some petty dispute, was deliberately kicked to death by an angry mob. Is this a fact of history? A year ago I should unhesitatingly have said "no." It was recorded by an eyewitness in some little-known memoirs;[12] but I had never seen it judged worthy of mention by any historian. A year ago Dr. Kitson Clark cited it in his Ford lectures in Oxford.[13] Does this make it into a historical fact? Not, I think, yet. Its present status, I suggest, is that it has been proposed for membership of the select club of historical facts. It now awaits a seconder and sponsors. It may be that in the course of the next few years we shall see this fact appearing first in footnotes, then in the text, of articles and books about nineteenth-century England, and that in twenty or thirty years' time it may be a well established historical fact. Alternatively, nobody may take it up, in which case it will relapse into the limbo of unhistorical facts about the past from which Dr. Kitson Clark has gallantly attempted to rescue it. What will decide which of these two things will happen? It will depend, I think, on whether the thesis or interpretation in support of which Dr. Kitson Clark cited this incident is accepted by other historians as valid and significant. Its status as a historical fact will turn on a question of interpretation. This element of interpretation enters into every fact of history.

May I be allowed a personal reminiscence? When I studied ancient history in this university many years ago, I had as a special subject "Greece in the period of the Persian Wars." I collected fifteen or twenty volumes on my shelves and took it for granted that there, recorded in these volumes, I had all the facts relating to my subject. Let us assume—it was very nearly true—that those volumes contained all the facts about it that were then known, or could be known. It never occurred to me to enquire by what accident or process of attrition that minute selection of facts, out of all the myriad facts that must have once been known to somebody, had survived to become *the* facts of history. I suspect that even today one of the fascinations of ancient and mediaeval history is that it gives us the illusion of having all the facts at our disposal within a manageable compass: the nagging distinction between the facts of history and other facts about the past vanishes because the few known facts are all facts of history. As Bury, who had worked in both periods, said, "the records of ancient and mediaeval history are starred with lacunae."[14] History has been called an enormous jig-saw with a lot of missing parts. But the main trouble does not

---

[12] Lord George Sanger: *Seventy Years a Showman* (London: J. M. Dent & Sons; 1962); pp. 188–9.

[13] These will shortly be published under the title *The Making of Victorian England*.

[14] John Bagnell Bury: *Selected Essays* (Cambridge University Press; 1930), p. 52. (lacunae: empty spaces or gaps. [Eds.])

consist of the lacunae. Our picture of Greece in the fifth century B.C. is defective not primarily because so many of the bits have been accidentally lost, but because it is, by and large, the picture formed by a tiny group of people in the city of Athens. We know a lot about what fifth-century Greece looked like to an Athenian citizen; but hardly anything about what it looked like to a Spartan, a Corinthian, or a Theban—not to mention a Persian, or a slave or other noncitizen resident in Athens. Our picture has been pre-selected and predetermined for us, not so much by accident as by people who were consciously or unconsciously imbued with a particular view and thought the facts which supported that view worth preserving. In the same way, when I read in a modern history of the Middle Ages that the people of the Middle Ages were deeply concerned with religion, I wonder how we know this, and whether it is true. What we know as the facts of mediaeval history have almost all been selected for us by generations of chroniclers who were professionally occupied in the theory and practice of religion, and who therefore thought it supremely important, and recorded everything relating to it, and not much else. The picture of the Russian peasant as devoutly religious was destroyed by the revolution of 1917. The picture of mediaeval man as devoutly religious, whether true or not, is indestructible, because nearly all the known facts about him were pre-selected for us by people who believed it, and wanted others to believe it, and a mass of other facts, in which we might possibly have found evidence to the contrary, has been lost beyond recall. The dead hand of vanished generations of historians, scribes, and chroniclers has determined beyond the possibility of appeal the pattern of the past. "The history we read," writes Professor Barraclough, himself trained as a mediaevalist, "though based on facts, is, strictly speaking, not factual at all, but a series of accepted judgments."[15]

But let us turn to the different, but equally grave, plight of the modern historian. The ancient or mediaeval historian may be greatful for the vast winnowing process which, over the years, has put at his disposal a manageable corpus of historical facts. As Lytton Strachey said in his mischievous way, "ignorance is the first requisite of the historian, ignorance which simplifies and clarifies, which selects and omits."[16] When I am tempted, as I sometimes am, to envy the extreme competence of colleagues engaged in writing ancient or mediaeval history, I find consolation in the reflexion that they are so competent mainly because they are so ignorant of their subject. The modern historian enjoys none of the advantages of this built-in ignorance. He must cultivate this necessary ignorance for himself—the more so the nearer he comes to his own times. He has the dual task of discovering the few significant facts and turning them into facts of history, and of discarding the many insignificant facts as

---

[15] Geoffrey Barraclough: *History in a Changing World* (London: Basil Blackwell & Mott; 1955), p. 14.

[16] Lytton Strachey: Preface to *Eminent Victorians*.

unhistorical. But this is the very converse of the nineteenth-century heresy that history consists of the compilation of a maximum number of irrefutable and objective facts. Anyone who succumbs to this heresy will either have to give up history as a bad job, and take to stamp-collecting or some other form of antiquarianism, or end in a madhouse. It is this heresy, which during the past hundred years has had such devastating effects on the modern historian, producing in Germany, in Great Britain, and in the United States a vast and growing mass of dry-as-dust factual histories, of minutely specialized monographs, of would-be historians knowing more and more about less and less, sunk without trace in an ocean of facts. It was, I suspect, this heresy—rather than the alleged conflict between liberal and Catholic loyalties—which frustrated Acton as a historian. In an early essay he said of his teacher Döllinger: "He would not write with imperfect materials, and to him the materials were always imperfect."[17] Acton was surely here pronouncing an anticipatory verdict on himself, on the strange phenomenon of a historian whom many would regard as the most distinguished occupant the Regius Chair of Modern History in this university has ever had—but who wrote no history. And Acton wrote his own epitaph in the introductory note to the first volume of *The Cambridge Modern History*, published just after his death, when he lamented that the requirements pressing on the historian "threaten to turn him from a man of letters into the compiler of an encyclopedia."[18] Something had gone wrong. What had gone wrong was the belief in this untiring and unending accumulation of hard facts as the foundation of history, the belief that facts speak for themselves and that we cannot have too many facts, a belief at that time so unquestioning that few historians then thought it necessary—and some still think it unnecessary today—to ask themselves the question: What is history?

The nineteenth-century fetishism of facts was completed and justified by a fetishism of documents. The documents were the Ark of the Covenant in the temple of facts. The reverent historian approached them with bowed head and spoke of them in awed tones. If you find it in the documents, it is so. But what, when we get down to it, do these documents—the decrees, the treaties, the rent-rolls, the blue books, the official correspondence, the private letters and diaries—tell us? No document can tell us more than what the author of the document thought—what he thought had happened, what he thought ought to happen or would happen, or perhaps only what he wanted others to think he thought, or even only what he himself thought he thought. None of this means anything until the historian has got to work on it and deciphered it. The facts, whether found in documents or not, have still to be processed by the historian

[17]Quoted in George P. Gooch: *History and Historians in the Nineteenth Century* (London: Longmans, Green & Company; 1952), p. 385. Later Acton said of Döllinger that "it was given him to form his philosophy of history on the largest induction ever available to man" (*History of Freedom and Other Essays* [London: Macmillan & Co.; 1907], p. 435).

[18]*The Cambridge Modern History*, I (1902), p. 4.

before he can make any use of them: the use he makes of them is, if I may put it that way, the processing process.

Let me illustrate what I am trying to say by an example which I happen to know well. When Gustav Stresemann, the Foreign Minister of the Weimar Republic,[19] died in 1929, he left behind him an enormous mass—300 boxes full—of papers, official, semi-official, and private, nearly all relating to the six years of his tenure of office as Foreign Minister. His friends and relatives naturally thought that a monument should be raised to the memory of so great a man. His faithful secretary Bernhardt got to work; and within three years there appeared three massive volumes, of some 600 pages each, of selected documents from the 300 boxes, with the impressive title *Stresemanns Vermächtnis*.[20] In the ordinary way the documents themselves would have mouldered away in some cellar or attic and disappeared for ever; or perhaps in a hundred years or so some curious scholar would have come upon them and set out to compare them with Bernhardt's text. What happened was far more dramatic. In 1945 the documents fell into the hands of the British and the American governments, who photographed the lot and put the photostats at the disposal of scholars in the Public Record Office in London and in the National Archives in Washington, so that, if we have sufficient patience and curiosity, we can discover exactly what Bernhardt did. What he did was neither very unusual nor very shocking. When Stresemann died, his Western policy seemed to have been crowned with a series of brilliant successes—Locarno, the admission of Germany to the League of Nations, the Dawes and Young plans and the American loans, the withdrawal of allied occupation armies from the Rhineland. This seemed the important and rewarding part of Stresemann's foreign policy; and it was not unnatural that it should have been over-represented in Bernhardt's selection of documents. Stresemann's Eastern policy, on the other hand, his relations with the Soviet Union, seemed to have led nowhere in particular; and, since masses of documents about negotiations which yielded only trivial results were not very interesting and added nothing to Stresemann's reputation, the process of selection could be more rigorous. Stresemann in fact devoted a far more constant and anxious attention to relations with the Soviet Union, and they played a far larger part in his foreign policy as a whole, than the reader of the Bernhardt selection would surmise. But the Bernhardt volumes compare favorably, I suspect, with many published collections of documents on which the ordinary historian implicitly relies.

This is not the end of my story. Shortly after the publication of Bernhardt's volumes, Hitler came into power. Stresemann's name was consigned to oblivion in Germany, and the volumes disappeared from circulation: many, perhaps

9

10

---

[19] Weimar Republic: the government of Germany, established in the city of Weimar after World War I (1919) and lasting until Adolf Hitler rose to power in 1933. [Eds.]

[20] *Stresemanns Vermächtnis*: this title may be translated as "Stresemann's Legacy." [Eds.]

most, of the copies must have been destroyed. Today *Stresemanns Vermächtnis* is a rather rare book. But in the West Stresemann's reputation stood high. In 1935 an English publisher brought out an abbreviated translation of Bernhardt's work—a selection from Bernhardt's selection; perhaps one third of the original was omitted. Sutton, a well-known translator from the German, did his job competently and well. The English version, he explained in the preface, was "slightly condensed, but only by the omission of a certain amount of what, it was felt, was more ephemeral matter . . . of little interest to English readers or students."[21] This again is natural enough. But the result is that Stresemann's Eastern policy, already under-represented in Bernhardt, recedes still further from view, and the Soviet Union appears in Sutton's volumes merely as an occasional and rather unwelcome intruder in Stresemann's predominantly Western foreign policy. Yet it is safe to say that, for all except a few specialists, Sutton and not Bernhardt—and still less the documents themselves—represents for the Western world the authentic voice of Stresemann. Had the documents perished in 1945 in the bombing, and had the remaining Bernhardt volumes disappeared, the authenticity and authority of Sutton would never have been questioned. Many printed collections of documents gratefully accepted by historians in default of the originals rest on no securer basis than this.

But I want to carry the story one step further. Let us forget about Bernhardt and Sutton, and be thankful that we can, if we choose, consult the authentic papers of a leading participant in some important events of recent European history. What do the papers tell us? Among other things they contain records of some hundreds of Stresemann's conversations with the Soviet ambassador in Berlin and of a score or so with Chicherin.[22] These records have one feature in common. They depict Stresemann as having the lion's share of the conversations and reveal his arguments as invariably well put and cogent, while those of his partner are for the most part scanty, confused, and unconvincing. This is a familiar characteristic of all records of diplomatic conversations. The documents do not tell us what happened, but only what Stresemann thought had happened, or what he wanted others to think, or perhaps what he wanted himself to think, had happened. It was not Sutton or Bernhardt, but Stresemann himself, who started the process of selection. And, if we had, say, Chicherin's records of these same conversations, we should still learn from them only what Chicherin thought, and what really happened would still have to be reconstructed in the mind of the historian. Of course, facts and documents are essential to the historian. But do not make a fetish of them. They do not by themselves constitute history; they provide in themselves no ready-made answer to this tiresome question: What is history?

11

---

[21] *Gustav Stresemann: His Diaries, Letters, and Papers* (London: Macmillan & Co.; 1935), I, Editor's Note.

[22] Grigory Chicherin (1872–1936): a powerful Russian diplomat. [Eds.]

At this point I should like to say a few words on the question of why   12
nineteenth-century historians were generally indifferent to the philosophy of
history. The term was invented by Voltaire,[23] and has since been used in
different senses; but I shall take it to mean, if I use it at all, our answer to the
question: What is history? The nineteenth century was, for the intellectuals of
Western Europe, a comfortable period exuding confidence and optimism. The
facts were on the whole satisfactory; and the inclination to ask and answer
awkward questions about them was correspondingly weak. Ranke piously believed that divine providence would take care of the meaning of history if he
took care of the facts; and Burckhardt with a more modern touch of cynicism
observed that "we are not initiated into the purposes of the eternal wisdom."
Professor Butterfield as late as 1931 noted with apparent satisfaction that "historians have reflected little upon the nature of things and even the nature of
their own subject."[24] But my predecessor in these lectures, Dr. A. L. Rowse,
more justly critical, wrote of Sir Winston Churchill's *The World Crisis*—his
book about the First World War—that, while it matched Trotsky's *History of
the Russian Revolution* in personality, vividness, and vitality, it was inferior in
one respect: it had "no philosophy of history behind it."[25] British historians
refused to be drawn, not because they believed that history had no meaning,
but because they believed that its meaning was implicit and self-evident. The
liberal nineteenth-century view of history had a close affinity with the economic
doctrine of *laissez-faire*—also the product of a serence and self-confident outlook
on the world. Let everyone get on with his particular job, and the hidden hand
would take care of the universal harmony. The facts of history were themselves
a demonstration of the supreme fact of a beneficent and apparently infinite
progress towards higher things. This was the age of innocence, and historians
walked in the Garden of Eden, without a scrap of philosophy to cover them,
naked and unashamed before the god of history. Since then, we have known
Sin and experienced a Fall; and those historians who today pretend to dispense
with a philosophy of history are merely trying, vainly and self-consciously, like
members of a nudist colony, to recreate the Garden of Eden in their garden
suburb. Today the awkward question can no longer be evaded.

QUESTIONS

1. Carr's essay answers the question, "What is a historical fact?" Summarize his
answer to that question.
2. In paragraph 7, Carr says the historian must "cultivate . . . ignorance." What

---

[23] Voltaire (1694–1778): French dramatist, philosopher, and social critic. [Eds.]
[24] Herbert Butterfield: *The Whig Interpretation of History* (London: George Bell & Sons; 1931),
p. 67.
[25] ALfred L. Rowse: *The End of an Epoch* (London: Macmillan & Co.; 1947), pp. 282–3.

does this expression mean in its context? What is the point of the discussion of Acton and Döllinger in that paragraph? How does this discussion contribute to the larger theme of the essay?

3. In presenting an argument, especially a controversial one, a writer must often seek to gain the confidence of the reader. How does Carr go about this? What sort of picture does he present of himself? What impression of him do you get from his references to himself in paragraphs 1 and 6, and how does that impression affect your evaluation of his position?

4. Carr's essay is an argumentative essay on interpretation. Locate the many uses of the words *interpret* or *interpretation* in the essay, and consider how they function in the larger discussion. What view of the relationship between facts and interpretation is presented here?

5. Carr's essay contradicts previously existing explanations of the relationship between historians and the facts they must deal with in writing history. Where does Carr summarize the opposing position? State in your own words the views of historical facts with which Carr takes issue.

6. Consider several facts generally known to you and your class. Limit your attention to recent facts, specifically from the last year. (You might first discuss in class what sorts of facts merit your attention.) Which of those facts has the best chance of becoming "a historical fact," in Carr's terms? On what does that process depend? Write an explanation of the historicity of a fact you choose, trying to convince your classmates that your fact will become a historical fact.

7. Using an accepted historical fact not mentioned by Carr, write an essay in which you argue why your chosen fact is a historical fact and what grounds we have for understanding it and accepting it as a fact.

MAKING CONNECTIONS

1. Read Linda Simon's "The Naked Source." Are Simon and Carr in essential agreement about the nature of history? What would they say about Phillip Knightley's "The First Televised War," in the context of a discussion about the televised coverage of that war being a step toward its history?

2. Compare Carr's and Simon's essays to Lewis Thomas's "The Art of Teaching Science." What commonalities do you find between Carr's and Simon's approaches to studying history and Thomas's ideal approach to studying science?

WHEN DOES HISTORY HAPPEN?

Barbara Tuchman

Like E. H. Carr, Barbara Tuchman is concerned with the role of facts. According to Tuchman, "the historian's task is . . . to tell what happened within the discipline of facts." The following essay comes from her collection, Practicing History: Selected Essays *(1981); in this particular selection, Tuchman offers a lucid argument for her attitudes toward history and historical research. For further biographical information on Tuchman, see the headnote on page 159.*

Within three months of the Conservative party crisis in Britain last October   1
[1963] a book by Randolph Churchill on the day-to-day history of the affair had been written and published. To rush in upon an event before its significance has had time to separate from the surrounding circumstances may be enterprising, but is it useful? An embarrassed author may find, when the excitement has died down, that his subject had little significance at all. The recent prevalence of these hot histories on publishers' lists raises the question: Should—or perhaps can—history be written while it is still smoking?

Before taking that further, one must first answer the question: What is history?   2
Professional historians have been exercising themselves vehemently over this query for some time. A distinguished exponent, E. H. Carr of Cambridge University, made it the subject of his Trevelyan Lectures and the title of a book in 1962.

Is history, he asked, the examination of past events or is it the past events   3
themselves? By good luck I did not read the book until after I had finished an effort of my own at historical narrative, otherwise I should have never dared to begin. In my innocence I had not been aware that the question posed by Mr. Carr had ever come up. I had simply assumed that history was past events existing independently, whether we examined them or not.

I had thought that we who comment on the past were extraneous to it;   4
helpful, perhaps, to its understanding but not integral to its existence. I had supposed that the Greeks' defeat of the Persians would have given the same direction to Western history whether Herodotus chronicled it or not. But that is not Mr. Carr's position. "The belief in a hard core of historical facts existing independently of the interpretation of the historian," he says, "is a preposterous fallacy but one that is very hard to eradicate."

On first reading, this seemed to me to be preposterous nonsense. Was it   5
some sort of recondite joke? But a thinker of such eminence must be taken

seriously, and after prolonged silent arguments with Mr. Carr of which he remained happily unaware, I began to see what he was driving at. What he means, I suppose, is that past events cannot exist independently of the historian because without the historian we would know nothing about them; in short, that the unrecorded past is none other than our old friend, the tree in the primeval forest which fell where there was no one to hear the sound of the crash. If there was no ear, was there a sound?

I refuse to be frightened by that conundrum because it asks the wrong 6 question. The point is not whether the fall of the tree made a noise but whether it left a mark on the forest. If it left a space that let in the sun on a hitherto shade-grown species, or if it killed a dominant animal and shifted rule of the pack to one of different characteristics, or if it fell across a path of animals and caused some small change in their habitual course from which larger changes followed, then the fall made history whether anyone heard it or not.

I therefore declare myself a firm believer in the "preposterous fallacy" of 7 historical facts existing independently of the historian. I think that if Domesday Book and all other records of the time had been burned, the transfer of land ownership from the Saxons to the Normans would be no less a fact of British history. Of course Domesday Book was a record, not an interpretation, and what Mr. Carr says is that historical facts do not exist independently of the *interpretation* of historians. I find this untenable. He might just as well say the Grecian Urn would not exist without Keats.

As I see it, evidence is more important than interpretation, and facts are 8 history whether interpreted or not. I think the influence of the receding frontier on American expansion was a phenomenon independent of Frederick Jackson Turner, who noticed it, and the role of the leisure class independent of Thorstein Veblen, and the influence of sea power upon history independent of Admiral Mahan. In the last case lurks a possible argument for the opposition, because Admiral Mahan's book *The Influence of Sea Power upon History* so galvanized the naval policy of Imperial Germany and Great Britain in the years before 1914 that in isolating and describing a great historical fact he himself made history. Mr. Carr might make something of that.

Meanwhile I think his main theme unnecessarily metaphysical. I am content 9 to define history as the past events of which we have knowledge and refrain from worrying about those of which we have none—until, that is, some archeologist digs them up.

I come next to historians. Who are they: contemporaries of the event or 10 those who come after? The answer is obviously both. Among contemporaries, first and indispensable are the more-or-less unconscious sources: letters, diaries, memoirs, autobiographies, newspapers and periodicals, business and government documents. These are historical raw material, not history. Their authors may be writing with one eye or possibly both on posterity, but that does not make them historians. To perform that function requires a view from the outside and a conscious craft.

At a slightly different level are the I-was-there recorders, usually journalists, whose accounts often contain golden nuggets of information buried in a mass of daily travelogue which the passage of time has reduced to trivia. Some of the most vivid details that went into my book *The Guns of August* came from the working press: the rag doll crushed under the wheel of a German gun carriage from Irvin Cobb, the smell of half a million unwashed bodies that hung over the invaded villages of Belgium from Will Irwin, the incident of Colonel Max Hoffmann yelling insults at the Japanese general from Frederick Palmer, who reported the Russo-Japanese War. Daily journalism, however, even when collected in book form, is, like letters and the rest, essentially source material rather than history.

Still contemporary but dispensable are the Compilers who hurriedly assemble a book from clippings and interviews in order to capitalize on public interest when it is high. A favorite form of these hasty puddings is the overnight biography, like *The Lyndon Johnson Story*, which was in the bookstores within a few weeks of the incident that gave rise to it. The Compilers, in their treatment, supply no extra understanding and as historians are negligible.

All these varieties being disposed of, there remains a pure vein of conscious historians of whom, among contemporaries, there are two kinds. First, the Onlookers, who deliberately set out to chronicle an episode of their own age— a war or depression or strike or social revolution or whatever it may be—and shape it into a historical narrative with character and validity of its own. Thucydides' *Peloponnesian War*, on a major scale, and Theodore White's *The Making of a President*, undertaken in the same spirit though on a tiny scale in comparison, are examples.

Second are the Active Participants or Axe-Grinders, who attempt a genuine history of events they have known, but whose accounts are inevitably weighted, sometimes subtly and imperceptibly, sometimes crudely, by the requirements of the role in which they wish themselves to appear. Josephus' *The Jewish War*, the Earl of Clarendon's *History of the Rebellion*, and Winston Churchill's *World Crisis* and *Second World War* are classics of this category.

For the latter-day historian, these too become source material. Are we now in possession of history when we have these accounts in hand? Yes, in the sense that we are in possession of wine when the first pressing of the grapes is in hand. But it has not fermented, and it has not aged. The great advantage of the latter-day historian is the distance conferred by the passage of time. At a distance from the events he describes and with a wider area of vision, he can see more of what was going on at the time and distinguish what was significant from what was not.

The contemporary has no perspective; everything is in the foreground and appears the same size. Little matters loom big, and great matters are sometimes missed because their outlines cannot be seen. Vietnam and Panama are given four-column headlines today, but the historian fifty or a hundred years hence will put them in a chapter under a general heading we have not yet thought of.

The contemporary, especially if he is a participant, is inside his events, which is not an entirely unmixed advantage. What he gains in intimacy through personal acquaintance—which we can never achieve—he sacrifices in detachment. He cannot see or judge fairly both sides in a quarrel, for example the quarrel as to who deserves chief credit for the French victory at the Battle of the Marne in 1914. All contemporary chroniclers were extreme partisans of either Joffre or Gallieni. So violent was the partisanship that no one (except President Poincaré) noticed what is so clearly visible when viewed from a distance, that both generals had played an essential role. Gallieni saw the opportunity and gave the impetus; Joffre brought the Army and the reinforcements into place to fight, but it took fifty years before this simple and just apportionment could be made. 17

Distance does not always confer objectivity; one can hardly say Gibbon wrote objectively of the Roman Empire or Carlyle of the French Revolution. Objectivity is a question of degree. It is possible for the latter-day historian to be at least *relatively* objective, which is not the same thing as being neutral or taking no sides. There is no such thing as a neutral or purely objective historian. Without an opinion a historian would be simply a ticking clock, and unreadable besides. 18

Nevertheless, distance does confer a kind of removal that cools the judgment and permits a juster appraisal than is possible to a contemporary. Once long ago as a freshman journalist I covered a campaign swing by Franklin D. Roosevelt during which he was scheduled to make a major speech at Pittsburgh or Harrisburg, I forget which. As we were leaving the train, one of the newspapermen remained comfortably behind in the club car with his feet up, explaining that as a New Dealer writing for a Republican paper he had to remain "objective" and he could "be a lot more objective right here than within ten feet of that fellow." He was using distance in space if not in time to acquire objectivity. 19

I found out from personal experience that I could not write contemporary history if I tried. Some people can, William Shirer, for one; they are not affected by involvement. But I am, as I discovered when working on my first book, *Bible and Sword*. It dealt with the historical relations between Britain and Palestine from the time of the Phoenicians to the present. Originally I had intended to bring the story down through the years of the British Mandate to the Arab-Israeli War and the re-establishment of the state of Israel in 1948. 20

I spent six months of research on the bitter history of those last thirty years: the Arab assaults and uprisings, the Round Tables, the White Papers, the cutting 21 off of Jewish immigration, the Commissions of Inquiry, the ultimate historical irony when the British, who had issued the Balfour Declaration, rammed the ship *Exodus*, the whole ignominious tale of one or more chapters of appeasement.

When I tried to write this as history, I could not do it. Anger, disgust, and   22
a sense of injustice can make some writers eloquent and evoke brilliant polemic, but these emotions stunted and twisted my pen. I found the tone of my concluding chapter totally different from the seventeen chapters that went before. I had suddenly walked over the line into contemporary history; I had become involved, and it showed. Although the publisher wanted the narrative brought up to date, I knew my final chapter as written would destroy the credibility of all the preceding, and I could not change it. I tore it up, discarded six months' work, and brought the book to a close in 1918.

I am not saying that emotion should have no place in history. On the   23
contrary, I think it is an essential element of history, as it is of poetry, whose origin Wordsworth defined as "emotion recollected in tranquillity." History, one might say, is emotion plus action recollected or, in the case of latter-day historians, reflected on in tranquillity after a close and honest examination of the records. The primary duty of the historian is to stay within the evidence. Yet it is a curious fact that poets, limited by no such rule, have done very well with history, both of their own times and of times long gone before.

Tennyson wrote the "Charge of the Light Brigade" within three months of   24
the event at Balaclava in the Crimea. "Cannon in front of them volleyed and thundered . . . Flashed all their sabres bare . . . Plunged in the battery-smoke . . . Stormed at with shot and shell . . . When can their glory fade? O the wild charge they made!" His version, even including the Victorian couplet "Theirs not to reason why / Theirs but to do and die," as poetry may lack the modern virtue of incomprehensibility, but as history it captures that combination of the glorious and the ridiculous which was a nineteenth-century cavalry charge against cannon. As an onlooker said, *"C'est magnifique, mais ce n'est pas la guerre"* ("It is magnificent, but it is not war"), which is exactly what Tennyson conveyed better than any historian.

To me who grew up before Bruce Catton began writing, the Civil War will   25
always appear in terms of

> Up from the meadows rich with corn,
> Clear in the cool September morn,
> The clustered spires of Frederick stand.

Whittier, too, was dealing in contemporary history. Macaulay, on the other hand, wrote "Horatius at the Bridge" some 2,500 years after the event. Although he was a major historian and only secondarily a poet, would any of us remember anything about Tarquin the Tyrant or Roman history before Caesar if it were not for "Lars Porsena of Clusium / By the Nine Gods he swore," and the rest of the seventy stanzas? We know how the American Revolution began from Longfellow's signal lights in the old North Church.

> "One, if by land, and two, if by sea,
> And I on the opposite shore will be,
> Ready to ride and spread the alarm
> Through every Middlesex village and farm."

The poets have familiarized more people with history than have the historians, and sometimes they have given history a push. Kipling did it in 1899 with his bidding "Take up the White Man's Burden," addressed to Americans, who, being plunged into involuntary imperialism by Admiral Dewey's adventure at Manila, were sorely perplexed over what to do about the Philippines. "Send forth the best ye breed," Kipling told them firmly, 26

> To want in heavy harness,
> On fluttered folk and wild—
> Your new-caught, sullen peoples,
> Half-devil and half-child.

> Take up the White Man's burden,
> The savage wars of peace—
> Fill full the mouth of Famine
> And bid the sickness cease;

> Take up the White Man's burden—
> Ye dare not stoop to less.

The advice, published in a two-page spread by *McClure's Magazine*, was quoted across the country within a week and quickly reconciled most Americans to the expenditure of bullets, brutality, and trickery that soon proved necessary to implement it.

Kipling had a peculiar gift for recognizing history at close quarters. He wrote "Recessional" in 1897 at the time of the Queen's Diamond Jubilee when he sensed a self-glorification, a kind of hubris, in the national mood that frightened him. In *The Times* on the morning after, when people read his reminder— 27

> Lo, all our pomp of yesterday
> Is one with Nineveh and Tyre!
> Judge of the Nations, spare us yet,
> Lest we forget—lest we forget!

—it created a profound impression. Sir Edward Clark, the distinguished barrister who defended Oscar Wilde, was so affected by the message that he pronounced "Recessional" "the greatest poem written by any living man."

What the poets did was to convey the *feeling* of an episode or a moment of 28

668

history as they sensed it. The historian's task is rather to tell what happened within the discipline of the facts.

What his imagination is to the poet, facts are to the historian. His exercise   29
of judgment comes in their selection, his art in their arrangement. His method is narrative. His subject is the story of man's past. His function is to make it known.

QUESTIONS

1. What position is Tuchman taking in declaring herself a firm believer in "the preposterous fallacy" (paragraph 1) of historical facts existing independently of the historian?

2. According to Tuchman, what advantage does the latter-day historian have over the contemporary historian? What does this advantage suggest about when history happens?

3. Tuchman tells her readers about the problems she had in working on her first book, *Bible and Sword*. Tuchman writes: "Anger, disgust, and a sense of injustice can make some writers eloquent and evoke brilliant polemic, but these emotions stunted and twisted my pen" (paragraph 22). What is the effect of these personal reflections? How do they serve to strengthen her argument?

4. Why does Tuchman choose to quote from Tennyson, Longfellow, and Kipling? How does this evidence from poetry support her argument?

5. How do you respond to Tuchman's claim that emotion "is an essential element of history" (paragraph 23)?

MAKING CONNECTIONS

1. Frances FitzGerald, Linda Simon, E. H. Carr, and Tuchman all ask, in one way or another, "What is history?" Outline the major areas of agreement and disagreement among these writers. Where do you find the most significant areas of agreement? Of disagreement?

2. Consider an episode or event you know a good deal about and think about how you might write its history. You could write of a recent year or season, a local political campaign, curricular reform at your high school or college, the birth of an organization in which you know some members, a recent criminal case, a school controversy. Any number of events might serve your purpose, which is to determine how you would approach that event if you were to write under the influence of Carr or of Tuchman. What would you have to know, discover, worry, and think about if you were to take Carr as your guide? What if you were to take Tuchman? Write an explanation of where your research, in one case or the other, would lead you.

3. Tuchman asks an important question: Should, or perhaps can, history be written while it is "still smoking"? Consider your responses to Carr and Tuchman. What is your position?

Social Sciences and Public Affairs

TWO VIEWS ON THE LABELING OF ALCOHOLIC BEVERAGES

Patricia Taylor
James C. Sanders

Both of these writers are encouraging responsible alcohol consumption, but they disagree over the effectiveness of warning labels in fostering safe drinking. Patricia Taylor is director of the Alcohol Policies Project of the Center for Science in the Public Interest, in Washington. James C. Sanders is president of the Beer Institute. Each has a different understanding about the role the government should play in this matter. These articles appeared together in 1988 in the New York Times.

IT'S TIME TO PUT WARNINGS ON ALCOHOL

Spuds MacKenzie is tending goal. It's the last shot of the game, and Spuds 1
makes an incredible save. The skillful maneuver by Anheuser-Busch's mascot is part of an Olympian effort to convince Americans that drinking is harmless and all-American. But during the next Olympiad, the ads may have a new twist. The bottle of Bud hoisted by the Spudettes may carry a message about the risks of alcohol.

Since 1977, when the Food and Drug Administration commissioner, Donald 2
Kennedy, first recommended warning labels on alcoholic beverages, more than one million people have died from alcohol-related problems, one-fourth due to drinking and driving. The costs have been equally staggering—over one trillion dollars.

Congress is now considering a bill that would require health warning labels 3 on all alcoholic beverages, much as cigarettes are now labeled. Drinkers would be alerted to the risks of alcohol, just as consumers of bubble bath, over-the-counter drugs, and other products are told about the health risks of those products.

While industry opponents deride the usefulness of warning labels, the United 4 States Public Health Service says, "Studies which have examined the impact of health warning labels in 'real world' situations have concluded that the labels did have an impact on consumer behavior."

Five different proposed labels would cover proven risks related to alcoholic 5 beverages, ranging from birth defects to auto crashes. In 1981 the Surgeon General of the United States first advised women who are pregnant or considering pregnancy not to drink. Last year the National Institute on Alcohol Abuse and Alcoholism concluded that alcohol is the leading cause of mental retardation caused by known teratogenic agents (those that produce birth defects).

Alcohol is still involved in more than 50 percent of traffic fatalities. For 6 those between the ages of 16 and 24, alcohol-related traffic deaths are the No. 1 killer. Warning labels would reinforce programs to reduce drinking and driving.

Another label, this one warning that alcohol is a potentially addictive drug, 7 would dispel any notion that some alcoholic beverages are as harmless as soft drinks. New "cooler" products barely taste of alcohol but contain more than beer. In many states, you can walk into your local grocery store and purchase alcoholic beverages off the fruit juice shelf with names that give no hint that the product contains alcohol.

And on beer labels there isn't a single word to indicate that the contents are 8 alcoholic. Many beer drinkers, especially teen-agers, think a can of beer is "safer" than a rum and Coke, even though the two contain equal amounts of alcohol.

Other labels would inform consumers about alcohol's contribution to liver 9 disease, hypertension, and cancer, and about the risk of drinking while taking prescription and over-the-counter drugs.

Alcoholic beverage producers certainly don't want consumers to associate 10 drinking with mental retardation, alcoholism, cirrhosis of the liver, and death on the highways. So instead of informing drinkers about health and safety risks, they bombard us with $2 billion worth of slick promotional campaigns annually. According to Neil Postman, professor of media ecology at New York University, and his colleagues, children see more than 100,000 beer commercials on television before they are old enough to legally drink and drive. The ads do more than sell particular brands; they sell the assumption that drinking is not just safe, but essential to a happy, successful life.

Some companies do sponsor occasional ads to remind us to drink "moder- 11 ately." Unfortunately, those ads are designed more to undercut prevention-oriented legislative initiatives than to educate drinkers about health risks. The fact is, the $70 billion-a-year booze industry simply can't afford moderate drinking. Its best customers are heavy drinkers, who account for half of all sales. If those drinkers drank less, sales—and profits—would plummet.

Industry officials often argue that warnings on their products would ultimately 12 lead to warnings on everything from eggs to underwear. It's a cute argument, but it just doesn't wash. Only two products—alcohol and tobacco—are potentially addictive and sold legally directly to consumers despite their destructive impact on our nation's health.

With some luck, Congress will see through the anti-warning propaganda and 13 respond to their constituents' concerns about alcohol.

Of course, health warnings alone won't eliminate alcohol problems. We 14 really need a comprehensive strategy that would include expanded educational programs, mass media campaigns to neutralize industry's huge ad campaigns, and sharply higher Federal alcohol excise taxes. But passage of the pending bill with its clear, concise label notices, is an important place to start.

Patricia Taylor

WE NEED ROLE MODELS, NOT LABELS

Warning labels on alcoholic beverages could shape up as the "Why not" 1 issue of 1988. And that would be a shame.

No one really knows what warning labels will accomplish. And if you cut 2 through all the rhetoric, it's apparent that no one expects them to accomplish much of anything. But why not?

There are several good answers, and they can be summed up in two sen- 3 tences. First, warning labels won't have the beneficial effects their advocates claim. And second, they could hamper efforts to provide legitimate and useful education about safe drinking. The battle against alcohol abuse is too important to be entrusted to the "it can't hurt and it might help" mentality that is moving warning labels up on some legislative agendas.

Because when all is said and done, warning labels can hurt. 4

Cultures that successfully encourage responsible alcohol consumption do so 5 by providing credible role models for safe drinking—not by condemning all drinking as bad. Our Government should emphasize the differences between moderate and abusive consumption rather than obscuring them through the use of warning labels.

Warning labels won't foster safe drinking among the general population. And 6 there's even less chance that they will have a beneficial effect on abusers. Alcohol has been a part of society for well over 5,000 years. No one can argue that alcohol abusers drink because they do not know abuse can be bad for them.

More important, almost everyone agrees that serious, chronic abuse requires 7 in-depth intervention. When Congress considered warning labels on alcoholic beverages in 1979, Dr. Jack H. Mendelson, director of the Alcohol and Drug Research Center at Harvard, testified that such labels could cause "immeasurable harm."

"The warning label approach would be a regressive step in that it would   8
emphasize the primary importance of individual 'willpower' to abstain," Dr. Mendelson said. In other words, it could make the barrier between abusers and the help they need higher than is already the case.

Can warning labels help educate underage drinkers? That's not very likely   9
either. Most counselors who work with adolescents agree that a vital factor in helping teen-agers deal with subjects like drinking is honesty. One-sided, black-and-white arguments will be dismissed as adult scare tactics—particularly since they ignore the fact that two-thirds of adults drink.

In fact, warning labels are likely to make alcoholic beverages even more of   10
an alluring "forbidden fruit" for adolescents than they already are. A few words on the side of a beverage container won't convince teen-agers who are already risking trouble with the law to put off drinking until they are 21. It is a lot more likely that such a label will act as a challenge, taunting adolescents to prove they can handle drinking no matter what the older generation says.

It makes no sense to brand all drinking as undesirable when the American   11
Journal of Public Health reports—as it did earlier this year—that women who drink moderately are about one-third less likely to be hospitalized than lifelong abstainers. And moderate male drinkers are about 25 percent less likely to be hospitalized than people who have never taken a drink.

Researchers concluded that while some causes of hospitalization are clearly   12
increased among abusive drinkers, "the overall acute care hospitalization experience of moderate drinkers appears to be favorable." If we're after legitimate education, we can't ignore this half of the story.

Massachusetts State Representative Suzanna Bump, who has sponsored a   13
warning label bill in that state, recently told the Associated Press that warning labels on alcoholic beverages "would contribute to public health education, much like warnings that already appear on cigarettes." But from a public policy perspective, there's a major difference between tobacco and alcohol. Before the imposition of warning labels on cigarettes, the Government decided that smoking in any amount could be hazardous. In sharp contrast, respected researchers have compiled considerable evidence that moderate consumers may benefit from their drinking.

No one within the alcoholic beverage industry would argue against productive   14
efforts to promote safe drinking practices in our society. In fact, our industry supports hundreds of programs around the country.

But the warning label advocates have completely failed to make their case.   15
"Why not?" is never a good reason to do anything. Ours is a free and open society. One in which most people would just as soon be left alone by govern-

ment unless there is a good probability that government intervention will provide a benefit.

In the case of alcoholic beverage warning labels, that justification simple   16
doesn't exist. "Why not?" just isn't good enough.

James C. Sanders

QUESTIONS

1. What is Taylor's argument in favor of requiring health warning labels on all alcoholic beverages? How does Taylor contend with the arguments of the opposition?

2. What is Sanders's argument against labeling alcoholic beverages? How does Sanders contend with the arguments of the opposition?

3. Compare the two arguments. On what central issue of the debate does each writer base his or her argument?

4. What methods of arguing do Taylor and Sanders use to bring their readers to their respective points of view?

5. What is your position on labeling alcoholic beverages? Write a response to either Taylor or Sanders.

6. Consumer activists are currently recommending to the Food and Drug Administration that they consider placing warning labels on other products. Do you think it is the government's responsibility to educate and protect consumers? Sanders writes: "Ours is a free and open society. One in which people would just as soon be left alone by government unless there is a good probability that government intervention will provide a benefit." What is your position on this issue? Write an essay arguing your position on the government's responsibility to educate and protect consumers.

MAKING CONNECTIONS

Imagine you are in Sanders's position, having to refute the proposals of someone like Taylor. But rather than Taylor, take Nathan Glazer, "Some Very Modest Proposals for the Improvement of American Education," or Jonathan Swift, "A Modest Proposal," as your opposition. Essentially, you need to argue that the proposals of your opponent do not address the real problem or fail to offer the answer needed. Mount such an argument against whichever of those opponents you choose.

SOME VERY MODEST PROPOSALS
FOR THE IMPROVEMENT OF
AMERICAN EDUCATION

Nathan Glazer

Nathan Glazer (b. 1923) is a New York City native, a professor of education and sociology at Harvard University, and coeditor of The Public Interest *magazine. His books include* The Lonely Crowd *(1950) with Reuel Denney and David Riesman,* Beyond the Melting Pot *(2nd edition, 1970) with Daniel P. Moynihan,* Affirmative Discrimination: Ethnic Inequality and Public Policy *(1975), and an essay collection,* Ethnic Dilemmas, 1964–1982 *(1983). The following essay appeared first in the magazine* Daedalus, *an interdisciplinary journal of The American Academy of Arts and Sciences (Fall 1984). By mentioning "modest proposals," Glazer refers to Jonathan Swift, whose famous essay appears later in this section. By that term, Glazer also suggests deceptively simple steps that go directly to the heart of the problem. How "modest" are his proposals?*

That we can do a great deal for the sorry state of American education with   1
more money is generally accepted. Even apparently modest proposals will, however, cost a great deal of money. Consider something as simple as increasing the average compensation of American teachers—who are generally considered underpaid—by $2,000 a year each. The bill would come to five billion dollars a year. A similar figure is reached by the report of the highly qualified Twentieth Century Fund Task Force on Federal, Elementary, and Secondary Educational Policy, which proposes fellowships and additional compensation for master teachers. Reducing class size 10 percent, or increasing the number of teachers by the same percentage would cost another five billion dollars. With present-day federal deficits, these look like small sums, but since education is paid for almost entirely by states and local government, these modest proposals would lead to substantial and painful tax increases. (I leave aside for the moment the views of skeptics who believe that none of these changes would matter.)

But the occasional visitor to American schools will note some changes that   2
would cost much less, nothing at all, or even save money—and yet would improve at least the educational *environment* in American schools (once again, we ignore those skeptics who would insist that even a better educational environment cannot be guaranteed to improve educational achievement). In the

676

spirit of evoking further cheap proposals, here is a small list of suggestions that, to my mind at least—and the mind I believe of any adult who visits American public schools—would mean a clear plus for American education:

1. *Disconnect all loudspeaker systems in American schools—or at least reserve* 3 *them, like the hotline between Moscow and Washington, for only the gravest emergencies.* The American classroom—and the American teacher and his or her charges—is continually interrupted by announcements from central head-quarters over the loudspeaker system. These remind teachers to bring in some form or other; or students to bring in some form or other; or students engaged in some activity to remember to come to practice or rehearsal; or they announce a change of time for some activity. There is nothing so unnerving to a teacher engaged in trying to explain something, or a student engaged in trying to understand something, as the crackle of the loudspeaker prepared to issue an announcement, and the harsh and gravelly voice (the systems are not obviously of the highest grade) of the announcement itself.

Aside from questions of personal taste, why would this be a good idea? As I 4 have suggested, one reason is that the loudspeaker interrupts efforts to com-municate complicated material that requires undivided attention. Second, it demeans the teacher as professional: every announcement tells her whatever she is doing is not very important and can be interrupted at any time. Third, it accentuates the notion of hierarchy in education—the principal and assistant principal are the most important people, and command time and attention even in the midst of instruction. Perhaps I have been softened by too many years as a college teacher, but it would be unimaginable that a loudspeaker, if one existed, would ever interrupt a college class except under conditions of the gravest and most immediate threat to life and limb. One way of showing students that education is important is not to interrupt it for band-rehearsal announce-ments.

2. *Disarm the school.* One of the most depressing aspects of the urban school 5 in the United States is the degree of security manifest within it, and that seems to me quite contradictory to what a school should be. Outer doors are locked. Security guards are present in the corridors. Internal doors are locked. Passes are necessary to enter the school or move within it, for outsiders and for students. Students are marched in groups from classroom to classroom, under the eye of the teachers. It is understandable that given the conditions in lower-class areas in our large cities—and not only lower-class areas—some degree of security-mindedness is necessary. There is valuable equipment—typewriters, computers, audio-visual equipment—that can be stolen; vandalism is a serious concern; marauders can enter the school in search for equipment, or teachers' pocket-books, or to threaten directly personal safety in search of money or sex, and so on. School integration and busing, at least in their initial stages, have contrib-

uted to increased interracial tensions in schools and have in part severed the link between community and school. The difference in ethnic and racial composition of faculty, other staff, administrators, and students contributes to the same end.

Having acknowledged all this, I still believe the school should feel less like   6
a prison than it does. One should examine to what extent outside doors must be closed; to what extent the security guard cannot be replaced by local parents, volunteer or paid; the degree to which the endless bells indicating "stop" and "go" are really necessary. I suspect that now that the most difficult period of school integration has passed, now that teachers and administrators and staff more closely parallel in race and ethnic background students and community owing to the increase in black and Hispanic teachers and administrators, we may be saddled with more security than we need. Here we come to the sticky problem of *removing* security measures whose need has decreased. What school board will open itself to suit or to public criticism by deliberately providing *less* security? And yet one must consider the atmosphere of the school and a school's primary objective as a reaching agent: can this be reconciled with a condition of maximum security? Perhaps there are lessons to be learned from colleges and community colleges in older urban areas, which in my experience do seem to manage with less security. One reason is that there are more adults around in such institutions. Is that a hint as to how we could manage better in our public schools?

3. *Enlist the children in keeping the school clean.* Occasionally we see a   7
practice abroad that suggests possible transfer to the American scene. In Japan, the children clean the school. There is a time of day when mops and pails and brooms come out, and the children sweep up and wash up. This does, I am sure, suggest to the children that this is *their* school, that it is not simply a matter of being forced to go to a foreign institution that imposes alien demands upon them. I can imagine some obstacles in the way of instituting regular student clean-up in American schools—custodians' unions, for example, might object. But they can be reassured that children don't do that good a job, and they will still be needed. Once again, as in the case of the security problem, one wants to create in the school, if at all possible, a common enterprise of teachers and students, without the latter being bored and resistant, the former, in response, becoming equally indifferent. The school should be seen as everyone's workplace—and participation in cleaning the school will help.

4. *Save old schools.* Build fewer new ones. It has often surprised me that   8
while in schools such as Eton and Oxford—and indeed well-known private schools and colleges in the United States—old buildings are prized, in so many communities older public schools are torn down when to the naked eye they have many virtues that would warrant their maintenance and use. Only a few

blocks from where I live, an excellent example of late nineteenth-century fine brickwork and carved stonework that served as the Cambridge Latin School came down for a remodeling. The carved elements are still displayed about the remodeled school, but why a building of such character should have deserved demolition escaped my understanding, particularly since one can take it almost as a given that a school building put up before the 1940s will be built of heavier and sturdier materials than one constructed today. Even the inconveniences of the old can possess a charm that makes them worthwhile. And indeed many of the reforms that seemed to require new buildings (for example, classrooms without walls, concentrated around activities centers in large open rooms) have turned out, on use, to be not so desirable. Our aim should be to give each school a history, a character, something that at least some students respond to. The pressures for new buildings are enormous, and sometimes perfectly legitimate (as when communities expand), but often illegitimate, as when builders and building-trades workers and contract-givers seek an opportunity or when state aid makes it appear as if a new building won't cost anything.

5. *Look on new hardware with a skeptical eye.* I think it likely that the passion 9 for the new in the way of teaching-hardware not only does not contribute to higher education achievement but may well serve as a temporary means to evade the real and hard tasks of teaching—which really require almost no hardware at all, besides textbooks, blackboard, and chalk. Admittedly, when one comes to high-school science, something more is called for. And yet our tendency is to always find cover behind new hardware. It's *fun* to get new audio-visual equipment, new rooms equipped with them in which all kinds of things can be done by flicking a switch or twisting a dial, or, as is now the case, to decide what kind of personal computers and software are necessary for a good educational program. Once again, foreign experience can be enlightening. When Japanese education was already well ahead of American, most Japanese schools were in prewar wooden buildings. (They are now as up-to-date as ours, but neither their age nor up-to-dateness has much to do with their good record of achievement.) Resisting the appeal of new hardware not only saves money, and provides less in the way of saleable goods to burglarize, but it also prevents distraction from the principal tasks of reading, writing, and calculating. When it turns out that computers and new software are shown to do a better job at these key tasks—I am skeptical as to whether this will ever be the case—there will be time enough to splurge on new equipment. The teacher, alone, up front, explaining, encouraging, guiding, is the heart of the matter—the rest is fun, and very helpful to corporate income, and gives an inflated headquarters staff something new to do. But students will have time enough to learn about computers when they get to college, and getting there will depend almost not at all on what they can do with computers, but how well they understand words and sentences, and how well they do at simple mathematics.

There is nothing wrong with old textbooks, too. Recently, reviewing some 10
recent high-school American history texts, I was astonished to discover they
come out in new editions every two years or so, and not because the main body
of the text is improved, but because the textbook wants to be able to claim it
covers the very last presidential campaign, and the events of the last few years.
This is a waste of time and energy and money. There is enough to teach in
American history up to 1950 or 1960 not to worry about whether the text
includes Reagan's tax cuts. I suspect many new texts in other areas also offer
little advantage over the older ones. There is also a virtue in a teacher becoming
acquainted with a particular textbook. When I read that a school is disadvantaged
because its textbooks are old, I am always mystified. Even the newest advances
in physics and biology might well be reserved for college.

6. *Expand the pool from which we draw good teachers.* This general heading 11
covers a number of simple and concrete things, such as: if a teacher is considered
qualified to teach at a good private school, that teacher should be considered
qualified to teach at a public school. It has always seemed to me ridiculous that
teachers accepted at the best private schools in New York City or top preparatory
schools in the country would not be allowed to teach in the public school
system of New York or Boston. Often, they are willing—after all, the pay is
better in public schools and there are greater fringe benefits. They might, it is
true, be driven out of those schools by the challenge of lower- and working-
class children. But when they are willing, it seems unbelievable that the teacher
qualified (or so Brearley thinks) for Brearley will not be allowed to teach at P.S.
122.[1] Greater use of part-time teachers might also be able to draw upon people
with qualities that we are told the average teacher unfortunately doesn't possess—
such as a higher level of competence in writing and mathematics.

Our recurrent concern with foreign-language teaching should lead us to 12
recruit foreign-born teachers. There are problems in getting teaching jobs today
in Germany and France—yet teachers there are typically drawn from pools of
students with higher academic skills than is the case in this country. Paradoxically, we make it easy for teachers of Spanish-language background to get jobs
owing to the expansion of bilingual programs—but then their teaching is confined to children whose Spanish accent doesn't need improvement. It would
make more sense to expose children of foreign-language background more to
teachers with native English—and children from English-speaking families to
teachers who speak French, German, Spanish, and, why not, Japanese, and
Chinese natively. This would mean that rules requiring that a teacher must be
a citizen, or must speak English without an accent, should be lifted for special
teachers with special tasks. Perhaps we could make the most of the oversupply
of teachers in some foreign countries by using them to teach mathematics—a

---

[1] Brearley: a prominent private school in New York City. [Eds.]

subject where accent doesn't count. The school system in Georgia is already recruiting from Germany. Colleges often use teaching assistants whose English is not native and far from perfect, including Asians from Korea and China, to assist in science and mathematics courses. (There are many state laws which would not permit them to teach in elementary and secondary schools.)

All the suggestions above eschew any involvement with some great issues of education—tradition or reform, the teaching of values, the role of religion in the schools—that have in the past dominated arguments over education and still do today. But I add one more proposal that is still, I am afraid, somewhat controversial: 13

7. *Let students, within reasons, pick their schools, or let parents choose them for them.* All those informed on school issues will sense the heaving depths of controversy under this apparently modest proposal. Does this mean they might choose parochial schools, without being required to pay tuition out of their own pockets? Or does this mean black children would be allowed to attend schools in black areas, and whites in white areas, or the reverse if each is so inclined? As we all know, the two great issues of religion and race stand in the way of any such simple and commonsensical arrangement. Students are regularly bused from one section of a city to another because of their race, and students cannot without financial penalty attend that substantial sector of schools—30 percent or so in most Northern and Midwestern cities—that are called "private." I ignore the question of whether, holding all factors constant, students do "better" in private or public schools, in racially well-mixed or hardly mixed schools. The evidence will always be uncertain. What is perhaps less arguable is that students will do better in a school that forms a community, in which teachers, parents, and students all agree that *that* is the school they want to teach in, to attend, to send their children to. I would guess that this is the kind of school most of the readers of this article have attended; it is the kind of school, alas, that our complex racial and religious history makes it harder and harder for those of minority race or of lower- and working-class status to attend. 14

I have eschewed the grand proposals—for curriculum change, for improving the quality of entering teachers, for checking on the competence of teachers in service, for establishing national standards for achievement in different levels of education—all of which now form the agenda for many state commissions of educational reform, and all of which seem reasonable to me. Rather, I have concentrated on a variety of other things that serve to remove distraction, to open the school to those of quality who would be willing to enter it to improve it, to concentrate on the essentials of teaching and learning as I (and many others) have experienced it. It would be possible to propose larger changes in the same direction: for example, reduce the size of the bureaucracies in urban school systems. Some of my modest proposals are insidiously intended to do this—if there were less effort devoted to building new schools, buying new 15

681

equipment, evaluating new textbooks, or busing children, there would be no need to maintain quite so many people at headquarters. Or so I would hope.

In the meantime, why not disconnect the loudspeakers?   16

QUESTIONS

1. Among Glazer's proposals, which seem to you the most helpful and which the least? Explain why.

2. Why do you think Glazer focuses so much on money in his first two paragraphs? Would his proposals "cost much less, nothing at all, or even save money," as he claims in paragraph 2? Explain why or why not.

3. What audience is Glazer addressing? What does he expect readers to do about his "modest proposals"?

4. How has Glazer ordered his seven proposals? Why do you think he arranged them as he did? What other methods of organization might he have used?

5. Glazer makes his suggestions "in the spirit," he says, "of evoking further cheap proposals" (paragraph 2). Offer a few of your own, with explanations.

6. Pool the proposals that you and your classmates have made for question 5. Select the best of these with the best possible explanations, and prepare a group report that you might even forward to Glazer, as well as to other possible audiences.

7. Proposals of this sort suggest parodies. Can you come up with a few comic or ironic proposals that you would like to make on behalf of "better education," something like sending all the teachers home for one day a week and leaving learning to the students? Or maybe all the administrators should become bus drivers, the bus drivers coaches, and the coaches administrators. Of course, you would need to advance reasons for your proposals.

8. In general, Glazer's proposals address public education in elementary and secondary schools, but by now you've had a taste of college. As either an individual or a group activity, make up a list of modest proposals for improving, inexpensively, the quality of education at your college. Present your list, if you wish, wherever you think it should go.

MAKING CONNECTIONS

1. To what extent does Glazer's essay play off of Jonathan Swift's "A Modest Proposal"? In what ways are they similar? How do they differ? Given these similarities and differences, why do you think Glazer selected the title he did?

2. Read Theodore R. Sizer's "What High School Is" in "Explaining." What effect do you think Glazer's proposals would have on high schools as described there? Would some proposals work better than others? Why do you think so? Can you think of related proposals that you might substitute for some of Glazer's? Write your own memo to American high schools, urging some very modest proposals on them.

THE IGNORED LESSON
OF ANNE FRANK

Bruno Bettelheim

Psychoanalyst Bruno Bettelheim, as the headnote on page 395 explains, himself survived imprisonment in Nazi concentration camps. Here he writes about Anne Frank, one of the better-known victims of World War II. Her family, after hiding in an attic in Amsterdam for two years, was betrayed to the Nazis, and Anne perished in a concentration camp. Her Diary, *kept during her time in hiding, was published in 1947 and later was turned into a play and a film. The following essay originally appeared in* Harper's *(November 1960) and was reprinted in Bettelheim's book* Surviving and Other Essays *(1979). In this essay, Bettelheim seeks to revise our moral understanding of Anne Frank's story.*

When the world first learned about the Nazi concentration and death camps, most civilized people felt the horrors committed in them to be so uncanny as to be unbelievable. It came as a severe shock that supposedly civilized nations could stoop to such inhuman acts. The implication that modern man has such inadequate control over his cruel and destructive proclivities was felt as a threat to our views of ourselves and our humanity. Three different psychological mechanisms were most frequently used for dealing with the appalling revelation of what had gone on in the camps:

(1) its applicability to man in general was denied by asserting—contrary to evidence—that the acts of torture and mass murder were committed by a small group of insane or perverted persons;

(2) the truth of the reports was denied by declaring them vastly exaggerated and ascribing them to propaganda (this originated with the German government, which called all reports on terror in the camps "horror propaganda"—*Greuelpropaganda*);

(3) the reports were believed, but the knowledge of the horror repressed as soon as possible.

All three mechanisms could be seen at work after liberation of those prisoners remaining. At first, after the discovery of the camps and their death-dealing, a wave of extreme outrage swept the Allied nations. It was soon followed by a general repression of the discovery in people's minds. Possibly this reaction was due to something more than the blow dealt to modern man's narcissism by the realization that cruelty is still rampant among men. Also present may have been the dim but extremely threatening realization that the modern state now has available the means for changing personality, and for destroying millions it deems undesirable. The ideas that in our day a people's personalities might be changed against their will by the state, and that other populations might be wholly or partially exterminated, are so fearful that one tries to free oneself of them and their impact by defensive denial, or by repression.

The extraordinary world-wide success of the book, play, and movie *The Diary of Anne Frank* suggests the power of the desire to counteract the realization of the personality-destroying and murderous nature of the camps by concentrating all attention on what is experienced as a demonstration that private and intimate life can continue to flourish even under the direct persecution by the most ruthless totalitarian system. And this although Anne Frank's fate demonstrates how efforts at disregarding in private life what goes on around one in society can hasten one's own destruction. 3

What concerns me here is not what actually happened to the Frank family, how they tried—and failed—to survive their terrible ordeal. It would be very wrong to take apart so humane and moving a story, which aroused so much well-merited compassion for gentle Anne Frank and her tragic fate. What is at issue is the universal and uncritical response to her diary and to the play and movie based on it, and what this reaction tells about our attempts to cope with the feelings her fate—used by us to serve as a symbol of a most human reaction to Nazi terror—arouses in us. I believe that the world-wide acclaim given her story cannot be explained unless we recognize in it our wish to forget the gas chambers, and our effort to do so by glorifying the ability to retreat into an extremely private, gentle, sensitive world, and there to cling as much as possible to what have been one's usual daily attitudes and activities, although surrounded by a maelstrom apt to engulf one at any moment. 4

The Frank family's attitude that life could be carried on as before may well have been what led to their destruction. By eulogizing how they lived in their hiding place while neglecting to examine first whether it was a reasonable or an effective choice, we are able to ignore the crucial lesson of their story—that such an attitude can be fatal in extreme circumstances. 5

While the Franks were making their preparations for going passively into hiding, thousands of other Jews in Holland (as elsewhere in Europe) were trying to escape to the free world, in order to survive and/or fight. Others who could not escape went underground—into hiding—each family member with, for example, a different gentile family. We gather from the diary, however, that the chief desire of the Frank family was to continue living as nearly as possible in the same fashion to which they had been accustomed in happier times. 6

Little Anne, too, wanted only to go on with life as usual, and what else 7 could she have done but fall in with the pattern her parents created for her existence? But hers was not a necessary fate, much less a heroic one; it was a terrible but also a senseless fate. Anne had a good chance to survive, as did many Jewish children in Holland. But she would have had to leave her parents and go live with a gentile Dutch family, posing as their own child, something her parents would have had to arrange for her.

Everyone who recognized the obvious knew that the hardest way to go underground was to do it as a family; to hide out together made detection by the SS most likely; and when detected, everybody was doomed. By hiding singly, even when one got caught, the others had a chance to survive. The Franks, with their excellent connections among gentile Dutch families, might well have been able to hide out singly, each with a different family. But instead, the main principle of their planning was continuing their beloved family life— an understandable desire, but highly unrealistic in those times. Choosing any other course would have meant not merely giving up living together, but also realizing the full measure of the danger to their lives. **8**

The Franks were unable to accept that going on living as a family as they had done before the Nazi invasion of Holland was no longer a desirable way of life, much as they loved each other; in fact, for them and others like them, it was most dangerous behavior. But even given their wish not to separate, they failed to make appropriate preparations for what was likely to happen. **9**

There is little doubt that the Franks, who were able to provide themselves with so much while arranging for going into hiding, and even while hiding, could have provided themselves with some weapons had they wished. Had they had a gun, Mr. Frank could have shot down at least one or two of the "green police" who came for them. There was no surplus of such police, and the loss of an SS with every Jew arrested would have noticeably hindered the functioning of the police state. Even a butcher knife, which they certainly could have taken with them into hiding, could have been used by them in self-defense. The fate of the Franks wouldn't have been very different, because they all died anyway except for Anne's father. But they could have sold their lives for a high price, instead of walking to their death. Still, although one must assume that Mr. Frank would have fought courageously, as we know he did when a soldier in the first World War, it is not everybody who can plan to kill those who are bent on killing him, although many who would not be ready to contemplate doing so would be willing to kill those who are bent on murdering not only them but also their wives and little daughters. **10**

An entirely different matter would have been planning for escape in case of discovery. The Franks' hiding place had only one entrance; it did not have any other exit. Despite the fact, during their many months of hiding, they did not try to devise one. Nor did they make other plans for escape, such as that one of the family members—as likely as not Mr. Frank—would try to detain the police in the narrow entrance way—maybe even fight them, as suggested **11** above—thus giving other members of the family a chance to escape, either by reaching the roofs of adjacent houses, or down a ladder into the alley behind the house in which they were living.

Any of this would have required recognizing and accepting the desperate straits in which they found themselves, and concentrating on how best to cope with them. This was quite possible to do, even under the terrible conditions in which the Jews found themselves after the Nazi occupation of Holland. It can be seen from many other accounts, for example from the story of Marga Minco, a girl of about Anne Frank's age who lived to tell about it. Her parents had planned that when the police should come for them, the father would try to detain them by arguing and fighting with them, to give the wife and daughter a chance to escape through a rear door. Unfortunately it did not quite work out this way, and both parents got killed. But their short-lived resistance permitted their daughter to make her escape as planned and to reach a Dutch family who saved her.[1] 12

This is not mentioned as a criticism that the Frank family did not plan or behave along similar lines. A family has every right to arrange their life as they wish or think best, and to take the risks they want to take. My point is not to criticize what the Franks did, but only the universal admiration of their way of coping, or rather of not coping. The story of little Marga who survived, every bit as touching, remains totally neglected by comparison. 13

Many Jews—unlike the Franks, who through listening to British radio news were better informed than most—had no detailed knowledge of the extermination camps. Thus it was easier for them to make themselves believe that complete compliance with even the most outrageously debilitating and degrading Nazi orders might offer a chance for survival. But neither tremendous anxiety that inhibits clear thinking and with it well-planned and determined action, nor ignorance about what happened to those who responded with passive waiting for being rounded up for their extermination, can explain the reaction of audiences to the play and movie retelling Anne's story, which are all about such waiting that results finally in destruction. 14

I think it is the fictitious ending that explains the enormous success of this play and movie. At the conclusion we hear Anne's voice from the beyond, saying, "In spite of everything, I still believe that people are really good at heart." This improbable sentiment is supposedly from a girl who had been starved to death, had watched her sister meet the same fate before she did, knew that her mother had been murdered, and had watched untold thousands of adults and children being killed. This statement is not justified by anything Anne actually told her diary. 15

Going on with intimate family living, no matter how dangerous it might be to survival, was fatal to all too many during the Nazi regime. And if all men 16

---

[1] Marga Minco, *Bitter Herbs* (New York: Oxford University Press), 1960.

are good, then indeed we can all go on with living our lives as we have been accustomed to in times of undisturbed safety and can afford to forget about Auschwitz. But Anne, her sister, her mother, may well have died because her parents could not get themselves to believe in Auschwitz.

While play and movie are ostensibly about Nazi persecution and destruction, in actuality what we watch is the way that, despite this terror, lovable people manage to continue living their satisfying intimate lives with each other. The heroine grows from a child into a young adult as normally as any other girl would, despite the most abnormal conditions of all other aspects of her existence, and that of her family. Thus the play reassures us that despite the destructiveness of Nazi racism and tyranny in general, it is possible to disregard it in one's private life much of the time, even if one is Jewish.

True, the ending happens just as the Franks and their friends had feared all along: their hiding place is discovered, and they are carried away to their doom. But the fictitious declaration of faith in the goodness of all men which concludes the play falsely reassures us since it impresses on us that in the combat between Nazi terror and continuance of intimate family living the latter wins out, since Anne has the last word. This is simply contrary to fact, because it was she who got killed. Her seeming survival through her moving statement about the goodness of men releases us effectively of the need to cope with the problems Auschwitz presents. That is why we are so relieved by her statement. It explains why millions loved play and movie, because while it confronts us with the fact that Auschwitz existed it encourages us at the same time to ignore any of its implications. If all men are good at heart, there never really was an Auschwitz; nor is there any possibility that it may recur.

The desire of Anne Frank's parents not to interrupt their intimate family living, and their inability to plan more effectively for their survival, reflect the failure of all too many others faced with the threat of Nazi terror. It is a failure that deserves close examination because of the inherent warnings it contains for us, the living.

Submission to the threatening power of the Nazi state often led both to the disintegration of what had once seemed well-integrated personalities and to a return to an immature disregard for the dangers of reality. Those Jews who submitted passively to Nazi persecution came to depend on primitive and infantile thought processes: wishful thinking and disregard for the possibility of death. Many persuaded themselves that they, out of all the others, would be spared. Many more simply disbelieved in the possibility of their own death. Not believing in it, they did not take what seemed to them desperate precautions, such as giving up everything to hide out singly; or trying to escape even if it meant risking their lives in doing so; or preparing to fight for their lives when no escape was possible and death had become an immediate possibility. It is true that defending their lives in active combat before they were rounded up to be transported into the camps might have hastened their deaths, and so, up to

17

18

19

20

a point, they were protecting themselves by "rolling with the punches" of the enemy.

But the longer one rolls with the punches dealt not by the normal vagaries 21 of life, but by one's eventual executioner, the more likely it becomes that one will no longer have the strength to resist when death becomes imminent. This is particularly true if yielding to the enemy is accompanied not by a commensurate strengthening of the personality, but by an inner disintegration. We can observe such a process among the Franks, who bickered with each other over trifles, instead of supporting each other's ability to resist the demoralizing impact of their living conditions.

Those who faced up to the announced intentions of the Nazis prepared for 22 the worst as a real and imminent possibility. It meant risking one's life for a self-chosen purpose, but in doing so, creating at least a small chance for saving one's own life or those of others, or both. When Jews in Germany were restricted to their homes, those who did not succumb to inertia took the new restrictions as a warning that it was high time to go underground, join the resistance movement, provide themselves with forged papers, and so on; if they had not done so long ago. Many of them survived.

Some distant relatives of mine may furnish an example. Early in the war, a 23 young man living in a small Hungarian town banded together with a number of other Jews to prepare against a German invasion. As soon as the Nazis imposed curfews on the Jews, his group left for Budapest—because the bigger capital city with its greater anonymity offered chances for escaping detection. Similar groups from other towns converged in Budapest and joined forces. From among themselves they selected typically "Aryan" looking men who equipped themselves with false papers and immediately joined the Hungarian SS. These spies were then able to warn of impending persecution and raids.

Many of these groups survived intact. Furthermore, they had also equipped 24 themselves with small arms, so that if they were detected, they could put up enough of a fight for the majority to escape while a few would die fighting to make the escape possible. A few of the Jews who had joined the SS were discovered and immediately shot, probably a death preferable to one in the gas chambers. But most of even these Jews survived, hiding within the SS until liberation.

Compare these arrangements not just to the Franks' selection of a hiding 25 place that was basically a trap without an outlet but with Mr. Frank's teaching typically academic high-school subjects to his children rather than how to make a getaway: a token of his inability to face the seriousness of the threat of death. Teaching high-school subjects had, of course, its constructive aspects. It relieved the ever-present anxiety about their fate to some degree by concentrating on different matters, and by implication it encouraged hope for a future in which such knowledge would be useful. In this sense such teaching was purposeful, but it was erroneous in that it took the place of much more pertinent teaching and planning: how best to try to escape when detected.

Unfortunately the Franks were by no means the only ones who, out of anxiety, became unable to contemplate their true situation and with it to plan accordingly. Anxiety, and the wish to counteract it by clinging to each other, and to reduce its sting by continuing as much as possible with their usual way of life incapacitated many, particularly when survival plans required changing radically old ways of living that they cherished, and which had become their only source of satisfaction. ²⁶

My young relative, for example, was unable to persuade other members of his family to go with him when he left the small town where he had lived with them. Three times, at tremendous risk to himself, he returned to plead with his relatives, pointing out first the growing persecution of the Jews, and later the fact that transport to the gas chambers had already begun. He could not convince these Jews to leave their homes and break up their families to go singly into hiding. ²⁷

As their desperation mounted, they clung more determinedly to their old living arrangements and to each other, became less able to consider giving up the possessions they had accumulated through hard work over a lifetime. The more severely their freedom to act was reduced, and what little they were still permitted to do restricted by insensible and degrading regulations imposed by the Nazis, the more did they become unable to contemplate independent action. Their life energies drained out of them, sapped by their ever-greater anxiety. The less they found strength in themselves, the more they held on to the little that was left of what had given them security in the past—their old surroundings, their customary way of life, their possessions—all these seemed to give their lives some permanency, offer some symbols of security. Only what had once been symbols of security now endangered life, since they were excuses for avoiding change. On each successive visit the young man found his relatives more incapacitated, less willing or able to take his advice, more frozen into inactivity, and with it further along the way to the crematoria where, in fact, they all died. ²⁸

Levin renders a detailed account of the desperate but fruitless efforts made by small Jewish groups determined to survive to try to save the rest. She tells how messengers were "sent into the provinces to warn Jews that deportation meant death, but their warnings were ignored because most Jews refused to contemplate their own annihilation."[2] I believe the reason for such refusal has to be found in their inability to take action. If we are certain that we are helpless to protect ourselves against the danger of destruction, we cannot contemplate it. We can consider the danger only as long as we believe there are ways to ²⁹

---

[2] Nora Levin, *The Holocaust* (New York: Thomas Y. Crowell, 1968).

protect ourselves, to fight back, to escape. If we are convinced none of this is possible for us, then there is no point in thinking about the danger; on the contrary, it is best to refuse to do so.

As a prisoner in Buchenwald, I talked to hundreds of German Jewish pris-   30
oners who were brought there as part of the huge pogrom in the wake of the murder of vom Rath in the fall of 1938. I asked them why they had not left Germany, given the utterly degrading conditions they had been subjected to. Their answer was: How could we leave? It would have meant giving up our homes, our work, our sources of income. Having been deprived by Nazi persecution and degradation of much of their self-respect, they had become unable to give up what still gave them a semblance of it: their earthly belongings. But instead of using possessions, they became captivated by them, and this possession by earthly goods became the fatal mask for their possession by anxiety, fear, and denial.

How the investment of personal property with one's life energy could make   31
people die bit by bit was illustrated throughout the Nazi persecution of the Jews. At the time of the first boycott of Jewish stores, the chief external goal of the Nazis was to acquire the possessions of the Jews. They even let Jews take some things out of the country at that time if they would leave the bulk of their property behind. For a long time the intention of the Nazis, and the goal of their first discriminatory laws, was to force undesirable minorities, including Jews, into emigration.

Although the extermination policy was in line with the inner logic of Nazi   32
racial ideology, one may wonder whether the idea that millions of Jews (and other foreign nationals) could be submitted to extermination did not partially result from seeing the degree of degradation Jews accepted without fighting back. When no violent resistance occurred, persecution of the Jews worsened, slow step by slow step.

Many Jews who on the invasion of Poland were able to survey their situation   33
and draw the right conclusions survived the Second World War. As the Germans approached, they left everything behind and fled to Russia, much as they distrusted and disliked the Soviet system. But there, while badly treated, they could at least survive. Those who stayed on in Poland believing they could go on with life-as-before sealed their fate. Thus in the deepest sense the walk to the gas chamber was only the last consequence of these Jews' inability to comprehend what was in store; it was the final step of surrender to the death instinct, which might also be called the principle of inertia. The first step was taken long before arrival at the death camp.

We can find a dramatic demonstration of how far the surrender to inertia   34
can be carried, and the wish not to know because knowing would create unbearable anxiety, in an experience of Olga Lengyel.[3] She reports that although

---

[3] Olga Lengyel, *Five Chimneys: The Story of Auschwitz* (Chicago: Ziff-Davis, 1947).

690

she and her fellow prisoners lived just a few hundred yards from the crematoria and the gas chambers and knew what they were for, most prisoners denied knowledge of them for months. If they had grasped their true situation, it might have helped them save either the lives they themselves were fated to lose, or the lives of others.

When Mrs. Lengyel's fellow prisoners were selected to be sent to the gas   35
chambers, they did not try to break away from the group, as she successfully did. Worse, the first time she tried to escape the gas chambers, some of the other selected prisoners told the supervisors that she was trying to get away. Mrs. Lengyel desperately asks the question: How was it possible that people denied the existence of the gas chambers when all day long they saw the crematoria burning and smelled the odor of burning flesh? Why did they prefer ignoring the exterminations to fighting for their very own lives? She can offer no explanation, only the observation that they resented anyone who tried to save himself from the common fate, because they lacked enough courage to risk action themselves. I believe they did it because they had given up their will to live and permitted their death tendencies to engulf them. As a result, such prisoners were in the thrall of the murdering SS not only physically but also psychologically, while this was not true for those prisoners who still had a grip on life.

Some prisoners even began to serve their executioners, to help speed the   36
death of their own kind. Then things had progressed beyond simple inertia to the death instinct running rampant. Those who tried to serve their executioners in what were once their civilian capacities were merely continuing life as usual and thereby opening the door to their death.

For example, Mrs. Lengyel speaks of Dr. Mengele, SS physician at Ausch-   37
witz, as a typical example of the "business as usual" attitude that enabled some prisoners, and certainly the SS, to retain whatever balance they could despite what they were doing. She described how Dr. Mengele took all correct medical precautions during childbirth, rigorously observing all aseptic principles, cutting the umbilical cord with greatest care, etc. But only half an hour later he sent mother and infant to be burned in the crematorium.

Having made his choice, Dr. Mengele and others like him had to delude   38
themselves to be able to live with themselves and their experience. Only one personal document on the subject has come to my attention, that of Dr. Nyiszli, a prisoner serving as "research physician" at Auschwitz.[4] How Dr. Nyiszli deluded himself can be seen, for example, in the way he repeatedly refers to himself as working in Auschwitz as a physician, although he worked as the assistant of a criminal murderer. He speaks of the Institute for Race, Biological, and Anthropological Investigation as "one of the most qualified medical centers of the Third Reich," although it was devoted to proving falsehoods. That Nyiszli

---

[4]Miklos Nyiszli, *Auschwitz: A Doctor's Eyewitness Account* (New York: Frederick Fell, 1960).

was a doctor didn't alter the fact that he—like any of the prisoner foremen who served the SS better than some SS were willing to serve it—was a participant in the crimes of the SS. How could he do it and live with himself?

The answer is: by taking pride in his professional skills, irrespective of the 39 purpose they served. Dr. Nyiszli and Dr. Mengele were only two among hundreds of other—and far more prominent—physicians who participated in the Nazis' murderous pseudo-scientific human experiments. It was the peculiar pride of these men in their professional skill and knowledge, without regard for moral implications, that made them so dangerous. Although the concentration camps and crematoria are no longer here, this kind of pride still remains with us; it is characteristic of a modern society in which fascination with technical competence has dulled concern for human feelings. Auschwitz is gone, but so long as this attitude persists, we shall not be safe from cruel indifference to life at the core.

I have met many Jews as well as gentile anti-Nazis, similar to the activist 40 group in Hungary described earlier, who survived in Nazi Germany and in the occupied countries. These people realized that when a world goes to pieces and inhumanity reigns supreme, man cannot go on living his private life as he was wont to do, and would like to do; he cannot, as the loving head of a family, keep the family living together peacefully, undisturbed by the surrounding world; nor can he continue to take pride in his profession or possessions, when either will deprive him of his humanity, if not also of his life. In such times, one must radically reevaluate all of what one has done, believed in, and stood for in order to know how to act. In short, one has to take a stand on the new reality—a firm stand, not one of retirement into an even more private world.

If today, Negroes in Africa march against the guns of a police that defends 41 *apartheid*—even if hundreds of dissenters are shot down and tens of thousands rounded up in camps—their fight will sooner or later assure them of a chance for liberty and equality. Millions of the Jews of Europe who did not or could not escape in time or go underground as many thousands did, could at least have died fighting as some did in the Warsaw ghetto at the end, instead of passively waiting to be rounded up for their own extermination.

QUESTIONS

1. As part of his evidence, Bettelheim repeatedly refers to and sometimes summarizes parts of the story of Anne Frank. What are the main outlines of her story? What makes it so important?

2. What is Bettelheim's thesis? What is his most urgent message?

3. At times Bettelheim's thesis bears on Nazi resistance during World War II; at times it appears more universal. When does it tip one way, and when another? How do these two messages work together in the essay to strengthen Bettelheim's argument?

4. Bettelheim writes in paragraph 15, "I think it is the fictitious ending that explains the enormous success of the play and movie." Why does Bettelheim suggest that the ending must be fictitious? What evidence does he provide to support this claim?

5. Bettelheim refers to four other stories in print, those of Minco, Levin, Lengyel, and Nyiszli, as well as the case of his own distant relatives. How do these stories serve as evidence? Why do you think Bettelheim decided to arrange them in the order in which they appear?

6. Have you ever observed or learned of a situation in which someone's inaction seemed to increase, rather than decrease, some form of persecution? If so, analyze this situation in light of Bettelheim's essay.

7. Bettelheim seeks to revise his readers' moral understanding of Anne Frank's story. Write an essay in which you argue to revise your readers' understanding of some belief or some conventionally understood situation or story.

MAKING CONNECTIONS

1. Read Robert Jay Lifton's "What Made This Man? Mengele." Bettelheim mentions Mengele, too (paragraphs 37–39). More than that, he offers at least a few hints of what else went into making that man. What would Bettelheim add to Lifton's explanation?

2. Considering the cases Bettelheim discusses in his essay, whatever you know about the struggles of South African blacks, your knowlege of other contemporary freedom movements, and the reasons Thomas Jefferson gives in the Declaration of Independence (which follows in this section), write a position paper on when, if ever, you find it proper to rebel. You may bring any other doctrine you like into this paper—whether it be political, religious, or moral—so long as you explain it clearly and relate its principles to your thesis.

RACIST ARGUMENTS AND IQ

Stephen Jay Gould

*Stephen Jay Gould, as the headnote on page 573 mentions,
is a geologist best known for his column in* Natural History
magazine. The following essay comes from his book Ever
Since Darwin: Reflections in Natural History *(1977). The
broad subject at issue here is "biological determinism," the
idea that nature, more than socialization and training,
makes us what we are.*

Louis Agassiz, the greatest biologist of mid-nineteenth-century America, 1
argued that God had created blacks and whites as separate species. The defenders
of slavery took much comfort from this assertion, for biblical proscriptions of
charity and equality did not have to extend across a species boundary. What
could an abolitionist say? Science had shone its cold and dispassionate light
upon the subject; Christian hope and sentimentality could not refute it.

Similar arguments, carrying the apparent sanction of science, have been 2
continually invoked in attempts to equate egalitarianism with sentimental hope
and emotional blindness. People who are unaware of this historical pattern tend
to accept each recurrence at face value: that is, they assume that each statement
arises from the "data" actually presented, rather than from the social conditions
that truly inspire it.

The racist arguments of the nineteenth century were based primarily on 3
craniometry, the measurement of human skulls. Today, these contentions stand
totally discredited. What craniometry was to the nineteenth century, intelligence
testing has been to the twentieth. The victory of the eugenics movement in the
Immigration Restriction Act of 1924 signaled its first unfortunate effect—for the
severe restrictions upon non-Europeans and upon southern and eastern Europeans gained much support from results of the first extensive and uniform
application of intelligence tests in America—the Army Mental Tests of World
War I. These tests were engineered and administered by psychologist Robert
M. Yerkes,[1] who concluded that "education alone will not place the negro [*sic*]
race on a par with its Caucasian competitors." It is now clear that Yerkes and
his colleagues knew no way to separate genetic from environmental components
in postulating causes for different performances on the tests.

The latest episode of this recurring drama began in 1969, when Arthur 4

---

[1] Robert M. Yerkes (1876–1956): American biologist and psychologist. [Eds.]

Jensen published an article entitled, "How Much Can We Boost IQ and Scholastic Achievement?" in the *Harvard Educational Review*.[2] Again, the claim went forward that new and uncomfortable information had come to light, and that science had to speak the "truth" even if it refuted some cherished notions of a liberal philosophy. But again, I shall argue, Jensen had no new data; and what he did present was flawed beyond repair by inconsistencies and illogical claims.

Jensen assumes that IQ tests adequately measure something we may call "intelligence." He then attempts to tease apart the genetic and environmental factors causing differences in performance. He does this primarily by relying upon the one natural experiment we possess: identical twins reared apart—for differences in IQ between genetically identical people can only be environmental. The average difference in IQ for identical twins is less than the difference for two unrelated individuals raised in similarly varied environments. From the data on twins, Jensen obtains an estimate of environmental influence. He concludes that IQ has a heritability of about 0.8 (or 80 percent) *within* the population of American and European whites. The average difference between American whites and blacks is 15 IQ points (one standard deviation).[3] He asserts that this difference is too large to attribute to environment, given the high heritability of IQ. Lest anyone think that Jensen writes in the tradition of abstract scholarship, I merely quote the first line of his famous work: "Compensatory education has been tried, and it apparently has failed."

I believe that this argument can be refuted in a "hierarchical" fashion—that is, we can discredit it at one level and then show that it fails at a more inclusive level even if we allow Jensen's argument for the first two levels:

Level 1: The equation of IQ with intelligence. Who knows what IQ measures? It is a good predictor of "success" in school, but is such success a result of intelligence, apple polishing, or the assimilation of values that the leaders of society prefer? Some psychologists get around this argument by defining intelligence operationally as the scores attained on "intelligence" tests. A neat trick. But at this point, the technical definition of intelligence has strayed so far from the vernacular that we can no longer define the issue. But let me allow (although I don't believe it), for the sake of argument, that IQ measures some meaningful aspect of intelligence in its vernacular sense.

Level 2: The heritability of IQ. Here again, we encounter a confusion between vernacular and technical meanings of the same word. "Inherited," to a layman, means "fixed," "inexorable," or "unchangeable." To a geneticist, "Inherited" refers to an estimate of similarity between related individuals based

---

[2] Arthur Jensen (b. 1923): American educational psychologist. [Eds.]
[3] Standard deviation: a measure of variability of any set of numerical values around their arithmetic mean. [Eds.]

on genes held in common. It carries no implications of inevitability or of immutable entities beyond the reach of environmental influence. Eyeglasses correct a variety of inherited problems in vision; insulin can check diabetes.

Jensen insists that IQ is 80 percent heritable. Princeton psychologist Leon J.   9
Kamin has done the dog-work of meticulously checking through details of the twin studies that form the basis of this estimate.[4] He has found an astonishing number of inconsistencies and downright inaccuracies. For example, the late Sir Cyril Burt, who generated the largest body of data on identical twins reared apart, pursued his studies of intelligence for more than forty years.[5] Although he increased his sample sizes in a variety of "improved" versions, some of his correlation coefficients remain unchanged to the third decimal place[6]—a statistically impossible situation.[7] IQ depends in part upon sex and age; and other studies did not standardize properly for them. An improper correction may produce higher values between twins not because they hold genes for intelligence in common, but simply because they share the same sex and age. The data are so flawed that no valid estimate for the heritability of IQ can be drawn at all. But let me assume (although no data support it), for the sake of argument, that the heritability of IQ is as high as 0.8.

Level 3: The confusion of within- and between-group variation. Jensen draws   10
a causal connection between his two major assertions—that the within-group heritability of IQ is 0.8 for American whites, and that the mean difference in IQ between American blacks and whites is 15 points. He assumes that the black "deficit" is largely genetic in origin because IQ is so highly heritable. This is a *non sequitur* of the worst possible kind[8]—for there is no necessary relationship between heritability within a group and differences in mean values of two separate groups.

A simple example will suffice to illustrate this flaw in Jensen's argument.   11
Height has a much higher heritability within groups than anyone has ever claimed for IQ. Suppose that height has a mean value of five feet two inches and a heritability of 0.9 (a realistic value) within a group of nutritionally deprived Indian farmers. High heritability simply means that short farmers will tend to have short offspring, and tall farmers tall offspring. It says nothing whatever against the possibility that proper nutrition could raise the mean height to six

---

[4]Leon J. Kamin: American psychologist at Princeton and author of *The Science and Politics of I.Q.* (1974). [Eds.]

[5]Sir Cyril Burt (1883–1971): British psychologist. [Eds.]

[6]correlation coefficients: a technical term having to do with determining variables that tend to change together systematically. [Eds.]

[7]I wrote this essay in 1974. Since then, the case against Sir Cyril has progressed from an inference of carelessness to a spectacular (and well-founded) suspicion of fraud. Reporters for the London *Times* have discovered, for example, that Sir Cyril's coauthors (for the infamous twin studies) apparently did not exist outside his imagination. In the light of Kamin's discoveries, one must suspect that the data have an equal claim to reality.

[8]non sequitur: it does not follow. This Latin term, common in logic, indicates a conclusion that is not derivable from the evidence produced. [Eds.]

feet (taller than average white Americans). It only means that, in this improved status, farmers shorter than average (they may now be five feet ten inches) would still tend to have shorter than average children.

I do not claim that intelligence, however defined, has no genetic basis—I regard it as trivially true, uninteresting, and unimportant that it does. The expression of any trait represents a complex interaction of heredity and environment. Our job is simply to provide the best environmental situation for the realization of valued potential in all individuals. I merely point out that a specific claim purporting to demonstrate a mean genetic deficiency in the intelligence of American blacks rests upon no new facts whatever and can cite no valid data in its support. It is just as likely that blacks have a genetic advantage over whites. And, either way, it doesn't matter a damn. An individual can't be judged by his group mean.   12

If current biological determinism in the study of human intelligence rests upon no new facts (actually, no facts at all), then why has it become so popular of late? The answer must be social and political. The 1960s were good years for liberalism; a fair amount of money was spent on poverty programs and relatively little happened. Enter new leaders and new priorities. Why didn't the earlier programs work? Two possibilities are open: (1) we didn't spend enough money, we didn't make sufficiently creative efforts, or (and this makes any established leader jittery) we cannot solve these problems without a fundamental social and economic transformation of society; or (2) the programs failed because their recipients are inherently what they are—blaming the victims. Now, which alternative will be chosen by men in power in an age of retrenchment?   13

I have shown, I hope, that biological determinism is not simply an amusing matter for clever cocktail party comments about the human animal. It is a general notion with important philosophical implications and major political consequences. As John Stuart Mill wrote,[9] in a statement that should be the motto of the opposition: "Of all the vulgar modes of escaping from the consideration of the effect of social and moral influences upon the human mind, the most vulgar is that of attributing the diversities of conduct and character to inherent natural differences."   14

QUESTIONS

1. Gould has at least three strands to his argument: an argument with Jensen's methods and data, an argument based on the concluding sentences of paragraphs 13 and 14, and an interpretation of the motives for an argument like Jensen's. What are the main strands of Gould's argument?

---

[9] John Stuart Mill (1806–1873): British economist and philosopher, noted for his utilitarian views and his support for social and political reform. [Eds.]

2. Which strand of argument does Gould develop at greatest length? Why?

3. Which strand of argument do you find most convincing? Why?

4. If you have given different answers for questions 2 and 3, what do you make of that?

5. Gould says in paragraph 4 that Jensen presents no new data, in fact no reliable data at all. Do you find that to be so?

6. What do you think John Stuart Mill meant by *vulgar* in the quotation that ends Gould's essay? Would Jensen's experiment be an example of a "vulgar" method? Why or why not?

7. Taking the quotation from Mill (paragraph 14) as a starting point, write an essay that either defends or refutes Mill's idea.

8. Surely you know someone who seems either smarter or a lot less smart than he or she is generally taken to be. On what basis is that person commonly measured? On what basis do you evaluate her or him? Write a paper in which you reveal the "truth" as opposed to the more common interpretation of that person.

MAKING CONNECTIONS

1. There is a second argument by Gould in this section, "Evolution as Fact and Theory." Read it and trace what the two essays have in common. Does Gould use similar strategies of argument in both cases? Does he treat the opposition similarly? Does he give more convincing arguments for his own position in one case or the other? What do you make of the similarities and differences you find?

2. Compare the structure of Gould's argument to one or two others in this section, for example, Nathan Glazer's "Some Very Modest Proposals for the Improvement of American Education," Phillip Knightley's "The First Televised War," and James Baldwin's "If Black English Isn't a Language, Then Tell Me, What Is?" Choose one of these essays and describe the similarities and differences in handling an argument that you find between it and Gould's essay.

A MODEST PROPOSAL

Jonathan Swift

Jonathan Swift (1667–1745) was born in Dublin, Ireland, of English parents and educated in Irish schools. A graduate of Trinity College, Dublin, he received an M.A. from Oxford and was ordained a priest in the Church of England in 1695. He was active in politics as well as religion, becoming an editor and pamphlet writer for the Tory party in 1710. After becoming Dean of St. Patrick's Cathedral, Dublin, in 1713, he settled in Ireland and began to take an interest in the English economic exploitation of Ireland, gradually becoming a fierce Irish patriot. By 1724 the English were offering a reward for the discovery of the writer of the Drapier's Letters, *a series of pamphlets secretly written by Swift, attacking the British for their treatment of Ireland. In 1726 Swift produced the first volume of a more universal satire, known to modern readers as* Gulliver's Travels, *which has kept his name alive for two hundred and fifty years. A* Modest Proposal, *his best-known essay on Irish affairs, appeared in 1729. In 1742 he was found to be of unsound mind and three years later he died, leaving most of his estate for the founding of a hospital for the insane.*

A Modest Proposal
for Preventing the Children of Poor People in Ireland
from Being a Burden to Their Parents or Country,
and for Making Them Beneficial to the Public

It is a melancholy object to those who walk through this great town,[1] or travel in the country, when they see the streets, the roads and cabin-doors crowded with beggars of the female sex, followed by three, four, or six children, all in rags, and importuning every passenger for an alms. These mothers, instead of being able to work for their honest livelihood, are forced to employ all their time in strolling, to beg sustenance for their helpless infants, who, as they grow up, either turn thieves for want of work, or leave their dear na-

---

[1] this great town: Dublin. [Eds.]

tive country to fight for the Pretender in Spain,[2] or sell themselves to the Barbadoes.[3]

I think it is agreed by all parties that this prodigious number of children, in the arms, or on the backs, or at the heels of their mothers, and frequently of their fathers, is in the present deplorable state of the kingdom a very great additional grievance; and therefore whoever could find out a fair, cheap, and easy method of making these children sound and useful members of the commonwealth would deserve so well of the public as to have his statue set up for a preserver of the nation.

But my intention is very far from being confined to provide only for the children of professed beggars; it is of a much greater extent, and shall take in the whole number of infants at a certain age who are born of parents in effect as little able to support them as those who demand our charity in the streets.

As to my own part, having turned my thoughts for many years upon this important subject, and maturely weighed the several schemes of other projectors, I have always found them grossly mistaken in their computation. It is true a child just dropped from its dam may be supported by her milk for a solar year with little other nourishment, at most not above the value of two shillings,[4] which the mother may certainly get, or the value in scraps, by her lawful occupation of begging, and it is exactly at one year old that I propose to provide for them, in such a manner as, instead of being a charge upon their parents, or the parish, or wanting food and raiment for the rest of their lives, they shall, on the contrary, contribute to the feeding and partly to the clothing of many thousands.

There is likewise another great advantage to my scheme, that it will prevent those voluntary abortions, and that horrid practice of women murdering their bastard children, alas, too frequent among us, sacrificing the poor innocent babes, I doubt, more to avoid the expense than the shame, which would move tears and pity in the most savage and inhuman breast.

The number of souls in Ireland being usually reckoned one million and a half, of these I calculate there may be about two hundred thousand couples whose wives are breeders, from which number I subtract thirty thousand couples who are able to maintain their own children, although I apprehend there cannot be so many under the present distresses of the kingdom, but this being granted, there will remain an hundred and seventy thousand breeders. I again subtract fifty thousand for those women who miscarry, or whose children die by accident

---

[2] Pretender in Spain: the Catholic descendant of the British royal family (James I, Charles I, and Charles II) of Stuart. Exiled so that England could be governed by Protestant rulers, the Stuarts lurked in France and Spain, preparing various disastrous schemes for regaining the throne. [Eds.]

[3] sell themselves to the Barbadoes: sell themselves as indentured servants, a sort of temporary slavery, to the sugar merchants of the British Carribean islands. [Eds.]

[4] shillings: a shilling used to be worth about one day's labor. [Eds.]

or disease within the year. There only remain an hundred and twenty thousand children of poor parents annually born: the question therefore is, how this number shall be reared, and provided for, which as I have already said, under the present situation of affairs is utterly impossible by all the methods hitherto proposed, for we can neither employ them in handicraft or agriculture; we neither build houses (I mean in the country), nor cultivate land: they can very seldom pick up a livelihood by stealing until they arrive at six years old, except where they are of towardly parts, although I confess they learn the rudiments much earlier, during which time they can however be properly looked upon only as probationers, as I have been informed by a principal gentleman in the County of Cavan, who protested to me that he never knew above one or two instances under the age of six, even in a part of the kingdom so renowned for the quickest proficiency in that art.

I am assured by our merchants that a boy or girl before twelve years old, is 7 no saleable commodity, and even when they come to this age, they will not yield above three pounds, or three pounds and half-a-crown at most on the Exchange, which cannot turn to account either to the parents or the kingdom, the charge of nutriment and rags having been at least four times that value.

I shall now therefore humbly propose my own thoughts, which I hope will 8 not be liable to the least objection.

I have been assured by a very knowing American of my acquaintance in 9 London, that a young healthy child well nursed is at a year old a most delicious, nourishing and wholesome food, whether stewed, roasted, baked, or boiled, and I make no doubt that it will equally serve in a fricassee, or a ragout.

I do therefore humbly offer it to public consideration, that of the hundred 10 and twenty thousand children already computed, twenty thousand may be reserved for breed, whereof only one fourth part to be males, which is more than we allow to sheep, black-cattle, or swine, and my reason is that these children are seldom the fruits of marriage, a circumstance not much regarded by our savages, therefore one male will be sufficient to serve four females. That the remaining hundred thousand may at a year old be offered in sale to the persons of quality, and fortune, through the kingdom, always advising the mother to let them suck plentifully in the last month, so as to render them plump, and fat for a good table. A child will make two dishes at an entertainment for friends, and when the family dines alone, the fore or hind quarters will make a reasonable dish, and seasoned with a little pepper or salt will be very good boiled on the fourth day, especially in winter.

I have reckoned upon a medium, that a child just born will weigh twelve 11 pounds, and in a solar year if tolerably nursed increaseth to twenty-eight pounds.

I grant this food will be somewhat dear, and therefore very proper for 12 landlords, who, as they have already devoured most of the parents, seem to have the best title to the children.

701

Infant's flesh will be in season throughout the year, but more plentiful in   13
March, and a little before and after, for we are told by a grave author, an
eminent French physician,[5] that fish being a prolific diet, there are more
children born in Roman Catholic countries about nine months after Lent than
at any other season; therefore reckoning a year after Lent, the markets will be
more glutted than usual, because the number of Popish infants is at least three
to one in this kingdom, and therefore it will have one other collateral advantage
by lessening the number of Papists among us.

I have already computed the charge of nursing a beggar's child (in which list   14
I reckon all cottagers, labourers, and four-fifths of the farmers) to be about two
shillings *per annum*, rags included, and I believe no gentleman would repine
to give ten shillings for the carcass of a good fat child, which, as I have said,
will make four dishes of excellent nutritive meat, when he hath only some
particular friend of his own family to dine with him. Thus the Squire will learn
to be a good landlord and grow popular among his tenants, the mother will
have eight shillings net profit, and be fit for work until she produces another
child.

Those who are more thrifty (as I must confess the times require) may flay   15
the carcass; the skin of which artificially dressed, will make admirable gloves
for ladies, and summer boots for fine gentlemen.

As to our city of Dublin, shambles[6] may be appointed for this purpose, in   16
the most convenient parts of it, and butchers we may be assured will not be
wanting, although I rather recommend buying the children alive, and dressing
them hot from the knife, as we do roasting pigs.

A very worthy person, a true lover of his country, and whose virtues I highly   17
esteem was lately pleased, in discoursing on this matter to offer a refinement
upon my scheme. He said that many gentlemen of this kingdom, having of
late destroyed their deer, he conceived that the want of venison might be well
supplied by the bodies of young lads and maidens, not exceeding fourteen years
of age, nor under twelve, so great a number of both sexes in every county being
now ready to starve, for want of work and service: and these to be disposed of
by their parents if alive, or otherwise by their nearest relations. But with due
deference to so excellent a friend, and so deserving a patriot, I cannot be
altogether in his sentiments. For as to the males, my American acquaintance
assured me from frequent experience that their flesh was generally tough and
lean, like that of our schoolboys, by continual exercise, and their taste disagreeable, and to fatten them would not answer the charge. Then as to the females,
it would, I think with humble submission, be a loss to the public, because they

---

[5] French physician: François Rabelais (1494?–1553), physician and satirist known for his *Gar-
gantua and Pantagruel*. [Eds.]
[6] shambles: slaughterhouses. [Eds.]

soon would become breeders themselves: and besides, it is not improbable that some scrupulous people might be apt to censure such a practice (although indeed very unjustly) as a little bordering upon cruelty, which I confess, hath always been with me the strongest objection against any project, howsoever well intended.

But in order to justify my friend, he confessed that this expedient was put 18 into his head by the famous Psalmanazar, a native of the island Formosa, who came from thence to London, above twenty years ago, and in conversation told my friend that in his country when any young person happened to be put to death, the executioner sold the carcass to persons of quality, as a prime dainty, and that, in his time, the body of a plump girl of fifteen, who was crucified for an attempt to poison the emperor, was sold to his Imperial Majesty's Prime Minister of State, and other great Mandarins of the Court, in joints from the gibbet, at four hundred crowns. Neither indeed can I deny that if the same use were made of several plump young girls in this town who, without one single groat to their fortunes, cannot stir abroad without a chair, and appear at the playhouse and assemblies in foreign fineries, which they never will pay for, the kingdom would not be the worse.

Some persons of a desponding spirit are in great concern about that vast 19 number of poor people, who are aged, diseased, or maimed, and I have been desired to employ my thoughts what course may be taken to ease the nation of so grievous an encumbrance. But I am not in the least pain upon that matter, because it is very well known that they are every day dying, and rotting, by cold, and famine, and filth, and vermin, as fast as can be reasonably expected. And as to the younger labourers they are now in almost as hopeful a condition. They cannot get work, and consequently pine away from want of nourishment, to a degree that if at any time they are accidentally hired to common labour, they have not strength to perform it; and thus the country and themselves are in a fair way of being soon delivered from the evils to come.

I have too long digressed, and therefore shall return to my subject. I think 20 the advantages by the proposal which I have made are obvious and many, as well as of the highest importance.

For first, as I have already observed, it would greatly lessen the number of 21 Papists, with whom we are yearly over-run, being the principal breeders of the nation, as well as our most dangerous enemies, and who stay at home on purpose with a design to deliver the kingdom to the Pretender, hoping to take their advantage by the absence of so many good Protestants, who have chosen rather to leave their country than stay at home and pay tithes against their conscience to an idolatrous Episcopal curate.

Secondly, the poorer tenants will have something valuable of their own, 22 which by law may be made liable to distress, and help to pay their landlord's rent, their corn and cattle being already seized, and money a thing unknown.

Thirdly, whereas the maintenance of an hundred thousand children, from 23
two years old, and upwards, cannot be computed at less than ten shillings a
piece *per annum*, the nation's stock will be thereby increased fifty thousand
pounds *per annum*, besides the profit of a new dish, introduced to the tables of
all gentlemen of fortune in the kingdom, who have any refinement in taste,
and the money will circulate among ourselves, the goods being entirely of our
own growth and manufacture.

Fourthly, the constant breeders, besides the gain of eight shillings sterling 24
per annum, by the sale of their children, will be rid of the charge of maintaining
them after the first year.

Fifthly, this food would likewise bring great custom to taverns, where the 25
vintners will certainly be so prudent as to procure the best receipts for dressing
it to perfection, and consequently have their houses frequented by all the fine
gentlemen, who justly value themselves upon their knowledge in good eating;
and a skilful cook, who understands how to oblige his guests, will contrive to
make it as expensive as they please.

Sixthly, this would be a great inducement to marriage, which all wise nations 26
have either encouraged by rewards, or enforced by laws and penalties. It would
increase the care and tenderness of mothers towards their children, when they
were sure of a settlement for life, to the poor babes, provided in some sort by
the public to their annual profit instead of expense. We should soon see an
honest emulation among the married women, which of them could bring the
fattest child to the market. Men would become as fond of their wives, during
the time of their pregnancy, as they are now of their mares in foal, their cows
in calf, or sows when they are ready to farrow, nor offer to beat or kick them
(as it is too frequent a practice) for fear of a miscarriage.

Many other advantages might be enumerated. For instance, the addition of 27
some thousand carcasses in our exportation of barrelled beef; the propagation
of swine's flesh, and improvement in the art of making good bacon, so much
wanted among us by the great destruction of pigs, too frequent at our tables,
are no way comparable in taste or magnificence to a well-grown, fat yearling
child, which roasted whole will make a considerable figure at a Lord Mayor's
feast, or any other public entertainment. But this and many others I omit, being
studious of brevity.

Supposing that one thousand families in this city would be constant custom- 28
ers for infants' flesh, besides others who might have it at merry meetings,
particularly weddings and christenings; I compute that Dublin would take off
annually about twenty thousand carcasses, and the rest of the kingdom (where
probably they will be sold somewhat cheaper) the remaining eighty thousand.

I can think of no one objection that will possibly be raised against this 29
proposal, unless it should be urged that the number of people will be thereby
must lessened in the kingdom. This I freely own, and it was indeed one principal

design in offering it to the world. I desire the reader will observe, that I calculate my remedy *for this one individual Kingdom of* Ireland, *and for no other that ever was, is, or, I think, ever can be upon earth.* Therefore let no man talk to me of other expedients: *Of taxing our absentees at five shillings a pound: Of using neither clothes, nor household furniture, except what is of our own growth and manufacture: Of utterly rejecting the materials and instruments that promote foreign luxury: Of curing the expensiveness of pride, vanity, idleness, and gaming in our women: Of introducing a vein of parsimony, prudence, and temperance: Of learning to love our country, wherein we differ even from* Laplanders, *and the inhabitants of* Topinamboo: *Of quitting our animosities and factions, nor act any longer like the* Jews, *who were murdering one another at the very moment their city was taken: Of being a little cautious not to sell our country and consciences for nothing: Of teaching landlords to have at least one degree of mercy towards their tenants. Lastly, of putting a spirit of honesty, industry, and skill into our shopkeepers, who, if a resolution could now be taken to buy only our native goods, would immediately unite to cheat and exact upon us in the price, the measure and the goodness, nor could ever yet be brought to make one fair proposal of just dealing, though often and earnestly invited to it.*

Therefore I repeat, let no man talk to me of these and the like expedients, till he hath at least a glimpse of hope that there will ever be some hearty and sincere attempt to put them in practice. | 30

But as to myself, having been wearied out for many years with offering vain, idle, visionary thoughts, and at length utterly despairing of success, I fortunately fell upon this proposal, which as it is wholly new, so it hath something solid and real, of no expense and little trouble, full in our own power, and whereby we can incur no danger in disobliging England. For this kind of commodity will not bear exportation, the flesh being of too tender a consistence to admit a long continuance in salt, *although perhaps I could name a country which would be glad to eat up our whole nation without it.* | 31

After all I am not so violently bent upon my own opinion as to reject any offer, proposed by wise men, which shall be found equally innocent, cheap, easy and effectual. But before some thing of that kind shall be advanced in contradiction to my scheme, and offering a better, I desire the author, or authors, will be pleased maturely to consider two points. First, as things now stand, how they will be able to find food and raiment for a hundred thousand useless mouths and backs? And secondly, there being a round million of creatures in human figure, throughout this kingdom, whose whole subsistence put into a common stock would leave them in debt two millions of pounds sterling; adding those who are beggars by profession, to the bulk of farmers, cottagers, and laborers with their wives and children, who are beggars in effect; I desire those politicians who dislike my overture, and may perhaps be so bold to attempt an answer, that they will first ask the parents of these mortals whether they would | 32 not at this day think it a great happiness to have been sold for food at a year old, in the manner I prescribe, and thereby have avoided such a perpetual scene of misfortunes as they have since gone through, by the oppression of landlords, the impossibility of paying rent without money or trade, the want of common sustenance, with neither house nor clothes to cover them from the inclemencies of weather, and the most inevitable prospect of entailing the like, or greater miseries upon their breed for ever.

I profess in the sincerity of my heart that I have not the least personal interest   33
in endeavoring to promote this necessary work, having no other motive than the *public good of my country, by advancing our trade, providing for infants, relieving the poor, and giving some pleasure to the rich.* I have no children by which I can propose to get a single penny; the youngest being nine years old, and my wife past child-bearing.

QUESTIONS

1. A proposal always involves a proposer. What is the character of the proposer here? Do we perceive his character to be the same throughout the essay? Compare, for example, paragraphs 21, 26, and 33.

2. When does the proposer actually offer his proposal? What does he do before making his proposal? What does he do after making his proposal? How does the order in which he does things affect our impression of him and of his proposal?

3. What kind of counterarguments to his own proposal does this proposer anticipate? How does he answer and refute proposals that might be considered alternatives to his?

4. In reading this essay, most persons are quite certain that the author, Swift, does not himself endorse the proposer's proposal. How do we distinguish the two of them? What details of style help us make this distinction?

5. Consider the proposer, the counterarguments the proposer acknowledges and refutes, and Swift himself, who presumably does not endorse the proposer's proposal. To what extent is Swift's position essentially that which his proposer refutes? To what extent is it a somewhat different position still?

6. To what extent does an ironic essay like this depend upon the author and reader sharing certain values without question or reservation? Can you discover any such values explicitly or implicitly present in Swift's essay?

7. Use Swift's technique to write a "modest proposal" of your own about some contemporary situation. That is, use some outlandish proposal as a way of drawing attention to a situation that needs correcting. Consider carefully the character you intend to project for your proposer and the way you intend to make your own view distinguishable from hers or his.

A MODEST PROPOSAL

MAKING CONNECTIONS

1. By calling his essay "Some Very Modest Proposals . . . ," Nathan Glazer strikes a relation to Swift and announces that his essay will be somewhat like Swift's. How much of a relation do you find between the two essays? Where is Glazer most like Swift? What does he gain from that association?

2. Another ironic essay in this collection is Horace Miner's "Body Ritual of the Nacerima," in "Reporting." How similar is it to Swift's essay? How different? Consider especially your sense of the person doing the reporting. Do you find any reason to connect Miner's reporter with Swift's proposer?

THE DECLARATION OF INDEPENDENCE

Thomas Jefferson

Thomas Jefferson (1743–1826) was born in Shadwell, Virginia, attended William and Mary College, and became a lawyer. He was elected to the Virginia House of Burgesses in 1769 and was a delegate to the Continental Congress in 1776. When the Congress voted in favor of Richard Henry Lee's resolution that the colonies "ought to be free and independent states," a committee of five members, including John Adams, Benjamin Franklin, and Jefferson, was appointed to draw up a declaration. Jefferson, because of his eloquence as a writer, was asked by this committee to draw up a first draft. Jefferson's text, with a few changes suggested by Franklin and Adams, was presented to the Congress. After a debate in which further changes were made, including striking out a passage condemning the slave trade, the Declaration was approved on the fourth of July, 1776. Jefferson said of it: "Neither aiming at originality of principles or sentiments, nor yet copied from any particular and previous writing, it was intended to be an expression of the American mind."

In Congress, July 4, 1776
The unanimous Declaration of the
thirteen united States of America

When in the Course of human events it becomes necessary for one people 1
to dissolve the political bands which have connected them with another, and to assume among the powers of the earth, the separate and equal station to which the Laws of Nature and of Nature's God entitle them, a decent respect to the opinions of mankind requires that they should declare the causes which impel them to the separation.

We hold these truths to be self-evident, that all men are created equal, that 2
they are endowed by their Creator with certain unalienable Rights, that among these are Life, Liberty and the pursuit of Happiness. That to secure these rights, Governments are instituted among Men, deriving their just powers from the consent of the governed. That whenever any Form of Government becomes destructive of these ends, it is the Right of the People to alter or to abolish it,

and to institute new Government, laying its foundation on such principles and organizing its powers in such form, as to them shall seem most likely to affect their Safety and Happiness. Prudence, indeed, will dictate that Governments long established should not be changed for light and transient causes; and accordingly all experience hath shewn that mankind are more disposed to suffer, while evils are sufferable, than to right themselves by abolishing the forms to which they are accustomed. But when a long train of abuses and usurpations, pursuing invariably the same Object evinces a design to reduce them under absolute Despotism, it is their right, it is their duty, to throw off such Government, and to provide new Guards for their future security. Such has been the patient sufferance of these Colonies; and such is now the necessity which constrains them to alter their former Systems of Government. The history of the present King of Great Britain is a history of repeated injuries and usurpations, all having in direct object the establishment of an absolute Tyranny over these States. To prove this, let Facts be submitted to a candid world.

He has refused his Assent to Laws, the most wholesome and necessary for the public good. 3

He has forbidden his Governors to pass laws of immediate and pressing importance, unless suspended in their operation till his Assent should be obtained; and when so suspended, he has utterly neglected to attend to them. 4

He has refused to pass other Laws for the accommodation of large districts of people, unless those people would relinquish the right of Representation in the Legislature, a right inestimable to them and formidable to tyrants only. 5

He has called together legislative bodies at places unusual, uncomfortable, and distant from the depository of their Public Records, for the sole purpose of fatiguing them into compliance with his measures. 6

He has dissolved Representative Houses repeatedly, for opposing with manly firmness his invasions on the rights of the people. 7

He has refused for a long time, after such dissolutions, to cause others to be elected; whereby the Legislative Powers, incapable of Annihilation, have returned to the People at large for their exercise; the State remaining in the mean time exposed to all the dangers of invasion from without, and convulsions within. 8

He has endeavored to prevent the population of these States; for that purpose obstructing the Laws for Naturalization of Foreigners; refusing to pass others to encourage their migration hither, and raising the conditions of new Appropriations of Lands. 9

He has obstructed the Administration of Justice, by refusing his Assent to Laws for Establishing Judiciary Powers. 10

He has made Judges dependent on his Will alone, for the tenure of their offices, and the amount and payment of their salaries. 11

He has erected a multitude of New Offices, and sent hither swarms of Officers to harass our people, and eat out their substance. 12

He has kept among us, in times of peace, Standing Armies without the   13
Consent of our legislatures.

He has affected to render the Military independent of and superior to the   14
Civil Power.

He has combined with others to subject us to a jurisdiction foreign to our   15
constitution, and unacknowledged by our laws; giving his Assent to the Acts of
pretended Legislation: For quartering large bodies of armed troops among us:
For protecting them, by a mock Trial, from punishment for any Murders which
they should commit on the Inhabitants of these States: For cutting off our Trade
with all parts of the world: For imposing Taxes on us without our Consent: For
depriving us in many cases, of the benefits of Trial by Jury: For Transporting
us beyond Seas to be tried for pretended offenses: for abolishing the free System
of English Laws in a neighboring Province, establishing therein an Arbitrary
government, and enlarging its Boundaries so as to render it at once an example
and fit instrument for introducing the same absolute rule into these Colonies:
For taking away our Charters, abolishing our most valuable Laws and altering
fundamentally the Forms of our Governments: For suspending our own Legislatures, and declaring themselves invested with power to legislate for us in all
cases whatsoever.

He has abdicated Government here, by declaring us out of his Protection   16
and waging War against us.

He has plundered our seas, ravaged our Coasts, burnt our towns, and   17
destroyed the lives of our people.

He is at this time transporting large Armies of foreign Mercenaries to com-   18
plete the works of death, desolation and tyranny, already begun with circumstances of Cruelty & Perfidy scarcely paralleled in the most barbarous ages, and
totally unworthy the Head of a civilized nation.

He has constrained our fellow Citizens taken Captive on the high Seas to   19
bear Arms against their Country, to become the executioners of their friends
and Brethren, or to fall themselves by their Hands.

He has excited domestic insurrections amongst us, and has endeavored to   20
bring on the inhabitants of our frontiers, the merciless Indian Savages, whose
known rule of warfare, is an undistingushed destruction of all ages, sexes, and
conditions.

In every stage of these Oppressions We have Petitioned for Redress in the   21
most humble terms: Our repeated petitions have been answered only by repeated
injury. A Prince, whose character is thus marked by every act which may define
a Tyrant, is unfit to be the ruler of a free people.

Nor have we been wanting in attention to our British brethren. We have   22
warned them from time to time of attempts by their legislature to extend an
unwarrantable jurisdiction over us. We have reminded them of the circumstances of our emigration and settlement here. We have appealed to their native
justice and magnanimity, and we have conjured them by the ties of our common

kindred to disavow these usurpations, which would inevitably interrupt our connections and correspondence. They too have been deaf to the voice of justice and of consanguinity. We must, therefore, acquiesce in the necessity, which denounces our Separation, and hold them, as we hold the rest of mankind, Enemies in War, in Peace Friends.

We, THEREFORE, the Representatives of the UNITED STATES OF AMERICA, in   23
General Congress, Assembled, appealing to the Supreme Judge of the world for the rectitude of our intentions, do, in the Name, and by Authority of the good People of these Colonies, solemnly publish and declare, That these United Colonies are, and of Right ought to be FREE AND INDEPENDENT STATES; that they are Absolved from all Allegiance to the British Crown, and that all political connection between them and the State of Great Britain, is and ought to be totally dissolved; and that as Free and Independent States; they have full Power to levy War, conclude Peace, contract Alliances, establish Commerce, and to do all the Acts and Things which Independent States may of right do. And for the support of this Declaration, with a firm reliance on the protection of Divine Providence, we mutually pledge to each other our Lives, our Fortunes, and our sacred Honor.

QUESTIONS

1. The Declaration of Independence is frequently cited as a classic deductive argu-ment. A deductive argument is based on a general statement, or premise, that is assumed to be true. What does this document assume that the American colonists are entitled to and on what basis? Look at the reasoning in paragraph 2. What are these truths that are considered self-evident? What does *self-evident* mean?

2. What accusations against the king of Great Britain are the facts presented meant to substantiate? If you were the British king presented with this document, how might you reply to it? Would you first attack its premise or reply to its accusations? Or would you do both? (How did George III respond?)

3. To what extent is the audience of the Declaration intended to be the king and people of Great Britain?

4. What other audiences were intended for this document? Define at least two other audiences, and describe how each might be expected to respond.

5. Although this declaration could have been expected to lead to war and all the horrors thereof, it is a most civilized document, showing great respect throughout for certain standards of civility among people and among nations. Try to define the civilized standards the declaration assumes. Write an essay that tries to identify and characterize the nature and variety of those expectations.

6. Write a declaration of your own, announcing your separation from some injurious situation (an incompatible roommate, a noisy sorority or fraternity house, an awful job, or whatever). Start with a premise, give reasons to substantiate it, provide facts that illustrate the injurious conditions, and conclude with a statement of what your new condition will mean to you and to other oppressed people.

MAKING CONNECTIONS

1. If Jefferson's declaration is a classic deductive argument, as the first question above suggests, Alice Walker's "Am I Blue?" might stand as a clear example of inductive arguing. Review the structure of her argument. Where does she express her thesis most precisely? Why does she not announce it more quickly? What would the Declaration look like if Jefferson were to have approached it inductively? Write an inductive version of the Declaration of Independence.

2. What if Jefferson, rather than writing the Declaration of Independence, had, instead, offered "a modest proposal" to the British king? What do you suppose he would have said? How would he have formulated his argument? Write your own "modest proposal" to the king, addressing him in the manner of Swift, more or less, but drawing on the evidence Jefferson provides in the Declaration.

REVIEW OF STANLEY MILGRAM'S EXPERIMENTS ON OBEDIENCE

Diana Baumrind

Diana Baumrind (b. 1927) is a developmental and clinical psychologist with the Institute of Human Development at the University of California at Berkeley. Her research specializations are "the effects of family socialization on the development of social responsibility and personal agency in children and adolescents" and "the ethics of research with human subjects." That last subject is her topic here as she discusses the experiment conducted by Stanley Milgram (pages 437–459). Her article appeared originally in 1964 in American Psychologist, *the journal of the American Psychological Association.*

Certain problems in psychological research require the experimenter to balance his career and scientific interests against the interests of his prospective subjects. When such occasions arise the experimenter's stated objective frequently is to do the best possible job with the least possible harm to his subjects. The experimenter seldom perceives in more positive terms an indebtedness to the subject for his services, perhaps because the detachment which his functions require prevents appreciation of the subject as an individual. 1

Yet a debt does exist, even when the subject's reason for volunteering includes course credit or monetary gain. Often a subject participates unwillingly in order to satisfy a course requirement. These requirements are of questionable merit ethically, and do not alter the experimenter's responsibility to the subject. 2

Most experimental conditions do not cause the subjects pain or indignity, and are sufficiently interesting or challenging to present no problem of an ethical nature to the experimenter. But where the experimental conditions expose the subject to loss of dignity, or offer him nothing of value, then the experimenter is obliged to consider the reasons why the subject volunteered and to reward him accordingly. 3

The subject's public motives for volunteering include having an enjoyable or stimulating experience, acquiring knowledge, doing the experimenter a favor which may some day be reciprocated, and making a contribution to science. These motives can be taken into account rather easily by the experimenter who is willing to spend a few minutes with the subject afterwards to thank him for 4 his participation, answer his questions, reassure him that he did well, and chat with him a bit. Most volunteers also have less manifest, but equally legitimate, motives. A subject may be seeking an opportunity to have contact with, be noticed by, and perhaps confide in a person with psychological training. The dependent attitude of most subjects toward the experimenter is an artifact of the experimental situation as well as an expression of some subjects' personal need systems at the time they volunteer.

The dependent, obedient attitude assumed by most subjects in the experimental setting is appropriate to that situation. The "game" is defined by the experimenter and he makes the rules. By volunteering, the subject agrees implicitly to assume a posture of trust and obedience. While the experimental conditions leave him exposed, the subject has the right to assume that his security and self-esteem will be protected.

There are other professional situations in which one member—the patient or client—expects help and protection from the other—the physician or psychologist. But the interpersonal relationship between experimenter and subject additionally has unique features which are likely to provoke initial anxiety in the subject. The laboratory is unfamiliar as a setting and the rules of behavior ambiguous compared to a clinician's office. Because of the anxiety and passivity generated by the setting, the subject is more prone to behave in an obedient, suggestible manner in the laboratory than elsewhere. Therefore, the laboratory is not the place to study degree of obedience or suggestibility, as a function of a particular experimental condition, since the base line for these phenomena as found in the laboratory is probably much higher than in most other settings. Thus experiments in which the relationship to the experimenter as an authority is used as an independent condition are imperfectly designed for the same reason that they are prone to injure the subjects involved. They disregard the special quality of trust and obedience with which the subject appropriately regards the experimenter.

Other phenomena which present ethical decisions, unlike those mentioned above, *can* be reproduced successfully in the laboratory. Failure experience, conformity to peer judgment, and isolation are among such phenomena. In these cases we can expect the experimenter to take whatever measures are necessary to prevent the subject from leaving the laboratory more humiliated, insecure, alienated, or hostile than when he arrived. To guarantee that an especially sensitive subject leaves a stressful experimental experience in the proper state sometimes requires special clinical training. But usually an attitude of compassion, respect, gratitude, and common sense will suffice, and no amount of clinical training will substitute. The subject has the right to expect that the psychologist with whom he is interacting has some concern for his welfare, and the personal attributes and professional skill to express his good will effectively.

Unfortunately, the subject is not always treated with the respect he deserves. It has become more commonplace in sociopsychological laboratory studies to manipulate, embarrass, and discomfort subjects. At times the insult to the subject's sensibilities extends to the journal reader when the results are reported. Milgram's (1963) study is a case in point. The following is Milgram's abstract of his experiment: 8

> This article describes a procedure for the study of destructive obedience in the laboratory. It consists of ordering a naïve S to administer increasingly more severe punishment to a victim in the context of a learning experiment. Punishment is administered by means of a shock generator with 30 graded switches ranging from Slight Shock to Danger: Severe Shock. The victim is a confederate of E.[1] The primary dependent variable is the maximum shock the S is willing to administer before he refuses to continue further.[2] 26 Ss obeyed the experimental commands fully, and administered the highest shock on the generator. 14 Ss broke off the experiment at some point after the victim protested and refused to provide further answers. The procedure created extreme levels of nervous tension in some Ss. Profuse sweating, trembling, and stuttering were typical expressions of this emotional disturbance. One unexpected sign of tension—yet to be explained—was the regular occurrence of nervous laughter, which in some Ss developed into uncontrollable seizures. The variety of interesting behavioral dynamics observed in the experiment, the reality of the situation for the S, and the possibility of parametric variation within the framework of the procedure,[3] point to the fruitfulness of further study [p. 371].

The detached, objective manner in which Milgram reports the emotional disturbance suffered by his subjects contrasts sharply with his graphic account of that disturbance. Following are two other quotes describing the effects on his subjects of the experimental conditions: 9

> I observed a mature and initially poised businessman enter the laboratory smiling and confident. Within 20 minutes he was reduced to a twitching, stuttering wreck, who was rapidly approaching a point of nervous collapse. He constantly pulled on his earlobe, and twisted his hands. At one point he pushed his fist into his forehead and muttered: "Oh God, let's stop it." And yet he continued to respond to every word of the experimenter, and obeyed to the end [p. 377].

> In a large number of cases the degree of tension reached extremes that are rarely seen in sociopsychological laboratory studies. Subjects were observed to sweat, tremble, stutter, bite their lips, groan, and dig their fingernails into their flesh. These were characteristic rather than exceptional responses to the experiment.

---

[1] S: stands for subject; E: stands for experimenter. [Eds.]

[2] dependent variable: that which changes as a result of other changes made in the experiment. [Eds.]

[3] parametric variation: statistical term suggesting variables within the experiment that would influence the results and so leave some questions unanswered. [Eds.]

One sign of tension was the regular occurrence of nervous laughing fits. Fourteen of the 40 subjects showed definite signs of nervous laughter and smiling. The laughter seemed entirely out of place, even bizarre. Full-blown, uncontrollable seizures were observed for 3 subjects. On one occasion we observed a seizure so violently convulsive that it was necessary to call a halt to the experiment . . . [p. 375].

Milgram does state that,

After the interview, procedures were undertaken to assure that the subject would leave the laboratory in a state of well being. A friendly reconciliation was arranged between the subject and the victim, and an effort was made to reduce any tensions that arose as a result of the experiment [p. 374].

It would be interesting to know what sort of procedures could dissipate the type of emotional disturbance just described. In view of the effects on subjects, traumatic to a degree which Milgram himself considers nearly unprecedented in sociopsychological experiments, his casual assurance that these tensions were dissipated before the subject left the laboratory is unconvincing.

What could be the rational basis for such a posture of indifference? Perhaps   10
Milgram supplies the answer himself when he partially explains the subject's destructive obedience as follows, "Thus they assume that the discomfort caused the victim is momentary, while the scientific gains resulting from the experiment are enduring [p. 378]." Indeed such a rationale might suffice to justify the means used to achieve his end if that end were of inestimable value to humanity or were not itself transformed by the means by which it was attained.

The behavioral psychologist is not in as good a position to objectify his faith   11
in the significance of his work as medical colleagues at points of breakthrough. His experimental situations are not sufficiently accurate models of real-life experience; his sampling techniques are seldom of a scope which would justify the meaning with which he would like to endow his results; and these results are hard to reproduce by colleagues with opposing theoretical views. Unlike the Sabin vaccine,[4] for example, the concrete benefit to humanity of his particular piece of work, no matter how competently handled, cannot justify the risk that real harm will be done to the subject. I am not speaking of physical discomfort, inconvenience, or experimental deception per se, but of permanent harm, however slight. I do regard the emotional disturbance described by Milgram as potentially harmful because it could easily effect an alteration in the subject's self-image or ability to trust adult authorities in the future. It is potentially harmful to a subject to commit, in the course of an experiment, acts which he himself considers unworthy, particularly when he has been entrapped into committing such acts by an individual he has reason to trust. The subject's

---

[4] Sabin vaccine: an oral vaccine against polio, developed by Albert Bruce Sabin (b. 1906), Polish-born American physician and microbiologist. [Eds.]

personal responsibility for his actions is not erased because the experimenter reveals to him the means which he used to stimulate these actions. The subject realizes that he would have hurt the victim if the current were on. The realization that he also made a fool of himself by accepting the experimental set results in additional loss of self-esteem. Moreover, the subject finds it difficult to express his anger outwardly after the experimenter in a self-acceptant but friendly manner reveals the hoax.

A fairly intense corrective interpersonal experience is indicated wherein the subject admits and accepts his responsibility for his own actions, and at the same time gives vent to his hurt and anger at being fooled. Perhaps an experience as distressing as the one described by Milgram can be integrated by the subject,[5] provided that careful thought is given to the matter. The propriety of such experimentation is still in question even if such a reparational experience were forthcoming. Without it I would expect a naive, sensitive subject to remain deeply hurt and anxious for some time, and a sophisticated, cynical subject to become even more alienated and distrustful. `12`

In addition the experimental procedure used by Milgram does not appear suited to the objectives of the study because it does not take into account the special quality of the set which the subject has in the experimental situation. Milgram is concerned with a very important problem, namely, the social consequences of destructive obedience. He says, `13`

> Gas chambers were built, death camps were guarded, daily quotas of corpses were produced with the same efficiency as the manufacture of appliances. These inhumane policies may have originated in the mind of a single person, but they could only be carried out on a massive scale if a very large number of persons obeyed orders [p. 371].

But the parallel between authority-subordinate relationships in Hitler's Germany and in Milgram's laboratory is unclear. In the former situation the SS man or member of the German Officer Corps, when obeying orders to slaughter, had no reason to think of his superior officer as benignly disposed towards himself or their victims. The victims were perceived as subhuman and not worthy of consideration. The subordinate officer was an agent in a great cause. He did not need to feel guilt or conflict because within his frame of reference he was acting rightly.

It is obvious from Milgram's own descriptions that most of his subjects were concerned about their victims and did trust the experimenter, and that their distressful conflict was generated in part by the consequences of these two disparate but appropriate attitudes. Their distress may have resulted from shock at what the experimenter was doing to them as well as from what they thought `14`

---

[5] integrated: a technical term in psychology suggesting the process by which we adjust to and incorporate traumatic experience. [Eds.]

they were doing to their victims. In any case there is not a convincing parallel between the phenomena studied by Milgram and destructive obedience as that concept would apply to the subordinate-authority relationship demonstrated in Hitler's Germany. If the experiments were conducted "outside of New Haven and without any visible ties to the university," I would still question their validity on similar although not identical grounds. In addition, I would question the representativeness of a sample of subjects who would voluntarily participate within a noninstitutional setting.

In summary, the experimental objectives of the psychologist are seldom incompatible with the subject's ongoing state of well being, provided that the experimenter is willing to take the subject's motives and interests into consideration when planning his methods and correctives. Section 4b in *Ethical Standards of Psychologists* (American Psychological Association, undated) reads in part: 15

> Only when a problem is significant and can be investigated in no other way, is the psychologist justified in exposing human subjects to emotional stress or other possible harm. In conducting such research, the psychologist must seriously consider the possibility of harmful aftereffects, and should be prepared to remove them as soon as permitted by the design of the experiment. Where the danger of serious aftereffects exists, research should be conducted only when the subjects or their responsible agents are fully informed of this possibility and volunteer nevertheless [p. 12].

From the subject's point of view procedures which involve loss of dignity, self-esteem, and trust in rational authority are probably most harmful in the long run and require the most thoughtfully planned reparations, if engaged in at all. The public image of psychology as a profession is highly related to our own actions, and some of these actions are changeworthy. It is important that as research psychologists we protect our ethical sensibilities rather than adapt our personal standards to include as appropriate the kind of indignities to which Milgram's subjects were exposed. I would not like to see experiments such as Milgram's proceed unless the subjects were fully informed of the dangers of serious aftereffects and his correctives were clearly shown to be effective in restoring their state of well being.

REFERENCES

AMERICAN PSYCHOLOGICAL ASSOCIATION.
Ethical Standards of Psychologists: A summary of ethical principles. Washington, D.C.: APA, undated.
MILGRAM, S.
Behavorial study of obedience. *J. abnorm. soc. Psychol.*, 1963, 67, 371–378.

QUESTIONS

1. Baumrind challenges Milgram's experiment on two grounds. Distinguish and summarize the two.

2. Baumrind speaks generally for a couple of pages before even mentioning the Milgram experiment. Why do you think she introduces her argument this way? Are there moments during this opening when the Milgram experiment is very much in mind, even without being mentioned?

3. What do you make of Baumrind's claim that "the laboratory is not the place to study degree of obedience or suggestibility" (paragraph 6)? Do Baumrind's reasons successfully undercut Milgram, or has he anticipated that worry?

4. At the end of her article, Baumrind challenges the applicability of Milgram's experiment to events in Hitler's Germany. Does Baumrind represent Milgram's thinking fairly? Do you agree with her that the application does not work? Explain your views.

5. Study Milgram's abstract, quoted by Baumrind in paragraph 8. How do you understand its next-to-last sentence? Do you really find the "nervous laughter" unexplained?

6. See whether your school has a policy about the use of human subjects in experiments. Assuming it has, and that its standards are available to the public, get a copy of them. After studying them, write a paper either supporting them or arguing for their amendment.

7. Have you ever been coerced by a situation to mistreat another person, or have you witnessed such mistreatment? Write an analysis of that situation as you remember it. Try to explain the degree to which the situation itself seemed to elicit the questionable behavior. How do you weigh individual responsibility against institutional or group responsibility in this instance?

MAKING CONNECTIONS

1. Since Milgram's professed aims included the question of why people obeyed their leaders in Nazi Germany as they did, read Robert Jay Lifton's essay, "What Made This Man? Mengele," and ask whether the Milgram experiment does help answer that question. How does Baumrind's criticism of Milgram contribute to the same question?

2. The ethical points Baumrind raises have certain connections with issues of animal rights addressed in: "Just Like Us: A Forum on Animal Rights," by Arthur Caplan et al. and Frederick A. King's "Animals in Research: The Case for Experimentation." What connections do you find among these selections? To what extent is Baumrind addressing something quite different?

JUST LIKE US:
A FORUM ON ANIMAL RIGHTS

Arthur Caplan, Gary Francione, Roger Goldman, Ingrid Newkirk

This discussion of animal rights was held at the Cooper Union for the Advancement of Science and Art, in New York City. The participants approach the subject from a variety of viewpoints. Arthur Caplan is the director of the Center for Biomedical Ethics at the University of Minnesota. Gary Francione is a professor at the University of Pennsylvania Law School and frequently litigates animal rights cases. Roger Goldman is a constitutional law scholar and professor at St. Louis University School of Law. Ingrid Newkirk is the national director of People for the Ethical Treatment of Animals, in Washington. The forum was moderated by Jack Hitt, a senior editor at Harper's Magazine. *The participants debate what qualities determine a right to life. They raise the question of what the proper relationship between humans and animals should be: Do animals have the same rights as humans? During the discussion they seek to expose the assumptions which underlie their opponents' arguments.*

The relationship of man to animal has long been one of sympathy, manifested in such welfare organizations as the kindly Bide-A-Wee or the avuncular ASPCA. In the last few years, the politics of that relationship have been questioned by a number of new and vociferous interest groups which hold to the credo that animals are endowed with certain inalienable rights. 1

Typically, when animal rights advocates are called upon by the media to defend their views, they are seated across the table from research scientists. The discussion turns on the treatment of laboratory animals or the illegal efforts of fanatics who smuggle animals out of research facilities via latter-day underground railroads to freedom. 2

Behind these easy headlines, however, stand serious philosophical questions: How should we treat animals? Why do humans have rights and other animals not? If animals had rights, what would they be? To address these questions, 3

720

Harper's Magazine asked two leading animal rights activists to sit down with a philosopher and a constitutional scholar to examine the logic of their opinions.

BUNNIES AND SEWER RATS

JACK HITT: Let me ask a question that many readers might ask: Gary, why   4
have you—a former supreme Court law clerk and now a professor of law at the University of Pennsylvania—devoted your life to animal rights?

GARY FRANCIONE: I believe that animals have *rights*. This is not to say that   5
animals have the same rights that we do, but the reasons that lead us to accord certain rights to human beings are equally applicable to animals. The problem is that our value system doesn't permit the breadth of vision necessary to understand that. We currently use the category of "species" as the relevant criterion for determining membership in our moral community, just as we once used race and sex to determine that membership.

  If you asked white men in 1810 whether blacks had rights, most of them   6
would have laughed at you. What was necessary then is necessary now. We must change the *way* we think: a paradigm shift in the way we think about animals. Rights for blacks and women were *the* constitutional issues of the nineteenth and twentieth centuries. Animal rights, once more people understand the issue, will emerge as *the* civil rights movement of the twenty-first century.

HITT: I want to see where the logic of your beliefs takes us. Suppose I am the   7
head of a company that has invented a dynamite new shampoo. It gives your hair great body; everyone is going to look like Lisa Bonet. But my preliminary tests show that it may cause some irritation or mild damage to the eye. So I've purchased 2,000 rabbits to test this shampoo on their eyes first. Roger, do you find anything offensive about testing shampoo this way?

ROGER GOLDMAN: As someone new to the animal rights issue, I don't find it   8
particularly offensive.

HITT: What if the only thing new about my shampoo is that it is just a   9
different color?

GOLDMAN: If everything else is equal, then I would say the testing is unnec-   10
essary.

INGRID NEWKIRK: I think Roger hit the nail on the head. The public has   11
absolutely no idea what the tests involve or whether they're necessary. I think Roger might object if he knew that there were alternatives, that a human-skin patch test can be substituted for the rabbit-blinding test. If consumers were informed, then no compassionate consumer would abide such cruelty.

FRANCIONE: The problem is that we can use animals in any way we like   12
because they are *property*. The law currently regards animals as no different from that pad of paper in front of you, Roger. If you own that pad, you can

rip it up or burn it. By and large we treat animals no different than glasses, cups, or paper.

ARTHUR CAPLAN: I know you lawyers love to talk about the property status of 13 these little creatures, but there are other factors. We treat animals as property because people don't believe that animals have any moral worth. People look at rabbits and say, "There are many rabbits. If there are a few less rabbits, who cares?"

NEWKIRK: Not true. Many people, who don't support animal rights, *would* 14 care if you stuck a knife in their rabbit or dog. They're deeply offended by acts of *individual* cruelty.

CAPLAN: Yes, but I suspect that if in your test we substituted ugly sewer rats 15 for button-nosed rabbits, people might applaud the suffering. There are some animals that just don't register in the human consciousness. Rats don't, rabbits might, dogs and horses definitely do.

NEWKIRK: Not always. If the test were done to a sewer rat in *front* of a person, 16 the average person would say, "Don't do that" or "Kill him quickly."

HITT: Why? 17

NEWKIRK: It's institutionalized cruelty, born of our hideous compartmentalized 18 thinking. If the killing is done behind closed doors, if the government says it must be done, or if some man or woman in a white coat assures us that it's for our benefit, we ignore our own ethical good sense and allow it to happen.

HITT: If the frivolity of the original test bothers us, what if we up the ante? 19 What if the product to be tested might yield a cure for baldness?

FRANCIONE: Jack, that is a "utilitarian" argument which suggests that the 20 rightness or wrongness of an action is determined by the *consequences* of that action. In the case of animals, it implies that animal exploitation produces benefits that justify that exploitation. I don't believe in utilitarian moral thought. It's dangerous because it easily leads to atrocious conclusions, both in how we treat humans and how we treat animals. I don't believe it is morally premissible to exploit weaker beings even if we derive benefits.

GOLDMAN: So not even the cancer cure? 21

FRANCIONE: No, absolutely not. 22

CAPLAN: But you miss the point about moral selfishness. By the time you get 23 to the baldness cure, people start to say, "I don't *care* about animals. My interests are a hell of a lot more important than the animals' interests. So if keeping hair on my head means sacrificing those animals, painlessly or not, I want it." It's not utilitarian—it's selfish.

FRANCIONE: But you certainly wouldn't put that forward as a justification, 24 would you?

CAPLAN: No, it's just a description. 25

FRANCIONE: I can't argue with your assertion that people are selfish. But aren't 26 we morally obliged to assess the consequences of that selfishness? To begin

722

that assessment, people must become aware of the ways in which we exploit animals.

Maybe I'm just a hopeless optimist, but I believe that once people are 27 confronted with these facts, they will reassess. The backlash that we're seeing from the exploitation industries—the meat companies and the biomedical research laboratories—is a reaction of fear. They know that the more people learn, the more people will reject this painful exploitation.

HITT: But won't your movement always be hampered by that mix of moral 28 utilitarianism and moral egotism? People will say, "Yes, be kind to animals up to a point of utilitarianism (so I can have my cancer cure) and up to a point of moral egotism (so I can have my sirloin)." There may be some shift in the moral center, but it will move only so far.

CAPLAN: I agree. Gary can remain optimistic, but confronting people with the 29 facts won't get him very far. Moral egotism extends even into human relations. Let's not forget that we are in a city where you have to step over people to enter this building. People don't say, "Feed, clothe, and house them, and then tax me: I'll pay." We have a limited moral imagination. It may be peculiarly American, but you can show people pictures of starving children or homeless people or animals in leg traps, and many will say, "That's too bad. Life is hard, but I still want my pleasures, my enjoyments."

NEWKIRK: There are two answers to that. First, people accept the myth. They 30 were brought up with the illusion that they *must* eat animals to be healthy. Now we know that's not true. Second, because of humankind's lack of moral—or even just plain—imagination, we activists have to tell people exactly what they *should* do. Then we must make it easier for them to do it. If we put a moral stepladder in front of people, a lot of them will walk up it. But most people feel powerless as individuals and ask, "Who am I? I'm only one person. What can I do?" We must show them.

HITT: Roger, I'm wondering whether your moral center has shifted since we 31 began. Originally you weren't offended by my using 2,000 rabbits to test a new shampoo. Are you now?

GOLDMAN: I am still a utilitarian. But if the test is unnecessary or just repet- 32 itive, clearly, I'm persuaded that it should be stopped.

NEWKIRK: Precisely Gary's point. Armed with the facts, Roger opts not to hurt 33 animals.

ENFRANCHISING ALL CREATURES

HITT: Art, what makes human beings have rights and animals not have rights? 34

CAPLAN: Some would argue a biblical distinction. God created humans in his 35 image and did not create animals that way. That's one special property. Another philosophical basis is natural law, which holds that inalienable rights accrue to being human—that is a distinguishing feature in and of itself.

Personally I reject both those arguments. I subscribe to an entitlement view, 36
which finds these rights grounded in certain innate properties, such as the
ability to reason, the ability to suffer—

FRANCIONE: Let's take the ability to suffer and consider it more carefully. The 37
ability to use language or to reason is irrelevant to the right to be free from
suffering. Only the ability to feel pain is relevant. Logically, it doesn't follow
that you should restrict those rights to human. On this primary level, the
question must be *who* can feel pain, *who* can suffer? Certainly animals must
be included within the reach of this fundamental right.

If you don't, then you are basing the right not to suffer pain on "intelli- 38
gence." Consider the grotesque results if you apply that idea exclusively to
human beings. Would you say that a smart person has a right to suffer less
pain than a stupid person? That is effectively just what we say with animals.
Even though they can suffer, we conclude that their suffering is irrelevant
because we think we are smarter than they are.

CAPLAN: The ability to suffer does count, but the level of thinking and con- 39
sciousness also counts. What makes us human? What grants us the right to
life? It is not just a single attribute that makes us human. Rather, there is a
cluster of properties: a sense of place in the world, a sense of time, a sense
of self-awareness, a sense that one *is* somebody, a sense that one is morally
relevant. When you add up these features, you begin to get to the level of
entitlement to rights.

FRANCIONE: And I am going to push you to think specifically about rights 40
again. What must you possess in order to have a right to life? I think the
most obvious answer is simply a *life!*

But let's play this question out in your terms. To have a right to life, you 41
must possess a sense of self, a recollection of the past, and an anticipation of
the future, to name a few. By those standards, the chimpanzee—and I would
argue, the entire class of Mammalia—would be enfranchised to enjoy a right
to life.

NEWKIRK: The question is, do they have an interest in living? If they do, then 42
one has an obligation to recognize their natural rights. The most fundamental
of these is a desire to live. They *are* alive, therefore they want to *be* alive,
and therefore we should *let* them live.

The more profound question, though, is what distinguishes humans from 43
other animals. Most scientists, at first, thought that what separates us from
the other animals is that human beings use tools. So ethnologists went out
into the field and returned with innumerable examples of tool use in animals.
The scientists then concluded that it's not tool use but the *making* of tools.
Ethnologists, such as Geza Teleki, came back with lots of different examples,
everything from chimpanzees making fishing poles to ants making boats to
cross rivers. One might think they would then elevate the criterion to making
tools in *union* workshops, but they switched to "language." Then there was

a discussion about what *is* language. Linguists, among them Noam Chomsky and Herbert Terrace, said language possessed certain "components." But when various ethnologists were able to satisfy each of these components, the Cartesian scientists became desperate and kept adding more components, including some pretty complicated ones, such as the ability to recite events in the distant past and to create new words based on past experiences. Eventually the number of components was up to sixteen! The final component was teaching someone else the language. But when Roger Fouts gave the signing ape, Washoe, a son, she independently taught him some seventy American hand-language signs.

CAPLAN: One of the sad facts of the literature of both animal and human rights is that everyone is eager to identify the magic property that separates humans from animals. Is it the ability to suffer? The ability to say something? The ability to say something *interesting*! I think the philosophers are all looking in the right place but are missing something. We have rights because we are *social*.   44

NEWKIRK: Since all animals are social, then you *would* extend rights to non-humans?   45

CAPLAN: It's not just sociability. Of course, all animals interact, but there is something about the way humans need to interact.   46

Suppose we were little Ayn Rands who marched about, self-sufficient, proud, and arrogant. If we were able to chop our own wood, cook our own meals, and fend off those who would assault us, then we wouldn't need any rights. You wouldn't need to have a right to free speech if there was no one to talk to!   47

My point is that our fundamental rights are not exclusively intellectual properties. They are the natural result of the unique way humans have come together to form societies, *dependent* on each other for survival and therefore respectful of each other's rights.   48

NEWKIRK: None of this differentiates humans from the other animals. You cannot find a relevant attribute in human beings that doesn't exist in animals as well. Darwin said that the only difference between humans and other animals was a difference of degree, not kind. If you ground any concept of human rights in a particular attribute, then animals will have to be included. Animals have rights.   49

CAPLAN: That brings up another problem I have with your entire argument. Throughout this discussion, I have argued my position in terms of *ethics*. I have spoken about our moral imagination and animal *interests* and human decency. Why? Because I don't want our relationship with animals to be cast as a battle of rights. Only in America, with its obsession for attorneys, courts, judges, and lawsuits, is the entire realm of human relationships reduced to a clash of rights.   50

So I ask you: Is our relationship with animals best conceived of under the   51 rubric of rights? I don't think so. When I am dispensing rights, I'm relatively chintzy about it. Do embryos have rights? In my opinion, no. Do irretrievably comatose people have rights? I doubt it. Do mentally retarded people below some level of intellectual functioning have rights? Probably not.

There is a wide range of creatures—some of them human—for whom   52
our rights language is not the best way to deal with them. I want people to deal with them out of a sense of fairness or a sense of humanity or a sense of duty, but not out of a claim to rights.

NEWKIRK: I don't like your supremacist view of a custodial responsibility that   53
grants you the luxury to be magnanimous to those beneath you. The rights of animals are not peripheral interests. In this case, we are talking about blood, guts, pain, and death.

FRANCIONE: Art, when you start talking about obligations without rights, you   54
can justify violations of those obligations or intrusions more easily by spinning airy notions of utility. The reason many of our battles are played out in rights language is because our culture has evolved this notion that a right is something that stands between me and an intrusion. A right doesn't yield automatically because a stronger party might benefit.

If a scientist could cure cancer—without fail—by subjecting me against   55
my will to a painful experiment, it wouldn't matter. I have a right not to be used that way.

CAPLAN: Ironically, I agree with you. That's exactly the role that rights lan-   56
guage plays. It defines the barriers or lines that can't be crossed. But if you hand out rights willy-nilly, you lose that function.

NEWKIRK: When should we stop?   57

CAPLAN: I'm not sure I know the answer, but if you cheapen the currency of   58
rights language, you've got to worry that rights may not be taken seriously. Soon you will have people arguing that trees have rights and that embryos have rights. And the tendency would be to say, "Sure, they have rights, but they are not *important* rights."

NEWKIRK: Art, wouldn't you rather err on the side of giving out too many   59
rights rather than too few?

CAPLAN: No.   60

NEWKIRK: So, according to your view, maybe we should take away some of   61
the rights we've already granted. After all, granting rights to blacks and women has deprived society of very important things, such as cheap labor. That a society evolves and expands its protective shield should not daunt us. That's like saying, if I continue to be charitable, my God, where will it ever end?

CAPLAN: It may not be rights or bust. There may be other ways to get people   62
to conduct themselves decently without hauling out the heavy artillery of rights language every time.

NEWKIRK: People have to be pushed; society has to be pushed. Those who   63 care deeply about a particular wrong have to pressure the general population. Eventually a law is passed, and then adjustments are made to correct past injustices. You have to bring these matters to a head.

HITT: Roger, from a constitutional perspective, do you think that rights are cheapened when they are broadened? 64

GOLDMAN: When you put it in a constitutional context, you invite conflict. That's inevitable. If you have a free press, you're going to have fair trial problems. If you start expanding rights of liberty, you run up against rights of equality. I don't think expansion cheapens them, but by elevating animal rights to a constitutional issue, you certainly multiply the difficulties. 65

HITT: You could argue that conflict strengthens rights. If you had no conflict over free speech, would we have the solid right to free speech that we have today? 66

GOLDMAN: It depends on who wins. What would happen if free speech lost? 67

FRANCIONE: Roger, you will have conflict and difficulties whether you cast our relationship with animals as one of obligations *or* rights. The real question is, are those obligations enforceable by state authority? If they are, there will be clashes and we will turn to the courts for resolution. 68

CAPLAN: Gary, I would like those obligations enforced by the authority, if you like, of empathy, by the power of character. What matters is how people view animals, how their feelings are touched by those animals, what drives them to care about those animals, not what rights the animals have. 69

FRANCIONE: I agree that you don't effect massive social change exclusively through law, but law can certainly help. That's a classic law school debate: Do moral perceptions shape law or does law shape moral perceptions? It probably goes both ways. I have no doubt that we could effect a great change if animals were included within our constitutional framework. 70

NEWKIRK: Great changes often begin with the law. Remember the 1760s case of the West Indian slave Jonathan Strong. Strong's master had abandoned him in England after beating him badly. The judge in that case feared the consequences of emancipating a slave. But the judge freed Strong and declared, "Let justice prevail, though the heavens may fall." 71

MOJO, THE TALKING CHIMPANZEE

HITT: Meet Mojo, the signing chimpanzee. Mojo is female and has learned more words than any other chimpanzee. One day you're signing away with Mojo, and she signs back. "I want a baby." Roger, are we under any obligation to grant her wish? 72

GOLDMAN: Since I am not persuaded animals have any rights, I don't believe there is any obligation. 73

HITT: Doesn't it follow that if this chimpanzee can articulate a desire to have 74 a child—a primal desire and one that we would never forbid humans—we have some obligation to fulfill it?

CAPLAN: You are alluding to a foundation for rights that we haven't yet 75 discussed. Is the requirement for possessing a right the ability to *claim* it? That is, in order to hold a right to life, one must be able to articulate a claim to life, to be able to say, "I want to live."

There may be animals that can get to that level, and Mojo may be one 76 of them. Nevertheless, I don't buy into that argument. Simply being able to claim a right does not necessarily entail an obligation to fulfill it.

FRANCIONE: But Mojo does have the right to be left alone to pursue her 77 desires, the right *not* to be in that cage. Aren't we violating some right of Mojo's by confining her so that she cannot satisfy that primal desire?

HITT: Is this a fair syllogism? Mojo wants to be free; a right to freedom exists 78 if you can claim it; ergo, Mojo has a right to be free. Does the ability to lay claim to a right automatically translate into the *possession* of such a right?

CAPLAN: You don't always generate obligations and duties from a parallel set 79 of rights, matching one with another.

Look at the relationship that exists between family members. Some people 80 might argue that children have certain rights to claim from their parents. But there is something wrong with that assumption. Parents have many obligations to their children, but it seems morally weird to reduce this relationship to a contractual model. It's not a free-market arrangement where you put down a rights chit, I put down an obligation chit, and we match them up.

My kid might say to me, "Dad, you have an obligation to care for my 81 needs, and my need today is a new car." I don't enter into a negotiation based on a balancing of his rights and my duties. That is not the proper relationship.

NEWKIRK: But having a car is not a fundamental right, whereas the right not 82 to be abused is. For example, children have a right not to be used in factories. That right had to be fought for in exactly the same way we are fighting for animal rights now.

CAPLAN: Gary, I want to press you further. A baby needs a heart, and some 83 scientist believes the miniature swine's heart will do it.

FRANCIONE: Would I take a healthy pig, remove its heart, and put it into the 84 child? No.

CAPLAN: I am stymied by your absolutist position that makes it impossible 85 even to consider the pig as a donor.

FRANCIONE: What if the donor were a severely retarded child instead of a pig? 86

CAPLAN: No, because I've got to worry about the impact not only on the 87 donor but on society as well.

FRANCIONE: Art, assume I have a three-year-old prodigy who is a mathematical 88 wizard. The child has a bad heart. The only way to save this prodigy is to take the heart out of another child. Should we *consider* a child from a low socio-economic background who has limited mental abilities?

CAPLAN: You're wandering around a world of slopes, and I want to wander around a world of steps. I have argued strongly in my writing that it is possible for a human being—specifically an infant born with anencephaly, that is, without most of its brain—to drop below the threshold of a right to life. I think it would be ethical to use such a baby as a source for organ transplants. I do not believe there is a slippery slope between the child born with most of its brain missing and the retarded. There are certain thresholds below which one can make these decisions. At some point along the spectrum of life—many people would say a pig, and I would go further to include the anencephalic baby—we are safely below that threshold.   89

FRANCIONE: You can't equate the pig with the anencephalic infant. The anencephalic child is not the subject of a life in any meaningful sense. That is to say, it does not possess that constellation of attributes—sense of self-awareness, anticipation of the future, memory of the past—that we have been discussing. The pig is clearly the subject of a meaningful life.   90

CAPLAN: But if it's a matter of saving the life of the baby, then I want a surgeon to saw out the pig's heart and put it in the baby's chest.   91

NEWKIRK: The pig can wish to have life, liberty and the pursuit of happiness, and the anencephalic baby cannot.   92

CAPLAN: But you must also consider the effect on others. I don't think it's going to matter very much what the pig's parents think about that pig. Whereas the child's parents care about the baby, and they don't care about the pig.   93

FRANCIONE: Then you change their reaction.   94

CAPLAN: I don't want to change their reaction. I want human beings to care about babies.   95

NEWKIRK: Like racism or sexism, that remark is pure speciesism.   96

CAPLAN: Speciesism! Mine is a legitimate distinction. The impact of this transplant is going to be different on humans than on lower animals.   97

NEWKIRK: "Lower animals." There comes speciesism rearing its ugly head again. Look, Art, I associate with the child; I don't associate with the pig. But we can't establish why that matters *except* that you are human and I am human.   98

If a building were burning and a baby baboon, a baby rat, and a baby child were inside, I'm sure I would save the child. But if the baboon mother went into the building, I'm sure she would take out the infant baboon. It's just that there is an instinct to save yourself first, then your immediate family, your countrymen, and on to your species. But we have to recognize and reject the self-interest that erects these barriers and try to recognize the rights of others who happen not to be exactly like ourselves.   99

CAPLAN: I think you can teach humans to care about the pig. The morally 100
relevant factor here is that you will never get the pig to care about *me*.

NEWKIRK: Not true, Art. Read John Robbin's new book, *Diet for a New* 101
America, in which he lists incidents of altruism by animals outside their own
species. Everybody knows about dolphins rescuing sailors. Recently a pig
rescued a child from a frozen lake and won an award!

CAPLAN: To the extent to which you can make animals drop *their* speciesism, 102
perhaps you will be persuasive on this point.

NEWKIRK: Art, if you don't recognize my rights, that's tough for me. But that 103
doesn't mean my rights don't exist.

FRANCIONE: If blacks, as a group, got together and said, "We're going to make 104
a conscious decision to dislike non-blacks," would you say that black people
no longer had rights?

CAPLAN: No, but I would hold them accountable for their racism. I could 105
never hold a pig accountable for its speciesism. And I am never going to see
a meeting of pigs having that kind of conversation.

NEWKIRK: That happens when the Ku Klux Klan meets, and the ACLU 106
upholds their rights.

CAPLAN: The difference is that there are certain things I expect of blacks, 107
whites, yellows—of all human beings and maybe a few animals. But I am
not going to hold the vast majority of animals to those standards.

NEWKIRK: So the punishment for their perceived deficiencies—which, inci- 108
dentally, is shared by the human baby—is to beat them to death.

CAPLAN: I didn't say that. I am trying to reach for something that isn't captured 109
by the speciesist charge. The difference between people and animals is that
I can persuade people. I can *stimulate* their moral imaginations. But I can't
do that with most animals, and I want that difference to count.

A WORLD WITH NO DANCING BEARS

HITT: How would you envision a society that embraced animal rights? What 110
would happen to pets?

NEWKIRK: I don't use the word "pet." I think it's speciesist language. I prefer 111
"companion animal." For one thing, we would no longer allow breeding.
People could not create different breeds. There would be no pet shops. If
people had companion animals in their homes, those animals would have to
be refugees from the animal shelters and the streets. You would have a
protective relationship with them just as you would with an orphaned child.
But as the surplus of cats and dogs (artifically engineered by centuries of
forced breeding) declined, eventually companion animals would be phased
out, and we would return to a more symbiotic relationship—enjoyment at a
distance.

FRANCIONE: Much more than that would be phased out. For example, there   112
would be no animals used for food, no laboratory experiments, no fur coats,
and no hunting.

GOLDMAN: Would there be zoos?   113

FRANCIONE: No zoos.   114

HITT: Circuses?   115

FRANCIONE: Circuses would have to change. Look, right now we countenance   116
the taking of an animal from the wild—a bear—dressing that bear in a *skirt*
and parading it in front of thousands of people while it balances a ball on its
nose. When you think about it, that is perverted.

HITT: Let's say that your logic prevails. People are sickened by dancing bears   117
and are demanding a constitutional amendment. What would be the language
of a Bill of Rights for animals?

NEWKIRK: It already exists. It's "life, liberty, and the pursuit of happiness."   118
We just haven't extended it far enough.

GOLDMAN: I am assuming your amendment would restrict not only govern-   119
ment action but private action as well. Our Constitution restricts only government action. The single exception is the Thirteenth Amendment, which
prohibits both the government and the individual from the practice of slavery.

HITT: To whom would these rights apply? Would they apply among animals   120
themselves? Does the lion have to recognize the gazelle's right to life?

NEWKIRK: That's not our business. The behavior of the lion and the gazelle   121
is a "tribal" issue, if you will. Those are the actions of other nations, and we
cannot interfere.

GOLDMAN: What if we knew the lion was going to kill the gazelle—would we   122
have an obligation to stop it?

NEWKIRK: It's not our business. This amendment restricts only our code of   123
behavior.

HITT: But what Roger is asking is, should the amendment be so broad as to   124
restrict both individual and government action?

FRANCIONE: It should be that broad. Of course, it would create a lot of issues   125
we would have to work out. First, to whom would we extend these rights? I
have a sneaking suspicion that any moment someone in this room will say,
"But what about cockroaches? Will they have these rights? Do they have the
right to have credit cards?" Hard questions would have to be answered, and
we would have to determine which animals would hold rights and how to
translate these rights into concrete protections from interference.

NEWKIRK: The health pioneer W. K. Kellogg limited it to "all those with   126
faces." If you can look into the eyes of another, and that other looks back,
that's one measure.

So the amendment shouldn't be limited, as some animal rights advocates   127
think, to mammals, because we know that birds, reptiles, insects, and fishes

all feel pain. They are capable of wanting to be alive. As long as we know that they have these primal interests, then I think we need to explore down the line—if we think it is down.

GOLDMAN: Let me go up the line. What about humans?   128

NEWKIRK: They would be just another animal in the pack.   129

GOLDMAN: But your amendment would massively expand the reach of the   130
Constitution for humans. For example, the Constitution does not require
states to provide rights for victims of crime. Under your proposal, if a state
decriminalized adultery, shoplifting, or even murder, the victim's *constitutional* rights would be violated.

CAPLAN: And if we take the face test, how is that going to affect the way we   131
treat the unborn? Must we enfranchise our fetuses? That's going to be the
end of abortion.

FRANCIONE: Not necessarily. I am fairly comfortable with the notion that a   132
fetus does not have a right to life. But that is not to say that a fetus doesn't
have a right to be free from suffering. Fetuses do feel pain and they *ought* to
be free from suffering, But it doesn't make sense to talk about a fetus having
a sense of the past, anticipation of the future, and a sense of interaction with
others.

CAPLAN: But a mouse?   133

FRANCIONE: Sure.   134

CAPLAN: I guess we can experiment on and eat all the animal fetuses we want.   135

FRANCIONE: I didn't say you had a right to inflict pain on animal fetuses. I   136
don't think you have a right to inflict pain on human fetuses.

CAPLAN: Are you suggesting that we can't inflict pain, but we can kill them?   137

NEWKIRK: You are talking about the manner in which abortions are currently   138
performed, not whether they should be performed. Our standard of lack of
suffering holds up if you apply it across the board, for human and nonhuman fetuses.

GOLDMAN: Let me see if I can bring together those who advocate animal   139
welfare with those who believe animals hold rights. What about a different
amendment, similar to the difference between the Thirteenth Amendment,
which is an absolute ban on slavery, and the Fourteenth Amendment, which
bans discrimination, but not absolutely. In fact, the Fourteenth allows us to
take race into account sometimes, such as affirmative action. Do the animal
rights activists see a role for a limited amendment similar to the Fourteenth?
It would broadly protect animals from unnecessary suffering, but allow for
some medical experiments.

FRANCIONE: Does your amendment simply expand the word "persons" in the   140
Fourteenth Amendment to include animals?

GOLDMAN: No, but it is modeled on Fourteenth Amendment jurisprudence.   141
It would not permit experimentation on animals unless necessary for a compelling need.

FRANCIONE: I would favor this approach if the experimenter had the burden   142
to show the compelling need. I would have only one problem with adjudication under this compelling-need standard. My fear is that the balance
would always favor the biomedical research community. Everyone agrees that
no one should needlessly use animals in experimentation. Yet we all know
that millions of animals are being used for frivolous purposes. That is because
the biomedical researchers have persuaded enough people that their experiments are so important they have become "compelling" by definition.

GOLDMAN: Of course the difference with this constitutional amendment is that   143
it wouldn't pass unless two-thirds of congress and three-fourths of the states
backed it. So if we're projecting a hundred years from now, you won't have
the problem of science experts always prevailing.

FRANCIONE: Roger, I would retire tomorrow if I could get your amendment.   144
The problem is that our society economically *benefits* from exploitation. The
animal industries are so strong that they have shaped an entire *value* system
that justifies and perpetuates exploitation. So I am not sure your compelling-
need test would result in anything substantially different from what we have
now. That's why I favor a hard rights notion, to protect the defenseless
absolutely. As soon as you let in the "balancers," people such as Art Caplan,
you've got trouble.

CAPLAN: The problem with your constitutional amendment is that, finally, it   145
is irrelevant to human behavior. When the lawyers, the constitutional adju-
dicators, and the Supreme Court justices aren't there, when it's just me and
my companion animal or my bug in the woods, where are the animal's rights
then?

There was a time when I was a little boy running around in the woods   146
in New England. It was just a bunch of Japanese beetles in a jar and me.
The question was: How is little Art going to deal with those Japanese beetles?
Pull their wings off? Never let them out of the jar? Step on them? What do
I do with those bugs? What do I think of bugs? No Supreme Court justice is
going to tell me what to do with them.

NEWKIRK: A lot of these conflicts of moral obligation result from the wide   147
variety of *unnatural* relationships we have with animals in the first place—
whether it's little Art with his jar of Japanese beetles, or the scientist in the
lab with his chimpanzee, or any one of us at home with a cat. Just take the
single issue of the sterilization of pets. We now have burdened ourselves with
the custodial obligation to sterilize thousands of animals because we have
screwed up their reproductive cycles so much through domestication and
inbreeding that they have many more offspring than they normally would.
What would happen if we just left animals alone, to possess their own dignity?
You know, you mentioned earlier that there is something cruel in the lion
chasing down and killing the gazelle. Well, nature *is* cruel, but man is
crueler yet.

QUESTIONS

1. One of the central questions of this forum, and of all discussions of animal rights, is the question "What makes human beings have rights and animals not have rights?" How do the various participants in the forum seek to answer this question?

2. Newkirk asks "What distinguishes humans from other animals?" (paragraph 43). How do the various participants respond to this question? What assumptions underlie these various responses?

3. Francione states in paragraph 70: "That's a classic law school debate. Do moral perceptions shape law or does law shape moral perceptions?" Do you think that massive social change can be influenced by legislation protecting animal rights? How would our society change, according to some of the forum participants, if we embraced animal rights?

4. Should all animals have rights? In paragraph 125, one of the forum participants discusses the question: "But what about cockroaches?" Are you persuaded by any of the participants' positions? If animals have rights, what kind of rights should they be? How do you respond to this issue?

5. Newkirk concludes the forum with this powerful thought: "Well, nature is cruel, but man is crueler yet." How do you respond to this thought? Write an essay in which you develop your position on animal rights in the context of this comment.

6. Thomas Jefferson opens the Declaration of Independence by stating directly the "self-evident" "truths" upon which his argument will be based. In fact, every argument depends on an appeal to certain unquestioned values, to a body of "truths" that the writer assumes the audience accepts (although not every writer states these "truths" as explicitly as Jefferson). Take two of the participants in this forum and try to determine the values these participants assume—not the views being argued, but the accepted "truths" on which their arguments depend. Write an essay in which you analyze the accepted truths that provide the basis for their positions.

MAKING CONNECTIONS

1. Frederick A. King, in "Animals in Research: The Case for Experimentation," draws Arthur Caplan, one of the participants of this forum, into his argument, using Caplan to support his case for using animals in experiments. Do you think Caplan would agree with the case King is making? Where, if anywhere, would Caplan quarrel with King?

2. The first paragraph of this forum alludes to the Declaration of Independence. Imagine a "Continental Congress" of animals preparing to declare its independence from humans. Imagine further that you are a delegate, cast as one of whatever species you prefer, and you have been assigned the role Jefferson once held, to draft an animals' Declaration of Independence. What would you say? What evidence would you bring to your task? Go ahead and draft it.

3. Several selections in this collection focus on the special human regard for animals, at least for some species. Farley Mowat's "Observing Wolves," Jane van Lawick-Goodall's "First Observations," William Booth's "The Social Lives of Dolphins," and Stephen Jay Gould's "A Biological Homage to Mickey Mouse" are examples. Imagine at least two of those writers participating in this forum. Where would they break in? What would they say? Rewrite a section of this forum including two of those writers as participants.

Sciences and Technologies

ANIMALS IN RESEARCH:
THE CASE FOR EXPERIMENTATION
Frederick A. King

Frederick A. King (b. 1925) is a neuroscientist and an educator. He is director of Emory University's primate research center and has served on many committees on animal research and experimentation. He has edited books on primate biology and primate social dynamics. In this essay, King argues that while humans have a moral responsibility to animals, animals do not share the same rights as humans.

The Mobilization for Animals Coalition (MFA) is an international network 1 of more than 400 animal-protectionist organizations that address themselves to a variety of issues, including hunting, trapping, livestock protection, vegetarianism, and pets. Their primary concern, however, is an adamant opposition to animal research. Some groups within the movement want to severely curtail research with animals, but the most visible and outspoken faction wants to eliminate it.

The astonishing growth of this activist movement during the past three years 2 has culminated this year in an intense attack on the use of animals in psychological research. This past spring, John McArdle of the Humane Society of the United States charged that torture is the founding principle and fundamental characteristic of experimental psychology, and that psychological experimentation on animals among all the scientific disciplines is "the ideal candidate for elimination. No major scientific endeavor would suffer by such an act." A recent pamphlet published by the MFA stated, "Of all these experiments, those conducted in psychology are the most painful, pointless, and repulsive."

The following specific allegations have been made by the MFA: Animals are 3 given intense, repeated electric shocks until they lose the ability even to scream in pain; animals are deprived of food and water and allowed to suffer and die from hunger and thirst; animals are put in isolation until they are driven insane or die from despair and terror; animals are subjected to crushing forces that smash their bones and rupture their internal organs; the limbs of animals are mutilated or amputated to produce behavioral changes; animals are the victims of extreme pain and stress, inflicted out of idle curiosity, in nightmarish experiments designed to make healthy animals psychotic.

Such irresponsible accusations of research cruelty have consistently charac- 4 terized the publications of the MFA. However, a recent study by psychologists D. Caroline Coile and Neal E. Miller of Rockfeller University counters these charges. Coile and Miller looked at every article (a total of 608) appearing in the past five years in journals of the American Psychological Association that report animal research. They concluded that none of the extreme allegations made by the MFA could be supported.

Coile and Miller admit that charges of cruelty may have gone unreported or 5 been reported elsewhere but, they say, if such studies did occur, "they certainly were infrequent, and it is extremely misleading to imply that they are typical of experimental psychology."

Furthermore, there are standards and mechanisms to ensure that research 6 animals are treated in a humane and scientifically sensible way. These mechanisms include the Federal Animal Welfare Act of 1966 (amended in Congress in 1970, 1976, and 1979); periodic inspection of all animal-research facilities by the Department of Agriculture; visits by federal agencies that fund animal research and are increasingly attentive to the conditions of animal care and experimental procedures that could cause pain or distress; and a comprehensive document, "Guide for the Care and Use of Laboratory Animals," prepared by the National Academy of Sciences. In addition, virtually every major scientific society whose members conduct animal research distributes guidelines for such research. Above and beyond all of this, most universities and research institutes have animal-care committees that monitor animal research and care.

The United States Public Health Service is revising its guidelines to require 7 institutions that do research with animals to designate even clearer lines of authority and responsibility for animal care. This will include detailed information about how each institution complies with the new regulations as well as a requirement that animal-research committees include not only the supervising laboratory veterinarian and scientists but also a nonscientist and a person not affiliated with the institution. These committees will review programs for animal care, inspect all animal facilities, and review and monitor all research proposals before they are submitted to agencies of the United States Public Health Service. The committees will also have the power to disapprove or terminate any research proposal.

This is not to say that research scientists are perfect. There will be occasional 8 errors, cases of neglect, and instances of abuse—as is the case with any human endeavor, whether it be the rearing of children, the practicing of a trade or profession, or the governing of a nation. But a high standard of humane treatment is maintained.

The choice of psychological research for special attack almost certainly stems   9 from the fact that such research is viewed as more vulnerable than are studies of anatomy, physiology, or microbiology. In the minds of many, psychology is a less well-developed science than the biological sciences and the benefits that have accrued from psychological research with animals are less well known. Hence, it is more difficult to grasp the necessity for animal research in behavioral studies than it is in biomedical studies.

Anyone who has looked into the matter can scarcely deny that major advances   10 in medicine have been achieved through basic research with animals. Among these are the development of virtually all modern vaccines against infectious diseases, the invention of surgical approaches to eye disorders, bone and joint injuries and heart disease, the discovery of insulin and other hormones, and the testing of all new drugs and antibiotics.

The benefits to humans of psychological research with animals may be less   11 well known than those of medical research but are just as real. Historically, the application of psychological research to human problems has lagged considerably behind the applied use of medical research. Mental events and overt behavior, although controlled by the nervous system and biology of an organism, are much more difficult to describe and study than are the actions of tissues or organ systems. To describe the complex interplay of perceptions, memories, cognitive and emotional processes with a physical and social environment that changes from moment to moment, elaborate research designs had to be developed. Since even a single type of behavior, such as vocalization, has so many different forms, a wide variety of ways of measuring the differences had to be developed. Finally, because much psychological research makes inferences from behavioral observations about internal states of an organism, methods were needed to insure that the interpretations were valid. Such complexities do not make the study of animal or human behavior less scientific or important than other kinds of research, but they do make it more difficult and slow its readiness for clinical applications.

Basic psychological research with animals has led to important achievements   12 in the interest of human welfare. Examples include the use of biofeedback, which had its origin in studies of behavioral conditioning of neuromuscular activities in rats and other animals. Today, biofeedback can be used to control blood pressure and hypertension and help prevent heart attacks. In the case of paralyzed patients, it can be used to elevate blood pressure, enabling those who would otherwise have to spend their lives lying down to sit upright. Biofeedback techniques also are used in the reduction and control of severe pain and as a method of neuromuscular control to help reverse the process of scoliosis, a disabling and disfiguring curvature of the spine. Biofeedback can also be a cost-effective alternative to certain medical treatments and can help avoid many of the complications associated with long-term drug use.

Language studies with apes have led to practical methods of teaching language skills to severely retarded children who, prior to this work, had little or no language ability. Patients who have undergone radiation therapy for cancer can now take an interest in nutritious foods and avoid foods that have little nutritional value, thanks to studies of conditioned taste aversion done with animals. Neural and behavioral studies of early development of vision in cats and primates—studies that could not have been carried out with children—have led to advances in pediatric ophthalmology that can prevent irreversible brain damage and loss of vision in children who have cataracts and various other serious eye problems.   13

Behavioral modification and behavioral therapy, widely accepted techniques for treating alcohol, drug, and tobacco addiction, have a long history of animal studies investigating learning theory and reward systems. Programmed instruction, the application of learning principles to educational tasks, is based on an array of learning studies in animals. These are but a few examples of the effectiveness and usefulness for humans of psychological research with animals.   14

Those opposed to animal research have proposed that alternatives to animal research, such as mathematical and computer models and tissue cultures, be used. In some cases, these alternatives are both feasible and valuable. Tissue cultures, for example, have been very effective in certain toxicological studies that formerly required live animals. For psychological studies, however, it is often necessary to study the whole animal and its relationship to the environment. Visual problems, abnormal sexual behavior, depression, and aggression, for example, are not seen in tissue cultures and do not lend themselves to computer models. When human subjects cannot be used for such studies, animals are necessary if the research is to be done at all.   15

Extremists within the animal-rights movement take the position that animals have rights equal to or greater than those of humans. It follows from this that even if humans might benefit from animal research, the cost to animals is too high. It is ironic that despite this moral position, the same organizations condone—and indeed sponsor—activities that appear to violate the basic rights of animals to live and reproduce. Each year 10,000,000 dogs are destroyed by public pounds, animal shelters, and humane societies. Many of these programs are supported and even operated by animal-protectionist groups. Surely there is a strong contradiction when those who profess to believe in animal rights deny animals their right to life. A similar situation exists with regard to programs of pet sterilization, programs that deny animals the right to breed and to bear offspring and are sponsored in many cases by antivivisectionists and animal-rights groups. Evidently, animal-rights advocates sometimes recognize and subscribe to the position that animals do not have the same rights as humans.   16

740

However, their public posture leaves little room for examining these subtleties or applying similar standards to animal research.

Within the animal-protectionist movement there are moderates who have 17 confidence in scientists as compassionate human beings and in the value of research. Their primary aims are to insure that animals are treated humanely and that discomfort in animal experimentation is kept to a minimum. It is to this group that scientists and scientific organizations have the responsibility to explain what they do, why and how they do it and what benefits occur.

I believe that the values guiding contemporary animal research represent 18 prevailing sentiment within the scientific community and, indeed, within society at large. And I believe that these values are congruent with those of the moderates within the animal-protectionist movement. As articulated by ethicist Arthur Caplan, rights, in the most realistic sense, are granted by one group to another based on perceived similarities between the groups. Plainly, animals lack those characteristics that would allow them to share in the rights we grant to humans. We do not grant domestic animals the right to go where they wish or do what they want because they are obviously unable to comprehend the responsibilities and demands of human society. In fact, we do not as a society even grant all domestic animals and pets the right to live.

This does not mean, however, that we do not have a moral responsibility to 19 animals. I believe, along with Caplan and the scientific research community at large, that we hold a moral stewardship for animals and that we are obliged to treat them with humane compassion and concern for their sentience. Many animal forms can and do feel pain and are highly aware of their environment. This awareness makes them worthy of our respect and serious concern. Caplan is certainly correct when he says that this moral obligation ought to be part of what it means to be a scientist today.

Science must proceed. The objective quest for knowledge is a treasured 20 enterprise of our heritage and culture. Scientific inquiry into the nature of our living world has freed us from ignorance and superstition. Scientific understanding is an expression of our highest capacities—those of objective observation, interpretive reasoning, imagination, and creativity. Founded on the results of basic research, often conducted with no goal other than that of increased understanding, the eventual practical use of this knowledge has led to a vastly improved well-being for humankind.

Extremists in the animal-rights movement probably will never accept such 21 justifications for research or assurances of humane treatments. They may reject any actions, no matter how conscientious, that scientists take in realistically and morally reconciling the advance of human welfare with the use of animals. But, fortunately, there are many who, while deeply and appropriately concerned for the compassionate treatment of animals, recognize that human welfare is and should be our primary concern.

QUESTIONS

1. King begins his argument by presenting the opposition's position. In paragraph 2, he offers the charge from a member of the Humane Society of the United States that "torture is the founding principle and fundamental characteristic of experimental psychology." Why does King begin by presenting the opposition's case? How does he characterize their claims? How does he use this information to strengthen his own argument?

2. King argues that "it is more difficult to grasp the necessity for animal research in behavioral studies than it is in biomedical studies" (paragraph 9). What examples does he offer to make his case that animal research in behavioral studies has had important human benefits? Do you find these examples convincing?

3. Summarize King's position. What *is* the case for animals in research?

4. What values does King appeal to? What assumptions underlie King's position?

5. Spend some time in a psychology lab at your school where animals are used for research. What do you observe about the conditions and treatment of these animals? Interview the researchers in the lab to learn about the kind of research conducted and the projected benefits for behavioral studies. Using this information as evidence and your own responses to the various readings on animal rights, write an essay supporting your position.

MAKING CONNECTIONS

1. King writes, "Many animals can and do feel pain and are highly aware of their environment. This awareness makes them worthy of our respect and serious concern." How would Alice Walker respond to this claim and to King's argument? Read her essay, "Am I Blue?" Would King call Walker an *extremist* as he uses that term in paragraph 16? Imagine a conversation between King and Walker, and compose a dialogue between them.

2. This argument by King suggests, in some ways, James C. Sander's reply to Patricia Taylor in the debate on labeling alcoholic beverages. However, the position parallel to Taylor's, though partially implied by King, is not given explicitly here. Compose such a position in response to King. You might begin by deciding whether you want to present yourself as a moderate or an extremist, or whether you would reject from the outset those labels for positions mentioned by King.

THE ART OF
TEACHING SCIENCE

Lewis Thomas

Born in 1913, Lewis Thomas is a medical doctor, biologist, researcher, professor, and writer. For most of his life, he has carried out laboratory research and served as an adminis-trator for medical schools and hospitals. Until his retirement in 1982, he was chancellor of Memorial Sloan-Kettering Cancer Center in New York City. Thomas is most widely known for essays that he published first in the New England Journal of Medicine *and that have been gathered since in collections entitled* The Lives of a Cell *(winner of the National Book Award in 1975),* The Medusa and the Snail *(1979), and* Late Night Thoughts on Listening to Mahler's Ninth Symphony *(1983). This piece, which was given as a talk at a conference sponsored by the Alfred P. Sloane Foundation, appeared in the* New York Times Magazine *in 1982.*

Everyone seems to agree that there is something wrong with the way science is being taught these days. But no one is at all clear about when it went wrong or what is to be done about it. The term "scientific illiteracy" has become almost a cliché in educational circles. Graduate schools blame the colleges; colleges blame the secondary schools; the high schools blame the elementary schools, which, in turn, blame the family. 1

I suggest that the scientific community itself is partly, perhaps largely, to blame. Moreover, if there are disagreements between the world of the human-ities and the scientific enterprise as to the place and importance of science in a liberal-arts education and the role of science in 20th-century culture, I believe that the scientists are themselves responsible for a general misunderstanding of what they are really up to. 2

During the last half-century, we have been teaching the sciences as though they were the same collection of academic subjects as always, and—here is what has really gone wrong—as though they would always be the same. Students learn today's biology, for example, the same way we learned Latin when I was in high school long ago: first, the fundamentals; then, the underlying laws; next, the essential grammar and, finally, the reading of texts. Once mastered, that was that: Latin was Latin and forever after would always be Latin. History, 3 once learned, was history. And biology was precisely biology, a vast array of hard facts to be learned as fundamentals, followed by a reading of the texts.

Furthermore, we have been teaching science as if its facts were somehow superior to the facts in all other scholarly disciplines—more fundamental, more solid, less subject to subjectivism, immutable. English literature is not just one way of thinking; it is all sorts of ways; poetry is a moving target; the facts that underlie art, architecture and music are not really hard facts, and you can change them any way you like by arguing about them. But science, it appears, is an altogether different kind of learning: an unambiguous, unalterable and endlessly useful display of data that only needs to be packaged and installed somewhere in one's temporal lobe in order to achieve a full understanding of the natural world.

And, of course, it is not like this at all. In real life, every field of science is incomplete, and most of them—whatever the record of accomplishment during the last 200 years—are still in their very earliest stages. In the fields I know best, among the life sciences, it is required that the most expert and sophisticated minds be capable of changing course—often with a great lurch—every few years. In some branches of biology the mind-changing is occurring with accelerating velocity. Next week's issue of any scientific journal can turn a whole field upside down, shaking out any number of immutable ideas and installing new bodies of dogma. This is an almost everyday event in physics, in chemistry, in materials research, in neurobiology, in genetics, in immunology.

On any Tuesday morning, if asked, a good working scientist will tell you with some self-satisfaction that the affairs of his field are nicely in order, that things are finally looking clear and making sense, and all is well. But come back again on another Tuesday, and the roof may have just fallen in on his life's work. All the old ideas—last week's ideas in some cases—are no longer good ideas. The hard facts have softened, melted away and vanished under the pressure of new hard facts. Something strange has happened. And it is this very strangeness of nature that makes science engrossing, that keeps bright people at it, and that ought to be at the center of science teaching.

The conclusions reached in science are always, when looked at closely, far more provisional and tentative than are most of the assumptions arrived at by our colleagues in the humanities. But we do not talk much in public about this, nor do we teach this side of science. We tend to say instead: These are the facts of the matter, and this is what the facts signify. Go and learn them, for they will be the same forever.

By doing this, we miss opportunity after opportunity to recruit young people into science, and we turn off a good many others who would never dream of scientific careers but who emerge from their education with the impression that science is fundamentally boring.

Sooner or later, we will have to change this way of presenting science. We might begin by looking more closely at the common ground that science shares with all disciplines, particularly with the humanities and with social and be-havioral science. For there is indeed such a common ground. It is called bewilderment. There are more than seven times seven types of ambiguity in science, all awaiting analysis. The poetry of Wallace Stevens is crystal clear alongside the genetic code.

One of the complaints about science is that it tends to flatten everything. In its deeply reductionist way, it is said, science removes one mystery after another, leaving nothing in the place of mystery but data. I have even heard this claim as explanation for the drift of things in modern art and modern music: Nothing is left to contemplate except randomness and senselessness; God is nothing but a pair of dice, loaded at that. Science is linked somehow to the despair of the 20th-century mind. There is almost nothing unknown and surely nothing unknowable. Blame science.

I prefer to turn things around in order to make precisely the opposite case. Science, especially 20th-century science, has provided us with a glimpse of something we never really knew before, the revelation of human ignorance. We have been accustomed to the belief, from one century to another, that except for one or two mysteries we more or less comprehend everything on earth. Every age, not just the 18th century, regarded itself as the Age of Reason, and we have never lacked for explanations of the world and its ways. Now, we are being brought up short. We do not understand much of anything, from the episode we rather dismissively (and, I think, defensively) choose to call the "big bang," all the way down to the particles in the atoms of a bacterial cell. We have a wilderness of mystery to make our way through in the centuries ahead. We will need science for this but not science alone. In its own time, science will produce the data and some of the meaning in the data, but never the full meaning. For perceiving real significance when significance is at hand, we will need all sorts of brains outside the fields of science.

It is primarily because of this need that I would press for changes in the way science is taught. Although there is a perennial need to teach the young people who will be doing the science themselves, this will always be a small minority. Even more important, we must teach science to those who will be needed for thinking about it, and that means pretty nearly everyone else—most of all, the poets, but also artists, musicians, philosophers, historians and writers. A few of these people, at least, will be able to imagine new levels of meaning which may be lost on the rest of us.

In addition, it is time to develop a new group of professional thinkers, perhaps a somewhat larger group than the working scientists and the working poets, who can create a discipline of scientific criticism. We have had good luck so far in the emergence of a few people ranking as philosophers of science and historians and journalists of science, and I hope more of these will be coming along. But we have not yet seen specialists in the fields of scientific criticism who are of the caliber of the English literary and social critics F. R. Leavis and John Ruskin or the American literary critic Edmund Wilson. Science needs critics of this sort, but the public at large needs them more urgently.

I suggest that the introductory courses in science, at all levels from grade 14 school through college, be radically revised. Leave the fundamentals, the so-called basics, aside for a while, and concentrate the attention of all students on the things that are not known. You cannot possibly teach quantum mechanics without mathematics, to be sure, but you can describe the strangeness of the world opened up by quantum theory. Let it be known, early on, that there are deep mysteries and profound paradoxes revealed in distant outline by modern physics. Explain that these can be approached more closely and puzzled over, once the language of mathematics has been sufficiently mastered.

At the outset, before any of the fundamentals, teach the still imponderable 15 puzzles of cosmology. Describe as clearly as possible, for the youngest minds, that there are some things going on in the universe that lie still beyond comprehension, and make it plain how little is known.

Do not teach that biology is a useful and perhaps profitable science; that can 16 come later. Teach instead that there are structures squirming inside each of our cells that provide all the energy for living. Essentially foreign creatures, these lineal descendants of bacteria were brought in for symbiotic living a billion or so years ago. Teach that we do not have the ghost of an idea how they got there, where they came from, or how they evolved to their present structure and function. The details of oxidative phosphorylation and photosynthesis can come later.

Teach ecology early on. Let it be understood that the earth's life is a system 17 of interdependent creatures, and that we do not understand at all how it works. The earth's environment, from the range of atmospheric gases to the chemical constituents of the sea, has been held in an almost unbelievably improbable state of regulated balance since life began, and the regulation of stability and balance is somehow accomplished by the life itself, like the autonomic nervous system of an immense organism. We do not know how such a system works, much less what it means, but there are some nice reductionist details at hand, such as the bizarre proportions of atmospheric constituents, ideal for our sort of planetary life, and the surprising stability of the ocean's salinity, and the fact that the average temperature of the earth has remained quite steady in the face of at least a 25 percent increase in heat coming in from the sun since the earth began. That kind of thing: something to think about.

Go easy, I suggest, on the promises sometimes freely offered by science. 18 Technology relies and depends on science these days, more than ever before, but technology is far from the first justification for doing research, nor is it necessarily an essential product to be expected from science. Public decisions about the future of technology are totally different from decisions about science, and the two enterprises should not be tangled together. The central task of science is to arrive, stage by stage, at a clearer comprehension of nature, but this does not at all mean, as it is sometimes claimed to mean, a search for mastery over nature.

Science may someday provide us with a better understanding of ourselves, but never, I hope, with a set of technologies for doing something or other to improve ourselves. I am made nervous by assertions that human consciousness will someday be unraveled by research, laid out for close scrutiny like the workings of a computer, and then—and *then* . . . ! I hope with some fervor that we can learn a lot more than we now know about the human mind, and I see no reason why this strange puzzle should remain forever and entirely beyond us. But I would be deeply disturbed by any prospect that we might use the new knowledge in order to begin doing something about it—to improve it, say. This is a different matter from searching for information to use against schizophrenia or dementia, where we are badly in need of technologies, indeed likely one day to be sunk without them. But the ordinary, everyday, more or less normal human mind is too marvelous an instrument ever to be tampered with by anyone, science or no science.

The education of humanists cannot be regarded as complete, or even adequate, without exposure in some depth to where things stand in the various branches of science, particularly, as I have said, in the areas of our ignorance. Physics professors, most of them, look with revulsion on assignments to teach their subject to poets. Biologists, caught up by the enchantment of their new power, armed with flawless instruments to tell the nucleotide sequences of the entire human genome, nearly matching the physicists in the precision of their measurements of living processes, will resist the prospect of broad survey courses; each biology professor will demand that any student in his path master every fine detail within that professor's research program.

The liberal-arts faculties, for their part, will continue to view the scientists with suspicion and apprehension. "What do the scientists want?" asked a Cambridge professor in Francis Cornford's wonderful "Microcosmographia Academica." "Everything that's going," was the quick answer. That was back in 1912, and scientists haven't much changed.

But maybe, just maybe, a new set of courses dealing systematically with ignorance in science will take hold. The scientists might discover in it a new and subversive technique for catching the attention of students driven by curiosity, delighted and surprised to learn that science is exactly as the American scientist and educator Vannevar Bush described it: an "endless frontier." The humanists, for their part, might take considerable satisfaction in watching their scientific colleagues confess openly to not knowing everything about everything. And the poets, on whose shoulders the future rests, might, late nights, thinking things over, begin to see some meanings that elude the rest of us. It is worth a try.

I believe that the worst thing that has happened to science education is that the fun has gone out of it. A great many good students look at it as slogging

19

20

21

22

23

work to be got through on the way to medical school. Others are turned off by the premedical students themselves, embattled and bleeding for grades and class standing. Very few recognize science as the high adventure it really is, the wildest of all explorations ever taken by human beings, the chance to glimpse things never seen before, the shrewdest maneuver for discovering how the world works. Instead, baffled early on, they are misled into thinking that bafflement is simply the result of not having learned all the facts. They should be told that everyone else is baffled as well—from the professor in his endowed chair down to the platoons of postdoctoral students in the laboratories all night. Every important scientific advance that has come in looking like an answer has turned, sooner or later—usually sooner—into a question. And the game is just beginning.

If more students were aware of this, I think many of them would decide to 24 look more closely and to try and learn more about what *is* known. That is the time when mathematics will become clearly and unavoidably recognizable as an essential, indispensable instrument for engaging in the game, and that is the time for teaching it. The calamitous loss of applied mathematics from what we might otherwise be calling higher education is a loss caused, at least in part, by insufficient incentives for learning the subject. Left by itself, standing there among curriculum offerings, it is not at all clear to the student what it is to be applied to. And there is all of science, next door, looking like an almost-finished field reserved only for chaps who want to invent or apply new technologies. We have had it wrong, and presented it wrong to class after class for several generations.

An appreciation of what is happening in science today, and how great a 25 distance lies ahead for exploring, ought to be one of the rewards of a liberal-arts education. It ought to be good in itself, not something to be acquired on the way to a professional career but part of the cast of thought needed for getting into the kind of century that is now just down the road. Part of the intellectual equipment of an educated person, however his or her time is to be spent, ought to be a feel for the queernesses of nature, the inexplicable thing, the side of life for which informed bewilderment will be the best way of getting through the day.

QUESTIONS

1. What is the thesis of Thomas's argument? What parts of the essay present evidence to support it? What parts of the essay offer alternatives to present methods of teaching science? Do you think Thomas presents valid reasons for adopting these alternatives?

2. In Thomas's view, what is wrong with the way science is taught now? What suggestions does he offer for the improvement of science teaching?

3. What does Thomas mean by giving poets responsibility for the future (paragraph 22)? Can he be serious? Or is this a rhetorical trick of some kind?

4. What would it take to be the kind of critic of science that Thomas mentions in paragraph 13?

5. Who is Thomas's audience? What is his attitude toward his audience?

6. Thomas concludes by saying, "Part of the intellectual equipment of an educated person . . . ought to be a feel for the queernesses of nature, the inexplicable thing, the side of life for which informed bewilderment will be the best way of getting through the day." What does he mean by "informed bewilderment"? How does one develop that?

7. What points made by Thomas apply to your experience in science courses you elected or were required to take? Drawing on your own experience and those points in the essay which are relevant to it, or those points you wish to take issue with, write a letter to a friend who is to attend your college, and present an argument either for or against taking a particular science course.

8. If Lewis Thomas were teaching a biology course at your school next semester, would you take it? Give reasons.

MAKING CONNECTIONS

1. Thomas's argument is a little like John Berger's in "Hiroshima" in that it depends in part on a complete inversion of common assumptions. Berger reverses the prevailing definitions of *terrorism* and *terrorists*, while Thomas would invert the order in which questions are raised in science courses. Are there any other common denominators of their thinking? Would it make sense to add that Thomas's argument is to some extent political? What political dimensions do you find in it?

2. If Thomas's call for a revision in science teaching were to be heeded, would it not lead to some of the developments we have seen in history and in teaching history, particularly as represented by Frances FitzGerald's "America Revised" and Linda Simon's "The Naked Source"? Do you think those would be fortunate or unfortunate developments? Explain.

THE CASE AGAINST MAN

Isaac Asimov

Isaac Asimov (b. 1920) is a professor of biochemistry at the Boston University School of Medicine and one of America's most wide-ranging and productive writers. His popular Foundation novels are science fiction, but he has also written mysteries, fantasies, and many nonfiction books about science, technology, and history. Asimov has said of his own writing, "Everything I write goes through the typewriter twice. But I have a completely unadorned style. I aim to be accurate and clear, and not to write great literature." The following essay comes from Science Past—Science Future *(1970). In this essay, Asimov's "case" draws on both the legal and medical uses of the term but expands beyond both to encompass larger, moral issues.*

The first mistake is to think of mankind as a thing in itself. It isn't. It is part 1
of an intricate web of life. And we can't think even of life as a thing in itself.
It isn't. It is part of the intricate structure of a planet bathed by energy from the
Sun.

The Earth, in the nearly 5 billion years since it assumed approximately its 2
present form, has undergone a vast evolution. When it first came into being,
it very likely lacked what we would today call an ocean and an atmosphere.
These were formed by the gradual outward movement of material as the solid
interior settled together.

Nor were ocean, atmosphere, and solid crust independent of each other after 3
formation. There is interaction always: evaporation, condensation, solution,
weathering. Far within the solid crust there are slow, continuing changes, too,
of which hot springs, volcanoes, and earthquakes are the more noticeable
manifestations here on the surface.

Between 2 billion and 3 billion years ago, portions of the surface water, 4
bathed by the energetic radiation from the Sun, developed complicated compounds in organization sufficiently versatile to qualify as what we call "life."
Life forms have become more complex and more various ever since.

But the life forms are as much part of the structure of the Earth as any 5
inanimate portion is. It is all an inseparable part of a whole. If any animal is
isolated totally from other forms of life, then death by starvation will surely
follow. If isolated from water, death by dehydration will follow even faster. If

isolated from air, whether free or dissolved in water, death by asphyxiation will follow still faster. If isolated from the Sun, animals will survive for a time, but plants would die, and if all plants died, all animals would starve.

It works in reverse, too, for the inanimate portion of Earth is shaped and molded by life. The nature of the atmosphere has been changed by plant activity (which adds to the air the free oxygen it could not otherwise retain). The soil is turned by earthworms, while enormous ocean reefs are formed by coral. 6

The entire planet, plus solar energy, is one enormous intricately interrelated system. The entire planet is a life form made up of nonliving portions and a large variety of living portions (as our own body is made up of nonliving crystals in bones and nonliving water in blood, as well as of a large variety of living portions). 7

In fact, we can pursue the analogy. A man is composed of 50 trillion cells of a variety of types, all interrelated and interdependent. Loss of some of those cells, such as those making up an entire leg, will seriously handicap all the rest of the organism: serious damage to a relatively few cells in an organ, such as the heart or kidneys, may end by killing all 50 trillion. 8

In the same way, on a planetary scale, the chopping down of an entire forest may not threaten Earth's life in general, but it will produce serious changes in the life forms of the region and even in the nature of the water runoff and, therefore, in the details of geological structure. A serious decline in the bee population will affect the numbers of those plants that depend on bees for fertilization, then the numbers of those animals that depend on those particular bee-fertilized plants, and so on. 9

Or consider cell growth. Cells in those organs that suffer constant wear and tear—as in the skin or in the intestinal lining—grow and multiply all life long. Other cells, not so exposed, as in nerve and muscle, do not multiply at all in the adult, under any circumstances. Still other organs, ordinarily quiescent, as liver and bone, stand ready to grow if that is necessary to replace damage. When the proper repairs are made, growth stops. 10

In a much looser and more flexible way, the same is true of the "planet organism" (which we study in the science called ecology). If cougars grow too numerous, the deer they live on are decimated, and some of the cougars die of starvation, so that their "proper number" is restored. If too many cougars die, then the deer multiply with particular rapidity, and cougars multiply quickly in turn, till the additional predators bring down the number of deer again. Barring interference from outside, the eaters and the eaten retain their proper numbers, and both are the better for it. (If the cougars are all killed off, deer would multiply to the point where they destroy the plants they live off, and more would then die of starvation than would have died of cougars.) 11

The neat economy of growth within an organism such as a human being is sometimes—for what reason, we know not—disrupted, and a group of cells 12

751

begins growing without limit. This is the dread disease of cancer, and unless that growing group of cells is somehow stopped, the wild growth will throw all the body structure out of true and end by killing the organism itself.

In ecology, the same would happen if, for some reason, one particular type of organism began to multiply without limit, killing its competitors and increasing its own food supply at the expense of that of others. That, too, could end only in the destruction of the larger system—most or all of life and even of certain aspects of the inanimate environment. 13

And this is exactly what is happening at this moment. For thousands of years, the single species Homo sapiens, to which you and I have the dubious honor of belonging, has been increasing in numbers. In the past couple of centuries, the rate of increase has itself increased explosively. 14

At the time of Julius Caesar, when Earth's human population is estimated to have been 150 million, that population was increasing at a rate such that it would double in 1,000 years if that rate remained steady. Today, with Earth's population estimated at about 4,000 million (26 times what it was in Caesar's time), it is increasing at a rate which, if steady, will cause it to double in 35 years. 15

The present rate of increase of Earth's swarming human population qualifies Homo sapiens as an ecological cancer, which will destroy the ecology just as surely as any ordinary cancer would destroy an organism. 16

The cure? Just what it is for any cancer. The cancerous growth must somehow be stopped. 17

Of course, it will be. If we do nothing at all, the growth will stop, as a cancerous growth in a man will stop if nothing is done. The man dies and the cancer dies with him. And, analogously, the ecology will die and man will die with it. 18

How can the human population explosion be stopped? By raising the deathrate, or by lowering the birthrate. There are no other alternatives. The deathrate will rise spontaneously and finally catastrophically, if we do nothing—and that within a few decades. To make the birthrate fall, somehow (almost *any* how, in fact), is surely preferable, and that is therefore the first order of mankind's business today. 19

Failing this, mankind would stand at the bar of abstract justice (for there may be no posterity to judge) as the mass murderer of life generally, his own included, and mass disrupter of the intricate planetary development that made life in its present glory possible in the first place. 20

Am I too pessimistic? Can we allow the present rate of population increase to continue indefinitely, or at least for a good long time? Can we count on science to develop methods for cleaning up as we pollute, for replacing wasted resources with substitutes, for finding new food, new materials, more and better life for our waxing numbers? 21

Impossible! If the numbers continue to wax at the present rate. 22

Let us begin with a few estimates (admittedly not precise, but in the rough   23
neighborhood of the truth).

The total mass of living objects on Earth is perhaps 20 trillion tons. There   24
is usually a balance between eaters and eaten that is about 1 to 10 in favor of
the eaten. There would therefore be about 10 times as much plant life (the
eaten) as animal life (the eaters) on Earth. There is, in other words, just a little
under 2 trillion tons of animal life on Earth.

But this is all the animal life that can exist, given the present quantity of   25
plant life. If more animal life is somehow produced, it will strip down the plant
life, reduce the food supply, and then enough animals will starve to restore the
balance. If one species of animal life increases in mass, it can only be because
other species correspondingly decrease. For every additional pound of human
flesh on Earth, a pound of some other form of flesh must disappear.

The total mass of humanity now on Earth may be estimated at about 200   26
million tons, or one ten-thousandth the mass of all animal life. If mankind
increases in numbers ten thousandfold, then Homo sapiens will be, perforce,
the *only* animal species alive on Earth. It will be a world without elephants or
lions, without cats or dogs, without fish or lobsters, without worms or bugs.
What's more, to support the mass of human life, all the plant world must be
put to service. Only plants edible to man must remain, and only those plants
most concentratedly edible and with minimum waste.

At the present moment, the average density of population of the Earth's land   27
surface is about 73 people per square mile. Increase that ten thousandfold and
the average density will become 730,000 people per square mile, or more than
seven times the density of the workday population of Manhattan. Even if we
assume that mankind will somehow spread itself into vast cities floating on the
ocean surface (or resting on the ocean floor), the average density of human life
at the time when the last nonhuman animal must be killed would be 310,000
people per square mile over all the world, land and sea alike, or a little better
than three times the density of modern Manhattan at noon.

We have the vision, then, of high-rise apartments, higher and more thickly   28
spaced than in Manhattan at present, spreading all over the world, across all
the mountains, across the Sahara Desert, across Antarctica, across all the oceans;
all with their load of humanity and with no other form of animal life beside.
And on the roof of all those buildings are the algae farms, with little plant cells
exposed to the Sun so that they might grow rapidly and, without waste, form
protein for all the mighty population of 35 trillion human beings.

Is that tolerable? Even if science produced all the energy and materials   29
mankind could want, kept them all fed with algae, all educated, all amused—
is the planetary high-rise tolerable?

And if it were, can we double the population further in 35 more years? And   30
then double it again in another 35 years? Where will the food come from?
What will persuade the algae to multiply faster than the light energy they absorb

makes possible? What will speed up the Sun to add the energy to make it possible? And if vast supplies of fusion energy are added to supplement the Sun, how will we get rid of the equally vast supplies of heat that will be produced? And after the icecaps are melted and the oceans boiled into steam, what?

Can we bleed off the mass of humanity to other worlds? Right now, the   31 number of human beings on Earth is increasing by 80 million per year, and each year that number goes up by 1 and a fraction percent. Can we really suppose that we can send 80 million people per year to the Moon, Mars, and elsewhere, and engineer those worlds to support those people? And even so, merely remain in the same place ourselves?

No! Not the most optimistic visionary in the world could honestly convince   32 himself that space travel is the solution to our population problem, if the present rate of increase is sustained.

But when will this planetary high-rise culture come about? How long will it   33 take to increase Earth's population to that impossible point at the present doubling rate of once every 35 years? If it will take 1 million years or even 100,000, then, for goodness sake, let's not worry just yet.

Well, we don't have that kind of time. We will reach that dead end in no   34 more than 460 years.

At the rate we are going, without birth control, then even if science serves   35 us in an absolutely ideal way, we will reach the planetary high-rise with no animals but man, with no plants but algae, with no room for even one more person, by A.D. 2430.

And if science serves us in less than an ideal way (as it certainly will), the   36 end will come sooner, much sooner, and mankind will start fading long, long before he is forced to construct that building that will cover all the Earth's surface.

So if birth control *must* come by A.D. 2430 at the very latest, even in an   37 ideal world of advancing science, let it come *now*, in heaven's name, while there are still oak trees in the world and daisies and tigers and butterflies, and while there is still open land and space, and before the cancer called man proves fatal to life and the planet.

QUESTIONS

1. In the opening paragraphs of this essay, Asimov seems to disapprove of our ability or willingness to stand apart from nature. How does that view of humankind relate to the larger concerns of his essay?

2. Does Asimov convince you that birth control is necessary? Why or why not?

3. The word *case* in the title has both legal and medical meanings. Which predominates? How do both contribute to Asimov's thesis?

4. In paragraphs 7 through 18, Asimov argues by analogy. What are some of his analogies? How do they function in the essay?

5. Asimov's most serious analogy is of humankind as a cancer. Trace the development of that analogy.

6. Write a "case" against some category of thing—against automobiles, athletics, insects, or whatever. Try to find an analogy or two that will help shape your presentation.

7. If you think of this essay as a quasi-legal case, with humans as defendants in a special trial, there could be a statement written in our defense. Write one.

MAKING CONNECTIONS

1. Asimov's case suggests the need of someone writing a "Declaration of Independence" for the earth. Who might write such a thing? What kind of "Continental Congress" would best authorize that writing? What would such a declaration say? Try your hand at a draft.

2. Read Virginia Woolf's "The Death of the Moth" in "Reporting." Does Asimov's essay trivialize Woolf's concerns? Write your own commentary on Woolf but from the point of view of someone, like Asimov, thinking of "the big picture."

EVOLUTION AS FACT
AND THEORY

Stephen Jay Gould

Stephen Jay Gould, well known for his monthly column in
Natural History *magazine, has written many scientific ar-*
ticles including those reprinted on pages 573–582 and pages
692–696. The essay reprinted here appeared first in Discover
magazine, a journal of popular science, in 1981.

Kirtley Mather, who died last year at age 89, was a pillar of both science   1
and the Christian religion in America and one of my dearest friends. The
difference of half a century in our ages evaporated before our common interests.
The most curious thing we shared was a battle we each fought at the same age.
For Kirtley had gone to Tennessee with Clarence Darrow to testify for evolution
at the Scopes trial of 1925. When I think that we are enmeshed again in the
same struggle for one of the best documented, most compelling and exciting
concepts in all of science, I don't know whether to laugh or cry.

According to idealized principles of scientific discourse, the arousal of dor-   2
mant issues should reflect fresh data that give renewed life to abandoned notions.
Those outside the current debate may therefore be excused for suspecting that
creationists have come up with something new, or that evolutionists have
generated some serious internal trouble. But nothing has changed; the creationists have not a single new fact or argument. Darrow and Bryan were at least
more entertaining than we lesser antagonists today.[1] The rise of creationism is
politics, pure and simple; it represents one issue (and by no means the major
concern) of the resurgent evangelical right. Arguments that seemed kooky just
a decade ago have re-entered the mainstream.

CREATIONISM IS NOT SCIENCE

The basic attack of the creationists falls apart on two general counts before   3
we even reach the supposed factual details of their complaints against evolution.
First, they play upon a vernacular misunderstanding of the word "theory" to
convey the false impression that we evolutionists are covering up the rotten core
of our edifice. Second, they misuse a popular philosophy of science to argue
that they are behaving scientifically in attacking evolution. Yet the same phi-

---

[1]Clarence Darrow (1857–1938): the defense attorney in the 1925 trial of John Thomas Scopes
for teaching evolution; William Jennings Bryan (1860–1925): an orator and politician who aided
the prosecution in the Scopes trial. [Eds.]

losophy demonstrates that their own belief is not science, and that "scientific creationism" is therefore meaningless and self-contradictory, a superb example of what Orwell[2] called "newspeak."[3]

In the American vernacular, "theory" often means "imperfect fact"—part of   4
a hierarchy of confidence running downhill from fact to theory to hypothesis to guess. Thus the power of the creationist argument: evolution is "only" a theory, and intense debate now rages about many aspects of the theory. If evolution is less than a fact, and scientists can't even make up their minds about the theory, then what confidence can we have in it? Indeed, President Reagan echoed this argument before an evangelical group in Dallas when he said (in what I devoutly hope was campaign rhetoric): "Well, it is a theory. It is a scientific theory only, and it has in recent years been challenged in the world of science—that is, not believed in the scientific community to be as infallible as it once was."

Well, evolution *is* a theory. It is also a fact. And facts and theories are   5
different things, not rungs in a hierarchy of increasing certainty. Facts are the world's data. Theories are structures of ideas that explain and interpret facts. Facts do not go away when scientists debate rival theories to explain them. Einstein's theory of gravitation replaced Newton's, but apples did not suspend themselves in mid-air pending the outcome. And human beings evolved from apelike ancestors whether they did so by Darwin's proposed mechanism or by some other, yet to be discovered.

Moreover, "fact" does not mean "absolute certainty." The final proofs of   6
logic and mathematics flow deductively from stated premises and achieve certainty only because they are *not* about the empirical world. Evolutionists make no claim for perpetual truth, though creationists often do (and then attack us for a style of argument that they themselves favor). In science, "fact" can only mean "confirmed to such a degree that it would be perverse to withhold provisional assent." I suppose that apples might start to rise tomorrow, but the possibility does not merit equal time in physics classrooms.

Evolutionists have been clear about this distinction between fact and theory   7
from the very beginning, if only because we have always acknowledged how far we are from completely understanding the mechanisms (theory) by which evolution (fact) occurred. Darwin continually emphasized the difference between his two great and separate accomplishments: establishing the fact of evolution, and proposing a theory—natural selection—to explain the mechanism of evolution. He wrote in *The Descent of Man*: "I had two distinct objects in view; firstly, to show that species had not been separately created, and secondly, that natural selection had been the chief agent of change . . . Hence if I have erred

---

[2] George Orwell (1903–1950): English journalist and novelist, author of *Animal Farm* and *1984*. [Eds.]

[3] "newspeak": the official language in Orwell's *1984*, devised to meet the ideological needs of the ruling party and to make all other modes of thought impossible. [Eds.]

in . . . having exaggerated its [natural selection's] power . . . I have at least, as I hope, done good service in aiding to overthrow the dogma of separate creations."

Thus Darwin acknowledged the provisional nature of natural selection while affirming the fact of evolution. The fruitful theoretical debate that Darwin initiated has never ceased. From the 1940s through the 1960s, Darwin's own theory of natural selection did achieve a temporary hegemony that it never enjoyed in his lifetime. But renewed debate characterizes our decade, and, while no biologist questions the importance of natural selection, many now doubt its ubiquity. In particular, many evolutionists argue that substantial amounts of genetic change may not be subject to natural selection and may spread through populations at random. Others are challenging Darwin's linking of natural selection with gradual, imperceptible change through all intermediary degrees; they are arguing that most evolutionary events may occur far more rapidly than Darwin envisioned.   8

Scientists regard debates on fundamental issues of theory as a sign of intellectual health and a source of excitement. Science is—and how else can I say it?—most fun when it plays with interesting ideas, examines their implications, and recognizes that old information may be explained in surprisingly new ways. Evolutionary theory is now enjoying this uncommon vigor. Yet amidst all this turmoil no biologist has been led to doubt the fact that evolution occurred; we are debating *how* it happened. We are all trying to explain the same thing: the tree of evolutionary descent linking all organisms by ties of genealogy. Creationists pervert and caricature this debate by conveniently neglecting the common conviction that underlies it, and by falsely suggesting that we now doubt the very phenomenon we are struggling to understand.   9

Using another invalid argument, creationists claim that "the dogma of separate creations," as Darwin characterized it a century ago, is a scientific theory meriting equal time with evolution in high school biology curricula. But a prevailing viewpoint among philosophers of science belies this creationist argument. Philosopher Karl Popper has argued for decades that the primary criterion of science is the falsifiability of its theories. We can never prove absolutely, but we can falsify. A set of ideas that cannot, in principle, be falsified is not science.   10

The entire creationist argument involves little more than a rhetorical attempt to falsify evolution by presenting supposed contradictions among its supporters. Their brand of creationism, they claim, is "scientific" because it follows the Popperian model in trying to demolish evolution. Yet Popper's argument must apply in both directions. One does not become a scientist by the simple act of trying to falsify another scientific system; one has to present an alternative system that also meets Popper's criterion—it too must be falsifiable in principle.   11

"Scientific creationism" is a self-contradictory, nonsense phrase precisely because it cannot be falsified. I can envision observations and experiments that   12 would disprove any evolutionary theory I know, but I cannot imagine what potential data could lead creationists to abandon their beliefs. Unbeatable systems are dogma, not science. Lest I seem harsh or rhetorical, I quote creationism's leading intellectual, Duane Gish, Ph.D., from his recent (1978) book *Evolution? The Fossils Say No!* "By creation we mean the bringing into being by a supernatural Creator of the basic kinds of plants and animals by the process of sudden, or fiat, creation. We do not know how the Creator created, what processes He used, *for He used processes which are not now operating anywhere in the natural universe* [Gish's italics]. This is why we refer to creation as special creation. We cannot discover by scientific investigations anything about the creative processes used by the Creator." Pray tell, Dr. Gish, in the light of your last sentence, what then is "scientific" creationism?

THE FACT OF EVOLUTION

Our confidence that evolution occurred centers upon three general arguments. First, we have abundant, direct, observational evidence of evolution in action, from both the field and the laboratory. It ranges from countless experiments on change in nearly everything about fruit flies subjected to artificial selection in the laboratory to the famous British moths that turned black when industrial soot darkened the trees upon which they rest. (The moths gain protection from sharp-sighted bird predators by blending into the background.) Creationists do not deny these observations; how could they? Creationists have tightened their act. They now argue that God only created "basic kinds," and allowed for limited evolutionary meandering within them. Thus toy poodles and Great Danes come from the dog kind and moths can change color, but nature cannot convert a dog to a cat or a monkey to a man. 13

The second and third arguments for evolution—the case for major changes— do not involve direct observation of evolution in action. They rest upon inference, but are no less secure for that reason. Major evolutionary change requires too much time for direct observation on the scale of recorded human history. All historical sciences rest upon inference, and evolution is no different from geology, cosmology, or human history in this respect. In principle, we cannot observe processes that operated in the past. We must infer them from results that still survive: living and fossil organisms for evolution, documents and artifacts for human history, strata and topography for geology. 14

The second argument—that the imperfection of nature reveals evolution— strikes many people as ironic, for they feel that evolution should be most elegantly displayed in the nearly perfect adaptation expressed by some organisms—the chamber of a gull's wing, or butterflies that cannot be seen in ground litter because they mimic leaves so precisely. But perfection could be imposed by a wise creator or evolved by natural selection. Perfection covers the tracks 15 of past history. And past history—the evidence of descent—is our mark of evolution.

Evolution lies exposed in the *imperfections* that record a history of descent.   16
Why should a rat run, a bat fly, a porpoise swim, and I type this essay with structures built of the same bones unless we all inherited them from a common ancestor? An engineer, starting from scratch, could design better limbs in each case. Why should all the large native mammals of Australia be marsupials, unless they descended from a common ancestor isolated on this island continent? Marsupials are not "better," or ideally suited for Australia; many have been wiped out by placental mammals imported by man from other continents. This principle of imperfection extends to all historical sciences. When we recognize the etymology of September, October, November, and December (seventh, eighth, ninth, and tenth, from the Latin), we know that two additional items (January and February) must have been added to an original calendar of ten months.

The third argument is more direct: transitions are often found in the fossil   17
record. Preserved transitions are not common—and should not be, according to our understanding of evolution (see next section)—but they are not entirely wanting, as creationists often claim. The lower jaw of reptiles contains several bones, that of mammals only one. The non-mammalian jawbones are reduced, step by step, in mammalian ancestors until they become tiny nubbins located at the back of the jaw. The "hammer" and "anvil" bones of the mammalian ear are descendants of these nubbins. How could such a transition be accomplished? the creationists ask. Surely a bone is either entirely in the jaw or in the ear. Yet paleontologists have discovered two transitional lineages or therapsids (the so-called mammal-like reptiles) with a double jaw joint—one composed of the old quadrate and articular bones (soon to become the hammer and anvil), the other of the squamosal and dentary bones (as in modern mammals). For that matter, what better transitional form could we desire than the oldest human, *Australopithecus afarensis*, with its apelike palate, its human upright stance, and a cranial capacity larger than any ape's of the same body size but a full 1,000 cubic centimeters below ours? If God made each of the half dozen human species discovered in ancient rocks, why did he create in an unbroken temporal sequence of progressively more modern features—increasing cranial capacity, reduced face and teeth, larger body size? Did he create to mimic evolution and test our faith thereby?

AN EXAMPLE OF CREATIONIST ARGUMENT

Faced with these facts of evolution and the philosophical bankruptcy of their   18
own position, creationists rely upon distortion and innuendo to buttress their

rhetorical claim. If I sound sharp or bitter, indeed I am—for I have become a major target of these practices.

I count myself among the evolutionists who argue for a jerky, or episodic, rather than a smoothly gradual, pace of change. In 1972 my colleague Niles Eldredge and I developed the theory of punctuated equilibrium [*Discover*, October]. We argued that two outstanding facts of the fossil record—geologically "sudden" origin of new species and failure to change thereafter (stasis)—reflect the predictions of evolutionary theory, not the imperfections of the fossil record. In most theories, small isolated populations are the source of new species, and the process of speciation takes thousands or tens of thousands of years. This amount of time, so long when measured against our lives, is a geological microsecond. It represents much less than 1 per cent of the average life span for a fossil invertebrate species—more than 10 million years. Large, widespread, and well-established species, on the other hand, are not expected to change very much. We believe that the inertia of large populations explains the stasis of most fossil species over millions of years. 19

We proposed the theory of punctuated equilibrium largely to provide a different explanation for pervasive trends in the fossil record. Trends, we argued, cannot be attributed to gradual transformation within lineages, but must arise from the differential success of certain kinds of species. A trend, we argued, is more like climbing a flight of stairs (punctuations and stasis) than rolling up an inclined plane. 20

Since we proposed punctuated equilibria to explain trends, it is infuriating to be quoted again and again by creationists—whether through design or stupidity, I do not know—as admitting that the fossil record includes no transitional forms. Transitional forms are generally lacking at the species level, but are abundant between larger groups. The evolution from reptiles to mammals, as mentioned earlier, is well documented. Yet a pamphlet entitled "Harvard Scientists Agree Evolution Is a Hoax" states: "The facts of punctuated equilibrium which Gould and Eldredge . . . are forcing Darwinists to swallow fit the picture that Bryan insisted on, and which God has revealed to us in the Bible." 21

Continuing the distortion, several creationists have equated the theory of punctuated equilibrium with a caricature of the beliefs of Richard Goldschmidt, a great early geneticist. Goldschmidt argued, in a famous book published in 1940, that new groups can arise all at once through major mutations. He referred to these suddenly transformed creatures as "hopeful monsters." (I am attracted to some aspects of the non-caricatured version, but Goldschmidt's theory still has nothing to do with punctuated equilibrium.) Creationist Luther Sunderland talks of the "punctuated equilibrium hopeful monster theory" and tells his hopeful readers that "it amounts to tacit admission that anti-evolutionists are correct in asserting there is no fossil evidence supporting the theory that all life is connected to a common ancestor." Duane Gish writes, "According to 22

Goldschmidt, and now apparently according to Gould, a reptile laid an egg from which the first bird, feathers and all, was produced." Any evolutionist who believed such nonsense would rightly be laughed off the intellectual stage; yet the only theory that could ever envision such a scenario for the evolution of birds is creationism—God acts in the egg.

CONCLUSION

I am both angry at and amused by the creationists; but mostly I am deeply   23
sad. Sad for many reasons. Sad because so many people who respond to creationist appeals are troubled for the right reason, but venting their anger at the wrong target. It is true that scientists have often been dogmatic and elitist. It is true that we have often allowed the white-coated, advertising image to represent us—"Scientists say that Brand X cures bunions ten times faster than . . ." We have not fought it adequately because we derive benefits from appearing as a new priesthood. It is also true that faceless bureaucratic state power intrudes more and more into our lives and removes choices that should belong to individuals and communities. I can understand that requiring that evolution be taught in the schools might be seen as one more insult on all these grounds. But the culprit is not, and cannot be, evolution or any other fact of the natural world. Identify and fight your legitimate enemies by all means, but we are not among them.

I am sad because the practical result of this brouhaha will not be expanded   24
coverage to include creationism (that would also make me sad), but the reduction or excision of evolution from high school curricula. Evolution is one of the half dozen "great ideas" developed by science. It speaks to the profound issues of genealogy that fascinate all of us—the "roots" phenomenon writ large. Where did we come from? Where did life arise? How did it develop? How are organisms related? It forces us to think, ponder, and wonder. Shall we deprive millions of this knowledge and once again teach biology as a set of dull and unconnected facts, without the thread that weaves diverse material into a supple unity?

But most of all I am saddened by a trend I am just beginning to discern   25
among my colleagues. I sense that some now wish to mute the healthy debate about theory that has brought new life to evolutionary biology. It provides grist for creationist mills, they say, even if only by distortion. Perhaps we should lie low and rally round the flag of strict Darwinism, at least for the moment—a kind of old-time religion on our part.

But we should borrow another metaphor and recognize that we too have to   26
tread a straight and narrow path, surrounded by roads to perdition. For if we ever begin to suppress our search to understand nature, to quench our own intellectual excitement in a misguided effort to present a united front where it does not and should not exist, then we are truly lost.

QUESTIONS

1. Summarize the difference between *fact* and *theory* as Gould uses those terms in paragraphs 3 through 12.

2. Why, in paragraph 13, does Gould return to the "fact of evolution"? What turn does his argument take there?

3. In paragraphs 18 through 22 Gould claims that the creationists have distorted his work. How well do you think Gould has substantiated this claim? Are all his examples and arguments convincing? If there are problems, what are they?

4. Consider the proposition that "a set of ideas that cannot, in principle, be falsified is not science" (paragraph 10). How does that proposition set evolution theory apart from creationism? What underlying notion does it point to in the history and nature of science?

5. Insofar as you can tell, does the teaching of evolution continue in schools in your area? Have the fears Gould voices at the end of his essay come to pass? Perhaps you can draw upon your own memory of high school, and write a report on this subject. Or perhaps you can interview one or more high school biology teachers.

6. Gould opens his essay with a reference to the Scopes trial in 1925. Do some library research about that trial and about the current debate. Write an essay arguing that the same battle continues or that significant differences exist between the two situations.

7. In paragraph 12 Gould criticizes Gish for assuming that God created the world, using "processes which are not now operating anywhere in the natural universe." Does this mean that to be a scientist, one must accept the opposite assumption, namely, that *natural processes are always the same throughout the universe*? Write an essay in which you consider a science that you have studied, exploring the extent to which it depends upon this assumption. What are the main theories and facts established by this science? Do they require this assumption? Is the assumption itself scientific? Or is it an article of faith?

MAKING CONNECTIONS

1. Compare Gould's essay with Lewis Thomas's "The Art of Teaching Science." To what extent does Gould approach science, and evolutionary theory in particular, in much the way Thomas recommends? Where do you find particular points of convergence? If the creationists criticize Gould, what do you think they would say of Thomas? What do you suppose Thomas would say to them?

2. This collection includes three essays by Gould; two are categorized as explanatory and one as argumentative. It is interesting to note that one argument and one explanation are located within the "Sciences and Technologies" section and the other explanation is placed within the "Social Sciences and Public Affairs" section. What similarities do Gould's scientific pieces share? What differences? What aspects of style and theme might determine the distinctions between argument and explanation, between an essay written about science and an essay written about social science? Do you find these distinctions logical or somewhat random?

TEST-TUBE BABIES:
SOLUTION OR PROBLEM?

Ruth Hubbard

*Ruth Hubbard, born in 1924 in Austria, is now an Amer-
ican biologist and professor of biology at Harvard University.
Her research interests include the chemistry of vision, the
sociology of science, and women's biology and health. She
is a member of the National Women's Health Network and
often writes for a general audience on women's health issues.
With Mary Sue Henifin and Barbara Fried, she edited*
Women Look at Biology Looking at Women *(1979), and
with Marian Lowe, she has edited* Genes and Gender II:
Pitfalls in Research on Sex and Gender *(1979) and* Woman's Nature: Rationalizations of Inequality *(1983).*

In vitro fertilization of human eggs and the implantation of early embryos   1
into women's wombs are new biotechnologies that may enable some women to
bear children who have hitherto been unable to do so.[1] In that sense, it may
solve their particular infertility problems. On the other hand, this technology
poses unpredictable hazards since it intervenes in the process of fertilization, in
the first cell divisions of the fertilized egg, and in the implantation of the embryo
into the uterus. At present we have no way to assess in what ways and to what
extent these interventions may affect the women or the babies they acquire by
this procedure. Since the use of the technology is only just beginning, the
financial and technical investments it represents are still modest. It is therefore
important that we, as a society, seriously consider the wisdom of implementing
and developing it further.

According to present estimates, about 10 million Americans are infertile by   2
the definition that they have tried for at least a year to achieve pregnancy
without conceiving or carrying a pregnancy to a live birth. In about a third of
infertile couples, the incapacity rests with the woman only, and for about a
third of these women the problem is localized in the fallopian tubes (the organs
that normally propel an egg from the ovary to the uterus or womb). These
short, delicate tubes are easily blocked by infection or disease. Nowadays the
most common causes of blocked tubes are inflammations of the uterine lining
brought on by IUDs, pelvic inflammatory disease, or gonorrhea. Once blocked,
the tubes are difficult to reopen or replace, and doctors presently claim only a

---

[1] in vitro: Latin for "in glass," that is, in a test tube. [Eds.]

one-in-three success rate in correcting the problem. Thus, of the 10 million infertile people in the country, about 600 thousand (or 6 per cent) could perhaps be helped to pregnancy by in vitro fertilization. (These numbers are from Barbara Eck Menning's *Infertility: A Guide for the Childless Couple,* Prentice-Hall, 1977. Ms. Menning is executive director of Resolve, a national, nonprofit counseling service for infertile couples located in Belmont, Mass.)

Louise Brown, born in England in July, 1978, is the first person claimed to 3 have been conceived in vitro. Since then, two other babies conceived outside the mother are said to have been born—one in England, the other in India. In none of these cases have the procedures by which the eggs were obtained from the woman's ovary, fertilized, stored until implantation, and finally implanted in her uterus been described in any detail. However, we can deduce the procedures from animal experimentation and the brief published accounts about the three babies.

The woman who is a candidate for in vitro fertilization has her hormone 4 levels monitored to determine when she is about to ovulate. She is then admitted to the hospital and the egg is collected in the following way: a small cut is made in her abdomen; a metal tube containing an optical arrangement that allows the surgeon to see the ovaries and a narrow-bore tube (called a micropipette) are inserted through the cut; and the egg is removed shortly before it would normally be shed from the ovary. The woman is ready to go home within a day, at most.

When the procedure was first developed, women were sometimes given 5 hormones to make them "superovulate"—produce more than one egg (the usual number for most women). But we do not know whether this happened with the mothers of the three "test-tube" babies that have been born. Incidentally, this superovulation reportedly is no longer induced, party because some people believe it is too risky.

After the egg has been isolated, it is put into a solution that keeps it alive 6 and nourishes it, and is mixed with sperm. Once fertilized, it is allowed to go through a few cell divisions and so begin its embryonic development—the still-mysterious process by which a fertilized egg becomes a baby. The embryo is then picked up with another fine tube, inserted through the woman's cervix, and flushed into the uterus.

If the uterus is not at the proper stage to allow for implantation (approximately 7 17 to 23 days after the onset of each menstruation) when the embryo is ready to be implanted, the embryo must be frozen and stored until the time is right in a subsequent menstrual cycle. Again, we do not know whether the embryos were frozen and stored prior to implantation with the two British babies; we are told that the Indian one was.

In sum, then, there is a need, and there is a technology said to meet that 8 need. But as a woman, a feminist, and a biologist, I am opposed to using it and developing it further.

HEALTH RISKS

As a society, we do not have a very good track record in anticipating the   9
problems that can arise from technological interventions in complicated biological systems. Our physical models are too simpleminded and have led to many
unforeseen problems in the areas of pest control, waste disposal, and other
aspects of what is usually referred to as the ecological crisis.

In reproductive biology, the nature of the many interacting processes is poorly   10
understood. We are in no position to enumerate or describe the many reactions
that must occur at just the right times during the early stages of embryonic
development when the fertilized egg begins to divide into increasing numbers
of cells, implants itself in the uterus, and establishes the pattern for the different
organ systems that will allow it to develop into a normal fetus and baby.

The safety of this in vitro procedure cannot be established in animal exper-   11
iments because the details and requirements of normal embryonic development
are different for different kinds of animals. Nor are the criteria of "normalcy"
the same for animals and for people. The guinea pigs of the research and
implementation of in vitro fertilization will be:

—the women who donate their eggs,
—the women who lend their wombs (who, of course, need not be the same as
    the egg-donors; rent-a-wombs clearly are an option), and
—the children who are produced.

The greatest ethical and practical questions arise with regard to the children.   12
They cannot consent to be produced, and we cannot know what hazards their
production entails until enough have lived out their lives to allow for statistical
analysis of their medical histories.

This example shows the inadequacy of our scientific models because it is   13
not obvious how to provide "controls," in the usual scientific sense of the term,
for the first generation of "test-tube" individuals; they will be viewed as "special"
at every critical juncture in their lives. When I ask myself whether I would
want to be a "test-tube person," I know that I would not like to have to add
those self-doubts to my more ordinary repertory of insecurities.

A concrete example of a misjudgment with an unfortunate outcome that   14
could not be predicted was the administration of the chemical thalidomide, a
"harmless tranquilizer" touted as a godsend and prescribed to pregnant women,
which resulted in the births of thousands of armless and legless babies. Yet
there the damage was visible at birth and the practice could be stopped, though
not until after it had caused great misery. But take the case of the hormone
DES (diethyl stilbesterol), which was prescribed for pregnant women in the
mistaken (though at the time honest) belief that it could prevent miscarriages.
Some 15 years passed before many of the daughters of these women developed
an unusual form of vaginal cancer. Both these chemicals produced otherwise

rare diseases, so the damage was easy to detect and its causes could be sought. Had the chemicals produced more common symptoms, it would have been much more difficult to detect the damage and to pinpoint which drugs were harmful.

The important point is that both thalidomide and DES changed the envi-   15
ronment in which these babies developed—in ways that could not have been foreseen and that we still do not understand. This happened because we know very little about how embryos develop. How then can we claim to know that the many chemical and mechanical manipulations of eggs, sperms, and embryos that take place during in vitro fertilization and implantation are harmless?

A WOMAN'S RIGHT?

The push toward this technology reinforces the view, all too prevalent in our   16
society, that women's lives are unfulfilled, or indeed worthless, unless we bear children. I understand the wish to have children, though I also know many people—women and men—who lead happy and fulfilled lives without them. But even if one urgently wants a child, why must it be biologically one's own? It is not worth opening the hornet's nest of reproductive technology for the privilege of having one's child derive from one's own egg or sperm. Foster and adoptive parents are much needed for the world's homeless children. Why not try to change the American and international practices that make it difficult for people who want children to be brought together with children who need parents?

Advocates of this new technology argue that every woman has a right to bear   17
a child and that the technology will extend this right to a group previously denied it. It is important to examine this argument and to ask in what sense women have a "right" to bear children. In our culture, many women are taught from childhood that we must do without lots of things we want—electric trains, baseball mitts, perhaps later an expensive education or a well-paying job. We are also taught to submit to all sorts of social restrictions and physical dangers— we cannot go out alone at night, we allow ourselves to be made self-conscious at the corner drugstore and to be molested by strangers or bosses or family members without punching them as our brothers might do. We are led to believe that we must put up with all this—and without grousing—because as women we have something beside which everything else pales, something that will make up for everything: we can have babies! To grow up paying all the way and then to be denied that child *is* a promise unfulfilled; that's cheating.

But I would argue that to promise children to women by means of an   18
untested technology—that is being tested only as it is used on them and their babies—is adding yet another wrong to the burdens of our socialization. Take the women whose fallopian tubes have been damaged by an infection provoked by faulty IUDs. They are now led to believe that problems caused by one risky,

though medically approved and administered, technology can be relieved by another, much more invasive and hazardous technology.

I am also concerned about the extremely complicated nature of the technology. It involves many steps, is hard to demystify, and requires highly skilled professionals. There is no way to put control over this technology into the hands of the women who are going to be exposed to it. On the contrary, it will make women and their babies more dependent than ever upon a high-technology, super-professionalized medical system. The women and their babies must be monitored from before conception until birth, and the children will have to be observed all their lives. Furthermore, the pregnancy-monitoring technologies themselves involve hazard. From the start, women are locked into subservience to the medical establishment in a way that I find impossible to interpret as an increase in reproductive freedom, rights, or choices.

HEALTH PRIORITIES

The final issue—and a major one—is that this technology is expensive. It requires prolonged experimentation, sophisticated professionals, and costly equipment. It will distort our health priorities and funnel scarce resources into a questionable effort. The case of the Indian baby is a stark illustration, for in that country, where many children are dying from the effects of malnutrition and poor people have been forcibly sterilized, expensive technologies are being pioneered to enable a relatively small number of well-to-do people to have their own babies.

In the United States, as well, many people have less-than-adequate access to such essential health resources as decent jobs, food and housing, and medical care when they need it. And here, too, poor women have been and are still being forcibly sterilized and otherwise coerced into *not* having babies, while women who can pay high prices will become guinea pigs in the risky technology of in vitro fertilization.

In vitro fertilization is expensive and unnecessary in comparison with many pressing social needs, including those of children who need homes. We must find better and less risky solutions for women who want to parent but cannot bear children of their own.

QUESTIONS

1. Briefly state Hubbard's argument in your own words.
2. What are the main strands of evidence, both social and scientific, that she draws upon?
3. Examine the order in which Hubbard presents her main points. Why do you think she arranges them this way?

4. One argument she ignores is the moral issue of humans playing God and interfering in nature. Why do you suppose she does not include that issue?

5. Would you care to counter her argument? Write a position paper for the mother who desires a test-tube baby. Without ignoring Hubbard's case, make a case for the opposition.

6. Find out from the library or from one or more adoption agencies the rules for adoption in your state. Then, using Hubbard's article as a small piece of additional evidence, write an argument for liberalizing those rules. Or argue the opposite, if your research leads you to believe the rules are already too lax.

7. In vitro fertilization isn't the only example of technology running ahead of our ability, as a society, to decide the moral issues it raises. Choose another example—such as medical transplants, the development of highly efficient feedlots, a specific aspect of space exploration, or some other technological feat. After investigating this example, write a paper explaining the dilemmas such a scientific advance poses for society. If you want, you may write your paper as an argument like Hubbard's, either for or against some particular advance.

MAKING CONNECTIONS

1. To what extent are the issues Hubbard raises issues of feminism? Read several other essays in this volume that express feminist concerns and write an essay in which you include or exclude Hubbard from this group. Essays by Alice Walker, Carol Gilligan, Susan Fraker, Joan Didion, and Tania Modleski—all in "Arguing" or "Explaining"— would be fruitful to explore.

2. To what extent do the issues Hubbard raises address the nature of problems of research science? Does Hubbard speak chiefly as a scientist? Review some of the essays by Banesh Hoffmann, Carl Sagan, Richard Selzer, and Loren Eiseley in "Reflecting," or Francis Crick, Oliver Sacks, Stephen Jay Gould, Frederick A. King, and Lewis Thomas in "Explaining" and "Arguing." Where do you locate Hubbard within an array of writers like these?

THE HISTORICAL STRUCTURE OF SCIENTIFIC DISCOVERY

Thomas Kuhn

Thomas S. Kuhn (b. 1922) is a professor of philosophy at the Massachusetts Institute of Technology. His best-known book is The Structure of Scientific Revolutions *(2nd edition, 1970). The following essay was abstracted, as his first note says, from its third chapter; the essay appeared originally in* Science *magazine in 1962. Other books of his include* The Essential Tension: Selected Studies in Scientific Tradition and Change *(1977) and* Black-Body Theory and the Quantum Discontinuity, 1894–1912 *(1978). He has made the process of scientific investigation his special subject; historians and philosophers of science are his chief audience.*

My object in this article is to isolate and illuminate one small part of what 1 I take to be a continuing historiographic revolution in the study of science.[1] The structure of scientific discovery is my particular topic, and I can best approach it by pointing out that the subject itself may well seem extraordinarily odd. Both scientists and, until quite recently, historians have ordinarily viewed discovery as the sort of event which, though it may have preconditions and surely has consequences, is itself without internal structure. Rather than being seen as a complex development extended both in space and time, discovering something has usually seemed to be a unitary event, one which, like seeing something, happens to an individual at a specifiable time and place.

This view of the nature of discovery has, I suspect, deep roots in the nature 2 of the scientific community. One of the few historical elements recurrent in the textbooks from which the prospective scientist learns his field is the attribution of particular natural phenomena to the historical personages who first discovered them. As a result of this and other aspects of their training, discovery becomes for many scientists an important goal. To make a discovery is to achieve one of the closest approximations to a property right that the scientific career affords. Professional prestige is often closely associated with these acqui-

---

[1] The larger revolution will be discussed in my forthcoming book, *The Structure of Scientific Revolutions*, to be published in the fall by the University of Chicago Press. The central ideas in this paper have been abstracted from that source, particularly from its third chapter, "Anomaly and the Emergence of Scientific Discoveries" [2nd ed., 1970].

sitions.[2] Small wonder, then, that acrimonious disputes about priority and independence in discovery have often marred the normally placid tenor of scientific communication. Even less wonder that many historians of science have seen the individual discovery as an appropriate unit with which to measure scientific progress and have devoted much time and skill to determining what man made which discovery at what point in time. If the study of discovery has a surprise to offer, it is only that, despite the immense energy and ingenuity expended upon it, neither polemic nor painstaking scholarship has often succeeded in pinpointing the time and place at which a given discovery could properly be said to have "been made."

That failure, both of argument and of research, suggests the thesis that I   3 now wish to develop. Many scientific discoveries, particularly the most interesting and important, are not the sort of event about which the questions "Where?" and, more particularly, "When?" can appropriately be asked. Even if all conceivable data were at hand, those questions would not regularly possess answers. That we are persistently driven to ask them nonetheless is symptomatic of a fundamental inappropriateness in our image of discovery. That inappropriateness is here my main concern, but I approach it by considering first the historical problem presented by the attempt to date and to place a major class of fundamental discoveries.

The troublesome class consists of those discoveries—including oxygen, the   4 electric current, X rays, and the electron—which could not be predicted from accepted theory in advance and which therefore caught the assembled profession by surprise. That kind of discovery will shortly be my exclusive concern, but it will help first to note that there is another sort and one which presents very few of the same problems. Into this second class of discoveries fall the neutrino, radio waves, and the elements which filled empty places in the periodic table. The existence of all these objects had been predicted from theory before they were discovered, and the men who made the discoveries therefore knew from the start what to look for. That foreknowledge did not make their task less demanding or less interesting, but it did provide criteria which told them when their goal had been reached.[3] As a result, there have been few priority debates

---

[2] For a brilliant discussion of these points, see R. K. Merton, "Priorities in Scientific Discovery: A Chapter in the Sociology of Science," *American Sociological Review* 22 (1957): 635. Also very relevant, though it did not appear until this article had been prepared, is F. Reif, "The Competitive World of the Pure Scientist," *Science* 134 (1961): 1957.

[3] Not all discoveries fall so neatly as the preceding into one or the other of my two classes. For example, Anderson's work on the positron was done in complete ignorance of Dirac's electron theory from which the new particle's existence had already been very nearly predicted. On the other hand, the immediately succeeding work by Blackett and Occhialini made full use of Dirac's theory and therefore exploited experiment more fully and constructed a more forceful case for the positron's existence than Anderson had been able to do. On this subject see N. R. Hanson, "Discovering the Positron," *British Journal for the Philosophy of Science* 12 (1961): 194; 12 (1962): 299. Hanson suggests several of the points developed here. I am much indebted to Professor Hanson for a preprint of this material.

over discoveries of this second sort, and only a paucity of data can prevent the historian from ascribing them to a particular time and place. Those facts help to isolate the difficulties we encounter as we return to the troublesome discoveries of the first class. In the cases that most concern us here there are no benchmarks to inform either the scientist or the historian when the job of discovery has been done.

As an illustration of this fundamental problem and its consequences, consider first the discovery of oxygen. Because it has repeatedly been studied, often with exemplary care and skill, that discovery is unlikely to offer any purely factual surprises. Therefore it is particularly well suited to clarify points of principle.[4] At least three scientists—Carl Scheele, Joseph Priestly, and Antoine Lavoisier[5]— have a legitimate claim to this discovery, and polemicists have occasionally entered the same claim for Pierre Bayen.[6] Scheele's work, though it was almost certainly completed before the relevant researches of Priestley and Lavoisier, was not made public until their work was well known.[7] Therefore it had no apparent causal role, and I shall simplify my story by omitting it.[8] Instead, I pick up the main route to the discovery of oxygen with the work of Bayen, who, sometime before March 1774, discovered that red precipitate of mercury

---

[4]I have developed a less familiar example from the same viewpoint in "The Caloric Theory of Adiabatic Compression," *Isis* 49 (1958): 132. A closely similar analysis of the emergence of a new theory is included in the early pages of my essay "Energy Conservation as an Example of Simultaneous Discovery," in *Critical Problems in the History of Science*, ed. M. Clagett (Madison: University of Wisconsin Press, 1959), pp. 321–56. Reference to these papers may add depth and detail to the following discussion.

[5]Carl Wilhelm Scheele (1742–1786): Swedish chemist; Joseph Priestley (1733–1804): British chemist and clergyman; Antoine Laurent Lavoisier (1743–1794): French chemist. Pierre Bayen (1725–1798), mentioned at the end of the sentence, was a French chemist. [Eds.]

[6]The still classic discussion of the discovery of oxygen is A. N. Meldrum, *The Eighteenth Century Revolution in Science: The First Phase* (Calcutta, 1930), chap. 5. A more convenient and generally quite reliable discussion is included in J. B. Conant, *The Overthrow of the Phlogiston Theory: The Chemical Revolution of 1775–1789*. Harvard Case Histories in Experimental Science, case 2 (Cambridge: Harvard University Press, 1950). A recent and indispensable review, which includes an account of the development of the priority controversy, is M. Daumas, *Lavoisier, théoricien et expérimentateur* (Paris, 1955), chaps. 2 and 3. H. Guerlac has added much significant detail to our knowledge of the early relations between Priestley and Lavoisier in his "Joseph Priestley's First Papers on Gases and Their Reception in France," *Journal of the History of Medicine* 12 (1957): 1 and in his very recent monograph, *Lavoisier: The Crucial Year* (Ithaca: Cornell University Press, 1961). For Scheele see J. R. Partington, *A Short History of Chemistry*, 2d ed. (London, 1951), pp. 104–9.

[7]For the dating of Scheele's work, see A. E. Nordenskjöld, *Carl Wilhelm Scheele, Nachgelassene Briefe und Aufzeichnungen* (Stockholm, 1892).

[8]U. Bocklund ("A Lost Letter from Scheele to Lavoisier," *Lychnos*, 1957–58, pp. 39–62) argues that Scheele communicated his discovery of oxygen to Lavoisier in a letter of 30 Sept. 1774. Certainly the letter is important, and it clearly demonstrates that Scheele was ahead of both Priestley and Lavoisier at the time it was written. But I think the letter is not quite so candid as Bocklund supposes, and I fail to see how Lavoisier could have drawn the discovery of oxygen from it. Scheele describes a procedure for reconstituting common air, not for producing a new gas, and that, as we shall see, is almost the same information that Lavoisier received from Priestley at about the same time. In any case, there is no evidence that Lavoisier performed the sort of experiment that Scheele suggested.

(HgO) could, by heating, be made to yield a gas. That aeriform product Bayen identified as fixed air (CO_2), a substance made familiar to most pneumatic chemists by the earlier work of Joseph Black.[9] A variety of other substances were known to yield the same gas.

At the beginning of August 1774, a few months after Bayen's work had appeared, Joseph Priestley repeated the experiment, though probably independently. Priestley, however, observed that the gaseous product would support combustion and therefore changed the identification. For him the gas obtained on heating red precipitate was nitrous air (N_2O), a substance that he had himself discovered more than two years before.[10] Later in the same month Priestley made a trip to Paris and there informed Lavoisier of the new reaction. The latter repeated the experiment once more, both in November 1774 and in February 1775. But, because he used tests somewhat more elaborate than Priestley's, Lavoisier again changed the identification. For him, as of May 1775, the gas released by red precipitate was neither fixed air nor nitrous air. Instead, it was "[atmospheric] air itself entire without alteration . . . even to the point that . . . it comes out more pure."[11] Meanwhile, however, Priestley had also been at work, and, before the beginning of March 1775, he, too, had concluded that the gas must be "common air." Until this point all of the men who had produced a gas from red precipitate of mercury had identified it with some previously known species.[12]

The remainder of this story of discovery is briefly told. During March 1775 Priestley discovered that his gas was in several respects very much "better" than common air, and he therefore reidentified the gas once more, this time calling it "dephlogisticated air," that is, atmospheric air deprived of its normal complement of phlogiston. This conclusion Priestley published in the *Philosophical Transactions*, and it was apparently that publication which led Lavoisier to reexamine his own results.[13] The reexamination began during February 1776 and within a year had led Lavoisier to the conclusion that the gas was actually a separable component of the atmospheric air which both he and Priestley had previously thought of as homogeneous. With this point reached, with the gas

6

7

---

[9] P. Bayen, "Essai d'expériences chymiques, faites sur quelques précipités de mercure, dans la vue de découvrir leur nature, Seconde partie," *Observations sur la physique* 3 (1774): 280–95, particularly pp. 289–91. (Joseph Black [1728–1799]: Scottish physician and chemist. [Eds.])

[10] J. B. Conant, *The Overthrow of the Phlogiston Theory*, pp. 34–40.

[11] Ibid., p. 23. A useful translation of the full text is available in Conant.

[12] For simplicity I use the term *red precipitate* throughout. Actually, Bayen used the precipitate: Priestley used both the precipitate and the oxide produced by direct calcination of mercury: and Lavoisier used only the latter. The difference is not without importance, for it was not unequivocally clear to chemists that the two substances were identical.

[13] There has been some doubt about Priestley's having influenced Lavoisier's thinking at this point, but, when the latter returned to experimenting with the gas in February 1776, he recorded in his notebooks that he had obtained "l'air dephlogistique de M. Priestley" (M. Daumas, *Lavoisier*, p. 36).

recognized as an irreducibly distinct species, we may conclude that the discovery of oxygen had been completed.

But to return to my initial question, when shall we say that oxygen was discovered and what criteria shall be use in answering that question? If discovering oxygen is simply holding an impure sample in one's hands, then the gas had been "discovered" in antiquity by the first man who ever bottled atmospheric air. Undoubtedly, for an experimental criterion, we must at least require a relatively pure sample like that obtained by Priestley in August 1774. But during 1774 Priestley was unaware that he had discovered anything except a new way to produce a relatively familiar species. Throughout that year his "discovery" is scarcely distinguishable from the one made earlier by Bayen, and neither case is quite distinct from that of the Reverend Stephen Hales, who had obtained the same gas more than forty years before.[14] Apparently to discover something one must also be aware of the discovery and know as well what it is that one has discovered.

But, that being the case, how much must one know? Had Priestley come close enough when he identified the gas as nitrous air? If not, was either he or Lavoisier significantly closer when he changed the identification to common air? And what are we to say about Priestley's next identification, the one made in March 1775? Dephlogisticated air is still not oxygen or even, for the phlogistic chemist, a quite unexpected sort of gas.[15] Rather it is a particularly pure atmospheric air. Presumably, then, we wait for Lavoisier's work in 1776 and 1777, work which led him not merely to isolate the gas but to see what it was. Yet even that decision can be questioned, for in 1777 and to the end of his life Lavoisier insisted that oxygen was an atomic "principle of acidity" and that oxygen *gas* was formed only when that "principle" united with caloric, the matter of heat.[16] Shall we therefore say that oxygen had not yet been discovered in 1777? Some may be tempted to do so. But the principle of acidity was not banished from chemistry until after 1810 and caloric lingered on until the 1860s. Oxygen had, however, become a standard chemical substance long before either of those dates. Furthermore, what is perhaps the key point, it would probably have gained that status on the basis of Priestley's work alone without benefit of Lavoisier's still partial reinterpretation.

I conclude that we need a new vocabulary and new concepts for analyzing events like the discovery of oxygen. Though undoubtedly correct, the sentence "Oxygen was discovered" misleads by suggesting that discovering something is

---

[14] J. R. Partington, *A Short History of Chemistry*, p. 91. (Reverend Stephen Hales [1677–1761]: British botanist and physiologist. [Eds.])

[15] phlogistic: from *phlogiston*, a New Latin coinage from the Greek word for inflammable, naming a substance formerly thought to escape when a material burns. Though a faulty theory, its investigation contributed to the discovery of oxygen. [Eds.]

[16] For the traditional elements in Lavoisier's interpretations of chemical reactions, see H. Metzger, *La philosophie de la matière chez Lavoisier* (Paris, 1935), and Daumas, *Lavoisier*, chap. 7.

a single simple act unequivocally attributable, if only we knew enough, to an individual and an instant in time. When the discovery is unexpected, however, the latter attribution is always impossible and the former often is as well. Ignoring Scheele, we can, for example, safely say that oxygen had not been discovered before 1774; probably we would also insist that it had been discovered by 1774; probably we would also insist that it had been discovered by 1777 or shortly thereafter. But within those limits any attempt to date the discovery or to attribute it to an individual must inevitably be arbitrary. Furthermore, it must be arbitrary just because discovering a new sort of phenomenon is necessarily a complex process which involves recognizing both *that* something is and *what* it is. Observation and conceptualization, fact and the assimilation of fact to theory, are inseparably linked in the discovery of scientific novelty. Inevitably, that process extends over time and may often involve a number of people. Only for discoveries in my second category—those whose nature is known in advance— can discovering *that* and discovering *what* occur together and in an instant.

Two last, simpler, and far briefer examples will simultaneously show how typical the case of oxygen is and also prepare the way for a somewhat more precise conclusion. On the night of 13 March 1781, the astronomer William Herschel made the following entry in his journal: "In the quartile near Zeta Tauri . . . is a curious either nebulous star or perhaps a comet."[17] That entry is generally said to record the discovery of the planet Uranus, but it cannot quite have done that. Between 1690 and Herschel's observation in 1781 the same object had been seen and recorded at least seventeen times by men who took it to be a star. Herschel differed from them only in supposing that, because in his telescope it appeared especially large, it might actually be a *comet!* Two additional observations on 17 and 19 March confirmed that suspicion by showing that the object he had observed moved among the stars. As a result, astronomers throughout Europe were informed of the discovery, and the mathematicians among them began to compute the new comet's orbit. Only several months later, after all those attempts had repeatedly failed to square with observation, did the astronomer Lexell suggest that the object observed by Herschel might be a planet.[18] And only when additional computations, using a planet's rather than a comet's orbit, proved reconcilable with observation was that suggestion generally accepted. At what point during 1781 do we want to say that the planet Uranus was discovered? And are we entirely and unequivocally clear that it was Herschel rather than Lexell who discovered it?

Or consider still more briefly the story of the discovery of X rays, a story which opens on the day in 1895 when the physicist Roentgen interrupted a well-precedented investigation of cathode rays because he noticed that a barium

11

12

---

[17] P. Doig, *A Concise History of Astronomy* (London: Chapman, 1950), pp. 115–16. (William Herschel [1738–1822]: German-born English astronomer. [Eds.])

[18] Anders Johan Lexell (1740–1784): Swedish astronomer. [Eds.]

platinocyanide screen far from his shielded apparatus glowed when the discharge was in process.[19] Additional investigations—they required seven hectic weeks during which Roentgen rarely left the laboratory—indicated that the cause of the glow traveled in straight lines from the cathode ray tube, that the radiation cast shadows, that it could not be deflected by a magnet, and much else besides. Before announcing his discovery Roentgen had convinced himself that his effect was not due to cathode rays themselves but to a new form of radiation with at least some similarity to light. Once again the question suggests itself: When shall we say that X rays were actually discovered? Not, in any case, at the first instant, when all that had been noted was a glowing screen. At least one other investigator had seen that glow and, to his subsequent chagrin, discovered nothing at all. Nor, it is almost as clear, can the moment of discovery be pushed back to a point during the last week of investigation. By that time Roentgen was exploring the properties of the new radiation he had *already* discovered. We may have to settle for the remark that X rays emerged in Würzburg between 8 November and 28 December 1895.

The characteristics shared by these examples are, I think, common to all the episodes by which unanticipated novelties become subjects for scientific attention. I therefore conclude these brief remarks by discussing three such common characteristics, ones which may help to provide a framework for the further study of the extended episodes we customarily call "discoveries."   13

In the first place, notice that all three of our discoveries—oxygen, Uranus, and X-rays—began with the experimental or observational isolation of an anomaly, that is, with nature's failure to conform entirely to expectation. Notice, further, that the process by which that anomaly was educed displays simultaneously the apparently incompatible characteristics of the inevitable and the accidental. In the case of X rays, the anomalous glow which provided Roentgen's first clue was clearly the result of an accidental disposition of his apparatus. But by 1895 cathode rays were a normal subject for research all over Europe; that research quite regularly juxtaposed cathode-ray tubes with sensitive screens and films; as a result, Roentgen's accident was almost certain to occur elsewhere, as in fact it had. Those remarks, however, should make Roentgen's case look very much like those of Herschel and Priestley. Herschel first observed his oversized and thus anomalous star in the course of a prolonged survey of the northern heavens. That survey was, except for the magnification provided by Herschel's instruments, precisely of the sort that had repeatedly been carried through before and that had occasionally resulted in prior observations of Uranus. And Priestley, too—when he isolated the gas that behaved almost but not quite like nitrous air and then almost but not quite like common air—was seeing something unintended and wrong in the outcome of a sort of experiment   14

---

[19] L. W. Taylor, *Physics, the Pioneer Science* (Boston: Houghton Mifflin Co., 1941), p. 790. (Wilhelm Konrad Roentgen [1845–1923]: German physicist. [Eds.])

for which there was much European precedent and which had more than once before led to the production of the new gas.

These features suggest the existence of two normal requisites for the beginning of an episode of discovery. The first, which throughout this paper I have largely taken for granted, is the individual skill, wit, or genius to recognize that something has gone wrong in ways that may prove consequential. Not any and every scientist would have noted that no unrecorded star should be so large, that the screen ought not to have glowed, that nitrous air should not have supported life. But that requisite presupposes another which is less frequently taken for granted. Whatever the level of genius available to observe them, anomalies do not emerge from the normal course of scientific research until both instruments and concepts have developed sufficiently to make their emergence likely and to make the anomaly which results recognizable as a violation of expectation.[20] To say that an unexpected discovery begins only when something goes wrong is to say that it begins only when scientists know well both how their instruments and how nature should behave. What distinguished Priestley, who saw an anomaly, from Hales, who did not, is largely the considerable articulation of pneumatic techniques and expectations that had come into being during the four decades which separate their two isolations of oxygen.[21] The very number of claimants indicates that after 1770 the discovery could not have been postponed for long.

The role of anomaly is the first of the characteristics shared by our three examples. A second can be considered more briefly, for it has provided the main theme for the body of my text. Though awareness of anomaly marks the beginning of a discovery, it marks only the beginning. What necessarily follows, if anything at all is to be discovered, is a more or less extended period during which the individual and often many members of his group struggle to make the anomaly lawlike. Invariably that period demands additional observation or experimentation as well as repeated cogitation. While it continues, scientists repeatedly revise their expectations, usually their instrumental standards, and sometimes their most fundamental theories as well. In this sense discoveries have a proper internal history as well as prehistory and a posthistory. Furthermore, within the rather vaguely delimited interval of internal history, there is no single moment or day which the historian, however complete his data, can identify as the point at which the discovery was made. Often, when several individuals are involved, it is even impossible unequivocally to identify any one of them as the discoverer.

---

[20] Though the point cannot be argued here, the conditions which make the emergence of anomaly likely and those which make anomaly recognizable are to a very great extent the same. That fact may help us understand the extraordinarily large amount of simultaneous discovery in the sciences.

[21] A useful sketch of the development of pneumatic chemistry is included in Partington, *A Short History of Chemistry*, chap. 6.

Finally, turning to the third of these selected common characteristics, note 17
briefly what happens as the period of discovery draws to a close. A full discussion
of that question would require additional evidence and a separate paper, for I
have had little to say about the aftermath of discovery in the body of my text.
Nevertheless, the topic must not be entirely neglected, for it is in part a corollary
of what has already been said.

Discoveries are often described as mere additions or increments to the grow- 18
ing stockpile of scientific knowledge, and that description has helped make the
unit discovery seem a significant measure of progress. I suggest, however, that
it is fully appropriate only to those discoveries which, like the elements that
filled missing places in the periodic table, were anticipated and sought in
advance and which therefore demanded no adjustment, adaptation, and assimilation from the profession. Though the sorts of discoveries we have here been
examining are undoubtedly additions to scientific knowledge, they are also
something more. In a sense that I can now develop only in part, they also react
back upon what has previously been known, providing a new view of some
previously familiar objects and simultaneously changing the way in which even
some traditional parts of science are practiced. Those in whose area of special
competence the new phenomenon falls often see both the world and their work
differently as they emerge from the extended struggle with anomaly which
constitutes the discovery of that phenomenon.

William Herschel, for example, when he increased by one the time-honored 19
number of planetary bodies, taught astronomers to see new things when they
looked at the familiar heavens even with instruments more traditional than his
own. That change in the vision of astronomers must be a principal reason why,
in the half century after the discovery of Uranus, twenty additional circumsolar
bodies were added to the traditional seven.[22] A similar transformation is even
clearer in the aftermath of Roentgen's work. In the first place, established
techniques for cathode-ray research had to be changed, for scientists found they
had failed to control a relevant variable. Those changes included both the
redesign of old apparatus and revised ways of asking old questions. In addition,
those scientists most concerned experienced the same transformation of vision
that we have just noted in the aftermath of the discovery of Uranus. X rays
were the first new sort of radiation discovered since infrared and ultraviolet at
the beginning of the century. But within less than a decade after Roentgen's

---

[22] R. Wolf, Geschichte der Astronomie (Munich, 1877), pp. 513–15, 683–93. The prephoto-
graphic discoveries of the asteroids is often seen as an effect of the invention of Bode's law. But
that law cannot be the full explanation and may not even have played a large part. Piazzi's discovery
of Ceres, in 1801, was made in ignorance of the current speculation about a missing planet in the
"hole" between Mars and Jupiter. Instead, like Herschel, Piazzi was engaged on a star survey. More
important, Bode's law was old by 1800 (ibid., p. 683), but only one man before that date seems to
have thought it worthwhile to look for another planet. Finally, Bode's law, by itself, could only
suggest the utility of looking for additional planets; it did not tell astronomers where to look. Clearly,
however, the drive to look for additional planets dates from Herschel's work on Uranus.

work, four more were disclosed by the new scientific sensitivity (for example, to fogged photographic plates) and by some of the new instrumental techniques that had resulted from Roentgen's work and its assimilation.[23]

Very often these transformations in the established techniques of scientific practice prove even more important than the incremental knowledge provided by the discovery itself. That could at least be argued in the cases of Uranus and of X rays; in the case of my third example, oxygen, it is categorically clear. Like the work of Herschel and Roentgen, that of Priestley and Lavoisier taught scientists to view old situations in new ways. Therefore, as we might anticipate, oxygen was not the only new chemical species to be identified in the aftermath of their work. But, in the case of oxygen, the readjustments demanded by assimilation were so profound that they played an integral and essential role— though they were not by themselves the cause—in the gigantic upheaval of chemical theory and practice which has since been known as the chemical revolution. I do not suggest that every unanticipated discovery has consequences for science so deep and so far-reaching as those which followed the discovery of oxygen. But I do suggest that every such discovery demands, from those most concerned, the sorts of readjustment that, when they are more obvious, we equate with scientific revolution. It is, I believe, just because they demand readjustments like these that the process of discovery is necessarily and inevitably one that shows structure and that therefore extends in time. 20

QUESTIONS

1. State in your own words the principle Kuhn identifies at the end of paragraph 2.

2. Distinguish the two kinds of scientific discoveries Kuhn outlines in paragraphs 3 and 4. Which is the subject of this article?

3. Summarize the three characteristics of scientific discovery that Kuhn reviews in paragraphs 14 through 20.

4. Why does Kuhn spend so much more time on the discovery of oxygen than on the comet or x-rays? Would that first example have been sufficient in itself? Do all three examples contribute substantially to "the characteristics of scientific discovery" that Kuhn goes on to outline?

5. If a single word were to distinguish the scientific discoveries that most interest Kuhn, that word might be *process* (as paragraph 10 suggests). Describe an event you know well—a class, a game, a meeting, an accident—as if it were a process rather than a single event. How does your description of that process allow you to understand the event in a way you had not understood it before?

6. Seen from one point of view, the papers you write are events, too. You hand

---

[23] For α-, β, and γ-radiation, discovery of which dates from 1896, see Taylor, *Physics*, pp. 800–804. For the fourth new form of radiation, N rays, see D. J. S. Price, *Science Since Babylon* (New Haven: Yale University Press, 1961), pp. 84–89. That N rays were ultimately the source of a scientific scandal does not make them less revealing of the scientific community's state of mind.

them in when due and get them back, graded, later. But in another sense, they are part of a process as well. Describe the process of the last paper you wrote. When did that process begin? What pattern did it take? What were the crucial moments, perhaps the turning points? And when can you say the process came to an end?

MAKING CONNECTIONS

1. Both Kuhn and Lewis Thomas (in "The Art of Teaching Science") suggest that we misperceive the nature and methodology of scientific work and thought. Write an essay comparing their two arguments. Which, in your view, goes further toward correcting this misconception? Why?

2. The process of scientific discovery, with its three stages as reviewed by Kuhn in paragraphs 14–20, might apply to other developments in our lives. Consider, for example, the several articles in this collection that report, reflect upon, and argue about the atom bomb: William L. Laurence's "Atomic Bombing of Nagasaki Told by Flight Member" and John Hersey's "Hatsuyo Nakamura," both in "Reporting"; Zoë Tracy Hardy's "What Did You Do in the War, Grandma?" in "Reflecting"; and John Berger's "Hiroshima" in "Arguing." What kind of discovery is made in the course of those investigations? What are the stages of its process? When can you say a discovery was made? What was it? Do you agree with it? Do you foresee more stages of discovery to come?

ACKNOWLEDGMENTS (continued from p. ii)

Berger, John, "Hiroshima." From *The Sense of Sight*, by John Berger, edited by Lloyd Spencer. Copyright © 1985 by John Berger. Reprinted by permission of Pantheon Books, a Division of Random House, Inc.

Bettelheim, Bruno, "Joey: A 'Mechanical Boy.'" Reprinted with permission. Copyright © March 1959 by Scientific American, Inc. All rights reserved.

Bettelheim, Bruno, "The Ignored Lesson of Anne Frank." From *Surviving and Other Essays* by Bruno Bettelheim. Copyright 1952, © 1960, 1962, 1976, 1979 by Bruno Bettelheim and Trude Bettelheim as Trustees. Reprinted by permission of Alfred A. Knopf, Inc.

Booth, William, "The Social Lives of Dolphins." From *Science*, Vol. 240, Page 1273, June 3, 1988. Copyright © 1988 by the AAAS. Reprinted with permission.

Brown, Michael, "Love Canal and the Poisoning of America." Copyright © 1979 by Michael H. Brown. Reprinted from *Laying Waste: Love Canal and the Poisoning of America*, by Michael H. Brown, by permission of Pantheon Books, a division of Random House, Inc.

Brunvand, Jan Harold, "Urban Legends: 'The Boyfriend's Death.'" Reprinted from *The Vanishing Hitchhiker, American Urban Legends and Their Meanings*, by Jan Harold Brunvand, by permission of W. W. Norton & Company, Inc. Copyright © 1981 by Jan Harold Brunvand.

Caplan, Arthur, et al., "Just Like Us: A Forum of Animal Rights." Copyright © 1988 by Harper's Magazine. All rights reserved. Reprinted from the August issue by special permission.

Carr, Edward Hallett. From *What Is History?* by Edward Hallett Carr. Copyright © 1961 by Edward Hallett Carr. Reprinted by permission of Alfred A. Knopf, Inc. and Macmillan, London and Basingstoke.

Crick, Francis, "Times and Distance, Large and Small." From *Life Itself* by Francis Crick. Copyright © 1981 by Francis Crick. Reprinted by permission of Simon & Schuster, Inc.

Damasio, Antonio R., "Face Perception without Recognition." From *Trends in NeuroScience* (March 1985). Reprinted by permission of the author.

Darwin, Charles, "The Action of Natural Selection," from *The Essential Darwin*, edited by Robert Jastrow. Copyright © 1984 by Robert Jastrow. Reprinted by permission of Little, Brown and Company.

Didion, Joan, "Georgia O'Keeffe." From *The White Album*. Reprinted by permission of Farrar, Straus and Giroux, Inc.

Didion, Joan, "Why I Write." Reprinted by permission of Wallace Literary Agency, Inc. Copyright © 1976 by Joan Didion.

Dillard, Annie, "Singing with the Fundamentalists." Reprinted by permission of the author and her agent Blanche C. Gregory, Inc. Copyright © 1984 by Annie Dillard.

Dinesen, Isak. "The Iguana." From *Out of Africa* by Isak Dinesen. Copyright © 1937 by Random House, Inc. and renewed 1965 by Rungstedlundfonden. Reprinted with permission of the publisher.

Eco, Umberto, "*Casablanca*, or the Clichés Are Having a Ball." From *On Signs*, 1985. Reprinted by permission of Georges Borchardt Inc.

Eiseley, Loren. "The Bird and the Machine." From *The Immense Journey* by Loren Eiseley. Copyright © 1957 by Loren Eiseley. Reprinted by permission of Random House, Inc.

Fineberg, Harvey V., "Education to Prevent AIDS: Prospects and Obstacles." From *Science*, Vol. 239, Pages 592–6, February 5, 1988. Copyright © 1988 by the AAAS. Reprinted with permission by the AAAS and Harvey Fineberg.

FitzGerald, Frances, "America Revised," from *America Revised* by Frances FitzGerald, pp. 7–17. Copyright © 1979 by Frances FitzGerald. Reprinted by permission of Little, Brown and Company, in association with the Atlantic Monthly Press.

Fraker, Susan, "Why Women Aren't Getting to the Top," *Fortune*, April 16, 1984. Copyright © 1984 Time, Inc. All rights reserved.

Freud, Sigmund, "The Moses of Michelangelo." From *Character of Culture*. Reprinted by permission of Basic Books, Inc.

Geertz, Clifford, "Of Cocks and Men." Reprinted by permission of *Daedalus*, Journal of the American Academy of Arts and Sciences, "Myth, Symbol and Culture," Winter 1972, Vol. 101, No. 1 & No. 2, Cambridge, Massachusetts.

Gilligan, Carol, "Woman's Place in Man's Life Cycle." From *In a Different Voice* by Carol Gilligan. Copyright © 1982. Reprinted with permission from the Harvard University Press.

Glazer, Nathan, "Some Very Modest Proposals for the Improvement of American Education." Reprinted by permission of *Daedalus*, Journal of the American Academy of Arts and Sciences, "Values, Resources, and Politics in America's Schools," Fall 1984, Vol. 113, No. 2, Cambridge, Massachusetts.

Gould, Stephen Jay, "A Biological Homage to Mickey Mouse" is reprinted from *The Panda's Thumb, More Reflections in Natural History*, by Stephen Jay Gould, by permission of W. W. Norton & Company, Inc. Copyright © 1980 by Stephen Jay Gould.

Gould, Stephen Jay, "Evolution as Fact and Theory." Copyright © 1981 by Stephen Jay Gould. Reprinted by permission of the author.

Gould, Stephen Jay, "Racist Arguments and IQ" is reprinted from *Ever Since Darwin, Reflections in Natural History*, by Stephen Jay Gould, by permission of W. W. Norton & Company, Inc. Copyright © 1973, 1974, 1975, 1976 and 1977 by the American Museum of Natural History.

Hardy, Zöe Tracy. "What Did You Do in the War, Grandma?" (*Ms.*, August, 1985). Reprinted by permission of the author.

Hawking, Stephen W., "Our Picture of the Universe." From *A Brief History of Time* by Stephen W. Hawking. Copyright © 1988 by Stephen W. Hawking. Reprinted by permission of Bantam Books, a division of Bantam, Doubleday, Dell Publishing Group, Inc.

Hemingway, Ernest, "A New Kind of War." Reprinted with permission of Charles Scribner's Sons, an imprint of Macmillan Publishing Company from *By-Line: Ernest Hemingway* by Ernest Hemingway (William White, Ed.). Copyright © 1967 by Mary Hemingway. (First appeared in NANA Dispatch April 14, 1937.)

Hersey, John, "Hatsuyo Nakamura." From *Hiroshima* by John Hersey. Copyright 1946, © 1985 by John Hersey. Copyright renewed 1973 by John Hersey. Reprinted by permission of Alfred A. Knopf, Inc.

Hevesi, Dennis, "Running Away." Copyright © 1988 by the New York Times Company. Reprinted by permission.

Hoffmann, Banesh, "My Friend, Albert Einstein." Reprinted with permission from the January 1968 Reader's Digest. Copyright © 1967 by the Reader's Digest Assn., Inc.

Hubbard, Ruth, "Test-Tube Babies: Solution or Problem?" Reprinted with permission from *Technology Review*, © 1980.

Jeans, James, "Why the Sky Is Blue." From *The Stars in Their Courses* by Sir James Jeans. Reprinted by permission of Cambridge University Press.

Jung, Carl G., "Sigmund Freud," from *Memories, Reflections, Dreams* by C. G. Jung, recorded and edited by Aniela Jaffe, translated by Richard and Clara Winston. Translation Copyright © 1961, 1962, 1963, by Random House, Inc. Reprinted by permission of Pantheon Books, a division of Random House, Inc.

King, Frederick A., "Animals in Research: A Case for Experimentation." Reprinted with permission from *Psychology Today* Magazine. Copyright © 1984 (PT Partners, L.P.).

King, Martin Luther, Jr., "Pilgrimage to Nonviolence" from *Strength to Love*. Reprinted by permission of Joan Daves. Copyright © 1963 by Martin Luther King, Jr.

Knightley, Phillip, "The First Televised War" from *The First Casualty* copyright © 1975 by P. Knightley, reprinted by permission of Harcourt Brace Jovanovich, Inc.

Kübler-Ross, Elizabeth, "On the Fear of Death." Reprinted with permission of Macmillan Publishing Company from *On Death and Dying* by Elizabeth Kübler-Ross. Copyright © 1969 Elizabeth Kübler-Ross.

782

Kuhn, Thomas, "The Historical Structure of Scientific Discovery." From *Science*, Vol. 136, Pages 760–64, June 1, 1962. Copyright © 1962 by the AAAS. Reprinted with permission by the AAAS and the author.

Laurence, William L., "Atomic Bombing of Nagasaki Told by Flight Member." Copyright © 1964 by the New York Times Company. Reprinted by permission.

Lawick-Goodall, Jane van, "First Observations." From *In the Shadow of Man* by Jane van Lawick-Goodall. Copyright © 1971 by Hugo and Jane van Lawick-Goodall. Reprinted by permission of Houghton Mifflin Company and George Weidenfeld & Nicolson Limited.

Lifton, Robert Jay, "What Made This Man? Mengele." Copyright © 1982 by the New York Times Company. Reprinted by permission.

Mead, Margaret, "A Day in Samoa" from *Coming of Age in Samoa*. Reprinted by permission of William Morrow and Company, Inc. Copyright © 1928, 1955 by Margaret Mead.

Milgram, Stanley, "Some Conditions of Obedience and Disobedience to Authority," *Human Relations*, Vol. 18, No. 1, 1965, pp. 57–76. Copyright © 1972 by Stanley Milgram. All rights controlled by Alexandra Milgram, library executor. Reprinted by permission.

Miner, Horace, "Body Ritual among the Nacirema," reproduced by permission of The American Anthropological Association from *American Anthropologist* 58:503–507, 1956. Not for further reproduction.

Modleski, Tania, "Soap Opera, Melodrama, and Women's Anger," from *Loving with a Vengenrance*. Reprinted with permission of Shoestring Press.

Momaday, N. Scott, "The Way to Rainy Mountain." First published in *The Reporter*, 26 January 1967. Reprinted from *The Way to Rainy Mountain*, © 1969, the University of New Mexico Press.

Mowat, Farley, "Observing Wolves," from *Never Cry Wolf*. Copyright © 1963 by Farley Mowat. By permission of Little, Brown and Company, in association with the Atlantic Monthly Press. Reprinted with permission of the author.

Orwell, George, "Shooting an Elephant" from *Shooting an Elephant and Other Essays* by George Orwell, copyright 1950 by Sonia Brownell Orwell and renewed 1978 by Sonia Pitt-Rivers, reprinted by permission of Harcourt Brace Jovanovich, Inc., and the estate of the late Sonia Brownell Orwell and Martin Secker & Warburg.

Orwell, George, "Politics and the English Language," copyright 1946 by Sonia Brownell Orwell and renewed 1974 by Sonia Orwell, reprinted from *Shooting an Elephant and Other Essays* by permission of Harcourt Brace Jovanovich, Inc., and the estate of the late Sonia Brownell Orwell and Martin Secker & Warburg.

Ross, Murray, "Football Red and Baseball Green." Reprinted by permission of the author.

Sacks, Oliver, "The Autist Artist" and "The Man Who Mistook His Wife for a Hat." From *The Man Who Mistook His Wife for a Hat* by Oliver Sacks. Copyright © 1970, 1981, 1983, 1984, 1985 by Oliver Sacks. Reprinted by permission of Summit Books, a division of Simon & Schuster, Inc.

Sagan, Carl, "Can We Know the Universe? Reflections on a Grain of Salt," from *Broca's Brain*. Copyright © 1979 by Carl Sagan. All rights reserved. Reprinted by permission of the author.

Sanders, James C., "We Need Role Models, Not Labels." Copyright © 1988 by the New York Times Company. Reprinted by permission.

Selby, Roy, Jr., "A Delicate Operation." Copyright © 1975 by *Harper's* Magazine. All rights reserved. Reprinted from the December issue by special permission.

Selzer, Richard, "The Discus Thrower" from *Confessions of a Knife*. Reprinted by permission of William Morrow and Company, Inc. Copyright © 1979 by David Goldman and Janet Selzer, Trustees.

Selzer, Richard, ["Why a Surgeon Would Write"], "The Exact Location of the Soul," from *Mortal Lessons*. Copyright © 1974, 1975, 1976 by Richard Selzer. Reprinted by permission of Simon & Schuster, Inc.

784

Rhetorical Index

ANALOGY

Discussed in "Explaining," pp. 303–310
Exemplified by "Atomic Bombing of Nagasaki Told by Flight Member," pp. 210–216; "Football Red and Baseball Green," pp. 331–340; "Joey: A 'Mechanical Boy,'" pp. 395–406; "Why the Sky Is Blue," pp. 515–517; "Times and Distances, Large and Small," pp. 518–526; "The Origin of the Universe," pp. 538–550; "A Biological Homage to Mickey Mouse," pp. 573–582; "Am I Blue?," pp. 599–603; "The Case against Man," pp. 750–755

ARGUING

Discussed in "Arguing," pp. 591–598
Exemplified by all selections in "Arguing," pp. 599–786

CASE STUDY

Discussed in "Explaining," pp. 303–310
Exemplified by "Joey: A 'Mechanical Boy,'" pp. 395–406; "The Autist Artist," pp. 407–423; "What Made This Man? Mengele," pp. 424–436; "The Man Who Mistook His Wife for a Hat," pp. 551–562

CAUSAL ANALYSIS

Discussed in "Explaining," pp. 303–310
Exemplified by "Sigmund Freud," pp. 371–394; "Two Reports of an Airplane Crash," pp. 287–299; "*Casablanca*, or the Clichés Are Having a Ball," pp. 321–326; "Joey: A 'Mechanical Boy,'" pp. 395–406; "Why Women Aren't Getting to the Top," pp. 462–470; "Woman's Place in Man's Life Cycle," pp. 471–488; "What Made This Man? Mengele," pp. 424–436; "Some Conditions of Obedience and Disobedience to Authority," pp. 437–461; "Why the Sky Is Blue," pp. 515–517; "The Origin of the Universe," pp. 538–550; "The Man Who Mistook His Wife for a Hat," pp. 551–562; "A Biological Homage to Mickey Mouse," pp. 573–582; "The Action of Natural Selection," pp. 583–597; "The Ignored Lesson of Anne Frank," pp. 683–693; "The Case against Man," pp. 750–755

COMPARISON AND CONTRAST

Discussed in "Explaining," pp. 303–310

Exemplified by "The Social Lives of Dolphins," pp. 254–259; "Urban Legends: 'The Boyfriend's Death,'" pp. 311–320; "Football Red and Baseball Green," pp. 331–340; "The Autist Artist," pp. 407–423; "Woman's Place in Man's Life Cycle," pp. 471–488; "On the Fear of Death," pp. 494–501; "A Biological Homage to Mickey Mouse," pp. 573–582; "Face Perception without Recognition," pp. 563–572; "Times and Distances, Large and Small," pp. 518–526; "Am I Blue?," pp. 599–603; "America Revised," pp. 638–645; "Evolution as Fact and Theory," pp. 756–763

DEFINITION

Discussed in "Explaining," pp. 303–310

Exemplified by "Urban Legends, 'The Boyfriend's Death,'" pp. 311–320; "What High School Is," pp. 341–350; "Soap Opera, Melodrama, and Women's Anger," pp. 352–366; "Some Conditions of Obedience and Disobedience to Authority," pp. 457–461; "The Origin of the Universe," pp. 538–550; "Face Perception without Recognition," pp. 563–572; "Hiroshima," pp. 604–611; "If Black English Isn't a Language, Then Tell Me, What Is?," pp. 615–618; "The Historian and His Facts," pp. 652–662; "When Does History Happen?," pp. 663–669; "Evolution as Fact and Theory," 756–763; "The Historical Structure of Scientific Discovery," pp. 770–780

DESCRIPTION

Discussed in "Reflecting," pp. 31–36, and "Reporting," pp. 151–158

Exemplified by "Graduation," pp. 37–47; "The Way to Rainy Mountain," pp. 86–91; "Shooting an Elephant," pp. 92–98; "My Friend, Albert Einstein," pp. 115–120; "Singing with the Fundamentalists," pp. 184–193; "The Death of the Moth," pp. 194–197; "Body Ritual among the Nacirema," pp. 233–238; "Atomic Bombing of Nagasaki Told by Flight Member," pp. 210–216; "'This Is the End of the World': The Black Death," pp. 159–169; "A Day in Samoa," pp. 217–220; "First Observations," pp. 225–232; "The Discus Thrower," pp. 264–267; "Football Red and Baseball Green," pp. 331–340; "The Moses of Michelangelo," pp. 371–394; "Joey: A 'Mechanical Boy,'" pp. 395–406; "The Autist Artist," pp. 407–423; "The Man Who Mistook His Wife for a Hat," pp. 551–562

EVIDENCE

Discussed in "Arguing," pp. 591–598

Exemplified by all selections in "Arguing," pp. 599–780

786

EXPLAINING

Discussed in "Explaining," pp. 303–310
Exemplified by all selections in "Explaining," pp. 311–587

EXPLANATORY CONTEXT

Discussed in "Explaining," pp. 303–310
Exemplified by all selections in "Explaining," pp. 311–587

FIRST PERSON PERSPECTIVE

Discussed in "Reporting," pp. 151–158
Exemplified by "Graduation," pp. 37–47; "Learning to Read and Write," pp. 71–76; "Pilgrimage to Nonviolence," pp. 77–85; "Shooting an Elephant," pp. 92–98; "Sigmund Freud," pp. 99–105; "What Did You Do in the War, Grandma?," pp. 106–114; "A New Kind of War," pp. 170–174; "Singing with the Fundamentalists," pp. 184–193; "Atomic Bombing of Nagasaki Told by Flight Member," pp. 210–216; "Observing Wolves," pp. 221–224; "First Observations," pp. 225–232; "The Discus Thrower," pp. 264–267; "Am I Blue?," pp. 599–603; "Calculating Machine," pp. 612–614

ILLUSTRATION

Discussed in "Explaining," pp. 303–310
Exemplified by all sections in "Explaining," pp. 311–587, and "Arguing," pp. 599–780

LOGIC

Discussed in "Arguing," pp. 303–310
Exemplified by "The Moses of Michelangelo," pp. 371–394; "Why Women Aren't Getting to the Top," pp. 462–470; "Our Picture of the Universe," pp. 471–488; "Racist Arguments and IQ," pp. 694–698; "A Modest Proposal," pp. 699–707; "Just Like Us: A Forum on Animal Rights," pp. 720–735; "The Case against Man," pp. 750–755; "Evolution as Fact and Theory," pp. 756–763

NARRATION

Discussed in "Reflecting," pp. 31–36, and "Reporting," pp. 151–158
Exemplified by "Graduation," pp. 37–47; "Learning to Read and Write," pp. 71–76; "What Did You Do in the War, Grandma?," pp. 106–114; "Pilgrimage to Nonviolence," pp. 77–85; "Shooting an Elephant," pp. 92–98; "Singing

POINT OF VIEW

PROCESS ANALYSIS

PURPOSE

REFLECTING

REPORTING

SCIENTIFIC AND TECHNICAL REPORT FORMAT

Discussed in "Explaining," pp. 303–310

Exemplified by "Two Reports of an Airplane Crash," pp. 287–299; "Some Conditions of Obedience and Disobedience to Authority," pp. 437–461; "Education to Prevent AIDS: Prospects and Obstacles," pp. 502–514; "Face Perception without Recognition," pp. 563–572

THIRD PERSON PERSPECTIVE

Discussed in "Reporting," pp. 151–158

Exemplified by "The Death of the Moth," pp. 194–197; "Body Ritual among the Nacirema," pp. 233–238; "Hatsuyo Nakamura," pp. 175–183; "'This Is the End of the World': The Black Death," pp. 159–169; "A Day in Samoa," pp. 217–220; "A Delicate Operation," pp. 260–263; "Love Canal and the Poisoning of America," pp. 239–253; "Two Reports of an Airplane Crash," pp. 287–299

TOPICAL SUMMATION

Discussed in "Reporting," pp. 151–158

Exemplified by "Two Reports of an Airplane Crash," pp. 287–299; "Some Conditions of Obedience and Disobedience to Authority," pp. 437–461; "Education to Prevent AIDS: Prospects and Obstacles," pp. 502–514; "Face Perception without Recognition," pp. 563–572

Author and Title Index